THE CONSTANCE SPRY
COOKERY BOOK

The Constance Spry
COOKERY BOOK

CONSTANCE SPRY
&
ROSEMARY HUME

J. M. Dent & Sons Ltd
LONDON

Printed in Great Britain by
Butler & Tanner Ltd, Frome and London
for
J. M. DENT & SONS LTD
91 Clapham High Street, London SW4 7TA

© Text revisions, Rosemary Hume and Anthony Marr, 1971
First published 1956
Reprinted 1956, 1957, 1958, 1960, 1961, 1964, 1967
Reprinted with corrections and minor revisions 1971
Reissued 1978
Reprinted 1983
Reissued 1990

ISBN 0 460 04382 x

For students past and present at Winkfield
Place and the Cordon Bleu Cookery School.

Contents

It will be seen that we have used the word butter in a great many of the recipes. This is a policy of perfection and is not intended to indicate that no substitute is ever to be considered. Where butter is essential—a substitute really undesirable—this has been made clear.

For the most part the quantities given in the recipes are for 4–5 people.

Acknowledgments

To express thanks adequately for all the help received in the writing of a book such as this is difficult. In the appropriate chapters grateful acknowledgment is made of permission to quote from certain favourite volumes, but when that is done there still remain the hundreds of books read and long forgotten, the good dishes eaten in the houses of friends, the inspiring ideas about food gained from unremembered sources. And it is on such books and such experiences that knowledge of food and cooking is built up.

Rosemary and I both hope that we have not quoted from the work of other people without proper acknowledgment, and we certainly have not done so consciously. Nevertheless it is not at all uncommon among cooks to find that what we thought was our own grandmother's exclusive recipe has already been made free to the public in more than one cookery book. Of course, in the long range of classic dishes, where it is right and proper that no change should be made in the formulae, tradition has been followed.

While we think fondly of the shades of Mrs Glasse, Sir Kenelm Digby, and all the other people who wrote recipes in such enchanting and elegant language, we want to thank warmly and in particular those contemporaries who have given us the benefit of their time and thought.

Marjorie Baron Russell and Valerie Pirie for reading, criticizing, and advising; Muriel Downes, our deputy principal at the Cordon Bleu Cookery School in London, and Jean Chaplin at Winkfield for testing, suggesting, and improving recipes; Daphne Holden for much laborious checking and sorting, various members of the staff for kindly help, and quite a few students whose questions have often revealed to us that what we thought was as clear as daylight was really not so at all, and finally, the publisher's reader for looking after the consistent presentation of the text and preparing the index.

For the appendix, 'Wines, their Choice and Serving,' which is a rather specialized subject for a cookery book, Rosemary is solely responsible. Thanks are due to Major Bruce Shand for his helpful suggestions and also for reading the manuscript of this section. I also thank the owners of the copyright and the publishers Methuen and Co. Ltd, and Doubleday and Co. Inc., for permission to quote an extract from *The Price of Love* by Arnold Bennett, and the author and William Collins Sons & Co. Ltd, for permission to quote an extract from *The Sword and the Stone* by T. H. White.

Introductory

In music-halls and places where they sing, it is common practice for the star to have a stooge—a 'feed,' I believe, is the term used in the profession—and it is his job to underline and illumine, as it were, the qualities of the star. In preparing a book of this kind it is not a bad idea to have a stooge, and that is the part that vis-à-vis Rosemary I have tried to play; if I have done so properly I believe that the plan will have served to make clear a lot of things that professionals, in their knowledge and experience, take for granted, matters which cookery books do not always mention, and things that you aren't born knowing. I really wanted to call this book *The Reason Why*.

But whatever the title, this book is an offering from Rosemary and me to the students of Winkfield Place and the Cordon Bleu Cookery School in London. She and I planned it, thinking it might provide an answer to any question left over when, their training finished, they scattered themselves over the world, as indeed they have done.

I have had the pleasure of gathering up the material and stringing it together, but the technical knowledge, the technique, and most of the recipes are hers, and anything I know that is worth knowing I have gained from her. Sometimes knowledge pours from her as she talks about cooking, sometimes on the other hand I've battered her with questions about things second nature to her, but mysteries to me.

I am sometimes asked, and I am sure she is too, how it comes that she, a professional cook, and I, whose primary interest lies in flowers, have become allied in this way, and I should like to tell you how it happened.

Before the war each of us was ploughing her respective though not lonely furrow—Rosemary had her 'Au Petit Cordon Bleu' restaurant and its attached school and I a shop and a flower school. Like snow in summer students melted away at the proclamation of war, but before the very last of mine disappeared into the war machine, an idea was voiced which bore fruit. 'After the war,' said one of them, as though that relief were just round the corner, 'could you not add cookery lessons to our flower programme?' and then added thoughtfully: 'I think we shall need it'; showing in this constructive suggestion a prophetic vision.

So when the end of war was in sight there came, like an echo from the past, the question: 'What about that promised cookery and flower school?'

When I began to sketch a curriculum I quickly realized that if I carried it out I should merely be following the trail blazed earlier by Rosemary in her school, which had also become a war casualty. Full of doubts and nervous apprehension, I went off to see how she felt about it. The result was an enthusiastic and practical co-operation that has resulted in the London and Winkfield schools and now in collaboration over a book which her real knowledge and experience of food and cooking has made possible.

Little did I realize what was at stake when I went to see her, for I did not realize, nor do I think did she, what a big part cookery was to play in the lives of women after the war. I was the amateur with homely ideas and limited knowledge, enough perhaps to meet simple war-time demands, but completely inadequate to deal with the overwhelming demand for and need of knowledge which have since become manifest. She was the professional, and I often wonder with a cold shiver, generally around two o'clock in the morning, what would have happened if I had gone on without the inestimable benefit of her co-operation, without what seems to me to be an inexhaustible mine of information.

That is how this combination of professional and amateur has come about, and I hope you will find the recipe a practical one. You see, what is clear as day and foolproof to Rosemary is often not so for me, and in writing this book I have been a pestilential 'why man.' 'But Rose, why not? Why can't you? Why do you?'—until I couldn't have blamed her if she had rationed me to five tiresome questions a day, or deflected her rolling-pin from her puff pastry to me, and with equal vigour.

Collecting the material has been fun; it has also been hard work, and I am praying that not many slips will escape into print—not many, for instance, like the one I lighted on when half a saltspoon of cayenne had been translated by a typist into half a pound. Until you have tried it you cannot think how many snares there are in cooking parlance; it has a verb all its own, and now and then I have found myself instructing you to stand in a bain-marie till dinner-time, to cook the saucepan, and to pour the pudding over the sauce, and I have clearly accredited you with three hands.

The incidence of French words is no snobbery, or I hope not. It is sometimes difficult to find a suitable English equivalent for them; if you try you will find that often the English words lack nicety of description. Sometimes a translation sounds downright unappetizing. Do you like the sound of 'paste of fat liver'? Would you not laugh if instructed to stand a pan in Mary's bath? Of course many French words have become part of our cooking language.

Impatient youth may criticize the frequent, almost nagging repetition of some words and instructions, words such as 'gently and slowly,' for example; yet judging from the often misapplied verve and dash to be witnessed in the kitchen, the emphasis is not really out of place. Rosemary says will I please add the word spooning to the list. This is not a joke; she says that all too often she sees a pan of sauce being sloshed over a dish so that the food is afloat. She also says that I must add in letters of fire *Please read your recipe*, and she says it with so much pathos that I wish modern printing made this possible.

To the over-meticulous, or to those who think cooking can be reduced to a series of scientific formulae, the word 'approximately' may be an irritation. The fact is that cooking is a combination of science, art, invention, and a few other things; it calls for individual taste and latitude in adjustment of the formulae. There is another word to be underlined—taste—taste of course in both its meanings, of discrimination of quality and perception of flavour, but primarily here the latter. If you won't taste as you work you will never be a first-class cook; what other possible guide have you to rely on for nicety of seasoning and flavouring and all the subtleties of a dish— even of what you may be pleased to call good, plain food? There can be a smug sound about these words as sometimes uttered, especially when they are used to cover the bad cooking that produces overcooked meat, gloy gravy, waterlogged vegetables, and heavy puddings. Good plain food can be the best, the apotheosis of good fare; it can be very expensive and still plain. Good cooking owes a great deal to attention to detail, whatever the exponents of a more slapdash method may aver.

Cooking is an art; it demands hard and sometimes distasteful work, but on the whole it is the creative side that prevails. The kitchen should be raised to the status of a studio, as indeed it is in some homes where the mistress of the house is a cook. If it should ever become universally so regarded, then to earn a living in a domestic kitchen would become a more attractive calling to young, educated, qualified cooks, who at present are more attracted to posts in commercial and institutional kitchens. This is a pity, for it is in the private kitchen that opportunity presents itself for experiment and invention. As it is, the contemporary cook-hostess has the best of it, for she sees her efforts appreciated and hears the dishes discussed, which is a pleasant innovation, for talk about food used to be taboo.

Something else is new too: the immensely better and fairer distribution of food among all grades of society. This is due to a variety of causes, not the least of which was the rationing system at which we grumbled so incessantly and to which we so thankfully said good-bye. Remembering as I do the days of immensely long, boring, wasteful dinners, remembering too the starvation which was all too often at our very doors, I cannot forbear to remind you how much respect ought to be paid to food, how carefully it should be treated, how shameful waste is. Forgive me for this, but you see it is fortunately unlikely that your hearts will be wrung or your consciences nudged by the sight of starving people.

Since it would seem to be the simple duty of any woman with a home to run, of those with any sort of civic conscience to understand about food and cooking, it is strange how low the subject ranks in the estimation of many academically minded people. The influence of good food in the bringing up of children, its importance in the building up of a strong people, the contribution it may make to the harmonious running of a home, may be acknowledged theoretically, but there is still a tendency to consider the subject suitable primarily either for girls who cannot make the grade for a university or for those who intend to become teachers. As a training for home life, as a necessity for civilized living, as a serious consideration for the mentally clever girls, it is not always accorded approval. Possibly many scholarly women remember, as I do, the fight made for equality in education, and it may be natural for them to see only certain of the bright facets of learning. In gaining so much, and gaining it with courage and tenacity, the homelier arts may have been eclipsed for a short space of time, but surely now intelligent people recognize them for what they are, the basis of balanced living.

There is a lot of nonsense thought and said about French cooking. There is an idea that it is 'high-falutin fancy,' overdressed and not suitable for good sound English taste. The fact is that Frenchwomen, for various economic and historic reasons, are good housekeepers and good shoppers, cooking with skill, economy, and imagination, wasting nothing, disregarding nothing that may be turned pleasantly and profitably to account. It is because of this, because of their attention to detail, that Rosemary and I both think French cooking the best basis for teaching and practice. This does not preclude appreciation of all that is good in English and other traditions. The marriage of our excellent materials to French methods is a good union.

The following is a translation of a letter written by a Frenchwoman to a young Arab cook entering the service of some friends in Tunisia, and because it expresses so much of the spirit of the subject of this book, Rosemary and I felt we must let you read it.

CONSTANCE SPRY.

Winkfield Place,
Windsor Forest.

MY FRIEND AND FELLOW COOK,

I should like to offer you some advice, and write down a few hints for you, because your career as a cook is only just beginning, and it rests with your own native intelligence to make it interesting, and even exciting.

Cooking is a multi-faceted art. It is as old as the hills, and yet there is always something new to be learned—something new to be invented.

Since the dawn of history kings and potentates have been interested in cooking, and Good King Henry IV of Navarre is always remembered in France as a good-tempered king and one who loved good food and wine . . . throughout the ages all sorts and conditions of men have delighted to gather their friends around them and spoil them by cooking delicious dishes for them, with the result that their guests, even if comparative strangers, would go on their way well fed and comforted, calling down blessings on their kind host in whose house they had found the spirit of order, of hard work, and of peace.

Cooking is a complicated art: not everybody understands it. Keep your ears open and be humble; keep your eyes open too. Think: for the more you learn, the more full of interest life becomes. You can always go on learning, and so you ought to do. For you are the stuff that good cooks are made of; you have a receptive mind, and it is for this reason that I am putting down a few remarks that may be of help to you.

A good cook is always exact, always clean, and above all conscientious. It is a matter of pride with him to keep his kitchen in spotless order. As it happens, your kitchen is big, clean, well lighted, and comfortable. You do not know how lucky you are, for it is a comparatively simple matter to turn out marvellous dishes when the right equipment is available.

A good cook is economical. He goes to endless trouble to turn out his best efforts without wasting a crumb . . . waste is a grievous sin, which fills the heart of the honest man or the good cook with horror. To make sure of using up everything to good effect it is absolutely essential for him to be able to plan ahead.

As soon as the washing up is done each evening, he should run his eye over his provisions. Opening the door of his Frigidaire, he stands in front of it, and thinks. He thinks rapidly, but that moment's reflection is absolutely necessary. How much butter is there? How much meat is left? How much cheese? What is there in the way of left-overs? At least twice each week he should go right through his capacious Frigidaire, and make as much space as he can afford for the needs of the morrow. His kitchen companions should be made to understand that he is the absolute master of the Frigidaire, and he must insist that everything in it shall be kept in absolute order. Raw fish must not be left for days in the refrigerator, dripping on top of a custard; no plates or bowls must be lodged in such a way that they will fall and break when the door is opened. A chef proves his worth by the scrupulous order in which he keeps his refrigerator, for which he is solely responsible.

As a result of his nocturnal meditation beside the Frigidaire the cook should have a mental grasp of everything that is needed for to-morrow's meals. He must make a mental note of anything that is missing, for he cannot afford to run short, seeing that he is responsible for the comfort of his masters. If he loves them and respects them, it is up to him to see that all goes well and smoothly. . . .

In a well-run kitchen common sense is just as important as organization, and there is always plenty for everyone to do. But what a reward it is for a cook when he is sufficiently master of his trade to be able to send at will to his master's table beautiful dishes, cleverly planned and perfectly cooked. Quick, quiet service at the table, as in the kitchen, everything well planned in advance, a carefully considered menu, fine food when guests are present, good wholesome fare for the family every day—all these are the responsibility of the good cook. His basic axiom should be the old French proverb, 'LE BONHEUR C'EST L'ORDRE.'

The Cocktail Party

PERHAPS a cookery book should start in a less frivolous fashion than with a chapter headed 'The Cocktail Party,' and should show in its initial stages a proper seriousness of purpose and general sober-mindedness. But I had an idea that perhaps a light-hearted approach might present a more immediate appeal. One never knows, indeed, what trifle may awaken the enthusiasm necessary to carry one beyond the early arduous tasks connected with cooking into those realms in which cookery is an art and a pleasure. Rosemary Hume and I have noticed that a lesson or a demonstration on cocktail savouries is always popular, conjuring up as it does a vista of successful parties to be held in the future, and imparting a touch of glamour to the basic realities of the kitchen. Well, if the desire to excel in making good bouchées encourages a student to achieve mastery with pastry, all is well. Maybe this chapter should be regarded as the jam with the powder, the carrot before the donkey, but no matter if it serves to lure anyone on in the kitchen. It is only fair to admit that neither R. H. nor I set great store by cocktails or their accompanying savouries, regarding them, as it were, as menaces to the appreciation of good food.

Some cocktails, particularly the more potent of them, may blunt the palate, and preliminary savouries the appetite. The basic idea that a cocktail is intended to stimulate the appetite loses its point when one considers the profusion of food and drink usually presented at a cocktail party. At this point I am reminded of a paragraph that struck me in one of three articles written by Rebecca West for the *New Yorker* early in 1953. The articles were called 'The Annals of Treason' and dealt with the case of William Martin Marshall, the radio telegraphist, who became involved with a Soviet agent in London and was tried for espionage. His parents felt that the whole trouble had started in Russia, where they thought he had followed a life to which he was not accustomed, and Rebecca West goes on:

There were continual parties. Cocktail parties. The sharp sound of the words, flung out after a preparatory pause, recalled that there was an age not so long ago when a cocktail was considered an immoral drink, as different from sherry as concubinage is from marriage, and a cocktail party meant an assembly of people who had abandoned normal restraints. A change in custom in one group may take a very long time to become known in other groups. There was, indeed, no reason for a household like this, which drank either beer or, more probably, only soft drinks, ever to have learned that cocktails had long since become respectable, and that cocktail parties had for many people moved up to the position, formerly occupied by tea parties, of social functions too stereotyped to be anything but tedious.

Whether one likes such parties or not, it appears that for the moment at any rate they have come to stay and have their uses, and that being so, if you give one at all let it be of the best, a best which is not necessarily achieved by serving too many or too strong drinks.

When in England we first adopted the cocktail party we were inclined to timidity, and the range of savouries offered was conservative as to size and variety. Even yet there is a tendency in this direction. Too many little mouthfuls, canapés, bouchées and suchlike, can be monotonous. I personally like better to have one or two main dishes of undeniable popularity, every bit of which will be eaten, and which will send no one home feeling blown up with starch. For instance, if I were feeling extravagant I should choose perhaps as my *pièce de résistance* the prawn dish with Alabama sauce, or if economically bent the cream cheese dish; and I should moderate the number of small savouries accordingly. One must of course differentiate between the various occasions for which cocktail savouries are required, and they may fall under the following headings:

(*a*) Small savouries served with drinks before a dinner party. These should not be too substantial and need not be greatly varied, and such things as nuts, olives, small cheese biscuits, and tiny canapés are adequate. The canapés should be of a size that can comfortably be eaten in one mouthful.

(*b*) Savouries for the cocktail party lasting perhaps from six to eight o'clock, at which may be offered a certain number of fairly substantial items.

(*c*) Savouries for the pre-theatre cocktail party, when you know your guests will not be eating seriously until much later, and a few fairly solid savouries will be welcome.

It may well be emphasized at the outset that the success of this type of food depends more on seasoning, flavouring, and pleasing contrast of texture than on elaborate and expensive materials, and that particular consideration should be given to presentation, and ease of serving and eating. Remembering the worst and the best of such parties clarifies my ideas, and I will tell of those features which made or marred them for me. On a less successful occasion I remember thinking it a great mistake to have so large a number of savouries of one type. The labour-saving device resorted to for this party of making one large batch of pastry and ringing the changes on the filling might possibly have been all right if some more refreshing and contrasting items had been offered, but the addition of filled bridge rolls and bread sandwiches to an array of pastry cases did not produce happy results. The sum total was stuffy and starchy. Too many similar textures are also tiresome; creamy fillings in bouchées and creamy spreads for canapés become extremely cloying. So bearing in mind the need for refreshment for the palate, it is well to vary the pastry, bread, or biscuit theme of these savouries, perhaps with celery as in the recipe on page 7, or by offering stuffed grapes or cherries; or by having a large bowl of raw vegetables—*les crudités*—which are a feature of one popular Paris restaurant in particular, where you may find a few small mushrooms among the young carrots, celery, radishes, spring onions, lettuce, and chicory. A bowl of rough salt should be at hand if this refreshment appears on the cocktail table. If it is chosen as a first course for luncheon on a hot day, it calls for fresh French or home-made rolls with ice-cold curls of butter.

At one of the best cocktail parties I remember, attention was centred on two large dishes, one hot and one cold. There was an adequate supply of these and there were not a great many little savouries, though there were a few: grapes filled with cream cheese, for instance, celery with Stilton cheese and so on; but the main attention had been focused on one or two popular things which proved successful.

The presentation of food at a cocktail party has importance. The larger dishes should look and taste exciting and are generally eaten to the last morsel. The smaller savouries, bouchées, canapés and so forth, may be arranged like a wheel on large platters, and this is at once more convenient and nicer to look at than a number of small plates. Small plates covered perhaps with paper doilies have a way of looking derelict as soon as the party is under way. Cheese sticks, sablés, and biscuits can be aligned on wire trays which emphasize that they are fresh from the oven. Filled bridge rolls and sandwiches also look well on trays. Those items of food speared on small wooden sticks—olives, stuffed cherries, cheese or fish marbles and so on—may be conveniently collected for serving by using firm hearts of red and green cabbage into which the picks are stuck, presenting a porcupine-like aspect. The cabbages should be trimmed at the base and the lower leaves turned out, so that the whole stands firm. Polished apples, grape-fruit, lemons, and small marrows may be used in the same way. It is convenient, too, to have one main table on which the dishes are assembled, and by the way they are presented you may add to the gaiety and interest of the party.

If you should decide on having no main dish, but choose instead a diversity of small things, these are best assembled in a generous way, avoiding too many small dishes. However many odds and ends you may choose to have, bear in mind the importance of contrast both of flavour and texture. Olives, nuts, and potato chips are always popular. The nuts should be freshly prepared and the chips properly heated through and salted. Certain types of savoury suitable for a cocktail party are equally suitable for serving as an after-dinner savoury, and the subject of this final course to a meal will be dealt with later. But the following general points may apply to both types of savoury and so I will give them here.

1. When toast is used as a basis, the bread should be evenly sliced and about three-eighths of an inch thick. It should be toasted to a good brown and the crusts removed. It should be made at the last possible moment and dried off a little to allow the steam to evaporate before buttering.

2. Fried canapés should be cut from evenly sliced rounds of bread about a quarter of an inch thick. They may be fried in shallow fat, in either butter or oil, according to the rules for shallow frying, i.e. the rounds should be turned once only. If they are fried in deep fat, they should be plunged into the smoking fat and turned about with a slice. Care should be taken not to let them become over-brown, or they will be hard and chippy.

3. Where bacon rashers are used they should be streaky and cut very thin; a number three cut on the grocer's bacon slicer is suitable. The rind is then removed with scissors and the rashers trimmed and spread out with the flat of a knife on a board. Half a rasher for each savoury is usually enough.

4. Where anchovy fillets are called for they may well be soaked for some hours in milk, particularly if they have been preserved in brine, or have become hard and dry. If they have been preserved in brine they must be washed before being soaked. Picked shrimps may be treated in similar fashion.

5. Cheese for grating should be dry, and the best all-round cheese is a dry, well-matured cheddar, or a mixture of gruyère and Parmesan. For Welsh rabbit or other toasted cheese dishes cheddar is most suitable.

MAIN DISHES (HOT)

The keeping of these really hot does present a problem to the cook-hostess, for although one may serve them on a large hot fireproof dish, the savouries obviously will not retain heat for long. A chafing-dish is a valuable possession, and a hot-plate will help. Recently there have come on the English market deep dishes holding night-lights and covered with a perforated metal lid; these are less expensive than the two foregoing.

A large hot fireproof dish filled with small mixed fritters is excellent, but it is difficult to keep them small enough to uphold the idea of 'No two bites at a cocktail savoury.' They should be made as small as is conveniently possible and reserved for a party where more substantial items are called for. They may be of vegetables, sprigs of herbs, prawns, mushrooms, onion rings and so forth. They should be well flavoured and seasoned individually, dipped in a light fritter batter, and fried in deep fat. Piquante sauce may be served apart in a bowl into which the fritters are dipped. For this purpose they should be speared on picks. The recipe for a fritto misto of vegetables given on page 276 will serve for this dish, and any one of the really piquante sauces may be chosen; in particular I think the one called Alabama sauce is very good, as is the alternative given on page 6.

If you want a small dish of one kind of fritter, I would choose mushrooms, for which you take small button mushrooms, season them well with salt and pepper and a dash of lemon juice, dip them into the fritter batter given on the opposite page, and then fry them in deep fat to a golden brown.

These again are served with a piquante sauce. Or your dish may be half these and half watercress puffs, for which you take sprigs of well-dried watercress, dip them in the batter, and fry.

Prawns, pieces of crawfish tail, and lobster may all be treated in the same way.

Small, dry, well-seasoned fishcakes containing a touch of curry-powder or paste are a popular hot dish. Like the fritters these may be served on picks and dipped into a bowl of suitable sauce.

A LIGHT FRITTER BATTER FOR THE VEGETABLE AND HERB FRITTERS

5 oz. flour
a level teaspoon salt

yeast about the size of a
  walnut
about ¼ pint water

When yeast is not available a substitute may be made of 1–2 tablespoons brown ale, in which event the amount of water may be reduced. The mixture should have the consistency of thick cream. Sift the flour and salt, dissolving the yeast in a little of the slightly warmed water and beating it into the flour with the remaining liquid.

Here is a recipe for the small fishcakes:

PETITES CROQUETTES DE POISSON

cold fish that has been cooked
  in court bouillon
1 oz. butter
1 tablespoon flour
1½ gills milk

4 oz. breadcrumbs
salt, pepper, nutmeg
a dash of curry-powder
egg and breadcrumbs for
  coating

Flake the fish, remove all skin and bone. Melt the butter, add the flour, and cook gently for a short time. Pour in boiling milk and whisk until the sauce thickens, add fish and breadcrumbs, season well with salt, pepper, nutmeg, and curry-powder. Spread the mixture on a plate to cool. Make into small croquettes, coat with egg and breadcrumbs, and fry golden brown in hot fat. Drain and serve hot.

MAIN DISHES (COLD)

One of the best of these I met with in Alabama. For this a large dish was filled with crushed ice, a hollow in the centre holding a glass bowl filled with Alabama sauce; all around, stuck in the ice, were picks holding Dublin Bay prawns; the prawns were dipped into the sauce and eaten. This is an admirable dish but by no means economical; however, the prawns may be replaced by the Norwegian frozen prawns, which are excellent, by pieces of crayfish or lobster, or even by dry, very well-seasoned fishcakes, such as those already given.

A recipe for Alabama sauce will be found on page 180; the following is an alternative:

AN ALTERNATIVE SAUCE TO ALABAMA
TO SERVE WITH FRITTERS OR SHELL-FISH

Make a good cream dressing or mayonnaise and add to it 1 dessertspoon wine vinegar, 1 tablespoon salad-oil, salt, freshly ground black pepper and made mustard to taste, 1 heaped teaspoon sugar, 2 teaspoons grated horse-radish, chopped chives and spring onions, a squeeze of lemon juice, and a dash of tomato ketchup. Beat all together and add finely chopped gherkins, capers, or sweet pickles.

Another good main dish is made with a form of home-made cheese beaten to a light cream, piled lightly on a dish, surrounded by chipped potatoes, radishes, gherkins, olives and so forth, and accompanied by a separate dish of plain hot biscuits, preferably salted. The cheese is either spooned on to the biscuits or scooped up with potato chips. The cheese for this dish may be made in a variety of ways, and here is one simple recipe:

HOME-MADE 'CREAM' CHEESE

cheddar cheese
butter up to an equal quantity with the cheese
hot milk, cream, or yoghourt, or a mixture of all three, may be used
    in place of part or all of the butter. Additional bulk may be given
    by the incorporation of home-made sour-milk cheese, as given on
    page 745 in the milk and cheese chapter.
flavourings added to taste: a dash of anchovy essence and/or Wor-
    cestershire sauce, chopped capers, olives, gherkins, sweet pickle,
    chives, crushed garlic
seasonings: salt, paprika, freshly ground pepper

Grate the cheese and pound, or put it through a wire sieve. Beat it well, adding the other ingredients. Taste for seasoning and flavouring. If this cheese is to be used in quantities as a main dish the flavouring should be fairly restrained. If, however, it is wanted for canapés the stronger form of it known as Liptauer may be made. See page 747 of the milk and cheese chapter or the good luncheon cheese given on page 746.

SMALLER SAVOURIES

Cheese enters into many cocktail savouries, ranging from tiny Welsh rabbits to sablés and cheese creams for filling savoury éclairs and choux, and recipes for some of these savouries are now given.

CAMEMBERT SAVOURY

trimmings of puff pastry	Camembert cheese
olives	cream
salt, pepper, and cayenne	

Roll the puff paste thin and cut in strips. Bake light brown in a hot oven, and sandwich with Camembert cheese worked with an equal quantity of whipped cream, seasoned with salt and pepper and a dash of cayenne, and mixed with a few stoned, chopped olives. Serve hot or cold.

CREAM CHEESE CANAPÉS (1)

Make a rich short crust with 3 oz. flour, 2 oz. butter, 1 oz. cheese, 1 egg yolk, and seasoning. Roll and stamp into rounds the size of half a crown and bake for 7 minutes. Pipe on to these, or put on with a teaspoon, a good creamed cheese such as Liptauer. Into this you may put chopped chives, pounded anchovies, tomato purée, and paprika to taste. Decorate the canapés with black olives, pickled walnuts, pickled onions, or gherkins.

CREAM CHEESE CANAPÉS (2)

Beat demi-sel or home-made cheese with a little cream to the consistency of whipped cream. Season well, pipe on to small rounds of cheese sablés (see recipe below), decorate with red-currant jelly or pickled cucumber.

A recipe for Cheese Marbles (Hot) will be found on page 361 (Salads).

CÉLERI FARCI

1–2 heads of first quality celery	2–3 oz. Stilton cheese
1–2 oz. butter	salt and pepper
brown bread and butter	pimento

Cut the root off the celery, carefully detach the stems, and wash well. Discard any stringy or discoloured stems. Put the remainder into cold water and leave to become crisp. Meanwhile cream or pound the Stilton with enough butter to make it taste mild and good—the quantity depends on the ripeness of the cheese—and season well with salt and pepper. Dry each stem of celery well, and with a small palette-knife spread the cheese mixture inside the stems, starting with the smallest and reshaping the stalks into two or three 'heads,' according to the size of savoury desired. Wrap each 'head' in grease-proof paper and put aside in a cool place to become firm. Then cut each 'head' crossways into slices about ¼ inch thick, and set each on a round of brown bread and butter stamped out to exactly the same size as the slice of celery. Garnish with a very small round of canned pimento put in the middle of each slice. The nozzle of a forcing-pipe about ¼ inch in diameter is a good cutter for the pimento.

N.B. Chicory may take the place of celery when the latter is not in season, but it is not so crisp.

CHEESE SABLÉS

3 oz. butter	3 oz. flour
3 oz. grated cheese	salt and pepper

Rub the butter into the flour and add the grated cheese and seasoning. Leave in a cool place for 10 minutes. Roll out to ¼-inch thickness and cut into wide strips, then into triangles. Bake 10 minutes in a fairly hot oven.

Almond sablés filled with a creamy filling are delicious, and a recipe for them will be found in the milk and cheese chapter (page 754).

WALNUT SABLÉS

3 oz. butter	beaten egg
3 oz. grated cheese	coarsely chopped walnuts
3 oz. flour	rock-salt
salt and pepper	

Rub the butter into the sifted flour and add the cheese with the seasoning. Knead together into a paste. Roll out thinly. Cut into strips about 2 inches wide. Brush over with beaten egg and sprinkle thickly with the walnuts. Grind a little salt over this and cut each strip into triangles. Bake on a tin lined with grease-proof paper in a moderately hot oven till golden brown, about 10 minutes.

CHEESE STRAWS

6 oz. flour	salt, pepper, and cayenne
3½ oz. butter or margarine	yolk of 1 egg or a little
1½ oz. grated Parmesan or	beaten egg
Parmesan and gruyère cheese	

Rub in the fat lightly, add the grated cheese and seasoning, and bind with the egg yolk or beaten egg, and a spoonful of water if necessary. Roll out and shape into a rectangle; cut across into strips and bake on a paper-lined baking-sheet.

A range of cocktail savouries made with choux pastry may be light, agreeable, and easy to vary:

TARTELETTES A LA MARJOLAINE

Line very small tartlet moulds with a savoury short pastry. Prick the bottom of each case and line with paper and beans to keep the shape. Bake 10–15 minutes in a hot oven.

Prepare a choux paste in the usual way (see page 843) with the addition of 2 oz. grated cheese at the last. Fill this into a bag with a small round pipe, and pipe round the bottom and sides of the tartlets so as to form a small well in the middle. Fill in with a thick creamy béchamel sauce, well seasoned, and with grated cheese added. Put the tartlets into a moderate oven for another 10–15 minutes, in order to cook the choux paste gently whilst browning the middle of the tartlets. Serve very hot, and immediately, when they become like a soufflé. In larger tartlet moulds these make a good savoury.

Béchamel sauce

Bring ¼ pint milk slowly to the boil with a bay-leaf, a slice of onion, and a blade of mace. Strain carefully on to a roux of a good ½ oz. each of flour and butter. Stir till boiling, simmer a minute or two, add cheese to taste, and plenty of seasoning.

As well as the following recipes there is one for Beignets Soufflés au Fromage in the milk and cheese chapter on page 754.

SAVOURY ÉCLAIRS OR CHOUX

Prepare a choux paste with ¼ pint water, 2 oz. butter, 2½ oz. flour, seasoning, and 2 eggs (for method see page 843). Lightly grease a baking-sheet and put the mixture on it in small teaspoons. Sprinkle with chopped almonds or grated cheese and bake until crisp, or you may mix savoury ingredients in the paste:

Choux paste as above, season with salt (no sugar), mix with a little chopped lean ham or, more delicious, smoked ham and shredded browned almonds, and fry in deep fat.

Or you may fill cooked choux paste:

Bake the paste plain as choux, or pipe into little éclairs, split and fill with cheese cream or other savoury mixture. Or you may like to incorporate a little cheese with the mixture to give added interest.

In Edwardian days these savoury éclairs and choux were called carolines when shaped like éclairs, and duchesses when formed like choux à la crème; they were finished off, after being filled, by a coating of chaudfroid sauce or by a light brushing of aspic jelly just on the point of setting, and they were then sprinkled with finely chopped pistachios or other salted nuts. This finish is not often carried out to-day and is indeed a job for experts. The addition of sauce or aspic, of course, makes these savouries suitable for the dinner table rather than the cocktail party. Some of the fillings used for them, however, will serve our purpose.

Chicken. Cold chicken, shredded and pounded in a mortar, mixed with an equal quantity of butter and seasoned with salt, freshly ground black pepper, a squeeze of lemon juice, and a few drops of tabasco. Finely chopped herbs, such as tarragon, chervil, and parsley, can be worked into the mixture to taste.

Ham. Lean ham, with a very little fat added, shredded and pounded with enough hot chutney to flavour, a drop or two of Worcestershire sauce, some French mustard, and an equal quantity of butter.

Tongue, shredded and pounded with a tablespoon of Cumberland sauce, salt and pepper, a touch of made mustard, and an equal quantity of butter. Chopped orange or lemon rind added to taste.

Salmon. Fresh or smoked salmon, pounded and mixed with horse-radish sauce, seasoned with salt, pepper, and lemon juice.

Sardine. Boned and skinned sardines pounded with lemon juice, plenty of freshly ground black pepper, a little salt, and a teaspoon or more of Worcestershire sauce.

N.B. Instead of butter, a small quantity of good béchamel or demi-glace sauce, according to the other elements chosen, may be used with these purées.

In the following three fillings cream is given as a binding medium. This is classic, but in these days, when the general range of foods is much less rich, it is advisable to consider a good béchamel in its place. This produces a lighter and to some people a more agreeable texture.

Smoked salmon. Well pounded and mixed with 2 tablespoons of thick cream to every 4 oz. of salmon. Passed through a fine sieve, seasoned with lemon juice and freshly ground black pepper. If the mixture tastes too strong, a little more whipped cream may be added.

Tunny. Well pounded and mixed with the same proportion of thick cream or butter as the previous filling. Passed through a fine sieve and seasoned with black pepper, salt, and a little anchovy essence; garnished with chopped fennel.

Chicken, ham, and tongue. Made according to the same proportions, seasoned and flavoured as for smoked salmon, passed through a fine sieve and mixed with a little extra whipped cream.

SAVOURY FRITTERS

Prepare a choux paste as described on page 843. When well beaten, add to this 2 oz. finely shredded lean ham and 1½ oz. shredded browned almonds. Fry in hot fat in ½-teaspoons. When well risen and firm, drain on soft paper and serve at once.

TOASTED SARDINE SANDWICH

Skin, bone, and mash up a small tin of sardines and add 4 tablespoons good thick cream salad-dressing, cole-slaw, or well-flavoured mayonnaise. Add ½ dessertspoon Worcestershire sauce, a dash of tabasco, ½ teaspoon finely chopped chives, 4–5 tablespoons finely chopped celery or cucumber, a tablespoon of finely chopped green peppers, ½ teaspoon lemon juice, salt and pepper. Mix this all together, beat it up, and spread it thickly between rounds of bread, then toast under a grill, turning carefully and toasting on each side; or the whole may be cooked in a frying-pan in butter.

The grilled sardines mentioned in the section on after-dinner savouries (page 33) may be made in small size and are an excellent hot cocktail savoury.

SARDINE CANAPÉS

small croûtes or rounds of brown bread and butter	slices of hard-boiled egg
sardines	slices of lemon
chopped parsley	chopped capers

Bone and skin the sardines and lay one on each croûte, cover with a slice of egg and a slice of peeled lemon. Dust with chopped parsley and chopped capers.

Here is a refreshing mixture for canapés:

1 cream cheese the size of a demi-sel	1 teaspoon green peppers, finely chopped
2 tablespoons thick cream	1 teaspoon lemon juice
12 olives, finely chopped	1 teaspoon Worcestershire sauce

Beat together and put on croûtes or biscuits or ice wafers brushed with butter and crisped in the oven.

ANCHOVY ROLLS

fillets of anchovy	mustard and seasoning
dry grated cheese	melted butter
thin white bread and butter	

Cut the crusts off the bread and butter, spread each slice with mustard, sprinkle with seasoning and cheese, lay on a fillet of anchovy, and roll up. Set on a tin, sprinkle lightly with melted butter, and bake in a hot oven for 7 minutes to a golden brown. Serve very hot. These must be cut to an even size, and the slice should be medium-sized to small, so that each roll is not too 'bready.'

ANCHOVY AIGRETTES

Prepare a French dressing with plenty of herbs, oil, and vinegar, chives and parsley. Marinade with this for as long as possible anchovy fillets, then drain, dip into fritter batter, and fry at once in deep fat. Or the fillets may be laid on thin pieces of short or puff pastry and turned over to form *allumettes*. They are painted with beaten egg and baked.

The following shell-fish canapés may serve either as cocktail savoury or first course for dinner according to their size. The recipes may be interchanged or used with other shell-fish. The difference between them is that the one given for crab is creamy and bland and that for lobster much more piquante.

CRAB CANAPÉS

1 shallot	1½ oz. butter
a scant oz. flour	salt and pepper
¼ gill cream or creamy milk	½ lb. crab meat
cayenne	lemon juice
fingers of toast or fried bread	1 tablespoon grated cheese
paprika	watercress to garnish

Chop the shallot finely, make ½ oz. butter hot in a frying-pan, and cook the shallot gently until light brown. Add the flour, off the heat, and blend well. Pour in the cream or milk and bring to the boil, add the flaked crab and season well with salt, pepper, cayenne, and lemon juice. Stir until boiling-point is reached. Spread the fingers of toast or fried bread with the mixture, work the cheese and the rest of the butter together to a paste with a fork or a palette-knife, and add plenty of paprika to make the paste a good red colour. Spread a little of this paste on top of each. Put for a second or two under a hot grill, and garnish the dish with bunches of picked watercress.

LOBSTER CANAPÉS (COLD)

the meat from 1 small lobster, or a small tin of lobster
French dressing
3 sprigs of parsley
1 rasher of bacon, thinly cut
mayonnaise or boiled dressing
salt and freshly ground black pepper

2 sticks of celery, finely chopped, or a good tablespoon chopped celeriac
6 chives
fingers of toast or fried bread
lettuce to garnish
sugar

Break up the lobster meat into small pieces with two forks and marinade for an hour or more in well-seasoned French dressing, to which a pinch of sugar has been added. Add the finely chopped celery or celeriac, the chives cut small with kitchen scissors, and finely chopped parsley. Cut rind from bacon, grill until brown and crisp, and break in small pieces. Add these to the lobster mixture when cold, and mix with mayonnaise or dressing. Season with salt and freshly ground black pepper. Pile on fingers of fried bread or toast and garnish with small lettuce leaves.

SHRIMP CANAPÉS (HOT OR COLD)

Simmer shrimps in a little butter with a pinch of curry-powder and a dash of cayenne. Arrange on croûtes and put a little chilli sauce on top.

DEVILLED CROQUETTES OR KROMESKI (1)

Cod's roe or devilled crab shaped into small balls and sandwiched between two halves of a walnut, floured, egged and crumbed, and fried in deep fat. (See also page 36.)

DEVILLED KROMESKI (2)

10–12 large prunes
stock
chutney
fillets of anchovy
bacon rashers

batter of 2 tablespoons flour, salt and pepper, and a piece of yeast the size of a pea

Soak the prunes overnight and simmer until just tender in a little good stock. Remove the stones carefully. Stuff with the anchovy fillets and a good ½ teaspoon chutney. Make a batter by dissolving the yeast in 2 or 3 tablespoons warm water, then beating in the flour with a little cold water to make a thick cream. Leave the batter for 15 minutes in a warm place before it is used. Roll the prunes in a piece of bacon, dip in the batter one by one, and then drop into smoking deep fat. Fry to a golden brown. Serve very hot in a napkin.

DEVILLED CHESTNUTS

These may be used as cocktail savouries or as a hot hors-d'œuvre. Take large chestnuts, scald them, and remove the outer peel and every bit of the inner skin without breaking the chestnuts. Stew gently in milk with a little salt, till they are soft enough to penetrate with a skewer without losing their shape. Roll each nut in oiled butter and then cheese mixed with a good sprinkling of pepper, salt, and cayenne. Roll in butter once more and then in fried breadcrumbs. Place on a dish in a fairly hot oven, pour a little oiled butter carefully over them, and leave them to brown, which takes a few minutes. Serve in little paper cases and sprinkle at the last minute with a little chopped chervil and a dust of cayenne. Serve very hot. This is one of the most popular of cocktail savouries.

CHESTNUT CROQUETTES

See page 645 in poultry chapter. These are excellent as a hot cocktail savoury and very popular.

MUSHROOM ROLLS

Take thin slices of streaky bacon, cut off the rind, flatten with a knife, and spread with a well-seasoned mushroom purée. Roll up, brush with beaten egg, dip in breadcrumbs or oatmeal, and fry in deep fat.

Purée

1 oz. butter	¼ lb. mushrooms, washed, peeled, and chopped
2 oz. shallots	2 oz. white breadcrumbs
seasoning	1 teaspoon chopped parsley

Cook first four ingredients gently for 10 minutes. Add breadcrumbs and chopped parsley.

If mushroom rolls are to be served as a savoury course at the end of a meal, they may be accompanied by watercress tossed in sharp French dressing.

BACON ROLLS IN DROPPED SCONES

Roll a thin rasher of bacon, or part of one, round a pickled onion, and cook until the bacon is thoroughly done. Make small, thin, unsweetened drop scones and fold them round the roll, holding together with a wooden skewer.

Small, unsweetened drop scones, freshly made, may be filled in a variety of ways, or spread with savoury pastes, such as Gentleman's Relish or good bloater paste, and served rolled up. They are excellent, if not economical, filled with pâté de foie gras.

There is one particularly delicious cocktail savoury, Guacamole, which one serves in this country only when avocado pears can be bought inexpensively, which sometimes happens, particularly in the French market in London in the summer.   For this the flesh of the avocado pear is beaten up with sour cream, onion juice, lemon juice, and seasoning, then well chilled and served with brown bread and butter on which it is spread, or with a dish of potato chips beside the bowl for dipping into the mixture.   This is a particularly delicious and epicurean dish.

CUCUMBER AND TUNNY FISH

Peel a large cucumber, cut in half (not lengthwise), scoop out seeds. Fill with mashed tunny fish flavoured with mayonnaise, paprika, and Worcestershire sauce.   Pack in well with spoon handle.   Leave several hours in refrigerator.   Cut in $\frac{1}{2}$-inch slices.   Serve on lettuce moistened with French dressing.

CUCUMBER FARCI

Pieces of cucumber stuffed with a cream cheese or mushroom purée and set on rounds of brown bread and butter.

STUFFED GRAPES

Pip large grapes.   Make a paper cornet (see page 53).   With this fill each grape with a soft cheese cream, well seasoned with black pepper and salt.   Allow the cheese cream to come well above the top and dip this into salted browned almonds.   Serve on picks or in small paper cases.

STUFFED PRUNES

Soak the prunes well overnight, then remove the stones.   Finely chop together 3 shallots, a chicken liver, and 1 oz. fat bacon.   Heat a nut of butter in a small sauté pan, add the onion, bacon, and liver, and simmer for about 5 minutes.   Season well, adding plenty of finely chopped parsley and sage or savory.   Bind together with the yolk of an egg and stuff into the prunes.   These may be served hot.

SALTED AND DEVILLED NUTS

Almonds and filberts are blanched, peanuts are slipped from their thin brown skins before salting.   Walnuts when fresh must not have the skin left on as it is very bitter.   The nuts are lightly fried in butter, then drained and tossed in salt sprinkled on kitchen paper; for devilled nuts, cayenne is added to the salt.

COCKTAIL SAUSAGES

These are always popular and are interesting if they are treated as follows:
Cook chipolatas, make an incision lengthways, but do not quite cut

through. Spread inside with French mustard and fill with cream cheese well flavoured with chutney or with devil sauce. Roll the edge in browned chopped almonds.

Tiny Vienna smoked sausages (bought in jars) may be wrapped in wafer-thin puff paste, baked, and served on picks, or one may take chipolatas, splitting them and encasing them in pastry in the same way. They are baked and served cut in short lengths, on picks.

FILLED ROLLS

There is a whole range of filled rolls, minute, medium, or sizable, according to the occasion, which are good as long as they are not overdone. Assembled in one large dish they may, if you so wish, make a central feature of the table. The fillings for them are capable of great variation and are a matter for the imaginative. If one chooses tiny French or home-made rolls these are easily handled, but it must be acknowledged that savouries are lighter and less bready if one uses starchless rolls bought in packets and called Energen. The trouble here is that even half of one of these is on the large side and they are inclined to crumble, and perhaps savouries made with these find a better place as a first course for luncheon or dinner.

From the rolls cut off a slice and hollow slightly; brush inside and out with flavoured butter, garlic-flavoured if you like. After brushing put them into a sharp oven until golden brown, and then they may be filled in a variety of ways: pieces of chicken in devil or curry sauce; crab with a sharp dressing of oil, vinegar, plenty of mustard, salt and pepper; devilled mushrooms, cheese, or any one of a variety of fillings you may choose. The great point about these rolls is that they shall be very crisp and the filling well seasoned. They may of course be lavish or economical as your purse allows.

Another kind of filled roll is made by making tiny home-made croissants and filling them before they are baked—that is to say the roll and filling are baked together. The filling may be of ham, mushroom, devilled hard-boiled egg, or anything you may choose.

Here is a good devil sauce for binding together such things as hard-boiled eggs, diced chicken, mushrooms, etc., for filling rolls.

DEVIL SAUCE

4 tablespoons Harvey sauce	a good pinch of cayenne
1 level teaspoon made English mustard	a dash of anchovy essence brown sauce, béchamel, or
4 tablespoons tomato sauce	mayonnaise

Cook all ingredients but the last together to make a sauce of coating consistency which tastes both sweet and sharp. Add to this mixture a gill of béchamel, or if to be served cold use a small quantity of mayonnaise sufficient to bind, or a thick brown sauce. Mix this with the hard-boiled egg or chicken, cut fairly coarsely, and put a dessertspoon of the mixture in each roll, putting back the top at an angle. The rolls may then be heated in a hot oven for 7–10 minutes.

POTATO STICKS

Potato sticks are excellent to eat by themselves or with cheese or salad, and they are liked by children as well as older people.

3 oz. freshly cooked sieved potato	salt, pepper
3 oz. butter	beaten egg
3 oz. flour	dill or caraway seed

Work the potato, butter, and flour to a soft dough, with plenty of salt and pepper. Then leave for half an hour to chill. Roll out, brush with beaten egg, sprinkle well with dill seed, cut into sticks. Bake in a moderate oven 10–15 minutes.

CHUTNEY BISCUITS

Take thin water-biscuits or the 'last-minute' biscuits given on page 787. Make a mixture of a little butter worked well with Worcestershire sauce, a teaspoon of sieved chutney, and a dash of paprika. Spread this mixture on the biscuits and bake in a quick oven for about 5 minutes. Serve very hot. With these may be served in a separate dish ice-cold mint and apple chutney which one spoons on to the biscuit. This contrast in temperatures is excellent.

The following biscuit has a covering of thin, highly seasoned jelly or aspic. It can be most refreshing in flavour and a good contrast in texture to other savouries, but the jelly must be really hotly seasoned.

BISCUITS WITH SAVOURY DEVILLED JELLY

¼ pint chilli, tomato, or A1 sauce	1 teaspoon powdered gelatine
a dash of Worcestershire sauce	salt, pepper, and cayenne
small thin water-biscuits	stoned olives stuffed with anchovy butter

Dissolve the gelatine in a tablespoon of water, and mix it with the bottled tomato, A1, or chilli sauce. Add a dash of Worcestershire sauce and season with salt, pepper, and a spot of cayenne. Pour on to a wet plate to set. When quite firm, cut in rounds with a pastry cutter, and put each round of jelly on a small round cheese biscuit. In the middle set a stoned olive stuffed with anchovy butter.

PIN-WHEELS OR ROULADES

These are made by taking small pieces of pastry left over from other bakings and rolling them out extremely thinly. The pastry is then spread with anchovy or bloater paste, or a highly seasoned paste such as Gentleman's Relish, and rolled up like a small Swiss roll. This should be allowed to chill thoroughly and then be finely sliced, the slices being baked in the oven.   This is a useful type of simple cocktail savoury for everyday use, for if the roll is wrapped in grease-proof paper and kept in the refrigerator it will keep for days and may be sliced and used as required.

BOUCHÉES

puff pastry	piquante sauce
lean ham	parsley
beaten egg	

Roll out the pastry, brush over with beaten egg, stamp out into rounds about the size of a five-shilling piece.   To imitate the appearance of larger bouchées mark a well-defined circle with a smaller cutter in the centre (these little bouchées are split for filling instead of being filled like the larger ones).   Bake in a hot oven till well risen and crisp.   In the meantime, chop the ham, mix it well with the chopped parsley and enough piquante sauce to moisten well.   Split the bouchées in two and fill well with the mixture.   Serve hot or cold.

Small tartlet cases filled in various ways are attractive.   Tunny-fish cream makes a good filling and the finish may be of a turned olive, or of a turned olive stuffed with pimento.   Olives associate particularly well with tunny fish, now generally available, and are most suitable for cocktail savouries of many kinds.

There is no need to set out a list of fillings for bouchées as a choice may be made from those already suggested, chicken, hard-boiled eggs, lobster, mushroom, etc., bound together by a good béchamel.

SAVOURY BUTTERS

This seems a not entirely unsuitable place to mention savoury butters. These are of course used in many dishes in what R. H. calls 'proper cooking,' but as they are often useful for some of the foregoing kickshaws they may reasonably come in here.

MAÎTRE D'HÔTEL BUTTER

1 oz. butter	1 teaspoon finely chopped parsley
1 teaspoon lemon juice	salt and pepper

Cream the butter well on a plate with a palette-knife, work in the lemon juice a few drops at a time with the parsley and seasoning.   When all is thoroughly mixed, form into pats or spread out on a small plate and cut into squares when hard.   Leave to harden well before using.

A pat is put on grilled sole, cutlets, tournedos, poached eggs, etc., immediately before serving.

MONTPELLIER BUTTER

1½ oz. butter
1 hard-boiled egg yolk
2 or 3 leaves of spinach
2 sprigs of tarragon

2 fillets of anchovy
a small handful of parsley
salt and pepper

Boil the herbs together for 5 minutes, drain, press, and pass through a wire sieve or strainer. Pound or sieve the yolk with the anchovy, work into the butter, adding the herb purée by degrees; the butter should be quite green. Season rather well.

Use as a sandwich filling, or with eggs, fried fish, and as maître d'hôtcl butter.

ANCHOVY BUTTER

1 oz. butter
anchovy essence
freshly ground black pepper

4 fillets of anchovy
½ clove of garlic

Work the butter on a plate with a palette-knife until creamy; pound the anchovies and add to the butter with the pepper and enough essence to colour a delicate pink and strengthen the flavour. Crush the garlic to a cream with a pinch of salt, and mix in thoroughly.

For boiled, grilled, fried, or poached fish, and for adding to a béchamel or velouté sauce to form sauce aux anchois. In this case, omit the garlic and use finely ground white pepper.

ORANGE BUTTER

finely grated rind of 1 orange,
   preferably blood
½ teaspoon paprika pepper
1 teaspoon or more orange
   juice

1½ oz. butter
1 slice of shallot well crushed
   with a pinch of salt

Cream the butter thoroughly and work in the other ingredients by degrees. Leave to harden and use as for maître d'hôtel, but principally for grilled sole. It is also good with stuffed chipolatas.

GARLIC BUTTER

Blanch 1 oz. garlic, pound in a mortar, work in 1 oz. butter, and put through a fine sieve. Use for flavouring sauces, etc.

CHIVRY OR RAVIGOTE BUTTER

Pound in a mortar 3 oz. (altogether) of parsley, chervil, tarragon, and chives, blanched for a few minutes, refreshed, and squeezed. Pound also 1 shallot, chopped and blanched. Add 1½ oz. butter and put through a fine sieve.

SHRIMP BUTTER

Pound peeled shrimps in a mortar to a paste. Add an equal quantity of butter, season with a squeeze of lemon juice, and pass through a fine sieve.

TARRAGON BUTTER

Blanch 1 oz. tarragon leaves for 2 minutes, drain, refresh, and squeeze. Pound them with 2 oz. butter and pass through a fine sieve.

MUSTARD BUTTER

Add 1½ tablespoons French mustard to 4 oz. softened butter, work together, and keep in a cool place. For fish, grilled ham, etc.

PAPRIKA BUTTER

Soften in butter a tablespoon of finely chopped onion. Add a dessert-spoon of paprika, work into 2 oz. butter, and pass through a fine sieve.

PIMENTO BUTTER

Pound 1 red pimento, tinned, cut in small pieces, with 3 oz. butter, salt, pepper, and cayenne, 1 tablespoon thick cream, and a squeeze of lemon juice. Pass through a fine sieve.

BEURRE A L'INDIENNE

Pound a good tablespoon of mango chutney with a teaspoon of curry-powder, add a teaspoon of made mustard, 3 oz. butter, a squeeze of lemon juice, salt, pepper, and a spot of cayenne. Add a few drops of Worcester-shire sauce and spread on the bread or toast used for chicken sandwiches.

LOBSTER BUTTER

Pound together equal parts of the coral from a cooked lobster and butter. Season and press through a nylon sieve. Sometimes a recipe calls for lobster butter made from uncooked coral; the method is the same.

FRUIT COCKTAILS

The selection and mixing of cocktails is outside the proper scope of this book; there are other more suitable sources of information. It is a good plan to have one short drink that is non-alcoholic and the most generally popular is tomato juice. Recipes for making this follow. Often a tin of a good brand of tomato juice is used and seasoning and lemon juice added to this.

TOMATO JUICE COCKTAIL

Simmer 12 tomatoes in $\frac{1}{2}$ cup water with a sliced onion, a small stick of celery (or celery salt), $\frac{1}{2}$ bay-leaf, 3 sprigs of parsley, and 4 sprays of basil. Strain and season with salt, paprika, a little sugar, a dash of Worcestershire sauce (optional), and a squeeze of lemon juice.   Chill well.

TOMATO COCKTAIL

To 1 pint good strong tomato juice, made from ripe tomatoes, add the pared rind and juice of half a lemon, a teaspoon of mint flavoured vinegar, a teaspoon of Worcestershire sauce, sugar, salt, and freshly ground pepper to taste, and a grating of nutmeg.   Chill for an hour or two in the refrigerator before removing the lemon rind.

ORANGE AND TOMATO COCKTAIL

Bruise 3 or 4 sprigs of pineapple mint, put into a jug and pour over them 1 pint good tomato juice, add $1\frac{1}{2}$ gills freshly strained orange juice, a good pinch of salt, and sugar to taste.   Chill thoroughly and allow to infuse for at least an hour before straining.

Other recipes for fruit cocktails will be found on pages 1187–8.

II

Hors-d'œuvre, First-course Dishes, and After-dinner Savouries

THE preparation and selection of mixed hors-d'œuvre as a first course is an interesting affair and calls for discrimination. Such a course may be stimulating to the palate and delicious, but it may also be dull as ditch-water, too acid or *fade,* and indigestibly heavy. In some hotels and restaurants it can also be unimaginative and boringly repetitive. A good selection of hors-d'œuvre, which by the way need not be many in number, should present a reasonable contrast in texture and should have sharp dishes offset by bland ones. The oiliness of such fish as sardines, anchovies, and herrings needs a sharp accompaniment. Fruit has come to play a much bigger part in the selection of hors-d'œuvre than was once the case, and a wide variety of vegetables is now included. With experience the selection becomes a simple matter.

The most usual way of serving hors-d'œuvre is of course to put a selection of them in small dishes, assembled together on one large dish or tray, but some of the choicer of them may be arranged with more imagination. For instance, a melon hors-d'œuvre may be served in the scooped-out half of a small melon, or a salad of finely shredded cabbage, apple, and celery looks well served in a hollowed-out heart of a good firm cabbage. In serving just as with choosing and preparing hors-d'œuvre there is scope for imagination. One point should be made and emphasized: there is nearly always a certain amount left over from an hors-d'œuvre course, and some of these dishes will keep perfectly well for a few days, while others, particularly those containing potato and other vegetables, will in hot weather be inclined to ferment. The early stages of fermentation are not entirely easy to detect, and care should therefore be taken that hors-d'œuvre are served fresh.

MIXED HORS-D'ŒUVRE

Although a selection of recipes follow it should be remembered that there is an infinite variety of ways in which these may be presented. The bland or sharp quality of a dish may be controlled by the dressing chosen and varied greatly by flavourings. French dressing may be softened by the addition of cream or mayonnaise and well flavoured with French and English mustard. The yolk of an egg is an excellent addition and holds oil and vinegar in an emulsified condition.

In addition to the dishes made in the kitchen it is customary to serve such items as filleted anchovies, sardines, smoked herrings and so forth. One may of course use fillets of home-soused herring, and a recipe for good herring salad is given.

MARINADED ONIONS

Take large mild onions and slice thinly. Make a brine with a tablespoon of salt to a generous gill of water. Soak the onion rings in this for an hour or so, then drain well. Soak for another hour in a mixture of vinegar and cider or, if you prefer it, vinegar only, then drain the onions and chill well. Arrange on a dish, sprinkle with freshly grated pepper. These are a good accompaniment to a fish hors-d'œuvre.

SWEDISH CUCUMBER

Peel a cucumber and slice thinly. Salt well and leave for half an hour; drain and cover with a French dressing, sprinkle with dill seeds or freshly chopped dill.

MASHED POTATO SALAD
to be served hot or cold

Boil some potatoes and mash in the proper way, through a fine wire sieve on to a cloth, beat up with cream and vinegar. mix in chopped chives or the green top of an onion, some capers or gherkin. Chopped or sieved cooked beetroot may be added to the potato.

MARINADED MUSHROOMS

Peel and trim 1 lb. small mushrooms, simmer 5 minutes in just enough salted water to cover, add the juice of a lemon. Cook together for 5 minutes 1 cup vinegar, $\frac{1}{2}$ clove of crushed garlic, 1 bay-leaf, thyme, a pinch of salt, a pinch of ground pepper, and 2 shallots, sliced finely. Cool, remove the garlic, add 3 or 4 tablespoons olive oil and 1 tablespoon tomato ketchup. Drain the mushrooms, marinade in the above mixture, and keep in the ice-box for several hours. Arrange in a dish and sprinkle with chopped chervil, strain a little of the dressing over them.

STUFFED BRUSSELS SPROUTS

Choose large firm sprouts and cook them very gently without allowing them to break. Scoop out the centres, put in a few drops of French dressing, fill with the following mixture: a little well-seasoned mashed hard-boiled egg, pounded, chopped chives, and chopped pickles, bound together with a little cream or good sauce. The sprouts may be served cold, or dipped in batter and fried.

TOMATO AND ORANGE SALAD

Take the smallest possible tomatoes, peel and quarter, season, and use with an equal quantity of orange quarters from which skin and pith have been removed, i.e. use the flesh only.   Serve with a delicate dressing and with brown bread and butter.

CURRIED POTATO SALAD

Take small new potatoes, boil, and while hot dress with a good French dressing, allow to cool, and cover with a light mayonnaise or cream dressing, well flavoured with curry.

BEETROOT

Beetroot as an hors-d'œuvre is sometimes served in a very harsh way, that is to say cut into cubes and served with a sharp dressing.   The delicate and melting beetroot salad mentioned on page 344 is suitable, and even more so are the whole small filled beetroots given on page 345.

SOUSED HERRING SALAD

Souse the herrings in the way described on page 513.   Lift off and arrange fillets in a dish; place round them chopped salted cucumber and a little grated onion.   Sprinkle with chopped dill or fennel.

SPRING ONION AND SWEET CORN SALAD

Take sweet corn, well flavoured with lemon juice and seasoned with salt and pepper.   Add cream and finely chopped spring onion.   Garnish the dish with spring onions and slices of pimento.

COLE-SLAW

Very finely shredded heart of cabbage as given in the recipe on page 340 (Cole-Slaw Salad) is dressed with cream dressing and may well be served in a scooped-out heart of cabbage.   Suitable additions to it are shredded or sliced dessert apple, celery or celeriac, nuts, and orange.   The dressing should be plentiful and the cabbage really shaved rather than shredded.

Aubergines Robert as given on page 28 is another good hors-d'œuvre, and some of the salads in the salad chapter may be adapted.

FRUIT HORS-D'ŒUVRE

Hors-d'œuvre of fresh fruits are among the most delicious, and are generally so good that one serves them as a first course alone rather than among a selection of mixed items; and it is in the next section of this chapter that detailed reference to them will be found. Nevertheless a dish of celery and orange or celery and shredded pineapple may suitably find its place in mixed hors-d'œuvre, as may apple, nut, and celery and sliced ripe pears and orange.

SOME DISHES OF THE HORS-D'ŒUVRE TYPE

SUITABLE FOR SERVING AS THE SINGLE DISH FOR A FIRST COURSE OF A LUNCHEON OR A DINNER

I suppose the most popular of first dishes in restaurants might be considered to be caviare, smoked salmon, and smoked trout, and although they are accepted luxuries and probably more often eaten out than at home, it is as well to know how to serve them.

CAVIARE

There are two principal kinds of caviare, the black or grey and the red. The former is more widely known in this country and is by far the more expensive; it should be eaten well chilled with hot toast, fresh butter, and quarters of lemon. It is often served in a deep dish of crushed ice; the fresh toast is handed separately, and sometimes a small dish of finely chopped onion and roughly ground black pepper. The red caviare, the flavour of which does not compare with that of the black, is naturally the less expensive, and it is well suited to the making of cocktail savouries. It may be served on rounds of toast or in small pastry boats. Properly, of course, caviare should be served with blinis, small buckwheat pancakes made with yeast.

Blinis

between ¼ and ½ oz. yeast	2 small eggs or 1 large
½ teaspoon sugar	1 oz. butter
½ lb. buckwheat flour	level teaspoon salt
a warm mixture of milk and water	milk or milk and water
½ lb. white flour	

Cream yeast and sugar together. Add to the buckwheat with enough milk and water to make a thick cream. Put to rise in a warm place for 20 minutes. Meanwhile make a thick batter with the white flour, egg yolks, melted butter, salt, and milk. Combine the two mixtures, and allow to rise in room temperature for 2 hours. Whip whites to a firm snow and fold into the mixture. Heat small pancake or omelet pan, drop in a nut of butter, add a good spoonful of the mixture. Cook as for pancakes. Spread with butter and/or sour cream and stack one on top of the other. Serve hot with caviare.

Smoked salmon. I once knew a young cook who, owing to the war, had not met with smoked salmon. She boiled it, with horrible results.

Smoked salmon is bought ready sliced from a good delicatessen store or fishmonger. It should be moist because dryness may indicate saltiness; allow about 1½–2 oz. per person according to how lavish you wish to be. The very thin slices are served directly on individual plates and accompanied by quartered lemon and brown bread and butter.

Smoked eel is extremely good, although rather rich, and it should not be eaten in large quantities. It may be bought from a good delicatessen shop, and it is prepared by skinning and detaching the fillets. It is served with quarters of lemon or, in some cases, with a sharp vinaigrette sauce, and brown bread and butter should accompany it.

Smoked cod's roe is becoming more popular, as indeed is smoked eel. It is served just as it comes from the delicatessen shop, the halves being slit lengthways and cut across into two or three pieces. It should be served on individual plates, one or two pieces per person being laid on a crisp lettuce leaf. It may be accompanied by quarters of lemon and fresh toast or brown bread and butter. Cod's roe can also be bought in small jars; in this form it is less wasteful for use as savouries and sandwiches.

Gulls' eggs are an admirable and popular first course for luncheon; they may be served in a strawberry punnet lined with moss or in a nest made of moss. They are bought from the fishmonger already boiled and should be served with powdered rock-salt, mixed with paprika, and brown bread and butter. Allow as a minimum two per person.

Smoked trout is also bought ready prepared and is good served with quarters of lemon or a delicate horse-radish sauce, well seasoned with mustard, salt, pepper, and lemon juice, piled up in a scooped-out cup of cucumber. To serve it is usual to remove the head of the trout, peel off the skin, and gently lift out the backbone. Serve with brown bread and butter.

Dublin Bay prawns are another popular course. These are usually bought ready cooked. Allow five or six per person, according to size, and slit down the underside with scissors to loosen the shells, so making them easier to handle at table. Heap them in a large dish and serve with a good sharp sauce. Alabama sauce is excellent for this. Serve also quarters of lemon and brown bread and butter.

The following two pâtés are good and suitable for serving as a first course:

CHICKEN LIVER PÂTÉ

1 medium-sized onion	parsley, bay-leaf, and a few sprigs
1 clove of garlic	of thyme or savory
3 oz. butter	seasoning
8 oz. chickens' livers	a dessertspoon brandy

Chop the onion, crush the garlic, and soften in 1 oz. of the butter, add the chickens' livers and sauter for 2 or 3 minutes. Sprinkle with the chopped herbs and seasoning, cook again for about a minute, cool, chop, and then pound well. Stir in the remaining butter melted and a dessert-spoon of brandy. Pack into a mould, chill, then turn out and serve with fresh toast, and butter separately.

LIVER PÂTÉ

¾ lb. liver
¼ lb. fat bacon
1 clove of garlic

5 fillets of anchovy or 1 teaspoon anchovy essence
3–4 thin rashers of streaky bacon
a good pinch of salt.

Béchamel sauce

1 slice of onion
1–2 blades of mace
1 bay-leaf
3–4 peppercorns

½ pint milk
1 oz. butter
¾ oz. flour
seasoning

Infuse the onion, spices, and bay-leaf in the milk until it is well flavoured. Make a roux of the butter and flour. Add the strained milk, and stir over a moderate fire until boiling. Season well and turn into a bowl to cool.

Mince the liver and bacon twice, pound the anchovies, garlic, and salt, add to the liver with the sauce, beat well, adjusting the seasoning. Line a terrine or bowl with the bacon rashers, fill with the mixture and set in a tin of hot water, cover with buttered paper and bake in a slow oven for 40–50 minutes. Press lightly and allow to cool. Serve when completely cold with hot toast and fresh butter. Run a little clarified butter over the top if not for immediate use.

GOOSE PÂTÉ

See Winkfield chapter, page 977.

SOME FIRST COURSES OF VEGETABLES

STUFFED RED PIMENTOS

These pimentos are bought in tins and have a delicate flavour. Take some well-boiled cold rice, mix with a spoonful or so of thick cream, finely chopped chives, and capers. Season with lemon juice, black pepper, and salt. Satisfy yourself that the rice itself is sufficiently piquant and well flavoured, then fill the pimentos. Serve with French dressing mixed with a little cream and chill well.

MUSHROOMS IN ROLLS

Take either light French rolls or the starchless Energen rolls. Cut a slice off the top, hollow out, brush inside with flavoured butter, and put in the oven till crisp. Fill with mushroom filling:

1 clove of garlic crushed with a little salt	1½ gills cream
1 good oz. butter	1 tablespoon finely chopped parsley
1 lb. mushrooms, peeled, washed, and chopped	seasoning
1 dessertspoon flour	lemon juice

Melt the butter, stir in the garlic, add the mushrooms, and cook gently. Stir in the flour and cook for a few minutes, then add the cream, parsley, seasoning, and lemon juice.

FILLED ROLLS

Take light French rolls or starchless Energen rolls as before. Cut a slice off the top, hollow French rolls completely, Energen rolls slightly. Brush inside and out with flavoured butter and put in a hot oven till crisp. Fill with sautéd mushrooms well seasoned, with a squeeze of lemon juice added, or with a whole cooked tomato, sprinkled with a little onion juice, pepper, and salt.

STUFFED TOMATOES (1) (TOMATES FARCIES PROVENÇALES)

Allow 1 tomato for each person.

Filling (for 4 tomatoes)

1 oz. butter	4 fillets of anchovy soaked in milk
1 onion, finely chopped	a level teaspoon each of chopped parsley, tarragon, and marjoram
1 clove of garlic, crushed	
½ cup breadcrumbs	
salt and freshly ground pepper	

Cut the tops off the tomatoes and put them aside. Scoop the insides of the tomatoes into a basin. Make the butter hot in a frying-pan and cook the chopped onion and garlic over gentle heat until quite soft, but do not let them colour. The cooking should take about 15 minutes. Add the scooped-out flesh of the tomatoes and cook until quite soft. Add the breadcrumbs, season well, mash the anchovy fillets with a fork and stir them into the mixture together with the herbs. Fill the tomatoes and put on their tops. Put them into a moderate oven for 20–30 minutes and serve hot.

STUFFED TOMATOES (2)

Fillings for tomatoes are numerous—far too many to give in detail here.

Pineapple, apple, shredded ham, shredded chicken, cheese, olives, or whatever you may have or like may be mixed together, bound with a suitable sauce, and used as a filling. Only be sure that everything is really well seasoned and fairly sharp, or the dish will be dull.

Filling I

Slice the tops off the tomatoes, scoop out seeds, and drain. Fill with a mixture of finely chopped cucumber, chopped celery, walnuts, and a little pickled onion. Toss the filling in either a French or cream dressing to which you have added a drop of Worcestershire sauce.

Filling II

Make a mixture with some finely chopped fresh or tinned pineapple, finely chopped celery, and chopped cocktail onion or gherkin. Add a little rice, a little whipped cream, and enough cream dressing or mayonnaise to sharpen.

Filling III

Finely diced cucumber, chopped mint, and French dressing.

Filling IV

Diced potato, bound with mayonnaise and flavoured with horse-radish.

MARINADED MUSHROOMS

Cut mushrooms in quarters and sauter quickly in butter. Add $\frac{1}{2}$ gill burgundy or claret with salt and freshly ground pepper. Cook rapidly until completely reduced. Marinade in a vinaigrette dressing for a few hours before serving.

AUBERGINES (AUBERGINES ROBERT)

Slice the aubergines thinly, soak for an hour or two in olive oil, then grill them. Lay them in a dish, sprinkle well with chopped chives and a good French dressing, put in the oven for a minute, take them out, allow to get cold, and chill thoroughly.

See also Aubergines Caviar in Winkfield chapter, page 978.

FRUIT FIRST COURSES

Besides the ubiquitous grape-fruit with a glacé cherry in the middle there are many fruits suitable as hors-d'œuvre. If grape-fruit is to be served it should be well and truly prepared, and the sections should be cut in the way described on page 46. It may be served plain or with a little kirsch and sugar, or you may use the skin-free sections with orange or pineapple to make a coupe. If you wish to be particularly elegant and they are in season, you may take those tiny oranges called cumquats, chop them, skin and all, and mix them with the grape-fruit sections. Ripe plums, ripe dessert pears, peaches, or nectarines, peeled and dressed with one of the dressings given below (under Melon 1 and Melon 2) or the delicate dressing for fresh fruit given on page 369—all are excellent. Ripe pomegranates make one of the nicest hors-d'œuvre. The seeds of the pomegranate must be carefully extracted from the skin and every fraction of the yellow bitter membrane taken away. A well-seasoned, well-flavoured French dressing, softened with a little cream, may be poured over the fruit and the whole chilled.

But the thought of fruit hors-d'œuvre takes me back in memory to the refreshment of eye and palate provided by those at the Embassy Club. Not only were they prepared by an artist, but they were arranged by one of real imagination, so when, in 1934, Herbert Jenkins Ltd published *150 Hors-d'œuvre Recipes*, by 'Pin' Baglioni, many people were delighted to be let into Mr Baglioni's secrets.

Remembering this, when I got to this chapter I wrote to find out if the book was still in print. Alas! It is not, so one's only hope of having all the recipes is to search among the books of second-hand dealers or to advertise. I then wrote to Mr Baglioni himself and obtained leave to publish some of his recipes. Among the six chosen there is a preponderance of those made with fruit, because among so many first-rate hors-d'œuvre these were memorably good.

The following six recipes are from *150 Hors d'œuvre Recipes*, by 'Pin' Baglioni, published by Herbert Jenkins Ltd.

MELON ('PIN' SPECIAL) (1)

Cut a honey-dew melon in basket shape. This is easily performed by cutting each side right across to about half an inch from centre. Make two perpendicular cuts downwards to meet previous incisions—this forms the handle of basket. Extract all pips and scoop out flesh. Cut same in inch squares and soak in vinegar for 15 minutes.

Make a dressing: 1 dessertspoonful curry-powder, 2 tablespoonfuls vinegar, the juice of half a lemon. Mix well together.

Squeeze this preparation through a muslin into a cupful of slightly whipped cream and add sugar to taste.

Place melon in basket after draining vinegar and pour dressing over.

(If one finds the making of the basket too difficult use an ordinary dish or glass bowl.)

MELON ('PIN' SPECIAL) (2)

Cut cantaloup melon in half, extract pips and scoop out flesh, dice and replace in melon.

Make a sauce: 1 dessertspoonful curry-powder, 1 teaspoonful ginger, 1 small glass of port, 1 dessertspoonful kirsch. Stir well and pass through muslin. Add 4 tablespoonfuls whipped cream, 1 tablespoonful apricot purée, sugar to taste; mix well and pour over melon.

POMEGRANATE ('PIN' SPECIAL)

Cut a slice off stalk end, extract all pips and separate them.   Mix them with 2 diced gherkins.

Make a dressing: 2 yolks of hard-boiled eggs crushed with knife blade, 1 dessertspoonful red-currant jelly, 2 teaspoonfuls French mustard, 3 tablespoonfuls vinegar, a suspicion of Worcestershire sauce.   Stir well and mix dressing with first preparation.

Fill pomegranate with mixture.

HAM AND PINEAPPLE ('PIN' SPECIAL)

Shred: 2 slices of York ham, 2 pickled walnuts, 1 slice of pineapple. Mix well together.

Make a dressing: 2 tablespoonfuls whipped cream, 1 dessertspoonful tomato ketchup, the squeeze of quarter of a lemon.

Season with cayenne pepper, stir well and mix with salad.

Place in dish over crisp Romaine salad leaves.   Serve very cold.

GRAPE-FRUIT ('PIN' SPECIAL)

Cut grape-fruit in basket shape.   Extract interior and squeeze out all its juice, use same mixed with 1 dessertspoonful fresh cream, add sugar to taste.

Take some tinned sweet corn, add equal quantity of chopped celery and apple (enough of the three to fill grape-fruit).

Mix this well with the prepared grape-fruit juice and cream and fill basket.

VEGETABLE SALAD ('PIN' SPECIAL)

Take 4 peeled raw tomatoes cut in quarters and 2 peeled oranges cut in sections, add 2 sliced pickled walnuts, season with salt and pepper.

Make a dressing: 2 tablespoonfuls walnut juice, add 1 dessertspoonful olive oil, 1 teaspoonful French mustard.   Stir well and mix with salad.

FIRST COURSES FOR A SUMMER DINNER

Melon prepared in a variety of ways makes one of the most popular first courses, and the two recipes of Mr Baglioni mentioned above are admirable.

It has long been a fashion to hand powdered ginger with melon, but I would say that if you choose to eat ginger with your melon, do be careful that every bit of it is well moistened before you put the melon into your mouth.   People have had embarrassing choking attacks through a speck of dry ginger catching in the throat.   Quarters of lemon are a pleasant accompaniment to a well-chilled melon.   There are, however, more exciting ways of dealing with this fruit as a first course than this.   In particular, if you are fortunate enough to have small hothouse melons, allow half for each person, and serve with quartered limes.   Hand sugar and a pepper-mill: freshly ground black pepper brings out the flavour of the melon just as it does with strawberries.   Larger melons may be treated in a variety of ways: the cubes may be served in some cases in the shell of the melon itself, and in others in glass cups, or they may be handed in a glass dish with suitably flavoured cream dressings.   As well as those given by Mr Baglioni we like one in which the flavour of fresh tarragon predominates.

Thick slices of honey-dew melon, with the centre cut out, may be the receptacle for a mint ice, which is one of the nicest courses for a hot night. The recipe for Mint Ice is given on page 983, and you may serve with this also, if you like, a half-slice of lime, sprinkling the juice over the circle of melon.

Another recipe.   Cut a melon in half, removing the seeds, scoop out the flesh, and either cut it in dice or use a ball cutter.   Put the pieces of melon into a bowl, add delicate fresh fruits such as raspberries, strawberries, peaches, or nectarines cut up into suitable pieces.   Dress with sugar and a liqueur, Cointreau or sherry and a dash of maraschino.   Chill this mixture well, and replace it in the half of the melon.   Equally well, you may cut up your melon, dress it with a plain French dressing, and serve it with brown bread and butter.   Melon and orange salad is excellent treated in the same way.   When the small, inexpensive pineapples begin to come into the market, there is an excellent starting course to be made with these.   Allow one small pineapple for every two people, cut in two, and scoop out the flesh, removing the hard and pithy centre.   Mix the flesh with a little orange or any other fruit—raspberries, sliced strawberries, or whatever you may have at hand.   Return to the halves of pineapple, which have been trimmed so that they will stand.   Dress with either a delicate cream or a French dressing and a little lemon juice.

Into our summer markets now come, more plentifully, avocado pears—delicious things if properly dressed.   In the countries where they grow I believe the ripe flesh is of so nutty and delicious a flavour that only a sprinkling of salt and perhaps a touch of fresh lime is called for.   In this country they seem to need a more decisive accompaniment, and perhaps the simplest and nicest way of serving them is to cut them in two without removing the peel and lifting out the central nut and filling the hollow with a sharp French dressing.   Brown bread and butter may accompany them. The pears should be served ice-cold.   Another method is to scoop out the flesh, crush it, then dress it with a salad-dressing and replace it in the pear. Some people like these pears dressed with rum and powdered sugar. Allow half a pear for each person unless the fruit is very small.   Some books suggest mayonnaise as a dressing, but the smooth texture, with that of the pear, can be unpleasing.

In the Winkfield chapter will be found a good first course of melon, cucumber, tomatoes, and avocado pears (page 981) and another of fresh pears and cream cheese (page 982).

SHELL-FISH

A recipe for potting shrimps at home is given on page 503. These may be served with fresh hot toast, with butter served separately, and freshly ground pepper.

In place of potted shrimps one may use nowadays the Norwegian frozen prawns which have been introduced into this country. They are excellent. A pound packet for ten shillings was bought as an experiment and found to be extremely sweet, and smelling of the sea, and these were potted and made enough to serve between sixteen and twenty people at a party. The prawns, already cooked, merely need to be heated through in butter which is seasoned with a pinch of paprika, ground mace, and a little freshly ground black pepper. They are then packed into jars and a little butter added to that in the pan, which is poured over them to seal them off. These are admirable for fillings for bouchées or as a first course with fresh toast.

SHELL-FISH COCKTAIL (1)

Break up the meat of prawns, crabs, or lobsters. Prepare a good French dressing well seasoned with English and French mustard, and well-crushed garlic. Put the flaked fish to marinade in this for an hour or so, then drain the fish and mix it lightly in the following sauce: a teacup of cream dressing or mayonnaise, mixed with a tablespoon of A1 or other piquante sauce or tomato ketchup, and a good tablespoon of grated horse-radish. Finally, fold in a cup of chopped celery, and serve in glasses or on glass plates, garnished with watercress, and accompanied by hot fresh rolls or brown bread and butter.

A RATHER RICH SHELL-FISH COCKTAIL (2)

To 3–4 tablespoons mayonnaise or cream dressing add 2 tablespoons good tomato ketchup and a dash of Worcestershire sauce. Season well with salt and pepper, then add cream to taste and a dash of lemon juice. When you are satisfied with the seasoning and sharpness of your sauce, put it to chill while you prepare the fish. Flake up lobster meat, crab, or Dublin Bay prawns, fold these into the cream mixture and put into glasses. Serve with brown bread and butter and quarters of lemon.

For other dishes suitable for first courses see pages 975–84.

AFTER-DINNER SAVOURIES

This course, which used inevitably to follow the sweet course in my young days, sometimes now takes the place of this, particularly for those whose taste lies in a savoury direction.

The savouries should be fresh, very hot, if to be hot, and well seasoned. Many after-dinner savouries resemble cocktail savouries and sometimes they resemble hors-d'œuvre, but they are more substantial in size. Sardines on toast, toasted cheese, cheese-straws, angels on horseback, devils on horseback, were, and still are, popular, though they more often find their place in an English menu than a French one.

SOFT ROES ON TOAST

Work together ½ teaspoon English mustard, a saltspoon of salt, and a large knob of butter.   Melt this, lay in it the soft herring roes, and cook gently for 5–10 minutes, according to size.   Have ready hot buttered toast, and when the roes are ready lay them on this and serve piping hot.

DEVILLED SOFT ROES

1–1½ oz. butter	salt, pepper, cayenne
½ lb. soft roes lightly rolled in a little seasoned flour	lemon juice hot buttered toast

Heat pan, drop in butter, and when this foams put in floured roes. Dust with a little of the seasoning.   When brown on one side turn and brown on the other, sprinkling again with seasoning.   Squeeze lemon juice over the roes; arrange on toast and serve at once.

HERRINGS ON TOAST

Clean, bone, and fillet the herrings.   Butter a frying-pan, lay in the fillets, cover with buttered paper, and cook gently.   Toast slices of bread, remove the crust, spread with butter with which is mixed a little mustard and pepper.   Lay the fillets on top of the toast and sprinkle with freshly ground pepper.   Serve very hot.

SARDINES ON TOAST

Instead of the usual sardines on toast, try the following:

Make the toast, cut in suitable pieces.   Make a paste as follows: Skin and bone 6–8 sardines, add a teaspoon of scraped onion, a teaspoon of French mustard, 3 teaspoons butter, a teaspoon of vinegar, and a pinch of salt.   Spread this mixture on the toast, then lay a boned and skinned whole sardine on top of it.   Finish off under the grill, and add a sprinkling of finely chopped fennel and some freshly ground black pepper.

FINNAN-HADDOCK

Flaked finnan-haddock, mixed with a little butter or cream, highly seasoned, put on buttered toast, and finished off in the same way as the sardines is excellent.

Or it may be pounded, very well seasoned, bound together with butter and a beaten egg, shaped into tiny cakes, rolled in egg and breadcrumbs, and fried in deep fat.   A good accompaniment to these is fried parsley. Aberdeen smokies are a greater delicacy than the ordinary finnan-haddock, and these should be flaked, mixed with butter, seasoned with black pepper, and served on hot buttered toast, with a knob of butter put on top at the last minute.

CHEESE SAVOURIES

Some of the best of these are made with Camembert. On a hot night iced Camembert, served on a bed of crushed ice and accompanied by water-biscuits which have been heated up in the oven, is delicious; but even better perhaps are pieces of Camembert, taken not too ripe, sieved, mixed with butter, reshaped, dipped in egg and breadcrumbs, and fried in deep fat.

These Camembert Croquettes are one of the best of all savouries:

CAMEMBERT CROQUETTES

1 medium ripe Camembert	1 egg yolk
1½ oz. butter	beaten egg, dry white crumbs
1½ oz. flour	and deep fat for frying
½ pint milk	grated Parmesan cheese
salt, pepper, cayenne or dash	
of tabasco sauce	

Scrape rind from the cheese; press through a wire sieve. Melt butter, add flour, then milk; stir until boiling, season well, and allow to cool. Work in the Camembert and lastly the yolk. Turn on to a plate and when absolutely cold shape into pieces the size of a walnut on a floured board. Dip into or brush with beaten egg and roll in the crumbs. Fry in deep fat until golden brown. Serve very hot, dusted with grated Parmesan cheese.

CAMEMBERT EN SURPRISE (ICED CAMEMBERT)

1 medium ripe Camembert	grated Parmesan cheese
3 oz. creamed butter	salt, pepper, and cayenne
2 tablespoons dry white bread-	paprika
crumbs	watercress, etc., for garnish
½ gill (or ¾ wineglass) dry	pretzels or small salted water-
white wine	biscuits
1–2 tablespoons cream	

Scrape most of the rind from the cheese and press through a sieve. Work into the butter, adding the wine by degrees, and the crumbs. Moisten with enough cream to make the mixture the consistency of a cake batter. Season highly. Turn into a lightly oiled mould, or flan ring, smooth the top, and chill in a refrigerator or on ice till firm. Turn out and coat all over with the Parmesan cheese, mixed with a little paprika. Mark the top with the back of a knife.

Set on a serving plate and surround with the biscuits. Garnish with 'bouquets' of watercress and, if liked, radishes cut into rosettes and black olives.

This can be made into quite a decorative dish for a lunch.

LADY MACDONALD'S CHEESE BISCUITS

3 oz. grated cheese	pepper
½ oz. butter	yolks of 2 eggs
1 tablespoon cream	

Mix the above together. Stir over a gentle heat until it thickens. Have ready plain ice wafer biscuits crisped in the oven. Put a layer of the cheese mixture between them and serve at once.

TOASTED CHEESE

4 oz. grated cheese	beer or cider
½ oz. butter	

Mix to a paste, season well with made mustard and freshly ground pepper. Spread on to buttered toast and grill to a golden brown.

HAM CORNUCOPIAS

Roll strips of good short crust round small cornet moulds, brush lightly with beaten egg, and bake to a golden brown in a hot oven. When cool fill with creamed ham, well seasoned, and sprinkle the top with chopped truffle.

HOT CHICKEN CROÛTES

1 gill good béchamel sauce	lemon juice
1 teaspoon curry-paste	fried bread
3 tablespoons cold chicken, diced	1 tablespoon grated Parmesan and gruyère cheese
3 tablespoons cold ham or tongue, diced	1 tablespoon butter
salt, pepper, and cayenne	fried parsley to garnish

Make the béchamel sauce (see page 155), add the curry-paste, and mix in the diced chicken and ham or tongue. Season with salt, pepper, a spot of cayenne, and a squeeze of lemon juice. Heap the mixture on small rounds of fried bread, put another round of fried bread on top, and spread over the cheese and butter, worked together to a paste. Brown quickly under a hot grill and serve hot, garnished with a heap of fried parsley.

DEVILS ON HORSEBACK

12 large prunes or French plums
½ bay-leaf
water or red wine to cover
stuffings of:
    (a) a fillet of anchovy curled round an almond, or
    (b) chopped mango chutney, or
    (c) an olive stoned and stuffed with pimento
½ thin rasher of bacon for each prune
buttered toast
watercress

Pour boiling water or hot red wine over prunes; leave half an hour. Simmer in same liquid with half a bay-leaf till tender. If wine is used allow it to be absorbed by the prunes until it has practically disappeared. Cool prunes and stone. Fill with any one of the fillings given.

Flatten each half-rasher on a board and wrap round a prune. Set on a tin, bake in a hot oven 7–10 minutes. Set each on a piece of hot buttered toast. Arrange a bunch of watercress in the centre of the dish.

ANGELS ON HORSEBACK

These are oysters rolled in bacon, fastened with a skewer, and either grilled or baked in a quick oven 5–6 minutes. Two rolls may be allowed per person and they are served on hot buttered toast.

The following recipe is substantial for an after-dinner savoury. It may be increased, by the addition of kidney, to a luncheon dish, and it is an economical way of using kidneys.

PRUNE AND DATE KEBABS

good prunes	dessert apple
dates	bay-leaves
walnuts or almonds	butter
chutney	stale bread
thin rashers of streaky bacon	watercress

Steam or poach the prunes, then stone them. Stone the dates. Brown nuts and chop coarsely, then mix with chutney. Fill into the fruit and wrap each one in a thin piece of streaky bacon.

Arrange on skewers with slices of apple and pieces of bay-leaf in between. Brush with melted butter.

Meanwhile grate or shred coarsely some stale bread, dry lightly in the oven, then fry in butter until crisp. Now grill the kebabs, pile on a hot dish with the crumbs, and garnish with watercress.

KROMESKI

These are a creamy mixture of diced cooked meat, ham, chicken, mushrooms, oysters, and hard-boiled egg, bound with a well-seasoned béchamel sauce and egg yolk. A little chutney or chopped herbs may be added to make them more piquant.

A teaspoon of the mixture is enclosed in a rasher (or half-rasher) of bacon, rolled up, dipped in fritter batter, and fried at once in deep fat.

III

Kitchen Knowledge

IT is sometimes assumed that a woman, by virtue of her sex, will know instinctively the meaning of technical terms in cookery, as though a girl child should have trailed along with her cloud of glory an embryonic knowledge of cooking.

Instructions such as make a purée, clarify the fat, reduce the gravy, make a roux, blanch this, glaze that, are not always amplified and to the novice in the kitchen can be puzzling.

If as a child you were allowed in the kitchen you probably imbibed some useful first-hand knowledge. What time you sieved the breadcrumbs, or turned the ice machine, you were no doubt registering a good deal of all that went on around you. The penetrating observation of an intelligent child seems to be acceptable to the cagiest of cooks, even to those who regard with suspicion innocent questions from adults. You perhaps were fortunate and free to learn as much as you liked or could, so that it is probably said now that, to you, cooking comes naturally.

Many of the present generation have missed such early experience, and it is for those who suffered this deprivation that the following notes have been compiled.

If one is possessed of certain basic information the use of recipe books is simplified and causes of failure more readily identified. It is hoped, therefore, that no apology is called for by reason of the elementary nature and detail of the information offered. The notes are divided in two portions; the first half concerns everyday processes and the second is devoted to necessary but less commonplace kitchen operations.

BREADCRUMBS

A jar each of dried white and of browned breadcrumbs should be kept in every kitchen. Dried white crumbs should be used for coating for frying. Browned breadcrumbs are for covering the surface of ham, for frying and serving with game (they have a good nutty taste), and for gratinés.

Fresh white crumbs are used for panades, for fish, meat, and vegetable creams, for stuffings and bread sauce, and for certain sweets and cakes. They will not keep as they soon become mouldy.

37

Fresh white breadcrumbs are prepared from stale bread: it must be at least a day old.   The crust is cut off and the remainder rubbed through a wire sieve with the palm of the hand.

Dried white breadcrumbs are made by slow and thorough drying of fresh crumbs.   This may be done in a slow oven provided they are not allowed to colour.   A better way is to set them in a warm place, say on the rack over a stove, cover them with a piece of kitchen paper, and leave them there, even for a day or so, until completely dry.   They will keep for some weeks stored in a screw-top jar.

Browned breadcrumbs should be prepared by drying and browning crusts of bread in the oven.   These are then put through a cheese-grater or crushed with a rolling-pin; the crumbs are then sifted through a sieve and stored in a jar.

Egging and crumbing.   This is done with dried white crumbs, fresh ones being too absorbent.   In a shallow dish or soup-plate beat an egg lightly, just until yolk and white are well mixed, season with pepper and salt, and add a little salad-oil and a spoonful of milk.   Have a well-floured board and a piece of clean paper covered with a layer of the crumbs.   Set these three alongside, first flour, then egg, then crumbs.   With the aim of obtaining a dry surface turn whatever is to be coated in the flour on the board.   In the case of croquettes the final shaping is now done.   Fish should be well dried with a cloth and turned on the board, patted and rolled lightly in flour, and then shaken well.   Avoid a thick coating of flour; it should be as thin as possible.   Set whatever you are coating on a clean plate and brush it with the beaten egg, turning it with the aid of a palette-knife so that no part of the surface is missed, and, lifting it on the palette-knife, allowing any surplus egg to drain back on to the egg plate. Transfer it to the crumbs, and by gentle movement of the edges of the paper roll it about sufficiently to cover the entire surface with a thin crust. Avoid touching with the fingers.   Pat the surface gently but firmly with the palette-knife to help the crumbs to adhere.   Renew the supply of crumbs in the paper as required.

If from any cause the egg soaks through the surface of the crumbs it may be necessary to give another light coating.   This is not a good thing as the result may be an over-thick, over-resistant surface.

TO GLAZE WITH BEATEN EGG

Egg-wash is the term given to a mixture of egg and salt used for glazing pastry, bread, and buns when a shiny surface is required.   One egg with $\frac{1}{2}$ teaspoon salt is lightly beaten with a fork.   The salt has the effect of making the egg more liquid, clear, and easy to apply.

EGGS

For notes on eggs see page 285 in egg chapter.

DUXELLES

This is a paste or mince made of mushrooms, or mushroom peelings and stalks.   It is used for flavouring sauces, soups, ragoûts, stuffings, stews and so forth.   One or more handfuls of mushrooms, not necessarily of the best quality (or stalks and peelings only), are washed well, squeezed to dry as much as possible, and finely chopped.   Chopped herbs may be added for flavouring.   A small piece of butter or other fat is melted in a sauté pan, salt and pepper added, and the chopped mushroom cooked till dry. Stirring must be constant to avoid burning.   The duxelles is then turned into a small jar, pressed down, covered, and kept in a cool place until wanted.

MIREPOIX

This is a mixture of vegetables, cut in dice and used either as a basis or a *fond* for a braise, or cut slightly smaller (about $\frac{1}{8}$ inch) and used as a garnish for cutlets or for a fish dish (see Filets de Sole Sylvette in fish chapter on page 481).   It should consist of such vegetables as onions, carrots, parsnips, leeks, peas, Brussels sprouts, etc., which must be arranged so that no one flavour predominates.   The mixture of vegetables is put into the braising-pan, as indicated in the recipe.   If the mirepoix is to be served as a garnish, the mixture is put into a sauce or stew-pan with a little melted butter.   Seasoning is added, the pan covered, and the mixture cooked on a slow heat for 5–6 minutes.   One to two tomatoes, skinned, pipped, and chopped, are then put in, a piece of buttered paper pressed down on the vegetables, the pan tightly covered, and the whole put into a moderate oven for 20–30 minutes, or until the vegetables are tender.

BRUNOISE

This is also a mirepoix, but consists of very finely diced vegetables, usually carrots, shallots, beans, and turnips, rissoléd gently in a nut of butter.   Used mostly as a soup garnish.

JULIENNE

Julienne is a term usually applied to vegetables cut into small, narrow strips about $\frac{1}{8}$ inch wide and 2 inches long.   They are used as a garnish for a clear soup, or for an entrée.   A julienne of vegetables consists of carrot, turnip, leek, and celery.   It is cooked in much the same way as a brunoise, i.e. rissoléd in a nut of butter until just beginning to change colour.   A very small quantity of liquid is then added, and the vegetables are gently simmered until cooked.

FAT

In the first flush of enthusiasm over the possession of a country cottage, a friend, inexperienced in farming, reared and killed a pig, proceeded to cure it (in his London flat), then, finding it so fat as to be inedible, gave it away to his friends; and this at a time when to collect enough fat for deep frying was almost impossible. 'To render down fat' meant nothing to him.

To render down fat. Cut fat in small cubes, remove coarse skin and gristle. Put in a strong iron saucepan, cover, and cook steadily over slow heat. At first when it heats the fat sizzles and makes a noise; when this ceases one must watch that it does not burn. The process should be slow and steady. When the contents of the pan have become a clear liquid remove from fire and pan and press through a strainer lined with muslin. The scraps which remain should have very little substance. The process may also be carried out in an uncovered baking-tin in a slow oven.

To clarify fat (1). Put fat into an iron saucepan and cover with water. (Do not put on a lid, for this reason: the water boils, the fat forms a coating, the steam is trapped, and there may be enough pressure to blow the lid off.) Bring to the boil, allow to simmer a short time. Remove from fire, allow to get cold, lift off solid fat, scrape the underside free of impurities and you have now a solid block of purified fat.

To clarify fat (2). The collection of drippings from baking-pans and from stock and soup skimmings will not keep sweet for long or be suitable for frying until clarified. Put the drippings into a pan with a cup of water. Allow to boil for 20 minutes. Strain off into a basin. The fat will then rise to the top and all impurities will be left below in the water. The fat thus obtained is more suitable for shallow than for deep fat frying, but may at need be added to the deep fat fryer.

To clarify fat (3) (Quick method). Slice a large potato. Put into the fat, bring the fat up to boiling-point, and allow to simmer until it becomes absolutely still. The potato will by now be dark brown. Strain off. Any impurities will have been absorbed by the potato. This also has the effect of removing flavours imparted by strongly flavoured foods.

These processes should be carried out on the top of the stove and not in an oven.

THE BLANCHING OF BACON AND SALT PORK

Bacon is blanched to remove excess of salt and to render it entirely clean before it is added to such dishes as ragoûts or braises; if this is not done the whole is apt to taste too strongly of bacon. Salt pork, which is sometimes used in place of bacon, is always blanched.

The bacon is put into cold water and brought slowly to boiling-point. It is then simmered gently 2–3 minutes according to the degree of saltness, then turned into a strainer and cold water run over it; it is drained well and, if the bacon is to be browned, dried completely.

Lardons, described under larding (see page 69), should be cut in the way described before being blanched and drained.

TO PREPARE BACON FOR FRYING

If bacon is so salt that it must be blanched, it must then be thoroughly dried.   The rinds and rust are first cut off with kitchen scissors and the rashers flattened out with the blade of a knife.

TO SCRAPE BACON FAT

Sometimes a recipe calls for the use of bacon fat in such a fine state that it has to be scraped.   This is done by scraping the surface of the bacon with a short, strong knife until the required amount is obtained.   It is easier to do this from a fair-sized slab of fat bacon than from a slice.

BLANCHING

The process of blanching is applied sometimes to kippers, if these are not of the finest quality, and to sweetbreads and calf's head.

Blanching of Sweetbreads and Calf's Head

This is done with the object of making the flesh firm and clean.   They are covered with cold water which is brought slowly to boiling-point; they are then drained and washed in cold water.

THE CLARIFICATION OF MARGARINE AND BUTTER

Margarine is clarified in order to eliminate moisture.   Salted butter is clarified with the object of eliminating salt.

To clarify margarine.   An ounce and a half of margarine will render approximately 1 oz. when clarified.   It is simpler therefore to clarify say $\frac{1}{2}$ lb. at a time, and to keep it in a jar in a cool place so that the quantity called for in a recipe is immediately available in net weight.

Heat the margarine in a small pan; after a short time the initial sizzling will cease and at this moment care must be taken to avoid burning.   The contents of the pan will now present the appearance of a clear oil.   Strain this through a piece of muslin, allow to cool a little, and pour into a jar.

To clarify butter.   (This process is not applied to fresh, unsalted butter; it is unnecessary and the good fresh taste would be lost.)   Clarified butter, as well as being called for in recipes, is used for sealing off potted shrimps, potted meats, duxelles and so forth.

Melt the butter in a stew-pan and cook gently without allowing it to colour, skimming off all scum and impurity as it rises to the top.   Strain through a strainer, lined with muslin, leave it in a basin to settle, then pour it gently into another basin, leaving the sediment behind.

To soften butter. Warm an earthenware bowl by pouring boiling water into it, emptying it, and drying it well. Avoid heating the bowl by placing it on the stove. This heats the bottom only, and every part of it should be warmed. Put in the butter, cut up in small pieces. Work it with a wooden spatula until it reaches the condition of a cream, smooth, even, and entirely without lumps.

To desalt butter. Put it into a basin and pour boiling water over it. Leave it to become quite cold. The butter rises to the top of the water (which has washed out all the salt), and can be lifted off.

To flavour butter. Soften as directed above, and incorporate the flavouring required by working it into the butter, either in a mortar or by manipulating the mixture with a palette-knife or a fork.

'*Monter au beurre*,' *or to add butter to cooked dishes*. A recipe sometimes requires that butter be added at the last moment to a sauce or a soup. It should in these circumstances be added off the fire, divided into small pieces and well incorporated. No sauce should ever be reboiled after the butter has been added. Such heat reduces the butter to oil, and the good flavour is lost. Therefore the dish in question should be quite ready for serving, and boiling hot, before the butter is added. If it is absolutely necessary to delay before serving, the sauce must be kept hot in such a way that the butter will not oil (for example in a bain-marie).

To improve the taste of tinned or slightly rancid butter. Break the butter into quite small pieces. Put these into fresh cold milk and leave for an hour, then wash in cold salted water.

TO OIL A MOULD

Oiled moulds are essential for certain cold dishes such as set creams, bavaroises, and parfaits, because oil does not set when cold. Tasteless oil is called for. This is applied with a brush as evenly as possible and with especial attention to corners, crevices, and indentations of fancy moulds. The mould should be turned upside-down and left so for a short time in order that any surplus oil may drain away.

CREAM

To whip cream. Pour the cream into a cool basin, whip gently at first, until the cream is light and frothy. Use a wire whisk and whip faster as the cream begins to thicken. Be careful not to over-whip; as soon as the cream is stiff enough to stand in a point, put it aside in a cool place until needed, or use at once.

Crème chantilly. The term chantilly indicates a slightly sweetened whipped cream, flavoured with vanilla. The sugar should be sweetened with real vanilla pod (see paragraph on the use of vanilla, page 44). By reason of the presence of specks of vanilla in the sugar this cream may present a slightly speckled appearance. Sometimes to a rich and thick chantilly whipped white of egg is added, one white to a pint of cream; this has the effect of lightening the cream and may be used when it is to be piled on top of a sweet dish. If the cream is to be piped the egg white should not be used.

To whip evaporated milk. The best method is to boil the tin for 20 minutes, chill it, open, pour out the milk, and whip vigorously. This will be firm enough for folding into creams and soufflés, but if something stiffer is required, add a level teaspoon of gelatine dissolved in a spoonful of water to the milk whilst still warm. Then whip over ice.

To make cream from fat and milk with a machine. This can only be done with an emulsifying machine, through which a mixture of milk and unsalted butter or margarine is forced. Unsalted margarine makes excellent cream for cooking purposes. To make just under half a pint of cream, take 4 oz. unsalted butter or margarine, melt it in a gill of milk. Cool the mixture by pouring it backwards and forwards from the pan to a jug until it is at blood-heat. Pour it into the bowl of the emulsifying machine until the bowl is half full. Pump with quick, hard strokes. The cream will come through into a basin placed underneath the machine. Stir it well with a fork, and leave it in the refrigerator to get quite cold. Stir again before using, as the thicker part of the cream rises to the top.

   For successful cream-making:
   Keep exact proportions, as given above.
   Keep the mixture at an even temperature, i.e. blood-heat or 98° F.
   Pump hard and evenly.
   Stir well before using.

   Cream made with an emulsifying machine is not easy to whip. It can be made of the right consistency by adding to the amount given above a sheet of gelatine or a teaspoon of powdered gelatine, dissolved in a spoonful of water and added to the milk before the butter or margarine is melted. The cream should be allowed to become quite cold, stirred, then whisked as directed above.

To reduce milk. This is done to make the milk richer in quality, and is a process called for in certain sauces and soups where it is used as a substitute for cream. In an uncovered pan the milk is simmered until the required reduction in quantity is reached.

GELATINE

The use of gelatine. So great is the improvement in the type of gelatine now obtainable that a note on this may seem unnecessary; yet some cooks retain an impression of difficulty. The old-fashioned thick sheets of this substance were slow to dissolve and it was possible to burn them during the process. Now, with gelatine in fine powder or extremely thin sheets, one can hardly go wrong.

Only the best kind should be used; cheap, poor gelatine has an unpleasant taste. This substance is generally used in small quantities. It should be thin, transparent, and brittle and be kept in an air-tight tin. Leaf gelatine should be washed in cold water before use, then soaked in a basin of cold water till soft. It is then dissolved in the quantity of liquid called for in the recipe by being placed in a small saucepan and gently warmed (it should not boil). It may then be strained through a fine wire strainer or a piece of muslin.

Powdered or granulated gelatine is soaked in the quantity of cold water or liquid indicated in the recipe and then dissolved over gentle heat. Gelatine is usually added to the substance it is required to set when this is lukewarm, and it is necessary to stir the whole gently until it reaches the point of setting. The following list of equivalent weights may be of use to the novice.

PROPORTIONS OF GELATINE USED FOR THE SETTING OF VARIOUS LIQUIDS

(a) For thin liquids such as fruit juices:

French leaf gelatine:	$1\frac{3}{4}$–2	oz. to set 1 qt liquid.
Powdered gelatine:	2 ,,	,, ,, 1 ,, ,,
Strip gelatine (a coarser variety):	$1\frac{1}{2}$,,	,, ,, 1 ,, ,,

(b) For moulded creams composed of eggs and cream, a smaller proportion, as little as half the above amounts. Reference should be made to individual recipes.

(c) For thick fruit purées: $\frac{1}{2}$ oz. gelatine to the pint.

In hot weather, and without the aid of an ice-box, it may be necessary to increase slightly the above amounts.

Instructions about gelatine vary in their wording in different books, and the following note may be of use:

6 medium sheets of gelatine as now sold, *or*
2 old-fashioned thick sheets, *or*
2 level tablespoons granulated gelatine

all equal 1 oz.

FLAVOURINGS AND SEASONINGS

Proper use and care of a vanilla pod. When buying choose those covered with white crystals, which indicate freshness. Keep in a covered jar containing sugar, which will then become flavoured with vanilla.

To use: a small piece may be cut off, or half a pod may be taken, according to the amount of liquid to be flavoured. Split the pod, scrape out some of the seeds, put both seeds and pod into the liquid, e.g. milk for custards and ice-cream mixtures. When the liquid is well flavoured remove pod, dip in warm water, dry, and return to sugar jar. In this way a pod will last two or three weeks at least.

Vanilla essence. Always buy the very best, which unfortunately is expensive, and use with economy.

SALT

Pure block salt should be used in the kitchen, as 'table' salt contains other substances included specially by the manufacturers to keep it free-running; block salt, therefore, may be more accurately measured and is the purer article. It is bought in bars or blocks of about 3 lb. or more and should be grated or ground down and stored in a covered jar for use as required. It is ground down:

(a) by using a coarse grater on the surface of the block, *or*
(b) by cutting the block in half and rubbing each half against the other.

Rock-salt. This may be bought from a chemist or a French or Italian grocer and consists of salt crystals for use in small wooden salt grinders. 'Freezing' salt, which is obtainable from a fishmonger, is also a rock-salt, but is less refined and is used principally with ice for freezing purposes.

PEPPER

A substitute for pepper, consisting of a mixture of other highly flavoured spices, is now widely sold in place of pepper, owing to the very high cost of peppercorns; but pure ground pepper, white and black, may still be bought. White pepper should be used in white or fine sauces and black for other savoury dishes where a more spicy and robust flavour is called for and where the colour is not so noticeable. White pepper (or white peppercorns) has a more delicate flavour than black. Peppercorns should always be at hand in the kitchen, either for use whole or for grinding in a pepper-mill. Pepper ground from a mill is excellent for many dishes, salad-dressings and so forth, but is not quite fine enough for adding to white or fine sauces, so a pure ground pepper is also necessary. For table use it is best to have ground white pepper in the pot, and a black pepper in the mill.

PAPRIKA

This is a red pepper ground from sweet red peppers or pimentos. It is spicy and only slightly hot. It is best to buy it loose in small quantities from a good store; comparatively large quantities may be used in dishes. The best paprika comes from Hungary.

CAYENNE

Cayenne is ground from red chillis and is very hot. A pinch or a *point* only is called for in a dish and it should be bought in very small quantities.

ALLSPICE (PIMENTO)

This is sometimes called Jamaican pepper. It is a spiced pepper and may be used whole or ground. It is mild and spicy in flavour and is used mainly for pickling and spicing, in pies, ragoûts, devils and so forth.

JUNIPER BERRIES

These are sold dried and may be finely crushed and added to a dish or put into a muslin bag with other spices for infusion. They are used principally for game sautés, marinades, etc.

SALTPETRE

This is nitrate of potash and is used for pickling meat, rendering it a reddish colour.

CLOVES

Cloves are very pungent and aromatic and should be used with care, usually not more than one or two in any dish. They are traditional in this country as a flavouring for apple tart and bread sauces, and in certain cases they may also be included in a bouquet garni. They are bought ground for use in conjunction with other spices in fruit cakes, and they are used also in a wide range of other dishes, such as jugged hare, cream soups, and strawberry jam.

GINGER

This is obtained ground or in root form. Root ginger is used whole, chiefly in pickles and chutneys, though in some curried dishes it may be grated and pounded; a root is sometimes known as a 'race' of ginger.

Ground ginger is widely used, mostly for puddings and cakes. Ginger in syrup and glacé and crystallized ginger are dessert sweetmeats and are used also for flavouring sweet sauces and garnishing cakes.

POT-HERBS

This is an old-fashioned term for mixed vegetables used as flavouring. They consist of onions, carrots, turnips, swedes and so forth. Sometimes in northern towns one may still see them offered for sale by the pound, ready sliced, in small vegetable shops.

THE PREPARATION OF FRUIT AND VEGETABLES

To prepare grape-fruit for breakfast. Cut fruit in half; take a curved saw-edged knife, cut round the outside of the fruit next to the skin and then in between each section. Slip the knife underneath the fruit and cut away the attachment of the core. Lift the core out, pushing the flesh well down. If you have not a saw-edged knife, take a stainless steel knife and cut between the sections and the membrane first, before cutting round, otherwise the knife will slip.

To cut grape-fruit and orange for fruit compôte or salad. This is made easier by a preliminary chilling of the fruit in the ice-box. Use a very sharp knife. Hold the grape-fruit firmly in the left hand with the tips of the fingers. Then begin to remove the peel at the top in a sawing circular movement, taking pith as well as peel. As you saw turn the grape-fruit in your fingers. When all peel is removed, if any bits of white pith remain saw these off, and if the fruit is soft it may now be chilled again. Now carefully cut each section free of membrane and lift it out. As you do so, put the layers of membrane together like the leaves of a book. This method is only suitable for grape-fruit and large oranges. When a small orange must be cut for a compôte proceed as follows: peel, removing as much of the pith as possible, as before. Cut in four vertically, then slice downwards the length of the quarters, so that the line of white membrane comes away and it is easy to remove the pips.

To cut lemons for serving with pancakes or fried fish. Wipe the lemon and cut it in four lengthways. Remove the line of white pith as before and the pips. If the lemon is large the quarters will probably need to be cut again. This is a convenient way of cutting a lemon, because the juice is directed, by the formation of the lemon, downward on to the food, and does not spurt all over the place.

Poaching and peeling of peaches for compôtes. Put the peaches into a bowl and pour boiling water over them. Leave up to a minute. Pour off the water and pour on cold. The skin may now be easily removed, using a silver or stainless steel knife. The peaches are then ready for poaching in thick syrup, and are either left whole or halved according to their ripeness and size.

To cut pineapple for compôte. With a sharp knife take slanting cuts downwards, between the eyes. It is then easy to remove the eyes with the skin. The pineapple is then cut in slices with a stainless steel knife and the core removed.

To cut pineapple for dessert. For dessert a pineapple should be torn apart with two silver forks.

To stone a cherry. There are cherry-stoners on the market; failing one of these the simplest way is to take a very small vegetable scoop and scoop out the stone, or fix a hairpin into a cork and scoop it out with the rounded end.

Zest of orange and tangerine. Take rough lumps of sugar and rub thoroughly all over the skin of the fruit until they are completely soaked with oil, roughly one or two lumps of sugar for each orange or tangerine. The sugar may be crushed and incorporated into butter for orange butter, or put into milk when it has reached boiling-point for the making of custard.   After the addition of the orange-soaked sugar to the milk, avoid boiling or the flavour will be spoilt.   Sometimes the sugar is added to a hot custard and allowed to dissolve in it.

To 'turn' an olive.   This applies only to green olives.   Hold the olive in the fingers of the left hand and with a small vegetable knife cut the pointed top nearly three-quarters through, then pare round the stone until the stalk end is reached, rather like peeling an apple.   Then cut straight across the bottom.   Carefully detach from the stone and reshape.   Black olives are merely partly split and the stone removed.

To peel, slice, and chop an onion.   See page 198.

To cut a radish for decoration.   There are two ways of cutting a radish: the first is to make four cross cuts after having cleaned it, cut off the root, and left on about $\frac{1}{4}$ inch of the green tip; if the radish is then left in iced water it will open like a flower.

The second and nicer way is to make small uneven cuts all round the outside of the radish; it is then left in iced water to open.

To curl celery.   With a potato-peeler take off slivers of celery about 2–3 inches long.   Put these into iced water for an hour or two.   Or choose tender stalks and make five or six incisions at the top for about a third of the length; or short pieces may be so cut at both ends.   Put in iced water and allow to stand overnight in a cold place, preferably in the ice-box.

TO BLANCH ALMONDS
See page 853.

TO PEEL CHESTNUTS (TWO METHODS)

(*a*) Put nuts into cold water and bring quickly to the boil, remove from fire, lift out with a spoon one or two nuts at a time.   The outer and inner skins may then be removed easily, but do not take all the chestnuts out of the water and let them get cold.   Do not keep the water on the boil.   It may be brought back to the boil if it gets too cold.   Any nut from which the inner peel cannot be removed may be replaced in the hot water.

(*b*) Cut a tiny piece off the top of the nut, put nut into a frying bath and dip into smoking hot fat for half a minute.   Both skins are then easily removed.

When a particularly dry purée is wanted for piping, for example for a Mont Blanc, the chestnuts may be baked.   A slit is made in the skin, the nuts baked in the oven till tender, the inside then scooped out and sieved.

TRUFFLES

These tuber-like fungi are expensive luxuries and are generally reserved for special dishes and occasions.   They are found in some parts of France and Italy and grow a few inches below the surface of the ground in the vicinity of oak-trees.   Périgord is famous for the black truffle and from

Piedmont comes a white variety. Truffles are sometimes found in England, but one rarely comes across a native truffle. Their size varies from a walnut to a hen's egg. If French truffles are available—and they are sometimes imported into this country in autumn and early winter—the rough skin is pared off and they are then stewed till tender. It is more usual for us to buy them in tins or bottles ready for use. They have a unique flavour which is readily imparted and the black slices also have a decorative quality. A traditional delicacy is a chicken or turkey *en demi-deuil*, for which thin slices of truffle are carefully inserted under the skin of an uncooked bird, which is then left overnight so that the flavour may penetrate the flesh before the bird is stuffed with veal force-meat and roasted.

PREPARATION OF SHRIMPS OR PRAWNS FOR GARNISH

Prawns or shrimps used for garnish have the tail or body shell carefully pulled off and the head left on. If to accompany a hot dish the heads may be lightly brushed or rubbed with oil, if for a cold dish brushed with cool aspic.

TO SKIN SAUSAGES

With a sharp-pointed knife draw a thin line down the length of the sausage and so split the skin. It may then be easily ripped off.

TO MAKE CROUSTADES

Cut rounds of stale bread 2 inches thick and about 3 inches in diameter; with a smaller cutter make an incision, taking care not to go through to the base; this will facilitate the removal of the centre after frying. Fry to a golden brown in deep fat, drain, scoop out the centre to form a hollow case. Fill with the mixture indicated in the recipe.

TO FRY PARSLEY

Unless it is absolutely necessary refrain from washing the parsley. If it is necessary to do so, do it some hours beforehand and see that it is perfectly dry before putting into the hot fat, otherwise the fat splashes in a violent way and is dangerous. Pick the sprigs from the main stalks of the parsley. Allow a really large handful of sprigs for four people. Put into a frying basket, and when the fat shows a faint blue haze plunge into the fat bath. Do not be deterred by the noise it makes. As soon as the hissing stops, lift out the parsley, which should be bright green.

TO IMPROVE CHOPPED PARSLEY

To make chopped parsley easy to sprinkle and a good colour, put it, after chopping, into a corner of a clean cloth or piece of muslin. Gather it up and hold for a few minutes under the cold tap or in a bowl of water, working it well with your fingers. Then squeeze it dry, and shake the parsley out of the cloth. It will be a brilliant green.

PREPARATION OF WATERCRESS FOR A GARNISH

Open the bunch and throw into plenty of cold water containing a little salt. Lift out and shake well. Lay on a clean cloth and dab dry, pick over, discarding faulty leaves and any white rootlets high on the stem. Lay all the stems in the same direction, arrange the sprigs in small bunches, shorten the stems a little so that you have neat little bunches of perfect sprigs. At the last moment dip each bunch in French dressing, shake gently to remove surplus, and put them on the dish with the grill or whatever food the garnish is to accompany. Do not return to the oven.

If the bunches are really young and good they may be washed as they are without being untied; the stalks are then shortened and little bouquets of the sprigs are picked out from the bunch.

SIEVING AND SIEVES

Wire sieves and hair sieves (or nylon which has now taken the place of hair) have each their proper uses and are not, generally speaking, interchangeable. The primary use of each is for the making of purées. A hair or nylon sieve produces the finer purée, but this is not invariably desirable. For acid fruits, when contact with the metal would cause discoloration, or when a very smooth purée is called for, a hair or nylon sieve is required. Sometimes the operation of making a fine purée may be expedited by making a preliminary coarser purée with a wire sieve and finishing it off through the finer medium.

Within reason a large sieve is more practical than a small one. It is easy to confine the material to the central part of the sieve and more comfortable to have plenty of space.

Speedy work is essential because it is easier to pass hot materials through a sieve than cold. A wooden spoon is suitable for this work, with the fingers placed in the bowl of it in order to exert adequate pressure. A specially curved wooden spoon is obtainable for this purpose, and also a presser known as a *champignon* which is frequently used for sieving potatoes.

The operation is one of crushing rather than rubbing, though this applies more to some substances than others; in the case of potatoes, for instance, rubbing will produce a gluey consistency, but with berried fruits short, sharp strokes from back to front of the sieve are required.

The sieve, shallow side uppermost, should fit easily over bowl or dish and be in no danger of slipping. When a dry purée is required, of potatoes, lentils, or chestnuts, a clean dry cloth may replace bowl or dish with advantage; it will absorb a certain amount of surplus moisture (see also Drying a Purée, page 51).

Sieve and saucepan should be close together, the contents of the latter being taken out in small quantities and the lid replaced each time. With certain materials, berried fruits for instance, the operation is helped by the addition from time to time of a little of the liquid in which they were cooked. At intervals, and of course at the end, the underpart of the sieve should be scraped free of purée with a metal spoon, palette-knife, or rubber scraper—not with the wooden spoon in use. Sometimes, if skins of fruit or dried vegetables accumulate on top of the sieve, impeding progress, they should be scraped together and discarded. It is perhaps unnecessary to point out that a strainer, either the pointed or round type, cannot suitably be substituted for a sieve. This utensil is for draining and straining, and it is unwise to try to make it do more than this, and the result in any case will be unsatisfactory.

DRYING A PURÉE

For certain dishes, for example for mashed potatoes, turnips, haricots, and other dried vegetables, a dry purée is required, and all possible moisture has to be driven off. To do this the purée should be gathered up in a cloth on to which it has been sieved, returned to a hot, wide-based saucepan, and set on good heat. The wider the base of the pan the thinner the layer of purée and the easier the process of drying.

The purée should be stirred with a square-tipped wooden spoon, turned steadily, and pressed first against the base of the pan and then at once turned all over again. Superfluous moisture is thus driven off in steam and the purée becomes increasingly thick. It is now ready for the incorporating of other ingredients such as butter, milk, or sauce.

CHOPPING

Such an everyday process hardly seems worthy of a note, yet if one watches a class of students it is surprising to see the degrees of apt and inept work. One will bang away with a knife, making little impression on the material, another will be moving her knife to and fro in a rhythmical rocking motion, reducing whatever is under it to fine shreds. A proper chopping-knife, by its shape, graduating from broad blade to narrow point, facilitates the action. If, for instance, a bunch of herbs is to be chopped, these should first be gathered together and roughly shredded. Then, holding down the tip of the knife in the left hand (the point used as the fulcrum of a lever), move the knife rapidly up and down with the right. A level board is, of course, essential. In big kitchens where work is done on a large scale a curved chopping-knife with two handles is used, and this, in combination with a chopping-block, is most efficient.

USE OF A MINCING-MACHINE

A mincer has many uses, apart from the mincing of meat. It can be used for chopping raw or dried fruits, apples, pears, stoned prunes, figs, sultanas, and raisins, particularly when such fruits are to be made into chutney, pickle, or bottled sauces. Baked crusts may be put through a coarse mincer, sieved, and used for raspings. This is a quicker and easier way than crushing them with a rolling-pin. Vegetables may be minced in this way, but experienced cooks prefer to grate or chop them, for then they are less crushed and less juice is extracted. Potatoes and artichokes become discoloured if put through a mincing-machine.

A cheese-grater is useful; it can be fastened on to the edge of the kitchen table in the same way as the mincing-machine, and it is used for nuts, cheese, crumbs, and other things.

SKIMMING

With certain classic sauces, soups, and stocks, perfection can only be attained by lengthy and meticulous skimming. This is carried out when the liquid has been gradually brought to the boil. It is at this point that impurities rise to the surface. To facilitate skimming a saucepan should be chosen which the liquid will fill almost to the brim.

When the liquid comes to the boil, it is drawn aside from the heat and any scum or grease that comes to the surface lifted off. From time to time a spoonful or two of cold water or reserved stock is added, which will bring more matter to the surface to be skimmed off. The pan should then be placed in such a manner that the heat gives rise to a gentle bubbling in one part of the saucepan only, and always at the same place. The pan should be left uncovered while the skimming is done from time to time. This is the process meant by the word *dépouiller*. (See also Sauce Demi-glace, page 143.)

REDUCING

It is sometimes necessary, in order to strengthen flavour or produce a thicker consistency, to reduce the quantity of a sauce or syrup. This is effected by boiling the liquid quickly in an uncovered pan. (See also general notes in chapter on sauces, page 135.)

GLAZING

A dish coated with sauce which has been glazed presents a lacquer-like surface. The operation has to be accomplished speedily so that the food is not subjected to further real cooking. Certain sauces would be spoiled if this were allowed. A shallow dish is desirable; the glazing is done by subjection to strong heat over the surface, a gas or electric grill or very hot oven.

Glazing cold meats such as galantines, brawn, etc., is a different process. In this case melted meat glaze or savoury jelly is brushed over the surface with a glaze brush. Each coat is allowed to dry before another is added. The process is repeated, coat upon coat, until the required thickness is obtained.

Sweet glazing for such dishes as flans and tartlets is done in much the same way. A thick purée of well-boiled apricot jam or melted red-currant jelly is applied to the surface with a brush. In this way a much more even coating is obtained (see page 856). The more homely way of pouring the glazing mixture over the fruit in the flan will often leave islands of uncovered fruit.

For oiling and greasing of tins see chapter on cakes, page 807.

THE FORCING-BAG *

This is a bag made of strong cotton, shaped like a cornet with the tip cut off. A short metal tube or nozzle fits into the open point. It is used for squeezing certain mixtures such as choux or meringue paste into the required shape on the baking-sheet. The mixture is transferred by the spoonful from bowl to bag, which should only be three-quarters filled. The top of the bag is held securely in the right hand and the weight is supported by the left, and it is the left hand which guides and steadies the bag. It should be lightly squeezed from the top by the right hand. The tip of the pipe or nozzle should be kept close to the baking-sheet. For a round shape the pipe is kept still while pressure is exerted, and for éclairs a line is drawn.

For icing (either royal or butter cream) it is usual to make a forcing-bag or cornet of paper to take the place of the forcing-bag described above. The opening at the top of the cone may be cut to the appropriate size and used with the various nozzles and pipes. For drawing a thin line of jelly or cream the cone may be used without a nozzle, but the paper would not be strong enough without the nozzle to support heavy icing.

To make the cornet proceed as follows: Take a double layer of best quality grease-proof paper and cut into a square. Fold diagonally to form a triangle. Holding this with the point uppermost fold the right-hand edges over to meet the centre line. Then take the left edges and bring them right over and round to the back until the two points of paper lie over one another. Tuck the flap thus formed inside the cone. Cut the point to the size required. For use, half fill the bag, and fold over the top of the bag so that the contents are enclosed, pressing a little so that the bottom of the bag is solidly filled. Pressure should be exerted steadily from the top.

SOME TERMS FREQUENTLY USED IN COOKING·

(N.B. These terms are defined in the culinary sense. Their actual meaning, generally speaking, is not the same.)

Arroser	to baste, to add liquid.
Aspic	(*a*) a savoury jelly.
	(*b*) cold entremets set in jelly, e.g. aspic de pommes.
Au blanc	to cook without colouring, as a rule in a white sauce or a velouté, e.g. poulet au blanc, or in a 'blanc,' a sort of white bouillon.

* *See plate 1*

Au bleu	to cook freshly caught trout in court bouillon so that the fish looks bluish, having been cooked without scaling.
Au gras	cooked with meat or meat stock.
Au gratin	method of cooking which usually gives a brown surface; the dish is covered with sauce, bread-crumbs, sometimes with grated cheese, and served in the vessel used for cooking.
Au maigre	cooked without any meat or meat stock.
Bain-marie	(a) a square or oblong vessel that will hold a number of smaller pans standing in hot water. Used to keep sauces, soups, etc., hot without further cooking. Temperature about 130°–140° F.
	(b) a baking-tin half filled with hot water in which steamed soufflés, custards, etc., stand while cooking at a temperature of about 180°–190° F.
Beignets	fritters.
Beignets soufflés	fritters made of choux pastry.
Beurre manié	butter and flour worked together to a paste. One of the liaisons.
Blanchir	(a) to put into boiling water for a moment, e.g. sweetbread, or scallops, to make firm before cooking.
	(b) to put in cold water and bring to the boil, in order to whiten or to reduce strong flavour.
	(c) to make less salt, and to clean, e.g. bacon or salt pork.
	(d) to cook partly, e.g. some vegetables.
Bouchées	small cases of puff pastry.
Bouillon	consommé, unclarified, or beef broth, veal broth.
Bouquet garni	a bouquet of herbs, usually parsley, thyme, and bay-leaf, tied together and used to flavour sauce, soup, etc. Other herbs may be called for by the recipe.
Canapé	a small platform of fried or toasted bread used as the foundation of a savoury or hors-d'œuvre.
Chaudfroid	cooked chicken or game or other meats, coated with brown or white chaudfroid sauce, then with aspic jelly.
Chinois	a wire strainer, conical in shape.
Concasser	literally to pound, crush, or grind. In cookery, to chop roughly.
Coulis	concentrated liquid, the result of long, slow cooking.

Couronne	*dresser en couronne*, to arrange in a ring.
Court bouillon	liquid used for cooking fish, made from boiling salted water, wine, or vinegar, carrots, onion, and bouquet garni.
Croquettes	cork shapes or cones, made of minced meat, fish, eggs, or vegetables, egged and crumbed and fried in deep fat.
Croustade	case of fried bread or pastry in which chicken, game, or minced meat may be served.
Croûte	crust, i.e. pastry or a crust of bread, fried, baked, or toasted light brown and used for serving small birds or for an entrée.
Croûtons	small dice or other shapes of fried or toasted bread, used to garnish some soups and other dishes.
Cuisson	the liquor in which something has been cooked, or which has been produced in the cooking process.
Dariole	dariole mould: a small mould in which a little pudding is steamed or baked—a dariole is a small pâté.
Déglacer	to dissolve with hot liquid, usually water, the solids at the bottom of a roasting or sauté pan.
Dégorger	to soak meat or fish, vegetables or fruit in water, to improve their colour, or to take away too strong a flavour. Often applied to aubergines and cucumbers, which are sprinkled with salt and left for some time so that harmful juices may be drawn out and washed away. This is said to make these vegetables taste better and to make them easier to digest.
Dégraisser	to skim off fat, or to remove superfluous fat from meat.
Demi-glace	brown sauce, semi-clear and syrupy in texture.
Dépouiller	to skim off every trace of fat while a sauce, soup, or stock is cooking.
Dorer	to gild or brown with beaten egg.
Entrée	side-dish, hot or cold, which is complete in itself, having vegetables and sauce or gravy on the same dish.
Entremets	sweet dishes.
Escalope	a thin slice of meat.
Étuver	to cook under cover with little or no liquid.
Faire revenir	to cook something so that it takes colour lightly without being completely cooked.

Farce	stuffing.
Fécule	potato flour, corn-flour, or arrowroot.
Flan	open tart, cooked in a ring.
Fleurons, feuilletons	small pieces of puff pastry, usually crescents, used as garnish.
Fonds de braise	fat bacon, sliced carrots, and onion, etc., used with bouquet garni to line a braisière.
Fontaine	*faire la fontaine*, to make a circle of flour on a marble slab or pastry board, before making French pâte or pastry.
Frappé	iced.
Frémir, frissoner	to come to simmering-point.
Friture	frying, or something fried.
Fumet	stock of game or fish, or meat, sometimes of mushrooms, greatly reduced, and used to give good flavour to a dish.
Garniture	garnish, i.e. the small ornamental items that can be eaten and that give colour and attraction to a dish, e.g. small glazed onions or carrots, sliced sautéd mushrooms and so on, or for a fried dish, fried parsley. Often a dish will be named after the garniture.
Glacer, glacage	(*a*) to reduce the gravy of a meat dish and use it, poured over the dish and exposed to great heat, to give a smooth, shining appearance.
	(*b*) to give the same appearance to a dish covered with sauce.
	(*c*) to ice a cake.
	(*d*) to freeze a mixture.
	(*e*) to dip fruit in very hot syrup and so give it a shining enveloping coat.
	(*f*) to cook fruits or nuts over and over again in syrup successively strengthened, so that they become soaked in sugar, e.g. marrons glacés, fruits glacés.
Hâchis	minced meat.
Hâtelet	ornamental silver skewer.
Hors-d'œuvre	appetizing morsels served at the beginning of a meal.
Infuser	to steep: to extract flavour from material into a liquid by leaving it steeped in that liquid in a warm place—the liquid need not boil.
Jus	gravy or reduced stock.

Kromeski	Polish name for a sort of croquette, sometimes dipped in fritter batter before being fried in deep fat.
Lard	bacon.
Larder	to lard the surface or interior of a piece of meat or of a bird. (*See* Larding, Chapter IV, page 69.)
Lardon	a small slice of fat bacon used for larding.
Liaison	an element used for the binding together of a sauce, soup, or other liquid; it may be a roux, white, blond, or brown, beurre manié, egg yolk and cream, fécule or blood.
Macédoine	vegetables cut in even-sized dice, or fruits evenly divided.
Macérer	to macerate: to soak a fruit in liqueur. The same process used for fish or meat is called *mariner* (q.v.).
Manier	to manipulate butter to be used in pastry-making; to make beurre manié.
Mariner, marinade	to steep meat, fish, or vegetables, before they are cooked, in an acidulated liquid containing vegetables and herbs (a marinade), which gives flavour and makes meat more tender.
Marmite	a stock-pot of earthenware.
Mask	to coat with sauce.
Menu	bill of fare.
Mijoter	to cook gently.
Mirepoix	the preparatory foundation for a braise, sauce, or ragoût: vegetables cut in dice, diced fat bacon, gently cooked in butter.
Monter	to increase, by beating, the volume of a substance or a sauce.
Mouiller	to add liquid to a dish in order to cook it; *à court mouillement*, with little liquid.
Mousse	a light mixture, savoury or sweet, which can be hot, cold, or iced.
Napper	to coat with sauce.
Navarin	a stew of lamb or mutton.
Noisettes	small rounds of meat taken from lamb or mutton cutlets; beurre noisette, nut-brown butter.
Pailles	straws: fried potatoes or cheese-straws.
Pain grillé	toast.
Panache	with bands or stripes of different colours; salade panachée, made of several ingredients.
Panade	paste of flour and butter and a little liquid, or of soaked crumbs, used as foundation for croquettes or soufflés.

Papillotes	literally curl-papers: paper cases in which food is cooked or served.
Passer	to sieve, strain, or put through a tammy cloth.
Pâte	dough or pastry.
Pâté	pie; patty case; raised pie or savoury mixture of game, liver, etc.
Pâtisserie	pastry made as by a pastry-cook, i.e. delicate and attractive in appearance.
Paupiette	a fillet of raw fish, or a thin slice of meat, spread with farce, rolled up, tied, and cooked.
Piqué	larded.
Plat	dish.
Pocher	to poach.
Pot-au-feu	traditional beef broth.
Poussin	baby chicken.
Praline	flavoured with almond rock.
Purée	a vegetable or other soup put through a sieve, or a sieved substance.
Quenelles	farce of meat or fish made into small oval shapes, poached, and used as a garnish or served as a dish.
Rafraîchir	to refresh: to pour cold water over vegetables, fruit, or meat after they have been blanched.
Ragoût	a stew.
Ravioli	small squares or triangles of nouille paste enclosing a savoury mixture, boiled and served with a sauce.
Réchauffé	a reheated dish, made with previously cooked food.
Réduire	to reduce by rapid boiling.
Relevé	remove: a course consisting of a large fish, a dish of venison or hare, or a joint.
Renversé	turned out from a mould on to a dish.
Rissole	minced mixture, usually of meat, enclosed in pastry and fried in deep fat.
Rissoler	to colour light brown in hot fat.
Rôti	roast: a course of meat, poultry, or game, plainly roasted.
Roux	hot butter or fat mixed together with flour and used as one of the liaisons; may be white, blond, or brown.
Ruban	ribbon: to beat to the ribbon is to beat yolks and sugar together until they fall like a ribbon from the spatula or whisk.
Saignant	underdone: almost raw.

Salamandre	salamander: used red-hot to brown the surface of a dish.
Salmis	game stew.
Salpicon	a mixture used to make croquettes, rissoles etc., made of diced chicken, veal, game, sweetbreads, mushrooms, truffles, etc. Also used to fill vol-au-vent, bouchées, and so on.
Sauter	to cook in hot fat, oil, or butter by tossing in sauté pan.
Socle	a pedestal of rice, bread, ice, etc., often not to be eaten, made to support an ornamental dish.
Soubise	purée of onions, sometimes mixed with a béchamel sauce.
Souchet	a fish dish served in a soup-plate, made with vegetables and herbs and cooked in salted water.
Suer	to sweat: to cook slowly in a covered pan.
Suprême	choice pieces of chicken, or of fish; a delicate sauce.
Tamis	sieve or tammy cloth.
Tartine	a slice of bread and butter.
Timbale	a mixture cooked in a high mould.
Tournedos	beef fillet.
Tourner, i.e. to turn	(a) to give a turn in pastry-making: that is, to fold and roll.
	(b) to cut vegetables in an oval shape or like olives.
	(c) to stone an olive by taking off the flesh in a spiral, and then re-forming the olive.
Tourte	a shallow open tart.
Travailler	to work: to mix a paste so that all its elements are combined; to reduce a sauce by rapid boiling in an uncovered pan, stirring and beating meanwhile so that the surface is kept smooth.
Tutti-frutti	a mixture of fruits
Vanner	to stir a sauce after it has been cooked until it is cool, so that no skin forms, and its texture remains uniform.
Velouté	one of the foundation sauces, usually made with meat stock.
Vol-au-vent	a case of puff pastry, large or small.
Zest	the thin coloured skin of an orange or lemon used to give flavour; very thinly pared without taking any of the bitter white pith. Also the oil extracted from the skin with loaf sugar. See page 47.

TABLES OF WEIGHTS AND MEASURES

French Weights and Measures

The following table is approximate only. 1 oz. = 28·352 grammes, but for practical purposes it is here taken as 30 grammes.

(a) *Weights:*

15 grammes	= $\frac{1}{2}$ oz.	
30 ,,	= 1 ,,	
50 ,,	= $1\frac{3}{4}$,,	
60 ,,	= 2 ,,	
75 ,,	= $2\frac{1}{2}$,,	approx.
100 ,,	= $3\frac{1}{2}$,,	
500 ,,	= 1 lb. $1\frac{1}{2}$ oz.	
1 kilogramme	= 2 lb. 3 oz.	
	(just under $2\frac{1}{4}$ lb.)	

(b) *Liquid Measures:*

1 litre	= $1\frac{3}{4}$ pts—35 oz.	
1 decilitre	= 3–4 oz. or 1 wineglass	approx.
1 demilitre	= $\frac{3}{4}$ pt (generous)	

American Measures

An American pint	= 16 fluid oz.
An English ,,	= 20 ,, ,,
An American cup measure	= 8 ,, ,,

All American spoon measures are a flat spoonful.
An American tablespoon = 3 flat teaspoons

	Weight of 1 American Cup	Weight of 1 American Tablespoon
Flour	$4\frac{1}{2}$ oz.	$\frac{1}{2}$ oz.
Sugar	7 ,,	$\frac{3}{4}$,,
Butter	7 ,,	$\frac{3}{4}$,,

Oven Temperatures

	Temp.	Regulo	Main Setting
Very slow	240°–280°	$\frac{1}{4}$–$\frac{1}{2}$	A–B
Slow	280°–320°	1	C
Warm	320°–340°	3	C
Moderate	340°–370°	4	D
Fairly hot	370°–400°	5–6	E
Hot	400°–440°	7	F
Very hot	440°–480°	8–9	G–H
	450°–500°		

N.B. Most modern electric stoves are fitted with thermostatic oven controls. The control knob may be set to the temperature required and a light shows when the oven is turned on; when the required temperature has been reached the light automatically goes out.

For those stoves which are not fitted with this device, the following scale may be useful:

Slow: Switch on at high for 7–10 minutes, then turn to slow.
Moderate: Switch on at high for 12–15 minutes, then turn to moderate.
Hot: Switch on at high for 20–25 minutes, and leave.

It should be noted that some stoves heat up more quickly than others, so that the above notes can only serve as a guide and should not be taken too literally.

IV

Kitchen Processes

Roasting—Grilling—Sautéing—To flamber with wine and brandy—
Braising and Stewing—Marinading—Larding—Barding—Boiling
—Simmering and Poaching—Steaming—Bain-marie—Frying—
Tammying—Boning.

NOTES on cooking processes divorced from actual recipes make dull
reading. The young cook will hardly be tempted to read this chapter;
nevertheless, time will be saved in the long run if she makes herself
familiar with general principles involved, and the recipes which follow on
for fish, meat, game, and poultry will assume a more familiar air.

ROASTING

The days of real roasting are gone by: no more roasting-spits and jacks,
no one with time to turn them and to baste unceasingly, not even the little
Dutch oven to hang on the bars of an open range, in which to cook the
smaller birds; even if one could find such a utensil and just use it modestly
to grill bacon as we used to do in my young days, where should we find the
open range, or if we did, think how we should be accused of roaring away
the fuel! No! What we do nowadays in the name of roasting is to bake,
really to bake, but as basting is part of the process we miscall it roasting.
For this the oven should be hot, an average temperature of 450°, with
certain exceptions noted in the recipes. The fat is heated in the baking-
pan, the meat put in, and basting carried out at regular intervals. Cooking
according to the size of the joint, allow 10–15 minutes per lb. for a small
joint, 20 minutes for a large one.
Some cooks set the meat on a grid in the pan, and this is good when
potatoes are to be cooked with the meat, and it was a common custom when
a Yorkshire or suet pudding was cooked with the joint. Potatoes should
be put in approximately three-quarters of an hour before the meat is done,
and the same amount of time should be allowed for a pudding cooked in
this way.

To baste. Lift the tin from the oven, place on a board on the table, and
close the oven door. Spoon the hot dripping several times over the meat,
using a basting-spoon. The object of basting is to keep the meat moist
and juicy.

Frothing. Flouring and salting of the surface of a joint to give additional crispness is carried out during the last quarter of an hour of cooking; a sprinkling of salt and a dredging of flour is made over the surface which is then immediately basted. This process applies particularly to game birds, pork, and mutton. This is known as frothing.

POT ROASTING

This is a method of cooking suited to meat which is on the tough and dry side. The method is simple: in a heavy saucepan heat a spoonful or two of dripping, add an onion stuck with one or two cloves and a bay-leaf. Put in the joint, baste, and cover tightly. Cook over very low heat or in the oven, allowing approximately 30 minutes to the pound.

GRILLING

This simple but excellent method of cooking is less good now as one is so rarely able to use an open fire, for perfect grilling is done over red-hot coals or over a charcoal grill. In the United States one buys such grillers for cooking in the open air, but nowadays most of our grilling is done with gas and electric grills.

The procedure requires a preliminary searing of the surface of the meat to keep the juices in, and continued cooking just long enough to achieve the degree of grilling required. The process, calling for strong radiant heat, requires that the heat shall be strong at the very outset. A fire is allowed to burn through until quite red, and a gas or electric grill should be heated until red-hot. The meat, to begin with, is put close to the heat, having first been brushed over with oil or butter. Each side having been cooked for the requisite time, gauged not by the weight but by the thickness of the piece of meat or fish, the griller may be put lower down, farther away from the heat, for any final cooking that may be called for. The turning of the meat should be done with a pair of tongs, or with two spoons, but never with a fork.

A grilled steak may be called for in one of three degrees of cooking. Some people like to have it brown on the outside, but practically raw inside; others like it well seared on the outside, and cooked throughout till pinkish red in colour and juicy; this is described as being cooked *à point*. When it is required to cook the steak to a further degree than this, the last few minutes of cooking are carried out an inch or two lower, away from the hot grill.

For white meat, veal, pork, or fish a more moderate heat throughout is required. These meats require thorough cooking to make them digestible, and if the fire is too strong to begin with, the hard surface formed will prevent the heat from reaching the innermost part of the meat. Fish should be scored across if round, and cut down nearly to the backbone if flat, and it may be lightly floured except for salmon, herrings, mackerel, and mullet, which are oily fish and not likely to be too much dried by the heat of the grill.   Then in every case the fish is brushed over with oil or melted butter.   When the flesh comes readily away from the backbone, the fish is cooked.

Here are some general points:

1. Steak or cutlets must be cut thick, never less than an inch, and they may be marinaded in a little sherry or brandy or good olive oil; or they may simply be brushed over with clarified butter or oil.

2. Salt should not be used as it will prevent browning and tends to harden the meat.

3. The grill should be red-hot before the griller is placed underneath it. Raise the griller to within two inches of the meat to sear, and then, if further cooking is required, the griller may be lowered slightly for an extra last minute before serving.

4. Grills should be served at once.   Tomatoes, mushrooms, etc., may be grilled to serve as an accompaniment.   Maître d'hôtel butter may accompany chops and kidneys.

MIXED GRILL

For mixed grill, cutlets, kidneys, sausages (especially chipolatas), tomatoes, bacon and so forth may be used.   Start with the ingredient which takes the longest time to cook.   Grill, for instance, the cutlet and the kidney and follow on with the chipolatas and tomatoes.   At the same time the mushrooms may well be sautéd on top of the stove.   The dish should be garnished with watercress, and the juices from the griller poured on.

See fish chapter (page 444) for the discussion of grilled herrings, mackerel, salmon, etc.

To grill over a fire.   Make the fire up beforehand so that a layer of red-hot coals is available.   Open the top of the grate and heat the grill thoroughly. When a thick piece of red meat is to be grilled, it is a good precaution to have some red-hot cinders available to add to the fire if the heat dies down.

To grill with a gas or electric grill.   Make the grill red-hot before starting, lay the object to be grilled on the heated rack in the grill pan, and when moderate heat is required for the actual cooking the gas or electricity may be turned down as the case requires.

SAUTÉING *

The word *sauter* is used to indicate two methods of cooking.   The first, pedantically correct, is a process by which meat is cooked in hot butter and/or oil, uncovered, in a sauté pan or *sautoir*, which is a deep, straight-sided frying-pan.

The second process to which this term is applied involves a preliminary cooking in this way which is followed by further cooking in a small quantity of liquid.

* *See plate 2*

Examples of the first method may be found in tournedos, escalopes, and some chicken dishes. The second method is often called for when meat requires slightly longer cooking, for example for rabbit, veal sauté, kidneys, and certain chicken dishes.

In the case of vegetables, some of these are sautéd by the first method only, in hot butter from start to finish, others, in particular root vegetables, are previously cooked before being finished in the sauté pan.

The pan. The correct pan is a deep, straight-sided pan called a *sautoir* or sauté pan; it should be heavy, and the straight sides are from $2\frac{1}{2}$ to $3\frac{1}{2}$ inches deep. While it is convenient to use a frying-pan for vegetables, the *sautoir* is more convenient for meat, because being deeper it will more readily hold the necessary gravy or sauce.

Fat. Clarified butter, or a mixture of clarified butter and the best olive oil, are the correct frying media for this purpose.

Liquids. The recipes indicate where white wine or red wine is required, and this, together with a rich stock, gives the proper results. It is required that the liquor shall reduce greatly during the simmering and finishing of the sauce, so that it acquires the texture of a demi-glace, becoming syrupy in consistency and clear in appearance.

Here are the stages of cooking for a sauté in order:

1. Birds or rabbits are jointed and the meat neatly cut up or sliced.

2. The pieces are browned on both sides, over moderate heat, in the fat; they must be laid flat on the bottom of the pan, and not superimposed one over another. The time required for this process varies according to the dish in hand. Chicken, rabbit, partridge, and chops may take 25 minutes, while escalopes de veau will call for much less, perhaps for 5 minutes. Actual times are given in the recipes.

3. After this cooking in the hot fat, some recipes indicate that meat is to be flambéd with brandy or sherry (see note on page 66).

4. If the meat is to be cooked by the first process only, that is to say entirely in the fat, it is dished when ready, and the process known as 'to déglacer' carried out, that is to say the pan is swilled out, after any remaining fat has been poured off, with a liquid, sherry, white wine or red, stock and so forth, in order to dissolve the sticky glaze which is left on the bottom of the pan. This liquid is then reduced a little and may be thickened in ways indicated in the different recipes. When the right consistency is reached the gravy is strained, and whatever garnish is called for in the recipe is added.

5. When further cooking is necessary, after this preliminary process of browning in hot fat, the pan is déglacéd in the way described with sherry or wine, though in this case the meat is usually left in the pan while the process is carried out, then barely covered with the liquid and simmered for the time given in the recipe. This process may be carried out on the stove top or in the oven.

6. When cooked the meat is dished; the gravy is rapidly reduced, the necessary liaison and garnish added, and the whole spooned over the dish.

Typical examples of the second method of making a sauté are:

> Poulet sauté à l'Estragon.
> Lapin sauté Chasseur.
> Sauté de Veau Marengo.
> Rognons sauté Turbigo.

These will be found in their proper chapters.

TO FLAMBER WITH WINE

This operation is called for in certain braises, sautés, and ragoûts. It has for its object the removal of any rough taste or harshness in the wine, and it burns out the alcohol. It is a process usually applied to vin ordinaire and the cheaper types of red wine, and it is not normally carried out when a vintage wine is called for in the recipe.

The wine is put into a saucepan, brought to the boil, and lighted. Boiling is continued until the flame burns out; the wine is then ready to add to the dish, or it may be added while flaming. Sometimes a recipe calls for reduction after flaming.

TO FLAMBER WITH BRANDY (OR SHERRY)

While the burning has the same result in that the alcohol is burnt out, in this process the liquid is poured flaming over the object being treated. The slight singeing of the surface of the flesh gives added good flavour. The brandy is heated in a silver spoon or in a very small saucepan (in which case the pan is shaken briskly), set alight, and poured over the birds or meat in the pan.

BRAISING

Braising is a method of cooking applied to meat, fish, game, poultry, and some vegetables; it involves the application of both top and bottom heat, and the process is long, rendering the object cooked extremely tender, so tender and melting that it can be cut with a spoon. While choice meats so cooked are among the classic dishes, it is obvious that this method has its particular value when the cheaper cuts of meat, the older game and poultry are concerned. It is excellent for thick cuts and whole fish, although English cooks seldom adopt this method; braised whole codling, for instance, is excellent. In the appropriate chapters will be found details of suitable joints for braising.

This process, which is really a combination of steaming and baking, is carried out, in France and in big kitchens, in a proper *braisière*, a pan with a concave lid which will hold hot charcoal or, in more modern fashion, boiling water. In domestic kitchens a heavy saucepan or *cocotte* is used, thick enough to ensure that the heat shall not become too fierce. Although for a part of the time cooking may be carried out on top of the stove, for the most part it is done in the oven.

Meat for braising, particularly if taken from a lean cut, is sometimes larded and barded (see pages 69–70) and sometimes subjected to a preliminary marinading (see page 730) which improves both flavour and texture.

The following gives an outline of the method when a whole joint is to be braised:

1. Heat the fat, brown the meat on all sides, then remove from pan.

2. Lay one or two slices of bacon on the bottom of the pan (this is optional, but improves the flavour); on this arrange a bed of sliced or diced root vegetables to the depth of $\frac{1}{2}$–1 inch, the vegetables chosen in such proportions that no one flavour will predominate. Allow these to sweat gently in the fat with the lid on until softened, without browning, about 10–15 minutes. This mixture of vegetables is called a mirepoix and is not usually served with the finished dish.

3. Season vegetables, lay the browned meat on them, moisten with the liquor called for in the recipe, wine or stock or both, which should come a quarter or more up the side of the joint. Add bouquet, cover, and allow to simmer anything up to an hour on top of the stove and then for 2–3 hours in the oven. The time depends, of course, on the size of the joint and is indicated in the recipe.

4. When the meat is cooked the gravy is strained, skimmed with a metal spoon of all fat, reduced if necessary, and poured over the meat in a deep dish with the appropriate garnish. In some cases the straining is done half way through the cooking, and vegetables added, this time to be served with the meat. In this way one ensures that the garniture does not get overcooked.

Braising is a method of cooking frequently used for ragoûts. In this case the meat is cut up into squares $1\frac{1}{2}$–2 inches in size; these are browned, the vegetables then added and browned also on a lower heat, a small quantity of flour stirred in, and the whole moistened with stock or wine. The pan is then put into the oven until the meat is thoroughly tender and the gravy rich and thick.

The word salmis indicates a mixture of two processes, roasting and braising, the roasting being done first for a short time so that the flesh is *saignant*. The sauce is added to the meat, together with all the juices from the bird. It is a suitable process for young birds.

STEWING

There are two main kinds of stew, white and brown, e.g. beef ragoût, a brown, Irish stew, a white stew. The chief difference between a brown stew and a braise is that the stewing may be carried out on top of the stove, but as it may also be done in the oven, it will be seen that the margin between certain braises and stews is narrow. The meat is cut up and, although vegetables enter into its composition, a stew does not involve the meat being cooked on a mirepoix. There is a certain elasticity about these terms, but this roughly marks out the difference between the two processes.

The principles are slow, gentle cooking either on top of the stove or in the oven; enough liquid to cover meat and vegetables; herbs and seasonings to flavour. Vegetables and herbs vary, of course, according to the main ingredient. Thickening is achieved by the use of potatoes or barley, as in the case of Irish stew, or by the addition of a small quantity of flour added in a brown stew after the meat has been coloured. In some cases rice or small suet or force-meat dumplings are added for both thickening and flavour.

Meat for stewing is usually from less good cuts; it should have a small quantity of fat; if it is entirely lean extra care has to be taken in its preparation or it may become hard and dry. Suitable cuts of meat for both braising and stewing will be found in the appropriate chapter.

BROWN STEW OR RAGOÛT

Choose a thick aluminium or iron casserole or stew-pan, that is to say a shallow pan, but not a frying-pan, which is too shallow (earthenware may well be used for this, but then the meat, vegetables, and flour must first be browned in a metal pan). The meat is trimmed and cut in large squares and a small proportion of fat left on. The pieces are browned in hot dripping or oil, 3 minutes on each side; a common fault is to over-brown, and then the meat becomes dry and chippy and the gravy too dark in colour. The meat is now taken out and any fat beyond a good table-spoon poured off, the heat lowered, and the vegetables browned lightly. Flour, ½–1 tablespoon, is now added and allowed to brown. The meat is returned to the pan with liquor, bouquet, and seasoning, and any other ingredients called for in the specific recipe. The whole should now be gently simmered on top of the stove or in the oven.

Navarin is the French word for a mutton ragoût or stew.

WHITE STEW

This is made in the same way as a brown stew except that the meat is not coloured in the hot fat. Irish stew is an example, as is also a blanquette. The latter is finished with a sauce velouté made from the liquor in which the meat is cooked. The following preliminary preparation has the effect of whitening the meat and removing any strong flavour. It may, in particular, be adopted for such cuts of meat as scrag or middle neck of mutton, and breast of veal, also for rabbit. Soak the meat, after it has been cut and trimmed, for some hours, preferably overnight, in salted water containing a little vinegar, approximately 1–2 tablespoons vinegar to 3 or 4 quarts water and a dessertspoon of salt. The effect of this is to whiten the meat and to remove any strong flavour. The meat is then rinsed and

dried with a cloth.   It is now put into enough water to cover it by about
an inch or two and brought slowly to the boil.   During this time ½ cup
cold water may be added to facilitate the rising of scum to the surface, and
careful skimming is carried out; this clears the liquid and helps to whiten
the meat.   When boiling-point is reached flavouring vegetables and salt
are added and the meat is simmered for the required time.   It is important
to emphasize the word simmer, for if the water gallops the meat will
immediately be toughened.   This cooking is always done on the top of the
stove.   Blanquette of Veal (see recipe on page 583) is an example of a stew
prepared in this way.

A goulash is an Hungarian stew in which paprika is sometimes used for
flavouring, though this is not invariably the case.

MARINADING

See Chapter XXIII, Devils, Barbecues, and Marinades, page 724.

LARDING

Larding is the introduction of thin strips of fat bacon into the surface of
meat or game with the object of supplying surface fat; it is a process used
therefore for lean meat and the drier birds, as, for example, fillet of beef,
veal, guinea-fowl, etc.   This preparation is sometimes carried out by the
supplier, or it can be done at home.   It has importance since it adds considerably to the quality of certain dishes.   If for instance one is cooking a
proper filet de bœuf rôti, one will try to do the whole thing properly.

Larding means the threading through, on the surface of the meat, of thin
strips of solid bacon called lardons.   These are cut from a small solid
block of fat bacon and are occasionally marinaded and flavoured before
being used.   As well as adding fat, they keep the meat moist and give extra
flavour.   One buys from the poulterer, provision merchant, or delicatessen
shop a small block of prepared bacon, entirely fat and salted; this,
blanched [1] and kept in a cool place (for it is easy to cut when cold and hard),
is ready for cutting into lardons.   The rectangle of fat is put on a board,
rind side downwards, then, with a sharp knife dipped into hot water, cuts
are made right down to the rind in regular slices of ⅛–¼ inch thick; next,
horizontal slices of the same thickness are made; the length of the block of
fat, which may be from 2 inches upwards, represents the length of the
lardons.

A larding-needle is used to introduce the lardons and to pull them
through the surface of the meat.   This needle is first plunged shallowly
into the meat, a very thin morsel only being taken up; then the lardon is
introduced into the split eye of the needle and pulled in a direction away

[1] If the larding bacon is strongly salted, and only if this is so, it may be blanched
by being put into cold water, which is brought slowly to the boil; the bacon is
boiled gently for 5–10 minutes, then plunged into cold water, drained, and dried.

from yourself. Repeat the process with the lardon left in the meat, working from right to left and leaving regular gaps, but each lardon almost touching the next. Larding is done across the grain of the meat.

BARDING

This is a process more commonly carried out to-day than larding, and in place of the special larding bacon an ordinary fat rasher may be used. This is securely fastened with string over the breast of the bird or the top of the meat in question, and it is employed for dry birds or lean, dry meat.

BOILING

Boiling is a term sometimes carelessly applied in cooking, for instance we talk of boiled beef, boiled fish, boiled fowl, when we really mean simmered beef, simmered fish, and so forth. If meat is subjected to fast boiling throughout the cooking process it becomes tough, ragged, and retains little nutritive value. It may be brought to boiling-point, 212° F., even kept at this temperature for a short time, but the subsequent cooking is carried out at a lower temperature.

Boiling is indicated as a short preliminary process in many recipes; for example, in the case of some meats the preliminary process of boiling is required to seal the surface in order to retain the juices; while, as an opposite example, salt meat will not be so sealed, because it is desirable to draw out and dissolve some proportion of the salt. Boiling is also required for certain of the heavier types of pudding, and for green and other vegetables. Boiling-point is a temperature essential for syrups, jams, jellies, and infusions. In addition, liquid is allowed to boil strongly when its reduction is required, when, in other words, water is to be driven off in the form of steam, rendering the ingredients, in consequence, more concentrated.

SIMMERING AND POACHING

A liquid is said to simmer when the movement on the surface may be described as a gentle agitation with possible bubbling at one point, but not the pronounced rapid bubbling and strong movement that starts when boiling-point is reached. Simmering temperature may be from 185° to 200° F., but a cook is generally guided by the appearance of the liquid rather than by a thermometer.

Poaching is a term used to indicate a gentler cooking still; the water or other liquid should show only the gentlest quivering movement and the temperature should be between 170° and 180° F. Either process may be carried out, according to the dish in hand, on top of the stove or in the oven. Poaching is a process used for materials of delicate consistency which might be spoiled if subjected to strong heat. It is used primarily for eggs, fish, meat, vegetable creams, gnocchi, etc. The recipe usually indicates whether the process is to be carried out in the oven or on top of the stove, but as a general rule eggs, gnocchi, and quenelles are poached in water on top of the stove, and fish, whole or filleted, whether in wine, water, or fish stock, is usually poached in the oven. Meat, fish, and vegetable creams, cooked in moulds, and custards, plain baked, or renversées, may be said to be poached when they are set in a tin of boiling water, put in the oven, and cooked gently until set.

STEAMING

Steaming is a long, slow, and thorough method of cooking in which food is directly exposed to and surrounded by concentrated steam. This process is carried out with a special utensil. The steamer itself has a per-forated base which fits tightly over a saucepan, and it is covered with a well-fitting lid. This method is employed for puddings, certain meat, fish, and vegetable creams, and potatoes and some other vegetables. The points to be observed in steaming are that the water in the saucepan should never be allowed to go off the boil, because cooking then ceases; it is therefore necessary to have at hand a kettle of boiling water for replenishment, which may be required once or twice during the cooking. The lid should fit tightly and it is inadvisable to remove it at frequent intervals for inspection. If it should become necessary to look at the contents of the steamer the lid should be lifted off quickly and immediately turned upside-down, so that the water condensed inside it does not drip on to the object being cooked, an occurrence which may give an un-pleasant surface, for instance, to a suet pudding. The basin or mould which is set in the steamer is covered with grease-proof paper, and this may be pleated down the centre to allow for expansion.

To facilitate the removal of the contents of a steamer it is a good plan to arrange a strip of cloth under the basin or mould, bringing the ends of the cloth over the edges of the steamer. It is also necessary to select a basin which fits easily into the steamer and allows reasonable space for the steam amply to surround the basin.

A method of gentle steaming is to place the tin or mould on a thick piece of paper in a saucepan, with water half way up the side of the mould; the pan, with the lid on, is then stood over the heat until the water boils; it is then drawn aside and only a quarter of it is allowed to stand over the heat. If the contents are to be turned out of the mould it should be allowed to stand for a few minutes after it is taken from the saucepan. This more gentle method is suitable for delicate meats, fish creams, and set custards, and it is an alternative to cooking au bain-marie in the oven.

Fish for invalids is sometimes cooked between two plates over a pan of boiling water. This too is referred to as steaming, but is also a gentler process. More elegantly this may be done with a bell-glass over the plate, the thick glass cover that is used for chicken or mushrooms sous cloche.

COOKING 'AU BAIN-MARIE' OR IN A HOT-WATER BATH

This is a process designed to protect food from strong direct heat, either on the stove or in the oven. The food is insulated from fierce, dry heat by being surrounded by hot water. The words *au bain-marie* call for a little explanation. The kitchen utensil called a bain-marie is properly used for sauces and liquids which are to be kept hot but must not be allowed to reboil, as for instance certain sauces which have been thickened with egg or cream. This useful piece of equipment, more often seen in the kitchens of catering establishments than in English homes, consists of a large shallow pan containing an array of small saucepans of different sizes. When we speak of cooking by bain-marie we really mean cooking in a water bath. This is usually done in the oven in order to get top heat. To cook in this way the mould or basin containing the ingredients is placed in a baking-tin of water; the water is brought up to the boil, and the tin then put in the oven. This method is used for such dishes as custards, crème caramel, and vegetable and delicate fish creams, and it is a slightly drier method than steaming. Cooking in a double boiler, a method much advocated in American cook-books, is another example of cooking by bain-marie, and it is applied to custards, sauces, frostings, etc.

FRYING

Frying is cooking in hot fat and it is done by two methods, shallow and deep fat frying. Shallow frying is carried out in a frying-pan with enough hot fat to come half way up the object to be cooked, or in some cases the fat may be much shallower. Deep fat frying is done in a deep saucepan, the object to be fried being submerged in the fat or floated on the surface, as the case may be. The following rules are common to both methods:

1. The fat should always first be heated to the degree indicated in the recipe, the heat being judged sometimes by the blue vapour or smoke rising from the centre of the pan, and sometimes by a test made with a small piece of bread; sometimes the heat is tested by a thermometer.

2. Moderation should be shown in the number of objects fried at one time. If too much is put into the pan at once the fat is cooled, and this may result in greasiness and heaviness.

3. For each batch of frying the fat must be reheated to the required degree, and in some cases it is necessary to strain the fat between each batch of frying to remove any crumbs or other objects which have become burnt.

4. The food should always be thoroughly drained on a wire rack or on crumpled kitchen paper.

5. When frying is finished the fat should be strained through muslin into a bowl when it is cool, and the pan then wiped out first with crumpled paper and then with a dry cloth.

The following rules are applicable to *shallow fat frying*:

1. Choose a heavy type of pan and heat well before putting in the fat.

2. The fat to be used may be clarified fat, dripping, lard, butter, oil, or oil and butter mixed.

3. Food cooked in this way must be turned when brown on one side, and care taken not to pierce the object during the cooking.

DEEP FAT FRYING

This is a more economical method of cooking, for the fat used can be strained for repeated use. The temperature of the fat becomes so high that no flavour of the food that has been cooked remains in it, whereas in shallow frying this is not always so. For this operation a deep, thick iron or aluminium pan is required, preferably with a basket which fits it. If too thin a pan is used, the fat heats too quickly and is liable to boil over and catch fire. It is necessary to have the pan deep enough to hold sufficient fat to cover the food completely. Particular care is required in this operation. If the fat bath is overfilled, and the food put into it causes the fat to overflow the sides, serious accidents may result. If wet objects are introduced into the fat they cause fierce crackling and spitting, and again sometimes cause the fat to overflow its bounds. It should always be borne in mind that this highly heated fat is extremely inflammable. The fat should be melted first over gentle heat and then submitted to greater heat and brought gradually to the right temperature for cooking. It should be closely watched while coming up to cooking temperature. Where much cooking of this type is to be done, a frying thermometer should be employed. This registers up to 400° F. It should be stood in a pan of hot water and carefully dried before being put into the frying bath. The hot water warms the glass so that there is not too great a shock when it is plunged into the fat, which may be well over 212° F.

Fats saved from the skimming of stocks and so forth are not recommended for deep fat frying, but may, at need, be added to other fats after clarifying. The following rules sum up the points to be observed in deep fat frying:

1. The pan should be thick iron or aluminium and never too thin; it should be ample in size and have, if possible, handles at each side which make it easier and safer to lift. It should be fitted with a frying basket in which the food to be cooked may be laid before immersion.

2. A wire skimmer or spoon should be at hand, so that crumbs or morsels of food detached from the main object cooking may be carefully removed; otherwise, remaining in the fat, they will burn and give a dark colour and bitter taste.

3. Suitable fats are clarified dripping, lard, or lard and dripping mixed, and oil (vegetable oil is excellent, especially for dishes cooked *au maigre*). A mixture of beef suet and lard is excellent. Two pounds of suet to one pound of lard is a suitable mixture. The fat in the pan must come half

way, or possibly two-thirds of the way, up the side, in order that the food fried may be totally immersed or can float easily as the case requires.

4. The fat must be perfectly clean and free from sediment and should always be strained after use.   It may be used many times, provided it does not get overheated and burnt and that reasonable care be taken of it.

Nearly all food requires a protective coating before being cooked in deep fat. This serves to keep in the moisture and to prevent the food from bursting under the high temperature; exceptions to this are potato chips, ribbons, etc.

5. Great care must be taken not to allow water or other liquid to get into the fat.

6. Great care must be taken in moving the pan of hot fat on the stove, as it is highly inflammable.

TEMPERATURES

Frying temperatures vary from 330° to 400° F. When frying food already cooked, such as fishcakes, all that is required is that the fat shall give a crisp coating and that the inside shall be heated through.   Therefore in these cases a hotter temperature may be employed.   But where the food has to be cooked through, as well as acquiring a crisp outside, a somewhat lower temperature will be called for, because the duration of cooking is longer.   It is important to test the temperature.   With a frying thermometer the temperature is easily judged, but in the average kitchen it is more usual to test in other ways.   When the fat is at its hottest, i.e. 390°–400° F., a blue haze will rise from the surface.   No other indication is necessary, and the fat is ready for small croquettes, fritters (other than apple), fillets of whiting, whitebait, and smelt, croûtons, game chips, and the final frying of French fried or chip potatoes.

For other foods the following test may be carried out:

1. Take a small cube of bread such as a soup croûton and drop it into the fat bath; if the bread sinks to the bottom and does not frizzle at all the fat is not ready for use.

2. If, however, the bread frizzles gently, the fat is ready for beignets and the first frying of potatoes.   This is just before haze point.

3. At haze point a light blue haze rises from the surface.   The fat is now at moderate heat and the croûton will brown in about a minute.   Large croquettes, rissoles, large fillets of fish, apple fritters, etc., may now be fried.

The following table of temperatures is intended to be a general indication; the recipes themselves will give more detailed instructions.

FRYING TEMPERATURES

Choux paste (beignets soufflés, etc.)	330° F.–375° F. (rising gradually, see recipe, page 934)
First frying of potatoes	330° F.–340° F.
Croquettes, rissoles, large fillets of fish, fruit fritters, cutlets	360° F.–390° F.
Second frying of potatoes, small fritters, croûtons, etc.	390° F.–400° F.

COATINGS FOR FRIED FOOD

Certain foods, if put directly into boiling fat without a coating of some kind, would disintegrate and the fat would boil over. If fish were put straight into hot fat, the agitation brought about by the introduction of the wet surface would cause the fat to boil up and overflow the sides of the pan. (Potatoes which have been soaked should be drained and thoroughly dried in a cloth before being introduced into hot fat.)

The simplest coating of all is seasoned flour and milk. The food to be fried is first brushed over with milk, then tossed in a cloth or a sheet of paper in flour mixed with salt and pepper, to which may be added flavourings in the form of grated lemon rind, chopped parsley, or other herbs.

Flour, beaten egg, and dried white breadcrumbs is another and usual coating (see Egging and crumbing, Chapter III, page 38), and a third method, suitable for fillets of fish and fritters both sweet and savoury, is to dip the food to be fried into batter. It should be noted that when batter is used as a coating the frying basket is not used, because scraps of the batter would cling to the wire and, exposing the raw surface of the food, possibly cause an accident, besides allowing the fat to penetrate the food. Moreover the particles so separated would become burnt and cause burning of the fat, spoiling both colour and flavour.

Certain foods for deep fat frying may be encased in pastry, which may be left plain or coated in egg and rolled in vermicelli (see recipe for rissoles, page 718).

GENERAL CARE OF THE FAT BATH

1. The fat should be allowed to cool and be strained through muslin into a clean, dry, enamel bowl. This should be done after every occasion of frying.

2. It should be covered when cold, and kept in a cool place.

3. The fat used should be perfectly clean (see instructions on clarifying fat, page 40).

OIL

This is more difficult to clean. It reaches a high temperature more rapidly than the solid fats and therefore may burn. It cannot of course be treated with water. The potato method is applicable, but must be carried out with care.

SOLID FAT

To clarify solid fat, for example the trimmings of cutlets, beefsteak, etc., cut into small pieces, put into a roasting-tin, and set in a slow oven until all the fat is extracted and the pieces of fat brown and crisp; then cool slightly and press.

TAMMYING

By this process certain liquids, such as the finer cream or velouté soups and sauces, which require to be particularly finely strained, are passed through a tammy cloth or a tammy strainer, whichever may be called for in the recipe. The process improves both gloss and consistency, and the use of the tammy cloth also helps to bind or amalgamate the liquid passed through it.

The tammy strainer. This is made of gauze and is conical in shape. It should be reserved exclusively for the use for which it is intended. After use it should be washed immediately and thoroughly in clean hot water. If this is not done the gauze becomes clogged and is then very difficult to clean. This strainer is used for certain stocks, especially fish, velouté soups, the juice from the bones for a salmis, and for any sauce where fine straining and good finish is wanted.

The tammy cloth. This is a piece of special material of slightly rough texture, like a hard non-hairy flannel. In the absence of this a piece of coarse linen is sometimes used. Before use the cloth is scalded and wrung out in hot water. After use it is well washed in warm water, then scalded again and well dried before being put away. For use the cloth is laid over a bowl, the liquid to be tammied is poured into the centre, the edges are folded neatly over, then the ends are twisted in opposite ways until all the liquid has been forced through. This process is applied to velouté and cream soups where a particularly fine and velvety finish is required, and to such sauces as cardinal or nantua in which lobster or shrimp butter is added. The process is carried out when the sauce has been completed, and it is then carefully reheated before being served.

BONING

For this process a small, sharp vegetable knife may be used.

TO BONE MEAT

Unless other instructions are given a small incision is made at the point where the bone is nearest to the surface, for example at the edge of the blade of a shoulder of mutton or at the edge of the chine bone of a loin or neck of lamb. The knife should be kept firmly against the bone the whole time and the flesh worked away in short, clean cuts. The fingers of the left hand should be kept well under the flap of meat being lifted, peeling it back gently from the blade of the knife. Generally speaking the object of boning is to make room for a force-meat or stuffing and the bone should be removed with a minimum amount of cutting, leaving as small a gap as is reasonably possible. In the case of a shoulder or leg of lamb, for instance, the space left by the removal of the bone should be as much like a pocket as is possible.

TO BONE GAME AND POULTRY

It is not necessary to draw the bird before boning; the process is easier if this is not done.

1. For a galantine when the flesh is to be rolled. The first cut is made down the centre of the back of the bird. The flesh is cut and worked off the bone in the way described above. When the leg is reached the bone is taken out from the thigh downwards. The working off is continued until the centre breast-bone is reached, then the process is repeated on the other side from the back cut, working again to the centre. When all the flesh is loosed and ready to be lifted right off the carcass, care must be taken not to cut through the skin at the edge of the breast-bone where it is thin.

2. When the bird is to be stuffed and reshaped. For this more stuffing is used and it is not easy to keep a good shape. Sometimes, to help to keep an attractive shape, the drumstick bones and wing pinions are left in. For this method start the boning at the wing joint and work the flesh backward towards the tail, working all round the bird, and turning the flesh and skin inside out. When all flesh is off the carcass the flesh and skin are turned back again and stuffed according to the recipe, then shaped and trussed as neatly as possible. After boning, the carcass is cleaned, washed, and broken up for making into stock with the giblets.

V

Soups and Soup-making

I. SOUPS IN GENERAL

R. H. and I both think it would be small wonder if young students thought soups and soup-making to be among the least interesting of culinary matters. In the last decade there have been some poor concoctions ladled out in the name of soup: quite enough to cause all interest in this course to die. We have passed through a period when we were short of materials, and we are still often short of time, and as a result what used to be a first-class item of food has deteriorated and is too often looked on as a mere fill-in.

In the days when soup was Beautiful Soup I do not believe a Victorian music-hall audience would have appreciated that crack of the late Billy Bennett: 'There were three kinds of soup, noodle, poodle, and cock-a-doodle. The soup was thrown in—it should have been thrown out.' I am not sure if that is the exact wording, but it is near enough.

We cannot, and I doubt if we want to, go back to the heavy richness of some of the Victorian recipes, but there is a half-way house between those and some of the uninteresting mixtures one meets with to-day.

It will, we think, be more generally helpful, more in keeping with contemporary taste, if, contrary to usual practice, we leave the subject of the preparation of stocks, consommés, and soups which call for meat as a main ingredient till later in the chapter, and pay primary attention to soups in which vegetables play a main part, and to those which may suitably be made in small quantities and do not call for lengthy preparation.

But it would, we think, be a pity if in our anxiety to be practical we were to restrict ourselves entirely to utility models. There is no fun, no inspiration in that, so although due attention is paid to what must be, there will be found later on recipes for some party soups as well as for a few of the great classics.

In all circumstances, one point cannot be over-emphasized: whether the soup be rich or plain, for dinner-party or homely luncheon, the classic method should be followed. Short cuts, unnecessary omissions will give disappointing results. We all know the kind of cook who, on being given the recipe for some dish which we have liked particularly, has indicated immediately that she thinks the whole process quite unnecessary, the

78

instructions too full of frills, and that she for her part could never be bothered with all that nonsense. We know also how often she fails to produce good food. I do assure you that no instructions are given for fun, for effect, to make it harder, or for any other reason than that it is by observing the details of preparation that one gets the best results.

To emphasize certain points in a practical way, I am using as an example the most simple recipe for a French potato soup, Potage Purée Parmentier, and after giving the ingredients and method I am taking the instructions apart and amplifying each one. To anyone with a little experience this may seem like making heavy weather over so small a matter, but a beginner may find it of use, and the instructions will serve as a model for other soups of a similar type.

POTAGE PURÉE PARMENTIER

1 lb. peeled potatoes	*Liaison*
1 medium-sized onion	1 egg yolk
1½ oz. butter	½ gill cream
1 bay-leaf	
salt and pepper	croûtons
1½ pints milk	

Slice the potatoes and onion finely and evenly, melt the butter in a stew-pan, add the vegetables, cover, and cook very slowly for about 7 minutes. The potatoes must on no account brown. When softened, draw the pan aside, add the bay-leaf and milk. Cover and simmer for 20 minutes. Then pass through a fine wire sieve. Return to a clean pan, season, reheat to boiling-point, whisk well with a sauce whisk, and add the liaison (see note on liaisons, page 138). Serve with an appropriate garnish.

This soup, containing butter, milk, cream, and egg, is moderately rich, but on page 81 there is another version of it which is simpler in procedure and is made principally with water or light stock and a small proportion of milk. It is possible, of course, to dilute the milk with water in the above recipe, but this sometimes causes the soup to curdle.

Here are the instructions taken apart and amplified so that they may be taken as a guide to the making of potages purées generally.

Instruction 1

Slice the potatoes and onion finely and evenly. The object of this is to facilitate the absorption by the vegetables of the butter. This is more thoroughly accomplished when the slices are evenly thin than when they are thick and uneven. Moreover the cooking process is completed sooner and more thoroughly.

Instruction 2

Melt the butter, add the vegetables, cover, and cook slowly. During this process the vegetables are required to absorb the butter. If the butter is too hot the surface of the slices will become fried and resistant, thus defeating this object. The butter therefore should not be too hot and the vegetables should cook slowly or, as cooks say, sweat. This will take about 7 minutes to accomplish. The vegetables should become soft but in no circumstances brown. The French have a good word to describe the appearance of vegetables so cooked, *fondant*, meaning 'melting.' Sometimes this process of sweating may be facilitated by the addition of a sheet of buttered paper pressed down closely over the top of the vegetables.

Instruction 3

Cover and simmer. Simmering a liquid means just letting it move gently, bubbling only in one part of the pan; this process usually continues for about 20–30 minutes. This may be taken as a general rule. Certain vegetable soups when overcooked lose a good deal of flavour, and in the case of green vegetables lose colour as well. There is a choice of liquids for this type of soup: in this recipe it is milk. Sometimes a vegetable stock is used, and in particular the water in which potatoes, carrots, artichokes and so forth have been boiled.

Instruction 4

Pass through a fine sieve. The correct way to sieve a soup is as follows: Take a sieve (the suitable type is generally indicated in the recipe; it may be wire, hair, or now nylon in place of hair); place this over a large bowl and pour all the liquid through from the pan, keeping the vegetables back with the lid; now place the sieve over an adequately sized plate or dish and rub or push a little of the vegetable through at a time with a wooden spoon or curved spatula. All the time you are doing this the lid should be kept on the pan, so that the heat is retained. When all the material has been pressed through, scrape every bit of purée from underneath the sieve with a wooden spoon, thoroughly rinse out the pan, and return the purée from the plate. Dilute this purée by degrees with the liquid from the bowl, adding gradually and stirring well. In this way you get a perfectly smooth soup. In this recipe a wire sieve is called for; when potatoes are being sieved there is danger that if they are worked too vigorously they will become gluey. The action is one of crushing and pressing rather than of rubbing.

Instruction 5

Add the liaison. A note on liaisons is given on page 138, but to complete these instructions it may be repeated here. The yolks should not be added directly to the boiling soup, or they will curdle. Put the yolks in a small bowl, beat them slightly, add the cold milk or cream, and mix well. Now remove the pan of soup from direct heat, take from it one at a time 3 or 4 spoonfuls of soup, and add them to the egg mixture. Now, with the soup still away from direct heat, strain into it the contents of the bowl. Serve the soup at once. There is no flour in this soup, so you will note that it is not reboiled after the liaison has been added.

The heat of a purée of this type is generally sufficient to cook the egg in the liaison.

In certain recipes there may be found an instruction to bring back to boiling-point a liquid to which a liaison of egg and milk has been added. That is because it is considered that the amount of flour, corn-flour, or fécule in the liquid is sufficient to prevent curdling.

When additional enrichment in the form of butter is to be added at the end of cooking, it is important that the process should be carried out properly if the texture, appearance, and goodness of the soup are to be right. The butter should be divided into fragments which should be whisked well into the soup with a sauce whisk.

Do I hear, ghost-like on the air, the words 'What a performance'? It certainly sounds rather like that, but once it is set out so that those who have 'never boiled an egg' cannot go wrong, we can leave it; for once you have carried out these rather minute instructions you will appreciate their relative value, and will carry them out in all the variants of potages purées, or, alternatively, skip or skimp them according to your will; but at any rate you will have a sort of measuring-rod to help you if you wonder one day why your purée falls short of perfection.

I want to go on with the recipes for purées, but first I will give the simpler version of the Parmentier. There are, of course, other soups with a base of potatoes, but with richer additions, and these will be found in the party section of this chapter, i.e. Potage Purée Bonne Femme and Crème Vichyssoise, a most delicious cold cream soup.

Here then is the simpler version of Parmentier:

POTAGE PURÉE PARMENTIER
simplified version

2 medium-sized onions	salt and pepper
¾ lb. potatoes weighed after peeling	1½ pints light stock or water or potato water
1 oz. butter	½ pint boiling milk
a pinch of mace	a piece of butter

Slice the onions and potatoes very thinly. Melt the butter in a thick stew-pan, add vegetables, cover and cook very slowly for 7–10 minutes, stirring from time to time, without allowing the vegetables to colour, add stock or water and seasoning, bring to boil, and simmer with the lid on 40–50 minutes. Adjust seasoning, add boiling milk, whisk in a piece of butter, and serve.

Chopped chives are a good addition; the soup should be creamy and should not resemble porridge.

A good simple potato soup is made by using a potato mousseline as thickening for a thin béchamel sauce. The sauce should be well seasoned and flavoured, and the amount of potato to be beaten in is judged as the mixing proceeds.

Certain root vegetables are lacking in starch, and though these may be treated in the same way as in the preceding recipes they call for the addition of a thickening ingredient; this may be flour, arrowroot, cream of rice, sago, or corn-flour.

POTAGE CRÈME AUX CHOUX

1 good green cabbage, weighing about 1 lb. when trimmed	¾ oz. flour
1¼ oz. butter	1¼ pints milk or milk and water, and a little extra milk if necessary
1–2 oz. onion, finely chopped	
1–2 oz. chopped potato	½ gill cream (optional)
a pinch of nutmeg or ground mace	1 tablespoon chopped parsley grated Parmesan cheese
salt and pepper	

Cut cabbage into four, trim away a little of the stalk. Blanch in boiling water for 6 minutes. Drain, refresh, drain again, and press well. Chop. Melt the butter in a pan, add the onion, and allow to soften without colouring. Add the cabbage and potato and stir over a moderate heat for a few minutes. Add the spice and seasonings, the flour and liquid. Bring to boil and simmer 10–12 minutes. Rub through a nylon sieve. Turn into a clean pan, reheat, adjust the seasoning, and the consistency by adding a little boiling milk if necessary. Lightly whip the cream, and just before serving add a spoonful to each soup-bowl. Scatter the top with a small spoonful of the parsley and a light dusting of the cheese over all.

A Cream of Brussels Sprouts may be made in the same way.

Here is a recipe for Potage Palestine where the same process is adopted as before in making the purée, and flour is added for thickening. This is followed by a second recipe for a richer Palestine, and then by a recipe for a carrot soup in which a small quantity of potato and cream of rice is used, and in addition a final liaison is made with yolk of egg.

POTAGE PALESTINE (1)

1–1¼ lb. Jerusalem artichokes (weighed before peeling)	1 pint boiling milk
2 medium onions	1 oz. corn-flour
1 oz. butter	½ gill cold milk
1 pint water or potato water	¾ oz. butter
a pinch of salt and sugar	2 dozen fried croûtons (stale bread)

Wash, peel, wipe, and slice the artichokes. Slice the onions. Cook the onions in butter for 5–6 minutes, do not colour; add artichokes and shake over gentle heat for 15 minutes. Add water and seasoning, cover, bring to the boil, and simmer for 15–20 minutes. Rub through a hair or a fine wire sieve and add boiling milk. Blend corn-flour with cold milk, add, bring to the boil, stirring with the sauce whisk, adjust seasoning, then simmer for a few minutes, adding butter in small pieces. Strain and serve with fried croûtons.

POTAGE PALESTINE (2)

1 lb. artichokes
1¼ oz. butter
3 oz. onion, finely sliced
6 hazel-nuts, grilled or baked to remove skins, and crushed and pounded
½ teaspoon salt
a good pinch of sugar
¾ pint warm water
¾ pint boiling milk

a level teaspoon arrowroot
2–3 tablespoons cold milk

Liaison
2 yolks of egg
3–4 tablespoons cream
or
1 oz. butter

soup croûtons served separately

Wash artichokes well, peel, dry, and slice thinly. Heat the butter in large thick pan, add the onion, and cook gently for a few minutes, then put in the artichokes, and continue cooking very gently on a low heat. On no account allow to colour. At the end of 10 minutes add the crushed nuts, salt, and sugar. Pour in the water, and simmer 15–20 minutes. Rub through a nylon sieve, return to the rinsed-out pan, boil the milk, and whisk into the artichoke purée.

Mix the arrowroot with the cold milk, pour into the soup, and bring to the boil, whisking all the time. Simmer 3–4 minutes. Adjust seasoning, skim if necessary, and add the liaison; if it is omitted, add the butter in small pieces off the fire, whisking vigorously.

CRÈME DE CAROTTES

2 oz. butter
2 onions
1 lb. carrots
1 clove of garlic, crushed, with a pinch of salt
salt and black pepper
1 potato

1 teaspoon cream of rice
1½ pints milk and water mixed in equal quantities
½ gill cream
1 yolk of egg
chopped parsley
small squares of dried toast

Melt the butter in a stew-pan. Add the finely sliced onions and carrots, and the crushed garlic. Season with salt and black pepper and cook slowly with the lid on for 10 minutes, stirring occasionally. Then add the sliced potato and cook for another few moments. Add the cream of rice and stir until smooth. Pour on the liquid and stir over the fire until it comes to the boil. Draw aside and simmer for 20 minutes. Rub through a nylon or fine wire sieve. Mix the cream and egg yolk and make the liaison. Return soup to the pan, add liaison, and stir over the fire until it thickens without boiling. Pour into the soup marmite. Sprinkle the top with freshly chopped parsley and serve with small squares of dried toast.

Here is a recipe for a simple carrot soup in which bread is used as thickening and no final liaison is required:

POTAGE CRÉCY

1 onion
½ lb. carrots (if these are old and large the red part only should be used, and weighed when cut)
2 oz. butter
a thick slice of crust of bread cut from the bottom or sides of a loaf, as it should not be too hard or brown, with

about ¼ inch of crumb attached and weighing about 3 oz.
3 pints vegetable stock
a pinch of sugar
seasoning
a bouquet of parsley
2 tablespoons rice
a little chopped chervil or mint

Slice and chop the onion finely. Slice the carrots thinly and evenly (or if using old carrots peel off the red part thinly as though peeling an apple and work down until the core is reached; this can be done most efficiently with a potato-peeler). Put half the butter with the onion and carrot into the pan, cover, and cook very gently till the carrot is quite soft, about 20 minutes. If the cooking is too fast and the carrot fried you will not get the best results. Cut the crust in dice and dry in the oven. Add the dried dice to the carrots with a quart of the stock, the parsley, and the pinch of sugar. Simmer gently 35–40 minutes. While the cooking proceeds, prepare the rice by boiling till tender in salted water. Put the contents of the stew-pan through a fine sieve and return to the rinsed saucepan. Add remainder of stock. Adjust seasoning and simmer again for 10–15 minutes, skimming frequently. Remove from the fire, whisk in the rest of the butter, add cooked, drained rice and chervil or mint, and serve.

CELERY SOUP

There is a possibility that soup made with heads of celery may curdle. For this reason many celery soups are made with root celery (celeriac) (see Potage Savoyarde, page 98). The following recipe calls for a head of celery and the procedure is arranged to minimize the risk of curdling, that is to say the celery is not boiled in milk but is made into a purée and then added to a creamy béchamel. A fresh, crisp head should be chosen, and the piece of root, so often thrown away, used.

POTAGE CRÈME DE CÉLERI (CREAM OF CELERY)

1 good head of celery
1 medium-sized onion
2¼ oz. butter
1½ pints milk, or milk and water
2 blades of mace
2 bay-leaves
6 peppercorns

1¼ oz. flour
salt

Liaison
2 yolks of egg
½ gill cream

croûtons

Slice celery and onion finely. Melt ¾ oz. butter in a stew-pan, put in the vegetables, cover with a buttered paper and the lid, and stew very gently 20–30 minutes, or until the vegetables are very soft.

Meanwhile put the milk into a saucepan with the spices and bay-leaves, bring very slowly to the boil with the lid on. When well flavoured strain and cool. Rinse out the pan, melt the remaining butter in this, and stir in the flour. Pour on the flavoured milk, blend well, and stir on the fire until boiling; reduce heat and simmer 4–5 minutes. In the meantime, rub the celery and onion through a nylon sieve; draw the sauce aside and whisk in the purée by degrees, adjusting the seasoning.

Work the yolks and cream together for the liaison and add as directed (page 80). Serve at once with the croûtons.

The following, a delicious soup made with young turnips, requires the addition of a liaison, as there is little thickening quality in the vegetable itself:

POTAGE FRÉNEUSE

¾ lb. young turnips (weighed when peeled)	1½ oz. butter
	1 oz. flour
2 oz. onion	2–3 yolks of egg
2 pints vegetable stock or potato water	2–3 tablespoons thick cream
	salt and pepper

Cut the turnips and onion in quarters and blanch for a few minutes in salted water. Meanwhile melt the butter in a stew-pan. Add the flour, mix, and pour on the liquid; stir until boiling. Then add the vegetables and simmer until absolutely soft, about 40 minutes. Pass through a nylon sieve. Rinse out the pan well, return the soup, mix the yolks and cream together and make the liaison in the usual way (page 140). Thicken carefully over a slow fire or in a bain-marie. Adjust the seasoning.

This soup should be very smooth and creamy and should be put through a hair or nylon sieve: a wire one would not give the right texture.

Serve with croûtons of fried bread or tiny crisp cheese profiteroles.

Thick soups are made with vegetables other than roots, and with these come variations in method.

POTAGE ST GERMAIN

a handful of spinach leaves and a head of lettuce	1 flat teaspoon salt
	1 good teaspoon sugar
2 leeks (green part only) or seedling leeks	3 oz. butter (this quantity may be modified)
1 quart large shelled peas	1 gill cold water
a bouquet of chervil, and some small sprigs for garnish	1 quart white or vegetable stock or water
pepper	1 cup small fresh green peas

Wash the spinach, lettuce, and green parts of the leeks and shred finely. Put these with the large peas, the bouquet of chervil, the pepper, salt, and sugar, 2 oz. of the butter, and the gill of cold water into the pan. Bring to the boil and draw away from heat. Cover and let the contents simmer gently and regularly for 35–45 minutes. Put the contents through a fine sieve. Return to a clean pan and add the white or vegetable stock or water. Stir thoroughly and bring to the boil. While this is going on, the small green peas should be cooked in boiling salted water till tender, then drained. Now add the remainder of the butter to the purée, verifying the seasoning; add the small green peas and serve in a hot tureen.

Here is a recipe for Danish Green Pea Soup, given to us by Lorna Francis:

DANISH GREEN PEA SOUP

1 pint shelled peas	20 baby carrots, or 2 large
2 sprigs of parsley	carrots cut in 16 pieces and
1 sprig of mint	shaped like baby carrots
1 quart good chicken stock	1 tablespoon finely chopped
1 oz. butter	parsley
1 oz. flour	1 gill cream or top of milk
salt and pepper	

Simmer peas in the stock till tender, with the herbs. Strain the peas from the stock and rub them through a nylon sieve. Melt the butter in a clean pan, mix in the flour, pour on the stock, stir until boiling, whisk in the purée, season, and simmer for a few minutes. Add the baby carrots, previously simmered in a little stock, and the parsley. Finish with cream or top of milk. Serve hot or chilled.

Celery, broad beans, French beans, cauliflowers, chestnuts, pumpkins are all vegetables which in season may suitably be used for soup.

Here are some further recipes:

POTAGE PURÉE DE FÈVES (BROAD BEAN SOUP)

1 lb. broad beans (weighed after shelling)	1 teaspoon arrowroot
	¼ pint milk or cream
1 pint light stock (veal or chicken)	1 oz. butter
2 sprigs of savory or thyme	seasoning

The thick skins of the beans would give a bitter taste to the soup; they would also give it a granulated appearance and a bad colour. They must therefore be removed and this should be done with a small pointed knife. Then cook the beans with the sprigs of savory quickly in boiling stock, with the lid off the pan, for 20 minutes. When the beans are beginning to break, take off and drain, keeping the liquor and reserving a few of the best beans for the garnish. Rub the rest of them through a fine sieve. Return to the pan with the liquor. Bring to the boil, season, simmer 10–15 minutes, skimming frequently. Mix the arrowroot with the milk, pour into the soup, and allow to boil up for a minute or two. Then add the butter in small pieces, and the broad beans kept back for garnish. A liaison of egg yolks may be added to the soup.

POTAGE PURÉE DE MARRONS

¾ lb. peeled chestnuts. (The small English ones will do. You will then need about 1¼ lb. unpeeled.)
2 oz. sliced onion
½ oz. butter or bacon fat
salt and pepper

1 sour apple, peeled, cored, and sliced
1 oz. carrot
a little thin cream or top of milk
chopped parsley
1½ pints stock or water

To peel the chestnuts put them into cold water and bring to the boil. Take off the fire, take 1 or 2 out of the boiling water at a time and remove the skins. Directly the water begins to cool and the chestnuts become hard to peel, bring the water up to the boil again. Put the peeled nuts in a stew-pan with the sliced onion, the carrot, and the stock. Cover, season, and simmer until the nuts are absolutely soft. Put all through a hair or fine wire sieve and return to the pan with the top of the milk or the cream. Reheat slowly.

If no hair sieve is available and a wire one must be used, put the chestnuts through as rapidly as possible, as they are apt to discolour in contact with metal.

When immature nuts are used the soup may need a little thickening—arrowroot, corn-flour, or an egg liaison will be suitable. This should be done before the addition of the cream.

For the garnish, melt the butter or fat in a frying-pan and fry the slices of apple in this quickly. They should be a nice brown. Add them to the soup just before serving and sprinkle the top of the soup with chopped parsley.

POTAGE ANDALOUSE (PUMPKIN SOUP)

2 lb. pumpkin
6 oz. potatoes
4 oz. onions
½ lb. tomatoes
1 quart water or potato water

salt and pepper
1½ oz. rice
1 pint salted water
½ oz. butter
½ gill cream

Peel and cut up the pumpkin, potatoes, and onions and chop the tomatoes. Put them into a saucepan with the quart of water, salt, and pepper. Bring to the boil and cook until tender, about 20 minutes. While the vegetables are cooking, boil the rice in a pint of salted water. When cooked, strain and rinse with cold water. Put the cooked vegetables through a fine sieve, return them to the pan, and reheat. Add the rice, a nut of butter, and the cream. The soup should be of a creamy consistency and a rich golden colour.

Small fried croûtons, served separately, may replace the rice if this is not available.

When green peppers are plentiful this Creole Soup is one of many good uses for them:

CREOLE SOUP

2 oz. butter	salt
2 heaped tablespoons finely chopped onion	pepper
	cayenne
4 heaped tablespoons finely chopped green peppers	a dash of vinegar
	2 teaspoons freshly grated horse-radish
1½ oz. flour	
1 lb. tomatoes	
1 quart stock, preferably vegetable	*Garnish* croûtons

Heat butter and cook onion and peppers gently for 5–7 minutes till softened; do not allow to brown. Sprinkle with flour and continue cooking for 3 or 4 minutes. Peel and chop the tomatoes, and add with stock. Simmer for 1 hour. Season very well. Add finally the dash of vinegar and horse-radish which may be modified to taste. Add the garnish and serve. This soup is sometimes put through a sieve but is nicer left unsieved.

In making a green vegetable soup with such materials as lettuce, spinach, cucumber and so forth there are variations in method. Sometimes the vegetables are boiled in water, drained, and pressed through a sieve, and the resulting purée added to a roux-thickened liquid, really a thin béchamel. In this case a roux is made with the addition of chopped onion or a vegetable mirepoix (see béchamel, page 155), liquid added, and the whole simmered 10–15 minutes. It is then strained and returned to the pan, the purée beaten in, and a liaison of fécule or egg added if desired. A rough guide to proportions is 1–1½ oz. each of butter and flour for each pint of liquid. This may vary to some small degree depending on the amount and strength of the vegetable purée to be added, and whether or not a liaison is to be used. If it is borne in mind that the consistency of a vegetable cream soup should resemble that of thin cream, it is easy after a little practice, using the above quantities as a guide, to experiment with various green vegetables. In some cases, e.g. Potage Crème de Laitue, the flour is added to the vegetables immediately after the preliminary softening.

To obtain a more creamy finish to purée soups, a little more butter than is given in the recipe may be used. This extra butter should be added in small pieces just before the soup is served, and stirred in, but on no account should the soup continue cooking after this addition has been made.

Sometimes a mixture of milk and water or milk and vegetable stock is called for in a vegetable soup. It should be observed that this mixture sometimes causes a slight granulation in the texture of the soup, and although this is not a very serious defect, it is advisable, when possible, to use all milk or stock and, particularly in the latter case, an egg liaison for finish.

POTAGE CRÈME DE LAITUE

2 large heads of lettuce
2 oz. chopped onion
1 oz. butter
¾ oz. flour
salt and pepper
1½ pints milk

Liaison
1 teaspoon arrowroot or 2 egg yolks
½ gill cream or top of milk

Garnish.
fried croûtons
freshly chopped mint

Finely shred the lettuce, melt the butter, add the lettuce and onion, cover, and stew gently 5–7 minutes. Draw aside, add the flour and seasoning. Add liquid and simmer 15–20 minutes, pass through a fine sieve. Return to the pan, add the liaison, and bring up to the boil. Sprinkle with freshly chopped mint and serve with fried croûtons.

POTAGE PURÉE D'ÉPINARDS

1 lb. spinach
½ oz. butter
½ oz. flour
¾ pint stock
1 teaspoon finely chopped shallot

¼ pint milk
a little nutmeg
½ gill cream or top of milk
quartered hard-boiled eggs
slices of lemon

Prepare the spinach and cook in plenty of boiling water until tender; drain well. Blend the butter and flour, add the stock, and stir until boiling. Add the prepared spinach and the shallot, and simmer gently 20 minutes. Pass through a fine sieve, return to the pan, adding the milk, a grating of nutmeg, and the cream. Reheat carefully and serve with quartered hard-boiled eggs and slices of lemon.

PARSLEY SOUP

2 oz. onion
¼ lb. good parsley
1½ pints stock or water
1 oz. butter

1 oz. flour
salt and pepper
3 oz. potato
1½ gills top of milk

Slice the onion and coarsely chop the parsley. Put the stock or water into a pan with salt and bring to the boil, add the onion and parsley and simmer 30 minutes uncovered. Rub through a nylon or fine wire sieve. Melt the butter in the pan, add the flour, pour on the liquid, season, and stir until boiling. Dice the potato, simmer them in the milk until soft with the lid on the pan, then add to the soup.

POTAGE CRESSONIÈRE (1) (WATERCRESS SOUP)

1 lb. potatoes
1 teaspoon salt
1½ pints milk

1 bunch of watercress
1 oz. butter

Peel the potatoes, quarter them, and boil them in salted water until tender. Drain, crush them with a potato-masher, and when free from all lumps add the boiling milk and the salt.   While the potatoes are cooking, wash and pick the leaves off the watercress and chop roughly.   Add to the soup and cook for 5–6 minutes.   Take off the fire and add the butter. Pour into a hot tureen and serve.

POTAGE CRESSONIÈRE (2)

2 bunches of good cress
2 oz. butter
1 chopped onion
1½ oz. flour
2 pints milk and water mixed

Liaison
1 heaped teaspoon arrow-
   root, slaked with ⅛ gill
   cream

Coarsely chop the cress.   Melt butter in a pan, add the onion, cover, and cook a few minutes.   Now add cress and cook a further 5–6 minutes. Draw aside, add flour and liquid.   Blend and simmer 15 minutes.   Rub through a fine sieve.   Rinse out pan, return the soup, and add liaison if called for.

Potage Germiny is a soup made of sorrel, spinach, and spring onions, but as it is particularly good made with chicken stock and calls for 3 yolks for the liaison, it will be found in the section on party soups; another sorrel soup, Soupe à l'Oseille à la Paysanne, is to be found in the section on peasant soups.

CREAM OF TOMATO SOUP

1 lb. ripe tomatoes or 1 small
   can of tomatoes
1–2 oz. onion
1–2 oz. carrot
1 oz. butter
1 oz. flour
1 pint water, or vegetable or
   potato stock
1 bay-leaf
2 lumps of sugar

a pinch of ground mace or
   nutmeg
salt and freshly ground black
   pepper
1 teaspoon arrowroot (if
   called for)
3–4 tablespoons cream or
   evaporated milk
cheese croûtes (see next page)

Wipe, slice, and pip the tomatoes.   Finely slice the onion and carrot. Melt the butter in a pan, add the onion and carrot, cover, and allow to soften for 5–6 minutes.   Draw aside from the heat, stir in the flour, add the tomatoes, liquid, bay-leaf, sugar, spice, and seasoning.   Stir until boiling, simmer for 20–30 minutes.   Rub through a nylon sieve or aluminium strainer, pour back into the rinsed-out pan, and reheat. Adjust seasoning and thicken slightly, if necessary, with a teaspoon or more of arrowroot slaked with a tablespoon of water.   Reboil.

Add cream or evaporated milk, or this may be added to each bowl of soup, with a little chopped chives sprinkled on the top.   If the tomatoes are not very full of flavour, a teaspoon of concentrated tomato purée may be added with them.

Serve cheese croûtes either separately or in the soup.

Cheese croûtes

1 oz. grated cheese	1–2 rounds of bread, cut
¼–½ oz. butter	¼–½ inch thick
pepper, salt, mustard, cayenne	

Work the cheese and butter together on a plate with a palette-knife. Season highly. Toast the bread fairly slowly on one side, spread the cheese mixture thickly on the other. Toast quickly to a golden brown, then cut each round into small squares (¼–½ inch), and serve at once.

Now follow some recipes where a slight variation of method, or more particularly some trick of flavouring or finish, gives results a little out of the ordinary, and while economical enough for everyday use, these soups are also good for special occasions.

In some of them long simmering is called for and this is done with the lid half off the pan. In this way some evaporation takes place and consequently the liquid is partially reduced and concentrated.

First comes a tomato soup made interesting by the addition of a garnish of blanched shredded orange peel. Then comes a piquante, spicy soup, very warming in winter and good for a party, and then another tomato soup called Potage Véronique, where the addition of fresh tomato at the end of cooking gives a refreshing taste.

The flavouring of the following soup is essentially delicate and is obtained in the first place by rubbing one lump of sugar on to the rind of an orange in order to get some of the richly flavoured oil which is the zest. It is important not to overdo this flavouring or the delicate balance of the final effect will be spoiled. It is all too easy to overdo the orange. The garnish, consisting of a small quantity of the rind thinly pared, shredded, and then blanched, adds the final delicate touch.

POTAGE DE TOMATES A L'ORANGE

2 lb. tomatoes, fresh or canned	1½ oz. butter
1 medium-sized carrot	1½ oz. flour
1 medium-sized onion	1 lump of sugar and a little
1 bay-leaf	additional sugar to taste
1 strip of lemon rind	1 gill cream or top of milk
6 peppercorns	orange rind for garnish
2½ pints stock, chicken or vegetable	
salt	

Choose ripe red tomatoes. Wipe, cut in half, and squeeze lightly to remove the seeds. Slice the onion and carrot finely and put in a stew-pan, together with tomatoes, bay-leaf, lemon rind, peppercorns, and stock. Add a little salt, cover, and simmer for about 1 hour with the lid half off. Rub through a fine sieve. Rinse out the pan. Melt the butter in it, add the flour, mix well, and dilute with the tomato pulp. Take the zest of orange on the lump of sugar, add, and put in a little more sugar to taste. Simmer 5 minutes, or longer if it is necessary to concentrate or thicken the soup a little more. Add cream gradually, stir round once, and pour quickly into bowls.

Serve with the following garnish: Shred finely a small quantity of the rind of an orange. Simmer for 6 minutes in boiling water, drain, and sprinkle over the soup.

The following is excellent:

SPICY TOMATO SOUP

½ oz. butter	1 teaspoon paprika
1 onion	1 lb. tomatoes
½ oz. flour	a bouquet garni
a blade of mace	1¼ pints chicken stock
4–6 peppercorns	½ oz. sago
1 clove	1 glass port or red wine
salt	

Melt butter, add sliced onion and soften. Add flour, spices, salt, paprika, and tomatoes, herbs and stock, and cook for 20 or 30 minutes. Strain, add the sago, and simmer until sago is transparent. Finally add the port.

Potage Véronique is a tomato soup to which the addition of a little fresh shredded tomato towards the end of cooking gives the distinguishing note.

POTAGE VÉRONIQUE

1 lb. ripe tomatoes	1 lump of sugar
1 clove of garlic, bruised	a teaspoon salt
2 bay-leaves	freshly ground black pepper
1½ oz. butter	1 oz. rice
2 onions	
½ oz. flour	*Garnish*
1½ pints vegetable stock or water	1 oz. grated cheese
	2 slices of bread
1 teaspoon tomato purée	mustard and pepper

Take three-quarters of the tomatoes, cut in quarters, and squeeze out the seeds. Put into a pan with the bruised clove of garlic, the bay-leaves, and ½ oz. butter. Simmer very slowly with the lid half off for about 40 minutes. Rub through a sieve or strainer. Meanwhile finely slice the onions, put into a stew-pan with ¾ oz. butter, cover, and stew slowly for 15 minutes without colouring. Add the flour off the fire, the stock, and the tomato purée. Season with the sugar, salt, and freshly ground black pepper. Add the rice and simmer for 20–30 minutes. Scald and skin the remaining tomatoes, cut in quarters and remove the seeds, cut in shreds and add to the soup. Spread the cheese on the slices of bread buttered with the remainder of the butter, season well with mustard and pepper, and brown under the grill. Cut into strips and serve separately.

POTAGE SOLFERINO

¾ lb. tomatoes
2 oz. onion
the white part of 2 leeks
1½ oz. butter
1 quart vegetable stock, water, or water
    potatoes or beans have been cooked in

1 clove of garlic
½ lb. potatoes
seasoning
cayenne

Wipe tomatoes, cut in two, remove all seeds and water, and cut out any hard stalk or core. Chop coarsely. Cut the onion and leeks into thin slices. Melt half the butter in a large saucepan, add the onion and leeks and cook gently until turning yellow, but do not allow to brown. Add the liquid and a little salt if the stock is not already salted. Boil, then add the tomatoes, the finely chopped garlic, and the potatoes cut into thin slices. Cover and simmer for a good half-hour. Pass through a nylon or fine wire sieve, rinse out the pan, pour back the soup, and stir until boiling, thinning down if necessary with a little stock or water. The purée should be clear-looking and the consistency that of cream. Draw aside and stir in the rest of the butter in small pieces. When thoroughly incorporated adjust the seasoning, adding a touch of cayenne.

A particularly good Tomato Soup is given on page 992, and a recipe for Cold Tomato Soup will be found on page 107.

Crème Olga is a delicate soup tasting of fresh mushrooms. Here a flavoured potato and milk broth is made, and then the raw mushroom added and cooked for 2 minutes.

CRÈME OLGA

¼ lb. spring onions
2 lb. potatoes
1 oz. butter
1½ pints milk
1 bay-leaf
3 oz. mushrooms

salt and pepper

Liaison
  1 egg yolk
  ½ gill cream

croûtons of fried bread

Slice the onions and potatoes and cook in the butter until soft but no coloured. Add the milk and bay-leaf and simmer for 20 minutes. Rub through a fine sieve, return to the pan, and add the raw sieved mushrooms. Stir, season, bring up to boiling-point, and simmer for 2 minutes. Remove the pan from the fire, and add the liaison of egg yolk and cream (see note on liaisons, page 138). Reheat carefully, correct the seasoning, and serve with croûtons of fried bread.

POTAGE CRÈME D'ASPERGES (ASPARAGUS CREAM SOUP)

1 bundle of asparagus, about 30
  medium-sized heads
1 shallot
1½ pints veal or vegetable stock
salt and pepper

Beurre manié
  1 oz. butter
  1 oz. flour

Liaison
  ¾ gill cream
  2 egg yolks

Wash and trim the asparagus, lightly scraping the white part of the stalks and reserving about half a dozen of the smaller tips for the garnish. Cut the stalks into inch lengths and slice the shallot finely. Put together in a pan with the stock. Cover and simmer 30 minutes. Meanwhile blanch the tips for 1 minute and cook in water until just tender. Rub the soup through a fine sieve, rinse out the pan and return it. Reheat and season. Work the butter and flour together to a soft paste (beurre manié), divide into small pieces and whisk into the soup off the fire. When thoroughly blended stir over a moderate fire until boiling. Beat the yolks, add the cream, and make the liaison in the usual way. Whisk for a minute or two over the fire, but do not allow to boil. Add the tips and serve.

CRÈME DE CONCOMBRES

1½ pints vegetable or light stock
1 large cucumber (or 2 small)
1 teaspoon chopped shallot
1 oz. butter
¾ oz. flour
salt and pepper
liquid green colouring

Liaison
2 yolks or 2 teaspoons arrowroot
½ gill milk or cream

Garnish
freshly grated cucumber
finely chopped mint

Boil up the strained stock and add the cucumber, peeled and cut in ½-inch slices, and chopped shallot. Simmer gently until the cucumber is soft (15–20 minutes) and rub through a hair sieve. Rinse the saucepan. Blend the butter and flour and add the sieved cucumber and stock. Stir until boiling and simmer for 5 minutes. Cool a little, add the liaison, and thicken the soup carefully. Colour delicately, correct the seasoning, add the garnish, and serve.

The following recipe is for a classic cream soup, having as a base milk thickened with crème de riz or cream of rice (not to be confused with ground rice). Crème de riz has not been easy to obtain lately, so a velouté base has had to be used: that is to say, a white stock in place of milk thickened with a roux.

POTAGE CRÈME DE RIZ

2½ oz. crème de riz
2 pints milk
1 small onion stuck with a clove
a bouquet of 2–3 parsley stalks, a sprig of thyme, and ½ bay-leaf

salt and pepper
6 oz. white mushrooms, cups or buttons
¼ pint single cream
a nut of butter

Mix the cream of rice to a smooth paste with a little of the cold milk. Put the remainder of the milk on to boil, and when boiling draw aside and whisk in the cream of rice. Add the onion, bouquet, and a little salt and pepper, cover and simmer very gently 12–15 minutes. Meanwhile peel the mushrooms and rub through a wire sieve with the stalks, reserving 2 mushrooms for a garnish. Cut these into fine 'filets' or julienne strips and cook in a nut of butter. Remove the bouquet and onion and strain soup through a fine or tammy strainer. Return to the rinsed pan, add purée, bring to the boil, and simmer for a few minutes, adding the cream. Add garnish and serve at once.

Attention is drawn to the cream soups given in the chapter on modern kitchen appliances, pages 1185–7. These soups made in an electric blender are particularly smooth and good, and for small quantities this is a practical method.

II. BROTHS AND PEASANT SOUPS

The following are the simplest soups of all. They are rustic but good, excellent for family meals, and in some cases, for example the Italian minestra, will serve as a substantial course for luncheon.

MINESTRA

This differs from the well-known minestrone in that it is made from vegetable stock and contains no meat.

1 tablespoon oil	6 French beans or a quarter of a
2 oz. carrot	cabbage or 6–8 Brussels sprouts
2 oz. onion	(or all three if available)
2 sticks of celery	2 oz. potato
1 oz. leek	2 oz. tomato
3 pints boiling water	1 clove of garlic crushed with ½
salt	teaspoon salt
½ bay-leaf	a spoonful chopped parsley
	grated cheese

Heat a tablespoon of oil in the stew-pan. Add the carrot, onion, celery, and leek, all cut into thick strips. Cook until just turning colour, shaking and stirring occasionally, then pour in about 3 pints boiling water (the liquid should well cover the vegetables). Add salt, bay-leaf, the cabbage and beans, also cut into strips, and the Brussels sprouts if available, then simmer 30–40 minutes with the pan covered. Add the potato cut in the same way and simmer again for another 20 minutes. Peel the tomato, cut in quarters, and add to the soup with the crushed garlic and a good spoonful of chopped parsley. Simmer another 10 minutes and then serve. More water must be added during the cooking if necessary, preferably during the early stages, but the soup should be thick with vegetables. Grated cheese is served separately.

On the whole cabbage is not carefully cooked in this country, and the recollection of the smell of its cooking is prejudicial to a general appreciation of cabbage soup.   Yet the French Soupe aux Choux is really excellent.

SOUPE AUX CHOUX

2 oz. butter	approximately 2½ pints vege-
4 small onions	table stock or water
a clove of garlic	salt and pepper
1 rasher	2 oz. French or runner beans
1 cabbage	French bread
	grated Parmesan cheese

Melt the butter in a casserole.   Add the sliced onions, crushed garlic, and coarsely cut-up bacon.   Sauter over a slow fire for a few moments, and add the cabbage, previously blanched and coarsely shredded.   Pour on the stock, season, and bring slowly to the boil.   Cover and simmer in a slow oven for 50 minutes.   Add the shredded beans, and continue cooking for another 50 minutes.   Take out and serve in the pot with slices of the toasted bread floating on the top.   Serve the grated cheese separately.

The following soup is simple, good, and really suitable for a *maigre* day:

POTAGE FERMIÈRE

3 carrots	1 quart boiling water
3 onions	seasoning
3 turnips	2 heaped tablespoons chopped mixed herbs
3 leeks	(chives, chervil, and parsley, with a little
5 or 6 potatoes	lemon thyme, summer savory, basil, and
1½ oz. butter	dill, make a good mixture)

Prepare the vegetables and cut all except the potatoes into neat dice; sweat the diced vegetables in the butter till softened but not coloured. This should be done over very gentle heat and takes about 20 minutes to half an hour.   Add the boiling water and simmer until the carrots are tender, then add sliced potatoes and cook another 20 minutes.   Season well, pour into a hot tureen, and sprinkle the surface with the finely chopped herbs:

The following excellent Garbure Paysanne is made interesting by the serving of the special croûtons described.

GARBURE PAYSANNE

3 oz. butter	4 oz. potatoes
2 large leeks (white part)	2 sticks of celery or ½ root of
4 oz. carrots	celeriac
3 oz. turnip	3 pints water or vegetable
the heart of a small cabbage	stock
2 oz. onion	1 French or breakfast roll
seasoning and a pinch of sugar	1 oz. gruyère cheese, grated

This garbure is made with certain basic vegetables, but other vegetables, such as broad beans, peas, and French beans, may be added when these are in season.

Melt half the butter in a stew-pan, slice the leeks, carrots, turnip, cabbage, and onion thinly. Add to the pan with a good pinch each of salt and sugar, cover and cook very slowly for 20 minutes. Moisten with half the liquid, bring to the boil, add the potatoes cut in slices and any other seasonable vegetables. Cover and simmer for 1 hour. Cut the bread into croûtons ⅓ inch thick, fry until a delicate brown in half the remaining butter, and set aside to keep warm. When the vegetables are soft take out 2 or 3 spoonfuls and push through a wire sieve to make a very thick purée. Heap this purée on the croûtons, smoothing it over with a knife, sprinkle on the cheese, and brown in the oven. Meanwhile sieve the remainder of the soup, return to the pan with enough of the remaining liquid to give a creamy consistency, and bring to the boil. Adjust the seasoning, add the rest of the butter off the fire, pour the soup into the tureen, and hand the croûtons separately.

The author of the letter in the preface gave us a recipe for a Garbure Basque, an all-the-year-round soup, to be made with whatever vegetables are in season, or available. It needs long cooking: 4–5 hours is not unusual unless one is using young vegetables early in the year. The measurements are in cups, as given to us, and the recipe calls for a great deal of garlic, which may be modified to suit English tastes, but by no means omitted. The soup is very thick and substantial and forms the main dish of a midday meal in the Basque country.

GARBURE BASQUE

a piece of butter the size of an egg	a coffee-cup of garlic, finely chopped
a breakfast-cup each of leeks, carrots, potatoes, peas, beans, turnips, tomatoes, etc. cut in small pieces	2 tablespoons olive oil chopped parsley a pinch of salt milk or butter to finish
a tea-cup each of onions and celery	1 tablespoon chopped chervil

Melt a piece of butter the size of an egg in an earthenware casserole. Gently cook the leeks in this and then add the other vegetables, the garlic, 2 tablespoons olive oil, chopped parsley, and a pinch of salt. Pour on enough water to cover well, put the lid on the casserole and cook on a very low fire 4–5 hours. Do not sieve. The garbure is finished when the vegetables have disappeared and the soup is a fairly thick purée. Finish with a piece of fresh butter or a cup of fresh milk added at the last minute. Sprinkle over a tablespoon of finely chopped chervil before serving.

SOUPE A LA SAVOYARDE

6 oz. celeriac, weighed after
  peeling
2 oz. potato
3 oz. onion
1 oz. leek (white part)
2 oz. dripping or butter
a flat teaspoon salt and a pinch
  of sugar

1½ pints warm water
½ pint freshly boiled milk
a dozen fingers of brown
  bread and butter
2 oz. grated gruyère cheese

Slice all the vegetables very thinly: this is important. Put all together into a saucepan with the dripping or butter, salt, and sugar. Soften the vegetables in the dripping or butter, cooking gently and not allowing them to brown. As they take about 20–25 minutes, it is necessary to stir and shake the pan frequently. At the end of this cooking they should be *fondant*—melting. Add the warm water, cover, and leave to simmer gently for 10 minutes. Then add the milk and continue simmering gently for 3 or 4 minutes.

Lightly brown the fingers of bread and butter in the oven, sprinkle them with cheese, and brown under the grill or in the oven. Adjust the seasoning of the soup and serve with croûtons on top.

The following is a slightly richer vegetable soup by reason of the addition of eggs:

POTAGE JULIENNE ST MAUR

3 oz. leek
8 oz. carrots
1 oz. turnip
2 oz. onion
2 sticks of celery
2 oz. butter
salt and pepper

1 very small cabbage or heart
  of a cabbage
3 pints stock or water
1½ oz. rice
1 very small lettuce
1 small handful sorrel
2 eggs

Cut the leek, carrots, turnip, celery, and onion into small julienne shreds. Melt 1½ oz. of the butter in the stew-pan, put the vegetables into this, and shake over a brisk fire for a few minutes; this is required to brown the vegetables lightly before the addition of the liquor. Add salt and pepper; cover and cook on a very slow fire for 10 minutes. Blanch the cabbage whole, then cut in shreds and add to the vegetables in the pan with the stock and rice. Simmer 30–40 minutes. Meanwhile shred the sorrel and lettuce, cook for a few minutes in the remainder of the butter, then add to the soup 5 minutes before serving. Beat the eggs in the tureen or soup marmite, re-season the soup if necessary and pour gently into the marmite, stirring briskly.

Sorrel and lettuce may be omitted when out of season, also lightly toasted bread or rolls may be put in the marmite when eggs are unobtainable. This, of course, alters the character of the soup, but the bread is quite a satisfactory substitute.

VEGETABLE BORTSCH OR SUMMER BORTSCH

raw beetroot
onion
carrot
celery or celeriac
parsnip
2–3 quarts ham or veal stock
a bouquet garni
2 cloves of garlic

cabbage
tomatoes or tomato purée
salt
sugar
chopped parsley or Hamburg
  parsley
sour cream
a little flour

The vegetables (except the cabbage and tomatoes) should be cut into coarse match-like pieces, and the beetroot should, for choice, be the round, deep red variety. Take a 2-pint pudding basin, fill a half with the cut-up beetroot, a quarter with onion, half the remaining quarter with carrot, and divide the rest of the space between celery (or celeriac) and parsnip. Put 2–3 quarts ham or veal stock into a large pan, and when boiling turn the bowl of vegetables into it. Add a bouquet of herbs and the garlic crushed with salt. Simmer for about 20 minutes. Fill up the bowl with coarsely shredded cabbage, turn this into the soup, and continue cooking for another half-hour. Now add fresh, peeled tomatoes, coarsely chopped (enough to fill a quarter of the pudding basin), or a large spoonful of concentrated tomato purée. Add also salt, sugar, and plenty of chopped parsley. Cook a little while longer. Take a little sour cream and blend it with a very small quantity of flour. Add to the bortsch off the boil, then reboil. This should not make it in any way thick, but should just take away the clear, watery look. If you wish, serve with more sour cream.

For Consommé Bortsch and Bortchok see pages 130 and 131 (Party Soups).

The following Soupe à l'Oignon is excellent and the brown sticky cheese top has a most appetizing savour. It is a good dish to serve after a theatre party. A real party onion soup is given on page 126.

SOUPE A L'OIGNON

½ lb. onions
1½ oz. butter or good dripping
½ oz. flour
1½ pints boiling water or vegetable stock

seasoning
bay-leaf
slices of French bread
grated cheese

Finely chop the onions. Melt the butter in a thick pan. Add the onions and brown slowly and well. This will take at least 15–20 minutes. Dust in the flour, and pour on the boiling water or vegetable stock. Simmer for about half an hour, adding seasoning and bay-leaf. Put several slices of French bread at the bottom of a casserole, pour on the boiling soup, first removing the bay-leaf. Dust thickly with grated cheese, then set the casserole in the oven for 15–20 minutes to brown. Serve very hot.

The following cream of onion soup is a speciality of the Île de France:

LE THOURIN

1½ pints milk	*Liaison*
4 oz. onions	2 tablespoons top of milk or cream
1½ oz. butter	2 egg yolks
¾ oz. flour	
	salt and pepper
	3–4 very thin slices of bread

Boil the milk and slice the onions finely.   Melt the butter, and when frothing add the onions and cook very slowly to soften completely, without colouring.   When the onions are almost cooked, add the flour and mix in well over the fire for 3–4 minutes.   Add the boiling milk a little at a time, stirring well to avoid lumps.   Bring to the boil and allow to simmer 15–20 minutes.   Remove from the fire, add the liaison of egg yolks and cream, reheat carefully, and adjust the seasoning.   Meanwhile cut the bread into rounds, bake to a golden brown in a cool oven, place at the bottom of a soup marmite, pour the soup over, and serve at once.

Potage Périgord is an interesting soup because of the farci which is added:

POTAGE PÉRIGORD

2 large onions	seasoning
1 oz. butter	farci (see below)
1 clove of garlic crushed with	1 egg
½ teaspoon salt	a few drops of vinegar or a
1¼ pints water or stock	little lemon juice

Slice the onions finely, and separate them into rings.   Make the butter hot in a saucepan, cook the onion rings in this over gentle heat, stirring them about with a wooden spoon so that all cook equally golden brown. Add the crushed garlic, the water or stock, salt, and pepper and simmer for 10 minutes.   Add farci and cook for half to three-quarters of an hour; take out.   Blend the egg yolk with a tablespoon of the soup, add a few drops of vinegar or lemon juice.   Pour this mixture into the soup and stir, but do not boil.   Put the egg white into a greased cup and steam until firm. Then chop finely and add to the soup.   Cut the farci into slices and serve in the terrine with the soup.

Farci

a slice of stale bread	1 clove of garlic
½ rasher of bacon, finely minced	pepper
1 teaspoon chopped parsley	1 egg yolk
1 teaspoon chopped chives	1 large cabbage leaf
1 teaspoon chopped thyme	
1 teaspoon chopped onion or	
shallot	

Make the slice of stale bread into fine crumbs, mix with it the bacon, the parsley, chives, thyme, and chopped onion or shallot, and the clove of garlic. Mix well together, add a little pepper, and bind with yolk of egg. Blanch the cabbage leaf and spread this farci over it; fold the leaf neatly and tie it up with thin string or cotton. Drop it into the soup and cook for half to three-quarters of an hour. Take out when the soup is ready for the liaison, remove the string, and cut the farci into slices. Serve a slice or two of farci in each plate of soup.

Some people consider that sorrel soup is an acquired taste. If so, I think it is worth acquiring, but perhaps for beginners, so to speak, it is wise to start with a soup made half of sorrel and half of spinach or young nettles, because this addition modifies the sharp flavour of the sorrel, and also improves the colour of the soup. Here is a recipe for the real thing, and another made half with sorrel and half with spinach:

SOUPE A L'OSEILLE A LA PAYSANNE

12 oz. roughly chopped sorrel	1 or 2 eggs (whole)
1½ oz. butter	1 gill milk
¾ oz. flour	croûtons or thin slices of
2½ pints boiling water or potato water	French roll dried in the oven
a good pinch of sugar and salt	

Put half of the butter and the sorrel together in a pan, cover and cook gently for about 25–30 minutes, stirring from time to time. Sprinkle with flour and allow this to colour, still stirring, add boiling liquid and salt and sugar. Cover and simmer for 15 minutes. Whisk in remaining butter, beat eggs with milk, strain, and add in the way described on page 140. Serve immediately with croûtons.

POTAGE DE SANTÉ

3 large handfuls spinach	2½ pints liquid (1¼ pints ham
2 large handfuls sorrel	stock, 1¼ pints of the water
1 bundle spring onions and/or	the herbs have been boiled
½ bundle watercress	in)
½ handful parsley	pepper
1½ oz. butter	cream
1½ oz. flour, scant weight	hard-boiled eggs or savoury fritters

Boil the spinach, sorrel, onions, and parsley in 3 pints boiling water for 5–7 minutes. Drain, press, and sieve, reserving the water. Melt the butter in a large saucepan, add the flour off the fire, pour on the liquid and bring to the boil. Season and simmer 5 minutes. Whisk in the purée, reboil, and serve with a spoonful of cream and a little chopped hard-boiled egg in each plate, or hand the savoury fritters separately. See page 10 (Savouries).

III. VEGETABLE PURÉES MADE FROM DRIED VEGETABLES

The following notes on the preparation and preliminary cooking of dried vegetables are applicable to any dish, not only to soups.

HARICOT BEANS, BROWN OR RED BEANS, LENTILS, GREEN PEAS, WHOLE OR SPLIT

Preparation

Dried vegetables should be washed well, picked over, weighed or measured for the dish in hand, and then soaked in plenty of water which should be just tepid. The more thorough the soaking (24 hours is not too long), the less time they will take to cook.

Cooking

Fresh water should be taken for this and the vegetables well covered in the pan. If the water is hard, a pinch of bicarbonate of soda may be added.

Boiling-point should be reached very slowly: this should take not less than 40 minutes. If this rule is not observed and the dried vegetables are allowed to cook fast in the early stages they are apt to harden.

When, after 40 minutes, boiling-point is reached, further gentle simmering for 1½–2 hours is required before the vegetables are treated for the final dish.

Probably the most generally popular of soups made from dried vegetables are those made from dried peas. There are various ways of making these taste and look something like soup made from the fresh vegetable. For one thing, the colour may be improved by the addition of some fresh spinach juice, which should be put into the bottom of the tureen and the hot soup poured on to it. It is not a good thing to put the spinach juice into the saucepan, as the boiling liquid will spoil the colour. This juice is obtained by pounding a good handful of spinach leaves and then squeezing out the juice through a fine strainer or a piece of muslin. The addition of a few young, canned peas as a garnish is another way of improving this soup, and chopped fresh mint added finally as well as a sprig used while cooking make all the difference to the flavour. In fact, the addition of fresh herbs and, where suitable, of fresh raw vegetables, such as carrot or celery finely grated, or the sprouted peas mentioned on page 104, gives an agreeable fresh taste to these soups.

Before giving recipes for these and other soups of dried vegetables, I ought to say that French authorities point out that this type of soup should be very carefully skimmed, and indicate that this should be done for the last half-hour before it is served; they say that unless this skimming is carried out carefully the soup will have a rough taste.   Other authorities make no reference to the necessity for this skimming, so it must be left to the individual cook to test the soup and decide whether she thinks it worth while or not.

I think it is doubtful whether the title Potage St Germain should be given to soup made of dried peas; so perhaps it would be best if the following were called Purée of Pea Soup.

PURÉE OF PEA SOUP (1)

½ lb. green split peas weighed before soaking (soaked in tepid water overnight)
1 quart boiling water
a bouquet garni
½ oz. butter
1 carrot

1 onion
green part of 2 leeks
1 piece of lump sugar
salt and pepper
croûtons
freshly chopped mint

Put the soaked peas into cold water and bring them to boiling-point. Strain off the first water, cover again with 1 quart boiling water without salt, and add the bouquet.   In another pan heat the butter, add the finely sliced carrot and onion, and cook gently for 10 minutes.   Then add with the finely sliced leeks to the liquid.   Add sugar, cover, cook gently till all vegetables are tender.   The peas will take anything between 2 and 3 hours to be adequately cooked.   Pass through a sieve, reheat, season with salt and pepper; put, if you wish, the spinach juice mentioned on the previous page in the bottom of the tureen, pour on the hot soup, and serve with small croûtons of fried bread.

PURÉE OF PEA SOUP (2)

1 oz. butter
1 carrot
1 onion
1 clove of garlic
½ lb. dried peas, weighed before soaking (soaked for 12 hours and cooked for 1–1½ hours)

2 pints stock
3 or 4 sprigs of mint
1 teaspoon sugar
½ pint single cream or good milk
a few cooked canned peas for garnish
salt and pepper

Melt the butter in a stew-pan.   Add the finely chopped carrot, onion, and garlic.   Cook for a few minutes and then add the strained peas. Pour on the stock, also the stock from the peas, add mint (reserving 1 sprig) and sugar.   Stir over the fire until it comes to the boil.   Draw aside and simmer until the peas are tender.   Remove mint.   Rub through a fine sieve and return to the pan.   Heat over a slow fire, adding the cream by degrees and lastly the cooked peas.   Add finely chopped mint and season. Approximate time 2½ hours.

PURÉE OF PEA SOUP (3)

1 pint dried peas measured before soaking (soaked overnight and cooked for 1–1½ hours)	1 large potato
	a lump of sugar
	½ teaspoon peppercorns
	1 bay-leaf
3 pints vegetable stock or water	1 oz. butter to add at end of cooking
1 carrot	
1 turnip	salt and pepper
1 onion stuck with cloves	spinach juice for colouring
1 head of celery or root of celeriac	croûtons

Proceed as in the previous recipe except that the vegetables are cut up and added raw, not cooked in butter. Colour with juice of spinach and serve with croûtons.

It is an old-fashioned trick, and a good one, to sow, early in the year, shallow seed trays thickly with seed peas (home-saved seed is economical). These are put in a warm corner of the greenhouse, and covered with paper, until they germinate, and when the tips are an inch or two high they are cut over like mustard and cress and used to give a fresh flavour to soups made with dried peas or beans.

PEA-LEAF SOUP

6 oz. green split peas	salt
1 onion	pepper
1 carrot	½ oz. flour
1½ oz. butter	½ pint milk
1 pint stock or water	2 handfuls green pea tops, grown in greenhouse
2 or 3 sprigs of mint	

Soak the peas overnight and give 1 hour's preliminary cooking. Slice onion and carrot and soften in half the butter. Drain the peas and add to the pan, cook for a few minutes, then add the stock with mint, salt, and pepper. Cover and simmer until the peas are tender. Rub through a fine sieve. Melt the remaining butter in a pan and add the flour, then add the pea purée, season, bring to the boil, and finish with the hot milk. Meanwhile cook the tops in boiling water for 10 minutes, drain and sieve. Add to the soup, reheat, and serve.

Here is a recipe for a soup made from little red beans known as 'rognons de coq.' It may also be made from brown Dutch beans or from the mature seeds of runner or French beans after these have been well dried.

POTAGE ROGNONS DE COQ (RED BEAN SOUP)

½ lb. red beans (weighed before soaking)	4 tomatoes
	a dessertspoon tomato purée
2 oz. butter	a bouquet of mixed herbs
1 carrot	3 pints water or vegetable stock
1 onion	
salt and pepper	grated cheese

Soak the beans for 12 hours, then drain.   Melt the butter in a casserole, add the sliced onion and carrot, the beans, and the seasonings.   Toss over the fire for a few moments, then add the skinned and quartered tomatoes, the tomato purée, and the herbs.   Pour on the water and simmer until the beans are soft (approximately 2–3 hours).   Remove the herbs, season, and serve with grated cheese.

Here is a recipe for a soup made from white haricot beans:

POTAGE DAUPHINOISE OR SOISSONAISE

1 oz. butter	3 pints vegetable stock (or ham stock when available is excellent)
¼ lb. onions	
½ lb. peeled potatoes	
a clove of garlic	1 dessertspoon chopped parsley
½ lb. white haricot beans (soaked overnight)	
salt and freshly ground pepper	1 gill cream or top of milk (optional)
a bouquet garni	croûtons

Melt the butter in a stew-pan, add onions, potatoes, and garlic, finely sliced, then the well-drained beans.   Cover the pan and sweat the vegetables gently over low heat for 10–15 minutes.   Add salt, freshly ground black pepper, the bouquet, and the stock.   Bring to the boil, cover, and simmer until the beans are absolutely soft (about 2–3 hours).   Then rub all through a fine wire sieve.   Return the soup to pan, bring to the boil, finish with chopped parsley.   A little cream or top of the milk added at the last moment is a great improvement.   Fried croûtons may be served with this soup.

And, finally, a recipe for Lentil Soup:

POTAGE PURÉE DE LENTILLES (LENTIL SOUP)

1 pint lentils	*Liaison* (optional)
3 oz. onion	2 yolks of egg
3 pints cold water	½ gill cream
¼ oz. salt	2 rashers of streaky bacon for the garnish (optional)
a small bacon bone, if possible	
mint, fresh or dried	croûtons

Pick over the lentils and wash well; they may either be soaked overnight or, since they are very small, cooked straight away.   Put into a stew-pan with the sliced onion, water, salt, and the bacon bone.   If they have not been previously soaked, add ½ gill cold water to the pan every half-hour, bringing the pan up to the boil each time.   This accelerates the cooking, though it is slightly more extravagant on fuel; but it is a useful method when time is short.

When the lentils are thoroughly soft, drain off the liquid into a bowl and pass them through a fine sieve.   Rinse out the pan, return the purée, and add the liquid by degrees.   If the soup is too thick add a little potato or vegetable stock to clear it; if too thin a very small quantity of arrowroot mixed with water may be used as liaison. Reheat and serve with finely chopped or dried powdered mint in the soup. The liaison of egg yolks and cream may be added if the soup is to be richer.

Dice the bacon finely, fry till crisp, and powder over the top of the soup when in the bowls or marmites. Fried bread croûtons may also be served.

Vegetable stock can be very good and is most useful. If made with care it can be an excellent clear soup. It may also be served with the garnishes appropriate to a real pot-au-feu bouillon, such as are called for in Croûte-au-pot, Julienne, and Paysanne. It is admirable as a basic stock for vegetable soups, a point of especial value when milk is in short supply. Vegetable bouillon or stock takes some time to make properly and has one drawback—it should not be kept beyond one day in hot weather, or two days at most in winter, for not only does it lose flavour quickly, but it is liable to turn sour.

VEGETABLE BOUILLON OR STOCK

½ oz. butter	a bouquet garni and a few pepper-
1 lb. carrots	corns
1 lb. onions	a level dessertspoon salt
½ head of celery	3 quarts hot water
a small piece of turnip	1 teaspoon Marmite (optional)

Melt butter in a large stew-pan. Peel and wash the vegetables, dry, and slice them in big pieces, add to pan and shake over a slow fire until brown. Add the peppercorns, salt, bouquet, and hot water. Bring to the boil, half cover the pan, and simmer 3 hours, or until the bouillon has a good flavour: it should reduce by about one-third. Strain off, and when cold remove any fat before using. Marmite may be added to improve colour and flavour.

Another recipe for this pot-au-feu bouillon will be found on page 121.

IV. COLD SOUPS

Probably on account of the exigencies of our climate, cold soups, with the exception perhaps of jellied consommé, are not so universally popular in this country as in America. This is a pity, for they can be so very good. Just as hot soup should be served very hot, so cold soups should be served really cold: they lose considerably if they are just 'room' cold rather than ice-cold. For special occasions, and in very hot weather, it is nice if one can serve the soup-cups surrounded by crushed ice, but this necessitates an outer bowl to hold the ice in which the soup-cup, marmite, or glass bowl sits. Or one can have all the soup-bowls arranged in a long entrée dish containing the crushed ice, and either handed in this or taken out at the last minute and put on saucers.

These soups are sometimes thick and creamy like Crème Vichyssoise (page 129), sometimes thin but with a final addition of cream as in Winkfield Tomato Soup (page 992), and sometimes in jelly form as in Consommé Madrilène or Consommé en Gelée (page 120). The two last-named should be accompanied by quarters of lemon, as the addition of fresh lemon juice is considered by many to be a great improvement.

The following is a delicious summer soup which may be made with outdoor cucumbers:

ICED CUCUMBER SOUP

1 large cucumber or 2 or 3 small outdoor ones	1 dessertspoon arrowroot
1 shallot	½ gill top of milk or thin cream
1½ pints water or light chicken stock	seasoning
1 sprig of mint	green colouring
	shredded mint

Thinly peel the cucumber and cut into small pieces. Chop the shallot and put it into a pan with the water or stock. Cover and simmer 10–15 minutes. Add the cucumber with the mint and cook until just tender. Rub through a fine sieve. Return to the pan, slake the arrowroot with the cream, strain into the soup, bring to the boil, season, simmer half a minute, then pour off into a bowl. Colour lightly and delicately with a little green colouring and chill thoroughly before serving. For the garnish have diced blanched cucumber or cucumber 'peas' cut out with a small vegetable scoop. Shake shredded mint over the soup at the last moment.

The final addition of grated lemon or orange rind to the following Cold Tomato Soup is refreshing:

COLD TOMATO SOUP

2 lb. ripe tomatoes	1 level tablespoon arrowroot
1 oz. onion	½–¾ gill cream or evaporated milk
1 bay-leaf	seasoning, including freshly ground black pepper
6 peppercorns	
2 cloves	lemon juice
1 strip of lemon rind	cayenne
2 pints potato water or vegetable stock or, when available, chicken stock set in a jelly (the arrowroot may then be cut down)	grated lemon or orange rind

Wipe tomatoes, cut into two, squeeze to remove seeds, and cut out any stalk or green part. Put into a stew-pan with onion, bay-leaf, peppercorns, cloves, lemon rind, and stock. Cover and simmer very gently for an hour. Rub through a fine sieve. Slake the arrowroot in 2 or 3 spoonfuls of water, add to the pan, and reboil. Adjust seasoning, adding some freshly ground black pepper, a squeeze of lemon juice, and a touch of cayenne. Pour off and cool. Then chill thoroughly. Serve in bowls with a spoonful of cream in each. Grate a little lemon or orange rind on top.

Soupe Verte is delicious green soup made either with a clear bouillon half of ham and half beef, carefully cleared and skimmed, or with vegetable or chicken stock. The soup may suitably have a whole hard-boiled egg served in the middle of each plate. Half an egg is given here, and this may be sliced or quartered if preferred. This soup may be served hot or ice-cold, and rolls of brown bread and butter are good with it.

SOUPE VERTE (RUSSIAN)

Have ready some bouillon: half ham, half beef is best. When hot put into it 2 parts of spinach, 1 part of green onions, and 1 part of sorrel, all finely chopped, and celery tops and parsley to flavour. Add a bouquet garni. Simmer for about 1 hour. Thicken with sour cream and flour mixed, season, and serve half a hard-boiled egg in the middle of the soup-plate.

This is not a precise recipe. One requires enough of the vegetables to impart a good flavour, and about three times as much liquid as solid in the finished soup. R. H. takes to each quart of liquid approximately a double handful of spinach, one each of onion and sorrel, and half that quantity of celery and parsley.

The following cold Spanish soup, Gazpacho, has not so much oil in it as is used in the real Spanish article. But it is difficult to get the thin, clear, perfect olive oil in this country, and in this recipe the oil is modified to suit English palates.

GAZPACHO ANDALUZ

1 cup breadcrumbs	½ glass salad-oil
red wine vinegar to taste	iced water
2 cloves of garlic	2 lb. tomatoes
salt	pepper
2 small outdoor cucumbers	croûtons of toasted bread and
1 green pepper	a bowl of cubes of ice
1 onion	

Soak the crumbs in 2 tablespoons vinegar. Pound the garlic to a cream with a teaspoon of salt. Chop roughly 1 cucumber, ½ the green pepper, and the onion and put them, with the crumbs, into the mortar. Pound to a paste, then rub the paste through a fine sieve. Add the oil a few drops at a time as for mayonnaise. Season with a little more vinegar if necessary and pour into a tureen. Add the iced water and the tomatoes rubbed through a sieve: the amount of water depends on the juiciness of the tomatoes, but the soup should be of fairly thin consistency. Season with salt and pepper and chill well. The remaining cucumber and pepper, cut up, may now be added to the soup or served separately. Small croûtons of toasted bread and a bowl of cubes of ice are also handed to be added to the soup.

CHERRY SOUP

Fruit soups are popular abroad, but little known here. They are refreshing and palatable, and deserve a trial. Cherry, perhaps, is one of the nicest in flavour, and may be made from fresh or canned cherries. For fresh choose a good red cherry, for canned, morellos.

1 lb. cherries (weighed when stoned)	1 glass red wine (optional)
	1½ pints water
4–5 lumps of sugar	1 dessertspoon arrowroot
1 orange	sugar to taste

Put the cherries into a pan. Rub the lumps of sugar over the orange to remove the zest. Add to the pan with the strained juice, the wine, and the water. Bring to the boil, simmer 5–6 minutes. Slake the arrowroot with a spoonful or two of water, add to the soup while just off the boil. Reboil and sweeten to taste. If the liquid is too thick with fruit, take out some and replace with a little water.

Crème Vichyssoise is so delectable a dish that it finds its place in the party section of this chapter, page 129; also it calls for chicken stock and at least ½ pint cream, so it is by no means a dish for every day.

Another party soup is a cold cream of curry soup which R. H. has kindly christened 'Crème Constance.' A recipe for it is to be found on page 991.

The advent of emulsifying apparatus has added to the possible repertoire of cold soups, and reference is made to these in the chapter on modern kitchen appliances, pages 1185–7.

V. MULLIGATAWNY AND CURRY SOUPS

The curry soups vary considerably in the degree of spiciness, but they should not, for the normal palate, be over-peppery—certainly not so peppery as a curry itself may be. Some of them may be quite bland in seasoning, tasting of nuts and spices and agreeable to the most sensitive palate. If you like cooking and like spices you will not be satisfied with having just a tin of curry-powder and one of paste in your store-room, but you will have, as mentioned in the curry chapter, the individual spices which together make the generally accepted curry-powder; and you will certainly have desiccated nuts of some kind, preferably coco-nut and almonds.

There are three distinct main types of mulligatawny; it can be in the form of

(a) consommé
(b) gravy broth
(c) thick soup

The base of the first is good bouillon or stock, and the flavouring is imparted to it by the infusion in it of whole spices. The following recipe calls for beef bouillon, but Mulligatawny Maigre, which is not the real thing, may be made in exactly the same way, using vegetable stock.

CONSOMMÉ MULLIGATAWNY

3 pints well-flavoured beef bouillon (see page 119)
½ lb. minced gravy beef
2 egg whites
2 tablespoons good Madeira

Spices for infusing
  ½ oz. each of coriander and cardamon
  ¼ oz. each of cumin seed and fenugreek
  12 peppercorns

1 clove of garlic
thinly peeled rind of 1 lemon
1 bay-leaf
seasoning

Garnish
  3 oz. rice
  ¼ oz. butter
  a little turmeric
  quarters of lemon

Bruise or pound lightly the spices and garlic, and put together with lemon rind and bay-leaf into a muslin bag tied tightly at the neck so that they cannot escape. Put the bag into the bouillon; bring to boil and keep at simmering-point until the liquid is well flavoured with the spices. This takes from 40 minutes to an hour. Remove the bag; allow the bouillon to cool, and clarify in the following manner. Put the minced beef into an enamel or tin-lined pan, add whites whipped to a froth and the bouillon. Whisk over moderate heat until it boils. Then stop whisking and allow the liquid to boil up. Draw aside and set on very low heat for half an hour. Strain carefully through a wet cloth, season, add Madeira, and reheat without allowing soup to boil. Hand boiled rice, mixed with butter and coloured lightly by the addition of a little turmeric, and also quarters of lemon.

See also reference to Oxtail Soup with addition of spices (page 123).

THICK MULLIGATAWNY (1)

1½ pints strong beef stock, flavoured with vegetables

Spices for infusing
  ¼ oz. cardamon, whole
  6 peppercorns, whole
  ¼ oz. coriander, whole
  ⅛ oz. fenugreek, whole
1 bay-leaf
the pared rind of ½ lemon

2 tablespoons desiccated coconut steeped in a tea-cup of boiling water
2 oz. onion or shallot
1 oz. butter or dripping
1 oz. flour
1 heaped teaspoon curry-powder
seasoning

Bruise all the spices lightly and put them into a muslin bag with the bay-leaf and lemon rind. Simmer for half an hour in the prepared stock, then remove bag and set stock aside. Pour the boiling water over the coco-nut and allow to steep for half an hour. When required strain it through muslin.

Chop the onion finely and fry slowly in the heated fat, add the curry-powder and continue frying for a few minutes. Add the flour off the fire, cook for a minute, then add the stock. Simmer a quarter of an hour, strain, add coco-nut milk. Return to pan to heat up, reduce a little if necessary, adjust seasoning, and serve.

THICK MULLIGATAWNY (2)

2 pints meat, fish, or vegetable stock
1½ tablespoons desiccated or 3 tablespoons freshly grated coco-nut
1½ tablespoons ground sweet almonds
½ pint boiling water
1 small clove of garlic
4 oz. finely chopped shallots
1½ oz. butter
1 oz. flour or cream of rice
1 tablespoon curry-powder or powder and paste mixed
lemon juice
salt and pepper

Spices for infusing
½ oz. each of cardamon and coriander
8 peppercorns
¼ oz. fenugreek

1 bay-leaf
the thinly peeled rind of ½ a lemon

Garnish
3 oz. boiled rice coloured with turmeric
quarters of lemon

As in previous recipe, bruise the spices, put with lemon rind and bay-leaf in a muslin bag, and infuse in the stock in covered pan for 30–40 minutes after boiling-point is reached. Mix the nuts together, pour over the boiling water, and leave to steep until required. Melt the butter in a large saucepan, keeping back ½ oz.; add shallots and garlic and fry slowly until turning colour, then add curry-powder and continue cooking slowly for 5 minutes, stirring constantly. Draw aside, stir in flour, and add stock by degrees; bring to boil, skimming from time to time, then simmer uncovered 10–15 minutes. Strain carefully. Return to a clean pan Strain the nut mixture through muslin and press to get as much milk as possible. Add this to the soup, reboil, adjust seasoning, and add a squeeze of lemon juice. If the soup is too thin, it may be reduced or thickened with a little arrowroot. Hand quarters of lemon and boiled rice into which you have stirred the remaining ½ oz. of butter cooked with the turmeric.

N.B. This soup may be enriched by the addition of a liaison of egg yolks.

THIN MULLIGATAWNY OR GRAVY BROTH

Proceed exactly as for the Thick Mulligatawny above, but use only ¾ oz. butter and ¾ oz. flour. Add 2 tablespoons boiled rice when the nut milk is added, and omit the liaison of egg yolks.

N.B. A good fish stock well flavoured with onion and herbs is excellent for this, as for instance the court bouillon in which salmon has been boiled. Stock made from a cod's head, plenty of root vegetables, and some lemon rind is also good.

The following soup is delicately flavoured and not at all hot, though of course the amount of curry-powder may be increased. Three or four ripe coriander seeds crushed and added to the broth before it is sieved give it a distinctive and, I think, delicious flavour.

POTAGE PONDICHERRY

3 leeks

½ oz. butter

½ teaspoon curry-powder

1 pint white stock

1½ oz. rice

1 gill milk

salt and pepper

Liaison (optional)

1 egg yolk

½ gill cream or ½ oz. butter

Blanch the leeks for 10 minutes. Melt the butter, add the finely chopped leeks, and cook them for a few minutes, shaking and stirring to help them to dry a little. Add curry-powder and continue cooking for some minutes. Add stock, rice, and milk and continue cooking gently for about half an hour. Put through a fine wire sieve, return to pan, season, and add the liaison or beat in a little extra butter. A little plain boiled rice, very dry, may be handed with the soup.

VI. FISH SOUPS

Fish soups are not, on the whole, greatly popular in England, except perhaps for lobster bisques and, before they became pearl-like in value, oyster soups. I had always had the idea that an oyster soup was only for very special occasions, something to be thought about beforehand, to be concocted with infinite care with silence in the kitchen. The first time I saw it made in an American kitchen I felt quite dazed. It was in the middle of a big cocktail party. From a fairly large room there led off a tiny kitchen; this kitchen was orderly, organized, equipped to the last degree with American ingenuity, and in it the cocktail savouries were laid out so that the guests ranged in and out helping themselves. In the middle of a bewildering noise of laughter and talk I heard my hostess ask a guest if he would like oyster broth instead of a drink; he accepted her suggestion, and then followed activity that seemed to me more like sleight-of-hand than plain cooking. This is what the hostess did, and in less time than it takes to write: she put a small double saucepan on the gas-ring, took from the ice-box a half-pint carton of milk, poured it in the pan, took another carton containing oysters, slipped a few of them into the boiling milk, added seasoning and cream, took a jar of small crackers from the shelf, crumbled them into the broth, and there it was, steaming, smelling good, and taking less time than making tea. It certainly revolutionized my ideas about oyster broths.

All the same I think that perhaps in an English cook-book a few recipes for fish soup will suffice: a fish stock that can be adapted to various soups, a shrimp and potato soup, practical and homely, a Soupe aux Moules and a simple Mussel Broth, and, reserved for the party section, a Lobster Bisque. The famous bouillabaisse, truly a fisherman's soup, is made from an assortment of Mediterranean fish which it would be difficult to get in this country, so it was decided that to include a recipe would be too unrealistic.

FISH STOCK

1 or 2 sole bones or good fish trimmings	salt
1 large bunch of parsley	8 peppercorns
1 bay-leaf	3 pints water
1 large sliced onion	(approx.)
white wine, $\frac{1}{2}$ bottle, is desirable; a	
smaller amount may be used	

Wash bones well and put all ingredients in a pan (the water should cover the contents). Simmer gently until liquid is reduced by about a third, then strain off and use.

POTAGE DE CREVETTES (SHRIMP SOUP)

1 lb. potatoes	1 oz. butter
2 oz. leek (white part only)	2 yolks of egg
2 pints fish stock (see above)	1 gill cream or top of milk
or milk	croûtons
fennel	2 oz. picked shrimps
salt	

Peel and quarter the potatoes; slice the leek, put both into a pan with the stock and add fennel and salt as required. Cover and simmer gently for 20 minutes. Rub through a fine wire sieve, rinse out the pan, pour in the soup, and bring slowly to the boil, stirring in the butter in small pieces. Mix the beaten yolks with the cream or milk, add to the soup off the fire in the way indicated for liaisons, page 140, and add the washed and coarsely chopped shrimps. Serve at once with the croûtons.

The following is a light cream soup suitable for dinner:

SOUPE AUX MOULES

sole or plaice bones	1 quart mussels (see note on
1½ gills white wine or cider	preparation of mussels,
1¼ pints water	page 499)
a bouquet garni	croûtons
a slice of onion	chopped parsley
a clove of garlic	
1 oz. butter	*Liaison*
¾ oz. flour	¾ gill cream or top of milk
salt and pepper	2 yolks of egg

Make a stock with bones in the following way. Put the washed fish bones into a pan with half the wine and all the water. Add the bouquet garni, onion, and garlic. Bring to the boil and simmer for 20 minutes. Melt the butter in a pan. Add, off the fire, the flour and seasoning. Stir until smooth. Strain on the fish stock and bring to the boil. Leave to simmer for 15 minutes. Wash and scrub the mussels. Put them into a pan with the rest of the wine. Cover and bring to the boil. Shake over the fire for 2 or 3 minutes, strain the liquor into the soup. Shell the mussels and remove the beards, add to the soup, and simmer for 5 minutes. Mix the yolks and the cream and make the liaison in the usual way. Add croûtons and serve sprinkled with chopped parsley.

MUSSEL BROTH

This soup, which is suitable for luncheon, is not a very 'fishy' one, though fish in place of vegetable stock may be used if a more pronounced flavour is wanted. The mixture of a small quantity of court bouillon (to taste) with the vegetable stock is excellent, as the former offsets the sweetness of the latter.

1 quart good mussels	1 oz. flour
6 peppercorns	1½ pints unsalted vegetable
1 large bouquet garni	stock
1 glass white wine or dry cider	½ lb. good tomatoes, peeled,
a squeeze of lemon juice	squeezed, and chopped
4 large tablespoons finely cut	1 clove of garlic, crushed
mirepoix (see page 39),	with salt
made with carrot, leek,	salt and pepper
turnip, celery	1 French roll
1½ oz. butter	1 tablespoon chopped parsley

Well wash and scrub mussels, removing all weed. Put into a large pan with the peppercorns, bouquet, wine, and lemon juice. Cover and bring to the boil, shaking frequently.

When the mussels are well opened, shell, removing the beards. Strain the stock through a fine muslin and leave to settle. Put mussels aside in a small covered bowl. Melt the butter in a large saucepan, add the mirepoix, cover with paper, then the lid, and sweat gently for about 7 minutes. Then carefully stir in the flour, add the vegetable stock, blend thoroughly, and pour in the mussel stock, being careful not to disturb the dregs in case of any sand. Stir until boiling, add the tomatoes and garlic, cover, and simmer 5 minutes or until the vegetables are quite tender. Draw aside, add mussels, and adjust seasoning.

Cut the roll into thin slanting slices, bake lightly in the oven, put in the bottom of the tureen with the parsley. Pour on the boiling soup and serve.

POTAGE POISSONIÈRE (CREAM OF WHITING)

2 medium-sized whiting	1 small glass white wine
2 pints milk or milk and water	1½ oz. butter
mixed	¾ oz. flour
1 teaspoon salt	seasoning
4 oz. carrots	a little grated nutmeg
1 oz. celery	2 tablespoons parsley sprigs
4 oz. onions	½ gill cream
1 oz. parsley roots	fried croûtons
1 tablespoon grated horse-radish	

Fillet and skin the whiting. Wash and break up the bones and heads of the fish, put bones with the skin into a pan. Add the milk and salt. Bring to the boil, skim, add the vegetables, sliced, with the parsley roots and horse-radish. Cover and simmer 30 minutes, then strain off through a fine strainer. Meanwhile poach the fillets of fish in the wine in a shallow pan, allowing the liquid to reduce well, and covering the fillets with a buttered paper. Then pound or beat the fish with half the butter until very smooth.

Melt the remaining butter in a saucepan, add the flour, mix, then add the strained stock. Stir until boiling, then whisk in the purée. Adjust the seasoning and add nutmeg. The soup may now be rubbed through a fine wire or nylon sieve to give a smoother finish. Blanch the parsley sprigs for 1 minute, and lightly whip the cream. Fold into the soup with the parsley just before serving. (If an egg liaison is used, mix in the usual way.) Serve croûtons separately.

VII. STOCKS, BOUILLONS, AND MEAT SOUPS

STOCKS

Ordinary household stock, which, it should be noted, can in no way replace the real bouillon made from pot-au-feu, may be made twice a week, or for large households, daily. It may contain cooked meat bones, chicken carcasses, vegetables and débris of vegetables which have been prepared for other dishes (the débris from tomatoes should be avoided as it may turn the stock sour), bacon rinds, and mushroom peelings. The carcasses of game and duck are best kept apart and used for separate stock or gravy.

The pot. A special pot, which may be of earthenware, enamel, or tin-lined copper, should be kept for stock. A small pot with a tap is most useful; the stock may then be drawn off and the fat and bits held back. The vegetables should form a third of the total raw materials of the stock.

The following household stock is suitable for the making of sauces, gravies, broths, and simple soups; as has already been said, it cannot replace proper bouillon. The vegetables may be varied according to supplies, but they should be so balanced that no one flavour predominates.

The bones. The bones should be broken up in as small pieces as possible, and browned before using, either in the stock-pot or in a roasting-tin in the oven. In neither case is fat added, as there is sufficient on the bones to prevent burning. It is inadvisable to mix raw and cooked bones, as the resulting stock is cloudy and does not keep well.

The vegetables. The stock is improved in flavour and colour if the carrots and onions are lightly coloured—fried in a little dripping—before being added to the stock-pot. The onions are stuck with two or three cloves each.

HOUSEHOLD MIXED STOCK

cooked meat bones	sliced vegetables (onion, carrot,
chicken carcasses	leek, celery or celeriac)
giblets	a bouquet garni
bacon rind	salt
mushroom peelings	a few peppercorns
	water to cover

N.B.   The sliced vegetables should form a third of the total materials of the stock.

Break up the bones in small pieces and brown in the oven or in the stock-pot.   Fry the vegetables lightly in dripping.   Put the bones, bacon rind, giblets, vegetables, mushroom peelings, bouquet, salt, and peppercorns into the pot and add the water.   Bring slowly to the boil, skim, and simmer, half covered, for 3–4 hours.   Strain at once, and when cold skim off all the fat.   This fat may be clarified and used for dripping, etc.

This stock should be used within a day or two of making, and should be kept in a cool place.   If the stock-pot is kept on the stove, so that the contents remains tepid for a long time, the stock will go sour.

BONE STOCK

Stocks made entirely from bones, or those in which bones play a predominant part, should be used only for sauces.   They are not suitable for clear soups and consommés, to which they would impart an unpleasant flavour and a gluey consistency.   A small amount of bone, preferably veal, is permissible.   One should use meat stock for real consommés and mixed household stock for simple soups.

Here follows a recipe for pot-au-feu suitable for bouillon and consommés.   This is the proper foundation stock for soups and consommés, and for some sauces.   From it derive such classic soups as Petite Marmite and Madrilène.

POT-AU-FEU

1 veal bone	5 oz. turnips
chicken giblets (optional)	2 leeks
2¼ lb. rolled ribs of beef, with	1 stick of celery
the bones	1 oz. parsnip
5½–6 pints water	3 onions, each stuck with 1
1 level dessertspoon salt	clove
cold water for skimming	a bouquet garni
6 oz. carrots	

Wash the bones and giblets, put into the bottom of a soup marmite, lay the meat on the top, pour over the water, and add the salt.   Set on a gentle heat, uncovered, and bring to the boil: this must not take less than half an hour.   Remove all the scum with a metal spoon as it rises to the surface, and when at boiling-point throw in a coffee-cup of cold water.   Bring again slowly to the boil, skimming well; throw in another coffee-cup of water and repeat this process.   This helps to clear the bouillon and removes any strong taste of meat or bone.   Add all the vegetables, whole or quartered according to their size, bring up to the boil, skim again, and wipe round the inside of the pot.   Put in the bouquet, and half cover with the lid; simmer continuously for 3 hours.   Strain off the liquid, leave until cold, and remove all fat.

If the meat is to be served separately it may be taken out of the bouillon after 1½ hours and served as boiled beef with the vegetables.   The bouillon is then left to simmer with the bones for another 1½ hours before straining, and it is strong enough for Croûte-au-pot, Julienne, and Paysanne.

If the bouillon is required for consommé, the meat should be left for the full time.

When a large quantity of meat can be used, say 5–6 lb., two different cuts should be chosen; for example, 3 lb. topside or top rump and 2 lb. brisket will give a lean piece with a fatter one, which will make the bouillon richer.   For this amount of meat ½–¾ lb. bones should then be added, and the proportion of carrots and other vegetables increased to double the quantity mentioned above.

Many recipes call for the meat to be cut up in small pieces for the making of consommé, the idea being to extract more juices, but after long cooking the bouillon will probably be cloudy.

In the early summer, when the winter vegetables are not obtainable, onions alone may be used, with 1 large clove of garlic, well crushed.

The colour of the bouillon may be improved by adding a well-grilled sliced tomato with the vegetables.   The slices of tomato should be sprinkled with sugar before grilling.

CROÛTE-AU-POT
for 1½–2 pints

1 long French roll	¼ of a small cabbage cooked
vegetables from the pot-au-feu	apart in a little bouillon
	chopped chervil

Slice the roll and bake lightly in the oven.   A little of the fat from the bouillon may be poured over the slices of bread before baking.   Cut the vegetables and the cabbage into neat, even-sized dice and put them into the tureen or soup marmite.   Boil up the bouillon and pour it over the vegetables; then add the croûtes with a good pinch of chopped chervil.

PETITE MARMITE

The stock for this classic soup is from a pot-au-feu well flavoured with chicken. Chicken giblets, together with the carcass of a raw fowl, preferably, or failing this that of a cooked chicken, are added with the other meat.

The stock can be clarified as for consommé, but if it is clear, strong, and of a good colour this can be omitted, the stock being merely strained and skimmed well.

The soup should be served in little marmites and have a traditional garnish of shredded chicken and a julienne of carrot, turnip, the white part of a leek, and shredded cabbage, all cooked in a little of the stock before being added to the soup. Rounds cut from a 'flute' and lightly baked are served separately, as sometimes is grated Parmesan.

The addition of long thin strips of vegetables to a bouillon confers the name of Julienne.

POTAGE JULIENNE

1 medium-sized carrot	salt and pepper
1 medium-sized onion	a pinch of sugar
1 leek	1½ pints bouillon
a small piece of turnip	a little chopped chervil
a spoonful or two of fat from the pot-au-feu	

Cut the vegetables in long thin strips lengthwise, *en julienne*. Put into a pan with the fat from the pot-au-feu, the seasoning, and the sugar. Cover as tightly as possible, put over gentle heat or into the oven, and cook until the vegetables are tender and slightly brown. Drain off any fat there may be. Add the thoroughly drained vegetables to the bouillon and leave on gentle heat for about 15 minutes. Serve with a little chopped chervil.

POTAGE PAYSANNE

Prepare in the same way as Julienne, but this time cut the vegetables into rounds the size of a shilling. They may be cooked in the bouillon itself instead of the fat in this case. Add chopped parsley in place of chervil.

CONSOMMÉ

To make a good consommé it is essential to have a specially strong, clear bouillon of a rich brown colour. This is usually taken from a pot-au-feu which has been made with the maximum quantity of beef, and simmered for the full length of time before straining and cooling. When economy in meat is called for, the following recipe is useful and will give a strong, clear bouillon. For this the addition of a chicken carcass or giblets is required, particularly if the bouillon is to form the base of a Consommé

Madrilène (a clear tomato soup with a strong chicken flavour) or a chicken consommé.   The carcass may be raw and well broken up; the meat from it can be used for a chicken cream, for galantines, suprêmes, and in other ways.

SIMPLE BOUILLON FOR THE MAKING OF CONSOMMÉ

1½ lb. shin of beef	a bouquet garni tied to a stick
1 chicken carcass	of celery
3 oz. onion	6 peppercorns
3 oz. carrot	2 quarts water
2 level teaspoons salt	

Cut the meat up into 6–8 pieces.   Break up the carcass and cut the onion and carrot into thick slices.   Heat a thick aluminium or iron pan, put in the meat and bones, and cook over moderate heat until thoroughly and evenly brown, adding the onion half way through the process.   Draw aside, add the bouquet, salt, peppercorns, and water.   Bring to the boil and simmer, uncovered, 3–4 hours, or until the liquid has reduced to a little over a quart.   Strain off and cool.

It is sometimes necessary to add a very small quantity of fat during the preliminary frying, if the meat is exceptionally lean.

After cooking the meat has little value; it can be made into rissoles or cottage pie, but in pre-war days it was not used again.

LE CONSOMMÉ

3 pints strong bouillon	whites of 2 eggs
¾ lb. lean minced shin of beef	additional sherry to add at
½ gill good sherry or Madeira	end

Put the bouillon into an enamel or tin-lined pan, with the beef and ½ gill sherry or Madeira.   Whip the whites to a light froth, add to the pan, then whisk over a moderate heat, whisking backwards, i.e. the reverse of the usual whisking movement, until the liquid is at boiling-point.   Then stop whisking and allow the soup to come right up to the top of the pan. Draw aside, then boil up carefully once more, taking care not to break the crust which will form on the top.   Draw aside and leave for a good hour on a very slow heat.   This is to extract all the flavour from the meat.   Scald a clean cloth, wring it out, place it over a bowl, and pour the soup through, at first keeping the crust back with a spoon, and then at the end sliding it out on to the cloth.   Pour the soup again through the cloth and through the filter of egg white.   (See notes on clarifying, page 120.)

The consommé should now be clear.   Add extra sherry at this point and any garnish called for.   Reheat but do not allow to boil.

Certain garnishes added to consommé give it various names.   For example, the addition of dice of a cooked savoury custard made with egg white gives it the name of Consommé à la Royale; with a garnish of tiny fine cooked dice of carrots, turnips, and celery it becomes à la Brunoise; and so forth.   (See garnishes for soup, page 132.)

CONSOMMÉ MADRILÈNE

1 lb. red, ripe tomatoes	½ gill good sherry or white
1 quart strong chicken bouillon	wine
¼ lb. minced gravy beef	1 strip of lemon peel
whites of 2 eggs	quarters of lemon

Put the prepared tomatoes (coarsely chopped but not skinned) into an enamel or tin-lined pan with the cold bouillon, minced beef, and the whites whipped to a froth.　Mix thoroughly, add the sherry or white wine and lemon peel, and whisk steadily over a moderate fire until boiling. Stop whisking and allow to boil up.　Draw aside and set to simmer very gently, so gently that there is barely any movement of the liquid, for half to three-quarters of an hour.　Take off the fire and after 10 minutes drain carefully through a cold, wet cloth.　Serve *en gelée* in soup-cups with small quarters of lemon handed separately (see Consommé en Gelée below).

Madrilène may also be served hot, in which case blanched tarragon leaves may be added when reheating.

N.B.　Add 1 teaspoon gelatine if the chicken bouillon is not sufficiently gelatinous.

CONSOMMÉ EN GELÉE

This is prepared as for ordinary consommé, but it is unnecessary to have the bouillon set to a jelly before clarifying.　To make it more gelatinous a slightly greater proportion of veal bone is required in the pot-au-feu. Bouillon should not be made to set by the addition of gelatine, which does not give the right consistency and detracts from the flavour.

A cold consommé should, when thoroughly chilled, barely set to a jelly; it should not be iced and should never be so firm that it can be cut with a spoon.　It should be served with quarters of lemon.

The following summary is given to emphasize the foregoing points.

NOTES ON CLARIFICATION OF BOUILLON *

1. The bouillon should be cold and, for a successful result, of clear brown colour.　It is impossible to clarify properly a grey, muddy bouillon.

2. The utensil.　An enamel or tin-lined pan should be used rather than one of aluminium, which is apt to cause the liquid to be cloudy.　Both pan and whisk should be scalded before being used.

3. The addition of raw minced beef.　The presence of albumen in the beef helps clarification, as it coagulates and helps in the precipitation of fine solid particles.　The beef also adds to the richness of flavour and is called for in the making of a fine consommé and of aspic.

4. The addition of wine.　Sherry, Madeira, white and red wines are called for in some recipes, and they help in the final clarification and improve the flavour.

5. Egg whites.　These are whipped to a froth only; the shells are sometimes added, but this is not essential, although adding to the efficiency

* *See plate 3*

of the filter.   Again it is the coagulation of the albumen which helps the precipitation of fine solid particles, the presence of which gives a cloudy appearance.   The white crust which forms on top of the bouillon as a result of adding egg whites must not be broken.   It should be gently slid from the pan on to the cloth or into the jelly-bag, as it acts as a filter.

6. *Method*.   The ingredients are all put together into the pan, the whites whipped to a froth, the pan set on a moderate fire, and the whole whisked steadily until the contents are on the boil.   The whisking should be backwards, i.e. the reverse of the usual movement; this results in a more thorough mixing of the egg white with the liquid.   Immediately the liquid boils whisking is discontinued and the liquid allowed to come right up to the top of the pan; the pan is then drawn aside and left on a slow fire for the time indicated in the recipe.

7. *Straining*.   For this purpose a clean cloth is used, although when a cloudy consommé is to be strained a jelly-bag is found more practical, as the liquid has to be strained several times.   The cloth should first be scalded, then wrung out and placed over a bowl.   The liquid is then poured carefully through, the crust being kept back at first and then tilted gently on to the cloth.   If the liquid is not absolutely clear directly it comes through, the cloth should be moved quickly over another bowl and the liquid put back into it for re-straining through crust and cloth.

The cloth must be neither squeezed nor pressed.   The liquid should drain through it slowly.

8. *When a jelly-bag is used* this should be well scalded before the liquid is poured in, then immediately a small quantity comes through it should be returned to the bag, and this should be continued until the liquid runs clear.

VEGETABLE BOUILLON OR STOCK

The following recipe for a bouillon de légumes, or a pot-au-feu made only with vegetables, gives a broth, or rather a bouillon, of good flavour. The quantities of vegetables are so balanced that no one flavour predominates, and the haricots are an important ingredient, forming as they do a good base.   Small white haricots should be chosen, as the larger ones are apt to break in cooking and spoil the clearness of the liquid.

POT-AU-FEU BOUILLON MADE WITH VEGETABLES

1 pint haricots	salt
6 oz. each of onions and turnips	½ oz. parsnip
(the onion should be stuck	1½ oz. butter
with cloves, 3 or 4 according	5 pints water
to size)	a bouquet of a good handful
4 oz. leeks	parsley stems, a sprig of
½ lb. carrots	thyme, 2 bay-leaves, and a
1 oz. celery	small clove of garlic

Although it is unnecessary to soak the haricots, nevertheless this broth takes 6 or 7 hours to make.

Cover the haricots with water and bring to the boil. Allow to boil for 2 minutes and then set aside for half an hour. Take half the number of carrots called for and slice. Cut the onions in thick slices and stick with cloves. Soften the sliced carrots and the onions in the usual way, allowing them to colour on a gentle heat and stirring and shaking from time to time so that they do not burn. They should colour to a deep golden brown, but not be allowed to catch. This will take anything from 15 to 20 minutes. When ready draw aside from the fire and add the 5 pints of water. Add the drained haricots and the salt and bring to the boil. Add the remainder of the vegetables (with the exception of the leeks and the remaining half of the carrots) and the bouquet. Bring to the boil and allow to simmer very gently for 3 hours. Now add the remainder of the carrots split in two (not diced) and the white part of the leeks tied up into a bundle. Allow the simmering to continue for another 3 hours. At the end of this time the saucepan should be taken away from the heat, but it may be left on the corner of the stove, so that it does not get entirely cold, and remain there during the night. When required for use next day, lift out gently the bundle of leeks and the long pieces of carrot. Strain the bouillon through a fine sieve, but be careful to take off the liquid without disturbing the deposit of fine vegetables and the thicker liquid at the bottom of the pan. Heat this clear liquid and serve with thin dry toast. At the same time the leeks and carrots may be handed separately.

N.B. This is an excellent and economical bouillon to use for the Iced Curry Cream Soup on page 991.

KIDNEY SOUP (1)

giblets of 2 chickens cut in pieces	salt
2 minced kidneys, and 1 sliced	1 bay-leaf
1 large sliced onion	a few peppercorns
4¼ oz. butter	¼ pint stock or water
1 quart stock or water	¾–1 oz. flour
a bouquet garni	½ gill reduced sherry or red wine
½ lb. unskinned tomatoes	chopped parsley
2 red peppers	croûtons of fried bread (shilling size)
1 clove of garlic, bruised	

Toss the giblets and minced kidneys with the onion in 2 oz. butter until brown. Pour on a quart of stock or water, add the bouquet, and simmer 40 minutes or until of good flavour and reduced by about a third.

Slice the tomatoes and red peppers and cook to a pulp with 1 oz. butter, garlic, salt, bay-leaf, peppercorns, and ¼ pint stock or water. Rub through a strainer. Strain the soup and add the tomato mixture. Work 1 oz. butter with ¾ oz. flour, or 1 oz. if the soup is very liquid. Add the kneaded butter in small pieces to the soup, whisking it well in. Reboil thoroughly, adding the sherry or red wine and the finely sliced kidney, sautéd in ¼ oz. butter, for the garnish. Dust the top with chopped parsley when serving, and hand the croûtons of fried bread.

The following second Kidney Soup is a good winter dish. The blanching of the kidneys in the way described obviates any possibility of an unpleasant flavour. The recipe is suitable for adaptation to game, and provides a good way of using a badly shot bird.

POTAGE PURÉE DE ROGNONS (KIDNEY SOUP) (2)

2 sheeps' kidneys
1½ pints well-flavoured stock
1 large dessertspoon dried mixed herbs
a pinch of ground mace
1 whole anchovy or 2 fillets (soaked in milk to extract the salt)
¾ oz. butter

¾ oz. flour
a small glass sherry
1 heaped teaspoon red-currant jelly
a good squeeze of lemon juice
salt and pepper
a little browning or caramel
croûtons of fried bread

Skin the kidneys, drop into boiling salted water, and blanch for 2–3 minutes. Drain and dry. Put into a pan with a cup of the stock, the herbs, and the spice, and simmer gently until very tender. Then remove and mince finely with the anchovy, or pound until smooth in the mortar. Rub through a fine wire sieve. Strain the stock back into the remaining stock.

Make a roux with the butter and flour, pour on the stock, stir until boiling, simmer a few minutes, then add the purée, the sherry, jelly, and lemon juice. Adjust seasoning, skim, add a little browning or caramel to deepen the colour, and serve with the croûtons.

PURÉE OF GAME SOUP

Use the above recipe with the following modifications: Substitute for the kidneys 4–6 oz. raw or cooked game, hare, grouse, or pheasant. Use the bones for making the stock. If the meat is cooked proceed straight away to mince and/or pound finely. The anchovy may be included or not according to taste.

OXTAIL SOUP

This soup may be thick or clear. The former is made in the same way as an oxtail stew, but with, of course, more liquid. Nowadays, when oxtails are difficult to come by, it is an economy to make thick soup from the remains of an oxtail stew, or to make a clear oxtail from a fresh tail, and in the next day or two follow with a thick soup or 'quick stew' made from the left-overs and second stock. A tail is fairly large and so easily provides these two dishes for a family of four.

Oxtail makes an excellent clear soup, a little more *recherché* than a thick one. Both clear and thick can, however, be made from one tail. The recipes given here are on those lines. (If a clear mulligatawny is wanted, a simple method is to infuse curry spices in the stock during the simmering process, removing them when the stock is sufficiently flavoured. The drawback here is that all the stock and meat is then so flavoured. The spices are: 1 tablespoon whole coriander, 1 teaspoon whole fenugreek, 1 dessertspoon whole cumin, 1 dessertspoon whole cardamon, 2 whole cloves of garlic. Tie in muslin before adding.)

CLEAR OXTAIL
to be made a day before it is needed

1 good-sized tail
1 oz. butter or bacon fat
4 oz. onions, sliced
4 oz. carrots, sliced
3 oz. swede or turnip, sliced
1 stick of celery, sliced
¾ pint good stock
1 glass good sherry or Madeira
about 3 quarts water or good clear stock (this improves the strength and quality of the consommé)

salt
4–5 parsley stalks, 1 bay-leaf, and 2–3 sprigs each of savory and lemon thyme, all tied together
4–6 peppercorns
½ lb. lean gravy beef
whites and shells of 2 eggs
cayenne
an extra glass sherry

Well wash and dry the tail, or it may be blanched for 3–4 minutes before being drained and dried. Cut into pieces and crush each piece slightly with the flat of a chopper. Choose a thick braising-pan, put in the butter, add the vegetables, and rissoler gently 5–10 minutes. Now add the pieces of tail and continue to rissoler, allowing them to take colour. Pour in the stock and sherry and allow to cook, swirling the pan around from time to time until the liquid has reduced practically to a glaze.

Now cover well with water, add salt, herbs, and peppercorns. Bring slowly to the boil, skimming well. Simmer 2–3 hours or until the stock is really strong and good. Then strain off, reserving the pieces of tail and vegetables for a second stock.

Next day skim off all fat from the stock and measure out a good 2 pints. Put into a pan with the finely minced or scraped beef, the whites of egg beaten to a froth, and the shells. Clarify as for consommé (see clarification of bouillon, page 120). When strained, reheat and serve with a little of the shredded meat from the tail in the soup as a garnish, and a dust of cayenne. An extra glass of sherry may be poured into the soup just before serving.

THICK OXTAIL

2 pints oxtail stock, either remains of the first, or the second stock, well strained and skimmed
the meat picked from the tail, together with a little lean ham or boiled bacon, about 4–5 oz. in all

1¼ oz. butter
1¼ oz. flour
1 glass sherry or Madeira
salt
pepper
cayenne

Make sure the stock is well flavoured and strong: reduce if necessary. Mince and pound the meat until smooth. Make a roux with the butter and flour. Pour in the stock, blend, bring to the boil, and simmer to reduce for 10–15 minutes. Now add by degrees to the meat, adjust seasoning, and rub all through a wire sieve. Return to the rinsed-out pan, and finish with the sherry.

If a mortar is not used, it is best to rub the meat through a sieve after mincing, before diluting with the liquid.

Turtle soup is rarely made in the domestic kitchen, and as it can be bought for those rare occasions when it is required it was thought unnecessary to include a recipe here. It may be either thick or clear, but the latter is considered the finer soup. The garnish of small pieces of the green fat floating in the soup is considered a delicacy.

Mock Turtle is also a good clear soup, made with calf's head, which gives it the correct gelatinous quality. The soup is clarified and served with small squares of the jelly part of the head as the garnish. Quarters of lemon are served separately. The head can be used for a dish, such as Devilled Head (see page 606), during the next day or two.

MOCK TURTLE SOUP
to be prepared a day before it is required

½ calf's head
1½ oz. bacon fat or dripping
1 gammon rasher of bacon
½ lb. veal trimmings, cut from the knuckle or shoulder
1 lb. lean gravy beef
1 stick of celery
4 oz. each of carrots, onions, and turnips, cut in quarters

a large bouquet garni, parsley, thyme, savory, marjoram, and bay-leaf
6 peppercorns
1 teaspoon salt
2–3 quarts water

For clarifying
the whites of 1 or 2 eggs, and the shells, and half the beef already mentioned

1 glass Marsala

Bone the head after soaking well, tie up the meat neatly with tape, and blanch for 5–10 minutes. Take out, plunge into cold water, drain, and dry. Break up the bones, and allow to brown in the oven.

Meanwhile heat the fat in a large pan, put in the bacon, veal, and half the beef cut into fairly large pieces. Fry briskly till turning colour, lower the heat and add the vegetables. Rissoler 5 minutes or so, then draw aside and add the herbs, peppercorns, salt, and water. Bring slowly to the boil, skimming thoroughly. Add the bones and the head, bring again to the boil, skim again, then simmer gently 3–4 hours. Take up the head and press gently under a weight.

Strain off the stock, and leave till next day, when it should be a firm jelly. Skim off all fat, measure out 1 quart and put into a pan with the remaining beef, finely minced. Add the egg whites whipped to a froth and the crushed shells and clarify as for consommé (see clarification of bouillon, page 120). Reheat, adding the Marsala, and small squares of the gelatinous parts of the head as a garnish.

SCOTCH OR MUTTON BROTH

1½–2 lb. neck of mutton, scrag
  or middle neck
3 pints water
1½ oz. pearl barley, previously
  soaked overnight
3 oz. each of carrot, leek, and
  turnip

2 oz. onion
2 oz. celery
freshly ground pepper
a level teaspoon salt
chopped parsley

Remove as much fat as possible and cut the mutton up into small pieces. Put into the cold water and bring slowly to the boil, skimming well. When all the scum has been removed add the barley and salt, and simmer 20–30 minutes. Now add the vegetables cut into small dice, and freshly ground pepper. Continue cooking gently about 1½ hours with the lid on the pan. Now remove the mutton, cut a few good pieces off the bone, and return these to the broth. Skim to remove any fat, adjust seasoning, and add parsley; the soup should be thick, and full of vegetables and barley.

CHICKEN BROTH

Use strong chicken stock as a base and the same vegetables as in above recipe, but cut into finer dice and substitute rice for barley. An excellent addition is 2–3 tablespoons thick cream stirred in just before serving.

VIII. PARTY SOUPS

Now come some recipes for soups which we hesitated to give in the general section of this chapter, being afraid they might be dismissed with remarks of 'no time,' 'too extravagant' and so forth—and that would be a pity. But the frustrations and restrictions of everyday life have a way of melting when a party is in question. So here they are.

The first recipe given is to me most interesting. It was given to us by R. H.'s mother and is quoted exactly as she gave it to us. It is an onion soup into which raw eggs are beaten at the last moment, one egg for each person. A good vegetable bouillon may at need be substituted.

SOUPE A L'OIGNON

A lunch or supper dish. By Baron de Grandmaison. Paris in the eighties or nineties.

'This must be served in marmites, red rough earthenware, glazed inside, large enough for one portion. The marmites are placed in a soup-plate, one before each guest.

1. Warm gently sufficient bouillon for total quantity.

2. Cut up onions in slices and place them in frying-pan; make them revenir to a golden colour, *not* brown: best butter should be used.

3. When the onions are ready, put them into the bouillon and bring to boil.

4. Have ready slices of French bread, toasted. In another plate gruyère and Parmesan cheese in equal parts, 15 grammes [1] of each per portion.

5. Put the bread into each marmite. Soak the bread with the bouillon *boiling* hot. Add, without stirring, the cheese in each marmite, heat above and below, or in the oven, and serve.

6. Alongside each soup-plate put a raw fresh egg, which must be broken by the guest into the marmite, and the whole stirred with a fork, adding pepper and salt to their taste.

7. It is wished that the dish should be served boiling hot, and that it should be eaten out of the marmite and not the soup-plate.

'The above was given to my aunt by her friend M. de Grandmaison, a frequent guest at her house at Dinard in the eighties and nineties. My aunt was a very good cook and entertained a great deal, especially the French society who went to Dinard in the summer. My uncle was a well-known gourmet and their house was very popular.'

The next two recipes are just plain expensive. The first is a Lobster Bisque, the second an American lobster soup.

BISQUE D'HOMARD (LOBSTER BISQUE)

2 oz. carrots	2 wineglasses white wine
2 oz. onions	3 oz. rice
1 shallot	3½ pints court bouillon *au vin*
2 oz. butter	½ gill cream
1 small uncooked lobster	seasoning, including cayenne
4 tablespoons cognac	

Cut the vegetables into a fine mirepoix. Melt half the butter in a large sauté pan, add the mirepoix, cook gently for some minutes, then put in the lobster split in two, cut side downwards. Keep out any spawn or coral and pound with the rest of the butter. Pass through a fine sieve and reserve. Increase the heat, cover, and sauter 2 minutes. Heat the cognac, flame, and pour over with the white wine, a pinch of salt, and a touch of cayenne. Cover tightly and cook very gently for 15 minutes, shaking the pan occasionally. Meanwhile cook the rice in about a pint of the bouillon for about 30 minutes until really soft. Shell the lobster, cut up the meat finely, and put into a mortar with the creamy part from the head and any spawn or coral. Drain the liquid from the sauté pan and reserve it, adding the mirepoix to the mortar. Pound thoroughly. Then add the rice by degrees, pounding all the time, and being careful not to add any liquid. When really fine, add the reserved liquid and turn into a clean saucepan. Dilute with about ½ pint of the bouillon, and pass through a fine sieve or tammy through a piece of butter muslin. Return again to the pan, add the remaining bouillon, reheat, draw off the fire, and beat in the lobster butter; whisk in the cream, season, and serve.

The soup may be reheated after the butter has been added, but must on no account boil, as this would ruin the texture and flavour of the soup.

[1] Approx. ½ oz.

The following recipe was given to us by the Arab cook mentioned in the Introduction:

SOUPE D'HOMARD A L'AMÉRICAINE

1 small uncooked lobster or 1 pint uncooked shrimps
1 oz. fresh butter or good oil
3 oz. onion
2 cloves of garlic
a large pinch of saffron, soaked overnight in an egg-cup of water
1 level teaspoon curry-powder
¾ oz. flour
1 glass red wine
1 tablespoon brandy

1 large tablespoon rice
1 quart good well-reduced court bouillon *au vin*
1 heaped teaspoon tomato purée
a bouquet garni
salt and pepper
1 dessertspoon freshly chopped parsley
croûtons of bread fried in butter
thin slices of lemon

Split the lobster in two and remove the bag from the head. Crack the claws. Melt the butter in a large sauté or stew-pan, put in the lobster split side downwards, cover, and cook on a low fire 7 minutes. Meanwhile slice the onion very finely and crush the garlic with a little salt. Then remove the lobster, and add the onions, garlic, and curry-powder. Sauter until brown. Add the flour, wine, brandy, saffron, rice, and court bouillon. Bring to the boil, add the bouquet, a little salt and pepper, and cook gently uncovered for about an hour. Meanwhile take the meat from the lobster and cut into small pieces. Add to the soup and leave to poach 20–30 minutes *without* boiling. Finish with the parsley and tomato purée, and serve the croûtons and slices of lemon separately.

If using shrimps do not sauter first, but add them to the soup when finished and leave to poach 30 minutes. Then remove, shell, and replace them in the soup. Press the shells well in a strainer to extract all the juice, which should be added to the soup.

Potage Purée Bonne Femme can fairly be described as a dinner-party soup. It is a smooth cream soup of which the main ingredients are leek and potato, but it is made with milk and a liaison of yolks of egg and cream is added.

POTAGE PURÉE BONNE FEMME

4 potatoes
6 leeks
1½ oz. butter
salt and pepper
¾ pint milk
¾ pint water

Liaison
2 yolks of egg
1 gill single cream or top of milk

croûtons of fried bread

Slice the potatoes and shred the leeks. Melt the butter in a stew-pan, add the potatoes and leeks, reserving 1 leek. Season with salt and pepper and stir over a slow fire until the vegetables are nearly soft. Add the milk and water and stir until boiling. Draw aside and leave to simmer for 15–20 minutes. Rub through a sieve, add gradually the yolks of egg beaten into the cream, and thicken over a slow fire without boiling. Serve in a marmite with the remaining leek, shredded, blanched, and drained, scattered over the top of the soup, and with croûtons of fried bread.

Crème Vichyssoise is a cold soup of particularly delicious flavour. This also is made with leeks and potato, but it calls for chicken broth and a certain amount of cream. When these ingredients are available it is well worth making as it is one of the best of cream soups. It should be eaten ice-cold with finely minced chives on the top.

CRÈME VICHYSSOISE

1½ oz. butter	parsley and chives
the white part of a dozen small leeks	1 quart strong chicken stock
3 or 4 potatoes	salt, pepper, and nutmeg
1 stick of celery (optional)	½ pint cream, or top of milk

Heat the butter slowly and add the finely sliced leeks. Cover and shake the pan gently over moderate heat for about 15 minutes, that is until the leeks are softened and pale yellow. They must not turn brown at all. You will need to watch and stir frequently. Add the finely sliced potatoes and celery, the chopped parsley, stock, and seasoning. Bring to the boil, stirring, and then simmer for 30 minutes or until all the vegetables are well cooked. Pass the whole through a nylon sieve and then through a tammy, for this soup should be velvet-smooth. Re-season, allow to cool, add cream, chill in the refrigerator or on ice, and serve with finely chopped chives sprinkled on top. It may be served hot, but is then less seductive, and a less rich soup might better take its place.

See also page 1185 for this soup made in an emulsifying machine.

Another soup which calls for chicken stock, this time with eggs as a liaison, is Potage Crème Germiny:

POTAGE CRÈME GERMINY

2 large handfuls sorrel	3 yolks of egg
3 large handfuls spinach	¼ pint thin cream or top of milk
1 handful spring onions	
¾ oz. butter	seasoning
1½ pints chicken stock, well strained	very small egg croquettes

Well wash the sorrel and spinach. Trim the spring onions, leaving the green tops. Cut all in fine shreds. Melt the butter in a stew-pan, put in the vegetables and stock, cover, and stew gently for 20 minutes. Rub through a fine sieve. Rinse out the pan thoroughly, return the soup, and bring it to the boil. Draw aside. Beat the yolks well, add a small quantity of the cream and then several spoonfuls of the hot soup by degrees. Pour back into the pan with the remainder of the cream and stir continuously until very hot. Adjust the seasoning. On no account boil or bring near to boiling-point: it is really better to do this final thickening in a double saucepan. The consistency should be that of thin cream, and the flavour pleasantly acidulated. Garnish with very small egg croquettes served separately.

To make a good bortsch with the proper accompaniments takes some time, so the following is a dish to try when you have a little leisure. It calls for strong, well-flavoured meat stock, but may be made with a liquid made with dried mushrooms and water in the proportion of ½ oz. dried mushrooms to 2 quarts water. The stock thus made should be cooked until the flavour is extracted from the mushrooms, and should be well seasoned. It is, of course, equally possible to make it with a good vegetable stock, but it cannot then be truly called a bortsch.

Here are recipes for Consommé Bortsch and a Bortchok:

CONSOMMÉ BORTSCH

whites of 2 eggs	1 quart strong, well-flavoured
½ lb. minced gravy beef	beef stock
1 raw beetroot, the round,	seasoning
deep red variety	sour cream
	piroshski (see below)

Whip the whites to a froth, mix with the beef, and put into an enamel or tin-lined pan. Peel and grate the beetroot, add to the pan with the stock. Whisk over the fire until boiling, draw aside carefully and simmer for 30–40 minutes, taking care not to disturb the crust. Take off the fire and leave for about 5 minutes before straining through a scalded cloth (see clarifying notes, page 120). Reheat carefully, season, and serve with a bowl of sour cream and piroshski.

Piroshski are small turnovers or Russian pies made with a light yeast dough and filled with minced meat, mushrooms, rice, hard-boiled eggs, etc. They are made quite small in the shape of a turnover and handed hot in a napkin with either clear bortsch or bortchok or any gravy soup.

PIROSHSKI

Dough

¼ lb. flour	¼ gill milk
½ teaspoon salt	1 egg
¼ oz. yeast	1 oz. creamed butter
½ teaspoon sugar	beaten egg

Sift and warm the flour and salt. Cream yeast with the sugar and dissolve in the warm milk. Beat the egg and add to the flour with the milk. Beat thoroughly. The dough should be fairly soft. Work in the creamed butter and set to rise 30 or 40 minutes in an even temperature. It may then be put aside in an ice-box or refrigerator for use when wanted. In any case this preliminary chilling makes for easy handling. Roll out on a floured board, stamp out into large rounds, brush with beaten egg, and put a teaspoon of filling on each. Fold over and pinch the edges well together, and flatten each one lightly on the board so that the join will make a ridge along the top. Put to prove 10–15 minutes, then brush lightly with egg and bake in a hot oven, 450° F. These may also be fried in the same way as rissoles.

Meat filling

¼ oz. butter	2 oz. cooked minced beef or
½ shallot	ham
½ oz. mushrooms	salt and pepper

Melt the butter in a small pan, add the shallot finely chopped, soften slightly, then add the chopped mushrooms. Cook briskly for a minute or two, then add the minced meat and seasoning and work well together. Cool before using.

Maigre filling

1 oz. mushrooms	½ hard-boiled egg
¼ oz. butter	salt and freshly ground black
½ handful small spring onions	pepper
1–1½ tablespoons boiled rice	

Wash and slice the mushrooms. Cook in the butter. Wash and trim the onions, keeping the green part, and cut in very small pieces with scissors. Mix everything together in a bowl and season well with salt and freshly ground black pepper.

BORTCHOK

1 quart strong, clear, well-flavoured beef stock	sour cream
1 large cooked beetroot	piroshski

Put the stock in a pan and bring to the boil. Grate the beetroot fairly finely and add to the pan. Infuse on a very gentle heat for about half an hour. When a good flavour of beetroot is obtained, strain through a muslin, rinse out the pan, return the soup, and reheat. Serve with sour cream and piroshski of meat or containing a *maigre* filling of hard-boiled eggs and parsley. The soup should be almost clear and a good red colour; therefore the stock must be well made, as for consommé.

In the Winkfield chapter will be found other party soups, a Cold Tomato Soup (page 991), a Cream of Curry Soup (page 990), and an almond soup, Potage Crème d'Amandes (page 989), etc.

SOUP GARNISHES

Garnishes for soups in the domestic kitchen are a simpler affair than the classic garnishes of the *haute cuisine*, as a glance at the subject in one of the important French cookery books will show. The important aspect of the matter in the domestic kitchen is really a comprehension of the principles that guide us in choosing a garnish. With this understanding there is plenty of opportunity for improvisation with the materials at hand. This section of the soup chapter, therefore, is chiefly concerned with these principles, but in passing we should note that however well we may experiment and invent, we should not misapply classic names. For example, the name Consommé à la Royale indicates a garnish of a firm, lightly cooked egg custard, added in small pieces or shapes to the clear soup; if in place of it you choose to use green peas, the correct garnish for Crème St Germain, or the asparagus tips for Consommé Princesse, there is no reason why you should not do so, but then the soup should not be labelled 'Royale.' This would be a misuse of a classic name.

Generally speaking, a garnish is added to a soup for one of the following purposes, or possibly for a combination of them: (1) to embellish, (2) to add flavour, (3) to give contrast of texture, (4) to make a more substantial dish. In attempting to achieve any one of these objects, it is necessary to observe certain precautions. It is important not to detract from some essential quality of the soup by choosing an unsuitable garnish; for example, a strongly flavoured garnish might overwhelm a subtly flavoured soup. An ordinary fried croûton added to a clear and limpid consommé might spoil these very characteristics by dispersing a slight trail of grease over the surface of the soup. On the other hand, sometimes, when a clear consommé is to contain a julienne of vegetables, the recipe may indicate that these are to be cooked to a very light brown in a nut of butter; then, should a little of the delicate beurre noisette escape into the soup, this is not considered a detraction. It is not so much a case of hard and fast rules as of discrimination.

Here are some examples of the purposes enumerated:

1. To embellish. In Consommé à la Royale the garnish, a small portion of a cooked egg custard, gives a pleasant appearance, as well as being of a good texture. A julienne added to a consommé is both an embellishment and an addition to the flavour; one has the agreeable colours of gold, green, and white from the carrots, green vegetables, and celery.

2. To add flavour. Croûtes Mornay are a piquant addition to a tomato soup; picked shrimps add flavour to a bland potato soup.

3. To give contrast of texture. Crisp croûtons provide a contrast of texture in any cream soup; shreds of raw celery do the same and are good also with a consommé.

4. To make a more substantial dish. With some garbures croûtes covered with a purée of the vegetables are served. With Potage Périgord cabbage leaves are filled with a stuffing and served with the soup. Cheese croûtes are served with Potage à l'Oignon. Sometimes tiny profiteroles made of choux paste, no bigger than a small marble, are split and filled with a mixture that will add contrast to a soup: for example, a tiny bit of beaten-up cream cheese or devilled cream (cream mixed with Worcestershire sauce, cayenne, and French mustard), a purée of mushrooms, a curry-flavoured cream, or a horse-radish cream. Even in these fillings there is scope for experiment. A plain broth may have croûtes the size of a two-shilling piece on which a purée of vegetables has been laid and then grilled; these are either put at the bottom of the soup-tureen or served separately. In certain cream soups a refreshing flavour is added by using the diced flesh of tomatoes or cucumber. As a garnish for a watercress soup a little dab of cream cheese added at the last moment is good: indeed, this is good in many soups needing a heightening of flavour.

In the domestic kitchen a garnish is almost bound to depend on what you may have at hand, and for this very reason there is opportunity for invention and cleverness. Here are a few more suggestions for your consideration: A bland soup, such as spinach, may have tiny egg croquettes served in it, eggs and spinach presenting a good combination of flavour. Some people like a sweet element in a potato soup, and shredded prunes, French plums, or almonds may be added. As well as egg custard for Consommé à la Royale and the julienne of vegetables for Consommé Julienne, vermicelli, various pastas, sago, profiteroles, green peas, and asparagus points are all commonly used, and when fried croûtons are not wanted, croûtons of toast are sometimes substituted.

CUSTARD FOR CONSOMMÉ A LA ROYALE

1 egg white
4 tablespoons cream
seasoning

Put the mixture into a dariole mould or a tea-cup and steam gently until set. For a yellow custard, take 2 egg yolks to 3 or 4 tablespoons cream, season, and cook in the same way.

CROÛTES MORNAY

Toast bread on one side only and on the untoasted side put a layer of mornay sauce; sprinkle with a little cheese and cook under the grill.

Croûtes or croûtons may either be fried in deep fat or in just enough hot fat almost to cover them in a frying-pan. For flavour butter should be used, preferably clarified, but frying-oil or lard may be substituted. The fat, in a frying-pan, is heated over moderate heat; when hot the croûtons or croûtes are put in, and when lightly coloured lifted out and drained. Only the surface of the bread should be coloured, and this should not be more than a light, golden brown. Fried bread deepens a little in colour when taken out of the fat, and this should be borne in mind. The whole of the cooking should be done over gentle heat, not too quickly.

TOASTED CROÛTONS

A slice of stale bread should first be lightly toasted, then cut in dice.

TO CUT POTATOES FOR POTATO CROÛTONS

Pare the potatoes thinly, cut in thick slices; cut these slices into sticks, put a bundle of the sticks together flat on a board and cut them across so that you have small dice; plunge these at once into cold water to wash away the starch, drain and dry them. Blanch the dice for 2 or 3 minutes, strain and allow to dry a little, then fry till golden brown and crisp in butter or oil; drain and sprinkle lightly with salt.

Unsweetened pancakes are sometimes used as a soup garnish; they may be cut into rounds or into thin strips. Little sprigs of chervil called *pluches* are used as a garnish for many soups.

The Russian garnishes for soups are of quite substantial proportions. Both pirogi and piroshski are served. Pirogi means a pie and piroshski is its diminutive, meaning a little pie. The paste for these may be of brioche type or puff paste, or the dough given on page 130, and the filling is of rice, meat, hard-boiled eggs, cabbage, etc. The shape of the pie is like our Cornish pasty. If a large pirogi is served it may be sliced. The little piroshski are served whole. These accompaniments are commonly served with bortsch, and they may equally form part of the cocktail savoury preceding the meal.

A short list of soup garnishes and the soups they usually accompany is added as a guide:

Garnishes	Served with
Bread and potato croûtons	Any purée, especially pea and potato
Brunoise	Consommé or soups from the pot-au-feu
Celery chips	Tomato, potato, lentil soup
Cheese profiteroles	As above, or any velouté creams
Cheese-straws	Tomato, carrot, potato soups
Chopped hard-boiled egg	Most purées, particularly green
Fish or chicken quenelles	Velouté cream soups
Force-meat balls	Game purées, e.g. hare, kidney
Fried sliced apple	Celery or chestnut soup
Julienne	Consommé or soups from the pot-au-feu
Liptauer or creamed cheese	Potato or other bland cream soups
Mornay croûtes	Tomato, carrot soup, or mixed purées
Picked shrimps	Any bisque, potato purée, tomato soup
Royale	Consommés
Salted cucumber or gherkin	Giblet, kidney soups
Shredded pancakes (fried till crisp)	Green soups
Small pats of green butter	Cream of celery soup
Tiny ravioli filled with any good force-meat	Gravy soups or consommé
Vegetable purée on croûtes	A clear gravy or game soup

VI

Sauces

I. GENERAL

WHAT A SAUCE CAN DO AND BE

1. A sauce may be the making of a dish, bringing out and enhancing the flavour of the food with which it is served, and often, by subtle contrast, making two flavours blend into one whole.

2. It may be an essential component of a dish, as when the liquid or 'cuisson' from meat or fish forms part of its composition; fricassées and blanquettes are examples of this.

3. It may be the foundation of a dish, as when a thick béchamel or velouté sauce is used to bind together fish, chicken, or eggs to form croquettes, or a demi-glace holds meat for rissoles and kromeski.

4. It may be an accompaniment only, in which case it is often in direct and sharp contrast to the dish with which it is served. For example, sauce tartare is served with fried fish, its piquancy offsetting the rich quality of fried food. Sauce béarnaise is served with tournedos, and, simpler examples still, mint sauce with lamb and apple sauce with pork or goose.

Many of these combinations are traditional; indeed, certain sauces are made to be served only with certain foods. Good sauces are generally rich and concentrated in flavour and should be served in reasonable measure, two tablespoons per person being a suitable allowance. Food should not swim in these sauces, nor should the flavour be lost beneath them.

5. A sauce should have so pleasant a flavour and be so discreetly blended that on tasting you feel it might be eaten by itself. Sauces that you do not feel that way about are the average English mint sauce with large pieces of mint floating in rough vinegar, and the thick brown gravy sometimes served with roast meat.

A sauce should not be used as a cloak for badly prepared or unpalatable food; for example, thick 'white sauce' blanketing watery marrow. Nor should it be an indeterminate flavourless liquid used without discrimination.

Do not I beg of you be offended and think that such direct words belittle your intelligence as students of cookery. It is precisely such culinary sins that have made the great mass of our countrymen suspicious of sauces, and caused them to talk in a belittling way of 'messed-up food.'

Of course we have lived through an era of makeshift, the natural reaction to which is a general wish for 'straight' food, for the roast and grilled meats that we have missed in our menus and lacked in our sustenance.   But even if one were called upon to cook for someone whose diet was restricted in such a way, the need to understand sauce-making would still remain.   I am not at this moment thinking of the great and classic sauces, but of the simpler ones such as ordinary gravy, well seasoned, and mint sauce, and the difference between the vinegary affair already referred to and the properly made article, creamy with finely chopped mint, not over-acid, and pale green in colour.   I think too of the difference between white sauce or gloy and the delicate béchamel.

A beginner may be reassured by the thought that in spite of an imposing array of names there is no deep mystery about sauce-making.   Its mastery lies in taking pains and following faithfully the guidance of experienced chefs.   Most of the sauces whose names are familiar to us—soubise, aurore, béarnaise, bordelaise, poulette and so forth—are for the most part the offspring of a few basic sauces called sauces mères.   If, in the earlier stages of your cooking career, you take these seriously, master and understand them, then the door to sauce-making will be open to you.   The day will arrive when you know so well what you are doing and why that you will feel free to experiment and improvise.   When a chef produces the finest of his sauces he will find it difficult to give you hard and fast rules about the making of it, because in the higher flights of this branch of cooking there is room for experiment and imagination.

If, in the earlier stages of learning to cook, the careful instructions are ignored, regarded as unnecessary frills, or quicker, easier ways are considered just as good, one may miss later on the pleasure of successful improvisation and invention, because the cause and effect of the various processes are imperfectly understood.

An enthusiastic cook will consider it worth while to collect, and care for, special equipment for sauce-making.   When she finds her special little sauce whisk has been taken for some unsuitably heavy process, or her shining little pans misused, she may in retrospect be sorry for R. H., remembering the occasions when such things happened at Winkfield.

There is one piece of sauce-making equipment which must be singled out for emphatic comment.   This is the bain-marie.   If you have seen a beautiful old-fashioned bain-marie made of shining copper and holding a battery of graduated copper pans you may pine to possess one, but the probability is that something simpler will have to serve.   You will probably improvise with a baking-tin filled with water holding a number of small pans.   The pans are small not only because of restricted space, but because by using them one avoids too large a surface of sauce over which skin can form.

The bain-marie or hot-water bath is used for two purposes in sauce-making, and sometimes the two are confused:

1. As a means of thickening delicate sauces which should not be exposed to direct heat.   For this the temperature of the water should be about 180°–190° F., that is to say just below boiling-point.   A double

saucepan is often used for this purpose. The common mistake is to allow the water to get beyond this temperature.

6. A bain-marie is used for keeping sauces warm for a reasonable time. For this the temperature of the surrounding water should be lower, about 130°–140° F. The sauce is kept warm but does not continue to cook. For a delicate sauce such as hollandaise the temperature of the water bath may be even lower.

After a sauce has been kept for some time in a bain-marie it must be well stirred or beaten before being served; possibly it may need reheating, and then special care is called for.

To prevent the formation of skin, some sauces may be covered with a piece of paper lightly pressed down on the surface, or, as for a panade, be lightly rubbed over with butter.

Traditionally certain sauces are served with certain dishes, and there is generally a sound gastronomic reason for this association. For this reason it is unwise to mix dishes and sauces in an uninformed way.

THE CONSISTENCY OF SAUCES

This varies according to their intended use:

'Flowing' for serving separately in a sauce-boat.

'Masking' for fillet of fish dishes, chaudfroids, blanquettes, hot creams, or mousses.

'Coating,' principally used for frying à la villeroy, e.g. for boned chicken or rabbit which is spread with very thick sauce, then coated in egg and breadcrumbs and fried. This is also used as the basis of croquettes, rissoles, and kromeski.

A panade has the thickest consistency of all; it is used as a foundation for meat and fish creams. See page 701.

The two principal basic sauces from which so many others derive are the sauces brunes and the sauces blanches. There is a third type, classed under the heading of sauce blanche, which needs separate consideration, because in ingredients and method it differs from what may be termed the flour sauces. This is the sauce au beurre, and under this heading come hollandaise and sauce blanche au beurre, or sauce bâtarde, and its derivatives.

In the following pages each of these sauces will be dealt with individually, but common in importance to them all are the various methods of thickening.

METHODS OF THICKENING

These processes apply, of course, to soups as well as to sauces, and are of sufficient importance to warrant a section of this chapter to themselves. Before dealing with methods which involve additional ingredients, and bearing in mind the student who, instructed to reduce a liquid by half, poured half down the sink, a note should be made on thickening by reduction.

THICKENING BY REDUCTION

A liquid is reduced by being boiled or simmered for a certain length of time so that, moisture being driven off in the form of steam, the liquid remaining is thicker in consistency, and more concentrated in flavour and seasoning.

Generally speaking flour sauces should be reduced in this way, and the effect of this treatment—the concentration of the seasoning—should be borne in mind when seasoning the preliminary roux; the tendency should be to under-season in the first stages and to adjust at the end.

The process of reducing takes place before the final liaison is made; the effect is to thicken the sauce and improve its flavour and gloss.   It is most important to taste and to avoid over-concentration of flavour.

The length of time cannot be stated with any rigidity, for something depends on the strength of the stock used and the thickness of the sauce when it comes to the boil, but with the exception of demi-glace and long-method béchamel a sauce is generally reduced over quick heat for about 4–5 minutes, and should be well stirred or whisked during the whole process.

THICKENING BY LIAISONS

1. Roux.
2. Beurre manié.
3. A la fécule.
4. With egg yolk.
5. With egg yolk and butter or cream.
6. Au sang
7. Enriching with butter and finishing with flavoured butters.

1. Roux

Roux differs from the other liaisons in that thickening is carried out at the beginning of the proceedings, while the others are added at the end. It is the most simple and everyday process, and for this reason is often done in a slapdash fashion detrimental to the finished dish.

Roux is flour gently cooked in fat.   According to the length of cooking and the heat of the fat the roux will acquire colour, and from the degree of colour the varieties are named blanc, blond, and brun.   Brun, however, is a misnomer, for even this, the darkest roux, should never be allowed to become darker than deep biscuit or café au lait.

The flour should be of the best quality and should be dry.

The fat.   For roux blanc and blond the fat should properly be butter, which if particularly salt may with advantage be clarified.   If it is necessary to substitute margarine this should be clarified, the effect of which is to produce a smoother roux.   The fat should only just be allowed to melt. When flour is added to margarine care should be taken not to overwork the mixture, or an over-solid roux is obtained which will not mix readily with the liquid.   Dripping is normally used for roux brun.

Proportion of fat to flour. Generally speaking the weight of fat may be slightly in excess of that of flour, although many recipes call for equal weights, and variations in this general rule may be found.

Liquid. The liquid should not be boiling when it is added to the roux or a granulated texture will result. It should be warm, and added off the heat.

Cooking. This should be carried out gently and in a thick saucepan of a size which will just comfortably hold the sauce. The butter is melted slowly and should not be allowed to get really hot, because if flour is added to hot fat it loses some of its thickening properties. For this reason too the flour is added off the fire. The sifted flour added to the melted butter is stirred until the mixture is smooth; the pan is then returned to the fire for 1 or 2 minutes to heat the mixture through. There should now be a smooth, liquid paste, with which the liquid for the sauce, added all at once, readily blends. This is a roux blanc, which is used as a basis of such sauces as béchamel and sauce crème.

Roux may be made in advance and will keep for a few days provided no other ingredients beyond butter and flour are added.

Roux blond

This is made in the same way as the foregoing, but the cooking time is longer and the roux is allowed to acquire a pale straw colour. When the pan is set back on gentle heat the mixture should be stirred from time to time, but should be watched. At first there is a general bubbling all over the surface, making it look like a thin crust. If the bubbling is too pronounced at any point the roux should be stirred at once to avoid burning. When the bubbling ceases the mixture becomes smoother and more liquid and the cooking really starts, and it should be timed from this point. Cook gently, otherwise the sauce may acquire a bitter taste; stir from time to time and allow about 7–10 minutes to acquire the pale straw colour indicated.

Roux blond is employed for velouté and piquante sauces and for various soups.

Roux brun

For this the procedure is as before, but usually dripping is taken in place of butter and cooking is continued until a pale nut-brown colour is achieved. Generally speaking the sauces for which a brown roux is used are cooked for a longer time than the white sauces, and the process of skimming and purifying is an extended one. Occasionally, in the interest of flavour, butter is called for in a roux brun, but dripping more easily acquires a brown colour.

2. Beurre manié, or kneaded butter

This liaison is butter and flour worked on a plate with a fork to a smooth paste, the proportion of butter being slightly greater than that of flour; the paste is then added in pieces by degrees to the dish it is required to thicken.

This may be sauce, soup, ragoût, fish fumet, or the liquor from cooked food.   After the beurre manié is added the pan should be gently shaken and turned (but not necessarily stirred) so that all is well blended.   For a soup or sauce a whisk may be used, but a spoon or a whisk would break up pieces of meat or fish in the dish being thickened.   The contents of the pan are brought gently to boiling-point, but not allowed to boil hard.

This form of thickening is frequently used to make a thin sauce from liquid in which certain foods have been cooked, or for binding such sauces as tomato and Bercy where the flavouring ingredients have first been cooked by themselves in wine or stock.

3. A la fécule

The word fécule really denotes any starch—flour, arrowroot, corn-flour— and in particular it is associated with potato flour.   This fécule, in France, used to cost a good deal less than arrowroot, and so was commonly employed and may be frequently met with in French recipes.   French cookery books sometimes point out that arrowroot is the most desirable fécule because it produces a brilliant finish.   Thickening by this ingredient is employed for some gravies and soups and for fruit juices and fruit sauces.   A very small quantity of arrowroot is needed to give a good result.

Allow 1 rounded teaspoon of arrowroot or potato flour to 2 tablespoons of cold water.   Mix well together and pour into the boiling liquid, stirring it thoroughly with a wooden spoon or whisk.   Boil only 2 or 3 seconds after adding arrowroot—a little longer for potato flour.   This quantity is enough to thicken ¾ pint of thin liquid.

4. With egg yolk

Where yolk of egg is used for thickening in any liquid in which there is no flour, the egg will curdle if the liquid is boiled, but where there is a small percentage of flour in the liquid, if the liaison is properly made the sauce will not curdle if brought to boiling-point.

Work the yolks thoroughly with a wooden spatula in a small bowl with 2 or 3 tablespoons cold cream, milk, fumet, or stock, according to what is to be thickened.   Take the sauce or soup from the fire and add, one at a time, 3 or 4 spoonfuls to the yolks.   When well mixed return it by degrees to the saucepan, beating it well in with a little whisk, then replace the pan on a moderate fire and reheat gently, stirring continuously till boiling.

When no other thickening is employed 4 egg yolks to each pint of liquid are required.

5. With egg yolk and butter or cream

For thickening sauces au beurre, hollandaise for example, egg yolks and butter alone are used.   To the egg yolks, well creamed in a bowl, flavouring and seasoning are added.   It is customary in some kitchens to add vinegar, which should first be reduced so that the necessary sharpening is acquired without too much liquid being added (some recipes call for lemon juice only, while some omit the acid ingredient altogether). After this the softened butter is incorporated by degrees with the sauce. The sauce is thickened in a bain-marie, and should be well worked all the time with a wooden spatula. Provided that the butter is added gradually at first the yolks will absorb it readily and the thickening process will proceed evenly and quickly. A sauce of this kind cannot be submitted to a final reducing process, for if it becomes too hot it will be spoiled, the butter will oil and the yolks solidify, and the whole will curdle. For this reason too it is cooked in a bain-marie and not over direct dry heat.

For certain sauces, e.g. suprême and velouté, a mixture of egg yolks and thin cream is stirred in just before serving. This gives smoothness of texture to the sauce as well as thickening it slightly.

6. *Au sang*

This liaison is used principally for game dishes, e.g. jugged hare (civet de lièvre), ragoût, sauté of venison, etc. The blood is reserved, that of the hare being found in a membrane behind the heart, and, if clotted, broken up as much as possible with a fork. If the quantity of blood is small and it is required to thicken a large amount of sauce, a level teaspoon of arrow-root may be added. Strain the blood and add a small quantity of the sauce to it by degrees, then return gradually to the casserole, turning and shaking it gently to mix it thoroughly. Simmer gently 2–3 minutes, then serve at once.

7. *Enriching and finishing with butter*

Butter may be added to a sauce at the end of cooking to enrich it. Flavoured butters are added to give variety. For example, lobster or shrimp butter may be added to certain sauces and fish soups (bisques). Such butters are beaten into the finished sauce, care being taken not to allow the sauce to boil after the butter is added, because this would cause it to oil and the flavour and texture of the sauce would be spoilt. Examples are sauce cardinal made with lobster butter, sauce nantua with shrimp butter, etc.

II. LES SAUCES MÈRES

Les sauces mères are the basic sauces from which many others are derived. Since sauces are essentially French in origin it seems suitable to keep the French names for the classics rather than to attempt translation. The busy woman of to-day may regard some of the longer sauces as outside her possibility, but for the student of cookery—the true *amateur* in the French sense—a knowledge of them is indispensable. In a later section of this chapter simpler sauces and quicker methods will be given, such as are referred to by R. H. as 'little sauces knocked up in a hurry.'

Les sauces mères comprise les sauces brunes, les sauces blanches, les sauces au beurre, and les sauces blanches au beurre.

LES SAUCES BRUNES

The most important of the sauces brunes might, by reason of the fact that it is not often prepared in the domestic kitchen, have been omitted from this book, but for students of cookery a knowledge of its proper preparation is desirable. It is known as sauce demi-glace and might be described briefly as a sauce made with a rich and gelatinous stock thickened with a brown roux, and skimmed and purified by a long process known as *dépouillement*. In effect it is not so simple as that by any means, but that is the essence of its construction. It is served in large restaurants with grills and roasts. It is replaced in the domestic kitchen by brown sauce or jus or the jelly to be found at the bottom of a basin of dripping poured from roast meat.

Sauce demi-glace is a rich-looking gravy, syrupy when hot, semi-clear in appearance, and setting to a jelly when cold. As well as being served as an accompanying sauce it is a component of other sauces, and these, according to the additions made, carry such classic names as bordelaise, chasseur, bigarade, and so forth.

FOND BRUN, THE STOCK FROM WHICH
SAUCE DEMI-GLACE IS MADE

This stock is made largely of bones. Sometimes in the interest of flavour a small amount of meat is used, but it is the proportion of bones in its construction that gives the essential glaze. In fact, when this stock is reduced beyond the degree required for a sauce it becomes the glaze known as glace de viande.

Although the making of demi-glace is usually reserved for large kitchens a fond brun is useful to have in reserve in a domestic kitchen, because it is handy for adding to small game, cutlets, and small roasts that do not yield much jus. Although the time of preparation is long the actual amount of work involved is not large.

2½–3 lb. mixed beef and veal bones, broken in pieces	3 or 4 peppercorns seasoning
1 oz. bacon rind, cut up	a small proportion of meat, if available
4–6 oz. onions, sliced	
4–6 oz. carrots, sliced	water to cover
a bouquet garni	

The bones and meat are first browned to give good colour and flavour, and this may be done in two ways, by baking slowly in the oven in a baking-tin or over the fire in the saucepan. There is generally enough fat adhering to the bones to prevent sticking, but if not a piece of fat the size of a hazelnut may be added. If the bones are browned in a saucepan, the bacon rind and vegetables are added to them a little before the end of the browning, and they are all finished together; the water is then added with the peppercorns, bouquet, and seasoning.

If the bones are browned in the oven the bacon rind and vegetables are first put in the pan and allowed to cook gently till lightly coloured, and the bones taken from the oven and added. Cover well with water, add bouquet and peppercorns, season and cover. Cook slowly 3–4 hours or until flavour is good. Strain, allow to get quite cold, and skim off all fat.

If the colour of the fond brun is poor this may be improved when the roux for the sauce demi-glace is made by the addition of a slice of tomato lightly sprinkled with sugar grilled on both sides to a dark brown. The addition of chopped mushroom peelings also improves the colour.

GLACE DE VIANDE (MEAT GLAZE)

A small quantity of this may be kept in the refrigerator, where it will keep for several weeks. It is of value for enriching gravies and stocks when good stock is not available. Take a portion of the completed fond brun (see above), strain and allow to get completely cold. Remove all fat and turn into a clean pan. Boil on steady heat, skimming occasionally. When syrupy in consistency watch and stir frequently with a metal spoon. When a good clear brown and the consistency of thick syrup, pour off into small pots. When cold tie down and keep in the refrigerator.

SAUCE DEMI-GLACE

The principal ingredients of a demi-glace are fat, flour, and fond brun.

The fat. Dripping, oil, or good fat free from moisture should be used. Butter or margarine is less suitable, and if employed must be clarified.

The flour should be dry and of good quality; it should not be browned too fast or too much in the fat. To obtain rich colour flour is sometimes over-cooked at this stage, and a bitter flavour imparted.

The use of the liquor from a pot-au-feu in demi-glace. Sometimes instead of fond brun the liquid from a pot-au-feu is employed. This has good flavour by reason of the meat and vegetables used, but lacks the gelatinous quality of the proper fond brun made with bones.

1 oz. flour	a handful of washed, chopped
1 oz. dripping or other fat	mushroom stalks and/or
2 pints fond brun or good	peelings, or a teaspoon of
brown stock	prepared duxelles
1 small teaspoon tomato purée	

Make a brown roux with the fat and flour, cooking gently till the right colour is acquired and stirring continuously. Reserve a gill of the fond brun and add the remainder to the roux, add tomato purée and mushroom. Bring to boil, stirring all the time with a whisk, set on low heat and allow to simmer very gently 1–1½ hours. The cooking must be slow, a gentle simmer, with movement only in one part of the saucepan. Do not stir, but skim from time to time.   The process of skimming is a special one, and as it applies also to sauce brune it should be set out in a separate paragraph.

The skimming or dépouillement of demi-glace.   After the first long simmering the sauce is strained through a fine strainer and returned to the rinsed-out pan.   It is now put on the fire, brought back to boiling-point, and simmered slowly as before.   The pan may, for the convenience of skimming, be slightly tilted by placing a skewer under one side.   Every trace of fat as it rises to the surface is skimmed off with a metal spoon.   At intervals a spoonful or so of the cold stock in reserve is added.   This has the effect of hastening the rising of fat to the surface.   This process, for the above quantity of sauce, will take about 20 minutes.

The following recipe is for a much simplified demi-glace suitable for ordinary domestic use.   It may be employed as the basis for the sauces for which the classic version is used.   The resultant sauces will not be so rich or so good in appearance, but may be improved by the addition of a piece of glace de viande the size of a hazel-nut.

SAUCE DEMI-GLACE (HOUSEHOLD OR QUICK METHOD)

½ oz. dripping
3 shallots or 1 oz. onion, finely chopped
1 rasher of bacon, diced
1 level dessertspoon flour
1 small teaspoon tomato purée (a few mushroom peelings and stalks, washed and finely chopped, may be added with this)
½–¼ pint stock
salt and pepper
1 teaspoon mixed chopped herbs

Heat the dripping in a small saucepan, add shallots or onion and bacon and cook slowly to a golden brown.   Add flour and allow it to colour. Draw aside, add the purée, stock, pepper, and salt.   Bring to boil, simmer 10–15 minutes.   Add herbs, adjust seasoning, and simmer for another 5 minutes.   If required as a basis to other sauces this may be strained.

The adding of ingredients to a demi-glace to make other sauces.   The additional ingredients given for the various sauces are usually cooked a little before being added to the finished demi-glace.   They may be sautéd or softened in butter or simmered in wine.   Then, after the addition, the whole is simmered for 10 or 15 minutes to blend the flavours.

The wine.   When wine is called for as an addition to a sauce it is usually reduced to half its original quantity before being incorporated.   There are, however, exceptions, as in the brown sauce on page 149, which calls for wine as a basic ingredient.

Now in alphabetical order follow some of the sauces deriving from demi-glace, which in the domestic kitchen may be made on the simpler base given above.

SAUCE A LA DIABLE

Basic sauce with brandy, shallots, tomato purée, chervil, cayenne, and Worcestershire sauce. Served with grilled meat and chicken

1 tablespoon chopped shallots	1½ gills demi-glace
a little butter	1 level teaspoon chopped chervil
1 small wineglass brandy	cayenne and Worcestershire
tomato purée to taste	sauce to taste

Soften shallots in a little butter, allow them to colour very slightly. Add brandy and reduce gently to half. Add demi-glace and tomato purée. Simmer for a few minutes. Add chervil, cayenne, and Worcestershire sauce.

SAUCE BIGARADE

Basic sauce with red wine, red-currant jelly, orange, and shallots. Served with wild duck, widgeon, and other game

2 shallots, finely chopped	rind and juice of an orange
a nut of butter	1 teaspoon red-currant jelly
1 glass red wine	1½ gills demi-glace
a small bay-leaf	

Soften shallots in butter in a small saucepan. Add wine and bay-leaf. Reduce gently by about a third. Add, with the juice and half the pared rind of the orange, to the demi-glace. Simmer 5–7 minutes. In the meantime shred remaining rind thinly, blanch for 5 minutes and drain. Strain the sauce, return to the pan with the shredded rind and jelly. Bring slowly to the boil, stirring frequently and allowing the jelly to dissolve.

SAUCE BORDELAISE

Basic sauce with red wine, shallots, and beef marrow. Served with roast beef, fillet, tournedos, certain game, and pigeons

1 tablespoon chopped shallots	a small sprig of thyme
a nut of butter	1½ gills demi-glace
¾ gill red wine	½ oz. beef marrow, cut in small
5 or 6 peppercorns	pieces

Soften the shallots in a little butter, add the red wine, peppercorns, and thyme. Reduce to half quantity. Add demi-glace and simmer 15 minutes. Skim, strain, and add beef marrow. Without allowing the sauce to boil, keep it very hot for about 10 minutes to allow the marrow to melt, and serve at once.

SAUCE CHASSEUR

Basic sauce with mushrooms, white wine, shallots, and tomato purée. For rabbit, chicken dishes, and various meats; sometimes served separately, sometimes added to the dish

3 oz. mushrooms, finely sliced
a little oil or butter
2–3 shallots, chopped
¾ gill white wine
1 dessertspoon tomato purée

1½ gills demi-glace
a nut of butter
a little chopped parsley and 2 leaves of tarragon, chopped

Fry mushrooms lightly in oil or butter. When lightly browned add shallots, cook a minute or two longer, then add white wine. Reduce to half and add demi-glace and tomato purée. Simmer a minute or two. Remove from fire, add butter in small pieces, and chopped parsley and tarragon.

SAUCE FINES HERBES

Basic sauce with white wine, tarragon, chervil, chives, parsley, shallots, and lemon juice. Served with eggs and various other dishes

1 gill white wine
¼ teaspoon each of tarragon, chervil, chives, and parsley, finely chopped
1 teaspoon finely chopped shallots

a few extra chopped herbs
a few drops of lemon juice
a nut of butter
1½ gills demi-glace

Bring wine to boil, add the first quantity of chopped herbs and the shallots. Simmer 10 minutes and strain. Add demi-glace. Simmer again, add the smaller quantity of freshly chopped herbs and the lemon juice. Remove from fire, add butter in small pieces.

Tarragon sauce. Proceed as above, using a teaspoon of chopped tarragon only, which is added all at once. This is excellent to serve with roast chicken.

SAUCE GENEVOISE

a red wine sauce to serve with boiled salmon, carp, or other freshwater fish

2 oz. onion, chopped
2 oz. shallot, chopped
2 oz. carrot, chopped
1 stalk of celery
¾ oz. butter
a bouquet of bay-leaf, parsley stalks, thyme

the head of the fish, well cleaned
½ pint red wine
salt and freshly ground pepper
1½ gills demi-glace or brown sauce
anchovy essence

Soften the vegetables slowly in the butter in a stew-pan, draw aside, add bouquet and the head roughly cut up. Cover pan and cook gently for another 5 minutes. Flamber the wine (see page 66), add, and allow to reduce to a little more than half. Season, pour on the demi-glace. Cover and simmer 15–20 minutes. Strain through a tammy strainer into a clean saucepan and bring to boil. Simmer a few moments, add a few drops of anchovy essence, and serve.

See also sauce genevoise for fish, page 161.

SAUCE ITALIENNE

Basic sauce with mushrooms, shallots, ham, white wine, and tomato purée. Used with pasta dishes, vegetables such as celeriac, Jerusalem artichokes, potatoes, etc.

2 oz. mushrooms, finely chopped	1 gill white wine
a little oil or butter	1½ gills demi-glace
1½ oz. cooked lean ham, cut in small pieces	1 dessertspoon tomato purée
1 shallot	1 teaspoon chopped parsley

Soften mushrooms in oil or butter, add lean ham and shallot. Cook gently 3 or 4 minutes, add white wine and allow to reduce to half. Add demi-glace, tomato purée, and chopped parsley.

SAUCE LYONNAISE

Basic sauce with chopped onion and white wine for meat and vegetables

2 oz. onion, finely chopped	¾ gill white wine
a little butter	1½ gills demi-glace

Chop onion finely and allow it to soften in a little butter. Add white wine, reduce to half, and add demi-glace. Simmer 10–15 minutes. Strain or leave as it is according to taste.

SAUCE MADÈRE

reduced Madeira and glace de viande. Served with meat, game, etc.

¾ gill Madeira	1½ gills demi-glace
a nut of glace de viande	a nut of butter

Put Madeira in a pan with the glace de viande. Reduce to half, add demi-glace, simmer a few minutes, remove from fire, add butter in small pieces.

If this sauce is to accompany pan-fried meat it may be made in the same pan in which the meat has cooked; in this way no flavour is lost. If the meat is grilled then the juice from the grilling pan may be strained and added.

See also sauce madère in Winkfield chapter, page 1000.

SAUCE PÉRIGUEUX

sauce madère with truffles to serve with tournedos, cutlets, etc.

½ pint sauce madère	1 large truffle and the juice from the tin

Prepare the sauce madère as above. Chop the truffle finely and add with the juice. Allow to stand covered for a short time before serving, so that the flavour of the truffle is absorbed by the sauce.

SAUCE ROBERT

Basic sauce with gherkins, onions, vinegar, and parsley; piquante in flavour.
Served with roast pork, grilled pork chops, kidneys, etc.

1 tablespoon onion, chopped	2 or 3 chopped gherkins
a little butter	1 heaped teaspoon French
¾ gill vinegar	mustard
1½ gills demi-glace	1 teaspoon chopped parsley

Soften onion in butter, add vinegar and reduce to half. Add demi-glace and simmer 15 minutes. Add immediately before serving the chopped gherkins, mustard, and parsley. Do not allow to boil again.

SAUCE ROMAINE

Basic sauce with caramelized sugar, vinegar, and raisins.
For game, tongue, beef, braised mutton, etc.

2 tablespoons granulated sugar	a handful of fine raisins,
1 wineglass vinegar	washed, dried, and stoned
½ pint demi-glace (approx.)	

Melt sugar in a saucepan and allow it to become brown. Add the vinegar off the fire. Reduce this until the sugar is on the point of caramelizing again. Add demi-glace and raisins. Simmer 5 minutes.

SAUCE ROUENNAISE

Basic sauce with onion, red wine, ducks' livers, and chopped parsley.
Served with duck

1 tablespoon chopped onion	a little chopped parsley
a little butter	seasoning
1 wineglass red wine	3 or 4 ducks' livers
1½ gills demi-glace	

Soften the onion in butter, add red wine and cook till the moisture has almost evaporated. Add demi-glace, seasoning, and chopped parsley.

Take ducks' livers, clean them well, cutting away any greenish part. Cut up fine and pass through a hair or nylon sieve. Keep in a cool place till immediately before using. Then take a few spoonfuls of hot sauce and mix with the liver. Add the mixture to the hot sauce, but on no account allow it to boil again.

TARRAGON SAUCE

See Sauce Fines Herbes, page 146.

From the foregoing list it will be seen what variety of sauces may be achieved with a good basis of demi-glace, even if in domestic kitchens the short method of making it has to be adopted. Now follow other brown sauces made in a different way.

On first looking at ingredients and method a sauce brune would not appear to differ greatly from a demi-glace. The latter has really a more gravy-like consistency, clear and limpid, while sauce brune is more of a sauce. This too may be used as a basis of other sauces as well as being served as it is. It is made with a mirepoix of vegetables and calls for ½ pint white wine. It takes 2 hours to prepare, must not be hurried, but presents no difficulties of technique. It may be prepared well ahead of time, will keep for a day or two, and may be reheated as required.

SAUCE BRUNE (1) (SOMETIMES CALLED ESPAGNOLE)

to accompany grilled steak, cutlets, vegetables, game, or eggs

for approx. 2 pints sauce

3 oz. fat
3½–4 oz. onions, sliced
3½–4 oz. carrots, sliced
3 oz. lean bacon, cut fine (optional)
4 stems of parsley, cut up and without leaves
2 oz. flour
3 pints good jellied stock (clear and well skimmed)

1 dessertspoon concentrated tomato purée
a handful of mushroom stalks and peelings (optional)
2 sprays of thyme
1 bay-leaf
½ pint white wine
½ gill sherry
seasoning

Gradually heat fat in a 4–5-pint saucepan. (It is desirable to have the liquid nearly to the top of the pan to facilitate the skimming process.) Add onions and carrots, bacon, and parsley stems and cook uncovered, stirring from time to time until the vegetables are softened and yellow. Sprinkle in the flour and stir well.

Withdraw pan from fire and set on gentle heat. Let the flour cook gently till it is golden brown, stirring from time to time. This should take about 12–15 minutes. Set aside a good gill of liquid for the *dépouillement* of the sauce, and add the remainder gradually to the mirepoix of vegetables, stirring all the time. Add tomato purée. Bring to boil, stirring continuously. Add mushroom peelings.

Move pan to gentle heat, add thyme, bay-leaf, white wine, and seasoning, allow to cook so quietly and regularly that there is only movement in one part of the saucepan. The appearance of a slow regular single bubble is a general indication of the cooking pace. Allow it to cook in this way, uncovered, for an hour. Skim regularly with a metal spoon. At the end of the hour carry out *dépouillement* (see page 144), and strain the sauce through a tammy strainer or chinois, pressing the mirepoix gently, just enough to press out the juice. Return to rinsed pan and carry out the skimming as described for demi-glace (page 144).

At the end of this process the sauce should be without a trace of fat and of a semi-clear consistency. The flavour should be strong and rich. The sauce may be further reduced if necessary. Add sherry and seasoning before serving.

SAUCE BRUNE (2)

to use as foregoing sauce

1½ oz. each of carrot and onion	1 teaspoon tomato purée
1½ oz. lean bacon	1 oz. mushroom peelings
1¼ oz. butter [1]	a bouquet garni of 2 parsley
1¼ oz. flour, sifted	stalks, a sprig of thyme, and
1¾ pints jus or stock	½ bay-leaf
1 wineglass white wine	¼ gill Madeira or sherry

Dice the vegetables and bacon very finely (a mirepoix). Melt the butter in a thick saucepan, add mirepoix, and cook over a slow heat for about 10 minutes with the lid off the pan, stirring occasionally.

Add flour and allow to brown very slowly; this should take not less than 15 minutes, and the mixture should be well stirred from time to time with a metal spoon.

Draw aside, add the stock (reserving ¼ pint), the wine, tomato purée, peelings, and bouquet garni. Bring to the boil and simmer with the lid off the pan for 30 minutes. Then strain and return to the pan. Bring to boil again.

Tilt the pan on the stove by means of a metal wedge, skim, then lower the heat so that the sauce will just simmer. Add half the reserved stock and bring slowly to the boil, skimming off any fat that comes to the surface. Simmer for 20 minutes more, skim, add the remaining stock, boil again and skim. Continue simmering until the right consistency. Strain once more into a clean saucepan and add the Madeira, which has been reduced (i.e. boiled) to half the quantity.

SAUCE POIVRADE

slightly piquante; for serving with game and marinaded meat

2 tablespoons oil	½ gill vinegar
1 oz. onion, chopped	½ oz. butter, good weight
1 oz. shallot, chopped	½ oz. flour
1 oz. carrot, diced	¾ pint good stock
3–4 parsley stalks, cut up	3–4 crushed juniper berries
½ bay-leaf	salt, freshly ground pepper
½ gill red wine	

Heat oil, add vegetables and herbs, simmer 3–4 minutes. Pour off any surplus oil, add the wine and vinegar and reduce to half. Set aside. Make a brown roux with the butter and flour. Pour on the stock, bring to boil, add the vegetables with the liquid and simmer half an hour. Add juniper berries and seasoning and continue to simmer 5–10 minutes. Strain through a tammy strainer. Return to the rinsed pan and simmer for a further 15–20 minutes, or until of syrupy consistency and good flavour. Skim from time to time, verify seasoning and serve.

[1] Butter is used here for flavour, and great care must be taken not to over-colour it.

SAUCE VENAISON

for serving with roast venison

the above quantity of sauce poivrade

2 large tablespoons red-currant jelly

3–4 tablespoons cream

seasoning

lemon juice

Have the sauce poivrade at boiling-point, add jelly and stir until melted. Boil rapidly, adding the cream. Continue boiling until the sauce is rich and syrupy. Adjust seasoning, add a few drops of lemon juice.

III. LES SAUCES BLANCHES

The two important sauces mères falling within the category of sauces blanches are sauce béchamel and sauce velouté. The simple basic difference between them is that béchamel is made with milk on a roux blanc and velouté with stock on a roux blond.

These roux are made with butter, preferably unsalted, and not with dripping as for a roux brun. If butter were cooked to the degree that one cooks dripping for a roux brun, its flavour would be altered and the good taste of fresh butter would not be imparted to the sauce.

The flour for the roux may with advantage be dried, for this helps in achieving a smooth texture and, for sauce velouté, the straw colour required.

SAUCE VELOUTÉ (OR, AS IT USED TO BE CALLED, SAUCE BLONDE)

This sauce may be used alone or as the basis of such sauces as suprême, poulette, duxelles, and vin blanc. It may be kept for 2 or 3 days in a refrigerator to be used as required. It will be considered first because it resembles a demi-glace not only in the reducing and skimming but also in its consistency. Just as after long cooking the liquid of demi-glace falls to a brown glaze, so should this sauce, made with a roux blond and a white stock, fall to a white glaze. R. H. interjects at this point: 'So many people think that a blanquette of veal, which is the dish for which this sauce is most commonly used, indicates a dish covered with a thick white blanket, whereas the veal should be lightly bound together with a velvet-smooth, light, rich sauce.'

Sauce velouté, then, is made with a white stock on a roux blond. There is, however, a possible exception about the roux. If margarine must be substituted for butter, it is then wiser to use a roux blanc for this sauce, the reason for the substitution being that margarine does not easily acquire the deeper colour. The stock for velouté may be made from veal, chicken, or fish.

FOND BLANC (WHITE BOUILLON OR STOCK)

2½ lb. knuckle of veal or veal
   bones, and cold water to cover
1–2 glasses white wine
a good squeeze of lemon juice
3 quarts cold water (approx.)
4–6 oz. sliced onions

4–6 oz. carrots
1 stalk of celery
a bouquet garni
1 teaspoon salt
2–3 white peppercorns

Wipe the knuckle with a damp cloth, put into large pan. Cover with cold water and bring to the boil, removing any scum which rises to the surface. Drain and rinse. Return to the pan, pour over the wine, and allow to reduce to about 2 tablespoons. Add lemon juice and water and bring slowly to the boil, skimming thoroughly. Add the vegetables, bouquet, salt, and peppercorns. Reboil, partially cover pan with lid, and simmer gently 2–3 hours. Taste towards the end of the cooking time, and when strong strain off and cool. More water may be added to the bones and vegetables that remain to make 'second' stock.

All fat must be removed from the fond when absolutely cold.

When veal bone or knuckle is hard to obtain a piece of calf's or pig's head is an excellent substitute, and can, moreover, be used for brawn afterwards.

SAUCE VELOUTÉ

1½ oz. butter
1¼ oz. flour

1½ pints white stock, strained and well skimmed
salt, pepper, and a few drops of lemon juice

Make a roux blond (see page 139). Add the stock. Bring to boil, cook over moderate heat, skimming frequently as any fat rises to the surface. To make this process easier the pan may be tilted by placing a skewer under one side. Continue cooking until the sauce is slightly syrupy and semi-clear. Add seasoning and lemon juice. The sauce is now ready for the addition of cream, or egg and cream according to the dish in hand.

After the adding of the liaison the sauce may be tammied, which will add extra brilliance and velvety finish. This should be done quickly, for if after this process has been carried out the sauce is reheated, some of the brilliant finish and smooth texture is lost.

Before the recipe for the making of a simpler velouté, attention should again be drawn to the clarification of margarine. In many kitchens this must be used in place of butter, and it is important that this process should be carried out exactly in the way described on page 41.

SAUCE VELOUTÉ (SIMPLE METHOD)

¾ oz. butter, good weight
¾ oz. flour (if the sauce is to be
   finished with an egg liaison
   the quantity of flour may be
   slightly decreased)

scant ½ pint strong stock, veal,
   chicken, fish, etc.
½ gill cream or creamy milk
a few drops of lemon juice
salt and pepper

Melt butter, add flour. Cook slowly to a pale straw colour. Pour on the stock, stir until boiling. Simmer 5 minutes, add cream or milk and continue to simmer for a further 2–3 minutes. Draw aside, add lemon juice and seasoning.

Sauces derived from Velouté

These are principally suprême, chivry, duxelles, and poulette; because it is the finest of these suprême will be considered first.

SAUCE SUPRÊME

a velouté finished with a good proportion of egg yolks and cream; used for some of the best veal dishes, for breast of chicken as in chicken suprême, and for chicken creams

scant ¾ pint velouté sauce (first recipe), made with veal or chicken stock according to the dish with which it is to be served	3 egg yolks 3–4 tablespoons thick cream salt, pepper, and a few drops of lemon juice

Heat sauce carefully. Mix yolks and cream together thoroughly. Add to velouté as for egg liaisons (see page 140). Reheat carefully over slow heat, stirring continuously. This is best done in a bain-marie or in a double saucepan; care should be taken not to have the water surrounding the pan at boiling-point. It should be off the boil. This ensures that the sauce will thicken slowly, and so have a perfect finish. When of good coating consistency verify the seasoning, adding lemon juice to taste. Tammy and use immediately.

For a suprême of chicken or veal creams, etc., the addition of sliced, cooked, or sautéd mushrooms is usual. These are generally scattered over the meat before coating with the sauce.

The following may be made with suprême for richness or with velouté for a simpler sauce:

SAUCE CHIVRY

served with chicken, poached fish, or eggs

½ pint sauce 2–3 sprigs each of tarragon, chervil, and chives	a handful of spinach

Boil the spinach and herbs rapidly for 5 minutes, drain and sieve. They should render about a dessertspoon of purée. Add this to the sauce so that it is coloured to a delicate green.

SAUCE DUXELLES

served with veal or rabbit dishes, vegetables, cauliflower, artichokes, salsify, and white fish

1 finely chopped shallot	½ pint velouté sauce
¼ gill white wine, or a little butter and a few drops of lemon juice	1 tablespoon duxelles (see chapter on kitchen knowledge, page 39)

Put the shallot in a small saucepan with the wine. Simmer until soft and the wine is reduced to about a tablespoon. Whisk into the velouté with the duxelles and reboil before using.

N.B. If this sauce is made without wine the shallot is softened without being allowed to colour in a little butter, and a few drops of lemon juice added.

If the sauce is to be used over a dish to be gratinéd it is necessary to omit the liaison of eggs in the basic velouté, as the heat of the oven will cause the egg to curdle.

SAUCE POULETTE

served with carrots, broad beans, new potatoes, or with boiled veal, calf's head, etc.

1 large teaspoon finely chopped parsley	1 dessertspoon mushroom juice or cuisson (optional)
1 teaspoon lemon juice	½ pint velouté sauce
a pinch of chopped savory	*Liaison* 1 yolk 2 tablespoons cream

Add all the ingredients, except the liaison, to the velouté sauce, mix thoroughly and reboil. Then make the liaison.

Half this quantity, i.e. ¼ pint, is usually enough for a dish of vegetables for 4–6 people.

SAUCE BÉCHAMEL

Opinions about this sauce differ. One authority dismisses it with a few words, saying it is so simple that little need be said about it. This may be the reason for its casual treatment by some cooks. Another discusses it at length, giving various methods of making it. The first method given below depends for its success on long, slow cooking during which the flavour of mirepoix and herbs is drawn out and the generous quantity of milk is reduced so that the sauce is enriched.

This long-method béchamel is a delicious sauce in itself; it is also a suitable basis for other sauces when the ingredients to be added are delicate in flavour, as in egg sauce or sauce à la crème. When, however, the base is to carry stronger flavoured ingredients, such as cheese for sauce mornay or onions for sauce soubise, then a less delicately flavoured base may be used, and for this béchamel made by the shorter method is suitable.

SAUCE BÉCHAMEL (LONG METHOD)

2 oz. each of onion and carrot
1 oz. leek, the white part only
½ oz. celery stalk
¾–1 oz. butter

Roux
  1 oz. butter
  1 oz. flour

1¼ pints hot milk

a bouquet garni (large sprig of
  parsley, thyme, and bay-
  leaf tied together)
a blade of mace
6 peppercorns
a pinch of salt
a few mushroom peelings, well
  washed
top of milk or cream to finish

Dice all the vegetables finely. Melt butter in a thick saucepan, add the vegetables, cover, and soften (or sweat) 5–7 minutes, stirring occasionally. Turn contents of pan on to a plate. Wipe out pan, melt in this the butter for the roux, add the flour, mix lightly, pour on the hot milk, blend thoroughly, then stir constantly until boiling. Return the vegetables to the sauce with the bouquet, mace, and peppercorns. Add a pinch of salt and the mushroom peelings. Simmer gently 40 minutes at least, uncovered, stirring occasionally. When the consistency of cream strain into another saucepan, pressing the vegetables well to extract all the liquid; reheat, adjust the seasoning, add a little top of milk or cream, and reduce to the required consistency.

SAUCE BÉCHAMEL (SHORT METHOD)

a blade of mace, a bay-leaf, a
  slice of shallot, and 4 or 5
  peppercorns
¾ oz. butter, good weight
¾ oz. flour

½ pint milk
2 tablespoons top of milk or
  cream
seasoning

Put mace, bay-leaf, peppercorns, and shallot into the milk in a covered pan on low heat and infuse 7–8 minutes. Melt butter in a thick saucepan, draw away from heat, add flour, cook for a minute or so, then pour on all at once the flavoured milk, strained and slightly cooled.

When thoroughly blended stir continuously over moderate heat until boiling. Simmer 2 or 3 minutes, adding the cream or top of milk, adjust the seasoning and use.

Sauces derived from Béchamel

SAUCE AURORE

for fish, meat, eggs, and vegetables

½–¾ gill much reduced tomato
  pulp

½ pint béchamel sauce, short
  method (see above)
top of milk or cream to finish

Add the pulp to the béchamel, adjusting the amount so that the colour is a good pink and the flavour delicate and fresh. Finish the sauce with a little cream or top of milk and adjust seasoning.

SAUCE AUX CHAMPIGNONS

for fish and vegetable dishes, and for general purposes

½ pint béchamel sauce, long or
   short method (see page 155)
3 oz. button mushrooms
¾ oz. butter

salt, pepper, a touch of cayenne
   pepper
a pinch of ground nutmeg
½ gill cream

Have the sauce ready prepared and at boiling-point.

Wipe or wash mushrooms, and trim the stalks level with the caps. Do not peel unless the skins are tough. Cut in quarters. Heat a frying-pan, drop in butter, and when foaming put in mushrooms. Cook over quick heat, shaking pan continuously, and adding the seasonings. Be careful not to overcook the mushrooms, as their flavour will be lost. After 3–4 minutes draw aside and add to the béchamel.

Add cream and simmer very gently 1–2 minutes. If not to be served at once keep in a bain-marie, not on the direct heat.

SAUCE CRÈME

for egg, vegetable, and delicately flavoured dishes

½ pint béchamel, long method
   (see page 155)
¼ pint cream

seasonings

Boil the cream 2 or 3 minutes to allow it to reduce a little. Add to the hot béchamel, adjust seasoning, and serve.

SAUCE MORNAY

for egg and vegetable dishes, gratins, fish, spaghetti, and gnocchi

½ pint béchamel (short method,
   page 155, will suffice)
1–1½ oz. grated cheese, preferably gruyère and Parmesan
   mixed, or failing this dry,
   full-flavoured cheese

1 small teaspoon French mustard
pepper and salt
a little cream or top of milk to
   finish, if required

Beat the cheese thoroughly into the hot sauce off the fire, adding seasonings. Cheese thickens the sauce considerably and extra liquid may have to be added. For this reason, if a basic sauce is being made especially for sauce mornay the amount of flour may be reduced from ¾ to ½ an ounce to ½ pint of milk. Reheat the sauce, taking care not to boil or the sauce will curdle.

SAUCE SOUBISE

onion sauce for eggs, artichokes, cauliflower, potato, or fish

½ pint béchamel sauce, short method (see page 155)
6–8 oz. onions, according to type used. Spanish onions, for example, are milder than the ordinary brown onions

a little butter for softening
½ gill cream or top of milk
seasoning

Slice and chop the onions, blanch, drain, and soften in butter, taking care that they do not colour. Season. Put through a sieve, add the purée to the béchamel with the cream or top of milk, and reduce for a minute or two. For economy the onions may simply be simmered in salted water till tender, drained, and then passed through a wire sieve.

SOUBISE PURÉE

for serving with mutton

1½ oz. butter
1½ oz. flour
½ pint flavoured milk (see béchamel sauce, short method, page 155)

8 oz. chopped, blanched onions
1 oz. butter
seasoning
1–2 tablespoons cream (optional)

Make a roux with butter and flour. Pour on flavoured milk, stir till boiling. Soften the onions in the ounce of butter and sieve, add the resulting purée to sauce, and cook together until the mixture will just leave the side of the pan. Season well.
Cream may now be added.

IV. LES SAUCES AU BEURRE

Sauces au beurre is a title given to certain delicate and rich sauces composed of butter and eggs and in most cases acidulated by the addition of lemon juice and vinegar. Some chefs employ only cream and butter and no acid. Examples of les sauces au beurre are hollandaise, béarnaise, choron, and mousseline. These sauces are not thickened with flour, and their construction calls for meticulous attention to detail. They are served lukewarm rather than hot.

SAUCE HOLLANDAISE (1)

served with salmon, asparagus, vegetable entrées, and fish dishes

3 tablespoons wine vinegar
6 peppercorns
½ bay-leaf
a blade of mace

3–4 oz. butter
2 egg yolks
seasoning

Put vinegar, spices, and bay-leaf into a pan and reduce to a small dessertspoon. Set on one side. Reserve a nut of butter and work the remainder until soft. Break the yolks into a small bowl, add the vinegar, and beat well with the nut of butter and a pinch of salt. Set the bowl in a bain-marie on gentle heat. The water in the bain-marie should be lukewarm to begin with, gradually increasing till very hot, about 170°–180° F., but on no account to boiling-point.

Using a small wooden spoon or spatula, work the yolks until thick, then add the softened butter, bit by bit, as the sauce thickens, taking the bowl out of the bain-marie if the sauce is thickening too quickly. When all is added season delicately, and if the sauce is too sharp add a little more butter. It should be lightly piquant, should barely hold its shape, and be lukewarm rather than hot.

SAUCE HOLLANDAISE (2)

This is a more homely version of sauce hollandaise and is a little easier for the student to manage.

2 yolks of egg	3½ oz. butter
1 small teaspoon arrowroot	salt and pepper
1 gill cold boiled milk	1 small tablespoon lemon juice

Put the egg yolks, arrowroot, half the milk, and 1 oz. of the butter into a small saucepan. Work well together off the fire. Now stir over gentle heat, or in a bain-marie, until beginning to thicken. Draw aside, add another nut of butter, and when dissolved again return to the heat to thicken slightly. Warm the rest of the milk and add to the sauce with the remaining butter in small pieces. Finish with the seasoning and enough of the lemon juice to give a pleasant acidity.

SAUCE BÉARNAISE
for steaks, tournedos, and grills

4 tablespoons white wine vinegar	3 oz. butter, softened, and an extra nut of butter
6 peppercorns	a piece of meat glaze the size of
½ bay-leaf	a hazel-nut, or a teaspoon of
1 sprig each of tarragon and chervil	very strong jus
1 small chopped shallot	1 small teaspoon each of chopped tarragon and chervil
2 egg yolks	seasoning

Put the vinegar, peppercorns, bay, tarragon and chervil sprigs, and shallot into a small saucepan. Reduce to a good dessertspoon. Cream the yolks thoroughly together with a nut of butter and a pinch of salt. Thicken slightly in the bain-marie, strain on the vinegar, mix well, and add the softened butter piece by piece as the mixture thickens, stirring continuously with a wooden spatula, and gradually increasing the heat of the bain-marie as for sauce hollandaise. When all the butter is added, stir in the meat glaze with the chopped tarragon and chervil. Adjust seasoning.

Béarnaise should be slightly thicker in consistency than hollandaise, and much more piquante in flavour.

SAUCE CHORON

The base of this sauce is a hollandaise made with white wine in place of vinegar and sharpened with orange juice. Chopped chives are sometimes added as a finish, with or without a little whipped cream. The addition of chives depends on what the sauce is intended for. The sauce is excellent with grills, meat or fish, or with sole meunière, in all of which cases the chives may be added. As an accompanying sauce to asparagus, omit chives and add the cream.

3 yolks of egg
finely grated rind and juice of an orange (blood for preference)
3½–4 oz. butter, slightly softened
¾ gill dry white wine

1 teaspoon finely chopped shallot
1 small teaspoon tomato purée, or a dash of tomato sauce
a few drops of lemon juice (optional)
salt and pepper

Work yolks together in a bowl, add the orange rind and strained juice and a good nut of the butter. Beat well. Put wine and shallot in a small pan, reduce to 1 tablespoon and add to the yolks with the purée. Stand bowl in a bain-marie and, stirring constantly, add a small nut of the butter. When beginning to thicken add the rest of the butter piece by piece. Finish with the lemon juice if required, and the seasoning.

If chives are added a heaped teaspoon, cut finely with the scissors, is enough.

When cream is called for, as for asparagus, add 1 large tablespoon lightly whipped.

SAUCE MOUSSELINE

for asparagus, sea-kale, and grilled sole

3 yolks of egg
juice of ½ lemon
seasoning of salt and pepper

3 or more oz. butter, unsalted
¾ gill cream

Break the yolks into a bowl, add half the lemon juice, a little salt and pepper, and a nut of the butter. Put the bowl in a bain-marie and work the sauce well with a small sauce whisk until quite thick. Take the bowl from the bain-marie and whisk in the softened butter. Put back in the bain-marie if the sauce gets too cool towards the end. Add the rest of the lemon juice. Season delicately, and lastly add the cream whipped to a stiff froth.

Serve as soon as possible, as the sauce is very light and delicate.

CUCUMBER SAUCE (HOT)
for fish, vegetable, and miscellaneous dishes

1 tablespoon tarragon vinegar	seasoning of salt, pepper, and a
2 yolks or 1 whole egg	dash of cayenne
3 oz. butter	2 tablespoons cucumber (approx.)

Reduce vinegar to half. Melt gently 1 oz. of butter, add egg, and stir with whisk in a bain-marie. Add reduced vinegar gradually, whisking well. Add remaining butter in small pieces. Season well. Add chopped, drained cucumber.

SAUCE BLANCHE AU BEURRE (SAUCE BÂTARDE)
for cauliflower, veal, eggs, etc.

Blanche here is the distinguishing word, for this, although a butter sauce, also contains some flour. Its other name, sauce bâtarde, is given because this sauce is a mixture of two types. It is really a mock hollandaise, but less rich in flavour and texture than the real thing. The butter used is generally smaller in quantity than that employed in the true sauce au beurre, though this may be increased at will. The liquid is water, and egg yolks are used, but may also be omitted. Briefly the way of making a sauce bâtarde is as follows: A roux is made, hot water is added with the egg yolks, the whole whisked rapidly and brought to the boil, and butter in varying quantities is then worked in off the fire in the same manner as for a sauce hollandaise. This sauce is the basis of such sauces as ravigote, aux câpres, and moutarde.

Roux	2 egg yolks (optional)
¾ oz. butter	2–3 oz. butter
¾ oz. flour, scant weight	lemon juice or vinegar
½ pint hot water	

Melt the butter for the roux in a small thick saucepan, and add the flour off the fire. Beat the water by degrees into the yolks and add all at once to the roux. Whisk the sauce briskly until just on boiling-point, draw aside at once and add in small pieces as much butter as you wish, stirring vigorously all the time. Reheat in a bain-marie, but on no account allow to boil after butter has been added. Finish with a good squeeze of lemon juice or a few drops of vinegar.

SAUCE BLANCHE
a sauce blanche au beurre without egg yolks; used as for sauce bâtarde

1 flat teaspoon salt	a pinch of grated nutmeg
½ pint boiling water	1 teaspoon lemon juice or a
Roux	few drops of vinegar
¾ oz. butter	1¼ oz. butter
¾ oz. flour	

Have ready a 2-pint saucepan and a smaller pan containing the boiling water and salt. Melt the butter for the roux in the larger saucepan over a gentle heat; draw aside from the heat and stir in the flour with a wooden spatula. Then take a small sauce whisk and, still keeping the pan off the fire, pour the fast-boiling water in a steady stream on to the roux, whisking vigorously all the time. Add the nutmeg, the lemon juice or vinegar, and whisk in the butter piece by piece. Serve at once or keep hot in a bain-marie.

SAUCE AUX CÂPRES

for serving with boiled turbot, cod, mutton, etc.

To $\frac{1}{2}$ pint sauce blanche or bâtarde add a tablespoon or more of capers, $\frac{1}{2}$ teaspoon finely chopped parsley, and a few drops of vinegar.

SOME SAUCES PARTICULARLY SUITABLE TO ACCOMPANY FISH

SAUCE GENEVOISE

$\frac{3}{4}$ oz. flour, scant weight	2 yolks beaten into a table-
$2\frac{1}{2}$ oz. butter	spoon cream
$\frac{1}{2}$ pint court bouillon, hot	1 teaspoon anchovy essence
	seasoning

Make a roux with the flour and $\frac{3}{4}$ oz. of the butter. Remove from the heat and pour on the hot court bouillon, whisking vigorously. Reboil. Off the fire again whisk in the remaining butter and stir in the egg yolks and cream in the way indicated for making this liaison (page 140). Add anchovy essence and season highly.

See also sauce genevoise under demi-glace, page 146.

SAUCE MOUTARDE

served with grilled herrings, mackerel, sautéd rabbit

To $\frac{1}{2}$ pint sauce blanche or bâtarde add a dessertspoon or more of French mustard and $\frac{1}{2}$ teaspoon tarragon vinegar.

SAUCE CARDINAL (LOBSTER BUTTER)

Use the coral or spawn of the lobster, preferably raw. The amount required is usually about a tablespoon, and it is pounded with the butter before being sieved. It may be added to a béchamel sauce in place of a velouté, depending on the dish.

SAUCE NANTUA (PRAWN SAUCE)

Sauce	*Butter*
$\frac{3}{4}$ oz. butter	1 large handful of prawn heads
$\frac{3}{4}$ oz. flour	and body shells, or the peel-
$1\frac{1}{2}$ gills good fish stock con-	ings from about $\frac{1}{4}$ pint
taining white wine	prawns
$\frac{3}{4}$–1 gill creamy milk	2 oz. fresh butter
salt and pepper	
	1 tablespoon cream

Well wash the prawn trimmings if inclined to be salty. Remove the eyes. Pound thoroughly in a mortar, adding the butter by degrees. Rub through a nylon sieve. Set the butter aside.

Prepare sauce by melting the butter carefully, adding flour off the fire, and pouring on the fish stock. Stir until blended. Return pan to heat, stir continuously whilst sauce thickens, then add the milk. Continue stirring until boiling, then allow to boil fairly rapidly until the consistency of cream. Draw aside and whisk in the butter, piece by piece. Add seasoning and finish with the cream. Reheat but do not boil.

SAUCE RAVIGOTE

slightly piquante and with herbs; served with grilled or boiled salmon, fried fish, grilled pork

2 finely chopped shallots
a liqueur glass vinegar
1 teaspoon each of chopped chives, tarragon, and chervil

a little French mustard
½ pint sauce bâtarde (page 160)

Add shallots to vinegar and reduce gently by half. Mix herbs, mustard, and strained vinegar into the sauce.

SAUCE VENITIENNE

for serving in particular with mackerel, salmon, or salmon trout

½ pint sauce bâtarde (page 160)
a little fish fumet reduced to a glaze
2 chopped shallots
1 wineglass white wine
a few drops of vinegar

1 dessertspoon green purée (approx.) (see sauces chivry or verte, pages 153 and 168)
if as an accompaniment to salmon trout, a heaped tablespoon of cucumber, diced, salted, drained, and blanched

Add to the sauce bâtarde enough fish fumet to flavour delicately. Put shallots into white wine and vinegar and reduce by half. Strain into the flavoured bâtarde. Beat in enough of the purée to colour and flavour well. The sauce should be rather sharp and more lemon may be added to taste. Add cucumber if required.

SAUCE VIN BLANC

1 glass (approx. ¾ gill) dry white wine
1 shallot, chopped
1 blade of mace
3–4 peppercorns
½ bay-leaf
¾ oz. butter (good weight)

½ oz. flour
¼ pint good fish stock
⅜ gill milk
1–2 tablespoons cream, salt and pepper, and ¼ oz. butter to finish

Add to the wine the shallot, spices, and bay-leaf; simmer until reduced to half quantity. Draw aside.

Make a roux with the butter and flour, pour on the fish stock and strain in the wine. Stir until boiling. Add the milk and allow to boil 2 or 3 minutes, adding the cream and seasoning. When of a syrupy consistency draw aside and beat in the butter.

Use at once or keep in a bain-marie until required. Veal, chicken, or vegetable stock may be used in place of fish stock according to the dish which the sauce is to accompany. For additional smoothness this sauce may be tammied.

A GOOD SAUCE FOR FISH

served with any boiled white fish, fried fish, or fish cooked à la meunière

½ oz. butter
1 tablespoon chopped onion
1 dessertspoon chopped shallot
1 tablespoon chopped mushroom peelings
a bouquet of tarragon, lemon thyme, and parsley
¾ pint strong fish stock, lightly seasoned
1 wineglass white wine

1 sherry glass Madeira or good sherry

Liaison
2 yolks of egg
1½ oz. butter
a good pinch of corn-flour
seasoning
1 teaspoon tomato purée or 1 tablespoon tomato sauce (2) (page 178)

Soften the onion and shallot in the butter. Add the mushroom, moisten with the stock and wine, and put in the bouquet. Simmer 25 minutes with pan uncovered, skimming occasionally. Strain, return to the pan, and boil rapidly until reduced to half. Add the Madeira and adjust seasoning. Work the yolks well with a nut of the butter and the corn-flour. Moisten with a little of the liquor, then pour back into the pan by degrees. Stand in a bain-marie, and stir well until the mixture begins to thicken. Work in the rest of the butter by degrees, season, and when the consistency of thick cream add the tomato purée, first diluting it with a little of the sauce.

WATERCRESS SAUCE FOR FISH

served with salmon, salmon trout, or grilled mackerel

2 bunches of watercress (or ¼ lb.)
1½ oz. butter
1 teaspoon anchovy essence, or 2 pounded anchovies
½ pint good fish fumet

Roux
¼ oz. butter
¼ oz. flour

¼ of a cucumber (1–2 oz.), finely diced and blanched
salt, pepper, and cayenne
lemon juice

Pick over watercress, boil in salted water until just tender. Drain, press well, and rub through a fine sieve. Cream butter, work the purée in by degrees, add pepper and a good dust of cayenne. Add the anchovies to the fumet. Make roux, pour on the fumet, stir until boiling, boil 5 minutes and skim well. Draw aside, add the green butter piece by piece, stirring it well in. Season very well and sharpen with lemon juice. Add the cucumber. Do not boil after 'mounting' or adding the butter.

LAST-MINUTE SAUCE
served with fish cutlets and grills

Take equal quantities of cream and A1 sauce, heat gently, add seasoning and a pinch of sugar.

APPLE AND MAYONNAISE SAUCE

¼ lb. tart apples, weighed when peeled and cored
1 sprig of mint
1 wineglass white wine or cider
1 large tablespoon freshly grated horse-radish

1 gill mayonnaise sauce (see page 166), or thick cream dressing (see page 363)
salt, pepper, French mustard, sugar

Slice apples.   Simmer them with the wine and mint with the lid off the pan, until the wine is reduced and absorbed and the apples are soft. Remove mint.   Mash or sieve the apples, mix with the horse-radish, and when quite cold beat into the mayonnaise, adding the seasonings to taste.

V.   COLD SAUCES

A chaudfroid is a coating sauce applied to cold food.   There are two kinds, white and brown.   Each is made with the appropriate sauce, stiffened with aspic suitable to the food to be coated.   The aspic is strengthened by the addition of a little extra gelatine.   After the food is coated with the sauce a further glazing of aspic is added to preserve the glossy appearance.   The coating should be delicately and carefully carried out: the food should not be blanketed.

A white chaudfroid is made with béchamel and aspic and is used for coating cooked chicken, fillets of sole, and eggs: food suitable for dance and buffet suppers.

A brown chaudfroid is employed for coating dark meat, game, cutlets, or duck and is made with a demi-glace sauce and aspic.

After the food has been coated, and glazed with aspic, the dish is carefully garnished.

WHITE CHAUDFROID SAUCE
for coating chicken, fish, eggs, etc.

1 oz. butter
1 oz. flour
¾ pint milk, flavoured as for a béchamel (see béchamel sauce, short method, page 155)

¼ oz. or level dessertspoon gelatine
½ gill aspic, chicken or fish
½ gill cream
salt and pepper

Make a roux with the butter and flour.   Pour on the warm flavoured milk.   Stir until boiling, simmer 4–5 minutes, stirring continuously.

Dissolve gelatine in the warm aspic and add to the sauce with the cream and seasoning. Tammy. Stir frequently whilst cooling to keep the sauce smooth and velvety. When of the consistency of thick cream it is ready for coating.

BROWN CHAUDFROID SAUCE

for game, duck, cutlets, etc.

¾ pint good demi-glace (page 143)
¾ gill aspic jelly

a good ¼ oz. or level dessert-spoon gelatine
½ gill Madeira, sherry, or port

Warm the demi-glace. Dissolve gelatine in the aspic jelly over gentle heat. Add to the demi-glace with the wine. Use when on the point of setting.

CUMBERLAND SAUCE

served cold with either hot or cold meat (ham, mutton, venison), and also with brawn

3 tablespoons red-currant jelly
1–2 lumps of sugar
1 orange
1 lemon

2 glasses red wine
1 teaspoon arrowroot or corn-flour

Put jelly into a saucepan. Rub sugar over the orange rind until the lumps are soaked with the oil, add to pan with the juice. Pare the lemon rind thinly and add half to the pan with the juice. Boil the wine, flame and add to the pan. Bring all to the boil. Simmer 5–7 minutes. Meanwhile shred remaining lemon rind finely and blanch. Slake arrowroot with a dessertspoon of water and add to pan while boiling. Draw aside at once and strain. Add shredded rind, stir, and allow to cool. This sauce improves if kept a day or two before use.

Traditionally Cumberland sauce should be made with port, but unless good port can be used a better result can be obtained with a vin ordinaire. A little more jelly or sugar can be added to taste if necessary. A recipe for a richer sauce will be found on page 173.

MAYONNAISE SAUCE

For this sauce oil is used for thickening in place of butter, and the principle of adding the thickening ingredient slowly should be observed. If the oil is added slowly and carefully during the first minute or two of mixing, and no more added until the first additions have been absorbed, there is little danger of the sauce curdling. Once thickening has begun the oil may be added more freely.

The following general notes may be of use to beginners. Contrary to the general idea, ingredients and equipment should not be very cold; for example, the eggs should not come straight out of the refrigerator, and the oil, if at all cloudy or chilled, should be slightly warmed. This may be done by putting the bottle into a pan of hot water for a short time, or on the stove rack. The mayonnaise will then be quickly and easily made, and the chances of curdling lessened. No special gadget is needed for pouring the oil: a small jug or a well-grooved cork in the oil bottle answers very well. For working the sauce a small sauce whisk is quicker and easier than a spatula or wooden spoon.

The quantity of eggs. Strictly speaking, 4 yolks should be employed to a pint of oil. For economy these may be cut to 3, and when a large quantity of mayonnaise is in hand this is the proportion generally used. If the sauce should curdle, a fresh yolk, with seasonings, must be put into a bowl and the curdled mixture incorporated very gradually before the addition of any further oil.

The addition of boiling water to a finished mayonnaise. If a small quantity of boiling water ($\frac{1}{2}-\frac{3}{4}$ gill per pint) is added to a finished mayonnaise, it will lighten it.

To keep mayonnaise for a short time. If the mayonnaise is not for immediate use, press a piece of paper over the top of the sauce, or turn into a glass jar with a screw top. If keeping for several days store in room temperature, not in the refrigerator.

MAYONNAISE SAUCE

served with lobsters, langoustes, and various salads

2 yolks of egg	a dust of cayenne
$\frac{1}{2}$ teaspoon French mustard	a few drops of lemon juice
$\frac{1}{2}$ teaspoon each of sugar and salt	$\frac{1}{2}$ pint best olive oil
a pinch of white pepper	2–3 tablespoons white wine vinegar (to taste)

Put the yolks into a small bowl, removing the thread if present. Add the seasonings and lemon juice and work with a small wooden spoon or preferably a sauce whisk for a minute or two. This thickens the yolks and prepares them for the oil. Now add about 2 tablespoons of oil 2 or 3 drops at a time. The mixture should now be very thick and must be diluted with about a teaspoon or dessertspoon of the vinegar to bring it to the consistency of cream. Continue adding the oil, carefully at first and then more quickly as the sauce thickens, so that finally the oil is being poured in in a steady stream. The sauce must be worked continuously and a little vinegar added from time to time to prevent it from becoming too thick. The amount of vinegar used depends on its acidity and must be regulated according to the taste and thickness of sauce required. Mayonnaise, when completed (without the addition of the cream), should be stiff enough to keep its shape, and to show the mark of the spoon or whisk. Adjust seasoning. The mayonnaise is then ready to be used as the base of a sauce or served as it is with the addition of a little cream.

MAYONNAISE AURORE

served as above, and also with eggs and cold fish dishes

½ pint mayonnaise
2 tablespoons cream
1–2 tablespoons tomato sauce,
    made by cooking and season-
ing 2 or 3 ripe tomatoes,
sieving, and reducing the
pulp
a good sprinkling of tabasco

Mix all together. The sauce should be blush-pink in colour and piquant in flavour. The tomato is required primarily to colour the sauce; it should be in the form of a thick purée so as not to dilute too much.

The following mayonnaise is most easily made if two people work together. It is an easy and, we think, a foolproof method, and is light and quickly made.

HOT WATER MAYONNAISE

2 egg yolks
salt, pepper, mustard (French
    or English)
1 tablespoon boiling water
½ pint oil
1–2 tablespoons vinegar

Put yolks and seasonings in a bowl and mix well. Add boiling water and immediately begin to whisk with a rotary beater. Without any cessation of the beating add the oil in a steady stream. It is of great help to have an assistant pour it in. Continue beating until all the oil is incorporated and the sauce thick. Then add vinegar.

MAYONNAISE COLLÉE

for coating eggs and fillets of sole

Sometimes, instead of a chaudfroid sauce, a mayonnaise reinforced with gelatine and aspic is used for coating food. This has certain points in its favour. It is of different texture, more of a dressing than a sauce; it is lighter, has a more piquant flavour, and it is easier for the beginner to get the right coating consistency. If a dish is made, say, in the morning for an evening party, and is coated with this sauce, it should be glazed with aspic so that its glossy appearance is preserved. The sauce may be flavoured in any of the ways suitable for mayonnaise, with herbs, tomato purée and so forth.

¼ oz. gelatine
1 gill aspic jelly (if aspic is not available use an extra teaspoon of
    gelatine, and dissolve all the gelatine in a gill of hot water)
½ pint mayonnaise

Dissolve gelatine in the aspic, but do not boil. Whisk into the mayonnaise.

For mock mayonnaise see cream dressing (thick), page 363.

SAUCE RÉMOULADE

served with grilled meat or fish

½ pint mayonnaise
2 teaspoons mustard (French
and English mixed)
1 teaspoon each of chopped
capers and gherkins

1 teaspoon chopped parsley,
tarragon, and chervil
2 fillets of anchovy chopped,
or 1 teaspoon anchovy
essence

Add the other ingredients to the mayonnaise. The sauce should be well flavoured with mustard.

SAUCE TARTARE

served with fried fish, grills, etc.

2 hard-boiled egg yolks
2 egg yolks
½ pint olive oil
1–2 tablespoons vinegar
salt and pepper
1 teaspoon chopped capers

1 teaspoon chopped gherkins
1 teaspoon chopped herbs
shredded white of 1 hard-
boiled egg
a little cream (optional)

Sieve hard-boiled yolks into a bowl, work with a wooden spoon, adding the raw yolks by degrees. When well incorporated begin to drop in the oil gradually. When beginning to thicken add oil more quickly, diluting with the vinegar when necessary. Season to taste. Then add the capers, gherkins, and herbs, and lastly the egg white. A little cream may be added if liked.

SAUCE VERTE

a thick pale green mayonnaise served with salmon, salmon trout, and other cold fish

1 handful of parsley
3–4 sprigs of tarragon
3–4 sprigs of chervil
½ handful of spinach

½–¾ pint mayonnaise
1–2 tablespoons cream
seasoning

Cook herbs and spinach in boiling salted water until just tender. Drain, press, and rub through a sieve. Add this purée to the mayonnaise only a short time before serving: if kept it tends to lose its colour. Season and finish with the cream.

SAUCE GRIBICHE

served with cold fish dishes and shell-fish

This is mayonnaise to which has been added one sieved hard-boiled egg yolk, mustard, chopped gherkins, chervil, tarragon, parsley, and capers, and the egg white cut into julienne strips.

VI. SIMPLE HOUSEHOLD AND
MISCELLANEOUS SAUCES

No cook can afford to neglect the sauces mères and their derivatives, and that is the reason for their primary place in this chapter. But in her repertoire there must be many others, some recognized and classic, simple editions of the great sauces, some of the kind to be 'knocked up in a hurry,' and some designed to give an unusual and exciting touch to a meal. Examples of all these are to be found in this section. Among the first-named one counts the delicious beurre noir and beurre noisette and the English bread, parsley, and apple sauces. Among the last I would name such sauces as Alabama, barbecue, and orange mint, and it is roughly under such headings that I have grouped them.

BEURRE NOIR (1)

for eggs, fish (especially skate), and some vegetables

2 oz. butter   1 tablespoon chopped parsley
1 tablespoon vinegar   a little pepper and salt

Melt butter and cook till nut-brown. (If literally cooked till black it would be burned.) Pour the cooked butter over the dish in hand. Put vinegar and pepper and salt into the saucepan, reduce to half, add parsley, and pour over the dish.

BEURRE NOIR (2)

used as above

same ingredients as for Method 1

Cook butter till brown and allow to cool. Put vinegar into a saucepan with pepper and salt, reduce to half, add parsley. Remove from fire, strain the butter on to the vinegar and heat without allowing it to boil. The addition of capers to this sauce is excellent for skate (see Raie au Beurre Noir, page 474).

BEURRE NOISETTE

for vegetables, fish, and eggs

2 oz. butter   salt, freshly ground pepper
juice of ¼ lemon

Heat a frying-pan or saucepan, put in butter, cook over moderate heat, swirling the pan from time to time until the butter is a light nut-brown and has a nut-like fragrance. Add lemon juice and seasoning to taste, and serve.

APPLE SAUCE

for pork, duck, goose, sausages, and other rich meats; also for roast rabbit

¼ lb. apples (a red-cheeked apple of the 'fluffy' kind, such as a ripe Bramley or Laxton)	½ gill water 1 heaped tablespoon sugar 1 strip of lemon or orange peel ½ oz. butter

Wipe the apples, cut in four, core and slice.   Put into a small pan with water, sugar, and peel.   Cover and cook gently to a pulp.   Rub through a sieve or strainer, rinse out the pan and return the purée to it.   Cook fairly rapidly, stirring continuously until the purée will just drop from the spoon. Stir in the butter and serve hot.

Apple sauce may be varied by the addition of a good tablespoon of grated horse-radish, or of finely chopped chives, mint, or dill.

It acquires a subtle and delicious flavour if quince is added to the apples:

APPLE AND QUINCE SAUCE

1 small quince	a nut of butter
1–2 tablespoons sugar	¼ pint cider or water
½ lb. red-cheeked apples	seasoning
a strip of orange or lemon rind	

Slice quince thinly, simmer till tender in covered pan with sugar and three-quarters of the cider or water.   Meanwhile core apples and slice thinly.   Cook to a pulp with remaining cider and rind.   Rub through a strainer and add to quince.   Simmer together 3–4 minutes until thick. Add butter and season lightly.

BREAD SAUCE

This is the traditional English sauce to serve with roast turkey, chicken, or pheasant.   Flavourless, lumpy, or unseasoned it can be unpleasant, and because it is a homely sauce it often carries all these defects.   During the time of infusion the milk should absorb the flavour of onion, clove, and bay-leaf, and the crumbs should not be long cooked or the whole affair takes on the texture of a poultice.

2 cloves	seasoning of salt, pepper, and,
1 medium onion	if liked, a dash of cayenne
¼ bay-leaf	½ oz. butter
½ pint milk	1 tablespoon top of milk or
3–4 heaped tablespoons fresh white breadcrumbs	cream

Stick the cloves into the onion and put it with the bay-leaf and milk into a saucepan.   Cover and set on a very low heat to infuse for at least 10 minutes, or until the milk is well flavoured.   Remove the onion and bay-leaf, bring to the boil, and shake in the crumbs.   Simmer 3 or 4 minutes until thick and creamy, draw aside, add seasoning, butter, and milk or cream. Reheat gently and use at once.

This sauce should be neither sloppy nor stodgy, and the necessary adjustment of crumbs or liquid must be made to produce the right creamy consistency. This consistency is not liked by everyone, and the addition of rougher crumbs crisply fried and scattered over the top of the sauce is considered an improvement.

SAUCE BRUNE PIQUANTE

a good sauce for vegetables such as artichokes, celery, potatoes, and onions, or to be served separately with sausages, bacon, rissoles, or fritters

½ pint quick demi-glace (see page 144)
1 teaspoon red-currant jelly

vinegar to taste
1 teaspoon chopped gherkins or capers

After the sauce has simmered 15–20 minutes add the additional ingredients. Reboil, adjust seasoning, and serve.

BROWN SAUCE

a simple domestic sauce

This is generally liked by children, served with mashed potatoes, batter pudding, mashed swedes and so forth. It is also a suitable base for a simple devil sauce (see next page).

Important additions to the above. Variants in flavouring are tomato ketchup or concentrated tomato purée, or mushroom ketchup and a glass of white wine. These are added after the cooking of the flour.

1½ oz. butter or margarine or 1¼ oz. dripping
2 oz. carrot
2 oz. onion
1¼ oz. flour
a slice of tomato, cooked, sprinkled with sugar, and lightly grilled (to give colour)

seasoning
1½ pints liquid, vegetable stock, potato water, or light meat stock
a bouquet of parsley, thyme, and ½ bay-leaf

Prepare and slice the vegetables and cook in the fat till a good brown. Sprinkle in the flour and cook for about 10 minutes, stirring from time to time; add slice of tomato. Set aside a gill of the liquid and add remainder to the pan with bouquet. Bring to boil, season, and simmer gently for an hour uncovered. Skim from time to time. Strain and press the vegetables to extract all juice. Bring liquid to boil again. Simmer for half an hour, skimming and adding a spoonful of the reserved liquid from time to time. If the sauce is too thin it may be reduced. The long cooking may be curtailed, but the result is less good.

BROWN SAUCE FOR SPAGHETTI

½ oz. butter or dripping
1 good heaped tablespoon chopped shallot
3–4 mushrooms, chopped
a lean rasher, finely cut

1 teaspoon concentrated tomato purée
2 tablespoons red wine
1 pint of the above sauce

Cook the shallot, mushrooms, and rasher in the heated fat. Drain, add all ingredients to the sauce, and simmer 15 minutes.

BROWN DEVIL SAUCE (SIMPLE)

for devilled dishes, chicken, turkey, etc.

½ oz. butter or dripping
1 heaped tablespoon chopped onion
1 clove of garlic crushed in salt
6 peppercorns, crushed and tied in a bit of muslin
a dash of cayenne
1 good teaspoon made mustard
1 dessertspoon French mustard

vinegar to taste
1 tablespoon chutney and 1 tablespoon Worcestershire sauce
chopped mixed herbs
1 pint of the simple domestic brown sauce given on the previous page

Cook onion and garlic in fat, drain and add with all other ingredients to the sauce. Cook for 15 minutes.

BROWN CHESTNUT SAUCE

The simple domestic brown sauce given on the previous page may be used as a base for chestnut sauce by the addition of cooked chopped chestnuts, or a chestnut sauce may be made as follows:

CHESTNUT SAUCE

for roast turkey

1½ oz. butter
1 oz. onion
1 oz. carrot
1 glass of sherry
1 oz. flour
¾ pint stock

a bouquet garni and ½ bay-leaf
seasoning of salt and fresh-ground pepper
½ oz. butter to finish
a short ½ pint boiled and chopped chestnuts

Heat fat, cook onion and carrot, add sherry and allow it to reduce a little. Add flour and cook gently 5 minutes. Add stock, bouquet, and bay-leaf. Simmer gently 20–30 minutes, season, finish with butter, and add chestnuts.

CASHEW NUT OR ALMOND SAUCE
for chicken or turkey

This sauce is a good alternative to gravy for a bird roasted in the French way. It may also be used for a boiled chicken.

2 oz. blanched almonds or cashew nuts
¾ oz. fresh butter
½ oz. flour
½ pint good chicken or turkey stock, or the gravy from the bird made up to ½ pint with stock
salt, freshly ground pepper, ground mace, and paprika
a few drops of lemon juice
2 tablespoons cream

Chop the nuts very finely. Melt the butter in a frying-pan, brown the almonds slowly and evenly in it. Draw aside, blend in the flour, add the stock, and stir until boiling. Simmer 4–5 minutes, adding salt, pepper, mace, and paprika to taste. When the consistency of thin cream add the lemon juice and cream. Boil rapidly to a light coating consistency. Pour over the jointed bird or serve separately.

The following gives a richer sauce than the recipe on page 165:

CUMBERLAND SAUCE

1 lb. red-currant jelly
the rind of 1 orange and 1 lemon
the juice of 2 oranges and 2 lemons
2 rounded teaspoons arrowroot
2 large glasses of port

Pare the rinds thinly, cut in fine shreds, blanch 5 minutes in boiling water, strain and refresh in cold.

Put the jelly into a pan with the strained fruit juice, bring to boil, simmer 3 minutes, add port. Slake arrowroot with a tablespoon of cold water, stir into boiling liquid in pan. Draw away from heat immediately. Strain and cool. Add blanched rind.

This sauce is best made a day before it is to be used. Once in a Paris restaurant a particularly good Cumberland sauce was served, and the *maître d'hôtel*, on being complimented, said: 'Madame, the secret is 2 tablespoons of Grand Marnier, it makes all the difference'—and it does.

CAPER SAUCE (SIMPLE METHOD)
for boiled mutton and boiled chicken

¾ oz. butter
¾ oz. flour
½ pint vegetable stock
1 teaspoon vinegar
½ teaspoon made mustard
salt and pepper
1 large tablespoon capers
1 tablespoon cream

Melt the butter in a thick saucepan, add the flour off the heat, pour in the stock, add the vinegar, mustard, seasonings, and capers. Stir until boiling and simmer 5 minutes. Adjust seasoning, add cream and serve.

SAUCE BERCY

1 tablespoon finely chopped shallots	salt and pepper
½ oz. butter	juice of ½ lemon
1 wineglass white wine	1 dessertspoon chopped parsley
2 wineglasses white stock, veal, chicken, or fish	*Thickening*
	a good ½ oz. butter
	½ oz. flour

Soften the shallots in the butter without colouring. Add wine and reduce to half quantity. Add stock, seasoning, lemon juice, and parsley. Boil and draw aside.

Work the butter and flour together to a smooth paste. Add to the pan in small pieces, stir until thoroughly blended. Continue to stir until boiling, and boil briskly for about a minute. Adjust seasoning.

Sauce bercy should be on the thin side and sharp in flavour, and may be used in the following ways:

1. Made with a veal or chicken stock—over poached eggs, escalope of veal, calf's head, artichokes, salsify, etc.

2. Made with fish stock—over raw fillets of whiting or sole; the dish is then cooked fairly rapidly in the oven for 10–15 minutes. It is served garnished in various ways.

EGG SAUCE

served with boiled cod or other plain boiled fish, and good with salsify

2 hard-boiled eggs
½ pint creamy béchamel sauce (long or short method, see page 155)
seasoning

Chop the eggs coarsely while hot, add to the sauce and adjust seasoning.

GREEN SAUCE (SIMPLE METHOD)

a spicy sauce, excellent over poached eggs on toast, vegetables, or fish

1 bunch of watercress	1 tablespoon cream
½ pint béchamel sauce (long or short method, see page 155)	seasoning and a dash of cayenne

Wash the whole bunch of watercress without trimming the stalks. Boil for 5–7 minutes. Drain and press well. Sieve or chop finely. Add to the béchamel with cream and seasoning.

PARSLEY SAUCE

A simple parsley sauce for chicken or rabbit may be made in the same way, substituting a handful of parsley for the cress.

GREEN SAUCE (COLD)

A cold green sauce is made in the same way on a base of mayonnaise in place of béchamel.

HORSE-RADISH SAUCE (COLD)

traditional English sauce for roast beef, and good with certain fish dishes

1 dessertspoon vinegar	sugar to taste
a squeeze of lemon juice	1–1½ heaped tablespoons fresh-
¼ teaspoon mustard	grated horse-radish
salt and pepper	¼ pint cream

Mix vinegar, lemon juice, mustard, seasonings, sugar, and horse-radish together. Whip cream till stiff, incorporate other ingredients, adjust seasonings. Add extra horse-radish if necessary.

HORSE-RADISH SAUCE (HOT)

good with roast or boiled beef, fried or grilled fish, fritters, poached eggs, and baked stuffed potatoes

1 good tablespoon fresh-grated horse-radish	a squeeze of lemon juice
¼ pint béchamel sauce (short method, see page 155)	½ teaspoon salt and a good pinch of pepper
½ teaspoon French mustard	1 tablespoon cream

Mix all ingredients together and serve hot.

MINT SAUCE

for roast lamb

1 large handful of mint leaves	a good ½ gill vinegar
2 tablespoons sugar	⅓ gill hot water

Pound the leaves in a mortar with half of the sugar. When quite fine add hot water and the rest of the sugar. When dissolved add vinegar. Leave an hour or two before serving. The sauce must be thick with mint. For orange mint and other mint sauces see page 182.

MUSTARD SAUCE

for herrings, eggs, rabbit, or white fish

1 oz. butter or margarine	salt and pepper
1 shallot or small onion, finely chopped	1 large teaspoon French mustard
¾ oz. flour	1 large teaspoon chopped parsley
2½ gills light stock	
½ bay-leaf	

Melt butter, add shallot, cook for a few minutes.   Add flour, continue cooking 4–5 minutes, add stock and bay-leaf, simmer 3–4 minutes. Remove bay-leaf, season, add mustard and parsley.   Serve.

If to be served with eggs or rabbit, tomato may be added: 1 large peeled tomato, the seeds removed, coarsely chopped.

MUSHROOM SAUCE (SAUCE DUXELLES)

for vegetables, eggs, veal, rabbit, white fish, etc.

This is a good sauce made from the washed peelings and stalks of mushrooms.

1 oz. butter or margarine	$\frac{3}{4}$ oz. flour
1 shallot or small onion, finely chopped	2$\frac{1}{2}$ gills light stock or potato water
2 tablespoons well-washed mushroom stalks and peelings, finely chopped	$\frac{1}{2}$ bay-leaf
	$\frac{1}{2}$ gill top of milk
	salt and pepper

Melt butter, add onion and chopped mushroom, cook 4–5 minutes. Add flour off fire, pour on stock and add bay-leaf.   Blend and stir till boiling.   Simmer 3 or 4 minutes to reduce slightly.   Add milk and seasoning.   Remove bay-leaf and serve.

This may be used as an accompanying sauce or be poured over raw fillets of fish in a fireproof dish.   The surface may then be sprinkled with brown crumbs and grated cheese and the whole baked in the oven.

ONION SAUCE (ENGLISH FASHION)

served with roast or boiled mutton

This may be made by adding boiled, roughly chopped onions to a thick béchamel sauce, or it may be made with a purée of onions (a sauce soubise) as given on page 157.

The following is a different type of onion sauce, and it is good to serve with réchauffés, fried or stuffed eggs, or chicken, game, or liver:

LA SAUCE AUX OIGNONS DE PÉRIGORD

1 tablespoon bacon fat or lard	seasoning
2 or 3 onions	$\frac{1}{4}$ pint boiling water or stock
2 oz. fat bacon	a bouquet of thyme, parsley,
1 dessertspoon flour	and bay-leaf

Make the fat hot, fry the onions golden brown with the bacon, add the flour, cook well, add water or stock, salt and pepper, and the bouquet. Cook gently for half an hour, then remove the bouquet.

OYSTER SAUCE
for boiled fish, cod or turbot

½ pint velouté sauce made with fish stock (either method, see page 152)

8–12 sauce oysters
seasoning
1 egg yolk for liaison

Heat the oysters through in the sauce without allowing to boil, season and make the liaison in the way described on page 140.

PARSLEY SAUCE
traditional English sauce for boiled chicken or calf's head

1 large handful of fresh parsley, free from stalks

½ pint velouté or béchamel sauce (short method, see pages 152 and 155)
seasoning

Boil parsley 5–7 minutes in slightly salted water with lid off the pan. Drain and press well. Rub through a fine wire sieve. This should give about a teaspoon of purée. Add to basic sauce and adjust seasoning.

PIQUANTE SAUCE
for grills, devils, etc.

¾ oz. butter
1 onion, chopped
¾ oz. flour, scant weight
1 teaspoon tomato purée or 2 tomatoes, peeled, pipped, and chopped
1½ tablespoons mushroom peelings, washed
a bouquet garni

½–¾ pint stock, or water with a teaspoon of consommé or meat extract
1 teaspoon tarragon vinegar
seasoning
2 gherkins, sliced
1 teaspoon chopped parsley
French mustard to taste

Melt the butter, add onion and soften slowly. Add the flour and brown lightly. Add tomato purée, mushroom peelings, bouquet garni, stock, and vinegar. Season, bring to the boil, and simmer gently 20–30 minutes. Strain, return to the pan, and reduce to about 1½ gills. Add sliced gherkins and chopped parsley, and French mustard to taste.

SAUCE PROVENÇALE
for liver, cutlets, croquettes, etc.

1 oz. washed mushroom peelings and stalks, finely chopped
1 oz. shallot, chopped
1 clove of garlic, crushed
1 tablespoon oil
1 teaspoon flour

¾ gill white wine or cider
¾ gill strong stock
seasoning
a bouquet garni
1 teaspoon tomato purée

Soften the chopped mushroom peelings and stalks, the shallot, and garlic in oil. Dust lightly with flour and moisten with the cider and stock. Add salt, pepper, and bouquet garni and allow to simmer for 20 minutes. Then add tomato purée. Simmer 2–3 minutes.

Tomato Sauces

TOMATO SAUCE (1)

simple fashion for croquettes, cutlets, etc.
for ½ pint of sauce

½ oz. butter	a bouquet garni
½ oz. flour	pepper and salt
1½ gills stock	½ oz. butter to finish
1 lb. tomatoes	

Melt butter in a saucepan, add the flour. Cook for 2–3 minutes and pour on the stock. Cut the tomatoes in two, squeeze to remove the seeds and water, and add to the pan with the bouquet garni, pepper, and salt. Cover and simmer for half an hour or longer. Rub through a hair sieve, rinse the pan, pour back the sauce and reheat. Add the last ½ oz. of butter off the fire before serving.

TOMATO SAUCE (2) (FAÇON MÉNAGÈRE)

1 oz. good dripping or lard	1 wineglass white wine
1 onion	a good pinch of salt and sugar
1 carrot	a small pinch of pepper
½ oz. flour	a large sprig of parsley
1 lb. tomatoes	

Heat the dripping in a stew-pan, add the onion and carrot cut in dice, brown slightly, dust in the flour and allow to colour. Cut the tomatoes in two, squeeze to remove pips, and add to the pan with the wine, salt, sugar, pepper, and parsley. Cover and simmer gently for half an hour. Pass through a hair sieve or aluminium strainer. Rinse the pan and pour back to reheat.

On page 1117 of 'The Store Cupboard' is a recipe for Tomato Purée 2, a much reduced tomato sauce which may replace a condensed tomato purée and is excellent for spaghetti and pasta dishes.

TOMATO SAUCE FOR GRILLS

1½ oz. butter	1 teaspoon French mustard
1 clove of garlic, crushed	½ teaspoon English made mus-
1½ gills strong tomato pulp	tard
2 teaspoons lemon juice	1 teaspoon sugar
1 saltspoon grated lemon rind	salt, freshly ground black pep-
1 dessertspoon Worcestershire	per, a touch of cayenne and
sauce	nutmeg

Add butter to garlic and cook until lightly brown, add tomato and remaining ingredients. Simmer 3–4 minutes until thick.

SAUCE DE TOMATES PROVENÇALE

good for fish (grilled lobster, red mullet)

12 large ripe tomatoes
2 tablespoons olive oil or 1 oz. butter
1 clove of garlic, crushed
1 bay-leaf

1 onion, chopped
1 carrot, sliced
a bouquet garni
seasoning

Cut the tomatoes in half, squeeze out pips, and cut in pieces. Put in a saucepan with olive oil, garlic, bay-leaf, onion, carrot, bouquet, salt, and pepper. Cook gently for at least half an hour. Remove bouquet and bay-leaf. Put through a sieve, and keep hot until wanted. Reduce if necessary.

Lastly, here is a good quick tomato sauce, of value in winter because it is made with concentrated tomato purée in place of fresh tomatoes.

WINTER TOMATO SAUCE

½ oz butter or dripping
½ oz. flour
a clove of garlic crushed in salt
½ pint stock or potato water
1 teaspoon concentrated tomato purée

½ bay-leaf
seasoning and a pinch of sugar
a nut of butter to finish

Make a roux of fat and flour, add garlic, stock, purée, and bay-leaf. Simmer a few minutes, remove bay-leaf, season, and finish with a nut of butter.

The following recipe is for a tomato coulis, much thicker than a sauce, really of the consistency of a purée, although it is not sieved. It is useful for pasta, vegetable, and other dishes.

TOMATO COULIS

1 lb. ripe tomatoes or 2 teacups tinned tomatoes
½ oz. butter
1 medium onion
¼ gill vegetable stock

1 bay-leaf and a little chopped basil or lemon thyme
salt, freshly ground pepper
½ teaspoon arrowroot

Blanch and skin the tomatoes, cut in quarters and remove the seeds. Slice the onion finely, sauter slowly in the butter. Add tomatoes, stock, herbs, and seasoning. Cover and simmer until the tomatoes are pulpy and rich-looking. Draw aside, remove bay-leaf, and add arrowroot mixed with a tablespoon of water. Reboil and serve. If tinned tomatoes are used proceed as above, but do not remove the seeds.

Two other recipes for tomato sauce will be found in the chapter on pastas, page 426.

The next few paragraphs might well be labelled 'Sauces for the cook-hostess,' for some of them, at any rate, will prove useful to those of us who can give neither much time nor undivided attention to the preparation of a meal. So often all we can accomplish is to add one or two final touches to make ordinary food a little more interesting. It may be just the addition to a simple salad-cream of sweet chutney or pickle finely chopped, or a spoonful of thick damson purée, or diced sweet apple and crisp celery. Such a sauce is served with fried fish, a grill, or sausages. The extra touch may be in a sauce with a difference such as the apricot and horse-radish, or perhaps, if you come home in the late afternoon bringing with you some Dublin Bay prawns or a lobster, you will have time to make the unusually good Alabama sauce. It takes only a minute or two to add orange and some red-currant jelly to a mint sauce to make it more interesting. These are indeed for the most part 'little sauces knocked up in a hurry.' Notwithstanding this they have their place.

ALABAMA SAUCE

for cocktail savouries, Dublin Bay prawns, and fish croquettes, and, diluted, it may be served with cold fish

½ green pepper, chopped
a small head of celery, chopped, or a small cucumber and a little celery salt
1 clove of garlic crushed with salt

1 good gill mayonnaise or cream dressing
a short ½ pint tomato chilli sauce (see page 1116)
1 large tablespoon grated horse-radish
a little cream

Mix all ingredients well and ice. For eating with cooked fish this is toned down with cream or mayonnaise.

APRICOT AND HORSE-RADISH SAUCE

for chicken and white meat

Make a purée of apricots. To a good gill of purée add:

lemon or orange juice to sharpen
sugar to taste

1 tablespoon horse-radish
1 level dessertspoon chopped herbs

The herbs may vary according to the dish in hand: tarragon or basil for chicken, mint for lamb, fennel for fish. The sauce may be served hot or cold.

In the chapter on devils and barbecues (page 724) will be found some excellent last-minute hot and spicy sauces, including a chutney sauce which will turn a dish of eggs into something special.

Yoghurt?

CUCUMBER SAUCE
served with cold fish, eggs, or salad   X

a few spoonfuls good salad-cream, cole-slaw dressing, or mayonnaise, all diluted with cream seasoning

a small cucumber, finely chopped, salted, and drained
a good pinch of finely chopped tarragon and mint

Mix all together and chill.

Another version of this is made with whipped cream, lemon juice or tarragon vinegar, seasoning, sugar, and chopped cucumber.

HOT CUCUMBER SAUCE
served with lamb or mutton

2–3 cucumbers
½ oz. butter
½ oz. flour
¼ pint strong veal stock

salt, pepper, orange juice, green colouring
½ oz. butter and 2 tablespoons cream to finish

Peel cucumbers and cut in chunks. Cook in boiling salted water till tender. Drain and rub through a sieve. Melt butter in a small saucepan. Add flour and cook to a pale straw colour. Pour on the stock, stir till boiling, simmer a few minutes, then add the cucumber purée. Reboil and reduce if necessary, add orange juice and a few drops of colouring. Adjust seasoning, add butter in small pieces, and the cream.

DILL SAUCE
for fish

1 oz. butter
¾ oz. flour
½ pint fish stock or light court bouillon
1 tablespoon white wine vinegar or half the quantity of ordinary vinegar

1 dessertspoon sugar
1 large tablespoon chopped dill or fennel
salt and freshly ground pepper
1 yolk of egg

Melt butter, add flour, pour on the liquid off the fire, blend, and stir over moderate heat until boiling. Simmer 2–3 minutes, draw aside, add vinegar, sugar, dill, and seasoning to taste. Beat yolk, add a small quantity of the hot sauce gradually to it, then return to the saucepan. Stir or whisk vigorously for a minute over gentle heat, then serve.

SAUCE ITALIENNE (SIMPLE)
for fried liver

1 oz. butter, good weight, or 1 tablespoon oil
½ medium onion
1 shallot
1 good teaspoon flour
2 oz. mushrooms
salt, pepper, nutmeg

2–3 tablespoons white wine
1 dessertspoon concentrated tomato purée
½ pint stock
1 dessertspoon mixed chopped herbs

Heat butter or oil, add finely chopped onion and shallot, cook until pale gold, sprinkle in flour. Slice and chop mushrooms as finely as possible, add to contents of pan, and cook for a few minutes, taking care not to burn. Season, add wine, and continue cooking to reduce a little. Add tomato purée and stock, simmer all for 10 minutes. Adjust seasoning; add herbs.

ORANGE MINT SAUCE
used in place of mint sauce

10–12 sprigs of mint	1 orange
1 level tablespoon castor sugar	2–3 tablespoons boiling water
2 lumps of sugar	2 tablespoons wine vinegar
1 heaped teaspoon red-currant jelly	

Strip sprigs, then bruise and pound leaves in a mortar until fine, or they may be chopped finely, but the former method is better. Add the castor sugar. Rub lumps of sugar over the orange rind until soaked with the oil and add to the mint with the jelly. Pour on the boiling water. Leave 5–10 minutes.

Add the strained juice of the orange and the vinegar, and a little more sugar if necessary. The sauce must be quite thick with mint and pleasantly sharp.

The first time R. H. made the following version of sorrel sauce was when we found a batch of wild sorrel in the garden, which on tasting proved to be not too harsh or acid. This may well be made with wild sorrel leaves that are not too mature and rough in taste.

SORREL SAUCE
for veal, fish, etc.

1 lb. sorrel	½ teaspoon sugar
½ oz. butter, good weight	1–1½ gills veal stock or water
½ oz. flour	½ teaspoon meat glaze or Marmite
a good squeeze of lemon juice	2 tablespoons sour cream
seasoning	

Wash and boil sorrel, drain, press, and rub through a sieve. There should be about 3 tablespoons of purée. Melt butter in a saucepan, add flour, and cook gently till straw-coloured. Add the purée but do not stir. Cover and leave in a warm place (stove rack or hot-plate) 10–15 minutes. Add lemon juice, seasoning, sugar, stock, and meat glaze. Simmer 4–5 minutes until the consistency of cream. Adjust seasoning and sugar and add cream.

SPANISH SAUCE FOR FISH

½ pint well-flavoured fish fumet or stock	spoon or more of chopped watercress and 2 oz. butter
1 dessertspoon arrowroot	2 tablespoons cucumber, diced and blanched
anchovy essence to taste	
2 oz. watercress butter, made by working together 1 table-	salt, pepper, and a squeeze of lemon juice

Slake arrowroot with a spoonful or two of the fumet. Bring remaining liquid to boil and add mixed arrowroot, reboil and draw aside. Flavour well with the anchovy. Whisk in the butter by degrees, add the cucumber, seasoning, and lemon juice. Reheat carefully but do not allow to boil.

The following sauce is less simple to make than the foregoing, and is for a cook with experience rather than a beginner. It is really an anchovy-flavoured hollandaise.

SAUCE HOLLANDAISE AUX ANCHOIS
for salmon, asparagus, sea-kale, and delicate vegetables

½ oz. butter	1 glass white wine
1 oz. onion, chopped	½ pint fish fumet
1 oz. shallot, chopped	1 glass Madeira or sherry
1 oz. mushroom peelings and stalks (or prepared duxelles)	2 egg yolks
	1½–2 oz. butter
1 dessertspoon mixed chopped herbs (parsley, thyme, and tarragon)	anchovy essence
	salt, freshly ground pepper

Melt butter in a saucepan, add onion, shallot, mushrooms, and herbs. Cover, simmer 5–7 minutes. Add white wine and fumet, simmer again 10–15 minutes, skimming occasionally. Strain and return to the rinsed-out pan. Now reduce rapidly by about a third (to approximately 1½ gills). Add Madeira and set pan in a bain-marie.

Beat yolks with a nut of the butter, add a spoonful or two of the liquid by degrees and pour back gradually into the pan. Add rest of the butter slowly in small pieces (as for sauce hollandaise, page 157). Finish with a few drops of anchovy essence and the seasoning.

For tamarind sauce and almond sauce see Winkfield chapter, pages 992–3.

VII. SWEET SAUCES

An earlier remark that food should not swim in a sauce applies also to this section of the chapter. Many sweet sauces are rich and concentrated in flavour, and about two tablespoons per person is generally an adequate allowance. This is just as well perhaps, as some of the best of the sweet sauces are not economical; but then it may be remembered that a little of them goes a long way.

Chocolate Sauces

Chocolate sauce is one of the most popular. Unfortunately it is not always so good as it should be: it is apt to be gluey, pallid, and reminiscent of cocoa. A chocolate sauce worth its name is dark, really sweet, and full of the essence of chocolate. The secret lies in simmering the chocolate, sugar, and water together for some time so that the proper, slightly sticky consistency is reached without the addition of corn-flour, which so often spoils the sauce.

A dash of coffee essence or Nescafé helps to improve both the colour and flavour, and a yolk of egg, though optional, will enrich and help to thicken.

Sweetened chocolate is best used for the following, but the brand chosen should not be over-sweet. A so-called 'bitter' chocolate is excellent. The proportion of sugar may be varied slightly, but if too little is added it is impossible to get the rich, sticky consistency a good chocolate sauce should have.

CHOCOLATE SAUCE (1)

3 oz. sweetened block chocolate
2 oz. vanilla sugar
1 teaspoon unsweetened chocolate powder or cocoa

$\frac{1}{2}$–$\frac{3}{4}$ pint water
a piece of vanilla pod or
vanilla essence to taste
1 egg yolk (optional)

Break up chocolate in small pieces, put into a scrupulously clean roomy saucepan with the sugar, cocoa, and half the water. Stir over a moderate heat until boiling and the chocolate has dissolved. Simmer 2 or 3 minutes, then add the rest of the water and the vanilla pod. Reboil and continue to simmer for 15–20 minutes or until the sauce is syrupy and rich-looking. Draw aside and add egg yolk as for a liaison (see page 140).

Keep covered in a bain-marie if the sauce is to be served hot.

CHOCOLATE SAUCE (2) (SAUCE SUCHARD)

This is the finest of the chocolate sauces, and is made with syrup in place of water. It is especially sweet and rich and is used mostly for ices and ice-puddings. It may be served hot or cold.

6 oz. finest sweetened block
chocolate
1$\frac{1}{4}$ pints vanilla-flavoured stock
syrup (see page 860)

rum to taste (optional)
1–2 egg yolks (optional)

Grate or shred the chocolate, put into a pan or bowl and set over boiling water. Stir well until melted, add syrup by degrees, stirring continuously. When chocolate and syrup are thoroughly blended the sauce is ready and rum may be added. If to be served hot, egg yolk may be added as for a liaison.

See also chocolate sauce with Crêpes au Chocolat, page 927.

Fresh Fruit Sauces

FRESH FRUIT SAUCE

served principally with meringue sweets, ices, cold soufflés, etc.

The fruits most suitable for this sauce are raspberries, strawberries, peaches, and currants, red or black, and they must be really ripe, though not necessarily of the first quality.

Crush the fruit with a silver fork, then rub through a nylon sieve or aluminium strainer. Sweeten well with icing sugar, and if too thick dilute with a light syrup or water. The sauce should pour easily. Kirsch or maraschino may be added. Chill well before serving.

FRUIT SAUCE (HOT OR COLD)

This is a change from the ordinary jam sauce, and is a good way to use up fruit compôtes or bottled fruit. Serve with sponge puddings, pancakes, rice creams, etc.

Rub the fruit with a little juice through a nylon sieve or aluminium strainer. Turn into a pan, sweeten, and dilute to taste with more juice, but keep it strong in flavour. Bring to the boil and simmer several minutes. Thicken with 1 teaspoon of arrowroot for every $\frac{1}{2}$-pint, and slake with a little extra juice before adding to the pan. Boil up quickly and serve.

PEACH SAUCE
served with cream ices, vanilla or praline

4 ripe peaches	2 teaspoons maraschino
2 tablespoons rum	icing or castor sugar to taste

Skin peaches. If the skin does not peel off easily scald as for tomatoes in boiling water. Crush with a silver fork and pass through a nylon or silk sieve. Put into a scrupulously clean saucepan with the rum and maraschino, sweeten to taste, and heat slowly until very hot but not boiling.

For pineapple sauce see page 973.

Hard Sauces

These are derived from the English 'senior wrangler' sauce and are popular in America. They are good with steamed puddings and may vary in flavour to contrast with that of the pudding. The following is a basic recipe, and the various flavours may be beaten in at the finish.

4 oz. unsalted butter	4$\frac{1}{2}$ oz. castor, soft brown, or icing sugar [1]

Flavourings

vanilla essence, or vanilla sugar and the seeds from a vanilla pod	the same of lemon
	2 tablespoons fresh raspberry or strawberry purée
grated orange rind and a tablespoon of the juice	coffee essence
	cinnamon and mixed spices

Cream butter very thoroughly. If hard, warm the bowl in hot water, but avoid putting it in the oven. Add sugar gradually, beating well. Before adding the last spoonful or two of sugar add the flavouring called for by degrees. Serve piled in a dish or spread out, hardened and cut into blocks.

[1] Any of the above sugars can be used for these hard sauces. It is a matter of taste whether a slightly gritty finish is preferred or a perfectly smooth one.

BRANDY BUTTER (SENIOR WRANGLER SAUCE)
traditional with plum pudding and mince-pies

3 oz. good unsalted butter	2–3 tablespoons brandy
3 oz. fine castor sugar	

Cream butter until white. Beat in sugar gradually; when thoroughly mixed add the brandy a few drops at a time, beating continuously. Add enough to flavour well, taking care towards the end that the mixture does not curdle. It should now look white and foamy. Pile up in a glass dish and leave to harden.

Alternatively the mixture may be spread about half an inch thick on a dish. When firm and set it is cut into small blocks and piled up in a small dish for serving.

RUM BUTTER
served with rich fruit puddings, baked apples, baked bananas, and mince-pies

3 oz. butter	a little grated lemon or orange
3 oz. soft brown sugar	rind
¼ gill rum (approx.)	a squeeze of lemon juice

Cream the butter thoroughly, beat the sugar in by degrees with the grated rind and lemon juice. Then add rum to flavour well.

Other Sweet Sauces

WALNUT BUTTERSCOTCH
served with apple compôtes, purées, or baked apples

2 tablespoons golden syrup	¼ pint water
1 tablespoon soft brown sugar	½ teaspoon custard powder
¼ oz. butter	2 tablespoons walnut kernels
the juice of ½ lemon	

Put the syrup, sugar, and butter into a small pan and cook to a toffee brown. Add the water, bring to the boil, and pour on to the custard powder slaked with a dessertspoon of water. Reboil, and add the lemon juice. Toast the walnuts, break them up and add to the sauce.

SAUCE SABAYON (1) (HOT)
for hot sponge or fruit puddings

3 yolks of egg	1 wineglass white wine, sherry,
3 oz. castor sugar	or fruit juice

Beat the yolks with the sugar until white. (A pinch of arrowroot may be added to the sugar to prevent the mousse falling.) Add the wine or juice and whisk vigorously, standing the bowl in a roasting-tin of hot water. Bring to the boil, still continuing to whisk until the sauce becomes thick. Remove from the heat and beat for another few minutes. Serve at once, as the mousse is likely to fall unless arrowroot has been added.

SAUCE SABAYON (2) (COLD)

served with sugared fruit, fruit jellies, and apple charlotte

This may be made with the above recipe plus an extra yolk.   Beating is then continued over ice until the sauce is thoroughly chilled.

SAUCE SABAYON (3) (COLD)

(alternative method)

2 yolks of egg
2 oz. sugar
½ gill water
the rind of ½ lemon and the
   juice of a whole

2 tablespoons rum or sherry
2 tablespoons or more whipped
   cream or evaporated milk

Put the sugar and water together in a small pan.   Boil until a thread will form between the finger and thumb.   Pour on to the beaten yolks and whisk until thick and mousse-like.   Add the grated lemon rind, the strained juice, and the rum or sherry.   Whisk for a minute or two, then gently whisk in the cream.   Chill well.

SAUCE SABAYON (4)

served with Fig Pudding (see page 1018) and other rich steamed puddings

2 tablespoons castor sugar
2 large eggs
1 teaspoon vanilla

the grated rind of 1 lemon
2 tablespoons sherry

Put sugar, yolks, vanilla, and grated rind into a bowl standing in a pan of hot water.   Beat until pale in colour and smooth.   Add sherry, renew the hot water in the pan, and whisk until light and fluffy.   Beat the egg whites till stiff and fold them in.

See also Iced Zabaione, page 944.

SAUCE MOUSSELINE (HOT)

served with steamed or baked sponge puddings; to be made immediately
before being served

1 whole egg
1 yolk
1¼ oz. castor sugar

2 large tablespoons sherry,
   rum, orange juice, or strong
   coffee, this last strengthened
   with coffee essence

Put all together into a bowl.   Whisk over very hot water until thick and frothy.   Use as soon as possible, but if it has to wait whisk it for a minute before serving.

CARAMEL SAUCE
for various sweets, ice-cream, and apple dishes, etc.

4 oz. loaf or granulated sugar, and enough water to form a syrup	an extra 1½ gills water a few drops of lemon juice

Put the sugar and water for the syrup into a thick saucepan, allow to dissolve over a gentle heat, stirring from time to time with a metal spoon. When completely melted boil rapidly without stirring until a pale golden colour. Decrease heat and continue boiling to a good caramel (a rich brown). Remove at once from heat and hold bottom of pan for a moment in cold water to check the boiling.

Add the 1½ gills water carefully and by degrees. Return to the heat and allow water and syrup to amalgamate. Then reboil and add lemon juice to flavour.

This sauce is generally used cold, when it should have the consistency of thick syrup. This is determined by the amount of water added, and if when boiling the liquid is too thin and watery it must be reduced until the right consistency is reached.

If a hot caramel sauce is called for it is best to make a butterscotch sauce (see page 186). Omit the walnuts and thicken with arrowroot in place of custard powder. This will give a clear sauce.

JAM SAUCE
for beignets soufflés, castle and steamed puddings, and various sweet dishes

When serving a jam sauce with a pudding, the best method is to warm the jam, taking care that it does not become too hot, and serve it as it is in a sauce-boat. If a more economical sauce is called for the following recipe may be used:

3 large tablespoons jam ¼ pint fruit juice or water	1 teaspoon arrowroot or corn-flour, slaked with a dessert-spoon of water a few drops of lemon juice

Put the jam and fruit juice or water into a pan. Bring to the boil, simmer a few minutes. Draw aside, add the arrowroot, reboil, and finish with the lemon juice.

For mincemeat sauce see page 973.

VII

Root Vegetables

In writing emphatically about the cooking of vegetables, I am half afraid that I may alienate a sympathetic ear, because so much has already been said and written on the subject. Perhaps when the young, for whom this book is intended, are grown up, great changes will have taken place in English kitchens, and cooking may have become an accredited art with all its component materials given proper and informed consideration. In the meantime it is not like that, and the general English public resignedly accepts badly cooked vegetables and is reluctant concerning new introductions, so perhaps I may be allowed to follow at least one line of thought for a moment.

Vegetables, for the most part, are in some degree edible before being cooked, a characteristic which does not distinguish all other foods. Although I know that children like to scrape out uncooked cake mixture from a mixing bowl, most of us could not contemplate testing uncooked fish, meat, or poultry, or even raw egg, and yet we eat raw peas, nibble a bit of juicy cabbage stalk, and eat grated raw root vegetables with pleasure. This may sound irrelevant, but is it? In the cooking of vegetables to make them more digestible, special care must be taken to avoid destroying their intrinsic fresh and delicate flavour.

Most root vegetables are delicious eaten raw in grated form (as indeed are cabbage, cauliflower, and sprouts), but not so easily digested as when cooked. If this quality of freshness and delicacy is borne in mind it may help us to avoid the common sins, such as choosing them when they are too old, keeping them too long in the store, overcooking them, and cooking them too soon and then keeping them half warm. I think one should start with the idea that all vegetables can be luxuries—not just asparagus and early peas, but even the common cabbage when treated with respect—and that their pre-eminent quality is that of delicacy. Think for a moment of one of the most universally eaten of all vegetables, the potato. Quite a few people think of this as a sort of filling, something to eat with meat to assuage hunger. Yet potatoes have a subtle flavour, a perfume almost, when perfectly cooked, which is particularly noticeable in a potato very well baked in its skin, or perfectly boiled. But certain culinary atrocities can give potatoes a nauseous taste. Even the delicate and delicious taste of asparagus can be rendered unpleasant by a careless cook. To take a further instance, consider the small Italian zucchini, like the smallest baby marrow, finished in a little butter with herbs, and compare

189

this with large slabs of mature vegetable marrow blanketed in a tasteless gloy.   Think of large Brussels sprouts, strong and watery, and then of tiny ones, slightly cooked and then sautéd; think even, if you like, of perfectly mashed potatoes, smooth, light, well flavoured, with perhaps a touch of grated orange, and then of the lumpy porridge which is sometimes offered under the same name.   I know that arguments of economy will be levelled, but they can only be accepted as just when some of the more glaring wastefulnesses of the ordinary English kitchen are eliminated. We are lucky that our climate produces good and tender vegetables, and now that the kitchen comes more closely under the personal concern of the mistress of the house, I believe that there is hope that criminology in the vegetable world will decline and the horrible joke of 'meat and two veg.' will no longer mean anything.

For convenience, the subject of vegetables is divided under the headings of root, green, and flowers and fruits.

Root vegetables should be washed and lightly scrubbed with lukewarm water with a vegetable brush to remove any sand or earth before peeling or scraping.   After this they should be put into fresh, cold water.   Except for onions, all root vegetables should be peeled with a potato-peeler, which is more economical than a knife, and a vegetable knife should be used for trimming.   A potato-peeler suitable for left-handed people is now on the market.   After peeling, root vegetables should be put into fresh, cold water immediately, and in the case of Jerusalem artichokes, salsify, and celeriac a teaspoon of vinegar or lemon juice may be added to the water to prevent discoloration.   When you are directed to slice the vegetables, this should be done on a board and not over a saucepan, and the slicing should be even and of the thickness indicated in the recipe.   For shredding, chopping, and dicing the instructions given for each should be followed. If one is tempted to adopt more casual and slapdash methods the results are apt to be less satisfactory.

Cooking and blanching

Generally speaking, root vegetables are put into cold water and brought to the boil, and salt is added in about 1–1½ teaspoons to a quart of liquid; they are simmered until cooked with the lid on the pan, then drained and returned to the pan to dry, and they are then ready for the addition of butter, seasoning, and flavouring, or to be finished off in any way called for in the recipe.   Certain root vegetables are submitted to a preliminary blanching.   This is done in order to eliminate a strong taste and, as in the case of celeriac, to whiten.   They are put as before into cold water, brought slowly to the boil, allowed to boil for two or three minutes or whatever length of time is indicated, and they are then ready to be used in various ways.

Root vegetables are particularly suitable for fritters and for soufflés of various kinds.   Not everybody knows how good are the shoots which spring from these roots when they have wintered in a sand-pit.   They are delicate in flavour and are excellent eaten raw in salads. They may be cooked in much the same way as asparagus—tied up in bundles and simmered in boiling salted water till tender. Noisette butter is a good accompaniment, or they may be served cold with a vinaigrette sauce.

As a rough guide it may be taken that one pound of root vegetables (with the exception of potatoes) will serve four people.

BEETROOTS

Small roots are better in texture and flavour than very large ones, and for those who have gardens it is a good idea to sow a small quantity in succession and pick them when of medium size. For winter storage, of course, they must grow to their full size. Beetroots should be washed carefully in tepid water, care being taken not to bruise or break the skin. The roots should not be cut and the leaves at the top should be shortened only. If one root should be cut by mistake, it may be sealed by singeing.

Beetroots may be put into boiling salted water, and they take anything from one to four hours to cook, according to size. The best test is to remove a root from the water, press gently with the fingers, and if the skin slides off cooking is complete. They may be baked in the oven, in which case they are wrapped in oiled paper and take roughly the same time to cook. Beetroots probably take their most elegant form in the Russian soup called bortsch. In the salad chapter (page 344) recipes will be found for beetroots served cold. When to be served hot they need for most palates some acidity to counteract their sweet taste.

'PIQUANTE' BEETROOT

2 large cooked beetroots	1 tablespoon sugar
2 tablespoons vinegar	freshly ground black pepper
1 teaspoon salt	½ oz. butter

Peel and chop or mince the beetroots. Put into a pan, add seasoning and vinegar, and cook over a moderate fire until really hot, stirring all the time. Allow to simmer rather than boil, draw off the fire, add the butter in small pieces, then taste and adjust seasoning. The best should be lightly piquant in flavour and very well seasoned. This is an excellent dish with a ragoût, cottage pie, or rissoles.

BEETROOT WITH CAPERS

2 large cooked beetroots or 12–15 baby ones	grated rind of a lemon
1 oz. butter	1 tablespoon chopped chives
salt	1 dessertspoon chopped parsley
freshly ground pepper	juice of ½ lemon
1 teaspoon sugar	1 large tablespoon capers

Dice the beetroots if large, but leave the baby ones whole, merely rubbing off the skins. Melt the butter in a stew-pan, and when just beginning to colour add beetroots, seasoning, sugar, and lemon rind. Shake and turn until thoroughly hot, then add chives, parsley, capers, and lemon juice, cook for another minute, and serve piping hot.

Here is a good nursery dish of beetroot and potatoes:

1 oz. butter	2 cooked beetroots, finely sliced
2 sliced onions, shallots, or leeks	1–2 tablespoons vinegar
1 oz. flour	mashed potatoes, a purée of potatoes and celeriac, or old-fashioned bubble-and-squeak
salt and pepper	
1 teaspoon sugar	freshly ground black pepper for the top
½ pint milk	

Put the butter in a frying-pan, add onions, shallots, or leeks, and cook gently to soften without allowing them to colour. Sprinkle in the flour and cook for a minute or two. Add seasoning, sugar, and milk. Simmer for a few minutes, put in the beetroots, sprinkle with the vinegar. Make a ring of mashed potato and pour the beetroot mixture into the middle. Make the whole thing very hot and sprinkle with freshly ground black pepper before serving.

Golden brown croûtons are an agreeable addition and make the dish more substantial. Or the beetroots may be cooked, sliced, and served with the piquante sauce given for carrots on page 194.

The flavour of orange associates well with beetroot and the flesh is a good addition to a salad; it may also be used with a little shredded peel and a little juice in the above dishes.

CARROTS

Old carrots are first washed, and then peeled thinly with a potato-peeler. This ensures a smooth surface and the minimum amount of peel being removed. When these large carrots are to be cut or shaped, it is desirable to avoid using the inner part of the core, which has very little flavour and not a very good appearance.

For shredding or cutting in julienne strips or in dice they should first be sliced lengthwise, the pithy core discarded, then with the flat surface downwards they should be cut into the shape required.

It may be noted that dice for a mirepoix are smaller than those for a macédoine. For the latter they are about the size of dice used in games, and for a mirepoix considerably smaller.

Old carrots are indispensable for the basis of soups and sauces, but perhaps are less suitable for vegetable dishes than the smaller ones. There are, however, some good dishes to be made from them. To boil old carrots is perhaps to serve them in the least attractive way. More satisfactorily they may be well flavoured and seasoned and made into a purée with potatoes, or served as Carottes Vichy or à la Poulette. They may also be cut, shaped, and cooked as for Carottes Glacées.

PURÉE OF CARROTS

A good purée may be made by boiling old carrots and adding an equal quantity of mashed boiled potato, plenty of black pepper and salt, chopped parsley, butter, and a little grated orange rind.

CAROTTES VICHY

1 lb. even-sized carrots	1 lump of sugar
1 gill water	chopped parsley
butter the size of a walnut	freshly ground pepper
seasoning	

Wash and prepare carrots. Cut into really thin rounds. Put into a pan with water at the bottom, add the butter, seasoning, and sugar. Press a piece of buttered paper down on to the carrots, cover the pan and cook gently until tender (about 20 minutes). By this time the liquid should have disappeared, and the carrots should have begun to cook gently in the butter and become lightly rissoléd. Now sprinkle with parsley and fresh pepper.

This dish may be made more important and, perhaps, suitable for a separate course if the carrots are surrounded by small glazed onions.

An alternative method of cooking is:

Take the same ingredients as above, and increase the amount of water, putting in sufficient just to cover the carrots. Cook fairly rapidly with the lid off the pan until the liquid is reduced to about a good tablespoon and the carrots are glistening. Finish as before.

CAROTTES A LA POULETTE

Cook carrots as for Carottes Vichy (second method), drain off liquid, add ¼ pint sauce poulette (see page 154). Shake gently to mix thoroughly and serve at once without reboiling.

Young carrots should have the green tops trimmed to within only a quarter of an inch of the top; they are scraped and not peeled. If they are really young it will probably be enough to rub them with a rough cloth. A little coarse salt will help, or they may be plunged for a moment into boiling water and then rubbed in a cloth. Young early carrots are a luxury and are best cooked quickly and with delicate flavouring. They may be glazed, that is to say blanched and finished off with butter, with a light sprinkling of sugar, and served mixed with finely chopped herbs (mint in particular is good) and a little lemon juice.

For these or for medium-sized carrots the following sauce is excellent, and it may also be used with other root vegetables.

PIQUANTE SAUCE FOR VEGETABLES

for carrots, turnips, zucchini, broad beans, etc.

1¼ oz. butter
2 oz. onion, finely sliced
¾ oz. flour
2 cloves of garlic crushed with salt
¾ pint vegetable stock
salt
1 saltspoon freshly ground pepper
a pinch of ground cloves

a pinch of ground allspice
the rind of ½ lemon, grated, and the juice of 1 lemon
a pinch of sugar

Liaison
1 egg yolk
½ gill cream

1 dessertspoon finely chopped parsley

Melt butter, add onion, and allow to soften without colouring. Add flour and cook gently to a roux blond, or straw-coloured roux. Draw aside, add the garlic, stock, seasoning, and spices. Return to heat and stir over the fire until boiling. Simmer 7–10 minutes, stirring occasionally. Add the lemon rind and juice and sugar. Continue simmering another 2–3 minutes. Mix the yolk and cream together, and add to the sauce off the fire. Adjust seasoning, reheat carefully, and finish with the parsley.

N.B. Wine vinegar may be used in place of lemon juice.

CAROTTES GLACÉES

Choose short, stumpy carrots for this, such as Sutton's Golden Horn. Large carrots may be used, but after peeling they must be cut into rounds about an inch long, then cut again into small quarters lengthways, shaped, and smoothed, the core part being trimmed off with care.

¾ lb. carrots, weighed after trimming
¾ oz. butter
½ pint good veal or chicken stock (approx.)

freshly ground black pepper
1 dessertspoon sugar
finely chopped mint (optional)

Put the prepared carrots into a saucepan with the rest of the ingredients. The stock should just cover, and for that reason it is best to use a deep rather than a shallow saucepan. Cover the pan and allow to cook on a moderate fire 20–25 minutes. By this time the carrots should be tender and the liquid practically reduced to a glaze. Watch carefully during the last part of the cooking to see that they do not catch or burn. They should be bright and glistening when finished. These carrots may with advantage be finished off with finely chopped mint.

CELERIAC OR ROOT CELERY

This is not an easy root to peel cleanly, because of its uneven surface. After being washed carefully it may be cut in thick slices, and then the peel is more easily removed and one can see exactly how much to take off. Celeriac is often used in hors-d'œuvres, being first blanched and brought just to boiling-point, then cut in julienne strips and served with a well-seasoned French dressing. It is valuable as a grated raw vegetable.

For hot dishes it is cooked first for about three-quarters of an hour, the time depending on the size of the roots and their age. It is excellent with the piquante sauce already given, or after cooking it may be finished off by being fried in a little butter and served with lemon juice and chopped parsley. If to be eaten as a purée it should be diluted with an equal quantity of purée of potato. Celeriac makes excellent fritters and is good as one of the ingredients in the dish Fritto Misto given on page 276.

CELERIAC PURÉE

Boil the celeriac unpeeled in salted water till quite tender when tested with a skewer. Peel and pass through a sieve. Mix the purée with an equal quantity of mashed potatoes and season very well. Pile in the centre of a hot dish, garnish with croûtons tossed in butter. Pour round it a little good gravy or brown sauce.

JAPANESE ARTICHOKES (CRÔSNES)
Stachys tuberifera

These are small, irregular tubers of delicate flavour which should be eaten while fresh, for they do not keep well. If newly taken from the ground the delicate skin may be removed by rubbing them well in a cloth with rough salt, or they may be plunged for a moment in hot water to soften the skin. They are difficult to peel because of their irregularity, but if this is necessary a small sharp-pointed knife is required. They may be plunged into a pan of boiling salted water and cooked for 10–15 minutes uncovered. It is easy to overcook them; they should be firm and not broken into pieces. After careful draining they are ready for finishing in butter (preferably beurre noisette with a little lemon juice) or with a good cream sauce.

JAPANESE ARTICHOKES A LA CRÈME

2 lb. Japanese artichokes	salt, pepper, and a touch of
1¼ oz. butter	nutmeg
lemon juice	½ pint rich milk
	2–3 tablespoons thick cream

Blanch the artichokes for 5–6 minutes in boiling salted water. Melt butter in a pan, add artichokes and lemon juice and cook gently 7–8 minutes. Add milk and seasoning, cover and simmer 10–15 minutes. Add cream and serve at once.

If to be cooked in a cream sauce, the following recipe is useful:

Cook them for 5 minutes in boiling water. To 1 lb. of crôsnes allow 1¼ oz. butter. Put this into a saucepan, put in the drained artichokes, add a few drops of lemon, and continue cooking for 7–8 minutes. Then add ½ pint thin cream, season with salt and pepper and a touch of nutmeg, cover the saucepan, and boil for 10–15 minutes.

These small and nutty crôsnes are good for salads.

JERUSALEM ARTICHOKES

This vegetable is not an artichoke, nor is it particularly associated with Jerusalem. It is a member of the sunflower family, and Jerusalem is probably a corruption of girasol, an old name for sunflower.

Writing a very long time ago, the great Soyer praised this vegetable highly, saying that it was not appreciated as it should be, and one wonders whether the position is really better now than it was then. All too often it is cooked in an unsuitable way, boiled in water and served in an indifferent white sauce, and then dismissed, as well it may be, as a slithery, unappetizing dish.

For those who grow their own vegetables it may be interesting to know that there is a good variety of this vegetable called Fuseau. In his list of 'Vegetables for Epicures' Mr George Bunyard of Maidstone refers to it as 'a very refined edition.' It is of slightly different texture and flavour from the common variety, closer and creamier, and it has a less uneven surface, which makes it easier to prepare.

When this root is to be used for fritters or a soufflé, or for any dish in which preliminary blanching is called for, the cooking may, at need, be done in water, but if it is to be served hot in a sauce it is better that the cooking should not be carried out in water.

The following recipe for cooking it in butter sounds extravagant, but it is not really so if you set aside the surplus butter poured off after the first stage of the cooking for use later.

1½ lb. artichokes	1½ oz. butter

Sauce

½ oz. flour	salt and pepper
½ oz. butter	nutmeg
a short pint of milk or milk and water	
a little freshly ground black pepper	

Cut the artichokes up into suitably sized pieces. Heat the butter in a pan, add the artichokes, and toss well over a good fire. After a few minutes cover the pan and put it over moderate heat, or preferably in a medium oven, for about 15–20 minutes, giving the contents an occasional gentle stir. In the meantime prepare the sauce as follows: Melt the butter, add the flour, cook for a minute or two. Add the boiling liquid, then salt and pepper and a dash of nutmeg, and bring to the boil. Now drain off the butter from the artichokes, pour the sauce over them, and let the whole cook gently for about 15–20 minutes. A little of the butter which was drained off earlier may be added at the last moment, and the pan shaken gently to mix the whole. Just before serving sprinkle with the black pepper.

If it is not possible to spare butter for this purpose, the artichokes may be simmered in milk (preferably) or milk and water and finished off with butter, lemon juice, and parsley.

Roast Jerusalem artichokes are excellent: they may be cooked round the meat, being put in the hot fat half an hour before the end of cooking; or the raw vegetable may be shaved thinly and cooked in deep fat in a frying basket like potato chips; or the root, blanched, may be dipped in batter or egged and breadcrumbed and turned into fritters. Slices of artichoke that have been cooked gently in milk make an excellent salad; they are also good raw. The French name for Jerusalem artichokes is 'topinambours,' and here is a French recipe for cooking them:

TOPINAMBOURS VELOUTÉS

1½ lb. artichokes	salt
½ pint water	2 tomatoes
¼ pint milk	1 oz. butter
8 'pickling' or button onions, well blanched for 5–7 minutes	1 oz. flour
	seasoning
¼ bay-leaf	chopped parsley

Wash and peel the artichokes, cut into pieces the size of a walnut, and, as you do so, put them at once into cold water containing a little vinegar. Have ready a saucepan containing ½ pint water and ¼ pint of the milk called for in the recipe. Add the onions, the bay-leaf, and the salt. Put in the artichokes, cover the pan, and simmer for 20–25 minutes. Peel the tomatoes, squeeze gently to remove the seeds, and slice. Melt the butter in a saucepan, add the flour off the fire, and strain off ½ pint of the liquor from the artichokes; reboil, add the remaining milk, re-season, and simmer for a few minutes. Drain the artichokes (removing bay-leaf), return to the pan, pour over the sauce, add the tomatoes and chopped parsley, and allow to simmer a minute or two before serving.

ONIONS

There are four principal kinds of onion: pickling onions, shallots, ordinary or all-purpose onions, and Spanish onions.

Pickling onions

These are small round onions and are always served whole; they are used chiefly for garnitures, braises, and sautés, besides being pickled.

Shallots

These are roughly the same size as pickling onions, but are oval in shape, slightly purple in colour, and of milder flavour.   They are nearly always used chopped and sliced for flavouring sauces, farces, sautés, etc., but the bigger and better-shaped ones may be used for garnitures.

Ordinary all-purpose onions

These are best when two to three ounces in weight, and are used for most purposes, chopped or sliced.

Spanish onions

These are very large but mild in flavour.   They are mostly used whole for boiling or braising, or they are cut into rings for frying.

Except for chopped shallots or onions used as a flavouring, all onions may be blanched, either whole if for braising or for garnishes, or when sliced if for frying.   To blanch onions put into cold water, bring to the boil, boil for 2–3 minutes, then drain and dry.

Cooking time: 20 minutes to an hour according to size; 2 hours for large braised onions.

Preparation

Slice the onion cleanly through at top and bottom and peel off the brown skin with a vegetable knife.   If strong they may be peeled under water, but they should not be kept there longer than is absolutely necessary. Small onions are not easy to peel and may be scalded in the same way as tomatoes, but first they must be topped and tailed; they are then placed in a colander and submerged in boiling water for a minute or two: this facilitates the removal of the skins and is less painful to the eyes.   There are two ways of cutting and slicing an onion and, where specific directions are not given, here are useful guiding points.

1. If, in the finished dish, you wish to see traces of onion, it should be cut as follows: Cut the onion longways from top to bottom.   Then slice in such a way that each piece has a small portion of the root end on it. This will hold the flesh together, and some portion of the onion will be visible in the finished dish.

2. If, on the other hand, you want all the onion to disappear and not be obvious in the finished dish, it should be cut in two as before from top to bottom, the flat side laid on the table, and slicing started at the crown end.

If you wish to cut your onion so that you have a complete set of slices and not half-slices, it is advisable to cut a thin piece off one side of the onion and lay the flattened side on the table; in this way the onion will not slip.

Where an onion is to be used in large pieces, as for a ragoût or goulash, it should be cut so that a small portion of the root end attaches to each piece. In this way the onion will not open out and disappear into the dish.

To chop an onion

The onion should be cut lengthwise from root to stem, then if the flat surface is put downwards on the board it will not slip about. It may then be sliced finely lengthwise, cut again in the opposite direction, and chopped to the required fineness. Or, having set the flat surface downwards, you may make a series of lengthwise cuts (but not quite the whole way through to the root end), then two or three horizontal cuts, and the onion will fall apart in neat cubes. This way of working is not just a frill. Some people find this proceeding trying to the eyes; the less cut surface of the onion exposed, the less tears.

BRAISED SPANISH ONIONS

Take good-sized Spanish onions, blanch, and cook them until tender in salted water for 1–1½ hours, according to the size. Drain, lift out the heart of the onion; chop this up, put it into a frying-pan with a little hot fat and allow it to colour, adding chopped mushrooms and a little salt and good seasoning. Put this back into the onion, dot with butter, and finish in a baking-pan in the oven. Or the onions may be blanched for 15 minutes, the centres taken out, the fillings put in, and the onions braised for 1½–2 hours in a little good brown stock in the oven.

BRAISED ONIONS (SIMPLE METHOD)

Parboil onions as above, drain well, set in a well-buttered dish, pour over melted butter—about 1½ oz. butter to 4 onions is a reasonable quantity, and this may be replaced by 1 oz. bacon fat—sprinkle with castor sugar and salt and pepper and bake in a moderate oven, basting well till tender and of good colour. A little stock may be added during cooking if the onions become dry.

FRIED ONIONS

Slice the onions as directed; blanch by putting into cold water, bringing to the boil, and boiling for 2 or 3 minutes. (Blanching is not necessary when a mild type of onion is being used.) Drain and dry thoroughly; heat dripping in a frying-pan, add the onions, cover with a plate, and cook slowly, turning from time to time until brown and thoroughly cooked— these are soft fried onions. To make crisp fried onions shred finely, heat fat in a deep frying-pan, put the onions in, turn constantly till brown and crisp, drain on kitchen paper, and dry off in a warm oven.

CRISP FRIED ONION RINGS

For crisp fried onion rings large Spanish onions should be taken, and it is not absolutely necessary to blanch first; if, however, they are blanched they should be made thoroughly dry. Cut the onions in ¼-inch slices, separating the rings; dip in milk, drain; dip in flour and fry in deep fat; drain again and sprinkle with salt; or the rings may be dropped into batter before being fried. These are particularly good with the Fritto Misto mentioned on page 276.

GLAZED ONIONS

Quantities for a garnish:

½ lb. small pickling onions or shallots	1 teaspoon sugar
¾–1 oz. butter	salt and pepper

Peel onions and blanch 5–7 minutes; drain well. Put into the pan with the butter, sugar, and seasoning. Cook gently with the lid on, shaking and stirring from time to time until the onions become tender and well glazed. Care must be taken that the cooking is slow or the sugar will burn.

For onions as a vegetable entrée see Chapter X, page 263.

PARSNIPS

I can remember the days when parsnips were very popular in the schoolroom. It is true that we then had plenty of good beef dripping, much more butter than we have to-day, and sugar was plentiful and cheap, so that we could do more with them without upsetting the balance of our rations. I suppose it is because of the shortage of these finishing ingredients that parsnips have fallen a little into disuse and are not so popular as they used to be, and yet in recent years we grow a much better type of this vegetable, smaller, finer in grain, and altogether less rough than they once were. But things are getting easier in every direction, and here are one or two recipes that we used to like long ago:

1. Prepare the parsnips, steam for 40 minutes to an hour till tender. Finish off in the oven in good beef dripping until brown. Sprinkle with salt and pepper, drain, and serve very hot with roast meat.

2. Boil the parsnips in their skins, thus retaining the maximum of flavour. When tender rub off the peel, brush with butter, and brown under the grill.

We particularly liked fried parsnips. After cooking, the vegetable was finished off in a frying-pan with a knob of butter and sprinkled with brown sugar. This gave it a particularly crisp and sweet taste.

Purée of Parsnips is made in the same way as Purée of Carrots. In the recipe for Fritto Misto (page 276) instructions are given for making little fritters of parsnips with half a shelled walnut on either side, but when we were young we used to have parsnips prepared in this way:

The parsnips were cooked and put through a sieve, and to a pint of purée 2 good tablespoons of butter were allowed, and plenty of seasoning. A little cream was added and the whole cooked in a pan with the lid off to allow the mixture to dry off a little. Then a beaten egg was added, the cakes were shaped, egged and breadcrumbed, and fried in deep fat. Or the purée was seasoned, beaten egg and flour added, and the cakes fried in shallow fat; or the mixture was put in scallop shells with crumbs and knobs of butter and finished off in the oven.

A purée of parsnips, dried off, may be mixed with a good béchamel sauce, and a small amount of mashed potato added.

PARSNIP GALETTE

1½ lb. medium-sized parsnips   castor sugar, salt, freshly
1½ oz. butter   ground pepper, lemon juice
2 shallots, finely chopped

Peel parsnips and boil them whole in salted water until tender. Drain. Cut them into thin slices. Take ½ oz. of the butter and cook the shallots in this until lightly coloured. Melt the remaining butter, and with part of it well brush the inside of a deep sandwich tin or small frying-pan. Dust lightly with castor sugar. Choose the larger rounds of parsnips, line the bottom and sides of the tin with them, arranging the slices in circles and allowing them to overlap. Fill the centre of the mould with the remaining parsnips, sprinkling each layer with salt, pepper, lemon juice, and the rest of the melted butter.

Cover the top with a piece of buttered paper and put to bake in a hot oven, 400° F., for 35–40 minutes or until well browned. Turn out into a hot dish. If wanted for a main course or a supper dish add thin slices of cheese when filling the mould, and pour round or serve separately tomato sauce, façon ménagère (see page 178).

POTATOES

The potato, probably because of its usefulness and cheapness, has almost become a Cinderella in the kitchens of to-day. Old-fashioned books lay much emphasis on the details of such a simple process as boiling a potato, giving instructions about careful drying off after boiling, and refraining from putting a cover on the dish for serving, lest steam should spoil both texture and flavour; and all agreeing that potatoes after peeling must lie for two hours in salt and water before being cooked. One recipe even recommends sea-water for cooking. All their advice leads towards one result, the production of mealy, white, delicately flavoured boiled potatoes. In Ireland, where potatoes are even more of a staple diet than with us, they are generally boiled in their skins, and there is no doubt that to get the utmost flavour out of a potato it should be cooked in its skin, whether boiled or baked, even if, ultimately, it is not to be served so. Mashed potatoes, for instance, have a particularly good flavour if the potatoes are baked rather than boiled before being sieved, and the base of potato soufflé is best made of baked rather than boiled potatoes.

Steaming is said to have advantages over boiling in that the vegetable loses less of its value and is more slowly cooked. On the other hand the liquor from boiled potatoes is useful in so many ways, for soups, for gravy, and even for the mixing of bread, that one could not adopt this process exclusively.

OLD POTATOES

There are three basic ways of cooking old potatoes:

    (*a*) peeled and boiled or steamed
    (*b*) boiled in their jackets
    (*c*) baked in the oven in their jackets.

(*a*) *Peeled and boiled or steamed potatoes*

Choose, if possible, potatoes of equal size. Peel them thinly with a potato-peeler. As you do so drop them into cold water containing a little salt and allow them to stay there at least half an hour, and preferably longer, before cooking. For cooking allow a tablespoon of salt to each 2 quarts of cold water. Put the potatoes into the water, bring to the boil, and allow to boil steadily and uncovered till cooked. The approximate time is from 20 to 30 minutes, or even 40 for very large potatoes. When cooked strain away the water, but do not throw it away. Return potatoes to the pan, lay a folded clean towel over the top, and set the saucepan over gentle heat for a few minutes. In this way the steam is absorbed and the potatoes dry and become floury. Towards the end of the potato season they sometimes become difficult to boil satisfactorily, disintegrating in the water before they are cooked. In this case they may be put into cold water, brought to boiling-point, allowed to boil for 7 or 8 minutes, then drained, covered with a clean cloth, the lid put on, and the potatoes allowed to finish cooking over very gentle heat. In this way they do not become waterlogged. It is customary to serve potatoes boiled plainly in this way with boiled or poached fish.

Where steaming is preferred to boiling, care should be taken that the water in the saucepan is at boiling-point before the potatoes are put into the steamer.

(*b*) *Potatoes boiled in their jackets*

Wash the potatoes, cut off a small piece at one end to prevent bursting, allow them to lie as before in cold water; put into cold salted water in a saucepan, bring to the boil, and cook until ready. Again, time according to size. Drain off the water, put a folded clean cloth over the potatoes, and dry off on a gentle heat. Allow them to dry for 5–15 minutes. Potatoes so cooked may be served in their jackets, in which case they should be dished on a clean napkin, or they may be peeled before being sent to table. The dish in which they are served should not be covered with a lid or they become watery.

Mashed potatoes and *Pommes Mousseline* differ from each other in their final texture. The method of preparation is much the same.

Pommes Mousseline may be considered mashed potatoes *in excelsis*. When finished the texture should resemble softly whipped cream. Mashed potato or potato purée is of stiffer consistency.

MASHED POTATOES (PURÉE OF POTATO) (1)

1½ lb. potatoes	1 gill boiling milk (approx.)
1 oz. butter	pepper and salt

Boil potatoes in the usual way, drain and dry thoroughly (or the potatoes may be baked in their jackets). The moment the potatoes are cooked, strain off the water and put the pan back on low heat, or in the oven for a few minutes, so that all the moisture is dried off. Have ready a folded cloth or warm plate and a wire sieve; it is important that the potatoes should be kept hot at each stage if the dish is to be perfect. Taking 2 or 3 potatoes at a time, and keeping the remainder covered, push them quickly through the wire sieve on to the cloth. Put them back into the hot saucepan and this back on to the stove. Now add a little of the hot milk, and the seasoning, and begin to beat with a wooden spoon or spatula. Add butter in small pieces and combine beating and adding milk by degrees. Beat thoroughly.

MASHED POTATOES (2)

Put the cooked potatoes through a sieve and mix with a little béchamel sauce and tomato sauce. Add finely chopped chives or watercress, or grated orange rind.

POMMES MOUSSELINE

1½ lb. potatoes	a good ½ pint boiling milk, possibly more
1 oz. butter	salt, pepper, a pinch of nutmeg

Proceed as for Mashed Potatoes 1, but by reason of the extra milk the final texture is much more liquid; indeed, enough milk to produce this effect must be added.

If butter cannot be used for Pommes Mousseline it is better to use milk only, and not to substitute margarine for butter.

Good flavourings for varying the above dishes are:

grated orange peel (excellent)	a pinch of nutmeg
finely chopped chives	finely chopped watercress
finely chopped green onion tops	

These should be put into the milk.

In the following recipe for Pommes Sicilienne the sieved potato, mixed with cooked orange, is formed into small cakes and finished in the oven. It is also very good without this final process, and pleasant to eat with salad.

POMMES SICILIENNE

½ lb. potatoes, freshly boiled	½ teaspoon sugar
1 small orange	2 tablespoons hot milk, if re-
2 shallots or 1 small onion	quired
1 oz. butter	beaten egg
salt and freshly ground black pepper	

Boil the orange in water 30 minutes. Drain. Chop the shallots finely and soften them without colouring in three-quarters of the butter in a small saucepan. Cut the orange into thin slices, remove pips. Chop finely and add to the shallots with the salt, pepper, and sugar. Cook slowly for another 7–10 minutes. Have the potatoes freshly boiled and pushed through a sieve or ricer. Add the orange mixture with the remainder of the butter and enough milk to make a firm purée. Adjust the seasoning. Divide the mixture into small pieces the size of a pigeon's egg, roll lightly between the palms of the hands, arrange on a buttered baking-sheet, flatten out with a fork, brush with beaten egg, and brown well in a hot oven 5–10 minutes. Lift off the sheet and serve overlapping, brown side uppermost.

POMMES A LA MAÎTRE D'HÔTEL

1 lb. potatoes	1 chopped shallot
1 oz. butter	salt and pepper
2 tablespoons chopped parsley	

Scrub the potatoes and boil or steam them in their skins until they are cooked, though quite firm. Remove the skin, cut the potatoes in thin slices. Melt the butter in a fireproof dish, lay in the potatoes, season, cover them with the parsley and the shallot, very finely chopped, cover, and make hot in a moderate oven for 10 minutes.

In the next recipe the potatoes are simmered in a thin milk sauce. This is a good dish to serve with salad for a simple lunch.

POMMES NORMANDE

1 lb. potatoes	chopped parsley
1 oz. butter	a sprig of thyme
2 onions	½ bay-leaf
1 tablespoon flour	freshly chopped parsley for
¾ pint boiling milk	garnish
salt and pepper	

Peel the potatoes and slice them very thinly. Heat the butter in a frying-pan, put in the chopped onions and cook to a light brown, stir in the flour, take off the heat and pour in the boiling milk. Stir until the sauce comes to the boil, add salt, pepper, parsley, thyme, and bay-leaf.   Add the potatoes to the sauce, cover, and cook very gently for half an hour.   When the potatoes are cooked remove the thyme and bay-leaf, pour all in a fire-proof dish, gratiné in a hot oven for 10 minutes, and serve in the same dish, with some freshly chopped parsley scattered on top.

POMMES A LA POULETTE

1 lb. potatoes	salt and pepper
1 oz. butter	1 egg yolk
½ pint hot milk	chopped parsley

Scrub the potatoes and boil them in their skins.   When they are barely tender remove the skins and slice the potatoes thickly.   Make the butter hot in a pan, add the potatoes and stir them very carefully for a minute or two, taking care not to break them up.   Add hot milk, salt, and pepper, cover and cook very gently for a quarter of an hour, until the liquid is reduced.   Just before serving take a little of the reduced liquid and add an egg yolk to it, return it to the pan, and reheat without boiling.   Turn out the potatoes and well sprinkle them with chopped parsley.

In Pommes Hongroise the potatoes are simmered in stock:

POMMES HONGROISE

This is good also for new potatoes.

a little butter	1½ lb. potatoes, weighed when
3 oz. finely sliced onion	prepared
1 large tablespoon tomato purée	1 teaspoon paprika
1 pint vegetable stock	salt and pepper

Place the butter in a saucepan and soften in it the onion.   Add tomato purée and stock.   Bring this to the boil and allow to simmer for a few minutes.   Then add the potatoes cut in rounds.   Season well, add paprika, cover, and cook for 20–30 minutes.

POTATO GALETTE

This is good with cold meat as an alternative to baked potatoes.

1 lb. potatoes	a little hot milk
2 oz. onion	salt and pepper
1 oz. butter	grated nutmeg
1 egg	

Boil the potatoes, drain and dry.   Push through a sieve or ricer.   Chop the onion finely, soften in three-quarters of the butter, add the potatoes, and beat up to a firm purée with the egg, hot milk, and seasonings.   Rub the remaining butter over the sides and bottom of a sandwich tin, fill with the potatoes, smooth over the top, and bake in a moderate oven for 1 hour. Turn out and cut into wedges.   The cake should be brown and crisp, and very well flavoured.

(c) Baked potatoes

Choose potatoes of an even size, the larger the better. Scrub well, bake in a hot oven 1½–2 hours. Do not have them ready too soon so that they have to be kept warm, and do not overcook them, as they shrivel and become unpalatable. If they have to be kept, cut a cross-shaped incision on the top with a sharp knife.

One of the nicest ways of baking potatoes is, after scrubbing and drying, to roll them in coarse salt and bake in the usual way. Just before serving cut a cross on the top with a sharp knife, squeeze gently so that the white of the potato appears, push in a knob of butter, and serve at once.

Here are some recipes for potatoes baked in their jackets and stuffed. Probably the nicest way of all is the following:

POMMES EN ROBE DE CHAMBRE SOUFFLÉES

6 large potatoes	3 dessertspoons cream or top
2 eggs	of milk
1½ oz. butter	salt, pepper, and a pinch of
	nutmeg

Bake the potatoes. When ready cut a thin slice off one side and take out the contents, taking care to keep the skins whole. Have a hot bowl and put the potatoes into this. Work the potatoes well with a wooden spoon, adding the butter a little at a time, then the slightly beaten yolks to which the cream has been added. Season well and finally fold in the beaten whites of egg. Refill the skins with this mixture, so that some of it appears above the top of the skin. Do not overfill the potatoes as they rise in cooking. Replace them in a hot oven for 10–15 minutes. The mixture inside will rise like a soufflé, and the potatoes should be served immediately or they will go down.

There are many ways in which baked potatoes can be turned into a satisfactory main dish for lunch. For instance, some slices of onion may be tossed in butter, the flesh of the potatoes mashed, and the onion added with other herbs and the whole returned to the skin. Of course the potato should be mashed properly with hot milk and well seasoned. Or, after the onion has been tossed in the butter, other vegetables may be added, e.g. diced carrots or turnips, a little stock poured on, and the whole simmered until the vegetables are cooked. This mirepoix, as it were, of vegetables can then be put back into the potato, either mixed in the purée or put first in the bottom of the skin and the mashed or soufflé potato put in on top.

The changes can be rung on stuffed baked potatoes. For instance, a rasher or so of bacon, fried, may be chopped up with the mashed potato; yolks of egg may be added to the purée; any kind of herb which seems useful may be added. Cheese may be incorporated with the mixture, or a little sprinkled on the top of the stuffed potato.

To roast potatoes round a joint

The potatoes should be peeled as before, parboiled for 7 minutes, dried thoroughly, heavily scored all over the surface with a fork, and then put into the hot fat round the meat, or into a separate pan of hot fat, and baked in the oven after being first basted well with the fat. If there is not sufficient good dripping from the meat, they are excellent roasted in this way in oil.

GRATIN DAUPHINOIS

1 lb. potatoes	1 small egg
1 clove of garlic	½ pint creamy milk
salt, pepper, grated nutmeg	½ oz. butter
1 oz. grated cheese	a little extra grated cheese

Butter a fireproof dish, then spread in it a clove of garlic crushed under the blade of a knife with a little salt. Peel the potatoes, slice them paper thin, and lay them in the dish in regular rows, seasoning between each row with salt, pepper, grated nutmeg, and cheese. Beat the egg, bring the milk to the boil and pour over it. Pour the mixture over the potatoes, dot with small pieces of butter and a little grated cheese, and bake in a moderately hot oven for three-quarters of an hour.

POMMES NOISETTE

In this the potatoes, after blanching, are cooked in a covered pan in beurre noisette (see page 169), and are soft and rich.

1 lb. potatoes	salt and pepper
2 oz. butter	a squeeze of lemon juice

Scoop out the potatoes with a potato cutter, put in cold salted water and bring to the boil. Blanch for 2–3 minutes, drain well, and dry off. Melt the butter in a shallow pan, and when just beginning to turn colour add the potatoes. Cover the pan and continue cooking, shaking the pan occasionally, for about 7 minutes. Remove the lid, increase heat, season lightly, add a squeeze of lemon juice, and continue shaking over the fire until the potatoes are a good brown.

For a second and quicker way the potatoes are cooked longer in water and only finished in beurre noisette. Scoop out the potatoes in the same way, blanch until just tender, drain and dry as before, and put into a noisette butter (see page 169).

POMMES RISSOLÉES

1 lb. prepared potatoes	chopped parsley
1½ oz. butter	

Choose large potatoes, peel, and scoop out from each with a large round potato cutter as many rounds as possible. The remains of the potato can be used up for soup. Keep the balls in cold water until wanted, then blanch in fresh cold water for 5–6 minutes. Drain and dry in a cloth. Take a large sauté or deep frying-pan, heat it, drop in the butter, and when foaming add the potatoes. Lower the heat and continue to sauté slowly, shaking the pan frequently, until the potatoes are an even golden brown. Dust with chopped parsley before serving.

POMMES CHÂTEAU

These are sometimes called Pommes Fondantes, and either old or new potatoes may be used.

1. Take 1 lb. prepared potatoes, 1½–2 oz. butter, salt, and freshly ground black pepper. If old, choose medium-sized potatoes, peel and quarter, then shape into large olives with a potato-peeler; if new, use medium-sized whole potatoes carefully scraped.

Dry the potatoes thoroughly in a cloth after peeling or scraping and shaping. Rinse them only if necessary, and do not soak in water. Heat a large sauté or stew-pan, put in the butter, and when really hot add the potatoes. Lower the heat and cook slowly and steadily for 20–30 minutes, shaking the pan slightly from time to time. For the first 2 or 3 minutes of cooking shake the pan gently and continuously to make sure the potatoes get well covered with butter and start to cook evenly. Season lightly during cooking. The potatoes when finished should be golden in colour and quite soft to the touch, but unbroken.

2. Use the same ingredients and prepare the potatoes in the same way. Put them into a pan of cold water to cover. Add ½ teaspoon salt, bring to the boil quickly, and boil gently 2–3 minutes. Drain well, dry, and put immediately into the hot butter. Add a pinch of salt, cover at once, and put into a slow oven 15–20 minutes. Drain, if necessary, from the butter, season lightly with salt and pepper, and sprinkle with chopped parsley.

It is advisable to use clarified butter for these potato dishes, to avoid sticking. For clarifying see page 41.

The following dish is really a potato mould, golden and crisp outside, melting inside. The potatoes are cooked throughout in butter and are not previously boiled or blanched. It is obvious therefore that the cooking has to be long and steady, and the potato slices should be cut extremely thin.

The recipe which follows gives the correct method, but with less butter than in the classic form, which calls for 5–6 oz. to 1 lb. of potatoes.

POMMES ANNA

1½ lb. potatoes   salt and pepper
2 oz. butter

Peel the potatoes thinly and shape them into cylinders, then slice finely. Butter well a small fireproof dish which has a lid, or you may use a small omelet pan. Cover the bottom of the dish with overlapping circles of potato. Arrange the first ring in the middle of the dish with the slices overlapping in one way, and in the next ring overlap the slices in the opposite way. Carry on in this manner until the whole surface of the dish is covered. Continue in this way, putting butter, pepper, and salt between each layer of potato, and have five or six layers in all. Have the butter well worked and softened, so that when you add it to the layer of potatoes it is not disarranged. Finish with butter and seasoning, and cover with a tightly fitting lid lined with a piece of buttered paper. The lid must be absolutely close-fitting. Bake in a moderate oven or on a hot-plate for about three-quarters of an hour. Test at the end of 35 minutes with a skewer. The potatoes should be soft throughout when ready. Turn out on to a fire-proof platter.

NEW POTATOES

New potatoes should be scraped and not peeled. If they are ripe and fresh the skin can be peeled off with the thumb or rubbed off with a rough cloth. If the skin is tough they may be peeled after cooking.

To boil. Put in boiling salted water with a good sprig of mint. Cook 15–20 minutes, according to size. Drain, dish, and add a piece of butter and finely chopped mint.

The following dish is good made with new potatoes and may be served on a hot side-plate to accompany cold meat for luncheon:

POMMES INDIENNE

1 lb. new potatoes (small)	1 pint milk
1 oz. butter	1 oz. flour, scant weight
1 small onion, chopped	bay-leaf, blade of mace, a few
1 level dessertspoon curry-powder	peppercorns
	salt

Parboil the new potatoes. Melt the butter in the saucepan, add the onion, cover, and soften slowly. Add the curry-powder, cook for a minute or two, add the flour off the fire, strain on to this the milk which has been brought slowly to the boil with the flavourings and salt. Stir until boiling, simmer for a few minutes, then add the potatoes and continue simmering until they are quite soft. The sauce should reduce to the consistency of cream. The bay-leaf can be left in during the cooking.

Various forms of Fried Potatoes

POTATO CROQUETTES

These must always be made with freshly boiled potatoes, never with cold left-overs.

1 lb. potatoes	additional flavouring such as
1 or 2 egg yolks	chopped herbs, grated orange
½ oz. butter	rind, picked shrimps, etc.
hot milk	beaten egg for coating
salt and pepper	dry white crumbs

Boil the potatoes and dry off well.   Push through a wire sieve, or ricer, into a warm bowl or clean warm pan.   Beat in the yolk, butter, and enough hot milk to make a fairly firm paste.   Season well.   Now add any of the additional flavourings.   Divide into small even-sized pieces on a lightly floured board and leave to cool.   Form into cork, cutlet, or ball shapes, brush over with beaten egg, and roll in the crumbs.   Before shaping, a small teaspoon of chutney may be pushed into the middle of the croquettes, and each one rolled lightly on the board to cover the filling completely. Fry in shallow or deep fat.   Use the croquettes as a garnish or as a simple first course, or serve them with salad and a suitable sauce for a simple luncheon.

POMMES A LA PROVENÇALE

Parboil 6 potatoes, cut in pieces ½ inch thick, and keep hot.   Prepare frying-pan with 2 oz. butter (or equivalent in oil) covering the bottom. Put in 2 crushed cloves of garlic, 2 sprigs of rosemary, and seasoning. Cook in the butter until golden brown in colour.   Add the potatoes and cook until golden brown on both sides.   Arrange in a pile in an earthenware dish and sprinkle with chopped parsley.   Serve hot.

The following dish of fried potatoes is good to eat with salad:

Peel and parboil some potatoes.   They should be half cooked so that they may be cut into thin slices without breaking.   Dip them first in flour, then egg and breadcrumb and fry.   They may be served with fried parsley.

For a good luncheon dish of potatoes and cheese see chapter on vegetable entrées, page 264.

POMMES LYONNAISE

1–1½ lb. potatoes	salt and pepper
2 medium-sized onions	chopped parsley
3–4 tablespoons olive oil (approx.)	

Boil the potatoes with their skins, peel and cut in thin slices.   Cut the onions in thin, even slices.   Heat the oil in a frying or sauté pan and fry the onions to a good, even brown.   Drain and keep hot on a plate.   Then add the potatoes to the pan and cook as for sauté potatoes, salting lightly. When golden brown add the onions.   Adjust seasoning and turn on to a hot dish.   Dust with chopped parsley.

SAUTÉ POTATOES

These are best made with old potatoes, new are apt to be too firm and soapy.

All butter should be used, but a mixture of oil and butter, in the proportion of ½ oz. butter to a tablespoon of oil, is quite satisfactory.   All the fat must be put into the frying or sauté pan at the beginning, and not added during the cooking.   The following quantities are approximate, and the fat should well cover the bottom of the pan. The potatoes should be freshly boiled. The difference between 'pan-fried' potatoes and sauté potatoes is clearly defined. The former are sliced cold boiled potatoes, fried quickly in a single layer in the pan and turned carefully so that they do not break. For sauté potatoes the pan may be half filled, and the whole mass of potatoes turned occasionally as they brown. The result is slightly broken potatoes, golden brown, crisp, and yet *fondant*.

1 lb. potatoes freshly boiled in their skins	salt
1½ oz. butter or 1 large table-spoon oil and ½ oz. butter	freshly ground black pepper chopped parsley

Peel the potatoes and slice them. Heat a frying or sauté pan, drop in the butter, and when foaming add the potatoes. Season well, and allow them to take colour before turning. Then turn occasionally, shaking the pan to prevent sticking, and cooking on a moderate fire. When golden brown finish with a good sprinkling of chopped parsley, and additional seasoning if necessary. Turn into a hot dish.

POTATOES FRIED IN DEEP FAT
chipped or French fried potatoes, game potatoes, straws, etc.

1. A small cube of bread dropped into fat at a moderate heat will frizzle immediately, but gently; very hot fat will show a strong blue haze.

2. If a piece of raw potato the size of an ordinary chip is dropped into fat at the higher temperature, the surface will brown quickly while the centre remains hard. For this reason chipped or French fried potatoes are usually started in fat at the lower temperature and finished in the higher.

3. If too large a quantity of potatoes is fried at one time, the temperature of the fat will be lowered too much, cooking will be slower, and you will get greasy results.

4. Whether the potatoes are being put into the fat bath in a frying basket or directly into the fat, great care should be taken not to splash. The pan should not be too full of fat or it will overflow. The basket should be lowered gently; at no time should you throw food into boiling fat.

5. Overflowing may also be caused by introducing imperfectly dried potatoes, hence the emphasis laid on drying.

6. The best kind of potatoes for frying are yellow-fleshed Dutch potatoes. One variety grown in England, called Kipfler, is especially good for this purpose.

French fried potatoes or Pommes Pont Neuf used to be sold at the corners of the streets in Paris. They are what are generally called in this country chipped potatoes. Prepared by a chef they are cut extremely carefully so that each piece is of the same thickness and length. By having all the pieces of equal dimensions one is sure of absolutely even cooking. In order to achieve this the chef peels the potato, then cuts off a slice at either end, and the rounded surfaces, so that he has an oblong brick of potato. Unless one has an immediate use for these pieces which have been cut away this is extravagant to-day, and the process is not usually carried out by the ordinary cook. The homely method, therefore, is to take the peeled potato, slice it in two, lay the flat surface on the table, and cut the potato into sticks. Better still is to cut each half into two, then into four, and then into eight. There is also a cutter which cuts a raw potato into even pieces; this can be bought quite cheaply.

The pieces should be between a quarter and half an inch thick and wide and about two to two and a half inches long. Authorities differ as to whether for chipped potatoes it is necessary to subject the pieces to preliminary soaking in cold water. If this is done they must be thoroughly dried. Washing is necessary where the potato is cut into much smaller pieces as for straw potatoes, because in such fine cutting a great deal of starch is released on the surfaces. Having peeled the potatoes and cut them into even sticks, soak and dry, or cook straight away, whichever method may be chosen. Have the fat heated to the lower temperature (i.e. the piece of bread should frizzle gently); lower the potatoes gently into this, put directly over heat to bring the fat back again to the temperature it was at when the potatoes were put in. Move the basket about very gently to stop the chips from sticking to one another. Cook at this heat for 7–8 minutes or until a stick of potato lifted out is soft under the finger. Another indication that the potato is cooked to the required degree is that the sticks float on the surface of the fat. The potatoes are removed from the fat in the frying basket and the pan returned to the fire. It is then heated to the required degree and the potatoes put back until golden brown and crisp. They are now lifted out carefully, drained, and salted, and they should not be covered. A lid over them will cause them to lose their crispness and become soft. A good plan is to have two fat baths: the first one a deep iron pan with its frying basket, which is kept at the first heat, the second, which need not be deeper than a deep frying-pan, for your hotter fat. Then take a few potatoes at a time from the first bath and finish them off in the hot fat. In many ways this is easier, the fat heating up much more quickly than if a larger quantity of potatoes had been fried.

Where very thin slices, or very thin sticks of potatoes (as in straw potatoes), are being cooked, only one frying is necessary, and the hotter temperature is required straight away. For instance, here is the method of making round wafers, sometimes called game chips, the variety often served with cocktails.

GAME CHIPS OR WAFERS

Peel the potatoes, shape into cylinders so that each slice will be approximately the same in diameter, and cut very finely, preferably on a cucumber cutter. Soak in cold water in order to remove the surface starch, and dry thoroughly. Drying is most important. Have the frying fat at the higher temperature (395° F.). Lower the slices of potato gently into this, or if a basket is not being used sprinkle them into the fat without splashing. Keep them moving about gently so that they do not stick together. After a minute or two the slices will begin to come back to the surface, which will indicate that they are nearly cooked. Watch them, and as they begin to change colour test one. They should be golden brown and crisp. Remove them gently from the fat, drain, sprinkle with salt, and serve on a folded napkin.

POTATO STRAWS (POMMES PAILLE)

Proceed in the same way as for potato chips, but this time the little sticks must be cut very much finer: about an eighth of an inch is big enough. The easiest way to cut is to slice the potatoes to the thickness of about one-eighth of an inch, lay the slices one on top of another, and cut down in widths of an eighth of an inch. The straws must now be soaked in cold water and dried thoroughly. The drying is best carried out by putting the straws into a dry cloth and swinging them to and fro as you would dry salad. After this they should be put into another dry cloth and patted until they are thoroughly dry. Lower the frying basket with the potatoes in it into the hot fat, which should be at the higher temperature. Agitate the basket gently to keep the straws as much apart as possible, and cook for 3–4 minutes. Lift the basket out, set it on a plate, reheat the fat, and lower the basket into the very hot fat for about a minute, or until the straws become golden brown and crisp. This, of course, should be done at the very last moment, and the potatoes must be served at once, as they quickly become soft.

Another variety of thinly fried potato is called Copeaux.

POMMES COPEAUX

In this case the potato is cut into fine ribbons; use a potato-peeler for this purpose, and cut round and round as you would pare an apple, as thinly as possible. Each strip may then be loosely knotted. These are fried in the same way as the straws: a preliminary cooking and a final finishing off in very hot fat a minute or two before serving.

For the following dish a firm yellow-fleshed Dutch potato or the variety called Kipfler is best.

POMMES SOUFFLÉES

These are thinly sliced raw potatoes which are fried in two lots of fat at considerably differing temperatures. They are really puffed-out chipped potatoes. The potato must be so prepared and cut that all the slices are of equal size. For this method two pans of fat are necessary, one being only at about 250° F., while the second and much hotter one must be as hot as 425° F. It is the change in temperature which causes the thin chip to puff out. The potatoes should be sliced very thinly, about an eighth of an inch, and either round or oval in form. After cutting put the slices into cold water and leave for 25 minutes. Take out and dry thoroughly, shaking first in a towel, and patting dry in a second dry towel. Put first into the fat with the lower temperature and cook there for about 3 minutes. The slices should soften but not colour. Lift them out with a skimmer, and allow them to drain and cool. A few minutes before serving plunge them into the pan of very hot fat, moving them about gently and watching for them to puff. Those which do not puff should be removed and may be put back into the fat for a second attempt. The slices should be a delicate golden colour; dry and salt before serving.

SALSIFY AND SCORZONERA

In England we separate salsify and scorzonera, or at least the seed catalogues do, and the chief attention is generally paid to the white-skinned, parsnip-like vegetable, while the black-skinned scorzonera is generally dismissed with very few words; and yet this is by far the better vegetable to eat. French authorities classify them all as 'salsifis,' putting forward very strongly the view that the black-skinned variety is the only good one to eat. There is no doubt, I think, that the flavour of the scorzonera is better than that of the white salsify. Many English books, assuming that it is the white salsify that is to be used, give directions for peeling before cooking; if, however, you have grown or bought scorzonera you should not attempt to take the black skin off at this stage. The roots are cooked and peeled afterwards and so retain all their flavour. They are then cut into three or four pieces and may be served with butter, lemon juice, and herbs, probably the nicest way of all. For this the butter should be cooked as for beurre noir (page 169). They may also be served in a really good cream sauce and, if you like, finished off *au gratin*. The root may be blanched, peeled, and used for croquettes, or the flesh may be broken up thoroughly with a fork, bound together with egg and béchamel sauce, then shaped, floured, egged and breadcrumbed, and fried in deep fat.

Here is a recipe for:

SCORZONERA A L'ITALIENNE

8 sticks of scorzonera	1 teaspoon tomato purée
juice of ½ lemon	½ gill white wine
1 oz. butter	½ pint stock
1 onion	2 tomatoes
2 mushrooms	chopped herbs or parsley
1 oz. cooked ham	a dish of grated Parmesan
½ oz. flour	cheese to hand separately
seasoning	

Cook the scorzonera in salted water with the lemon juice, simmering 45–60 minutes till tender. Then remove black skin. In the meantime melt the butter in a casserole, add the chopped onion, mushrooms, and ham, and cook slowly, stirring frequently, for 7–10 minutes. Draw aside, mix in the flour, tomato purée, and seasoning, pour on the wine and stock, and bring to the boil. Simmer 10–15 minutes with the lid off. Add the scorzonera cut in pieces, and the tomatoes skinned, quartered, and pipped, and cook for another 5 minutes. Serve sprinkled with herbs in the casserole or in a fireproof dish, and serve a dish of grated Parmesan cheese with it.

N.B. This is a good way of cooking artichokes, chicory, sea-kale, potatoes, and other root vegetables.

If scorzonera is to be served as a gratin or a purée it is better to break it up with a fork rather than put it through a sieve. It may then be mixed with a béchamel sauce, dotted with butter, sprinkled with breadcrumbs, and finished off in the oven. One pound of scorzonera serves three people.

SWEDES

These are cooked in all ways that are suitable for turnips.

TURNIPS

Young turnips may be dealt with in the same way as young carrots; they may be glazed, using the same method as that given for Carottes Glacées (page 194), blanched and finished off in butter, or fried slightly and served with lemon juice and chopped herbs. An agreeable way of serving young turnips is to peel and boil them, scoop out the centres so as to form the outer part into a cup, fry the bottom of the cup in butter in a frying-pan, make a purée with the remainder of the turnip which was scooped out, mix it with a little purée of potatoes, season very well and return it to the cup, dot with butter, add a little scraped onion, and finish off in the oven. The addition of a little lemon juice and beurre noisette is good. A sprig of rosemary fried in the pan with the butter gives a delicious flavour to this dish.

Old turnips are suitable for mashing, and when this is done the purée should be placed in a clean cloth, in order to get rid of as much moisture as possible. On the whole, for the purposes of a purée, swedes are to be preferred, but in either case the addition of a certain proportion of mashed potato is an advantage, giving a drier, lighter type of purée.

For vegetable soufflés on a base of root vegetables see section on soufflés, page 327.

VIII

Green Vegetables

GENERAL NOTES ON THE COOKING OF GREEN VEGETABLES

GREEN vegetables such as cabbage, Brussels sprouts, kale, cauliflower and so forth should be well washed in plenty of cold water and allowed to remain in salted water for a short time before cooking, then well drained on a sieve or in a colander before being plunged into boiling salted water. The reason for the draining is that, if the vegetables are introduced into the boiling water while very wet, the temperature is reduced and cooking delayed, and for most green vegetables quick cooking is desirable. Particular attention has to be paid to the washing of spinach, and this will be described in the paragraphs dealing with that vegetable (page 229). On the other hand, peas and beans gathered at home and carefully shelled may be cooked without washing, unless there are signs of insects in the shells, in which case they must be rinsed in a colander under the tap.

As a general rule green vegetables are cooked or blanched in plenty of boiling salted water with the lid off the pan, and exceptions to this are indicated in the appropriate paragraphs.

As with root vegetables, the blanching may be used to remove any strong taste, as well as to keep or improve the colour, or it may be the whole process of cooking. Sometimes, after blanching, a vegetable is refreshed in cold water (see note below on refreshing vegetables). After this blanching of perhaps 5–15 minutes the vegetables are drained, dried, and are ready for further cooking according to the recipe—braising, stuffing, or sautéing. Or the blanching may in some cases be prolonged and be the only cooking called for; in this case the vegetables are ready for finishing with butter and final seasoning. It is important not to overcook green vegetables, for they lose both taste and colour, and they should never be left, even for a moment, in the water in which they have been blanched, but should be drained immediately they are ready.

To refresh vegetables (rafraîchir)

After blanching, vegetables are sometimes submitted to cold water. This is commonly but not exclusively reserved for strong-tasting vegetables, as it takes away a certain amount of flavour. It also (and this is of importance) helps to bring up the colour of vegetables, the fresh colour of beans for example, or the redness of carrots.

216

A note may be made here of conservative methods of cooking vegetables. Modern cooks and some health specialists recommend what they call conservative cooking of vegetables, in which these are cooked in the minimum amount of water and sometimes under pressure; in this way it is considered that most vitamins and the maximum of taste are preserved. R. H. and I both like the old-fashioned method of cooking in plenty of boiling salted water, followed by draining, drying, and finishing off with butter and pepper and salt. We think it produces a delicate taste and a digestible vegetable. When butter is added to a finished vegetable in the pan care should be taken to avoid overheating, or it will oil and the good flavour will be lost. In some cases cooked butter—beurre noisette—is poured over a vegetable. The quick-drained, thoroughly dried vegetables are returned to the pan and tossed gently, so that they absorb the butter without its being allowed to get very hot; if vegetables are overcooked and imperfectly drained the butter is wasted. Excellent additions to vegetables cooked in this way are chopped herbs, lemon juice, and cream.

The recipes that follow are for vegetables to be served as an accompaniment to other dishes. Recipes for dressed vegetables, that is to say vegetables suitable for serving as a separate course, such as asparagus, sea-kale, and globe artichokes, will be found in the chapter on vegetable entrées and luncheon dishes (page 250).

BRUSSELS SPROUTS

Brussels sprouts come in for a great deal of criticism from both a gardening and a cooking point of view. Even our most appreciative and complimentary friends from overseas have told us that, though we may convert them to dishes more popular with us than with them, they will never become reconciled to Brussels sprouts. That means either that they have listened to travellers' tales about them, or that they have tasted them as one sometimes may, coarse, large, badly cooked, and probably sloppy. I suppose it is because they are fairly easy to grow, and amongst the cheaper vegetables, that they are so casually and carelessly treated by many cooks. They should be regarded, I think, as minute and delicate little cabbages, mostly heart. Cooked in the way described in Choux de Bruxelles en Cassoulettes they are fit food for a luncheon-party, and might well be served as a first course for a simple dinner. Those who have gardens and can grow this vegetable for themselves would be well advised always to look in the seedsman's catalogue for small varieties. The sprout should be solid, not at all loose or soft to the touch.

Prepare by trimming and cutting the stalks and removing two or three of the outer leaves; do not make a cross-way cut at the base of the stem as this spoils the shape and allows juice to escape. Wash well, blanch in plenty of boiling salted water for 10 minutes or until just tender. Drain thoroughly at once.   The sprouts are then ready for turning into other dishes, e.g. a la Crème, Provençale, aux Marrons, or if for a plain vegetable to be tossed up in a little butter and seasoning.   The cooking time is from 8 to 12 minutes.

BRUSSELS SPROUTS A LA CRÈME

1–1½ lb. baby Brussels sprouts   a nut of butter, salt, freshly
¼ pint single cream   ground pepper

Blanch sprouts 7 minutes in boiling salted water.   Drain thoroughly. It is very important that the sprouts are absolutely dry when added to the cream.   Care must therefore be taken not to overcook them and to allow time for draining.

Meanwhile put the cream in the pan and reduce to about half.   Add the sprouts, butter, and seasoning.   Cover pan and shake well to mix the contents thoroughly.   Set on a very low heat and simmer for a few minutes to allow the flavour of the cream to mix with that of the sprouts.

CHOUX DE BRUXELLES SAUTÉS

After cooking the sprouts drain with great care.   Heat a little butter in a saucepan, put in the well-drained sprouts, and proceed to toss and shake over a brisk fire for 4–5 minutes.   Do this by shaking the saucepan and not by using a fork or spoon.   Season well with freshly ground pepper and salt.   The sprouts will then be crisped very lightly on the outside.   Add finely chopped parsley, a squeeze of lemon, and a nut of butter divided up small.

CHOUX DE BRUXELLES AUX MARRONS

Allow half as many chestnuts as sprouts and peel as described on page 48.   Place them in a saucepan, just cover with vegetable or light meat stock, add a piece of celeriac or a stick of celery, and a teaspoon of sugar. Bring to boil, allow to simmer gently until the nuts are soft (35–40 minutes according to the size of the nuts; cooked too quickly the nuts will break up).   Remove celery, drain if necessary, mix the cooked nuts with the cooked sprouts and toss them over the fire with a little butter, as in the foregoing recipe.

PURÉE OF BRUSSELS SPROUTS

Blanch sprouts, drain, sauter in butter until tender, sieve.   Allow one part of potato purée to two of sprouts.   Mix together and beat well; add seasoning, grated nutmeg, and a little hot milk.

This purée might also be used as a base for a soufflé.

BRUSSELS SPROUTS WITH CELERIAC OR CELERY

1–1½ lb. sprouts	1 oz. flour
1 celeriac root or 1 stick of celery	¾ pint milk
1½ oz. butter	a little extra butter, melted
1 medium onion	breadcrumbs

Cook the Brussels sprouts, parboil the celeriac and chop. If stick celery is used blanch for 1 minute. Melt butter, soften onion and celeriac for a few minutes, sprinkle in the flour, dilute with the milk, add the cooked sprouts, continue cooking for a few minutes to blend the whole, and turn into a fireproof dish. Sprinkle with melted butter and crumbs and finish in a hot oven.

Towards the end of the season, when the sprouts are getting big and open, they may suitably be used for Pain de Choux de Bruxelles (made as Pain d'Épinards, page 266), or they may be creamed as for Choux à la Crème (page 220), or served in the following way:

BRUSSELS SPROUTS WITH CROÛTONS

2 lb. sprouts	seasoning
1 shallot	lemon juice
½ clove of garlic	fried croûtons
1 oz. butter	

Cook, drain, press, and chop the sprouts and set aside. Chop the shallot, crush garlic in salt. Put butter in a frying-pan, add shallot and garlic, cook gently without browning too much. Add the chopped sprouts, season well with salt, freshly ground pepper, and a good squeeze of lemon juice. Serve garnished with fried croûtons.

CABBAGES

The preliminary remarks about Brussels sprouts may apply also to cabbages. The ordinary methods of treating cabbage in England can be greatly improved upon. There are three principal kinds of cabbage, spring or summer cabbage, winter cabbage, a hard green drumhead variety, and the Savoy cabbage.

Spring cabbages are in season from May to September. This cabbage is rather pointed in shape, bright green in colour, and a more tender variety than the winter cabbage. It is, therefore, good for serving plainly boiled with melted butter, and chopped herbs as an accompanying vege-table. It is cut into quarters or eighths and blanched; the blanching is continued until the cabbage is completely cooked. It is then drained well and finished off according to the recipe. It is best served in the quarters and not cut or broken up in any way. The time for blanching is from 10–15 minutes.

Winter cabbage is in season from October to February. This might be described as an all-purpose cabbage, fairly large, hard, and round. It is suitable for salads, for stuffing, for braising, to make creamed cabbage and so forth. For an accompanying vegetable it is usually cut into coarse shreds before being blanched and cooked. When cooked it may be chopped again and well stirred over the fire with butter and seasoning. When required for braising or stuffing it may be cut into larger pieces, or even left whole, blanched for 10 minutes, then drained and refreshed. After refreshing (see note on refreshing on page 216) it should be drained and well dried before further cooking. When the white heart of winter cabbage is required for salad, it should be cut in quarters, the centre stalk partially removed, and the quarters cut across the grain in the finest possible shreds. It is then soaked for an hour or two in iced, salted water, drained, dried, and mixed with a good dressing. The cooking time for plain boiling is from 15 to 20 minutes, and for braising 40 minutes to 1 hour.

Savoy cabbage is in season from November till February and is essentially a winter cabbage. It will stand frost better than the plain variety. It is excellent for creaming or serving with a béchamel sauce. It may be used for a salad, but is not quite so good as the hard, white heart of the winter cabbage. It shrinks a good deal in cooking. The cooking time is approximately 20 minutes.

Red cabbage is in season from November to March. This cabbage is cooked differently from green cabbage and is the usual accompaniment to hare, partridge, rabbit, and sausages. It is never blanched or boiled in water, but is shredded and cooked in a casserole (an earthenware one preferably), with butter or dripping, a dash of vinegar, and a very small quantity of water or stock. The whole is well covered and stewed slowly. In some recipes apples are added towards the end of the cooking, in others dill-seed or red wine is used to flavour. Red cabbage, of course, is also used for a pickle. Cooking time is approximately 2 hours.

CHOUX A LA CRÈME

cabbage (1 large or 2 small)	1 gill cream, or ½ pint milk
2 oz. butter	reduced to 1 gill
seasoning and nutmeg	2 tablespoons boiling cream
½ oz. flour	for finishing
	fried triangular croûtons

Blanch the cabbage as described above and then chop it finely on a board. Melt 1 oz. of the butter in a wide saucepan, add the cabbage, and cook for a few minutes on the fire, stirring continuously. Remove from the fire and add seasoning, grated nutmeg, and flour, mixing all well together. Then add the cream or reduced milk, stir in, bring to the boil, and allow to simmer very gently for 20–30 minutes. Before serving add the rest of the butter in small pieces, and pour over 2 tablespoons boiling cream when the cabbage is in the dish in which it will be served. Garnish with croûtons.

CHOUX AU GRATIN

1 medium cabbage (or 2 small) 1½–2 gills béchamel sauce (long or short method, see page 155) seasoning and nutmeg	2 oz. grated gruyère cheese *For the top* breadcrumbs melted butter

Prepare cabbage and cook in plenty of boiling salted water. Drain, refresh, press well between the hands. Chop moderately finely and mix with the sauce, using sufficient to give a creamy mixture. Season well, add a little nutmeg, and simmer for 10 minutes. Add grated cheese, reserving a little for the top. Put mixture in fireproof dish, sprinkle with cheese, crumbs, and melted butter, and brown in a hot oven.

The two following recipes are for braised cabbage:

CHOU A LA LORRAINE

1 cabbage 4 oz. onions 1 tablespoon oil or 1 oz. butter 2 large tomatoes, skinned, pipped, and chopped ¼ oz. flour, scant weight	¼–½ pint stock finely chopped parsley seasoning 3 or 4 tablespoons sour cream or yoghourt

Cut cabbage in quarters, blanch 5–10 minutes. Drain well, pressing gently to remove water. Arrange in a fireproof dish. Slice onions finely, soften in oil or butter. Lift from fat, draining well, and spoon over cabbage. Put tomatoes into the fat in which the onions were fried, dust in the flour, add stock, and bring to boil, stirring continuously. Season, add parsley, and spoon over the cabbage. Cook in a moderate oven till tender, basting occasionally, for about an hour. Fifteen minutes before serving pour over yoghourt or sour cream.

The following is a recipe for red cabbage:

CHOU ROUGE A LA FLAMANDE

1 red cabbage 1 chopped onion seasoning 3 tablespoons vinegar 3 tablespoons water	4 sour apples, peeled and sliced 1 tablespoon sugar a nut of beurre manié (see page 139)

Finely shred the cabbage, put it into a very well-buttered casserole or thick pan with the onion. Season it well and pour over the vinegar and water. Cover and cook gently for 2 hours. After 1 hour's cooking add apples, together with sugar. Finish cooking and just before serving bind with beurre manié.

SAUERKRAUT (SOUR-CROUT)

This is a form of fermented cabbage much esteemed in Germany, and a classic accompaniment to Frankfurter sausages, knuckle of pork, and boiled ham or bacon. Its sourness offsets the richness of such foods, and it is considered good for digestion. It is unusual in this country to prepare the sauerkraut at home, although a method of doing so will be given; more often it is bought at good delicatessen stores or in tins.

To cook sauerkraut

(1 lb. kraut is considered sufficient for 4–5 people.) Plunge sauerkraut into boiling salted water or stock. Boil 30–40 minutes. Drain well, return to the pan with a knob of butter or bacon fat and plenty of freshly ground pepper.

Alternative method. Boil the sauerkraut as above for 10 minutes only. Drain well. Take (for about 1 lb. sauerkraut):

½ oz. bacon fat (or a slice of pickled pork or a blanched rasher of streaky bacon cut into lardons)
1 medium-sized onion, finely sliced
1 medium-sized carrot, finely sliced

seasoning
1 bay-leaf
1–1½ gills stock (approx.) (a small quantity of white wine or cider may be used with the stock, half and half)

Choose a thick pan or casserole. Melt the fat, add the vegetables, and rissolé gently 5–6 minutes. Now put in the well-drained kraut with plenty of seasoning and the bay-leaf. Moisten with the stock, put a round of buttered paper firmly over the cabbage, cover the pan tightly, and simmer on a low heat or braise in a slow oven about an hour.

For those who like their kraut fairly sharp, the preliminary boiling for 10 minutes is omitted.

If prepared sauerkraut is bought in tins it is improved by a little further cooking at home.

To make sauerkraut at home it is essential to have the proper solid white cabbage. Cut each cabbage in quarters. Cut out the stalk and shave the cabbage into wafer-thin slices. Put in layers in a wooden tub or jar, strewing well with salt, and with a light sprinkling of coriander (optional). Put a cloth or piece of muslin on the cabbage, a large plate or cover on the top, and a moderate weight on that. Leave to ferment about 4–6 weeks, turning every few days.

CELERY

Celery is supposed to be in season from September to February, but is always at its best after the first few frosts. Probably it is most popular eaten raw, and for this purpose should be prepared as follows: All outer or broken sticks should be removed, and the root shortened and cut to a slight point. (No portion of this solid part, beyond the surface parings, should be discarded. If not required to be eaten raw it may be sliced or diced and lightly cooked as a garnish for soups or a salad.) The celery should be cut directly in two and then in quarters. It must be washed with great care, the stems being pulled apart so that the water from the tap can pour through them. The green tops should be cut off, and the moment the celery is prepared it should go into ice-cold water until it is served.

For curled celery see page 48.

Cooked celery

Cooked celery is one of the most delicious of vegetables, but suffers a little from the maltreatment of some cooks, who take the view that the stems removed from the heart are good enough for braising. When we were young children in the nursery we used to be given these sticks braised or boiled, or cooked in white sauce, and they gave me a distorted view of what braised celery could be like. The outside stems should be scrubbed clean, put into cold water, and used for soups and stock. In whatever way it may be cooked, celery should first be blanched by being plunged into boiling water and allowed to remain in it for 10 minutes after boiling-point has returned, undisturbed in the pan. It should then be drained and dried and have the tops lightly tied together before further cooking. The very simplest way of preparing it is to continue the blanching until the celery is cooked, and then to serve it with a good white sauce. The disadvantage of this is that celery cooked without any fat in the preliminary stages is apt to be dry. When the celery is properly braised, fat is incorporated with it in the cooking at an early stage; this has the effect of making it very luscious and soft.

Braised celery

Here is a classic method of braising which illustrates this point. Take for choice short heads of celery, as these fit better into the saucepan. According to the thickness of the root allow a whole or half a head per person: 1 head per person if very small. Remove the outer leaves as before, shorten the green tops down to the white part, and pare the root, shaping it to a point (keep débris for soups and stocks). Plunge the prepared heads whole into boiling water for blanching, and allow 10 minutes after boiling-point is renewed. To 6 heads of celery allow 2–3 oz. dripping or chopped-up bacon rind, a small carrot, 2 onions, a mixed bouquet, a quart of stock, and if you have it a few spoonfuls of the grease taken from the top of stock. Put the fat or bacon rind in the bottom of a suitably sized saucepan. On this put the sliced onion and carrot; arrange the heads of celery head to tail on these. Put in the bouquet garni, season well with pepper, add the stock and the spoonfuls of fat from the top. The liquid should just cover the celery and no more. Bring to boil. Lay a piece of greased paper directly on to the celery, cover the saucepan. Put over slow heat and allow to simmer gently. This gentle simmering should go on for $1\frac{1}{2}$–$1\frac{3}{4}$ hours, according to the thickness of the celery sticks used, and may be done in the oven.   Lift out the heads of celery and drain on a sieve.   Cut the celery in two or three pieces longwise and arrange on a fireproof dish.   Keep it warm while you prepare the finishing sauce.   This may be a good béchamel, or some of the liquid in which the celery was cooked, treated in the following way: Skim the juice thoroughly. Take a good pint of this liquid and put it into a clean saucepan, reduce it by half over quick heat.   Make a brown roux with $\frac{1}{2}$ oz. butter and a little less than this weight in flour.   Cook this in the way described on page 139, dilute with a little of the boiling reduced liquid, return to pan, bring back to boil, cook for 8 or 9 minutes, and serve the celery in this sauce, re-heating altogether if necessary, or merely pouring the sauce over the already reheated celery.   Another method of thickening this juice is to make a liaison with egg yolk and cream (see page 140).

Another method of making a type of braised celery, though not really the proper dish, is as follows: When you have prepared the celery heads, cut each in two and sauter in butter in a saucepan until both sides are golden brown.   Then add stock to cover, a bouquet garni, and seasoning, and simmer gently till cooked.

Celery, dipped in batter and fried after preliminary blanching, makes excellent fritters, and is very good in the Fritto Misto of Vegetables given on page 276.   Another good method is to continue blanching until the heads are tender, then cut into suitably sized pieces, allow to get cold, dip in egg and breadcrumbs, and fry in butter.   (The piquante sauce given on page 194 is good served with this dish if it is to be used as an entrée.)

A dish of celery and mushrooms as a separate course is given on page 260 (Vegetable Entrées and Luncheon Dishes).

CHICORY (ENDIVES BELGES)

There is confusion over the name of this vegetable.   In England when we say endive we generally mean a curly-leaved salad plant.   By chicory we mean what the French call endives.   The long heads looking like white, slender cos lettuces are generally imported into this country from Holland or Belgium.   This whiteness is achieved by forcing the roots in darkness.   We can grow chicory in the garden; when the plants are full grown in the autumn the big heads of green leaves are twisted off and the roots packed tightly in boxes of light soil.   The boxes must then be brought in and all light excluded from them; this is sometimes done under the staging of a greenhouse, in a cellar, or in a mushroom house.   Failure to achieve real darkness will result in green-tinted heads, and this means that they will have a bitter flavour.   A good deal of bitterness can be got rid of by a preliminary blanching in boiling water, after which the vegetable may be finished off, but the greenish heads are not good for salads.

Sometimes, especially towards the end of the season, even the imported heads may begin to have a trace of greenness and bitterness, and although this is not at all disagreeable to those of us who are addicted to this delicious vegetable, it does not please the young and unaccustomed palate. It is important, therefore, to remove this before cooking by preliminary blanching in boiling water.

There are two principal ways of cooking chicory: the first the classic way in which the heads, whole, are braised in butter, the second a more domestic way for which the heads are sliced in rounds before cooking. Chicory is in season from November to February and is prepared by having the outer leaves taken off; generally there are only one or two of these to be removed, and very little washing is required. If to be served as salad the heads are cut lengthways in halves or quarters, and should be put into cold water with a little lemon juice or vinegar in it if they have to be kept waiting.

BRAISED CHICORY (1)

1–1½ lb. chicory	1 teaspoon lemon juice or
2 oz. butter (approx.)	vinegar
3 tablespoons water	salt

Blanch chicory if this is necessary, throw water away and drain the heads well. Take half the butter to spread over the bottom of the saucepan. On this lay the heads of chicory, lightly packed together, and spread the rest of the butter in little bits over the top. Add the cold water and lemon juice or vinegar and a good pinch of salt. Bring this quickly to the boil, cover the chicory with a piece of greased paper, put the lid on the pan and cook gently, preferably in an oven. A gentle simmer is the utmost that is required. Cook for 1–1¼ hours. Lift out the heads with care, serve with a little of the liquor from the pan, and sprinkle with pepper, or drain the heads and heat them in a cream or brown sauce or in gravy.

BRAISED CHICORY (2)

Cut the chicory in rounds. Smear with butter the whole of the inside of a saucepan, which should be just the right size to be filled by the quantity of chicory taken. Cover the slices with a sheet of greased paper and put the lid on, and if it does not fit really closely put an iron on top to hold it down firmly, or fit a piece of paper between lid and pan. A well-sealed pan is needed to hold the steam in, for it is in this and their own juice that they cook, as no liquid is added. Put the pan into a moderately slow oven and allow about 1½–2 hours for cooking. Sometimes the chicory is ready in 1½ hours, but it may take a little more. At the end of the time no liquid should remain; if it does, leave the pan uncovered in the oven for a few minutes to allow this to evaporate. The chicory should turn out in a mass, slightly brown on the surface and not at all sloppy. Sprinkle with pepper and salt and serve.

CURLY GREENS, SCOTCH KALE, AND
TURNIP TOPS

All these may be cooked in the same way as creamed cabbage (page 220), so no separate recipes are called for. Or they may be cooked, drained, chopped, and finished off in a little butter in which some grated onion has been tossed over heat, with a final addition of lemon juice and freshly ground pepper.

KOHLRABI

Kohlrabi, a turnip-shaped vegetable, is included here because it is really a swollen stem base rather than a root. It has a delicate flavour, and may be cooked in all ways that are suitable for turnips: for fritters, purées, *au gratin*, or boiled and finished off by sautéing in butter. It is also excellent finely shredded in a root-vegetable salad.

LEEKS

One may get the impression from French books on cookery that the leek is a vegetable primarily used for the flavouring of soups and stews. Scant attention seems to be paid to its value as a vegetable dish. Yet it is delicate in flavour, can be tender and of excellent texture, and it is often easily digested by those who find onions unwholesome. Too often a dish of leeks is watery, and sometimes too heavily blanketed in sauce; and if preparation has been inadequate there may remain specks of sand or grit between the tightly folded layers. The following details of preparation need to be observed.

Cut off the roots, then shorten the green tops, leaving about 2–3 inches of the green part. Peel off the outside layer, then make two cuts, about $1\frac{1}{2}$–2 inches long, first one way and then the other on the top of the leek. This makes it easy to ruffle back the layers a little when washing, so facilitating the removal of any particles of grit which lie between the leaves.

One of the nicest ways to eat leeks is to choose those of medium size, blanch them till tender, drain well, cut them in short lengths, and sauter them in a little butter, or serve with beurre noisette. Another good way is to braise them. Prepare the leeks, throw them into well-salted water (if very large cut in two). Blanch for 3 or 4 minutes, drain, sauter in a little butter in a saucepan for about 5 minutes, then add stock or water, a bouquet garni, and a bay-leaf. Cook in this way for about an hour, or longer if the leeks are big. When ready lift out, keep hot, strain the liquor, reduce it, thicken it with brown roux, and pour over the leeks.

Leeks make a delicate soufflé; a recipe for this will be found on page 328, and a recipe for Leek Pie on page 281.

If you grow your own vegetables take care to retain the row of seedling leeks from which planting out is done. From this, later in the year, may be pulled small leeks no thicker than a finger, and these make one of the most delicious salads. A recipe will be found in the salad chapter, page 347.

LETTUCE

Although lettuce is commonly used as a salad plant, it is an excellent cooked vegetable. And cooking it has this advantage: sometimes in a spell of hot weather the lettuce plants will begin to bolt, and are then not good to eat raw, but excellent cooked, provided they are not bitter. Cos lettuce, which can, after its first freshness, be a little coarse in texture when eaten raw, makes an excellent dish served braised.

BRAISED LETTUCE (1)

4–6 lettuces, according to size
  (cos lettuce if possible)
1 oz. butter (approx.)
1 fat rasher of bacon
1 carrot

1 onion
a bouquet garni
1–1½ gills good stock
seasoning
finely chopped parsley

Wash the lettuces, keeping them whole, and taking care to remove all grit. Pare the base of cos lettuce to a point without detaching the lower leaves. Have ready a pan of boiling salted water. Plunge the lettuces into this, bring back to the boil, and allow to boil 5 or 6 minutes. Take out and plunge into cold water, drain, and then dab gently in a clean cloth. Butter thickly a fireproof dish, lay the rasher of bacon in the bottom, chop the carrot and onion finely and sprinkle over the bacon. Fold the tops of the lettuces under so as to make a neat shape and lay them on top of the bacon. Pour over the stock, add the bouquet and seasoning, cover with buttered paper, cook in a moderate oven 40–45 minutes. When ready arrange the lettuces on a dish, reduce the stock in which they were cooked and strain over them, sprinkle with chopped parsley, and serve.

BRAISED LETTUCE (2)

4–6 lettuces
2 oz. butter
4 small onions
2 lumps of sugar

a bouquet garni
salt and pepper
1 heaped teaspoon flour

Wash lettuce and chop roughly in inch-wide slices. Place in alternate layers in a thick saucepan with three-quarters of the butter divided into small pieces. Press down, make a little hollow in the middle and place onions, sugar, and bouquet in it. Season with salt and pepper. Cover and cook three-quarters of an hour on moderate heat. Work reserved butter with the flour, remove bouquet, add the beurre manié and reboil. Turn into a hot dish and serve.

When a row of cos lettuce has run to seed, a good dish can be made of the centre stems, in the same way as cabbage stems are sometimes used. In this case the leaves are stripped off, and the harder parts of the stem cut away, the stems are then boiled, and peeled more finely than can be done before they are softened in cooking. The centre soft part is cut up into slices and finished off in butter. In some cases the outer leaves may be made into a cooked dish, creamed for example, and these pieces of the inside of the stem added. Or, after being finished off in butter, they may be put on to slices of buttered toast, seasoned with ground black pepper and salt, and sprinkled with finely chopped parsley, or any other herb, such as chives, that may be liked.

SEA-KALE

Notes on this vegetable will be found in the chapter on vegetable entrées and luncheon dishes, page 265.

SORREL

If you find this in English catalogues at all it is listed as a herb, and it would certainly be an enterprising greengrocer who would offer it for sale in England. This is a pity, as everyone will agree who has enjoyed oseille à la crème in France, served probably with escalopes de veau or a perfect sorrel soup. Picked wild from our meadows the leaves have an over-sharp taste, though even these are not to be despised as a salad ingredient; but it is with milder forms of cultivated sorrel that we are concerned. This useful plant may be grown from seed or be propagated by root division; the best varieties come from France, as for example the Oseille de Belleville. The sharp quality in sorrel may be ameliorated for those who do not like it by using it mixed with other vegetables such as spinach, young nettles, or lettuce.

SORREL A LA CRÈME (1)

2 lb. sorrel (or sorrel mixed with spinach)	salt and pepper
5–6 tablespoons water	1 egg
1 oz. butter	1 tablespoon milk
1 level tablespoon flour	an extra nut of butter
1 teaspoon sugar	2 or 3 tablespoons cream to finish (optional)

Wash the sorrel thoroughly and drain it. It is unnecessary to remove the stems. Put a handful of leaves into the pan with 5–6 tablespoons water. Start on a slow fire. As the first leaves begin to soften down add more and stir. Continue until all leaves are in the pan. Put the lid on and simmer gently for 5 minutes. Take care that the sorrel does not burn on the bottom of the pan.   Turn the whole out on a wire sieve and drain for 15–20 minutes.   Press the sorrel through the sieve.

In the meantime melt the butter in a saucepan, add the flour, and cook for 3 or 4 minutes.   Add sorrel, sugar, and seasoning.   Stir until it boils, cover with a round of greased paper, and put in a slow oven for 1–1½ hours. At the end of this time have ready the egg beaten with milk.

Strain this mixture into a basin and add to it gradually a little of the hot sorrel—2 or 3 tablespoons.   (This is to prevent the egg from curdling, which it will do if you add it suddenly to the whole hot mixture.)   Pour the mixture in the basin into the pan and let all cook without boiling for 5 minutes, stirring well.

Immediately before serving add a nut of butter, and pour over the surface the cream, heated and seasoned with a little salt and pepper.

SORREL A LA CRÈME (2)

2 lb. sorrel	½ cup cream
½ oz. butter	1 small egg
scant ½ oz. flour	seasoning
1 tea-cup thick béchamel	

Wash sorrel well, blanch in boiling water 10 minutes.   Drain, press, and rub through a wire sieve.   Melt the butter in a thick pan, add flour, and allow to colour to a delicate brown.   Lay the sorrel in this without mixing, cover and leave in a warm place 40 minutes—on the stove rack for example; this has the effect of softening the flavour.   Mix and beat with the béchamel, cream, and beaten egg.   Season, heat up over moderate heat, stirring well.   When the sorrel will just hold its shape, serve.

SPINACH

Spinach is in season all the year round.   There are three main kinds, summer, winter, and perpetual.   Summer spinach is pale green and delicate in flavour; winter and perpetual spinach are a darker green and need slightly longer cooking.   The summer spinach can be used whole, that is to say the stems need only be shortened, but the coarser varieties need more careful preparation and each stem has to be pulled off backward, taking with it part of the midriff.   It is in the washing that the preparation of spinach needs a great deal of care.   The simplest way to wash it is to have two bowls of cold water, and to plunge it alternately into each, lifting it out with the hands from one bowl to another, until no sediment remains at the bottom of either bowl.   The water has to be changed, of course, between each rinsing.

There are two main ways of serving spinach, in a purée and *en branches*. It should be remembered that spinach reduces greatly in cooking, even by as much as two-thirds. Two pounds is enough for four people. There are two schools of thought about methods of cooking spinach. The French school, which R. H. and I like, cook it in plenty of salted water, after which it is drained, well pressed, and finished off in a variety of ways. In the second method, often advocated by English and American cooks, the spinach, after washing, is put into the pan with only the water, which clings to the leaves, and the spinach is cooked in this and in its own juice. To cook it by the first method proceed as follows:

Prepare the leaves in the way described, then wash in as many waters as may prove necessary to get rid of all grit. In rainy weather when the leaves have been splashed this needs particular care. Drain well on a sieve. Have ready a large enamel pan of boiling salted water, put in the spinach, continue for 7–12 minutes after boiling-point is regained, according to the type and age of the spinach. Drain and press. Lift it out a little at a time, sieve or chop well, then put the spinach into a pan, lightly buttered to prevent sticking, and shake over heat.

SPINACH A LA CRÈME (CRÈME D'ÉPINARDS) (1)

2½ lb. spinach
2 oz. butter
1 good tablespoon flour
1½ gills milk
seasoning
a pinch of sugar and a dash of
    nutmeg

lemon juice
freshly ground pepper
fried croûtons
a spoonful or two of hot cream
    (optional)

Prepare and cook the spinach as above, and after drying over the fire with half the butter add flour mixed with seasoning and sugar, cook for a few minutes, and remove from heat. Add milk gradually, bring to boiling-point, cover, put on low heat and simmer for a quarter of an hour, adjust seasoning and add nutmeg. Immediately before serving add the remaining butter in small pieces, a dash of lemon juice, and freshly ground pepper and dish with the croûtons. A good addition is a spoonful or two of hot cream just before serving.

SPINACH A LA CRÈME (2)

Prepare spinach. Dry off in a buttered pan as described above, add a spoonful or two of béchamel sauce. Add salt, pepper, and a pinch of sugar and finish off with a spoonful of hot cream.

SPINACH EN BRANCHES

For cooking spinach *en branches* the leaves are prepared in the same way, cooked in boiling salted water for about 10 minutes, drained, and pressed.

They are then finished off in butter, which is melted first in the saucepan. A little cream, nutmeg, sugar, and seasoning may be added.

For Subrics à l'Italienne, Spinach Fritters, and Pain d'Épinards see Vegetable Entrées and Luncheon Dishes, page 250.

SPINACH BEET

This is the wide midriff of a large leaf and may be cooked like spinach or sea-kale; and served plain with melted butter; or it may be braised. The stalks take from 20 to 30 minutes to cook, and the leaves 15 minutes.

IX

Vegetables: Flowers and Fruits

THE GLOBE ARTICHOKE

THIS plant, with its fine grey foliage and great purple thistle-like flowers, has garden and decorative as well as kitchen value. It is the bud of the plant which is eaten, and this is formed of overlapping fleshy scales, the swollen bases of which are edible. In order not to be pedantic these are referred to as 'leaves' in cookery books. Under the last layer of this conical cap of leaves lies, first, a hairy structure called the choke, which in time becomes the purple part of the flower and is quite inedible, and below this again the base or *fond*, which is the *bonne bouche* of the whole. One wonders in what circumstances it was first found that the fleshy bases of the leaves were good to eat, and it was learned to avoid the spiny, even dangerous choke and to come again to the delicious base. French cookery books give recipes in which this *fond* is used with greater abandon than is customary in this country—we are more inclined to use the whole artichoke. Abroad, where so much attention is paid to young and delicate vegetables —*les primeurs*—artichokes are sometimes cut in quite small bud, so young indeed that the choke is practically undeveloped and need not inevitably be discarded. In England one commonly meets the large and more developed artichoke. This is cooked whole, the base of the leaves eaten, and the choke lifted out, after which the *fond* is reached.

Since the whole artichoke is used as a separate course, and not as an accompaniment, notes on it will be found in the chapter on vegetable entrées and luncheon dishes, page 250.

It is perhaps sufficient to say on the subject of the *fonds* that they may be bought in tins, may be seasoned, dipped in batter, and made into fritters, or used as a base for hors-d'œuvre and cocktail savouries.

AUBERGINE OR EGG-PLANT

The aubergine has become better known and appreciated of late, and now it is not unusual to find the shining purple fruits in many shops. General preparation consists merely in wiping the fruit with a damp cloth and removing the stem and calyx. Some recipes call for the fruit to be cooked whole, others indicate slicing, and generally call for the slices to be sprinkled with salt and the liquid drawn from them to be discarded. It is considered that this process—to dégorger—improves the flavour of the finished dish.

The aubergine lends itself to various dishes, which on the whole are more suited for a separate course than for an accompanying vegetable. Simple fritters may be offered with grilled fish or chicken, and Aubergines Caviar may be used, as will be seen in the Winkfield chapter, page 978, in three ways. Beyond this the recipes for Aubergines Hongroise, à la Boston, and Gratinées, three good ways of eating this vegetable, will be found in the next chapter, pages 252–3.

Here is a recipe for aubergines served hot:

AUBERGINE FRITTERS

After the preliminary slicing, salting, draining, and drying they may be dipped in fritter batter and fried in deep fat, or be brushed over with oil and cooked under a hot grill. They should be well seasoned. For additional flavour a pinch of turmeric may be added to the batter. These are good to serve with fish, chicken, or rice dishes.

BROAD BEANS

There are three stages at which broad beans are edible. First, when the young pods are still so small (roughly about two inches or so long) that the flower has only just withered. These miniature beans may be cooked whole, or roughly cut into two or three pieces each, and they have all the flavour and tenderness and none of the coarseness of a big broad bean. The next stage to eat them is when the beans are about as big as a good-sized pea. Later, when the beans are considerably bigger, they should be slipped out of their skin after cooking, so that only the delicate green inside is eaten. When they are big this skin is coarse and has an unpleasant taste. Just as mint is the classic herb for flavouring peas, so is savory for beans, and a sprig of this may be put into the water for cooking. The beans should be boiled till tender, the length of time depending on size. They are then drained and reheated with a little butter, and may be finished with a little finely chopped savory. The nicest way of serving small beans is to toss them in a little butter and sprinkle them with a little finely chopped parsley. When they get larger they may be blanched, cooked, and served in a white sauce, or a cream sauce with chopped parsley. In the largest state of all they are best skinned and made into a purée.

CREAM SAUCE FOR BROAD BEANS

¾ oz. flour	¾ pint milk
1 oz. butter	a sprig of savory
salt	a good gill cream
pepper	a bunch of parsley
a little nutmeg	

Make a white roux with flour and butter, season with salt, pepper, and nutmeg. Dilute with milk. Bring to boil, add a sprig of savory, and cook gently on low heat. Strain the sauce into a clean saucepan. Stir over a brisk heat until sufficiently reduced to be of a good creamy consistency. Add the cream. Do not allow to boil. Finely chop the parsley, add it to the sauce, and pour over the drained beans.

FRENCH BEANS

These should be picked young and cooked whole: topped, tailed, washed, and blanched in rapidly boiling salted water until soft, 10–15 minutes. They are then ready for reheating with butter and seasoning for a perfect dish. Larger beans may be cut in two or three pieces and finished off after blanching in various ways, none of which is so good as that given above.

HARICOTS VERTS (FRENCH BEANS) A L'OIGNON

1 lb. haricots verts	1 medium-sized onion
1 oz. butter	salt and pepper

Prepare and cook the beans. When they are ready drain them, rinse out the pan, make the butter hot in it, and fry the finely chopped onion brown. Pour the flavoured butter over the beans and season. Haricots verts may be finished with a sauce poulette (see page 154). The beans are cooked and drained and the sauce added.

RUNNER BEANS

These beans, being larger and of rougher skin, are not cooked whole or even broken in pieces, but after washing, topping, and tailing should be finely sliced, either with a bean slicer or a sharp knife. Any stringy bits at the sides must be cut away. Some of the modern varieties of runner bean are alarmingly large; the test of edibility, however, is to snap a bean in two, and if it is juicy and free from strings it will be good to eat.

The sliced beans are cooked and served like French beans. The cooking time is approximately 20 minutes. Late in the season, as the beans become mature, the following is a good method of cooking:

Slice the beans and parboil in salted water, drain, and finish cooking in a tightly lidded casserole in the oven with butter, savory, sliced onion, seasoning, and enough vegetable stock to cover. Allow them to simmer for about an hour. Another way of finishing off these beans is to fry some finely shredded onion gently to a pale gold in butter, then add a little finely chopped savory, and pour this over the beans when they are cooked.

Runner beans in the garden should be picked over every day, and any not required for immediate use put down in a jar with salt, roughly a good handful of salt to each double handful of beans. They may be sliced first or left whole. They should be kept covered. The salt will eventually turn to brine and the beans will be preserved. When required for use they should be put in cold water and brought to the boil. Sometimes this has to be done twice, with different water, but the beans can be tested for saltiness at the end of the first boiling. They are then ready for cooking and finishing off in the same way as fresh beans.

BROCCOLI

The large white broccoli which looks like a small cauliflower can be cooked in any of the ways given for cauliflower (see below). Sprouting broccoli, green, white, and purple, are treated somewhat differently. The shoots of these may be tied up into bundles, blanched in boiling water, and served like asparagus, or they may be blanched, dipped in fritter batter, and fried in deep fat. The most interesting of the sprouting broccoli is a green early variety called Italian broccoli or Calabresse. This is in season towards the end of July, and during August and September. First of all the green central head is cut; this looks like a small green cauliflower and is of exceedingly delicate flavour. It is best to blanch this until tender and to serve it with butter. After this come the side-shoots, and they need rather more careful preparation. Each shoot should be peeled from the butt of the stem upwards to remove all leaf. When this is done the stem is of pale translucent green. The delicate stems are now tied in bundles, blanched in boiling water until ready, and served with noisette butter (see page 169).

CAULIFLOWER

There are two ways, or two main ways, of preparing cauliflower for cooking. The first is the method usually adopted in England. For this the cauliflower is carefully washed, stripped of coarse leaves, and plunged head downwards in cold water containing vinegar. The stalk is trimmed crosswise. The flower is next plunged into boiling water with the head uppermost and cooked gently until just tender, then lifted out and thoroughly drained.

An alternative adopted by some cooks is to stick two skewers through the stalk at right angles, and put the head downwards with the skewers resting on the edges of the pan.   In this way part of the stalk is not cooked.   This preserves the whiteness of the flowers but deprives one of a portion of the stalk.

The French method, more complicated, produces the best results.   For this break up the cauliflower in flowerets, peel off any stringy bits that may remain.   Trim and split the main stem.   Choose and trim as many young green leaves as possible.   As you proceed put the pieces into a bowl of salted water, or water containing vinegar, to remove green fly or any other insects that may remain.   Plunge the pieces into rapidly boiling water, bring them to the boil, and boil fast for a quarter of an hour.   Immediately they are tender drain in a colander.   They are now ready for finishing off. If you wish the cauliflower to come to the table looking whole, butter a basin thickly, and arrange first the leaves then the flowerets head downwards.   Press lightly and turn them out as though from a mould so that they retain the shape of a cauliflower.

CHOU-FLEUR A LA POLONAISE

cauliflower
2 oz. butter
1 heaped tablespoon dry white
   breadcrumbs

sieved yolk of 1 hard-boiled
   egg
chopped parsley

Prepare and cook cauliflower in the French way.   Heat the butter and cook crumbs to a golden brown.   Dish the cauliflower, pour over the butter and crumbs, sprinkle over the egg yolk and parsley.

CAULIFLOWER WITH MINT SAUCE

This is a good vegetable to serve with mutton or as a separate dish.

1 good cauliflower
¼–½ oz. butter
1 yolk of egg
½ gill creamy béchamel

1 gill orange mint sauce (see
   page 182)
2 rounds of freshly made hot
   buttered toast

Prepare the cauliflower sprigs by the French method.   Cook and arrange in a pudding bowl so that the original shape is re-formed (see above).   Melt butter and pour over the cauliflower, cover and keep hot. Beat the yolk of egg with the béchamel and add the mint sauce by degrees. Thicken in a bain-marie to the consistency of cream.   Remove crust from toast and cut in four from corner to corner.   Turn out the cauliflower on to a hot dish, pour over it the sauce, and surround with the pieces of buttered toast.

This may have sautéd tomatoes as a garnish, and makes a good first course for luncheon.

Pain de Chou-fleur, Cauliflower Fritters, Chou-fleur Toscana, and other recipes will be found in the next chapter, page 250.

CUCUMBER

The early summer cucumbers, grown in a hothouse, are expensive for cooking, although they are delicious.   Later, when frame cucumbers and outdoor ridge cucumbers are available, there are some admirable dishes to be made from them.

Many French recipes advise that the seeds should be removed, but this is only necessary when one is using the mature ridge cucumbers, which have a quantity of rather large seeds.   Greenhouse and frame varieties usually need not have the seeds removed.

The following dish is excellent and may be served as a separate course:

CUCUMBERS A LA CRÈME

2 medium cucumbers	½ gill hot cream
½ pint béchamel sauce, made	chopped tarragon and dill
with ¾ oz. butter, ¾ oz. scant	salt and freshly ground black
weight flour, and ½ pint milk	pepper

Peel the cucumber thinly, split in two, and cut up into longish pieces— each half-cucumber into four pieces is about right.   Blanch these in salted water until just tender, approximately 5 minutes.   Make a béchamel sauce by the short method (page 155).   Add cucumber, the cream, the tarragon, dill, salt and pepper.

Another way is to blanch the pieces until cooked, and finish them off with beurre noisette (see page 169).   Or they may be blanched and lightly sautéd in butter.

VEGETABLE MARROWS

It may seem odd in an English book to make reference at the very beginning of this subject to the tiny Italian marrows called zucchini.   But these are one of the high lights of the vegetable year, a luxury in the same category as asparagus and the first garden peas.   Gardeners have told me on occasion that these delicate finger-long fruits are nothing more or less than ordinary bush marrows picked young.   But it seems to me that some varieties produce better babies and more of them than others, and whenever it is possible I get a packet of seed from Italy or America.   Should a time come when this proves too difficult, I shall have to grow small bush marrows and, doubtless in the face of opposition, cut the fruits while they are still minute.   Except for purposes of jam-making and possibly harvest festivals—and then only to fill up space—large ripe marrows have little value.   The ordinary garden marrow for table use should be cut young, while the skin is tender and the seed hardly formed.   Seedsmen now offer in their catalogues a wide choice of marrows and courgettes; Miss Kathleen Hunter lists twenty-four varieties, and the seed list of 'Vegetables for Epicures' of Bunyards of Maidstone, suggests several unusual kinds.

Preparation and cooking

According to their tenderness and the dish in hand, marrows may be peeled or not, and they may be boiled, baked, sautéd, fried, or stuffed. They may be blanched for 5 minutes and then finished off in a variety of ways.

To cook from beginning to end in water, as is often done, robs them of taste and produces an over-watery dish. It is perfectly possible to cook marrows in their own juice as follows:

Peel the marrow, split, scoop out seeds with a sharp metal spoon, cut in pieces. Put in pan with ½ oz. melted butter, seasoning, and freshly chopped herbs (parsley, chives, marjoram, or savory). Press over them a piece of buttered paper, cover pan, and cook gently 7–10 minutes, shaking vigorously from time to time.

Marrows cooked in the above way but without herbs may well be finished with the following flavoured butter:

A BEURRE NOISETTE FOR MARROWS, COURGETTES, AND ZUCCHINI

2 oz. butter	1–2 tablespoons herbs as follows:
2 tablespoons tarragon vinegar	equal quantities of parsley, fennel, marjoram, and thyme
	pepper and salt to season

Melt the butter and fry to nut-brown. Add vinegar, herbs, and seasoning while still frothing and pour over hot vegetable.

Here is a recipe for a marrow dish which may be made from a slightly larger marrow, though never an old one:

VEGETABLE MARROW HONGROISE

1 medium marrow	a pinch of dill seed, finely crushed, or fresh dill leaves, chopped
1 oz. butter	
1 tablespoon onion, finely chopped	salt, pepper
1 tablespoon wine vinegar	1 teaspoon paprika
	1 teaspoon sugar
	1 heaped teaspoon flour

Peel marrow, cut in two, scoop out seeds, cut into slivers. Heat three-quarters of the butter in large stew- or frying-pan, add marrow. Cook over moderate heat, shaking pan frequently and turning marrow over with a fish slice. When soft and melting lift out with the slice. Put onion in pan, allow to soften, return marrow to pan with vinegar, dill, seasoning, and sugar. Continue cooking for a few minutes, draw aside. Work remaining butter into flour, add, and when melted reboil. Turn into a hot dish.

COURGETTES PROVENÇALE

4–6 courgettes or baby marrows	1 shallot
(according to size)	1 lb. tomatoes
2 tablespoons salad-oil or 2 oz.	3 oz. grated cheese
butter	seasoning

Cut the courgettes in two-inch slices and sauter them in hot salad-oil for 10–15 minutes with the finely minced shallot. Skin the tomatoes, cut them in quarters, and sauter them also. Put into a fireproof dish first a layer of tomato, then one of courgette; sprinkle with grated cheese between each layer. Season with salt and pepper. Let the top layer be of tomatoes, sprinkled with cheese. Cook for about three-quarters of an hour in a moderate oven.

The little zucchini referred to earlier are at perfection when they are cut just as the flower fades. At this stage they require little cooking; it is generally enough to put them with a piece of butter and without any liquid in a tightly covered pan and cook them very gently for about 15 minutes. They may then be dished with their own juice, a dash of lemon, and chopped herbs.

They are so good that they take their proper place as a vegetable entrée.

MUSHROOMS

Field mushrooms are in season during August and September, cultivated mushrooms all the year round. Field mushrooms have more flavour but are more fragile and juicy than the forced ones, and so less firm for slicing and garnishing; they are good for frying or grilling with bacon for break-fast or on toast as a savoury. All mushrooms should be fresh, and the cultivated ones, though drier than those from the field, should not be kept over-long or they will shrivel. The skin of the cultivated mushrooms is tender and need not necessarily be removed. Field mushrooms are peeled and the stalks of all mushrooms cut off level with the caps. Do not pull out the stem or the cap will shrink too much in cooking. To peel mush-rooms, take the edge of the skin which overhangs the cap between the knife and your thumb and pull the skin towards the centre of the cap. The peel should not be cut off with a knife. For certain dishes mushrooms may be steamed; cooked in this way they retain their shape.

Mushrooms required for a dish in which they are to be sieved or chopped are not peeled, but rubbed with a dry cloth and a little salt, and the stems trimmed. The peelings and stalks of mushrooms should not be thrown away as there is a great deal of flavour in them, and they should be made into a preparation known as duxelles (see next page) which is kept for flavouring savoury dishes.

DUXELLES

Wash the peelings and stems well.   Squeeze tightly to dry, chop finely, put into a pan with a nut of butter, or some other suitable fat, and cook until dry, stirring frequently.   Turn into a jar, press down, and keep in a cool place until wanted for use.   They may be covered with a little clarified butter and will keep for a week or more.

MUSHROOMS COOKED IN THE OVEN

One of the simplest and nicest ways of cooking mushrooms is to lay them in a fireproof dish with a spot of butter and a teaspoon of cream inside each cap.   Season well, put a little milk in the bottom of the baking-dish, cover closely, first with paper then with a lid, and cook them in the oven.   In this way all the flavour and fragrance of the mushroom is kept, and the lid should not be taken off until immediately before serving.

STEWED MUSHROOMS

1 oz. butter	½ pint milk
½ lb. mushrooms	seasoning of salt, pepper, and
1 oz. flour	a dash of nutmeg
bay-leaf	

Melt the butter, add the prepared mushrooms and cook gently until lightly brown.   Sprinkle the flour carefully over the mushrooms.   Put a bay-leaf into the milk and bring to the boil.   Remove the bay-leaf, add the milk gradually to the mushrooms in the pan, add seasonings and continue cooking for 10 minutes.

GRILLED MUSHROOMS

Prepare the mushrooms, brush over the caps very lightly with butter, put dome side upwards on a grill pan and grill for 4 or 5 minutes.   Now turn the caps so that the hollow side is upwards and put in the middle of each a little butter; sprinkle with salt.   Return to the grill and finish off. Lift carefully on to buttered toast so that none of the juice from the cap of the mushroom is lost.   Sprinkle with freshly grated pepper.

For other mushroom dishes see next chapter, page 262.

GREEN PEAS

If peas are shelled a little time before being cooked they should not be thrown into water, but may be kept moist with a covering of the shells. The shells of early peas are excellent for a green pea soup.

The variety known as Mangetout is eaten whole before the peas begin to swell.   It is important to pick and use these before they have grown tough and stringy.   They are boiled in salted water, drained, and finished with butter.

There are two principal methods of cooking peas, the English and the French.   For the first early garden peas and the young marrowfats there is no better way than the simple English method.   For this the peas are cooked until tender (about 10 minutes) in slightly salted water containing a sprig of mint and a teaspoon of sugar, then drained and finished with a piece of butter shaken into them in the pan.   No dish of peas can be better than this, but it is not easy to produce with bought peas and one rarely meets with it in restaurants.   In fact, peas offered in restaurants are very often a disappointing vegetable.

The French method for Petits Pois à la Française gives an excellent dish of different flavour, the peas being mixed with lettuce and spring onions. French cooks use very small, specially graded peas for this, but the method may well be applied to more mature peas and produces, if not quite such a delicate dish, at least something better than is generally to be met with. In this dish the fresh green colour is lacking, but this is made up for by the good flavour.

The quantity of peas for four people is from two to three pounds according to the fullness of the pods; we buy peas unshelled, but French cooks buy them shelled and graded.   One pint of shelled peas serves four people.

PETITS POIS A LA FRANÇAISE

1 pint shelled green peas	a good pinch of salt, freshly
heart of a lettuce, shredded	ground pepper, and sugar
6–8 spring onions	bouquet of parsley and mint
¾ tea-cup cold water	stalks
1 oz. butter	

Put all into a medium-sized pan with half the butter.   Cover tightly or set a soup-plate filled with hot water on top of the pan.   (This water may be used for adding to the peas if additional liquid is required during the cooking.)   Cook on moderate heat till peas are just tender, 15–20 minutes. Draw aside, remove bouquet, adjust seasoning, and add remaining butter. Turn into a hot dish.

Some recipes indicate that the remaining butter is to be creamed with a teaspoon of flour—beurre manié; this is then added to the cooked peas off the fire and when melted the whole brought back to boil.

PETITS POIS A LA BONNE FEMME

This is a dish suitable to serve as a first course.

1½ oz. butter	seasoning
2–3 rashers of streaky bacon	heart of a lettuce, shredded
cut in lardons and blanched	¾ tea-cup water
12 spring onions	1 pint shelled peas
1 teaspoon flour	

Heat 1 oz. butter in stew-pan, add bacon and onions, and cook gently till coloured. Add flour, seasoning, lettuce, water, and peas. Cover and cook till just tender. If too much liquid remains take off lid and reduce rapidly. Add remaining butter and serve.

PETITS POIS A LA CHANTILLY

This is excellent with an omelet or young chicken or as a first course for a summer lunch.

1 bunch of new carrots	freshly ground black pepper
1 tea-cup cold water	a pinch of sugar
1 oz. butter	1 pint shelled young green peas
1 sprig of mint	2 tablespoons whipped cream
salt	

Scrape and trim carrots. Put into a pan with the water, half the butter, the mint, salt, sugar, and pepper. Cover the pan and allow to simmer for 7–10 minutes. Add peas with remaining butter and additional seasoning if necessary and cook fairly rapidly until tender. There should be only a tablespoon of liquid left. If more remove lid and reduce rapidly. Remove mint, add the cream, and serve.

The following two recipes are good for mature peas:

PETITS POIS A LA FLAMANDE (1)

1 pint green peas	a bouquet of parsley
20 tiny new potatoes	salt and pepper
1 onion	2 oz. fresh butter, melted

Put the peas on in boiling salted water, add the potatoes, the onion, and the parsley. Cook over moderate heat for 25 minutes. Peas and potatoes should be tender at the same time. Drain, season, pile on a hot dish, and pour over melted butter.

PETITS POIS A LA FLAMANDE (2)

6 small carrots	1 pint green peas
salt and pepper	a bouquet of parsley
2 oz. butter	

Scrape the carrots and form in olive shapes. Cook them with just enough water to cover, salt, pepper, and 1 oz. of the butter. Boil fairly fast for 15 minutes, then add the peas and bouquet, and cook, still fairly fast, for 25 minutes. The liquid should disappear at the same time that the vegetables are cooked.

If the vegetables are tender and some liquid still remains, take the lid off the pan and reduce by rapid boiling. Add the remaining ounce of butter off the heat, in small pieces, and serve.

SWEET CORN, INDIAN CORN, OR MAIZE

The ears of this corn should be eaten when green or just turning yellow. When they have become a bright shining yellow they are generally too ripe and rather hard. The usual way of cooking in England is to plunge them into boiling salted water and boil them for 20 minutes. One good American way is to put them into cold water and bring them up to boiling-point. Continue boiling for 2–3 minutes before draining. Corn should be cooked as soon after being picked as possible.

Whole ears of corn are served as a separate course, and reference to them will be found in Chapter X, page 269.

It is comparatively recently that varieties of quickly maturing corn, suitable to our climate, have been introduced, and only now is it finding a regular place in our gardens. While its popularity increases rapidly there are still some people who regard it as an acquired taste. This is surprising when its fresh, delicate, sweet flavour is considered. It would seem essentially a food for young and sensitive palates. Because of its some-what high cost in shops, we have not acquired as a common habit the American way of eating the grain cut from the cob. For those who grow it I would advise that the dishes mentioned be tried.

To remove the grain from the cob

Remove the husk and the silk. With a sharp, pointed knife slit down the middle of each row of grain. Then with a sharp knife cut off the grain from the cob, working first on the lower portion, and then turning it upside-down and scraping off the rest. In other words, do not try to cut off the full length of grain in one swoop. Scrape off any pulp and milk that may remain on the ear. Tinned corn 'off the cob' and grain taken from tinned whole corn may be used in place of fresh. The result, however, lacks the freshness of newly cut grain.

In the following dish a delicious flavour of fresh corn is retained without the trouble of biting it off the cob. Cut the grain from 6–8 large ears of freshly cut corn in the way described, taking care to scrape off all the milk from the cob. Season with salt, pepper, and a pinch of sugar. Put into a double saucepan with a piece of butter the size of a large egg and a little milk, and cook gently till tender, about 20 minutes. Serve on rounds of fresh-buttered toast.

An alternative method

8 ears of corn, scraped from the cob	½ oz. sugar
	1 oz. butter
1 gill cream	seasoning
½ gill milk	croûtons or fresh toast

Heat the milk and cream and stir in the corn and sugar. Cook for 20 minutes, then add the butter and seasoning. Stir for a minute or two over heat and serve with croûtons or fresh toast.

The following corn fritters are really good, light and of fresh flavour. They may be eaten with roast meat, chicken, or as an accompaniment to a salad luncheon.

CORN FRITTERS

This takes from 2 to 3 cobs. The grain scraped from the cob may be cooked as described above, or if particularly tender may be used raw.

1 cup fresh-cooked corn	1 teaspoon baking-powder
2 eggs	½ cup fresh breadcrumbs
salt and a pinch of sugar	fat for frying

Separate the yolks and whites, beat the yolks well and add to corn. Season. Beat the whites stiffly and fold in. Add baking-powder and enough breadcrumbs to make your mixture thick enough to handle. Form into little cakes. Heat the fat, lift the cakes with a palette-knife, and fry till brown on each side.

Tinned corn may replace the fresh but is not so good.

SWEET GREEN PEPPERS

This delicate vegetable is quickly gaining popularity in English kitchens, and the shining irregular green fruits are found in many shops. The flesh is a good addition to salads, curries, and rice and chicken dishes. Whole sweet peppers may be stuffed in the same way as tomatoes and are then usually served as a separate dish. Recipes for these will be found in Chapter X, page 270.

Preparation. Remove a slice from the stalk end and scoop out the seeds and pithy veins. If the peppers are really young and tender they may now be shaved thinly for use in salads. If not really tender they should be blanched.

To blanch. Put the cups, emptied of seeds and veins, into a basin, and sprinkle with salt and a pinch of bicarbonate of soda. Pour boiling water over them and allow to stand a few minutes. Drain and rinse. Or they may be put in a pan of cold water and brought to boiling-point.

The peppers, after slicing, are now ready to add to various suitable dishes. If they are to be served whole they may be parboiled and are then stuffed.

Tinned pimentos are good as an hors-d'œuvre.

TOMATOES

Varieties. For those who must buy from shops a tomato is just a tomato, and beyond choosing firm fruit, small or medium-sized, there is little to be done. But with a garden there is much more to it. In addition to the red and the delicately flavoured yellow fruits there is a small range of decorative varieties valued not only for flower arrangement but for garnishes and salads. Dishes such as the first course of melon and cucumber given on page 981 are better made with the tiny whole fruits, because not only do they look better, but the dressing is not diluted by juice. Before the war one could buy in this country seed of pear, plum, cherry, and currant tomatoes in both red and yellow; these are now again obtainable from Miss Kathleen Hunter, of Wheal Frances, Callestick, near Truro.

To serve tomatoes. Served whole, uncooked, and unpeeled they should be wiped gently with a cloth, and the green stalk should not be removed. If they are to be served whole and peeled they should be kept in the ice-box until the moment of serving.

To skin tomatoes. Put them into a bowl, pour over enough boiling water to cover, leave for a moment only and then put immediately into cold water; the skin can then be pulled off cleanly.

To empty. Certain dishes require that the seed and juice shall be eliminated and the firm flesh only used. For a purée it is enough to halve the fruit and squeeze out the seeds and juice. This is then strained and the juice added to the purée.

To quarter. For a garniture the fruit is quartered and the core cut out with a sharp knife, the seeds being removed at the same time. The seeds of tomatoes sometimes have a bitter quality.

To fry tomatoes. Peel and thickly slice tomatoes. Fry in butter, sprinkling with a little sugar till brown. Or cut in half, sprinkle the cut side with sugar, and fry on both sides.

To grill tomatoes. Leave whole or cut in two, brush with oil, and brown under the grill. If cut grill rounded side first.

For stuffed tomatoes, salads, and other dishes see appropriate chapters.

DRIED VEGETABLES
butter beans, haricot beans, brown and red beans, lentils, green peas, whole or split

Dried vegetables should be well washed and picked over and then put to soak in plenty of tepid water, that is to say the water should just have the chill taken off and no more. The more thorough the soaking the less will be the time taken for cooking. Fresh water is taken for the cooking, not that in which the vegetables have been soaked, and the important points to be noted are:

1. The vegetables should be put to soak in tepid water and may be left all night; alternatively, if this is inconvenient, they must be soaked in warm water for 2 hours.

2. Always cook with the lid on the pan. Cover with plenty of warm water; if the water is hard a pinch of bicarbonate of soda may be added.

3. The vegetables should be brought very slowly to boiling-point, taking for this not less than 40 minutes, after which they are simmered very gently for about an hour. They are then drained.

4. After draining the vegetables are covered, this time with boiling salted water, and fresh vegetables and herbs added for flavouring. They are now simmered until tender.

If the vegetables are to be made into a purée the final water should be just sufficient to cover, so that when they are tender all liquid has been absorbed. For a finished purée the vegetables are put through a wire sieve, and returned for a minute or two to the fire. A nut of butter, seasoning, and possibly cream are then added. Sometimes a little crushed garlic is softened in butter in the pan before the purée is put back.

BUTTER BEANS (OR SMALL HARICOTS)

These are a useful vegetable in winter, and when thoroughly cooked and mixed with plenty of butter and parsley are very good. Traditionally they should accompany roast or braised mutton, but they go equally well with a ragoût of rabbit, or a dish of eggs *sur le plat*.

Allow approximately ¾ pint of the butter beans or ½ pint of the smaller haricots for four people. Soak for 2–3 hours in tepid water. Drain, put into a pan, and cover again with warm water; bring very slowly to the boil, draw aside and soak for 1 hour. Strain off all the liquid and throw into boiling salted water with an onion stuck with a clove, a carrot, a small piece of celery, and a bouquet garni. Cover and simmer gently until the beans are tender. Approximate time 1½ hours, possibly a little longer for butter beans.

BUTTER BEANS PERSILLÉS (OR MAÎTRE D'HÔTEL)

¾ pint butter beans, cooked as above	1 dessertspoon finely chopped parsley
1½ oz. butter	freshly ground black pepper, salt
1 clove of garlic crushed with ½ teaspoon salt to a cream (or chopped chives may replace garlic)	juice of ½ lemon

When beans are cooked drain and return to the pan. Dry for a few minutes over the fire. Draw aside, add butter in small pieces, creamed garlic, parsley, and plenty of seasoning. Shake gently without stirring to mix thoroughly. Finish with the lemon juice and serve.

N.B. Garlic here is optional but goes well with the beans; chopped chives may be added in place of garlic.

BUTTER BEANS MÉNAGÈRE

In this recipe the beans are mixed with a light sauce; it is a good dish if the beans are inclined to be dry.

½–¾ pint beans	juice of ¼ lemon
¼ pint of the cooking liquor (approx.)	salt, freshly ground black pepper
1½ oz. butter	a little cream (optional)
1 oz. flour	chopped parsley and chives

Prepare and cook beans as indicated in above notes. Drain, reserving a small quantity of the liquor. Work butter and flour together, adding the lemon juice and seasoning. Add 2–3 tablespoons of the reserved stock to the beans with the butter mixture in small pieces. Shake pan thoroughly to mix, adding a little more stock. Bring to the boil, simmer a few moments, adjust seasoning, adding a spoonful or two of cream. Turn into a hot dish and dust well with the chopped parsley and chives.

The beans may also be mixed with a well-flavoured tomato sauce, and finished with a knob of butter.

Haricot and Other Dried Beans

HARICOT BEANS WITH TOMATO SAUCE

1½ pints beans	1 tablespoon lard
3 pints water	chopped parsley
1 teaspoon rough salt	

Tomato sauce

1 lb. tomatoes	1 clove of garlic
1 heaped tablespoon chopped onion	a pinch of black pepper and nutmeg
bouquet of 3 or 4 sprays of parsley, 1 of thyme	½ teaspoon salt
½ bay-leaf	1 tablespoon butter

Put the haricots in boiling water after preliminary blanching (see directions for cooking dried vegetables); half cover with the lid. Boil gently for about 1½ hours, then add salt and lard and continue cooking for another 30 minutes. Watch that the beans do not stick to the pan. Test between your fingers to see if they are done. Meanwhile prepare the tomato sauce. Cut up the tomatoes, chop the onion and garlic, tie up the bouquet. Heat the butter and cook the onion in it for a few moments till pale gold, add the tomatoes, and stir over good heat for 5 or 6 minutes. Then add the other ingredients. Put the lid on and set over a slow heat for about 45 minutes, stirring now and then. Remove bouquet. Rub through a hair sieve and keep hot. You should now have a creamy sauce; if by any chance it is too thick you can thin it with a little of the haricot water.

Drain the haricots and replace in pan, adding the sauce. Shake over fire for a minute or two to mix all together, dish up and sprinkle over with chopped parsley.

PUCHERO

This is a rich bean stew of Spanish origin. The version given here is an anglicized one; no doubt the real thing has other, and different, ingredients. The one I have is made with red or brown beans, and the saveloy obviously replaces some type of smoked sausage. Beef or mutton may be used instead of pork.

¾ lb. red or brown beans, previously soaked overnight
1 large tablespoon olive oil
1 large onion
1 large carrot
2–3 cloves of garlic, chopped
2 red peppers, seeded and shredded, or canned peppers
1 teaspoon tomato purée or conserve
a large bouquet garni

1½ pints stock or water (approx.)
½ lb. salt pork, previously blanched and boiled for a good ½ hour
2 saveloy sausages, blanched and cut into thick slices
½ lb. good ripe tomatoes, peeled and halved
salt and pepper
chopped parsley

Put the beans on to cook (see directions for cooking dried vegetables). Simmer for about 1–1⅓ hours, then drain. Heat the oil, add onion, carrot, garlic, and peppers. Cook 5–7 minutes, then add beans and after a further 5–6 minutes the purée, bouquet, and stock just to cover. Bring to the boil and allow to simmer gently for about 2 hours or until the beans are soft. At the end of the first half-hour add the pork. Half an hour before serving put in the sausages and the tomatoes. If canned peppers are used add these with the tomatoes. Adjust seasoning. To serve remove pork and bouquet, slice, arrange in the bottom of a serving dish, dish the stew over, and dust with chopped parsley.

Stock must be added from time to time during the cooking if necessary, and the puchero can be thickened slightly if wished with a little kneaded butter. Add this just before the tomatoes.

CASSOULET

This is a French regional dish and comes from the Languedoc district. There are several local varieties, but in principle the cassoulet is composed of haricot beans, strongly flavoured with tomato and garlic and simmered with a small quantity of meat which is served with the dish. The meat again varies according to the district, but is generally goose or mutton, with the addition of pork or bacon, garlic or smoked sausages. The goose is often a piece of confit d'oie, or pickled goose. After being stewed for several hours the cassoulet is dished and put to gratiné in the oven. Like so many of the French regional dishes it is a little difficult to reproduce over here owing to some of the ingredients being specialities of the district, but the recipe given here is a composite and simplified one. Cassoulet is an excellent dish for a cold day, and one that can be put on to simmer and then left.

1½ lb. haricot beans, soaked for 12 hours
¼ lb. streaky salt pork, or blanched streaky bacon
5–6 cloves of garlic, chopped
1 lb. shoulder of mutton or ¼ of a goose
good dripping or butter
a large bouquet garni

pepper, salt
6 oz. garlic sausage
1. lb. good ripe tomatoes, peeled and cut in thick slices
1 dessertspoon tomato purée or conserve
a pinch of sugar
browned crumbs

Blanch beans (see directions for cooking dried vegetables). Put to cook in salted water with the port or bacon and the garlic. Cover and simmer for a good hour. Drain, reserving the liquor. Bone mutton and cut into pieces, or leave the goose whole. Fry till golden in the dripping, add beans and pork to the pan with the bouquet, plenty of pepper, a little salt, and some of the bean liquor to moisten well. Cover and stew slowly for 3–3½ hours. Add a little liquor from time to time if necessary. After 2½ hours add the garlic sausage. When beans are cooked take up the meats and slice. Arrange in a deep dish with the beans, removing the bouquet. Cook tomatoes to a pulp, then add the purée, with salt, pepper, and sugar. Spoon this over the dish, sprinkle with crumbs, and put into the oven for a further ¾–1 hour.

For salads made with lentils and beans see Salads of Cooked Vegetables (pages 345 and 348).

X

Vegetable Entrées, Dressed Vegetables, and Simple Luncheon Dishes

WARS and rationing have brought about many changes in the culinary world, none greater, perhaps, than in the food which we may now serve with propriety for a luncheon party, or indeed for everyday family fare. It is amusing to look through old-fashioned books and study the menus; one is beset by a constant wonder as to how they did it.

But I do not need to go to books to recall a luncheon menu of considerable proportions. When I was about the age of some of our Winkfield students, that is to say had put up my hair and was therefore 'out,' I was invited to a family luncheon before a concert at the Albert Hall. Borne in the arms of a stiffly capped maid came first of all an enormous tureen of rich oyster cream soup, very full of oysters. This rich soup was followed by roast turkey with all the trimmings, including a separate dish of chestnuts—and it was not Christmas, mind you. Then there was apple pie or treacle pudding, cheese, celery, and dessert. Of the concert afterwards I remember nothing, but after all these years I recall the food and think of it when I pass the great block of flats which has replaced the imposing Victorian house near the concert hall.

If such a menu were considered necessary for a luncheon party to-day we should think twice before asking our friends, and I find it fortunate that simplicity is in fashion. Friendliness and easy hospitality are more important than grandeur.

In the chapter on menus and parties (page 1066) a few menus are suggested, and in this one various vegetable dishes are indicated which are suitable either as first or as main courses for a modern luncheon. In addition to these, others will be found in the chapters on eggs, pastas and batters, rice and curry dishes, cheese, and devils.

THE GLOBE ARTICHOKE

For general notes see page 232.

To serve hot or cold as a first course or as an entrée. To prepare artichokes cut off the stem close under the leaves, remove any old outside leaves, and if the artichokes are big shorten the tips with scissors. Plunge the heads into a large pan of boiling salted water and cook for 30–40 minutes, according to size; the test of readiness is to pull gently one of the leaves, which should come away easily. Drain well. You may now, if you wish, lift off the whole cap of leaves, thus exposing the choke; cut this away without spoiling the base and then put back the cap. This takes a little time, and unless the artichoke is to be served cold it is probably better for the beginner to adopt the homelier method—sending the drained artichokes straight to table, dished in a napkin, together with a tureen of sauce. Then as each member of the party pulls off the leaves, dipping the base of each in sauce, the choke may be removed when reached, and discarded. It is a good thing to provide a side-plate for débris. Hot globe artichokes may be served with melted or, better, with noisette butter, with hollandaise sauce, or with a piquante sauce. Cold artichokes are excellent with a good vinaigrette.

ASPARAGUS

I suppose it will be considered *lèse-majesté* to say that English garden asparagus is the best in the world, the most delicately flavoured and the sweetest. Already I think I hear ghostly voices calling 'Argenteuil, Argenteuil,' and a vision springs up of a stately waiter in an expensive restaurant bearing a dish of gigantic stems of pale out-of-season asparagus to his most rich and valued clients. I am not going to say that I wouldn't like to eat it too, because I would eat asparagus whenever I had an opportunity, but it is a moment when I feel sorry for people who have to feed chiefly at hotels and who do not have a vegetable garden of their own, for the difference between the taste of these two kinds of the same vegetable is great. They are indeed poles apart. Early forced bunches of large stems are expensive and succulent, but lack the delicious flavour of the fresh green stems from the garden asparagus bed. Freshness with asparagus is a *sine qua non*; even this delicate vegetable can acquire an unpleasant flavour if it has been kept too long at the vegetable shop. It is a vegetable which requires careful cooking; if the water races at boiling-point, the heads will drop off before the stems are cooked. It is as well to remember that the tips cook far more quickly than the stems, and that is why the bundles are put upright in a saucepan with the tips just above the surface of the water. Special asparagus containers may be bought, which simplifies cooking. If the bundles are laid in the pan horizontally they must be watched for overcooking.

According to the size, allow eight to ten stems per person. Cut all stalks of the same length, lightly scrape the white part of each with a sharp knife, and put into a large bowl of salted cold water. With large imported asparagus you may find isolated leaf points fairly low down the stem. These should be removed with the point of a sharp knife, as they sometimes contain grains of sand. Arrange in moderate bunches, not bigger than your hand can hold, tie in two places, trim the ends again, plunge into boiling salted water. Cook only until just tender, lift out at once and drain well. The time for cooking varies according to the age and size of the asparagus; after the water has returned to boiling-point allow from 12 to 14 minutes. Freshly cut small garden asparagus may take a shorter time.

Hot asparagus is piled neatly on a hot dish on a folded napkin and may be served simply with melted butter, which should be handed separately, or with beurre noisette (see page 169); or with hollandaise (see page 157). Cold asparagus may be served with a vinaigrette sauce, or with a cream sauce flavoured with tarragon or other herbs according to taste.

AUBERGINES

A description of this vegetable will be found in the previous chapter, page 232.

AUBERGINES A LA BOSTON

4 aubergines
2 onions, chopped and soft-
    ened in ¼ oz. butter
1 egg

2 oz. grated cheese
¼ pint thin béchamel sauce or
    cream
seasoning

Cut unpeeled aubergines in half lengthways. Run the point of a knife round the inside of the skin to a depth of 1 inch, and make several cuts across the fleshy part. Sprinkle with salt and allow to stand for half an hour. Dry them with a cloth and sprinkle with flour, then fry them, preferably in oil, on the cut side only. When they are cooked through, which will take about 8–10 minutes, lift them out of the frying-pan and allow to cool. With a metal spoon scoop out the inside flesh and chop up, adding softened onions, salt and pepper, egg, and grated cheese. Fill the empty cases with this mixture, place in a fireproof dish, and bake 10 minutes in a hot oven. Serve in the same dish and pour over thin béchamel sauce.

AUBERGINES HONGROISE

4–5 aubergines
yoghourt, sour milk, or sour
    cream
about ¼ pint oil
1–1½ lb. tomatoes
2–3 cloves of garlic

1 bay-leaf
1–2 sprigs of thyme or basil
paprika, salt, pepper
paprika sauce, optional (see
    next page)

Slice aubergines. Sprinkle with salt and leave half an hour. Fry quickly in hot oil. Prepare a well-reduced tomato pulp with ripe tomatoes, and the garlic and herbs to flavour, the whole simmered to a thick pulp, strained, and further reduced if necessary. Lay the slices of aubergine in a cake tin in shallow layers with the tomato pulp, yoghourt, and plenty of salt, pepper, and paprika. When the tin is full cover with buttered paper and bake in a moderate to hot oven 30–40 minutes. Turn out and serve as it is or pour over more yoghourt, sour milk or cream, or paprika sauce.

Paprika sauce

1 oz. butter	a bouquet garni
1 medium onion, finely chopped	seasoning
	1 gill stock
1 teaspoon paprika	2 tablespoons cream
1 teaspoon flour	lemon juice
¼ lb. tomatoes	

Melt the butter, add onion, cover, and cook till soft, about 2 minutes. Add paprika and cook a further 2 minutes; dust with the flour, add tomatoes, bouquet, seasoning, and stock and bring to boil. Simmer gently 20–30 minutes and strain. Reheat carefully, adding cream and lemon juice.

AUBERGINES GRATINÉES

4 aubergines	1 oz. fine breadcrumbs
flour for coating	½–¾ oz. butter
oil for frying	3 oz. grated cheese
½ pint tomato sauce, 1 or 2 (see page 178)	

Slice, salt, and drain the aubergines, wipe well and dip in flour, coating well. Have the oil very hot, put in the slices, and turn them after a few seconds. Take out, drain, and keep hot until all are fried. Put a layer of sauce in a fireproof dish, then grated cheese, then the aubergines. Continue putting these in layers until the dish is full, and finish off with tomato sauce, breadcrumbs, cheese, and melted butter. Put in a very hot oven to heat thoroughly and to brown on top.

AUBERGINES AVIGNONAISE

2 large aubergines	1 gill well-reduced tomato sauce (page 178), strongly flavoured with garlic
5 large firm tomatoes	
4 oz. mushrooms	
2 oz. black olives, halved and stoned	olive oil for frying
	salt, freshly ground pepper

Peel aubergines, cut into rounds a good ¼ inch thick and cover with salt, drain well. Fry on both sides in hot oil. Lay in a fireproof dish. Scald and skin tomatoes, cut off tops, scoop out and season inside.

Slice mushrooms, cook in a tablespoon of oil 2 or 3 minutes. Remove and add to olives. Moisten with sauce. Fill the tomatoes, arrange on the aubergines, dust with salt and pepper, sprinkle with olive oil, and cook in a moderate oven 7–10 minutes. These are good served with tomato sauce and sauté or lyonnaise potatoes.

AUBERGINES FARCIES PROVENÇALE

2 aubergines	2 cloves of garlic, crushed
4 tablespoons salad-oil	1 teaspoon chopped herbs
1 oz. butter	seasoning
4 medium-sized onions, finely sliced	grated cheese
	brown crumbs
4 large ripe tomatoes, peeled and emptied of pips	a little melted butter

Cut the aubergines in half, and with a knife slit round the edge and several times across. Sprinkle well with salt and leave 30 minutes. Drain, dry, and place them face downwards in the oil, which has been heated in a frying-pan. Fry 7 minutes, turning them once or twice and adding more oil if necessary. Lift out when brown and scrape the meat carefully from the skins; chop coarsely.

Melt the butter in a pan, add onions, and cook slowly without colouring until soft. Add the tomatoes, garlic, aubergine meat, herbs, and seasoning and simmer 5 minutes. Fill the mixture into the skins, dust well with the cheese and crumbs, sprinkle over each a little melted butter, and brown well under the grill or in the oven.

For Aubergines Caviar, an excellent dish, see Winkfield chapter, page 978.

BRUSSELS SPROUTS

In Chapter VIII reference was made to an economical use of the leaves of Brussels sprouts taken from a dish in which only the hearts were used. Equally this dish can be made from sprouts which are not so small as one would wish, perhaps towards the end of the season. It can also be made with various kales. This is the type of dish known in French books as 'pain,' and in American books often referred to as a vegetable mould.

PAIN DE CHOUX DE BRUXELLES

1½ lb. Brussels sprouts	1½ oz. fresh breadcrumbs, soaked in a wineglass of hot milk and passed through a wire sieve
1½ oz. butter	
seasoning	
nutmeg	1 egg yolk
	1½ gills sauce mornay (page 156) or sauce crème (page 156)

Boil the sprouts, drain, and press in small handfuls to extract all the water. Pass through a wire sieve. Put the purée into a pan, add the butter, reserving a small piece for greasing the mould. Mix, adding salt, pepper, and a grating of nutmeg. Stir well on a very low fire in order to melt the butter, then add the soaked bread and the egg yolk and adjust seasoning. Turn into a buttered charlotte mould and cook in the oven in a bain-marie for 40 minutes. Turn out and pour over a sauce crème or a sauce mornay.

CABBAGE

It is unusual to regard cabbage as a vegetable suitable to be eaten as a separate course, but the following is worthy of being offered in this way:

STUFFED CABBAGE

1–2 lb. cabbage	2 heaped tablespoons chopped
2 oz. butter or bacon fat	parsley and herbs
2 oz. onion, finely chopped	2 beaten eggs
3 oz. fresh white breadcrumbs	salt, freshly ground pepper

For finishing

1 oz. fresh white crumbs fried to a golden brown in ½ oz. butter	½ pint tomato sauce 1 (see page 178) or quick demi-glace (see page 256)

Trim cabbage but leave whole. Plunge it into a large pan of boiling water. Boil 3–4 minutes. Lift out into a colander, drain. Carefully detach the outside leaves (4–6) and put on one side. Cut the cabbage into quarters, cut away a little of the stalk, then slice and chop finely. Melt butter in a stew-pan, add onion, cover and cook gently 1–2 minutes. Add cabbage, press a piece of buttered paper on the top, cover pan and cook on slow heat 25–35 minutes, stirring thoroughly once or twice during the cooking. The cabbage should then be soft and golden all through. Draw aside, stir in the crumbs, herbs, eggs, and plenty of seasoning. Line a pudding basin with a piece of butter-muslin or clean cloth. Arrange the outside leaves in this, stalks uppermost. Fill with the mixture, fold over and tie the ends of the cloth as for a pudding. Lift out of the basin, and plunge the cabbage into a pan of boiling salted water or vegetable stock. Boil gently and steadily for 45 minutes to 1 hour. Turn it over once or twice during the cooking. Lift out into a colander, drain well, untie the cloth, and turn the cabbage over on to a hot dish. Sprinkle over the breadcrumbs, pour round the tomato sauce, and serve at once.

CHOU FARCI AUX MARRONS

1 medium-sized cabbage	¼ pint good stock
18 good chestnuts, peeled	a nut of butter
1 stick of celery	

For braising

2 rashers of bacon	½–¾ pint good stock
1 sliced onion	salt, pepper
1 sliced carrot	a bouquet garni

Garnish

¼ lb. chipolata sausages	chopped parsley
grilled rashers of bacon	sauce demi-glace (see next page)

Trim and blanch the cabbage. Put the chestnuts into a pan with the celery, stock, and butter. Simmer until just tender and the stock is absorbed.   Take out the heart of the cabbage, put in the chestnuts, and tie round with a piece of thread.   Lay the rashers on the bottom of a stew-pan or casserole, add the vegetables, cover and cook for a few minutes. Then lay the cabbage on this, pour round the stock.   Add seasoning and bouquet garni.   Cover and braise until tender, about 40 minutes.   Meanwhile fry or grill the sausages and grill the bacon.   Drain the cabbage and arrange in a serving dish.   Have ready the sauce and pour over.   Garnish with the chipolatas and bacon, and sprinkle over the chopped parsley.

Sauce demi-glace (quick method)

⅛ oz. dripping or butter	½ pint good stock
3 shallots, finely chopped	salt and pepper
1 rasher of bacon, finely chopped	1 teaspoon chopped mixed herbs
1 level dessertspoon flour	½ gill sherry
1 small teaspoon tomato purée	2 chopped mushrooms
a few mushroom peelings	

Heat the dripping in a small saucepan, add the shallots and bacon, and cook slowly to a golden brown.   Add the flour and allow to colour. Draw aside, add the purée, peelings, stock, and seasoning, bring to the boil, simmer 15 minutes; add the herbs, adjust seasoning, and boil for another 5 minutes.   Strain.   Reduce sherry in a saucepan to half, add the mushrooms, simmer 3–4 minutes.   Add the strained sauce, reboil, and simmer another 2–3 minutes.

CHOU FARCI LORRAINE

1 medium-sized cabbage	¼ pint stock or cider
½ lb. onions, sliced	1 bay-leaf
1 small head of celery	salt and freshly ground pepper
1 clove of garlic crushed with salt	½–¾ lb. chipolata or ordinary sausages
1 oz. good dripping or bacon fat	1 dessertspoon chopped parsley

Cut cabbage into four.   Blanch 7 minutes.   Drain well.   Cut quarters in half and arrange in a casserole.   Soften onions and celery in the dripping and when turning colour add the garlic, stock, and bay-leaf.   Season well, bring to boil, and simmer 5 minutes.   Pour over the cabbage, cover with a piece of buttered paper and the lid, and cook gently in the oven for about an hour.   The cabbage should be tender and succulent.

About 10 minutes before serving grill or fry the sausages.   Arrange round the cabbage and sprinkle over the parsley.

CABBAGE AND MUSHROOM DOLMAS

1 medium-sized cabbage	6 oz. rice
2 oz. onion	¾–1 pint stock or water
1½ oz. butter	salt and pepper
6 oz. mushrooms, chopped or sliced	½ pint milk
	grated cheese

Blanch the cabbage in boiling water for 2–3 minutes. Drain and carefully detach the leaves; replace the cabbage in the boiling water directly the leaves become stiff and difficult to detach. Chop the onion finely, soften in ½ oz. of the butter, add the mushrooms, and fry briskly for a few minutes; draw aside. In another pan fry the rice in ½ oz. of the butter, then join the two together. Add the water and seasoning, cover, and cook in the oven until the rice is tender and the stock absorbed. Lay the cabbage leaves out on a board, cut out any tough stalk, put a dessert to a tablespoon of rice on each leaf and roll up into a fat sausage, tucking in the ends. Finely slice any remaining cabbage, lay in the bottom of a fireproof dish, arrange the dolmas on this, pour over the milk, dot over the remaining butter, and scatter grated cheese over the dish. Cook in a moderate oven for at least 1 hour.

CAULIFLOWER

For general preparation of cauliflower see page 235.

CRÈME DE CHOU-FLEUR

1 large or 2 small cauliflowers or broccoli weighing 1¼–1½ lb.
1 bay-leaf
1¼ gills béchamel sauce made with 1 oz. butter, 1 oz. flour, 1¼ gills milk

2 eggs
1 tablespoon cream
salt and pepper
a little ground mace
a handful of good spinach leaves
sauce mornay (see page 156)

Prepare cauliflower as on page 235. Cook until tender in boiling salted water with the bay-leaf, then drain well, remove the bay-leaf, and rub cauliflower through a fine wire sieve. Weigh the purée; it should weigh 12 oz.–1 lb.

Make the béchamel according to the directions given on page 155. Dip the spinach leaves into boiling water for a minute or two, well butter a deep sandwich tin, charlotte mould, or shallow cake tin. Line the tin or mould with the leaves, laying the outside of the leaf against the tin.

Add the purée to the sauce, beating well. Season well with salt and pepper and flavour delicately with the mace. Beat in 1 egg and 1 yolk, reserving 1 white. Now add the cream, and lastly fold in the white, stiffly whipped. Fill into the mould, cover lightly with buttered paper, stand it in a tin of hot water, and put into a slow to moderate oven 20–30 minutes, or until firm to the touch. Turn out on to a hot dish and surround with a light sauce mornay.

CAULIFLOWER AU GRATIN

This dish can be absolutely delicious but also very disappointing. There should never be any hard bits of stalk or half-cooked cauliflower, and the sauce should be creamy and the whole dish melting. Although it will come to table looking like a whole cauliflower, in point of fact it is carefully prepared in the French way, so that every bit of the stalk is properly cooked. For a cauliflower weighing 2 lb. take:

Roux
1¼ oz. butter
1¼ oz. flour (scant)
¾ pint milk
salt, pepper, nutmeg

1¼ oz. gruyère cheese
1¼ oz. Parmesan cheese
2 large tablespoons fresh white breadcrumbs
1½ oz. butter

Prepare, wash, and cook the cauliflower in the French way (see page 236). Make the roux in a thick saucepan; add the milk, salt, pepper, and nutmeg. Stir till boiling and leave to simmer 4–5 minutes. Meanwhile grate the cheese and add 2 spoonfuls of each kind to the crumbs. Add the remainder of the cheese to the sauce and beat well until perfectly mixed and very creamy. Add the remaining butter off the fire, with the exception of a piece the size of a nut for the gratin. Adjust the seasoning. Arrange the sprigs of cauliflower in a buttered pudding basin (the flowers outwards and the stalks inwards), fill up the middle with sprigs, and, using a metal spoon, spoon in just enough sauce to bind the cauliflower. Turn out on to a fireproof dish and spoon over the rest of the sauce carefully. Sprinkle over the crumb mixture, and dot over with the butter. Brown quickly in a hot oven 8–10 minutes.

CHOU-FLEUR A L'ITALIENNE

1 cauliflower
½ pint sauce italienne, made with 1 oz. butter, 1 chopped onion, 2 mushrooms, 1 oz. cooked ham or bacon, shredded, ½ oz. flour, 1 teaspoon tomato purée, seasoning, ½ gill white wine, ¼ pint good brown stock

Prepare the cauliflower in the French way (see page 236). Cook until tender in boiling salted water, drain thoroughly. Oil or butter a warm basin and arrange the cauliflower sprigs in it, adding a spoonful of the sauce. Press lightly with the hand and turn out on a hot dish. Coat with remainder of the sauce.

Sauce. Melt the butter, add the onion, mushrooms, and ham (or bacon) and cook slowly, stirring frequently, for 7–10 minutes. (If using bacon in place of ham it should be blanched first.) Draw aside, mix in the flour, purée, and seasoning, pour on the wine and stock and bring to the boil. Simmer 10–15 minutes with the lid off.

N.B. This sauce is also good with scorzonera and celeriac. For classic recipe for sauce italienne see sauce chapter, page 147.

PAIN DE CHOU-FLEUR

¾ lb. cooked cauliflower
¾ pint thick béchamel sauce
  (see page 155)
4 eggs

3 oz. grated cheese
salt, pepper, and grated nutmeg
tomato sauce (see page 178)

Put the cauliflower through a sieve, then mix it with the sauce, add beaten eggs, grated cheese, salt, pepper, and nutmeg. Put into a well-greased mould and cook in a saucepan one-third full of boiling water for 40 minutes; turn out and mask with a tomato sauce.

CHOU-FLEUR TOSCANA

1 large cauliflower
1½ oz. butter
1 teaspoon chopped chives
2 oz. chopped mushrooms
1¼ gills stock

seasoning
2 yolks of egg
½ gill thin cream
2 rounds of hot buttered toast
1 teaspoon chopped parsley

Prepare the cauliflower in the French way (see page 236) and blanch for 7 minutes. Drain, return to the pan with half the butter, the chives, chopped mushrooms, stock, and seasoning. Cover with a buttered paper and the lid and simmer 15–20 minutes. Beat the yolks with the cream and seasoning in a pan, pour on the strained juice from the cauliflower, and thicken carefully over the fire without boiling, adding the rest of the butter by degrees. Cut the buttered toast into squares, lay them on a hot dish, arrange the cauliflower sprigs on the top, and coat over the sauce. Scatter over the chopped parsley and serve at once.

N.B. It is easy to curdle this sauce, and a good pinch of corn-flour may be added to the egg to prevent this.

The following is a delicious dish for a first course for luncheon:

CAULIFLOWER FRITTERS A LA VILLEROY

1 cauliflower, medium to large
1½ gills well-flavoured béchamel
  sauce, made with 1 oz. flour,
  1 oz. butter, ½ gill milk

1 egg yolk
1 teaspoon chopped parsley
fritter batter
deep fat for frying

Have ready a good fritter batter (see page 441).

Prepare the cauliflower in the French way (see page 236). Cook until tender but firm. Make the béchamel sauce and beat in the egg yolk while still warm, add parsley. Turn on to a plate to cool, spread on to each sprig of cauliflower a fairly thick coating of béchamel. When all are ready heat the fat till it smokes slightly, dip the sprigs quickly into the batter and straight into the fat. When golden brown drain and serve with a good sauce, such as tomato (page 178) or mushroom (page 176).

On page 236 is a recipe for cauliflower and mint sauce, which with certain garnishes is good to serve separately.

CELERY

CELERY AND MUSHROOMS ON TOAST

2 heads of celery	1 gill rich milk or cream
¼ lb. mushrooms	seasoning and a bay-leaf
½ oz. butter	rounds of buttered toast
1 dessertspoon flour	

Cook the celery till tender in salted water. Prepare and chop the mushrooms and toss them in butter. Sprinkle with flour. Drain and dry the celery. Chop roughly and add to the mushrooms. Add a whole bay-leaf, seasoning, and the cream. Mix well, heat gently, remove bay-leaf, and serve on buttered toast.

CHESTNUTS

The following croquettes of chestnut may be served as an accompaniment to turkey or chicken, as part of the dish of Fritto Misto, or, if made sufficiently small, as cocktail savouries. If offered as a first course for luncheon they should be accompanied by a good sauce.

CROQUETTES DE MARRON

Prepare some chestnuts as usual (see page 48) and boil them till soft. Rub through a sieve, season with salt and pepper, a pinch of cayenne, and a little very finely minced parsley or fresh marjoram. Mix in a walnut of butter and enough top of milk or good cream to make a fairly thick paste. Spread on to a board to cool, and then shape. Dredge with flour, dip in beaten egg, roll in fine breadcrumbs, and fry in deep fat till a golden brown. Pile high on a folded napkin and garnish with bunches of fried parsley. Serve with a demi-glace, piquante, or tomato sauce (see pages 143, 177, and 178).

CHICORY

STUFFED ENDIVES (CHICORY)

6 good heads of chicory	a few drops of lemon juice
1–2 oz. onion, finely chopped	2 tablespoons fresh bread-crumbs
1 oz. butter	
3 oz. chopped mushrooms	½ pint tomato sauce (see next page)
seasoning	
1 tablespoon mixed chopped herbs	1 heaped tablespoon Parmesan cheese
grated rind of 1 orange or lemon	½ oz. melted butter for finishing

Trim the heads of chicory. Blanch 3–4 minutes, then drain and dry. Split each head three parts through and lay in a buttered fireproof dish dusted out with some of the cheese.

Soften the onion in the butter. Add the mushrooms and cook another minute or two, then turn into a bowl. Add seasoning, the herbs, orange rind, lemon juice, and breadcrumbs. Fill this mixture into the heads of chicory. Heat sauce and pour over. Scatter on the rest of the cheese and sprinkle with the extra ½ oz. butter. Put into the oven for 15 minutes.

Tomato sauce for endives

1 lb. red, ripe tomatoes
a bouquet of a stick of celery, 1 clove of garlic crushed with salt, basil or lemon thyme, parsley stalks, and ½ bay-leaf

salt and freshly ground black pepper
a nut of butter
1 wineglass stock or water

Wipe the tomatoes and cut into small pieces, first removing the seeds. Put into a saucepan with the remaining ingredients, cover and simmer for a good hour. Then remove the bouquet and rub through a strainer. Turn into a small saucepan, reheat, and reduce further if necessary. The sauce should be a rich dark red.

VEGETABLE MARROWS

A large marrow may have to be split lengthwise, stuffed, and then tied together again for cooking. A medium fruit is better not split; a slice is cut off from the stalk end and the centre scooped out with the handle of a spoon. The marrow may then be blanched in boiling salted water for 2–3 minutes. After stuffing it may, according to size and age, be either braised or baked and well basted with a little butter or good dripping. It may also be cooked in the sauce which is to accompany it. Stuffed marrow should be accompanied by good tomato or brown sauce or gravy.

Sometimes the marrow is peeled, cut in slices 1½–2 inches thick, and the seeds stamped out with a cutter. After blanching, the slices, drained, are arranged in a buttered fireproof dish and then filled with a suitable filling.

Various fillings may be taken from the chapter on force-meats and stuffings (page 691), and the following unconventional one is good in the late summer:

STUFFED MARROW

Use young marrows or courgettes for this dish.

1–2 marrows, according to size
1 oz. butter, melted
salt and freshly ground black pepper
1½ gills creamy béchamel sauce: ¾ oz. butter, ¾ oz. flour, 1½ gills flavoured milk (see béchamel sauce, short method, page 155), 1 table-spoon cream

3 hard-boiled eggs, coarsely chopped
½ lb. runner or French beans, sliced or trimmed, boiled and well drained
½ oz. butter for finishing the beans and tomato
½ pint thin brown or tomato sauce or good gravy
2 tomatoes
chopped parsley

Peel and split marrows. Scoop out the seeds. Blanch 1–2 minutes. Drain well. Sprinkle with the melted butter and seasoning, pack closely together in a buttered fireproof dish, cover with buttered paper, and slip into a moderate oven 10–15 minutes, or until barely tender. The paper may be removed after 5 minutes and the marrow basted with the butter. Meanwhile make the béchamel and add the hard-boiled eggs to it. Have ready the beans. Season them and add a nut of butter. Take the marrow from the oven, pour off any liquor from the dish. Add to the brown or tomato sauce.

Fill half the marrow with the egg mixture and half with the beans. Pour round a little of the brown sauce, cover with buttered paper and set in a moderate oven 5 minutes. Halve the tomatoes and fry or grill quickly in the remaining butter. Take out the dish and set a piece of tomato at the end of each half-marrow. Dust well with chopped parsley and serve with the rest of the brown sauce.

MUSHROOMS

Forced mushrooms, available all the year, are very useful, but it is when the field mushrooms come in that the following dishes are at their best.

FIELD MUSHROOMS IN CREAM SAUCE (FOR 4–6)

1–1½ lb. mushrooms	1 gill rich milk or cream (good
a little butter	measure)
salt	finely chopped parsley
a sprinkle of flour	freshly ground black pepper
	rounds of buttered toast

Peel and prepare the mushrooms. Well butter a frying-pan and lay in it the mushroom caps with the hollow side upwards. Put a little butter and salt into each one, sprinkle over the flour, add milk or cream and cook slowly, shaking over finely chopped parsley and pepper before serving on buttered toast.

The above may be used in the following way:

MUSHROOM-FILLED FRENCH ROLLS

Take small fresh French rolls, cut a slice off the top, pull out the crumb, butter lightly inside and out, bake in the oven till crisp, and fill with the hot mushroom mixture.

When mushrooms are brought in from the fields they often vary a good deal in size and perfection; the following dish makes good use of all:

FIELD MUSHROOMS ON TOAST

Put the better-shaped mushrooms, hollow side up, in a buttered dish. chop finely and season well with salt and pepper a number of imperfect ones. Fill the cups with this filling, dot with butter, and bake till done, about 15 minutes. These may be served on buttered toast and should be served hot.

BEIGNETS DE CHAMPIGNON

Choose small mushrooms, not opened out—in other words, button mushrooms. Do not peel but rub with a clean cloth dipped in salt. Have ready a good light fritter batter (page 441), well seasoned. Dip each mushroom into this and fry in deep fat. They should be accompanied by a sharp sauce, sauce tartare or devil sauce (see pages 168 and 145). They are suitable for a cocktail savoury or for a last course at dinner, or they may make part of the dish of Fritto Misto given on page 276.

ONIONS

The following dish of stuffed onions and mushrooms is good:

ONIONS AND MUSHROOMS

4 Spanish onions, peeled and blanched	2 hard-boiled eggs
1 pint water (approx.)	1 tablespoon cream
juice of ½ lemon	1 teaspoon chopped savory or sage
1 oz. butter	1 tablespoon Parmesan cheese
seasoning	¼ lb. mushrooms

Put in a saucepan water, lemon juice, and half of the butter, pepper and salt. Cook the onions in this for about 10 minutes. Take them out, scoop out the centres, chop these finely, and add the chopped hard-boiled eggs, chopped savory, and cream. Stuff the onions with this mixture and tie round with string. Put in a fireproof dish and pour over half the stock in which the onions were cooked. Sprinkle over cheese, cover with grease-proof paper, cook for 1½ hours, and serve in the dish they were cooked in with the mushrooms, which have been cooked in the rest of the butter between two plates in the oven.

ONIONS AND POTATO

This is a simple luncheon dish liked by children.

4 large onions	6 medium-sized potatoes, mashed, and butter and milk for mashing
½ pint stock or milk and water	
bay-leaf and bouquet of herbs	seasoning

Parboil peeled onions in salted water 10 minutes. Drain. Scoop out centres, leaving ¼-inch shell. Put stock or milk and water with bay-leaf and bouquet in baking-pan and put in the onion shells. Bake and baste till tender. Meanwhile boil and mash potatoes in the proper way (see pages 202–3), beat and season well. Fill onions with mashed potato. Fry the scooped-out onion and scatter over the top.

POTATOES

POTATO AND CHEESE FRITTERS

¾ lb. potatoes, weighed after cooking
2 eggs
2 tablespoons cream, or rich milk and butter
seasoning and a speck of cayenne

1½ oz. grated cheese, Parmesan if possible
a pinch of chopped parsley
a pinch of curry-powder (optional)

Sieve the potatoes, keeping hot. Beat egg yolks and add to cream. Incorporate with potato, cheese, and seasoning. Beat the egg whites and fold in. Drop into hot fat from a spoon and fry till golden brown; or take the same mixture, omit the beaten whites, form into cakes, coat lightly with flour and egg and crumb, and fry.

The following dish is a mixture of potatoes and cheese cooked in a frying-pan. Melting and golden, it is good for a simple luncheon with salad.

POTATO AND CHEESE PANCAKE

This is really a winter dish as it must be made with old potatoes.

Peel about 8 good-sized potatoes and slice into ¼-inch rounds. If the potatoes are peeled some time before they are needed and are put into water, they must be well dried before slicing. Have ready about 3 oz. grated cheese. Melt a little butter or lard in a large frying-pan, just enough to prevent the potatoes from burning. Cover the whole pan with an overlapping layer of potato rings, arranging them in diminishing circles round the pan. Sprinkle with salt, pepper, and one-third of the cheese. Repeat two more layers of potatoes and seasoning, ending with cheese. Cover with a lid or large metal plate, and cook slowly on moderate heat for about three-quarters of an hour, till the potatoes are soft. Run a palette-knife under the cake to loosen it from the pan. Turn over or slide on to a serving dish. It should turn out firm and compact and golden on both sides.

When we were young there was a potato and tomato dish much liked by us all:

NURSERY POTATOES

1–1½ lb. potatoes
the grated rind of 1 orange
seasoning
tomato coulis (as given for Spinach Galette, page 267) or a tin of tomatoes heated, reduced a little, and well

seasoned with pepper, salt, and sugar; in either case a good squeeze of orange juice may be added
chopped parsley
finely shredded blanched orange rind (optional)

Boil the potatoes, drain, and return to the pan to dry well. Add the orange rind and plenty of seasoning. Put through a potato ricer and with a spoon arrange lightly in a ring in a hot dish. Have ready the tomato and pour it into the centre of the ring. Sprinkle the dish well with the parsley. Orange rind can also be scattered over the top.

The following potato and cheese mixture may be used in the same way:

Make some mashed potatoes, add grated cheese (2 oz. to 1½ lb. potatoes), mix well together, pile in a fireproof dish in a ring, and brown lightly in a hot oven or under the grill. Put tomato in the centre.

POTATOES MONTE CARLO

6 large even-sized potatoes	salt, pepper
4 cobs of green corn or a small	hot milk and a nut of butter
tin of creamed corn	6 oz. cooked flaked fish
¾ oz. butter	browned crumbs
1 dessertspoon chopped chives	1 oz. grated cheese
or 1 chopped shallot	melted butter

Sauce

½ oz. butter	1½ gills milk
½ oz. flour	salt, pepper, mustard

Roll potatoes in salt and bake until soft. Meanwhile cut or scrape the corn from the cob. Melt butter, add corn, and cook slowly until turning colour. Draw aside, add chives and seasoning. Prepare sauce by melting butter and adding flour off the fire, pour on the milk and stir until boiling. Draw aside, add seasoning and mustard. Cut top off the potatoes lengthways, scoop out the pulp, mash with hot milk and a nut of butter. Season. Set potato skins firmly on a baking-sheet. Put the corn mixture at the bottom of each, arrange fish lightly on the top, and pour over the sauce. Pile the creamed potato high on the top, sprinkle with browned crumbs, grated cheese, and melted butter, and brown in a hot oven.

SEA-KALE

This is another vegetable probably more appreciated in England than in France. Sometimes early in the season one may unfortunately buy forced heads which have perhaps been cut for several days and are not crisp and juicy as they should be. These are not calculated to win enthusiasts. Small crisp heads, the stems of which snap off when lightly bent, are a different thing. In the old days when people had large gardens, good gardeners, and adequate help, sea-kale was one of the most appreciated vegetables of winter and early spring. Early in the winter it would be brought in from the greenhouse where it had been forced in darkness under the staging; later, batches might come from boxed roots grown in dark sheds or cellars. Last of all it came in from outside. Here it might be grown in beds edged with planks which held in place the thick covering of leaves used to blanch it.   In smaller gardens triangular groups of three plants covered with weathered, sifted ashes serve the same purpose.   On a cold March day it is always an excitement to see the first cracks in the cone of ashes which on examination show first the purplish leaf tip and then, after a gentle scrabbling, the white, crisp heads.   The usual way to eat it in earlier days was as a vegetable entrée: blanched, finished with butter, and served on buttered toast with a sauce-boat of melted or noisette butter, or hollandaise sauce.

The white heads require very little preparation, only trimming at the root and washing under running water.   They may be shortened a little if necessary and tied into little bundles.   The water in which they are cooked should be slightly acidulated so that the heads remain white.   The nicest way to eat sea-kale is to blanch it till tender, 20–30 minutes according to age and size, drain it well, and serve it as described.   Another method is to blanch it till tender, drain it, and allow it to cool.   Cut the stems into suitable lengths, dip them in flour and egg and breadcrumbs, and fry in deep fat.   Or equally the pieces may be dipped into fritter batter and fried.   Sea-kale, of course, may also be blanched and served in a good white sauce, though this is not the most interesting way of presenting it.

SPINACH

PAIN D'ÉPINARDS

1½ lb. good spinach
1½ oz. butter
salt, pepper, a grating of nut-meg

1½ oz. fresh breadcrumbs soaked in a wineglass of hot milk
1 egg yolk
1½ gills sauce (sauce mornay or sauce crème, page 156)

Cook the spinach, drain, and press well to extract all the water.   Pass through a wire sieve.   Put the purée into a pan, add the butter, reserving a small piece for greasing the mould.   Mix, adding the salt, pepper, and nutmeg.   Stir well on a low fire in order to melt the butter, then add the soaked bread and egg yolk and readjust the seasoning.   Turn into a buttered charlotte mould and cook in the oven in a bain-marie for 40 minutes.   Turn out and pour over a sauce crème or mornay.

SPINACH CREAM WITH MUSHROOMS

2 lb. spinach
½ pint béchamel sauce (made with 1 oz. butter, 1 oz. flour, and ½ pint flavoured milk)

2 beaten eggs
1 tablespoon cream
salt, pepper, and nutmeg
salpicon (see next page)

Boil the spinach, drain, and press well. Sieve. Have ready the béchamel sauce, add the spinach purée, mixing thoroughly. Stir in the eggs and cream, season with salt and pepper and a small grating of nutmeg.

Turn into a well-buttered ring or savarin mould. Stand in a roasting-tin on a doubled piece of paper, surround with boiling water, lay a piece of buttered paper over the top and cook in a moderately slow oven until firm to the touch, 30–40 minutes. Turn out on to a hot dish and fill the centre of the mould with a salpicon of mushrooms.

Salpicon

¾ oz. butter
1 dessertspoon finely chopped
  onion
6–8 oz. mushrooms, trimmed
  and peeled
a squeeze of lemon juice

1 dessertspoon flour
¾ gill vegetable stock
½ gill sherry
salt, pepper, a pinch of ground
  mace

Heat a frying-pan, drop in butter, and when foaming add onion. Cook a minute or two, add mushrooms, quartered, and cook briskly 4–5 minutes, shaking pan frequently and adding the lemon juice. Draw aside, mix in the flour, add stock and sherry. Bring to boil, season well, and boil rapidly until creamy; use at once.

EGG AND SPINACH GALETTE (HOT)

4 eggs
4 tablespoons spinach purée
  (see page 230)
2 tablespoons milk or cream
salt

pepper
1 oz. butter
tomato coulis (see below)
½ pint sauce mornay (see page
  156)

Beat the eggs with a fork, add purée, cream, and seasoning. Heat a small omelet pan (6–7 inches diameter on the bottom), drop in a nut of the butter and a quarter of the egg mixture and cook like a pancake, turning carefully. Repeat with the remaining butter and mixture, making four rounds. Turn into the serving dish as each one is done, spreading with a spoonful or two of the coulis, and make thoroughly hot in the oven for a minute or two. Then pour over a light mornay sauce and cut like a cake before serving. This may be garnished with bread snippets fried in garlic butter to a golden brown.

Tomato coulis for Egg and Spinach Galette

½ lb. red, ripe tomatoes
1 bunch of spring onions
½ oz. butter

salt
pepper
a pinch of ground mace

Peel the tomatoes. Slice and remove the seeds. Melt the butter in a stew-pan, add the onions, cook for a minute or two, then add the tomatoes and seasoning. Cover and simmer to a pulp, 20–30 minutes.

In place of tomato coulis other salpicon mixtures may be used, or you may use a good mushroom sauce for the spreading, or prawns tossed in butter.

The galette itself may be made with a firm purée of other vegetables, carrots or onions, provided you keep the proportion of purée and eggs the same.

EGG AND SPINACH ROULETTE

1 lb. good spinach	4 eggs
½ oz. butter	grated Parmesan
salt, pepper	

Filling

6 oz. mushrooms	¾ gill milk or veal stock
½ oz. butter	⅛ gill (2 tablespoons) cream
½ oz. flour	grated nutmeg

Cook spinach in boiling salted water, drain well, rub through a sieve. Stir in butter, salt, pepper, and the yolks of the eggs, one at a time. Whip the whites to a firm snow, fold into the mixture. Have ready a Swiss roll tin lined with buttered paper, or make a case with firm white paper (see note on Swiss roll, page 808). Spread mixture quickly on this, about ¼ inch thick, and dust well with the Parmesan. Bake in a hot oven about 10 minutes. Meanwhile prepare filling. Slice the mushrooms thinly. Sauter in the butter, add the flour off the fire with seasoning, pour on the milk and bring to the boil. Simmer to a creamy consistency, draw aside, add a dusting of grated nutmeg and the cream. Turn the soufflé out on to a piece of grease-proof paper laid on a warm enamel tray or board. Quickly peel off the paper, spread with the mushroom mixture, and roll up. Serve on a hot dish; for serving cut in slices.

FRIED SPINACH

This is a simple and very good luncheon dish. Left over spinach can be used: it need not be specially cooked for this purpose. Take rounds or squares of bread, spread with butter, heap with cooked well-seasoned spinach, add a little grated onion to the top. Place in a frying-pan in hot fat and fry till the bread is golden brown. Then with a palette-knife lift gently and turn over and fry the top of the spinach. Season well with black pepper and serve very hot.

SUBRICS A L'ITALIENNE

½ oz. butter	seasoning, nutmeg
1 lb. cooked spinach	1 beaten egg
1 teaspoon flour	sauce italienne

Put butter in pan, add spinach, cook quickly to dry off. Add flour, seasoning, a grating of nutmeg, and egg. Fry tablespoons of the mixture in a little hot oil, turning once very gently. Arrange in a dish and serve with sauce italienne as for Chou-fleur à l'Italienne (see page 258).

SPINACH FRITTERS

½ pint well-seasoned spinach
purée (page 230), thoroughly
dried with a nut of butter

2 small eggs
1 dessertspoon grated Parmesan
a grating of lemon peel

Prepare the purée and dry off well with a nut of butter in the pan over the fire. Allow to cool a little, then add yolks of egg, cheese, and grated peel. Allow to get almost cold, then fold in the egg whites, stiffly beaten. Drop in spoonfuls into hot fat in a shallow frying-pan, turn once, drain and serve.

For pancakes filled with spinach see Crêpes d'Épinards, page 435.

SWEET CORN

Corn on the cob may be boiled or baked. The outer husks are removed except for the innermost layer, which may remain on and be taken off at table. The silk is pulled off in a downward movement.

To boil. Twenty minutes in boiling salted water or 3–4 minutes if the corn starts in cold water should suffice. The corn is then served on a folded napkin. Beurre noisette (page 169) may be offered, or fresh pats of cold butter may be spread on the hot corn at table.

To bake. Very tender ears should be chosen for this purpose. The husks are not removed before cooking. The whole ears with husks and silk complete are baked in the oven for about half an hour, after which these are removed at table.

The following is a good luncheon dish made with tinned corn off the cob:

1 onion, finely chopped
1 oz. butter
3 or 4 tomatoes, peeled and
quartered
½ oz. flour
seasoning of salt, pepper, and
paprika

1 small teaspoon made mustard
1 gill hot milk
a small tin of corn
yolk of an egg
freshly fried small croûtons

Soften onion in butter, add tomatoes, flour, seasonings, and mustard, cook for a few minutes and add hot milk gradually, reserving a spoonful to mix with the egg yolk. Stir into this the corn. Thicken with the yolk mixed with reserved milk. Serve with the croûtons laid on top. The mixture may be turned into a fireproof dish, sprinkled with breadcrumbs and melted butter, and browned in the oven.

SWEET PEPPERS

STUFFED SWEET PEPPERS

To prepare. Remove a slice from the stalk end and scoop out seeds and pithy veins. Put the hollowed peppers into boiling salted water and cook uncovered till tender. They may also be parboiled and finished off in the oven. After parboiling and filling they should be arranged in a baking-tin containing a little water to prevent scorching, and some recipes call for the skin to be rubbed with butter before baking.

Stuffings

For 6–8 peppers

1 large onion, sliced and softened in a little butter or oil
1½ lb. tomatoes, skinned and
   emptied of seeds

seasoning of salt, pepper, and
   celery salt
the flesh of 2 outdoor cucumbers, chopped

Soften onion and add other ingredients. Cook all together till soft, fill the peppers, and finish off in the oven for a few minutes.

Other fillings

1. Cooked mushrooms and breadcrumbs added to a softened sliced onion with a little cooked rice, seasoning, and a spoonful or two of gravy may be filled into the blanched peppers. The top is then dotted with butter and the whole baked in the oven.

2. Fresh corn filling is good. For this the fresh grain may be scraped from the cob and cooked in a double boiler with a nut of butter, seasoning, and a little milk till tender (or tinned corn seasoned and mixed with cream may be used). Fill the peppers with this mixture, sprinkle with freshly ground pepper, and finish off in the oven.

3. For each pepper allow 1 hard-boiled egg; chop the eggs and mix with a good béchamel sauce, season well. Add crisply fried bacon broken in small pieces to the mixture. Parboil the peppers, fill with the mixture, sprinkle with freshly ground pepper and crumbs, dot with butter, and bake till soft.

Other fillings may be taken from those given for tomatoes (page 271). Peppers may be parboiled, dipped in batter, and deep fat fried. They may also be blanched, dried, fried in butter, and served with a sharp dressing.

PIMENTO DOUX FARCIS (RED SWEET PEPPERS STUFFED)

6 large, red, sweet peppers
1–2 oz. onion
¾ oz. butter
4 oz. mushrooms
4 oz. lean ham or tongue
2–3 oz. fresh white breadcrumbs
1 dessertspoon chopped mixed
   herbs

¼ pint demi-glace sauce
   (approx.) (see page 256)
1–2 tablespoons sherry
seasoning
melted butter
brown crumbs

Cut the tops off the peppers and remove the seeds. Put into boiling salted water and simmer 15 minutes. Meanwhile chop the onion finely and soften in the butter, add the mushrooms, also chopped, and cook for a few minutes. Draw aside, add the finely shredded ham or tongue, the crumbs and herbs. Moisten with the sauce and sherry and adjust the seasoning. Fill this mixture into the peppers and lay in buttered baking-dish. Brush over with melted butter, sprinkle with brown crumbs, and finally sprinkle with more melted butter. Bake in a moderate oven 15 minutes.

A piperade is a dish of eggs and vegetables. In the following recipe peppers, tomatoes, and eggs are cooked together slowly so that the flavours merge. A piperade may be served hot or cold: hot with a garnish of garlic toasts or croûtes and cold with boiled rice. The whole may be served inside a hollowed-out French loaf for a picnic.

PIPERADE

2 red sweet peppers	4 eggs
⅓ lb. good ripe tomatoes	2 tablespoons milk
2 oz. butter	croûtons of bread spread with
1 shallot, finely chopped	garlic-flavoured butter and
2 cloves of garlic, finely chopped	grilled until crisp
seasoning	

Prepare and shred the peppers, and blanch. Scald and skin the toma-toes, squeeze to remove the seeds, and chop. Heat a sauté or stew-pan, drop in the butter, and when frothing put in the shallot and garlic. When turning colour add the peppers, and after 4–5 minutes the tomatoes. Season well and leave to simmer. Meanwhile beat the eggs up with a fork, add milk and seasoning. When the peppers and tomatoes are soft and well reduced, pour in the eggs. Cook a further 3–4 minutes. Turn on to a hot dish and surround with the garlic-flavoured croûtons of bread. If to be served cold, turn into a long French roll, with the top cut off, the crumb scooped out, and the case spread with garlic butter and baked lightly.

TOMATOES

TOMATES AU GRATIN A LA PROVENÇALE

3 large onions	chopped lemon thyme and
oil or dripping for frying	coarsely chopped tarragon
6–7 tomatoes, peeled and	leaves
sliced	browned crumbs
seasoning and grated nutmeg	melted dripping
2–3 potatoes, boiled but only	
just cooked, and cut in very	
thin slices	

Cut onions into thin rings. Lightly brown in oil or dripping in a frying-pan. Put a little of the hot fat in a fireproof dish, add a layer of tomatoes, season, and cover with a third of the fried onion. Add the potatoes. Season. Add half the remaining fried onion, the nutmeg, and then another layer of well-seasoned tomatoes. Add the rest of the fried onion, the lemon thyme, and the tarragon leaves. Finish with some browned crumbs, sprinkle with melted dripping, and bake for half an hour in the oven.

TOMATOES FILLED WITH MUSHROOMS AND BAKED

6 even-sized tomatoes	1 dessertspoon capers
½ lb. mushrooms	1 tablespoon chopped parsley
1 oz. butter	seasoning
2 tablespoons breadcrumbs, fried	a little cream
	a clove of garlic
3 large rashers of bacon	

Slice or chop the mushrooms, sauter in two-thirds of the butter, and use the remaining one-third for frying the crumbs. Grill bacon till crisp, cut into small pieces and add to the mushrooms with the capers and parsley. Season well and bind with a little cream. Peel the tomatoes, cut off the tops and scoop out the seeds and core. Rub a deep fireproof dish with a little butter and a clove of garlic. Fill the tomatoes with the mixture, place the crumbs on the top, set tomatoes in the dish, lay over a piece of grease-proof paper, and bake in a moderate oven 10–15 minutes.

The following dish may be used as a garnish to meats, but is good eaten separately with salad or another vegetable dish:

TOMATOES AND PEPPERS AU GRATIN

3 large tomatoes	1 oz. butter
1 cupful each of:	salt, pepper, sugar
finely sliced onion	grated Parmesan cheese
finely sliced green peppers	a little melted butter

Slice tomatoes 1 inch thick, lay on a buttered dish. Sauter the onions and peppers separately in the butter. Sprinkle the slices of tomato with sugar, salt, and pepper and cover thickly with the onions and peppers. Scatter over the Parmesan cheese, sprinkle with a little extra melted butter, and bake in a hot oven 10–15 minutes.

STUFFED TOMATOES A LA SOUBISE

The garnish of crisp onion rings is an agreeable feature of this dish.

4 oz. mushrooms	¾ oz. flour
2 oz. butter	scant ¼ pint milk
seasoning	3 Spanish onions
½ oz. grated cheese	½ egg white
1 large slice of stale bread	seasoned flour
6 large firm tomatoes	frying fat
½ lb. onions	

1. Wash the mushrooms, chop finely. Melt ¼ oz. of the butter, add the mushrooms, cook 4–5 minutes, draw aside, season, and stir in the cheese. Cut the bread into small dice (croûtons) and fry in deep or shallow fat until golden brown. Drain and add to the mushroom mixture. Set aside.

2. For the soubise sauce: Chop the onions, blanch 5 minutes. Drain well and return to the pan with 1 oz. of the butter and salt and pepper. Cover tightly and cook slowly until quite tender, without allowing them to colour. Rub through a sieve or strainer. Melt the remaining butter in a saucepan, add the flour off the fire, pour on the milk and stir until boiling. Add the onion purée and simmer until thoroughly blended and creamy. Adjust seasoning, cover, and keep hot in a bain-marie.

3. Meanwhile slice the Spanish onions into thick rounds, push out into rings, and coat thoroughly with the lightly beaten egg white. Dust well with seasoned flour, coat again, and leave until ready to fry.

4. Scald the tomatoes, skin, cut off the tops and carefully scoop out the seeds. Fill with the mushroom mixture, replace the tops, arrange in a fireproof dish, and set in a moderate oven 5–7 minutes until thoroughly hot. Meanwhile fry the onion rings in smoking hot deep fat. Drain well. To dish spoon the soubise sauce over the tomatoes, and surround with the onion rings.

TOMATOES, CORN, AND SWEET PEPPERS ON TOAST

3 onions	4 tablespoons finely chopped
2 oz. butter	celery or cucumber
3 sweet green peppers, finely	seasoning
chopped	1 teaspoon sugar
3 cobs of corn	buttered toast
3–4 tomatoes	

Slice onions thinly, soften in butter, add peppers and celery, cook 5 minutes. Scrape corn from cobs in way described on page 243. Peel tomatoes, squeeze out seeds, and slice. Cook all together in a double boiler with seasoning and sugar for about 1 hour (or in a thick saucepan on low heat, but then it must be watched). Serve on rounds of buttered toast.

If this is made with fresh corn it is very good. Tinned corn may be used, a small tin for this quantity.

TOMATES FARCIES DUXELLES

4 large, firm, ripe tomatoes	1 dessertspoon finely chopped
4 good, even-sized mushrooms	herbs (parsley, lemon thyme,
1–2 shallots	basil)
1 stick of celery	seasoning
2 tablespoons breadcrumbs	1 egg yolk
a little milk	bread and garlic butter
1½ oz. bacon fat, good dripping,	
or margarine	

Clean mushrooms with a cloth dipped in salt, peel, cut off stems, and chop stalks and peelings finely. Chop shallots and celery and put crumbs to soak in milk. Heat half the fat in a small sauté pan, put in shallots and chopped mushroom peelings, simmer slowly 5–7 minutes, add herbs, seasoning, and crumbs. Continue cooking gently till the mixture will leave the sides of the pan clean, draw away from heat, add egg and adjust seasoning. Cut off the tops of the tomatoes, scoop out seeds and juice. Heat remaining fat and fry the mushrooms. Fill the tomatoes with the mixture from the pan, put a mushroom on top of each. Spread bread with garlic-flavoured butter, toast well, arrange a tomato on each slice, cover with buttered paper and cook 10 minutes in the oven.

TOMATES FARCIES PROVENÇALE

4 large tomatoes
1 oz. butter or 1 tablespoon olive oil
1 onion, finely chopped
1 clove of garlic, chopped
3 or 4 tablespoons fresh bread-crumbs

salt, freshly ground pepper
2 anchovies, well washed and mashed to a paste
½ oz. butter to finish

Cut tomatoes in half and strain the scooped-out insides into a basin. Set the halves in a greased fireproof dish. Heat oil or butter in a frying-pan and in it cook onion and garlic gently until soft. Add the strained tomato pulp and continue cooking till all is softened and blended. Add enough breadcrumbs to make a firm, moist mixture; add the anchovies. Stir well, season with pepper and very little salt. Put the mixture into the halves of tomato, dot with butter, and bake about 30 minutes in a moderate oven.

TOMATOES STUFFED WITH CUCUMBER AND BAKED

4–6 good-sized tomatoes, scalded and peeled
1 onion, sliced, and ½ clove of garlic, crushed
½ oz. butter
¾ oz. flour

seasoning and sugar
1 medium cucumber, peeled and diced
½ pint thin béchamel sauce or cream
fried white breadcrumbs

Scoop out tomatoes and invert to drain. Season inside with pepper and salt and a dusting of sugar. Sauter onion and garlic in butter, add flour and seasoning. Continue cooking for a few minutes. Add cucumber, cook for a little longer. Add liquid and cook till slightly thickened. Adjust seasoning. Fill tomatoes, sprinkle with fried breadcrumbs, and bake in oven till tender.

COLD STUFFED TOMATOES

apple and celery stuffing

6 large tomatoes
2 apples
1 stick of celery or ½ head of celeriac
lemon juice
salt

1 or 2 spoonfuls French dressing
1 or 2 spoonfuls thick cream (sweet or sour)
chopped chives and tarragon

Scald, peel, and empty tomatoes. Chop apple and celery, sprinkle with a pinch of salt and lemon juice, and leave 20 minutes. Mix French dressing and cream and add to apple and celery. Adjust seasoning, add herbs, and fill tomatoes with this mixture. Chill well.

SOME DISHES OF MIXED VEGETABLES

The following is good enough to offer as a main dish for a simple luncheon party. It is a *mélange* of vegetables, each individually cooked and the whole served in a béchamel sauce, made by the long method (see page 155). Its quality depends on three things: the judicious choice of vegetables, the flavours of which blend well, the cooking of these, each in a proper way, and the combining of them with a first-class béchamel properly flavoured. This dish is not quickly made, so you will modify your variety of vegetables to suit the time in hand.

Here are examples of what is meant by individual cooking:

If peas are included they should be cooked with mint and sugar; if mushrooms, in the oven with butter and milk. Small onions and carrots should be glazed. If tomatoes are to be used they should be emptied of seed and juice or they dilute the sauce. Sweet corn is an admirable ingredient in this dish, and if it can be taken fresh from the cob and cooked in the way described it is particularly good. If tinned corn be used, it should be warmed with a little butter or cream and seasoned.

VEGETABLES IN BÉCHAMEL SAUCE

Make a selection of vegetables, e.g. new potatoes, peas, mushrooms, sweet corn, onions, and baby carrots. Cook each in the way directed:

Potatoes with mint
Peas with mint and sugar
Mushrooms with butter in the oven
Sweet corn scraped from the cob and cooked with butter and milk
Onions and carrots glazed.

Arrange the cooked vegetables in heaps in a shallow fireproof dish. Pour over the béchamel which should coat lightly, so that the colour of the vegetables is just revealed. Sprinkle with crumbs, pour over a little melted butter, and finish in the oven.

In winter one might select from:

Potatoes, shaped into olives
Sprouts, the hearts blanched and cooked in butter
Leeks, blanched and sautéd
Onions, glazed
Carrots, shaped into small sizes and glazed
Tinned corn, warmed with a little butter or cream and seasoned
Mushrooms, prepared as above
Jerusalem artichokes, cooked gently in a little milk.

A SPANISH DISH OF MIXED VEGETABLES

oil for frying
2 or 3 rashers of bacon
1 large onion
1–2 cloves of garlic, crushed
a mixture of green vegetables
   in equal proportions, all
   finely cut or shredded:
     lettuce
     zucchini or baby marrow
     young French beans
     cucumber
     peas

chopped parsley
salt, pepper, nutmeg
a gill or more white wine
tomato sauce (see page 168)
fresh rolls of French bread

Fry together bacon, onion, garlic. Then add vegetables and parsley. Cook gently, season, add nutmeg, and moisten with wine. Cook till tender and add tomato sauce to hold all together. Serve with fresh rolls of French bread.

A similar mixture of vegetables may be served with scrambled egg, the egg at one end of the dish and the vegetables at the other.

MIXED VEGETABLES AND SCRAMBLED EGG

1 onion
2–3 rashers of bacon
oil for frying
1 young marrow or zucchini,
   diced

1 lb. tomatoes, emptied of
   seeds and cut in pieces
4 sweet peppers, green or red,
   well blanched and shredded
seasoning

Heat oil, fry bacon and onion to pale gold, add marrow and cook 5 minutes, then tomatoes and peppers. Cook till tender and season well. Dish with the scrambled egg.

The following Fritto Misto of vegetable and herbs is a good luncheon dish:

FRITTO MISTO OF VEGETABLES

For this one wants vegetables of various types, some of which are cooked in a good light fritter batter (No. 1, page 442), some egged and crumbed, and some fried without any coating; this gives contrast. Some of the vegetables are marinaded before being coated to give them a slight piquancy. It is the herb fritters which lend the special quality to this dish. These may be made of any tender sprigs of herbs, but there must be no woody stems. Chervil, mint, thyme, savory, parsley, dill, tarragon, fennel, sorrel are all good. The lemon fritters given in the Winkfield chapter, page 1007, may accompany this dish.

A selection of the following may be used:

Potato croquettes (see page 209), made in small size.

Cauliflower fritters. These may be made à la Villeroy (see page 259), or be sprigged, cooked, marinaded in French dressing, and dipped in batter.

Carrots 'panés.'   Take small whole carrots; if very young leave on green tops.   Cook *à la Vichy* (page 193), then flour, egg and crumb, or shred and fry like chipped potatoes.

Parsnips.   Boil, drain, cut in slices, marinade in French dressing, and dip in batter, or make a stiff purée of parsnips bound with a little egg and well seasoned.   Divide into small pieces.   Put half a shelled walnut on either side of each piece, then egg and breadcrumb.

Beetroot.   Cook beets, slice or quarter them, marinade in French dressing. Drain and dip in batter.

Brussels sprouts.   Small firm hearts blanched for a moment, then dipped in batter.

Spinach.   Blanch the spinach leaves for 5 minutes, drain, marinade in French dressing, roll several leaves together to form a 'cigar,' roll in flour and dip in batter.

Green beans.   String, leave whole, boil, drain well.   Marinade in French dressing.   Dip 3 or 4 together in fritter batter 1 (page 442) and drop carefully into hot fat, or egg and breadcrumb singly.

Mushrooms.   Choose small unopened mushrooms, do not peel, wipe with a cloth dipped in a little salt and use fritter batter 1 (page 442).   They may be marinaded first in French dressing and a little red wine.

Onion rings.   Take a Spanish onion, one-third of an egg white lightly beaten, and a little seasoned flour.   Cut onion in slices ⅛ inch thick. Separate the rings, put on a plate, moisten with egg white, making sure each ring is coated.   Toss in seasoned flour and fry immediately.   Another method is to soak the rings in milk for half an hour, drain, and then toss in flour.

Cos lettuce.   Stalks prepared as on page 228, blanched, salted, and dipped in batter.

Chestnut croquettes.   As on page 260.

Herb fritters

These are delicious and a refreshing addition to either vegetable or fish fritto misto.

Take any tender sprigs of herbs, mint, parsley, marjoram, dill, fennel, spring onions and so forth.   Marinade in French dressing and shake before dipping in fritter batter 1 (page 442): 2 or 3 sprigs of herbs may be bunched together and dipped in the batter.

RATATOUILLE (1)

2 aubergines	salt, pepper, and a clove of garlic
2–3 tomatoes	2 tablespoons oil
1 green pepper	grated Parmesan cheese (optional)
1 zucchini or small marrow	

Peel, slice, and dégorger the aubergines and zucchini. Skin the tomatoes, squeeze out the pips, and cut into rough slices. Slice the pepper, removing the core and all the seeds. Heat the oil until smoking, add the aubergine and zucchini and sauter quickly until soft. Crush the garlic with salt, add to the pan with the sliced pepper, tomatoes, and seasoning and continue cooking for about three-quarters of an hour, stirring occasionally; or place in a fireproof dish, sprinkle with the grated cheese, and bake in a moderate oven for 1 hour.

RATATOUILLE (2)

4 aubergines	2 or 3 outdoor cucumbers
6 large tomatoes	seasoning
1 lb. potatoes	oil
1 large sweet pepper	a clove of garlic, crushed
1 onion, chopped fine	(optional)
3 or 4 zucchini or a small marrow	

Prepare the vegetables: peel, slice, and dégorger the aubergines. Peel, pip, and slice tomatoes, peel and slice potatoes. Chop onion. Blanch, empty, and slice pepper. Cut marrow in pieces, unpeeled. Peel cucumbers and cut in thick slices. Brown each vegetable in turn, lay in a deep fireproof dish or casserole. Begin with potatoes, then aubergines, then onions, pepper, cucumber, and finish with tomatoes. Season each layer. Cook in slow heat in covered dish (or casserole) 1½–2 hours.

N.B. A crushed clove of garlic may be added to the oil before the vegetables are fried.

VEGETABLE DISHES FOR WHICH PASTRY OR A CROUSTADE IS REQUIRED

The croustade for the next dish is a crisp shell made of thin slices of bread (or of hollowed-out rolls or a small loaf) brushed over with butter and baked in the oven. Delicious cases for a variety of fillings, these may, if you wish, be brushed with garlic-flavoured butter.

SUMMER CROUSTADE

This pretty dish looks like an open tart of vegetables.

Croustade

medium stale white bread	1–2 cloves of garlic (optional)
2 oz. butter (approx.)	salt

Filling

summer vegetables: peas, broad beans, baby carrots, new potatoes, tiny beetroots, etc.
chives or finely chopped mixed herbs
French dressing for marinading the vegetables
any good cream dressing, to be handed separately
if a more substantial dish is required for a main course, slices of ham or tongue may be added

Chop the garlic and crush with salt, and cream this into the butter. Cut the bread into thin slices, removing the crusts, spread with the butter, and as far as possible cut into $2\frac{1}{2} \times 3$ inch squares. Butter a deep sandwich tin (or, to avoid difficulty in turning out, use a buttered fireproof dish which can be taken direct to the table). Arrange the squares, slightly overlapping, cornerwise round the edge, so that one corner will project above the top of the tin. Cover the bottom of the tin with more squares, also overlapping, then fit another smaller tin inside the lined one to keep the bread in place and bake to a golden brown 30–40 minutes in a moderate oven. Cool and turn out very carefully. In the meantime prepare and cook all the vegetables separately. Marinade each kind for an hour or longer in a good French dressing. To serve this croustade lay it on a flat dish, drain the vegetables from the marinade, and arrange them. Scatter the finely chopped herbs over the whole and serve with a cream dressing handed separately. If ham or tongue is to be used, line the croustade with small thin slices before putting in the vegetables.

CROUSTADE OF TOMATO AND SWEET PEPPER

Make the croustade as in the preceding recipe.

Filling

1 green pepper	dressing of lemon juice, sugar,
1 lb. tomatoes	and freshly ground black pepper

Cut the pepper in half, remove the core and seeds, and shred finely. Skin the tomatoes, cut in four, and squeeze gently to remove the seeds. Toss each piece of fruit in the dressing. Arrange the green pepper in the centre of the croustade and surround with the tomatoes.

KOULIBIACA

This is a Russian speciality and is generally served hot at the beginning of the meal, as an accompaniment to a clear soup or consommé, or it may be included in the 'zakouska' or hors-d'œuvre. It is also a good dish for a lunch, picnic, or buffet served hot or cold. The shape is that of a long roll, the outer covering of which may be either a rich yeast dough or puff pastry. The fillings vary: chicken, fish, and egg are the best known over here.

CHICKEN KOULIBIACA (FOR 8–10)

Dough

2 oz. butter	$\frac{1}{2}$ teaspoon sugar
$\frac{1}{2}$ lb. flour	1–2 eggs
$\frac{1}{2}$ teaspoon salt	about a cup of warm milk
$\frac{1}{4}$–$\frac{1}{2}$ oz. yeast	

Filling

1 oz. butter	seasoning
1 medium-sized finely chopped	2 hard-boiled eggs
onion	1 tablespoon chopped parsley
2 oz. chopped mushrooms	4–5 thin pancakes
½ gill chicken stock	1 beaten egg mixed with a large
½–¾ lb. finely diced or minced	pinch of salt for brushing
chicken	

Dough. Cream the butter. Sift the flour and salt together into a warmed basin. Cream the yeast and sugar together, add the beaten eggs and about half the warm milk. Mix into the flour, adding the remaining milk if necessary to make a fairly soft paste. Beat thoroughly with your hand. Work the creamed butter into the paste. Cover the bowl with a cloth and leave to rise in a warm place 30 minutes. Now cover with a plate and put into the refrigerator for about an hour or more to firm. Alternatively the dough may be made the night before and put into the refrigerator or in a cool place until the next day.

Filling. Heat the butter in a sauté or frying-pan, add the onion, and cook gently until beginning to soften, add the mushrooms, cook for a little longer. Now add the chicken and season well, moisten with the stock and continue simmering, stirring frequently until the mixture will bind lightly together. Turn on to a plate to cool. Chop the hard-boiled eggs, and cut the pancakes into wide strips. Knead the prepared dough lightly on a floured board, cut off a small piece of about 1–2 oz. and put on one side. Roll out the remaining dough to a rectangle about ½ inch thick. Lay this on a lightly floured cloth and brush the edges with beaten egg. Put half the chicken mixture down the middle of the dough, arrange half the pancake strips on this, then the eggs and parsley. Cover with the remaining strips, and then the rest of the chicken. Bring the edges of the dough up over the top of the chicken mixture, folding them well over, and pressing in the ends of the roll. Lift the cloth and turn the roll right over on to a greased baking-sheet.

Brush the roll with a dry brush to remove any surplus flour, then paint with the beaten egg. Roll out the reserved piece of dough thinly. Cut into fine strips. Lay two of these at a time close together over the roll at intervals of about two inches, tucking the ends of the strips well down underneath the roll. Brush them lightly with the beaten egg. Bake in a hot oven about 30 minutes. Cool slightly before cutting into slices for serving.

N.B. It does not seem necessary here to prove the koulibiaca after shaping, as is usual with yeast mixtures. Should the dough, however, be over-firm it would be as well to prove for 5–7 minutes. But this should be left to the discretion of the cook.

LEEK PIE

8 young leeks
bay-leaf
3 oz. unsmoked bacon or salt
   pork (or smoked bacon
   blanched)
freshly ground black pepper

stock or water
1 egg
1–2 spoonfuls cream
short or flaky pastry (see
   page 835)
beaten egg for brushing

Cut leeks in small pieces, put them into a shallow casserole or pie plate with a bay-leaf and the unsmoked bacon or salted pork cut into small dice. Add pepper and cover with stock or water. Simmer on the stove on a mat or cook in oven until the liquid has almost evaporated. Draw aside, cool slightly, and stir in a beaten egg and a spoonful or two of cream. Cover the dish with a layer of flaky or short pastry rolled out thinly. Press down well round the edges, brush over with beaten egg, and bake quickly until a golden brown. This is excellent either hot or cold.

MUSHROOM FLAN

short pastry (see page 835),
   made with 6 oz. flour
1 onion, medium size
1½ oz. butter
1¼ oz. flour
seasoning

½ pint milk
1 bay-leaf and 2 blades of mace
4–6 oz. mushrooms
2 tablespoons cream
1 egg yolk
beaten egg for binding

Line a 6-inch flan ring with pastry. Chop or slice the onion, and soften it in the butter without colouring. Add the flour off the fire and season. Bring the milk to the boil with the bay-leaf and mace and strain on to the roux. Blend thoroughly and stir over the fire until boiling. Cut the mushrooms into quarters and sauter briskly for 2 or 3 minutes. Add to the mixture with the cream and egg yolk. Cool, fill into the flan, and with the trimmings of the paste make a lattice-work over the top. Brush with salted beaten egg and bake in a hot oven 20–30 minutes.

MUSHROOM PIE

1 lb. mushrooms
2 oz. butter
3 hard-boiled eggs, sliced
seasoning

1 gill cream or rich milk
short or flaky pastry (see page
   835)
beaten egg for brushing

Prepare mushrooms and cook them quickly in butter in a frying-pan. Add the sliced eggs and seasoning. Add the liquid and put mixture into a pie dish, cover with a good short or flaky crust. Brush over the top with a little egg and bake until the crust is cooked, about 15 minutes.

ITALIAN PIZZA

The base of a true pizza is a dough.   This is covered with such mixtures as tomato, herbs, onions, and anchovies, with sometimes the addition of black olives and cheese.   The whole is then baked.   Pizza, a village near Naples, grows and grinds a special flour for this dough; in England we substitute a bread dough.   A fairly rich bread dough, which is suitable to the purpose, is given below.

8 oz. flour	a good ½ gill warm milk
1 teaspoon salt	1–2 eggs
1 teaspoon sugar	2 oz. butter
½ oz. yeast	

Sift flour and salt into a warmed basin; cream yeast and sugar and add to milk with the beaten eggs; add all liquid to flour and beat thoroughly. Have butter ready creamed and work into the paste.   Cover and rise 40 minutes.   Then flour and pat out with your fist on a floured baking-sheet to the size of a large bread board.   Cover with the tomato mixture, prove 10 minutes, bake in hot oven for 20–30 minutes.

For the top:

1 lb. ripe tomatoes	1 tablespoon chopped basil or
8–10 anchovy fillets	marjoram
1 dessertspoon oil	3 oz. Bel Paese or Italian cream
1 tablespoon chopped spring onions	cheese, diced or shredded

Peel and squeeze the tomatoes, cut each into four or five pieces.   Split the anchovy fillets.   Melt the oil in a hot frying-pan, sauter the onion, tomato, and herbs briskly for 2–3 minutes.   Cool slightly, drain off any surplus liquid, and scatter the tomatoes over the flattened dough, then the cheese, and finally arrange the anchovies in strips over the pizza.

PISSALADIERA

Pissaladiera is a form of the Italian pizza.   It is much the same in appearance, and has the addition of black olives.

½ lb. bread dough (½ lb. flour, ¼ oz. yeast, salt, and warm water to mix)	12 fillets of anchovy
	1–1½ lb. ripe tomatoes, peeled, pips removed, and sliced
¼ pint good olive oil (approx.)	¼ lb. black olives, stoned and
⅓ lb. onions, finely shredded	quartered
2–3 good cloves of garlic, finely chopped	salt, freshly ground pepper

Have the dough made and well risen (see page 759).   Roll out to a strip on a floured board.   Brush with oil, fold in three, turn to bring the open edge towards you, and roll out again.   Brush with oil, fold, and roll out once more.   Leave for 15 minutes, then repeat.   Roll or pat out to a large round, slip on to a baking-sheet.   Heat 2 or 3 tablespoons of the oil, cook onions and garlic in this until just coloured.   Drain from the oil and sprinkle over the dough.   Arrange the anchovy fillets on the dough in the form of a star, and in between the 'rays' the tomatoes and olives. Season well and sprinkle with oil. Leave in a warm place 7–10 minutes, then bake in a hot oven.

A pizza may also be made with pastry in place of dough. Line a pastry ring with short crust:

Pastry

8 oz. self-raising flour	4 oz. butter
a pinch of salt	cold water to mix

Filling

1 lb. tomatoes	½ oz. butter
1 onion	2 eggs
1 clove of garlic	4 oz. grated cheese
3 sprigs of parsley	1 dessertspoon anchovy essence
3 sprigs of thyme	seasoning

Peel the tomatoes, squeeze to remove seeds, peel and chop the onion, crush the garlic under the blade of a knife, put tomatoes, cut in quarters, onion, garlic, parsley, thyme, and butter into a pan, cook gently for about half an hour. Add the beaten eggs and the cheese, mix in anchovy essence, season with salt and pepper, and pour the mixture into the pastry ring. Bake in a hot oven (450° F.) for 30 minutes.

QUICHE LORRAINE

short or flaky pastry (see page 835), made with 4 oz. flour	1 gill single cream or milk
	½ oz. butter
1 egg and 1 yolk	2 oz. bacon, blanched and
1½ oz. grated cheese	diced
seasoning	2 oz. onion or 12 spring onions

Make short or flaky pastry. Line into a 6-inch flan ring. Fill with this mixture: Beat the eggs and cheese together in a bowl, add seasoning and the milk. Melt the butter in a small saucepan, add the bacon and the onion finely sliced. Keep spring onions whole. Cook slowly till just turning colour, then turn the contents of the pan into the egg mixture. Mix and pour into the pastry case. Bake in a moderate to slow oven till firm and a golden brown. Serve hot or cold.

SAVOURY STRUDELS

Savoury fillings for strudels are not so well known in England as on the Continent. If the paste is good and the filling well flavoured and seasoned a savoury strudel is a good luncheon dish. The making of the paste is described on page 840, and here are some fillings:

CAULIFLOWER, CHEESE, AND MUSHROOM STRUDEL

1 large cauliflower	2 oz. dry grated cheese
2 heaped tablespoons fresh white breadcrumbs	salt, pepper, paprika
1 dessertspoon chopped parsley	a light mornay or tomato sauce (see pages 156 and 178)
2 oz. (or more) sliced cooked mushrooms	

Break the cauliflower into tiny sprigs and blanch till just tender.   Drain thoroughly and toss lightly in a bowl with the breadcrumbs, parsley, mushrooms, cheese, and seasonings.   Serve the strudel with a light cheese or tomato sauce.

SPRING ONION, HARD-BOILED EGG, AND TOMATO STRUDEL

4–6 large tablespoons fresh white breadcrumbs (approx.)
seasoning
1 teaspoon fresh tarragon leaves, chopped
3 hard-boiled eggs, coarsely chopped

1 lb. spring onions, cut into inch lengths and stewed in a little butter until soft
4–5 tomatoes
a light mornay or green sauce (see pages 156 and 174)

Put the crumbs into a bowl, add seasoning, the tarragon leaves, the eggs, and the onions.   Scald the tomatoes, squeeze them lightly and cut into shreds.   Add them last to the mixture and use at once.   Serve the strudel with a light cheese or green sauce.

CABBAGE STRUDEL

1 cabbage
2 onions
2 tablespoons bacon fat or dripping

a few tablespoons sour cream or yoghourt
seasoning
paprika
caraway seeds

Chop cabbage finely, chop onions.   Heat the bacon fat or dripping, sauter the onion, then put in the cabbage, season well, add paprika and caraway seeds, and simmer till tender.   Add sour cream and when cool fill strudel.

For vegetable soufflés see next chapter, page 327.
For other luncheon dishes see chapters on eggs, cheese, pastas, and rice and curries.

XI

Eggs and Savoury Soufflés

IT has to be admitted that we are a cake-minded country. Even at moments when it might seem expedient to use all the eggs obtainable for the production of main courses to replace meat and expensive poultry, there is a tendency to take them for cakes. This, perhaps, is not economically the soundest use to make of them when they are not plentiful. We are less knowledgeable than our French friends about the great range of egg dishes, and we are apt to cook them with less attention to detail. A young cook does well to learn some of the many delicious dishes to be made from eggs, and to use them cleverly in her repertoire of menus. To do this with distinction it is necessary to practise, for even the basic ways of cooking eggs are far from foolproof.

To some students the detailed instructions concerning egg cookery may seem unnecessary. If so I suggest they be skipped until a moment comes when perhaps a rather special dish of œufs mollets is in hand, or an egg is to be coddled to exactly the right degree for an invalid, or, on the other hand, until you have found the hard-boiled eggs for your picnic or salad rather tough in consistency and have wondered why. As though one imbibed knowledge of cookery with a mother's milk the scornful say: 'My dear, she can't even boil an egg,' the implication being that all you have to do is to put it in boiling water for four minutes and there you are. Well, yes, so you are, but did you by chance bring the egg from a cold place and put it straight into boiling water and wonder why it cracked? Or have you ever turned a nice little aluminium saucepan black by boiling eggs in it? Or have you ever found your hard eggs soft in the middle, although you thought your timing had been right? Well, these things have happened to me, and now I'm glad to know the reasons why, and if the next few paragraphs sound like lessons in a kindergarten you must forgive them.

GENERAL INFORMATION

The average weight of a hen's egg is 2 oz. A duck's egg weighs about 3 oz., and a goose's egg from 8 to 10 oz. Duck and goose eggs are excellent for many dishes calling for hens' eggs, and in particular for cakes. Recipes may be adapted if one bears in mind the relative weights; for example, a recipe calling for six eggs means twelve ounces of egg (weighed with shells).

A simple test for freshness is that a fresh egg placed in a bowl of cold water will sink.

EGG PRESERVATION

There are three main ways of preserving eggs:

1. The old-fashioned way, claimed by those who use it to be absolutely reliable and one of the simplest. The eggs should be fresh and perfectly clean and dry. They should be wiped clean. If they are washed some of the protective film is removed. They are then well rubbed all over with a buttered paper—real butter should be used. Care must be taken to ensure that the eggs are completely covered with a thin film of grease which will exclude air. They may then be packed away in boxes and stored for future use.

2. In this method the principle of preservation, the exclusion of air, is the same as in the foregoing, but a solution is used in place of the butter. One suitable solution is on the market under the name of Oteg. The eggs, perfectly clean, and some hours old, are dipped into the solution, laid on racks of wire netting, and allowed to dry thoroughly. After half an hour or so they may be stored in boxes as before.

3. In the last and popular modern method of preservation the eggs are submerged in a solution of water-glass. For this a prescribed amount of water-glass is mixed with boiling water and the liquid allowed to get cold. The eggs are carefully laid in a pail or crock and the cold liquid gently poured over them, or if the water-glass solution is already in a pail the eggs are placed in it with a long baking-spoon. Special egg-preserving pails with a fitted wire basket are available. The pail is half filled with the solution and the basket containing the eggs gently lowered into it. By this means the risk of cracking eggs is lessened. Eggs, of course, may be added from time to time to the pail, and care must be taken to see that the containers are always kept full and that the eggs are well below the surface. If the pail is kept tightly covered there will be less diminution of the liquid by evaporation.

The following rules should be observed for all three methods of preservation:

1. Non-fertile eggs should be used for preservation whenever possible.

2. Eggs should be at least twelve hours old before being placed in Oteg or water-glass solution.

3. Eggs must be perfectly clean and dry and wiped over with a damp cloth before being put down.

4. When stored in boxes or pails they should not be packed too deeply, as the weight of eggs may crack the bottom layer.

5. If the butter or Oteg method is used the eggs should be stored with the broad end uppermost.

6. Boxes for storing should not be air-tight. Cardboard boxes with holes in the lid are suitable. They should be kept in a cool place.

Preserved eggs may in many cases be used in place of fresh eggs. They are generally unsuitable for boiling as the shells are apt to crack.[1] When they have been kept for a long time the whites become rather thin and watery and the separation of yolks from whites is less easy and complete than with fresh eggs, so that for such dishes as meringues or angel cake they are less satisfactory than fresh eggs, though not out of the question.

TO REMOVE THE THREAD

The thread which attaches the yolk to the shell is seen as a small opaque spot in the white. This may readily be taken out with a small section of egg-shell. Removal may not be necessary for all cakes and puddings, but is advisable when eggs are used in soups and sauces and for scrambled eggs and omelets. This is the reason for the instruction sometimes given to strain the beaten eggs.

THE WHIPPING AND BEATING OF EGGS

The whipping of egg whites

This heading takes me a long way back in memory: to the open kitchen door on a hot summer's morning when I struggled to beat egg whites for meringues. This confection was considered rather special in those days, and a party was afoot. My weapons were a soup-plate and a knife, and I was assured that if I beat well and long enough, and didn't slack off in the middle, all would be well. I suppose I did achieve some sort of froth that would stand up, because I seem to remember an agonized and mainly unsuccessful struggle to get some flat sticky-looking objects off the baking-sheet. I even think we tried to eat them and I am sure I blamed the recipe, and perhaps that was not altogether unjust, for explicit and fool-proof instructions were not always to be found. For example, I remember being told, or reading, that the beaten whites were stiff enough if they would support a whole egg in its shell. Alternatively, if I could turn the plate upside-down and the froth adhered and did not fall to the ground, I had got there. I could see with half an eye just what was going to happen if I applied either of these tests.

Remembering my own lack of knowledge and the disappointments I suffered I propose to 'go on' a bit about the whipping and beating of eggs.

Certain dishes such as soufflés, sponge cakes, and meringues require that egg whites shall be whipped to a stiff snow, and the criterion of this is that the mixture will form an unbending stiff pyramid of snow, like a dunce's cap, on the end of the whisk when this is lifted out of the bowl.

[1] Two suggestions concerning the boiling of preserved eggs:

(a) Prick the egg with a pin.

(b) Wrap it in a screw of paper containing a good pinch of salt. If cracking should occur the salt tends to harden the escaping white.

To achieve this certain conditions are necessary:

(*a*) freedom of the whites from any yolk or grease
(*b*) the use of suitable utensils
(*c*) method in carrying out the operation.

The eggs should be broken one at a time over a cup or small basin so that an unfresh one, or one spoiled by having the yolk broken, can be avoided. (A very small speck of yolk among the whites can be removed with a sharp fragment of shell.) Each perfect white is then put in the whipping bowl.

It is a long way from my soup-plate to the proper utensil for the whipping of egg whites, and probably, until you become so kitchen-proud that you must be perfectly equipped, you will make do—and quite reasonably—with a kitchen mixing bowl which should be washed anew before being used, perfectly dried, and may with advantage be rubbed over with lemon or with a cloth dipped in a spot of vinegar. The object of this is to secure that there is no trace of grease anywhere. The proper, the ideal utensil for this purpose is an unlined copper bowl. There is possibly some chemical reaction between egg whites and copper, because the result of using a copper bowl for this process is very marked. One gets a greater bulk of snow. There is less tendency to grain (graining is a state where the froth divides into fine particles and liquid) and the whole affair is expedited. A thin wire balloon whisk, kept exclusively for this work, is desirable. These whisks are sold in various sizes to fit the copper bowls. Both bowl and whisk must be kept meticulously clean, preferably without the use of soap, which contains fat.

In big kitchens a copper bowl may be kept exclusively for egg whites and be cleaned after use by being rubbed well with a clean cloth and not washed at all. But in smaller kitchens the bowl has to serve also for beating whole eggs and yolks. It may then be rinsed with clean water and dried, but should be rubbed with a piece of cut lemon dipped into salt immediately before being used for whites. It should be well cleaned inside and out with the salt and lemon, then rinsed and dried with a perfectly clean cloth. At no time should any form of metal polish be used for cleaning. The wire of the whisk may be cleaned in the same way.

The whites are beaten gently at first, the pace being increased as their consistency changes from a viscous mass to froth and from froth to white snow. Towards the end the movement should be vigorous, air being beaten well into the whole mass. The operation should be continuous. When the test of the whisk indicates that the required stiffness has been reached the whites should be used at once. They will not stand satisfactorily for any length of time unless a proportion of sugar has been incorporated into them; if this has been done they will remain firm for a limited time.

The incorporation of egg whites *

The incorporation of the whites with other substances needs care. So

* *See plate 4*

light and airy a mass will lose its quality if too heavily mixed into other ingredients, and the word folding is applied to this process.

If the whites are lighter than the mixture with which they are to be incorporated, and they usually are, they should be laid on top of the firmer mixture and folded in with a metal spoon. To do this cut through the whole mixture with the spoon, bringing the lower layers over the top, and folding it all over, using the spoon with the right hand as the bowl is turned slowly round with the left. The turning and folding should continue until the mixture is complete. For soufflés special care has to be taken that the mixing is not overdone.

The beating of egg yolks

Neither of the instructions 'beat till pale yellow' and 'beat till thick' really indicates to the beginner the exact degree required for, say, a sponge mixture. The French description *en ruban* gives a better idea, indicating, as it does, that the mixture when ready should run in a steady stream, like a ribbon, from the whisk. To achieve this result you may adopt the following method.

Put the sugar required in a bowl and make a well in the centre. Drop one yolk into this and stir with a spatula, drawing in only a little of the sugar but working the mixture well. Add more yolks and draw in more sugar. This gradual process enables the yolks to dissolve the sugar. When ready the mixture will stream steadily from the spatula in an unbroken satin-like pale yellow ribbon.

This method is suitable for such dishes as crème à la vanille where a perfectly smooth mixture without froth is required. For cake-making a thick wire whisk may be used instead of a spatula.

TO BOIL EGGS

Wash the shells or wipe with a damp cloth. Choose a pan large enough to hold sufficient water to cover the eggs completely. This should not be of aluminium as eggs discolour this badly. Eggs brought in from a cold temperature and plunged straight into boiling water are apt to crack. It is advisable, therefore, to warm them a little before boiling. When a number of eggs are to be boiled it is convenient to use a frying basket.

Method 1. Bring water to boil, draw pan aside, lay the eggs gently with a spoon on the bottom of the pan. Cover the pan and cook for $3\frac{1}{2}$-4 minutes at simmering-point.

Method 2. Put the eggs into cold water and bring fairly slowly to the boil, when they will be lightly cooked.

These timings are for those who like eggs cooked so that the white is just set and the yolk creamy; for those who like them more firmly set allow $4\frac{1}{2}$ minutes in the first method, and in the second allow them to boil for 1 minute.

In the times allowed for the cooking of eggs the degree of freshness must be taken into consideration. According to whether the egg is to be soft, 'mollet,' or hard-boiled from ½ to 2 minutes of extra time may be allowed.

Sometimes the rounded end of the egg is lightly tapped to effect the immediate cessation of cooking. Another safeguard is to dip the egg quickly in cold water—just in and out at once.

When eggs are boiled for dishes which call for œufs mollets or for hard-boiled eggs they must, after cooking and shelling, be kept in water, warm or cold according to whether the final dish is to be hot or cold. If they are left exposed to the air they will toughen.

Method 3. Coddled eggs. Bring the water to the boil, lay in the eggs, remove pan from heat and cover, keeping in a warm place on the stove for 8–10 minutes without further boiling.

An old-fashioned way of cooking an egg for an invalid was to warm it first in a hot damp cloth, then put it in a warm basin and pour boiling water over it; the basin was then covered with a plate and the egg left for about 12–15 minutes.

Hard-boiled eggs

These should be cooked so that both yolks and whites are firm but not tough; if overcooked the whites will be tough and the yolks encircled with a blackish line.

Method 1. Put the eggs into fast-boiling water and, according to size and freshness, allow 10–12 minutes after the water has returned to boiling-point. Plunge immediately into cold water; this helps to prevent dis-coloration of the yolks and facilitates peeling. Use a frying basket when a number of eggs are to be cooked.

Method 2. Put the eggs into fast-boiling water, but do not allow it to return to boiling-point and keep the eggs in this for 30–40 minutes. This is less easy to gauge in that the temperature must get neither too low nor too high. Some cooks claim that this method avoids toughness.

After boiling and peeling, the eggs should go straight into cold water if required whole. If to be stuffed they should be cut, the yolks taken out, and the whites put into cold water and kept there until the eggs are stuffed. They are then taken out and laid on a clean cloth, cut side downwards, to drain all the water away.

TO FRY EGGS

To get the perfect result necessary if one is to serve fried eggs in different fashions for a major dish, it is as well to follow the classic method. Have ready a small omelet pan, the extra depth of which is an advantage. The eggs may be fried in butter, oil, or bacon fat. Have ready the eggs, a saucer, and the oil or fat heated until it is just sending off a pale blue smoke. (If butter is used, this is not made as hot as the oil and the cooking time is slightly longer. Baste with the hot butter while cooking.) Break each egg into a saucer. Slip the egg from the saucer into the fat. Take a metal spoon, put it into the hot fat for a second, and then use it to baste a little of the white of the egg over the yolk. Baste a second time, then turn the egg carefully if you wish both sides to be brown. Lift with an egg-slice and drain on paper.

Deep-fried eggs

This method is often used for egg entrées, and is an easier way than turning the egg over in a shallow pan in order to fry it on both sides. Moreover the shape is better. The fat used may be oil, lard, or dripping, and the best utensil a small saucepan rather than the deep fat bath, which would get overheated, as the eggs should be fried one at a time. The eggs must, of course, be very fresh. Break them one at a time into a cup or small saucer. Heat the fat to smoking-point, stir gently, and carefully slide in the egg. If properly done and the egg really fresh the white should at once envelop the yolk; if it is reluctant to do so help it with a metal spoon. Allow 2–2½ minutes for frying. Drain well, season with salt and freshly ground pepper, and use for whatever dish is called for. These eggs cannot be kept as poached eggs can, but must be cooked and served at once.

To make fried eggs into a main dish they may be served on fried croûtons with a good appropriate sauce such as tomato, périgueux, piquante, etc. Cooked rice heated up in a little curry sauce makes a good base for fried eggs, and this is a good way of using up the remains of curry and rice.

One of the best simple luncheon dishes is fried eggs *au beurre noir*.

ŒUFS AU BEURRE NOIR

The correct amount of butter for this dish is an ounce for four eggs—one cannot successfully substitute margarine because it does not colour well. Use three parts of the butter for frying the eggs. Melt the butter and heat in a frying-pan, add the eggs, baste well with the hot butter. When set turn over with an egg-slice and cook for a minute. Lift the eggs when fried on to a hot dish, add the remainder of the butter to that in the pan, and cook until nut-brown. Pour the butter over the eggs, take a dessertspoon of vinegar, put into the hot pan, swill it round, and pour over the eggs. Finely chopped parsley is a good addition, as are a few capers, added while the butter is cooking. See page 169 (Sauces).

For Œufs Frits Cubanos see Winkfield chapter, page 985.

ŒUFS FRITS FLORENTINE

6 eggs
2 large thin slices of ham
oil or dripping for frying

½ pint sauce crème (page 156),
    sauce velouté (page 152), or
    made with chicken stock

Spinach subrics

1 lb. good spinach
a large nut of butter (at least
    ¼ oz.)
1 teaspoon flour

salt, pepper, nutmeg
1 small beaten egg
oil, butter, or good dripping

First prepare subrics. Cook spinach in water, drain well, press and chop finely. Heat butter to a good *noisette*, add the spinach, and cook quickly until dry, stirring frequently. Draw aside, add flour, seasonings, and egg. Fry full even tablespoons of this mixture in smoking hot oil or hot butter or dripping, turning once gently. When a delicate brown dish on a hot serving dish. Cut six rounds out of the ham, pass quickly through the hot fat (about half a minute), and set one on each subric.

Heat oil to smoking-point in a small saucepan (half to three-quarters full), break each egg on to a saucer and slide in carefully. Spoon white round yolk if necessary. Cook 2–3 minutes, drain well on paper, sprinkle with salt and pepper, and place an egg on each subric. Serve at once with the sauce handed separately.

POACHED EGGS

Eggs for poaching should be new-laid or the white will tend to come apart from the yolk. Do not cook too many eggs at a time; they should be able to cook without touching each other. Fill a frying or sauté pan three-quarters full of water, add 1 tablespoon vinegar to each quart of water. Some authorities hold that the addition of salt to the water tends to harden the whites. Bring just to boiling-point. Break each egg separately into a cup, slip it into the water. Allow to poach 3 minutes. Lift out with an egg-slice.

To trim. Cover your left hand with a clean dry cloth, lift each egg into the palm of this hand and trim with a sharp knife. Then slip the egg either on to the dish or on the toast, according to how it is going to be served.

French poached eggs

Chefs have another way of poaching eggs. The boiling water in the saucepan, containing vinegar as before, is stirred round until there is a small whirlpool. Into this an egg is dropped, the circular or oval shape is preserved, and the yolk is entirely in the white.

Luncheon or Supper Dishes made with Poached Eggs

Poached eggs on crisp croûtons may be covered with a good béchamel or mornay sauce, sprinkled with finely grated cheese, and browned in the oven. They are also good masked with a creamy tomato sauce and garnished with grilled or fried mushrooms and with fried parsley.

ŒUFS POCHÉS CAPRICE

eggs poached, served in a circle of pommes duchesse, coated with a sherry cream sauce, and garnished with sautéd tomatoes

1½ lb. potatoes, made into a duchesse with a little grated cheese	4–5 poached eggs sautéd tomatoes for garnishing, half for each person

Sauce

1 good red carrot	1½ gills milk
¼ oz. butter	½ gill cream
½ gill sherry	seasoning

Roux

¾ oz. butter
¾ oz. flour (scant weight)

Pipe or shape the potatoes round a fireproof dish, brown in the oven. Have ready the poached eggs and the tomatoes. Finely shred the carrot, rissoler in the butter, then add the sherry; cook a few minutes. Make the roux, pour on the milk, stir till boiling, add cream, seasoning, and prepared carrot. Arrange eggs in centre of dish, coat over the sauce, and garnish with tomatoes.

N.B. The potatoes can be omitted if wished.

In Œufs Pochés Soubise 1 the eggs are set on croûtons, coated with an onion sauce, and surrounded by crisp onion rings.

ŒUFS POCHÉS SOUBISE (1)

6 eggs	egg white
2–3 large Spanish onions for garnish	well-seasoned flour, and a little milk if wished
	6 rounds of bread

Sauce

½ lb. onions	½–¾ pint milk
2 oz. butter	salt and pepper
¾ oz. flour	

To make sauce chop and blanch onions and soften in 1 oz. butter. Sieve. Melt remaining butter, add flour, then milk. When boiling season, add onion purée and simmer gently till creamy. Cut Spanish onions into rings, separate, moisten each with egg white, and toss in well-seasoned flour (or sprinkle well with milk and then with flour). Fry in deep fat, fry also the rounds of bread. Poach the eggs and drain well. Set an egg on each croûte. Coat with sauce and garnish with onion rings.

The following is a cold version of Œufs Pochés Soubise.

ŒUFS POCHÉS SOUBISE (2) (COLD)

6 eggs	2 tablespoons cream
½ lb. onions	6 rounds of fried bread or croûtons
¾ pint milk	
seasoning	thin strips of sweet pepper
1 oz. butter	watercress
½ oz. flour	

Poach the eggs in the way described and slip into cold water. Finely slice the onions and put into a pan with the milk, salt, and pepper. Bring slowly to the boil and simmer until tender. Rub all through a fine sieve. Then melt the butter in a pan, add the flour. Pour on the onion and milk and stir over the fire until it comes to the boil; pour into a bowl to cool and beat in the cream.

Arrange rounds of fried bread on a dish. Remove the eggs, trim with scissors, and dry carefully in a cloth. Place the eggs on the croûtons, mask each with the sauce, and decorate with thin strips of sweet pepper and watercress.

Another excellent way is to mix the onion purée with mayonnaise or cream dressing, omitting the flour sauce. In this case add 1 teaspoon of gelatine for each ½ pint of finished sauce. (See mixing and addition of gelatine, page 43.)

In the following dish the poached eggs are served in baked potato shells containing a mixture of prawns, tomatoes, and onion and are masked with sauce.

ŒUFS POCHÉS GEORGETTE
for 5 small eggs

5 large potatoes	1 pint prawns, shelled
a nut of butter	a level teaspoon flour
seasoning	3 large tomatoes, skinned,
1 or 2 spoonfuls of milk	pipped, and shredded
1 oz. butter	1 teaspoon chopped herbs
1 onion	

Sauce

¾ oz. butter	seasoning
½ oz. flour	1½ gills stock or milk
1 oz. cheese, grated	1 bunch of watercress

Potatoes. Bake the potatoes 45–60 minutes. Cut a slice off the side lengthways and scoop out most of the inside; mash well with a fork or push through a wire sieve, beat in a nut of butter, seasoning, and a spoonful or two of hot milk. Keep warm. Melt 1 oz. butter in a pan, add the finely sliced onion, and simmer 5–6 minutes without colouring. Add the prawns, the teaspoon of flour, the tomatoes, and seasoning. Rub the débris from the tomatoes through a strainer and add the juice to the pan with the herbs. Boil, draw aside, and keep warm.

Sauce. Melt ½ oz. of butter in a saucepan, add the flour, pour on the milk, and season. Stir until boiling, then whisk in the rest of the butter and simmer for a few minutes.

Eggs. Poach the eggs and slip into a basin of warm water.

To serve. Put the potato purée into a forcing-bag with a rose pipe. Put a spoonful of the prawn mixture at the bottom of each potato. Drain the eggs, trim them, and fit them into the potatoes; mask each with the sauce and pipe round the edge with the potato. Scatter over the grated cheese and brown quickly under the grill. Serve in a napkin, garnished with watercress.

ŒUFS POCHÉS A L'OSEILLE

4–5 eggs

a croustade for each egg (see page 49) (use an oval cutter if possible)

butter or oil for frying

sorrel purée (see below)

Purée

1 oz. butter

1 lb. sorrel or spinach

1 egg

½ oz. butter and a good ¼ oz. flour made into beurre manié

salt and pepper

First prepare the purée. Shred the sorrel or spinach finely. Melt the butter in a stew-pan, add sorrel, and allow to 'melt' over a slow fire for 12 minutes, stirring frequently. When completely soft beat the egg, add a little of the sorrel, and when mixed add by degrees to the pan with the beurre manié. When thoroughly incorporated add seasoning and set pan on a gentle heat or in the oven for a further 10 minutes. Meantime poach the eggs and fry the croustades. Hollow them out and set a well-drained and dried egg on each. Pour the sorrel purée in the middle of a fireproof dish and arrange the eggs round with the points in the middle.

This dish can be made also with œufs mollets.

The next dish, for cold poached eggs, is good for summer luncheons. The eggs are laid on a bed of seasoned watercress and coated with a pale green cream sauce.

ŒUFS CRESSONIÈRE (COLD)

4–5 eggs

2 bunches of watercress

French dressing

¼ pint mayonnaise sauce or cream dressing

lemon juice, cayenne

Poach the eggs and slip into cold water. Boil three-quarters of one bunch of the cress for about 5 minutes, drain and press to remove superfluous liquid, then sieve. Add to the cream dressing with a squeeze of lemon and a touch of cayenne. Chop the remaining cress, mix lightly with a little French dressing. Arrange down a dish, drain and dry the eggs and set them on the watercress. Coat over the sauce and serve.

The next two recipes are luncheon-party dishes. In the first poached eggs, coated with a chaudfroid sauce (see sauce chapter, page 164), are arranged on a prawn mousse. The sauce must be very smooth and is put through a tammy (see page 76). This is a dish for a practised cook. The second, provided one is a good hand with pastry, is more perhaps a matter of care in detail.

ŒUFS POCHÉS RICHELIEU (COLD)

5 eggs

5 thin slices of truffle

Prawn or shrimp mousse

¼ lb. picked prawns or shrimps

2 oz. creamed butter

3 tablespoons cool thick béchamel sauce (may be taken from the chaudfroid sauce before the addition of the aspic)

carmine

1–2 tablespoons lightly whipped cream

Chaudfroid sauce

¾ pint creamy well-flavoured béchamel (allowing for sauce for mousse), made with:

¼ oz. butter
1¼ oz. flour, scant weight
¾ pint milk and the usual flavouring as for béchamel
salt and pepper

3 tablespoons liquid aspic jelly
1 small teaspoon gelatine
2 tablespoons cream

1½ pints fish or light chicken aspic jelly (see page 736)

Mince or pound the prawns. When smooth work in the creamed butter by degrees, then add the béchamel a little more quickly. Colour a delicate pink and fold in the whipped cream. Spread smoothly down the centre of an oval serving dish. Set aside. Prepare chaudfroid. Have ready the béchamel which must be creamy and thick. Dissolve gelatine in the aspic and add to the sauce, beating well over gentle heat. When smooth, tammy and add cream. Cover and set aside, but do not allow to get completely cold. Poach eggs, slip into iced water. When quite cold dry, trim, and put on a fine wire rack. Coat with the chaudfroid. If this is of right consistency one coat only should be given, otherwise the covering is too thick. When almost set decorate each egg with a slice of truffle. When completely set cover with some of the cool aspic, which should be put on in two or three coats to ensure complete covering. Leave if possible for half an hour or more before dishing. Then arrange eggs on the prawn mousse. Set the remaining aspic. Cut out 10–12 triangular blocks and chop the remainder. Put the chopped jelly round the mousse, and arrange the blocks round the edge.

Cold salmon or lobster is excellent in place of prawns or shrimps, if these are difficult to obtain.

In the following dish, also cold, the eggs are served in cheese-flavoured pastry shells on cooked green peas, and have a sharp mayonnaise sauce as accompaniment.

ŒUFS POCHÉS CLAMART (COLD)
for 5–6 small eggs

Pastry

¼ lb. flour
1 yolk of egg
1 dessertspoon water

2½ oz. butter
½ oz. grated cheese
salt and pepper

1½ lb. peas
2 tablespoons cream or French dressing

chopped mint
salt and freshly ground black pepper

Sauce

2 yolks
2 tablespoons vinegar
1 teaspoon French mustard
salt and pepper

lemon juice
1½ gills oil
2 tablespoons cream
2 tablespoons sieved peas

watercress

Pastry. Pile the flour on a slab or board; make a well in the middle and add the butter, yolk, water, grated cheese, salt, and pepper. Work all up to a smooth paste and leave for 1 hour. Roll out fairly thinly, cut into large rounds with a fluted cutter, and line into tartlet tins. Bake blind in a hot oven for about 20 minutes.

Peas. Cook the peas until just soft and leave to cool in the water, first sieving enough to give 2 tablespoons of purée for the sauce. Drain and mix in the cream or dressing, the chopped mint, salt, and a little pepper.

Sauce. Into the yolks stir vinegar, French mustard, salt and pepper, and a little lemon juice. Beat in the oil slowly. Add cream and sieved peas. Keep cool.

Eggs. Poach the eggs as described on page 292.

To serve. Place the cases down a dish. Fill each with peas and set a neatly trimmed egg on the top. Mask with the sauce and decorate at each end of the dish with the watercress.

ŒUFS POCHÉS NANTUA

4 eggs
1 pint prawns
¼ pint béchamel sauce (¾ oz. butter, ¾ oz. flour)
1 oz. creamed butter

½ gill whipped cream
carmine
¼ pint aspic jelly, flavoured and coloured a delicate pink with tomato purée

Poach the eggs and leave in a bowl of cold water until wanted. Pick the prawns and keep a few on one side for the garnish. Mince the remaining prawns and pound with the béchamel and butter. Colour and mix in the whipped cream with a tablespoon of cool aspic. Fill into small *cocottes*, place an egg on the top, decorate with the remaining prawns, and coat over with the semi-liquid aspic.

ŒUFS EN COCOTTE

Eggs may be gently cooked in the oven in individual dishes, in cream, in broth, or in a thin vegetable purée. This is really a method of poaching in liquid other than water. In this way they are called œufs en cocotte. Allow a tablespoon of liquid for each egg, bring to the boil, and put a spoonful of the boiling liquid into each heated *cocotte*; break in the egg, add two scraps of butter, and set the *cocotte* in a baking-dish, allowing hot water to reach half way up the *cocotte*. Cover and put in a medium oven for 6–7 minutes, or 8–9 according to the thickness of the *cocotte*. Eggs so cooked are a little more firmly set than œufs sur le plat.

CONVENT EGGS (ŒUFS EN COCOTTE A LA CRÈME)

This is a classic and was very popular at one time. Convent eggs were often presented in one dish, but more correctly should be cooked and served in individual fireproof or china *cocottes*.

6 new-laid eggs	½ oz. butter
a good ¼ pint cream to allow a	salt and freshly ground pepper
tablespoon of cream per egg	china or fireproof *cocottes*

Warm the *cocottes*, then set them in a large roasting-tin. Bring the cream to the boil, put a spoonful of cream into each and break in an egg. Season, divide the butter into small pieces and put on the top. Pour hot water into the baking-tin to come half way up the sides of the *cocottes*. Put a baking-sheet to cover them all. Set the tin carefully in a moderate oven for 6–8 minutes. The white should be nicely set and the yolk creamy, as for a poached egg. Take out the *cocottes*, dry, and serve at once on a large dish covered with a folded napkin.

ŒUFS SUR LE PLAT

Œufs sur le plat are, correctly, cooked so lightly that they are barely set. While they are sometimes served individually in small shallow fireproof dishes, there is a traditional type of dish for serving a number. This may be of copper, shallow, with handles, or fireproof with ears. The eggs should just cover the bottom of such a dish. The procedure is to put a little butter in it, heat it—which starts off the cooking—then to break in the eggs, season with salt, add a little cream or melted butter, and put in a sharp oven for 4–5 minutes, or until eggs are just set. The yolks should be creamy and thinly covered with a film of white, the whites slightly solidified; a teaspoon of cream over each egg yolk helps keep the yolk soft. Melted butter has the same effect and is more easily distributed.

Many additions are suitable to a dish of eggs cooked *sur le plat*—cooked peas, spinach, asparagus points, glazed pickling onions and baby carrots, purées of onion and other vegetables, frizzled bacon, chipolata sausages and so on—but they must be added in a suitable way and special attention paid to the seasoning. Here are some suggestions: all the quantities given are for 6 eggs.

Aux champignons

Take 4 oz. mushroom, chop finely with the stalks, and toss in a little butter in a saucepan. Put the softened mushrooms into a buttered fireproof dish, into which the eggs are to go, season, sprinkle with finely chopped parsley, add the eggs, put into the oven, and cook as described.

Italienne

Blanch, skin, and slice finely half a green pepper, add the flesh of 2 tomatoes, peeled, pipped, and chopped, and 2 fillets of anchovy, chopped. Lay this mixture on the base of the fireproof dish, sprinkle with a little olive oil, and cook very gently for a few minutes. Add the eggs and bake.

A l'estragon.

Put into a saucepan a gill of fresh tomato juice and a good tablespoon of rich jus. For this you may substitute a tablespoon of natural gravy from the roast. Add a bouquet garni, a bay-leaf, and 3 or 4 leaves of blanched tarragon. Cook in the pan rapidly, until the liquid is reduced to a thickish syrup. Strain, put in fireproof dish, add the eggs, sprinkle the white parts of the eggs with salt, the yolks with melted butter, and cook in the oven.

Aux asperges

Take cooked asparagus tips. Lay them in a fireproof dish, sprinkle with a little oil or butter, and cook just enough to heat. Add the eggs and bake in oven.

One can go on at great length with different variants of this dish. Chopped onion, slices of zucchini or of very young baby marrows, first softened in butter, may go into the bottom of the dish, as may slices of grilled kidney, grilled or fried tomato, creamed spinach, or even a base of crisp fried croûtons. There are certain additions which can be made after the eggs are cooked, such as little crisp rolls of bacon, small pieces of fried sausage, or simply well-chopped herbs.

ŒUFS SUR LE PLAT AUX ANCHOIS

4 oz. rice	paprika
chicken or vegetable stock or water	bay-leaf
	crushed garlic
4–6 eggs	cream
¾ lb. peeled tomatoes	anchovy fillets
tomato purée	grated Parmesan cheese
butter	

Boil the rice in the stock or water, drain, rinse with a cup of boiling stock or water, drain again and return to the pan with a nut of butter. Cut tomatoes and stew to a pulp with a little purée, garlic, paprika, a bay-leaf, butter, and a little stock or water. Arrange the rice in a flat dish and hollow out a place for each egg. Cover the rice with the tomato pulp, break an egg into each hollow, cover each with a spoonful of cream and anchovy strips, and sprinkle the whole dish with the grated cheese. Set in a moderate oven 7–10 minutes.

ŒUFS SUR LE PLAT BERCY

Good luncheon or supper dish. They are usually served in individual fireproof dishes.

5 new-laid eggs	10 baby chipolata sausages
¾ oz. butter	1 teaspoon chopped mixed herbs
¼ pint tomato sauce 2 (see page 178), or a little tomato purée diluted with strong stock or gravy	salt and pepper

Rub the dishes with a little of the butter.   Break an egg into each.   Melt the remaining butter and sprinkle over each yolk.   Season lightly.   Have ready the tomato sauce, well seasoned; add the herbs.   Put the eggs into the oven and grill or fry the sausages.   When the eggs are just set take out, pour a tablespoon of the sauce round the yolk of each, garnish each with 2 chipolata sausages, and serve at once.

ŒUFS SUR LE PLAT FLAMENCO

4–5 eggs
2 potatoes
2 oz. butter
2 smoked sausages (such as
    frankfurters or saveloys)
seasoning
2 tablespoons cooked peas

2 fresh or tinned sweet red
    peppers, cut into shreds
2 tomatoes, peeled, quartered,
    and pipped
chopped parsley
2 tablespoons cream
cayenne

Vegetable mixture.   Cover potatoes with cold water and bring slowly to boil.   Strain, dry in a cloth, and cut into small even cubes.   Melt the butter, add potatoes and sausages, cut into slices.   Shake over the fire until the potatoes begin to brown.   Add salt and pepper, peas, and the sweet peppers.   Cook for a little longer, then add the tomatoes with the parsley.   Put the mixture in the bottom of a flat earthenware dish. Break the eggs on the top.   Season with salt and pepper and place in a moderate oven until set.

To serve.   Remove and pour over the cream.   Sprinkle each egg with a little cayenne pepper and serve at once.

ŒUFS SUR LE PLAT LORRAINE

Delicious, an elegant form of eggs and bacon, which may be cooked in individual dishes or one large eared dish.

5 new-laid eggs
¾ oz. butter
3 oz. lean bacon in thin rashers
1½ oz. gruyère cheese

¾ gill cream
finely chopped parsley
salt and freshly ground pepper

Cut the rind from the bacon, cut crosswise into pieces about 1–1½ inches in length.   Blanch in boiling water 3–4 minutes, then drain well. Cut the cheese in wafer-thin slices.   Rub the butter thickly over the dish or dishes, lay the bacon over the bottom and cover with the slices of cheese. Break in the eggs and season with pepper and a little salt.   Pour over the cream, sprinkle with parsley, and bake in a moderate oven for 6–8 minutes.

ŒUFS SUR LE PLAT MARIE-ANNE

4–5 eggs
1½ lb. young broad beans
1 oz. butter
1 onion, sliced
1 teaspoon chopped parsley

seasoning
1 tomato, skinned, pipped, and
    shredded
2 tablespoons thin cream
½ oz. grated cheese

Beans. Shell the beans and simmer till tender in salted water. Drain. Melt the butter in a pan, add the onion, simmer for 4–5 minutes without colouring, put in the beans with parsley, seasoning, and tomato. Shake over the fire for a minute or two and turn on to a well-buttered, flat, fire-proof dish.

Eggs. Break the eggs on the top, pour the cream on to the yolks, scatter the cheese over the dish, and set in a slow oven (7–10 minutes).

Œufs au miroir are a form of 'sur le plat.' For these nothing is put over the yolk, neither cream nor butter. The eggs are cooked *sur le plat*, then cut out and set on rounds of something suitable—in the following recipe it is rounds of foie gras. The baked yolks have a shiny appearance, hence 'au miroir.' The following recipe is elaborate, a party dish, but if you have chickens' livers not extravagant, and we have tried it successfully with a well-flavoured purée of chestnuts. If this is used follow recipe for Chestnut Croquettes in poultry and game chapter, page 645.

ŒUFS AU MIROIR FOIE GRAS

½ lb. tinned purée of foie gras, or the following pâté in its place:

    2 or 3 chickens' livers
    2 oz. fat bacon
    1 shallot, chopped

1½ gills béchamel for panade, made with:

    1 oz. flour
    1 oz. butter
    1½ gills flavoured milk

1 egg	5–6 eggs
1 yolk	sauce périgueux (see below)
cream and seasoning	a slice of truffle for each egg
a large nut of butter	

Sauter the livers and bacon lightly with the shallot. Pound together, adding the béchamel sauce, the egg, the yolk, cream, and seasoning. Butter a flat shallow dish and fill in the mixture; poach in the oven in a bain-marie, or steam gently until set. Turn out and stamp into rounds with a plain cutter.

Butter a fireproof dish thickly; break in the quantity of eggs, cover with buttered paper, and place in the oven. When set stamp out each with a cutter. Take particular care that the fireproof dish chosen is of the right size, for if the egg whites are too thinly spread it will be difficult to cut them out. Arrange foie gras or home-made pâté rounds on dish, place an egg on each, pour over the sauce périgueux, and garnish each with a slice of truffle.

Sauce périgueux

Heat 2 tablespoons oil in a pan, add an onion, a carrot, and a stick of celery, all sliced. Fry until brown, add a large tablespoon of flour and brown slowly. Add ½ teaspoon tomato purée, salt, and ¾ pint strong stock.

Simmer until required consistency and add ½ gill well-reduced sherry, a teaspoon of finely chopped truffle, and a little of the truffle liquor. Reduce again and use.

The following dish of eggs on a high-piled mound of light, carefully mashed potato is popular for luncheon.

ŒUFS MONT D'OR

Make a well-seasoned purée of potato, beating it well so that it is really light (see page 203). Flavour with a little onion tossed in butter, with chopped celery or celery salt, or with grated orange rind. Make a lightly piled mound of this and with a spoon make hollows for as many eggs as you wish to cook. Drop a raw egg into each hollow, pour a little melted butter over the whole, sprinkle well with grated cheese, and bake in the oven. Serve with a richly flavoured tomato sauce (see page 178) and/or with grilled mushrooms.

CHACHONKA

This dish comes from Hammamet from Violet Henson, whose Arab cooks produce delicious food, particularly of the light well-flavoured kind so much appreciated in a warm climate; although this particular one, Violet says, they like to eat on what they call a chilly day.

3½ oz. butter	a pinch of salt
¾ lb. onions	½ glass cold water
1 lb. tomatoes	6 or 8 eggs
½ lb. sweet peppers	

Prepare vegetables: slice onions, skin tomatoes, and wash peppers in cold water; cut them in thin slices and dry them in clean cloth just before they are wanted.

Melt butter in saucepan, add onions with pinch of salt, stir over gentle heat till nearly brown, add tomatoes, stir and turn till nearly cooked, put in peppers, stir for a few more minutes, throw in the cold water, and cook 10 minutes more. Turn vegetables into a fireproof dish, break 6 or 8 eggs on top of them, and put in oven till latter are cooked.

ŒUFS MOLLETS

Certain dishes call for boiled eggs which are something in between a hard-boiled egg and the lightly boiled or coddled egg already mentioned. These are called œufs mollets. In this case it is required that the white should be solid while the yolks are still soft, and they require careful handling. Eggs should be chosen all of approximately the same size, and those of medium size are best. The simplest way to secure that they are all boiled exactly to the same degree is to put them in a frying basket and lower them into boiling water, counting between 5 and 6 minutes from the moment the water reboils according to the freshness of the eggs. This timing should be observed with care. Lift the frying basket at the end of cooking time, plunge into a large bowl of cold water, and leave 7–8 minutes. If you have not a frying basket suitable for this purpose the eggs may be cooked in a saucepan in the ordinary way, but then, in order that they shall all be cooked to the same degree, the pan must be put under the cold tap at the end of 5–6 minutes to stop further cooking. The eggs are immediately shelled, and if required at once for a hot dish are put straight into the sauce, or they may be kept in cold water until required. If necessity arises to reheat, they may be put into a bowl of hot salted water to warm them through. The eggs must not in any circumstances be left exposed to the air.

To shell. Take the egg in the palm of the hand, tap it gently all over with the back of a teaspoon or the blade of a large knife, and shell very gently. Some cooks, after cracking the egg all over, strip off a band from the middle and then pull off the shell at either end.

Eggs cooked in this way may be lightly floured and egged and bread-crumbed, or dipped in batter and fried in deep fat. They make an excellent addition to a dish of hot fritters.

Œufs mollets may be served on a bed of rice mixed with a good curry sauce. They are then well sprinkled with grated cheese, finished off with a little butter, and browned under a hot grill for about 2 minutes. A good accompaniment is made by cutting light starchless Energen rolls in slices with a sharp knife, dipping the slices in melted butter, putting them in a sharp oven till crisp, and then spreading them with chutney.

The following is a simple and good dish for œufs mollets:

ŒUFS EN ROBE DE CHAMBRE

Choose full, soft, French bread rolls. Cut a slice off the top and tear out the crumb, so as to leave a case of thick crust. Brush this inside and out with butter, season the inside with salt and pepper. (If liked garlic butter, not too heavily flavoured, may be used.) Cook these rolls in a sharp oven till golden and crusty. Heat up the shelled eggs in salted hot water, and drop one egg into each roll. Melt a little butter in a pan till golden brown (beurre noisette), add a good spoonful of very finely chopped mixed herbs, mix in with the butter, and pour over the top of each egg.

The two following recipes bear the same name but the ingredients differ. The first is a good supper dish, the second suitable for a party.

ŒUFS MOLLETS BENEDICTINE (1)

5 new-laid eggs
½–1 oz. butter
2 cloves of garlic crushed with salt
1 lb. cooked flaked fresh haddock, pounded lightly until smooth

1 gill béchamel sauce (½ oz. butter, ½ oz. flour)
½ gill boiling cream
sauce crème (see next page)
French roll
butter or oil for frying

Place eggs in boiling water and boil for 6 minutes from the time they come to the boil.   Put immediately into cold water and leave 7–8 minutes. Then peel carefully and slip into lukewarm water until wanted.   Melt the butter in a pan, add the garlic, cook for a few moments, then add the fish.   Work over the fire, adding the béchamel by degrees.   When smooth add the cream.

Turn on to the bottom of a hot serving dish, drain eggs and arrange on the fish cream.   Coat over with a cream sauce, and garnish with slices of French roll fried in butter.

Sauce crème

¾ oz. butter	½ gill cream
½ oz. flour	salt
1½ gills milk	pepper

Melt the butter, add flour, pour on the milk, and stir over the fire until boiling.   Cook rapidly for a few minutes.   Then add cream and seasoning.

ŒUFS MOLLETS BENEDICTINE (2)

puff pastry (see page 836)	a little butter or stock
4 eggs	hollandaise sauce (see below)
4 slices of lean ham	

Prepare a large bouchée case for each egg from the pastry.   Boil the eggs for 6 minutes and then plunge into cold water for 7–8 minutes. Heat the ham in a little butter or stock and place a slice at the bottom of each pastry case.   Shell the eggs and rewarm in a little hot water, place on the ham and coat with hollandaise sauce.

Hollandaise sauce

2½–3 oz. butter	½ bay-leaf
3 tablespoons wine vinegar	a blade of mace
6 peppercorns	2 yolks of egg

Make sauce as described on page 157.

ŒUFS MOLLETS DUCHESSE

4 eggs	4 croustades of potato, made by
1 oz. butter	piping potato purée containing
2 onions	egg yolks into shallow, round
2 oz. mushrooms	cases, and browning in the
paprika	oven.

Horse-radish sauce

¼ oz. butter	seasoning
¼ oz. flour	mustard
¾ gill creamy milk	cream (optional)
1 tablespoon grated horse-radish	

Cook eggs in the way described on page 302.   Soften the finely sliced onions and mushrooms in the butter, season, add paprika, and place a spoonful of this mixture at the bottom of each baked croustade of potato. Peel and dry the eggs carefully, reheat in the way described, place in the prepared cases, and spoon over a hot horse-radish sauce.

Horse-radish sauce

Melt the butter, add the flour off the fire, and add the milk. Return to the heat and stir until boiling. Add the horse-radish and adjust the seasoning, adding mustard to taste and a little cream.

This may also be made in a large dish with sauce both below and above the eggs, and the potato piped round the edge.

The following is a cold version of the above:

ŒUFS MOLLETS DUCHESSE (COLD)

4–6 eggs

Short pastry

3 oz. flour	1 oz. grated cheese
1½ oz. butter and lard mixed	seasoning

Sauce

½ oz. butter	a level teaspoon flour
1 small shallot, finely chopped	3–4 tablespoons milk
2–3 oz. mushroom stalks and peelings, or whole mushrooms, finely chopped	¼ pint mayonnaise
	1–2 tablespoons grated horse-radish
seasoning	a little extra cream or milk if necessary

slices of cucumber or pimento for garnish

Make up the pastry, line into boat or round moulds and bake blind. Cook eggs in the way described, then plunge immediately into cold water for 6–7 minutes. Peel and keep in cold water until wanted. Melt the butter, add the shallot, simmer 2–3 minutes. Then add the mushrooms and continue to cook, stirring frequently, for a further 4 minutes. Season well, dust with the flour, and add the milk. Cook for another half-minute, then turn out to cool.

Put a spoonful of this mixture into each croustade, place an egg on the top. Add the horse-radish to the mayonnaise with a little extra cream or milk to thin it slightly if necessary. Coat over each egg and garnish with sliced cucumber or pimento.

ŒUFS MOLLETS CRÉCY

6 eggs of even size	a large pinch of sugar
1¼ lb. carrots	a pinch of salt
1 oz. butter	chopped parsley

Mornay sauce

¾ oz. butter	1¼ oz. grated gruyère cheese
scant ½ oz. flour	
1½ gills milk	salt and pepper

Peel or scrape the carrots, trim off the ends, and cut into rounds. Put into a shallow stew-pan or sauté pan with water barely to cover, add the butter, sugar, and salt. Cover and cook gently until tender and the liquid reduced to 3–4 tablespoons. Remove lid and cook rapidly until the liquid has further reduced to a tablespoon. Add a good sprinkling of the parsley, shake over the fire for a few minutes, then turn into a fireproof dish.

Cook the eggs in the way described and immerse in cold water for 7 minutes. Peel carefully and slip into warm water until wanted. Make the sauce by melting the butter in a saucepan, adding the flour, and cooking for a minute or two. Draw aside, cool slightly, pour on the milk and stir until boiling. Simmer a few minutes, draw aside, season, and beat in 1 oz. of the cheese by degrees. Drain and dry the eggs, set on the carrots, coat with the sauce, sprinkle over the remaining cheese, and brown in a quick oven for 7–10 minutes.

N.B. The carrots for this dish must be good, red, and even-sized. Those of the 'stumpy' variety are best, and ideally this dish should be made with these at their prime; care must be taken in the cooking of them. It is a very good dish and one suitable for a main course for a light meal. The dish need not necessarily be browned; it may be served immediately after the sauce has been poured over.

ŒUFS MOLLETS MAINTENON

Œufs mollets served on a soubise purée and coated with a sauce mornay. An excellent dish and one that may be served individually in *cocottes*, pastry tartlet shells, or croûtes, or as one dish in a gratin dish, flan case and so on.

6 eggs, new laid

Purée

½ lb. onions	¾ gill vegetable stock or milk
½ oz. butter	salt and pepper

Béchamel

1 oz. butter	1 blade of mace
¾ oz. flour	1 oz. grated cheese, gruyère
scant ¾ pint milk	for preference
½ bay-leaf	1 tablespoon cream
a sprig of thyme and parsley	salt and pepper

First prepare purée: Slice onions thinly, put into boiling water, and boil 7–10 minutes. Drain well. Melt the butter in a stew-pan, add onions, and cook gently on the fire to dry off a little. Now add the stock, salt, and pepper. Cover and simmer 30–40 minutes, when the onion should be very soft and the liquid completely reduced. Rub through a nylon sieve and return to the rinsed-out pan. Meanwhile prepare the béchamel by bringing the milk slowly to the boil with the herbs, mace, and bay-leaf. Strain and cool. Pour on to the roux, blend, and stir over the fire until boiling. Simmer for 5–6 minutes. Season. Add ¾–1 gill of this to the onion purée, then reduce over a moderate fire, stirring frequently, until it will leave the sides of the pan. Cover and set aside.

Prepare eggs according to instructions given for œufs mollets. Drain and dry carefully. Spread the purée in the centre of a hot gratin dish. Arrange the eggs on this. Beat three-quarters of the cheese into the remaining béchamel with the cream. Coat this sauce over the eggs, sprinkle with the rest of the cheese, and brown quickly under the grill. Serve at once.

For Œufs Mollets en Soufflé en Surprise, see Winkfield chapter, page 988.

SCRAMBLED AND BUTTERED EGGS (ŒUFS BROUILLÉS)

The term 'buttered eggs' is a little old-fashioned and is only used here to simplify the difference between two points of view. Argument wages round the question as to whether any liquid at all should be added to scrambled eggs; some experts say emphatically none. Others, however, hold that the richness of the dish made with butter and eggs alone is much too cloying for some tastes, and that the addition of a little milk and/or cream has a lightening effect. The argument is resolved if the term 'buttered eggs' is reserved for the dish made without the addition of milk or cream, and 'scrambled eggs' for that containing either of these. Whichever dish is in hand the rules concerning the cooking remain the same. There is probably no more delicate or digestible way of preparing eggs, but it is all too easy to overcook them, in which case the dish, instead of being soft and creamy, will probably present a dry and granulated appearance. It is useful to remember that the cooking which continues after the pan has been withdrawn from direct heat is enough to overcook this delicate dish, so that the pan has to be withdrawn from the fire before the eggs are à point. A thin pan is unsuitable for this, as for many dishes: the eggs are liable to burn or in any case to cook unevenly. A thick sauté or shallow pan should be used, and for stirring a silver spoon, as with this it is easier to scrape the egg well from the bottom of the pan.

Butter. The amount to be used must depend to some extent on what can be spared, and is, of course, in the case of buttered eggs a little more than for scrambled eggs, when cream may be added. It may be from ¼ to ½ oz. per egg and may be added in two parts, the main part to the pan before the eggs and the rest in small bits at the end of cooking. If cream is to be employed—and in addition to lightening it adds a good flavour to the dish —allow in proportion of a tablespoon to 3 eggs. This is added when the eggs have finished cooking and has the advantage also of arresting cooking. Gentle cooking throughout is essential. In the following two methods the advantages are divided. In the first the initial butter is spread with the fingers over the inside of the pan and the strained eggs poured in, so that from the start the heat is applied gradually. In the second the butter is melted before the eggs are added. This is less trouble.

Buttered eggs

Beat the eggs slightly, just enough to break up yolks and whites. Season lightly with salt and pepper. Spread half the quantity of the butter over the bottom and sides of the pan with your fingers. Pass the eggs through a strainer into the pan. This not only removes the thread but helps to mix whites and yolks without producing froth. Add remaining butter in small pieces, cook over gentle heat, and begin stirring immediately with a small silver spoon, scraping the bottom of the pan with each movement. As soon as the eggs begin to thicken and are in soft creamy flakes, remove the saucepan from the heat; continue stirring. The heat of the saucepan will soon finish off the cooking of the eggs. Serve at once.

Scrambled eggs

Melt half the butter in a saucepan, strain in the beaten and seasoned egg, and stir from the first with a silver spoon. When the eggs form into large flakes add remaining butter in small pieces. Remove from heat, add cream, and serve at once.

Scrambled eggs may be served in many ways. Suitable ingredients are either used as a garnish or incorporated with the egg when cooked. Grilled or fried mushrooms, croûtons, crisp bacon rolls, asparagus tips and so forth all make good garnishes, while chopped herbs, small croûtons, and cheese may be lightly folded into the scrambled egg.

Hollowed-out fried croûtons may be filled with a variety of ingredients and used to turn scrambled eggs into a more important dish. Long fingers of bread fried, sprinkled with grated cheese, and finished in the oven are a good accompaniment, and the slices of Energen rolls already mentioned may be used in the same way.

The following are two particularly good recipes for scrambled eggs. The first especially is suitable as a first course for a party luncheon.

ŒUFS BROUILLÉS (CRÉCY A L'ORANGE)

2–3 medium-sized carrots
the rind of 1 orange
1½ oz. butter
1 glass Madeira or good sherry
seasoning

4 eggs
2 tablespoons cream or creamy milk
buttered toast or fried croûtes
bouquets of watercress

The carrots must be red, juicy, and firm. Slice off the red part in thin even slices, discarding the yellow core, then cut across into fine needle-like shreds. Pare the rind from the orange and cut into the same-sized shreds. The proportion should be two of carrot to one of orange rind, and about 3–4 tablespoons in all. Blanch the orange rind for about 5 minutes, then drain.

Melt half the butter, add the carrot and orange rind, put a piece of paper right down on them, cover the pan and cook gently, *without colouring*, 5–7 minutes.   Now add the wine and continue simmering until the orange and carrot are tender, and the liquor slightly reduced.   Meantime break the eggs into a bowl and beat up with a fork, season, add cream, and add to the pan with remaining butter.   Finish as for buttered eggs, keeping them very smooth and creamy.   Serve on hot buttered toast or fried croûtes of bread, with bouquets of fresh watercress.

ŒUFS BROUILLÉS AUX SALSIFIS

Use the scorzonera, or black salsify, for this.   It has a better and more delicate flavour than the white.

2–3 roots of scorzonera	salt
a squeeze of lemon juice	freshly ground white pepper
4–5 eggs	triangular croûtons of bread
1¼–1½ oz. butter	fried to a golden brown in
2 tablespoons cream or creamy	butter
milk	

Scrub and wash the scorzonera.   Boil in salted water till tender, then peel and cut into small pieces the size of a pea.

Heat a sauté or stew-pan, drop in half the butter and when foaming add the scorzonera, sauter and shake over a moderate fire 4–5 minutes, seasoning well and adding a good squeeze of lemon juice.   Meantime beat eggs with a fork, adding the cream or milk, salt and pepper.   Pour into the sauté pan and cook gently, scraping up the mixture with a silver or metal spoon.   When set, but creamy, turn into a hot dish and surround with the croûtons.   Serve at once.

SCRAMBLED EGGS WITH CREAM CHEESE

A good savoury.

1 cream cracker for each person, and butter to spread them	seasoning of salt, freshly ground pepper, and a dash of cayenne
2 small cream cheeses, e.g. Petit Gervais or Petit Suisse	6 eggs
½ oz. butter	1 teaspoon finely chopped herbs, chives, chervil, or basil
5–6 tablespoons rich milk	

Heat and butter a cream cracker for each helping.   Beat up the cheese with a fork, adding a spoonful or so of the milk.   Melt butter and add rest of milk, seasoning, and herbs.   Beat the eggs lightly and add.   Cook carefully for a minute or so until the eggs begin to 'seize.'   Add the softened cheese.   Adjust seasoning and serve at once on the buttered biscuits.

DISHES MADE FROM HARD-BOILED EGGS

These may be substantial enough for a main dish for luncheon, or suitable for savouries or as a first course for dinner.

Hot Dishes

ŒUFS A LA TRIPE

4 eggs	1 oz. flour
1–1½ oz. butter	seasoning of salt and pepper
½ lb. spring onions, cut in pieces, *or*	¾ pint milk (approx.)
½ lb. ordinary onions, finely sliced	grated cheese

Hard-boil the eggs. Separate the whites from the yolks. Cut the whites into slices and rub the yolks through a strainer. Keep in separate small basins, well covered. Put butter in a saucepan, melt, add the onions, cover, and simmer till the onions are soft. It is important to cook the onions well. Partially cooked they may cause the sauce to curdle. Do not allow to colour. Add, off the fire, flour and seasoning, mix well and pour on ¾ pint milk; stir till boiling and simmer for a few minutes. The sauce should be thick and creamy: add more milk if necessary. Put the egg whites on the bottom of a small buttered gratin dish. Scatter over the yolks and spoon over the sauce. Sprinkle thickly with grated cheese and brown in a very hot oven.

ŒUFS DURS AUX CHAMPIGNONS

4–6 hard-boiled eggs	seasoning
6 small onions	cheese
1 oz. butter	breadcrumbs
a little béchamel sauce (or use that in Œufs à la Tripe above)	a little melted butter
	6–8 sautéd mushrooms

Slice, blanch, and drain onions, heat butter in saucepan and put in the onions to soften. When really tender season well and mix with sauce. In a hot fireproof dish put first a layer of onion mixture, then a layer of sliced eggs. Season each layer. Finish off with crumbs, melted butter, and cheese and brown in oven. Surround with the mushrooms.

ŒUFS GRATINÉS PORTUGAISE

A simple, popular, first-course luncheon dish. If required in a more substantial form, allow one whole egg per person instead of half.

3 eggs	½ lb. tomatoes
1½ oz. butter	½ oz. butter or margarine
1 heaped tablespoon finely chopped herbs	béchamel sauce
salt, pepper	½ oz. grated cheese

Béchamel sauce

½ pint milk	6 peppercorns
1 slice of onion	salt
carrot	¾ oz. butter
bouquet garni	¾ oz. flour

Hard-boil the eggs and cut in two lengthways. Sieve the yolks, mix with the creamed butter, chopped herbs, and seasoning to taste, and refill the egg whites with this mixture. Skin and slice the tomatoes, fry quickly in the butter, and place at the bottom of a serving dish. Arrange the stuffed eggs on this, coat over with the béchamel sauce, sprinkle with the cheese, and brown in a quick oven or under the grill.

ŒUFS FARCIS A LA REINE

3 eggs	a little thick béchamel sauce
3 oz. mushrooms	(see above) or cream
a nut of butter	beaten egg and dry white
3 oz. cooked chicken, finely	crumbs for coating
diced	tomato sauce

Hard-boil the eggs and cut in two lengthways. Wash the mushrooms in salted water and chop finely; cook in a nut of butter until soft and tender. Add the chicken, a little thick béchamel sauce to bind, and the pounded egg yolks. Reshape each half-egg into a whole with the mixture, coat with egg and crumbs. Fry in deep fat until golden brown and serve with a tomato sauce handed separately.

ŒUFS FARCIS CANTALIENNE
stuffed eggs on braised cabbage

3 hard-boiled eggs	¼ pint stock
1 small cabbage	seasoning
2 oz. butter	2 shallots
½ gill white wine	

Sauce

½ oz. butter	½ oz. grated cheese
½ oz. flour	¼ teaspoon mustard
1½ gills milk	salt and pepper

Finish

browned crumbs	grated cheese

Shred and blanch the cabbage, drain and return to the pan with 1 oz. of butter, the wine, and the stock. Season, cover with buttered paper and the lid, and simmer or cook in oven until the cabbage is just tender. Chop the shallots and cook slowly until soft in the remaining ounce of butter with seasoning.

Melt the ½ oz. of butter in a pan, add the flour, and pour on 1 gill of milk; stir until boiling, draw aside, and mix in the cheese, seasoning, and mustard.

Split the eggs lengthways, remove the yolks and rub through a strainer. Turn the shallots with the butter into a basin, beat in the yolks with a table-spoon of the sauce. Arrange the whites down the middle of a fireproof dish, sticking a little of the yolk mixture on the bottom to prevent them from sliding. Fill the whites as full as possible with the mixture; add the rest of the milk to the sauce, reheat, and mask the eggs with it. Put the cabbage down each side of the dish, sprinkle the eggs with browned crumbs and grated cheese, and brown lightly under the grill or in the oven. Approximate time 50 minutes.

The following is a good way of using up fresh mushroom stalks. (See Duxelles, page 240.)

ŒUFS A LA CHIMAY

eggs stuffed with mushrooms and covered with mornay sauce

6 hard-boiled eggs
½ oz. butter
1 tablespoon oil
1 oz. finely chopped onion
3½ oz. finely chopped mushrooms or mushroom stalks
  and peelings

1 dessertspoon tomato purée
1 teaspoon chopped parsley
seasoning
½ pint mornay sauce (see page
  156)
grated cheese

Hard-boil the eggs. Heat the oil and butter together and sauter the onion without colouring. Add the mushrooms and cook quickly for a few minutes. Then mix in the purée, parsley, and seasoning. Cut the eggs lengthways, remove yolks, and pound with the mixture. Fill back into the whites, arrange in a dish, coat over the sauce, dust well with grated cheese, and brown in a quick oven.

ŒUFS COQUILLES

A simple and good supper dish.

Make a béchamel sauce by the short method (see page 155). Season the sauce with a little anchovy essence but do not over-flavour. Cut the eggs in two lengthwise, carefully take out the yolks and cut into slices; cut the whites in long thin strips. Put the whites into the sauce, half fill a coquille shell with the mixture, then sprinkle with pieces of egg yolk. Put another layer of the sauce, fill the shell well, rounding it up in the centre, sprinkle with grated cheese, and finish under the grill, or in the oven, just long enough to melt and brown the cheese.

EGG CROQUETTES

3 hard-boiled eggs, chopped
1 yolk
1½ gills panade, made with:
  1½ gills milk
  1 slice of onion
  3–4 peppercorns
  1 blade of mace
  1 small bay-leaf
  1¼ oz. butter
  1¼ oz. flour (scant weight)

seasoning
seasoned flour, beaten egg, and
  dry white crumbs for coating

To prepare the panade put onion, spices, and bay-leaf in milk, infuse well, and bring gently to boiling-point. Strain and cool. Make a roux with butter and flour and pour on the milk, blend well and stir over heat till boiling. Draw aside, season with salt and pepper, add the eggs and lastly the raw egg yolk. Turn on to a plate to cool and leave for some hours in a cold place. A quick method is to turn the mixture into an empty refrigerator ice drawer, slide it back into place, and leave for half an hour or so to harden. Now shape mixture into small croquettes, roll in seasoned flour, brush with beaten egg, and roll in the crumbs. Fry in deep fat until golden brown and crisp. Serve with any good piquante or tomato sauce. N.B. If the croquettes can be left to dry and harden slightly before frying, they will be drier and crisper.

ŒUFS KROMESKI

Proceed in the same way as for egg croquettes, but add if you like some chopped cooked mushrooms. Make some thin unseasoned pancakes. You may either make very small pancakes or cut large ones into strips about 3 inches wide. Spread the pancakes with the mixture, roll them up, allow to chill, dip them in fritter batter (page 441), and fry in deep fat. Serve with one of the sauces recommended for egg croquettes. Or put mixture in thin bacon rashers, roll up, dip in batter, and fry.

Cold Dishes

The yolks of hard-boiled eggs may be taken out of the whites, pounded, flavoured, softened with butter or liquid in a variety of ways, and returned to the whites. They may be accompanied by a suitable sauce.

Cream or mayonnaise and tarragon vinegar or lemon juice with chopped mint or other herbs, with chutney, curry-paste, anchovy, capers, sweet pickles and so forth give a simple range of cold savoury dishes, which may be made more important by having a base of croûtons and an accompanying sauce of the cream type.

The following dish of hard-boiled eggs and anchovy has a fresh tomato salad, and the eggs are served in boats of short pastry.

ŒUFS FARCIS AUX ANCHOIS

4 hard-boiled eggs	1 lb. tomatoes
short pastry (see below)	French dressing
8 fillets of anchovy	1 tablespoon cream
a little anchovy essence if necessary	chives, dill, and grated lemon rind
2 oz. butter	anchovy fillets for garnishing
2 tablespoons thick béchamel sauce	

Short pastry

4 oz. flour	1 yolk of egg
2 oz. margarine	cold water
seasoning	

Prepare pastry: rub fat into flour, add seasoning, yolk, and water to mix to a firm dough. Roll out, line into large boat moulds, and bake blind.

Peel eggs, split lengthways, remove yolks, sieve, and pound till smooth with the anchovies, butter, and sauce. Add a few drops of the essence if necessary. Set the whites in the pastry cases, fill well with the mixture. Garnish with 2 thin strips of anchovy laid crosswise on top of each. Arrange on a serving dish with the tomato salad in the centre:

Peel the tomatoes, cut in thin slices. Mix the cream with the French dressing and marinade the tomatoes in a little of this for about half an hour. Then arrange down the serving dish, pour over the rest of the dressing, and scatter over the chopped chives, dill, and shredded lemon rind to taste.

N.B. The pastry boats can be left out and the eggs set on the serving dish, a little of the filling being used to stick them on.

ŒUFS DURS NORVÉGIENNE OU SUÉDOISE

A cold lunch or supper dish; could be served as an hors-d'œuvre for a lunch.

short crust pastry, rich or ordinary, made with 6 oz. flour (see page 835)	castor sugar
	1–2 tablespoons cream or evaporated milk
4–5 new-laid eggs, hard-boiled	¼ pint picked shrimps, well washed and dried
1 gill French dressing	6 anchovy fillets
English mustard	2 pickled cucumbers

Roll out the pastry, line into a flan ring, and bake blind. Cool. Prepare French dressing, adding about a teaspoon of made mustard and a heaped teaspoon of castor sugar. These two ingredients should be added to taste—the dressing must be sweet but rather hot. Lastly beat in the cream. Set aside when thick.

Carefully remove the whites from the yolks of egg, wash and cut into strips. Mix with the shrimps. Sieve yolks through a bowl strainer. Wash anchovy fillets, dry, and cut into thin strips. Slice cucumber into thin rounds.

A short while before serving mix the shrimps and egg whites with enough dressing to moisten well. Fill the centre of the flan case with this and garnish round the edge with the sieved yolk and sliced cucumber. Arrange a lattice-work of anchovy fillets over the top. Hand the remaining dressing separately.

If for a main course, a beetroot salad should be served. (See Beetroot Salad, page 344.)

CURRIED EGGS (COLD)

Suitable for a first course for luncheon.

6 hard-boiled eggs	salt and pepper
1 teaspoon curry-powder	extra mayonnaise thinned with
1 tablespoon tarragon vinegar	cream and sharpened with
1½ tablespoons mayonnaise	lemon juice
½ teaspoon chopped tarragon leaves	brown bread and butter

Hard-boil eggs. Slice in two lengthwise. Remove yolks and put through a fine wire sieve. Mix curry-powder with tarragon vinegar. Squeeze through muslin cloth and mix with mayonnaise. Add to the egg yolks and mix well. Add chopped tarragon leaves, and salt and pepper to taste. Fill the centres of the whites with this and stick the eggs together. Lay them in a dish and cover lightly with the extra mayonnaise. Serve with brown bread and butter.

For Curried Eggs see also pages 415 and 1016.
For Egg and Spinach Galette see page 267.
For Egg and Spinach Roulette see page 268.
See also Winkfield chapter (pages 984–9) for other egg dishes.

OMELETS

If you are not sure of yourself in the making of omelets there are several points worth consideration. The first perhaps is the matter of the pan. There are some who say they can make an omelet in any old frying-pan, but experts take a different view. An omelet pan should be thick and of the right size to hold a reasonable number of eggs: a pan with a 7-inch base, for instance, will take 3–4 eggs. When buying such a pan choose either thick aluminium or iron, wash it well, and then cover the bottom with salad-oil and leave it for at least 12 hours. Pour off the oil and wipe the pan thoroughly. After this preliminary washing the pan should not be washed again, but wiped over after use with a damp cloth. This treatment helps to maintain an absolutely smooth and slightly greasy surface which prevents the omelet from sticking. If such a pan is used for other purposes, for frying bacon or fish for instance, at some time or other the surface may have to be scoured to remove burnt particles, and any consequent roughness of the surface is detrimental to perfect omelet-making. If by some mischance an omelet pan is misused and must be washed, dry it well, polish it with a clean cloth dipped in coarse salt or with very fine wire wool, and oil it again.

It is inadvisable to make omelets too big, certainly not with more than 6 eggs, and preferably 4 at a time, because an omelet larger than this is difficult to cook to perfection. A pan with a base 7 inches in diameter will serve for 3–4 eggs, and one of 9 inches will take 6. Omelets may be cooked in butter. They take various flavours, fillings, and forms. Sometimes the additional ingredient is added to the egg mixture, sometimes it is used as a filling. For example, in Omelette Fines Herbes the herbs are added to the egg mixture, while in Omelette Alsacienne the cooked, shredded cabbage is used as a filling, and in this way one has an omelette fourrée or filled omelet.

A Spanish omelet is a more solid affair with a mixture of cooked vegetables added to the eggs; it is not perhaps really to be admitted as an omelet by the true amateur.

If garlic is called for in flavouring it may be added in various ways calculated to control the strength of this potent herb. The bowl in which the eggs are beaten may be rubbed round with the cut surface of a clove of garlic; very subtle and refined, this. Or the clove may be crushed with half a teaspoon of salt and a portion of the salt only used according to taste. Care should be taken that the garlic is so thoroughly creamed with the salt that it will mix with the egg without leaving small particles in it.

For certain sweet omelets called omelettes soufflées the yolks and whites are beaten separately and cooking is carried out in the oven. Recipes for these will be found in the chapter on sweets, pages 938–41.

Cooking. An omelet should not be overcooked; the word *baveuse* is sometimes used to indicate the degree of semi-liquidness. This obviously must be adjusted to suit individual taste, and an omelet may even be cooked so as to be firm throughout, though this idea would shock many a good cook. For those who like a really firm omelet it is probably better to adopt the method for omelettes soufflées, which is usually considered suitable only for sweet omelets, but is often pleasing in savoury form to children and to those who find eggs in a liquid state unpleasant. In addition a recipe for a dry omelet is given on page 317.

When eggs are plentiful 2 per person may be allowed. This may be modified to 4 eggs for 3–4 people. The eggs are beaten lightly with a fork, just enough to mix whites and yolks well without making them foamy, seasoning is added, and if herbs are to be used these are also added now. The pan is made really hot so that the butter smokes slightly as soon as it is put in; when it begins to foam the eggs are poured in. It is from this point that the beginner may need help, and while nothing is so good as an ocular demonstration the following will perhaps be better than nothing.

As soon as the eggs are poured in begin to shake the pan and to stir slowly with the back of a fork rather as if you were stroking the mixture, scraping up as you do so large creamy flakes. Then pause for a second or two to let cooking proceed; now tilt the pan a little away from you and begin to fold the edge well over. As you do this some of the liquid will escape from the middle of the omelet and come into contact with the hot base of the pan. Set the pan flat again, and when you judge that cooking is enough in that the omelet has begun to set lightly, draw aside, add any filling called for, tilt the pan again away from you, and fold the omelet right over quickly. The omelet is now half-moon in the pan. To turn it out have ready a hot dish in your right hand; change the position of your left hand so that it is underneath the handle of the pan, which enables you to tilt the pan well and slip the omelet over on to the dish. The whole operation should be quick, a question of 2–3 minutes.

PLAIN OMELET (FOR 3–4)

½ oz. butter	seasoning
4 eggs	1 tablespoon water

Break the eggs into a basin, beat with a fork until well broken, the yolks and whites just mixed but not foamy; add seasoning and water. Proceed in the way described above.

OMELETTE FINES HERBES

Add to the above egg mixture 1 large dessertspoon finely chopped herbs: chives, parsley, chervil, and tarragon are all suitable.

CHEESE OMELET

Sprinkle the omelet thickly with grated cheese whilst in the pan and before folding over. Some French recipes also incorporate little dice of good gruyère with the egg mixture.

BACON OMELET

Take 2 or 3 thin rashers for 4 eggs. Well cook until crisp, break in very small pieces, add to the egg, and cook all together. In place of the bacon very small crisply fried croûtons may be used.

TOMATO OMELET

4–5 ripe tomatoes	½ clove of garlic crushed with
a little olive oil	salt
1 tablespoon finely grated onion	seasoning
	a little cream or brown sauce

Peel and quarter, seed and chop the tomatoes, put them in a saucepan with a little olive oil, the onion, and the garlic. Cook these rapidly, stirring and shaking all the time. Rub through a sieve, put the purée back into a saucepan to reduce until it is a thick sauce. Season well and put about three-quarters of it into the omelet before folding. Dilute the remainder with a little cream or brown sauce, pour over and around the omelet.

For those who like a dry omelet the following recipe is suitable:

Separate the whites and yolks of the eggs. Beat the yolks, add the stiffly beaten whites and a spoonful of cream. Season with garlic crushed with salt, add finely chopped mixed herbs or chives cut up in small pieces. Cook gently, turn, and when ready fold in the usual way and serve with mornay, mushroom, or tomato sauce (see pages 156, 176, and 178).

STUFFED OMELETS (OMELETTES FOURRÉES)

These are made in the same way with the mixture spread quickly over the omelet before folding over. The following are some good fillings:

Alsacienne. Finely shredded and blanched cabbage cooked in a little butter and stock until tender with a flavouring of chopped dill.

Dieppoise. Shrimps or prawns heated in a little mornay sauce with the addition of some cooked mussels.

Champignons. Mushrooms cut in four and cooked for 5 minutes in a little water and lemon juice. A nut of butter worked into a little flour (beurre manié), then added off the fire; the mixture well stirred and reboiled with the addition of a little cream.

Parmentier. Diced potatoes well tossed over the fire in a little butter, and a few leaves of rosemary added with plenty of seasoning. Used when crisp and golden brown.

Chasseur. Two or three chicken or rabbit livers sautéd in butter and cut in slices, dusted with flour, a dash of sherry added, and the whole moistened with stock. Simmered until creamy. Use kidney in the same way.

OMELETTE GERMINY

3 eggs	a little chopped onion
seasoning	a light mornay sauce (see page
¾ oz. butter	156)
lettuce	spring onions sautéd in butter
¾ gill single cream	to garnish

Break the eggs into a bowl, beat up with a fork, season well, adding a spoonful of cream. Shred the lettuce and soften in a quarter of the butter with a little chopped onion; add the rest of the cream and simmer till thick. Make the omelet, using the remaining butter, fill with the lettuce, fold over, turn out and coat quickly with mornay sauce. Garnish with spring onions.

A good omelet is made with cooked smoked fish, finnan-haddock for example, which is mixed with cream or béchamel sauce, parsley, and, if liked, grated cheese. This mixture should be well seasoned and put into the omelet before folding.

The following is an epicurean dish. Like many good dishes it is a little extravagant, being rich in the proportions of butter and cream.

OMELET ARNOLD BENNETT

3 eggs	2 oz. butter
1 gill cream	seasoning
3–4 tablespoons cooked flaked smoked haddock	2–3 tablespoons grated Parmesan cheese

Toss the haddock over a quick fire with half the butter and 2 tablespoons of the cream and allow to cool. Separate the eggs, beat the yolks with a tablespoon of the cream and season. Whip the whites lightly, fold into the yolks with the haddock, add half the grated cheese. Cook omelet in the usual way in the rest of the butter. Do not fold but slide on to a hot dish, scatter over remaining cheese, pour over remaining cream, and brown quickly under a hot grill.

SPANISH OMELET

A Spanish omelet is more solid in texture than the classic dish. Small diced vegetables cooked as for a mirepoix in the proportion of 1 tablespoon for each egg are put into the pan with a little of the heated butter or oil; the seasoned egg is poured on the top and the whole fried as a flat cake. The vegetables may be left-overs, but needless to say the flavour is better if the mirepoix is freshly made. Choose the vegetables with an eye to colour as well as flavour; any or all of the following: aubergines, tomatoes, green and red peppers, onions, carrots, peas, turnips, potatoes. All should be well seasoned and flavoured with garlic.

3–4 eggs	salt, pepper, and crushed garlic
3–4 tablespoons mixed and diced	to taste
or shredded vegetables	2 tablespoons butter or good oil

Heat half the butter in a saucepan, add the vegetables, garlic and, seasoning. Press a piece of buttered paper down on to the vegetables. Cover the pan tightly and cook slowly, shaking the pan occasionally until the vegetables are tender. Adjust seasoning. Break the eggs into a bowl, beat up with a fork, adding salt and pepper. Heat a large omelet pan, add the remaining butter or oil, turn in the vegetables which should be nicely juicy. Pour in the eggs, stir round once or twice and shake the pan. Leave to set on gentle to moderate heat, and after about 3–4 minutes turn the omelet over with a couple of palette-knives and leave for about a further 1–2 minutes to set. Slide at once on to a hot dish and cut into slices before serving.

Alternatively, after the first 3–4 minutes the omelet can be put into the oven for a couple of minutes to set. It should then be slid bottom side up on to a hot plate and served.

N.B. The omelet is usually between $\frac{1}{2}$ inch and $\frac{3}{4}$ inch thick, and is not folded but served flat.

The following recipe calls for more garlic than suits English palates, but may be adjusted, and this is a rustic, agreeable dish. It is quite good eaten cold for outdoor meals.

POTATO OMELET

2 eggs	6 cloves of garlic
1 lb. potatoes	a nut of butter
oil and butter	seasoning of salt and pepper
parsley, finely chopped	

Peel the potatoes, slice about the thickness of a shilling, and fry in a little hot oil and butter until golden brown on both sides. Add the parsley, garlic, and seasoning; push the potatoes together in the centre of the pan to form a cake.   Take care not to burn the garlic.   Drop a nut of butter round the sides of the pan and heat the pan well.   Run in the beaten, seasoned eggs and when set turn the contents of the pan over like one large pancake, using a wide palette knife or a fish slice.   Allow the second side to colour slightly and dish.

An omelet may be made into a more important dish for a main course by the addition of small hollowed croustades containing suitable fillings. For example, a tomato omelet may be garnished with croustades filled with one of the following mushroom mixtures:

(a) Take cooked mushrooms, chop them, and finish off in a little good well-seasoned white sauce.

(b) Chop raw mushrooms, cook for a few minutes only in a little sauce so that the taste of fresh mushrooms is preserved.

A plain omelet or a 'fines herbes' might have croustades filled with tiny glazed onions or baby carrots finished off in butter and sugar.   Another good filling is made with finely sliced onions blanched for 7 or 8 minutes, drained, dried a little over a hot fire, and mixed with a curry-flavoured white sauce.   A cheese or plain omelet may have the croustades filled with melted cheese.   There are possibilities in plenty here for the inventive cook.

To make these croustades cut slices of bread about $\frac{3}{4}$ inch thick.   Stamp out rounds with a cutter, and then with a smaller cutter mark out about $\frac{1}{4}$ inch from the edge an inner ring, but do not cut to the bottom.   Fry the croustades in deep fat, lift out the centre portion with a small knife or with your fingers, leaving a hollow into which the filling will go.

For omelet inside French roll see page 1077.

Recipes for sweet omelets will be found in the chapter on sweets, pages 938–41.

SAVOURY SOUFFLÉS

As in many other cooking processes the achievement of a good soufflé depends on attention to detail: not difficult, not even boring detail, for a soufflé is quickly prepared.   What is needed is a clear mental picture of what you are doing and why you are doing it.   Since every student is proud when she produces a perfect soufflé, light in texture, delicate in flavour, neither dry nor dull, you will perhaps have patience with these details if they seem unduly emphasized.

First of all it should be remembered that there are two main elements in a soufflé: (1) the base which carries the flavour and (2) the egg whites which supply the raising power.   When once the preparation and combination of these two elements are comprehended many changes may be rung. This is one reason for making yourself proficient, another is that while a soufflé is considered suitable for a party it is often made with simple and inexpensive ingredients. Perhaps it is helpful to consider each process separately.

1. The base

This is the element which carries the principal flavour. For savoury soufflés it may be composed of cooked fish, meat, poultry, or game, of a purée of vegetables, or of cheese. The principal flavouring ingredient is mixed with a good béchamel containing yolk of egg. Later on the quantities for a typical basic mixture will be indicated, but one should bear in mind that much depends on the degree of moisture of the base. A vegetable purée may contain more moisture than a meat or fish base, and necessary adjustment has to be made, for if the final mixture for the base is too wet the beaten whites will be unable to carry out their function. This base may be prepared ahead of time, for it is only when the beaten whites are incorporated that all must go forward without delay, but if the base is allowed to become absolutely cold it will have to be slightly warmed in order to facilitate the incorporation of the white. Bearing in mind that this base is to be incorporated with a considerable bulk of beaten whites, it will be clear that seasoning and flavouring will need emphasis. Far too often this point is insufficiently considered, and a soufflé beautiful to look at proves disappointing, and of indistinguishable flavour.

For this reason a cook may add French mustard and cayenne to the base of a cheese soufflé, or crushed garlic to a vegetable base; or flavour the béchamel rather more than usual by cooking perhaps a little onion or garlic in the butter before adding the flour, or by adding grated celery to the sauce at boiling-point. This is perhaps why a strongly flavoured vegetable such as a swede makes such a good soufflé, producing as it does an almost nut-like flavour in the finished dish; and why tomatoes, *douce* in flavour, need a lot of seasoning and flavouring and reduction of the basic pulp.

2. The egg whites

These, usually exceeding in quantity that of the yolks, must be properly beaten and incorporated in the way described on page 287, whipped exactly to the required degree, and folded into the base lightly and quickly.

3. The soufflé case

The modern soufflé case is made of fine fireproof china, thin, much thinner than ordinary fireproof ware, so that it allows the ready penetration of heat and is not so retentive of it that cooking will go on for some time after it has left the oven. These cases are a valuable part of a cook's equipment and should not be used for a generality of purposes—a practice of the inexperienced which irritates the true cook. For individual soufflés special little china cases or small paper *cocottes* are to be bought. For the American type of soufflé to be mentioned later a fireproof dish is sometimes used.

4. The preparation and filling of the case

The case must first be well buttered and this is best done with the fingers. Then a piece of buttered paper is tied round the outside and the ends secured with a paper clip. This paper must project above the rim— ordinarily by about 2 inches.

When the paper is removed at the end of cooking, if the soufflé has risen well the effect is good. Sometimes a deeper band of paper is used, projecting even more above the rim and so giving an impressive effect; this is usually done when something rather special in the way of sweet soufflés is in hand. (See Soufflé Rothschild, page 938.)

5. The filling of the case

Usually the case is filled approximately two-thirds full; if the wider band of paper is used then it may be filled more nearly to the top. If the consistency of the mixture permits it may be put in in large spoonfuls in pyramid form. Sometimes a cook will make a crosswise cut across the top with the back of a knife with the object of facilitating the penetration of heat. It may be convenient to note that a soufflé should rise about 2–3 inches. The case filled, cooking must proceed at once.

6. Timing

Since in serving a soufflé there is no leeway in the matter of time one's planning has to be well considered. For a big soufflé, that is to say one to serve 4–5 people, from 30 to 35 minutes may be allowed after the basic elements have been prepared, which includes 6–7 minutes for beating the whites, 2–3 to mix them with the base and to turn into the soufflé case, and 20–25 minutes for baking. In other words you may prepare the base of your dish early in the day and know that you need only allow 30–35 minutes for finishing off and baking.

7. Baking

All the care in the world in making the mixture is wasted if the baking is improperly carried out; that is why the wise cook will test the heat of her oven, which must be given up entirely to the soufflé, before she folds in the egg whites. If the heat is too great a crust will quickly form which not only deters rising but will prevent the inside from cooking, so that the moment the serving spoon goes in the whole thing will fall in a discouraging way. If the soufflé is overcooked it will be too dry and will shrink, which is also discouraging. It should be said here, though, that even for a perfectly cooked soufflé there are permissible variations; some people like them to be creamy in the middle, while some prefer a spongy consistency. Either may be achieved without going to disappointing extremes. The oven should be moderate to hot, 375°–400° F. The heat is required to come from below, so that a soufflé is put in the oven at the point where bottom heat is strongest. In an Aga the middle shelf should be removed and the soufflé put on the floor of the oven. If the oven is too hot it may be cooled in one of two ways. The door may be left ajar for a few minutes or, better, a large pan of cold water may be put in it 20–30 minutes before it is required; this is probably a more foolproof way of cooling the oven moderately.   For gas or electric stoves the bottom or middle shelf is used. In ovens in which the shelves are in the form of racks it is sometimes useful to set the soufflé on a preheated metal sheet or shallow cake tin.   This, put into the oven early so as to become really hot, presents a solid sheet of metal at oven temperature.   This is of particular use in handling the soufflé, and it may also serve to give that initial kick, as it were, of bottom heat that starts a soufflé on its rising way.   A too hot oven will cause the soufflé to rise too suddenly and to harden.   The cooking should be constant; rising and cooking proceeding together, and particular care being taken not to overcook.   If, towards the end of cooking, the top of the soufflé shows signs of becoming too brown, a thin sheet of greased paper may be laid over it.

A practised cook will not need to test her soufflé, but for those who find need for reassurance a long thin darning-needle or a fine steel knitting-pin may be used to discover the texture of the inside of the dish.   A thick cold skewer may have disastrous results.

8. Serving

I need hardly say that a hot soufflé is served in the dish in which it is cooked, so this should be placed on a folded napkin in another dish for handing.

STEAMED SOUFFLÉS

A soufflé may also be steamed, and old-fashioned cooks often prepared such a dish as one of the courses for luncheon, and it was also a favourite form of invalid food.

The base is usually uncooked, fish, liver, chicken, or veal.   The basic method of all is the same, so the one recipe given will serve as a typical example.   The texture of the finished dish is somewhat firmer than that of a baked soufflé, and by reason of this it may be, and often is, turned out of the case and coated with a light sauce.

A 'layered' soufflé is reasonably substantial, and useful therefore as a main course for luncheon.

Some typical recipes will follow, and those for cheese, vegetable, and sweet soufflés will be found in the appropriate chapters.

It is perhaps risky to offer a typical basic mixture for a savoury soufflé because so much depends on the moistness or otherwise of the base, but for those who wish to experiment the following may be taken as a guide:

For 3 egg yolks and 4 whites allow between $1\frac{1}{2}$ and 2 gills of creamy sauce made with a good $\frac{1}{2}$ oz. each of butter and flour, $1\frac{1}{2}$ gills milk, and 5–6 oz. vegetable, fish, or other purée.

Causes of failure

Those who teach and write about cooking are all too familiar with questions about the failure of dishes they have never had an opportunity of seeing. In particular do questions arise concerning soufflés. Not being gifted with second sight we find such diagnoses difficult, and the following questionnaire, self-applied, may be of use:

1. Did you employ the proper utensils, a copper bowl, or at least a mixing bowl, and a balloon whisk for the egg whites, or did you try to work magic with a knife and a soup-plate?

2. Did you satisfy yourself that the beaten whites stood up like a peak on the whisk, or, alternatively, did you beat them too much so that they presented a rocky texture and began to disintegrate?

3. Was the base of good creamy consistency or did you omit to dry off, perhaps, a vegetable purée, and so use a sloppy mixture that no whites, however well beaten, could hope to raise?

4. Was your timing well planned, or did you leave your soufflé to stand when ready for baking while you played about with the oven?

5. Was the oven too hot so that a crust formed all too quickly, preventing the inside from getting cooked?

6. Did you overcook and so achieve a dry and shrunken soufflé?

7. Did you secure adequate bottom heat?

8. Did you open the oven door too often?

9. Or was the soufflé perfect in texture, beautiful to the eye, but dull, lacking in taste, because in judging the seasoning and flavouring you failed to take into consideration the bulk of egg whites to be added?

Before proceeding to recipes, I think a note might be made here on the American type of soufflé, which is of somewhat different consistency. This often calls for equal quantities of yolks and whites, and the basic ingredients are sometimes added to a thick cream sauce while the sauce is boiling; the heat is then reduced and the egg yolks added. Sometimes breadcrumbs soaked in hot milk replace the sauce. These soufflés are baked at a lower temperature, often in an ungreased soufflé case, generally for a slightly longer time, usually from 35 to 40 minutes, do not rise quite so high, and do not fall so readily. Typical recipes will be given at the end of the chapter (page 332).

CHICKEN SOUFFLÉ
with cooked chicken

10–12 oz. cooked minced chicken	1 oz. butter
1¼ gills well-flavoured béchamel	3 egg yolks
sauce (½ oz. butter, ½ oz. flour)	salt and pepper
(see page 155)	4 egg whites

Have the béchamel sauce ready prepared and cold. Mix this with the chicken and pass through a wire sieve. Turn into a pan, add the butter, and warm over gentle heat. Draw aside and beat in the egg yolks one at a time. Season well. Whip whites to a stiff froth, cut and fold into the mixture. Turn into a buttered soufflé case and bake for 25 minutes in a moderate oven, approximately 375° F. This soufflé is suitable for invalids and children and may be steamed, though the result is then better if raw chicken is used.

CHICKEN, VEAL, OR RABBIT SOUFFLÉ (STEAMED)

Panade

1 oz. butter	2 small eggs
1 oz. flour	½ lb. raw veal, chicken,
1 gill milk	or rabbit, weighed when
a pinch of ground mace	minced
salt and pepper	1 tablespoon thick cream

Velouté sauce

1 oz. butter	½ gill milk
½ oz. flour	salt and pepper
1½ gills strong stock	½ gill cream

First prepare the panade. Make a roux with the butter and flour, pour on the milk and stir until boiling. Draw aside, add seasonings, and allow to cool. Beat in the egg yolks and the minced meat. Mix thoroughly and rub a little at a time through a medium mesh wire sieve. Return to a bowl and stir in the cream. Whip the whites to a stiff but not rocky froth and fold carefully into the mixture. Pour the panade into well-greased oval dariole moulds or individual china soufflé cases. Set in a steamer and steam over moderate heat until well risen and firm to the touch. Meantime prepare the sauce (see page 152). Set in a bain-marie to keep hot. Leave the soufflés in the steamer for a few minutes before turning on to a hot dish, and pour the sauce round and over them. If the mixture has been cooked in the cases, send to the table as they are with a little of the sauce poured over each one. This mixture may also be turned into a buttered soufflé case with a band of paper tied round it. In this case increase the quantities by half and allow 30–40 minutes' steaming. Send to the table in the case, first removing the paper, and serve with an appropriate sauce, such as demi-glace, mushroom, or tomato (see pages 143, 176, and 178).

N.B. This recipe is more of a cream than a soufflé, and the mixture may be turned satisfactorily out of the moulds.

CRAB SOUFFLÉ

¾ oz. butter	¼ pint béchamel (see page 155),
1 teaspoon paprika pepper	made with ½ oz. butter and
1 small teaspoon curry-powder	½ oz. flour
(optional)	1–2 tablespoons cream
12 oz. crab meat (preferably	3 egg yolks
white)	4 egg whites
a few drops of tabasco sauce or	grated cheese
chilli sherry	a few browned crumbs
salt and freshly ground black	
pepper	

Melt the butter in a stew-pan, add paprika and curry-powder, and cook 1 minute. Draw aside, add crab meat and tabasco and season well. Warm over the fire, adding the béchamel and cream. Draw aside and mix in the yolks. Whip whites to a firm snow, cut and fold into the mixture, and turn into a prepared soufflé case. Scatter the top well with the cheese and a few crumbs. Bake in a moderate oven until well risen and firm to the touch, 20–25 minutes.

A prawn or shrimp soufflé may be made in the same way, using a pint of shelled prawns and ¾ pint béchamel.

HERRING ROE SOUFFLÉS

8 oz. good soft roes
a little hot milk for poaching them (enough just to cover)
¼ pint creamy béchamel sauce, made with ½ oz. butter, ½ teaspoon paprika pepper, ¼ oz. flour, and ¼ pint milk,
flavoured as for béchamel (see page 155)
2 yolks of egg
1 oz. grated gruyère cheese
2 stiffly whipped whites
salt, pepper, cayenne

Lay roes in a buttered fireproof dish, pour over hot milk. Poach in oven until firm, 3–4 minutes. Drain and lay in small individual soufflé or Pyrex dishes.

Make up the béchamel, cooking the paprika in the butter for half a minute before adding the flour. When sauce is well cooked draw aside, beat in the yolks one at a time, add half the cheese and plenty of seasoning. Lastly fold in the whites. Cover the roes with a spoonful of the mixture, sprinkle with the remaining cheese. Bake in a moderately hot oven 7–10 minutes.

FISH SOUFFLÉ

½ gill boiling milk
1 oz. breadcrumbs
½ lb. cooked fish
lemon juice, if necessary
½ pint thick béchamel sauce (see page 155), with at least
2 tablespoons less milk or fish stock than usual
salt and paprika
3 yolks of egg
3–4 egg whites
chopped parsley and fennel

Pour the boiling milk over the breadcrumbs and leave them to soak. Divide the fish finely, or if it is at all fibrous pound it in a mortar with the lemon juice. Make the béchamel sauce; stir the fish, chopped parsley and fennel, and bread-crumbs into it, season with salt and paprika, and beat in the yolks. Beat the egg whites stiffly and fold them into the mixture. Turn the soufflé into a well-buttered case; set in a baking-dish of hot water, and bake 30 minutes in a moderate oven (350° F.). Serve at once.

Vegetable Soufflés

MUSHROOM SOUFFLÉ

8 oz. mushrooms
½ oz. butter
1 shallot, finely chopped
1 good teaspoon chopped mixed herbs
1 good teaspoon chopped parsley
¼ pint béchamel sauce (1½ oz. each of butter and flour, ¾ pint flavoured milk) (see page 155)

3 egg yolks
3 oz. grated Parmesan or gruyère
1–2 tablespoons cream
a pinch of ground mace
salt and pepper
4 egg whites
grated cheese and a few browned crumbs

Wash the mushrooms, peel, and cut the stalks off level with the caps. Chop these trimmings finely. Slice or quarter the mushrooms. Melt half the butter in a frying-pan, throw in the mushrooms and cook quickly 3–4 minutes. Turn on to a plate. Put the rest of the butter into the pan, add chopped trimmings with the shallot and after 2 or 3 minutes the herbs. Stir continuously whilst cooking.

Have ready the béchamel; while still warm add the chopped mixture with the yolks and cheese by degrees. When well beaten add the cream and mace and adjust seasoning. Whip the whites to a firm snow and cut and fold into the mixture. Pour a third of this into a prepared soufflé case, scatter over half the mushrooms, pour in another third of the mixture; add the remaining mushrooms and finally the rest of the soufflé mixture. Sprinkle the top well with the grated cheese and a few browned crumbs. Bake in a moderately hot oven (390°–400° F.) 20 minutes.

SOUFFLÉ AUX ÉPINARDS

1 oz. butter
½ oz. flour
4 large tablespoons spinach purée made from 1 lb. picked spinach (see Spinach à la Crème, page 230)
¾ gill single cream or top of milk

salt, pepper, nutmeg, browned crumbs
2 oz. grated gruyère cheese
3 yolks of egg
4 whites of egg

Melt half the butter in a saucepan, add the flour, and cook for a few minutes. Put in the spinach purée and stir vigorously over a moderate fire until it comes well from the side of the pan. Add the cream, cover, and leave on a gentle heat 15 minutes. Draw aside, beat in the remaining butter, salt, pepper, and grated nutmeg to taste. Add the cheese and egg yolks one at a time. Whip whites, fold into the mixture. Turn into a prepared soufflé case, sprinkle top with crumbs, and bake in a moderate to hot oven 20 minutes.

This recipe may be taken as a basic one for most vegetable purée soufflés. Nearly all need cheese or some addition such as chopped cooked ham or mushrooms to give flavour, otherwise they are apt to be insipid.

Sorrel soufflé is made as above.

LEEK SOUFFLÉ (FOR 5–6)

8 good-sized leeks	4 eggs
2 oz. butter	salt, pepper, grated nutmeg,
1½ oz. flour	browned crumbs
½ pint milk	

Wash leeks and cut in pieces. Cook till just tender in boiling salted water. Drain well. Chop roughly and return to the pan with ½ oz. of the butter. Season lightly. Dry off on a slow fire. Meanwhile melt remaining butter in a saucepan, add flour off the fire, and when well mixed add the milk. Stir till boiling, draw aside, add seasoning, nutmeg, and the egg yolks. When well beaten turn on to the leeks and mix gently together. Whip whites till stiff, mix in a large spoonful and fold in the remainder. Turn into a prepared soufflé dish, dust over with the crumbs, and bake in a moderately hot oven for 20 minutes.

SWEET CORN SOUFFLÉ

1½ oz. butter	corn rinsed in a colander
1½ oz. flour	under the tap
½ pint milk	1 teaspoon onion juice
seasoning	1 teaspoon chopped parsley
1 cup fresh corn prepared as	3 egg yolks
for corn fritters (see page	4 egg whites
244), or a small tin of sweet	

Make the base with butter, flour, and milk. Season. Add corn, onion juice, and parsley, adjust seasoning, and cook all together for a few minutes. Add egg yolks one at a time. Whip whites and fold into the mixture. Bake as in previous recipes.

Soufflés made from Root Vegetables

Excellent soufflés may be made from certain root vegetables, in particular Jerusalem artichokes, parsnips, potatoes, and swedes. The basic sauce or panade may be as for spinach soufflé, or the vegetable base may be mixed with a béchamel sauce. Sometimes cream is also added. Here are some typical recipes.

POTATO SOUFFLÉ

In order that this soufflé shall have a nut-like flavour, which it can have, the potatoes should be baked in the oven and not boiled.

¾ lb. potato pulp	¼ gill thin cream or top of milk
¼ oz. butter	2 egg yolks
seasoning of salt, pepper, and a dash of nutmeg	3 egg whites
a little grated orange rind or any suitable chopped herbs for flavouring	a little melted butter

Bake potatoes in the oven. Remove them one at a time, scoop out the insides, weigh, put through a ricer into a saucepan. Beat well, adding butter, seasonings, and orange rind or other flavourings. Return to gentle heat to reduce a little, taking care not to burn. This drying permits the absorption of the cream without the purée being rendered too moist. Add the cream by spoonfuls, beating continuously. Remove from fire and allow to cool. Add slightly beaten yolks one at a time, then fold in stiffly beaten whites.

Have ready a buttered soufflé dish or earthenware casserole and with a large spoon put in the purée, allowing it to rise in the middle to a dome, which you may smooth off with a palette-knife. Brush lightly over with melted butter. Put in a moderate oven and bake about 15–20 minutes.

ONION SOUFFLÉ (1)

Onions make too sloppy a base for a soufflé, so must be mixed with some thickening. Many recipes give flour for this purpose, but here is a recipe in which rice and a few breadcrumbs are used.

2 oz. rice	seasoning
½ lb. onions	2 cloves
1 oz. butter	1½ gills cream or top of milk
2 tablespoons stale bread-crumbs	2 egg yolks, beaten slightly
	2 egg whites, beaten firmly

Stick the onions with cloves and parboil for 5 minutes, then remove cloves. Chop onions finely. You should have approximately ¾ pint of onion pulp. Boil the rice. Melt the butter in a saucepan and add the pulp. Cook gently without browning until soft. Mix together rice, onion, breadcrumbs, seasoning, and cream. Add the yolks, fold in the whites. Proceed as for other soufflés.

Here is another method for Onion Soufflé which may also be used with turnips in place of onions:

ONION SOUFFLÉ (2)

1 lb. onions	the water in which the
2 oz. butter	onions were boiled)
1 oz. flour	seasoning
1 gill liquid (which can be half	4 cloves
cream or good milk and half	3 eggs

Stick the onions with cloves and boil till tender, remove cloves and put onions through a sieve. Make a roux of butter and flour, diluting with the liquid. Add the purée of onion and bring to boiling-point. Season well and add the slightly beaten egg yolks. Beat the whites of egg stiff and fold in. Put into a buttered soufflé dish and bake for 20 minutes.

SWEDE SOUFFLÉ

One of the best and most delicate soufflés is made by the method of the above recipe, substituting as a base 4 tablespoons good swede purée, well seasoned and with plenty of pepper. A little cream used in the preparation of the purée is excellent.

SOUFFLÉ AU FROMAGE

1 oz. butter	1½ oz. each of grated Parmesan
½ oz. flour	and gruyère cheese mixed
1 gill milk	salt, cayenne and paprika
3 egg yolks	pepper
4 egg whites, stiffly whisked	a little extra grated cheese

Prepare a soufflé case. Melt the butter in a pan, stir in the flour, add the milk, and stir until boiling. Cool slightly, beat in the yolks, adding salt and a little cayenne pepper. Work in the cheese and 1 spoonful of the egg whites to soften, then fold in the remainder. Turn the mixture into the prepared case and bake in a moderate oven for about 20 minutes. Remove paper and serve *at once* sprinkled with grated cheese and paprika pepper.

This quantity halved may be baked in small ramekin or soufflé cases for a savoury.

In the chapter on cheese (page 755) will be found a cold gruyère soufflé.

'Layered' Soufflés

The following recipe for tomato and macaroni represents a more substantial dish than the ordinary soufflé. It is really a layered soufflé and is capable of much variation. It is an excellent way of using up cooked food: fish, vegetables and so forth.

TOMATO AND MACARONI SOUFFLÉ

For the layers

1–2 oz. macaroni, boiled till tender

2 large ripe tomatoes, peeled, seeded, and thinly sliced

1 large tablespoon chopped basil or mint

For the soufflé

1½ oz. butter

1½ oz. flour, scant weight

¾ pint milk

3–4 eggs

1 oz. grated Parmesan cheese

salt, pepper, and browned crumbs

Prepare macaroni and tomatoes, chop herbs, and mix all together. Melt butter in saucepan, take from fire, add flour, and pour on the milk. Stir until boiling. Draw aside, cool, season well, and beat in yolks one at a time. Whip whites stiffly and fold into the mixture. Turn a third of the mixture into a prepared soufflé case, put a layer of half the macaroni, tomato, and herb mixture on the top, and a third of the grated cheese. Cover with half the remaining soufflé mixture. Make another layer of the remaining macaroni mixture and cheese, but reserve a little cheese to scatter on the top of the soufflé. Add the remaining soufflé mixture, finish with a scattering of cheese and browned breadcrumbs. Bake in a moderate oven 25–30 minutes.

VARIANTS OF THE ABOVE 'LAYERED' SOUFFLÉ

The basic soufflé may be plain or tomato- or cheese-flavoured, according to the filling to be used; for example:

1. A cheese soufflé with layers of cooked flaked finnan-haddock. Follow the recipe given above, but take half the quantity of butter and flour and 2½ oz. grated Parmesan; or the recipe for Soufflé au Fromage on the previous page may also be used.

2. The layered soufflé as above, with cooked peas or sprigs of cauliflower for the layer, and the milk in the soufflé base replaced either by tomato juice and stock or by concentrated tomato purée diluted with juice and stock. Chopped mint or basil is a good flavouring for this soufflé.

3. Cooked leeks with strips of blanched bacon on a cheese soufflé base.

4. A plain basic soufflé made with milk flavoured as for béchamel and with layers of sautéd mushrooms, the mushrooms dusted as they are added with a little ground mace or nutmeg.

In soufflé-making an extra white of egg is often called for to give additional lightening, and though it may be used in the above dishes it may also be dispensed with.

Recipes for two American Soufflés

AUBERGINE AND MUSHROOM SOUFFLÉ

1½ cups cooked aubergine
1 oz. butter
2 oz. mushrooms (approx.)
a clove of garlic
1 oz. flour

¼ pint milk
salt, pepper, and cayenne
3 eggs
2 tablespoons crumbs browned
in butter

Peel the aubergine, cut it in dice, and cook it in boiling salted water until quite soft.   Quarter the mushrooms and cook them in a little of the butter until soft.   Crush the garlic, or chop it finely, cook it for a few minutes in the rest of the butter, add the flour, pour on the milk, and make a thick sauce.   Season well with salt, pepper, and a pinch of cayenne.   Cook for a minute or two and beat in the aubergine and mushroom, crushed together with a fork.   Beat in the egg yolks.   Beat up the whites in the way described on page 287, fold them in, pour the mixture at once into an un-buttered soufflé case, with a band of paper tied round the outside.   Bake in a moderate oven (325° F.) for 35 minutes, increasing the heat to 350° after 10 minutes, or keeping the heat at 325° and leaving the soufflé to bake for 40 minutes.   Scatter crumbs on top before serving.

CHICKEN SOUFFLÉ

1 good tablespoon chopped onion
1 oz. butter or bacon fat
1½ cups breadcrumbs
½ cup milk
a clove of garlic
1 oz. mushrooms, sliced and cooked in an extra ½ oz. butter

2 cups minced chicken
1 tablespoon finely chopped herbs, thyme, parsley, and tarragon
salt and pepper
3 eggs

Cook the onion in the butter or bacon fat over gentle heat until soft, but do not allow to colour.   Stir in the breadcrumbs and add the milk. Crush the garlic and cook it with the mushrooms in the extra ½ oz. of butter.   Add, with the chicken, to the mixture and cool.   Add the chopped herbs and season very well.   Beat in the yolks, whip the whites in the way described on page 287, and fold them in.   Pour into an un-buttered soufflé case and bake 35 minutes at 325° F.

XII

Salads

THERE are certain solid-flesh devotees who regard salads as kickshaws at best, at worst as raw poison; there are also unrestrained vitamin-conscious raw-food enthusiasts who regard a taste for uncooked foods as praiseworthy. In the ranks of such extremes no true epicure would find himself.

There are, of course, manifestations of this form of food calculated to drive one to the ranks of the anti-salad section. One, to be met with at certain eating-places, is composed of slices of tomato, seeds and juice escaping, couched on a bed of lettuce shredded with a steel knife, the whole having a tinny, fish-like flavour, reminiscent of last night's hors-d'œuvre. Another unpleasant and misnamed dish is a conglomeration of cooked root vegetables gloyed together with unpleasant sauce and be-glamoured, or otherwise, by the name of Russian salad. There is, of course, a good salad of this name.

It was about a hundred years ago that someone said that a salad was 'the glory of every French dinner, and the disgrace of most in England.' While we have improved a little in the intervening years, there is still some truth in this sweeping assertion. In this, as in most culinary affairs, the French excel, although now that Englishwomen are less remote from the cooking-pot and stove than once they were, French supremacy may not continue for ever.

The subject of salads in my mind divides itself geographically. Generally speaking I think of it in terms of England, France, and America: England, the home of potato, beetroot, and mixed salad; America, the sponsor of a great variety of salads, many of them suitably served as a separate course; and France, epicurean France, where, with unerring simplicity of taste, fresh green salad is served as a matter of course as an accompaniment to roast and grilled meat and poultry. This, the serving of a piquant salad with hot dishes, is done not only with the object of refreshing the palate, but always, in effect, to enhance the flavour of the main dish.

So this chapter may well be divided in this way, even if here and there it overflows its geographical boundaries.

I remember a restaurant in Paris (could it have been the Auberge Père Louis?) where one could eat excellent poulet à la broche. Now chicken roasted on a spit before a glowing wood fire is a dish of such perfection that to serve it with concocted gravy or sauce of any kind, however rich and rare, would be an affront.   Nor is it something to be eaten with 'two veg.' and bread sauce.   There it was served simply with pommes frites and a piquant green salad.   While we may never again hope to cook in this way, before an open fire, creating Lucullean smells and tastes, we can adopt the same restraint when we serve roast chicken, and, if you like, follow the excellent French way and serve afterwards a green vegetable as a separate *plat*.

In France the range of materials commonly used for green salads is wider than one generally finds with us.   In addition to the more usual lettuce, watercress, curled endive, and batavia it is usual to be offered a salad of mâche (corn salad or lamb's lettuce) or blanched dandelion leaves, slightly bitter and very good, and sometimes purslane, sorrel, and other less well-known plants.   Moreover French cooks have a pleasant custom of serving certain cooked and chilled vegetables in salad form: spinach, beans, cauliflower, aubergines, artichokes and suchlike; and although these figure perhaps more often among their hors-d'œuvre than as an accompaniment to a main dish, there is no reason why they should not be adapted in any way that suits our purpose.   Cooked chilled spinach, for instance, is popular with us, as is also a salad of young French beans and the flowers of cauliflower or broccoli.

For most of the salads so far named a simple French dressing is generally the best, the basic ingredients of which are oil, French wine vinegar, salt, and pepper, supplemented at times to suit purpose or palate with crushed garlic, French mustard, onion juice, chopped herbs, crushed yolks of hard-boiled egg, and sugar.   Vinegar may be flavoured with tarragon or other herbs or be replaced in part or whole by lemon juice; cream may take the place of oil, and pleases some palates better.   In using some of these additions one may be getting a little far from the classic French dressing which, simple as it is, is perhaps the best, although improperly prepared it can be very bad.

A word must be said on the subject of garlic, for opinions on this pungent bulb are apt to be very definite.   You may hate it, or you may find tame a green salad from which it has been omitted.   One meets sometimes, in English cook-books, a timorous recommendation to rub garlic round the inside of the salad bowl.   I do not deny that if you put your head well over the bowl you will be able to detect its presence with your sense of smell, but for those who like it this is an inadequate way of using it.   If, however, you like a little flavour of garlic, but find too much the use of a small piece crushed in the dressing, you may prefer an in-between course.   In this event you will rub garlic, or spread a little of it, crushed, on a crust of bread, and lay this in the bottom of the salad bowl, tossing it with the salad; the crust, called in France a 'chapon,' may then be removed or left in the bottom of the bowl as you please.   This bread crust, I may say, is not intended to be eaten, but if you really are a garlic addict there is a way of introducing it into a salad on croûtons which is particularly whole-hearted.   This is probably of peasant origin and comes, I think, from the region of Languedoc; it is suitable only for uninhibited enthusiasts.

Croûtons, or small rounds of fried brown bread, are rubbed over on either side with the cut surface of a clove of garlic; these are then put in the salad bowl and sprinkled with a well-seasoned French dressing. To these highly flavoured pieces of bread the rest of the salad is added, and the whole dressed and well tossed together. Young blanched dandelion leaves or curled endive are often used for this.

From France let us turn to England and a more restricted salad outlook. Like most things, the old-fashioned mixed salad can be very good, but I have heard it described as an incongruous mess. It is worth paying attention to details of preparation. Its ingredients vary according to taste. I prefer to leave out beetroot and also sliced tomatoes: the appropriate herbs and dressing for both of these are, from a gourmet's point of view, sometimes so different from those suitable to a mixed salad. With a mixed salad many people like an old-fashioned 'cooked' dressing, and very good, simple, and appetizing this may be.

Beetroot is another variable salad. In thick slabs, slices, or cubes, harshly dressed, it has limited appeal. Paper-thin, ice-cold, and melting, suitably dressed, prepared hours before it is to be eaten, it is a very different affair.

Tomatoes too need special preparation to be really good, and I think taste best served apart, sometimes whole, sometimes sliced, but whenever possible flavoured with the appropriate herb, sweet basil.

Potato salad can be unpleasant in the form of slabs of cold potato glued together, but it can also be creamy, melting, and delicious. It depends mainly on attention to detail.

The first time I met a range of American salads at a party I was thoroughly nonplussed, and it was not until I had travelled about a little, used my eyes, and asked a few questions that I began to get the hang of American ideas on this subject. The occasion was a buffet supper. On the table was a great array of food, turkey, chicken, ham, and various familiar salads, along with others quite unfamiliar in the form of jellies, mousses, and fruit which I took to be part of the sweet course. In this I was mistaken: these were intended to be eaten with the savoury course, and so I omitted on that occasion to try the range of jellies and fresh fruit salads dressed in various ways and intended to accompany the turkey, the ham, and the chicken.

The American housewife is both inventive and adventurous, and I am everlastingly grateful that I learned to use fruit, beyond the limits of orange with wild duck, as the basis of salad. And some of the recipes counted here among our most epicurean, and for this reason placed in the Winkfield chapter, would never have been thought out, added to, and played with, without this opportunity of learning from American ways. And how grateful I was to them, during the more rigorous rationing days, for many a good idea with which to supplement what would otherwise have been meagre fare. So I think, if I were you, that I would bear in mind the range of possibilities which are only indicated in this chapter, but from which many varieties of salad are to be devised.

EQUIPMENT

A perfectly good salad is to be made with a minimum of equipment—a bowl and a fork—but for the salad-minded there are certain things which it is a pleasure to use.

Salad basket. A wire salad basket for drying the leaves of lettuce and other salad plants is invaluable. The washed leaves are placed in this and it is then swung to and fro vigorously. As a result the leaves are dried without being crushed. Failing this useful piece of equipment a clean dry cloth may be used.

Wooden bowl. This is a suitable dish in which to serve most green salads as well as some others. It is best to choose a bowl on the large side for one's needs, so that the contents may be well turned over and tossed ('fatigued') without splashing or spilling. Do not, for a green salad, if I may venture to advise you, use, in the name of prettiness or party effect, a crystal or ornamental china bowl, or seek to improve the look of the whole by arranging the salad ingredients in a pattern. A green salad should be well tossed and well anointed with dressing. This wooden bowl should not be washed after use, but be wiped round with crumpled soft paper, and it may if you wish be finished off with a dry rough cloth.

Small wire sauce or rotary whisk. This is useful for emulsifying the various dressings easily. A particularly quick and effective emulsifier in the form of a china or glass cylinder with a metal piston is often sold as an egg-beater, and can also be found at the chemist's.

Salad tray. If you like, as I do, to dress the salad yourself on a side table, a well-equipped salad tray is practical. It may carry, as well as oil, French wine and flavoured vinegars, mustard, pepper, salt, and sugar, a small wooden bowl for mixing the dressing, a wooden plate for the various herbs, the whisk or emulsifier, a small knife for cutting the garlic, and a lemon squeezer. So equipped you may vary your salad to the need of the moment.

INGREDIENTS SUITABLE FOR GREEN SALADS OR 'SALADES DE SAISON'

Lettuce, cabbage or cos; the latter is sometimes called Romaine.

Endive, curled or batavian.[1]

Chicory.[1]

[1] The respective French and English names for chicory and endive are confusing. The blanched white heads sold in English shops as chicory are called in France endives or endives belges, and are so named in many menus in English restaurants. Chicorée in France corresponds to our endive, and chicorée frisée to our curled endive. It is these two green vegetables that we refer to as curled endive and batavian endive, and we reserve the name chicory for that blanched white salading which is available during the winter.

Mâche (corn salad or lamb's lettuce), particularly useful as a winter salad because it needs no protection, but lives outside through the cold weather.

Watercress and garden cress. The latter is sometimes called American cress and is a little hotter in flavour than watercress.

Blanched dandelion leaves. The blanching is done by placing an inverted plant pot (with a flat stone or slate over the hole) over a good-sized dandelion plant. Plants may be covered in rotation and the centre leaves picked when pale in colour.

Sorrel. Both garden and wild varieties are used, the latter being more acid.

Blanched stems of certain root vegetables. If left too long in the sand in which root vegetables are stored during the winter, the roots of turnips, parsnips, swedes and so on will send up blanched growths. These are delicate in flavour, generally juicy and crisp, and added to other salads lend variety of flavour.

Celery and celeriac. The latter is used cut in thin strips, either raw or blanched in boiling water for a few moments.

Sea-kale. This has a crisp nutty flavour in its raw state, and used in moderation is a good addition to various mixed salads. It may be used alone in its cooked state to make a most delicate salad.

GREEN PEPPERS OR PIMENTOS

Sweet peppers are neither grown nor used sufficiently in England. Not only are they good in many cooked dishes, but they are a valuable addition in their raw state to salads. Plants may be grown from seed in the greenhouse. The peppers are prepared by being cut in two, and the seeds and pith removed; if the fruit is young and tender it may then be finely sliced and added to the salad without further preparation. Less tender fruits may be blanched in the following way:

The peppers are put in a small basin with a pinch of bicarbonate of soda in each. Boiling water is poured over them and allowed to stand for a few moments; they are then rinsed and shredded.

HERBS

Chopped herbs are an important ingredient in salads and these are dealt with in a separate chapter (page 371).

VINEGARS

The normal French dressing calls for three parts of oil to one of vinegar. If these proportions are used with the ordinary vinegar in general commerce in this country the result may be an over-strong taste of oil for English palates. The vinegar called for in French recipes is a strong wine vinegar, something which cuts through the oil and sharpens the taste without over-diluting the oil. Failing this lemon juice may be used to replace the vinegar in whole or in part. It should, however, be observed that many of the recipes given can only be carried out successfully with French wine vinegar. Flavoured vinegars lend interest and variety, and for those who agree that a salad should appear at some meal on every day of the year the recipes for these given on pages 1107–9 will help to ring the changes, and may be of interest.

OIL

Pure olive oil of the first pressing, known as 'huile vierge,' is much sought after by connoisseurs. It is by no means easy to find or to buy. Unfortunately it is all too easy to buy oil of an inferior quality and of unpleasant flavour, and if this is used for dressing salads it may ruin a taste for salad-oil for a long time. Good olive oil and certain tasteless vegetable oils are now obtainable.

One can also now buy rape and other seed oils which have been treated, that is to say deodorized so that they are rendered free of unpleasant taste or smell. Rape seed produces a limpid oil, good for use in the kitchen. For those who do not like oil, however good it may be, fresh or sour cream is a valuable substitute, as is yoghourt.

GREEN SALADS ('SALADES DE SAISON') AND OTHER RAW SALADS

It is of importance that green salads should never be dressed any length of time before they are required. It is best, when possible, to do this at the moment of serving.

Batavian endive is good alone or with sections of orange prepared in the way given on page 47, and with either French or a cream dressing.

Curled endive is usually dressed with a French dressing, but is particularly good with the bacon dressing on page 362.

LETTUCE

Lettuce salad, plain. Break the lettuce leaves apart with the fingers, wash if necessary, carefully examining each leaf; dry thoroughly in salad basket or clean cloth, put leaves in salad bowl, dress with French dressing, toss and turn until dressing is thoroughly dispersed over the leaves. Grind black pepper over the surface and toss once more. Chopped chives, chervil, or a mixture of herbs may with advantage be added.

Hearts of lettuce. Cut solid crisp hearts of lettuce in wedges with a stainless steel knife. The cream dressing on page 363 is suitable for this, and the addition of orange is good. A mixture of cream, lemon juice, sugar, pepper, and salt, alone or with such herbs as chervil, basil, and tarragon, is excellent.

Cos lettuce may be treated in either of the above ways, and if I wanted to persuade children to eat green salad I should probably make it with the crisp leaves of cos lettuce and serve it with the nursery dressing given on page 365, perhaps making the affair more amusing by serving the dressing in little cups made of halves of lemon from which the flesh has been scooped out, and letting them dip each leaf in it.

Mâche (or lamb's lettuce) is an excellent winter salad; seeds of this are sown in the summer and the leaves are best after the first frosts have been on them. As this plant lies close to the ground it is apt to be splashed with grit, and exceptional care must be taken in washing it. It is usually served plain with French dressing and may also accompany beetroot.

OLD-FASHIONED MIXED SALAD

Lettuce, spring onions, chicory, radishes, cucumber, celery, or what you will may go into this salad, including hard-boiled eggs. An old-fashioned boiled dressing, such as one of those given on pages 369–70, is generally popular. This may be almost a meal in itself served with brown bread and butter. In American restaurants such a salad is offered as a separate course; it usually contains also small pieces of highly tasting cheese such as Roquefort.

SORREL AND BLANCHED DANDELION LEAVES

These make a good early spring salad; wash the leaves, put them in cold water in the ice-box to crisp for an hour or two, dry, break up with the fingers, dress with French dressing. Wild sorrel is suitable but sharper than the cultivated variety, and raw, young spinach may be mixed with it.

OTHER RAW SALADS

Celery and apple salad is excellent; sweet dessert apples should be used and nuts may be added. Celeriac may be used raw, cut in julienne strips, or these may be blanched (see page 190). In the first case they should be chilled by being put into ice-cold water in a cold place for a few hours.

Curled celery and orange salad is also excellent, and may be dressed simply with a little orange juice, a pinch of salt, and a little grated rind. To curl celery see page 48.

CHICORY

The heads of this make a first-class salad.   Late in the season there is a tendency to bitterness, not necessarily unpleasant.   Outer, greenish-tinted leaves should be removed.   Orange is a particularly good addition to chicory.   For this most refreshing and delicate of salads the oranges are peeled and prepared in the way described on page 47, and the heads of chicory are split longitudinally in halves or quarters according to size; an orange-flavoured dressing such as that on page 365 is delicious.

Chicory may be cut across into small pieces and mixed with dessert apples peeled and cut up; for this a similar dressing with lemon instead of orange is suitable.   Alternatively any good cream dressing will serve; for example, a few spoonfuls of cole-slaw dressing diluted with milk, cream, or Yoghourt is excellent.

SALADE NIÇOISE

A rustic and substantial salad suitable as a first course for summer luncheons.

1 large lettuce	1 small cucumber, sliced
½ head of celery, chopped	½ hard-boiled egg per person
1 large tomato, sliced	(approx.)
2 anchovies per person (approx.)	a small tin of tunny fish
12 black olives	1 green pepper, seeded and sliced
1 medium-sized onion, chopped	

Dressing

3 tablespoons olive oil ('huile de Provence')	½ teaspoon freshly grated pepper
1 dessertspoon wine vinegar	1 flat teaspoon salt
1 teaspoon French mustard	1 clove of garlic crushed with salt (optional)

The salad can be served with anchovies alone, without tunny; if this is done use twice as many anchovies, or more.

Line a salad bowl with leaves of lettuce, and arrange over them, in layers, chopped celery, slices of tomato, fillets of anchovy, black olives, chopped onion, slices of cucumber, and hard-boiled eggs cut in halves or slices.   Put the tunny fish on top, in large pieces, scatter over the finely sliced green pepper, and pour over the dressing.   The chopped celery, onion, and cucumber may be served in separate small bowls, for the benefit of those who dislike the flavour of any one of them, or who find one of them difficult to digest.

COLE-SLAW OR RAW CABBAGE SALAD

It is sometimes possible to buy for this a creamy-white cabbage which I think comes from Belgium.   It has a particularly sweet and nutty flavour, and I have always wondered about the complete absence of green colouring.

One winter when we lived in Kent there was heavy and deep snow which lay over the land for weeks; the cabbages in the fields near us were quite hidden from sight, and when at last the snow melted these were blanched white. The farmer told me to take all I wanted, for he would have to plough them in; no one, he said, would accept them for sale. They too had this sweet, nut-like taste.

Choose a solid heart of cabbage, cut this in quarters, lay the flat surface of a quarter downwards on the table, then with a very sharp thin knife shave it in wafer slices. Put the shreds into ice-cold salted water and put in a cold place (possibly on a stone floor) for a few hours and preferably all night. Lift out, drain, and dry thoroughly. The drying is of importance, for no drop of water must dilute the dressing.

Thin slices of dessert apples are a good addition, as are nuts, celery, or thinly sliced celeriac. Plenty of dressing is required, and one may vary the dressings given by adding finely minced onion, sprouted onion tops, or various herbs, dill being particularly suitable. Provided the cabbage is really shaved, this salad is not indigestible for most people, but it may be made more tender by a preliminary blanching of the cabbage shreds, and also of the celeriac if this is used. For this purpose the shreds are plunged into a large pan of boiling salted water, and left until the water comes back to the boil. They are then drained, dried, and treated as before.

The large black Spanish radish is useful for winter salads; it may be grated and added to other raw vegetables, or be shaved in paper-thin slices and dressed.

CUCUMBER SALAD

The English method is to slice the cucumber thinly either with or without its peel (for very tender greenhouse cucumbers it is an advantage to retain the skin, which is said to act as a digestive), to sprinkle with salt and pepper, dress with a French dressing, and finish with chives or other herbs. The French way is somewhat more complicated and is particularly suited to outdoor cucumbers, which are tougher than our English greenhouse varieties. For this the cucumbers may be peeled, sliced, or cut in dice, then placed in a soup-plate, sprinkled with a tablespoon of salt, and turned over until the salt is well mixed in. A plate is fitted over them and pressed down on top of the cucumbers, which are allowed to stand for an hour, and then the juice is drained away. (The effect of salting is to render the slices or cubes pliable and soft; it also draws out any bitterness that may exist.) For this a good French dressing with plenty of freshly ground black pepper (but no salt) and 2 good tablespoons chopped parsley or dill is suitable. A little of the liquid drained from the cucumber may be added to the dressing if liked. A variant from Sweden gives a similar dressing with sugar and no oil. A recipe may be found on page 367.

SALAD OF GRATED RAW VEGETABLES

The following are all suitable: turnips, carrots, kohlrabi, swedes, Jerusalem artichokes, celeriac, parsnips, Brussels sprouts, and cauliflower. These may be finely shredded or grated and arranged in separate heaps on a flat dish, with a small heap of grated onion in the middle for those who like it. Some people like the vegetables coarsely shredded, but in this case they are less easy to digest.

Thin slices of dessert apples and curled celery hearts are a good addition. Such a salad should have the dressing served apart, and one of the boiled dressings given on pages 369–70 and the cole-slaw dressings on page 369 are equally suitable.

TOMATO SALADS

Red or yellow tomatoes and the smaller decorative varieties may all be used. Tomatoes are peeled by being plunged into boiling water for 30–60 seconds according to their ripeness, and they should then go immediately into cold water before being skinned.

SMALL WHOLE-TOMATO SALAD

Choose small tomatoes, peel them, removing the pith at the stem with a sharp-pointed knife. Place in a basin, marinade in French dressing in the ice-box for a few hours. Lift them out, arrange in a single layer in a deep platter or glass dish, add a little cream to the basic French dressing of three parts oil, one part vinegar, French mustard, salt, sugar, and garlic, and pour over the tomatoes. Sprinkle with chopped basil. Large tomatoes peeled and sliced may be dressed in the same way, or with a plain French dressing without the use of cream. In this case chopped chives or onion are a good addition. One of the nicest ways of serving tomato salad is to dress the chilled tomatoes with plenty of lemon juice, sugar, and salt and to grate over at the last moment a little of the lemon peel. This is sharp, cool, and refreshing.

TOMATOES WITH ASPARAGUS, DICED CUCUMBER, MELON, OR PEAR

Allow 1 medium-sized tomato for each person. Cut a slice from the stem end, remove seeds, invert to drain, season well inside with salt and freshly ground black pepper. Marinade cooked asparagus tips or diced cucumber, melon or pear, or a mixture of these in a French dressing for an hour before filling the tomato. Fill with the mixture, dress with a cream dressing or a watercress or mint dressing (see page 368). This may be served on a thickish small slice of bread and butter or on a fried croûton. A small roll with the inside pulled out may have the crust buttered, be made crisp in the oven, and have the tomato served in it. Tomato salad with cream and horse-radish dressing is very good.

TOMATOES WITH HORSE-RADISH CREAM

Skin and chill tomatoes. Cover with the cream horse-radish sauce given on page 364, well iced.

TOMATO AND FRUIT SALAD (AS A FIRST COURSE)

4 ripe, even-sized tomatoes and
    salt, pepper, and lemon juice
    to season them
5 oz. grapes
2 oranges or tangerines

2 dessert apples
new brown bread and butter
    sprinkled with chopped nuts
    and rolled

Scald and skin tomatoes, skin and pip grapes, cut, peel, and remove pith from oranges and cut out the sections. Peel, core, and dice the apples.

Dressing

3–4 tablespoons cream
1 tablespoon oil
sugar to taste

lemon juice to sharpen
salt and freshly ground black
    pepper

Mix well, add fruit, and set aside.

Cut tomatoes in the following manner. Stand stalk side down and make eight cuts through the flesh, taking care not to cut through to the base. Press back the 'petals.' With a sharp knife or scissors cut away the central core and remove seeds. Set each tomato on a small glass dish. Season well inside with salt, pepper, and a squeeze of lemon juice. Put a large spoonful of the fruit in each. Chill well. Serve with brown bread and butter rolls.

N.B. Pear, pineapple, or banana is also suitable as a filling. A stainless steel or silver knife should be used for preparing fruit and tomatoes.

TOMATO, RAISIN, AND HERB SALAD

4–6 tomatoes
2 tablespoons in all of the following herbs, measured after mincing:

        lemon thyme   basil
        tarragon   fennel
        marjoram   savory
        chives

2 oz. stoned, roughly chopped raisins

Mince the herbs very finely. Peel and quarter tomatoes, add raisins, sprinkle with herbs. Dress with the following dressing and chill well:

1 teaspoon French mustard
2 tablespoons oil
the juice of ½ lemon

1 dessertspoon sugar
salt and freshly ground pepper
    to taste

SALADS OF COOKED VEGETABLES

Now we come to salads of chilled, cooked vegetables. Among the most popular, apart from potato, are those made of cauliflower or broccoli, spinach or young Brussels sprouts, French beans, the zucchini described in the vegetable chapter, which may either be split or served whole, and, perhaps best of all, very small leeks. Any of these may be dressed with a French dressing or with a boiled or cream dressing, but it is necessary to remember that whatever dressing is used should be highly seasoned and well salted, otherwise the salad is apt to have a somewhat flat taste. It is also a good plan to marinade the cooked vegetables for an hour or two in a little French dressing, then to drain, arrange, and cover with the final dressing chosen.

ARTICHOKE SALAD

1½ lb. Jerusalem artichokes	1 teaspoon sugar (approx.)
¼ lb. firm ripe tomatoes	a slice of lemon and a squeeze
1 bottle yoghourt	of lemon juice
½ gill cream	1 dessertspoon chopped chives
salt and pepper	

Peel artichokes, cut into pieces the size of a walnut. Cook until barely tender in salted water with a slice of lemon. Drain and refresh. Drain thoroughly. Peel and quarter tomatoes, remove seeds and shred. Turn the yoghourt into a bowl, whip cream to a froth, add plenty of salt and pepper, a squeeze of lemon juice, and the sugar. Mix and add the tomatoes and chives. Add the artichokes to this, stir carefully, turn into a salad dish and serve as a first course with brown bread and butter, or as part of the hors-d'œuvre.

BEETROOT SALAD

Beetroots may be either baked or boiled. The flavour is considered better when they are baked. (For this purpose one needs a very slow oven, and they may take as much as 3 hours to cook. They should be rolled in grease-proof paper before being put into the oven.) Slice the cooked beetroot as thinly as possible, one might almost say shave it; arrange it on a dish, sprinkle it with a tablespoon each of brown sugar and vinegar, and a teaspoon of salt. Put aside in a cold place for at least 8 hours, at the end of which time some of the juice will have run out of the beetroot. Rearrange the slices on the dish on which it is to be served. Make a dressing with a little oil, some vinegar, and some of the beetroot juice. Extra sugar will probably be needed. Sprinkle the top of the salad liberally with chopped chives, or the green tops of onions finely minced.

Several dressings for beetroot salads will be found on page 363. Small cooked beetroots may be cut in two, hollowed out, marinaded inside and out in a French dressing, then filled with finely chopped beetroot, grated horse-radish, celery, and onion to taste and dressed with a sweetened French dressing and a little cream.

BEETROOT, ONION, AND CELERY SALAD

Here is an old-fashioned salad in which cooked onions and celery are added to the beetroot.

Slice 3 or 4 large onions and cook gently in well-salted milk and water; when quite tender drain and chill thoroughly. An alternative way of preparing the onions is to slice them, lay them in a bowl, and pour over boiling water, let them stand for 30–40 minutes, then drain, soak in cold water with a lump of ice, and allow to become crisp. Mix sliced onions and beetroot (in equal quantities), add shredded celery. Some hours before serving pour over it one of the dressings given on page 363. If to be eaten as a separate dish, hand brown bread and butter.

WHOLE SMALL FILLED BEETROOTS

1 small beetroot for each person	French dressing
seasoning and lemon juice	horse-radish
chopped celery	onion juice
orange sections freed of skin	sugar

Hollow out the beetroots, season with salt and pepper, and sprinkle with lemon juice. Fill with celery and orange. Sprinkle with French dressing containing grated horse-radish, onion juice, and sugar to taste.

BROWN BEAN SALAD

½ lb. brown beans, Italian or Dutch, soaked overnight	2 ripe, firm tomatoes
a bouquet garni of a bay-leaf, a stick of celery, and 4 or 5 parsley stalks	1 dessertspoon chopped parsley
1 medium-sized onion, finely sliced	salt, freshly ground black pepper
	lemon cream dressing (see below)

Simmer beans until tender in slightly salted water with the bouquet. (See rules for cooking dried vegetables, page 245, or this may be done in a pressure cooker.) Cool slightly in the liquor, then drain. Simmer onion in salted water until just tender (3–4 minutes), then drain. Scald and peel tomatoes, cut in half, remove seeds and hard core, and slice each half into four. Put the beans into a bowl with the onion, tomatoes, parsley, and seasoning. Moisten well with the cream dressing and serve as an accompaniment to cold lamb or mutton, or as an hors-d'œuvre. Do not chill.

Lemon cream dressing

1 tablespoon lemon juice	salt, pepper, and sugar to taste
1 tablespoon oil	3 tablespoons single cream or evaporated milk
a grating or two of lemon rind	

Mix ingredients in the order given, then adjust seasoning and if too thick dilute with a little more cream.

CAULIFLOWER AND BROCCOLI SALAD (1)

cauliflower or broccoli	capers
French dressing	watercress dipped in French
cream dressing	dressing
chervil, chives, or green onion tops	

Prepare and cook the broccoli or cauliflower in the French way (see page 236), in branches, taking care not to overcook. Drain, pile in a bowl, and chill. Sprinkle first with French dressing, leave for an hour or so, finish with a good cream dressing, adding chopped chervil or chives or green onion tops and capers. Surround this with watercress which has been dipped into a French dressing.

CAULIFLOWER AND BROCCOLI SALAD (2)

cauliflower or broccoli	mustard
mayonnaise or cream dressing	tomato pulp or purée
a little curry-paste (optional)	

Having prepared and cooked the branchlets in the French way (see page 236), take 2 or 3 together at a time, forming them into little bouquets, and press them lightly in a clean cloth so that they will hold their shape; arrange these suitably in the dish and dress with a mayonnaise or cream dressing highly seasoned with the addition of plenty of mustard and some strong tomato pulp or purée. The cream dressing on page 363 is suitable. The addition of a little curry-paste is excellent. Watercress dressing is very good with cauliflower salad. Recipes will be found on page 368.

The following is a more substantial dish with an anchovy dressing:

CAULIFLOWER AND WATERCRESS SALAD

cauliflower	French dressing
tomato- and anchovy-flavoured dressing	cold hard-boiled egg, croûtons, ice wafers, or cheese marbles
chervil or parsley	(optional)
watercress	

Prepare the cauliflower in the French way (see page 236), pour over the dressing given on page 370. Sprinkle with finely chopped parsley. Surround with a good watercress salad which has already been dressed with French dressing; add, if you like, cold boiled egg and triangular croûtons of bread which have been fried in butter, or serve with ice wafers which have been spread with a little butter, sprinkled with cheese, and crisped in the oven, or with cheese marbles (see page 361).

SALADE BELLE HÉLÈNE
a classic of celeriac and beetroot

celeriac	cooked beetroot
mayonnaise	French dressing

Cut celeriac in julienne strips, cook till tender in boiling salted water. Drain and when cool dress with mayonnaise and pile in the centre of the serving dish. Slice the beetroot very finely and cut in crescents, sprinkle it lightly with French dressing and arrange it round the celeriac.

An alternative dressing in the absence of mayonnaise is:

½ teaspoon mustard	2 tablespoons evaporated milk
a pinch of castor sugar	1 tablespoon vinegar
a pinch of salt	2 tablespoons oil
a pinch of pepper	

Mix well together and emulsify thoroughly. This salad is improved by the addition of a handful of walnut kernels, halved, blanched, and peeled.

LEEK SALAD

leeks	French or cream dressing
freshly ground black pepper	

Choose young thin leeks, preferably those taken from the unthinned seedlings left over after planting. Blanch in boiling salted water for 5 or 6 minutes: they are very quickly cooked. Lift out, drain carefully, chill well, sprinkle with freshly ground black pepper, and dress with French or cream dressing.

LEEK AND SHRIMP SALAD

8–12 young leeks	2 hard-boiled eggs (optional)
½ pint mayonnaise	1–2 tablespoons top of milk or
¼ pint picked shrimps or prawns, cooked for about ½ an hour in a little cold water to remove the salt	single cream
	salt and black pepper
	lemon juice
	paprika

Clean and wash leeks thoroughly. Tie up in two bundles and trim the ends neatly. Plunge into boiling salted water and boil until just tender, approximately 10 minutes. Take out, remove string, and allow to drain until cold on a piece of muslin or clean cloth. Prepare mayonnaise and lighten with the cream to a good coating consistency. Drain the shrimps and dry on a piece of muslin, add to the mayonnaise. Peel the eggs, carefully remove the whites from the yolks. Wash the whites, dry and cut into shreds. Crush yolks through a bowl strainer. Arrange the leeks in an oval salad dish, seasoning them well with salt, black pepper, and a squeeze of lemon juice. Coat with the sauce, scatter the whites of egg over, and arrange a border of the sieved yolks round the dish. Dust the whites with paprika. Do not chill this salad.

BEAN AND ANCHOVY SALAD

Choose butter beans for this dish.

½ pint butter beans, cooked as
    described on page 246
12 fillets of anchovy
1 shallot, finely chopped
2 tablespoons vinegar, prefer-
    ably red wine vinegar

3 tablespoons oil, more if
    necessary
2 tablespoons cream
1 teaspoon sugar
salt, freshly ground pepper,
    and a touch of cayenne
1 dessertspoon chopped chives

Leave beans to cool in cooking liquor when tender. Then drain
thoroughly.

Soak fillets in a spoonful or two of milk for half an hour. Meantime
put shallot in a bowl with vinegar, oil, and cream. Mix thoroughly
together with a small whisk or fork; if it does not thicken (or emulsify) add
a little more oil. Add sugar, peppers, and a small pinch of salt. Drain
anchovies, cut into pieces and add. Well moisten the beans with this
dressing. Serve in a china dish and sprinkle with chives.

This salad may be part of a selection of hors-d'œuvre, in which case use
half quantities, or it may be served with cold mutton or veal.

LENTIL SALAD
*good with roast chicken, as a winter salad, or as a first course with
brown bread and butter*

lentil purée
pickled onions
tomatoes
celery and lemon

French dressing and freshly
    ground black pepper
1 clove of garlic crushed with
    salt

Make a lentil purée (see page 246). Add the crushed garlic, season
highly with French dressing and plenty of black pepper. Mix into it
slices of pickled onion and the tomatoes, peeled, pipped, and roughly
chopped. Surround with curled celery and lemon quarters.

Potato Salads

Salad potatoes

Except for a salad to be made with mashed potato it is best to use new
potatoes, special salad potatoes, or some other waxy potato. Certain
continental types particularly suitable for salads and for frying are sometimes available in this country. We get our supplies from Messrs Bunyard of Maidstone. Among them is a particularly good one called Kipfler,
a small yellow-fleshed potato. Then there is the Himalayan 'black' potato
which we get from Messrs Wallace & Barr, Tunbridge Wells. This is
dark purple in colour, with lighter-coloured flesh and a nutty flavour. If

one is driven to making potato salad from old potatoes there is an old-fashioned trick which is worth trying. Do not peel the potatoes but scrub them, then boil in the ordinary way. When cooked cover them with cold water completely for a minute or two, then peel and put back into the pan for a few minutes to dry off. This has the effect of reducing the flouriness, although one cannot perhaps claim more than that for it.

POTATO SALAD

Two points are of importance in making a potato salad. The dressing should be poured over the cooked potatoes while these are still hot in order that it may penetrate into the slices. The salad itself should be garnished with some sharp ingredient such as capers, sliced gherkin, or sliced pickled walnuts to relieve the somewhat cloying taste of potatoes. The addition of a little white wine or claret to the dressing is good, and a recipe will be found on page 366. Sliced dessert apples and celery may suitably be added to a potato salad.

Prepare a sharp French dressing to which is added plenty of mustard and salt. Make also some mayonnaise or cole-slaw dressing (see page 369). Boil the potatoes, slice them while hot, and immediately pour over the French dressing; set aside to cool. When cold and well chilled arrange in a mound on a large dish, surround the mound with slices of dessert apple and, if you like, little heaps of capers or finely sliced gherkins; if you wish to be extravagant you will add sliced truffles. Add to your dressing some thick cream and pour this over the mound immediately before serving. Finish with finely chopped chives, green sprouted onion tops, or chervil. For special occasions this potato salad may be finished off with a sprinkling of chopped nuts, fresh or browned slightly in the oven, or better still salted, that is to say browned in a frying-pan with a little butter, then salted while hot and chopped.

POTATO VINAIGRETTE

This is a salad made with baby new potatoes boiled and while still hot mixed with a vinaigrette dressing. The potatoes are left whole and should be really tiny. Failing these, waxy salad potatoes will serve, but they must be sliced after boiling. When cold and just before serving the salad is sprinkled with a herb suited to the dish in hand: freshly chopped parsley, chives, spring onion tops, stalks of watercress, etc.

HOT POTATO SALAD

Cook the required number of potatoes in their jackets. Peel, slice, and pour over them while hot bacon dressing 2 on page 362.

POTATO SALAD (FOR 6–8)

1½ lb. potatoes
½ oz. butter
salt, pepper
hot milk
2 or 3 tablespoons finely chopped cooked beetroot
1 teaspoon finely chopped onion
1 clove of garlic crushed with salt

boiled dressing or mayonnaise
French dressing
1 whole or ½ a hard-boiled egg for each person
endive, watercress, or lamb's lettuce
chives or green onion tops, when available

Boil the potatoes, drain, dry, and push through a sieve. Turn into a warm bowl, beat in butter, salt, pepper, and enough hot milk to make a soft consistency. Cover with cloth and allow to get quite cold, beating from time to time. Now add enough beetroot to colour a good pink, the onion, garlic, and more seasoning if necessary.

Arrange down the middle of a large platter, split the eggs in half lengthways and stick them slantwise two by two down the potato. Coat over with the cream dressing, dip the cress or endive in bouquets in the French dressing, shake and arrange down each side of the dish. Serve at once.

When chives or green onion tops are available, chop them with scissors and scatter thickly over the whole dish.

HAM AND RICE SALAD

May be served as a main dish or accompany an egg mayonnaise.

4 oz. Patna or Carolina rice
4 oz. lean thinly sliced ham
2 oz. diced French beans
2 oz. diced carrots
2 oz. shelled green peas
4 even-sized tomatoes
1 dessertspoon chopped parsley

1 dessertspoon chopped chives or 1 teaspoon onion
French dressing, well flavoured with mustard
1 bunch of watercress, trimmed and washed

Boil rice, drain, rinse, and drain thoroughly. Meanwhile trim the ham and cut into dice or shreds. Boil the vegetables till just tender, drain and refresh. Scald and skin the tomatoes. Quarter and remove the seeds and juice. Strain this and reserve. Now turn the rice (if thoroughly dry) into a bowl. Add ham, beans, peas, and carrots. Stir lightly together with a fork, adding the parsley, chives, tomato juice, and enough dressing to moisten nicely. Pile up in the centre of a dish, arrange the quartered tomatoes round the sides and the watercress at each end. Extra dressing may be handed separately. As an alternative way of serving, the tomatoes may be hollowed out and filled with the vegetables moistened with a little French dressing or mayonnaise. The tomatoes are then arranged round the salad as before. This makes a nice buffet luncheon dish.

A SIMPLE BUT GOOD RUSSIAN SALAD

This is a mixture of cold cooked vegetables with the addition of sharpening ingredients, to which may be added white meat of chicken, mixed herbs, or, if liked, cold fish.   Suitable vegetables would be potatoes, beetroot, carrots, celery or celeriac, French beans, green peas, and cauliflower. Sharpening ingredients might be pickled cucumbers, gherkins, capers, olives, pickled walnuts, and anchovies; suitable herbs are chervil, chives, tarragon, and others.   The ingredients are all bound together with a French dressing and then coated with mayonnaise, but the mayonnaise should be sharp in flavour.   The cream dressing given on page 363 is suitable.

ICED SPINACH SALAD

Blanch spinach leaves, well season, dip into French dressing, roll, and shape into little parcels; these are arranged in a dish and dressed with the sour cream dressing on page 370 and quarters of lemon.   They are very good served on crisp croûtons.

SALADS OF FRUIT TO BE EATEN WITH SAVOURY DISHES, OR SUITABLE FOR FIRST COURSES

In England the words 'fruit salad' indicate a mixture of fruit in syrup served as a sweet dish.   With the exception of orange salad, eaten with wild duck, one meets infrequently fruit used as the basis of a real salad, and this is a pity, for not only is it very good, it is also refreshing to the palate and so may enhance the flavour of a main dish; cherries are particularly good in such a salad.   In some cases the fruits are dressed with delicately flavoured dressings; others will take an ordinary French dressing. A pineapple salad, properly seasoned and flavoured, is excellent with roast mutton and with cutlets.   Prune salad is served with Irish stew or a ragoût of beef.   There is an especially good salad of ripe dessert plums, one of dessert pears, and another of pear, melon, and cucumber, all of which may serve as excellent first courses for a summer luncheon.   Recipes for these and others will be found in the Winkfield chapter, pages 981–2.   In the winter, or when ripe fresh fruit is scarce, tinned fruits separated from their juice may be used; in this case the fruit should be very well drained from the syrup, and the dressing on the whole may be sharper than is necessary for fresh fruit.   Tinned apricots, cherries, pineapple, peaches, and pears, among others, are entirely suitable.   Here are one or two suggestions:

APRICOT SALAD
very good to eat with hot or cold ham

Blanch fine ripe apricots.   Peel, split, and remove stones.   Crack and remove kernel.   Lay fruit in a dish, cover with a tarragon-flavoured cream dressing, and sprinkle with kernels and tarragon leaves, both chopped.

N.B. If apricots are very firm and blanching is therefore insufficient, cook in a spiced and sweetened syrup till tender. Allow to cool in syrup and drain.

CHERRY SALAD
to be eaten with game, pigeon, rabbit, etc.

Choose ripe sweet cherries as large as possible, or tinned cherries, to which may be added, if available at the same time, a small proportion of the ripest of morello cherries. (These slightly bitter, sharp cherries come in later than the main crop of sweet cherries, and it is only late in the season that one is able to combine the two.) Dress with any well-seasoned cream dressing and arrange a few blanched tarragon leaves on the fruit. Blanched, split, sweet almonds may also be added.

GRAPE SALAD

Grapes, being particularly sweet in themselves, will take a sharp dressing and make an excellent salad, though since they have to be skinned and pipped, they take a little time to prepare. They may be used alone, are excellent with cucumber, and may be served with lettuce hearts or in crisp lettuce leaves. They are good as an accompaniment to roast fowl. In America they are often served as a first course with chilled cream cheese and hot, fresh rolls.

GRAPE-FRUIT AND ORANGE SALAD

Cut out the sections of fruit in the way described on page 46, arrange in a glass dish, dress with a mint dressing (see page 364).

GRAPE-FRUIT BAR-LE-DUC

choose heavy, smooth-skinned grape-fruit (allow ½ per person)	1 pot Bar-le-Duc currants, red or white a little kirsch

Cut fruit in half, leaving a plain or serrated edge. Prepare as described on page 46. Sprinkle each half grape-fruit with sugar and a teaspoon of kirsch. Put a teaspoon of the Bar-le-Duc currants in the centre of each half. Chill well before serving. Serve the grape-fruit on leaves on small glass plates.

Bar-le-Duc is a brand of special conserves put up in small pots; the currants in this range of jams are pipped.

For grape-fruit and mint ice see page 983.

LETTUCE AND FRUIT SALAD

This is good when firm hearts of lettuce are available.   Take lettuce hearts, slice with a stainless steel knife, and allow:

2 slices per person
2 thin slices of pineapple per person
sections of grape-fruit and orange to taste

1 green pepper for 4–6 helpings
French dressing flavoured with grated horse-radish, and seasoned and sweetened to taste

Arrange the slices of pineapple and lettuce in layers on individual plates, with the sections of orange and grape-fruit in between.   Seed, blanch, and finely slice the green peppers and add them.   Pour over the dressing.

ORANGE SALAD FOR ROAST DUCK

choose large seedless oranges, allowing 1 for each person
French dressing

castor sugar
freshly ground black pepper

With a potato-peeler peel the yellow part of the rind of 1 orange as thinly as possible.   Cut this into fine shreds with a sharp knife or scissors, put into cold water, bring to the boil, and boil for 5 minutes.   Drain and refresh.   Now prepare remaining oranges in the way described for cutting for a compôte (see page 47).   Lay the sections in a glass or china dish, dust with castor sugar and black pepper, and sprinkle over the blanched orange rind.   Pour over a well-mixed French dressing and allow to stand an hour or two before serving.

When a smaller type of orange has to be used, remove the rind and pith with a potato-peeler and then cut across in thin slices, removing the pips.

N.B. Curled celery may be used to garnish this salad; it should be arranged in a thick circle round the edge of the dish.

FRESH PEAR AND WATERCRESS SALAD

Allow half a ripe pear for each person, and for 4 pears allow 2 bunches of good watercress.   Prepare the dressing first and peel the pears and cut in two just before serving.   Make a good French dressing:

6 tablespoons oil to:
2 tablespoons best wine vinegar
2 teaspoons French mustard
1 teaspoon English mustard
freshly ground pepper and salt

Mince the watercress finely, using as much of the stalk as possible, and add to the dressing immediately before using.   Arrange the peeled half-pears on a lettuce leaf on individual plates.   Pour the dressing over, seeing that each pear gets its adequate share of watercress, and chill for a few minutes before serving.

PINEAPPLE AND LETTUCE SALAD

Take the compact heart of a lettuce. With a silver or stainless steel knife cut in thick slices crosswise. Lay slices of pineapple on the lettuce. Dress with cream and lemon juice or French or cream dressing. This is best served on glass plates, not in a salad bowl. A leaf or two of tarragon may be chopped finely and added to the dressing, or whole blanched leaves arranged on top. With tinned pineapple a sharp French dressing is probably the better.

PRUNE SALAD

The prunes may be stewed but preferably should be steamed, as they are then much plumper. The stones are removed and the cavity filled with chopped raisins, or raisins and apple or nuts. The prunes may be dressed with either a French or any simple cream dressing, and chopped herbs added to taste. Dill is good with this salad. This is excellent for children and is well liked by them if dressed with a sweet cream dressing.

Here are some miscellaneous salads suitable for first courses for luncheon, though not perhaps sufficiently piquant in taste to serve as hors-d'œuvre. A number of piquant salads for this purpose will be found in the chapter on first and last courses, page 21.

AN AMERICAN SALAD TO SERVE AS A SEPARATE COURSE

ripe or tinned pears	lettuce
grapes or black cherries	herbs
cream or milk cheese	a little French dressing, or the
a little butter	watercress dressing with
cream	chilli sauce on page 368
seasoning	rolled bread and butter

Peel, slice in two, and core ripe pears, or use tinned ones. Take either large grapes or very ripe or tinned black cherries. Pound some good cream or milk cheese with a little butter, cream, seasoning, and chopped herbs. Stone the cherries and stuff with the cheese (or slice and pip the grapes and put the cheese between the halves). Take crisp lettuce leaves, arrange half a pear in each, and fill the hollow centre with a mound of the cheese-stuffed fruits. Chill well, dress with a little French dressing or the watercress dressing, to which a spoonful of cream may be added. Serve with rolled bread and butter.

Another American salad comes, like those on page 357, from *The Boston Cooking School Cook Book*.[1] This is a frozen fruit salad.

FROZEN FRUIT SALAD

½ cup grape-fruit pulp	⅓ cup chopped almonds
1 cup mixed canned fruit	½ cup mayonnaise
¼ cup diced celery	¾ cup heavy cream, whipped
½ cup sliced dates	

---

[1] Fannie Merritt Farmer, *The Boston Cooking School Cook Book* (Little, Brown & Co., Boston).

'Drain fruit thoroughly, cut in small pieces, combine with celery and almonds. Add cream to mayonnaise, fold in first mixture. Freeze. This is good served with hot rolls or water-biscuits.'

For Pear and Cream Cheese Salad see Winkfield chapter, page 982.

AVOCADO PEARS

Last in this section we come to what is perhaps the most epicurean of fruit salads, that made with the avocado pear. This fruit, a commonplace perhaps in America, is still a luxury with us.

Perhaps because it is so easily bought in America it is treated there in ways which seem to be rather a gilding of the lily. Cubed, cut up, served with crab, shrimp, cheese, and various fruits, even mashed to make a mousse, it is served in many ways: some good, as for instance when it is combined with grapes or sections of orange or filled with shrimps; others less good, less respectful, as it were, to its subtle, delicate flavour. It may with advantage be prepared very simply.

AVOCADO PEAR SALAD

Allow half a pear for each person. Leaving the skin on, cut the fruit in two and lift out the large stone, fill each cavity with a sharp French dressing. This salad is served on a plate apart, and eaten with a teaspoon.

On occasion we can buy the fruit of the tree tomato, the edible part of which is the inside mass of seed and pulp. This pulp is used to fill the hollows of the avocado pears. Fresh passion fruit makes a particularly good filling.

The recipe given for fresh pears on page 353 may also be taken for avocado pears, and the piquant dressing given on page 368 is suitable when a shrimp filling is used.

For other fruit salads as first courses see Winkfield chapter, pages 981–2.

JELLIED SALADS

Although I had eaten a tomato chartreuse before the American party mentioned earlier, I had not until then met with other jelly salads, so that it was natural for me to mistake the pale green, yellow, and pink jellies filled with fruit or tomatoes or shreds of pimento, cucumber and so forth for sweet dishes rather than savoury. So on that occasion, by my ignorance, I was the loser. Later on I ate many good salads of this kind, and they are refreshing in hot weather and make a very good first course for luncheon on a summer's day. The best of them are those made on a really piquant base, and served with a sharp dressing. If they lack the quality of piquancy these salads may be insipid. In the recipe for Tomato Chartreuse which we like at Winkfield it will be seen that the celery and walnut salad as well as the watercress garnish has a French dressing, while lemon slices are served to squeeze over the chartreuse; this gives just the touch required: without this zest the dish would be flat and unpalatable.

TOMATO CHARTREUSE WITH CELERY AND WATERCRESS SALAD

Chartreuse

1 pint tinned tomatoes	1 teaspoon sugar
1 teaspoon tomato purée	water
3 or 4 peppercorns	½ oz. gelatine
salt	a squeeze of lemon juice
½ bay-leaf	freshly ground pepper
1 small clove of garlic	extra sugar if required

Salad

1 head of celery	a well-seasoned French dress-
1 small handful of fresh-shredded walnuts	ing with extra mustard and sugar
1 bunch of watercress	lemon and brown bread and butter

N.B. Watercress only may be used and the celery omitted

Make chartreuse ingredients into a pulp as follows: Simmer tomatoes, purée, peppercorns, salt, bay-leaf, garlic, and sugar together 5–7 minutes; press through a strainer into a measuring jug and make up to ¾ pint with water or additional tomato juice. Soften the gelatine in 2 tablespoons water and a squeeze of lemon juice. Add to pulp and adjust seasoning, adding freshly ground pepper and more sugar if required. Pour into a ring mould and leave to set. Meanwhile prepare the salad: Cut the stalks of a head of celery into 2-inch lengths, then cut down into fine shreds. Leave in iced water for an hour. Blanch the fresh walnut kernels. Drain and dry the celery thoroughly, toss celery and nuts in the dressing. Dip the mould for a moment into hot water, turn out and fill the centre with the celery and walnut salad. Garnish with small bouquets of watercress which have been dipped in the dressing. Serve with brown bread and butter and quarters of lemon.

Sometimes instead of a purée a clear liquid is used as a base; in this case the jelly may well have suitable solid ingredients set in it, just as one has in jellies for the sweet course. Diced cucumber or melon, small whole tomatoes or strips of tomato flesh, gherkin, celery, nuts, and so on are all suitable.

While there would be no point in giving a range of detailed recipes—the whole idea is a matter of well-seasoned, acidulated, and sweetened liquid, set with gelatine in the proportion of ¾ oz. gelatine to 1 pint liquid—those following are typical and will serve as a guide. Any of these jellied salads may either be made in small moulds, one for each person, or in ring moulds, in which case the centre may be filled with some other appropriate salad; for instance, a tomato jelly ring may carry a potato, celery, or green salad in the middle, a cucumber jelly may have fresh grape salad. As these jelly salads are so typically American I have taken advantage of the kind permission given by Mrs Dexter Perkins to quote two of them from

The Boston Cooking School Cook Book by Fannie Merritt Farmer, and here is her recipe for Cucumber Jelly Salad:

CUCUMBER JELLY SALAD

2 large cucumbers
½ cup cold water
1¼ tablespoons [1] granulated gelatine soaked in ½ cup cold water
a few drops of onion juice

1 tablespoon vinegar
a few grains of cayenne
salt and pepper to taste
green vegetable colouring

'Peel and slice cucumbers, add cold water and cook slowly until soft. Force through purée strainer. Add gelatine, onion juice, vinegar, cayenne, salt, and pepper. Colour green, strain and mould. If desired garnish with thin slices of cucumber shaped with small, round, fluted cutter. Arrange circular pieces of truffle on each. Arrange halved tomatoes around mould, each garnished with cucumber and truffle. Serve with mayonnaise coloured with tomato purée.'

And a second from the same source:

GINGER ALE FRUIT SALAD

2 tablespoons [1] granulated gelatine soaked in 2 table-spoons cold water
⅛ cup boiling water
¼ cup lemon juice
2 tablespoons sugar
a few grains of salt
1 cup ginger ale

⅓ cup Malaga grapes, skinned, seeded, and cut in halves
⅓ cup celery, thinly sliced
⅓ cup apple, cored and cut in julienne-shaped pieces
¼ cup pineapple cubes [2]
2 tablespoons chopped candied ginger

'Dissolve soaked gelatine in boiling water. Add lemon juice, sugar, salt, and ginger ale. When mixture begins to set fold in other ingredients. Turn into ring mould and chill. Unmould, garnish, fill centre with mayonnaise.'

GRAPE ASPIC SALAD

½ lb. grapes [3]
2 teaspoons [1] gelatine
2 tablespoons water
½ cup lemon squash
3 dessertspoons sugar

¼ cup lemon juice
¼ cup water
1 dessertspoon finely chopped or pounded mint
green colouring

---

[1] See American measures, page 60.
[2] Tinned pineapple should not be replaced by fresh pine for filling jellies, as the fresh fruit may prevent the jelly from setting.
[3] Cucumber may replace grapes and is prepared as for French Cucumber Salad (see page 341).

Peel and pip grapes.   Dissolve gelatine in the 2 tablespoons water, then add the squash and sugar, the lemon juice and remaining water.   Finally stir in the mint and colour lightly.

Turn into a ring mould and fill the centre with quartered tomato tossed in French dressing; or set in individual moulds, serve in crisp lettuce with fresh cucumber or in hollowed tomatoes, and accompany by a well-seasoned dressing.

N.B. Fruit or cucumber should both be well drained on muslin, otherwise the juice from them may prevent the jelly from setting.

PINEAPPLE AND ORANGE JELLY SALAD

¼ pint pineapple syrup from freshly poached or canned pineapple

juice of 2 large oranges
2 tablespoons white wine
1 tablespoon white wine vinegar

1 teaspoon sugar
½ gill water
½ oz. gelatine
2 tablespoons cut-up pineapple (canned, see footnote 2 on previous page)

Dressing

½ teaspoon sugar
a pinch of salt
½ teaspoon dry mustard
½ gill evaporated milk

½ gill oil
1½ tablespoons wine vinegar
1 level teaspoon paprika

2 tablespoons shredded celery

1 dessertspoon shredded pimento, blanched if fresh

Mix the syrup, orange juice, wine, and vinegar together with the sugar. Warm the water, adding the gelatine.   Stir to dissolve, then add to the liquid.   Pour into a measure to test for quantity (a good ½ pint).   Rinse out a ½-pint ring mould into cold water, put the pineapple round the bottom, then carefully pour in the liquid.   Leave to set.

Put the sugar, salt, and mustard into a small bowl, add the evaporated milk and gradually beat in the oil.   Then beat in the vinegar.   Adjust the seasoning, adding the paprika.   Stir in the shredded celery and pimento.

Dip the mould quickly into hot water, turn out and fill the centre with pimento and celery well mixed with dressing.   Pour any remaining dressing round the ring.

BEETROOT AND CELERY IN JELLY (FOR 8–10)

1 oz. granulated gelatine
3 tablespoons cold water
¾ pint boiling water
3 tablespoons wine vinegar
extra vinegar or a little lemon juice if required
1 tablespoon golden syrup

1 dessertspoon salt
1 pint chopped cooked beetroot
2 tablespoons chopped celery
2 tablespoons grated horse-radish
lettuce leaves
a sharp dressing

Soften gelatine in cold water for a few minutes.   Add boiling water, vinegar, syrup, and salt.   Test for flavour, add extra vinegar or lemon juice if not sharp enough. Allow to cool a little, add beetroot, celery, and horse-radish. Rinse out a shallow dish or tin. Pour in the mixture and allow to set. Cut in squares, set on lettuce leaves, and serve with a sharp dressing.

CRAB AND SHRIMP JELLY SALAD

1½ pints chicken broth, very well seasoned	3 oz. diced celery or cucumber
lemon juice to taste	2 red sweet peppers, finely shredded
1¼ oz. gelatine	lettuce leaves
2 or 3 tablespoons warm water	quarters of lemon
4 oz. each of crab meat and picked shrimps or prawns, well soaked to remove salt	mayonnaise, tabasco, and cream

Heat broth and sharpen with lemon juice. Dissolve gelatine in warm water; add to broth. Cool, arrange crab and shrimps with celery and peppers in mould. Fill carefully with cooled broth. Leave to set. Turn out on to dish and surround with crisp lettuce leaves and quarters of lemon. Serve with light mayonnaise well flavoured with tabasco and a little cream.

For Pear and Cream Cheese Salad as a first course see Winkfield chapter, page 982.

ACCOMPANIMENTS TO SALADS WHICH ARE BEING SERVED AS A SEPARATE COURSE

A salad served as a separate course may well be accompanied by some special bread, sandwich, or savoury. The following suggestions are offered as a basis for experiment.

For those who like garlic the following loaf or rolls will probably prove a first favourite.

GARLIC LOAF

a light loaf such as Procea or milk bread
sufficient butter to spread on both sides of the slices when cut, and
   to leave a little over for top and sides
1 clove of garlic

With a sharp knife cut the loaf in slices to within ½ inch of the bottom, taking care not to sever them. Crush the garlic with a teaspoon of salt and work it into the butter with a spatula. (For those who like only the faintest suggestion of this flavour it will be sufficient to cut the garlic in quarters, allow it to lie in the creamed butter for half an hour, and then to remove it, taking care to recream the butter before use in order to equalize the flavour.) Spread the flavoured butter on each side of the slices, press them firmly together again, spread top and sides with remaining butter, put in a sharp oven until thoroughly heated through and crisp all over.

This is also excellent without garlic if butter mixed with French mustard is used. French or Energen rolls may be treated in the same way and are useful if only a small amount of bread is wanted.

On baking day a fresh loaf may be torn to pieces for Pulled Bread (page 764), or the Grissini or Bread Sticks on page 765 may be brushed over with melted butter, dipped in grated cheese as well as a little rock-salt, and put back into the oven for a few minutes. Last Minute Biscuits (page 787) may be treated in the same way.

Cheese rolls are popular and quick to make: Cut thin bread and butter, spread with a well-beaten mixture of grated cheese and butter, season, flavour with a little Worcestershire sauce or other relish, add a few chopped capers or small cocktail onions, roll up, brush over with melted butter, and toast. Crisp stalks of celery may be filled with a similar cheese mixture.

Substantial but very good is a filled French roll. Cut a fresh French roll in half, scoop out the crumb, butter and season it inside and out, crisp it thoroughly in the oven, and fill with shredded chicken mixed in a little béchamel or a seasoned cream dressing.

The popular 'cheese dream' has many variants; the following is a good one:

CHEESE DREAMS
for 4 medium helpings

4 slices of stale bread ¼ inch thick

Home-made cheese

½ oz. butter
2 oz. ordinary cooking cheese
2½ oz. soft processed or cream cheese
½ teaspoon paprika
1 small clove of garlic crushed
a pinch of mace and of caraway seed

freshly ground black pepper
2 shallots, finely sliced and fried in a little butter till soft (or spring onions may be used)

Cream butter, grate cheese, add cream cheese, and beat well; add seasoning ingredients one by one, beating them in. (This is best done when possible in a mortar, as one gets a smoother mixture.) Add lastly the shallots, folding them in with a spatula. Spread the mixture thickly over 2 slices of bread, lay the other slices on top, trim edges, cut in two, and fry in shallow fat. The same mixture may be used for a plain toasted sandwich.

The following 'sandwich' is particularly good either as an accompaniment to salad or as a savoury, and may be eaten hot or cold, but preferably hot:

SAVOURY PAIN PERDU

4 slices of bread ½ inch thick soaked in a savoury custard

Custard

1 egg yolk
½ pint milk

salt and pepper

Beat egg slightly, pour the boiling milk over egg and seasonings. Soak the bread in this, drain, and fry in deep fat (olive oil is excellent for this). Make a filling as follows:

¾ oz. butter	3 oz. ham, finely shredded, or
¾ oz. flour	similar quantity of grated
½ pint milk, scalded with a	cheese or sautéd mushrooms
blade of mace, a slice of onion,	
and 6 peppercorns	

Make a sauce of the butter, flour, and milk, reduce till thick and add the ham, cheese, or mushrooms.

Fried croustades of bread filled with suitable mixtures are excellent as an accompaniment to salads. They should be served fresh and crisp but not necessarily hot. For the making of croustades see page 49 (Kitchen Knowledge). Fill with any of the following: chopped hard-boiled egg bound with béchamel or whipped, seasoned cream; mushrooms in a similar sauce or a whole mushroom, grilled, or spiced button mushrooms; milk cheese beaten up with a little rich milk or cream and well seasoned; chopped onions cooked in a little butter or margarine and sprinkled with grated cheese.

A different type of croustade may have the bread treated in the same way as for pain perdu, that is to say the rounds soaked in a mixture of egg and milk, drained, deep fat fried, and filled with a variety of fillings: any of those given above as well as prawns, shredded crab, lobster, or tunny fish in a suitable binding sauce.

Little cheese croquettes are good; any cream or soft milk cheese may be beaten up with seasoning, flavoured with Worcestershire sauce, chilli sauce, crushed garlic, paprika, or with a little port or sherry, rolled into shape, egged and crumbed, and fried in deep fat. Chopped nuts and herbs may be added to the cheese to taste.

Cream cheese treated in this way may be shaped, rolled in chopped nuts, and served iced without being fried.

Here is a recipe for cheese marbles made with household cheese:

CHEESE MARBLES

½ tablespoon flour	egg yolk and breadcrumbs for
½ pint grated cheese	coating
seasoning of salt, pepper, and	deep frying fat
a pinch of cayenne	chopped browned almonds
2 egg whites	(optional)

Mix flour, cheese, and seasoning. Beat egg whites till stiff and add to mixture, roll mixture into shape about the size of a walnut, egg and breadcrumb, fry in deep fat to golden brown. If chopped browned almonds are added to the breadcrumbs an extra interest is given.

Small potato croquettes egged and coated with a mixture of crumbs and browned chopped almonds in equal quantities give a *de luxe* note to a salad luncheon dish. The cheese biscuits given on page 35 are generally useful.

CREAM CHEESE ROLLS

½ clove of garlic crushed in salt
butter for spreading
Energen rolls, at least 1 per person
1 small milk cheese

a little cream or butter
1 tablespoon chopped chives and 1 tablespoon chopped pickled gherkins
seasoning

Chop the garlic and crush thoroughly. Incorporate with the butter. Cut the Energen rolls lengthwise in two, spread all over with the butter, and put in a sharp oven for 10–15 minutes to become crisp. Beat the cheese with the cream or butter, add chives, seasoning, and gherkins. Put a spoonful on the top of each half-roll and serve.

TANGERINE STRIPS

Allow 1 slice of bread per person. Toast bread on one side, cut off the crusts. Spread untoasted side lightly with butter, cut into 3 fingers, and make a three-tiered sandwich with the following mixture between the layers:

2 oz. sugar
2–3 tablespoons grated tangerine rind

juice of 2 tangerines

Brush the tops of each with a little butter, put back again under the grill and heat through thoroughly.

UNCOOKED DRESSINGS

BACON DRESSING FOR CURLED ENDIVE SALAD

Cut up 2 or 3 rashers of bacon in small pieces, fry gently to extract the maximum of fat; when the scraps of bacon are quite crisp, lift them out with a strainer and sprinkle over the endive. To the fat in the pan add enough vinegar to sharpen well; season with salt. Pour over the endive and sprinkle with freshly ground black pepper.

BACON DRESSING FOR COOKED OR RAW SPINACH SALAD

Proceed as in foregoing recipe, but fry half a finely chopped onion with the cut-up bacon.

Both of these are also good with celery and potato salad.

BEETROOT SALAD DRESSING

yolks of 2 hard-boiled eggs, sieved
1 good teaspoon made English mustard
1 good teaspoon French mustard
salt and a touch of cayenne
3 tablespoons oil
1 tablespoon vinegar
2 or 3 tablespoons cream
a little lemon juice
sugar if liked

Mix in the usual way, add sugar if liked and finish off with cream.

SCANDINAVIAN DRESSING FOR BEETROOT

Take 1 teaspoon caraway seed (or substitute dill seed), pound well and scald with a gill of boiling water.   Cool and strain.
Take:

2½ tablespoons of above extract
1 teaspoon salt
1½ tablespoons vinegar
2 teaspoons sugar

Slice beetroot very thin and dress while warm.   Allow to stand for 8 hours.

BEETROOT DRESSING (RICH)

2 raw egg yolks
2 teaspoons made mustard
3 tablespoons oil
1 tablespoon French wine vinegar
1 teaspoon chopped tarragon (or replace ½ wine vinegar with tarragon vinegar)
1 tablespoon onion juice or chopped and pounded onion
salt and pepper
4 or 5 tablespoons cream

Mix thoroughly in the usual way, testing for seasoning and finishing off with the cream.

CONDENSED MILK DRESSING

3–4 tablespoons sweetened condensed milk
½ teaspoon salt
fresh black pepper
1 dessertspoon salad-oil
1 good teaspoon made mustard
5 tablespoons French wine vinegar
chopped herbs to taste

Add salt and pepper to condensed milk, mix well.   Stir in mustard and oil and beat.   Finally add vinegar and chopped herbs.

CREAM DRESSING (THICK)
a good substitute for mayonnaise

1 level teaspoon French or English mustard
½ teaspoon salt
1 teaspoon sugar
¼ teaspoon white pepper
¼ pint evaporated milk
¼ pint olive oil
2–3 tablespoons wine vinegar

Put the seasonings into a bowl and add the milk. Mix and beat in by degrees the olive oil. Then add the vinegar gradually and adjust seasoning.

N.B. The dressing will thicken when the vinegar is added—how quickly depends on the acidity of the vinegar.

CREAM DRESSING WITH HORSE-RADISH

½ pint thick cream dressing (see above)

1–2 tablespoons freshly grated horse-radish

a squeeze of lemon juice

1 teaspoon sugar

freshly ground pepper

a little cream or top of milk to thin the dressing if required

Mix all well together, adding the last spoonful of horse-radish with caution. The dressing must have a distinct flavour of horse-radish, but not so strong as to resemble horse-radish sauce. Horse-radish varies in strength according to whether or not it is freshly dug.

CUCUMBER DRESSING

1 or 2 ridge cucumbers

1 gill cream

salt, paprika (sugar optional)

1 tablespoon lemon juice (approx.)

Seed, peel, and finely chop cucumber and allow to drain half an hour. Beat cream and add seasonings and lemon juice to taste; add sugar if liked and fold in cucumber.

FRENCH DRESSING (CLASSIC)

Basic recipe

3 parts oil

1 part wine vinegar

a good ½ teaspoon each of salt and freshly ground pepper

Crushed garlic, French and English mustard, chopped herbs in variety and various other additions are suitable and will be found among the following recipes. It is, however, difficult to be exact in the matter of quantities as much depends on taste, and those given are approximate. Garlic, salt, pepper, and mustard are first mixed with the oil, then vinegar is added and all well emulsified. Herbs are added last.

LEMON DRESSING

See page 345.

MINT DRESSING

Pound a good handful of mint leaves with 2 tablespoons brown sugar. Add 2 tablespoons boiling water to dissolve the sugar, then add vinegar or lemon juice to taste; or make a classic French oil and vinegar dressing and add sugar and a heaped tablespoon of finely chopped mint.

DAVIS'S SALAD-DRESSING

A typical English butler's dressing and very good.

yolk of 1–2 hard-boiled eggs
seasoning
2 tablespoons best Lucca or olive oil
1 dessertspoon Worcestershire sauce

1 teaspoon vinegar
English made mustard to taste
2–3 spring onions, chopped finely
¾ gill single cream (approx.)

Crush the yolks well with seasoning, add the oil by degrees, then add the Worcestershire sauce, vinegar, mustard, and onions. Finish with the cream; whisk or shake thoroughly in a jar.

If a thick creamy dressing is wanted, the cream may be whipped to a froth before adding.

NURSERY DRESSING

2 tablespoons brown sugar
2 or 3 tablespoons hot water
lemon juice or vinegar

pale green tops of sprouted onions, finely chopped (or grated orange rind)

Dissolve sugar in boiling water, add lemon juice to taste, add onion tops.

There is nothing in this to offend the delicate palate of a child, although orange rind is sometimes preferred to onions. I always thought that this was our own special nursery recipe until I met it in another form in a Persian cookery book, in which honey was used as a sweetening, and the whole flavoured with lemon flowers. The mixture was poured into little bowls into which the lettuce leaves were dipped:

PERSIAN HONEY DRESSING

3 tablespoons honey
½ pint wine vinegar
a pinch of salt and freshly ground pepper

a good squeeze of lemon juice
orange-flower water or orange or lemon flowers
crisp cos lettuce leaves

Boil honey and vinegar together for 10 minutes, adding seasonings. Cool and add lemon juice and a few drops of orange-flower water or the flowers. This is good with crisp cos lettuce. It may be served in little bowls or in cups made of half a lemon or orange, and the leaves dipped in.

N.B. A small quantity of water may be added to this dressing before the orange-flower water if it is considered too strong. Both the above dressings keep well in a screw-top jar.

ORANGE-FLAVOURED DRESSING FOR CHICORY AND OTHER SALADS

a small piece of garlic (optional)
1 teaspoon French mustard
1 tablespoon sugar
4 tablespoons cream
grated rind of half an orange, and a little of the juice

oil and vinegar to taste, but in the proportion of 3 of oil to 1 of vinegar
salt and pepper

Crush the garlic in the mixing bowl, add the mustard, sugar, and salt and pepper. Mix well. Add cream, orange juice, and rind and mix again. Taste and adjust the ingredients if required. Add oil and vinegar mixture in the amount required to suit the taste. Lemon juice and peel may replace orange for a chicory and apple salad.

POTATO SALAD DRESSING (WITH WINE)

This amount of dressing is sufficient for a salad made of $1\frac{1}{2}$ lb. of potatoes weighed raw and unpeeled, if these are salad potatoes or of a waxy variety, or 1 lb. of floury potatoes.

the yolk of 1 raw egg	2 tablespoons white wine or
the yolk of 1 hard-boiled egg	claret
2 teaspoons French mustard	1 heaped tablespoon pounded
1 teaspoon salt	cooked beetroot
1 clove of garlic, crushed	1 heaped tablespoon chopped
1 tablespoon onion juice or	and pounded gherkin
crushed onion	a little cream added just before
freshly ground pepper	serving
3 tablespoons oil	extra oil or cream if desired
2 tablespoons French wine	sugar (optional)
vinegar	

Mix in the usual way, pour over hot potatoes some hours before required. Reserve a few spoonfuls of the dressing, which, mixed with a little cream, should be added just before serving. If this is too sharp extra oil or cream may be used, and sugar may be added if liked.

HOT POTATO SALAD DRESSING

4 rashers cut up small or 2	4 tablespoons vinegar
tablespoons bacon fat	1 teaspoon sugar
2 tablespoons chopped onion	$\frac{1}{2}$ teaspoon salt
2 tablespoons chopped celery	1 saltspoon paprika
2 chopped gherkins	1 teaspoon made mustard
2 tablespoons water	

Fry the bacon, or melt the bacon fat, add onion, celery, gherkins. Fry till bacon and onions are crisp. Mix together water, vinegar, sugar, salt, paprika, and mustard. Pour these ingredients into the pan. Combine with the potatoes and serve at once.

POTATO DRESSING (DRESSING THICKENED WITH POTATO)

1 potato, baked or boiled	3 tablespoons vinegar
1 tablespoon sugar	1 teaspoon chopped chives or
1 tablespoon made mustard	any other suitable herb
salt and pepper to taste	cream or milk (optional)
1 tablespoon oil	sugar (optional)

Put potato through a wire sieve, add sugar, mustard, and seasoning to part of it, then beat in oil and vinegar and add chives. Add more potato if the mixture is not thick enough. This is best made while the potato is hot. Cream or milk may also be added, in which case the addition of sugar is an improvement.

SOUR CREAM DRESSING FOR FRUIT SALAD

4 tablespoons thick sour cream
3 tablespoons vinegar or slightly
  less of lemon juice
sugar to taste (at least 1 tablespoon)
salt and pepper to taste

Mix in the usual way.

SPANISH DRESSING

suitable for potato salad or for certain cooked vegetable salads

2 onions
1 fresh sweet green pepper
1 clove of garlic
3 tinned red pimentos
½ teaspoon salt
½ teaspoon paprika
2 tablespoons sugar
freshly ground black pepper
1 teaspoon French mustard
5–6 tablespoons vinegar
2 tablespoons tomato, A1, or
  Worcestershire sauce
8 tablespoons olive oil
lemon rind and juice to taste

Chop the onions, seed and chop sweet green pepper, crush garlic, chop pimentos, add dry seasonings and mustard, mix well. Add vinegar and tomato or other sauce, stir well, beat in oil. Add lemon rind and juice to taste.

SWEDISH DRESSING FOR CUCUMBER SALAD

2 tablespoons sugar dissolved
  in 1 tablespoon warm water
¼ teaspoon black pepper
2 tablespoons chopped dill
6 tablespoons French wine
  vinegar

Mix and allow to stand half an hour.

VINAIGRETTE DRESSING

4 tablespoons vinegar (½ wine
  and ½ tarragon vinegar), *or*
1 tablespoon each of tarragon
  and wine vinegar and 2
  tablespoons lemon juice
1 gill oil
a clove of garlic
1 teaspoon sugar
1 teaspoon, or more, made
  mustard
chopped herbs: chervil, tarragon, parsley, chives, or the
  sprouted top of an onion, or
  onion juice
½ teaspoon salt (approx.)
1 tablespoon finely chopped
  onion
black pepper

Mix the ingredients, the seasonings and the herbs, add the oil, beating with a spoon or whisk, and finally the vinegar or vinegar and lemon juice.

WATERCRESS OR MINT DRESSING

2 yolks of hard-boiled egg
1 teaspoon French mustard
½ teaspoon English mustard
1 clove of garlic, crushed
1 teaspoon salt
4 tablespoons chopped water-
    cress

basic French dressing
lemon juice (optional)

For mint dressing
    a little boiling syrup of sugar
        and water
    green colouring

Sieve the yolks, mix to a paste with mustard, garlic, and salt and a little of the French dressing, beat in remainder of dressing, add watercress. Add lemon juice if required. This method may be used for mint, in which case sugar is necessary. The mint may either be chopped or crushed and then infused in a little boiling syrup of sugar and water. This is then strained and coloured with a very little green colouring.

PIQUANT SALAD-DRESSING

2 tablespoons grated horse-
    radish
2 tablespoons tomato chilli
    sauce (see page 1116)
1 tablespoon lemon juice

½ teaspoon Worcestershire
    sauce
a good pinch of salt
a dash of tabasco
1 gill sour cream

Mix well together and chill.

WATERCRESS DRESSING WITH CHILLI SAUCE
good with pear, grape, and cream cheese salads

6 tablespoons oil
3 tablespoons tarragon vinegar
1 teaspoon salt
freshly ground pepper

1½ gills tomato chilli sauce
    (see page 1116)
2 gills chopped watercress
a few chopped chives

Beat together the oil, vinegar, and seasoning. Add the chilli sauce, watercress, and chives. Chill on ice.

Other dressings may be found in the Winkfield chapter; they are included in the salad recipes given on pages 981–2.

COOKED DRESSINGS

The following dressings will all keep for several days, especially when stored in an ice-box. The cole-slaw dressings will keep longer if they are put away before extra cream or milk is added. The quantities given are suitable for an ordinary household, and it is economic to make up the recipes as given and use in the required amounts.

COLE-SLAW DRESSING (1)

suitable for cabbage, celery and apple, and potato salads, or as a base for other cream dressings

2 tablespoons sugar
1 tablespoon flour
2 teaspoons salt
1 tablespoon made mustard
½ pint vinegar or vinegar and water mixed

2 eggs (1 egg will suffice, or no eggs need be used)
½–1 oz. butter
cream or good milk for final dilution, or French dressing

Mix dry ingredients together, moisten with a little water, add mustard; add to vinegar and cook thoroughly for about 15 minutes. Beat eggs, add butter, pour the hot vinegar over these and beat thoroughly. (One egg will suffice, or the dressing may be made without eggs.) When cool add a cup of cream or good milk and beat again. This keeps well in the ice-box, and it is a good plan to put it away (before the cream is added) and to take out a small quantity at a time, diluting this with cream, good milk, or French dressing, to suit your need of the moment.

COLE-SLAW DRESSING (2) (WITH SOUR CREAM)

1 dessertspoon sugar
1 dessertspoon flour
1 teaspoon mustard
1 teaspoon salt
a few grains of cayenne

1 teaspoon butter
yolk of 1 egg
⅓ cup vinegar
½ cup thick cream, sour (or sweet)

Mix dry ingredients and mustard, add butter, egg, and vinegar. Cook over boiling water, stirring till mixture thickens. Cool, add cream, and beat thoroughly.

DELICATE DRESSING FOR FRUIT SALADS

1 egg
2 tablespoons sugar
3 tablespoons tarragon vinegar

rich milk or cream
¼ pint thin well-flavoured béchamel sauce (optional)

Beat egg and sugar. Add vinegar. Cook in a basin put in a pan of boiling water. Stir until thick and dilute with top of milk or cream. The addition of the béchamel sauce, properly made and tammied, gives the dressing a different texture—somewhat smoother and blander. It is also an economy.

OLD-FASHIONED BOILED SALAD-DRESSING (1)

1 tablespoon flour
1 dessertspoon salt
2 tablespoons sugar
½ teaspoon pepper
2 tablespoons made mustard (English or French)

1 pint milk
1 tablespoon salad-oil
1 or 2 eggs
1 gill vinegar

Mix all the dry ingredients together, add mustard, milk, oil, and beaten egg. Cook very gently, stirring all the while, until the mixture reaches boiling-point. Continue cooking for 3 or 4 minutes, stirring constantly, and at the last moment add the vinegar, gently whisking it in.

Here is a richer boiled salad-dressing:

OLD-FASHIONED BOILED SALAD-DRESSING (2)

1 tablespoon melted butter	1 teaspoon mixed mustard
½ teaspoon salt	3 eggs
1 tablespoon sugar	½ pint milk or cream
¼ teaspoon black pepper	1 gill vinegar

Beat the melted butter, salt, sugar, pepper, and mustard until smooth. Add the well-beaten eggs and the milk. Put into a double saucepan over hot water and cook until thick. Add vinegar gradually at the moment of thickening and continue cooking for a few moments, stirring all the time. Various herbs may be added, or flavoured vinegars used. Bottled, these dressings keep well.

Another old-fashioned recipe was thickened with mashed potato. This was usually made with a little cream (or thin béchamel sauce), vinegar, pepper, salt, and mustard, and the whole thickened with mashed potatoes. This is another dressing which appeals to children.

SOUR CREAM DRESSING

8 tablespoons sour cream	1 tablespoon sugar (more if
2 tablespoons vinegar	required)
1 teaspoon made mustard	1 egg, lightly beaten
seasoning to taste	herbs to taste

Mix all ingredients together. Cook until mixture thickens, taking care not to boil. This may with advantage be made in a double saucepan.

TOMATO- AND ANCHOVY-FLAVOURED DRESSING FOR CAULIFLOWER SALAD

yolks of 2 hard-boiled eggs	½ pint old-fashioned or cole-
1 teaspoon French mustard	slaw dressing (see page 369
2 tablespoons strong tomato	and above)
purée or sauce	seasoning
1 anchovy	3 or 4 spring onions or sprouted
	onion tops

Crush egg yolks, add mustard, tomato purée, and finely pounded anchovy, add to the ½ pint of dressing. Adjust seasoning, add well-chopped onion.

A store of flavoured vinegars is of value in making salad-dressings; prepared at the moment when herbs are available, these may be kept for general use, and recipes for them will be found in Chapter XXXV, 'The Store Cupboard' (pages 1107–9). In this chapter also will be found a recipe for salad-dressing for bottling and keeping.

XIII

Herbs

SOMETIMES on a warm summer night I have used herbs as a decoration for the dinner table, a low dish heaped with little sweet-scented bunches making a centre-piece. My hopes that my friends would take the bunches from the dish after dinner have not been disappointed, and the sweet scent of the leaves has hung on the air for hours. If this were not a prosaic cookery book it would be of balm and southernwood, rosemary and bergamot, that I should be writing, but even though some sweet-scented herbs have their culinary uses, it is with the more utilitarian plants that we are chiefly concerned here, and from the dinner table we must get back to the kitchen.

It is not uncommon for the young and inexperienced to judge and condemn a herb all too hastily. Even qualified cooks have been known to state, and state with pride, that they never use the things; an admission which opens up fields of speculation concerning their real knowledge and appreciation of good food. To nibble a leaf in the garden and to come to a conclusion about its suitability as a flavouring is foolish. No one would judge, for instance, the final effect of vanilla in a dish by tasting the undiluted essence in the bottle. If they did they might never use it. Herbs, like other flavouring materials, are often pungent and harsh in the raw. Their value can only be assessed when they have been blanched, chopped, crushed, prepared in any one of the approved ways, and incorporated, and above all used in balanced and suitable proportion.

The most everyday use of herbs is in the form of the bouquet called for unremittingly in recipes for sauces, soups, and savoury dishes. This, the classic bouquet, is made up of half a bay-leaf, three or four stems of parsley (used with the full length of the stalk, which holds the chief flavouring quality), and a spray of thyme. To these may be added other herbs as called for in individual recipes. It is outside the scope of this book to discuss all the herbs, decorative, aromatic, and medicinal, that may be grown in an English herb garden. If such a garden is in contemplation, other factors than culinary values have to be considered.

For a kitchen herb garden on a liberal scale, the number and variety of plants to be grown might hardly exceed a dozen and a half, and one may manage well on considerably less. To take a conservative view, a cook

371

would be at a disadvantage without bay, basil, chives, chervil, dill, horse-radish, parsley, marjoram, mints in variety, savory, tarragon, and thyme. To these the enthusiast will probably add coriander, fennel, and rosemary, and should space permit may consider growing angelica, borage, caraway, garlic, and lovage. With a greenhouse one will probably add for flavouring purposes plants of sweet-scented geranium and verbena.

Before considering the uses of each of these, there is a point which may well be underlined. Should you be, or become, greatly interested in your herb garden, it would be a mistake to allow enthusiasm to lead you to excessive use of herbs in the kitchen. Restraint and balance may well be the watchword, unless you wish to be considered a bit of a crank or, what is worse, a spoiler of good food. Too much of some of the more potent herbs—sage, bay, and rosemary, for example—can be dreadfully putting off, and I remember a horrid soup featuring marigolds. A woman of taste does not drown herself even in the most expensive of scents, and a discriminating cook will not overwhelm a dish with flavouring.

You see how the balance of these paragraphs swings, first wooing you to use the herbs, and then warning against their over-use. So let us settle for this: you can never be a first-class cook if you fail to employ these wonderful natural flavourings, and if you are a first-class cook you will have them under control and at your informed command.

Now is come the moment to discuss herbs individually, and instead of making an alphabetical list it will possibly be more interesting to take them in some order of their distinction, and discuss first, for example, tarragon, the subtle sweet basil, and the scented mints. The letter A against the following herbs indicates that they are annual, B biennial, and P perennial, and the letters HHA indicate half-hardy annuals.

TARRAGON (P)

This is an aristocrat among herbs, but it is important to acquire for your garden the true French variety. My plants have all come from the Herb Farm at Seal, but for many years before I found these I suffered from a variety of this plant which really was of no use at all. It grew and flourished more vigorously than the true French variety, but to no purpose. The true French tarragon needs a light soil and a certain amount of shelter. It is not over-hardy, and it is as well to plant either in early autumn, to let it get well rooted before the cold weather, affording it possibly a little protection, or in the spring. Tarragon is used for such dishes as the delicate Poulet à l'Estragon, for adorning the cold salmon trout to be seen on a cold table, and for infusing in fine vinegar to make tarragon vinegar. It may also be employed in salads, although it is usually introduced through vinegar for this purpose. The use of the raw leaves requires discretion, for these have a pungent taste which at need may be modified by blanching. For this they are threaded on to a darning-needle and plunged for a minute only into boiling water. For winter purposes, as well as being used as a flavouring for vinegar, tarragon may be bottled. The leaves and tender

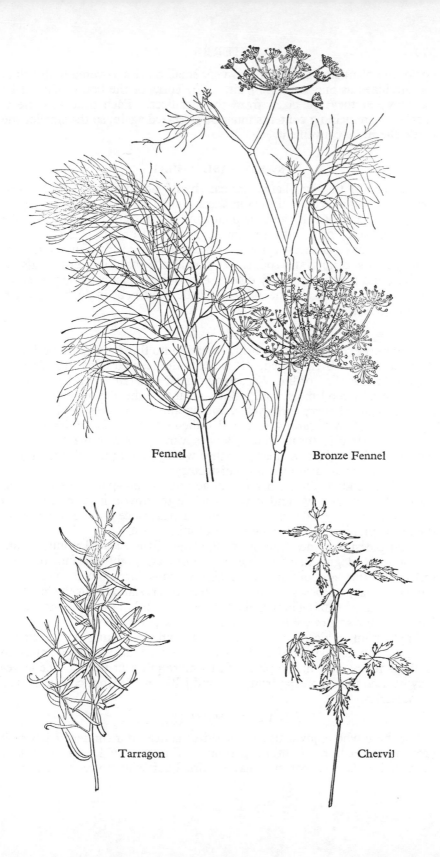

Fennel

Bronze Fennel

Tarragon

Chervil

tips of the plant should be put into very small bottles, covered with brine, and sterilized as one sterilizes fruit.   The corks of the bottles should be waxed when they are taken from the sterilizer.   Each time a bottle is opened the remaining contents must be sterilized again, so the smaller the bottle the more convenient.

SWEET BASIL (HHA)

The seed of this half-hardy annual should not be sown outside until danger of frost is over, and then in warm, moist earth, or sowings may be made in boxes in warmth and the plants put out in May.   The leaves have a fragrant, spicy taste with a slight suggestion of orange peel and clove. Sweet basil has a dedicated use; it is a classic ingredient of many tomato dishes, salads, drinks, and soups.   It may also be used in green salads, in omelets, and in many savoury dishes, and is traditionally a component of turtle soup.   It is an elegant and useful little plant to be in the herb garden of an enthusiastic cook.

MINTS (P)

It may seem out of place to bring so early into this catalogue a herb that grows in many a back garden.   It is really the scented mints that deserve such priority.   The ordinary spearmint most generally used by the cook does best in a good moist soil.   With advantage the site of the mint bed may be changed every three years, and an annual top dressing is of help. If, in spite of such care, it is found difficult to keep spearmint in good condition, Mentha rotundifolia (Bowles variety) may replace it.   This mint is a robust plant with large, rather woolly leaves; it will often thrive in places where spearmint is not satisfactory.

Not everybody realizes what a great addition to pot-pourri are the dried leaves of mint, and we find it worth while to grow a large bed for this purpose alone.   Dried mint has a delicious fragrance and does not make the pot-pourri in the least reminiscent of mint sauce.

Great pleasure comes from growing some of the scented mints.   Both the eau-de-Cologne and the pineapple mints are highly perfumed.   For this reason they are, of course, valuable in pot-pourri, but they are good too for culinary purposes.   The leaves may be crystallized for the finishing off of various gâteaux; a bunch of either adds a subtle and surprisingly good flavour to any sort of wine cup, and both make good tisanes.

Apple mint, a decorative variety, with white marking on variegated foliage, has a faint suggestion of sage, and may be used with advantage in stuffings for poultry in the place of this more pungent herb.   The leaves may be used for flavouring fruit cups and jellies made from crab-apples or gooseberries.

PEPPERMINT (P)

For those who enjoy a tisane instead of coffee after dinner, it is worth growing a small batch of peppermint.   The variety known as 'black peppermint' is excellent and may be dried for winter use, or the fresh

Bay

Sweet Basil

Bush Basil

leaves may be infused. It has excellent digestive properties, and as well as this is a soothing and pleasant after-dinner drink.

Tisanes of herbs. These are infusions made with various herbs and boiling water. Certain of them, those made with different mints and limeflowers in particular, make pleasant after-dinner drinks appreciated by those who do not drink coffee in the evening. Mints may be used fresh or dried; limeflowers are dried. Dried peppermint is sold by herbalists for this particular purpose.

A separate teapot should be kept for tisanes. For fresh tea take a good handful of mint leaves of any variety liked—we find both pineapple and eau-de-Cologne mints particularly good while young and fresh—pour on fresh boiling water, and allow to infuse 6–7 minutes. You may add sugar and lemon, but the tisane enthusiast does not generally do this. For tilleul take a small handful of the dried flowers, infuse 3–4 minutes, and add a small teaspoon of orange-flower water. Dried peppermint is good for winter use. One or two good teaspoons are generally sufficient; this is allowed to infuse 5–7 minutes.

I referred earlier to the possibility of growing plants of the scented-leafed geranium and verbena in the greenhouse for flavouring. These may be made into jellies in the way described in the chapter on the store cupboard (pages 1097–8), or used for the flavouring of sponge cakes as described on page 806.

DILL (A)

I have read that William the Conqueror introduced dill to his cook and rewarded him highly for a soup in which the herb was used. It is said to have been appreciated by the Romans, but I have also read that dill has no culinary reputation to-day. That surprises me, for we find that no matter how much dill we grow there always seems to be a demand for more. It has a delicate flavour, again with a slight suggestion of orange peel, and some other spicy touch, and the seeds have a strong fragrance with a distinct flavour of anise. The leaves are used for sauces for fish, and mixed with herbs for omelets and salads and for certain pickles, in particular those made with cucumber. In that old book, Parkinson's *Paradise in Sole*, the association of cucumber with dill is mentioned. Dill, by the way, should be sown where it is to stay, as it dislikes being transplanted, and it is necessary to thin the seedlings to give the plants sufficient room to expand.

SWEET MARJORAM (HHA)

This again is a half-hardy annual, and the seeds should be sown under glass and transplanted after danger of frost is over. It has a pungent spicy flavour, slightly reminiscent of nutmeg. It is used with mixed herbs for flavouring salads, and the tips of the shoots are suitable for herb fritters. When the leaves are dry they have a delicious scent and are excellent to put among the pot-pourri.

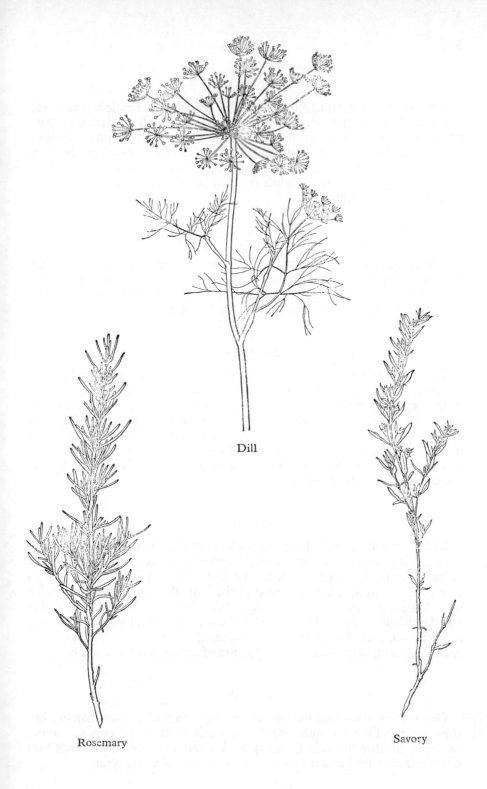

Dill

Rosemary

Savory

SAGE (P)

This is one of the strongest of the herbs, and has as its main use sage and onion stuffing for rich meat; it also makes a good flavoured jelly with gooseberries or crab-apples to serve with such dishes. Its place is sometimes taken by winter or summer savory, which have a similar taste but are much less strong. There is a charming red sage with purplish foliage and a pineapple sage called *Salvia rutilans*, but this, alas, is not hardy and must be given protection.

SUMMER SAVORY (A) AND WINTER SAVORY (P)

The summer savory is an annual, the winter savory a perennial. They are similar in taste, with a delicate suggestion of sage, which they may suitably replace. Their proper use is in conjunction with beans, and they may be introduced with discretion into 'fines herbes' for omelets and salads.

CHIVES (P)

This is one of the most useful of all the herbs in the kitchen garden. It is a pleasant-looking plant and may well be used as an edging to small beds in the vegetable garden. It is used for salads, soups, egg dishes, and for any dish in which a very delicate flavour of onion is required. The grass of the chives, which is the part of the plant used, will keep in good condition for a longer period of time if the flowers are cut back. As these are so pretty, it is probably better to keep a large number of plants going and not sacrifice the flowers of all.

GARLIC (A)

This is grown annually from small cloves pressed two inches down into the soil; it is one of the most useful flavouring ingredients of the whole range of herbs, for even if you do not like what may be described as its direct taste, it may be used to enhance the basic flavour of a dish in such a way that its presence remains undetected. On the whole it is probably simpler to buy garlic than to grow it, for it is easily come by and keeps well, and after all, even though it is used frequently in the kitchen, a large crop is not required, since such a small portion of the bulb is used at a time.

CARAWAY (B)

One usually associates the use of caraway seeds with cake-making, but they are excellent for some salads, particularly those of cucumber and beetroot, and for cheese. Caraway seeds should be sown in the late part of the summer for bearing flowers and seeds the following year.

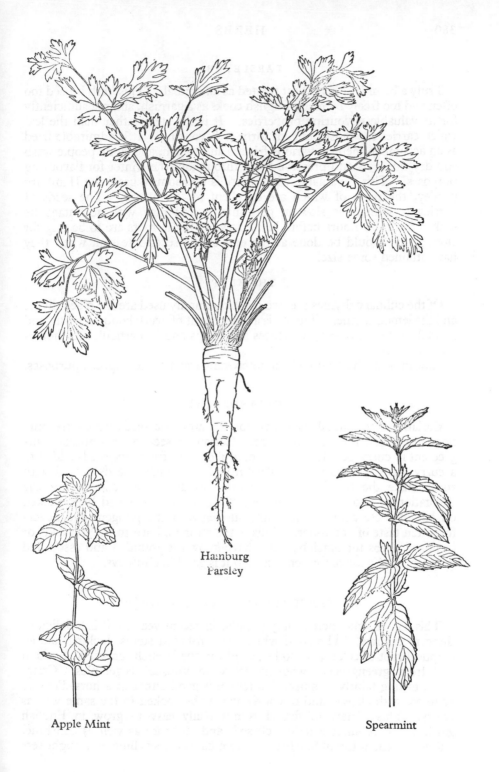

Hamburg
Parsley

Apple Mint

Spearmint

PARSLEY (B)

Truly a biennial, this is best treated as an annual. This herb is used too often and too freely by many English cooks as a garnish, and not sufficiently for its valuable flavouring properties. It is the stem rather than the leaf which carries the most pungent form of flavouring. It is admirable fried as an accompaniment to various fritters and to fish, and some people wash and dry the roots and preserve them throughout the winter for flavouring purposes. This is valuable when there is no room to grow the Hamburg parsley, the roots of which are excellent for flavouring. The seeds of parsley is sometimes slow in germination and may with advantage be soaked for a few hours before being sown. If the roots are to be dug for storing this should be done at the end of the second season, when they have attained some size.

THYME (P)

Of the culinary thymes the two most commonly used are the black thyme and the lemon thyme. Thyme is a component of every bouquet garni, and is used for the flavouring of sauces and soups and in particular for home-made cheeses.

Now for some herbs used in an interesting way for a few special purposes.

CORIANDER (A)

Coriander, an annual, is grown for the aromatic seeds which are only fit to use when they become ripe. Coriander seed is an important in-gredient in curry-powder, and a spoonful or so of fresh ripe seeds added to a curry gives it an admirable flavour. The aromatic seeds coated with sugar make the little coriander comfits used by confectioners for the decoration of cakes. In childhood, when all the sugar had been sucked off one of these comfits, one came suddenly on the pungent and never-forgotten taste of coriander. This is too strong a herb to use in salads or in mixed herbs for omelets, but I have known it pounded and associated with lemon in a sauce for venison, and it is good in chutneys.

FLORENCE FENNEL (FINOCCHIO) (A)

This has become increasingly popular in recent years. It is a delicious thing to eat raw. The solid white swollen-based stems, looking like an elliptical root of celery, are to be bought in the French market in London and from greengrocers who specialize in unusual vegetables. Crisp, juicy, tasting faintly of anise, this fennel is good either as a hors-d'œuvre or to eat with cheese, and of course it may be cooked in the same way as celery. This variety of fennel is not really easy to grow in English gardens. It requires a light rich soil, and moisture as well as sunshine, and too often, at the time when the stem bases are swelling, a drought sets

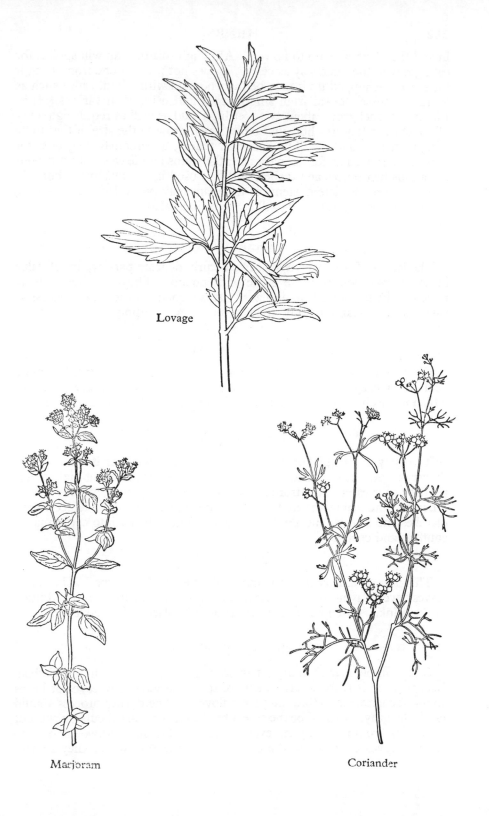

Lovage

Marjoram

Coriander

in and the plant runs up to flower. Although this mishap will spoil it for eating raw in the same way as celery, it does not prevent one from using it for sauces—chopped up it may be incorporated with a light sauce such as a sauce mousseline—or from shredding it and using it in various salads. Florence fennel grows about two feet high, and as well as requiring plenty of moisture it requires hot sun before it will grow to the size of that to be bought in the market. The common fennel, a perennial, is grown for decorative as well as for culinary use; the stems and leaves impart flavour to various fish sauces and dishes, and it is used in the making of bortsch. The young tender lateral stems of the plant may be peeled, thinly sliced, and served among mixed hors-d'œuvre or in a salad.

CHERVIL (A)

The leaves of this, which look like a curly delicate parsley, are of value in soups, particularly those made with potato. They are used, too, in mixed herbs for omelets and salads. It is a good plan to make successive sowings from March to July, to keep up a regular supply.

LOVAGE (P)

For a long time this herb has been neglected in gardens, but it is coming back into use again. It has aromatic leaves with a definite celery flavour, which makes it valuable in summer when celery itself is not available.

ANGELICA (B OR P)

This may be biennial or perennial according to whether it is allowed to flower or not. It is a handsome plant of from four to five feet high, and is perhaps of greater value from a decorative than a culinary point of view. The stem and leaf stems are used for candying and then for the decoration of cakes and sweets, and the flavour may be introduced into certain jams, soufflés, and creams.

BORAGE (B)

This is used chiefly in the making of wine and fruit cups. The rough leaves have a flavour of cucumber and the blue flowers are a pretty addition to the drink. Often cucumber peel is used in place of borage leaves.

DRYING OF HERBS

It is a simple matter to dry a few herbs for use in the domestic kitchen. Except when it is the seeds which are to be garnered the leaves of herbs should be gathered before the plants flower. The drying process should not be lengthy, as would be the case if the leaves were dried outside without protection from morning and evening dews. The method we adopt is to lay the leaves on racks in the cool oven of the Aga where they remain

(12–24 hours) until brittle, and they are then rubbed through a wire sieve and stored in dry, sterilized jars.

Another method suitable for larger quantities is to spread the leaves on canvas trays, Hessian stretched on wooden frames, and set these in a cool place out of the sun. During the drying the herbs should be turned. They may also be hung up in loose bunches in a cool dry place, until ready for stripping, sieving, and storing.

The seeds of coriander, fennel, and caraway are allowed to dry partially on the stems; they are then stripped and finally dried and stored for winter use.

XIV

Rice, Risottos, Pilaffs, and Curries

WHEN the following chapter on rice and curries, pastas and batters came back in first rough type it looked uncommonly long. I must, I thought, have put down a lot of nonsense which will now have to be cut out. And yet, on rereading, I found that for the most part I had only written of things that as an amateur I should at one time or another have been glad to know about.

To gain confidence I took a look at my early edition of Mrs Beeton to see what that Sibyl of our grandmothers had to say, for instance, about macaroni, and found there no precedent for my own wordiness. Her comment on macaroni ('As it is both wholesome and nutritious it ought to be much more used by all classes in England than it is') can have raised little enthusiasm in a day when the best meat cost no more than 11*d.* per lb. The addendum 'It generally accompanies Parmesan cheese to the tables of the rich, but is also used for thickening soups and making puddings' does little to reflect the culinary possibilities of this 'favourite food of Italy.'

Some of the dishes in the following pages contain little but inexpensive basic ingredients accompanied by good sauces and flavourings; others call for chicken, game, or fish, and so at first sight seem to indicate no economy, until one reflects that the use of the rice or pastas stretches considerably the more expensive ingredient.

A cursory glance at the following recipes may bring cooks with defeatist tendencies, in particular defeatists who live in the country, into enthusiastic opposition. Where, they will exclaim, are *we* to get these things, the pimentos, green ginger, and sweet peppers; the coriander, cardamon, and cumin, to say nothing of lychees, water chestnuts, and mangoes? Do their voices have just an edge of insularity, or just a touch of the 'foreign kickshaw' theme? The soft answer to their irritation is simply—just in the same way as we do. A few things we grow in the garden, and for the rest an occasional morning of intensive shopping, in person or by letter, keeps us supplied with enough odds and ends to lend the desirable variety for many a long month.

I kept at hand and have before me now one list resulting from a morning's shopping in Soho. A lavish expenditure of two pounds odd gave us variety of flavour and interest in experiment for many months. If this

sounds a good deal to spend on flavourings and frills, compare it with the
cost of salmon, enough for one party of six, or one restaurant meal at which
you entertain a guest or two because you feel you can't manage to have
them to dine at home.

For a regular demand a local grocer may be induced to stock slightly
out-of-the-ordinary items, and the big London stores carry many of them;
and in case it is of use to you, a note of this particular morning's shopping
in Soho has been added at the end of this chapter.

RICE

Although there are many different kinds of rice, our choice in this
country is limited, and it is only necessary here to discuss the types needed
for different dishes.   For rice which is to be boiled in water (such as is
served with curry) a thinnish grain is desirable because it absorbs less
liquid than one of thicker grain, and the one most commonly used is Patna
rice.   For the making of risotto, when the grain is cooked in liquids of
varying richness, one looks for a particularly absorbent grain, and this may
be found in Italian rices; a husked but not polished rice, sometimes called
'red' from a pinkish line running through the grain, is good, as is a
variety from Piedmont.   The same type of thick-grained rice is good
for pilaff, though Patna rice is frequently used for this purpose.   The
particularly white rice from Carolina is generally reserved for sweet
dishes.

We rarely get in this country the delicious wild rice, popular in America,
but in case some of it comes your way, I may mention that it needs longer
boiling than ordinary rice, after which it is drained and is delicious mixed
with mushrooms, chopped onions, and a clove of garlic, all first sautéd in
a little good dripping or butter.

Rices vary in their powers of absorption, so that the amounts of liquid
given in recipes for risottos and pilaffs must of necessity be approximate,
and if after the rice is half cooked it is apparent that the liquid is insufficient, more may be added; equally, if at the end of cooking the dish
should contain surplus liquid, this may be driven off by a few minutes
extra cooking with the lid off the pan.

Plain boiled rice is the classic accompaniment to curry and presents an
ideal vehicle for the flavours of this dish.   Indeed, rice may reasonably be
regarded as a vehicle for flavours, for when used in risotto or pilaff it is
cooked in rich liquids with this object in view.

When boiled, rice just about trebles its bulk; 1½–2 oz. of uncooked rice
per person is a good normal allowance.   A dish of boiled rice should
present a snowy mound of well-defined grains, on the dryish side and
never sticky, mushy, or lumpy.   This is a matter of attention to detail:
proper washing, fast boiling in plenty of water, proper draining and
drying.

Washing

This is done in order to remove loose surface starch.   Put the rice in the deep part of a nylon sieve or in a muslin cloth, and submerge in a basin of clear, cold water, gently moving the rice about or rubbing it softly between the palms of the hands.   Lift the rice out, throw the cloudy water away, and repeat the process until the water remains clear.   In this way you are sure of removing any loose starch on the surface of the grain, which if left may make the cooked dish sticky.   As a short cut, perhaps for the less important dishes, the rice may be put in a conical strainer and held under running water from the cold tap.

Certain of the very finely polished rices packed in cellophane bags which come over from America do not require so many washings, but rice bought loose may want as much as five or six different lots of water.

Cooking

Allow 1½–2 oz. rice per person; if in doubt it is as well to choose a larger proportion, for drying is more successfully achieved with a large than with a small quantity, and there are many uses for any that may be left over.   For 6 oz. of rice allow 6 pints of water and put it into a pan which gives plenty of room.   Bring the water to boiling-point, add a level tablespoon of salt and the juice of half a lemon, which helps to keep the rice white.   Sprinkle the washed rice into the fast-boiling water and continue stirring until the water is again at full fast boil.   The point of this fast boiling is that the agitation of the water tends to keep the grains apart.   The time of cooking varies according to the size of the grain and is from 15 to 18 minutes.   Testing should begin after 12 minutes: a grain pressed between thumb and forefinger or bitten through should prove soft right through, neither mushy nor hard at the centre.   This is the moment at which to catch it.   Beyond this point very little further cooking will render it mushy.   It is a good plan, when the rice is at this point, to check boiling by throwing in a cup of cold water.   Drain thoroughly and return to the pan, in which a small lump of butter has been melted (this helps to prevent the rice from adhering to the bottom and sides of the pan). Cover with a clean napkin and shake from time to time, giving about 10–15 minutes in a warm corner of the stove to dry.   Some cooks think it is helpful to put the rice in the colander under the cold water tap before returning to the pan.   Here is R. H.'s note on the matter:

'Pour over the cooked rice a jug of boiling water; leave the rice in the colander, make holes through it with the handle of a wooden spoon, and leave for 15 minutes or longer.   Return to hot pan and proceed as before. If over gas or electricity use an asbestos mat and very low heat.'

Some authorities allow it to dry for much longer—as much as 1½ hours.

Sometimes for the sake of variety one may serve boiled rice, half plain and half fried.   For this purpose a small proportion of the boiled rice is taken and treated as follows.

Fried rice

Fry, in dripping or butter, a little onion and crushed garlic in a frying-pan; add a sprig of rosemary. When the onions are softened put in the cooked rice, season well, stir, and cook until it begins to colour. Add a good tablespoon of finely chopped herbs, chives, chervil, fennel and anything else you may like, or use turmeric or paprika in place of herbs. This may either be put in heaps around the central mound of white rice or the two may be served separately.

Saffron is a suitable flavouring ingredient for boiled rice dishes and for risottos. Half a teaspoon or more according to taste may be soaked overnight in a few spoonfuls of cold water, or for half an hour in boiling water; either the whole mixture or the liquid may be added to the dish in hand.

DISHES WITH PLAIN BOILED RICE

Plain boiled rice forms a basis for many good, simple luncheon dishes, and the following recipes may be varied in many ways to suit individual taste. The rice may be boiled specially for the dish in question, or left-over boiled rice may be substituted. The following is excellent and economical when tomatoes are in season:

TOMATOES WITH RICE

2 cups boiled rice	1 small onion, chopped
¾ cup milk	seasoning of salt, pepper, and
2 bay-leaves	a little sugar
1 egg	1 heaped tablespoon mixed
1½ lb. tomatoes	herbs, finely chopped
1 tablespoon strong tomato purée	the grated rind of a small lemon
1 oz. butter or margarine	a squeeze of lemon juice
1 clove of garlic, crushed	(optional)

Put rice, milk, bay-leaves, and a little salt into a pan, simmer till milk is absorbed, about 5–7 minutes. Beat egg and stir into rice. Pack the mixture into a ring mould and set aside in a warm place while you prepare the tomatoes. Skin, empty, and chop the tomatoes. Melt butter and in it cook garlic and onion till the latter is softened and pale gold in colour; add tomatoes and seasoning and simmer for 15 minutes, add tomato purée, herbs, and grated lemon rind and cook for a minute or two longer. Put ring mould of rice into the oven for about 15 minutes; turn out on to a dish and pour the tomato mixture in the middle, and if liked add a squeeze of lemon juice.

Reheated rice or freshly boiled rice may be used for the following dish:

TOMATO RICE

1 oz. butter or margarine	2 cups boiled rice (reheated as
1 clove of garlic, crushed	in foregoing recipe in ¾ cup
1 onion, chopped	milk)
seasoning	1 cup strong tomato pulp
	2 oz grated cheese

Heat the butter, add garlic and onion and cook for a few minutes, add the rice and tomato pulp, season well, heat thoroughly. Immediately before serving stir in the cheese. This is a particularly good dish when Parmesan and gruyère cheese can be used in equal proportions.

The following Riz à l'Espagnole is a very good dish:

RIZ A L'ESPAGNOLE

1½ pints cooked rice (or 8 oz. uncooked boiled for the purpose)
3 medium onions
1 clove of garlic
1½ oz. dripping or 3 table-spoons olive oil
a few celery stalks or ½ head of celeriac, cut up
¼ lb. mushrooms, sliced
1 outdoor cucumber, diced, or fresh green pepper, seeded and sliced

1 large tin of tomatoes (a generous pint), or an equal quantity of stewed fresh tomatoes
2 red tinned pimentos, sliced
seasoning
1 tablespoon chopped mixed herbs, including for choice basil and marjoram
4 oz. cheese (optional)

Slice onions, crush garlic, heat fat and cook them until golden in colour. Put on low heat and add celery, mushrooms, and cucumber or pepper. Allow to continue cooking gently for 15 minutes. Add tomatoes, pimentos, and seasoning. Add rice, adjust seasoning, add herbs. Turn into a fireproof dish and serve. If cheese is to be used, sprinkle over the top and brown under grill or in oven.

The following dish of rice with fried bananas is excellent and liked by children:

RICE AND FRIED BANANAS

½ lb. rice
1 large onion, shredded
2 cloves of garlic crushed with salt
2 oz. good dripping or mar-garine
¼ pint tinned or an equal quan-tity of fresh tomatoes, skinned, emptied, and chopped
salt to taste and freshly ground black pepper

1 sweet green pepper, seeded and shredded (optional)
1 canned red pepper (pimento)
1 tablespoon mixed chopped fresh herbs
1 pinch of saffron (optional) soaked overnight in an egg-cup of water or ½ an hour in hot water
1 pint water (approx.)
4 bananas split and fried in butter

Heat fat, cook onion and garlic till soft and turning colour, add rice and cook for a few minutes, add remaining ingredients (except the bananas) and simmer for 25–30 minutes. Turn into a fireproof dish and arrange bananas round the mound.

RICE CROQUETTES

¾ pint boiled rice
2 oz. grated cheese
1 level tablespoon finely chopped chives
1 teaspoon onion juice or grated onion

½ oz. self-raising flour
2 eggs
2 tablespoons good milk
seasoning to taste

Mix together rice, cheese, chives, grated onion or juice, flour, and seasoning. Beat egg yolks well, add milk, then add to mixture. Beat the whites till stiff and fold into mixture. Drop the mixture a spoonful at a time into deep hot frying fat, or they may be cooked in a frying-pan if the fat is deep enough. Drain and serve with fried parsley (see page 49) or with any good tomato sauce, e.g. tomato sauces 1 and 2 on page 178.

STUFFED PIMENTOS

6 even-sized peppers, red or green
1 medium-sized onion
1 clove of garlic
1 oz. butter or bacon fat
2–3 oz. chopped mushrooms (or an equal quantity of diced ham)

6 oz. rice
1 dessertspoon finely chopped parsley
¾ pint good stock, meat or vegetable
salt and pepper
½ pint tomato sauce, simple fashion (see page 178)

Blanch peppers for 5 minutes in salted water, drain, cut off the tops and scoop out the seeds. Finely chop the onion and garlic, soften in the butter or bacon fat and add the chopped mushrooms. Sauter for a few minutes, add the rice, continue sautéing to fry the rice a little, then add the parsley, stock, and seasoning. Bring to the boil, cover, and set the pan in the oven for 20–25 minutes, until the rice is tender and the stock absorbed. Fill the peppers well with the rice and replace the tops. Arrange any remaining rice in a fireproof dish and set the peppers on the top. Coat over with the sauce and set in a moderate oven 30 minutes, basting occasionally. The dish may be garnished with croûtons of bread first spread with garlic crushed with a teaspoon of salt and then fried in olive oil.

Shrimps or prawns which have been sautéd in a little butter may be added to plain boiled rice or fried rice, in which case this may well be a little drier than in the foregoing recipes. Boil the rice, drain it and fry, or use reheated rice.

SHRIMPS AND RICE

1 oz. butter
2 tea-cups boiled rice
1 teaspoon turmeric
anchovy sauce mixed with 3 or 4 tablespoons cream or rich milk

chopped fennel
seasoning
½ pint shelled shrimps or prawns, sautéd in a little butter

Melt butter, stir in boiled rice, add turmeric. Mix enough anchovy sauce into the cream to season it fairly strongly, add this to rice and simmer for a minute or two.   Add fennel, season well, turn on to a dish.   Arrange shrimps on top of the rice.

In the Winkfield chapter (page 1015) will be found a recipe for Pine-apple Nut Rice which is delicious.

A risotto is an important dish; if properly made it is delicious.   It may be used as the main dish of a simple meal or, enriched with additional ingredients, be suitable for a more important one.

RISOTTOS

In risotto we should have a rich, creamy dish, not a dry mound of white separate grains as in boiled rice for curry.   This indicates a different technique in its preparation.   To begin with it is not necessary to wash the rice in order to remove surplus starch.   Indeed, if in the interests of clean-liness preliminary washing is required, the grains should be thoroughly dried again before being cooked.   Nor is the rice allowed to absorb water by being boiled as a preliminary process; neither is fast boiling with the object of keeping the grains apart called for.

The points which should be observed in making a risotto are as follows:

The dry rice is first subjected to the high temperature of hot fat, after which it must be cooked gently by slow simmering.   This is best done with such low heat as the simmering ring of an Aga, a slow oven, or the lowest heat of an electric plate, or, in the case of gas, with an asbestos ring.

After the preliminary frying of the rice in hot fat, and after the liquid is added, the mixture in the pan is stirred unceasingly till it boils, after which point there is some diversity of opinion.   Some authorities maintain that after boiling-point is achieved the contents of the saucepan should by no means be touched again until the rice is cooked; in other words throughout the simmering period the rice is not stirred.   Other cooks say stir from time to time.   R. H. and I both think that if the cooking is really slow enough, carried out for instance on the simmering ring of the Aga, the first system has much to be said for it, for unless the stirring is carefully done it may cause the rice to become sticky.   If, however, the cooking must perforce be done on stronger heat than is ideal, then stirring will have to be resorted to or the rice may stick to the bottom of the pan.   Some cooks prefer to add the stock gradually, starting with the liquid just covering the rice and adding more as required at intervals.   Here is a recipe for the simplest of all risottos, on which may be built many varieties of excellent dishes:

RISOTTO (FOR 3–4)

6 oz. rice	1 pint stock
1½ oz. butter and 1 oz. to finish	a pinch of nutmeg
2 oz. onion, chopped	bouquet garni
1 clove of garlic, crushed (optional)	seasoning
	1½ oz. grated cheese

Pick over but do not wash or wet the rice.[1]   Heat butter, add chopped onion and garlic, stir continuously over low heat until onion is soft but not brown.   Add rice, continue to stir until the rice has become soaked in the hot butter and takes on a slightly milky appearance.   After about 4 or 5 minutes draw the pan away from the heat and pour on the stock, add seasoning, bouquet, and nutmeg.   Stir gently till boiling, taking care that no rice sticks to the bottom of the pan.   When boiling-point is reached cover the pan tightly, weighting the lid if necessary, and continue cooking by gentle simmering.   The risotto should be ready in 25–30 minutes, the rice tender and all the liquid absorbed.   Since some kinds of rice take less time than others, it is as well to look at it after 20 minutes' cooking.   When ready remove bouquet, add cheese and butter broken into small pieces, mix in lightly and carefully with a fork.

Tomato purée and garlic are both good additions to the above ingredients, the garlic being put in with the onion and cooked in the hot fat, the tomato purée being added with the stock.

This plain risotto, if well made, is very good, and it can be enriched in many ways by the addition of mushrooms, tomato sauce, or kidneys; and the following Risotto à la Milanese is one of the best of dishes.   It will be noted that beef marrow is called for, but this of course may be replaced by butter or margarine, and the good beef stock replaced by whatever stock one may have at hand.

RISOTTO A LA MILANESE

6 oz. Italian rice
1 oz. beef marrow
1½ oz. butter
1–2 oz. onion, finely chopped
1 clove of garlic, crushed
2 oz. mushrooms, sliced
   (optional)

1 gill white wine (optional, and
   may be replaced with an
   equal quantity of stock)
a good pinch of saffron soaked
   ½ an hour in an egg-cup of
   hot stock
¾ pint good beef stock (approx.)
2 oz. grated cheese

Pick over the rice without washing.   Chop the marrow finely, put it into a saucepan with half the butter and when melted add the onion and garlic. Cook slowly until pale golden in colour, add mushrooms, and continue cooking for a few minutes, add rice and stir over a gentle heat 4 or 5 minutes.   Add wine, saffron, and half the stock, stir continuously till the mixture boils.   After 5–6 minutes' simmering add the remaining stock, bring back to boiling-point, and allow to simmer gently without stirring until the rice is cooked and the liquid absorbed.   Draw the pan aside, scatter the cheese on top, dot over the remaining butter, cover and leave for a few minutes, then stir lightly with a fork and serve at once.

N.B. This risotto should be creamy enough to spread gently on the plate when dished.   The mushrooms may be added to this after the onion is cooked, but then it is no longer *à la Milanese*.

---

[1] If there is reason to think that the rice is not clean it may be washed, but must then be thoroughly dried before being submitted to the hot fat.

RISOTTO A LA NAPOLITANA

1½ oz. butter
4 oz. onions, sliced
1 clove of garlic crushed with salt
6 oz. rice
1½ cups skinned, emptied, and chopped tomatoes or 1 cup canned tomatoes

1 teaspoon chopped basil or lemon thyme
a scant pint vegetable stock or water (approx.)
salt and pepper
1 oz. grated cheese
Parmesan cheese to hand separately

Melt 1 oz. butter in a stew-pan, gently fry the sliced onions in this to a delicate brown.   Add the garlic and the rice and fry again for a few minutes.   Add the tomatoes, herbs, and half the liquid.   Season well and cook slowly until thick.   Add the remaining stock and continue simmering until the rice is tender.   The risotto should still be fairly liquid, so add a little more stock if necessary.   Scatter over the cheese, and dot small pieces of the remaining butter over the top.   Cover and draw aside to stand for a few minutes.   Stir round once or twice lightly with a fork and turn immediately into a serving dish.   Serve a dish of Parmesan cheese separately.

RISOTTO A LA BOLOGNESE

1 oz. onion
1 oz. mushrooms or mushroom peelings (see note on duxelles, page 240)
3 chickens' livers
1½ oz. butter
1 teaspoon tomato purée

1 clove of garlic crushed with salt
6 oz. rice
salt and pepper
¾–1 pint stock
grated cheese

Chop the onion and mushrooms finely.   Slice the livers.   Heat three-quarters of the butter, sauter the onion in this for a few minutes.   Add the livers and mushrooms and cook quickly for a minute or two.   Draw aside, add the purée, garlic, rice, and seasonings.   Cook again for a minute or two, pour on half the stock and cook gently until the mixture begins to thicken, then add the remaining stock and continue simmering gently until the rice is tender and the stock absorbed.   Scatter a handful of cheese over, dot the remaining butter on the top, cover, and leave for a few minutes off the fire before stirring round with a fork.   Serve with grated cheese.

BROCHETTES A L'ITALIENNE

Use small silver or wooden skewers for this dish.

¼ lb. calf's liver
2 oz. mushrooms
¼ lb. small sausages (chipolatas)
sage
2 oz. bacon fat or butter
freshly ground black pepper

dry white breadcrumbs
freshly boiled well-dried rice or a Risotto à la Milanese (see previous page)
slightly thickened gravy or piquante sauce

Cut the liver into inch squares, the mushrooms into quarters, leave the sausages whole. Pick about a dozen sage leaves off the stalks. Melt the fat on a plate, roll the pieces of liver in it, and season with freshly ground black pepper. Push the liver on to the skewers with the sausages, mushrooms, and sage leaves at regular intervals between. Draw the skewers through the melted fat, roll in the crumbs, and put under an even hot grill for about 3½ minutes on each side. When brown lower the heat slightly for the rest of the time. The brochettes can be brushed with the remainder of the fat whilst grilling. Have ready the rice or risotto, arrange on a dish and lay the brochettes on top. Pour round gravy or piquante sauce and serve very hot.

PILAFF OR PILAU

Generally speaking a pilaff is a dish in which chicken or meat is so cooked that it falls apart easily and the juices are absorbed into the rice. In addition to this the rice itself may be suitably flavoured with spices, green ginger, chopped, pieces of mango chutney, almonds, raisins, sweet peppers, slivers of chilli, turmeric, and in some cases saffron, tomato, and tomato sauce. Some pilaffs consist of richly flavoured rice served with mushrooms or shell-fish, and some recipes for this dish call for a preliminary blanching of the rice in boiling water for 3 or 4 minutes. It is then drained, added to hot fat in a second pan, and stirred and shaken for a few moments, after which the liquid is added gradually.

CHICKEN PILAFF

1 boiling fowl	6 peppercorns tied in a bit of
2 rashers of bacon for pre- liminary cooking	muslin
water	1 large onion
a bouquet garni	2 oz. butter or chicken fat, more if necessary
1 onion, 1 carrot, and 2 or 3 celery stalks, all cut up	2 oz. almonds, blanched and split
salt	2–3 oz. raisins
	½ lb. rice

Make the bird tender by a preliminary cooking, without liquid, in the way described on page 634. When this process is completed draw pan from heat and after a few minutes add enough water just to cover the bird, add bouquet, onion, carrot, and celery cut up, salt and peppercorns. Simmer until very tender. Draw aside. Finely slice the onion, soften half of it in half the butter, add half the almonds and half the raisins; add rice, continue cooking a few minutes, then moisten with about 1¼ pints of the chicken stock; season, bring to the boil, and put the pan into the oven until the rice is tender and the stock absorbed. Add more stock, if necessary, after 10–15 minutes.

Meanwhile take the chicken out of the pot, carve the flesh from the bones in fairly large pieces. Melt the rest of the butter in a frying-pan, add the pieces of chicken and fry until turning colour. Dish the rice, arrange the chicken round, and put in the oven to keep hot.   Fry the remaining onion in the butter and when half done add the remaining raisins and almonds. Fry briskly until brown, adding more fat if necessary, then scatter over the rice and serve at once.

PILAFF AUX MOULES

For the rice

6 oz. rice
3 oz. onion
1 oz. butter
as much saffron as will cover a
  sixpence, soaked overnight
  in an egg-cup of cold water

if possible, or ½ an hour in
  boiling water
¾ pint vegetable, light veal, or
  chicken stock, more if necessary
seasoning

For the mussels

3 pints good mussels
a bouquet garni, including a
  short stalk of celery

a large glass wine or water
a slice of onion and of carrot
6 peppercorns

For finishing

1 oz. butter
½ oz. flour
a spoonful of cream

1 heaped teaspoon chopped
  parsley
seasoning

1. Chop the onion, soften in the butter, add the rice, stir over the fire for a minute or two, but without colouring.   Add the saffron and pour on the stock; season lightly, bring to the boil, cover, and set the pan in the oven until the rice is tender and the stock absorbed, about 20 minutes. Do not stir while cooking, but add a little more stock if necessary towards the end of the time.

2. Meanwhile scrub and wash the mussels well in cold water, rejecting any that are not tightly closed.   (See note on preparation of mussels, page 499.)   Put them into a pan with the bouquet garni, wine or water, onion, carrot, and peppercorns.   Cover tightly and bring to the boil, shaking the pan once or twice with an upward movement.   As soon as the mussels are open draw the pan aside, shell and, if wished, remove the beards.   Set aside to keep hot.   Strain the juice through a muslin.   Measure and make up to ½ pint if necessary with the light stock used for the rice.

3. Work the butter and flour together, add piece by piece to the mussel liquor, whisking it well.   Bring to the boil, simmer till creamy, then finish with the parsley, cream, and seasoning.   Add the mussels to the sauce and draw aside.   Butter a charlotte or plain mould, fill with the rice, packing it down lightly, then remove 2 or 3 spoonfuls from the middle.   Fill in with some of the mussels without much sauce, cover completely with the rice and leave for a few minutes.   Turn on to a hot dish and surround with the remaining mussels.

The following dish may be made with chicken or pigeon.   Where pigeons are plentiful and appear often on the menu it is possible to get very tired of them and to wish for new ways of dressing them; here at least is one good way of doing so.   The dried apricots, raisins, almonds, pistachios, and coco-nut milk give the dish a refreshing flavour, though at need some of these ingredients may be omitted.

PILAFF OF PIGEONS WITH APRICOTS AND NUTS

2–3 pigeons
3 oz. butter or dripping
3 medium onions, sliced
3 cloves of garlic
1 teaspoon each of coriander, cardamon, and fennel seed lightly bruised and tied in muslin
2 pints stock (approx.)
seasoning
¾ lb. rice
1 dessertspoon green ginger, grated, or preserved ginger

a good pinch of saffron, soaked overnight in an egg-cup of water or ½ an hour in boiling water
6 dried apricots soaked for an hour or two and cut in slices
2 oz. raisins
1 dozen almonds, 1 dozen pistachios, all blanched and shredded
1 tablespoon freshly grated coco-nut
½ pint first infusion of coco-nut milk (see page 403)

Prepare the infusion of coco-nut and the grated coco-nut. Blanch and shred the other nuts. Heat half the butter in a saucepan, brown the pigeons all over, remove, cut in two, and set aside. Soften half the onions in the hot fat, cooking gently for 5 or 6 minutes. Add garlic, pigeons, spices (tied in muslin), and stock to cover. Season. Cover pan tightly, weighting lid if necessary, simmer for an hour.

In another large pan melt the remaining butter, cook remaining onions till golden brown, add rice, cook for a few minutes till lightly coloured, add liquor from pigeons (about 1¾ pints), ginger, saffron with the liquid it soaked in, apricots, raisins, nuts, grated coco-nut, and finally the pigeons. Cover, cook slowly until rice is tender. Examine after 15 minutes or so and add extra stock if needed. The rice should be rich and creamy. If at the end of cooking there is too much liquid, cook for a few minutes with the lid off; finally add the infusion of coco-nut, adjust seasoning and serve. The flesh of the pigeons should fall away from the bones.

Here is another dish in which dried fruits play an important part, this time from Greece. The final cooking is done in an earthenware casserole in which the pilaff is served, and this is most important.

PILAFF A LA GRECQUE

2 oz. good prunes, 1 oz. dried apricots, and 2 oz. raisins, soaked separately overnight, the prunes and apricots then cut into strips, and the raisins stoned
½ lb. rice
1½ oz. butter
1 large onion
2 cloves of garlic crushed with salt

1½ cups Italian tinned tomatoes, or ripe tomatoes skinned, pipped, and chopped
1 bay-leaf
juice of ½ lemon
a pinch of saffron
1½ cups stock (approx.)
salt and freshly ground black pepper
finely shredded and blanched orange rind

Cook the rice in plenty of boiling salted water for 12 minutes only. Drain, rinse with hot water, and drain again.   Meanwhile melt 1 oz. of the butter in a stew-pan, add the onion, finely sliced, with the garlic and sauter slowly for 5 minutes.   Now add the prunes, apricots, and raisins. Simmer for 3 or 4 minutes.   Add the tomatoes, bay-leaf, and lemon juice and set aside.   Heat a third of the stock and pour on to the saffron, leave to soak.   Rub the remaining butter round a deep earthenware dish or casserole.   Put a third of the rice at the bottom, spoon over half the fruit mixture, first adding the saffron with plenty of seasoning.   Add another third of rice, the remaining fruit mixture, and finish with the last of the rice.   Moisten with the stock, cover with a piece of thickly buttered paper and then the lid, and cook in a slow oven about 1 hour.   At the end of that time stir round with a fork, adding more stock if necessary to keep it moist. Scatter the shredded orange rind over before serving.

This pilaff can be served with kebabs of lamb, or as a dish to accompany a vegetable such as fried aubergine, zucchini, etc.

N.B. The kinds of fruit may vary, both figs and dried peaches being suitable.

FOIE DE VEAU AUX ORANGES

Sautéd liver garnished with orange and served with a rice pilaff.

6 slices of liver	2 cloves of garlic, crushed
seasoning of salt, pepper, dry mustard, and cayenne pepper	1 tablespoon (altogether) chopped parsley and thyme
1½ oz. butter	½ gill red wine
1 onion, finely chopped	¾ gill strong stock

Garnish

1 orange browned in hot oil or butter and sprinkled with sugar

Pilaff

1 oz. butter	¾ pint stock (approx.)
1 onion, finely sliced	a little grated cheese
5 oz. rice	

Dust the slices of liver very lightly with flour and seasoning.   Heat half the butter in a pan and brown quickly both sides of the liver; remove and keep warm.   Melt the remaining butter in the pan, add the onion and garlic and cook until soft and golden brown.   Moisten with the wine and stock, add chopped herbs and simmer 1 minute.   Pour the sauce over the liver which has been arranged on a serving dish.   Cut the orange in thin slices with the peel on and brown quickly on both sides in hot oil or butter, sprinkling with sugar.   Garnish the liver with this and serve with rice pilaff.

Pilaff.   Melt three-quarters of the butter, add the onion, cover, and cook slowly until soft but not coloured.   Add the rice, sauter for a few minutes, stirring all the time.   Pour on the stock, season, bring to the boil, cover tightly, and put into a moderate oven 20–25 minutes.   Stir in the remaining butter with a fork, and add a little grated cheese.

MOULDED PILAFF

A dish which may be simple or rich according to the nature of the centre filling or sauce.

1¾ oz. butter
3 oz. onion, finely sliced
6 oz. rice
1–1½ pints stock
2 bay-leaves
6 coriander or cardamon seeds, bruised and tied in muslin (optional)

a pinch of saffron soaked over-night in an egg-cup of water, or put for ½ an hour in boil-ing water, or
1 saltspoon paprika
any good tomato or mushroom sauce or a suitable salpicon (see below)

Melt 1 oz. of the butter, add the onion, cook till golden brown, add rice, and continue cooking for 5 or 6 minutes. Add stock, bay-leaves, seeds in muslin, and saffron or paprika, bring to boil, cover, and set pan in oven until rice is tender and stock absorbed (approximate time 30 minutes). Remove muslin bag of seeds and bay-leaves. Butter well either a ring or a charlotte mould with the remaining butter, fill with rice, leave for a few moments to settle, turn out on to a hot dish, and, in the case of a ring mould, fill the centre and pour round a suitable sauce or salpicon.

When a charlotte mould is used it may be filled completely with rice, and a hollow then made in the centre into which the salpicon is put to within an inch or two of the top; this is then covered with rice and the mould left for a moment or two to settle, then turned out and the rest of the salpicon poured round.

Salpicon (1) (Mushrooms and Chicken Livers)

2 chicken livers (or kidneys may be used)
4 oz. mushrooms
8 pickling onions
¾ oz. butter
¾ oz. flour
1 wineglass red wine
1 wineglass stock or water

bouquet of bay-leaf, sprig of lemon, thyme, parsley stalk, blade of mace
salt and freshly ground black pepper
½ teaspoon concentrated to-mato purée

Trim the mushrooms, wash well and cut into quarters, blanch the onions 5 minutes. Melt butter in a sauté or shallow stew-pan; put in the livers and sauter briskly for 4–5 minutes. Remove, slice into 2 or 3 pieces, and set aside. Put into the same fat the onions, and allow to colour. Add the mushrooms and shake over a quick fire 4 or 5 minutes. Draw aside, shake in the flour, add the wine, stock, bouquet, seasoning, and purée. Bring to boil, replace the pieces of liver, and simmer un-covered 5–6 minutes. At the end of this time the sauce should be rich-looking and well reduced.

Salpicon (2) (Lobster)

2 cups sliced lobster meat or Dublin Bay prawns
¾ pint sauce aurore (page 155)
¼ lb. button mushrooms

a little butter
a few drops of tabasco sauce or lemon juice

Add the lobster to the sauce and leave on low heat or in a bain-marie for 15–20 minutes.   Do not let it boil.   Sauter the mushrooms briskly in a little butter and add to the sauce with the tabasco.

N.B. The liquid for the pilaff with which this particular salpicon is to be served should be vegetable stock, or water to which is added a glass of white wine.   For a richer dish use sauce cardinal (see page 161) instead of the sauce aurore.

PILAFF AUX FRUITS DE MER

2 oz. butter	2 scallops
1 onion, finely sliced	1 wineglass white wine
2 shallots	a bouquet garni
salt and pepper	6 Dublin Bay prawns, shelled
½ lb. rice	2 oz. mushrooms, sliced, and a
1¼–1½ pints stock	nut of butter for cooking them

Sauce

1 oz. butter	½ pint fish fumet or stock
¾ oz. flour	½ gill top of milk

Melt two-thirds of the butter, add the onion and 1 shallot, cover and cook slowly until soft but not coloured.   Add the rice, sauter for a few minutes, then add seasoning and the stock and bring to the boil.   Cover and place in the oven for about 20 minutes.   Stir the remaining butter lightly into the pilaff with a fork.   In the meantime place the scallops in a pan with a little water and the white wine, the second shallot, chopped, the bouquet garni, and seasoning.   Cook very gently for 5 minutes, remove scallops from the liquid, slice and keep warm.   Toss the prawns in the same pan, drain and keep warm with the scallops.

Melt the butter for the sauce, blend in the flour and add the fish stock. Bring slowly to the boil, add the top of milk, adjust the seasoning, adding all the fish and the previously cooked mushrooms.   Shake the pan over the fire till heated through.   For serving mould the rice in an oiled savarin tin or ring mould and turn on to a hot dish.   Spoon the fish in its sauce in the centre, serving separately any remaining sauce.

N.B. The sauce should be very light and creamy, and can have an egg yolk added to enrich it if liked.

CURRIES

It would not, I think, be an exaggeration to say that the word curry denotes to some English cooks a done-up dish, something inevitably hot and, as inevitably, deep yellow in colour.   This being so, those who do not like hot (in the sense of peppery) dishes will probably flick over these pages as being of no interest to them.   I should, however, like to persuade them to wait for a moment and, if you like, be converted, because some at least of their ideas are ill founded, and as long as they are allowed to prevail curries will not take the valuable place in our menus that they should.   So first let it be said that, according to the spices used, curries may be deep yellow in colour or they may not, also that some may be as hot as any fire-eater can take, while other dishes, suitably included under this heading, can be extremely delicate in flavour, tasting of nuts and the gentler spices.   As examples of these you may like to look for a moment at the recipe for Coronation Chicken on page 1012 or the Banana and Melon Curry on page 1014.   It would be safe to serve either of these to the most sensitive of palates, while if you are looking to please your retired Indian Army uncle you may like to try the Red Almond Curry on page 1017. But this is going ahead too fast, and I should first explain what reasons there are for wishing to arrest a reluctant attention to a group of dishes which originate in lands far distant from our own.   Briefly they are these:

It is possible with very simple, easily come-by ingredients to make appetizing and interesting dishes.   Moreover it is attention to detail rather than a high degree of culinary skill that is required to make a good curry, and added to this a gift of imagination, so that this is essentially a dish for an amateur to learn about.   Next, and perhaps the most important reason of all in these days, such a dish is a particularly practical affair for the cook-hostess, in that not only is it possible for a curry to be prepared the day before it is wanted, but there is definite advantage in doing so, since a reheated curry is in many ways the best.   The reason for this is that the blending of the various ingredients is perfected, and the staple used, the chicken, meat or what-have-you, is more thoroughly impregnated with the flavour of the curry sauce.   And finally, curries are suitable to eat in hot weather, just at that time of the year when people, particularly those of us who live in the country, want to entertain.   On this point it is interesting to note that countries with hot climates often have, as a national dish, something highly spiced and very hot indeed; for example, the Arab kous-kous in which the hottest of chillis are employed, and the hot pepper sauces of Mexico and their chilli con carne.   And British people living in such countries will tell you that there seems to be something in high temperatures that makes such highly spiced dishes particularly welcome. Be that as it may, this section is not intended to coax anyone to eat dishes too peppery for their normal taste, but to show the range of possibility to be found under its heading.   In this connection it may also be said that quite mild curries are often served with hot accompaniments, with, for instance, chutneys containing plenty of chillis or a hot pickle such as lime pickle, as well as with milder kinds, and in this way a dish may be adapted to different tastes.

Serving a curry

A word may be said on the usual way of serving a curry.   First the rice is handed; this should be white, dry, each grain defined.   A mound of this is put on the plate, then the curry is handed, sometimes with only a little sauce, in which case more sauce is handed separately, except in the case of dry curries (see page 417). The accompaniments may be put in small dishes which are arranged together on a flat dish or tray for convenience in serving, or they may be arranged in little saucers or hors-d'œuvre dishes and set at each place. Poppadums or the large flat 'last-minute' biscuits that we sometimes use in their place may be heaped up on a sieve or wire tray; these are crisp and friable and are usually broken up over the curry. Bombay duck may be bought from the same place as the curry spices, and the pieces are usually toasted before being sent to table. Curry is eaten with a dessertspoon and fork and never with a knife.

MATERIALS USED IN MAKING CURRIES

1. A staple ingredient such as chicken, rabbit, shell-fish, fresh or smoked fish, eggs, vegetables, fruit, and meat.
2. Rice, plenty of it and immaculately cooked.
3. Curry-powder, paste, and various spices.
4. A sauce in which the main ingredient is either cooked or reheated, the basis of which is shallots or onions, fat, and a suitable liquid.

In addition to these basic requirements there are many other ingredients employed in concocting this dish; these include among other things the following:

1. Various nut milks.
2. Something known as sweet-sour, that is to say red-currant or crab-apple jellies, certain seedless jams, lemon juice combined with sugar, tamarind, and chutneys.
3. Peppery or heat-giving materials such as chillis, fresh and dried, fresh and ground ginger, and mustard seed.
4. Herbs in variety.
5. Thickening agents.

The liquids employed in the making of the sauce may vary considerably, and then there are the various accompaniments and fresh and store chutneys, relishes and suchlike; and altogether there is so vast a range of things which may be brought into the making of a curry that the mere giving of recipes is not enough and it is worth discussing these items individually.

STAPLE INGREDIENTS

Chicken either raw or cooked: recipes will be given for both. Young birds are naturally preferable, but if an older fowl is to be used it may be made tender in the way described on page 634.

Young rabbits are excellent, and if treated in the way described on page 671 may be almost indistinguishable from chicken in flavour.

Shell-fish. All kinds of shell-fish are used for curries; most popular is the prawn and in particular the large Dublin Bay prawn. These and other shell-fish are usually first cooked and then gently heated up in the curry sauce.   Recipes for curries of lobster and crayfish often call for a certain weight of cooked flesh, so that in buying this must be borne in mind. Crayfish tails render more meat in proportion to weight in the shell than do lobsters and langoustes: a rough guide is that about 2 lb. gross weight of the latter would give approximately ¾ lb. of flesh, whereas two crayfish tails weighing 1 lb. each would yield about 1¾ lb. of flesh.

Fresh, salt, or smoked fish may all be employed, preferably lightly fried before being finished off in the sauce.   Care, however, must be taken in the final cooking, or the fish will break up into small pieces.

Eggs.   Hard-boiled eggs used plain or stuffed in the way given in the recipe on page 415 may be used alone or in association with vegetables.

Vegetables may either be blanched and finished off in a curry sauce or be cooked altogether in the sauce.   Almost all vegetables may be employed, in mixture or alone; cucumbers and small zucchini are particularly suitable as additions to curries of shell-fish.

Fresh fruits.   Certain fresh fruits are excellent additions to many curries; banana, melon, firm-fleshed peaches or plums, even orange, grape-fruit, and pineapple, all find their place and add that refreshing quality which offsets the effect of the spices.   Bananas and melon and the firmer peaches may be lightly fried before being added to the rest of the curry, or the fruit may be served apart in a little of the curry sauce reserved for the purpose. At Winkfield we have a curry made exclusively of fruit which we like to serve as a first course at luncheon.

Dried fruits.   Raisins, sultanas, and other dried fruits are all suitable ingredients.

Meat.   Mutton is probably the most commonly used meat for curries, though both veal and pork are sometimes called for; the meat is usually partially cooked by frying and then finished off in the sauce.   If cold meat is to be employed it should be carefully trimmed of fat, skin, and gristle, cut in small pieces, and marinaded for some hours in the curry sauce before being gently heated up.

Rice.   The subject of rice and its cooking calls for something more than a short paragraph, and has already been dealt with (page 385).

Curry-powder, paste, and other spices

Reliable blends of curry-powder and curry-paste are essential.   The paste contains some ingredients not in the powder, and recipes often call for the use of both.   These should be bought in such quantities as may be used up in reasonable time; an old powder or one that has not been kept in an air-tight container loses much of its value.   In countries from which curries come the various spices are used individually in variations of both kind and quantity, the cook adjusting and blending to suit the dish in hand.

In this country we are apt to rely on a bought mixture, and while this may be excellent, the exclusive use of it tends to make all our curries taste alike. Now that one can buy separately many of the various concomitants, the cook who is interested will see that her store contains a small quantity of each of them as well as the more usual commercial mixture. (We have been able to obtain a wide range of these ingredients from the Bombay Emporium, 70 Grafton Way, London, W.1.)

In addition to this she will make a home-made curry-powder which has the great advantage of tasting fresh, and which may be used alone or in association with a bought brand. It would be tiresome perhaps for the Englishwoman to follow the example of the native cook and make this powder every time it might be required, and it is convenient to make in moderate quantities and keep in air-tight jars.

Here is a good standard recipe:

2 tablespoons each of turmeric, cumin, and coriander seed	2 teaspoons each of fenugreek, chillis, cardamon seed, and mace
1 tablespoon each of powdered ginger and ground pepper	1 teaspoon each of mustard seed, cloves, and poppy seed

The measuring of the seeds should be made after they are ground and sifted, and it is not serious if one or other of them has to be omitted. Coriander, cumin, pepper, cardamon, chillis, mustard, and poppy seed should be ground or crushed by pounding in a mortar, then sifted. Add them to the cloves, mace, fenugreek, dry ginger, and turmeric, which are usually bought in powder form. Then sieve again all together, but with as little movement as possible or everyone in the kitchen will fall to sneezing.

In addition to these bought seeds and spices we find it convenient to grow in the garden fresh coriander and dill seed. The latter is good to add to a curry when fish is the main ingredient, and for certain delicately flavoured curries. Fresh ripe coriander seeds are a really excellent addition to a large range of curry and rice dishes. The important word there is ripe: unripe coriander seed has an unpleasant taste. It may still be green, but should be fully grown, and becoming firm.

The heating or pepper agent

It is inadvisable, with the intention of heightening the 'heat' of a curry, to increase to any great degree the amount of curry-powder called for in a recipe. It is true that the strength of these commercially prepared powders varies, and what may be an adequate amount of one kind will be inadequate of another; but once this adjustment is arrived at it should be remembered that in thus seeking to increase the pepperiness one is also adding to the proportion of other spices, some of them of pungent and pervading qualities, and an unpleasant taste may result. It is by the use of such things as chillis, fresh, dried, or preserved, chilli powder, cayenne, green ginger, and mustard seed that one may get the required effect. Chillis may be bought fresh in good fruit shops; the hot ones may be grown in a cool greenhouse along with the valuable sweet peppers, and these may be easily preserved, the simplest method being to fill a bottle with the long thinnish fruits, packing it reasonably tight, adding sherry to cover and corking well—after a few weeks both chillis and sherry may be used and will keep for years; and chilli powder may be kept in air-tight jars. It may be noted here that the effect of chillis is increased in proportion to the length of time they remain in the sauce; for example, a curry made to-day may be reasonably hot at the finish of the cooking, but if it is allowed to stand overnight with the chillis in the sauce it will be a great deal hotter on the morrow. Additional fresh green ginger, thinly sliced, chopped, or pounded, or powdered ginger, a touch of cayenne, and additional ground mustard seed, may each and all of them be used to the same effect.

Nut milks

In these we have one of the most delicious concomitants of curry, and for a long time our cooking in this direction faltered because it was almost impossible to get the most important of these, the coco-nut, nor was it easy for some years to replace this by fresh ground almonds or brazil-nuts or even by the ground almonds and desiccated coco-nut that one buys in tins. But now the appearance of the coco-nut in the fruit shops is a signal to the cooks. Nut milk is not, as you might think, the juice which is poured out of a coco-nut. It is an infusion of the grated nut meat in very hot milk, water, or stock, and the infusion is made in such a way that the last possible flavour of the nut is extracted. Here is one way of making it:

Grate the flesh of half a coco-nut into a basin and add ½ pint boiling water, stir well and allow to stand for half an hour or longer. Strain, and squeeze through a muslin. The result of this is a very rich highly flavoured creamy substance, something which, added to the curry at the end of cooking, so that its flavour will not be lost, will give subtlety to the dish. A further infusion may be made by using the grated flesh a second time; this time it may be diluted with as much as a pint of boiling liquid. Again it is strained and squeezed to the last drop through a muslin. This second infusion is often used in the cooking of the curry rather than as a last-minute addition, that is to say as the liquid with which one dilutes the sauce. When coco-nuts are not available, or when for some reason almond milk is required, the following recipe is suitable: 4 oz. sweet almonds, 2 bitter almonds thoroughly pounded, ½ pint boiling liquid, water, milk, or stock. The infusion should stand for 20–30 minutes before being strained and squeezed through muslin. This again should be added at the end of cooking, for it has a delicate flavour easily dissipated.

For ground almonds or desiccated coco-nut 3 tablespoons of either of these or a mixture of the two to ½ pint of boiling liquid will serve. Brazil-nuts may be pounded and treated in the same way as coco-nuts or fresh almonds, and make an excellent substitute.

Herbs

Any of the following may be called for and it is useful to grow them all: bay-leaf, basil, fennel, thyme, marjoram, savory, coriander, and dill. Dried herbs may at need be substituted.

Sweet-sour

This is an essential part of a curry in that it produces a refreshing taste, a sharpness to offset the rich flavour of the spice. A simple way to introduce it is by the addition of a little lemon juice and sugar to the curry. Jellies, seedless jams (apricot, plum and suchlike), and chutneys are excellent, and may be used to replace the more correct and more acid tamarind; indeed, if tamarind is used extra sugar is required. An excellent tamarind sauce for a chicken curry will be found in the Winkfield chapter (page 993). Dried fruit, such as seedless raisins and sultanas, thin slices of ripe dessert apples, and sections of orange and grape-fruit cut from the skin as for a fruit salad, are all good; the two last should be added just before the end of cooking.

Sweet peppers are excellent for many dishes and good in most curries, and when possible it is worth growing a few in a cool greenhouse; they may also be bought from good fruit shops.

The liquid with which the sauce is made

This varies according to the dish in hand, and may be chicken, fish, or meat stock, tomato juice or vegetable liquor (i.e. the water in which such vegetables as potatoes, rice, asparagus, and green peas have been cooked). In some cases sweetened fruit juice is excellent. Some Indian cooks hold that water is the only suitable liquid for the purpose, and there is also the second infusion of nut milk already mentioned.

Thickening agents

When the staple part of the dish has to be cooked for some time in the curry sauce a thin or thinnish liquid will probably be called for, but for the simple warming through of already cooked ingredients (particularly if, as in the case of hard-boiled eggs, they are non-absorbent) a creamier sauce may be required; for this purpose a thickening agent will be needed. Ordinary flour, rice flour, and potato flour are all suitable. Some recipes call for ground rice, some for the use of liquid in which the rice has been cooked, and which, when reduced, becomes creamy and thick. In certain vegetable curries a little freshly cooked potato may be mashed up and added to the sauce.

COLD CURRIES

Certain shell-fish, hard-boiled eggs, chicken, and fruit in particular make excellent cold curries, and may be served with perfectly cooked well-seasoned cold rice. In this case a cold creamy sauce is often handed separately as for Œufs Durs Soleil d'Or, page 987.

The various chutneys and sauces that are served with curries will be dealt with in a separate section of this chapter, so that now we come to the making of the curry sauce.

In order to emphasize the simplicity of the base on which the range of dishes may be built up, here is a recipe for the most elementary form of curry sauce:

1–1½ oz. good dripping, butter, oil, margarine, or other good frying fat	¾–1 pint liquid (according to what is used, and whether for reheating or cooking en-
4 oz. shallots or onions	tirely) of the kinds named
1 tablespoon curry-powder	above
1 tablespoon flour (if thicken- ing is required)	seasoning

Heat the fat gently (all the cooking should be unhurried); add the sliced or chopped onions and cook until golden, add curry-powder and continue cooking for 3 or 4 minutes longer, add flour and cook for another minute or so. Withdraw saucepan from the fire, add liquid gradually, stirring briskly. Bring to boil, adjust seasoning, simmer 15–20 minutes. The subjection of the curry-powder to the heat of the fat is important; when the powder is merely added to the boiling liquid one often gets a rough taste. You will now have the simplest form of curry sauce for vegetables, eggs, chicken or what you will. This, as you see, is childishly simple, and it is in the addition and adjustment of all the other interesting and suitable ingredients that the art of curry-making lies.

Here is another simple basic curry sauce, a little more complicated than the foregoing.

1½ oz. butter, margarine, or dripping	juice of ½ lemon and 1 dessert- spoon sugar, or
4 oz. shallots or onions	1 dessertspoon red-currant
a crushed clove of garlic	jelly or apricot jam
1 tablespoon curry-powder	¼ pint nut milk (use 1 large
1 teaspoon curry-paste	tablespoon ground almond
1 tablespoon flour	or desiccated coco-nut [1] and
¾ pint liquid	1 tea-cup boiling water;
seasoning	make 1 hour before using and squeeze well through a muslin)

1. Melt the fat in a saucepan.

2. Add chopped shallots or onions and garlic, cook gently for a few minutes until they begin to turn colour, but do not allow to burn.

3. Add curry-powder and paste and continue cooking 3 or 4 more minutes.

4. Add flour, cook again for 1 minute.

5. Add the liquid gradually, adjust seasoning, and simmer for 20 minutes.

6. Add the sweet-sour, i.e. the lemon and sugar or red-currant jelly, and simmer another minute or two.

The sauce should have the consistency of cream. Skim the surface if necessary. It is now ready for the addition of cooked vegetables, eggs,

[1] Or see method with fresh coco-nut on page 403.

prawns, or what you will.   Heat up such ingredients slowly in the sauce, add the nut milk a few minutes before serving.   Vegetables may with advantage be simmered for some time in the curry sauce in order that they shall absorb as much of the flavour as possible.   Such prolonged cooking would not be suitable for eggs or prawns.

If a curry is prepared the day before it is to be eaten and is cooked in a metal saucepan, it should be taken out of this and allowed to remain overnight in a glass, fireproof, or china dish.   When cold meat or cold chicken is to be used for curry it is a good plan to allow it to marinade for some time in the sauce before being finally heated up.

N.B. A curry is a dish which can be 'stretched' by the addition of ingredients of a secondary nature—fruits, vegetables, hard-boiled eggs, for instance—so it would be a mistake to be too precise about the numbers that any dish will serve.   It may be borne in mind that a $2\frac{1}{2}$-lb. chicken adequately serves 4 and a $3\frac{1}{2}$-lb. chicken 6 people.

Here are two recipes for chicken curry made with raw chicken: the first moderate, the second quite hot; the first plain, the second richer.   Both dishes should be started well ahead of time, and may with advantage be made a day in advance.

CHICKEN CURRY (1)

a roasting chicken cut up as directed on page 636, flour and a pinch of turmeric to sprinkle with, and oil or butter for frying

Stock

2 onions, 1 carrot	seasoning
a bouquet garni with a bay-leaf	$1\frac{1}{2}$ pints water
6 peppercorns	

Curry sauce

6 oz. shallots	1 tablespoon curry-powder
1 clove of garlic, crushed	1 dessertspoon curry-paste
$1\frac{1}{2}$–2 oz. dripping, butter, or margarine	1 level tablespoon flour

Finishing

nut milk made of $\frac{1}{2}$ a fresh coco-nut, grated, or 3 tablespoons desiccated coco-nut or ground almonds and $\frac{1}{2}$ pint water (see page 403)
1 tablespoon red-currant jelly or other sweet-sour

Put the pieces of chicken in cold water.   With the débris, feet, neck, liver, etc., and the stock ingredients given above make a rich broth, either by simmering for 30–40 minutes or by cooking with a pressure cooker (see page 1168), which is quicker and gives a richer broth.   Strain and skim. Make an infusion of nut milk in the way described and set aside.

Take a pan large enough to hold everything.   With the ingredients given above proceed to make the curry sauce.   Melt fat, cook shallots and garlic, add powder and paste, cook again, add flour, continue cooking, dilute first with a pint of broth, bring to the boil and allow to simmer while chicken is prepared.   The remaining broth may be added during cooking if required.   Take out pieces of chicken, dry thoroughly, sprinkle with a little flour mixed with a pinch or two of turmeric, fry the pieces in a frying-pan in butter or oil to a pale gold, lift out, drain, and add to curry sauce. Allow them to marinade in this for 30–40 minutes before cooking is continued. Then over low heat bring to boil, simmer in covered pan for 45–50 minutes or until chicken is thoroughly cooked. Ten minutes before the end of cooking add the infusion of coco-nut milk and the sweet-sour. Adjust the seasoning and the dish is now ready to serve. Serve with two varieties of chutney at least, poppadums or 'last-minute' biscuits, and Bombay duck, if available. Both sweet peppers (emptied of seed and finely sliced) and bananas are good additions to the curry and will help out the main ingredients.

CHICKEN CURRY (2)

A hot curry made richer by the addition of almonds and cream.

a roasting chicken cut up as directed on page 636
1 small fresh coco-nut
½ lb. sweet almonds, blanched and fried till brown
grated rind of 1 lemon
4 oz. onions, 1½ oz. fat for frying, preferably clarified butter
2 tablespoons curry-powder

salt
3 bay-leaves
2 small hot chillis
juice of 2 lemons and 2 table-spoons sugar
a few tablespoons cream to finish
2 chutneys and poppadums or 'last-minute' biscuits (see page 418)

Infuse grated nut in 1 pint boiling water and set aside. Pound almonds to a paste with the grated rind of lemon in a mortar, or chop finely and crush with a wooden spoon. In a good-sized pan melt fat and cook onions gently until turning colour, add curry-powder and cook for a few minutes, add the pint of coco-nut milk and salt to taste, the pounded almonds, bay-leaves, chillis, and lemon juice and sugar; simmer a few minutes and add chicken, bring to boil and simmer 45 minutes. Finish off with cream at last moment. Serve with two chutneys and perhaps lime pickle, and poppadums or 'last-minute' biscuits. If the chicken is a large one a little extra liquid may be required and may be obtained from a second infusion of the grated nut.

CHICKEN CURRY (3)
made with water and no stock

1 uncooked chicken cut up as directed on page 636
4 oz. onions
1 clove of garlic, crushed
1½ oz. dripping or butter
1 dessertspoon curry-powder
½ lb. ripe tomatoes
a few thin slices of green ginger, pounded

1 pint water or nut milk
salt
1 tablespoon red-currant jelly or other sweet-sour
1 dessertspoon fresh ripe coriander seed (if possible)
2 seeded, shredded sweet peppers
a little cream

Proceed as in previous recipes, adding ginger, sweet peppers, and tomatoes (peeled and quartered) with the liquid, the coriander seed towards the end of cooking, and the cream just before serving.

CHICKEN CURRY (4) ('MRS MACKENZIE'S CURRY')

made with spices and no mixed curry-powder

1 small chicken
2 dessertspoons turmeric
1 breakfast-cup cream
4 oz. onions
1½ oz. dripping
½ teaspoon powdered cloves
½ teaspoon cardamon seed,
   1 teaspoon coriander seed,
and 1 teaspoon pepper, all
   crushed or in powder form
1 breakfast-cup stock or vegetable liquor
salt
a few tablespoons almond or
   coco-nut milk, made as
   described on page 403
freshly made chutney

Cut chicken in small pieces.   Mix turmeric and cream, pour over chicken, and leave an hour or so.   Fry onions to pale yellow in the fat, add cloves, coriander, cardamon, and pepper.   Continue to fry a few minutes, add stock, then chicken and cream and turmeric mixture, and allow to simmer an hour or more.   Add seasoning and nut milk and serve with a freshly made chutney.

Ideally, young birds should be used for curry-making, but a good curry can be made from an old bird if it is either cooked in a pressure cooker (see page 1172) or subjected to a preliminary cooking as described in the poultry chapter (page 634).   Then remove from heat, being careful on account of steam, and when the pan has slightly cooled off add about a pint of water. Allow to cook for about half an hour with the lid on.   Set aside all liquid, cut up chicken, skinning and trimming each piece, and make a curry sauce with the following ingredients in the way described on page 405, adding tomatoes and coriander during cooking.

4 oz. onions
2 oz. margarine or dripping
1 large, sweet dessert apple to
   be fried with the onion
1½ tablespoons curry-powder
1 tablespoon flour
1 pint chicken stock
4 tomatoes, skinned and sliced
2 teaspoons salt
3 tablespoons chutney
1 tablespoon fresh ripe coriander seed, crushed (if
   possible)
a little cream to finish

COLD CURRIED CHICKEN

2 small roasting birds
tarragon (1 or 2 sprigs for
   each bird)
2 oz. onion and 2 oz. carrot (if
   to be poached) *or*
butter for roasting

Sauce

to be prepared the day before the dish is required

1 large onion
3–4 tablespoons butter
2 tablespoons good curry-
   powder
3 tablespoons flour

boiled rice
1½ pints chicken stock
lemon juice
2 tablespoons red-currant jelly
   or apricot jam
½–1 gill cream

'last-minute' biscuits (see
   page 418)

Put a sprig or two of tarragon inside each bird and either poach in water with vegetables to flavour or gently pot roast with butter. Joint when cold.

Prepare this sauce the day before: Finely chop the onion, soften it in butter, add curry-powder, fry for a few minutes, add flour, mix and pour on chicken stock. Simmer 30–40 minutes. Add a good squeeze of lemon juice and red-currant jelly. Mix well and strain. When cold beat in enough cream to soften the flavour. Pour over the chicken and leave for some hours before serving. Serve with boiled rice, well chilled, and 'last-minute' biscuits.

The following cold curry dish was popular in my young days for picnic parties. Then chickens were cheap and plentiful and we used only the white flesh of plump young birds for the dish itself, using all dark meat to make the rich broth. Now, however, we are of necessity less choosy and use the dark meat, sometimes eking it out with the choice portions of young wild rabbit, but if this is done the flesh from the back only is used, and no rabbit meat goes into the stock, which is made of chicken only.

COLD CHICKEN CURRY

This dish must be made the day before it is wanted.

1 large or 2 medium young birds (if any rabbit is to be added it must first be soaked in vinegar and water in the way described on page 671)	cucumber salad fresh sweet peppers gherkins (optional)

Cut the flesh from the bones. Set aside.

Stock

all the trimmings and bones of the raw chicken	2 carrots, sliced
a slice of raw ham or bacon	1 onion, sliced
a head of celery or celeriac, sliced, or 1 teaspoon celery seed	a bouquet garni
	1 pint water

Allow this to simmer with the lid off until it is reduced to ½ pint, or alternatively make this stock in a pressure cooker with ½ pint water only. Strain, cool, and skim.

Curry

4 oz. shallots	shredded sweet pepper, 24 finely chopped almonds, 1 teaspoon chopped tarragon, and 1 teaspoon grated ginger
1 ripe dessert apple	
1 dessertspoon curry-powder	
1½ oz. butter or margarine for frying	lemon juice
to this may be added 2 heaped tablespoons seedless raisins or sultanas, a seeded,	1 teaspoon sugar, or more to taste
	seasoning

Fry the shallots, apple, and curry-powder in the usual way, add raisins, pepper, almonds, tarragon, and ginger, and the chicken flesh finely chopped up. Allow the mixture to lie for half an hour, then add the stock. Simmer for half an hour, add lemon juice and sugar, adjust seasoning. Cook a few more minutes. Turn the whole into a basin which has been rinsed in cold water. Allow to get completely cold. The following day it may be turned out on to a dish, for it should retain its shape, the strong stock having turned into jelly. It is garnished with heaps of dry, cold cucumber salad, shredded fresh sweet peppers, and, if you like, sliced gherkins.

N.B. A little sherry from the preserved chilli bottle is a good addition to the liquid.

Here is a good way of making a mild curry with chicken already cooked.

MILD CHICKEN CURRY

Mix together:

1 dessertspoon turmeric	1 tablespoon Worcestershire
1 dessertspoon pounded green	or Harvey sauce
ginger (optional)	1 teaspoon salt
2 saltspoons cayenne or a fresh	
chilli, pounded	

Cut up the cold chicken in suitable pieces. Score the flesh and rub this mixture well in. Leave the pieces in it several hours, overnight if possible.

Take:

2 oz. almonds, and a nut of	2 shallots, sliced
butter for frying them	1 clove of garlic
the rind of a lemon, grated	

Fry the almonds to a golden brown and pound with shallots, garlic, and lemon rind to a paste.

Put all the above except the chicken into a pan, and add ¾ pint water. Simmer gently for 10 minutes, add the chicken and continue to simmer 15 minutes. Finish off with 4–5 tablespoons thick cream, the juice of half a lemon, and a little chopped chutney. If this recipe is required for un-cooked chicken the liquid must be increased, and 45–50 minutes of simmer-ing will be necessary.

In the Winkfield chapter there will be found a very rich curry made with almonds called ·Almond Chicken Curry (page 1013) and 'Coronation' Chicken Curry (page 1012), a delicately flavoured, bland dish.

Rabbits

Young rabbits make excellent curry, and if treated in the way described on page 671 may be hardly distinguishable from chicken. Do not include any part except the back, shoulders, and legs. After the preliminary all-night soaking in water and vinegar, wash and dry the pieces of rabbit. Cook them gently for 1–1½ hours in salted water with sliced onion and 2 bay-leaves. When cooked remove flesh from bones and cut up in pieces.

Make a curry sauce as described on page 405, with onion, garlic, curry-powder and paste, and thickening, using either water or the rabbit stock for dilution. Simmer 15–20 minutes, adjust seasoning. While this is simmering take 4 large onions, slice, soften in a little fat, add to the sauce, boil up, and skim if necessary. Put in the rabbit, warm up slowly. Finish off with a gill of cream or coco-nut milk and a good squeeze of lemon juice.

Now that conserve of tamarind is available again the following curry of rabbit is worth consideration. It may with advantage be prepared one or even two days ahead of time. This curry is best if the rabbit is allowed to lie in the sauce for at least 24 hours, and it may be heated up at least once in the interim in order to achieve a complete blend of flavours. In this case the lemon and cream or coco-nut milk must be reserved for adding just before serving.

2 young rabbits prepared as above	2 tablespoons flour mixed with 1 tablespoon curry-powder fat for frying the rabbit

Cut up rabbits and allow to lie for an hour in the seasoned flour. Fry the pieces of rabbit to a golden brown.

Stock

2 onions	1–2 peppercorns
2 bay-leaves	a bouquet garni
1 carrot	1 quart water

Simmer rabbit in the stock for 1–1½ hours.

Curry mixture

4 oz. onions	2 cloves of garlic
1½ oz. dripping	2 tablespoons curry-powder
1 tablespoon flour	3 tablespoons chutney
1 good tablespoon tamarind conserve worked with 1 tea-spoon sugar	1–1½ pints of the strained rabbit stock

Make the sauce in the way described on page 405, adding tamarind and chutney after it has simmered 15 minutes; add pieces of rabbit and finish off with lemon juice and if you like cream or coco-nut milk.

Shell-fish

Prawns, Dublin Bay prawns, lobsters, and langoustes are all excellent material for *de luxe* and classic curries. The cooked flesh of these may be gently warmed through in any one of the curry sauces already given, but there are some recipes particularly suitable to shell-fish. Some are mild and nutty in flavour, qualities in keeping with the delicate flesh of Dublin Bay prawns or young hen lobsters. Here is a classic prawn curry of such delicacy. It may be composed of prawns only or is better still with the addition of cucumber. Dublin Bay prawns are best, and 3 or 4 should be allowed for each person. For a dozen prawns 2 medium-sized tender cucumbers will suffice.

PRAWN CURRY (CLASSIC)

1 dozen Dublin Bay prawns
2 medium-sized cucumbers
1 coco-nut

1 teaspoon lemon juice
1 dessertspoon finely chopped
   dill or fennel

Sauce

6 oz. shallots or onions
1 clove of garlic
1½–2 oz. butter
¼ teaspoon each of cloves and
   cinnamon

1 teaspoon each of turmeric
   and sugar
salt
1 dessertspoon flour

Prepare the two infusions of coco-nut as described on page 403. Prepare the prawns: remove heads, cut down the inner side of the shell and lift out the flesh. With the point of a sharp knife remove the black line running down the back. Dust with flour.

Peel cucumbers, cut in large pieces, and cook partially in water or milk, or if very tender sweat in a little butter and cook in its own juice. Make the curry sauce as described on page 405, using cloves, cinnamon, and turmeric in place of curry-powder, and diluting with the second infusion of coco-nut milk. To the simmering sauce add:

1 tablespoon green ginger,
   pounded

1 sweet pepper seeded and
   sliced

Continue simmering all together 30 minutes. Add prawns and cucumber and allow them to marinade in the sauce for half an hour. Finally bring all gently to boiling-point, add the lemon juice, the first infusion of coco-nut, and the dill or fennel.

SIMPLE PRAWN CURRY

½ lb. ordinary prawns or the
   required number of Dublin
   Bay prawns cut in pieces
4 oz. onions or shallots, sliced
2 oz. butter
1 clove of garlic, crushed
¼ lb. tomatoes, skinned and
   quartered

a short ½ pint water, tomato
   juice, or vegetable liquor
seasoning
1 dessertspoon curry-powder
lemon juice
cream or a little nut milk
chopped dill or fennel

Fry the onions or shallots and garlic in butter, add curry-powder and seasoning and after 3 or 4 minutes the tomatoes and the water, tomato juice, or vegetable liquor. Cook these well together, verify flavouring and seasoning, add the cooked prawns, and heat through. Finish off with lemon juice and cream or a little nut milk, and the dill or fennel. This is suitable for prawns alone or prawns and tomato or prawns and cucumber.

The following recipes are equally suitable for lobsters or crayfish. For other fish curries it is necessary first to cook the fish, preferably by frying, after it has been washed, dried, and sprinkled with flour mixed with a little turmeric. The cooked fish is added to the curry sauce and gently simmered for a few minutes. One must be careful not to overcook the fish or it will break up, and the curry will neither look nor taste very good.

Here is a particularly good curry of shell-fish suitable for a party. It comes, not from India, but from Malaya.

LOBSTER CURRY (1)

2 lb. cooked lobster, crayfish, prawns, or a mixture of these (see note on weight of shell-fish on page 493)
1 small cucumber
3 gills coco-nut milk made in the way described (page 403)
1 clove of garlic, crushed
2 medium-sized onions, sliced
2–3 oz. butter
1½ gills stock made from the trimmings and shells of the fish cooked with an onion

a bouquet garni
a small quantity of water if necessary, to which may be added a gill of white wine
1 dessertspoon strong tomato purée
1 oz. green ginger, sliced and pounded, or grated or preserved ginger may be used instead
1 tablespoon lemon juice
1 teaspoon sugar
boiled rice

Mix together the following:

1 tablespoon curry-powder
½ teaspoon salt
½ teaspoon cinnamon
¼ teaspoon ground cloves

1 small saltspoon ground cumin seed
a pinch of ground chilli powder or cayenne

Prepare the cucumber as described in the recipe for the classic prawn curry. Cut up the cooked lobster meat into suitably sized pieces and set aside. Take a large pan, melt in it the butter, and cook onions and garlic to a pale golden colour, add the mixture of powders given above and continue cooking for a few minutes. Add the lobster stock, the bouquet, and stir in the tomato purée. Continue cooking for 10 minutes, then add the lobster meat, cucumber, grated or pounded ginger, and coco-nut milk. Simmer very gently for 25 minutes. The sauce should be creamy, and if not sufficiently so allow it to reduce a little, and if too thick add a little liquid. Add lemon juice and sugar. Serve with boiled rice.

N.B. Fresh green peppers, seeded, blanched, and shredded, are an excellent addition to this dish.

LOBSTER CURRY (2)

2 small lobsters
1 small cucumber, blanched
4 oz. mushrooms, sliced
1 pint water or white wine and water

a bouquet garni
1 sliced onion
2 shallots
2 oz. butter

Mix together the following:

1 dessertspoon each of ground ginger, turmeric, coriander, and cumin seed

2 large cloves of garlic crushed with salt
3 pounded chillis or ½ saltspoon cayenne

Cut the lobsters into small pieces, sprinkle over the above mixture, mix thoroughly and set aside. Make a stock with the pounded shells and heads of the lobsters and a pint of liquid (water or white wine and water as in previous recipe), a bouquet, and a sliced onion. Cook shallots in butter, add mushrooms, cucumber, and stock, add the lobster and all the spices in which it has been lying. Cover and simmer gently until the vegetables are cooked. Take care not to overcook. This should not be a sloppy curry, and if at the end of cooking there should be too much liquid it should be reduced by further cooking with the lid off the pan.

Here is an admirable sauce for cold curries, lobster, prawn, or egg, served with cold rice.

DELICATE SAUCE FOR COLD CURRIES

2 oz. butter	1 teaspoon flour
1 ripe dessert apple	a little liquid
4 shallots	mayonnaise or thick cream
1 teaspoon fresh ripe coriander seed	salad-dressing
	seasoning
1 good tablespoon curry-powder	a little lemon juice
	1 teaspoon sugar (optional)
a few sultanas	

Proceed in the usual way, frying apple with shallots, adding coriander seed with curry-powder and flour, and the sultanas with the liquid. Add this a tablespoon at a time, using just enough to make a thick paste: milk, water, or vegetable liquor will do, and coco-nut milk is best of all. Cool and mix this thickish paste with the mayonnaise or salad-dressing. Adjust seasoning, add lemon juice, and if liked the sugar.

This is a sauce of delicate flavour; the base of it, before the addition of the mayonnaise, may be used as the basis of a good cream soup.

Vegetable Curries

Many vegetables are suited for the main constituent of a curry dish. They may be cooked, or partially cooked, and finished off in a suitable sauce, and any of the above sauces may be used for this purpose. Care should be taken not to overcook the vegetables before the final simmering in the curry sauce. Cucumbers are excellent, as are young marrows, or better still the little zucchini mentioned in the vegetable chapter. Young and tender root vegetables in mixture, cauliflower, and broccoli are all suitable. Tomatoes or potatoes alone may form the main ingredients of a curry; the latter absorb a good deal of liquid.

TOMATO CURRY

1 lb. tomatoes, peeled and quartered	1 tablespoon grated green ginger
2 oz. butter or good beef dripping	coco-nut milk made in the way described (page 403) or vegetable liquor
4 oz. onions	seasoning
a clove of garlic	jelly or chutney
1 tablespoon curry-powder	boiled rice
1 dessertspoon flour	

Proceed in the usual way, frying the onions, curry-powder, and flour, then adding ginger and tomatoes. Simmer for a few minutes, dilute with coco-nut milk and simmer 15 minutes. Add jelly or chutney and adjust seasoning. Serve with plenty of boiled rice.

POTATO CURRY

Potatoes may be used alone or mixed with tomatoes as the main ingredient of the curry. The procedure is the same as before, the cooked, sliced, and sautéed potatoes being added to a thin curry sauce.

One final remark with regard to vegetable curries. In making the curry sauce the liquid to be used may be vegetable liquor, tomato juice, or, with advantage, the sweetened juice of stewed fruit such as gooseberries and plums, or even of tinned fruit. This adds a remarkably fresh taste to the curry, but it is necessary then to adjust the amount of chutney, jam, or other sweet-sour to be added, as this is already present in some degree in the liquid. Cooked chestnuts and chopped dessert apples are a good addition to vegetable curries.

CURRY OF MIXED VEGETABLES

2 lb. in all of cauliflower, Brussels sprouts, artichokes, peas, beans, celery, or whatever is available	2 or 3 tablespoons curry-powder
1 tablespoon flour mixed with 1 tablespoon turmeric powder	1 small tin of tomatoes (or ½ lb. fresh tomatoes and a little stock)
2 oz. fat for frying	2 teaspoons salt
2–3 onions	1 tablespoon coriander seed
2 apples	3 tablespoons chutney
	extra tomato juice or liquid if necessary
	a few tablespoons cream

Cut all vegetables except onions in suitable pieces; roll them in mixture of flour and turmeric powder. Fry them lightly in hot fat for a few minutes and set aside. Cut up onions and apples and fry. Add curry-powder and continue cooking a few minutes longer. Add tomatoes keeping back the juice if canned. Cook a little, adding finally tomato juice or stock. Season, add vegetables, coriander seed, and chutney, and simmer till vegetables are tender. Extra juice or liquid can be added if the sauce is too thick, and this will depend on the nature of the vegetables being cooked in it. Add cream immediately before serving.

Fruit Curries

Certain fruits make excellent mild curries which may be served alone or as accompaniments to hotter curries. Recipes for these will be found in the Winkfield chapter (pages 1014–15).

Egg Curries

Plain hard-boiled eggs may be warmed through in any of the curry sauces given, but better still is a stuffed hard-boiled egg in a creamy curry sauce.   For this purpose boil the egg hard and slice a piece off the top, just sufficient to enable the yolk to be taken out without breaking the white.   Pound the egg yolk, add a little cream, salt, pepper, a little curry-paste, some chopped chutney or chutney juice, and a touch of cayenne; adjust seasoning and flavours generally.   A little Worcestershire sauce is sometimes a good addition.   Pack the yolks, thus treated, carefully back into the egg, put back the slice cut off.   These are excellent cold coated with a cold sauce.   If to be hot they must be carefully warmed through in the curry sauce.   This is a particularly good type of curried egg, and more digestible to many people than a curry of plain hard-boiled eggs.

The following dish of poached eggs on fried bread surrounded by a creamy curry sauce is excellent, and liked by those who prefer poached eggs to hard-boiled:

POACHED EGGS IN CURRY SAUCE

Prepare the following sauce (it may with advantage be made a day in advance):

1 small onion or shallot, shredded	¾ pint vegetable stock, or water and tomato juice in equal proportions
1 oz. butter	
1 dessertspoon each of curry-powder and paste	1 dessertspoon sweet chutney
1 dessertspoon flour	1 dessertspoon fresh or desic-cated coco-nut
	1 teaspoon salt

Melt butter, fry onion till pale brown.   Add curry-paste and powder and cook slowly for 15 minutes.   Add flour, cook another 3 or 4 minutes. Dilute with liquid.   Add chutney, coco-nut, and salt.   Simmer for about an hour.   Fry slices of bread a quarter of an inch thick till crisp.   Keep hot.   Poach eggs, lay on fried bread.   Pour the sauce around and over the eggs.

Meat Curries

There is danger to curries from cooks who regard a curry as a réchauffé, which it should not be.   If for some reason or other cold cooked meat is to be used, it should be marinaded for some hours in the sauce before being gently warmed up.   Cooked meat may be used for curries in the same way as chicken, lean meat, preferably mutton or veal, being used.   It is cut in small squares, all fat and gristle being removed, and one of the most interesting ways of using it is in kebabs.

KEBABS

Mutton or veal probably serves the purpose best.   The raw meat is cut in thick slices about an inch square and half an inch thick.   To these are added pieces of parboiled onion, thin slices of green ginger, and bay-leaves.   These are arranged on wooden or silver skewers in the following order: mutton, onion, ginger, and bay-leaf, repeating until the skewer is filled. They are then lightly fried in butter in a frying-pan with an ounce of finely chopped onion and a teaspoon of salt. When brown on all sides they are put in a good curry sauce, allowed to lie in it for half an hour at least, and then simmered in it until completely cooked. They may be served with any of the usual curry accompaniments.

Another method of making kebabs gives a drier dish. Cut the meat into thick slices or squares as before, use small pickling onions either whole or cut in two. Sprinkle with a good curry-powder, and allow to lie in this for half an hour before cooking. Heat 3 oz. butter (or half butter and half margarine) in a frying-pan, and fry the kebabs in this. When brown lift out, put on to a dish, and pour what butter there remains in the frying-pan evenly over each of them.

DRY CURRIES

A dry curry may be made by cooking the basic ingredients in a thin curry sauce until the sauce is entirely, or almost entirely, reduced. This is done over an extremely slow heat, and by reason of the evaporation and consequent reduction the peppery ingredients, undiluted with liquid, give a hot curry. Make a curry sauce in the ordinary way, but without flour or any other form of thickening. Put the meat or chicken or whatever is required into this and simmer it until cooked. Set it aside to marinade for half an hour. Take a fresh saucepan, put in it a dessertspoon or so of butter and allow it to melt. Lift out of the curry sauce the chicken or meat with a little of the sauce adhering to it. Arrange this on the bottom of the saucepan in which the butter has been melted, stir gently and carefully until such time as the sauce is nearly evaporated or entirely so, in which case the surface of the meat will become slightly powdery.

DRY MUTTON CURRY

1 lb. uncooked mutton cut into ½-inch squares	1 tablespoon curry-powder
1 oz. butter	1 teaspoon curry-paste
2 oz. onion or shallot	1 tablespoon grated coco-nut
1 clove of garlic, crushed	1 teaspoon green ginger
	1½ gills mutton stock

Melt butter. Fry onion or shallot and garlic to golden brown. Add curry-paste and powder and continue cooking for a few minutes. Add coco-nut and ginger and cook for a few more minutes. Add meat and mutton stock and cook exceedingly gently with the lid off till stock has reduced almost completely, or, if preferred, until dry and powdery. This may take 1–1½ hours. The pan must be shaken from time to time to prevent meat from sticking.

For other curries and curry sauces see Winkfield chapter, pages 1012–18.

ACCOMPANIMENTS TO CURRY
rice, poppadums, Bombay duck, chutneys, etc.

RICE

The dish of rice which is handed before the curry itself should present a white pyramid of grains of rice, each one separate from the other.

Directions for cooking rice will be found on page 386.

BOMBAY DUCK, POPPADUMS, AND 'LAST-MINUTE' BISCUITS

Bombay duck. The pieces should be toasted before being sent up to be handed with the curry.

Poppadums may be toasted, put in the oven, or, best of all, plunged into hot fat for a moment, then drained and served hot and crisp. When these are unobtainable we replace them by a 'last-minute' biscuit which only resembles them in its thinness and crispness, for the ingredients for poppadums are not obtainable in this country. The 'last-minute' biscuits are made as follows:

Take 3 or 4 tablespoons flour, season well with salt, and if you like add a few caraway seeds and a little red pepper. Mix with cream or milk to a stiff paste. Knead well, roll out a little, then cut into cubes of about 1–1½ inches diameter. Take each cube and roll it and fold it and roll it again, finally beating it with the rolling-pin until it is paper thin and the size of a tea-plate. Prick each slice all over with a fork, lay on a lightly greased and floured baking-sheet, and bake for 3 minutes or so in a very hot oven. Because of the size of these biscuits they have to be cooked in relays. They should blister and be absolutely thin and crisp, breaking at a light touch. The name 'last-minute' biscuits is a slight misnomer, in that they take quite a little time to beat and roll and prepare. The only short time concerned is that of baking.

N.B. 'Last-minute' biscuits should be paper thin and uneven in shape, just as they come when beaten and rolled.

CHUTNEYS

In a great many English households the general idea about chutney is that it is something either to be bought or made from fruit at home, bottled, and kept during the winter. Many chutneys are excellent, and recipes will follow in the chapter called 'The Store Cupboard.' It is not perhaps so generally accepted that chutney may be made at the time that the curry is being cooked, but it is a good plan to do this. These fresh-tasting adjuncts are not troublesome to make and add greatly to the dish. The late Mrs Mackenzie, who lived long in the East, gave me the recipe for chicken curry quoted on page 408, and added at the same time the following list of chutneys which she said it was customary to serve among many others; and I quote them here as she gave them to me, though we sometimes add sugar to certain of them. Store chutneys are sweet, sugar being a preservative, and sweet chutneys please many English palates. The fresh chutneys are often unsweetened, though of course sugar may be added. It is a good plan to offer both, perhaps two fresh and one store chutney with a curry, although a great many more are served in countries where curry is the national dish, together with pickles, nuts, and relishes of many kinds.

Fresh Chutneys from Mrs Mackenzie

TOMATO CHUTNEY

Skin and cut up a tomato, cut up celery and a little onion. Moisten with salad-oil and vinegar. Mix all together with 1 green chilli cut up small.

MINT CHUTNEY

Finely chop 2 handfuls of mint with a pinch of sugar. Moisten with a little vinegar, a small clove of garlic, and a chopped green chilli. (We pound the mint with sugar and garlic.)

APPLE CHUTNEY

Cut apple into shreds, add minced onion, moisten with vinegar, and sprinkle with parsley and 1 chopped green chilli.

GREEN PEPPER, APPLE, AND RAISIN CHUTNEY

2 apples	salt
2 sweet green peppers	juice of 1 lemon, more if
2 tablespoons seedless raisins	required
1 small saltspoon cayenne	sugar (optional)
1 small saltspoon paprika	

Core and peel apples, seed and scald peppers, add raisins, chop all together very finely or put them through the mincer; they may then with advantage be pounded in the mortar. Add lemon juice and seasoning, adding sugar if liked and more lemon juice if required.

TAMARIND CHUTNEY

Pound together 1 tablespoon tamarind pulp, ditto green ginger, season with salt, minced green chillis, and 1 tablespoon mustard seed roasted in butter. Mix thoroughly.

BEETROOT CHUTNEY

Grate horse-radish and chop beetroot finely. Mix in equal proportions; add salt and sugar to taste and moisten with vinegar. This is very hot.

CUCUMBER CHUTNEY

Prepare in the same way as apple.

To these we add the following fresh chutneys:

SHREDDED APPLE

Mix dessert apples, finely shredded and well sweetened, finely chopped mint, and a little vinegar.   This is sweet-sour and minty in flavour.

TOMATOES

These are skinned, emptied of seed, and chopped up with chives, fresh chilli, and celery, and a little vinegar, pepper and salt, and sugar to taste.

MASHED POTATO

This is made with well and lightly mashed potato, finely chopped chives or the top of a sprouting onion, grated green ginger, seasoning, sugar, vinegar, and chilli, all mixed with potato while hot but allowed to cool. Garlic crushed with salt may be added.

Here is a fresh chutney which we use for general purposes:

1 apple, grated	1 tablespoon horse-radish, grated
1 onion, grated	
3 tomatoes, chopped	1 clove of garlic crushed with
3 stalks of celery, chopped	1 teaspoon salt
1 tablespoon mint	1 fresh chilli, seeded and
1–2 tablespoons vinegar	chopped, or a bottled one,
1 tablespoon chopped fennel	or paprika

All these are heated together to boiling-point and served either hot or cold.
We also like to add the flesh of an orange to a fresh chutney.   The orange is peeled, all the white pith removed, and then with a sharp knife the flesh is cut out of the sections from between the membranes.   This adds a particularly good taste.

And finally something which may be described as a 'last-minute' chutney:

2 or 3 tablespoons jelly or jam, seedless for choice, apricot or plum being very good	1 tablespoon fennel seed, or any other herb which may be liked
1 onion, finely chopped	chilli, fresh or preserved, or
1 clove of garlic, crushed	cayenne
	salt, pepper, and a little vinegar

Heat all until well mixed and serve hot or cold.
The Eastern cook sends up many other side-dishes with his curry: nuts, fish pastes, shrimps, fried ham, and pickles, particularly pickled lime. With us so many accompaniments would probably prove too much, but there are two additions much liked, the first a slice of pineapple with a sharp dressing, the second a dish of spiced prunes (see page 1106) stuffed with a salted or devilled almond round which is wrapped a fillet of anchovy.
For store chutneys see Chapter XXXV, pages 1121–6.

Here is the shopping list referred to on page 384:

		s.	d.
1. Tinned pimentos, large size		3	6
good for rice dishes, hors-d'œuvre, and for salads			
2. Chinese mushroom sauce		2	9
for rice and pasta dishes			
3. Tinned water chestnuts		4	0
crisp and sweet-tasting for curries and rice dishes			
4. Okra, large tin		4	6
for rice and pasta dishes and sauces			
5. Mangoes, large tin		7	0
to add to curries or to make a salad to go with them			
6. Mango pulp, medium		3	9
to add to curry sauce			
7. Green ginger, 1 lb. (in season March and April)		4	0
admirable in curries and other dishes; when out of season replaced by preserved ginger			
8. Jar of guava jelly...		3	0
a frill for adding to curries or rice dishes, excellent with hot water-biscuits and cream cheese as a luncheon finish			

9. Poppy seed, 2 oz. ⎫ 1 0
 Cardamon seed, 2 oz. ⎪ 4 0
 Whole coriander, 2 oz. ⎬ all used for curry and 8
 Chilli powder, 2 oz. ⎪ rice dishes 1 6
 Turmeric, 4 oz. ⎪ 1 0
 Cumin seed, 2 oz. ⎪ 1 0
 Tamarind, 1 lb. ⎭ 2 0

All the above were from the Bombay Emporium, 70 Grafton Way, W.1, and the following from Del Monicos, 64 Old Compton Street, W.1.:

Tinned lychees	2	9
delicious in a fruit curry and even more so in an accompanying salad, mixed perhaps with ripe pears		
Small tin of Italian roast pimentos	1	6
Jar of pickled green peppers	1	10
For use when fresh peppers are out of season. (We grow a few of these in a cool greenhouse each year, canning any that may be spared, but they are not sufficient for our needs.)		

With such materials and others on your shelves you can be sure of variety and interest, and even if you have to resort to the tin-opener for a main dish, you will have the wherewithal to vary the contents of the tins with good effect.

In the herb chapter will be found notes on such flavouring ingredients as may easily be grown in an average garden.

XV

Pastas, Pasta Dishes, and Batters

PASTAS

UNDER this heading we are again concerned with a type of food which, having little flavour of its own, may be used as a vehicle for other flavours. With macaroni, spaghetti, nouilles and suchlike it is customary to serve sauces containing cheese, tomato purée, or onions, or to cover them with a rich coulis containing mushrooms or chicken livers. Macaroni, spaghetti, canneloni, etc., are prepared commercially, nouilles and ravioli also, though these may be made at home; gnocchi are made at home.

Spaghetti is the long thin form of pasta, macaroni is in thickish pipe-stem tubes, and canneloni present short lengths of wide diameter which may be filled with a variety of stuffings. Vermicelli, one of the finest of the pastas, is used more often in soups and stews than as a separate dish. Macaroni, spaghetti, nouilles, and canneloni are first boiled in water before being dressed with a sauce or made up into a dish.

As with rice the pastas should be boiled in quantities of water, allowing 2–3 quarts for every ½ lb. of pasta. Neither macaroni nor spaghetti should be broken up. If they are introduced gradually into fast-boiling salted water it is a simple matter to coil them round the pan as they soften. After this the water must be brought to boiling-point again, but from that time onwards should be allowed only to simmer. A pasta should be allowed to poach rather than to boil. This is a definite point of difference between pastas and rice. It is necessary, from time to time, to move the pasta about very gently to prevent it from sticking together or to the bottom of the pan. An average time for cooking is 20 minutes, and it should have a creamy and opaque appearance and be neither clear nor rubbery in texture. A simple test is to see whether a piece of it can be readily severed with the thumb nail. If it is overcooked it will become sticky and floury. As soon as the pasta is ready it should be turned into a colander, a large jug of hot water poured over it, and it should then be well drained. The pan is now rinsed out, a lump of butter put into it, and the pasta turned back and tossed over the fire for a minute or two, and seasoning of salt and freshly ground pepper added. It is now ready to serve and may be piled up in a dish with the sauce handed separately, or the mixing of sauce and pasta may be done in the saucepan. Sometimes, after this, such a mixture is turned into a dish, sprinkled with crumbs and cheese, and browned in the oven. Pastas may be dished in different ways and with different sauces. A sauce such as a reduced tomato or a mornay is usually mixed with the pasta while it is still in the pan; but when it is a question of a coulis containing pieces of mushroom or chicken liver, this is usually poured over the dish of pasta or handed separately. All pastas should be served as soon as they are cooked; grated dry cheese should accompany them. Equal quantities of Parmesan and gruyère grated and mixed together are the most suitable.

Many of the best-known dishes take their name from the sauce accompanying them, as for instance 'à la Bolognese,' a rich brown sauce with liver, Marsala (or sherry), and tomato purée; 'à la Milanese,' mushroom sauce with shredded ham; 'à la mornay,' béchamel sauce with cheese; and 'à la Napolitana,' tomatoes flavoured with onion or garlic.

For simplicity the following recipes are given under the heading of one kind of pasta, but since the preliminary cooking of each is the same, the variant lying in the sauce or coulis which accompanies it, it would be tiresome repetition to set out each recipe for each type of pasta separately; so it should be noted that *all the following recipes are interchangeable, and may be used indiscriminately for spaghetti, macaroni, nouilles, gnocchi, and ravioli.*

SPAGHETTI A LA BOLOGNESE

1 large onion
1 oz. dripping
¼ lb. liver (chicken, calf, or pig)
½ oz. flour
1½ gills stock
seasoning
a bouquet garni
1 teaspoon concentrated tomato purée or 1 tablespoon reduced tomato pulp

1 clove of garlic, crushed with a large pinch of salt
freshly ground black pepper
a dash of sherry or Marsala
½ lb. spaghetti
a little melted butter
chopped parsley and grated cheese

Finely chop the onion. Melt the dripping in a sauté pan or shallow saucepan, add the onion and sauter slowly till turning colour, then put in the liver (whole if chicken liver, diced if otherwise) and cook briskly for a few minutes; draw aside. (If chicken liver is used it must now be removed, sliced, and returned to the pan.) Sprinkle in the flour, mix, pour on the stock, season, and bring to the boil. Add the bouquet, tomato, and clove of garlic, and finish seasoning with some freshly ground black pepper. Simmer, stirring occasionally, until thick and syrupy-looking. Remove the bouquet and add the sherry. Meanwhile cook the spaghetti as directed on page 422 and return to the pan, add a little melted butter, cover with a cloth, and leave to stand in a warm place until sauce is ready. Pile the spaghetti up in a hot dish and pour over the sauce. Serve at once, well dusted with chopped parsley, and with a dish of cheese handed separately.

SPAGHETTI A LA NAPOLITANA

½ lb. spaghetti	salt and freshly ground black
1 oz. grated Parmesan cheese	pepper
1 oz. butter	extra grated cheese for handing
tomato sauce 2 (page 426)	

Cook the spaghetti as directed on page 422, drain and rinse. Return to the pan with the butter and enough of the sauce to coat well each length of spaghetti, but no more. Shake over the fire until very hot, add salt and pepper, then quickly stir in the cheese, mixing and lifting with a fork. Serve at once with more grated cheese in a small dish.

N.B. Some people prefer not to add the cheese to the spaghetti, but to have it all served separately.

SPAGHETTI A LA MILANESE

8 oz. spaghetti	tomato pulp (see tomato
1½ oz. butter	sauce 2, page 426)
1 oz. mushrooms, finely sliced	seasoning
1½ oz. lean cooked ham	1 oz. grated Parmesan cheese
1½ oz. cooked tongue	additional grated cheese
1 gill strong, well-flavoured	

Cook the spaghetti as directed on page 422. Meanwhile melt the butter in a large saucepan, add the mushrooms, cook for a few minutes, then add the ham and tongue cut into julienne strips. Add the cooked spaghetti, the tomato pulp, and the seasoning. Shake up over the fire until piping hot, then quickly stir in the Parmesan cheese. Serve at once and hand with a dish of additional grated cheese.

SPAGHETTI WITH AUBERGINES

1 aubergine	if required (or anchovy
½ lb. spaghetti	essence may replace the
a nut of butter	fillets, though this is not so
seasoning	good)
1 green pepper	½ lb. red, ripe tomatoes,
1 clove of garlic crushed with	skinned and cut in slices
salt	chopped basil
2 tablespoons olive oil	1 glass white wine
2 fillets of anchovy, chopped,	grated Parmesan cheese
and a little anchovy essence	

Cut the aubergine into short strips without peeling, sprinkle with salt and leave 15–20 minutes, drain. Cook the spaghetti as directed on page 422. Turn back into the pan with a nut of butter and seasoning. Meanwhile shred the pepper, first removing the seeds, and fry with the aubergine in the oil until turning colour. Draw aside, add the garlic, the anchovies, the tomatoes, and the essence if on tasting this is required. Season highly, add a good sprinkling of basil and the wine. Simmer for about 7 minutes to a rich-looking vegetable salpicon. Pile the spaghetti

Plate 1. Method of filling forcing-bag and correct way to hold bag for piping (see page 53)

1. Hold bag firmly in left hand with top turned well over. Push mixture down into bag with the spatula and clean it off against fingers of left hand.

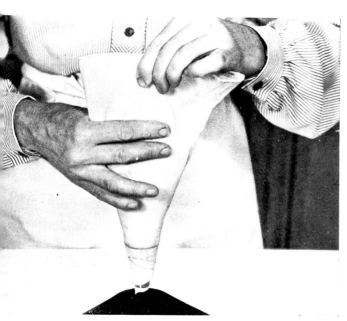

2. Hold bag upright with top closed and pack mixture well down into bag with a sliding movement of the right hand.

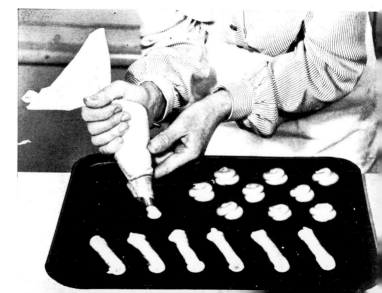

3. To pipe choux paste for éclairs, hold bag tightly in right hand, keeping first finger and thumb firmly closed. Apply pressure on bag with remaining fingers. Use left hand to guide.

Plate 2. Sautéing (see page 64)

1. Showing the correct amount of liquid in the pan for a sauté. The chicken has been sautéd in butter, the wine and stock called for in the recipe added, and the whole simmered for a short time.

2. The completed dish, Chicken Sauté Chasseur, with its garnish of mushrooms and fried croûtons. When the pieces of chicken are dished, boil the gravy rapidly for a minute or two before pouring over the chicken.

Plate 3. Clarifying
(see page 120)

Basic method illustrated by aspic jelly.

1. Immediately liquid begins to boil stop whisking and allow it to rise to the top of the pan. Turn off gas or remove from heat to settle. Repeat this process twice more to ensure good result.

2. After the third boiling. Here the liquid has been allowed to stand 5–7 minutes, and has broken well to show the clear liquid and solid filter of egg white.

3. The aspic has now been strained through the scalded cloth and has been lifted across to a second bowl. The liquid in the Pyrex bowl will be poured over the filter in the cloth to ensure a sparkling clear jelly.

Plate 4. Correct method of mixing egg whites into a soufflé mixture (see page 288)

1. Beaten egg whites, whether whisked by hand or mechanically, should reach the stage shown here, a smooth firm snow making a good peak on the whisk. These are for incorporating into a soufflé base.

2. When mixing them into a firmer substance always fold in a small portion completely before adding the main bulk. This will ensure the maximum lightness.

3. For a soufflé be careful not to fold the whites in too thoroughly. When turning the mixture into the prepared soufflé case draw the spoon through the centre. This helps the mixing but avoids over-stirring.

Plate 5. Boning a sole for stuffing whole (see page 446)
(*See:* Soles fourrées)

1. With a sharp thin-bladed knife raise the fillets on each side of the backbone with a clean sweeping movement. Draw the knife up to the edge of the backbone only.

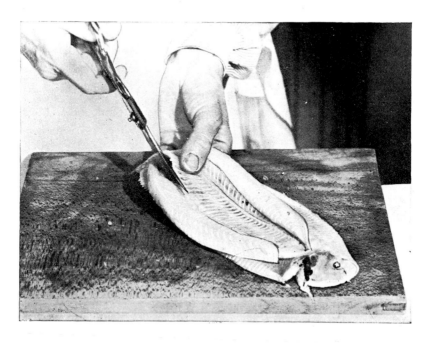

2. This process completed on each side of the fish, cut along the edge of the bone with the scissors, nicking it through at the tail and head. Remove bone and trim carefully round the fins with the scissors.

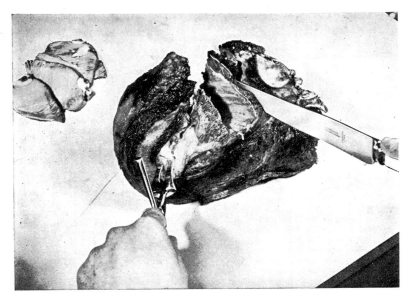

Plate 6. Carving a sirloin of beef (see page 527)

1. Insert the fork into the fat or streaky part of the joint. Turn it over as shown and slice out the undercut in ¼-inch slices. These slices of undercut are, as will be seen, slightly thicker than those of the top part of the sirloin.

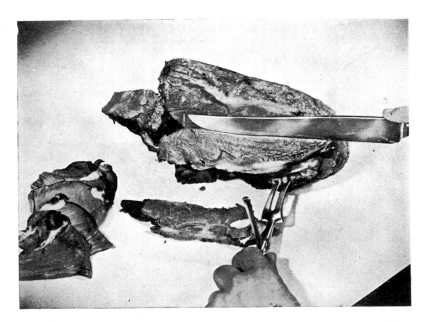

2. Turn the joint back again, i.e. upright, and begin to slice the top part of the sirloin in long, thin, even slices. It will be noted that the end bone has been slightly pushed down to facilitate the carving. It is usual to serve one slice of each cut for a portion.

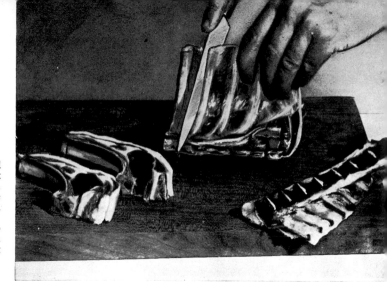

Plate 7. Cutting and trimming of cutlets, and slicing and trimming of tournedos (Cutlets: see page 551. Tournedos: see page 530)

1. When dividing the best end of neck into cutlets the joint should first be chined only. The chine bone is shown on the board. Cut down cleanly and evenly between the bones. When the neck is small two bones may be taken for each cutlet, the second bone being removed when trimming.

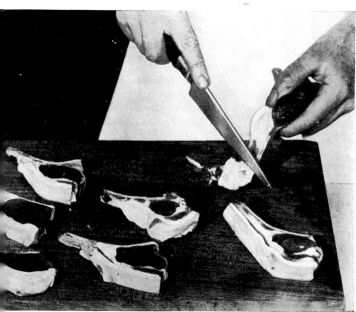

2. Trim off the surplus fat, leaving a rim round the edge of the meat and scraping the bone well. If the ends of the rib bones have not already been sawn off by the butcher the bones must be chopped off evenly at this stage.

3. For tournedos it is usual to trim the fillet, first removing the coarser-grained piece of meat adhering to it. This is here shown on the plate and is known as the 'skirt.' It is excellent for pies, stews, etc. Cut tournedos as shown; they need no further trimming.

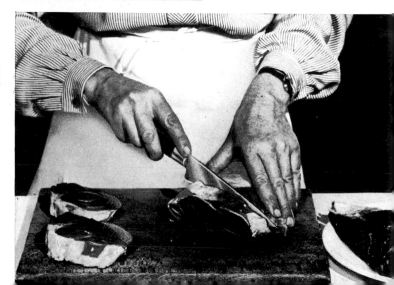

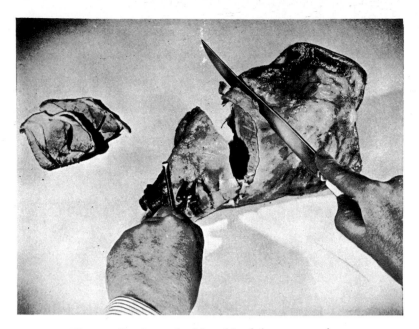

Plate 8. Carving a shoulder of lamb (see page 551)

1. Again ascertain where the bone lies and choose the fleshy part of the shoulder to make the first cut.   To begin with cut in the same way as for the leg, and as the carving progresses gradually incline the knife.

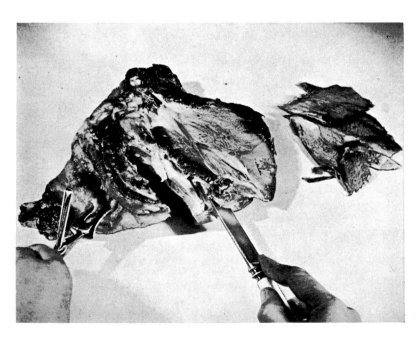

2. To reach some of the sweetest slices of meat, turn the shoulder over as shown in the picture and slice the meat from the blade bone.   The slices here will be thinner than those taken from the top part of the shoulder.

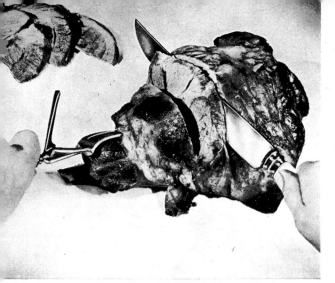

Plate 9. Carving a leg of lamb
(see page 551)

First ascertain where the bone of the leg runs, then insert the fork firmly into the knuckle end, tilting the joint towards you. Now make a cut into the fleshy part of the leg down to the bone, keeping the knife as straight as possible. Cut two or three slices out in this manner, tapering them slightly down on to the bone so that each slice is slightly wedge-shaped and $\frac{1}{4}$ to $\frac{1}{2}$ inch thick. Continue slicing, gradually inclining the knife slantwise until the end bone has been reached.

Carving a saddle of lamb
(see page 551) ·

Here the slices are carved with the grain of the meat. Insert the fork into the fat part of the saddle, and with the carving-knife make a long cut down each side of the backbone. The slices should be slightly wedge-shaped. This makes the lifting of them from the bone much easier. The whole of the slice is usually served, but if the saddle is a large one the slices may be cut in half.

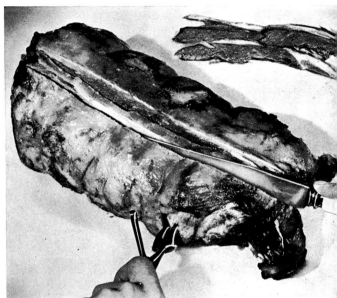

Carving a spare rib of pork

Insert carving-fork into the meat and bone to hold the joint securely, and cut down in pieces about $1\frac{1}{2}$ inches thick. The knife should go between the cutlet bones. Carve either the crackling or the plain end first, according to which side the spare rib is taken from.

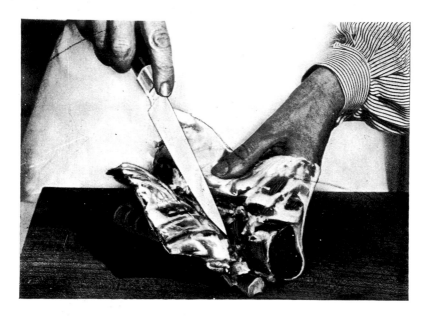

Plate 10. Cutting and shaping of noisettes (see page 553)

1. Here the chine bone may be left on before boning out the best end of neck. Keep the knife on the bone, making short clean strokes to cut away the meat.

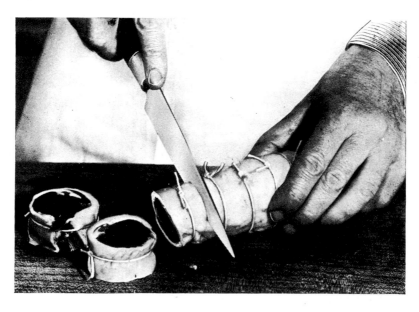

2. Roll the meat up tightly and tie firmly at intervals of about 1–1½ inches. Now cut between the string. The string around the noisette is removed before serving.

Plate 11. Lining of basin with suet crust (see page 535, Beefsteak and Kidney Pudding)

1. Showing the pleating of the dough, already rolled out and doubled over.

2. Rolling out the point to form a 'bag.'

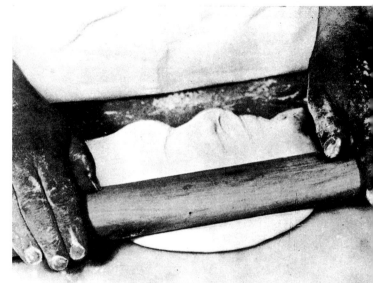

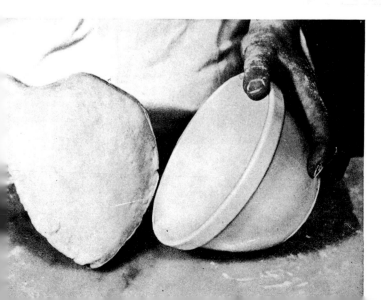

3. Inserting the 'bag' into the greased basin.

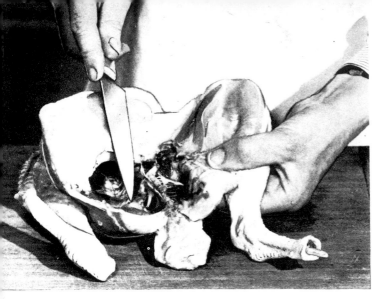

Plate 12. Jointing a chicken
(see page 636, under carving)

1. With a sharp knife cut the skin round the leg joint, and grasping it firmly pull it away from the carcass with an outward and downward movement. This will break the thigh joint. Remove the 'oyster' at the same time. Remove other leg in the same way.

2. Hold chicken firmly and cut the wing off, taking a line from the *top* end of the breast-bone and continuing down through the bone. Once the flesh has been cut through the scissors may be employed to cut the wing off neatly.

3. The joints are shown here with the remaining small portion of carcass on the right. The legs may be cut again according to size, usually when cooked to avoid undue shrinkage. At this stage the 'oyster' or carcass bone may be gently drawn out.

Plate 13. Carving a roast chicken (see page 636)

1. Insert the carving-fork into the leg and cut the skin with the carving-knife, then push the leg out, pressing the knife against the carcass to help this. This should remove the 'oyster' with the leg.

2. Now remove the wing by making a cut fairly high up in the breast and drawing the knife straight down on to the knuckle joint, which is easily cut through.

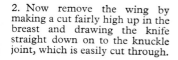

3. Now insert the fork into the carcass to hold it firmly and slice the breast down in thin slices. After one side of the bird is carved the other is then dealt with. The leg may be cut in half and a portion of this served with a slice of breast.

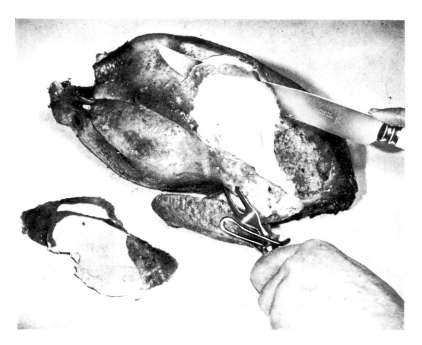

Plate 14. Carving turkey

1. The wing is not detached in a turkey. Start carving in slices about ¼ inch thick from the breast and wing as shown, taking a piece of the stuffing.

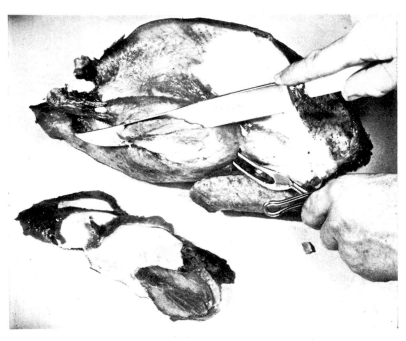

2. If carving a large bird, the drumstick and thigh are also carved in slices as shown, and a portion of the dark meat served with the breast.

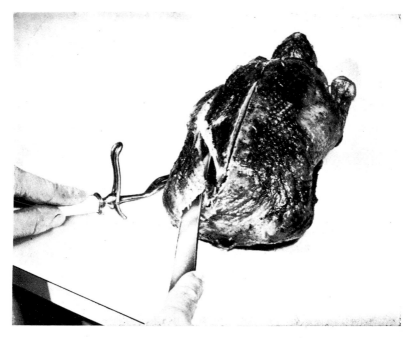

Plate 15. Carving duck (see page 657)

1. There are two methods of carving duck. In one the wing is detached before the breast is cut in slices; in the other, used more in restaurants than in the home, the whole of the breast and wing meat is cut off through the wing bone. It is then cut into slices for serving. Here the knife has been inserted along the breast-bone and carried down into the breast and wing to loosen the meat slightly. The wing is then detached.

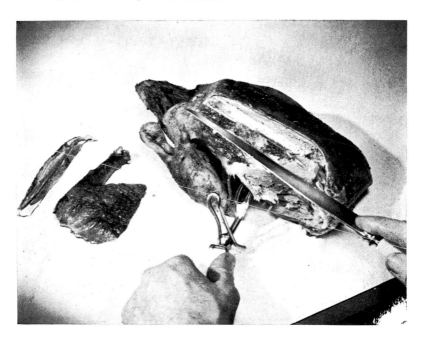

2. The breast is then carved in long wedge-like slices. The leg may be detached and cut in half before being served with a portion of the breast.

Plate 16. Pâte sucrée, or French flan pastry (see page 838)

1. Ingredients on slab, tilting in the last yolk.

2. Pinching up the sugar, butter, yolks, and gradually drawing in the flour.

3. Pressing out the mixture and drawing it up together to form a paste.

up at one end of a hot dish, turn the aubergine mixture into the other, and serve with a dish of grated Parmesan cheese.

MACARONI

Here are two simple dishes of macaroni:

6 oz. macaroni	seasoning of salt and freshly
1½–2 oz. butter or margarine	ground black pepper
2 oz. grated cheese	

Cook macaroni in way directed on page 422.   Return to pan, add 1 oz. each of butter (in small pieces) and grated cheese.   Stir carefully and shake the pan.   Finish off with the remaining butter and cheese added in the same way.   Season well, add freshly ground black pepper.   Serve very hot.

6 oz. macaroni	½ pint well-seasoned tomato
1 onion	sauce, 1 or 2 (see page 426)
1 clove of garlic crushed with	seasoning
a pinch of salt	extra cheese for serving
1 oz. butter	separately
1½–2 oz. cheese	

Fry onion in a little of the butter without allowing to colour.   Add garlic, cooked macaroni, rest of the butter in small pieces, seasoning, and just before serving stir in cheese and tomato sauce.   Reheat without allowing to boil.   Hand extra cheese separately.

MACARONI CHEESE

The ordinary English macaroni cheese is sometimes served in too dry a state; this may be the result of adding the sauce after the macaroni has been laid in the pie dish, when it is difficult to judge or to mix properly. The cooked macaroni should be put in a large bowl and mixed with a good mornay sauce and plenty of it.   During the mixing salt and freshly ground pepper are added.   All this is then laid in a greased fireproof dish, grated cheese and breadcrumbs are sprinkled over the top, and little pieces of butter dotted over it before finishing it off.   All that is required is a thorough heating through and browning of the top; 7–10 minutes in a really hot oven should suffice.

N.B. Half a teaspoon made mustard and 1 teaspoon Worcestershire sauce are good additions.

MACARONI WITH OYSTERS (FOR 6)

½ lb. macaroni	a few drops of tabasco sauce
1 dozen or more sauce or tinned oysters	½ oz. grated Parmesan cheese

Sauce

a slice of onion	1 oz. butter
a blade of mace	¾ oz. flour
4 peppercorns	seasoning
½ bay-leaf	2–3 tablespoons cream
¾ pint milk	

Cook the macaroni as directed on page 422.   Meanwhile prepare the sauce.   Put the onion, mace, peppercorns, and bay-leaf in the cold milk, bring to boiling-point, remove from heat, cover, set aside in warm place for 10 minutes, strain and cool.   Melt the butter, add the flour, season, pour on the milk, and stir continuously over the fire until boiling.   Simmer for a few minutes, add the cream and adjust the seasoning.   When bland and creamy draw aside and add the oysters and tabasco.

Stir the sauce into the macaroni and turn into a buttered gratin dish. Scatter over the cheese and brown in a quick oven for 10 minutes.

N.B. This used to be a favourite first-course luncheon dish in an Irish house.   A handful of picked shrimps were sometimes used instead of oysters.   The whole dish was very creamy and had a crisp brown top.

The two following tomato sauces are of a particularly suitable type for pasta dishes:

TOMATO SAUCE (1)

Owing to the length of cooking this sauce becomes fairly thick and creamy, although it contains no thickening agent.   It is suitable to add to any pasta dish.

2 lb. tomatoes	1 clove of garlic, crushed
1 bay-leaf	3 sprigs of thyme
2½ oz. butter	2 cloves
2 onions, chopped	3 sprigs of parsley
salt and pepper	grated nutmeg
a pinch of sugar	1 gill water

Quarter the tomatoes.   Make the butter hot in a saucepan, add onion and stir until soft, add tomatoes and stir over brisk heat for 5 minutes. Add herbs and garlic, bay-leaf, salt, pepper, sugar, nutmeg, cloves, and water.   Cook very gently, covered, for an hour.   Put through a sieve.

The second tomato sauce is of a consistency too thick to pour and may be suitably used as an addition to another sauce; for example, if some chopped onion and crushed garlic are cooked in a little butter, and diluted with a few spoonfuls of stock, the addition of a little of this sauce will give excellent results.

TOMATO SAUCE (2)

2 lb. red, ripe tomatoes	1 clove of garlic crushed with
a bouquet of a stick of celery,	salt
basil or lemon thyme, pars-	salt and freshly ground black
ley stalks, and ½ bay-leaf	pepper
	a nut of butter

Wipe the tomatoes and cut into small pieces.   Put into a large saucepan with the remaining ingredients, cover and simmer for a good hour.   If the cooking is too rapid the sauce will not be good, therefore if cooked over gas an asbestos mat should be used.   Remove the bouquet and rub sauce through a strainer.   Turn into a small saucepan, reheat and reduce further if necessary. The sauce should be a dark rich red and just drop from the spoon. It may be prepared in a larger quantity, and turned into small pots and covered with a film of oil to preserve it. It can then be kept for some time and used when required.

N.B. This sauce or purée is used principally for Italian pasta dishes and for adding to sautés, ragoûts, etc.; in fact, it may replace the condensed tomato purée.

GNOCCHI

There are three main varieties of gnocchi, French, Italian, and potato, and all require careful attention to detail, particularly the French and potato ones.

1. *French gnocchi* or gnocchi parisienne are made like a choux paste with water or milk, flour, butter, and eggs, and are then poached, drained, covered with a mornay sauce, and glazed under the grill or browned in the oven.

GNOCCHI PARISIENNE (1)

2 oz. butter	2 eggs
¼ pint water, or milk for richness	1 oz. grated cheese
	seasoning
3¼ oz. flour	mornay sauce (page 156)

Boil butter and water together, add flour all at once off the fire, beat well till smooth. When cool beat in the eggs, add cheese and plenty of seasoning. Poach[1] in spoonfuls[2] until firm. Drain, dish in a buttered gratin dish, and mask with mornay sauce. Brown in oven for 10 minutes or finish under grill.

GNOCCHI PARISIENNE (2)

4 oz. butter	2 oz. grated cheese
1½ gills milk	seasoning
6 oz. flour	mornay sauce (see page 156)
4 eggs	

Follow the method given for Gnocchi Parisienne 1.

N.B. This pasta will rise like a soufflé during the final baking, but if left a minute or two will subside and the gnocchi remain whole.

[1] It is to be noted that the poaching of all gnocchi should be carried out with care, for if the movement in the water is too great the paste will break. For this reason attention is drawn to the note on poaching on page 70.

[2] This is done by heating two dessertspoons in boiling water, and taking a spoonful of the mixture in one spoon and smoothing it over with the inverted bowl of the other. It is wise to make sure there are no cracks before putting the gnocchi into the water.

The gnocchi will detach themselves from the spoon if this is gently knocked on the bottom of the pan under the water. The time of poaching for dessertspoon size is 10–12 minutes, when they should feel firm when pressed with the finger.

For smaller gnocchi a bag and plain forcing-pipe about ¼ inch in diameter are used. The paste is squeezed out over the pan of water and cut off in lengths of half an inch with a hot wet knife, and poaching time is 7–10 minutes.

CROUSTADE OF GNOCCHI

Prepare a good short crust (see page 835), roll out paper thin, and with it line a flan ring or deep tartlet tins; bake blind (see page 844). Make the French gnocchi paste as described, using the smaller gnocchi for the tartlet tins. Drain well before filling into the pastry case or croustade. Coat with a good mornay sauce (page 156). A half-pint will be required. Scatter with grated cheese and brown in a quick oven or under the grill. N.B. Other sauces may be used besides mornay. Duxelles or shrimp or tomato sauce makes a good alternative.

This is not really an easy dish to make and to be good it must be well made. It is really a contrast in textures: thin, crisp, friable pastry, firm, creamy gnocchi, and soft, creamy sauce.

2. *Italian gnocchi*, or gnocchi à la Romana, are made with polenta (maize meal) or, as a substitute, coarse semolina. This ingredient is cooked to a thick paste in milk, then strongly flavoured with cheese and spread out to cool. It is then cut into squares, covered with grated cheese, and browned in the oven, or it may be egged and crumbed and fried. This is usually served with a tomato sauce (see page 426) or sauce italienne (see page 181).

GNOCCHI A LA ROMANA

1 onion	seasoning
1 bay-leaf	1½ oz. grated cheese
1 pint milk	½ oz. butter
5 tablespoons polenta or semolina	1 teaspoon French mustard
	extra grated cheese for dusting

Put onion and bay-leaf in liquid, bring slowly to boil with lid on pan. At boiling-point remove flavourings, sift in polenta or semolina, and season well. Simmer 15–20 minutes till creamy, stirring frequently. Remove from fire. Stir in cheese, butter, and mustard. Spread out about ¾ inch thick and allow to cool. When quite cold and set cut in squares or crescents, lay in a buttered fireproof dish, dust well˙with grated cheese, and brown in the oven.

FRIED GNOCCHI

Make a gnocchi à la Romana according to the recipe above. When cooked spread it out about an inch thick to cool. When quite cold cut into fingers about 2 inches long and 1 inch wide. Lightly flour, brush over with beaten egg, and roll in breadcrumbs. Fry in deep or shallow fat, or clarified butter. Serve with a strong piquante tomato sauce such as winter tomato sauce (see page 179).

3. *Potato gnocchi* require a little practice and experience, for while they may be good, they may also be heavy in the same way that potato scones sometimes vary. The reason for this is that the absorbent qualities of potatoes vary greatly, and one has to judge, within limits, how much flour

is required to make the perfect paste. In giving quantities the amount of flour can therefore be only approximate, and it is as well, before embarking on the cooking of the whole of the paste, to cut off a small piece and test it by poaching.

These gnocchi are made with potato freshly boiled and sieved, to which is added flour in quantities varying from one-third to one-half of the quantity of potato. The two are worked together to a light un-sticky paste, shaped into a long roll, and cut off in the following way: With a sharp knife cut diagonally across the roll, then placing the knife in an opposite slant to form a V cut again; this will give a triangular-shaped piece of paste—the base of the triangle should be approximately half an inch. These pieces are poached carefully, drained, and tossed in butter and chopped parsley. They may be served separately or with a ragoût or goulash, or they may be covered with 'Bolognese,' 'Italienne,' or tomato sauce, or with grated cheese and browned in the oven.

POTATO GNOCCHI

2 or 3 potatoes, boiled, drained, and sieved	flour from $\frac{1}{3}$ to $\frac{1}{2}$ the quantity of potato (see above note)
	salt

Put potatoes on floured board, work flour and salt in lightly as though you were kneading bread. When the dough is light and not sticky roll out under the palms of the hands into a long thin sausage. Then cut off in the way described above. Poach in salted water 5–10 minutes, when the gnocchi will rise to the surface. Take out with a skimmer and drain well. Test to see that they are cooked through and serve in the way described above.

RAVIOLI

One may buy ravioli in provision shops or make them at home, when they will be fresh as well as more economical. If, however, one is not prepared to practise and to take trouble over them it is probably better to follow the line of least resistance and buy them.

$\frac{3}{4}$ lb. flour	1 teaspoon salt
1 egg and 1 egg yolk	Bolognese or tomato sauce (see
1 tablespoon oil	pages 423 and 426)
1 gill tepid water (approx.)	

Filling

$\frac{1}{2}$ lb. spinach	$1\frac{1}{2}$–2 oz. Parmesan cheese
4 oz. milk cheese	seasoning

To make the paste sieve the flour with the salt, put it on a board and make a well in the middle. Into this put the egg, egg yolk, oil, and half the water. (It is not possible to say exactly the amount of water that will ultimately be needed, as different flours vary in their powers of absorption; the aim in making this dough is to use a minimum of liquid.) Work flour and liquids together, adding remaining water as required, kneading as for bread to a smooth, firm dough. (R. H. says this should be kneaded for

7–10 minutes and should look like a piece of chamois leather.) Leave for 15 minutes.

Filling. Blanch spinach for 5–7 minutes, drain and sieve. Sieve the milk cheese and stir into the spinach. Season well. Mix into this enough of the grated Parmesan cheese to form a paste. Roll out the dough as thinly as possible to form a large square, brush over half the square with cold water and on the wetted part arrange at regular intervals, about $1\frac{1}{2}$ inches apart, little heaps of the spinach filling. Fold over the other half of the paste and press firmly with the fingers around each mound. Take a small fluted cutter of convenient size (or use a pastry wheel) and cut out the mounds. Leave for some hours before cooking, preferably overnight. Cook in plenty of salted boiling water or in stock for 20–30 minutes; test at the end of 20 minutes and continue cooking if necessary. Serve with a tomato or Bolognese sauce.

The ravioli may also be suitably filled with various farces, such as those made with liver and smoked ham. The paste itself may be made richer by the addition of extra eggs. Any remaining paste may be rolled out, cut into strips, dried, and used as nouilles.

CANNELONI

$\frac{1}{2}$ lb. canneloni	filling, either 1 or 2
1 pint any good tomato sauce	grated cheese
(approx.)	chopped parsley

Cook the canneloni in boiling salted water for about 5 minutes. Drain well. Fill each piece with the prepared filling. Place in a casserole, cover with tomato sauce, and sprinkle with grated cheese. Bake in a moderate oven for about half an hour, dust with chopped parsley and serve.

Filling 1

a small tin of pâté de foie gras	1 oz. margarine
(mock pâté is used for this)	1 oz. flour
1 gill milk	seasoning
1 onion, chopped	French mustard
1 sprig of parsley, thyme, and	
a bay-leaf	

Heat milk slowly with onion and herbs; allow to infuse for 10 minutes and strain. Melt the margarine in the rinsed pan, stir in the flour, cook for a minute or two, then add the flavoured milk. Bring to the boil, stirring continuously, season well. Cream the pâté de foie gras with the sauce and add French mustard to taste.

Filling 2

1 lb. spinach	1 beaten egg
1 demi-sel cheese	seasoning

Cook the spinach in plenty of boiling water for 5 minutes, drain well and chop finely. Beat in the cream cheese and the beaten egg. Season well.

The following farces are suitable either for ravioli or as fillings for wide short tubes of canneloni.

FARCES FOR RAVIOLI OR CANNELONI

The quantities must be gauged to suit the amount of pasta to be filled.

Farce 1

chicken livers	chopped marjoram and thyme
shallots	seasoning
bacon	

Sauter the livers, sliced shallots, and bacon, add herbs and seasoning and pound to a paste.

Farce 2

| diced ham and/or sausage-meat | herbs as above |
| | seasoning |

These sautéd ingredients may be chopped or pounded. Veal may be used in place of liver or ham and sausage.

BATTERS AND THE DISHES MADE FROM THEM
puddings, pancakes, cassoulettes, fritters, etc.

Whether one cooks for a schoolful of small boys or for a critical gourmet, a knowledge of batters, their possibilities and their tricks is of real importance to a cook. There is a wide range of dishes, both sweet and savoury, to be made from them, which may be either economical or otherwise. These dishes vary from the popular Yorkshire pudding to the delicate shell-like case of a cassoulette; from the old-fashioned Shrove Tuesday pancake to a lacy, liqueur-flavoured morsel fit for any feast. In cassoulettes alone we have the basis of delicate dishes which combine economy with the party spirit in an uncommon way. As for fritters, their possibilities are legion, and I can promise that if you like the commonplace apple or banana fritter you will be impatient to try one summer's day the fruit fritto misto described in the chapter on sweets (pages 932–3), as well as some of the more complicated beignets soufflés.

It is one thing to choose a recipe and try it, another to know the whys and wherefores of its method and ingredients. As in other cooking affairs there is more fun to be got out of understanding what you are doing than in taking the line that any fool can toss up a pancake.

PANCAKE AND PUDDING BATTER

This is a mixture from which pancakes, cassoulettes, and batter puddings both boiled and baked are made. The basic ingredients of flour, egg, and milk or milk and water remain generally the same, though batters may vary in thickness according to the dish in hand, and butter and oil may also be employed.   By the use of extra butter and eggs the degree of richness may be increased.   Pancakes vary greatly from what may be described as family fare to something as exotic as the crêpe suzette, a lacy pancake tasting of orange juice and curaçao and finished off in the great restaurants under your eyes at table.   The additional ingredients for pancakes therefore vary greatly, and recipes may call for such items as chopped nuts, crushed ratafia biscuits, various liqueurs, rum, cream, orange-flower water, zest of lemon and so forth.

The following are the principles to be observed in batter-making:

1. The flour and seasoning are sieved together into a bowl and if a sweet batter is required sugar is added.

2. A well is now made in the flour right to the bottom of the heap, exposing the surface of the bowl.   Into this well the eggs are broken, and a small quantity of milk or water or a mixture of both is added and stirred into the eggs before any flour is incorporated.   The mixing is done with a small sauce whisk or wooden spatula; it begins with a rapid stirring, restricted at first to the eggs and liquid, and only gradually extended to incorporate the flour; as more and more flour is drawn in extra liquid is gradually added.   This stirring and addition of liquid goes on until the mixture has the consistency of thick cream; at this stage, and not before, beating may take the place of stirring and the mixture can be thoroughly beaten with a whisk.

3. If butter or oil are called for they are now added.   Butter should be melted but not hot, and immediately after its addition or that of oil any remaining liquid required is poured in, and the batter now becomes a thin cream.

4. The batter should now be allowed to rest, and anything from half an hour to three or four hours may be indicated.   The point of this is that the starch cells swell and are therefore more easily broken down in the cooking. During this time the batter thickens, and sometimes more liquid may be required to bring it to the right consistency.

5. Batter for puddings and thick pancakes requires less liquid than that for thin, lacy pancakes.   For batter puddings it should be of a consistency that will just drop from the spoon, for thick pancakes a little less thick, and quite thin for lacy pancakes.   Some recipes call for stiffly beaten white of egg to be added; in this case it is incorporated with the mixture just after the resting period and just before using.

6. Strong heat is essential in the cooking of batters.   It causes a further breaking down of the soaked starch cells and a release of air bubbles within the mixture which produces lightness of texture.   A tepid oven or pan, or cool fat for cooking, is detrimental to any batter.

A good pancake batter should contain a fair proportion of butter, though in the interests of economy oil may replace this, particularly for savoury pancakes, butter or margarine being preferable for sweet ones.   Water may replace some portion of the milk called for, and this not only in the name of economy but also of lightness.   Egg white stiffly whipped and added to the batter just before cooking gives a slightly fluffy pancake. By omitting fat a dry pancake is produced, and in this case a little extra fat is called for in the pan for cooking. When the proportion of fat in the batter is high, very little greasing of the pan is required; indeed, after the first greasing no more will be needed until the fifth or sixth pancake has been cooked.

The pan

A proper pancake pan is made of cast-iron and has straight edges about three-quarters of an inch high which make the tossing of a pancake easy. Such a pan, like an omelet pan, should never be washed; after being used it is cleaned with a piece of oiled cloth. If for some reason a pan should become burned or sticky, the simplest way of cleaning it is to take a damp cloth dipped into salt and rub the pan well with this. For a new pan it is a good plan to fill it with oil and allow it to stand for twenty-four hours.

If a pancake pan is not available a cast-iron omelet pan with base about five and a half inches in diameter will serve, though tossing with this is less easy and the pancakes will probably have to be turned with a spatula.

Greasing the pan

The pan is first heated and then wiped over with clarified butter or oil: wiped rather than brushed, because a brush is inconvenient as one is apt to burn and spoil it. A good weapon for the purpose may be made with several layers of clean linen tied over a wooden stick or spoon handle, rather like an artist's mahlstick. This is dipped into the melted fat and rubbed over the inside of the pan. In small kitchens a little jug of melted fat may be kept at hand; a few drops of fat are poured into the pan and any surplus after the pan is filmed over poured back into the jug. The only disadvantage of this is the possibility of using too much—pancakes should not be fried in the ordinary sense, the fat is merely to prevent sticking.

Cooking and turning

When the pan is thoroughly hot and greased test the batter for consistency; it should be possible to make one full tablespoon spread evenly over the base of a pan of the above size. Adjust the batter if it should prove too thick and then proceed with cooking, taking one full tablespoon for each pancake and turning the pan clockwise and shaking it gently to spread a thin film of batter over it. The pancake should be paper thin.

Allow it to cook until golden brown on one side, loosen the edge carefully with a palette-knife, then lifting the edge farther with the fingers slip the palette-knife right under and turn. The knack of tossing is a little more difficult to put into words; for this the edge is loosened, and the pan given a quick little shake and a quick movement upwards, outward, and back. Ocular demonstration and a little practice rather than description in words are really needed. A beginner needing confidence may spread a sheet of paper on the kitchen floor, by way of protecting both pancake and floor. Cook about half a minute on the turned side, then turn out on to a rack.   If the pancakes are not required for immediate use they may be piled one on another and covered with a cloth; they may be kept in this way for several hours and are reheated as follows.   A tin or oven sheet is brushed over with melted butter, and the pancakes peeled off one by one and arranged on it, overlapping closely.   They are lightly brushed over with melted butter, and are then ready to be put into a hot oven for 4 or 5 minutes.   They may then be taken off, filled with the appropriate mixture, and dished.

YORKSHIRE PUDDING

4 oz. flour	2 or 3 tablespoons smoking
1 large or 2 small eggs	hot dripping, or the dripping
1½ gills milk	round a roasting joint
salt and pepper	

Make the batter according to the directions on page 432.   Allow to stand for the given time.   Heat the dripping in a Yorkshire pudding tin until smoking, pour in the batter and put back into the oven at once. Cook for 30–40 minutes until risen and a good brown.   By that time all the dripping should be absorbed and the pudding crisp.   The consistency of this batter should be that of a very thick cream, just dropping from the spoon.   If a very puffy batter is liked the white of one of the eggs may be kept back, beaten, and added to the mixture just before using.

Some old-fashioned cooks make their batter pudding with milk and water mixed instead of with milk, and by this means obtain a crisper but less rich pudding.

STEAMED BATTER PUDDING

Steamed batter pudding may also be served with or before roast meat. The recipe given on page 926 for a sweet steamed batter is suitable; the sugar is omitted, salt and pepper added, and chopped herbs may be used for seasoning.

SIMPLE PANCAKE BATTER
for 10–12 medium pancakes

4 oz. plain flour	1 egg
½ oz. or more oiled butter	1 yolk
a pinch of salt	½ pint milk (approx.)

Mix and cook according to instructions on page 432.

N.B.   It is not uneconomic to make up the above quantity of batter even if so many pancakes are not immediately required.   Any that are left over may be cut up and turned into pancake chips (see page 436), much liked by children.   Surplus batter may be made into cassoulette cases, which will keep for a short time in an air-tight tin.

Savoury Pancakes

CRÊPES NIÇOISE

Pancakes with a savoury filling—an excellent way of using up chicken or ham.

pancake batter as given above

Filling

2 oz. butter	¼ lb. cold chicken, meat, veal,
3 oz. mushrooms	or ham, chopped
seasoning of salt and pepper	2 hard-boiled eggs, finely
¾ oz. flour	chopped
1 gill stock	1 teaspoon chopped parsley
	1 tablespoon cream
grated cheese	

Make the pancake batter mixture, which should have the consistency of thin cream, so if necessary a little more milk may be added after the batter has stood. It should stand for 1 hour in a cool place.

Filling. Melt half the butter. Finely chop or slice the mushrooms and add to the butter with the salt and pepper. Cover the pan with the lid and cook slowly 3–4 minutes. Remove lid and stir in the flour, then the stock. Bring to the boil. Add the chopped chicken, meat, veal, or ham, the hard-boiled eggs, parsley, and cream. Keep warm.

Cook the pancakes as directed on page 432. Put a spoonful of the filling in the middle of each, fold over and arrange overlapping down a fireproof dish. Dust well with grated cheese, sprinkle with remaining butter, melted, and brown under the grill.

CRÊPES D'ÉPINARDS A LA MORNAY (FOR 6)

Pancakes arranged with layers of well-seasoned spinach and covered with sauce mornay.

10–12 thin pancakes	1 teaspoon sugar
2 lb. spinach	a dash of nutmeg
½ oz. butter or margarine	2–3 tablespoons top of milk
1 dessertspoon flour	grated cheese
seasoning	

Wash and dry the spinach leaves, put into a pan with plenty of boiling salted water and cook 10 minutes. Drain well, return to pan, add butter, sprinkle with flour, add seasoning, sugar, nutmeg, and milk and shake well over fire until creamy and cooked.

Sauce mornay

2 shallots	½ pint milk
¾ oz. butter or margarine	2 oz. cheese, finely grated
¾ oz. flour, scant weight	mustard and seasoning

Chop the shallots, melt the butter in a saucepan, add the shallots and cook till soft. Add the flour off the fire, pour in the milk, stir until boiling and simmer till a creamy consistency. Draw aside, add cheese, mustard, and seasoning.

Make the pancakes and arrange them in layers with the spinach mixture between. Coat with the sauce, powder with grated cheese, and brown in a hot oven or under the grill for 5 minutes.

CRÊPES FARCIES AUX CHOUX

Pancakes with a highly seasoned cabbage filling, and covered with a cheese sauce.

basic batter as given on page 432	a handful of stoned raisins
1 lb. cabbage (net weight), finely shredded	a sprinkling of dill seed
	salt, pepper, sugar
1½ oz. dripping	a little vinegar
1 large onion, finely shredded	sauce mornay (see previous recipe) or grated cheese

Prepare the batter and allow to stand as long as possible. Melt half the dripping in a thick saucepan or casserole. Put in the cabbage. Cover tightly, cook 10–15 minutes. Lift cabbage out with a fish slice, add remaining dripping to the pan, add the shredded onion, raisins, and dill seed. Fry until turning colour. Put back the cabbage, season well with salt, pepper, sugar, and a sprinkling of vinegar, press a piece of buttered paper on the top, cover tightly and cook slowly for another 15 minutes. Cook the pancakes, fill with the mixture, coat with mornay sauce, or sprinkle well with grated cheese and brown under the grill.

PANCAKE CHIPS

An excellent way of using up cooked pancakes.

left-over pancakes	Parmesan cheese
tomato coulis (see page 179)	

Take 10–12 pancakes. Pile them one on top of another and cut in four. Cut into strips with a pair of scissors. Fry in deep fat until golden brown and crisp. Drain well. Pour a tomato coulis on to the serving dish, arrange the chips in the centre and scatter with Parmesan cheese. These chips are very crisp and good.

For children the chips may be dredged with icing sugar and served with a jam sauce or custard.

For Crêpes Farcies au Jambon et aux Champignons see Winkfield chapter, page 977.

CASSOULETTES

These are fragile, crisp, delicious cases made in various shapes in which individual portions of food are served. They are so delicate in texture that they can usually safely be eaten by those who do not readily digest fried food. A little practice is required in making them, but if the points given below are carefully observed cassoulettes present no real difficulty, and they are well worth mastering and great fun to make. They may be made ahead of time for a party and are a good solution for using any batter that may be left over and for presenting small portions of left-over food pleasantly. They will keep quite well for several days in an air-tight tin, but must then be heated up in a sharp oven before being filled.

As well as providing a means by which left-over food may be presented in an elegant way, cassoulette cases enable expensive foods, such as oysters, lobsters, chicken livers and so forth, to be used economically and well. Mushrooms, egg mixtures, delicate vegetables, and sweetbreads all find a place in them.

These thin, shell-like cases are made by pouring batter over a specially constructed mould. These moulds are made of metal and are attached to a long handle. (If they are not now obtainable it is possible, without much trouble, to provide a substitute. This is done by having a metal madeleine case, bouchée cup, or shell or brioche mould securely fastened to a long handle.) The case has first to be heated up in the frying fat before the batter is poured over it, and this is the procedure. Fill a small saucepan three parts full with oil or lard. Place the cassoulette mould in this and heat the fat up until it begins to smoke. Remove the mould, and holding it upside-down over the bowl of batter baste it quickly with the mixture, making sure that the edges are well coated, then reverse it and plunge it back into the hot fat. When fried to a golden brown lift out, shake off any surplus fat, and detach case carefully with the back of a knife. If the batter is thin enough the case should be crisp throughout. Set on a rack while frying the remainder of the cases. To fill and serve the cassoulettes heat them in an oven for 1 minute before filling. Arrange in a hot serving dish, fill in with the prepared mixture, and serve immediately.

The following points should be carefully observed:

1. A small pan of fat as mentioned above and not a large frying bath should be used. The reason for this is that each case is cooked separately, so only a very small portion of the frying bath is in use at a time. There is always the fear that a beginner at any rate may get the fat too hot and cause it to burn.

2. The mould must be thoroughly heated in the way described above, otherwise the batter will not make an adequate coating or, when cooked, the case may stick.

3. It is necessary to see that the texture of the batter is just right. It should be liquid enough to form a thin coating over the mould, so that it can be cooked through very rapidly.

4. The cases should be arranged in a dish and the filling put in at the very last moment before serving.

5. Where a sauce is used to bind the filling, this should not be too liquid, otherwise the case will disintegrate.

The cases may be served hot with either hot or cold fillings, and they may also be served cold, but should always be freshly crisped.

It will be seen that from small quantities of delicacies a substantial dish may be made.

Fillings for Cassoulette Cases

(a) Hot

BASIC SAUCE FOR SALPICON FOR DIFFERENT FILLINGS FOR CASSOULETTES

N.B. It may be reckoned for a salpicon that $\frac{1}{4}$ pint sauce will bind approximately $\frac{1}{4}$ lb. meat, although this naturally varies according to the absorbent qualities of the meat.

$\frac{1}{2}$ oz. butter	stock (or all stock), which
1 small onion	must be suitable to associate
seasoning	with the filling, i.e. fish
1 green fresh pepper or tinned	stock, chicken stock, vege-
pepper, or 3 stalks of celery	table stock
or $\frac{1}{2}$ cucumber, all shredded	3 tomatoes, skinned, quar-
1 heaped teaspoon flour	tered, and seeded, but not
3 tablespoons dry white wine,	chopped
together with 4 tablespoons	1 tablespoon cream (optional)

Take a shallow pan to expedite evaporation. Sauter onion in butter, add shredded pepper and continue cooking 3 or 4 minutes, add flour, then liquid and simmer to the consistency of cream for about 7 minutes. Add tomatoes, reboil, draw aside, season, and the sauce is now ready for the addition of the main ingredients, crab meat, shredded lobster, crayfish and so forth, and of the cream. For this amount of sauce, which will fill 6 cases, $1\frac{1}{2}$ cups crab meat, fresh or tinned, will be about right. If one wishes to use a smaller amount of crab meat or other shredded fish, then the amount of sauce to be added must be adjusted until the right consistency is achieved, bearing in mind that an over-wet mixture is unsuitable.

SAUTÉD CRAB MEAT FILLING

Sauter the crab meat, add a little cream and butter, and season well with a little tabasco, Worcestershire sauce, or sherry.

MUSHROOM FILLING

Mushrooms sautéd in a little butter and lightly sprinkled with beurre noisette (page 169), chopped dill, and seasoning make an excellent filling. Choose small button mushrooms. Do not peel but rub them with a clean cloth dipped in a little salt. Cook lightly in a little butter, arrange in the cases, sprinkle with chopped dill, seasoning, and finally with beurre noisette.

CHICKEN OR CALF'S LIVER FILLING

3 chicken livers or 6 oz. calf's liver
½ lb. mushrooms
¾ oz. butter

2 large ripe tomatoes, peeled, pipped, and chopped
chopped parsley
seasoning

Clean mushrooms with a little salt on a dry cloth; quarter but do not peel. Sauter the livers whole in the butter for about 3 minutes. Lift them out, sauter the mushrooms. When the mushrooms are ready slice the liver and add to the pan with the tomatoes. Sauter a minute longer on strong heat, sprinkle liberally with chopped parsley and seasoning.

FILLING OF SHREDDED COOKED CHICKEN

1 teaspoon chopped onion
¾ oz. butter
½ oz. flour
a pinch of salt
a pinch of nutmeg
1½ gills chicken stock or milk
2 or 3 mushrooms, sliced

1 small egg yolk
1 tablespoon cream
¼ teaspoon chopped tarragon or a squeeze of lemon juice
3–4 oz. cooked chicken
a dash of sherry

Soften onion in butter, add flour and seasonings, liquid and mushrooms, cook 3–4 minutes; add liaison of egg and cream (see liaisons, page 140), and tarragon or lemon juice. Shred the chicken small with a fork, add to the mixture, and add the dash of sherry at the end. This recipe may also be used with sauce or tinned oysters instead of chicken. In this case fish stock or milk should be employed and not chicken stock. The oysters are added at the end of the making of the sauce, poached for a moment or two, and the egg yolk added finally.

FILLING OF ASPARAGUS WITH BEURRE NOISETTE

Choose small green asparagus. Trim the heads and cut into 2½-inch lengths. Tie in small bundles (one for each cassoulette) and cook in boiling salted water until just tender. Drain well on a piece of muslin. Cut rings from a medium-sized tomato, one for each bundle. Remove the centres and thread a small bundle of asparagus through the tomato ring, then set each one in a cassoulette case and arrange on a fireproof dish. Pour a teaspoon of beurre noisette over each and serve very hot.

Beurre noisette (for 8 cassoulettes)

a good oz. butter
1 dessertspoon lemon juice
1 teaspoon chopped parsley

salt and freshly ground black pepper

Heat a small pan, drop in the butter; when golden brown quickly add the lemon juice, parsley, and seasoning. Use at once.

CHICKEN AND PIMENTO FILLING (FOR 6–8 CASSOULETTES)

1 oz. butter
2 oz. onion, sliced
1 level tablespoon flour
1½ gills milk
salt and pepper
a large pinch of paprika

1 oz. canned pimento or fresh
    green or red pepper
2 oz. chicken
a squeeze of lemon juice
1 tablespoon cream or top of
    milk

Melt the butter in a small saucepan, add the onion and soften slowly. Stir in the flour, pour on the milk, add seasonings, and stir until boiling. Simmer for a few minutes, then draw aside and add the shredded pimento and chicken.   Reheat, adjust seasoning, and finish with the lemon juice and cream.

If using fresh pepper, shred and blanch well before using.

Flaked cooked smoked haddock is good in place of chicken.

WATER CHESTNUT AND CHICKEN FILLING
(FOR 6–8 CASSOULETTES)

1 oz. butter
2 oz. onion
1 oz. mushrooms, sliced
1 gill chicken stock or water
2 oz. cooked chicken, shredded
1–2 oz. water chestnuts, sliced

juice of ½ lemon
salt, freshly ground black
    pepper
a large pinch of sugar
1 level teaspoon arrowroot

Melt the butter in a small saucepan, cut the onion into rings and soften in the butter without colouring.   Now add the mushrooms, cook for a minute or two, pour on the stock or water and bring to the boil.   Put in the chicken and chestnuts with the lemon juice and plenty of seasoning. Cook over a quick fire for a minute to reduce slightly, then draw aside and add the arrowroot slaked with a dessertspoon of water.   Bring to the boil, and adjust seasoning before serving.

This is enough to fill 6–8 cassoulettes, according to size.

Water chestnuts are bought in tins from stores carrying Chinese and Indian materials.

TUNNY FISH AND MUSHROOM FILLING

1 oz. butter
3 oz. mushrooms, finely sliced
1 heaped teaspoon flour
1 gill milk
Liaison
   1 egg yolk
   2 tablespoons cream

4 oz. tunny fish broken into
    large flakes (or a dozen or
    more sauce or tinned oysters
    or ¼ pint picked shrimps or
    prawns)
salt and pepper
a squeeze of lemon juice

Melt the butter in a saucepan, add the mushrooms, sauter 2 or 3 minutes, then draw aside, stir in the flour, pour on the milk and stir until boiling.

Simmer to the consistency of thin cream. Draw aside, season, and add the liaison. Return to fire and reheat carefully, stirring continuously; do not reboil. Draw aside, add the tunny fish, adjust seasoning, and finish with the lemon juice; or use a dozen or more sauce or tinned oysters in place of tunny fish, or ¼ pint picked shrimps or prawns. If using the latter it is advisable to add 1 or 2 hard-boiled eggs coarsely chopped to give bulk to the sauce. Soak the shrimps or prawns after picking in a little tepid water to extract the salt.

Hearts of Brussels sprouts cooked in the way described on page 217 and sprinkled with noisette butter (see page 169) make an excellent filling, as do asparagus tips treated in the same way.

(b) Cold

Cold fillings in hot crisp cases are excellent. Here are two or three suitable ones:

COLD CRAB, LOBSTER, OR CRAYFISH FILLING

4–6 oz. shredded fish
French dressing (see page 364)

Sauce
 ¼ pint cream
 4 tablespoons of any cream
 salad dressing

chilli sauce
mushroom ketchup
a little grated horse-radish
a tablespoon or so of celery, finely shredded and curled (see page 48)

Shred the fish, marinade in a sharp French dressing and drain. Mix together the cream, whipped, and the salad-dressing and flavour well. Add a little chilli sauce, mushroom ketchup, grated horse-radish, and celery. Mix all together.

HARD-BOILED EGG FILLING

Boil the eggs hard, shred the whites. Pass the yolks through a fine sieve. Mix with a little whipped cream. Season with salt, paprika, lemon juice, chopped chives, and, if possible, a little shredded pineapple and garnish with stoned black olives.

TINNED SALMON OR TUNNY FISH FILLING

Shred tinned salmon or tunny fish. Add celery in equal proportions to the fish. Mix with a little French dressing or other piquante sauce and chopped dill, or, if preferred, mix with cole-slaw dressing (see page 369) flavoured with chilli sauce and seasoning.

FRITTER BATTERS

The method employed in mixing the batter for fritters is for the most part the same as has been described for pancake batter (see page 432). The ingredients vary according to the type of dish in hand. The purpose of this batter is to form a light, crisp covering for various foods which, unlike pancakes, are to be fried in deep fat. The texture of the batter should be that of thick cream, coating the back of the spoon. In the first basic recipe which follows it will be seen that neither milk nor egg yolk is employed, and the result is a crisp, light, rather than a rich covering. Some recipes call for both yolks and whites: yolks add richness, whites lightness. The liquid may be water, beer, wine, milk, or some of these in mixture. Wine is sometimes used in sweet fritters; beer gives lightness but must be given time to work, and this may be anything from 3 to 4 hours. For the basic batter given below, mixed only with water and lightened with yeast, the resting time is from 30 to 40 minutes. This resting period is important and greatly improves the coating quality of the mixture. Yeast is an eminently useful ingredient in fritter batter and dissolved in warm water produces a particularly crisp coating. When both yeast and a small proportion of white of egg are used a particularly light, crisp batter is achieved.

When a recipe calls for butter, this ingredient is melted in the liquid, which must therefore be hot; it must then be allowed to cool down before being added to other ingredients. The addition of oil gives crispness.

Sometimes a small portion of batter is kept for a few days to be used as the lightening ingredient for a new batch. Such a batter, containing yeast or beer, will begin to ferment in this interval; it is then added to the fresh mixture. No further yeast is called for, but it is desirable to add beaten white of egg.

Complete coating is essential; a small bowl of batter is convenient, and the material to be coated may be lifted with the fingers or in the curve of a fork or flat whisk, submerged in the batter, lifted out, and gently and immediately plunged into the hot fat. A frying basket is not employed, the fritters being turned and taken out with a fish slice or curved wire whisk, and well drained before being served piping hot.

FRITTER BATTER (1) (BASIC RECIPE)

4 oz. flour
a pinch of salt
(1 heaped teaspoon castor
  sugar for sweet fritters)
1 piece of yeast the size of a
  hazel-nut

½ gill warm water
½ gill tepid water, ale, or cider
  (approx.)
1 dessertspoon olive oil
½ egg white (optional)

Sift flour and salt into a warm bowl, add sugar if called for. Dissolve yeast in warm water, pour into well made in the flour, stirring briskly, drawing the flour in by degrees, and adding tepid water and oil gradually. When of cream-like consistency begin beating. For some flours a little extra liquid may be required. Stand in a warm place on top of stove or near the fire for 30–40 minutes or time indicated in recipe. The batter should have risen a little at the end of this time. Fold in the stiffly beaten egg white just before using.

FRITTER BATTER (2)

4¼ oz. flour
a pinch of salt (1¾ oz. sugar for
   sweet fritters)
1 large egg, and yolk and white,
   separated, of a second egg,
the second white to be added
   at the last
1 tablespoon noisette butter
8–10 liquid oz. milk

N.B. The noisette butter, prepared by melting it and allowing it to brown, is strained through a muslin before being added to the mixture.

Make the batter in the way indicated (page 442), adjusting the amount of milk that may be required to give the thickness described; fold in the stiffly whipped white of egg just before using.

N.B. This batter may also be used for pancakes.

For these batters butter and not margarine should be used. A good quality oil is a suitable substitute.

Savoury fritters may be made of fish, vegetables, herbs, or a mixture of brains, kidney, sweetbreads, etc. They may also be made of fruit and of a stiff crème patissière. Each of the types is served with an appropriate sauce: piquante for the savouries and a fruit sauce, possibly liqueur-flavoured, with the sweet fritters. Recipes will be found in the appropriate chapters.

The following sauce is good with these, and indeed with many fried foods:

SHARP SAUCE FOR FRIED FOODS

½ pint cream dressing
1 tablespoon finely chopped
   pickles
1 tablespoon finely chopped
   parsley
1 clove of garlic, crushed
1 teaspoon grated onion
1 tablespoon each of chopped
   capers and olives, when
   possible
seasoning

Season well, and mix all together.

XVI

Fish

BEFORE embarking on this chapter it would be appropriate first to mention a notable book on the subject of fish, namely *Mme Prunier's Fish Cookery Book*,[1] selected, translated, and edited by Ambrose Heath. A sentence in the note to the original French edition is particularly apposite: 'Up to the present time [1929] fish has been insufficiently understood and its value almost unknown. . . .   It has happened that the present crisis of the high cost of living has created new problems for solution. . . .'

If that were so in France in 1929, how much more was it so in England during the war.   It is true that the odour of fried fish is no longer the exclusive prerogative of towns, and that certain of our country lanes are redolent of this popular form of food—not as you might think from the cottage frying-pan, but from the travelling fried-fish van.   Labour-saving this may be, and indicative, if you like, of extended distribution of food, but of real fish cookery we average Englishwomen know comparatively little.   'Eat more fish, eat more fish,' a friend overheard in a bus while fat was still rationed; 'what's the good of them keep on telling us that when you can't get enough fat to fry it?   You can't keep *on* eating boiled fish.'   Clearly the limitations for the irritated pair were fried or boiled, and yet all the basic methods of cooking are applicable to fish, as this noted Frenchwoman shows us.

In some ways it seems to me we are not individually all to blame for our lack of enterprise.   The distribution of fish in our country has its oddities. I am sure there are adequate though not good reasons for the fact that if one eats fish at the seaside, more often than not it has had a look at London before being served up in its own home town—misguided travel which may have broadened its mind but has not improved its quality as food.

It may be that I have a sense of smell too acute for easy living, but I confess I sometimes find provincial fish a little putting off.   And there are others too, I notice, who aren't madly keen on preparing bought fish. No criticism inherent in this for the fishmonger, who amongst the ice and salt which freezes his hands does miracles of legerdemain with boning,

[1] 'Selected, translated, and edited with an introduction and notes from *Les Poissons, Coquillages, Crustacés et leur préparation culinaire par Michel Bouzy*.' By Ambrose Heath (Nicholson & Watson).

skinning, and filleting in the coldest and most uncomfortable of circum-stances, and is more than obliging about doing things that one longs to avoid doing oneself. It is just, I suppose, 'a matter of distribution.'

But alas, the fact remains that fish fresh from its native element and 'fresh fish' from shops can be very different things. Fishermen, whether of the salt or the fresh water, often tell with reverent enthusiasm and a light in the eye not only of the weight of their catch but of how it tastes treated in this way and in that. I confess I have not always noted this same gleam in the housewife's eye over a pound and a half of cod.

The young student is not to conclude at this point that she either catches her own fish or never bothers with the subject at all. It is her skill that will be noted and appreciated when what she has to cook is not beglamoured with the glory of the sport. And there is an astonishing amount to be learnt about fish, more kinds than you even thought of and more ways of preparing them.

At Winkfield we have three copies at least of Mme Prunier's book, one for students, one for kitchen, and one 'not to be taken away.' The first time I read it I inclined to linger round the marble slabs of the fish shops, not, as may have been suspected, in order to abstract a juicy piece of hake, but to identify those fishes unfamiliar to me. After awhile my nervous dislike for skate in the raw abated a little, sufficiently at any rate for me to be willing to learn to cook it *au beurre noir*, and to appreciate this most excellent fish dish.

There are many fish not regarded as luxury food which by careful cook-ing may be turned into such, and while it is good to afford sole and salmon, lobster, Dublin Bay prawns and suchlike, it is not with these that a cook may show her skill so much as with the duller fish. One need not there-fore languish in between whiles because the budget will only run to cheaper varieties.

In the book I started to talk about there are to be learnt hundreds of ways of dealing with fish, and no sensible student of cooking will wish to overlook this store of knowledge.

In the following pages there are, as well as general notes, a number of recipes, but they are few indeed compared with all that are available. It may, however, be remembered that, particularly in the matter of white fish, the recipes are for the most part interchangeable, the method given for one fish being also suitable for another.

GENERAL NOTES ON THE CHOICE AND PREPARATION OF FISH

The eyes should be bright and clear. If they are dull the fish is not fresh. The gills should be bright scarlet in colour, and the flesh firm. If the flesh is flabby, and when pressed with the fingers retains the dent, this is another sign that the fish is not fresh. The fish should smell salt and not unpleasant.

Normally the preparation of fish is done by the fishmonger, that is to say it is usually cleaned, scaled, and filleted if required. For those who wish

to deal with freshly caught fish, or that which has been sent by rail uncleaned, a method must be given.　It should be said, however, that a great
deal of time will be saved if the novice can see these processes actually
carried out even once, either by the fishmonger or by an experienced cook.

Scaling

Lay the fish on a board, tail towards you.　Hold the fish firmly by the
tail and with a knife scrape vigorously upwards from tail towards the head,
that is to say against the grain of the scale.　Rinse the fish thoroughly
before beginning to clean it.

Cleaning

Cut off the head, unless the fish is specifically to be cooked with the head
on.　Pull out the gills.　Make a cut down the middle of the underside of
the fish and scrape out the intestines with a spoon.　With the corner of a
cloth dipped in rough salt remove any blood that remains, for if this is left
the fish becomes discoloured when cooked.　Wash the inside of the fish
well under the cold water tap, then dry and cook at once, or keep in the
refrigerator until ready to cook.

Filleting and skinning

In the case of filleting and skinning in particular an ocular demonstration is of the greatest possible help.

To fillet flat fish.　For this work a really sharp, thin, and flexible knife is
required.　Have ready a bowl of cold water to receive the fillets and a
clean cloth on which to dry them.

Lay the fish on a board with the tail towards you; it is not necessary to
remove the head or to trim before filleting.　Make first an incision straight
down the backbone from head to tail, cutting through the flesh right down
to the bone.　Start from the head on the left-hand fillet, and working from
right to left make a series of short sharp cuts between bone and flesh,
keeping the knife flat on the bone, working in clean even strokes, and taking
care not to cut into the flesh itself.　Lift off the fillet and put it into the
bowl of water.　Now turn the fish round, and working this time from tail
down to head remove the second fillet.　Turn the fish over and remove the
other two fillets.

Skinning of flat fish.　In the case of sole fishmongers usually remove the
black skin from the fillets, leaving the white unless specifically asked to skin
on both sides.　Before cooking both skins should be removed.　Dover or
black sole may be skinned before filleting, lemon sole or plaice are best
skinned after.

To skin a whole sole, or other flat fish. *　Make an incision at the tail and run
the thumbs between the skin and the flesh round the fins to loosen the skin.
Dip finger and thumb in salt, take hold of the loosened skin at the tail and
with a quick movement rip it off.　Do the same with the white skin,
holding the tail firmly.

* See plate 5

To skin fillets. Lay the fillet on a board with the skin side down, tail towards you, and with the filleting knife cut the flesh from the skin at the tip of the tail. Dip the fingers of the left hand in salt and take a firm hold of the skin, then work the knife along the fillet, tilting it slightly downwards towards the skin. The fillet is then trimmed and washed.

With very thin-skinned fish such as whiting and haddock care has to be taken not to cut or break the skin.

After skinning and washing, the fillets are drained, laid out evenly on one half of the clean cloth, and the other half is folded over to cover them and lightly patted and pressed. The cloth may then be rolled up and the whole put into the ice-box or other cold place till it is to be cooked.

This process of washing and drying before cooking is important and should not be neglected.

It may be noted here that fish received from the fishmonger is improved, made more crisp and white, by being lightly sprinkled with salt and left so until the moment of preparation. Fillets of cod for frying may be soaked in milk, in which case they must be well dried before cooking.

Round fish

Round fish such as mackerel, haddock, and whiting are filleted as follows (these fish give only two fillets each instead of four): Lay the fish on the board, the head to the right and the back towards you. With a sharp knife make a clean cut from the back of the head to the tail, making sure that the point of the knife rests on the backbone. With the knife, using clean even strokes, raise and work off the top fillet; detach the fillet from the head and turn the fish over. Again insert the knife with the point resting on the bone and work down from head to tail, detaching the fillet as before. During the process keep the left hand on the fish to hold it firmly to the board. Skin as for fillets of flat fish.

Herrings

Method 1. For splitting, filleting, or boning herrings other methods are adopted. Still keeping the head on split the fish down the belly from gills to tail; remove roe and gut, turn over so that the cut side lies on the board, then beat lightly along the backbone with an empty bottle, which will help to loosen the backbone so that it may be pulled out, together with the side bones. Care must be taken or the flesh will be bruised and broken.

Method 2. Split the herring down the back as for filleting. First nick the bone from the fillet just to give yourself enough bone to take hold of, then gently strip the bone from the fish, starting from the tail, cut off the head, either divide into fillets or leave whole, wash and dry.

Scoring

Scoring is only necessary when a fish is to be cooked whole. The object of scoring is to prevent the skin from bursting when heat is applied to it, and to help the penetration of heat and of flavour from seasoning and sauces.　Score diagonally with a sharp knife two or three times on each side about one-eighth of an inch deep, but not so far as to reach the backbone.　Round fish is more often scored than flat, because the flesh is thicker and therefore less able to absorb flavour.

Certain fish to be cooked whole are, for the sake of appearance, not split to be cleaned but are cleaned through the gills.　These are first removed, and if this is done carefully part of the gut will come away with the gills. Further cleaning is then carried out by inserting the fingers to loosen the gut, which is gently drawn out.　The fish is then washed, and all blood and membrane removed.

METHODS OF COOKING FISH

Poaching

Under this heading should come also what we call boiled fish, for in point of fact fish should never be boiled, for this may cause the flesh to break up and the final dish to be watery.　A slow cooking in the liquid just below boiling-point is required.　The poaching may be carried out on top of the stove or in the oven.　Both temperature and time are important; if the poaching is carried out in the oven this should be set at 350° F.　On top of the stove the water is kept just at simmering-point (approx. 180° F.). See notes on simmering, page 70.

The following approximate times apply to both methods:

Large whole fish up to 6 lb.　Allow 8–10 minutes to the pound.

Fillets of fish.　8–12 minutes.

Steaks or cutlets.　10–20 minutes according to thickness (slices about 1 inch thick 12–15 minutes).　When the bone can easily be detached from the flesh the fish is cooked.

Whole small fish such as whiting, sole, or plaice.　15–20 minutes in all.

The test of appearance is that the flesh should be white and curd-like, the eyes, in a whole fish, quite white.　Overcooking, or keeping for an undue length of time after cooking, may make the fish tough and, if the bones are in the fish, slightly bitter.

The liquid

The amount of liquid is usually indicated in the recipe; generally speaking it should be sufficient barely to cover the fish.

Fillets of fish, particularly those to be coated with a sauce, are poached in wine and water or water sharpened with lemon juice.　Examples will be found among the recipes.　Large pieces or whole fish should be poached in a liquid called court bouillon, which is prepared in advance and set aside for cooking.　It may be used several times provided it is strained and kept in a cold place.　In a refrigerator it would probably keep for a week or ten days, possibly longer.　It is really a salted, acidulated, seasoned, and flavoured liquid.　The simplest form of it is salted water to which vinegar is added, with seasoning of peppercorns and flavouring of carrots, onions, and celery, a bouquet garni and a bay-leaf. In some cases wine and cider form a large part of the liquid. The ingredients are boiled up together and the liquid then set aside to cool; the fish is usually put into the cool liquid, which is then brought up to boiling-point and allowed to simmer. There are, however, certain exceptions to this when fish is plunged straight into boiling liquid. Sliced fish, for example, is put straight into boiling liquid for purposes of sealing, otherwise the juices of the fish would escape into the water. Certain shell-fish are plunged into boiling water, and this is also used in the case of fish which has had to be kept, which has travelled, or is perhaps in danger of going off quickly because of hot or stormy weather, as the long slow cooking would otherwise cause the deterioration of the flesh to go too far.

SIMPLE COURT BOUILLON

2 quarts water	1½ oz. salt
1 lb. carrots, sliced	¼ pint cider vinegar or wine
3 shallots or 2 medium onions,	vinegar, or ½ gill malt vinegar
sliced	1 bunch of parsley
1 bay-leaf	12 peppercorns
1 sprig of thyme	

Put all ingredients in the saucepan except the peppercorns, which are reserved until 10 minutes before the end of cooking. Simmer for 1 hour, strain and cool.

COURT BOUILLON
suitable for salmon and trout

3 quarts water	a bouquet garni and a bay-leaf
½ bottle white wine	12 peppercorns
1 tea-cup tarragon vinegar	a blade of mace
2 onions and 2 carrots, sliced	

The peppercorns and the blade of mace are tied up in a bit of muslin, and the whole simmered for half an hour.

This court bouillon has a good flavour and may be reduced and used as an ingredient in a fish aspic.

FISH STOCK

1¼ lb. sole bones, preferably	1 teaspoon salt
from Dover sole	a blade of mace
1 onion	2½ pints water or court bouillon
1 carrot, red part only	1 wineglass white wine
a bouquet garni	a small strip of lemon rind
6 peppercorns	

Wash the bones, break up in two or three pieces, put into a pan with the sliced vegetables and all the other ingredients. Partly cover and simmer for about 30 minutes. Strain off and cool.

FISH FUMET

Fish fumet is a concentrated stock-like jus and is prepared by reducing to a syrupy consistency a stock such as the one given above.

FISH ASPIC

1¾ pints stock as above	1¾ oz. gelatine
2 egg whites	½–1 glass white wine or sherry

Put the stock into an enamel or tin-lined pan, add the gelatine and the white of egg whipped to a froth. Whisk over a moderate fire until boiling, allow to boil well, then draw aside and leave 15 minutes before straining carefully through a wet cloth. Add white wine or sherry after straining. See clarifying notes, page 120.

Poaching large pieces of fish such as cod or turbot

For convenience in handling it is a good plan to place the fish on a single layer of muslin and tie it at the top; particularly is this the case if an ordinary saucepan has to be used. It is then easy to lift out a large piece of poached fish and to keep it unbroken. The wrapped fish is put into a warm court bouillon, cooked, drained well, and dished on a folded napkin. An appropriate sauce, egg, oyster, shrimp, or prawn, is served apart.

Fish poached in this way is generally served with plain steamed or boiled potatoes, and may be garnished with sprigs of fresh parsley.

Grilling

This method of cooking is suitable for fish steaks and cutlets and such small whole fish as sole, plaice, whiting, mackerel, herring, etc.

Preparation for grilling. The flesh should be slashed diagonally to allow heat to penetrate, except in the case of very small flat fish. Mackerel and herring may be split open and the cut side grilled first. To protect the fish from too strong direct heat the surface is brushed over with melted butter or oil, or in some cases brushed with milk and lightly rolled in flour, a covering which not only protects from heat but produces a pleasant thin crust. Fish to be grilled should not first be seasoned with salt, as this not only draws out the natural juices but it detracts from the perfect browning, which looks attractive.

Cooking times. Fish should be grilled in moderate heat which should be controlled not by lowering the heat of the grill but by judging and controlling the distance of the fish from it. It is basted throughout cooking with melted butter or oil. The time depends not on the weight but on the thickness of the fish to be grilled:

½ inch thick allow approximately 7–8 minutes
1 inch thick allow 10 minutes
1½ inches thick allow 15–18 minutes

Cook first for 2 minutes on each side, then turn from time to time, increasing if necessary the distance between heat and fish should the surface become too brown before cooking time is accomplished.

Serving and accompaniments. Serve on a very hot dish garnished with crisp watercress. Small pats of a savoury butter of one kind or another melt and provide the seasoning omitted in the cooking.

Savoury butters are prepared by creaming butter until quite soft, incorporating seasoning and flavouring, shaping into small pats, and chilling in a cool place. The following are suitable:

Maître d'hôtel: flavoured with lemon juice and finely chopped parsley and seasoned with salt and cayenne. Good for delicately flavoured fish such as sole.

Orange butter: flavoured with orange juice, finely grated rind, salt, and freshly ground pepper. Excellent with skate (see Raie a l'Orange, page 474).

Anchovy butter: stronger in flavour, good with coarser types of white fish. The butter may be flavoured with pounded and sieved anchovy fillets or with prepared essence and lemon juice and cayenne. No salt is required.

Frying

Preparation for frying. Fish, as in the case of other articles of food to be fried, must have a coating which not only protects the flesh from the great heat of the fat but also preserves the fat from absorbing the flavour of whatever is cooked in it, so that it may be used for different kinds of food. There is also the possible danger of the fat boiling up and overflowing if uncoated fish is plunged into it. Usual coatings are:

Milk and seasoned flour
Beaten egg and dry white crumbs with a preliminary coating of flour
Seasoned batter
Pastry

With a few exceptions which will be noted in the recipes, the fish should be plunged into the fat bath, and there should be enough fat to cover it completely. The actual time of cooking depends on the thickness of the piece to be fried, which should not be too great. Provided this is so one may judge that the fish is cooked through when the coat is a good golden brown. Fillets of fish, thin slices, and small whole fish are suitable.

Temperature of fat. The temperature of the fat is most important; it must be hot enough to seal the protective coating immediately and so keep in the flavour and the juices of the fish. The temperature may be roughly gauged by the appearance of faint blue smoke rising from the pan, and a simple test is made by putting in an inch cube of stale bread, which will become brown in one minute if the fat is ready. The fat should be quite still; spluttering or spitting indicates the presence of water, and this must be allowed to disperse before the fat is used.

Fat if overheated burns quickly, and if the contents of the pan are smoking too freely a large crust of bread or a slice of raw potato should be added in order to lower the temperature.   Oil or fats with a high burning point, and not butter or margarine, are used for deep fat frying.   See also notes on frying (Kitchen Processes, page 72).

Slices, fillets, small white fish
   such as sole or plaice   340°–380° F. according to thickness
Whitebait   400° F.
Fritters and fish croquettes   370°–390° F.

For care of the fat bath see page 75 (Kitchen Processes).
For shallow frying see page 73 (Kitchen Processes).

Dishing and garnishing.   Drain the fish thoroughly, first over the pan in the frying basket or on a flat whisk, then on a wire rack or on crumpled kitchen paper.   Fried fish will not remain crisp if it has to be covered, so if it must be kept hot after cooking avoid this.   The sauce accompanying it should be served apart.   Parsley used as a garnish may be chopped for fish fried in shallow fat, but the sprays are kept whole for deep-fried fish (see Fried Parsley, page 49).   This if properly prepared is all that a garnish should be, delicious to eat and a pleasant colour contrast to the fish.

Fried fillets of fish.   These may be fillets of sole, Dover or lemon, plaice, or whiting.   All with the exception of whiting should be skinned.   After skinning the fillets are trimmed, washed, and dried as directed on page 447.   They are then rolled in seasoned flour, dipped in or brushed with beaten egg, and rolled and pressed in dry white crumbs.

Directions for coating with egg and crumbs are given on page 38.

Fillets may be fried in shallow or deep fat, though the latter gives a better result and is easier to accomplish.   The fat must be smoking hot, and in the case of deep frying the fillets are twisted before being dropped into it. They should be fried to a deep golden brown before being lifted out and drained on a wire rack or crumpled paper, and they are served with an appropriate sauce or butter.

Fillets coated in batter are fried in much the same way.   They are rolled in flour, dipped in fritter batter, and dropped immediately in smoking fat.

Fillets Orly.   This name denotes thin strips of fish fried in batter.   Fillets of whiting or plaice are cut into long strips, floured, dipped into batter, and then given a firm twist just as they are dropped into the smoking fat.

Fish à la meunière

This method of cooking, particularly suitable for delicately flavoured fish such as sole or fillets of plaice, is carried out in butter in a frying-pan, but the cooking is gentler than what is generally understood by frying. The gentle cooking, the butter, the finishing touches of beurre noisette, lemon juice, and fresh parsley or herbs combine to make a particularly delicious dish, and there are also some excellent suitable garnishes.

Spread some seasoned flour on a board or dish, season each piece of well-dried fish lightly with pepper and salt, dip the fish in the flour, then hold up and shake well to remove any surplus.

Cooking. Butter is required for this, and clarified butter should be used when a fairly large fish is in question, because in the longer cooking time called for the sediment from unclarified butter may burn and cause the fish to stick to the pan. For this reason also margarine is unsuitable. Heat the pan and put in enough butter to cover the bottom—a general guide is 2 oz. butter for 3 medium-sized fish. Do not allow this to colour. While still foaming lay in the fish and cook gently, taking care that the whole surface is in contact with the butter. Cook first on one side to a delicate brown, then turn with fish slice or palette-knife and continue. Allow for fillets about 4–5 minutes on each side, 8 or 9 minutes for fish such as medium-sized sole, and 10–12 minutes for larger fish still or for thick fish steaks. If there is any doubt about the fish being cooked through take a palette-knife and at the head end lift a little of the fish very gently away from the bone; if it comes away easily and cleanly the fish is cooked.

Serving. Serve as soon after cooking as possible, and immediately before the fish goes to table anoint it with beurre noisette (see page 169), a good squeeze of lemon juice, and chopped parsley or herbs.

See Sole à la Meunière, page 476.

Some of the garnishes suitable for fish cooked *à la meunière* are: cucumber cooked in butter, sautéd mushrooms, olives and anchovies, slices of aubergine fried, muscat grapes peeled and pipped, orange and grape-fruit sections lifted out of their covering membrane, tomatoes fried in butter, slices of zucchini and others.

For soused and spiced fish see page 512.

For fish cooked *en matelote* see page 508.

For fish cooked *au bleu* see page 506.

Sea Fish

BRILL, OR BARBUE

BARBUE A LA DURAND

Whole fish or fillets cooked and served with vegetables *à la paysanne,* and masked with a sauce of wine and cream. Excellent dish and full of flavour.

Vegetables

½ oz. butter	a bouquet garni
2 medium-sized carrots	1 wineglass (¾ gill) white wine
1 medium-sized turnip	or vegetable stock
1 medium-sized onion and/or	salt
leek	freshly ground pepper

Fish

1 brill, 1½–2 lb., or 4 large fillets of brill	1 dessertspoon chopped herbs and parsley mixed
butter	salt and pepper
4 medium-sized tomatoes, skinned, pipped, and chopped	2 wineglasses (1½ gills) white wine, or wine and water mixed
2 shallots, finely chopped	a squeeze of lemon juice

Sauce

1 oz. butter	1 teaspoon or more lemon juice
¾ oz. flour	1 gill cream or top of milk

Prepare the vegetables. Rub the butter well round a small stew-pan or sauté pan. First cut the turnip in quarters and then slice with all the vegetables in thin rounds. Put the vegetables into the pan, adding seasoning and wine. Lay the bouquet on the top, cover with a piece of buttered paper and a lid. Cook gently on the top of the stove or in the oven until the vegetables are tender and the wine absorbed.

Meanwhile trim the brill. To facilitate serving, the brill may be cut into 4 or 5 pieces after being trimmed. If using fillets skin them and cut in half if wished. Lightly butter a large fireproof dish, turn the vegetables into this, removing the bouquet. Lay the fish on the top, scatter over the tomatoes, shallots, and herbs. Season and moisten with the wine and lemon juice. Cook in a slow to moderate oven 25–30 minutes for the whole fish and 12–15 minutes for the fillets. Baste from time to time. Carefully strain off the liquor, which should measure ½ pint, into a saucepan.

Sauce

Work the butter and flour together, add by degrees to the liquor and when absorbed bring to the boil. Pour in the cream and boil well for a few minutes. Add the lemon juice to sharpen slightly. Coat the dish with the sauce.

The following recipe for Barbue aux Concombres is a good example of fish served in a perfectly plain sauce, and it has a garnish which may be varied as required. It will serve for any delicate white fish. In this case the garnish is of cucumber, a vegetable that goes particularly well with fish.

FILETS DE BARBUE AUX CONCOMBRES
brill with cucumber garnish

4–6 fillets of brill	seasoning
water sharpened with a little lemon juice	chopped dill or fennel
1½ oz. butter	¾ oz. flour
1 large cucumber or 2 or 3 small ones	½ pint milk
	1 dessertspoon grated cheese

Skin the brill, fold the fillets and lay them in a buttered dish. Cover barely with water containing the lemon juice. Cover with paper and poach in the oven 12–15 minutes. Peel the cucumbers and cut in small chunks. Melt a good ½ oz. of the butter in a stew-pan, add the cucumber, cover closely, and simmer till just tender, about 6–7 minutes. Adjust seasoning and add dill.

Sauce. Melt remaining butter in a saucepan, add flour off the fire, strain on the liquor from the fish, add milk, bring to boil and reduce rapidly to the consistency of cream. Adjust seasoning.

Dish the fish, coat with sauce, sprinkle with cheese, brown under the grill, and surround with the cucumber.

Another vegetable which is good with fish is aubergine. In the following recipe this vegetable is mixed with mushrooms, but the dish may be done entirely with aubergines. Rosemary describes this as not *haute cuisine*, but quite a party dish.

BARBUE JULIETTE

1½–2 lb. brill	a little flour, and butter or oil
6 oz. finely sliced mushrooms	for frying the aubergine
seasoning	5–6 tomatoes
1 gill white wine	a little butter to sauter them
1 aubergine	chopped parsley
	sauce (see below)

Fillet and skin the brill, reserving the carcass, lay the fillets in a long baking-dish. Season, cover with the mushroom slices, pour over the wine and lay the carcass on top. Poach 15–20 minutes. Meanwhile slice the aubergine diagonally, sprinkle with salt, leave for 15 minutes, drain, flour and fry in butter or oil. Cut tomatoes in half, scoop out the pips and sauter in butter.

Arrange the aubergine down a long dish, put the fillets on top with the mushrooms, coat over the sauce, and arrange the tomatoes round the edge sprinkled with chopped parsley.

The sauce should be a good rich béchamel finished off with the fish cuisson (reduced to approximately 2 tablespoons) and cream.

Sauce

1 oz. butter	½ pint milk
1 shallot	a little cream
¾ oz. flour	salt and pepper

Melt butter, add finely chopped shallot, cook till soft but not coloured, sprinkle in the flour, add milk, stir till boiling and reduce a little. Finish with the cuisson from the fish, adjust seasoning, and add cream to bring sauce to right consistency.

COD, OR CABILLAUD, AND CODLING, OR COLIN

Cod is generally agreed to be one of the duller fish, and although slices of codling fresh caught from the sea are delicious just grilled, on the whole cod from the fishmonger needs a little help. If codling is available the first recipe, for Cabillaud au Four Flamande, makes a particularly good dish, and the same recipe used for more delicate fish makes it suitable for special occasions. The effect of the lemon slices is to render the flesh very white. This recipe is also suitable for salmon. It may be regarded as a delicate version of sousing.

CABILLAUD AU FOUR FLAMANDE

4 slices of cod or codling, not too thickly cut	seasoning of salt and freshly ground pepper
2 large onions	vinegar and cider to cover
1 large lemon	($\frac{1}{3}$ vinegar to $\frac{2}{3}$ cider, or
2 or 3 sprays of parsley	acidulated to taste)
$\frac{1}{4}$–$\frac{1}{2}$ oz. butter	browned crumbs
	a good nut of butter

Cut onions into thin rounds. Blanch 1–2 minutes, drain and turn into a bowl. Add the grated rind of the lemon. With a sharp knife cut away the white pith, cut the lemon in four, slice away the central line of membrane, removing any pips. Cut these quarters into thin slices, add to the onion together with the leaves stripped from the parsley stems. Season well with salt and freshly ground pepper. Butter thickly the bottom of a fireproof dish, put in half the onion mixture and arrange cod on this. Season again with salt and pepper and scatter over remainder of onion mixture. Pour over vinegar and cider, which should just come level with the fish. Dust over with brown crumbs, scatter with tiny pieces of butter, and cook slowly in the oven about 40 minutes or until the liquid has reduced by two-thirds.

This is also good cold; in this case omit the crumbs and allow a little longer cooking.

In the following dish a slightly acid touch is given by the use of white wine or cider with a little lemon juice; in other words, the fish is served in a slightly piquante sauce, sauce bercy (see page 174). This is a good plain dish suitable for any white fish.

CABILLAUD BERCY

1–1$\frac{1}{2}$ lb. cod fillet or steaks	1 heaped teaspoon chopped parsley
2 shallots, finely chopped	a good squeeze of lemon juice
1 oz. butter	$\frac{3}{4}$ oz. flour, scant weight
1 wineglass white wine or cider	browned breadcrumbs
salt, pepper	

Skin fillets and make a strong fish stock with the trimmings. Measure a $\frac{1}{2}$ pint. Soften the shallots in a quarter of the butter, add the wine or cider and reduce to half. Pour on the $\frac{1}{2}$ pint of stock, boil, add seasoning, parsley, and lemon juice to sharpen. Work the rest of the butter with the flour (beurre manié). Add piece by piece off the fire. Reboil and simmer a few minutes. Arrange the fish in a buttered dish, spoon over the sauce, scatter lightly with the crumbs, and bake in a moderate oven about 15–20 minutes, or until the dish is nicely browned.

COLIN A LA BOULANGÈRE

1½ lb. cod steak	12 pickling onions
salt and pepper	lemon juice
3 oz. butter	chopped parsley
1 lb. potatoes, weighed when peeled	

Trim, wash, and dry the cod. Season with salt and pepper and lay in a buttered fireproof dish (use extra butter for this). Melt 1½ oz. of the butter, sprinkle over the fish, and set in a moderate oven to cook for half an hour, basting occasionally. Meanwhile cut the potatoes into four lengthways, trim into ovals and blanch, i.e. put into cold salted water, bring to the boil and drain. Melt 1 oz. of the butter in a deep frying-pan, add the potatoes, and shake gently over a moderate fire until they are golden brown and half cooked. Melt the remaining butter in a small saucepan, add the onions and brown well over a moderate fire. Then cover the pan and continue cooking for some minutes to ensure that the onions are soft.

Take out the fish, put round it the onions and potatoes, pouring over any butter left in the respective pans, and season well. Put the dish back into the oven for a further 10–15 minutes to finish cooking. Then baste again, squeeze over a little lemon juice, and sprinkle well with chopped parsley. Serve very hot.

The following simple dish involves a court bouillon and serves to remind beginners that fish should always be poached in this and not in plain water.

COLIN GRATINÉ

1½ lb. cod or codling (fresh haddock or whiting are also suitable)

Court bouillon

1½ pints water	salt
2 tablespoons vinegar	6 peppercorns
1 carrot, sliced	bouquet of parsley, thyme, and
1 onion stuck with a clove	bay-leaf

Sauce

1 oz. butter	½ pint fish liquor and milk
¾ oz. flour	mixed
	salt and pepper
1 oz. grated cheese	breadcrumbs

Prepare the court bouillon and cook for half an hour. Allow to cool. While it cooks wash and prepare the fish. Lay it in the bouillon and cook 20–25 minutes over gentle heat. Take out the fish carefully, skin, lay in a dish and keep warm while the sauce is prepared.

N.B. For a large fish steak the centre bone may be carefully detached.

Sauce

Melt the butter in a small pan, add the flour, pour on the boiling liquid and beat with a sauce whisk until the sauce boils. Continue cooking gently for 3 minutes, adjust seasoning, then pour over the fish.   Sprinkle with grated cheese and breadcrumbs and brown in a hot oven or under a red-hot grill.

DARNES DE CABILLAUD BRETONNE

An excellent dish for luncheon or supper.

4 cod steaks	1 bay-leaf
2 oz. each of carrot, onion, and celery	a nut of butter
	2 shallots
1 oz. butter	¾ oz. flour and ¾ oz. butter for the sauce
2 wineglasses cider	
½ gill water	salt and pepper

Finely shred the carrot, onion, and celery, cook in the butter in a closely covered saucepan till tender.   Put the steaks into a fireproof dish, moisten with a wineglass of cider and the water, add a bay-leaf.   Poach in oven for 20 minutes.   Melt the nut of butter in a saucepan, add the shallots finely chopped.   Cook a minute or two, add remaining cider, reduce to half and strain on the liquor from the fish.   Add the butter and flour already worked together to a paste.   Reboil, season, add the julienne of vegetables and pour over the dish.

Before two wars had revolutionized our menus it was unusual for a green vegetable to be served with fish, unless perhaps green peas with salmon.   Now that fish has so often to be a main course green vegetables are very commonly handed with it.   I still dislike the mixture of flavours, yet the following may be counted an exception.   'Florentine' indicates the inclusion of spinach.   This dish is useful in that it can be prepared ahead of time and is suitable for luncheon or supper.

FILETS DE COLIN FLORENTINE
suitable for any white fish

4 fillets of cod	spinach, cooked *en branches* in salted water and sautéd in butter (see page 230)
a little fish stock, or very little water sharpened with lemon juice	
	sauce mornay (see below)
	grated cheese

Skin and trim the cod.   Poach about 15 minutes in a little good fish stock.   Drain, dish on a bed of spinach cooked *en branches*.   Mask the whole with a creamy sauce mornay.   Scatter with grated cheese and brown under grill or in oven.

Sauce mornay

¾ oz. butter	French mustard
¾ oz. flour	1 oz. grated cheese
½ pint milk	a little cream or top of milk if required
seasoning	

Make in the usual way (see page 435).

Under salt cod several recipes are given which are equally suitable for fresh cod.

SALT COD, OR MORUE

Salt cod should be soaked for 24 hours or more before being cooked. During this time the water should be changed 6 or 8 times. One of the classic dishes is brandade de morue. This is a mixture of salt cod, olive oil, garlic, and cream, all pounded together to a fine white purée which should be soft and creamy like mousseline potatoes, and it is piled up and surrounded by croûtes; or it may be served as in the following recipe, inside scooped-out rolls or a loaf. This dish generally contains more olive oil and garlic than is agreeable to English palates, and the recipe given below is modified, having less oil and garlic, and the addition of mashed potato and a little béchamel sauce.

BRANDADE A LA PARISIENNE

1½ lb. salt cod
6 oz. potatoes
2 tablespoons olive oil
2 cloves of garlic

1½ gills béchamel sauce, short
    method (see page 155)
hot milk
seasoning
sautéd tomatoes

Croustades

5–6 small rolls or a small tin-
    shaped loaf
1 clove of garlic

salt
2 or 3 tablespoons olive oil

Soak the cod as directed. Poach for 30 minutes. Drain well, flake and chop finely. Have the potatoes freshly boiled and push through a sieve or ricer. Add to the fish and turn both into a fair-sized saucepan. Heat the oil in a little saucepan, crush the garlic lightly and fry in it until turning yellow, then remove garlic carefully.

Beat the flavoured oil into the fish and potato with the béchamel sauce, adding seasoning and hot milk until the mixture has the consistency of a potato mousseline. Sauce, oil, and milk must be added slowly, and the whole beaten over a slow fire or in a bain-marie until thoroughly hot.

Take small fresh rolls or a tin-shaped loaf (Procea bread is good for this). Cut off the top, scoop out all the crumbs, crush garlic with salt and mix it with 2 or 3 tablespoons of oil. Warm this and brush it well all over the rolls and lids, both inside and out. Set them in a tin and bake in a moderate oven till a light golden brown. Fill to overflowing with the brandade, replace lids at an angle, and garnish with sautéd tomatoes.

A similar dish may also be made with fresh haddock, though not then correctly called a brandade.

MORUE ANGEVINE

This is a regional *maigre* dish, good if you like salt cod.   It may also be made with smoked haddock.

1–1½ lb. salt cod, soaked for 24 hours, *or*	2–3 hard-boiled eggs, chopped seasoning
4–5 steaks of fresh cod or hake	lemon juice and rind if spinach is used
1½ lb. sorrel or spinach	
2 finely chopped shallots	2–3 tablespoons thick fresh cream
1 teaspoon each of chopped parsley and thyme	

Cut the sorrel into shreds.   Well butter a fireproof dish, put half the sorrel in the bottom with half the shallots, herbs, and eggs.   Put the fish on top, season well, and cover with the rest of the mixture.   If using spinach grate over a little lemon rind and sprinkle with the juice.   Poach in the oven 15 minutes.   Dish the fish and sorrel, pour off the juice and reduce slightly, adding the cream.   Reboil and pour over the fish.

MORUE FRITE A LA PROVENÇALE

Salt cod *à la provençale* (fresh cod may also be used).
Soak the salt cod as directed.

1 lb. steak of cod	¾ lb. tomatoes
seasoned flour	salt and freshly ground black pepper
oil for frying	
1 medium onion	chopped sage, thyme, and parsley
1 clove of garlic crushed with 1 teaspoon salt	
	3 oz. black olives

Cut the fish into 2-inch squares, removing the skin and bones; roll in seasoned flour and fry briskly in the oil until a golden brown.   Then remove and keep warm.   Slice the onion thinly, add to the pan with the crushed clove of garlic, cook slowly to soften, then add the tomatoes skinned, sliced, and the seeds removed.   Add salt, freshly ground black pepper, and a little chopped sage, thyme, and parsley.   Simmer 4–5 minutes.   Add the olives, stoned and quartered, simmer another minute and turn into a hot fireproof dish.   Arrange the cod in the centre and serve very hot.   This may be cooked and served in a copper or an enamelled omelet dish, and is very good.

The following very simple luncheon dish may be made with salt or smoked cod or with smoked haddock fillets.

MORUE A LA MÉNAGÈRE

1 lb. salt cod, soaked as directed, or smoked cod or haddock, unsoaked	1 lb. potatoes, boiled or steamed béchamel sauce (see next page) chopped chives

Cut the cod into square pieces and poach for 15–20 minutes. Have ready the boiled or steamed potatoes, cut them into quarters, arrange in a dish for serving, put the drained fish over the top or in the middle of the dish, and pour over a creamy béchamel sauce. Sprinkle well with the chives.

Béchamel sauce

1 oz. butter	a slice of onion
¾ oz. flour	a blade of mace
¾ pint milk	3–4 peppercorns
1 large bay-leaf	salt and pepper

Make the sauce, which should be creamy but not too thick, in the usual way (see page 155). If liked grated cheese may be added to it.

In spring a good addition may be made to this dish. Take 12–16 spring onions, boil 4–5 minutes, and either add to the fish before pouring on the sauce or use as a garnish, in place of chives. Two heaped table-spoons of leeks, green and white part, may replace the spring onions.

For spiced or pickled cod see page 514.

HAKE, OR MERLUCHE

The recipes given for other white fish will also serve for hake.

HALIBUT, OR FLETAN

This is a delicate and good fish. There is no point in putting special recipes in for it, as those recommended for turbot, cod, brill, and sole are applicable.

HERRINGS, OR HARENGS

Mme Prunier in her book says that there has always been a definite prejudice against herrings in the politer English kitchens, and gives 9 or 10 recipes proving well that the herring makes no 'poor and uninteresting dish.' One possible reason for such prejudice is the oily richness of this fish, a quality which makes it a valuable food, but not easy of digestion for everyone. Many a highland crofter lays in a barrel of salted herrings for his staple winter fare, but the salt offsets much of the oiliness, in the same way as does the vinegar in soused herring. Another discouragement is the aspect of herrings in the average fish shop. To the fastidious they lack allure. A herring fresh caught from the sea, split and boned, rolled in oatmeal, and fried is of the best of food, as is an equally fresh fish cooked *à la meunière*. The travelled herring, remote from his native element, may require embellishment. Mustard sauce is popular and herrings spread with mustard and grilled are good, and this again offsets the oiliness of the fish, as does the lemon in the following recipe.

One or two recipes follow, but if you are in any sense a serious cook you will have Mme Prunier's book beside you and will try all her ways with this, even now, inexpensive fish.

A note on the boning and preparation of herrings will be found at the beginning of the chapter (page 447). By the way, I do not believe it is generally known that for a small sum a fishmonger is generally willing to bone herrings, a great saving of labour and time for the cook.

HARENGS A LA MEUNIÈRE

4 fresh herrings
seasoned flour
¾–1 oz. butter
salt and freshly ground pepper
juice of ⅛ lemon
1 dessertspoon chopped parsley

1 lb. potatoes
chopped parsley for finish
1–2 fried apples to accompany
oil or butter for tossing and
frying

Fillet the herrings, wash and dry. Reserve the roes, and roll them with the fillets in seasoned flour. Heat a thick frying-pan, drop in half the butter, and whilst still foaming lay in the fillets, skin side uppermost. When a golden brown turn and fry on the other side. Salt whilst cooking, then serve at once on a hot dish; allow remaining butter to colour to a nut-brown, then at once add the pepper, half the lemon juice, and the parsley and pour over the fish.

Peel, quarter, and trim the potatoes. Blanch for 7–15 minutes, drain, toss well in oil or butter, and if not completely cooked cover and continue cooking for a few minutes. Finish with plenty of chopped parsley and the remaining lemon juice.

Core but do not peel the apples and cut in thick rings. Fry them quickly in hot oil or butter, then fry the roes in the same pan. Arrange round the fillets of herring.

Serve potatoes separately.

Both Harengs Calaisienne and Harengs Normande are good homely dishes:

HARENGS CALAISIENNE

4 fresh herrings with soft roes
1 tablespoon finely chopped
  onion
1 dessertspoon chopped parsley and lemon thyme
2 hard-boiled eggs
1 clove of garlic crushed with
  salt

salt and freshly ground pepper
1 thick slice of bread soaked in
  a little milk or vegetable
  stock
1 oz. butter, melted
tomato sauce (see page 178)
grated rind of ½ lemon

Cut off the heads of the herrings, split down the back and remove the backbone and roes. Wash and dry well and fill with this stuffing: Chop the roes, put into a bowl with the onion (previously softened in half the butter), herbs, chopped eggs, garlic, and seasonings. Squeeze the bread, chop and add to the mixture. Mix well to bind. Fill into the herrings neatly, place in a fireproof dish, pour over the rest of the butter, cover with a piece of buttered paper, and cook in a moderate oven for about 20–25 minutes. Have ready a tomato sauce, pour this on to a serving dish, arrange the herrings on this and garnish with rind of lemon. Serve.

The next is a good nursery dish with a crispish quality liked by children:

BAKED HERRINGS NORMANDE

4 herrings
1 onion
1 large apple
1 dessertspoon chopped herbs
(parsley, chives, thyme)
salt and freshly ground black
pepper

1 oz. butter or oil
2 tablespoons mild vinegar
(apple or fruit vinegar), or
vegetable stock sharpened
with lemon

Split and bone herrings. Wash, dry, and lay flat. Chop the onion very finely, dice the apple, and mix all together with the herbs. Season the inside of the herrings with salt and freshly ground black pepper, and sprinkle on the onion mixture. Roll up head to tail. Melt the butter, brush the inside of a fireproof dish with it, put in the herrings and the rest of the butter with the vinegar, and bake in a slow to moderate oven 45–50 minutes.

YORKSHIRE HERRING PIE

4 fresh herrings
4 potatoes blanched whole for
a few minutes
2 sour apples

1 shallot
salt and pepper
1 gill water (approx.)

Wash and bone the herrings. Cut into fillets and soak for a little while in salted water. Slice the potatoes thinly. Well butter a pie dish and line thickly round with the potato. Chop the apples and the shallot very finely. Place a layer of herring fillets in the dish. Season and cover with the apple mixture and so repeat until the dish is full. Finish with a layer of potato slices, add liquid, cover and cook in a moderate oven for $\frac{3}{4}$–1 hour. This is a very homely supper dish, much liked by some people.

Herrings with mustard sauce are generally popular; the dish looks good and bones are avoided.

HARENGS MOUTARDE

4 herrings split and boned
4 oz. onions
2 oz. butter
salt and freshly ground black
pepper
$\frac{1}{2}$ oz. flour

1 large teaspoon French mustard
a pinch of sugar
$\frac{1}{2}$ pint water
$\frac{1}{2}$ gill cream or top of milk
1 oz. grated cheese

Cut the onions in half, put them face downwards on a board, then slice finely. Melt $1\frac{1}{2}$ oz. of the butter in a stew-pan, put in the onions, cover and simmer until soft. Lay the herrings flat down a buttered dish, season well with salt and freshly ground black pepper, cover with a piece of buttery paper, and cook in the oven 15–20 minutes. Melt the remaining butter in a saucepan, add the flour off the fire, with the mustard, seasoning, and a pinch of sugar. Pour on the water, stir until boiling, simmer 4 or 5 minutes, add the milk and half the cheese off the fire. Take the herrings from the oven, remove the paper, and scatter the onions over the dish. Spoon over the sauce, sprinkle with the rest of the cheese, and glaze under the grill.

HARENGS PARAME

grease-proof paper	4 even-sized herrings
1½ oz. butter	4 croûtes of fried bread to fit
pepper and salt	the herrings
4 shallots, finely chopped	4 teaspoons chopped parsley
4 heaped tablespoons chopped	finely shredded or grated
mushroom stalks and peel-	lemon rind
ings, or whole mushrooms	

Cut ovals out of the paper, each large enough to wrap round a herring, spread well with half the butter and sprinkle with pepper and salt.　Melt the remaining butter, add shallot, mushroom, and seasoning; cover and cook slowly until soft, add half the parsley.

Split the herrings down the backbone, spread the inside with the mixture and reshape.　Put each one on the prepared paper, fold over and twist round the edge.　Set in a fireproof dish and bake in a slow to moderate oven 30–40 minutes.　Have ready a long croûte of fried bread to fit each herring.　Unwrap the fish and lay each one on a croûte.　Dust with remaining chopped parsley and the lemon rind.　Serve very hot.

N.B.　If wished, the roes may be chopped and added to the mixture before spreading it into the herrings, otherwise they may be used for a savoury.

For Soused Herrings see page 512.
For Herrings and Herring Roes on Toast see Savouries, page 33.
For Potted Herrings see page 514.

MACKEREL, OR MAQUEREAUX

When the mackerel come up into the salt sea lochs of the Highlands the water seethes with them; then they are caught easily and that is the time of times to eat them.　They again are fish rich in oil but of delicate flavour, and they should always be eaten perfectly fresh.　Again perhaps the best way of all is to roll the fillets in oatmeal, fry them or brush them with butter, and grill.　They are particularly good soused and served very cold. Mme Prunier gives over a dozen recipes for them, stuffed, cooked *en papillotes*—which sounds more exciting than paper bags—with force-meat, mussels and so on.　Fritters of fennel go well with mackerel, as well as fennel sauce.

GRILLED STUFFED MACKEREL

Wash, clean, and remove the heads of the mackerel.　Take out the roes and simmer them in salted water until cooked.　Break them up and bind them with the yolk of an egg.　Season with grated lemon peel, finely chopped dill or fennel, parsley and a little lemon thyme, and salt and pepper. If the mixture is too soft mix with a little fine breadcrumb. Stuff the mackerel with this, flour the fish and grill. Beurre noisette is good served with this, and beurre noisette with capers is excellent.

FILETS DE MAQUEREAUX MIREILLE

This is excellent for luncheon, almost a 'beurre noir' dish.

4 good fillets of mackerel
2 tablespoons butter or bacon fat
a handful of chopped mushrooms
1 chopped onion
1 chopped clove of garlic

1 tablespoon wine vinegar
seasoning
4 tomatoes, skinned, pipped, sliced, and sautéd in a little hot dripping
chopped parsley

Season and flour the fillets. Heat a tablespoon of the butter or bacon fat in a frying-pan, and when smoking fry the fillets in this till brown and crisp. Arrange in the serving dish and keep hot. Pour off the butter in the pan and wipe it round. Reheat the pan, add another spoonful of butter, and when foaming add the mushrooms, onion, and garlic. Sauter these well, sprinkle with wine vinegar and seasoning, and pour over the fish. Surround the dish with the sautéd tomatoes. Dust the dish well with chopped parsley and serve very hot.

In the next recipe a classic green sauce, venitienne, is used:

FILETS DE MAQUEREAUX VENITIENNE

Fillet 2 good-sized mackerel. Poach the fillets in white wine or cider with sprigs of tarragon and chervil. Pour off the liquor into a saucepan, add 2 chopped shallots and reduce to a syrupy consistency. Set aside to add to the sauce. Skin and dish the fillets, pour over a sauce venitienne, scatter chopped tarragon over the dish and surround with steamed or boiled potatoes.

Sauce venitienne

a handful of good spinach
a few sprigs of tarragon and chervil
½ oz. butter
½ oz. flour

½ pint hot water
seasoning
the yolks of 2 eggs
3 oz. butter
a squeeze of lemon juice

Boil spinach with sprigs of tarragon and chervil. Drain, press, and pass through a sievě. Put on one side. Melt the ½ oz. of butter in a saucepan, add flour off the fire, pour on water, add salt, pepper, and yolks. Stir briskly with a whisk until coming up to the boil, then draw aside and stir in by degrees the 3 oz. of butter. Strain in the reduced fish liquor, and mix in enough of the green purée to make a good colour and flavour. Finish with a squeeze of lemon juice. This is an excellent sauce for serving with fish, particularly mackerel, salmon, and salmon trout. For the latter a small quantity of diced blanched cucumber is a pleasant addition to the sauce at the end.

RED MULLET, OR ROUGET

This fish comes from the fishmonger whole and it should be scaled. It is usually cooked whole and with the head on. It may weigh from 6 to 12 oz.; small or medium fish are to be preferred, and one allowed for each person. The common practice is to cook the fish uncleaned but with the gills removed. It is said that the 'trail' has no bitterness and imparts good flavour; this fish is sometimes referred to as the woodcock of the sea. For those who dislike the look or taste of the trail the cleaning must be carried out through the gills. Sometimes all the gut is removed and the liver only replaced. This fish has a delicate flavour and calls for simple cooking and a sauce or accompaniment of a slightly piquante nature. Red mullet is excellent grilled or cooked *à la meunière* or *en papillotes* (enveloped in paper), a method which is said to preserve the delicate flavour.

Grey mullet or *mulet*, is a much larger fish weighing from 3 lb. upwards. In appearance it is not unlike salmon, with firm white flesh and of excellent flavour. It should be cooked plainly and served with any of the appropriate fish sauces, or slices of it may be grilled.

ROUGETS DUXELLES

1 oz. butter
4 large tablespoons chopped mushrooms
2 large tablespoons chopped parsley
1 large tablespoon chopped shallots or chives
4 nice-sized red mullet

salt and pepper
juice of ½ lemon
1½ gills good strong fish fumet containing white or red wine (if using a ready-made fumet add wine to flavour well)

Melt the butter in a pan, put in the mushrooms and herbs, cook over a moderate fire for a few minutes. Turn into a gratin dish and spread evenly over the bottom. Prepare fish by removing the gills, washing and drying. Lay them on the mushrooms, season well, sprinkling with lemon juice. Pour over the fumet. Cover with buttered paper, set in a moderate oven, and after 5 minutes remove paper and baste fairly frequently. Allow 20–25 minutes' cooking, when the liquor should have reduced by about half. (There should be enough for each person to have a tablespoon of cuisson.) The fish should be slightly glazed. Wipe dish round carefully and serve with plainly boiled potatoes.

ROUGETS NIÇOISE

2 tablespoons olive oil
1 clove of garlic
1 teaspoon paprika
1 teaspoon concentrated tomato purée
1 wineglass white wine

4 red mullet
a sprig of thyme
seasoning of salt and freshly ground pepper
4 oz. black olives
quarters of lemon

Heat the olive oil in a small saucepan, add the finely chopped garlic and the paprika and cook slowly until soft. Add the tomato purée and moisten with the wine. Wash the fish, remove the gills, dry and place in an earthenware dish with a sprig of thyme. Season with salt and freshly ground pepper. Spoon over the sauce and cook in a moderately hot oven 15–20 minutes. Baste well, adding the stoned black olives to the dish when cooked. Replace in the oven to heat through. Serve quarters of lemon separately. Good cold.

ROUGETS A LA PROVENÇALE

4–5 red mullet, about 6 oz. each
seasoned flour
lemon juice
oil for frying
2 tablespoons olive oil
2 shallots, finely chopped
1 clove of garlic, finely chopped
¾ lb. ripe tomatoes, peeled, squeezed, and sliced

½ teaspoon chopped parsley
salt and freshly ground pepper
1 wineglass white wine or strong fish stock
a pinch of saffron, soaked for ½ an hour in an egg-cup of water
French bread for croûtes

Scale the fish, remove the gills and clean, if wished; wash and dry thoroughly. Roll in seasoned flour and fry until golden brown on both sides. Arrange down an earthenware dish and sprinkle with lemon juice. Heat the olive oil in a stew-pan, add the shallots and garlic. Cook a few minutes, then add the tomatoes, parsley, salt and pepper, wine or stock, and saffron. Simmer 20–30 minutes with the pan uncovered. Pour over the sauce and surround with the croûtes toasted, or fried in the oil.

ROUGETS GRILLÉS MAÎTRE D'HÔTEL

5 red mullet, medium-sized
olive oil
1½–2 oz. butter
1 dessertspoon finely chopped parsley
lemon juice

a touch of cayenne
garlic
salt and freshly ground pepper
quarters of lemon and brown bread and butter

After scaling the mullet and removing the gills, brush well with the oil and grill on both sides. Meantime work the butter with the parsley, sharpen with lemon juice and add cayenne. Arrange the fish in an earthenware dish, well rubbed with garlic. Spread each mullet well with the butter, season, and serve with quarters of lemon and brown bread and butter.

ROUGETS AUX CÂPRES

4–5 even-sized red mullet
seasoned flour
2 oz. butter
lemon rind
2 tablespoons slightly chopped capers

salt and freshly ground pepper
1 dessertspoon lemon juice (approx.)
1 tablespoon chopped parsley

Scale mullet, remove gills, wash and dry. Roll lightly in seasoned flour. Heat half the butter in a large frying-pan, put in the mullet and fry till golden brown on both sides. Just before taking from the pan grate over a little lemon rind. Scatter over the capers. Season well. Arrange down a hot dish, pour on any juice from the pan, and slip into the oven to keep hot. Wipe out the pan, reheat, and drop in remaining butter. When a good *noisette* quickly add the lemon juice and parsley. Pour at once over the fish and serve.

PLAICE (CARRELET OR PLIE)

carrelet may indicate flounder or plaice; plie also means plaice

The prevalence of fried plaice on the menus of popular restaurants is in some degree an indication of our unadventurous spirit in the cookery world. It is one of the duller fish and relies on accompaniments for flavour and cooking for texture. Except for the more complicated, the recipes given for sole (pages 475–86) are suitable also for plaice.

FILETS DE PLIE GRATINÉS

1–2 lb. plaice, filleted
1 glass white wine
½ glass water
salt
1 bay-leaf
a blade of mace
peppercorns
½ oz. butter
2 shallots, chopped
3–4 oz. mushrooms, finely chopped
1 dessertspoon chopped parsley

1 large raw potato, grated and soaked in cold water ½ an hour
1 handful of fresh breadcrumbs
2–3 tablespoons oil or butter for frying
Roux
  1 oz. butter
  ¾ oz. flour
½–¾ gill cream or top of milk
fried croûtons or sautéd tomatoes for garnish

Skin plaice, wash and dry. Fold fillets. Lay in a buttered fireproof dish and pour over the wine and water, add seasoning, bay-leaf, and spices. Poach in oven 15 minutes. Melt butter in a pan, add shallots and after a few minutes the mushrooms. Cook 3–4 minutes, season well, add parsley. Drain and dry potato. Fry in the oil until crisp, remove and fry crumbs in same way. Set aside. Pour off liquor from fish. Make the roux, add liquor, stir until thickening, add cream or milk. Boil and then simmer a few minutes.

Arrange mushroom mixture on bottom of serving dish. Place fillets on top, coat with the sauce, and scatter over the fried potato and crumbs. The dish may be garnished with fried croûtons or sautéd tomatoes.

CARRELET AUX OIGNONS

1 oz. butter	1 wineglass white wine or dry
½ lb. onions, thinly sliced	cider
1 level teaspoon each of salt	½ gill water or mushroom liquor
and sugar	a squeeze of lemon juice
freshly ground pepper	½ oz. butter and good ¼ oz.
1–1½ lb. whole plaice (or fillets	flour for beurre manié
may be used)	chopped parsley

Melt butter in a stew-pan, add onions, salt, sugar, and plenty of pepper. Cover and cook gently until the onions are soft but not brown. Now lay the onions on the bottom of a fireproof dish, spreading them to the sides. Wash, trim, and dry the fish, score across the bone and lay in the dish, seasoning well. Pour over the liquids, add lemon juice, bring slowly to the boil on the top of the stove. Cover with buttered paper and cook in a moderate oven 20 minutes, basting every 6–7 minutes with the juice. Then lift out the fish, remove dark skin, and lay on a hot dish. Strain liquid from the onions, and scatter them round. Thicken the liquid with the beurre manié, boil up well and spoon over the dish. Dust well with chopped parsley.

The recipe given on page 481 for Filets de Sole Sylvette may also be adapted for plaice.

In the following recipe for Danish Plaice given to us by Mrs Francis, contrast of texture is obtained by poaching half the fillets and frying the rest. These are served in a rich sauce, and the dish is good, if a little lavish.

DANISH PLAICE

A suitable dinner-party dish.

2 plaice weighing 1–1¼ lb.	beaten egg and dry white
each, filleted	crumbs for coating
seasoning	deep fat (or butter for shallow
white wine (or lemon juice and	frying)
water) to cover	potato purée
flour	

Sauce

1 oz. butter	2–3 oz. mushrooms, sliced and
¾ oz. flour	cooked in a tablespoon of
1½ gills creamy milk	water and a little lemon
1 small tin of asparagus tips or	juice
a bunch of small fresh as-	
paragus	

Skin fillets, wash and dry. Take 4 of them, fold and lay in a buttered dish. Season and moisten well with white wine (or lemon juice and water) ready for poaching. Cut the remaining fillets into three lengthwise; flour and egg and crumb them. Now poach the first 4 fillets for 10–15 minutes. Take them up, strain off the liquor, and keep the fish hot.

Sauce. Melt the butter, add the flour, pour on the liquor, thicken, and add the milk. Stir until boiling and simmer to a creamy consistency. Draw aside, adjust seasoning, and add the asparagus tips and cooked mushrooms. Keep sauce hot in a bain-marie.

Fry the crumbed fillets in deep fat, or in butter in a frying-pan, until golden brown.

Have ready a potato purée, pipe at each end of a hot dish, lay the poached fillets in the middle, coat over the sauce, and arrange the fried fish down each side.

ROCK SALMON

The following recipe for this somewhat ambiguous fish is suitable for any form of white fish, just as the recipes given for these may in turn be used for rock salmon. There is one, for example, Turbot Piedmontaise, (page 487), which is particularly applicable. The following is a good supper dish:

ROCK SALMON PAPRIKA

1 lb. rock salmon	1 heaped teaspoon paprika
water with lemon juice or a	½ pint milk or milk and water
little vinegar for poaching	1 canned pimento or fresh
a bouquet garni	sweet pepper blanched
2 oz. mushrooms	salt and pepper
1 oz. butter	freshly boiled noodles
¾ oz. flour	

Cut the fish into neat steaks or fillets and poach in acidulated water with a bouquet garni 15–20 minutes. Meantime prepare the sauce. Wash the mushrooms, slice finely, melt the butter in a saucepan, add mushrooms, cover and simmer for 2 minutes. Then add the flour and paprika off the fire, pour on the milk, and stir until boiling. Reduce for a minute or two, then season and add the pimento or sweet pepper finely sliced. Arrange the fish on the serving dish, pour over the sauce, and serve at once with a dish of freshly boiled noodles.

ROCK SALMON WITH A MACÉDOINE OF VEGETABLES

Any firm white-fleshed fish is good for this dish.

1 lb. rock salmon	*Macédoine*
a little milk	carrots, celeriac, peas, and
flour (seasoned)	beans or sprouts, ½–¾ lb.
½–1 gill oil	in all, cut in dice
seasoning	¾ gill creamy béchamel (see
	page 155)

First prepare a good macédoine of vegetables, carrots, celeriac, peas, and beans. Boil the vegetables, separately. Peas and beans may be tinned,

but in the summer the macédoine should be made with all young vegetables. When cooked and well drained, mix them together with the
béchamel, season and keep hot.

Cut the fish into pieces the length and size of a little finger, dip into the
milk, toss in seasoned flour, taking care that each piece is well covered.
Heat the oil smoking hot in a frying-pan and fry a few at a time until
golden brown and crisp. Pile the macédoine in the centre of a dish and
surround with the fish.

SALMON, OR SAUMON, AND SALMON TROUT, OR TRUITE SAUMONÉE

Salmon cooked straight out of the water has a thick creamy curd
between the flakes of fish which does not appear in fish which has been kept
for 2–3 days. There are people who dislike the look of this curd and some
think it unwholesome, so a practice has arisen of keeping salmon 2–3 days
before cooking. This is not accepted by everyone, many people preferring
the fresh fish. In England we are inclined to restrict ourselves to a limited
number of salmon dishes, boiled salmon (hot or cold), grilled salmon
steaks, salmon mayonnaise, kedgeree, and salmon mousse covering this
fish in the average kitchen. Perhaps this is because we do not eat this
luxury fish very often, therefore no great variety is needed. Some
friends of mine, incarcerated in the precincts of Dublin Castle during the
1916 rebellion in Ireland, found themselves restricted to a diet of un-
relieved salmon for almost a week. What a blessing to them would have
been Mme Prunier's book giving around thirty ways of dealing with this
delicious but rich fish. As it was, their close friends were prayed to avoid
salmon when entertaining them for long months afterwards.

BOILED SALMON

As with all other 'boiled' fish, this should really be called poached
salmon, for the court bouillon should only just have a slight movement and
not be bubbling at all. For time one must be guided slightly by the
thickness of the fish, roughly about 8 minutes to the pound when the fish
is over 6 lb. in weight. A 10-lb. salmon takes about 1¼ hours. The
court bouillon given on page 473 is suitable.

Hot salmon may be accompanied by plain boiled potatoes, by a cucumber
salad, and by a variety of sauces, usually those of a slightly piquante nature:
hollandaise, mousseline, or a venitienne.

Cold salmon may be accompanied by cucumber salad, various mayonnaise sauces, hot cream sauce and so forth. If for a main dish plain
boiled potatoes are suitable.

Salmon trout is a more delicately flavoured fish than salmon, smaller in
size and usually served whole. It is cooked in the same way as salmon

and served with similar accompaniments. Sometimes when fishermen bring in small fish weighing as little as 1–1½ lb.—a size not seen with the fishmonger—they may be split, brushed with butter, and grilled, an epicurean experience. Salmon trout, which generally weigh 3–6 lb., may be poached as salmon, but sometimes their length causes inconvenience if no fish-kettle is at hand. In this case they may be poached in the oven, preferably in a fireproof dish in court bouillon or wine. In the following recipe the red wine makes an excellent sauce:

SALMON TROUT POACHED IN THE OVEN

Butter a fireproof dish well. Curl the trout a little to fit the dish, pour over the best red wine you may (burgundy for choice, about ½ a bottle for a fish of 3–4 lb.), add a bouquet garni, 2–3 blades of mace, 6 peppercorns, and salt and freshly ground black pepper. Poach, basting frequently—this is important, for if it is neglected, or if the heat is too great, there is fear that the skin will crack—for 45–60 minutes in a slow to moderate oven. Strain off the liquid, measure off between ½ and ¾ pint (but see note below) and thicken to the consistency of thin cream with beurre manié made with approximately 1 heaped teaspoon each of flour and butter, then add a good ½-cup of cream and boil up rapidly. Serve the sauce apart.

N.B. Reference may be made here to the note 'To flamber with wine' on page 66, but if a good wine has been used the liquid from the cooking will be delicate in flavour and suitable for use as it is. If, however, a harsher wine has been employed the whole of the liquid may be reduced to the required quantity of ½–¾ pint so as to ameliorate any crudity. Taste the liquid, therefore, and decide whether it is suitable to use as it is or if it must first be reduced.

SALMON TROUT IN ASPIC (FOR 8–10)

salmon trout, 3½–4½ lb.
1½ pints court bouillon (approx.), or a mixture of white wine and water, with onion, peppercorns, and bay-leaf to flavour
1 quart good fish aspic for glazing and decorating

12 good prawns
thin slices of cucumber with the skin left on
tarragon or dill
an appropriate cold sauce to accompany, such as mayonnaise or sauce verte

Clean the trout carefully, well brushing and scraping the cavity, particularly near the backbone. Leave on the head. Curl the trout nicely and lay in a big fireproof dish or tin. Pour in the liquid. Lay over a piece of paper, taking care that it does not touch the fish. Put into a slow to moderate oven and cook gently, basting frequently, about 45–60 minutes. The paper may be removed towards the end of the poaching, provided the oven does not get too hot. Remove and allow fish to cool well in the liquor, basting occasionally. When quite cold carefully strip off the skin, leaving on the head and tail.

Loosen the flesh along the ridge of the backbone, and with the scissors nick the bone just below the head and above the tail. Gently pull and ease out the bone. Glaze with cool aspic and allow to set. Remove shells from the tails of the prawns, leaving on the heads. Lay on a wire rack and brush with the cool aspic. Run a little aspic on to the bottom of a large flat oval silver dish, to the depth of about ⅛ inch. Leave to set.

Lift trout carefully on to the dish. Decorate the flat of the dish with the cucumber and sprays of dill or tarragon. Coat over with aspic. Arrange a line of prawns down the backbone of the trout, garnish the edge of the dish with blocks of aspic, chopped aspic, and any remaining prawns. Serve a mayonnaise or sauce verte separately.

N.B. For a beginner the boning of the trout may present a difficulty, in which case omit altogether, or bone on the dish for serving. Glaze and allow to set before adding the cucumber, etc. This is not an ideal practice, but can be done by the inexperienced and if the fish is friable and inclined to break.

SKATE, OR RAIE

This was once a cheap and neglected fish seen only in our island in fried-fish shops where it could be rendered unrecognizable by a ballooned covering of fried batter. It has become now more popular and in consequence more expensive. Ugly and unpleasing as it certainly appears in its raw state, it has nevertheless a delicate flavour, and properly prepared is considered a suitable *plat du jour* in the more expensive hotels and restaurants that pride themselves on their cuisine. Before the war this fish was usually prepared by the fishmonger, so that it was to all intents and purposes ready for cooking, but though this may still happen it does not do so invariably. For this reason somewhat full instructions are given here.

The surface should be gelatinous, shiny, and moist. If completely dry it is not fit for consumption. It is the wings or side pieces only which are eaten, each of these weighing from 1½ to 2½ lb. according to the size of the fish. Skate is generally bought by the wing, one of medium size serving 3–4 people. If it has not been prepared by the fishmonger the wing must be well scrubbed with a coarse brush and then thoroughly rinsed. It is trimmed to remove the fringe of gristly bone round the edge. After this it is cut again longitudinally into wide strips 3–4 inches long and 2–3 inches wide. This cuts through the bone, which is really more gristle than bone. The pieces are then poached in court bouillon, milk, or water according to the recipe in hand. The classic and perhaps best dish is Raie au Beurre Noir, although the other dishes given are also good.

COURT BOUILLON FOR SKATE

1 quart water
1 level dessertspoon salt
1 wineglass vinegar
4 oz. onions, thinly sliced

5–6 parsley stalks, a sprig of
  thyme, and a bay-leaf
6 peppercorns

Put all ingredients in a stew-pan, bring to boil and simmer 5 minutes. Pour liquid over the skate. Bring again to boil, draw aside and allow barely to simmer 25–30 minutes. Lift out the pieces with a fish slice, drain very well on a piece of muslin or clean linen rag, and gently scrape the skin from both sides. The fish is then ready for finishing in the way required.

RAIE AU BEURRE NOIR (FOR 4–6)

1 wing of skate weighing about 2 lb.	2 large tablespoons vinegar
court bouillon as above	salt and pepper
beurre noir (black butter):	1 dessertspoon capers
2 oz. butter	1 teaspoon chopped parsley

Prepare as indicated above, arrange in a serving dish and keep hot. Heat a frying-pan, drop in the butter and cook to a deep nut-brown. Pour over the skate. Add vinegar to the pan with seasoning and reduce to half. Sprinkle capers and parsley over the fish and pour over the reduced vinegar. Serve at once. Plain boiled potatoes usually accompany this dish.

N.B. The term 'black butter' may be misleading; if the butter were cooked to so dark a colour it would be burnt. In fact, it is only cooked to a good rich brown, darker than 'noisette.'

RAIE A L'ORANGE

A good dish, to be served piping hot.

1–1½ lb. skate	1 teaspoon each of chopped
1 onion	parsley and thyme
1 oz. butter	salt and pepper
2 oranges	a few drops of vinegar
1 teaspoon sugar	

Prepare and cook skate as directed, about 25–30 minutes. Drain very well, skin, arrange in dish and keep hot. Chop the onion very finely, melt half the butter in a small frying-pan, add the onion and soften slowly without browning. Peel 1 orange and slice into rounds. Add the rest of the butter to the pan, put in the orange, dust over with sugar and fry rather quickly until turning colour. Then add the juice of the other orange, the herbs, seasoning, and a few drops of vinegar. Boil up and pour over the fish.

RAIE AU FROMAGE

1½–2 lb. skate	a pinch of sugar
¾ pint milk	salt
a clove of garlic	
a slice of onion	*Sauce*
a blade of mace, a sprig of thyme, and a bay-leaf	¾ oz. butter
	¾ oz. flour
4–5 parsley stalks	seasoning
12 button onions	
¼ oz. butter	1½ oz. grated cheese
	triangular croûtons (and a little oil for frying these)

Prepare the skate as directed and lay the pieces in a stew or sauté pan. Add to the milk the garlic, slice of onion, mace, and herbs and allow them to infuse gently. When the milk is well flavoured strain it on to the skate, cover, simmer till tender. Lift out the fish, drain, skin, and keep hot. Melt the ¾ oz. of butter, add flour and the flavoured milk, blend and stir till boiling. Simmer till creamy, adjust seasoning. Blanch the onions for 7–10 minutes, drain, return to pan with the ¼ oz. of butter, the salt and sugar. Shake over moderate fire until lightly brown. Scatter half the cheese over the bottom of the serving dish, arrange the fish on this, coat with the sauce, sprinkle with the remaining cheese, allow to brown under the grill, and garnish with onions and croûtons.

FRITÔT DE RAIE

a wing of skate, approx. 2 lb.
  (cut in pieces and cooked in
  court bouillon as described)
1 onion
juice of ½ lemon
1 tablespoon oil

salt and black pepper
fritter batter 2 (see page 443)
sprigs of parsley
quarters of lemon and a sharp
  sauce to accompany

Drain and skin the pieces of cooked skate. Slice the onion and mix with the lemon juice, oil, and seasoning. Put the skate into this mixture and allow to lie in it 2–3 hours. Drain the fish and the slices of onion, toss the latter in flour, fry them in deep fat, and keep hot. Fry the parsley. Dip the pieces of skate in batter and fry to golden brown. Arrange in a serving dish, scatter over the onion and fried parsley. Serve very hot with quarters of lemon and any sharp sauce, such as tartare or rémoulade.

SOLE, OR SOLE

Once on arrival at a very northerly point in Scotland we went, a party of us, after seeing the fishing fleet come in, to dine at the hotel. Just before us a large party from a charabanc had gone into the dining-room. When the mannerly but exhausted waiter came to us he began apologetically to prepare us for a shock. He could not, he regretted, serve us all with roast beef, for the party before had left a mere two portions. Would we, could we, contemplate the possibility, one or two of us, of eating instead a grilled Dover sole! 'Just in from the quay,' he said, in palliation of so second-rate an offer. We assured him that one and all we would prefer to eat the sea-fresh fish. I have never, I think, eaten a fish quite so good as that; it may sound a little eccentric in a chapter on fish to say it was so un-fishy! It had a sweetness of nuts, tasted of the sea, and was so Lucullean a dish that it needed no frills of any sort or kind, though it was bedewed with fresh butter cooked to a golden brown.

It always seems to come back to that—fresh fish out of the sea needs little of sauces or trimmings, and yet, of course, every dish to be made is glorified by having such to cook. Having said so much I should add that Mme Prunier gives, I think, about one hundred and twenty-four ways of cooking sole, and reading her recipes one feels it would be sensible to live where the fishing fleet comes in and try each of them in turn.

The flesh of sole is delicate and firm—the best variety is the black Dover sole; a slip sole is a black sole not weighing over ½ lb. After black sole comes in merit the lemon sole. At the end of the chapter (page 520) is a note on Florence or root fennel served with fish. The method mentioned there is admirable for sole.

A la meunière is, as has been said, a perfect way of cooking delicately flavoured fish straight from the sea. It is a classic, and although garnishes may be added of sautéd mushrooms or of tomatoes, it is really best perfectly plain.

FILETS DE SOLE MEUNIÈRE

two 1¼-lb. soles, filleted	1 large teaspoon chopped
a small quantity of seasoned	mixed herbs, including
flour	parsley
2 oz. butter	1 teaspoon lemon juice
	quarters of lemon

The fish may be served plain, or with sautéd mushrooms, tomatoes, or other suitable garnish. Alternatively, a crisply grilled rasher of streaky bacon can be laid between each fillet when dishing. If a garnish is to be served, prepare this first, as the actual cooking of the sole takes very little time.

Skin the fillets, wash and dry thoroughly. Roll in seasoned flour. Heat a thick frying-pan and drop in a little less than half the butter. When foaming lay in the fillets with the skinned side uppermost. Cook over a moderate heat until golden brown, then turn and brown on the other side. Lay the fillets, without draining, in a hot dish, allowing them to overlap slightly. Add the garnish (if called for) and slide the dish into a cool oven to keep hot. Wipe out the frying-pan, reheat, drop in the rest of the butter. Allow to colour a delicate nut-brown, then quickly add the herbs and lemon juice. Pour over the fish and serve at once with quarters of lemon.

N.B. Herbs are sometimes omitted and chopped parsley only scattered over the dish before serving.

SOLE COLBERT

This is an excellent variant of fried sole in which the two top fillets are gently and partially lifted away from the bone so that after cooking the bone may be gently lifted out and the cavity filled with maître d'hôtel butter. One large sole may be used, or a small one for each person.

a sole weighing 1–1½ lb., or 4	dry white crumbs
slip soles	deep fat
seasoned flour	2 oz. maître d'hôtel butter,
beaten egg	well chilled (see page 17)

Skin and trim soles, leave on the head. With a sharp knife make a cut down the centre of the backbone on one side of the fish. Raise the fillets on this side only. Then with the scissors cut the backbone through just below the head and above the tail. Wash and dry thoroughly. Roll in the flour, shake well to remove any surplus, and brush with beaten egg, taking care that the egg coats the inside of the raised fillets. Roll and press in the crumbs. Fry in the smoking hot fat to a rich golden brown. Drain, then carefully pull out the backbone. Fill the cavity with the maître d'hôtel butter, dish and serve immediately.

When a recipe calls for sole to be poached this may be done in a fish stock or fumet, sometimes in a mushroom fumet or in wine, or in a mixture of all these liquids. Cider is sometimes used in place of wine, but it should preferably be draught cider for this and for all fish so cooked.

The following recipe is suitable for any white fish:

FILETS DE SOLE AU CIDRE

4 large fillets of sole
1 shallot, chopped
1 bay-leaf
seasoning
1 wineglass draught cider

½ wineglass water
a little fish fumet [1] or other additional liquid (a good simple fumet may be found in the recipe for Sole Mornay, see below)

Sauce

¾ oz. butter
¾ oz. flour

1 heaped teaspoon chopped parsley

Skin the fillets and lay them in a fireproof dish with shallot and bay-leaf. Season and pour over cider and water. Poach 20–30 minutes. Pour the liquor off the sole, measure and make up to between ½ and ¾ pint liquid with fish fumet. Melt butter in a saucepan, add flour and liquid off the fire. Stir till boiling, simmer till the consistency of thin cream, add chopped parsley, season, and pour over fish.

Sole Mornay is a classic and the recipe given may be used for any white fish. It is poached in a fumet and masked in a well-seasoned cheese sauce. It is a useful recipe also for fillets of haddock or plaice.

SOLE MORNAY

a sole weighing 1–1½ lb., filleted and sent from the fishmonger with the bones

Fumet

bones and trimmings from sole
1 small onion
1 small carrot
a bouquet of herbs
½–¾ pint water

a small handful of mushroom stalks and peelings (optional)
6 peppercorns
a pinch of salt

---

[1] Fumet is the proper liquid to use as it gives the right texture, but cider, wine, or water may be used instead, or cream, but *not milk*.

Sauce

1 oz. butter	salt and pepper
¾ oz. flour	a dust of ground nutmeg
½ pint milk	½ teaspoon made mustard
1–1½ oz. grated cheese	

Skin fillets, wash, dry, and set aside.   Prepare fumet with ingredients given, simmer 20–25 minutes.   Strain and cool.   Fold under tips of fillets, lay in a buttered fireproof dish.   Pour over enough fumet barely to cover. Cover with a piece of buttered paper and poach in oven 15–20 minutes.

To prepare the sauce.   Allow butter just to melt, add flour off the fire, pour on milk, blend thoroughly.   Stir till boiling.   Reduce for a minute or two, draw aside, beat in cheese by degrees.   Add seasoning.   Re-dish fish, coat with sauce and glaze under grill.

This dish may be garnished with sautéd mushrooms, or sliced cooked mushrooms may be scattered over the fillets before masking with the sauce:

FILETS DE SOLE DUGLÉRÉ

a sole weighing 1–1½ lb., or fillets (if the latter the backbone should be sent with them)	¾–1 oz. butter
	¾ oz. flour
	½ gill cream or rich milk
1½ gills strong fish stock prepared from bones, skin, bouquet, and shallot, or alternatively:	1 teaspoon finely chopped parsley
	2 small tomatoes peeled, pipped, and chopped
½ gill water	salt and pepper
1 gill white wine	
a bouquet garni	
a sliced shallot	

Skin and fillet the fish, place in a buttered fireproof dish and pour over the stock.   (If the alternative referred to above is used, cover the fish with the backbone and add the ingredients mentioned.)   Poach in a slow to moderate oven 10–15 minutes.   Melt the butter, add the flour, blend well, and pour on the strained liquor from the fish.   Stir till smooth, season, and cook, stirring till the mixture thickens.   Add the cream and bring to boil.   Reduce rapidly for about 2–3 minutes, draw aside, add parsley and tomatoes.   Arrange the fillets in a dish, coat with the sauce and serve immediately.

In the following dish the poached fillets are served on a salpicon of prawns inside the shell of a baked potato.   An excellent luncheon dish.

FILETS DE SOLE GEORGETTE

4 large, long-shaped potatoes	a blade of mace, bay-leaf
1–1¼ lb. sole	scant ¾ oz. flour
1 glass water	¾ oz. butter
½ glass white wine	½ gill milk or thin cream
a slice of onion	½ pint prawns, shelled
salt and pepper	

Bake the potatoes in their skins. Fillet and skin the sole. Fold the fillets and poach in the water and wine, with the onion, salt, pepper, bay-leaf, and mace to flavour. Drain off the liquor and reduce to 1½ gills. Strain. Make a roux with the butter and flour, pour on the fumet, thicken, add the milk, season, and stir continuously until boiling. Simmer a few minutes. Add a spoonful or two of this sauce to the shelled prawns. Cut the tops off the potatoes lengthways and scoop out the pulp. Rub the skins and tops over with buttered paper, put a spoonful of the salpicon in the bottom of each, lay a fillet of sole on top, coat over with the sauce, and replace the cover. Reheat for a few minutes in the oven, then serve on a napkin. If the potato pulp is firm, a small quantity can be diced and added to the prawn salpicon, or shredded tomato or sliced cooked mushroom can be added.

FILETS DE SOLE A LA DIABLE

The devil sauce made with cream given on page 725 is suitable to dress small poached fillets. It is good also with cooked smoked finnan-haddock, with filleted kippers, and with salmon.

FILETS DE SOLE NELSON

A good luncheon dish, suitable when there are soft roes to use up.

1–1½ lb. sole	¾ oz. butter
¼ pint fish fumet	scant ¾ oz. flour
3 or 4 potatoes	¼ pint milk
oil for frying	salt and pepper
¼ lb. soft roes	finely chopped parsley

Fillet and skin the fish, poach in fish fumet. Drain and keep warm. Scoop out as many large potato balls as possible from the potatoes. Blanch, dry, and sauter in the oil. Drain well. Flour the soft roes and fry in the same oil. Drain and keep hot. Make a velouté sauce (see page 152) with the butter, flour, fish liquor, and milk. Reduce well, season, and tammy. Re-dish the fillets, coat over with the sauce, arrange round the dish 'bouquets' of soft roes and the potatoes. Dust the garnish well with parsley.

Alternative method: The roes are laid down the length of the fillets when both are raw, and the fillets are poached in the same way. Dish as before —garniture only of potato, which must therefore be increased in quantity and arranged at each end of the dish.

FILETS DE SOLE ALPHONSE XIII
fillets of sole with aubergine

This is an excellent lunch dish, and fillets of other white fish may be used in place of sole.

a sole weighing 1 lb., filleted and skinned	½ lb. firm ripe tomatoes, peeled, pipped, and coarsely chopped
seasoned flour	2 cloves of garlic crushed with
1¼ oz. butter for frying	½ teaspoon salt
1 teaspoon lemon juice	1 large teaspoon chopped basil
2 medium-sized good auber- gines	or lemon thyme
	salt and pepper
½ oz. butter	4–5 tablespoons olive oil
1–2 oz. onion, finely sliced	chopped parsley

First prepare aubergines. Split in two lengthways. Make an incision round the edge of each half and criss-cross the centres with a sharp knife. Sprinkle with salt and set aside for half an hour. Melt butter in a saucepan, add the onion, cook till turning colour. Add tomatoes and garlic, simmer until rich and pulpy, about 15–20 minutes. Add herbs, season, and set aside. Drain and dry the aubergines, heat half the oil until lightly smoking in a frying-pan, lay in two halves cut side downwards and fry until golden brown, turn and fry for a shorter time on the skin side. Lift out and drain. Fry the other two halves in the same way in the remaining oil. Scoop out the flesh with a dessertspoon and chop coarsely. Add to the tomato mixture and adjust seasoning. Simmer 3–4 minutes. Lay the skins of the aubergines down an oval fireproof or copper dish. Fill equally with the mixture. Keep hot. Wipe out the frying-pan and reheat. Have ready the sole fillets rolled in seasoned flour. Drop in half the butter, when foaming lay in the fish, skinned side uppermost, and fry moderately quickly until golden brown on both sides, turning once only. Lift out and lay each fillet on a half-aubergine. Wipe out pan, reheat, drop in remaining butter, and when a light brown add lemon juice. Pour a little on each fillet, scatter over the chopped parsley, and serve at once.

The following recipe is suitable for fresh haddock as well as sole:

FILETS DE SOLE MACONNAISE

4 fillets of sole	a slice of onion
1 wineglass burgundy	½ lb. button onions
¼ wineglass water	¼ oz. butter
peppercorns	½ teaspoon sugar
bay-leaf	¼ lb. mushrooms
	a little butter or oil for frying

Sauce

½ oz. butter	½ gill creamy milk or cream
½ oz. flour, scant weight	salt and pepper

Trim and skin the fish. Wash and dry. Fold over and lay in a buttered fireproof dish. Pour over the wine and water, add the peppercorns, bay-leaf, and slice of onion with a pinch of salt. Cover with a buttered paper.

Set in a slow oven to poach for 20 minutes.   Then blanch the onions for
5 minutes.   Drain and return to the pan with the ¼ oz. of butter, a pinch
of salt, and the sugar.   Cover and cook gently until the onions are tender
and a light brown. Peel and trim the mushrooms.   If button mushrooms leave whole, otherwise cut in quarters.   Fry quickly in the extra
butter or the oil.   Keep both onions and mushrooms hot.   Arrange fillets
on a hot dish.   Melt the remaining ½ oz. of butter in a saucepan, mix in the
flour and strain on the liquor from the fish.   Stir until boiling, simmer to a
creamy consistency, add the milk and adjust seasoning.   Coat the fish.
Surround the dish with the onions and mushrooms.   Serve very hot.

In the next dish, which is substantial and suitable for a main course, care
must be taken to get the mirepoix of vegetables well cooked.   The amount
should not exceed 1 large tablespoon of cooked mirepoix for each fillet.
This recipe is often given as a test to our students to observe their care in
the matter of quantities and dishing.

FILETS DE SOLE SYLVETTE

1½ lb. sole, filleted, and the bones	1½ oz. butter
	seasoning
4 oz. carrots	water or fish stock
2 oz. turnips	a slice of onion
1 stem of celery	1 bay-leaf
2 oz. fresh beans or Brussels sprouts	a few peppercorns
	¾ oz. flour
2 tomatoes	¾ gill creamy milk

Dice all the vegetables except the tomatoes finely.   Melt ½ oz. of the
butter in a saucepan, put in the vegetables, season, and cover.   Cook
gently 3–4 minutes on the fire, then add the tomatoes skinned, pipped, and
cut in dice.   Cover tightly and put pan in oven for about 20 minutes.

Skin fish, lay in buttered dish, cover with water or fish stock, and the
bones; add onion, bay-leaf, and peppercorns and poach in the oven 15
minutes.   Melt the rest of the butter in a saucepan, add the flour off the
fire, strain on the liquor from the fish (this should measure 1½ gills).
Thicken, add the milk, season, and simmer for a few minutes.   Turn the
vegetable mirepoix on to the serving dish, arrange the fillets on this and
coat over the sauce.

Soles Fourrées aux Crevettes calls for a slip sole (a small black one) for
each person.   The sole is filled with a farce of prawns and mushrooms.
This is an excellent dish for a luncheon or dinner party.

SOLES FOURRÉES AUX CREVETTES

small black slip soles, 1 for each person	prawn filling (see next page)
	white crumbs
butter	watercress

For this dish the backbone has to be removed but the shape of the fish is
kept intact.   Do not remove head or tail—these serve to keep the fish in

shape.   Skin the fish whole and with a sharp knife raise the two top fillets without detaching them.   Cut backbone with scissors and pull it out. Lay fish in a buttered fireproof dish, fill them with the prawn mixture, reshape, brush over with melted butter, and scatter well over with white crumbs.   Sprinkle again with melted butter, then bake in a moderate oven, basting occasionally, for 20–30 minutes.   Pass under a hot grill to finish browning.   Serve with bouquets of crisp watercress.

Prawn filling: Allow 1 heaped tablespoon picked prawns, 1 oz. button mushrooms, 1 tablespoon cream, and 1 tablespoon sauce blanche or béchamel (see pages 160 and 155) for each sole.   Quarter the mushrooms, toss quickly in butter over the fire, then add seasoning, the prawns, sauce, and cream, and use.

Sole Marguery is named from a restaurant in Paris.   It is a very good dinner-party dish.

SOLE MARGUERY

6 fillets of Dover sole	1 carrot
fish fumet made from the bones	a bouquet garni
1 quart mussels	¼ pint picked or frozen shrimps
white wine	a little butter
1 onion	black pepper

Sauce

1 oz. butter, scant ¾ oz. flour for the roux	1 wineglass white wine
1½ gills milk	1 egg yolk
salt and pepper	2 tablespoons cream
1 chopped shallot	½ oz. butter

feuilletons (see page 56)

Skin fillets, poach them in fumet made from the bones.   Have ready the mussels well scrubbed, put into a pan with a little wine, the onion, carrot, and bouquet.   Cover and bring quickly to the boil.   Shell mussels when opened and remove the beards.   If picked shrimps soak to remove salt, then drain.   Toss over the fire with a little butter and black pepper. Carefully drain the fumet from the sole, and reduce to a syrupy consistency to make the ½ gill required for the sauce.

Sauce. Make the roux, pour on the milk, bring to boil and season. Meantime simmer the shallot in the white wine until reduced to half.   Add to the sauce with the fumet, simmer for a few minutes, and draw aside. Beat the yolk with the cream, add carefully to the sauce, finish with the butter, season, and strain before using.

Arrange fillets on the serving dish, scatter over the mussels and shrimps, and coat over the sauce.   The dish may be glazed or not as required. Garnish with feuilletons.

Certain fruits associate well with fish; one has orange with skate, gooseberry sauce with certain fish dishes, fried bananas with many.   Grapes, particularly muscats, are a good addition to sole, and the following is a delicious dish:

FILETS DE SOLE VÉRONIQUE

a sole of 1¼–1½ lb., filleted, and sent from fishmonger with the bones	1 onion, sliced
	3 or 4 peppercorns
	½ bay-leaf
white wine and water, or all wine if desired	4–6 oz. white grapes

Sauce

½–¾ oz. butter	½ gill very strong fish stock or fumet reduced from the liquor of the fish
1 oz. flour	
1½ gills milk	
	salt and pepper

Skin the fish, wash and trim the fillets. Dry. Lay in a buttered fire-proof dish and just cover with a mixture of white wine and water, approximately half and half, or all wine can be used if desired. Lay the slices of onion round, also peppercorns and bay-leaf. Cover with the washed bones of the fish and poach in a slow oven for 15–20 minutes. Meanwhile peel and pip the grapes, sprinkle with white wine, put in a warm place between two plates to get hot. Then strain off the liquor from the sole and reduce to just over 2 tablespoons.

Melt a good half of the butter in a saucepan, add the flour and milk and stir in the fumet, boil, reducing to the right consistency. Adjust seasoning and add off the fire the remaining butter. Arrange the fillets on a hot dish, coat with the sauce, arrange the grapes at the side, and serve immediately.

FILETS DE SOLE CUBAT

1 sole weighing 1¼–1½ lb. seasoning and a squeeze of lemon juice	1 wineglass white wine or water

Mushroom purée

4 oz. mushrooms
béchamel sauce (see page 155):

1¼ oz. butter	¼ pint milk
1¼ oz. flour	salt and pepper

Mornay sauce (see page 156)

¾ oz. butter	1½ oz. grated cheese
½ oz. flour	salt and pepper
½ pint milk	

Garnish

sliced truffle or mushroom

Fillet and skin the sole (reserving the backbone), place in a buttered fire-proof dish, season, add a squeeze of lemon and the wine, cover with the backbone and poach in a moderate oven 8–10 minutes. Meantime sieve the raw mushrooms and add to the béchamel. Reduce well.

Cover the bottom of a serving dish with the reduced sauce and lay the fillets of fish on the top. Decorate each with slices of truffle or mushroom and coat with the mornay sauce. Glaze under the grill.

The next three recipes are for somewhat complicated dishes to be attempted by the accomplished and perhaps ambitious cook. In Filets de Sole Gustav the poached fillets are laid on a light purée of potatoes and vegetable marrow. R. H. says she prefers this dish without the purée but that it is then considerably less substantial. The sauce is hollandaise containing asparagus tips, mushrooms, and tomatoes.

FILETS DE SOLE GUSTAV

4 fillets of sole
white wine to cover
a purée of vegetable marrow
    and potato, well seasoned
hollandaise sauce

a few asparagus tips, cooked
3 mushrooms, sliced
2 tomatoes sliced, quartered,
    pipped, and cut into shreds

Poach the fillets in the wine and lay on the purée.

Hollandaise sauce

2 yolks of egg
3 oz. butter
3 tablespoons vinegar reduced
    to 1 dessertspoon with herbs
    and peppercorns

3 tablespoons white wine re-
    duced to half
2 tablespoons thick cream
salt

Make the hollandaise according to directions on page 157, adding wine and cream. It should be, when finished, of the consistency of cream, so the wine must be added judiciously. Add the asparagus tips, mushrooms, and tomatoes. Coat sauce over fish and glaze lightly under the grill.

SOLE A LA BONNE FEMME

This is a famous and classic dish suitable for a dinner party, in which the contrast of the two sauces, one a creamy white wine, the other a piquante hollandaise, is particularly pleasing. This dish has also an advantage in that preparation to the point of dishing, though not the final glazing, may be done in advance. It is well worth the work entailed but is not a dish for a beginner to tackle.

1 sole weighing 1¼–1½ lb.,
    filleted, and the bones
1 gill white wine
¾ gill strong well-flavoured fish
    fumet made from the bones

and trimmings (see fish
    fumet, page 477)
a squeeze of lemon
2 oz. mushrooms, and a nut of
    butter and squeeze of lemon
    for cooking

Hollandaise sauce

2 tablespoons tarragon vinegar
a slice of onion
2–3 peppercorns
a blade of mace

1 egg yolk
2–2½ oz. butter
salt

Sauce vin blanc

1 oz. butter
¾ oz. flour
1½ gills liquor from the fish

½ gill cream or rich milk
salt and pepper

The procedure is first to prepare the sole, to set it aside while the hollandaise is made, to poach the fish, then to prepare the garnish, and finally to make the white wine sauce.

To prepare the fish. Skin, wash, and dry the fillets. Fold under the ends and lay in a buttered fireproof dish, pour over the wine and fumet, add lemon juice, cover with buttered paper.

To prepare the hollandaise. Reduce vinegar with onion and spices to about a teaspoon, strain on to the well-beaten yolk, stand the bowl in a bain-marie and add butter slowly as the mixture thickens, beating well. When it becomes the consistency of thick cream remove from the bain-marie, season, cover and set aside.

To poach the fish. Put the fish in oven to poach 15–20 minutes. Cook the mushrooms in butter and lemon juice. When fillets are ready take up, strain off the liquor.

To make the sauce vin blanc. Melt the butter in a saucepan, add flour off the fire, pour on 1½ gills of the liquor from the fish, stir until thickening, add cream or milk, season, and bring quickly to the boil. Boil rapidly till of coating consistency and adjust seasoning.

To dish. Dish the fillets, spoon over the white wine sauce, scatter the mushrooms over each fillet and mask each one with a spoonful of the hollandaise, glaze under the grill and serve at once.

The following dish of Filets de Sole Paillard belongs quite certainly to *haute cuisine*, and in a way is perhaps a little out of place here in that it is a dish for an accomplished cook and not for a student. It is interesting all the same to have a few examples for study and consideration of dishes in which neither time nor material is spared.

In Filets de Sole Paillard the real freshwater crayfish should be used for the garnish, but these, although possibly to be obtained, are not easily come by, so are sometimes replaced by Dublin Bay prawns. These are almost always bought already cooked. For the following dish they are best bought uncooked.

FILETS DE SOLE PAILLARD (FOR 8)

fillets of sole garnished with crayfish, mushrooms, truffle, and fish quenelles

2 Dover soles weighing 1–1½ lb. each, filleted
8 raw crayfish (or Dublin Bay prawns, see note in previous paragraph)
1 shallot
1 carrot
½ oz. butter
1½ gills white wine

½ gill sherry
a bouquet garni
mousseline farce (see page 700)
12 button mushrooms
a squeeze of lemon
2 nuts of butter
1 or 2 tablespoons water

Sauce

2½–3½ oz. butter
2 egg yolks
salt and pepper
sliced truffle

2–3 tablespoons cream
¼ pint white wine sauce (see previous recipe)

If crayfish are used the intestine must be removed in the way described on page 493.

Chop shallot and carrot, soften in butter. Add to the pan the raw crayfish (or Dublin Bay prawns in their shells), bouquet, wine, and sherry and cook 8 minutes (if cooked Dublin Bay prawns are used cook 3–4 minutes only). Take up, remove flesh, taking care to keep head shells whole. Wash these shells and set aside. Reserve also body shells. Skin fillets of sole, spread each with mousseline farce. Fold over and fix the tip of each fillet into the head shell of the crayfish or prawn, cementing well with some of the farce. Lay the prepared fillets in a lightly buttered dish, strain over the stock from the crayfish. Cover with a piece of buttered paper and poach gently 15–20 minutes.

Meantime prepare the garnish. Select a button mushroom for each fillet, quarter remaining mushrooms, and cook all together with a squeeze of lemon juice, a nut of butter, and a tablespoon or two of water. Shape remaining farce into quenelles and poach. Toss crayfish in a nut of butter, set aside.

Sauce

Pound shells of crayfish with butter and put through a fine sieve. Strain off cuisson from sole, reduce by a third, pour on to beaten yolks, stand bowl in bain-marie. Season, work in the flavoured butter, and when the consistency of thick cream add cream and white wine sauce.

To serve (in an oval dish). Dish the fillets with the heads of crayfish towards the centre in a crescent. Coat with the sauce and lightly brush head shells with a little oil. Garnish each fillet with a whole button mushroom and a slice of truffle. Arrange garnish of quenelles, crayfish, and quartered mushrooms in the hollow of the crescent of fillets.

The crayfish butter is troublesome to prepare and may be omitted and replaced by a spoonful or two of hollandaise sauce.

TURBOT, OR TURBOT

Turbot is one of the best of white fish and appreciated for its firmness and whiteness of flesh and its delicate flavour. The small fish or fillets from the larger ones are most suitable for domestic cooking. Turbot is neither skinned nor trimmed before being cooked. The skin is considered by some people to be a delicacy, as is the gelatinous matter found in the fins.

The following recipe for Turbot Piedmontaise is good and may well be used for any white fish, being suitable, for example, for the humbler rock salmon:

TURBOT PIEDMONTAISE

4 slices of turbot	2 pints vegetable stock
oil or butter for browning	6 oz. rice
seasoning	1 small onion
1 clove of garlic, chopped	1 stem of celery
chopped parsley	4 thick slices of tomato and
a pinch of thyme	butter to fry them
a pinch of basil	a nut of butter

Brown the fish slices quickly in oil or butter, lay in a buttered dish, season well and sprinkle with chopped garlic, the parsley, and herbs. Pour over ½ cup of the vegetable stock and set the dish in a slow oven 15–20 minutes. Meantime boil the rice in remaining vegetable stock with the sliced onion and celery, and dry the sliced tomato. Drain the rice thoroughly, season well, add a nut of butter and pile up in the centre of a dish. Put the fish and tomatoes round. Serve very hot.

TURBOT ARLÉSIENNE (SAUCE BERCY)

A good dish for a whole piece, or steaks, of turbot or halibut.

1½ lb. piece of turbot, or 4–5 steaks of turbot	¾ oz. flour
	1 wineglass white wine
1¼ gills strong well-flavoured fish stock	1 large teaspoon chopped parsley
2 shallots, finely chopped	a squeeze of lemon juice
1½ oz. butter	salt and pepper

Garnish
4–5 medium-sized tomatoes, skinned, cut in half, lightly baked, and filled with glazed button onions and fried parsley

Lightly butter a fireproof dish, put in the turbot and pour over the stock. Poach in a slow to moderate oven, basting occasionally, 25–30 minutes for a whole piece and 15–20 minutes for steaks. Meantime soften the shallots without colouring in a little less than half of the butter, add the wine and reduce to half quantity. Strain on the liquor from the fish when cooked. Boil for a few minutes to concentrate the flavour. Work the rest of the butter and the flour together, add to the liquor off the fire, and when dissolved reboil. Simmer for a few minutes, adjust seasoning, add parsley and lemon juice. Have the garnish ready. Re-dish the turbot, if wished remove the black skin, and coat over the sauce. Surround the dish with the tomatoes.

TURBOT SALVATOR

Suitable for a whole small fish or fillets of a larger one.

1¼–1½ lb. steak of turbot	3 tomatoes, skinned, pipped and chopped
2 teaspoons finely chopped mixed herbs	a squeeze of lemon juice
2 chopped shallots	

Sauce

1 oz. butter	1 finely chopped shallot
a good ½ oz. flour	½ gill strong fish stock
1 gill top of milk	salt and pepper
¾ gill white wine	

Place the turbot in a buttered fireproof dish, surround with tomatoes, herbs, and shallots. Add a squeeze of lemon juice, cover with a buttered paper, and bake in a moderate oven 20–30 minutes. Meantime prepare the sauce.

Melt a good half of the butter in a saucepan, add flour off fire, pour on the milk, blend and stir till boiling. Draw aside. Reduce wine to ½ gill with shallot, strain, add the fish stock and liquor from fish, add all this to the sauce by degrees, adjust seasoning. Cook to consistency of cream, add remaining butter off fire and spoon sauce over fish.

FILETS DE TURBOT NOVAROFF

Haute cuisine and a rich dinner dish.

2 lb. turbot	a little grated Parmesan
white wine	6–8 oz. crab meat
a bouquet of herbs	a nut of butter
1 small onion	seasoning
rich velouté sauce (see page 152)	paprika

Divide turbot into eight fillets, poach with white wine, herbs, and onion. Prepare a rich velouté sauce, adding the cuisson and a touch of Parmesan cheese. Heat the crab meat with a nut of butter, seasoning, and paprika. Put on the bottom of the serving dish. Lay the turbot on the top, pour over the sauce, brown quickly and lightly under the grill or mark with a red-hot skewer. Serve immediately.

WHITEBAIT, OR BLANCHAILLE

WHITEBAIT

1 pint whitebait	brown bread and butter
seasoned flour	quarters of lemon
deep fat fryer and fat	

Pick over the whitebait; do not wash. Roll lightly in the seasoned flour, a small quantity at a time. Heat the pan of fat until a *faint* blue haze comes from it. Put a handful of the floured whitebait in the frying basket, plunge into the fat and fry 2–3 minutes. Drain and turn on to crumpled paper or fine wire rack. Continue until all are fried. Reheat the fat until a strong blue smoke arises. Put all the whitebait together into the frying basket. Plunge into the fat and fry 1–2 minutes until crisp. Drain well

in the basket.   Turn on to a hot serving dish and serve at once with the
bread and butter and lemon.

BLANCHAILLE A LA DIABLE

Cook the fish as above and before serving dust liberally with cayenne,
pepper and salt, and a touch of Nepal pepper.

WHITING, OR MERLAN

Whiting, a small fish with rather friable flesh, is usually prepared whole,
although it is sometimes filleted as in the first recipe given.   It may be
grilled, fried, cooked *à la meunière*, baked, or served in a variety of sauces
and with different garnishes.   The first recipe is considered by R. H. to be
one of the particularly good dishes taught to students.   It is also an exception to the idea that green vegetables do not generally accompany fish, but
in this the cabbage is slightly crisp and one gets contrast of texture.

MERLANS ALSACIENNE

Cabbage

1 small firm cabbage	1 oz. butter
2 oz. onion, finely sliced	½ gill vegetable stock or cider

Fish

4–5 large fillets of whiting	1 bay-leaf, sprig of parsley and
4–6 peppercorns	thyme
	½ gill fish or vegetable stock

Sauce

¾ oz. butter	1 oz. grated cheese
¾ oz. flour, scant weight	salt, pepper, and mixed mustard
1½ gills milk	

Cut cabbage into quarters.   Remove hard core.   Shred and blanch in
boiling water 2–3 minutes.   Drain very well.   Melt the ounce of butter
in a stew-pan, add the onion, allow to soften slowly, then add the cabbage,
moisten with the stock, season, and cover with a piece of buttered paper
pressed on to the cabbage.   Put the lid on the pan and cook slowly until
quite tender.   Draw aside when done.   Meantime skin, fold or roll the
fillets.   Lay on a buttered dish, put round the peppercorns and herbs, and
pour over the stock.   Cover with a piece of buttered paper and poach in
the oven 15 minutes.   Melt the butter in a saucepan, stir in the flour off
the fire, pour on the milk, blend and stir until boiling.   Strain liquor from
the fish, add to the sauce, and simmer 3–4 minutes until creamy.   Draw
aside, season with salt, pepper, and mustard, add the grated cheese.
Arrange the cabbage down the centre of an oval dish, lay the fillets on top,
and mask with the sauce.   Brown under the grill or in a quick oven.

In Merlans Gratinés Bonne Femme the raw fish is cooked directly in the sauce with no preliminary poaching. This gives a complete dish suitable for supper and may well be made by a beginner.

MERLANS GRATINÉS BONNE FEMME

6 small whiting, or fillets	1 oz. butter
seasoning of salt and freshly ground black pepper	¾ oz. flour
2 oz. onion	¾ pint fish or vegetable stock
2 oz. mushrooms, or peelings and stalks of mushrooms	½ bay-leaf
	browned crumbs

Wash the fish, score them, season well. Lay in a buttered fireproof dish. Slice the onion finely and chop the mushrooms. Melt the butter in a pan, add the onion and mushrooms, cover and cook slowly for 3 or 4 minutes to soften them. Draw aside, mix in the flour, pour on the liquid, season, and stir until boiling. Boil quickly for a minute or two, add the bay-leaf, and pour over the fish. Sprinkle well with the crumbs and bake in a moderate oven about 20 minutes.

FILETS DE MERLAN DIEPPOISE

A good dish, not in quite such a fine sauce as that given for Sole Marguery, but containing mussels and shrimps and therefore good for those who like shell-fish.

2 whiting ½–¾ lb. each, filleted	3 or 4 mushrooms quartered and cooked with a nut of butter, a squeeze of lemon juice, and seasoning
¼ gill white wine	
½ pint well-flavoured fish fumet	
a few shrimps tossed in a little butter	
	mussels cooked in ¼ pint fish fumet, or as for Moules à la Marinière (page 500)

Sauce

1 oz. butter	½ gill milk
¾ oz. flour	

Skin the whiting. Lay the fillets in a lightly buttered dish. Pour over the wine and fish fumet and poach in the oven for about 15 minutes. Have ready the shrimps tossed in a little butter; the mushrooms quartered and cooked with a nut of butter, a squeeze of lemon juice, and seasoning; the mussels brought to the boil in ¼ pint fish fumet, or as on page 500, shelled and the beards removed.

Sauce. Melt the butter in a saucepan, add the flour and pour on the strained liquor from the whiting; stir until boiling and reduce rapidly to a syrupy consistency. Add the milk, season, and simmer for a few moments. Surround the fillets with the garnish, coat over the sauce and glaze quickly under the grill.

For Merlans à la Meunière see recipe for herrings cooked in this way on page 462, but take 4 tomatoes in place of apples.

Shell-Fish

CRAB, OR CRABE

Medium- to large-sized heavy crabs are the best. Very big crabs are sometimes coarse in texture and occasionally hollow. Little crabs have very little content. Crab is usually bought from the fishmonger cooked and dressed. If fresh from the sea it has to be killed and boiled.

To kill

The most humane way to kill the crab is to drive a sharp skewer into the brain, which lies on the underside of the body. The fish should then be plunged into boiling water.

A second method is to turn the fish at once into fast-boiling water, which kills it instantaneously. The third method, which is said by some to stun and stupefy the fish, is to put it into tepid salted water containing a small amount of vinegar and bring the water slowly to the boil. The crab may be cooked in this water or in a simple court bouillon (see page 473), allowing a quarter of an hour per pound.

To dress cooked crab

First remove big claws and set aside. Twist off the small claws, removing at the same time the under-shell or body of the crab. Set aside. Take out and throw away:

(a) the small sac that lies in the top of the big shell;

(b) any green matter in the big shell;

(c) the lungs or spongy fingers that lie round the big shell.

With a teaspoon scrape out into a small bowl all the brown creamy part which lies round the sides of the big shell. Take a cloth and, holding the big shell firmly, break down the sides, which are marked naturally. Wash and dry the shell thoroughly.

Remove the small claws and set aside. Cut the body of the crab in two and with a skewer pick out all the white meat into a bowl, taking care not to break off fine pieces of shell. Crack the big claws and shred all the meat, breaking it up well, again taking great care not to include any small pieces of shell.

Put all white meat together. Cream the brown part thoroughly. Season it well with pepper, salt, and mustard. Add dry breadcrumbs, about 2 tablespoons, and if mixture is stiff add a spoonful of cream. Arrange this mixture across the middle of the shell and pile white meat up at each side. The crab may be decorated with sieved hard-boiled yolk of egg and chopped parsley. The shell is laid in the middle of the ring of claws made by sticking the small claws one into another. Surround with crisp lettuce leaves, radishes, etc. Serve with mayonnaise, tartare sauce, or sharp French dressing and brown bread and butter. Pats of Montpellier butter and hot toast or devilled water-biscuits may replace the bread and butter.

AN EXCELLENT DRESSING FOR CRAB

Allow 2 dessertspoons cream for each person. Add chopped gherkins and capers or mixed pickles and season well. Add mustard, enough vinegar to sharpen, and a little sugar, about a teaspoon for ½ pint dressing. Serve in a sauce-boat.

CRABE GRATINÉ DIABLE

A very good hot crab dish.

1 dressed crab	mustard, cayenne, salt, pepper
1 oz. butter	a dash of anchovy essence
2 large tablespoons white breadcrumbs	Worcestershire or Harvey sauce thin hot biscuits
1 tablespoon dry grated cheese	fried bananas
top of milk	

Put the crab meat into a bowl. Melt the butter and add to the bowl with the grated cheese, keeping back a teaspoon, the top of milk, mustard, cayenne, salt and pepper, anchovy essence, and sauce to taste.

Mix well, replace in the shell or in a gratin dish, dust with crumbs and the extra grated cheese and bake 5–10 minutes in a hot oven. Serve with thin hot biscuits. This should have fried bananas, sliced lengthwise, laid on top before serving.

Crab meat makes excellent croquettes if well seasoned, flavoured with lemon juice, and mixed with a good béchamel sauce, then egged and breadcrumbed and fried in deep fat.

CRAWFISH, OR LANGOUSTES

Langoustes (crawfish) may be served in any of the ways given for lobster (page 493). The flesh is not quite so tender as that of small lobsters, but very good. One can get now imported crawfish tails which are economical, as they are solid, good tails weighing about 1 lb. each, giving about ¾ lb. meat. Small pieces of the flesh are excellent in the Fritto Misto dish given on page 520, and are useful also as hot hors-d'œuvre.

CRAYFISH, OR ÉCREVISSES

Crayfish are small freshwater shell-fish which used to be caught in the small rivers of this country. The fashion for crayfish picnics has gone, and now if one orders these from a London fishmonger he will probably have them flown over from France, the journey, of course, being reflected in the cost. Preparation of them consists in washing and gutting. Gutting is carried out by twisting off the middle tail fin, which draws away the intestine with it. The fish are then cooked in fast-boiling water containing a little vinegar, the flesh is removed from the shell and served as for lobster or prawns. It makes an excellent salad and is a classic ingredient in certain dishes of the *haute cuisine*, for example in Filets de Sole Paillard.

LOBSTER, OR HOMARD

As with other fish there is a wide difference between a fresh-caught lobster cooked at home to exactly the right degree and the cooked lobster bought in shops. It is true that a good fishmonger will boil the fish freshly for you, but even so it is better to buy lobsters alive and cook them yourself, for then there is no fear that they will be overcooked or have been kept on ice, which does not improve their flavour, though they may be perfectly wholesome. It is the killing of this fish that deters the inexperienced from taking such advice. There are two ways of doing this. If the lobster is to be boiled it may be plunged straight into fast-boiling water (or court bouillon) and killed instantly, and thereafter cooked for the proper length of time, 10–15 minutes to the pound, at simmering point. A court bouillon is best, but this should contain little vinegar or the colour of the shell will be spoiled. Ideally, part court bouillon and part sea-water are used.

To kill a lobster by putting it into cold water and bringing it gradually to boiling-point is recommended by some as being humane, but it must be said that it has certain culinary disadvantages; this process is inclined to draw out the juices, which show in the water in the form of creamy flakes.

For hot dishes the boiling water method is unsuitable, and the lobster in this case is killed by driving the point of a sharp knife right through the natural cross on the head under which the brain lies, death being instantaneous. A good point R. H. makes is that it is better when you are buying this fish at the sea to get it if possible straight from the lobster-pots and not from the reserve box, or what she calls the condemned cell in the bay, in which the fish from a large catch are kept fresh. The reason for this is that the fish in the reserve box grow thin in a few days, and hollow-shelled lobsters are the result. A lobster should be heavy in weight in proportion to its size, and the smaller hen lobsters are more delicate and tender. A good 2-lb. lobster should give about $\frac{3}{4}$ lb. meat. The number of persons it will serve depends to a large extent on the way in which it is to be prepared. A freshly boiled lobster split in two, served cold with a piquante sauce, or a half-lobster grilled, are both good ways of savouring the delicate nutty flavour of the fish, but not the most economical dishes.

The only inedible parts of a lobster are the bag in the head and the intestine. After the lobster has been split this bag and the intestine, a thin grey or black line running down through the tail meat, should be

removed and discarded. The green or creamy part of the lobster is the
liver, and it is perfectly good and wholesome. The coral is greeny black
when raw, bright red when cooked. When a raw lobster is being prepared for a hot dish the coral is usually removed and reserved for adding
to the sauce as lobster butter (see page 19); or it may be kept for a sauce or
soup for the next day. For dressing a cold lobster see Lobster Mayonnaise, page 498.

GRILLED LOBSTER (FOR 2)

a medium-sized live lobster	1 oz. butter, and a little extra
1 tablespoon oil	for the top
salt and cayenne	lemon juice

Kill the lobster in the way described, split lengthwise and remove the
bag lying in the head. Brush each half all over with oil, including the
shell. Grill cut side uppermost 8–10 minutes, turn and grill the shell side
5–6 minutes. Put a few pieces of butter on top, sprinkle with a touch of
cayenne and a little salt. Make a little beurre noisette with butter and
lemon juice and serve separately.

Devilled Lobster is excellent for a men's luncheon. It is possible to
use this recipe with imported crawfish tails, and although this may be
regarded as a good imitation it has not, of course, the same flavour or
texture.

DEVILLED LOBSTER

2 lobsters approx. 1 lb. each	1 gill cream
butter to sauter these	a few sprigs of watercress
sherry to flamber them	boiled rice (4–6 oz. uncooked)
devil sauce (see below)	

Devil sauce

3 tablespoons Worcestershire sauce	2–3 slices of lemon, halved
	freshly ground black pepper
2 tablespoons mushroom ket-chup	1 bay-leaf
1 dessertspoon tarragon vinegar	2 or 3 skinned and chopped tomatoes
1 teaspoon finely chopped onion	1 wineglass court bouillon or
1 clove of garlic crushed with 1 teaspoon salt	red wine

Put all ingredients for the sauce in a pan, simmer 10–15 minutes, pour
off and cool. Remove lemon.
Split the lobsters in two. Sauter in butter 4–5 minutes, flamber with
the sherry, moisten with the devil sauce, cover and cook in oven 10
minutes. Then take up, remove meat from claws and tail. Slice tail into
scallops and replace with the claw meat. Boil up the sauce, adjust
seasoning, and add cream; dish the lobsters, pour the sauce over, garnish
with watercress, and serve with boiled rice.

HOMARD THERMIDOR

2 live lobsters weighing ½–¾ lb. each	1 teaspoon chopped parsley
1 tablespoon oil	1 wineglass white wine
1½ oz. butter	1¼ gills béchamel sauce (see page 155)
1 good tablespoon chopped shallot	¼ pint single cream or rich milk
a pinch of chopped tarragon	mustard, salt, paprika
1 teaspoon chopped chervil	3 tablespoons grated Parmesan
	brown crumbs

Split the lobsters, heat the oil and butter (reserving a nut of the latter), put cut side down into the pan. Sauter gently 5 minutes, cover and put in the oven 15 minutes. Melt the nut of butter in a sauté pan or shallow saucepan, add a good spoonful of chopped shallot and the chopped herbs. After a minute's cooking add white wine and after 5 minutes the sauce and thin cream or milk. Simmer to a creamy consistency and add the cuisson from the lobsters. Remove the meat from the shells, chopping coarsely the shell and head meat and cutting the tails into thick scallops. Add the chopped meat to the sauce with mustard, salt, paprika, and 2 tablespoons of the Parmesan cheese. Arrange this in the shells, putting the tail scallops on top with the rounded side up. Sprinkle with the remaining cheese and the crumbs. Bake 5 minutes and pass under the grill to glaze. Serve very hot on a napkin.

HOMARD A L'AMÉRICAINE (1) (FOR 6)

2 live lobsters about 1½ lb. each	1 small glass cognac
2 tablespoons oil	1 glass dry white wine
1 small shallot, chopped	salt, pepper, cayenne
2 tablespoons onion, chopped	1 oz. butter
1 clove of garlic	1 teaspoon each of chopped chervil, tarragon, and parsley
3 medium tomatoes skinned, pipped, and chopped	

Kill the lobsters by putting the point of a knife through the cross on the head under which the brain lies. Cut off the head, split it and remove the bag. Crack the claws and extract the meat. Divide the body into 3 or 4 slices crosswise, leaving on the shell. Make the oil hot in a sauté pan and cook shallot, onion, crushed garlic, and tomato. Add lobster, reserving the coral and the soft greenish part found in the head. Cook until the flesh is quite firm (4–5 minutes). Flame with the cognac, add white wine, season, cover and simmer 12–15 minutes. While the lobster cooks pound the coral and green part and work into it the butter.

Pile the lobster in a hot dish; reduce the liquor, add the coral butter. Cook for a few minutes and add the chopped herbs. Spoon over the meat. Serve very hot.

HOMARD A L'AMÉRICAINE (2)

1 live lobster weighing 1½ lb.	reduced tomato pulp (see
1½ oz. butter	tomato sauce 2, page 178)
2 oz. each of carrot and onion, finely diced	¼ pint good fish fumet or light court bouillon
¼ oz. celery, finely diced	a bouquet garni
1 small glass brandy	salt and cayenne
1 glass white wine	½ oz. butter to finish
3 tablespoons strong well-	chopped parsley

Split lobster in two, remove the bag and set aside the coral and creamy parts from the head. Heat butter in a stew-pan, put in the pieces of lobster, flesh side downwards, and sauter gently until turning colour, add the vegetables and bouquet garni and continue cooking for 4–5 minutes. Flame with the brandy and cook for a few minutes. Add wine, tomato pulp, and fumet. Cover and simmer 7–10 minutes. Pile lobster in hot dish and continue to simmer the sauce. Work the coral with the creamy parts from the head and the remaining butter. When thoroughly smooth add to the sauce, reboil, adjust seasoning, remove vegetables and bouquet, and spoon over the lobster. Sprinkle with chopped parsley.

Either of the above dishes may be accompanied by plain boiled rice.

In Lobster Newburg one has a classic American dish, popular for luncheon parties and popular also because it can be made in a chafing-dish, a form of cooking which holds an element of excitement. On the whole it is perhaps more practical to prepare it in the kitchen.

There are two divergent opinions about the lobster for this dish. Should it be raw or cooked before being committed to the final processes? The French, Escoffier in particular, advocate the use of a live lobster in order to get the best results. The Americans—and after all the dish is American in origin—usually take a cooked lobster. R. H. says she has tried both ways many times and is all in favour of buying a live lobster, so ensuring perfect freshness, cooking it in court bouillon, and then preparing it in the Newburg fashion. If this is done, she says, the meat from claw and tail is less likely to break up and the final process is easier for the amateur. A recipe for each follows, but in either case it should be observed that the right ingredients, real butter, good cream, Madeira or good sherry, are essential for Lobster Newburg. The authentic flavour will not be achieved with substitutes, and it is a mistake to waste a lobster if the proper ingredients for the dish are not available.

LOBSTER NEWBURG
made with live lobster

1–1½ lb. live lobster	1½ gills cream
2½ oz. butter	yolks of 2–3 eggs
2 tablespoons brandy	salt, pepper, cayenne
2 sherry glasses Madeira or good sherry	boiled rice

Kill the lobster, cut the tail in its shell into 4 or 5 pieces, crack the claws. Remove the bag from the head and reserve the creamy parts. Heat two-thirds of the butter in a sauté pan and put in the lobster. Sauter the pieces 3–5 minutes over moderate heat, seasoning well. When the shell has turned red flamber with the brandy; add the Madeira. Allow to reduce by about half. Add the cream, reserving ½ gill, cover and simmer gently 15 minutes. Remove the pieces of lobster, take the meat from the shell and claws and put into a double saucepan to keep hot. Work the yolks with the remaining cream and butter and the creamy parts from the head. Pour on the liquor from the pan, mix thoroughly and strain over the lobster. Season well. Set pan over a moderate fire, and stir gently until the mixture thickens and has the consistency of cream. Turn at once into a hot dish and serve the boiled rice separately.

LOBSTER NEWBURG
made with cooked lobster

1–1½ lb. live lobster	1 oz. butter
court bouillon (see page 473)	

Sauce

1 gill Madeira or good sherry	salt, freshly ground pepper,
2–3 egg yolks	paprika and cayenne
	1½ gills cream

2 rounds of hot buttered toast cut into four

Boil the lobster 25–35 minutes in the court bouillon. Allow to cool in the liquor, then drain. When cold cut the soft shell down on the under-side of the tail with the scissors and carefully detach the tail meat in one piece. Cut in fairly thin slanting slices. Crack claws and remove the meat as whole as possible. Rub butter over bottom and sides of a shallow stew-pan or sauté pan. Lay in the pieces of lobster, season well, and allow to heat very gently 5–6 minutes, *without colouring*. Now pour over the Madeira, cover the pan, and continue to cook a little more quickly until the wine has reduced to about half.

Beat the yolks with a little seasoning, add the cream, and pour this over the lobster off the fire. Shake and swirl the pan gently to mix well, put back on slow heat and continue to shake and turn the pan until the sauce has the consistency of cream. Adjust seasoning and turn at once on to the hot buttered toast arranged in an eared fireproof dish.

HOMARD PROVENÇALE

1 large lobster or 2 small, boiled	salt, freshly ground pepper
2 oz. butter and 2 tablespoons oil	a pinch of saffron
1 clove of garlic crushed with salt	boiled rice (3–4 oz. before
2 shallots, finely chopped	cooking) and finely chopped
½ pint tomato pulp or coulis	chives for final addition
a bay-leaf, a sprig of thyme, and	eighths of lemon
a pinch of rosemary	

Take out the meat from the lobsters, cut up in large pieces. Put butter and oil in pan and heat well, add the garlic and shallot, cook gently till soft. Add tomato pulp, herbs, seasoning, and saffron. Add lobster and cook very gently till hot. Make a mound of the boiled rice, sprinkle with chives, arrange on this the lobster, and spoon over the sauce. Serve with lemon eighths.

LOBSTER MAYONNAISE

1½ lb. lobster, or 2 lobsters ¾ lb. each	1–2 good lettuces watercress
court bouillon (see page 473)	radishes and tomatoes
¾ pint good thick mayonnaise	paprika pepper
2 large tablespoons cream	chopped chives
a few drops of tabasco or Harvey sauce	hard-boiled eggs

Have the lobsters freshly boiled in court bouillon and cooled in the liquor. If the lobsters are small it is nicer to serve them in the shell, in which case it is advisable to tie the tails in position before boiling. Take out the lobsters and drain well. When cold lay a lobster on a chopping-board with the head towards your left hand, and the tail spread flat out on the board to your right. Hold the head firmly in position with your left hand, and with a strong chopping-knife in your right push the point strongly down through the cross on the top of the head to the board. Bring the blade of the knife down through the tail, thus splitting it in two. Turn the lobster round and divide the rest of the head. Now remove the bag in the head and leave the creamy parts in place. Carefully lift out the pieces from the tail shells. Set aside. Crack claws and remove the meat as whole as possible. Set the shells down a long dish or platter, wipe and oil the antennae. Fill the head shells with the claw meat. Cut the tails into slanting slices and fill back into the opposite tail shell from which they were taken, thus bringing the rounded (and red) side uppermost.

Add the cream to the mayonnaise, with a few drops of tabasco or Harvey sauce and a little paprika. Coat a little over each half-lobster and send the rest of the mayonnaise to table in a sauce-boat. Garnish the centre of the dish between the halves with the lettuce hearts cut into four.

Decorate the dish well with bunches of watercress, quartered hard-boiled eggs, 'rose' radishes, and 'dent de loup' or quartered tomatoes (see page 245). Scatter over the paprika and chives. Hand a potato salad separately. If a large lobster is used, the pieces may be laid on a rice salad well moistened with French dressing, or on lettuce leaves, before being coated with the mayonnaise.

HOMARD PARISIENNE

This is a well-known classic. The lobster may be served simply without garnish, or may, by the addition of this, be turned into a more elaborate dish suitable for a buffet. For the more elaborate dish aspic may be added to the mayonnaise, the filled lobster shells coated with cool aspic before they are dished, and blocks of aspic jelly and sliced truffle used to garnish the dish.   According to taste other garnishes may also be used.

one 1½-lb. lobster or two ¾-lb.   ½ pint mayonnaise or mayon-
    lobsters   naise collée
court bouillon or salted water   1 tablespoon single cream or
a handful of parsley   rich milk
3–4 sprays each of tarragon   seasoning
    and chervil

Cooked vegetables for salad: diced carrots, potatoes, and turnips, peas or diced beans.   Cook all separately and then mix together. Allow 2 tablespoons per person.

Garnish

3 large, even-sized, ripe toma-   2–3 hard-boiled eggs
    toes, or 5–6 tartlet cases   watercress or lettuce
    made with rich short crust

Tie the tail of the lobster in position.   Plunge into boiling court bouillon and simmer 25–30 minutes.   Allow 18–20 minutes for the smaller lobsters.   Cool in the liquid, drain, and when quite cold split in two, remove the bag from the head, and carefully lift out the tail meat. Crack claws and remove meat as whole as possible.   Boil the parsley and herbs for 5–7 minutes.   When tender drain, press, and rub through a fine sieve.   Add to the mayonnaise with the cream.   Mix a small quantity of this with the vegetables.   Season well.   Wash and dry the shells, oil the outsides lightly, and the antennae.   Line the bottom of the shells with the vegetable salad.   Prepare the garnish: Scald tomatoes and cut in half, scoop out the centres and fill with the salad.   Alternatively the pastry cases may be used in place of the tomatoes.   Quarter the eggs, or they may be cut in half, and the yolks scooped out and sieved back into the whites.

Cut the tail meat slantwise into neat scallops, arrange this in each half of tail shell, the rounded side uppermost.   Lay the claw meat in the head shell.   Coat with the sauce, arrange in a flat oval dish, garnish the top and bottom with the cress or lettuce, and arrange the tomatoes and eggs round the sides.

Recipes for Lobster Barcelona, Lobster '31,' and Lobster Armoricain will be found in the Winkfield chapter (pages 993–4).

MUSSELS, OR MOULES

Mussels should, of course, be absolutely fresh and the shells tightly closed.   They must be thoroughly washed and scrubbed before being cooked, because the water in which they are cooked is, in most cases, part of the finished dish.

Preparation.   Take a short, strong knife and scrape the joint of the shell to remove the filament, scraping away also any foreign body attached to the shell. Put each mussel as you prepare it into a bowl. If you find one with the shell ever so slightly open, test to see whether it is alive by giving it a sharp tap with the back of the knife. If it is alive the shell will immediately shut up. If it does not the mussel is dead and must certainly be thrown away. When each has been scraped and washed and put into a bowl, fill the bowl with water and quickly stir them about with your hands, not allowing them to remain still. Lift them out a handful at a time and put them into a colander. Repeat this two or three times. The last water should have no sand at the bottom of it and should be absolutely clean. Mussels are usually served in the half of the shell to which they are attached; the empty half is removed after they have opened. This should be done over the saucepan so that no liquor is lost. Mussels are eaten from soup-plates, and additional plates should be put on the table for the shells. Finger-bowls with a small piece of lemon in the water should be provided.

Moules à la Marinière is one of the most popular ways of serving them, and the recipe gives the process of preparation in detail.

MOULES A LA MARINIÈRE

2 quarts mussels	freshly ground pepper
1 onion	1½ oz. butter
1 shallot	1 small glass dry white wine
1 clove of garlic	1 dessertspoon finely chopped
bouquet of parsley and thyme	parsley
a little salt	

Put cleaned mussels in a large pan with onion, shallot, and garlic chopped together, the bouquet, salt and pepper, butter, and white wine. Cook quickly over fairly strong heat for about 5 minutes, shaking the pan as you do so. The mussels will open as they cook. When all are open take them out, retaining the half of the shell to which they are attached. Strain the liquor over them and sprinkle well with chopped parsley.

In this recipe the liquor is unthickened. Many people prefer it to have the consistency of single cream. In this case a heaped teaspoon each of flour and butter may be worked into beurre manié and added carefully till the exact consistency required is obtained. For special occasions the thickening may be made with egg yolks.

MOULES AU CITRON

2½ quarts mussels	salt, pepper, and grated
2½ oz. butter	nutmeg
2 oz. carrot, finely chopped	juice of 4 lemons
1 tablespoon chopped shallot	½ oz. flour
a bouquet garni	

Wash and clean the mussels. Take a large pan, put in it 1 oz. butter, add the chopped carrot, shallot, and bouquet. Cook gently, season with salt, pepper, and grated nutmeg. When soft add the lemon juice, cook for a minute or so and add the mussels. Cook quickly, shaking all the time, till the shells open. Keep them hot. In another pan brown the flour slightly with ½ oz. butter, moisten with the strained liquor from the mussels and boil for several minutes. Add the rest of the butter in small pieces, dish the mussels in the half-shells, and pour over the sauce.

FRIED MUSSELS

Clean the mussels, and cook as described in the recipe for Moules à la Marinière for 5 or 6 minutes, then take them out of their shells, remove the beards (if wished), dip them into a good fritter batter, and fry in deep fat.

For Pilaff of Mussels see page 394.
For Soupe aux Moules see page 113.

OYSTERS, OR HUÎTRES

In this country oysters are for the most part eaten uncooked. English oysters are considered to be perhaps the best in the world, particularly Whitstable natives and of late those from Cornwall. Connoisseurs are rarely willing to consider the cooking of them to be a good thing. Certain of the foreign oysters are good too, and being cheaper may well be considered for hot oyster dishes. 'Sauce' oysters are small and are less expensive than the finest natives. Oysters to be served raw should be opened as shortly as possible before being eaten. They are served in the deep half of the shell, embedded in crushed ice, and are accompanied by quarters of lemon, cayenne, and brown bread and butter.

HUÎTRES GRATINÉES A LA CRÈME

A particularly good dish of hot oysters for which one of the large foreign kinds is suitable.

oysters	grated Parmesan
1 dessertspoon thick cream for each shell	melted butter

Open the oysters, detach from the shell, put a dessertspoon of cream in each, dust with Parmesan, sprinkle with melted butter, and grill under a hot grill 3–4 minutes.

An alternative to this is to use mornay sauce (see page 156) in place of cream, sprinkle with grated cheese, and bake in the oven.

GRILLED OYSTERS

1 dozen oysters in the ½-shell	salt and freshly ground pepper
1 oz. butter	quarters of lemon
1 teaspoon Worcestershire sauce	brown bread and butter

Put oysters in grill pan. In a small saucepan melt the butter, add Worcestershire sauce, pour a spoonful over each oyster, season, and put under a hot grill till oysters begin to curl at the edges. Serve at once with lemon and brown bread and butter.

HUÎTRES GRATINÉES

'Sauce' or tinned oysters may be used for this dish.

1 clove of garlic crushed with salt	12 'sauce' oysters or 1 tin of oysters
1½ oz. butter	1 rasher of bacon cut in thin strips
4 tablespoons breadcrumbs	
salt and pepper	

Cook the garlic for a minute or two in the butter, add breadcrumbs, salt and pepper and brown lightly. Drain the oysters and put them in a shallow fireproof dish, cover all over with brown crumbs and put the strips of bacon on top. Put in a hot oven until bacon is crisp and brown. Serve very hot.

For Angels on Horseback see page 36.

PRAWNS AND SHRIMPS, OR CREVETTES

PRAWNS

These when freshly caught are boiled 3–4 minutes in salted or sea-water and allowed to cool in the liquid. They may be bought as follows:

(*a*) By the pint, usually at a moderate price, generally imported and somewhat salt, and for this reason they are improved by soaking for about 10–15 minutes after picking. They are admirable for filling bouchées, for croquettes, fritters, mousses, etc.

(*b*) by the dozen, generally English and unsalted, and more expensive; suitable for eating plain as hors-d'œuvre and for special dishes, very good served with Alabama sauce as given on page 180.

A particularly good hors-d'œuvre, Prawns with Alabama Sauce, is given in the chapter on cocktails (page 5).

SHRIMPS

These are bought by the pint. If required for sauce they may be obtained ready picked, but in this case they are rather salt and should be soaked in a little water or milk before being used. Frozen shrimps are to be bought and are excellent and not salt.

Potted shrimps are usually bought in small pots or cartons and served straight from the pot on the table, or they may be turned out. They should be accompanied by hot fresh dry toast and butter.

To prepare potted shrimps from the raw fresh fish

Boil the shrimps 3–4 minutes, cool, drain and pick them. For every pint of picked shrimps allow:

2 oz. (or more) fresh butter	a pinch of salt
1 teaspoon freshly ground pepper	½ teaspoon ground mace
a good dust of cayenne	(approx.)

Heat a third of the butter in a stew-pan, add seasoning and mace. When hot add shrimps and stir well with a wooden spoon. Heat them through but do not allow them to sauter. Pack into small pots. Heat remaining butter and when it stops foaming (do not allow it to brown) skim it quickly and pour it over the shrimps. There must be enough barely to cover the shrimps. Leave till quite set, tie down. They will keep in a cool place at least a week.

Lobster cut in small pieces and treated in the same way is excellent.

DUBLIN BAY PRAWNS, OR LANGOUSTINES

These are usually bought cooked and are really one of the great luxuries of the shell-fish tribe, more delicate in texture than lobster or langouste and of sweeter taste, though curiously enough less popular or well known. Perhaps the nicest way of serving is to have them cold with a piquante sauce. They vary greatly in size, and according to this one must judge how many to allow for each person, possibly 4–6. They are best served in the shell, but the following preliminary preparation is advisable. Make a cut with scissors down the centre of the under-shell, loosen the flesh slightly and lightly crack the claws.

Arrange piled up in a circle on a large dish, tails to the centre. Accompany by brown bread and butter, a piquante sauce or dressing served separately, and quarters of lemon, and put a slice of lemon in the finger-bowls which should be provided. Shelled, they are also excellent dipped in fritter batter, fried in deep fat, and served with quarters of lemon and brown bread and butter. They make a first-class curry and are a suitable ingredient of a fritto misto.

SCALLOPS, OR COQUILLES ST JACQUES

These are usually prepared for cooking by the fishmonger. It is advisable to ask him for the deep shells or one may find that the shallow sides only are sent, and this is inconvenient as they are too shallow to hold garnish and sauce. For a main dish with little or no accompanying garnish one may require 2 scallops per person, or it may be useful to note here a suitable economy. Small pieces of cooked Jerusalem artichoke used to fill out the shell absorb the flavour of the sauce, and being of suitable texture are in no sense a regrettable addition.

The first recipe given is a classic and very good, though not perhaps quite so good as 'Parisienne' which follows it.

COQUILLES ST JACQUES ARMORICAINE

3 good carrots	6 or 8 scallops according to size
1 shallot or a small onion	1½ gills water
2 stalks of celery	½ gill white wine or cider
a small turnip	¾ oz. flour
a large handful of Brussels sprouts or French beans	2 tablespoons cream or top of milk
1½ oz. butter	1 tablespoon chopped parsley
seasoning	browned crumbs
½ cup tinned tomatoes, or the equivalent in chopped fresh tomatoes	melted butter

Finely dice the first four vegetables and shred the sprouts. Melt ½ oz. of the butter in a small pan, put in the carrots, shallot, celery, and turnip with seasoning, press a buttered paper on the top, cover tightly and cook for about 5 minutes on the stove, then add the sprouts and tomatoes, cover again, and put the pan in the oven for another 15–20 minutes. Meantime put the scallops into a small pan with the water and wine barely to cover; simmer 4–5 minutes, then take out the scallops, cut each into 4 pieces. Strain off the liquor, melt the rest of the butter in the pan, add the flour and pour back the scallop liquor. Bring to boil, simmer to a creamy consistency, adjust seasoning, and add the cream or milk. Replace the scallops. Take out the vegetables. Add the chopped parsley and divide the mirepoix amongst 4 or 5 deep scallop shells. Put a spoonful of the scallop mixture on top, scatter over browned crumbs, sprinkle with melted butter, and colour in a quick oven.

COQUILLES ST JACQUES PARISIENNE

4 or 6 scallops according to size	1 shallot
½ gill white wine	4 oz. mushrooms
1 gill water	1 oz. flour
salt and pepper	½ gill milk
2–3 parsley stalks	browned crumbs
a bay-leaf	a little melted butter
6 peppercorns	a little cream or top of milk
1 oz. butter	(optional)

Put the scallops into a pan, cover with wine and water, add salt and pepper and the parsley, bay-leaf and peppercorns. Simmer for 5 minutes. Take out and cut each one into 4 or 5 pieces. Melt the butter in a saucepan, add the shallot finely sliced and the mushrooms cut in quarters, cover and cook about 5 minutes. Draw aside, add the flour and the liquor from the scallops. Stir till boiling, simmer a few minutes, add the milk by degrees, then reduce rapidly till the right consistency. Season, add the scallops, and fill into the deep shells. Scatter over browned crumbs and a little melted butter and brown under the grill. A little cream or top of milk added to the sauce at the end is a great improvement.

When scallops are plentiful the following ways of cooking them are excellent. In these recipes no garnish is given, so that one must allow 2 scallops per person, or 3 large scallops for 2 people.

COQUILLES ST JACQUES A LA CRÈME

6–8 large scallops	½ oz. flour
1 glass white wine	¼ pint cream
½ glass water	salt, freshly ground pepper, a
a squeeze of lemon juice	dust of cayenne
½ oz. butter	1 oz. grated gruyère cheese

Poach the scallops in the wine, water, and lemon juice for 8–10 minutes. Cool, strain off the liquor, and slice the scallops. Melt the butter, add the flour, and pour on the liquor, stir until boiling and cook rapidly 4–5 minutes. Add cream and boil again until syrupy. Season, add the scallops, turn into the deep shells. Scatter over the cheese and brown in a quick oven or under the grill.

FRIED SCALLOPS

2 large scallops per person	deep fat
white wine and water mixed,	fried parsley
or fish stock	brown bread and butter
seasoned flour	quartered lemon
beaten egg and breadcrumbs	
for coating, or fritter batter	
2 (page 443)	

Poach scallops in the liquid, which should barely cover. Cool, take up and dry scallops. Roll in seasoned flour, coat with egg and crumbs or dip in the fritter batter. Fry in deep fat till golden brown, drain on a rack or on paper and serve at once garnished with plenty of fried parsley. Accompany with the bread and butter and lemon. A sauce may be made if wished with the liquor from the scallops. Finish with chopped parsley and lemon juice. In this case the fried parsley, bread and butter, and lemon are unnecessary.

For Coquilles St Jacques Gratinées Duxelles see Winkfield chapter, page 995.

Freshwater Fish

The most delicate of freshwater fish is the trout. When this is brought straight in from the river the simplest forms of cooking are the best. First of all perhaps one might choose the classic method of *à la meunière* as described on page 452, or the fish may be brushed over with butter or oil and grilled or fried, or dotted with butter and baked in the oven.

Since a delicate flavour of fennel associates well with trout it may not be out of place to mention here a method of introducing this described in Mme Prunier's book for grilled John Dory. In this the grilled fish is lifted and placed on a grill with legs large enough to fit over a large dish on which a heap of dried fennel is laid and lighted. The fish is gently turned over so that each side may absorb some of the subtle flavour of the burning herb. The difficulty in turning without breaking is reduced when a double grill with legs on both halves is available, but these are seldom seen in domestic kitchens.

FISH COOKED 'AU BLEU'

This is one of the simplest and at the same time most effective methods of cooking a variety of freshwater fish. It is applied to fish (and in particular to trout) just taken from the river. In riverside hotels in France trout arc often kept swimming in a tank. Taken straight from the water and killed by a knock on the head, they are then cleaned, the smallest possible incision being made for the purpose (or this may be done through the gills, which in any case must be removed as they would make the dish bitter); the trout are neither scaled nor dried, but put straight into a saucepan and sprinkled with a little boiling vinegar. A boiling court bouillon is then added and the fish poached gently for about 15–20 minutes or until cooked.

The trout may be served hot curled round upon themselves and dressed in a folded napkin, usually with steamed potatoes and sometimes with a sauce-boat full of noisette or melted butter mixed with a little lemon juice. They are also served cold with a sharper sauce such as vinaigrette.

TRUITE AU BLEU

trout
simple court bouillon (see page 449—the quantities given may be
   modified to suit the number of fish to be cooked)
a little boiling vinegar

Clean the freshly killed trout, leaving on the head. Put in a pan and sprinkle with a little boiling vinegar. Add boiling court bouillon. The fish will curl. Reduce the heat and poach 15–20 minutes according to size. Serve as directed above.

The following dish is suitable for a luncheon party:

TRUITE A LA NORMANDE

4 even-sized trout	chopped parsley
1 tablespoon water	½–¾ gill cream
juice of a lemon	a few white breadcrumbs
seasoning	a little melted butter
chopped chives	

Wash and dry the trout and lay them down a well-buttered fireproof dish. Add the spoonful of water, the lemon juice, seasoning, and a good scattering of the chives and parsley. Cook the trout in the oven for 10 minutes. Meantime boil the cream for a minute or two, pour over the trout, powder over with the crumbs, sprinkle with melted butter, and brown under the grill.

A good cold dish of trout:

TRUITE DE RIVIÈRE EN GELÉE

4–6 trout	a few picked shrimps
1 glass white wine	a little mayonnaise
1 pint good fish aspic	1 bunch of small asparagus
4–6 small tomatoes	

Aspic (see aspic-making, page 735)

¾ pint strong, well-flavoured fish stock	½ gill sherry
	1 oz. gelatine
1 glass white wine	white of 1 egg

Poach trout in white wine. Allow to cool in the liquor, then drain. Have ready the aspic. Pour a little on the serving dish and allow to set. Arrange the trout on this, and decorate round with the tomatoes stuffed with the shrimps bound with mayonnaise, and little bundles of asparagus. Coat with the aspic and leave to set.

Such freshwater fish as pike and carp may also be cooked *au bleu*. Small fish under half a pound in weight are generally plunged into boiling court bouillon after having been treated with the hot vinegar. Larger fish are placed in cold or tepid court bouillon.

CARP OR WHITE FISH WITH CELERIAC (COLD DISH)

1 medium-sized carp, 2–3 lb.	3 medium-sized onions, thinly sliced in rings
2–3 pints court bouillon (see page 473)	¾ oz. gelatine
1 large root of celeriac	finely chopped parsley, salt, freshly ground pepper
1 lemon, thinly sliced, and 1 extra slice	

Well clean, scale, and wash carp. Leave whole or cut in steaks. Arrange in a large shallow pan. Pour over hot court bouillon just to cover. Poach gently 25–35 minutes. Meantime peel celeriac, cut into quarters and slice thinly. Cook the celeriac in court bouillon for 5–6 minutes, drain carefully and keep in cold water with a slice of lemon. Blanch onions and simmer in water until just tender. Blanch the lemon 1–2 minutes. Drain. Allow fish to cool in the court bouillon, then take up, drain well. Reduce the liquor to a good flavour, adjusting seasoning, strain through a muslin. Measure a pint and dissolve the gelatine in it. (This liquid may be clarified for attractive appearance, see page 120.) Cool. Pour enough into a large dish to cover the bottom. Allow to set. The fish may be brushed over with a little of the jelly, melted.

Arrange carp on this and garnish down the sides of the whole fish, or the steaks, with the celeriac. Surround the edge of the dish with the onion rings and sliced lemon. Add parsley to the remaining liquor and pour carefully over the whole dish. Leave to set well. Serve with plainly boiled potatoes.

There is a German way of serving carp with a garnish of herbs and hard-boiled egg. The carp, poached in court bouillon and drained, is served on a folded napkin. On a dish apart are arranged, in generous heaps, chopped parsley, chopped spring onions, chopped fennel, and the sieved yolks and shredded whites of hard-boiled egg. With this is served a slightly piquante sauce, blanche, bâtarde, au câpres and suchlike.

CARPE BRAISÉE MATELOTE
braised carp, sauce matelote, with red wine, onions, and mushrooms

one 3-lb. carp	a blade of mace
vegetables for braising: 2 onions, 2 carrots, 1 stick of celery, all sliced	a few peppercorns
	white wine
¼ oz. butter	wine vinegar
a bouquet garni	a little beurre noisette

Sauce matelote

1 large onion, finely chopped	½ oz. each of butter and flour worked together (beurre manié)
½ oz. butter	
¼ pint red wine	
a large bouquet garni	seasoning
¼ pint fish stock or court bouillon	

Garnish

freshly boiled new potatoes tossed in butter and parsley, button mushrooms, glazed button onions (see page 200)

Clean the carp. Put the braising vegetables into a large pan with the butter, allow to sweat slowly, then add herbs and spices and set the carp on the top. Moisten with the wine and vinegar, cover with a piece of well-buttered paper, cover the pan closely and set to cook on a slow heat, or in the oven, for about 1 hour. Baste occasionally.

Meantime prepare sauce. Brown the onion in the butter, add wine and bouquet and reduce to half. Add the stock and thicken with the beurre manié. Season well, and if wished enrich with a further ½ oz. butter.

Have ready the garnish: the potatoes boiled and tossed in butter and parsley, the mushrooms sautéd, and the onions glazed. Dish carp, pour over a little beurre noisette, surround with the garnish, and serve separately.

MATELOTES

Sometimes a matelote is a ragoût of beef cooked with red wine, mushrooms, and onions, but generally speaking the name is applied to a fish stew—a fisherman's dish. It may be made with one kind of fish, with eels for instance, but is more often taken as a method for cooking an assortment of fish, and particularly perhaps those generally considered to be lacking in flavour. Correctly, freshwater fish are used for this dish, but in England, where these are not so readily obtainable as in France (although both carp and pike are now sometimes to be found in our shops), it is useful to adapt the method to a miscellaneous collection of sea fish. An adapted recipe is given. Of fresh fish one may take eel, carp, pike, tench, or river bream, and in her recipe for using sea fish R. H. has suggested hake, sole, plaice, mackerel, or bream. The liquid for poaching is highly seasoned and flavoured and should preferably be a good wine, red, white, or a mixture of both. If only wine of less good quality is available it is best to use only a small proportion of wine and to make up with fish stock or good consommé. When wine is used the fish may with great advantage be flambéd with brandy. The essentials of a good matelote may be summed up as follows: fish freshly caught, good wine, plenty of good butter, and careful attention to cooking, for if the fish is broken up and an assortment of bones set free in the liquid, the result is unpleasant. Sometimes the stew is accompanied by a dish of small fish no bigger than whitebait, dipped in batter and fried, which give contrast of texture.

It should be remembered when cooking a mixture of fish that it is necessary to put the larger and more firm-fleshed fish in first, and to add the others later when a little cooking has taken place—to stagger the cooking in fact. At the end of the cooking the liquid is usually thickened with beurre manié (see page 139), and the garnish made of fried croûtons, or mushrooms, or small glazed onions, cooked separately and finished with a little of the matelote sauce.

It will be seen that this is no part of a menu for a *diner à deux*, not even for a small family meal: it is a main dish for a hungry party; but while the recipes may look formidable at a casual glance, they do not, in fact, present any real difficulty, and are less troublesome than may at first appear.

MATELOTE MÉNAGÈRE

2 lb. mixed fish, eel, carp, pike, etc.
2 oz. butter
2 large onions, sliced
1¼ pints good red or white wine (burgundy or Bordeaux excellent) (the wine should be sufficient just to cover the fish)
a bouquet garni
a small clove of garlic crushed with salt

peelings from the mushrooms
freshly grated black pepper
1 glass brandy
1 oz. butter, ¾ oz. flour (beurre manié)
a few drops of vinegar
12 glazed onions (cooked as described on page 200)
6 oz. mushrooms cooked with a nut of butter and lemon juice
slices of French bread

Cut the fish in thick slices keeping heads on, clean and dry. In a large sauté or shallow pan make the butter hot, put in the onions and the pieces of eel and sauter 6–7 minutes, shaking the pan and turning the pieces about. Add the liquid, bouquet, garlic, mushroom peelings, and a grating of pepper. Cook over strong heat 7–8 minutes. Flamber with the brandy (provided that wine only has been used as liquid). Add the rest of the fish. Cook over moderate heat until the fish comes away easily from the bone.   Take out all the fish with a fish slice and strain the liquid through a pointed strainer.   Rinse out the pan, put back the liquid, and thicken it with the beurre manié.   Adjust seasoning and add vinegar. The sauce should be fairly thin, only thickened just enough to coat the fish.   Put the fish back in the sauce and simmer very gently for 10 minutes. Toast the bread, lay it in a serving dish, arrange fish on top, removing the heads of the eels only.   Surround with the glazed onions and mushrooms. (Crayfish cooked in court bouillon may also be used as a garnish.)

MATELOTE WITH SEA FISH

This dish should be made for a fairly large party.

2–3 lb. mixed sea fish, such as hake, sole, plaice, mackerel, or bream
seasoned flour
deep fat for frying
¾ oz. butter
1 large onion, thinly sliced
2–3 oz. bacon (streaky), cut into strips and previously blanched

¼ pint white wine
1¼ pints strong fish stock, made from the heads and trimmings of the fish
a bouquet garni
1 clove of garlic, crushed
salt and pepper

Garnish

2 rounds of stale bread
¼ lb. button mushrooms, trimmed, washed, and cooked in a nut of butter and a squeeze of lemon juice
12 button onions, glazed (see page 200)
½ lb. good sprats

6–8 Dublin Bay prawns or 1 crawfish tail cooked in fish stock or court bouillon
1 oz. butter, 1 oz. flour (beurre manié)
¼–½ oz. butter
1 teaspoon anchovy essence
chopped parsley

Prepare and trim fish.   Wash and dry well.   Cut into large slices. Roll in seasoned flour.   Plunge in smoking hot deep fat for 2 minutes. Drain and set aside.   Melt butter in a very large shallow or sauté pan. Put in the onion and bacon, sauter gently 6–7 minutes, add wine and boil vigorously 3–4 minutes.   Draw aside, add stock, bouquet, garlic, seasoning, and fish.   Cover and simmer until the fish is tender but intact. Meanwhile prepare garnish.   Cut bread into triangular croûtes, fry in deep fat.   Cook mushrooms in the butter and lemon juice.   Cook onions. Flour sprats and fry till golden brown in the fat.   Cook prawns or tail in fish stock or court bouillon.   Drain.   Keep all hot.   Lift out the fish carefully, drain and pile in a large platter.   Strain liquor and reduce if necessary to about 1¼ pints.   Thicken with the beurre manié, reboil, add butter and anchovy essence worked together, off the fire.   Add the mushrooms and onions.   Spoon over the fish and garnish round with the croûtes, sprats, and prawns.   Dust over with chopped parsley and serve very hot.

N.B. Mussels could be substituted for prawns or crawfish.

Smoked Fish

The most important items in this category are smoked salmon, smoked trout, cod's roe, eel, finnan-haddock, smokies, kippers, and bloaters. The first two named are luxury dishes and are referred to in the section dealing with first courses, as are cod's roe and smoked eel. Finnan-haddock is good provided the fish is neither too large nor too coarse. It may be bought whole or in fillets, but particular care should be taken over the preparation of the latter as these are taken from larger fish and are sometimes much stronger than the whole smaller fish. If the fish is large or strongly flavoured it may be soaked overnight in cold water. This is an excellent fish for fish cakes and puddings and kedgeree. The simplest way to cook it whole is in the oven in a baking-dish with a little milk and water, and a few thin slices of onion laid on top. When the fish is cooked the liquid is thickened as for a sauce, with a little flour and butter, or the fish may be anointed with melted butter.

An excellent breakfast dish may be made by flaking the flesh from a cooked haddock, mixing it with butter, and piling the mixture piping hot on buttered toast. A variant of this is to soak a haddock in water for an hour or so, lift it out and put it into a pan of fresh water, and bring it to boiling-point. Butter a fireproof dish, wipe the fish and cut in pieces, arrange in the buttered dish, dot with bits of butter, grate over fresh black pepper, and add enough milk to cover the bottom of the dish. Bake 15–20 minutes and finish off with sour cream and finely chopped parsley.

Finnan-haddock also makes a good filling for a strudel (for the strudel paste see page 840).

SMOKED HADDOCK AND CHEESE

1–1½ lb. smoked haddock	seasoning
water	chopped chives
1–2 hard-boiled eggs	grated cheese
6 tablespoons fresh white breadcrumbs	mornay sauce (see page 156)

Simmer the haddock in water until tender; bone and flake and put into a basin with the hard-boiled eggs, chopped, and breadcrumbs. Add seasoning, chopped chives, and the grated cheese. Scatter over the strudel paste according to directions given on page 841. Serve a light mornay cheese separately.

SMOKIES

Smokies are small fine-fleshed haddock which are smoked closed and not flat like finnan-haddies. Brush them over with butter and heat through in the oven or on both sides under the grill, split and insert a pat of butter, close up tight again and finish off with a few moments' more cooking.

An American friend, normally most appreciative of English food, says, when he comes to stay, that he bars only two things, Brussels sprouts and kippers. I know just what that indicates: he has been served with large and watery sprouts and town kippers of henna-like complexion and un-refined flavour. I find myself getting quite sad to think that his prejudice will become so set that even when he comes up to the Highlands he will deny himself the luxury of eating a properly smoked, delicately flavoured, small Scotch kipper. These are delicacies: not commonplace food. Most people do not cook kippers enough; they do not take long to cook through, but too often the outside is insufficiently done. This should be dark brown, crisp—almost burnt—a degree of cooking that brings out the smoky flavour. I have seen cooks in London give kippers a preliminary moment or two in boiling water—and watched the colour come out; such treatment is not necessary for the real thing, unless in the case of very delicate digestions a preliminary moment or two in boiling water, which reduces the oiliness, is found of advantage. Kippers, of course, are best grilled: wiped over first with a damp cloth, rubbed over with a tiny piece of butter, and grilled to crispness. They may be fried or cooked in the oven. The flaked or pounded flesh of the properly smoked kipper, well seasoned and mixed with butter, makes an excellent sandwich filling or spreading for a canapé.

These, being 'closed' fish, may well be scored to allow heat to penetrate readily. Brush over with butter or oil and grill. Serve with mustard butter (see below) or maître d'hôtel butter (see page 17).

Mustard butter

Allow a teaspoon of made English mustard to an ounce of butter. Season with a pinch of sugar and salt and work in a few chopped chives. See savoury butters, page 17.

Soused and Spiced Fish

Sousing and spicing are suitable methods of preparation for fish rich in oil. The acid of the marinade or cooking liquid not only offsets the rich-ness of the fish but has the effect of softening the smaller bones of such fish as herrings, pilchards, and sprats. When spiced fish is kept for a few days the bones become quite soft, and this is often a recommendation to children, who often fear fish-bones. Some of our old-fashioned English recipes calling for undiluted vinegar, and that of a strong kind, have raised a prejudice among certain people of sensitive palate, and this is unfortunate, for harshness and extreme acidity are in no sense essential.

The liquid in which soused fish is prepared may consist largely of wine or cider, with the addition of lemon juice and a small proportion of good French wine vinegar.   The addition of such herbs as bay-leaf (in larger proportions than usual), tarragon, and fennel gives the fish a subtle flavour. A dish of soused herrings, pilchards, or fresh mackerel slowly cooked and served ice-cold can be delicate enough for the most critical epicure.   But the ingredients of the sousing liquid must be good.

In addition to the pleasant quality of such dishes there is the point that certain of these are best eaten two or three days after cooking, and so advantage may be taken of a glut of good fresh fish.   When the water of the sea lochs seethes and shows silver and the mackerel are to be caught with any bait at all, when the herring fleet is in, even when the luxury of a too large salmon comes your way or the fishmonger tells you that he has a fine fresh cod, this is the moment to turn up your recipes for sousing and pickling.   But do not use coarse vinegar—sharp, yes, as good French wine vinegar is—and dilute it with wine, water, or cider and possibly a little lemon juice, not by any means forgetting the herbs and spices.

Here are two methods for soused herring, pilchard, or mackerel.   In recipe 1 a court bouillon is made first and the fish cooked in it afterwards. This is a suitable way when the fish is to be eaten either hot or shortly after cooking.

Method 1

1 carrot and 2 onions, finely sliced	a little freshly ground pepper
parsley, 1 small sprig of tarragon, 3 bay-leaves, 12 peppercorns, a blade of mace	1 good teaspoon salt
	white wine or cider to cover
	juice of a lemon
	8–10 herrings

Cook vegetables, herbs, and spices with seasonings in the wine/cider and lemon juice until vegetables are cooked.   Arrange herrings in a pie dish, pour over liquid and cover.   Bake in the oven slowly till herrings are done, about 1½ hours in a cool oven.   Serve hot or ice-cold.

Method 2

Lay 8–10 cleaned herrings or split and cleaned mackerel in a dish. Cover with a mixture of three parts vinegar and one part water, or a mixture of wine and vinegar.   Add 4 bay-leaves, 2 cloves, 12 allspice, 2 blades of mace, a good teaspoon of salt.   Cook in slow oven 3–4 hours in a covered dish (the liquid must not boil).   To serve pour strained liquid over the fish and allow to get ice-cold.

The long slow cooking assists in the softening and dissolving of the bones.   This dish when cold will set to a light jelly.

HERRINGS BAKED IN COURT BOUILLON

8 herrings   grated nutmeg
rock-salt and freshly ground
   black pepper

Court bouillon

1 pint dry white wine or cider   2 large carrots, sliced
¼ pint water   a bouquet garni of parsley and
juice of 1 lemon   thyme
3 onions, sliced   4 bay-leaves
3 cloves of garlic crushed with
   salt

Clean the herrings and cut off heads and fins.   Lay them head to tail in
a fireproof dish with a close-fitting cover and season with rock-salt and
freshly ground black pepper.   Make the court bouillon and simmer it
three-quarters of an hour.   Strain over the fish, which should be just
covered.   Grate a little nutmeg over the top.   Cover the dish and cook
in a really slow oven (300° F.) for 6 or 7 hours.

Potted herrings are excellent for sandwich fillings and are prepared in much
the same way, except that in this case the vinegar is used undiluted and the
roes are added.   Remove the heads and tails and clean the herrings,
sprinkle with salt and pepper inside and out.   Place herrings and roes
together in a dish, cover with vinegar, adding bay-leaves and seasoning as
in the previous recipe, bake slowly for 2–3 hours.   The flesh is then
pounded or put through a fine wire sieve and pressed into pots.   If the
paste is to be kept beyond a day or two it should be covered with clarified
butter.

Eel is a fish very rich in oil and may well be used to make a paste similar to
that given above.   It is cooked in the same way, then skinned, boned, and
sieved.   It may also be cooked as for soused herrings.

The following Spiced Fish is delicious and is best kept for 2 or 3 days
before being eaten.   The fish is first cooked by frying, then covered with
the spiced marinade and allowed to stand in a cold place for a few days
before being served.

SPICED FISH (6–8 PORTIONS)

Preparations must begin 2 or 3 days in advance.

2–3 lb. fresh cod or other large   4 oz. flour mixed with 1½ tea-
   white fish   spoons salt and ½ teaspoon
                                            pepper
                                         fat for frying

Sauce

¼ oz. flour   3 or 4 bay-leaves
1 tablespoon curry-powder   2 or 3 sprigs of fennel
3 good tablespoons sugar   (optional)
1 pint vinegar   1 dozen peppercorns, tied in
¾ pint water   muslin
2 large onions, finely sliced

Prepare cod, cleaning and cutting into suitably sized pieces.   Dip fish into seasoned flour.   Heat fat well and fry fish till golden brown and cooked thoroughly, taking care not to break the pieces.   Lift out, cool, and lay in a deep dish or bowl.

Prepare pickling liquid as follows: Combine flour, curry-powder, and sugar and mix to a paste with a tablespoon or two of the vinegar.   Heat remaining vinegar and the water with the onions, bay-leaves, fennel, and peppercorns and cook till onions are soft.   Add prepared paste to boiling liquid and cook for a few minutes longer.   Pour boiling liquid over fish, cool, and set in a cold place for 2 or 3 days.

This method is also suitable for herrings and mackerel, and the dish will keep for some time.

Another recipe for Spiced Fish will be found in the Winkfield chapter, page 994.

Fish Creams and Miscellaneous Fish Dishes

PAIN DE POISSON

This may be a plain homely dish or be garnished and made more elaborate.

$\frac{3}{4}$ lb. hake or cod weighed, skinned, boned, and minced

Panade

2 oz. butter
2 oz. flour
$\frac{1}{2}$ pint milk

2 eggs
$\frac{1}{2}$ gill cream
salt and pepper

Fish velouté

$\frac{3}{4}$ oz. butter
$\frac{3}{4}$ oz. flour
$1\frac{1}{2}$ gills fish stock
$\frac{1}{2}$ gill milk
seasoning

a squeeze of lemon
a little top of milk if necessary
garnish of mushrooms and prawns or glazed little onions and carrots

Make the panade with butter, flour, and milk, stir till boiling.   Season well and cool thoroughly.   Pound well with fish, beat in eggs and cream and adjust seasoning.   Put into buttered mould and steam or poach till firm, about 40 minutes.   Leave for a few minutes before turning out. Pour over a fish velouté sauce (made as for next recipe) and garnish.

The following recipe is for a finer cream.   Containing no flour, it is suitable for invalids if the garnish is omitted.

MOUSSELINE DE POISSON

$\frac{3}{4}$ lb. whiting or haddock weighed when boned and minced
3 egg whites
$1\frac{1}{2}$ gills cream

salt and pepper
garnish of crab or shrimps, mushroom and tomato
velouté sauce (see below)

Put the minced fish into a bowl, beat well. Break the whites very slightly with a fork, then beat them into the fish by degrees. Pass through a fine wire sieve. Return to the basin. Beat in the cream, also by degrees, adding seasoning (plenty of salt after cream is in). Turn into a buttered oval dish or ring mould, poach in the oven until firm. Leave for a moment or two before turning out; then turn on to serving dish, surround or cover with a salpicon of crab or shrimps, mushrooms and tomato, and pour over a good velouté sauce.

Velouté sauce

¾ oz. butter
¾ oz. flour
1½ gills fish stock
½ gill single cream

salt and pepper
a squeeze of lemon
a little top of milk if necessary

Melt the butter in a saucepan, add the flour off the fire. Pour on the stock and stir until thickening, then add single cream, season, boil, and simmer for a few minutes. Add a squeeze of lemon juice and an extra spoonful or two of top of milk if necessary.

In the following recipe similar ingredients are called for but in different proportions. The sauce is richer and the mixture is cooked in individual moulds.

SUPRÊMES DE POISSON PARISIENNE
little fish creams

½ lb. haddock weighed when
    boned and minced
whites of 2 small eggs

1 gill cream
salt and pepper

Sauce suprême

¾ oz. butter
½ oz. flour

1½ gills fish fumet
a squeeze of lemon juice

Liaison

2–3 yolks and ¾ gill cream

Garnish

3–4 oz. whole (button) or sliced mushrooms cooked in a nut of
butter, a teaspoon of lemon juice, and a dessertspoon of water

Put the minced fish into a bowl and beat well. Break the whites lightly with a fork and beat into the fish gradually. Pass through a fine wire sieve and return to the basin. Beat in the cream slowly, adding seasoning. Put into buttered cutlet or quenelle moulds with a palette-knife (see paragraph 8, page 700). Poach or steam 7–10 minutes.

Sauce. Melt butter, add flour off the fire, pour on the fumet and stir till boiling. Add a squeeze of lemon and simmer for a few minutes, add the liaison of yolks and cream (as directed for liaisons, see page 138), and finally stir in the mushrooms. Turn out, dish the creams *en couronne*, and mask with the sauce.

The next recipe is for a simple fish cream, less elaborate than Salmon Mousse, but good.

FISH CREAM SUÉDOISE (COLD)

½ lb. cold cooked white fish
½ pint well-flavoured béchamel sauce, made preferably by the long method (see page 155)
1 level dessertspoon gelatine
1 large tablespoon whipped cream or 1 stiffly whipped egg white or 1 tablespoon cream dressing (see page 363)

1 cup cole-slaw dressing or mayonnaise
1 teaspoon chopped gherkins and capers, mixed
¼ teaspoon finely chopped onion
½ teaspoon chopped parsley
sliced beetroot or sliced dill cucumber
Scandinavian dressing (see page 363)

Put the fish into a mortar or bowl, pound or beat well, adding the sauce by degrees. Then add the gelatine dissolved in 2 tablespoons water and lastly the whipped cream, egg white, or mock mayonnaise. Turn into a small charlotte mould and leave to set. Unmould and coat over with the thick cole-slaw dressing to which has been added a teaspoon of mixed chopped gherkins and capers, a touch of onion, and ½ teaspoon chopped parsley. Surround with thinly sliced beetroot *en couronne* and spoon over a good Swedish dressing.

N.B. The sauce or dressing should only coat the cream and not fall down into the dish.

SALMON MOUSSE (COLD)

Béchamel sauce

½ bay-leaf
a blade of mace
3–4 peppercorns
a slice of onion

1½ gills milk
1 oz. butter
1 oz. flour
salt and pepper

Mousse

½ lb. cooked salmon weighed when skinned and boned
2 oz. well-creamed butter
1–2 tablespoons whipped cream
1 tablespoon sherry

a drop or two of carmine if necessary
½ pint aspic jelly (see page 736)
sliced cucumber, shredded tomato, or prawns for garnish

Prepare the sauce by infusing the bay-leaf, spices, and onion in the milk. When well flavoured strain and cool slightly. Melt the butter in a saucepan, add the flour off the fire and pour on the milk. Stir until boiling, cook for a minute or two, season, then turn on to a plate to cool.

Pound the salmon in a mortar, or cream and pound well in a bowl with the end of a rolling-pin. Add the sauce by degrees, with plenty of seasoning. Fold in the creamed butter, the whipped cream and sherry. Add a little carmine if necessary. Turn into a soufflé dish, filling three parts full. Smooth over the top and decorate. Leave in a cold place a quarter of an hour. Run over it a little liquid aspic to set the garnish, and when that is set fill to the top of the dish with the rest of the aspic.

Only those who really like garlic will be interested in the following recipe. It is for a Basque dish characterized by the highly seasoned mixture of garlic and onion.

CHIORRO

3 tablespoons good oil
3 large onions, thinly sliced
½–1 small coffee-cup of garlic (according to taste), very finely chopped
¾ oz. flour
1 heaped teaspoon tomato purée or 2–3 tomatoes skinned, pipped, and chopped
2 teaspoons paprika
a pinch each of cayenne and ground mace

2 wineglasses red wine
¼ pint water
1–1½ lb. white fish: turbot, cod, large haddock or such-like divided into cutlets
salt and freshly ground black pepper
lemon juice or tarragon vinegar for poaching fish
bread for croûtes
oil for frying

Heat the oil in a shallow pan, add the onions and chopped garlic; allow to soften slowly. Remove lid and increase heat to allow the onion to brown lightly. Add the flour, purée, and seasonings and when well mixed the wine and water. Bring to the boil and simmer 30–35 minutes with lid off. Adjust seasoning and set aside.

Meantime wash, dry, and trim the fish. Lay in a buttered fireproof dish, add salt and freshly ground black pepper; sprinkle with lemon juice or vinegar and cook in a moderate oven 15–20 minutes. Cut a croûte of bread to fit each cutlet, and fry in oil until golden brown on both sides. Arrange in a hot serving dish, set a cutlet of fish on each, and spoon the sauce over each piece. Serve very hot.

The next dish is Spanish and should properly be served in a large round dish called a paella, and garnished with some of the prawns, cockles, or mussels in their shells.

PAELLA VALENCIANA

1 lb. conger eel
2 lb. Dublin Bay prawns, cooked
¼ lb. prawns or shrimps, cooked
1½ cups rice
2 tablespoons salad-oil
1 small onion

1 clove of garlic
lemon juice
¼ lb. cockles, cooked
saffron
1 tomato
seasoning, if necessary

Wash the eel, trim it, and set the trimming aside. Peel half the Dublin Bay prawns and all the shrimps or prawns and set them aside in cold water. Pound the shells of the prawns and the fish trimmings in a mortar, then put them in a saucepan, cover them with water, and boil them fairly fast for 20 minutes or so. Strain off the stock and use it for cooking the rice later. There should be three times as much stock as rice, i.e. 4½ cups. If the fish stock does not provide enough, make up with water.

In a large shallow earthenware or iron pan make the oil very hot. Put in the chopped onion and cook golden brown; add the chopped garlic and cook also. Put in the rice and turn it about in the hot oil. Pour in the fish stock and the lemon juice, then add the eel (which takes the longest time to cook). After 20 minutes add the shelled Dublin Bay prawns and the shrimps and cockles. Add the saffron and the tomato, peeled and squeezed through a sieve or strainer. Continue cooking for a few minutes. Taste and season if necessary. Serve in the paella. Arrange the remaining Dublin Bay prawns in their shells on top.

A paella may also be made with vegetables, with chicken, or with chicken and fish together. Shell-fish should always be used, and some should be put in in their shells. Mussels, for example, can take the place of Dublin Bay prawns or cockles, or all of them may be used. Conger eel is almost indispensable, and freshwater eel could be used. Skate can be substituted if absolutely necessary. The beginning of the paella is always the same. Oil is made hot in the pan, onion and garlic are cooked in it, then the flavoured liquid is added with the main ingredient. The finished dish may be served with a browned top (done in the oven or under the grill) or rather moist, according to taste.

The following dish is improved if made the day before it is required so that the fish has time to absorb the flavour of the sauce. The preliminary frying of the fish and potatoes is to brown rather than to cook through, and that is why deep fat is satisfactory. The amount of ginger is given but must be adjusted to taste; the dish should be fairly hot. The sauce may be softened by the addition of a little cream or evaporated milk before being sent to table.

INDIAN FISH

1½ lb. cod or other firm white fish (in the piece)

Stock

1 sliced carrot	salt
1 sliced onion	4–6 peppercorns
a bouquet garni	1 pint water (approx.)

¾ lb. peeled potatoes	seasoned flour

deep fat bath, or if this is not available shallow fat frying may be substituted, and for this oil or dripping is required

4 medium onions, finely chopped	1 tablespoon flour
	salt and pepper
1 large tablespoon finely grated root ginger	

Remove skin and bone from fish. Put into a pan ingredients for stock, simmer uncovered until reduced by about one-third, strain. Meantime cut fish into pieces the size of a large walnut, cut potatoes to the same size, roll fish in seasoned flour, fry quickly to a golden brown in oil or deep fat. Fry the potatoes in the same way. Blanch the onions, mix with the ginger and pound to a paste, add flour and dilute with a little of the stock. Turn into a shallow pan or casserole, add rest of stock, bring to boil and season. Add fish and potatoes, cover and cook gently in the oven 40–50 minutes.

FISH WITH FENNEL

Both fennel and dill are herbs which associate well with fish, and the following way of serving any of the choicer white fish is one of the most delicious. For this the root of Florence fennel (finocchio) is required (see page 380). Nowadays it is often to be seen in the French market in Soho and in vegetable shops which sell unusual vegetables. Slice the fennel very finely, sauter the slices in butter in the frying-pan. Lift out and set aside. Add a little more butter to the pan and cook the fish *à la meunière* (see page 452). Arrange the slices of fennel in a dish, lay the cooked fish on top. Wipe out the frying-pan, drop in a little butter, and make a beurre noisette with lemon juice (see page 169).

FRITTO MISTO

The true fritto is made of different kinds of fish, some coated in batter, some egged and breadcrumbed, all fried in deep fat. The dish is accompanied by a suitable sharp sauce such as vinaigrette, tartare, ravigote, or gribiche, or served simply with slices of lemon. Brown bread and butter is handed with it.

Choose 4–6 different kinds of fish, treating each in the appropriate way. Prawns, Dublin Bay prawns, oysters or mussels, slices of lobster, crab made into croquettes, sole, whiting, mackerel, whitebait are, among others, suitable.

Prawns. Shell and marinade in French dressing for an hour, then dip in fritter batter.

Mussels. Cook to open (see page 499), shell, dip in fritter batter.

Oysters. Marinade in lemon juice with plenty of seasoning; dip in batter.

Lobster or crawfish tails. As for prawns.

Crab croquettes. See page 12 (Devilled Croquettes).

Sole. Choose slip soles, fillet, cut in strips, flour, egg and breadcrumb.

Whiting. Fillet the whiting, cut each fillet in half lengthwise, flour, dip in batter, and fry, twisting each strip as it slips into the pan.

Whitebait. Cook according to instructions on page 488.

Where fritter batter is called for use recipe 1 (page 442). Where egging and breadcrumbing is called for follow instructions given on page 38. In every case fry to a golden brown.

A few fritters made of herbs (see page 277) may with advantage be added. Pile up all the fritters in a hot dish.

Some recipes call for a preliminary marinading of the fish, except of course for the oysters and mussels. The fish is laid in a bath of white wine with seasoning and a bouquet of herbs and is left in this for about three-quarters of an hour, after which it is drained, coated, and fried.

Reheated Fish

FISHCAKES (ENGLISH METHOD)

equal parts of cooked flaked fish and freshly boiled potatoes, the latter put through ricer or sieved
seasoning
a nut of butter
1 egg
1 tablespoon finely chopped parsley
egg and breadcrumbs

Mix potatoes and fish in a warm bowl. Season well, add butter, and work well in with a wooden spoon. Add the beaten egg and chopped parsley. Spread on a plate to chill thoroughly, shape on a floured board into flat cakes. Egg and breadcrumb and fry in shallow fat.

The following croquettes, the French counterpart of fishcakes, are a more delicate dish. They should be crisp on the outside and very creamy within. They may with advantage be prepared for frying well ahead of time, and the mixture placed in the ice drawer so that it is thoroughly hard for coating. In this way it is possible to use a particularly soft mixture and have in the result a very creamy croquette.

CROQUETTES DE POISSON A LA CRÈME

1½ gills milk
1 bay-leaf
1 blade of mace
1½ oz. butter
1 slice of onion, chopped
1½ oz. flour
seasoning
8 oz. picked cooked fish
1 egg
dried white breadcrumbs and 1 beaten egg for coating
deep fat for frying

Bring milk slowly to boil with bay-leaf and mace and allow to cool slightly. In a saucepan melt the butter and soften the onion thoroughly, but without allowing it to colour, add flour off fire, season, strain on the milk all at once. Stir over the fire till boiling and simmer for a minute or two. Add the fish gradually, beating well, adjust seasoning, then add the egg. When thoroughly mixed turn on to a plate to get quite cold. If convenient allow to rest in ice-box for a time. Then divide into equal portions, roll and shape into croquettes on a floured board, brush with egg, roll and press lightly in the crumbs. Fry in deep boiling fat. Drain well. Serve with a sauce blanche or velouté, or a tomato sauce.

TARTE AU POISSON (FISH FLAN)

A Tunisian recipe.

6 oz. quantity of good short or flaky pastry (see page 835)
3 large ripe tomatoes
1 tea-cup onions, finely sliced
1 oz. butter
1 tea-cup single cream or rich milk
salt, pepper, grated nutmeg
2 eggs
1 heaped tea-cup flaked cooked fish: fresh or smoked haddock, kipper, salmon, etc.
a little grated cheese

Roll out pastry and line a flan ring.   Bake blind (see page 844).   Scald and skin the tomatoes, cut in half, remove seeds, slice and set aside. Soften onion in butter and add cream.   Stir until hot, draw aside, add seasoning and beaten eggs.   Arrange the tomatoes and fish on the bottom of the cooked pastry case, season highly, and pour in the onion and egg mixture to fill well.   Sprinkle with grated cheese and bake in a moderate oven till well set and golden brown.

FISH PIE

1½ lb. mashed potatoes	2 tablespoons chopped parsley
1 lb. cooked flaked fish	seasoning
½–¾ pint boiling milk	a little grated nutmeg
2 oz. butter	

Boil and mash potatoes, mix with flaked fish.   Add butter and boiling milk gradually, beating well.   Add parsley, seasoning, and nutmeg.   Pile into a greased pie dish and brown in a hot oven.

A good fish pie may also be made with layers of flaked fish, slices of hard-boiled egg, a béchamel or cream sauce, a good sprinkling of parsley, and a top of creamy mashed potatoes.

FISH PUDDING

¾ pint mornay sauce (see page 156)	chopped parsley and fennel
12 oz. cooked fish	browned breadcrumbs
12 oz. mashed potato	extra chopped parsley for garnish
salt and pepper	

Make the mornay sauce, mix with it the fish, mashed potato, seasoning, parsley, and fennel, put into a buttered fireproof dish, sprinkle with a few browned breadcrumbs, and bake three-quarters of an hour in a hot oven. Sprinkle with chopped parsley and serve.

KEDGEREE

Kedgeree is at its best when butter can be freely used, and it should be noted that fish and rice ought to be in equal proportions.   The rice should be very well dried, and in consequence becomes particularly absorbent, so that a good deal of butter may be used before the dish becomes really creamy.   It will be noted that a little cream is used in the following recipe; cream is a good addition, but properly speaking except for this no other liquid should be added.

Suitable fish for this dish include any white fish, salmon, tinned or fresh, and in particular smoked haddock, which is excellent.   Kedgeree, so popular now in England either for breakfast or luncheon, derives from India. When well made it is suitable for a party dish for luncheon or supper, and it has always been popular for breakfast.   Before the war one London hostess used to give a luncheon party each month during the winter with kedgeree as her main dish, followed by a rich and sticky toffee pudding, and very popular it was.

6 oz. rice
1 small onion, finely chopped (see note below)
2–3 oz. butter (see note below)
6 oz. cooked fish, flaked and free from skin and bone

1–2 hard-boiled eggs
seasoning
1–2 tablespoons cream (see note below)
1 tablespoon chopped parsley

Boil the rice in plenty of boiling salted water. Drain thoroughly (see page 386). Meantime chop onion finely, soften in the butter without browning. Add the fish and chopped hard-boiled egg. Mix and heat thoroughly. Season well, add rice, and stir with a fork till very hot. At the last moment stir in the cream, turn at once into a hot dish, and sprinkle with chopped parsley. The mixture must be creamy, but not dry.

The Indian version is coloured a delicate yellow with turmeric, and has thin strips of chilli pepper and green ginger in the rice, the whole garnished with crisply fried onions and hard-boiled eggs. The cream is left out.

N.B. For a breakfast dish the onion may be omitted. If butter has to be used sparingly or if a less rich dish is required, a beaten raw egg may be stirred in at the same time as the cream and the amount of butter reduced. The cream gives a good texture and should be thick, but single cream may be substituted at need.

For fish sauces see sauce chapter, page 163.

XVII

Meat—Beef, Mutton and Lamb, Pork, Veal

GENERAL

IT is desirable that the recipes in the following chapters should be read in conjunction with the chapter on kitchen technique and with the notes in other parts of the book on such matters as the use of butter in cooking, clarifying, and the substitution of margarine or oil; thickening and liaisons, and the browning of meats for ragoûts and braises; mirepoix; coulis and salpicons, etc.

It is impossible for those of us who have cooked or kept house over a long period not to be price conscious about all foods, but particularly so about meat. We remember an old boarding-school complaint that only beef and mutton were served to the unfortunate pupils, and hark back to earlier days when meat cost from sixpence to elevenpence per pound. It is natural then that while we feel that the classic recipes must be in the hands of all students of cookery, they must be balanced by considerations of economy.

It is not a bad thing to observe some of the ways in which, without spoiling its intrinsic qualities, meat may be stretched, so to speak, to go as far as possible. There are many ways, varying in their degree of simplicity, that are worth consideration.

It used to be the fashion among country folk to cook, under the rack of the Sunday roast, a suet pudding; this substantial dish, impregnated with the drippings and gravy from the meat, was rich and satisfying, and, served in slices before the meat itself, took the edge off large and healthy appetites, so that less meat was demanded. For the children in particular, this pudding, with gravy and vegetables, was considered adequate, the meat being reserved for the grown-ups. Some people went further, serving the pudding as the main part of the meal and keeping the meat until the next day, so that it was not cut until cold, when, of course, it could be carved much more economically than is possible with hot meat; moreover the slices (in particular of beef) were pinker and juicier than one gets with cold meat which has first been cut while hot. Yorkshire pudding was also cooked and used in the same way. There are other and perhaps more modern ways of stretching this part of our food; some English, some of American origin, others from European countries, especially from those which have not known long periods of plenty. Not all of them were necessarily originally conceived in the spirit of economy perhaps, but many are worth taking into consideration and adapting. The custom of serving fruit with certain meats has an American flavour; although spiced prunes with Irish stew and hot-pot, apple sauce with pork, and orange with duck are homely enough, fried pineapple with mutton and glazed crab-apples and spiced peaches with meat sound a newer note. Then there are the various fruit and savoury stuffings, the mirepoix, the purées of vegetables served as a part of the meat dish itself. As a simple example of economy, compare the ordinary dish of stew with the carbonnade of beef on page 547, in which the seasoned bread on top of the pot is considered by many to be more delicious than the meat itself, and just the sort of food that appeals to young palates.

The Pain Farci on page 714 is a better way of using up cold meat than the mince of my childhood days. Altogether we have opportunity for originality and inventiveness which may be greeted with greater appreciation to-day than might have been the case when meat was a good deal cheaper.

CHOOSING AND HANGING MEAT

All meat should hang for a certain time after it is killed; a good butcher sells meat already hung and ready for cooking. Home-killed pork or mutton should hang for 5–7 days according to weather. Except for certain kinds of game which are eaten slightly high or 'well hung,' all meat and poultry should be hung head downwards and used absolutely sweet. Should meat become slightly tainted, it must be either washed or soaked for a little while in vinegar and water before being cooked. Meat from the butcher should be kept either in a refrigerator or under a fine wire cover or a piece of clean muslin.

Offal, that is to say liver, kidney, heart, and sweetbreads, is not hung, but eaten when freshly killed.

How to choose meat

Good meat, beef or mutton, should have a marbled appearance produced by the distribution through the flesh of small veinings of fat. It should be neither too pale nor too dark in colour and should be firm and elastic to the touch; excessive moisture or flabbiness is a sign of poor meat, as is any unpleasant smell: good meat should have little odour.

Joints with too much fat are unprofitable, although the surplus fat may be cut off and rendered down. Generally speaking, meat for roasting should have a certain proportion of fat running through or around it.

FROZEN MEAT

Frozen meat should be thoroughly defrosted before cooking, otherwise it will be tough and of poor flavour; this point is not always sufficiently observed. A joint which has been kept for some time in a refrigerator may be brought into the warmth of the kitchen, covered with a clean cloth, and allowed to remain for 3 or 4 hours before being cooked. Meat arriving frozen from the butcher may take much longer to thaw, anything up to 24 hours.

GENERAL PREPARATION

Broadly speaking, meat is prepared for cooking by cutting off excess fat, tendons, and any gristly or inedible portions; the particular treatment for each kind of meat will follow under separate headings.

BEEF

The flesh should be open-grained, of good red colour, not too dark, and the fat firm and cream or yellowish in colour.

Joints for roasting: round, fore-ribs, sirloin, fillet, which is the undercut from the sirloin, aitch-bone, wing-ribs, and topside.   The best are fillet, sirloin, and rolled ribs.

To roast

Cover the joint with dripping and put into a hot oven (450°–500° F.). If the meat is liked underdone, which is the correct way to serve roast beef, allow 15 minutes to the pound and decrease the heat slightly after the first half-hour.   Baste every 15–20 minutes.   See page 62 for basting and roasting.

Roast beef should be a delicate to deep shade of pink inside when it is cut, and a crisp dark brown outside.

Classic accompaniments to hot roast beef: Yorkshire pudding, gravy, horse-radish sauce, and a garnish of thin slivers of plain horse-radish.

Gravy

Pour the fat gently from the pan, taking care to leave the juice from the meat behind, add a little pepper and salt, and if thickening is required add a sprinkling of flour and allow it to cook until coloured; if extra colouring is wanted, put into the pan a slice of onion or tomato sprinkled with sugar and allow this to brown (if this is overdone bitterness will be produced). Some cooks brown this sugared slice on the hot-plate of an electric stove before adding it to the contents of the pan.   Now add boiling liquid, stock, potato water, or water.   As one rarely has good beef stock, potato water is generally used and is excellent.   Strain and serve.

N.B. Gravy for roast beef should not really be thick and it is a common fault to add too much flour.

COLD ROAST MEAT

The joint should be allowed to become completely cold before carving; if it is cut into while hot it loses colour, juiciness, and flavour.   This may be a policy of perfection, but cold meat from a joint, part of which has been cut into while hot, is less good.

Classic accompaniments: cold creamy horse-radish sauce, a garnish of thin slivers of horse-radish.

To carve roast beef *

Choose a long, thin-bladed, sharp knife and cut as thinly as possible across the grain of the meat; the exception to this is the undercut, which is carved thickly, in quarter-inch slices, with the grain of the meat.

BOILED BEEF

In England it is customary to use salted beef for boiling, and the classic dish is boiled beef and dumplings. For the French classic, pot-au-feu, unsalted beef is used.

Suitable pieces are round and silverside, brisket and aitch-bone.

Salted brisket is used for cold pressed beef because it has a largish proportion of fat and would be wasteful if used for hot boiled beef. Salted silverside, being a leaner joint, is used for boiled beef and dumplings. Both thick and thin flank, salted, are used for pressed beef. If salting is to be done at home it is done in a mixture of salt and saltpetre (see recipe below), and preparation has to be made ahead of time, as three days at least are required for the salting.   In the case of spiced beef it is an advantage to salt at home as some of the spicing may be done at the same time.

BRINE BATH FOR LARGE QUANTITIES
suitable for home-killed meat

Rub each piece of meat to be pickled with salt and leave for 24 hours. Dry and pack closely in a jar or vat.

Make the following solution: To 2 gallons of water add 2 oz. saltpetre, 5 lb. salt, and 1 lb. brown sugar.   Boil for 15 minutes and skim.   When cold pour on to the meat, putting a weight on top to hold the meat well under the pickle.

BRINE SPECIFIC

¼ lb. white peppercorns	½ oz. juniper berries
2 oz. root ginger	¾ oz. mint
¼ oz. garlic	1½ oz. bay-leaves

Tie the above in a muslin bag.

In 5 gallons of water dissolve:

4 lb. coarse salt	¼ lb. saltpetre
¾ lb. cane sugar	

Stir well to ascertain that all the above are completely dissolved, add bag containing spices and herbs and stir it round for a few minutes, bruising the bag gently with a wooden spoon.   Add the piece of meat to be salted and leave for 2 or 3 days.

* See plate 6

The following is an alternative recipe from our butcher. To 2 pails of cold water take:

14 lb. rough salt	1 oz. Primla
2 oz. saltpetre	6 bay-leaves

Crush the saltpetre, Primla, and bay-leaves into a powder and pour on about 1 pint boiling water. When mixture is cold put into vat with salt and cold water. Settle for 3 hours and then skim. Primla may usually be bought from a butcher's sundriesman or chemist.

To boil salt beef

Put the joint in sufficient unsalted water to cover, bring slowly to boil, skimming frequently (see note on skimming in recipe for pot-au-feu, page 117). Simmer in half-covered pan for a preliminary hour, and the chosen root vegetables, bouquet, and seasonings, and continue cooking (see specific recipe, page 545).

Classic accompaniments: dumplings and carrots.

To serve salted boiled beef cold: Allow it to cool in the liquor in which it was cooked. It should cut like butter. Serve with grated raw, red cabbage and grated onion, with a sharp French dressing.

Grilling

Pieces suitable for grilling: rump steak, entrecôtes (sirloin steaks), and contrefilets (rib steaks). Fillet of beef cut into slices $1\frac{1}{2}$–2 inches thick provides tournedos; they may be brushed over with oil or clarified butter before being grilled, or grilled dry, that is without oil or butter (the way they are done in restaurants over a 'silver grill'), and sometimes they are marinaded in brandy or sherry. (See specific recipes.) For 'entrecôte minute' the steak is cut into slices $\frac{1}{4}$ inch thick; these are grilled for about 3 minutes on each side under a hot grill, should be brown on the outside, faintly pink inside, and are served with their own juice from the grilling pan. (This entrecôte is sometimes fried in butter and served with the juice from the pan.) (See specific recipes and notes on grilling, page 63.)

Braising

Sirloin and other ribs may be boned and braised; chuck steak and clod and other inexpensive stewing meats are all suitable. It should, however, be borne in mind that for braising a certain proportion of fat is needed, otherwise the dish becomes too dry. Sometimes two different cuts, one lean, one fat, are combined in the same dish. Often for a braise the meat is left whole and not cut.

Stewing

The same joints are used as for braising, and generally speaking the cheaper cuts of meat: second or buttock steak, chuck, topside, or rump, flank, skirt, and shin. For stewing the meat is generally cut up.

See notes on braising and stewing on pages 66 and 67. It may be noted that slices of quince or damson cheese are excellent eaten with beef stews and ragoûts.

BEEF TEA

Shin of beef, being lean and containing gelatine, is suitable for this purpose.

Other pieces of meat—head, knucklebones, etc.—are used in the making of stock and glaze.

In Filet de Bœuf Rôti we have what may be considered the most *recherché* of beef dishes.

FILET DE BŒUF RÔTI

2½–4 lb. fillet of beef	*Gravy*
larding bacon cut into strips ¼ inch wide by 2½ inches long	beef stock or bouillon seasoning
good dripping	watercress

Trim the meat slightly, but leave on a reasonable proportion of fat. With a larding-needle thread the lardons into the fillet all along the top of the meat, staggering the rows (see note on larding, page 69) and trimming the ends evenly with scissors. Melt 2 or 3 large spoonfuls of dripping in the roasting-pan, put in the meat and baste. Put in a hot oven (450° F., see oven chart, page 60), allowing 15 minutes to the pound. Baste frequently, every 10 minutes or so. Fillet should be rather underdone, and since to make a test by sticking in a skewer is to lose some of the juice of the meat, this is best done by pressing the meat with the finger. If softly springy (R. H. says 'feeling like a pincushion') the meat is underdone; if resilient and firm the joint is well done. This, I am afraid, is a matter of experience to some extent, but if the recipe is followed a beginner will not go far wrong.

To dish. Pour the fat from the pan, add beef stock or bouillon, using about ½ tea-cup (it is a common fault to use too much liquid); salt lightly, taste, reduce if necessary, strain and pour a little round the meat, serving the rest in a sauce-boat. Do not thicken the gravy for this dish. Sherry may be added to the pan with the bouillon. Garnish with little bouquets of watercress, which may be dipped in French dressing and shaken lightly before being arranged in the dish; this should be done immediately before serving. Pont Neuf potatoes are the usual accompaniment.

Note on the larding of a small fillet. (The lardons may be marinaded in chopped herbs before being used.) When larding small joints such as the above it is better to work across the grain of the meat, otherwise in carving in thinnish slices the lardons may disappear. For larger joints such as a piece of topside in braised beef, the larding may be done with the grain of the meat, which is an easier process.

Tournedos come from the same delicate fillet of the meat, this time cut in slices for grilling.

TOURNEDOS *

Tournedos are slices of meat not less than 1–1½ inches thick, cut from the heart of the fillet.   When cut they are tied round with a piece of strong cotton or thread to keep them firmly in shape; just, in miniature, as a round of beef is tied.   Usually this part of the meat, especially in the case of a large fillet (known in France as a noix), has a surround of ordinary meat which is trimmed away and is excellent for a ragoût, a salpicon, or a sauce such as Bolognese.   In addition to this, the noix itself is surrounded by a covering of thin skin which is removed by sliding a knife under it and carefully peeling it off.   Sometimes a piece of the fat which lies around the fillet is fried or grilled and put on the top of each piece of meat after it is done, and this should be cut and prepared at the same time as the fillets are trimmed.   Generally tournedos are served on a croûton of bread fried in butter, or on slices of buttered toast, and it is essential to have these freshly made and to set the tournedos on them at the last minute, otherwise the juice from the meat is too much soaked into the bread.   Any juice from the grill should be poured over.

It is usual to brush a tournedos over with melted glaze after it is cooked (¾ oz. glaze dissolved in 1 large tablespoon hot water).   In place of the glaze a dab of plain or maître d'hôtel butter may be used.   The dish is garnished with watercress.

To grill

After trimming, grill just as they are over an open fire or under a gas or electric grill previously well heated.   Strictly speaking they should be turned only once, 7–10 minutes being allowed for the whole operation. For a tournedos 1½ inches thick this should give, if the grill has been properly heated, a good medium pink colour to the inside flesh.

To fry

Choose a thick iron pan.   Take a small quantity of butter, oil, or good dripping, according to the garnish to be served.   Heat this till sizzling or smoking hot, put in the tournedos, cook on moderate to hot fire, turning once only.   Serve Pont Neuf potatoes.

Tournedos dishes may take their name from the sauces or garnish which accompany them; for example:

Tournedos Chasseur, served with sauce chasseur.

Tournedos Rossini, served with foie gras and mushrooms.

Tournedos Cyrano, served with chestnut purée and demi-glace sauce.

Tournedos Dubarry, served with bouquets of cauliflower and demi-glace sauce.

* See plate 7

TOURNEDOS SAUTÉS CHASSEUR

1 tablespoon oil and ½ oz. butter
3 oz. button mushrooms
2 shallots very finely chopped
1 teaspoon flour
1½ gills good bouillon or stock
1 teaspoon concentrated tomato purée
salt and pepper
6 tournedos cut 1 inch thick from approx. 1½ lb. beef fillet

2 tablespoons oil and 1 oz. butter to sauter
6 croûtons of bread about ½ inch thick, the same size as the tournedos
oil or butter for frying these
1 large wineglass white wine
1 teaspoon chopped tarragon
a nut of butter
½ teaspoon chopped parsley

Trim the mushrooms by cutting off the ends of the stalks level with the caps, wash, dry, and cut in fine slices. In a small sauté pan heat the butter and oil, add mushrooms, and cook quickly until lightly coloured. Add the shallot and sauter for a few minutes, taking care it does not burn. Add flour and leave on the side of the fire 3–4 minutes. Add bouillon, purée, and a light seasoning. Stir until boiling, simmer gently 15–20 minutes. Now fry croûtons and keep hot. Heat the oil and butter for the tournedos in a *sautoir* or deep frying-pan, and when just smoking put them in, first seasoning lightly with salt and pepper. Sauter on a quick fire 4–5 minutes on each side. This should bring them to the stage known as *à point*, that is to say brown on the outside and when cut a nice pink inside. If liked red allow only 4 minutes on each side. Remove from pan and keep hot between 2 plates. Drain off the fat and, adding the white wine, stir well, so that all the caramel-like substance on the bottom is dissolved (déglacer in fact). Boil quickly for a minute or two to reduce, then add the mushroom mixture, reboil, and draw aside. Put the tournedos on the croûtons, arrange round a dish; add tarragon to the sauce and pour this into the centre of the dish. Rub a lump of butter lightly over the tournedos to make them glisten, and sprinkle with chopped parsley. Melted glaze may be used instead of butter.

TOURNEDOS PROVENÇALE

For this dish croûtons are omitted and the tournedos are arranged on slices of aubergine which have been fried in oil with a crushed clove of garlic. They are served with a tomato coulis (see page 179) and sauté potatoes.

TOURNEDOS WITH MUSHROOMS

For this the tournedos are set on large grilled mushrooms in place of croûtons. They are glazed with butter or glaze and served with sauce bordelaise or italienne served separately, and the dish is garnished with pommes pailles.

ENTRECÔTES

Although technically entrecôte is from the ribs of beef (entrecôte, without bone; côtes de bœuf, with), it is more usually, on account of suitability of size, cut from the top part of a sirloin or 'faux filet.' Except for 'entrecôte minute' it should be cut in slices of about ¾ inch thick.

Grilled entrecôte, or rump steak, which is sometimes used instead of an entrecôte proper, is prepared as follows:

Allow 3–4 oz. per person and grill. After grilling rub lightly over the surface either with a lump of butter on the point of a knife, or cream the butter (plain or maître d'hôtel), put half of it in a warmed dish, and spread the remainder over the steak.

The following are classic garnishes for entrecôtes:

A la Béarnaise. Grilled, with sauté potatoes at each end of a long dish and a jus poured over, with béarnaise sauce served in a sauce-boat.

Aux marrons. Grilled or sautéd (see notes on sautéing, page 64). Served on a long dish with maître d'hôtel butter, surrounded with braised chestnuts and, at each end of the dish, quarters of tomato sautéd in butter.

Mirabeau. Grilled, with a jus poured over and anchovy butter served separately. Garnished with strips of anchovy fillets laid criss-cross over the meat, and a bouquet of watercress at each end.

Aux champignons. Grilled or sautéd. Served with Pont Neuf potatoes at each end of the dish. Surrounded with mushrooms, sautéd, and finished with a little garlic butter.

N.B. With all grills a jus should be served. It may be of good bouillon, veal for preference, to which a small piece of meat glaze has been added.

ENTRECÔTE MACON

This consists of an entrecôte grilled to taste and served in rich sauce made as follows:

1 tablespoon finely chopped onions	½ teaspoon tomato purée
½ oz. butter	2 cloves of garlic crushed with
¼ oz. flour (good weight)	½ teaspoon salt
1½ wineglasses red wine (Macon)	1 tablespoon Madeira or dark sherry
4 tomatoes, peeled, pipped, and chopped	1 bay-leaf
	salt and pepper

Fry onions in butter until lightly coloured, add flour, fry gently for a few minutes, add wine and tomatoes. Add remaining ingredients, seasoning lightly. Simmer gently with the lid on the pan 15–20 minutes. Remove bay-leaf, pour sauce, which should be rich, red, and not too thick, over the steak. Serve with pommes paille.

ENGLISH STEAK AND ONIONS

1 lb. or more very tender rump
    steak about 1½ inches thick
clarified butter for brushing

5 or 6 medium-sized onions
¾ oz. good dripping (approx.)
salt, pepper, and sugar

Trim steak and brush all over with clarified butter, set aside. Slice onions thinly, heat dripping till lightly smoking and add the onions all at once, then cover pan with plate or saucer; cook over moderate heat 5–6 minutes, then remove cover and add salt, pepper, and a good pinch of sugar. If there appears to be any surplus fat it may be drained off at this stage. Mix onions up lightly with a fork and continue cooking for a further 5 minutes or until just tender. If the onions are to be slightly crisp, this final cooking is done without the cover and the onions are turned occasionally with a fork until sufficiently brown. If onions are to be soft and melting they should be kept covered except for the last minute or two.

The grilling of the steak should be started after the onions have been put on to cook. Allow 6–7 minutes for each side; this should produce a rich brown outside and a medium pink inside. Brush occasionally with the clarified butter.

To dish, arrange the onions either as a bed or as a surround to the steak; arrange steak and dot it over with the ½ oz. butter. Serve at once. If gravy is required a small nut of meat glaze may be dissolved in ½ gill stock or potato water.

Another recipe for grilled steak:

GRILLED STEAK

Crush a very small piece of garlic under a knife with salt. Finely slice and chop 3 or 4 shallots, or a small onion. Melt a bit of butter in a saucepan and cook these gently 5–7 minutes. Grill the steak and put the mixture from the pan on top. Then quickly melt a little butter in the pan, add a tablespoon of chopped parsley, seasoning, and a dash of lemon juice and pour over the whole.

BŒUF STROGONOFF

At first blush this looks an easy recipe, but R. H. in her note points out that this is not so. She says its success depends on how perfectly the onions are fried, neither burned nor underdone, on the proper cooking of the strips of beef, which should be brown but not frizzled (a matter of having the fat at the right temperature), and on the reduction of the cream by just the right amount: these things being a matter of practice.

1½–2 lb. fillet of beef
3 medium-sized onions
6–8 oz. button mushrooms

1–2 oz. butter
¼ pint sour cream
salt and freshly ground pepper

Choose a sauté or deep frying-pan. Cut the beef in strips 1½–2 inches long and ¼ inch wide. Slice the onions finely. Wash or clean mushrooms (see note, page 239), cut stems level with caps and slice finely downwards. Heat pan, put in about half the butter, add onions, and fry rather slowly until coloured, add mushrooms and fry for a few minutes, adding more butter if necessary. Now remove onions and mushrooms, add remaining butter, allow to get thoroughly hot, put in beef and fry briskly 3–4 minutes. Now put back onions and mushrooms with plenty of seasoning, shake all together over the fire for a minute; add the cream, cook 1 minute over full heat, and serve at once.

BEEFSTEAK AND KIDNEY PIE

1½–2 lb. beefsteak cut in a thick piece	½ lb. ox kidney
salt, pepper	2 shallots, finely chopped
1 tablespoon chopped mixed herbs, parsley predominating	seasoned flour
	water
	flaky pastry
	a little good stock

Slice the steak in small, even strips about 3 inches long by 1½–2 inches wide. Flatten them out on a wet board, season each piece with salt, pepper, and chopped shallots and herbs. Cut the kidney in pieces, removing the core, and lay a piece on each slice of meat. Roll up and lightly roll each piece in seasoned flour. Pack, not too tightly, into a pie dish. The rolls should fill the dish and rise in a slight dome above it. Fill the pie dish three parts full with water and cover with flaky pastry (see Veal and Ham Pie, page 630, for pastry and method of covering and decorating meat pies). Put into a moderately hot oven to bake (pastry oven, 425°–450° F.) until pastry is well risen and a good brown, about 30 minutes. Lower the heat, envelop the pie completely in a piece of wet grease-proof paper, and continue cooking gently (375°–400° F.) for a further 1–1½ hours. Before serving remove the top piece of pastry decoration and fill up with a little good, hot stock.

If the pie is to be eaten cold it is a good plan to use, in place of water, some good jellied stock, or alternatively a little gelatine may be dissolved in the liquid used to fill up the pie after cooking. Additions to the filling of this pie may be hard-boiled eggs, quartered, sliced, or whole, or sliced mushrooms. It is not essential to roll the steak in the way described; it may simply be sliced, rolled in flour with the sliced kidney, and put in the dish with herbs and seasoning. But whatever the method, do not pack the pie too tightly or the result will be dry.

BEEFSTEAK AND KIDNEY PUDDING (FOR 6-8) *

1½ lb. beefsteak
½ lb. ox kidney
1 dessertspoon finely chopped
  mixed herbs

salt, pepper
flour
suet crust

Crust

1 lb. flour, self-raising, or plain
  flour with 1 large teaspoon
  baking-powder
a pinch of salt

8-10 oz. suet, chopped or
  shredded
½ pint cold water for mixing
  (approx.)

Sift flour with salt (and with baking-powder if plain flour is used). Rub in the suet lightly with the fingers for a minute or two, then mix to a fairly soft dough with the water. Cut off two-thirds of the paste, roll out to a round about an inch thick, dust with flour, and fold in two. Now begin to pull, in a direction away from you, the ends of this double piece of paste; the object is to shape it into a bag so that it will line the basin nicely without folds. Work gently to avoid uneven stretching of the paste. When you have formed this into the required shape, roll it lightly to flatten slightly. Line with this a well-greased basin. Cut the meat into ½-inch squares, leaving on a small proportion of fat, cut the kidney in pieces, carefully removing all the core. Roll lightly in seasoned flour, arrange in the basin, sprinkling herbs between the layers. Add cold water till the basin is three parts full. Roll out the rest of the paste ½ inch thick and cover right over the rim of the basin, pressing well round the edges. Trim the edge. Tie a scalded floured cloth over the pudding and set into a large pan of boiling water. Boil steadily for 3 hours; have at hand a kettle of boiling water to replenish from time to time, as the water evaporates. (The pudding may also be steamed; allow 4 hours for this size. See notes on steaming, page 71.)

To serve remove cloth, tie or pin a folded white napkin round the basin. Send in with the pudding a jug of boiling water, so that when the first slice is cut a small quantity of water may be added to the meat before any of it is served.

Mushrooms, either small whole ones or large ones quartered, may be added to the pudding; oysters also are a satisfactory addition (and sauce oysters are suitable).

BŒUF A LA MODE (1)

Preparation to be made a day or two before dish is required.

Marinade

salt, pepper
¼ oz. mixed spice
¾ pint red wine (generous
  measure)
6 oz. carrots, sliced

5 oz. onions, sliced
a bouquet of herbs containing
  6 parsley stems and 2 bay-
  leaves
6 peppercorns

* *See plate 11*

For the dish

3–3½ lb. braising beef, boned and trimmed (rolled ribs, top side, or top rump)

5 oz. larding bacon (and a little pepper, salt, and mixed spice and a clove of crushed garlic for seasoning this)

1 large calf's foot, cleaned, skinned, and boned (see footnote on page 537)

1 oz. dripping or fat from skimming the stock

1 quart stock

24 pickling onions

24 baby carrots (or large carrots cut into small shapes)

1 pint stock in which to cook these

Cut the bacon into lardons approximately ¼ inch wide and 6 inches long. Lay them for half an hour or more in a mixture of salt, pepper, spice, and crushed garlic, turning them about so that they absorb the flavours. Insert these along the grain of the beef (see note, page 69). Now rub the beef over with salt, pepper, and spices. Tie it firmly into shape with string, place in a deep bowl, adding the wine, sliced carrots and onions, bouquet of herbs, and peppercorns. Allow it to remain in this a minimum of 12 hours and preferably 24. Lift out, drain, wipe over with a piece of muslin. Heat the dripping and fry all sides of the meat to a golden brown. Pour off the dripping, add marinade, stock, and calf's foot, bring to boiling-point and simmer gently 3–4 hours. While this is cooking prepare the little onions and carrots by half cooking them in a little stock (they must not be completely cooked, as they are to be finished off with the beef towards the end of cooking). When the beef is cooked lift it out on to a dish, pour the liquid into a bowl (there should be about a pint), skim away all possible fat. Rinse the pan, put the beef and the liquid back. Add the partly cooked little onions and carrots and put back in the oven, uncovered, for 20–30 minutes, during which time the beef should be well basted. During this time the liquid should reduce further until it is of a syrupy consistency. Serve the beef, whole or sliced, surrounded with the vegetables. (This may also be served cold, in which case arrange meat surrounded by vegetables in a deep dish, skim the liquid from time to time as it cools, taking care to clear it of all fat, strain it and pour it into the dish. Chill thoroughly.

Some recipes call for young turnips and braised lettuce to be served with hot bœuf à la mode.

BŒUF A LA MODE (2)

Preparation to be made a day or two before dish is required.

Although this dish is, perhaps, preferably served cold it may also be eaten hot, and is therefore included here rather than in the chapter on *pièces froides*. It is in the accessories and minutiae of its preparation that it may be regarded as a luxury dish; it is not, in point of fact, an extravagant use of meat, for when eaten cold it may be cut up economically and is without waste. The meat, having absorbed the flavours of the marinade and of the good bouillon, is delicious, and the long slow cooking renders it perfectly tender. The calf's foot gives the necessary jelly-like consistency to the cold dish, and a rich glazed quality to the hot sauce. It is inadvisable to make this dish with anything less than 3 lb. of meat, and the recipe given is for a large joint.

For the dish

marinade as for Bœuf à la Mode 1

5–5½ lb. topside or top rump of beef, boned and trimmed

5–6 oz. larding bacon, cut approximately ¼ inch wide and 2–3 inches long

1 oz. fat from the skimming of stock, or good dripping

½ gill brandy

a piece of bacon rind about 4 inches square

a large calf's foot, scalded, cleaned, boned, and cut up[1]

½ lb. of the red flesh of carrots. (These are prepared by peeling round as an apple is peeled; the yellow core is rejected. Weigh after preparation)

3 oz. onion, sliced

a bouquet garni of 6 parsley stems, thyme, and 2 bay-leaves

3 or 4 cloves

1 quart good bouillon or stock seasoning

a little gelatine for cold dish (if necessary)

2 egg whites (for clearing liquor for cold dish)

Garnish

24 small, young carrots (in winter 12 stumpy carrots of the Golden Horn variety may be used instead)

Mix the ingredients of the marinade and lay the meat in this, together with the lardons, for 24 hours, basting with the liquid from time to time. Then with a larding-needle lard the piece of beef, working with the grain of the meat (see note on page 69). Heat the dripping in a large saucepan and brown each side of the meat well; this will take anything from 20 minutes to half an hour. Now heat the brandy and flamber the beef with it (see note on page 66). Lift up the beef and lay in the bottom of the pan the piece of bacon rind, fat side up. Replace the beef on this, add prepared calf's foot, carrot, onion, bouquet, cloves, bouillon, and all the marinade. Adjust seasoning, bring to boiling-point, and allow to simmer very gently for 4½ hours. Towards the end of this process cook the small carrots separately, taking care not to overcook. At the end of this time lift out the beef, strain the liquor, and, as it cools, skim away every bit of fat and reduce if necessary to a syrupy consistency.

Dish the beef whole or sliced, surrounded by the carrots, and pour over the gravy.

If the dish is to be served cold: With such a proportion of calf's foot as is given here the liquid ought when cold to set perfectly, but if the dish is to be served cold it is as well to test for setting, and if necessary to add a small proportion of gelatine to make sure of this. The liquor, when strained and skimmed of all fat, should be cleared with egg whites (see page 120), then the procedure is as follows:

Line the sides of a mould with long slices of the whole small carrots.

---

[1] Calf's foot is generally sent from the butcher prepared and split; it should be thoroughly scrubbed and cleaned and is then boned and cut up.

Mask these with the cool liquid which has not quite set, allow this to set to a jelly in a cold place, preferably the ice-box. Cut the beef in thick slices, arrange these alternately with carrots in the jelly-lined mould till full, finishing off with the beef. Chill thoroughly, unmould and serve.

The following spiced, marinaded beefsteak is a good way of using steak which is not of the first quality. Preparation should be made a day or two before the dish is required.

SPICED, MARINADED BEEFSTEAK

2 lb. steak

Marinade

6 peppercorns	6 cloves
1 bay-leaf	a few juniper berries, if
a sprig of rosemary	available
a small bunch each of thyme,	salt
marjoram, and parsley	2 tablespoons each of tarragon
a few slices of onion	vinegar and oil
dripping for frying	stock

Crush the peppercorns. Bruise the herbs. Mix all the ingredients of the marinade together. Allow the meat to lie in this, turning from time to time, for at least 12 hours. At the end of this time lift out and drain. Put a little dripping into a hot pan and fry the steak lightly on each side. Now add the marinade and a little stock and simmer gently till done. Lift out the steak and keep hot. Skim and strain the stock, reduce it in a small saucepan and pour over the steak.

RAGOÛT DE BŒUF BOURGUIGNONNE

This is a classic dish and one of the best ragoûts. It should have a rich brown sauce and calls for burgundy. According to the piece of beef and the quality of wine used, it may vary in its degree of excellence, but even with the cheaper cuts and a rough wine it can be very good. When a fillet of beef and a vintage wine are employed, then you have indeed a party dish. In this event the meat may be braised whole and probably a shorter duration of cooking will be required. The mushrooms and onions, increased in quantity, will be cooked separately and arranged as a garnish around the meat.

The following recipe is for the dish in a modified form:

1½–2 lb. braising beef	1 good teaspoon flour
1 tablespoon good dripping	2 wineglasses or more burgundy
12 pickling onions	good stock
1½ oz. fat bacon	seasoning
4 oz. small firm mushrooms	a bouquet garni containing a
cut in quarters	whole bay-leaf and a stalk
a good pinch of sugar	of celery
	croûtons of fried bread

Cut the meat into 2-inch squares (but see preliminary note). Take a thick iron or aluminium casserole and in this heat a good tablespoon of dripping. Put in the pieces of meat and brown them quickly. Lift the meat out on to a plate, put onions, bacon, and mushrooms into the pan with a good pinch of sugar, and allow all to brown rather slowly, then dust with flour. Take out onions and mushrooms and set aside. Put the meat back into the casserole, heat the wine in a small saucepan, set it alight and pour over the meat. Add enough stock barely to cover, season and add herbs. Cover tightly and cook very slowly in the oven for an hour or more. Now add the onions and mushrooms which were set aside earlier and continue cooking for another hour. Dish the meat, reduce the gravy a little, and spoon it carefully over. Garnish with croûtons of fried bread.

BŒUF ESTOUFFADE D'AVIGNON

A peasant dish made with marinaded braising beef, pig's trotter, olives, and tomatoes.

Preparation for this dish to begin 3–4 days before it is required.

Marinade

a large onion and a carrot, chopped	enough red wine (a vin ordinaire for choice) to cover meat, about 1 bottle
a fairly large bouquet of thyme, parsley, celery stalk, bay-leaf, and a sprig of rosemary	

For the dish

3 lb. beef for braising	salt and pepper
dripping for frying	1 teaspoon arrowroot
2 or 3 rashers of lean bacon or 3–4 oz. pickled pork	1 lb. tomatoes
1 pig's trotter	12 green olives
3 cloves, 6 peppercorns, 1 level teaspoon coriander seed	a little butter
	mashed potatoes

Cut the meat in 2-inch squares; marinade these in the mixture given, allowing them to stand in this for 3 days. Then lift out the pieces of meat, drain them, and strain the marinade. Brown each piece of meat in the hot fat and when brown continue cooking gently for a quarter of an hour. Take a casserole, put in the pieces of meat, the rashers of bacon, and the pig's trotter; tie the vegetables and herbs from the marinade securely in a piece of muslin and add. Add all the juice from the pan in which the meat was fried, the strained marinade, seasoning, and spices. If this does not cover the meat add a little extra liquid, stock, wine, or water. Lay a sheet of greased paper over the top of the saucepan and secure it firmly with the lid, weighting this if necessary.

The cooking, which must be very slow (the slowness can hardly be over-emphasized), is done preferably in a slow oven, and should take from 2½ to 3 hours.

Lift out the trotter and the bacon. Bone the former and cut up the flesh into small cubes, cut up the bacon into small pieces. Lift out the muslin containing the vegetables, press well to extract juice, pour off the gravy carefully from the meat, strain it, allow it to stand a few minutes to bring fat to the surface, skim this off thoroughly.   Thicken the gravy by adding a teaspoon of arrowroot mixed in a little cold water.   Pour back the strained gravy, adjust seasoning, and add the cut-up pieces of the trotter and the bacon.   Stone the olives, fry them lightly in a little butter; peel, empty of seeds, and chop the tomatoes; add both to the contents of the casserole.   Bring back to boil and simmer for a few minutes.   Serve with mashed potatoes.

BŒUF EN DAUBE MARSEILLAISE (1)

Preparations to begin the day before this dish is wanted.

2 lb. lean beef
1½ oz. fat bacon
2 onions, chopped

8 black olives
red-currant jelly

Marinade

1 sliced onion
2 sliced carrots
2 cloves of garlic crushed with
    a little salt
bay-leaf, a sprig of rosemary,
    3 sprigs of parsley

2 cloves
salt and pepper
a strip of orange rind
1 dessertspoon wine vinegar
2 glasses red wine

Cut the meat in square pieces and lay them in the marinade overnight. In the morning cut the bacon in small pieces and brown it in a saucepan. Add the chopped onions and colour them over gentle heat.   Then brown the meat lightly on both sides, pour the marinade over, and cook gently for about 2½ hours.   Stone the olives, skim the fat off the gravy, add the olives, and serve with red-currant jelly as an accompaniment.

DAUBE MARSEILLAISE (2)

Preparation to be made a day or two before dish is required.

A savoury braise of beef or pork.   Also frequently eaten cold, sliced and covered with the gravy, which sets to a jelly.   Marinade the meat for as long as possible; this gives additional flavour and makes it more tender.

Marinade

1 onion and 1 carrot, sliced
the pared rind of 1 orange or
    1 lemon
6 peppercorns and 6 allspice
    berries lightly crushed
a sprig of rosemary

3–4 parsley stalks and 2 bay-
    leaves
1 pint white wine (cider is
    possible as a substitute if a
    few drops of lemon juice or
    vinegar are added)

2–3 lb. braising beef (topside
    or top rump)
1–2 tablespoons oil or bacon
    fat for frying
2–3 oz. lean bacon, cut in strips
1 large onion, sliced
1 large teaspoon flour
¼ pint stock or water
salt

a bouquet garni (a sprig of
    thyme, parsley, and bay-
    leaf tied together)
3–4 large ripe tomatoes,
    peeled, squeezed to remove
    seeds, and sliced
6–8 green stoned olives
    (optional)
potato purée or spaghetti

Bring all ingredients for marinade to boil and allow to get cold. Leave meat whole or cut into large squares. Soak in marinade 6 hours to 2 days, basting and turning occasionally. Drain well. Heat fat in a large stew-pan, fry meat quickly till brown on both sides, remove, add bacon and onion. Cook till turning colour, dust with flour, strain marinade, add with stock, salt to taste, and bouquet. Boil and replace meat; meat and liquor may be transferred here to an earthenware casserole for cooking in oven if more convenient.

Cover with grease-proof paper and the lid and put pan or dish in slow oven 3–4 hours. Add tomatoes and olives after 2 hours. Serve hot with a potato purée or plainly boiled spaghetti.

BŒUF BRAISÉ A L'ITALIENNE

A more bourgeois dish than the Bourguignonne, this is good family fare; the addition of gnocchi makes it substantial and potatoes need not be served with it. The meat for this dish may with advantage be marinaded for a day or two beforehand (see note on marinading, page 730). In this case one of the glasses of wine called for may be replaced by a glass of the marinade. The meat, whole, should be drained and wiped with a piece of muslin before being browned in the hot oil.

2 lb. topside or top rump of beef (or other braising meat may be used)	1 teaspoon tomato purée
	2 cloves of garlic crushed with a little salt
1 tablespoon olive oil	a bouquet garni
2 oz. onion, finely chopped	2 wineglasses red wine
2 oz. button mushrooms, wiped and cut in quarters	¾ pint good stock (approx.)
½ oz. flour	seasoning
4 oz. tomatoes, peeled, emptied of seed and water, and chopped	gnocchi paste of polenta or semolina (see page 428), treated as given below

Take a stew-pan or *cocotte* and in it heat the oil. Brown the beef all over in this, then remove it; put in the onion in the hot fat, allow to colour, then add the mushrooms, fry briskly for a minute or so, add flour and allow this also to brown. Draw pan aside, add remaining ingredients, bring to boil, replace beef, cover with a piece of paper and the lid, cook in a slow oven 2–3 hours. In the meantime prepare the gnocchi paste in any of the ways described below. Take out the beef, slice and dish; reduce the gravy rapidly, adjust seasoning, spoon gravy carefully over the meat and garnish with the gnocchi.

Gnocchi

(a) Make the paste, turn into a bowl, allow to cool partially, but while still warm and pliable shape into small balls, roll in flour, egg and bread-crumb, and fry in deep fat; *or*

(b) Shape into flatter cakes and fry in shallow fat; *or*

(c) Spread out ¾ inch thick on a flat dish or tray, cut in slices or fingers and place in a buttered fireproof dish, sprinkle with melted butter and grated cheese and brown in a quick oven.

If this method of cooking is chosen, it is a good plan to choose a platter large enough for serving the whole dish. The gnocchi are then arranged in a circle, overlapping so as to form a raised border; they are cooked as described and the beef served within this ring.

RAGOÛT OF BEEF WITH HERB DUMPLINGS

1–1½ lb. beefsteak or top rump
¾ oz. bacon fat or dripping
12 pickling onions
4–6 small carrots
seasoning

¾ oz. flour
1 wineglass cider or red wine
a clove of garlic crushed with
    salt
a bouquet garni
1–1½ pints stock or water
fruit cheese such as damson or
    quince

Herb dumplings

2 oz. self-raising flour
2 oz. fresh breadcrumbs
2 oz. chopped or shredded suet

1 tablespoon or more chopped
    mixed herbs
a small egg
salt and pepper

Cut the beef into large squares, heat the fat, fry the beef until brown on each side, turning the pieces once only. Remove from pan and put in the onions, carrots, and seasoning, lower the heat and cook these gently until just coloured. Draw aside, remove vegetables, pour off the excess fat if necessary, and sprinkle in the flour; allow to brown slowly, draw aside from the heat and add cider or wine, garlic, bouquet, and stock. Stir until boiling. Replace meat and vegetables, simmer gently 1½–2 hours. Skim occasionally.

In the meantime prepare the dumplings: mix all dry ingredients together, add the beaten egg to bind. Divide the mixture into small pieces, roll between the palms to shape, then add to the stewpan 40 minutes before the ragoût is done. Baste with the gravy once or twice during the simmering.

To serve. Turn the ragoût into a deep dish. Alternatively it may be turned into a casserole at the moment when the dumplings are added and cooking continued in this, then towards the end of cooking time the lid may be removed so that the dumplings acquire a pleasant brown colour. Basting should continue during the final cooking and the dish be served *en casserole.* Serve with a fruit cheese such as damson or quince.

The following is unusual and refreshing by reason of the celery, nuts, and orange rind:

RAGOÛT OF BEEF WITH CELERY, WALNUTS, AND SHREDDED RIND OF ORANGE

1–1½ lb. beef, topside or stewing steak
1–2 tablespoons dripping or bacon fat
12 button onions
1 dessertspoon flour
1 wineglass red wine
a bouquet garni (thyme, parsley, bay-leaf)
a clove of garlic crushed with salt

stock, meat or vegetable, enough to cover (about 1¼ pints)
seasoning
1 oz. shelled walnuts
1 head of celery
a nut of butter
1 tablespoon finely shredded and well-blanched orange peel

Cut the beef into large squares, heat a thick iron or aluminium casserole, put in the fat and when smoking lay in the pieces of meat. Fry to a golden brown. Remove the meat, add the onions, whole, and fry rather more slowly until beginning to colour. Draw off the fire, dust in the flour, cook slowly for a few minutes, then add the red wine, meat, bouquet garni, garlic, and barely cover with stock, season, bring slowly to the boil, cover and simmer for about 1½–2 hours. After cooking about an hour add the following mixture to the casserole and continue cooking until the beef is tender.

Cut the best part of a head of celery into slices crossways, add the shelled and skinned walnuts. Heat a nut of butter in a frying-pan, throw in the walnuts and toss over the fire with salt until crisp. Then add the celery and shake over the fire for a moment (the celery should remain slightly crisp). Add to the casserole. Send the dish to the table with a good scattering of orange rind on top.

PAUPIETTES DE BŒUF

6 thin slices of lean beef, or rump steak, approx. 3½ × 4 inches
freshly ground black pepper

Farce

2 shallots
6 green olives
2 oz. lean ham
3 oz. minced pork or sausage-meat

a small beaten egg
a sprig or two of thyme, chopped
seasoning

vegetables for mirepoix (see page 39)
1 oz. butter or fat bacon
¾ pint stock
a bouquet garni

1 good teaspoon flour and 1 good teaspoon butter (for beurre manié)
a suitable garnish (see next page)

N.B. If no good stock is available water or vegetable stock may be used, and a little duxelles and ½ teaspoon tomato purée may with advantage be added to the liquid.

Beat out the slices of meat on a wet board with the flat side of a meat chopper or the blade of a heavy, wet knife. Season one side with freshly ground black pepper. Chop shallots finely, stone and chop olives, chop ham, put all into a basin with pork, beaten egg, and thyme. Mix thoroughly, season well. Make a mirepoix of the vegetables, about a cupful. Melt half the butter or fat bacon in a sauté or stew-pan, put in the mirepoix and fry and shake gently for a few minutes. Draw aside. Spread the farce thinly on one side of the meat, roll up from the wider edge and tie with cotton. In another pan sauter these paupiettes gently with the remaining butter until turning colour, then lay them on the mirepoix, cover with the stock, add bouquet, bring to boil, and cook gently for about an hour. Have ready a good potato purée, arrange down the centre of a hot dish, remove the cotton from the paupiettes and lay them on the potato. Strain the liquor from the pan, skim well of all grease. Work the butter into the flour (beurre manié) and add piece by piece to the liquor. Stir until boiling, adjust seasoning, and reduce to a syrupy consistency. Spoon enough gravy over the dish to coat well and serve the rest in a gravy-boat; decorate with appropriate garnish.

Suitable garnishes: Chestnut purée in place of potato purée and the dish garnished with bundles of braised celery and baby Brussels sprouts; purée of celeriac and potato with a garnish of sautéd tomatoes; purée of potato and a garnish of carottes Vichy.

Another similar dish:

ALOUETTES SANS TÊTE
stuffed beef rolls

¾ lb. lean beef	1 glass red or white wine
1 onion, sliced	1 cup good stock
1 carrot, sliced	a bouquet garni
5 or 6 small pieces of fat bacon	1 tablespoon tomato sauce or
salt and pepper	coulis

Farce

1 rasher of lean bacon, chopped	grated rind of ½ orange
a crushed clove of garlic	salt, pepper
1 dessertspoon chopped parsley	grated nutmeg
2–3 tablespoons breadcrumbs	

Cut the beef very thin, beat it well on both sides and cut it in pieces 1½–2 inches wide and 3–4 inches long. Make the farce by cooking the chopped bacon light brown, adding all the other ingredients and stirring well together. Put a teaspoon of this farce on each piece of beef, roll lengthwise, and tie neatly with string or thread. Put the sliced onion and carrot into a stew-pan, with 5 or 6 small pieces of fat bacon. Lay the 'alouettes' on top, season with salt and pepper, cover the pan, and cook over moderate heat until the 'alouettes' are brown and sticky. Then pour in the stock and the wine, add bouquet garni, cover with piece of grease-proof paper, and cook in a moderate oven with the lid on until the 'alou-ettes' are tender and the sauce reduced (about $1\frac{1}{2}$–2 hours). Untie the 'alouettes,' put them back in the pan, moisten them with tomato sauce or coulis (such as the one given on page 179), cook again for a minute or two, and serve with the sauce strained over.

This dish can also be made with thin pieces of veal. In that event use onion instead of garlic, and add a few mushrooms.

BOILED BEEF AND DUMPLINGS

4–5 lb. salt silverside or topside	5 or 6 medium onions (whole)
a bouquet garni of 1 bay-leaf, 4–5 parsley stalks, and a sprig of thyme	5 or 6 medium carrots, cut in quarters lengthways
6 peppercorns	2 turnips cut in quarters
1 medium onion stuck with a clove	dumplings (see below)

Put beef into a large pan and cover well with unsalted cold or lukewarm water. Bring slowly to boil, skimming frequently. Add bouquet, peppercorns, and the onion stuck with a clove. Set the lid half over the pan and simmer $1\frac{1}{4}$ hours. Remove bouquet and onion, skim again and add the vegetables. Continue simmering 40–50 minutes until the meat and vegetables are just tender. Dumplings may now be added and simmering continued for a further 15–20 minutes with the pan now com-pletely covered. Alternatively the dumplings may be cooked separately in some of the beef stock.

To serve set the beef on a large dish, surround with vegetables and dumplings, and hand the liquor, skimmed, in a sauce-boat, and if liked with horse-radish sauce, though this is not traditional.

Dumplings

4 oz. suet, shredded or finely chopped	a pinch of salt
8 oz. self-raising flour (or plain flour with 1 teaspoon baking-powder)	1 tea-cup cold water (approx.)

Sift flour with salt, add suet, mix well. Moisten with water to make a good light dough. Divide into small pieces the size of a pigeon's egg. Roll between the palms of the hands and drop into the boiling stock. Cover and simmer 15–20 minutes (longer if the dumplings are larger than the size indicated). Lift out from the stock with a perforated spoon or skimmer.

OXTAIL STEW

choose a small to medium-sized oxtail, 2½–3½ lb.

Vegetables for braising
2 onions, 2 carrots, ½ head of celery
a thick rasher of streaky bacon
1–2 tablespoons good dripping
1 tablespoon flour (approx.)
bouquet garni of parsley stalks (or root of hamburg parsley), bay-leaf, thyme

2–3 pints stock
salt
4–5 peppercorns

Vegetables for garnish
small carrots and turnips, either young or cut into small shapes, pickling onions, and, if wished, small hearts of Savoy cabbage
chopped parsley
boiled potatoes

Cut the oxtail through where jointed, put to soak in plenty of water for 3–4 hours, or preferably overnight. Then blanch slowly, putting into cold water, bringing gradually to the boil, and skimming regularly as the scum rises to the surface. Allow to simmer 10–15 minutes. Drain the pieces and dry with a clean cloth. Slice the braising vegetables thinly and dice the bacon. Heat dripping in a thick stew-pan, put in the pieces of tail and brown well, shaking the pan from time to time so that the pieces brown evenly. Remove the pieces, put in the braising vegetables and bacon, and shake over the fire for a minute or two. Pour off most of the fat and sprinkle in enough flour to absorb the remainder without making it too dry or sticky. Put back the oxtail, add the bouquet, add stock to cover, salt and peppercorns, bring to boil. Now cover with a thick piece of paper (either a double round of grease-proof, or white kitchen paper lightly greased) and fix the lid firmly over this. Simmer very gently 3–4 hours or until the meat is just about to fall off the bone. This simmering may be done in the oven.

While the oxtail is cooking prepare and cook the garnish: the carrots, turnips, and onions should be gently simmered in a small quantity of the stock, then drained and the stock reserved and used if required to dilute the oxtail gravy, if this proves too thick. The cabbages should have most of the outer leaves removed (these may be set aside and used for a vegetable dish) and the hearts blanched and braised (see Braised Lettuce, page 227).

To serve. Take out the pieces of oxtail and arrange in a hot dish *en timbale*, that is piled up in the middle, strain the gravy into a pan, boil up, skim, and spoon over the meat. Arrange the garnish of vegetables, onions, carrots, and turnips at the sides, cabbage hearts at each end. Dust over with chopped parsley. Serve with plain boiled potatoes.

N.B. If the stock used is not very strong the gravy, after being strained and boiled, may be reduced and slightly thickened with arrowroot or corn-flour, to compensate for the deficiency in natural glaze.

SAVOURY MEAT LOAF

1 lb. minced raw beef
¼ lb. fat salt pork
1 pint fresh white breadcrumbs
2 oz. onion, finely chopped
1 teaspoon mixed chopped herbs (chives, chervil, fennel, and tarragon)
a green pepper very finely sliced and chopped (optional)
1 tablespoon each of Worcestershire sauce and mushroom ketchup

1 dessertspoon French mustard
1 good teaspoon each of salt and celery salt
freshly ground pepper
2 eggs
a little dripping for baking
tomato sauce (see page 178), or tinned tomatoes heated with a bouquet garni

Mix all ingredients except the last two together and bind with beaten eggs. Mix thoroughly and pack into a greased bread or cake tin. Chill for an hour or more, preferably in the ice-box. Melt a little dripping in a baking-tin, turn 'loaf' out of tin into this and bake an hour. Serve with a good tomato sauce or with tinned tomatoes heated up with a bouquet garni and very well seasoned.

The following Carbonnade de Bœuf is a simple and economical type of dish; at the same time it is good enough for a winter luncheon party. It is the bread that is so particularly good, having an excellent flavour: a sort of nursery 'bread and gravy' *de luxe*. The trouble is that there is seldom enough of the bread to meet the demand. It ought to be said that one meets with prejudices on the subject of ale in a dish of meat, but in the final result this amount cannot be detected. It has an enriching, nut-like flavour.

CARBONNADE DE BŒUF

1½ lb. braising beef
1 or 2 tablespoons dripping
6 oz. onions
½ oz. flour
a clove of garlic crushed with salt
½ pint brown ale
½ pint hot water
a bouquet garni

seasoning of salt and pepper
a pinch of nutmeg and of sugar
a dash of vinegar (optional)
4–5 squares of bread, ¼ inch thick and about 2 inches square, with crust removed, or slices of French roll with the crust left on
French mustard

Cut the meat into large squares. Heat dripping in a stew-pan, put in the meat and colour quickly on both sides. Cut onions in thin slices, add to the pan and allow to brown well. Pour off a little of the fat, dust with the flour, and add garlic. Add hot water to the beer, pour on to the beef, add the bouquet, and season with salt, pepper, nutmeg, sugar, and vinegar. Turn into a fireproof casserole, cover closely and cook gently in the oven for about 1½ hours. Fifteen minutes before serving skim off any surface fat from the gravy and pour the fat on to the squares of bread. Spread these thickly with a good French mustard and place on top of the pot, pushing the bread down below the surface and thus ensuring that it is soaked with gravy. It will float again to the top. Remove lid and put back in the oven for another 15–20 minutes, or until bread is a good brown.

A good and economical dish:

BITKIS A LA RUSSE

1 lb. lean minced beef	seasoning
1 oz. minced fat	dripping for frying
1 onion, finely chopped	a little sour cream (½–1 gill, to
1 tablespoon chopped parsley	taste) or yoghourt
4–6 oz. bread	tomato sauce (see page 178)
¼ pint water (approx.), and additional water for soaking bread	

Good accompaniments are carottes Vichy and sauté potatoes; fried parsley is a delicious garnish.

Put the beef into a bowl with the fat, onion, and parsley. Cut the bread into pieces and cover with the cold water. Leave until soaked through. Squeeze as dry as possible, mix with the meat and put all through the mincer. Return to the basin and work thoroughly, adding the water by degrees, and plenty of seasoning. When light and short in consistency, shape into cakes on a wet board and fry in hot dripping until brown on both sides. Arrange in a fireproof dish, pour over a little sour cream and/or tomato sauce and bake for about 20 minutes in a moderate oven. Serve the rest of the tomato sauce separately.

DOLMAS

It is important in this dish that the cabbage leaves shall be adequately blanched. It is therefore necessary to pay special attention to the instructions given about blanching (page 190).

1 small onion	1 cabbage
2 lb. minced beef	stock
salt and freshly ground pepper	1 bay-leaf
¼ gill water (approx.)	tomato sauce (see page 178)
2 tablespoons boiled rice or barley	freshly chopped parsley

Chop the onion very finely, put into a bowl with the meat and seasoning. Work well together, adding the water by degrees until the mixture is well beaten and pliable. Add the barley and adjust the seasoning.

Trim a cabbage, blanch it whole for 2 or 3 minutes, lift it out and begin to detach the leaves with care. As the heart of the cabbage is approached the leaves will be found to be stiff, and the cabbage must be returned to boiling water to complete the softening of the remaining leaves. Lay the leaves in front of you, remove any hard stalk, and put a small tablespoon of mixture on each leaf; roll up in a parcel to form a sausage. Roll them very lightly in flour and arrange in criss-cross layers in a thick stew-pan or casserole. Barely cover with stock, bring carefully to the boil, season, add a bay-leaf, and simmer gently 45–50 minutes on the stove or in the oven. Meantime prepare a good, rather thin tomato sauce. Lift the dolmas into a fireproof dish, draining well from the liquor, spoon over the tomato sauce and set in a fairly moderate oven for another 20–30 minutes. Serve with a good dusting of freshly chopped parsley over the dish.

BEEF TEA

½ lb. shin of beef   1 tea-cup cold water
a small pinch of salt

Cut the beef into small cubes, removing all fat. Put beef and water into a 2-lb. jam jar or stone gallipot. Cover the jar and set it in a deep pan containing water. Put into a slow oven or on top of the stove on very slow heat for 10–12 hours. Salt lightly half way through the cooking. Strain and cool. Before serving remove any particle of grease that may remain. The beef may be used again for second quality tea or for stock.

For cold pressed and spiced beef, etc., see 'Pièces Froides,' page 617.

MUTTON AND LAMB

Joints for roasting: saddle, leg, shoulder, best end of neck. The saddle is the prime joint; leg and shoulder come next, the leg being the more economical; both of these may be boned and stuffed.

For boiling: leg, breast, and neck.

For braising: leg and shoulder. The breast is also stuffed and braised.

For grilling: cutlets from the best end of neck, chops from chump end of loin or from loin.

For stewing and the making of ragoûts: breast, scrag end and middle of neck, head.

Mutton has more fat both around the joints and embedded in the meat than beef. The loin and neck in particular carry a large proportion of fat, and the shoulder a large proportion of bone; for these reasons mutton and lamb are generally considered rather wasteful meat. Every scrap of fat that may be trimmed off cutlets or chops, as well as any superfluous fat trimmed from the roasting joints, should be rendered down for dripping. It is a common fault to send shoulder, loin, or cutlets of lamb to table with far too much fat attached, which is then left on the dish or on individual plates. Adequate and careful trimming should be carried out before the meat is cooked. If wished the fat cut away from the joint may be put in the oven with the joint and rendered down for dripping at the same time.

The meat of good mutton is short in fibre, and when cooked should be tender and somewhat dry. Mutton and lamb, whether roasted or boiled, should be well cooked: lamb, being immature meat, particularly so; grilled cutlets should show no deeper colour than a faint pink.

To roast

After trimming, mutton may be roasted as for beef, but allowing 20 minutes to the pound and 20 minutes over, the joint being frequently basted. For lamb a little longer may be called for. There is, however, another school of thought which calls for different treatment, especially for lamb and for imported mutton. This involves a much longer time. The meat is put into a cool, even cold oven, and the temperature brought up slowly to roasting heat, the whole process being gradual. This has proved very successful with legs of mutton of uncertain age, R. H. having committed them to the oven soon after luncheon in order to have them tender and ready by dinner-time. Another treatment for the larger and older pieces of mutton is to marinade a joint in the way described on page 558, then to wrap it in a thick paste of flour and water, place it on a grid in the roasting-tin so that the crust will not soak up the drippings, and roast it in a hot oven, allowing 25–30 minutes to the pound. After cooking the paste is removed, and the joint returned to the oven and well basted with a little hot dripping until the surface is nicely browned.

A few sprigs of rosemary put in the pan with a joint of mutton greatly add to the flavour. Another good addition is the introduction of small pieces of garlic into the fatty portion of the joint and near the bone; this not only helps to make the meat more tender, but the flavour, gently permeating the meat, is not strong, and is generally liked by any but those with a strong antipathy to this herb.

Another old-fashioned and good trick is to make as many as 20–25 incisions with a sharply pointed knife into the meat and to insert stalks or small sprigs of parsley; these must be well pressed in with the knife, for if too much remains above the surface it will become burnt during the roasting. This gives excellent flavour. On page 728 will be found a recipe for a barbecue of mutton; not only is this a good dish in itself, and generally very popular, but the effect of this treatment is to render the meat more tender.

Gravy

Mutton and lamb give less gravy than beef, so that to satisfy the demand for plenty of gravy a certain amount of fortifying may be needed. This is not difficult if you have at hand a good supply of bouillon or meat glaze, and a recipe for simple brown sauce is given on page 171. A more homely plan is to slice a small onion finely and to add it with a little sugar to the pan after the fat has been drained off. This should be allowed to brown well, then a sprinkling of flour may be added to take up the fat and a good cup of stock or potato water poured on; the whole is then seasoned, reduced, and strained into the gravy-boat. This will give you a good, simple gravy. Although mutton gravy may be thicker than that served with beef, it should not have the gloy-like consistency so often met with. Particular care should be taken to avoid a layer of grease on top of the gravy, which indicates either insufficient care in draining off the fat or that the finished gravy is thin and too watery and needs further reducing and skimming.

To carve *

Mutton should not be carved so thinly as beef; the leg and shoulders are cut into wedge-like slices $\frac{1}{4}$–$\frac{1}{2}$ inch thick, and the neck and loin divided down between the bones. When carving the knife must be kept straight and the cuts made right down to the bone. In the case of a saddle the slices are made parallel with the centre bone.

Classic accompaniments: to roast lamb, mint sauce or mint jelly. To a perfectly made mint sauce the juice and grated rind of an orange may be added (see orange mint sauce, page 182).

To roast mutton, onion purée (soubise) or red-currant jelly; or quince or damson cheese, sliced; or a stiff purée made of tart apple with raw diced celery stirred into it at the last moment, the purée well seasoned and finished off with a large nut of butter.

Fried slices of pineapple may accompany either mutton or lamb.

It may also be noted here that a slice or two of quince added to a ragoût of mutton improves it greatly, and that steamed, stuffed prunes are excellent with an Irish stew. The stones are taken out and each prune is stuffed with the flesh of another.

ROAST KID

This is included here because it resembles lamb. Put a sprig or two of rosemary in the pan, roast as for lamb, cooking thoroughly. Serve with red-currant jelly, with or without grated rind and juice of orange.

THE PREPARATION OF LAMB OR MUTTON FOR CUTLETS ‡

(The following notes will be made more clear if it is imagined that the piece of meat in question, the best end of neck, is placed in front of you on a table with the half-backbone on your right and the flap of thin meat on your left.)

The joint for this purpose should be neither too large nor too fat. Best end of neck is used for cutlets and it consists of 5–6 bones. It is better to order in this way from the butcher, stating the number of bones required rather than the weight. There is a point to be stressed when ordering: it is a common practice for the butcher to chop the chine bone (the split backbone) at intervals down its length, and this custom makes it difficult for the cook to divide the cutlets neatly; in addition a small ugly piece of bone is left at the end of each cutlet. The butcher should be asked to chine the meat only; this means the sawing through of the long bone on your right (the split backbone) so that it may be easily removed when the cook is ready to divide and trim the cutlets. Another saw cut is made right through the series of rib bones on your left, some inches down from the backbone, and in this way the cutlets are readily separated from the meat called the flap (on your left). This thin meat which is around the further pieces of rib is sometimes used for épigrammes, and an old-fashioned and economical practice was to serve these with the dish of cutlets.

* *See plates 8 and 9* ‡ *See plate 7*

The joint arrives from the butcher with the bones mentioned sawn but not completely detached, and before the cutlets are divided the chine bone should be completely detached and the whole piece skinned, if this has not already been done by the butcher.   The flap is then removed and the thick meat of the neck divided into cutlets.   A good cutlet, one that will not present a hollow cheek after cooking, or become dried up, should be thick; the actual heart of the meat, described as the noix, should not be less than ¾ inch thick.   In order to obtain this it is sometimes necessary to take two bones for one cutlet; this is so if the animal is small or if the bones do not run particularly straight.   If two bones are taken the second is cut out with a sharp knife when the cutlet is trimmed.   To divide the neck into cutlets a sharp knife should be employed, and the cut made close to one side of the bone and not in the middle of the flesh between two bones. The cut should be carried down in a clean stroke, right through the meat. The noix is now flattened slightly with the flat of a knife and the fat lightly trimmed round it, and practically all fat removed from the end of the bone.   This trimming should leave ⅛ inch of fat round the noix of meat and a small piece where this joins the bone.   The fat may also continue down the bone for about ¾ inch.   The rest of the bone, for about 2–2½ inches, should be bare and clean; any length of bone beyond this should be chopped off.

The cutlets are now ready for further preparation and should be all of the same size and shape, as this adds to the appearance of the finished dish.

TO PREPARE A BEST END OF NECK FOR BRAISING OR ROASTING

Remove the chine bone and flap as before, then with a sharp knife cut the fat away from the ends of the bones.   It is easiest to hold the cutlet or meat end in your left hand with the ends of the rib bones on the board, and then to pare off the fat down to the board with the knife held in the right hand.   Now make a series of cuts between the lower ends of the rib bones for about 2–3 inches, removing the trimmings of meat between the bones, and cleaning and scraping them generally.   This should still leave ¾–1 inch of fat before the actual meat.   This way of trimming and preparing makes for economy and easy carving.

ÉPIGRAMMES

The flap of meat referred to in the note on the preparation of cutlets (it is really the end of the rib bones) is often used by the cook for rendering down for fat, or it is sometimes roasted with the meat if the piece of best end is being served as a roast.   It may with advantage be made into a dish called Épigrammes d'Agneau.   If the meat is being used for a dish of cutlets, these may be served arranged alternately with the cutlets.   This is an old-fashioned and economical use of this meat.   The dish is also made from the leaner meat of breast of mutton, and may then be served as a separate dish accompanied by a sharp sauce such as piquante, tomato, bercy, or Robert.

TO PREPARE NOISETTES *

Noisettes make a good party dish: one takes for them exactly the same meat as for cutlets (the best end of neck), but also the meat of the flap. The butcher should be asked to chine the meat as before, but not to cut through the rib bones as in the case of cutlets. The cook removes the chine bone, skins the meat, and then removes all the rib bones. Thus completely free of all bone the meat is seasoned inside with salt and freshly ground pepper; in some cases chopped herbs are added. The piece of meat is then tightly rolled up, starting from the thick end and rolling towards the flap; the thin meat of the flap should wrap round the thick meat once or once and a bit. This roll is now tied securely with fine string at intervals of $1\frac{1}{2}$ inches, each tie being independent. With a sharp knife the meat is cut through in slices exactly half way between each string. Noisettes may then be treated as for cutlets.

LOIN OF LAMB OR MUTTON AND THE PREPARATION OF LAMB OR MUTTON FOR CHOPS

Chops are cut from the loin of lamb or mutton. The loin is sent from the butcher with the bone chopped at regular intervals, at the natural divisions of the bone, and it is then cut into chops at home. These are trimmed of much of the fat, but as in the case of cutlets a nice rim of fat is left round the noix of meat, and care is taken to leave the small piece of fine quality fat which lies at the base of this. There is, of course, no rib bone, but a piece of fat and meat take its place. As for cutlets the piece of meat should not be too fat, and for mutton not too large or coarse.

Loin chops or the whole loin may be braised, or the loin may be boned, stuffed, and roasted. This method is a good way for mutton; lamb is better served plain, as grilled chops, or roasted whole with the proper accompaniments. Loin of mutton may also be marinaded and will make a good barbecue.

Reference to the old-fashioned and economical use of a poor part of mutton or lamb for making épigrammes nerves me to mention in contrast, in conclusion of these general notes, a delicacy which has long ago disappeared from our tables. This was real 'baby' lamb, so small that one used to order and cook a whole fore or hind quarter; indeed the butcher would not commonly cut anything smaller. This, called Pauillac, was imported from France and was to be obtained on occasion from the very highest of high-class butchers. The meat was white and the fat exceedingly delicate. It was indeed one of the real luxuries of pre-war days. If days of plenty return to the earth it may well be seen again, in which case it will be roasted to perfection, and served with its own delicate and unthickened juice, and perfect mint sauce combined with melted red-currant jelly and a dash of orange rind. More probably, however, it will become more legendary than roast peacock, which can't have been a patch on it.

* See plate 10

SADDLE OF MUTTON OR LAMB

This joint, comprising both loins together from ribs to tail, may weigh in the case of mutton anything from 8 to 11 lb., and in that of lamb from 4½ to 7 lb.   It is the prime joint for roasting and used to take its place at city banquets; it is a particularly choice dish.   The smaller saddle of lamb is considered by some people to be the greater delicacy, but a saddle of Welsh or Scotch mutton is preferred by others, for its shortness of texture and richer, gamier flavour.

The classic method of cooking is roasting.   Lamb, which nevertheless should be cooked through, may be delicately pink, but mutton should be well cooked.   The kidneys are sometimes sent attached to the saddle and may be roasted and served with the joint, a slice being served with each portion, or they may be removed and used for another dish.   Roast the saddle in a moderate oven with plenty of good dripping, basting well.   It is advisable to start roasting with a piece of paper over the joint, to be removed after the first half-hour or so.   Allow 20 minutes to the pound.

Serve with gravy and mint sauce for lamb, red-currant jelly for mutton.

There are many recipes for saddle of lamb, garnished in various ways; sometimes it is stuffed after roasting, and the slices laid on top and glazed. But the best way with the joint is the simple one of roasting.   Nevertheless it may be necessary for one reason or another to keep such a joint for several days, and if this should happen in hot or thundery weather, and one is not certain that it will keep safely, the following marinade is worthy of it:

1 quart water	a sprig of thyme
¾ oz. salt	1 bay-leaf
1 carrot, finely chopped	6 peppercorns, 2 or 3 cloves,
2 medium onions, chopped	and a blade of mace
a few parsley stems	1 gill vinegar

Boil all together for half an hour.   When cold add:

1½ pints red wine	a glass of sherry and a glass of brandy

Put the saddle in a deep dish, cover with the marinade; keep 4 or 5 days, even longer if necessary, in a cool place, and preferably in the ice-box. When required wipe with a clean cloth, roast with a sprig or two of rosemary in the pan.   Reduce a little of the marinade to make a sauce with red-currant jelly dissolved in it, and thicken slightly with a nut of beurre manié (see page 139).

As an offset to this English classic, I follow it with two recipes for an excellent bourgeois dish of leg or shoulder of mutton carrying the name of 'à la boulangère.'   This, I like to think, derives from the practice, common apparently in French villages as once it was in the English countryside, of carrying the Sunday joint to the baker, who for a few pence would roast it in his bread oven still hot from the baking.   The potatoes, absorbing the fat and juice from the meat, are rich and melting and the cooking should be steady and moderate, as of course it would have been in the days of the baker's oven.

GIGOT OU ÉPAULE DE MOUTON A LA BOULANGÈRE

a shoulder or leg of mutton	a bouquet garni
8 or more potatoes	seasoning
3 or 4 onions	a little butter or dripping
2 cloves of garlic split into pieces	a small quantity of stock

Slice potatoes and onions finely. With a sharp-pointed knife make incisions near the bone and press into these the pieces of garlic. Grease well a long fireproof or copper dish, arrange the potatoes and onions neatly, leaving a space in the middle for the meat. Add the bouquet and seasoning, put in the meat with a few pieces of dripping or butter on top, moisten the potatoes with a little stock. Put into a moderate oven and roast, allowing 15–20 minutes to the pound. If the dish begins to get too brown before the meat is sufficiently cooked, cover it with a piece of paper. Serve in the dish in which it is cooked.

N.B. The actual amount of stock needed will vary according to the absorbent quality of the potatoes. More may be added during cooking; the potatoes should not be sloppy.

The following recipe is for Neck of Lamb à la Boulangère, and this, being a more delicate cut of meat, is suitable for a simple luncheon party. The joint being smaller, the cooking time is shorter. In this recipe the vegetables are cooked apart from the meat.

NECK OF LAMB A LA BOULANGÈRE

1½ lb. best end of neck of lamb, chined only	1–1½ lb. potatoes
dripping	salt and pepper
1 apple	a bay-leaf
2–3 sprigs of rosemary	1 dessertspoon flour
3 medium-sized onions	stock
	½ teaspoon tomato purée

Trim the meat, cutting away the fat from the ends of the bones. Set in a small roasting-tin, cover with 2–3 large spoonfuls of dripping, and cook in a slow to moderate oven 40–45 minutes. When the dripping has melted add the apple wiped, cored, and cut in fair-sized pieces, with the rosemary and 1 onion, sliced. Baste frequently during the cooking. In the meantime slice the remaining onions and the potatoes very thinly. Grease a fireproof dish well with the dripping, arrange the onions and potatoes in layers, finishing with potatoes and adding plenty of salt and pepper and the bay-leaf. Three parts fill the dish with stock. Set in the oven for 40–50 minutes, or until the potatoes are cooked and well browned.

Take up the meat, strain off the fat, dust a level dessertspoon of flour into the pan and brown carefully. Pour in about a cup of stock, add the tomato purée and bring to the boil. Simmer to a good consistency, then strain. For serving the meat may be carved, arranged on the top of the potatoes, and the gravy served separately.

The following dish is a roast of best end of mutton larded with fillets of anchovy and accompanied by a garnish of glazed onions and tomatoes.

CARRÉ D'AGNEAU A LA CONTI

2 lb. best end of mutton or
   lamb, chined only
6 fillets of anchovy
1 good teaspoon mixed chopped
   herbs and a little finely
   chopped shallot
dripping or butter for roasting

Garnish
½ lb. pickling onions
1 oz. butter
sugar
¾–1 lb. tomatoes
salt and freshly ground
   pepper

sauce provençale (page 177) or
   demi-glace (page 143)

Remove chine bone and skin, trim and prepare as explained in the note on page 550. Cut the fillets of anchovy in half lengthways, roll them in part of the chopped herbs and shallot and lard the joint with them (see note on larding, page 69). Melt dripping or butter in roasting-tin, put in the meat, baste and roast in a moderate oven 40–50 minutes, basting every 10 minutes.

Prepare the garnish as follows: Blanch the onions, drain, return to pan with ½ oz. butter, salt, and ½ teaspoon sugar. Sauter over moderate heat, shaking the pan frequently until well glazed and tender. Peel the tomatoes, cut in thick slices, melt remaining butter in a frying or sauté pan, add a level teaspoon of sugar, season with salt and freshly ground pepper. When sizzling hot lay in the slices of tomato; cook quickly on each side till brown. Draw aside and sprinkle over the remaining herbs. Lay the meat in a hot dish, arrange onions on one side, tomatoes on the other. Pour round a little sauce provençale or demi-glace, serving the remainder in a sauce-boat.

The following recipe for stuffed loin of mutton is a family dish; the use of stuffing ekes out the meat and is therefore an economy.

CÔTE DE MOUTON BRAISÉE MÉNAGÈRE

2½–3 lb. loin of mutton
2 large onions and a little
   dripping
¾–1 lb. sausage-meat
1 tablespoon chopped parsley
1 tablespoon chopped mixed
   herbs, thyme, marjoram,
   and savory

seasoning
2 tablespoons dripping
1 dozen little onions and about
   4 carrots
1 pint water
a clove of garlic
1 lb. potatoes (approx.)

Bone the mutton and trim off a little of the fat. Chop the onions, sauter them in a spoonful of dripping to soften, and add them to the sausage-meat with the herbs, parsley, and plenty of seasoning. Spread this farce on the inside of the loin, roll up and tie with fine string.

Heat 2 spoonfuls of dripping in a thick casserole, brown the meat in this, then add the carrots cut in quarters and the onions whole. Shake over the fire for a few minutes to allow the vegetables to colour slightly, drain off as much fat as possible into a frying-pan, and pour over the water. Add the clove of garlic, season, cover, and braise in the oven about $1\frac{1}{2}$–2 hours.

Cut the potatoes in quarters, dry them well and rissoler to a crisp golden brown in the dripping that was poured out of the casserole before the liquid was added. When the meat is done take it up and remove the fat from the gravy, reduce it a little if necessary, carve the meat and lay it on the serving dish, surround it with the vegetables and pour over the gravy.

This dish can be done with a shoulder of mutton, or a piece of loin or shoulder of veal.

Here is another stuffing for a boned leg of lamb or mutton:

2 medium-sized cucumbers, peeled and diced	1 tablespoon finely chopped herbs, dill, parsley, tarragon
12 spring onions	2 egg yolks
1 oz. butter or dripping	seasoning
a clove of garlic	
1 pint freshly grated bread-crumbs	

Blanch the cucumber for 5 minutes. Soften the chopped onion in the butter or dripping. Crush the garlic under salt and add it to the onion. Mix all ingredients together and stuff the boned mutton with this. Tie firmly with string and roast. A little piquante sauce such as A1, Harvey, or Worcestershire may be added to the gravy for serving with roast lamb with this stuffing.

SHOULDER OF MUTTON WITH TURNIPS

This dish is one of the nicest ways of eating turnips. Allow equal quantities of mutton and turnips, say 3 lb. of each (a rolled shoulder is suitable), some good fat and a quart of stock or water, a little sugar and seasoning.

Brown the meat on each side in hot fat. Pour away the fat, add the stock and seasoning and simmer for about 2 hours. Peel the turnips; if they are small ones cut in half, if they are large slice thickly. Roll them in a little sugar and allow them to brown thoroughly in fat in a frying-pan. If the turnips are very young it is sufficient to add them to the meat about half an hour before the end of cooking. If older add them about half way through. Serve the joint surrounded by the turnips and hand a good brown gravy.

SHOULDER OF LAMB A LA TURQUE

a small shoulder of lamb
salt and freshly ground pepper
1 oz. butter or bacon fat
4 oz. liver
1 large onion, finely sliced
2 cloves of garlic crushed with
    salt
1 large handful of stoned raisins
1 dessertspoon chopped mixed
    herbs (thyme, marjoram,
    parsley)

3 oz. boiled rice (approx.)
3 or 4 large basting spoonfuls
    of dripping
2 or 3 sprigs of rosemary
1 heaped teaspoon flour
1 teaspoon tomato purée
¼ pint stock or water

Bone the shoulder and season the inside of the meat well.   Melt the fat in a *sautoir* or frying-pan, cut the liver in fairly large dice and sauter briskly for a few minutes (the pieces should be lightly browned on the outside and juicy within).   Remove them with a wire slice into a bowl. Put the onion into the pan with the garlic and sauter these gently for 4–5 minutes, now add the raisins and after a minute or two put back the liver with the herbs.   Shake all together over the fire for half a minute, then turn back into the bowl.   Add the rice and stir all together with a fork. Season as required.   Cool slightly and then put this stuffing inside the meat, sewing it up securely with coarse thread and a darning-needle.

Set the joint in a roasting-pan, pour over the melted dripping, add the sprigs of rosemary to the pan and roast in a moderate oven 1½–2 hours, or according to the size of the joint, which must be thoroughly cooked. During the last part of the cooking it may be necessary to lower the heat considerably, as the stuffing sometimes oozes out and is liable to get over-brown in a very hot oven.   Serve the meat on a hot dish, pour off the fat, add the flour to the pan and when well mixed add the purée and water. Stir well, bring to boil, simmer for a few moments, add seasoning.   Strain enough over the lamb to moisten the dish and serve the rest separately.

N.B. This is a useful recipe for a small shoulder of mutton or for part of the loin.   Avoid overfilling with stuffing and be discriminating about the amount of rice; if too much is added the stuffing will be dull.

The following is an excellent marinade used for a leg of mutton to be cooked like venison; it is useful when meat has to be kept over-long, and excellent for older meat as it helps to make it tender.

MARINADE FOR LEG OF MUTTON
to be cooked like venison

4 oz. carrots, chopped
4 oz. onions, chopped
2 oz. celery or celeriac, sliced
1 gill oil
short pint wine vinegar
1½ pints wine and water
    (mixed) or cider

a sprig of thyme and ½ bay-leaf
a clove of garlic
6 peppercorns
8 juniper berries, if possible
    (or a sprig of rosemary), and
    a few parsley stalks, cut up
salt and pepper

Brown the vegetables in oil, add liquids, herbs, spices, and seasoning, bring to the boil and simmer 30 minutes. Allow to get quite cold before pouring over the meat. Lay the leg in as deep a dish as possible, season it with salt and pepper, pour over the cold marinade, unstrained. Turn and baste twice a day, and keep in the marinade two days in warm weather, three days in cool or winter weather. Use cheap red or white wine if available, substitute home-made wine or cider if necessary.

To cook. Take out the meat and wipe it thoroughly, lay it in a roasting-pan, pour 2 or 3 spoonfuls of oil over it and roast in a hot oven, turning and basting several times. Cook on the top shelf to get well browned, then put on a lower shelf to finish.

Sauce. Take some of the marinade and reduce it over the heat, add red-currant jelly to taste. If the mixture has to be made without wine, and is a little poor in flavour, mix it with a little brown sauce, or thicken it with brown roux.

The following recipe for cutlets makes a luncheon-party dish; the purée of potatoes should be perfect, the sauce soubise creamy, the onion rings crisp. This combination of textures is its essence and if you fall down on these it will not be good. R. H. says it is typically a dish that can be damned by bad cooking, in which event someone will be sure to say—or perhaps more politely think without saying—'I don't like messed-up food.' Let a prentice hand try it once or twice on the family before producing it for a party, but it would be a pity to leave it out of the repertoire.

CÔTELETTES D'AGNEAU SOUBISE

1½–2 lb. best end neck of lamb or mutton, chined only
1½ oz. butter or dripping
1⅛ oz. chopped onion, blanched for 5 minutes and drained
seasoning
a bay-leaf
1 wineglass stock or white wine (approx.)

½ pint creamy béchamel sauce (see page 155)
a purée of potatoes

Garnish
2 large Spanish onions
⅛ of an egg white lightly beaten with a fork (or milk may be substituted)
a little flour
deep frying fat

Remove the chine bone and divide into cutlets, prepare as note on page 551. Shape and trim neatly. Melt 1 oz. of the butter or dripping in a sauté pan, put in the cutlets, cover and simmer 10 minutes, turning once only. They must not be allowed to brown. Take out, add the extra ½ oz. butter or dripping to the pan, put in the onions, cover, and allow them to soften but not colour. Season, replace the cutlets on top of the onions, add the bay-leaf and moisten with the stock or white wine. Cover with a piece of paper and the lid, put the pan into the oven for 20–30 minutes. Take out, remove the cutlets and keep hot. Put the onions and the liquor through a fine sieve or strainer; add this purée to the béchamel sauce, simmer together 3–4 minutes and adjust seasoning.

For the garnish cut the onions into slices ⅛ inch thick, push out into rings, moisten these with the egg white. Dust over with flour and mix well, so that the rings are coated with a kind of dry batter. Then fry in deep fat until crisp. Have ready a purée of potatoes, arrange down the centre of the serving dish, set the cutlets on the top, mask with the soubise and garnish with the onions.

The following may also be considered a dish for a luncheon party and is of simpler preparation. The cucumber and spring onions are an excellent accompaniment to the cutlets. This is a suitable dish with which to combine the épigrammes already referred to, for which a recipe will follow on page 562.

CÔTELETTES D'AGNEAU A LA DORIA

1½–2 lb. best end of neck of lamb or mutton, chined and prepared as described on page 552
flour
seasoning
beaten egg
fine white breadcrumbs, well dried

a good cucumber
12 spring onions trimmed to within an inch of the bulb
½ oz. butter
freshly chopped mint
dripping or butter for frying
gravy, or a mousseline or light soubise sauce

Roll the trimmed cutlets in seasoned flour, brush with egg and roll and press in the crumbs. Peel the cucumber, split it into four, then cut it into 2-inch lengths. Blanch it quickly and drain well; prepare the spring onions and blanch. Melt the butter in a pan, add cucumber and onions, season and cover; simmer 5–10 minutes, shaking the pan occasionally. When the cucumber and onions are tender draw aside and add the mint. Fry the cutlets in hot fat, turning once only. Arrange them *en couronne* in a serving dish and pile cucumber and onions in the centre. Hand the gravy or sauce separately. (A little of it may be poured on the dish before the cutlets are arranged to keep them in place.)

The following again is a dish that requires care and a little practice, but it is worth while, being very good and generally much appreciated by men. It consists of cutlets sandwiched between layers of a very good farce and wrapped in light and very flaky pastry.

CÔTELETTES D'AGNEAU EN CUIRASSE

1–1½ lb. best end of neck of lamb, chined only
oil or butter for frying
6 oz. mushrooms
½ oz. butter or margarine
2 oz. cooked ham
seasoning
chopped parsley

2 teaspoons tomato purée
¼ lb. flaky pastry (see page 835) or puff pastry trimmings
beaten egg
pommes parisienne or new potatoes
tomato coulis (see page 179)

Prepare the cutlets in the way described on page 551.   Fry or grill them and allow to cool.   Mince finely the mushrooms and ham and mix well with the butter, add seasoning and chopped parsley and moisten with the tomato purée.   Roll out a piece of pastry the size of your hand, brush the edge with water, spread a spoonful of farce in the middle, lay cutlet on this and spread with another layer of farce on top.   Fold over the pastry, leaving a piece of the cutlet bone showing.   Brush with beaten egg and cook in hot oven 20–30 minutes.   Arrange *en couronne* with pommes parisienne or new potatoes and serve a coulis of tomato.

The following recipe for mutton cutlets has for accompaniment a purée of peas.   The peas may be tinned, dried, or fresh.   The dried must be well soaked and cooked until absolutely soft before serving.   If using fresh choose peas not too young, but rather floury: it is an excellent way to use them up.

CÔTELETTES DE MOUTON FONTANGE

4–6 bones middle or best end of neck of mutton (approx. 1¼ lb. in
    the piece), prepared in the way described on page 551

dripping	¼ pint thick béchamel sauce
½ lb. small onions, blanched	(¾ oz. butter, ¼ oz. flour, ¼
1 rounded dessertspoon flour	pint milk, seasoning, and a
1 teaspoon tomato purée	dust of nutmeg)
½ pint stock	butter or dripping
a large tin of peas	seasoning

Heat the dripping in a sauté pan and brown the cutlets quickly on each side.   Remove, add the blanched onions.   Lower the heat and allow to brown.   Dust in the flour, cook for a few minutes, draw aside and add the tomato purée and stock.   Bring to the boil, then replace the cutlets, cover and simmer 30 minutes.

Meantime drain and rinse the peas and pass them through a wire sieve. Make the béchamel (see page 155), then add the purée with a nut of butter and plenty of seasoning.   Beat over the fire until thoroughly hot, then set aside in a bain-marie.   When the meat is cooked pile the purée up in the centre of a dish, arrange the cutlets and onions round.   Skim the gravy and reduce to a syrupy consistency, strain and spoon round the dish.

The next recipe is good for a women's luncheon party; it is excellent when young broad beans are in season, and frozen ones may be used in place of these.   It is not a difficult dish to prepare.

CÔTELETTES D'AGNEAU MARIE-ANNE

2 lb. best end of neck of lamb or mutton, chined only

Garnish

1 pint small shelled broad beans and a sprig of savory	a nut of butter
	salt and a little sugar and water
a dozen or more baby carrots, young and small enough to be left whole	¼ pint sauce poulette (see next page)

Prepare the cutlets as described on page 551. Cook the beans with a sprig of savory until just tender, drain and keep hot. Cook the carrots in a covered pan with a spoonful or two of water, a nut of butter, and a pinch of salt and sugar. By the time the carrots are tender the liquor should be reduced to a small quantity of glaze. Mix beans and carrots together and bind with the sauce poulette. Grill the cutlets, arrange in a semicircle, with the garnish in the centre.

Sauce poulette

½ oz. butter
¼ oz. flour
¼ pint milk
1 teaspoon chopped parsley

a pinch of chopped savory
lemon juice
yolk of egg (optional)

Make in the usual way (see page 154) and finish with a squeeze of lemon juice and, if liked, the yolk of an egg.

The following recipe is an example of the use of the flap made into épigrammes accompanying the cutlets:

ÉPIGRAMMES D'AGNEAU A LA FLAMANDE

N.B. It is best, if possible, to prepare the flap in the way described the day before the dish is required.

2 lb. best end of neck of lamb, chined only
1 medium onion, sliced
1 medium carrot, sliced
1 stalk of celery (or a piece of lovage in the bouquet)
a bouquet garni
flour
beaten egg
dry white crumbs
seasoning
olive oil or dripping for frying

Garnish
¼ lb. carrots
1 lb. small Brussels sprouts, or as an alternative, according to the season, 1 pint shelled peas and ½ lb. baby carrots

½–¾ oz. butter
salt and pepper

sauce espagnole or provençale (see pages 149 and 177)

Prepare the meat in the way described on page 552. Put the flap into a stew-pan with the cut-up carrot, onion, and celery. Add the bouquet, a little salt, and enough water to cover. Put the lid on the pan and simmer gently until the meat is so tender that the bones may easily be pulled out. Remove from the pan, take out the bones. Put the meat between two dishes with a weight on top so that it is well pressed and leave till quite cold. Cut the meat into neat shapes (épigrammes); a heart shape is the classic, but large crescents or cutlet shapes are easier. Roll in seasoned flour, egg and breadcrumb, and set aside for frying while the cutlets are being cooked.

The cutlets. These may either be egged and breadcrumbed and fried, or brushed over with clarified butter and grilled. As the épigrammes are rather fat, and must be egged and crumbed and fried or they would fall to pieces, it makes a better contrast of texture if the cutlets are grilled.

The garnish. Cook the carrots *à la Vichy* (see page 193). Trim the sprouts and cook 5 minutes in boiling salted water, drain, return to pan with the butter and seasoning, continue cooking gently, shaking from time to time, for about 5 minutes. The sprouts should be just tender and not at all mushy. Add carrots and shake the pan to mix them. (If peas and baby carrots are used instead of sprouts add them to the carrots when these are half cooked, with butter, seasoning, and a cup of water.)

Dish the cutlets with an épigramme between each, *en couronne,* with the garnish in the middle. Pour round a little of the sauce and serve the rest apart.

N.B. The épigrammes may also be used for a dish apart, and if, as in this case, they are made with the flap and not with a piece of breast of mutton, they may need some addition to make the dish more substantial. Chipolata sausages or savoury force-meat cakes would be suitable. An appropriate sauce such as espagnole, provençale, or soubise and a garnish of vegetables are called for in either case. It should be noted that épigramme dishes contain much fat, more so with the flap than with breast of mutton, and therefore need consideration in the matter of accompaniments. They are not suitable for those who cannot digest fat.

In noisettes of lamb one has a delicate dish in which part, at any rate, of the thin flap of meat is included, and the bones, not cooked with the meat, are set free for stock. The appearance of this dish is of importance, and all the points of preparation given on pages 551 and 552 should be observed.

NOISETTES D'AGNEAU ARLÉSIENNE

1–1½ lb. best end of neck of lamb	olive oil for frying
2 aubergines	4 tomatoes
1 heaped teaspoon freshly chopped herbs	salt and pepper
¾ oz. butter	a clove of garlic crushed with salt
	3 large onions, sliced

Slice the aubergines and dégorger while preparations are continued. Bone the lamb completely without removing the flap (see notes on pages 233 and 553). Sprinkle well with freshly chopped herbs, roll up tightly, tie in the manner described at intervals of 1½ inches. Heat the butter in a frying-pan and sauter the noisettes 3–4 minutes on each side. Heat olive oil in the frying-pan and fry the slices of aubergine briskly, add quartered tomatoes, toss up together with salt, pepper, and crushed garlic. Fry the onions in a separate pan. Arrange the aubergine mixture in the centre of the dish, surround with the noisettes, with a round of fried onion on top of each and a little heap of fried onion between.

NOISETTES D'AGNEAU HENRI IV

1–1½ lb. best end of neck
canapés of fried bread for each
   noisette
1 wineglass bouillon, or stock
   made with meat glaze or
   vegetable extract

1 small glass sherry
béarnaise sauce (see page 158)
spinach cooked *en branches*
   (see page 230)
potato croquettes (see page
   209)

Prepare the noisettes in the way described (see page 553), grill or fry. Dish each on a canapé of fried bread cut to fit. Pour off the fat from the pan, add bouillon (or a little meat glaze or vegetable extract dissolved in water) and the sherry. Boil up and reduce slightly. Dish the noisettes, pour round the gravy, put a teaspoon of béarnaise sauce on each noisette, or if preferred serve this in a sauce-boat. Serve the spinach in the centre of the dish and the potato croquettes separately.

The following recipe needs a little more skill in preparation; the noisettes are served in pastry cases filled with a purée of peas, and the pastry must be very short and crisp, the noisettes very neat and not too large, and the whole carefully and precisely dished, or it may look messy.

NOISETTES D'AGNEAU A LA CLAMART

1–1½ lb. best end of neck of
   lamb
1 pint shelled peas (the peas
   may be past their first youth
   —floury)

3 or 4 sprigs of mint
a pinch of sugar
2 oz. butter
seasoning

Short crust pastry
   4 oz. flour
   1½ oz. margarine

½ oz. lard

good plain gravy or sauce
   espagnole (page 149) or
   demi-glace (page 143)

noisette potatoes (see page 207)

Cook the peas with a sprig of mint, seasoning, and a pinch of sugar. Make the pastry in the way described on page 835. Roll out very thinly and line into deep tartlet tins. Line again with paper, fill with beans and bake till crisp (see baking blind, page 844). Remove paper and beans, take the cases out of the moulds and return to the oven for a few minutes to dry. Drain the peas, rub them through a wire sieve, put them into a saucepan with a quarter of the butter, seasoning, and the rest of the mint, chopped finely. Beat and heat thoroughly over moderate heat. Prepare the noisettes in the way described (page 553), heat the remaining butter and fry 3 or 4 minutes on each side. Fill the pastry cases with the pea purée and set a noisette on top of each. Arrange in the dish with the noisette potatoes in the centre and serve with the gravy or sauce.

The following noisettes are served with spaghetti well flavoured with tomato and onion, and are accompanied by a sauce italienne or piquante, so that they present a fairly substantial dish.

NOISETTES OF LAMB A LA MILANESE

1½ lb. best end of neck of lamb, boned and prepared in the way described on page 553.
flour
beaten egg and dry white crumbs
6 oz. spaghetti
½ oz. butter
1 small onion, chopped
a clove of garlic crushed with 1 teaspoon salt

1–2 teaspoons tomato purée (or 1 lb. tomatoes, wiped, cut up, and cooked to a pulp with salt, pepper, and a nut of butter)
½ gill strong stock
seasoning
oil or butter for frying noisettes
sauce italienne (see below) or piquante (see page 177)

Cut the prepared meat into noisettes, flour, egg and crumb, and set aside. Poach the spaghetti in boiling salted water, when tender drain and rinse with boiling water. Melt butter in the pan, add onion and garlic, cover and cook for a few minutes to soften. Add the tomato purée with the stock, bring to boil, season well. Add the spaghetti and toss up well together over the fire.

Heat the oil or butter in a frying-pan and when very hot put in the noisettes, fry to golden brown on each side. Pile the spaghetti in the centre of a hot dish, arrange the noisettes round and serve a sauce italienne or piquante separately.

Sauce italienne (quick method)

1 oz. butter
1 onion, chopped
2 mushrooms, chopped
1 oz. cooked ham, chopped (if bacon is used in place of ham it should first be blanched)

½ oz. flour
1 teaspoon tomato purée
seasoning
½ gill white wine
½ pint good brown stock

Melt the butter, add onion, mushrooms, and ham, cook slowly, stirring frequently, 7–10 minutes. Draw aside, mix in the flour, purée, and seasoning, pour on the wine and stock and bring to boil. Simmer 10–15 minutes with the lid off.

The following dish of chops, with onions, apples, and potatoes, is good and homely.

CÔTES DE MOUTON CHAMPVALLON

4 mutton chops
2 oz. butter
8 potatoes, thinly sliced
4 onions, thinly sliced
salt and pepper
4 apples, peeled, cored, and quartered

1 dessertspoon flour
½ pint stock or gravy
small glass white wine or cider
½ oz. grated cheese

Trim some of the fat from the chops and brown them quickly in the hot butter in a frying-pan. Take them out and keep them hot while frying the thinly sliced onions and potatoes. Put a layer of the vegetables in a fireproof dish, lay the chops on top, cover them with the rest of the vegetables, season with salt and pepper. Peel, core, and quarter the apples, and arrange the quarters round the top of the dish. Sprinkle the frying-pan with the flour, brown it in the fat, pour in the stock and boil up. Add the wine and strain the liquid into the dish. Scatter with grated cheese, put into a moderately hot oven (380° F.) and cook for 1 hour. Serve in the dish.

A GOOD WAY OF STUFFING MUTTON OR LAMB CHOPS

Trim the chops and split the lean part of the meat lengthwise with a sharp knife. Fill with the following stuffing and either secure with two cocktail sticks or sew with strong thread. Grill and serve with a good tomato sauce.

Stuffing for 6 chops

2 tablespoons chopped onions	1 tablespoon chopped parsley
a little fat	or chives
2 tablespoons finely chopped	seasoning
celery or mushrooms	yolk of egg, or enough milk or
2 tablespoons fresh white	cream to moisten
breadcrumbs	

Soften the onion in a little fat, add the celery or mushrooms, the bread-crumbs, herbs, and seasoning, bind with yolk of egg or mix with a little milk or cream.

NAVARIN OR RAGOÛT OF MUTTON (GENERAL NOTES)

This is an excellent homely dish if properly made. It is often served in an unappetizing way, the gravy greasy and the vegetables overcooked. To avoid these faults the following points should be observed.

The gravy should be rich and full-flavoured, and carefully skimmed at the point indicated in the recipe, and, as in the case of all hot dishes containing fat, the navarin should be served on piping hot plates. The meat should be tender and about to fall from the bones, the potatoes and other vegetables tender and melting, but retaining their shape and not in a state of mush. To ensure this it is desirable to cook the navarin in two stages in the way to be described. The meat used may be middle neck, breast, part of a shoulder, or, as the breast is fat, a mixture of breast and shoulder. In this way one obtains a proper proportion of both fat and lean. The vegetables for the navarin may vary according to the season; sometimes only one variety is used, sometimes a mixture as in Navarin Printanière (page 568).

The two stages of cooking are carried out as follows:

1. The meat is browned, flour, liquid, bouquet, and seasoning added, and the whole simmered for 40 minutes to an hour.

2. The meat is then taken from the gravy and the latter strained through a fine strainer. This serves to remove any small splinters of bone which may have become detached during cooking. Now, tilting the bowl, skim the gravy with a metal spoon. Meat and gravy are then returned to a clean pan (if the same pan is to be used again it must be washed out first). Then the vegetables, previously fried, are added; if some take longer to cook than others, this must be taken into consideration and proper intervals allowed. For instance, root vegetables will go in first, and after an interval peas, beans, or other vegetables requiring a shorter cooking time. Simmering is now continued for a further hour or until meat and vegetables are tender.

NAVARIN OF MUTTON (1)

$1\frac{1}{2}$ lb. middle neck of mutton
freshly ground pepper and salt
  for seasoning
1 oz. good dripping
$\frac{1}{2}$ oz. flour
$1\frac{1}{4}$ pints warm water or stock
1 clove of garlic crushed with
  $\frac{1}{2}$ teaspoon salt
1 teaspoon tomato purée
a bouquet garni
$\frac{1}{4}$ oz. dripping for frying the
  vegetables

1 teaspoon sugar
8 pickling onions
2 large carrots cut in pieces $1\frac{1}{4}$
  inches long by $\frac{1}{4}-\frac{1}{2}$ inch
  wide
1 turnip cut in the same way
a good purée of potatoes,
  lightly seasoned with nutmeg

Divide the mutton into neat pieces, season lightly with freshly ground pepper and a small pinch of salt. Heat the dripping in a stew-pan or *sautoir* and when smoking put in the meat. Fry quickly until a good brown on both sides, then draw aside and pour off about half the fat. Sprinkle with flour, and with a wooden spoon turn the pieces of meat over and about to get them well coated. Allow to cook gently till the flour is well coloured. Add water or stock, garlic, and purée and bring to boil, stirring gently all the time. Season, add bouquet, cover, and simmer gently three-quarters of an hour. Meantime heat the $\frac{1}{4}$ oz. dripping in a frying-pan until smoking, add sugar and put in the vegetables, fry to a good colour, turning frequently; when a good brown turn them on to a plate.

Lift out the meat on to a plate, strain the gravy through a fine strainer into a bowl, and with a metal spoon skim off as much fat as possible (it is easier to do this if the bowl is tilted). Rinse out the pan, return meat and gravy and add the vegetables. Cover pan and simmer another hour, skimming from time to time.

When meat and vegetables are tender remove pan from heat and leave for a few minutes, then skim again. Pile meat and vegetables in a deep dish, boil up the gravy and spoon over them. Serve with a good purée of potatoes, lightly seasoned with nutmeg.

NAVARIN OF MUTTON (2)

2 lb. mutton cut from the breast and shoulder
seasoning
1 oz. (scant) dripping
1 level teaspoon sugar
½ oz. flour
1½ pints warm water or stock
1 tablespoon tomato purée or ½ lb. good tomatoes, peeled, pipped, and chopped
1 clove of garlic crushed with ¼ teaspoon salt

a bouquet garni
¼ oz. dripping
8 pickling onions
1 lb. even-sized potatoes, peeled, quartered, and trimmed into the shape of large olives. (These should be 'soapy' or new; floury potatoes spoil the gravy)
chopped parsley

Follow the preceding recipe but with this difference. After seasoning the meat add to the hot dripping with the sugar and fry, turning frequently until a good brown; pour off a little of the fat if necessary, then add the flour and proceed as in the first recipe to the end of the first process of simmering and straining, browning the onions carefully in the ¼ oz. dripping and adding them to the navarin after the straining. Cover, continue simmering, and after 15 minutes add the potatoes, which have been well dried in a cloth; cover the pan again and continue gentle simmering for another 40 minutes or until all is well cooked. After a final skimming serve in a casserole or deep dish scattered with chopped parsley.

NAVARIN PRINTANIÈRE

Use either of the preceding recipes, adding a garnish of spring vegetables.

a little dripping
6–8 spring onions (the round-bulbed variety)
6 small new turnips
a little castor sugar

2 oz. French beans
1 tea-cup shelled peas
12 baby new potatoes
6 small new carrots
salt and pepper

Brown the onions and the turnips in the dripping (cut into quarters if not very small), dusting them lightly with a little castor sugar; set aside. Cut beans into inch lengths, blanch for 2 minutes in boiling water and drain. Add these with the remaining vegetables to the navarin after the preliminary cooking and straining, season and continue simmering as in other recipes.

HARICOT OF MUTTON (1)

The word haricot is a corruption of 'halicot,' from *halicoter*, to cut in small pieces. Haricot beans of any kind are not therefore necessarily a part of this dish, although they are often included.

1½–2 lb. mutton, shoulder, breast, or middle neck
salt and pepper
¾ oz. good lard or dripping
2–3 oz. streaky bacon
3 medium-sized onions
½ oz. flour
1¼ pints water
1 clove of garlic crushed with ¼ teaspoon salt

a bouquet garni
¼ lb. haricot beans which have been soaked overnight
a pinch of bicarbonate of soda
½ lb. tomatoes, peeled, pipped, and coarsely chopped
chopped parsley

Cut the mutton in pieces, season lightly, set aside. Heat the fat in a heavy saucepan until lightly smoking. Cut the bacon into lardons (if very salt these may first be blanched), put in the pan with the onions, quartered. Shake and stir over the fire until coloured. Lift out the pieces on to a plate with a slice and set aside. Now fry the mutton until brown, pour off about half the fat and sprinkle in the flour, cook gently to colour, add water, garlic, bouquet, and seasoning. Bring to boil, cover, simmer gently for about $1\frac{1}{4}$ hours. Meanwhile prepare the haricots; cook them in lightly salted water with a pinch of bicarbonate of soda until three parts done. Now, as in the navarin, remove the pieces of meat, strain the gravy, rinse out the pan, and put back the meat, onions, and bacon, add the haricots, strained, and the tomatoes. Cover and simmer another hour, when the beans should be quite tender, serve in a hot dish, well sprinkled with parsley.

N.B. A haricot may with advantage be cooked in the oven.

HARICOT OF MUTTON (2)

$1\frac{1}{2}$–2 lb. mutton, shoulder, breast, or middle neck
1 oz. good dripping or bacon fat
$\frac{1}{2}$ oz. flour
$1\frac{1}{2}$–2 pints water
1 large clove of garlic
a bouquet garni
salt and pepper
2 medium-sized onions
4 medium-sized carrots
1 small cabbage, Savoy for choice
1 level teaspoon sugar
$\frac{1}{2}$ pint haricot beans which have been soaked overnight and three parts cooked
1 tablespoon tomato purée or $\frac{1}{2}$ lb. good ripe tomatoes, peeled, pipped, and chopped

Cut the meat in even-sized pieces. Heat half the dripping in a saucepan, brown the pieces all over in this, draw aside, dust over with flour, continue cooking a few moments to brown the flour evenly. Add water, garlic, bouquet, and seasoning. Bring to boil, stirring all the time, and simmer 30–40 minutes. Remove meat, strain the gravy and skim. Slice onions thinly, cut carrots in rounds and the cabbage in quarters. Rinse out the pan, heat in it the remaining dripping, add onions, carrots, and sugar and allow to colour. Replace the meat and put the cabbage round the sides of the pan. Put the partially cooked haricots and the tomatoes or tomato purée with the gravy into the pan. (If purée is used it should be well incorporated with the gravy.) The mixture should just cover the contents: if needed a little more water may be added. Cover tightly first with thick grease-proof or greased kitchen paper, then with lid, and cook on a low fire or in the oven for another 2 hours.

The last part of the cooking may be done in an earthenware casserole in which the dish may be served.

BREAST OF MUTTON WITH ONIONS

N.B. It is best to braise the meat for this dish the day before it is to be eaten.

1-2 breasts of mutton
½ oz. dripping
1 large breakfast-cup of sliced root vegetables for the mirepoix
1 teaspoon tomato purée
1-1½ pints stock
a bouquet garni
4-6 peppercorns

4-6 onions, thinly sliced
1 oz. butter
2 rounds of stale bread with crusts removed
a little flour
seasoning
1-2 tablespoons grated cheese
purée of potatoes

Braise the mutton as follows: Cut meat into even-sized pieces, allowing 1 or 2 for each person. Brown all over in the dripping, remove from the stew-pan and throw in the mirepoix, allowing the vegetables to sweat gently 5-6 minutes. Put back the mutton on top of the bed of vegetables, add the tomato purée and enough stock barely to cover, add bouquet and peppercorns. Bring to boil, cover, and braise in the oven till the meat is tender and the bones can be pulled out. Remove bones, press the pieces of meat between 2 plates with a weight on top and set aside. Strain the gravy well and when cool skim carefully of all fat.

Now prepare the coating: Soften the onions in two-thirds of the butter in a sauté or frying-pan, allow to colour to a delicate brown. Crumble the bread in pieces, sprinkle with flour and seasoning and rub lightly together in a cloth till fairly fine. Add the cheese. Arrange the pieces of mutton on a large fireproof dish, cover each with a spoonful of onion, press on to this a covering of breadcrumbs and cheese. Sprinkle with the remaining butter just melted, pour round the dish enough of the strained and skimmed mutton gravy to moisten. Put into a fairly hot oven until well browned, basting occasionally. Serve with a purée of potatoes and a sauce-boat of the gravy, which may, if wished, be slightly thickened with a little beurre manié.

IRISH STEW

To each pound of meat allow 2 lb. potatoes, ½ lb. onions, and just enough water to cover. (A little mushroom ketchup or a few spiced mushrooms is a good, but not classic, addition.)

say:
2 lb. scrag or middle neck of mutton
4 lb. potatoes
1 lb. onions

seasoning and 1 pint water
a bunch of mixed herbs
2 bay-leaves

Cut the meat into cutlets. Trim off the fat, cut the potatoes in half and slice the onions thickly. Put in the pan a layer of potatoes, then the meat, then more potatoes and all the other ingredients. Cover tightly and simmer gently for 2–2½ hours. Watch that it does not stick, and shake the pan from time to time. This dish should not be sloppy; the consistency should be thick and creamy and it should be very well seasoned. Spiced or stuffed prunes are excellent with this. If stuffed they are stoned and stuffed with the flesh of prunes.

For a recipe for Lancashire Hot Pot see Winkfield chapter, page 996.

DAUBE AVIGNONNAISE

1–1½ lb. mutton or veal	2 rashers of fat bacon,
1 onion, finely chopped	chopped small

Marinade

1 onion, sliced	6 peppercorns
1 bay-leaf	2 cloves of garlic, crushed
6 allspice berries	3 sprigs of parsley
a thin strip of orange rind	2 cloves
¾ pint dry white wine	1 dessertspoon olive oil
1 carrot, sliced	1 teaspoon salt
a sprig of rosemary	

Lay the meat, which may be left whole or cut in square pieces, in the marinade. Leave it for 5–6 hours, turning and basting it several times. Take it out and drain it. Put the chopped bacon into a stew-pan and brown it lightly; add the chopped onion and brown that also. Put in the meat, add the marinade, and cook in the oven in slow heat for 3–4 hours. (Three hours if the meat is cut up, 4 hours if it is left whole.) Dish, strain the marinade, reduce it if necessary and serve it with the meat.

PORK

Pork should be particularly carefully chosen and is best served in cool or cold weather. Small pork is generally preferred. Pork is a close-grained meat and to some people may be indigestible. It takes longer to cook than other meats, and should not be served underdone. When of good quality it has a smooth, thin rind and firm flesh of very pale pink colour, with white fat. It should be quite odourless. If there are signs of uneven flesh in the form of enlarged glands or kernels in the meat, it should be avoided.

The most popular method of cooking pork is to roast the larger joints and to grill the chops which are taken from the loin or the best end of neck. The legs, loin, and spare rib are usually roasted: the loin may be boned and stuffed. Generally the skin is scored through with a sharp knife before cooking, to form the crackling.

Pork is a rich, fat meat and it is natural for the palate to appreciate an accompaniment of something refreshing and sharp. In England this may be in the form of apple sauce, sauce Robert, or apples baked in the way to be described on page 575.   In America one finds extensions of the idea, and there pork, ham, and bacon are sometimes accompanied by various fruits other than apple.   Tinned apricots drained of syrup, dotted with butter, and sprinkled with sugar are grilled and served round a joint of pork or with hot baked ham; pineapple is another accompaniment, and many people find a sharp cranberry sauce agreeable.   Sausages with fried apple or pineapple, pigs' feet with sauerkraut, and pickled peaches with ham are variants of the same theme.

Savoury stuffings have the same effect of tempering the richness of the dish, and while one made of bread, herbs, and onions is a commonplace, others containing dried fruits, examples of which are given in Chapter XXI, are also suitable.

To roast

Score the skin with a sharp knife in cuts about ¼ inch apart.   Cook in a moderate oven, allowing 30–35 minutes to the pound.   The surface of the skin should either be rubbed with olive oil or well spread with dripping; the former in particular helps to produce crisp crackling.   Serve with a purée of apple flavoured with a little grated lemon rind.

It is a good plan also to roast a few crab-apples in the baking-dish with the meat; when cooked these may be rubbed through a sieve and a proportion of them added to the gravy.   This must be done with discretion, as crab-apples can be bitter, but they give the necessary zest to this rich meat.

BASIC RECIPE FOR STUFFING

8 oz. fresh white breadcrumbs	1 small onion, sliced and browned in dripping or parboiled and chopped
3–4 tablespoons mixed finely chopped herbs (sufficient to make the stuffing really green)	2 oz. suet or melted butter
	1–2 eggs, or milk
	seasoning

Where eggs are not required for binding, milk may be used in quantities sufficient for moistening properly.   Brown or parboil onion, incorporate with crumbs, herbs, seasoning, and chopped suet or melted butter, and bind with egg or milk.   This may be used to stuff a joint or be cooked and served separately.

The recipe on page 695 for sage and onion stuffing with pickled walnuts is good.

FRIED PORK CHOPS WITH APPLES

The chops should be cut ¾–1 inch thick.   Wipe well with a damp cloth, sprinkle with salt and pepper and give a light dusting of flour.   Have the fat in the frying-pan thoroughly hot, and cook well for about 7–10 minutes on each side, until well browned.   Peel, core, and slice some apples, fry these well, adding towards the end a sprinkling of brown sugar on each slice, allow the sugar to brown slightly and serve the apples with the chops.

PORK CHOPS POLONAISE

Trim the chop and cut the meat away from the bone. With a sharp knife make an incision at the side in the middle of the lean part of the meat, fill with the stuffing given below and sew up again with strong thread. Brown each side of the chop in hot fat in a frying-pan, add a few spoonfuls of milk, then cover and finish cooking in a moderate oven, from 50 to 60 minutes according to the thickness. Remove the thread and serve with fried slices of apple and a little gravy made from the dripping in the pan, or with barbecue sauce (page 728).

Stuffing

To the basic stuffing given above add a little extra chopped onion softened in fat, a tablespoon of sweet chutney, and a full tablespoon of chopped celery; season well. One egg will be sufficient for binding in this case.

BROCHETTES OF PORK

Choose tender and fairly lean pork, loin or fillet. Cut into pieces 1 inch square, allowing 2 or 3 brochettes per person.

1 or 2 bay-leaves	sauce Robert (page 148) or
Madeira or brown sherry	barbecue sauce (page 728)
freshly ground pepper	apple and mint ice (page 706)
fried onion rings (see page 200)	

Skewer the meat alternately with small pieces of bay-leaf on small wooden or silver skewers, being careful that the pieces of meat do not touch each other. Sprinkle liberally with Madeira or brown sherry and freshly ground pepper. Leave for $\frac{1}{2}$–1 hour.

Heat the grill and set the brochettes either over it, or under it at a moderate distance away. Allow a full 7 minutes, turning once during the grilling. When thoroughly cooked and a good brown serve piled up on a hot dish, surrounded with fried onion rings. Serve a sauce Robert or barbecue sauce separately, and an apple and mint ice.

CÔTE DE PORC AUX PRUNEAUX

An excellent dish, rich and good.

1½–2 lb. good small loin of pork	1 oz. butter
½ lb. good prunes soaked overnight in a good ½ pint white or red wine	1 teaspoon red-currant jelly
	1½ gills cream
	seasoning
seasoned flour	potato purée

Simmer the prunes gently in the wine for about half an hour, or until they are quite tender. Bone and trim the pork and cut into slices between

$\frac{1}{4}$ and $\frac{1}{2}$ inch thick.   Dust with seasoned flour and cook thoroughly in the hot butter, colouring well on both sides; remove and keep warm.   Drain the juice from the prunes into the pan, first draining off some of the fat; reduce a little, add the jelly, cream, and seasoning to taste.   Boil quickly until thick.

Dish the slices of pork on a bed of potato purée, surround with the prunes and strain over the sauce.

GREEN PIMENTOS STUFFED WITH PORK AND RICE

6 green pimentos
$\frac{1}{4}$ lb. rice
$\frac{1}{4}$ lb. pork (6 oz. pork chop)
1 teaspoon chopped herbs

salt and black pepper
1 pint tomato sauce (simple fashion, page 178)

Cut the tops off the pimentos, scoop out the seeds and blanch the skins for 3 minutes in boiling water.   Boil the rice until just tender, drain, rinse, and drain again.

Mince the pork and mix with the rice, herbs, and plenty of seasoning. Fill the pimentos with this, lay in a buttered casserole, pour over the tomato sauce, cover with a buttered paper and the lid, and cook in a slow to moderate oven for 1–1$\frac{1}{2}$ hours.

SUCKING-PIG

Sucking-pig is undoubtedly pork in its most delicate form; unfortunately served in the traditional way it can look unpleasantly realistic, and to children in particular may be almost horrifying.   One English method is to stuff and roast the pig, then to remove the head and split it, then to split the body of the pig down its length.   The pig is then dished back to back with half its head at each end.   Another way is to serve it whole with a lemon or apple in its mouth; yet another calls also for raisins in the eye sockets and even a green-leaf necklace.   All of this is still, to me, distasteful, although the first method is not so bad if the head is omitted; but personally I prefer a sucking-pig to be carved out of sight, that I may never see it whole as a dish.   It is carved by separating first shoulder then legs from the carcass.   This is done by making a circular cut round each of the joints, very much in the same way that one starts to carve a turkey; this leaves the ribs clear for carving in the same way as is done for a similar joint in lamb: in other words the meat is cut down into chops.   Another argument for carving the pig privily is that it is not particularly easy to do without some practice.   On this subject Mrs Beeton makes a pleasing remark; she says: 'The truth is the whole of the sucking-pig is delicious, delicate eating, but in carving it the host should consult the various tastes and fancies of his guests, keeping the larger joint generally for the gentlemen of the party.'

To roast a sucking-pig clean and wipe the pig thoroughly, fill with a chosen stuffing and sew it up. Skewer the hind legs backwards, the fore-legs forwards, in order to expose the carcass thoroughly for browning. Brush with good olive oil, which will give a crisper crackling than any other fat, and sprinkle the surface with salt. Allow 30–35 minutes per pound in a moderate oven, baste every 15 minutes, and towards the end of cooking sprinkle well with flour and continue basting. Serve with apple sauce or with baked apples prepared as given in the recipe below. Make gravy in the usual way.

Stuffing

The most usual stuffing for sucking-pig is sage and onion, but any other stuffing suitable for pork may be substituted.

Baked apple is served with roast pork or sucking-pig. Choose good cooking apples, do not peel but wipe and core. Fill the space left by the removal of the core with a mixture of sugar, lemon juice, and grated rind. Arrange in a baking-dish, put a little boiling water in the bottom of the dish and bake until soft, basting from time to time. With a sharply pointed spoon remove as much as possible of the soft baked apple without breaking the skin and mix with apricot jam or purée. Add extra lemon juice and sugar to taste, then put back into the skin of the apple.

A GOOD SAUCE FOR SUCKING-PIG

2 oz. seedless raisins or sultanas	gravy
2 tablespoons sherry	1 tablespoon granulated sugar
	a nut of meat glaze

Soak the raisins in the sherry for an hour or two, place them in a sauce-pan with the sugar and warm thoroughly, then add the meat glaze, allowing this to melt but not boil; set aside until the pork gravy is made, then mix both together.

FRESH SALT PORK OR PICKLED PORK

This is belly of pork and is thin; it is sometimes called poor man's bacon. Sometimes it is cut in lardons and cooked with rabbit, or it may be cooked in two or three pieces according to its size; these are then laid one on top of the other and the whole pressed. It is eaten cold cut in very thin slices. It is fat but very sweet, and used to be bought in delicatessen shops as pressed pork.

Pigs' feet are usually prepared for cooking before being sold. They are also frequently sold already boiled. If to be boiled at home they may be split, put into water containing pot-herbs (carrot, turnip, onion, and a dozen peppercorns, a bay-leaf, and a level teaspoon of salt), brought to the boil and simmered for 3–4 hours. After this they may be grilled or egged and breadcrumbed and fried, and served with a piquante sauce or with a dish of sauerkraut (see next page).

CHOUCROUTE ALSACIENNE

1–1½ lb. sauerkraut	freshly ground black pepper
1 oz. dripping or pork fat	1–2 knuckles of ham, accord-
2 carrots, sliced	ing to size
1 onion, sliced	2–3 saveloys or frankfurters
1 pig's trotter	chopped parsley
¼ lb. pickled pork, blanched	boiled potatoes
good stock	brown or piquante sauce, or
a bouquet garni	gravy
salt	

Blanch the kraut 10 minutes in boiling salted water. Drain well.
Heat the dripping in a braising pan, add the vegetables and allow to brown
slightly.   Add the trotter, pork, and kraut.   Moisten with the stock, add
bouquet and seasoning.   Cover tightly and braise about 1–1½ hours.
Meantime boil the knuckle, blanch, and grill the sausage.   Pile the
sauerkraut in a fireproof dish, arrange the meats, cut into slices, around
and on top.   Sprinkle well with parsley.   Serve boiled potatoes and a
brown or piquante sauce or gravy, either on the dish or separately.

On page 248 will be found a recipe for Puchero, which has pork as an
ingredient.

SAUSAGES

The following recipes are for sausage dishes for luncheon or supper.
Earlier in the chapter reference was made to the American way of eating
fruit as an accompaniment to certain meats; this applies also to sausages
and dishes made with sausage-meat, and the first recipe comes from *The
Boston Cooking School Cook Book* by Fannie Merritt Farmer (Little,
Brown & Co., Boston).

SAUSAGE-STUFFED PRUNES

½ lb. large prunes	⅓ cup soft breadcrumbs
½ lb. sausage-meat	salt, pepper, poultry seasoning

'Cook prunes in water to cover till tender but not soft.   Remove pits,
fill generously with sausage mixed with crumbs and seasonings.   Bake
in lightly greased pan in hot oven (400° F.) about 25 minutes or until
sausage is well browned.   Serve with sauce made with 1 tablespoon fat
from pan, 1 tablespoon flour, 1 cup prune juice, 1 tablespoon lemon juice,
1 tablespoon grated lemon rind, salt to taste.   Serves 4 as a main dish or
may be used as a garnish on a platter with roast turkey.'

We replace the poultry seasoning with fresh, finely chopped herbs, marjoram and savory, thyme and sage, or a pinch or so of mixed dried herbs, and we serve it with fingers of fried bread or the breakfast dropped scones given on page 1049.

SAUSAGE CAKES WITH PINEAPPLE

½ lb. sausage-meat
4 tablespoons fresh bread-crumbs
1 tablespoon finely chopped herbs, including mint
salt and pepper
flour

egg and breadcrumbs for coat-ing, fat for frying
slices of tinned pineapple, 1 for each cake
French mustard and sugar
2 teaspoons finely chopped chives

Mix thoroughly sausage-meat, breadcrumbs, herbs, and seasoning. Shape into cakes, dip into flour, egg and breadcrumb, and fry. Drain the slices of pineapple, carefully spread with a little French mustard and sugar, and fry these after the sausage cakes are ready. Arrange in a dish with the sausage cakes laid on the top of the pineapple, and sprinkle with finely chopped chives.

APPLE CAKE (TO SERVE WITH SAUSAGES)

6–8 firm cooking apples
2 oz. butter
castor sugar

wine vinegar
salt
freshly ground pepper

bacon and chipolata sausages

brown sauce, such as the demi-glace on page 143, or gravy

Peel and core apples, cut into rings ¼ inch thick. Heat a frying-pan, drop in ½ oz. of the butter, when foaming dust heavily with castor sugar and put in enough apple slices to lie flat on the bottom of the pan. Cook rapidly till brown, turn and brown on the other side. Butter a sandwich tin, dust with sugar and lay in the cooked apple rings, slightly overlapping. Reheat the pan and fry the remaining rings in the same way. Pack them into the tin, sprinkling the layers with vinegar, salt, and pepper. When the mould is full place in a hot oven 20–25 minutes to brown.

Turn out on to a hot dish and garnish with crisp curls of grilled bacon and grilled chipolata sausages. Hand a good brown sauce or gravy separately.

SAUSAGE-ROLLS

6 oz. quantity flaky pastry (see page 835)
¾–1 lb. sausages or sausage-meat

a little finely chopped onion and parsley
salt and pepper
1 beaten egg with a pinch of salt

Skin sausages, incorporate onion, parsley, and seasoning with the sausage-meat. Shape into rolls. Roll out pastry fairly thin into a long strip equal in width to the shaped meat. Place the first roll of meat at one end of the strip, leaving about 1½–2 inches of pastry to turn over. Brush the edge lightly with beaten egg. Fold over, press down firmly, and cut off with a knife. Continue till all meat is used. Brush rolls with egg. Bake near top of hot oven (425° F.) 25–30 minutes.

SAUSAGE BARBECUE

This is a good dish for fresh sausages or for tinned hamburgers.   Allow
1½ or 2 sausages per person according to size.

Sauce for 12 sausages

2–3 tablespoons oil or approx. 2 oz. margarine, the quantity depending on the amount of fat left in the pan after frying sausages

2 or 3 shallots or 1 small onion, finely chopped

1 gill good store sauce (A1, tomato ketchup) or home- made plum sauce (page 1118), mixed with an equal quantity of water

a good pinch of salt and pepper

⅛ gill vinegar

1 dessertspoon Worcestershire sauce

1 dessertspoon chutney

1 dessertspoon French mustard

Fry the sausages to a good brown all over; remove from pan.   Add
additional fat or oil to that left in the pan and in this cook the onions to
golden brown.   Mix all the other ingredients in a bowl, then add them to
the onions.   Boil up this sauce until slightly reduced.   Split the sausages,
add to the sauce, and continue cooking for about 5–7 minutes, or until
sausages are thoroughly cooked through.

PORK SAUSAGES FLAMANDE

Red Cabbage Flamande (page 221)

1½ lb. pork sausages (6 to the pound)

2 or 3 tablespoons good dripping or bacon fat

sauce demi-glace, short method (page 144)

Prepare the cabbage according to the recipe.   When nearly cooked
begin frying the sausages.   Do not prick these, but roll them lightly on a
board or between the hands.   Use a heavy frying-pan and when just hot
put in the dripping or bacon fat.   When melted but not hot put in the
sausages and fry slowly, gradually increasing the heat.   Turn them over
occasionally; allow at least 10 minutes' cooking time.   When a good
glistening brown draw aside.   Dish the cabbage, arrange the sausages on
the top and pour the sauce round.

N.B. Be careful not to pierce the sausages while they are frying.

HAM AND GAMMON

There are various kinds of ham.   York and Cumberland hams, unsmoked, are particularly sweet and delicate in flavour.   Bradenham hams,
often smaller in size, are specially treated, being black on the outside and
having redder flesh than either of the others.

A gammon of bacon (approximately 12 lb.) is a smaller joint, convenient for a small household, and one can also buy a corner of gammon, a still smaller cut, approximately 3–4 lb. It provides sweet and delicately flavoured meat, may be cooked as ham, and is the piece used for classic English boiled bacon. There is an old-fashioned dish called Stuffed Chine in which this piece of meat or collar is cut and stuffed with mixed herbs and lots of parsley, then tied in muslin and boiled; the flavour is excellent. The surface of the meat is cut in long slits and the stuffing pressed in.

BOILED HAM

If necessary scrub the surface with a stiff brush. Soak overnight in cold water. Have ready a large saucepan of cold water, place the ham in this, bring to boiling-point and simmer, allowing 20 minutes to the pound. When cooked allow the ham to cool in the water. When cold remove, peel off the skin, then finish off by covering the surface with brown bread-crumbs.

To boil a ham Alabama way

Soak a ham 48 hours, boil up enough water to cover and add 1 pint vinegar. Allow 25 minutes to each pound. When cooked allow the ham to cool in the water in which it has simmered, then remove skin and trim. Mix ½ lb. brown sugar with a beaten egg to a smooth paste and spread over the surface of the ham. Place this in a baking-tin with 1 pint vinegar, bake for 1 hour, basting frequently.

An alternative coating

½ pint stale breadcrumbs	1 tablespoon French mustard
6 oz. brown sugar	

Bind the ingredients with a little fruit juice or cider and spread over the surface of the peeled ham. Bake as before, basting with the vinegar or with cider if preferred.

BAKED HAM LISSANOURE

ham	cloves
3 onions	sugar, preferably dark brown
3 carrots	Barbados
a bunch of celery stems	1 or 2 bottles of stout or cider
a wisp of hay	

Soak the ham and boil, with the vegetables and wisp of hay, in the usual way, allowing 25 minutes to the pound, but do not cook it completely to the end of the time, bearing in mind the subsequent baking. The addition of the hay gives the ham a faint fragrant flavour. Drain, skin, stick with cloves and cover thickly with sugar. Put into a baking-tin, surround with stout, and bake about 40 minutes, basting with care.

It was in America that I first saw ham cooked in what I thought the perfect manner, and though we finish our boiled and baked hams nowadays in various and similar fashions, I am giving an American recipe in its entirety. It is the ham boiled and baked from *The Joy of Cooking* by Irma S. Rombauer. The following preliminary note is given: 'For a ham, that is to be boiled and then baked allow twenty-five minutes' simmering to the pound for a medium-sized ham, and slightly more for a small ham and slightly less for a large ham.'

HAM BOILED AND BAKED[1]

'Scrub well:

A smoked ham.[2]

Place it in a kettle of fresh simmering water that barely covers it.

Add:

> Vegetables suitable for soup
> 1 bay-leaf
> 8 peppercorns
> 6 allspice (optional)

Simmer the ham. Permit it to cool partly in the water in which it was cooked, drain it and strip off the skin. Cover the top of the ham with:

> Brown sugar
> A little dry mustard (optional)

Stud it with:

> Whole cloves

Bake the ham in a hot oven, 425° F. for 20 minutes.

Baste it with a choice of:

> 1 cup of cider, pineapple or orange juice, the juice of pickled peaches, cooked prunes, or apricots, wine, ginger ale, or molasses

Dredge it with:

> Brown sugar

Sprinkle it with:

> Grated orange rind

Lower the heat to 350° F. Cook it without basting for 30 minutes.

For the last 15 minutes put into the pan:

> Pineapple slices

[1] Copyright 1931, 1936, 1943, used by special permission of the publishers, the Bobbs-Merrill Co.

[2] [Mrs Rombauer's footnote] Processed hams need not be boiled. They are sold ready to be baked.

Garnish the ham with the pineapple and:

        Maraschino cherries
        Parsley

Serve it with:

        Raisin Cider Sauce
        Sour cream and horse-radish sauce
        Barbecue sauce or horse-radish mixed with Currant jelly.

Mrs Rombauer recommends that this ham be served with various sauces, among them Raisin Cider Sauce, which we quote from the same book.

'About $1\frac{1}{2}$ cupfuls. Good with hot or cold ham or ham sandwiches.

Combine in a saucepan:

        $\frac{1}{4}$ cup brown sugar (firmly packed)
        $1\frac{1}{2}$ tablespoons cornstarch [1]
        $\frac{1}{8}$ teaspoon salt

Stir in:

        1 cup fresh or bottled cider
        $\frac{1}{4}$ cup raisins cut in halves
        8 whole cloves
        1 2-inch stick of cinnamon

Cook and stir these ingredients for 10 minutes. Add:

        1 tablespoon butter

Remove the spices. Serve very hot.'

She also recommends a horse-radish sauce made with sour cream, a barbecue sauce, or horse-radish mixed with currant jelly.

HAM BAKED IN A CRUST

Make a paste of flour and water, enough to cover the ham thickly. Soak the ham overnight, wipe well, then cover it completely with the paste, taking care that the paste is neither thin nor broken in any place. Bake between 3 and 4 hours according to size, in a moderate oven. Remove the crust, pull off the skin, and cover with brown breadcrumbs. This method of cooking may be applied to a corner piece of gammon, served hot with broad beans in traditional English fashion.

BARBECUED HAM

This is a good recipe for cooking a thick slice of ham. First brown the ham on each side. Make the barbecue sauce given on page 728. Place the ham in a fireproof dish with a cover. Pour over and around it the barbecue sauce and bake in a moderate oven for $1-1\frac{1}{2}$ hours until thoroughly cooked. If the sauce becomes too thick during the cooking a little extra water may be added.

        [1] Cornstarch = corn-flour.

JAMBON BRAISÉ MADÈRE

A piece of collar, slipper, or corner of bacon answers well for this. (A slipper weighs 2–2½ lb. and consists almost entirely of lean meat.) Preparations must begin a day in advance.

2–2½ lb. bacon
1 good dessertspoon dripping or bacon fat
4 tablespoons Madeira or brown sherry, and an extra spoonful or two for finishing
4 tablespoons mirepoix
a small handful of mushrooms, or mushroom stalks or peelings, well chopped (optional)
a large bouquet garni
freshly ground pepper
¾ pint good strong stock
1 teaspoon beurre manié or arrowroot (approx.), if necessary
spinach à la crème (page 230)

Soak the bacon for 12 hours. Drain and dry well. Heat the dripping in a stew or braising pan, put in the bacon and sauter slowly, turning the joint over from time to time, for about 7 minutes. Flamber with the Madeira, then remove the bacon, add the mirepoix, cover and allow to sweat gently for 5–7 minutes. Set the bacon on the top of this, add the mushrooms, bouquet, some freshly ground pepper, and the stock. Put a piece of paper under the lid, cover tightly, bring to the boil, then braise in the oven 1–1½ hours or until tender. Take up, carve as much bacon as required, and dish on a purée of spinach à la crème. Strain the gravy, skim well and thicken slightly, if necessary, with the beurre manié or arrowroot, boil rapidly for a minute or two and finish with an extra spoonful or two of Madeira. Spoon some of the sauce over the dish and serve the rest in a boat.

For Cornets de Jambon see Winkfield chapter, page 999.

VEAL

Veal, which is young beef or calf, is specially treated when killed. It should be the faintest delicate pink in colour. It has very little fat and is often larded. Being young, immature meat it should be very well cooked; underdone veal is unpleasant.

The leg and fillet. The fillet should come from what the French call the noix de veau, a long piece cut lengthwise from the leg of veal just above the knuckle, but this is difficult to get from English butchers because they cut the leg up differently. This, a tender part, is used for escalopes, grenadins, and fricandeaux.

The absence of fat in the meat makes larding a necessary preparation for most dishes.

The loin for chops, roasts, sautés, and small braises; on occasion used for a fricandeau. It is also possible to cut escalopes yourself from this piece of meat.

The neck as above, and also for cutlets and for stuffing and roasting.

The shoulder (including the oyster). The shoulder may be stuffed and roasted, the oyster is the best part for blanquettes, ragoûts, braises, and an economical fricandeau.

The knuckle and feet. The top part of the knuckle as cut by English butchers will supply a suitable piece for a fricandeau, the knuckle as a whole may be used for sautés, ragoûts, and blanquettes, and the feet are suitable for gelatine, and for calf's foot jelly, and are included in such large braises as bœuf à la mode.

Middle and top end of neck and breast for ragoûts, stuffing, braising, and for galantine.

The head may be braised or boiled; this joint includes tongue and brains, the latter often incorporated in the accompanying sauce.

To roast. The same method is used for roasting veal as for other meat. It should be thoroughly cooked and should be well basted during the cooking to counteract the natural dryness of the meat. Cook 20–25 minutes to the pound, according to the thickness of the meat.

To carve. Cut in thin slices. In the case of fillet, when it is cut raw and then sautéd or fried, it must be wafer thin. For blanquettes and ragoûts the meat should be cut in thick cubes.

Classic accompaniments. Purée of sorrel or spinach; force-meat balls, sautéd prunes, glazed onions; veal stuffing or force-meat is a savoury mixture of herbs with flavour of lemon thyme or grated lemon rind predominating.

Classic dishes. Blanquette of veal; fricandeau with sorrel or spinach purée; escalopes; Wiener Schnitzel.

BLANQUETTE DE VEAU

1–1½ lb. veal from the shoulder
or knuckle
water
2 medium-sized onions or 6–8
pickling or baby onions
2 medium-sized carrots
a good squeeze of lemon juice
or a glass of white wine

a bouquet garni
seasoning of salt and pepper

Roux
1½ oz. butter
1½ oz. flour, scant weight
seasoning

Liaison
1 or 2 egg yolks
½ gill creamy milk or cream

Cut the veal in large square pieces, blanch them, then rinse in fresh cold water. Return to the pan with sufficient water just to cover. Add onions and carrots cut in quarters (if the onions are small leave them whole), the lemon juice or wine, bouquet and seasoning. Cover and simmer until tender. Then strain off all the liquid, keeping the meat and vegetables covered in the pan, and measure 1¼ pints. Melt the butter in a thick saucepan, add the flour off the fire and pour on the 1¼ pints of liquid. When thoroughly blended stir over a moderate fire until it boils. Allow to boil fairly rapidly until it becomes thick and syrupy, draw aside, adjust the seasoning and add the liaison of egg yolk and milk or cream. Then reboil over a gentle heat, pour over the meat and vegetables in the pan. Draw to the side of the stove for 10 minutes or so before serving, so that the flavour of the sauce may penetrate the meat. Then dish in a china casserole or fireproof dish.

LE FRICANDEAU

This is a classic. It may have several different garnishes, but the best known is a purée of sorrel—fricandeau à l'oseille. On occasion spinach, braised celery, lettuce, or a purée of soubise may take its place, but sorrel remains the best accompaniment to the fricandeau. Its smoothness and pleasant acidity contrast well with the rich gelatinous quality of the meat.

A fricandeau differs slightly from the more homely braise, the un-thickened gravy being so reduced as to become a real jus, the essence of the meat, semi-clear and pale gold in colour. The amount of this gravy or jus served with the meat is small, 1–2 tablespoons per person, or about ½ pint for the whole dish.

In the first recipe given you have the classic; the method of cooking ensures that the meat is not dry—a common fault with veal—but it involves careful cooking and practice. Impossible to describe exactly in a recipe just at what intervals the liquid should be added, and for how long it should reduce to get exactly the right degree of syrupiness; for this one must have practice or be able to watch a skilled cook at work. The second recipe, not the classic, but still in the tradition, is not so technical or so difficult and is therefore more suited to a beginner; it is also slightly more economical, and as is the case with most economies does not give quite the result that may be obtained by the first method. It is neverthe-less good.

Veal for the fricandeau should be cut from the noix.[1] It should always be larded and may be cooked in one piece or cut into slices about 1¼ inches thick, each slice then larded before being cooked. There is an advantage in choosing the smaller cuts because a fricandeau should be cooked until you can 'cut it with a spoon,' and this makes the carving of a large piece difficult. The meat may be served either on the purée or separately.

For reasons of economy a different piece of meat is sometimes used for this dish, a cut taken from the best part of the shoulder, but the meat is

[1] If the noix is unobtainable (and English butchers cannot always supply it), then a long piece from the top of the knuckle makes a good substitute; it must be boned.

drier and the resulting dish therefore less succulent. A recipe for each follows:

LE FRICANDEAU (THE CLASSIC)

2½ lb. veal without bone (see preceding note)
3 oz. larding bacon (approx.), cut into lardons
2 oz. pickled pork or streaky bacon, blanched and diced
3 oz. onions, finely sliced

3 oz. carrots, finely sliced
1 wineglass white wine
1 pint good stock (approx.), of veal if possible, very lightly seasoned
a bouquet garni

Cut the meat into slices about 1–1¼ inches thick and lard on one side. Choose a good pan, a large *sautoir* is the best. Scatter the pork and sliced vegetables on the bottom, lay the pieces of meat side by side on these with the lardons uppermost. Cover tightly, set on a very low fire to sweat for 15–20 minutes. Pour over the wine, cover and sweat again for the same length of time, but seeing that the reduction is not overdone. Add a wineglass of stock, cover and repeat the process. Do this once again with another wineglass of stock. It is most important that throughout the whole cooking the *fond* of vegetables shall not brown. Each time the liquid is added it must be allowed to reduce to a syrupy consistency, and it is during this time that watchfulness is needed. Now add the remaining stock, which should come just level with the pieces of meat but should not cover them; then add the bouquet garni. Bring up quickly to the boil, cover closely with a piece of paper and then the lid, put into a very moderate oven 1½–2 hours, basting every 20 minutes. The meat must be absolutely tender. Within half an hour of serving carefully remove meat on to a hot plate, strain the gravy into a bowl, scraping the pan well. Replace the meat, skim gravy thoroughly of all fat and pour it over. Set the pan on fairly quick heat or if preferred in the oven, cook fairly rapidly, basting every 2 or 3 minutes. During this process the meat will become lightly glazed and the gravy be reduced to about ½ pint. It is on account of this reduction that it is important to season the bouillon very lightly in the first place, otherwise the final rich jus will be over-salty.

Serve the meat in a hot dish with the jus poured over and the garnish with it, or this may be handed separately.

The following recipe is for the piece of meat referred to as being more economical, and the recipe is an easier one for a beginner:

FRICANDEAU A L'OSEILLE

2½ lb. veal cut in a long, slightly tapering piece from the shoulder
2 rashers of streaky fat bacon
3 oz. larding bacon, cut in lardons
1 large carrot cut in thin rounds

1 large onion cut in thin rounds, alternatively 3 or 4 shallots, sliced
1 wineglass white wine
1½ pints stock
a bouquet garni

Trim and skin the veal and lard it (see page 69); if necessary tie it up. Lay the rashers on the bottom of a shallow stew-pan or *sautoir*, put the sliced vegetables on top and the veal on these. Add the wine, a pint of the stock, and the bouquet. Bring to boil, put the pan in a moderate oven and braise for at least an hour with the lid off, basting well. Add the extra stock by degrees as the gravy in the pan reduces; do this with judgment, not adding more than you think necessary. (This is a point of cooking where the recipe can only indicate and the cook must decide.) Decrease the heat at the end of cooking. When quite tender take up the meat, strain and skim the gravy. Return both to the pan and continue cooking 10–15 minutes on a brisk fire, basting well. When the meat is a little glazed and the gravy of good consistency and flavour it is ready and may be dished on a purée of sorrel.

Purée of sorrel

2 lb. sorrel	½ cup cream
½ oz. butter	1 small egg
scant ½ oz. flour	seasoning
1 tea-cup thick béchamel sauce	

Wash the sorrel well in the way described for spinach on page 229. Blanch in boiling water 10 minutes. Drain, press, and rub through a wire sieve. Melt the butter in a thick pan, add flour, allow to colour a delicate brown. Lay the sorrel on top of this without mixing, cover and leave in a warm place for 40 minutes. At the end of this time mix well and beat in the béchamel sauce, the beaten egg, and cream; season and reheat over moderate fire, stirring well; when thick enough just to hold its shape it is ready to serve.

ESCALOPES

After a discussion on the matter of escalopes and the greatly varying dishes now served under this name, it was decided to put in an elementary note for students. If you think for a moment of a leg of mutton you will recall that there is one part of the flesh, under the bone, which is lighter in colour and more tender than the rest of the meat. This, in veal, is the true noix, and you can see that in order to get a piece of it, apart from the rest of the meat, the butcher would have to cut the leg longwise and, having disposed of this special delicacy, would be left with only the less attractive part of the leg. Escalopes should be cut from the noix, the best part of the leg of veal; they should be between ¼ and ½ inch thick, unless otherwise stated in the recipe, and they should be cut across the grain of the meat. The escalopes that one may get in English restaurants are sometimes cut from across the whole leg, trimmed, and cut into suitably sized pieces, so that they contain, at most, only a percentage of the true noix. The result may be good, but of course cannot be quite so good as when the noix only is used, as is customary in the best French kitchens.

Owing to the difficulty, to say nothing of the expense, of getting the proper cut of veal, one may take as substitute the best end of neck or, as second choice, loin. This is boned and cut in slices from $\frac{1}{4}$ to $\frac{1}{2}$ inch thick, which are well beaten with the flat of a heavy knife. The escalopes thus made are not so large as they should be, but are tender and good. The bone left over is excellent for a strong stock.

When veal is plentiful and we can choose what we will buy, no better dish can be made of this noix than the following classic and delicious one, Escalopes de Veau à la Crème: its perfection depends on having the right ingredients.

ESCALOPES DE VEAU A LA CRÈME (1)

5–6 thin escalopes
1 good oz. or more of butter
salt and freshly ground white
  pepper

a sherry glass Madeira or good
  sherry
1 gill cream
8–10 tarragon leaves

Heat a large *sautoir* or frying-pan, put in two-thirds of the butter. Allow this to get hot, taking care not to overheat it, for the escalopes should be very lightly browned. Lay into the butter as many escalopes as will fit into the pan, cook over moderate heat 3–4 minutes on each side. Remove on to a hot plate, add the remaining butter and cook the rest of the escalopes. When all are done, lightly browned on each side, pour off a little of the butter from the pan, leaving behind only a small quantity. Add the wine, swilling the pan well round. Reduce by a third, then add the cream and the tarragon leaves, boil up well, season, replace the escalopes, cover and simmer for 1 minute. Dish. Reboil the sauce, reducing a little if necessary, and pour over the escalopes.

In a simpler form one may omit the sherry and sprinkle instead with a little lemon juice. In this case one must be careful not to use too much, because it may curdle the cream.

The second recipe for Escalopes de Veau à la Crème is very good also, but may be described as being more of a sauce dish.

ESCALOPES DE VEAU A LA CRÈME (2)

4–5 thin escalopes
$\frac{3}{4}$ oz. butter
1 shallot, finely chopped
4 oz. button mushrooms, white
  and small, thinly sliced
1 wineglass white wine
$1\frac{1}{2}$ wineglasses veal stock or
  bouillon

1 wineglass ($\frac{3}{4}$ gill) cream
1 teaspoon flour
1 teaspoon butter (flour and
  butter to be worked to-
  gether for beurre manié)
a little chopped tarragon

Bat out slightly and trim the escalopes. Heat a *sautoir* or deep frying-pan, drop in the butter and when foaming lay in the escalopes. Over a moderate fire fry 3–4 minutes on each side. Take them out and put on a plate. Reduce the heat a little, put in the shallot and allow to soften without colouring. Then add the mushrooms and cook gently, turning frequently, 5–6 minutes; lift out on to the plate. Add the wine to the pan and allow to reduce by half, swilling it well round. Add the stock, boil up and strain. Now return the liquor to the pan with the cream, boil for a minute or two, draw aside and add the beurre manié bit by bit. Allow this to dissolve, then reboil. Replace the mushrooms and escalopes, cover with a piece of buttered paper and leave on the side of the fire 4–5 minutes to simmer gently. Arrange the escalopes down a long dish, spoon over the sauce, which should have the consistency of cream, and sprinkle over with chopped tarragon.

It is also good to cook these escalopes in butter in a frying-pan, frying them on each side, then adding a squeeze of lemon juice, and after dishing them to déglacer or swill out the pan with a little cream; this is poured over the escalopes, which are served immediately.

ESCALOPES DE VEAU HOLSTEIN

This is a good dish and can be made when one cannot get the true noix of veal.

5 large thin escalopes	lemon juice
seasoned flour	freshly ground black pepper
clarified butter for frying	chopped parsley
a nut of fresh butter	

Garnish

3 hard-boiled eggs	$\frac{1}{2}$–$\frac{3}{4}$ oz. butter
5 fillets of anchovy	16 turned (stoned) olives
1 large clove of garlic crushed with salt	sliced lemon (rind and pith removed before slicing)

To prepare garnish. Divide the yolks from the whites of the hard-boiled eggs. Rub the yolks through a strainer, rinse the whites in cold water and chop them; keep separate. Split the fillets of anchovy in two lengthways. Mix the garlic with the butter, and with a small paper cornet (see page 53) fill the olives with it.

Bat out the veal to flatten it well; roll and press it in the flour, and shake each piece to remove the surplus. Heat the butter in a thick frying-pan, put in the veal and sauter over a moderate fire, allowing 4 minutes on each side.

Lay the veal on a long dish, arrange the yolks and whites in a neat pattern down each side and pile the olives at each end. On each escalope lay 2 strips of anchovy crosswise, and on the top a very thin slice of lemon. Reheat the pan, drop in the fresh butter, when foaming add a good squeeze of lemon juice, freshly ground black pepper, and a sprinkling of chopped parsley, and pour over the escalopes. Heat the whole for a minute in the oven and serve.

WIENER SCHNITZEL (ESCALOPES VIENNOISES)

5 thin escalopes of veal measuring about 5 inches by 3 inches
seasoned flour
1 beaten egg, seasoned, and with a few drops of oil added
dry white crumbs
clarified butter for frying, or more economically a mixture of oil and butter

for each escalope a thin slice of lemon, and ½ teaspoon capers, a slice of gherkin cut lengthwise, or a turned olive
a squeeze of lemon juice
chopped parsley

If the escalopes are not already paper thin, beat each one with the flat of a heavy knife, roll in flour, shake, brush with egg, and roll and press in crumbs.   Heat the butter in a large frying-pan, lay in the escalopes and fry over a moderate to slow fire for about 7–10 minutes, turning once only. At the end of this time they should be a deep golden brown.   Serve at once on a hot flat dish and garnish the middle of each schnitzel with a slice of lemon, and the capers, gherkin, or olive on top of the lemon.   Add a squeeze of lemon to the butter remaining in the pan and strain over the dish.   Dust with chopped parsley and serve immediately.

CÔTELETTES DE VEAU FOYOT

This excellent dish is named from the restaurant Foyot in Paris, where it was created.   It is one of the best of the veal cutlet dishes and is relatively easy to prepare.

4 veal cutlets cut from the best end of neck, which ensures that they are large and of even size. The butcher should be asked to cut them about ½ inch thick
salt and pepper
2 oz. butter

3 oz. onion, finely chopped
1 oz. fine fresh white breadcrumbs
1¼ oz. grated Parmesan cheese
1 wineglass white wine
a good ½ pint veal stock
sauce périgueux (see next page)

Trim the cutlets by cutting out the end piece of bone (chine bone) and chopping the rib bone to within 2½ inches of the noix.   Salt and pepper lightly.   Heat 1½ oz. of the butter in a deep frying-pan or *sautoir*.   Brown the cutlets on each side over moderate heat.   Lift them out on to a plate, add the onion to the pan, lower the heat and allow it to soften and colour lightly, stirring frequently.   Cover each cutlet with about a dessertspoon of the onion; this should leave about a third of the onion in the pan.   Mix the cheese and crumbs together and press the mixture well on top of the onion on each cutlet, using a palette-knife.   Replace the cutlets, cheese side up, on the onion remaining in the pan; pour round the white wine and enough of the stock to moisten well.   Oil the rest of the butter and with a small pastry brush or a small bunch of feathers sprinkle this over the cutlets.   Bring to boil and put into a slow to moderate oven for about 1½ hours.   Baste frequently with a small spoon every 15 minutes for the first hour, adding the remaining stock as that in the dish reduces.   Do not baste for the last half-hour, for during this time the cutlets should brown well.   Serve carefully on a large hot dish, reduce the liquid in the pan, strain and add to the sauce.

Sauce périgueux (quick method)

1 sherry glass Madeira or dark brown sherry
1 dessertspoon chopped truffle

½ wineglass good bouillon
1 teaspoon arrowroot

Put the Madeira into a little saucepan with the truffle, simmer to reduce to a tablespoonful, add the bouillon, reboil, add to the jus from the cutlets, adjust seasoning and thicken with the arrowroot.

The following is good, and is not a 'made-up' dish.   It is more economical of meat than the foregoing recipes.

FRICADELLES A LA GRECQUE

1 lb. lean veal weighed when minced
2 oz. fat from the veal, minced
2 oz. onion, finely chopped
2–3 sprigs of parsley, 2 sprigs of lemon thyme, the leaves of each stripped from the stems and chopped
5 oz. white bread with crust removed soaked in milk for ¼ an hour

1½ gills water (approx.)
salt, pepper, paprika
flour
butter for frying
tomato sauce (simple fashion, page 178)
2 or 3 spoonfuls sour cream
black olives and quarters of lemon

Mince the veal, weigh, add by degrees the fat, onion, and herbs. Squeeze the bread between the hands and add to mixture.   Pass all again through the mincer.   Work with the hand with the same movement as for making bread, adding the cold water by degrees.   It is important that the water be gradually absorbed; if added too quickly the mixture may become sloppy, and what is required is that it shall change its consistency, gradually becoming firm yet light.   The amount of water that it will absorb varies depending on how much the meat has been worked beforehand.   Season highly with salt, pepper, and paprika.   Roll into very small balls about the size of a marble, roll lightly in flour and fry quickly in the butter till brown.   Lay in a *sautoir* or deep fireproof dish, pour over the tomato sauce, which should just cover.   Poach in the oven 15–20 minutes.   Add 2 or 3 spoonfuls of sour cream, shaking the pan gently to mix in the cream without breaking the fricadelles.   Pile up carefully in the serving dish and garnish with black olives and quarters of lemon, or serve in the fireproof dish in which it is cooked.   Château potatoes are a good accompaniment.

ROAST STUFFED VEAL NIÇOISE

3½–4 lb. shoulder of veal, cut from the knuckle end and boned
8 fillets of anchovy, chopped
2 cloves of garlic, crushed
3 oz. butter or bacon fat
3 bay-leaves
2 shallots

½ pint water or stock
1 orange with the rind removed, thinly sliced
¼ oz. butter and flour worked together (beurre manié)
a good ½ gill cream
slices of orange, fried
chopped parsley to garnish

Stuffing

2 tablespoons fresh white crumbs
2 tablespoons chopped parsley
5 oz. raisins, stoned and split
grated rind and juice of 1 large orange

seasoning
1 oz. butter
2 shallots, finely chopped
2 tablespoons shelled walnuts, coarsely chopped
beaten egg

Crush the anchovy with the garlic to a paste, then with a sharp-pointed knife make 12–16 incisions all over the surface of the joint. Work the paste well into these. Prepare the stuffing as follows:

Put the crumbs, parsley, raisins, and orange rind together and season well. Heat the butter in a small pan, add the shallots, soften slightly, add the walnuts and allow to colour. Cool a little and then add to the crumbs. Bind with beaten egg and orange juice to make a good moist mixture. Stuff into the joint and sew up with a coarse thread or string. Heat the butter or fat for roasting in a roasting-tin, put in the meat, baste, add the shallots, bay-leaves, liquid, and sliced orange. Put into a moderate oven and cook, basting fairly frequently, for about 2 hours. If the liquid in the pan reduces too much, add a little extra water or stock to keep the quantity to about 1½ gills. Serve the meat on a hot dish, then draw out the threads with care. Strain the gravy into a small saucepan, déglacer the tin with a little stock or water and add to the gravy. Thicken very slightly with beurre manié, reboil, add the cream, boil hard for a minute or two, then pour into a sauce-boat.

Garnish the dish with slices of fried orange, and finish with a sprinkling of chopped parsley.

PAIN DE VEAU FERMIÈRE

Ingredients for the veal cream

¾ lb. raw minced veal, weighed when minced
1½ oz. butter
1½ oz. flour

1½ gills water
seasoning
2 eggs

Garnish

½ a cabbage heart
1 oz. butter
2 large carrots
3 tomatoes

seasoning and chopped herbs
a handful of pickling or spring onions

Sauce

½ oz. butter	lemon juice
½ oz. flour	1 yolk of egg
1½ gills veal stock	¼ gill top of milk

To make the veal cream.   Melt the 1½ oz. butter in a pan, stir in the flour and the seasoning off the heat.   When quite smooth pour on the water. Stir until boiling, then turn on to a plate to cool.   Add this to the veal, beating well.   Break in the eggs one at a time and mix thoroughly. Season again and rub all through a wire sieve.   Then fill this mixture into a well-buttered charlotte or plain mould and steam until firm to the touch (see note on steaming, page 71), approximately 30–40 minutes.

For the garnish.   Shred the cabbage and blanch it for 10 minutes.   Drain and return to the pan with a nut of butter.   Cut the carrots into thin rounds, blanch, return to the pan and finish cooking in a little butter. Peel and quarter the tomatoes, empty of seed.   Toss the quarters in a little butter over the fire, add seasoning and chopped herbs.   Blanch the onions for 5 minutes.   Drain and return to the pan with a nut of butter. Season and finish the cooking.

For the sauce.   Melt the ½ oz. butter in a pan, add the flour off the fire. When smooth pour on the stock and stir until boiling.   Simmer 4–5 minutes, draw aside, add a squeeze of lemon juice and the yolk of egg mixed with the milk.   Stir again for a minute or two over the fire, but do not allow to boil.

To serve.   Leave the cream for a minute or two in the mould before turning it on to a hot dish.   Then with a spoon mask it with the sauce and pour a little of this round, serving the rest separately.   Arrange the vegetables neatly round the dish.

N.B.   This cream may be made in exactly the same way with fish, chicken, and ham.

VEAL GOULASH

1 lb. veal, shoulder or leg free from bone	2 teaspoons tomato purée
1 lb. onions	1 cup sour cream or fresh cream made sour with lemon juice
¾ oz. lard	
1 cup stock (veal bouillon if possible)	1 teaspoon flour
seasoning of salt, pepper, and paprika	accompaniment of rice, spaghetti, macaroni, or nouilles, or boiled or mashed potatoes

Slice the onions finely.   Heat the lard and cook the onions until soft but not browned.   When cooked rub through a sieve.   Cut the veal in 2-inch squares, add to the onions in the pan and cover with the stock. Add salt, pepper, and paprika to taste and simmer gently 45 minutes to 1 hour, or until tender.   Then add the tomato purée and the flour slaked with the sour cream.   Reboil and serve with boiled or mashed potatoes or rice, spaghetti, macaroni, or nouilles.   A small wineglass of white wine added just before the cream is an improvement.

SAUTÉ DE VEAU MARENGO

1 lb. veal fillet, or oyster or
  knuckle of veal
1 good dessertspoon each of oil
  and clarified butter
2 medium onions, sliced
1 wineglass white wine
1 teaspoon flour
a clove of garlic crushed with
  salt

a scant ½ pint stock
a bouquet garni
salt and pepper
½ lb. tomatoes, peeled, cut in
  thick slices, and the seeds
  removed
4 oz. mushrooms
fried bread croûtons
chopped parsley

Cut the veal into large squares.   Heat the oil and butter in the sauté
pan, add the veal and onions and sauter fairly quickly to a good brown.
Add the wine, simmer for a few minutes, dust with flour, add the crushed
garlic, stock, bouquet, seasoning, and tomato, cover and simmer gently
till the veal is tender, 30–40 minutes.   Cut the mushrooms in quarters
and sauter separately.   Dish the veal, removing the herbs, reduce the
sauce, spoon over the meat, and garnish with bouquets of the mushrooms,
surround with the croûtons and scatter parsley over the dish.

VEAU EN CASSEROLE

½ lb. fillet of veal
¾ oz. dripping
½ a small onion
¾ oz. flour
½ pint stock
a little Worcestershire sauce

seasoning
1 or 2 tomatoes or 2 teaspoons
  tomato purée
1½ oz. bacon, blanched
¾ lb. potatoes, blanched
shavings of butter or dripping

Cut the veal into strips.   Fry these in dripping to a golden brown a
few pieces at a time and remove.   Add the sliced onion and fry gently
until soft.   Add the flour and allow to brown.   Add the stock, Worcestershire sauce, and seasoning and bring to boil.   Add the peeled, sliced
tomatoes and simmer for 10 minutes.   Put layers of veal, blanched bacon,
and blanched sliced potatoes into a casserole.   Strain the stock over these.
Add a few shavings of dripping or butter and cover with a lid, stand the
casserole in a baking-tin with a little water in it.   Bake in a moderate oven
for 1½ hours, removing the lid for the last half-hour.

For Veal and Ham Pie see page 630.

XVIII

Meat—Les Abats

THE word offal has unpleasant connotations, although during and for some years after the war it was used more appreciatively than was once the case. In fact, esteem for the butcher was for a time in direct ratio to the amount of offal he could provide. All the same, an out-of-date prejudice still holds, and cover is taken under the French name, which at any rate assails the ears less distastefully.

Les abats comprise generally liver, kidney, brains, head, tongue, sweetbreads, heart, tripe, and trotters. It is not necessary to hang offal, as it must be eaten while absolutely fresh. The calf furnishes most of these at their best, but it may be well to tabulate and estimate these products under each of our principal food-producing beasts.

THE CALF

Head. This is usually first cooked by boiling and is then served with a variety of sauces, and it may be eaten hot or cold. It produces a rich gelatinous meat, is easily digested, and is generally served with slices of the tongue and sometimes with a sauce made of the brains. Brown, poulette, vinaigrette, or tomato sauces are also usual accompaniments. It is used also as a basis for soup and is the principal ingredient of a mock turtle.

Brains. These are considered a delicacy, and after preliminary boiling may be served in a variety of ways.

Liver. This is tender and of good flavour.

Kidneys. These are less delicate than lambs' kidneys and are larger in size; frequently used for entrées and sautés.

Tongue. This is delicate in texture and flavour. Approximate weight 1–2 lb.

Sweetbreads. These are of delicate flavour and much esteemed; the usual allowance is one pair for two people.

Calves' feet. Used for making jelly or to add to the gelatinous consistency of certain meat dishes, as in Bœuf à la Mode.

SHEEP AND LAMB

Head. Chiefly used for broth.

Sweetbreads. Used as calves' sweetbreads, but much smaller; they are generally sold by the pound and are good for ragoûts.

Kidney. Lambs' kidneys are delicate and particularly suitable for grilling.

Heart. Generally weighs about 12 oz. to 1 lb. and may be stuffed and roasted.

Tongue. Approximate weight 8–12 oz.

THE PIG

Head. This is used for brawn.

Kidneys and Liver. These are used in certain dishes but are larger than those of calves and sheep. They are used for sautés and ragoûts and may be grilled.

Trotters. Called also pettitoes or crubeens; they are usually sold cooked.

Pigs' blood is used for making black puddings.

THE OX

Heart. This is large, weighing about 3–4 lb., and is hard and indigestible. If it must be used it requires soaking overnight in vinegar and water (2 tablespoons vinegar to each quart of water).

Liver. This is coarse and strong and is best used as one of the ingredients in a terrine.

Kidneys. These are sometimes used with other things, for example with steak in a pie or pudding, but are not usually served alone.

Tongue. This is excellent in texture and flavour, weighing 4–6 lb. raw, and is bought either fresh or salted.

Tail. Used for soups and stews.

Tripe. Is usually sold cleaned and blanched, but requires further cooking for another hour. It is particularly easily digested.

KIDNEYS

Kidneys should come from the butcher surrounded with their fat, which is known as kidney suet. That of sheep or lamb is excellent for rendering down for frying and roasting, while the fat round ox kidney is the suet used for suet crust for puddings and, rendered down, gives the purest of fats for deep fat frying. Sheep or lambs' kidneys are generally employed either in mixed grills or as a breakfast dish.

Pig or pork kidney. Pigs' kidneys resemble those of lambs or sheep in appearance, but are larger. They are prepared in the same manner, though on account of their size they are usually cut right through for grilling. They are also used for sautés and ragoûts.

Veal kidneys. These are as much of a delicacy as lamb kidneys. They are, however, used for the most part in sautés, quick braises, or as entrées with rice and so on. Again they should not be overcooked, and, if cooked in a sauce, particular care must be taken that the cooking is carried out gently or they will become hard. Veal kidneys are unlike sheep's kidneys to look at in that they are divided as it were into small sections on the surface, and they have a larger and thicker core. They are skinned as for lambs' kidneys, but care must be taken that the initial cut does not penetrate the flesh if these are to be cooked whole, as is often the case. On the other hand, they are sometimes cut in slices from $\frac{1}{4}$ to $\frac{1}{2}$ inch thick. (See Rognons de Veau, page 600.)

Ox kidney. Ox kidney is used only for stews and for savoury puddings; it is considered too strong in flavour to be served alone, and unlike other kidneys calls for long, slow cooking. It is bought by weight and is cut off the core by the butcher.

GENERAL NOTE ON COOKING OF KIDNEYS

There are two generally accepted and opposing degrees in the cooking of kidneys: brown on the outside and a delicate pink within, as when they are perfectly grilled, or, as in the case of a braise or a ragoût, very well cooked throughout and completely tender.

In the recipes for sautés it will be seen that it is recommended that any juice which may run from the kidneys after they have been fried and while they are being kept hot for finishing should be added to the sauce in preparation. This instruction applies only to kidneys of first quality. If these are not of the first quality or are in the least coarse or strong, such juice should not be added.

Allow per person approximately:

2 lambs' kidneys
1 sheep's kidney
$\frac{1}{2}$ veal kidney (according to size)

To prepare kidneys for grilling. Peel off the fat and set aside. Lay the kidney on the chopping-board, the rounded side to the right hand. With a sharp knife make a nick in the skin at the side of the kidney in the middle of the curve. Draw the skin right back on each side and then, pulling all of it together gently, draw out as much of the core as possible. Cut it off close to the kidney. Lay the kidney on the board as before, and holding it flat under your left hand slice through to the core, beginning at the nick or cut first made. Now lay the kidney opened, with the cut side upper-most, on the board, and if necessary extend the cut a little to ensure that the kidney lies flat, but do not cut it completely in two. As kidneys tend to curl very much in grilling it is desirable to skewer them through to keep them as flat as possible. One used to get a wooden skewer like a large toothpick for this purpose, and the larger size of cocktail stick will serve; sometimes tiny silver skewers were used for the purpose, one for each kidney. More often now an ordinary kitchen skewer is employed on which two kidneys are impaled. The point of the skewer is stuck through one half of the kidney, starting about the middle of the cut side, and then, as it were, a big stitch is taken bringing the point of the skewer out on the other half, thus keeping the kidney open and flat.

To grill. Brush the kidneys with clarified butter and grill over fairly quick heat, starting with the cut side uppermost; 3 minutes on each side is usually enough. Kidneys should be slightly underdone or they are apt to become tough and leathery.

When the kidneys are done take the ends of the skewers in the left hand, and with the back of a knife, held in the right, push them off gently on to a round of freshly made toast either buttered or dry. A pat of green, maître d'hôtel, or anchovy butter well chilled is put in the middle of each kidney. This dish, which should be served immediately, may be garnished with watercress dipped or not, as you please, in a little French dressing. This garnish is not used if the kidneys are being served for breakfast.

ROGNONS SAUTÉS TURBIGO

4–6 sheep's kidneys, skinned
1½ oz. butter
¼ lb. chipolata sausages
2 dozen button onions, well blanched. (Put in cold water, bring to boil, boil 2 minutes)
4 oz. peeled mushrooms
seasoning
1 teaspoon tomato purée
1 level dessertspoon flour
1 tablespoon sherry
1½ gills jellied stock
1 bay-leaf
rectangular croûtons fried in a little hot oil
chopped parsley

Kidneys. Melt the butter in a sauté pan. Skin the kidneys, cut in half and remove the core. Brown first the kidneys and then the sausages quickly in the hot butter. Remove them and add to the pan the blanched button onions and the mushrooms cut into four. Season and cook 5–6 minutes, stirring occasionally. Then add the flour and leave to brown a little. Add the sherry, tomato purée, and stock. Return to the fire and stir until it boils. Replace the sausages and the kidneys, with the bay-leaf. Adjust seasoning. Cover the pan with paper and the lid and simmer gently on the fire 15–20 minutes.

Croûtons. Cut bread into rectangular pieces and fry in a little hot oil until golden brown.

Serving. Pile the kidneys on to a hot dish, surround with the croûtons and sprinkle the top with parsley.

KIDNEY IN BAKED POTATO

allow 1 large potato for each   black pepper
  person   salt
allow 1 kidney for each potato   mustard
allow 1 rasher for each kidney

Scrub the potatoes as for roasting. Bake in oven about 1 hour. Take a slice off the top and, making a hollow inside the potato, put in a kidney, skinned, seasoned with mustard, and rolled in a rasher. Season with black pepper and salt. Replace top slice. Wrap each potato in a piece of buttered paper and bake for another good hour. In this way flavour and richness are conserved and the potato is filled with the gravy.

KIDNEYS SAUTÉD WITH SHERRY

6–8 lamb kidneys
½ oz. butter or 3 tablespoons oil
  in which to sauter them
pepper and salt

Sauce
  ½ oz. butter
  scant ½ oz. flour
  1 gill clear stock (veal for
  preference)

1 heaped tablespoon finely
  chopped herbs
3 oz. mushrooms (optional)
1 oz. butter (optional)

3 tablespoons sherry
½ oz. butter to finish

Prepare the kidneys, divide in two or if preferred cut into slices, season with pepper and salt. Heat butter or oil, put in the kidneys, cook quickly on either side for 2–3 minutes until the slices become firm and turn colour, a matter of 5 or 6 minutes. Lift out of the fat, put in a dish, and cover to keep hot. Pour off the fat from the pan. Make a roux of butter and flour, cook gently until brown. Add the stock and bring to the boil, stirring constantly. Cook 4–5 minutes. Put in the kidneys with any juice that may have run from them, add the sherry, cover the pan and allow to stand for a few minutes. Continue cooking very gently for a few more minutes. Finish the sauce with the butter divided into small pieces. Adjust final seasoning. Serve in a hot dish and scatter with the chopped herbs.

Three ounces of mushrooms, sliced and sautéd in an ounce of butter, may be added as a finish to this dish.

KIDNEYS IN A WHITE WINE SAUCE

6–8 kidneys
1 oz. butter in which to sauter
  them
seasoning
2 tablespoons finely chopped
  onions
½ gill white wine
1 gill stock

½ clove of garlic
½ bay-leaf
¾ oz. butter blended with 1
  heaped teaspoon flour to
  make beurre manié
1 level tablespoon chopped
  parsley

Prepare the kidneys, slice and season them. Heat the butter in a frying-pan, cook the onions till pale gold in colour, then add the kidneys. As soon as the slices have become firm and are slightly coloured on either side, lift out, put in a hot dish, and cover. Into the pan with the onions put wine, stock, garlic, and bay-leaf. Bring to the boil, cover, and simmer for 6 or 7 minutes. Remove garlic and bay-leaf, return the kidneys and any juice that has escaped from them, add the beurre manié and blend well. Continue cooking for 3 or 4 minutes, without allowing the mixture to boil. Serve on a hot dish, spoon over the sauce, and sprinkle with chopped parsley. This dish may be surrounded with fried croûtons.

KIDNEYS COOKED IN A CHAFING-DISH

Three veal kidneys cooked partially and quickly in butter as in the foregoing recipes till brown on all sides. They may be done in the kitchen and brought to the dining-room in a hot fireproof dish. In the dining-room mix together a tablespoon or two of sherry, the juice of half a lemon, a small teaspoon of mustard, and a dash of cayenne. Warm these in the chafing-dish, add the finely sliced kidneys and continue cooking, being careful not to overcook. They should be slightly pink on the inside. Add a little finely chopped parsley just before serving.

KIDNEYS WITH ONIONS

6–8 lamb kidneys or 4–6 sheep
   kidneys, sliced finely
4 large onions
butter or oil for frying
approx. ¼ pint strong well-
   reduced stock, or demi-

glace sauce, short method
   (see page 144)
1 level tablespoon chopped
   parsley
juice of ¼ lemon
fried croûtons

Slice the onions finely, cook them in butter or oil until a good golden brown. Remove from pan and keep warm. Put in the kidneys, add more butter if necessary, and fry quickly 4–5 minutes, then add the stock, parsley, and lemon juice. Heat all together, pile the onions in the centre of the dish, surround with kidneys and croûtons.

KIDNEYS AU VIN BLANC '31'

6 sheep kidneys
1½ oz. butter
a clove of garlic
1 shallot
½ oz. flour
salt and pepper

2 oz. mushrooms
1 teaspoon chopped herbs
¼ pint white wine
¼ pint stock
3 large tomatoes
croûtons

Melt the butter in a sauté pan, add the chopped garlic and shallot and sauter 3–4 minutes. Skin the kidneys, prepare them, and cut across in thick slices. Add to the pan and cook quickly, shaking well, 4–5 minutes; draw aside, stir in the flour, seasoning, sliced mushrooms, herbs, wine, and stock. Bring to boil and simmer 10 minutes. Skin, quarter, and pip the tomatoes, and add to the pan a minute or two before dishing up. Turn the contents of the pan into a deep dish and surround with croûtons. Serve at once.

ROGNONS DE VEAU AU VIN BLANC

2–3 veal kidneys
1 oz. butter (scant weight)
1 dessertspoon olive oil
3 finely chopped shallots
1 wineglass dry white wine

½ pint demi-glace sauce, short method (see page 144)
chopped parsley
garnish (optional) of button mushrooms and baby tomatoes.

Skin the kidneys in the way described (page 596), cut into slices ⅛ inch thick. Heat a sauté or frying-pan and drop in the oil and butter. When foaming put in the kidneys and sauter rapidly for a few minutes until turning colour (just tinged with brown). Remove on to a hot plate. Add the shallots to the pan, sauter a minute or two, déglacer the pan with the wine and reduce to half. Now add the demi-glace and simmer 5 minutes. Skim and strain into a fresh pan, add the pieces of kidney, reheat gently but do not boil. Serve *en timbale* in a hot dish with a garnish of sautéd button mushrooms and baby tomatoes. Dust over with chopped parsley. Serve with rissolé potatoes.

For Rognons d'Agneau Marsala see Winkfield chapter, page 1002.

KIDNEYS SAUTÉD WITH A DEVIL CREAM SAUCE

6–8 lambs' or sheep's kidneys
1 oz. butter
2 oz. finely chopped shallots
1 wineglass white wine or good stock
salt, freshly ground pepper (cayenne)

¼ pint cream
1 teaspoon anchovy essence
1 tablespoon each of Worcestershire and Harvey sauce (or mushroom ketchup)

Skin the kidneys in the way described (page 596). Cut them in slices about ⅛ inch thick. Heat a sauté or thick frying-pan, drop in the butter and when foaming put in the kidneys. Sauter over full heat 3–4 minutes until the pieces have thickened and are turning colour. Take them out at once and turn into a small gratin dish.

Put the shallots into the frying-pan. Cook for a few minutes, then déglacer the pan with the wine, stirring well. Reduce the wine to half, then pour it over the kidneys. Season well. Whip the cream, adding the essence and sauces during the process. Season highly and when a light creamy consistency coat over the kidneys. Bake in a hot oven to a light brown. Serve at once as a first course or as a savoury.

STEAK AND KIDNEY PIE (AND PUDDING)

See Beef, pages 534–5.

LIVER

GENERAL NOTES

Take calf's liver for choice, failing this sheep's or lamb's. In calf's liver choose the palest—avoid a bluish tint in all liver.

Allow approximately 3–3½ oz. per person.

Wipe with a damp cloth and remove the thin outside tissue and any veins. Cut in slices from ¼ to ½ inch thick; cut evenly or they will cook unequally.

Ox liver is coarse in flavour and texture, and if this is to be used the slices may be soaked in salted water (a dessertspoon to the quart) for an hour or more before being blanched for 5 minutes as a preliminary to final cooking.

Grilling. Cut the liver into slices, brush over with oil or melted butter, season well with pepper, and cook for 4–5 minutes on each side under a really hot grill. A second brushing with oil or butter during cooking is strongly advised.

Frying. Slice the liver, season with salt, pepper, and a squeeze of lemon juice. Coat with flour to give the slices a crisp surface. Fry on each side in hot butter, bacon fat, dripping, or oil for 3–4 minutes. Serve on a hot dish.

Fried liver may be accompanied by fried bacon, onion, tomatoes, and a variety of hot sauces which, too, should be well flavoured and seasoned, and of not too bland a nature. It should be borne in mind that liver is rich and that a sauce tending towards piquancy is called for.

Liver with the sauce italienne (simple) on page 181 is good. Cook the liver in the way required, arranging the slices round a dish, pour the sauce in the centre, and serve with quarters of lemon.

BROCHETTES OF LIVER AND MUSHROOMS
WITH CRISP ONION RINGS

¾ lb. calf's liver	4 tablespoons oil for rolling
4 lean rashers	skewers
2 oz. mushrooms	seasoning, lemon juice, and
½ oz. butter and 1 tablespoon	chopped parsley
oil	2–3 large onions sliced and
4 tablespoons breadcrumbs	cooked as for onion rings
	(page 200)

Cut the bacon and liver in squares and peel the mushrooms. Heat the butter and oil till smoking and sauter the liver over a quick fire 2 minutes. Lift out and put on to a hot plate. Cook the mushrooms in the fat in the pan for about 2 minutes on each side.

Thread liver, mushroom, and bacon on skewers, putting a square of liver last.   Roll the skewerfuls in the oil and then in breadcrumbs.   Set aside for 10 minutes or until ready to grill.   Sprinkle with remaining oil. Grill gently 10–12 minutes.   Sprinkle with seasoning, lemon juice, and chopped parsley.   Pile up the onion rings on a dish and surround with the skewers of liver.

Another method

Marinade the liver and mushrooms in a good devil sauce before grilling, and put a sage leaf between each layer on the skewer.   Serve with a devil sauce.

BROCHETTES A L'ITALIENNE

See rice chapter, page 384.

LIVER AND BACON

¾–1 lb. calf's liver	2 or 3 thin slices of onion
seasoning and flour	hot water
butter or bacon fat for frying	lemon juice
1 or 2 rashers per person	chopped parsley

Slice the liver ½ inch thick.   Season with salt and pepper and dip in flour.   Heat the butter or bacon fat.   Fry the slices of liver 3–4 minutes on each side.   Put on a hot dish.   Fry the bacon till crisp and arrange over the liver.   Put the thin slices of onion into the hot fat and cook until golden brown.   Remove them, drain, and arrange on dish.   Put a little seasoning and a few tablespoons of hot water in the pan to make a little brown gravy.   Sprinkle the liver with lemon juice, gravy, and chopped parsley and arrange in dish with bacon on each slice.

CASSEROLE OF LIVER WITH OLIVES AND MUSHROOMS

1 lb. liver	3 or 4 medium-sized onions, finely sliced and chopped and browned in a little dripping or oil
4 rashers	
4 oz. mushrooms, sliced	
1 oz. butter	
¾ oz. flour	1 dozen turned olives
¼ pint good stock	juice of ½ lemon
seasoning	

Trim and slice the liver.   Fry the rashers and cut up into small pieces. Fry the liver brown on each side, in the bacon fat, for about 2 minutes. Put the liver in a casserole.   Sauter the sliced mushrooms in bacon fat till lightly brown, lift out and set aside.   Add the butter to the fat in the pan and heat.   Add flour and make a brown roux.   Add stock and seasoning.   Bring to boil, skim well, and strain over liver in casserole.   Add browned onions and chopped bacon.   Cover and cook very gently in the oven 40–50 minutes.   Then add sautéd mushrooms and olives.   Cook for another half-hour.   Add lemon juice, adjust seasoning, and serve in casserole.

FOIE A LA BONNE FEMME

a little bacon fat or butter	1 dozen small onions
1–1½ lb. liver	1 dessertspoon flour
¼ lb. lean bacon or ham	½ gill white wine or cider
2 or 3 potatoes or 6–8 tiny new potatoes	½ pint stock
	seasoning
2 mushrooms	a bouquet garni

Heat the fat in a thick pan or casserole, put in the piece of liver whole and sauter it quickly on all sides for about 5 minutes. Meantime cut the bacon into lardons, the potatoes into olive shapes, and the mushrooms in quarters. Then remove the liver from the casserole and put in the mushrooms, bacon, onions, and potatoes. Rissoler them lightly, scatter over a dessertspoon of flour, mix well and pour on the wine and stock. Bring to the boil, season, add the bouquet and the liver and simmer or braise in the oven for about 40–50 minutes. Take up, carve the liver in thin slices, lay on a serving dish, boil up the sauce and spoon it carefully over the liver.

FOIE DE VEAU AUX ORANGES

See rice chapter, page 384.

SWEETBREADS

Allow 2 pairs of calf's sweetbreads or about 1 lb. lamb's sweetbreads for 4 people. Soak in cold water for about 4 hours. As soon as the water becomes tinged with pink change it; this may be necessary several times. The sweetbreads should not be cooked until all trace of blood has been removed.

Blanch the sweetbreads by putting into a pan of cold water and bringing to boil; allow to boil 2 minutes. Lift out the sweetbreads with a strainer and put into cold water (throw away the water in which they were blanched); dry on a clean cloth. Remove as much skin and membrane as possible.

The sweetbreads are now ready to cook in a variety of ways. They may be braised with sherry and lemon juice, or cut into small pieces, mixed with a thick béchamel, and used in cassoulettes or as a filling for vol-au-vent cases. They may be fried: seasoned, dipped into egg and breadcrumbs and fried in butter in a frying-pan, and served with sauté mushrooms.

BRAISED SWEETBREADS

2 pairs sweetbreads blanched in the way described above	yolk of 1 egg
	2 tablespoons cream
½ pint stock	salt and freshly ground pepper
2 tablespoons sherry	squeeze of lemon juice
4 oz. mushrooms	12 turned olives (see page 48)
1 oz. butter	

Break up the sweetbreads, season with freshly ground pepper and salt, put into a fireproof dish. Mix stock with sherry and pour over sweetbreads. Slice mushrooms and sauter in butter. Arrange them round and over sweetbreads, cover with buttered paper and cook in moderate oven 15 minutes. Drain off the liquid into a small pan, reduce a little, make a liaison with yolk of egg and cream and add to liquor (see page 140). Reheat if necessary, but do not boil. Squeeze a little lemon juice over the sweetbreads, pour over the sauce. Allow to stand 5–10 minutes to blend flavours. Garnish with turned olives and serve.

BRAISED SWEETBREADS WITH FRENCH PLUMS

2 pairs calf's sweetbreads	1 wineglass red wine
1 oz. butter	$\frac{1}{2}-\frac{3}{4}$ pint strong veal stock
1 doz. button onions	1 bay-leaf
1 doz. French plums (if prunes, soak overnight)	chopped parsley
	potato purée (page 203)
$\frac{1}{2}$ oz. flour	croûtons

Prepare sweetbreads as described above (i.e. blanch and drain). Heat a sauté pan or shallow stew-pan. Drop in the butter and when foaming put in the sweetbreads, sauter on both sides until a pale golden brown. Remove them, add the onions, and when turning colour add the plums. Shake and stir over the fire for another few minutes, then remove. Add the flour and allow to colour slowly. Draw aside, add the wine, stock ($\frac{1}{2}$ pint to begin with), and bay-leaf. Bring to the boil, add the sweetbreads, onions, plums, and more stock, if necessary, barely to cover the sweetbreads. Put a piece of paper under the lid, cover and braise in a moderate oven for 40 minutes to 1 hour.

The stock should be well reduced and the sweetbreads have a glazed and shiny appearance. If this is not so reduce the sauce further.

Remove the sweetbreads carefully and cut each into three or four slanting slices. Dish these on a good potato purée and spoon over the sauce and garnish.

The sweetbreads may be dished *en couronne* as an alternative, with the garnish in the centre and the sauce over. Surround with 6–8 croûtons of fried bread, crescent- or heart-shaped. Dust over with chopped parsley.

CALF'S HEAD

There are two main methods of preparation:

1. The head may be boned out before cooking. The advantage of this is that the bones can be browned and cooked as for a fond brun, thus giving an extra quantity of good brown stock for use as a soup or for a sauce for the head. In this method the head is cooked apart, collared, braised, *à la poulette*, etc., and is more easily and economically sliced.

2. The head is cooked with the bones in. It can then be served whole

(or halved, if a half-head only is required) or, when cooked, the bones may be gently pulled out before pressing and serving. The only real advantage of this method is that it saves a little time.

The old-fashioned way was to serve the head whole so that it could be carved at the table. In this way each person was helped to a piece of the choicest morsels, both fat and lean, the tongue and brains were served on a separate dish, and the appropriate sauce in a boat. Nowadays people shudder at the thought of seeing a head on a dish, and it really looks more palatable and appetizing dished as an entrée.

N.B. Pig's head may be treated in the same way.

The number of people a calf's head will serve depends to some degree on whether it is to be eaten hot or cold—like other meats it goes further when carved cold—and on whether the tongue and brains are served with it. It may be said roughly that a whole head will serve 8–10 people.

CALF'S HEAD A LA POULETTE

½ or a whole small calf's head
1 medium-sized onion
1 medium-sized carrot
a bouquet garni
a few peppercorns

1 pint poulette sauce (approx.)
(see page 154)
freshly ground pepper
salt
boiled potatoes

Well scrub the head, first removing the brain. Soak for about half an hour in salted water, then rinse and put into a pan with the vegetables and herbs and cold water just to cover. Add peppercorns, bring to the boil, cover the pan and simmer until the bones can be detached easily from the head, about 2–3 hours. Take up, remove the bones, skin the tongue and cut into slices. Cut the rest of the head into 2–inch squares. Place the head and tongue in a pan, season with salt and freshly ground pepper, add enough sauce to moisten well and reheat slowly and carefully without reboiling. A double saucepan or bain-marie is best for this.

To serve pile the pieces of head on a very hot dish, coat with a little more sauce if necessary. Serve with boiled potatoes.

An alternative way of dishing is to reshape the head after boning, lightly press and leave until the next day. It can then be cut up as before and reheated in the sauce.

CALF'S HEAD VINAIGRETTE

½ or whole calf's head
sauce vinaigrette (page 367)

lemon quarters
brown bread and butter

Prepare the calf's head as for 'à la Poulette.' Shape and press lightly after cooking, and leave until the next day. Slice thinly and cover with a good sauce vinaigrette. Allow to marinade some hours before serving.

This may be served with lemon quarters and brown bread and butter and is used for a first course.

For Collared Head see 'Pièces Froides,' page 619.

DEVILLED CALF'S HEAD

½ calf's head, cooked as for 'à la Poulette,' boned and lightly pressed
1 beaten egg
browned breadcrumbs
1½ oz. butter

1½ gills stock from the head
barbecue sauce (page 728) or sauce Robert (page 148)
quarters of lemon and boiled potatoes

Trim the head, brush over with the egg and roll in the crumbs, pressing them well on. Set it in a roasting-tin, melt the butter and sprinkle half over the head. Add the stock and put into a hot oven for 20–30 minutes, or until a rich brown, basting occasionally with the liquor in the pan. Five minutes before it is done sprinkle over the rest of the butter.

Dish either as it is or cut in slices. Pour round a little of the sauce to cover the dish and serve the remainder in a sauce-boat.

Accompaniment. Quarters of lemon and boiled potatoes.

RAGOÛT OF CALF'S HEAD
with onions, mushrooms, and red wine sauce

½ calf's head, cooked as for 'à la Poulette' and pressed
1 oz. dripping or oil, good weight
1 dozen button onions
4–6 oz. mushrooms
1 oz. flour
1 dessertspoon tomato purée or ¼ pint fresh tomato pulp

¾ pint good, strong veal stock (the liquor from the head may be used)
1 glass red wine (optional)
¼ of an orange
chopped parsley
triangular croûtons of fried bread

Cut the head into 2-inch pieces. Prepare the sauce by heating the dripping in a shallow stew-pan or sauté pan, add the onions and sauter briskly until turning colour. Then add the mushrooms and continue to cook for 3 or 4 minutes. Sprinkle in the flour, lower the heat and allow to colour. Draw aside, add the tomato, stock, and wine (1 pint of liquid in all). Bring to the boil and simmer, uncovered, skimming when necessary, for 10–15 minutes or until syrupy. Add the pieces of head and reheat gently.

Serve the head *en timbale* (i.e. piled up in the middle of the dish). Reduce the sauce rapidly for a minute or two, finish with a squeeze of orange juice. Spoon the sauce and garnish over the head, sprinkle with chopped parsley and surround with the croûtons.

BRAINS

Brains are very easily digested. One pound serves 4 people. Calves' brains are best, those of sheep or lamb second best. Soak brains at least 4 hours in cold water, changing it frequently. Pull off the skin. Put brains in tepid water to remove any remaining traces of blood.

Preliminary cooking. Method 1.

Make a court bouillon with:

1 quart water	2 tablespoons vinegar
1 teaspoon salt	a bouquet garni and 6 pepper-
1 onion stuck with 2 cloves	corns

Strain this bouillon over the brains in a stew-pan and bring to boil. Simmer very gently, for sheep's brains 15 minutes, for others 20–25 minutes. Drain.

Method 2 (quicker way).

Soak and prepare as indicated above. Poach 15–20 minutes in water sufficient to cover them well, to which has been added salt and a tablespoon or two of vinegar. In no circumstances must the water be allowed to boil. Cool the brains in the liquor before using for final dish.

They may now be served in a variety of ways:

(*a*) *Au beurre noir.*

(*b*) Marinaded in lemon juice, parsley, oil, and seasoning, then drained, egged and crumbed, and fried in butter, or dropped in fritter batter and fried in deep fat.

(*c*) Mixed with a good béchamel they may fill cassoulettes or vol-au-vent cases.

FRITOT OF BRAINS (FRITOT DE CERVELLES)

calves' or sheep's brains, 1 or 2 sets, prepared as above	sauce Robert (page 148), rémoulade (page 168), or
1 tablespoon lemon juice	tomato (page 178)
salt and pepper	lemon quarters
several large sprays of parsley	

Batter

4 oz. flour	1 egg white
1 tablespoon melted butter or oil	salt and pepper
1 egg yolk	¼ pint ale

Make up the batter in the usual way (see page 432), reserving the egg white. It must be thick and just drop nicely from the spoon. Leave to stand. Meantime divide the brains into pieces (about 8–10), marinade for half an hour in the lemon juice, salt and pepper. Whip the white of egg and fold into the batter.

Put the pieces of brain in a bowl, pour over enough batter to cover them. Have a pan of smoking hot fat ready, lift out the pieces of brain with a fork and drop into this. Fry till golden brown and drain well on crumpled paper. Dip the parsley into the batter and fry also.

Dish brain and parsley fritters together and serve very hot with an accompanying sauce and quarters of lemon.

FRITTO MISTO OF BRAINS, KIDNEY, SWEETBREADS, ETC.

All ingredients must be prepared in the ways already described. Brains, after cooking, should be cut up into suitably sized pieces and egged, breadcrumbed, and fried.

Liver may be fried or grilled.

Sweetbreads may be dipped in batter and fried.

Lemon fritters (see page 1007) are admirable as a part of this dish, and the whole should be served with a sharp sauce such as rémoulade (page 168) or piquante (page 177).

HEARTS

GENERAL NOTES

To prepare cut away veins and arteries. Wash well in cold water. In the case of ox hearts soak for some hours or overnight in water with vinegar (1 tablespoon per pint of water).

The flesh is lean, dry, and close in texture, and basting therefore is of importance; it has not much flavour so a good stuffing is essential. Hearts are generally stuffed and roasted, and served with gravy and red-currant jelly, but ½-inch slices of the meat may also be sautéd.

The amount of stuffing required may be from 1 gill for each small calf's or sheep's heart to four or five times this quantity for an ox heart. Highly seasoned and highly flavoured stuffings containing plenty of herbs and fruit are suitable.

BAKED STUFFED HEART

2 or 3 hearts of calves or sheep according to size (1 lb. of flesh
serves approximately 3 people)

Wash and prepare the hearts. Make a suitable stuffing, e.g. prune and apple, or sage and onion with pickled walnuts, or orange and anchovy. Fill in the heart cavities and sew up with a needle and thread. Put the hearts in a baking-tin with about ½ pint stock. Cover with buttered paper. Bake 1½–2 hours, basting well. Make a simple gravy in the pan by thickening the liquor with beurre manié (a heaped teaspoon of flour and a dessertspoon of butter worked together). Serve with red-currant jelly.

N.B. Put ½ pint stock in to begin with and add more as this evaporates.

TRIPE

This is usually bought partially cooked or blanched and requires further cooking in salted milk and water for an hour to an hour and a half. It may be served with the onion sauce, soubise, given on page 157 and in other ways.

TRIPE JARDINIÈRE (TO SERVE 6 OR MORE)

2 lb. tripe (already blanched before buying)	1 oz. butter
	1 tablespoon oil
1 medium onion	seasoning
1 carrot	¼ pint stock
1 leek	¼ pint tomato sauce
½ root of celeriac	a bouquet garni
6 mushrooms	1 clove of garlic, crushed

Slice all vegetables finely, cook in butter and oil, adding mushrooms after the others have softened. Add tripe cut in strips, continue cooking 2 or 3 minutes, season. Barely cover with stock and tomato sauce, add bouquet and garlic. Bring to boil, reduce heat. Cook gently 1–1½ hours. Skim carefully and serve.

FRIED TRIPE AND ONIONS

1½ lb. cooked tripe [1]	1 clove of garlic
1½ tablespoons flour	a touch of cayenne
seasoning	1 tablespoon chopped parsley
3 onions	juice of 1 lemon and 1 lemon
1 oz. butter	cut in quarters
1 tablespoon oil	brown bread and butter

Cut tripe in strips, season and toss in flour. Fry in deep fat till golden and crisp. Drain.

Slice the onions, heat butter and oil in pan, fry onions and crushed garlic till pale gold. Add tripe, season well and add cayenne. Cook all together for a few minutes, add parsley and lemon juice and serve with lemon quarters and brown bread and butter.

Tripe may also be cut 2 inches wide by 3 inches long and dipped in flour, egged and breadcrumbed, and fried in deep fat; serve with sauce Robert (page 148), or tomato barbecue sauce (pages 178 and 728).

TRIPE IN THE GENOESE MANNER

2 lb. tripe previously cooked [1]	1 lb. tomatoes peeled, pipped, and chopped, or 2 table- spoons tomato purée
1 onion (large)	
1 gill oil	
1 bay-leaf	1 clove of garlic
1½ oz. dripping	seasoning, rosemary, and chopped parsley
a few dried mushrooms soaked first in boiling water and well chopped (optional)	a little nutmeg
	a little stock or water
1 gill dry white wine or dry cider	a few small potatoes (optional)

[1] Although bought partially cooked, the tripe must be cooked at home for a further hour in salted milk and water before being fried.

Cut the tripe into fine strips about 3½–4 inches long. Cut up the onion. Put the oil into a deep pan, add the onion, bay-leaf, dripping, and mushrooms, if available. Cook until the onion turns colour, add the tripe and white wine or cider and cover the pan, allowing the wine to reduce gradually. Add tomatoes or tomato purée, crushed garlic, chopped parsley, a pinch of chopped rosemary, seasoning, and grated nutmeg. Allow to cook slowly for about 1 hour. From time to time add a little stock or plain water. When cooked the tripe should have absorbed all the moisture and be of a rich, creamy consistency. If potatoes are to be added they should go in with the tomatoes and then extra liquid will be needed for the cooking. Otherwise the potatoes can be served separately, plainly boiled.

TONGUES

Ox tongue

If an ox tongue has not already been salted by the butcher the process may be carried out at home. The tongue is put into a brine bath of the type given on page 612 and left in the pickle for 5–10 days according to size. If the tongue is to be served cold it may be treated in either of the following ways. After the tongue has been salted it is rinsed in fresh cold water.

For a round. Curl the tongue gently round, place it in a suitably sized saucepan, and cook in the manner to be described.

If the tongue is to be arched and glazed proceed as follows: Stick a skewer firmly through the root of the tongue; to the skewer tie tightly a piece of tape, pass the tape over the tongue to the tip, tie it firmly to the tongue just above the tip, drawing the tongue into a slightly arched position. Put the tongue into a saucepan large enough to allow it to be covered with water.

In either case proceed with the cooking as follows:

Having covered the tongue with cold water, add vegetables and herbs called for in the recipe, bring gently to the boil and simmer 4–5 hours, depending on the size of the tongue. The cooking must continue till the tongue is extremely tender; one indication is that the small bones at the root almost detach themselves, another is, as Mrs Beeton says, that the tongue may be readily pierced by a straw. Allow the tongue to cool slightly in the liquor before lifting it out and draining. Skin carefully.

If for a round the root must be trimmed, the bones removed, and the tongue tightly curled and fitted into a circular tin; a 9-inch cake tin will serve the purpose for a tongue of average size.

If a jellied tongue is called for, a little good clear jellied stock or aspic is now poured into the tin. It is probable that the stock in which the tongue was cooked will be too salt for the purpose. A plate is now put on the top and must just fit inside the tin; a heavy weight—at least 7 lb.—is placed on top. This is left in position overnight.

For a glazed arched tongue. Skin the tongue, and remove the bones at the root. Set it on a board and fasten the root securely to this by means of a skewer or carving-fork. Take a moderately heavy weight, cover it with grease-proof paper and set it on the tip of the tongue to keep the whole in a slightly arched position. When all is firm the tape may be taken away. Some authorities dispense with tape altogether, cooking the tongue as it is, then skinning and boning and finally pressing it into position on the board in the way described. This has an advantage in that there is then no fear of the tape cutting or marking the tip, which can happen in a particularly tender tongue. After shaping in this way the tongue is left fastened to the board overnight and is then well glazed (see glazing, page 52). In serving a glazed tongue the slices are cut about $\frac{3}{4}$ inch thick across the grain, and the carver should take slices both from the centre and the root end for each individual helping.

For hot dishes fresh, unsalted tongue is sometimes used; in this case it is thoroughly cleaned and given a preliminary soaking in cold water, then cooked as for salted tongue. It is skinned, sliced, and used as the recipe indicates, or it may be pressed and left until cold to be sliced as required and warmed up gently in an appropriate sauce. Another method of cooking is to simmer the tongue until three parts cooked and then to finish off by braising.

It should be noted that the proper way to prepare hot dishes of tongue is to carry out the process described: in other words, to cook fresh tongues expressly for the purpose. In these days, however, it is a more common practice to buy slices of cooked salted tongue. If these are to be heated the process must be gentle, and any one of the appropriate sauces given for fresh tongue is suitable.

Smoked tongues

Ox tongues are sometimes sold smoked; they are then soaked for 12 hours before simmering as for a salted tongue.

Calves' or pigs' tongues are generally served hot and so are used unsalted. They salt well, however, and are good cold. They should be treated in the same way as for ox tongues, but only half the time allowed in the brine or pickle. For serving cold they are best pressed into a round. Use two or three and pack them into a cake tin, filling it with jellied stock which serves to keep the tongues together when turned out. Then put on the plate and weight. Approximate weight of a calf's tongue is 1–2 lb.

Lambs' or sheep's tongues are invariably served hot and unsalted. The tongues are thoroughly washed and scrubbed, given a short soaking, and simmered until they can be skinned easily and are quite tender (about 1–1½ hours in a good well-flavoured stock). They are then skinned, split, pressed between two plates with a weight on top, and left until cold. They may then be braised, sautéd, etc., and served with an appropriate garnish. Average weight 8–12 oz.

Carving

Slice cold, pressed tongues very thinly across the top of the round.   As the carving progresses gently incline the knife, so that the top of the round has a slanting surface.   This enables all the tongue to be sliced thinly, without waste, down to the last fragment.   Glazed tongues or tongues served hot, whether ox or calves', are cut in slices about ⅜ inch thick against the grain of the meat.   Sheep's tongues are usually split in two lengthways either during the cooking or just before dishing.

PICKLE FOR BEEF OR TONGUE

3 lb. kitchen salt	6 oz. brown sugar
½ oz. saltpetre	1 gallon water

Dissolve solid ingredients in water, boil for half an hour.   Skim and cool.   Put the meat or tongue into this, turning every day or two.   Allow 8–14 days for beef, according to the size of the joint, and 4–6 weeks for ox tongues.

DRY PICKLE

6 oz. salt	½ teaspoon ground cloves
2 oz. bay salt	½ teaspoon ground cinnamon
½ oz. saltpetre	½ teaspoon ground ginger
8 oz. brown sugar	½ teaspoon black pepper
1 teaspoon ground mace	

Mix spices together, then mix with the other ingredients.   Lay the tongue or meat in this mixture and rub it well in.   Leave a tongue in this 14 days, beef about 7 days, turning every day.

TO COOK AN OX TONGUE

tongue	a large bouquet garni
water	2 medium onions
salt	2 carrots
6 peppercorns	1 stalk of celery

If the tongue is salted it should be rinsed in fresh water before cooking, but if fresh soak in water with a handful of salt for about an hour.

Tie the tongue securely as described, or put it as it is into a large pan or fish-kettle (see note, page 610).   Add cold water to come 2 or 3 inches above the tongue.   If the tongue is fresh add salt to the water.   Add peppercorns, bouquet, onions, carrots, and celery.   Bring slowly to boil, skimming if necessary.   Cover the pan tightly and simmer gently about 4 hours.   Allow to cool for about an hour in the liquid.   Take out, put on a dish, remove the bones from the root of the tongue and clean off the skin. Now shape the tongue either for a pressed round or for glazing, and leave until the next day.   If tongue is required for a hot dish it may be left without shaping until quite cold and then sliced as directed.

BAKED TONGUE

Tongue, like ham, may be baked instead of boiled.   It is more interesting if it is salted or pickled first: a dry pickle may be used.   Rinse the
tongue and dry it and make a flour and water crust.

Rub a large baking-tin or dish thickly with butter or good bacon
dripping.   Lay the tongue in this and brush thickly with melted butter
or dripping; this is easier than attempting to rub the tongue over with
butter.   Roll out the paste about ½ inch thick and cover the tongue with
it, tucking it well down but not enveloping the tongue completely.   Bake
in a slow oven about 4 hours or until really tender.

Allow to cool a little in the crust before shaping and redishing for
serving cold.   For serving hot slice when cool and reheat in the sauce
chosen.   Serve with the appropriate garnish.

BRAISED TONGUE

The most satisfactory method of braising a tongue is to simmer it first
in water until about three parts cooked, or until the moment when the skin
may easily be removed.   It is then trimmed and treated as follows:

½ oz. butter or good dripping
2 rashers of bacon (optional)
6–8 oz. mixed vegetables, diced
   carrot, onion, celery, parsnip, or turnip (see mirepoix, page 39)
¼ lb. tomatoes, peeled, squeezed
   to remove seeds and water,

and chopped, or 1 teaspoon
   tomato purée
good stock
1 bouquet garni
4–6 peppercorns
beurre manié or fécule for thickening, if stock is poor in
   quality

Melt the butter in a stew-pan, lay the bacon on the bottom, add the
mirepoix, cover, and allow to sweat for 15–20 minutes on a low heat.

Set the prepared, partially cooked tongue on the mirepoix, add tomatoes,
bouquet, peppercorns, and enough stock to come half way up the side of
the tongue.   Cover with a round of paper and tightly fitting lid.   Braise
slowly for 1–1½ hours.

Lift out the tongue, set on a serving dish and keep hot.   Strain the
liquor from the mirepoix into a small saucepan and reduce rapidly to a
syrupy consistency.   If the stock is salty and poor in quality and there is a
fear of the reduced liquid being over-salt, it may be thickened (instead of
being reduced) with beurre manié or fécule.   Strain enough of this juice
over the tongue to moisten well, and serve the rest in a sauce-boat.   The
dish may be garnished with such vegetables as French beans, peas, new
potatoes, potato croquettes, etc., and should be served very hot.

See also Garnishes for Tongue, page 615.   Fresh tongues are better for
braising than salted ones.   Calf's tongues are particularly good and may
be sliced before being dished.

TONGUE WITH ALMONDS AND WHITE GRAPES

Ox or calf tongue can be used for this dish, either fresh or slightly salted.

½ oz. butter
2 oz. blanched, shredded almonds
4–6 oz. muscat or sweet white grapes
freshly ground black pepper
salt and lemon juice

¾ pint demi-glace sauce (page 143)
1 teaspoon tomato purée
1 glass Madeira or sherry
feuilletons made of puff pastry (see page 836) or croûtons of fried bread

Simmer the tongue as described on page 610. When very tender cool in the liquid, then take up, skin, trim, and slice as directed for hot tongue, that is to say across the grain of the meat. Allow 2–3 slices per person, according to the size of the tongue.

Have ready the grapes, peeled and pipped. Heat a sauté or frying-pan, drop in the butter, and when foaming put in the almonds, sauter to a light brown, then add grapes. Increase the heat and shake over the fire for 2 or 3 minutes, adding plenty of freshly ground black pepper, a small pinch of salt, and a few drops of lemon juice. Put the demi-glace in a small saucepan, add the tomato purée, bring to boil and add the contents of the sauté pan. Into the sauté pan itself put the Madeira, and reduce to half. Now add this to the contents of the small saucepan. Stir the whole and adjust the seasoning. Lay the sliced tongue in the sauté pan, pour the sauce over it and reheat gently, bringing it up to boiling-point.

Dish the slices *en couronne*. Lift out the grapes and almonds with a spoon and lay in the centre of the dish. Spoon the sauce itself over the tongue and round the dish. Surround with the feuilletons or croûtons and serve very hot with rissolé potatoes or baby new potatoes tossed in butter and plenty of chopped parsley.

A similar recipe, Langues d'Agneaux Braisées aux Raisins, will be found in the Winkfield chapter, page 1002.

LAMBS' TONGUES SAUTÉD

6 lambs' or sheep's tongues prepared and cooked as described (page 611)
1 oz. butter
2 medium-sized onions, finely sliced
4 oz. mushrooms, peeled and quartered
½ oz. flour

1 wineglass burgundy
2 wineglasses good strong stock, veal or beef (more if necessary)
seasoning
chopped parsley
croûtons in either triangular or crescent shapes

Heat a sauté pan, drop in the butter, and when foaming add the tongues and sauter them gently for 5–6 minutes. Then lift them out and keep hot.

Add the onions to the pan and sauter 4–5 minutes. Throw in the mushrooms, increase the heat and cook briskly 3–4 minutes. Now draw aside, stir in the flour and when well mixed add the wine and stock. Season lightly and bring to the boil. Draw aside, add the tongues, arranging them neatly so that the liquor just covers them. If necessary a little extra may be added. Cover with a round of grease-proof paper and simmer very gently 30–40 minutes. Shake the pan and turn the tongues over occasionally.

Arrange the tongues *en timbale* in a hot dish and coat over with the jus. There should be just enough to moisten the dish nicely. Dust with chopped parsley and surround with the croûtons.

GARNISHES FOR TONGUE

For cold tongues, pressed or glazed:

Cherry compôte (see Caneton aux Cerises, page 659)
Orange and celery salad (page 339)
Sliced fresh pineapple with cream dressing
Beetroot salad spiced with caraway seeds (page 363)
Cucumber with Swedish dressing (page 367)
Cumberland sauce (page 165)

For hot tongue

1. Spinach purée, either plain or à la crème, on which the slices of tongue may be arranged. Sauce chasseur may be poured over them and rissolé potatoes served as an accompaniment.

2. Slices of tongue may be arranged on a purée of potato delicately flavoured with nutmeg, with a sauce madère or demi-glace (pages 147 and 143) or tomato sauce poured over them, and sautéd or fried salsify served as an accompaniment. Parsnip may be substituted for the salsify.

3. 'A la bourgeoise'—braised and sliced tongue arranged on a tomato purée with a reduced gravy poured over. Glazed, quartered carrots and turnips, glazed baby onions, and small baked tomatoes may surround the dish.

4. 'A l'allemande'—braised tongue, sliced and dished with the following sauce poured over. To ¾ pint of the strained jus add 2 oz. dried currants simmered in a little stock to plump them up, and 1 tablespoon red-currant jelly. Reboil, stirring well to dissolve the jelly. Serve with red cabbage and a purée of potato.

5. 'A l'orange'—boiled tongue, fresh or salt, sliced and carefully warmed in the following sauce: ¾ pint well-reduced demi-glace, 1 teaspoon tomato purée, the juice of an orange, a dessertspoon of red-currant jelly, and a glass of burgundy. Simmer together until a syrupy consistency. Dish the sliced tongue on a pureé of potato, spoon over the sauce and

garnish with thinly cut half-slices of orange, well sautéd in butter, sprinkled with a teaspoon of castor sugar, and a little ground black pepper added while the slices are being sautéd.

An excellent sauce for tongue:

SAUCE FOR TONGUE

Take a little demi-glace sauce (page 143), add a good pinch of ground allspice, a little cinnamon, ginger, and sugar, and 1–2 tablespoons currants or sultanas which have been put in water and brought to the boil to plump them up.

XIX

Pièces Froides

THE cold table is essentially an indication of a certain degree of plenty. The dishes on it, the pressed beef, the brawn, the glazed tongue, the pork pies and all the rest, are not contrived out of pennyworths of meat. Nor can they be prepared in the few moments eked out of a busy day away from the kitchen. You may say, if you like, that the cold table is a period piece now only to be represented perhaps on the stage by succulent-looking papier mâché pieces borne high on the raised arms of suitably gorgeous pages, with a peacock's tail somewhere in the picture. But this is not really an escapist chapter. If, for example, you are in the lucky position of having your own pigs, you may want a recipe for pork pie or brawn; and at Christmas it may come your way to spice a piece of beef. In any case it is worth bearing in mind that meat cooked and not carved until cold goes further than hot meat. The pies, the pâtés, and the game dishes are by no means out of reach, and one or two of the recipes given are really economy dishes.

In private life the true cold table is disappearing along with big houses and house parties; only the tradition of the preparation of the individual dishes remains. But how well worth while to remember how good things should be prepared. Preparation for cold dishes must be started in plenty of time: this is far from being last-minute cookery. Spiced beef is a case in point; this has to be thought about, ordered, and prepared for days and days before it is to be eaten. If the spicing and pickling preliminaries are hurried the meat, instead of being melting and creamy, will be hard and unpleasing. If you kill a pig you will have the necessary genuine lard for the crust of a pork pie, which should be crisp on the outside, creamy within, and the jelly, not too firm in texture, should be well seasoned.

Aspic, which seems to have acquired almost a snobbish value in cookery, can really be an unpleasant garnish for cold dishes if it is not made of good stock and really well seasoned, and this takes time and care.

The details of the simpler, more economical dishes such as the addition of stuffed prunes to a rabbit pie, anchovies to a liver pâté, the cherries in the Savoury Flan, the mint with aspic for Lamb Cutlets, are small things which make more than a small difference in the finished dishes.

As these recipes are for large dishes such as one has for a cold buffet party, or for special occasions, they are obviously for more people than four, and the actual numbers are not given.

For good old-fashioned spiced beef both the pickling and the spicing may be done at home. There is no difficulty beyond that of remembering to start in time. The piece of meat to be chosen depends on individual taste. Brisket will give a mixture of fat and lean. Aitch-bone (a very big joint if the whole is taken) is leaner, and topside and silverside are lean.

SPICED BEEF (1) (FOR 6 LB. BEEF)

Preparations must begin a week in advance.

3 bay-leaves	6 lb. beef
1 teaspoon cloves	3 carrots
6 blades of mace	2 or 3 onions, according to size
1 level teaspoon peppercorns	a bunch of mixed herbs, in-
1 clove of garlic	cluding savory, marjoram,
2 oz. brown sugar	and a sprig of rosemary
1 lb. salt	another teaspoon of pepper-
1 oz. saltpetre	corns

Pound together the bay-leaves, cloves, mace, peppercorns, garlic, and sugar thoroughly in a mortar. Mix them with the salt and saltpetre. Rub them well into the meat and lay the meat in a bed of them. Rub this into the sides of the meat every day for 7 days. Then wash the meat and prepare for boiling. Slice and prepare carrots and onions. Tie a bunch of mixed herbs with a sprig of rosemary. Cover the meat with water, put in the vegetables, herbs, and peppercorns and bring to boiling-point. Simmer for 5 hours. The meat may then be pressed between two suitable dishes, a heavy weight being placed on the upper. This dish may be coated with meat glaze.

SPICED BEEF (2)

Preparations must begin a week in advance.

beef, say 3–4 lb.	¾ oz. saltpetre (optional)
garlic	chopped bay-leaf (optional)
2 oz. sugar, brown if possible	4 oz. salt
1 oz. pounded allspice	flour and water paste

Split the garlic and insert into the meat, rub the surface of the joint well with the sugar and leave for about 12 hours. Then rub with mixture of allspice, saltpetre, and finely chopped bay-leaf, and rub over well with salt. Keep for a week, turning and rubbing each day. Make a paste of flour and water, wrap the meat in this and bake for about 2 hours in a baking-tin with a little water in the bottom. Allow to cool, strip off the crust, let meat get absolutely cold before carving.

COLLARED BEEF

Preparations must begin a week in advance.

a thin piece of flank of beef, 4–5 lb.
6 oz. salt
1 oz. saltpetre
a bunch of parsley, including the stalks
a few sprigs of savory or leaves of sage, the same of lemon thyme and
 marjoram, and 2 or 3 small, tender sprigs of rosemary, all chopped
 extremely fine
a little celery seed
freshly ground black pepper
salt
a clove or two of garlic crushed thoroughly with a teaspoon of salt
meat glaze

Rub the piece of beef well over with salt and saltpetre. Lay it in a dish. Turn it and rub it every day for 6 or 7 days. Lift it out of the pickle, wash it over with cold water and trim well of all bone, gristle, and the inside skin. Spread the finely chopped herbs, the seasoning, and the crushed garlic on the inside of the meat, and roll up as tightly as possible. Tie in a cloth, put into the water and simmer gently 5–6 hours. Remove from the liquid, place a heavy weight on the meat, and when cold take off the cloth and glaze.

BŒUF A LA MODE

See Beef, pages 535–8.

COLLARED HEAD (FOR 8 OR 9)

Preparations must begin a day in advance.

1 calf's head	4 shallots, finely chopped
pot-herbs	grated rind of 1 lemon
6 peppercorns	1 teaspoon ground mace
salt	4 hard-boiled eggs, chopped
freshly ground pepper	meat glaze
2 gammon rashers, thinly cut	
2 large handfuls of parsley, finely chopped	

Remove the brains, wash the head thoroughly and soak for an hour in salted water. Rinse and cover with salted water, add the pot-herbs and peppercorns and simmer for 1–1½ hours, or until the bones can be detached easily. Remove the bones. Skin the tongue and cut in dice. Put the head, skin side down, on a board, season liberally with salt and freshly ground pepper. Cut the bacon into strips and scatter over the head in layers with the parsley, shallots, lemon rind, mace, eggs, and tongue. Roll the head up as tightly as possible and tie at intervals with fine string. Wrap in a cloth and tie securely. Return to the pot, making sure that the liquid completely covers the head. Simmer for 3–4 hours. Remove from the liquid, tighten the cloth, and press for 12–24 hours under a moderately heavy weight. Remove cloth and glaze.

N.B. Although this makes a fairly large joint, it is easier to do this dish with a whole head rather than a half. It keeps well.

BRAWN

Note from R. H.

'My mother used to make the following dish for us when we were children—a Cumberland habit, I think! We liked lemon juice better than the vinegar, but then not so much was used. It had *lots* of black pepper. Also, not liking fat we used shin of beef in place of brisket.'

1 pig's head, split; if large ½ a head will serve	1 large onion
1½–2 lb. shin or brisket of beef	6 peppercorns
a bouquet garni	pepper
	sauce (see below)

(Calf's head may be substituted for pig's head)

Have the pig's head salted from the butcher, or salt for a day in brine. Wash and clean it well. Put into a large pan with the beef cut in half, the bouquet, onion, and peppercorns. Just cover with water, put the lid on tightly and simmer until the meat will come off the bone, about 2 hours. Lift out the head and beef and strain the stock. Skim and put back to simmer while the meat is pulled into small pieces. Put all the pieces into a brawn mould, peppering liberally, moisten with the stock to come just level with the meat. Put on the weighted lid and leave till next day. Turn out, cut in wafer-thin slices, and serve with the following sauce.

Sauce for brawn

2 tablespoons brown sugar	½ teaspoon salt and ground black pepper
3 tablespoons vinegar (cider or white wine)	a pinch of ground cloves or nutmeg
4 tablespoons oil	
1 teaspoon English mustard, made	

Work all well together and shake or stir well before using.

GALANTINE OF BEEF (BEEF ROLL)

2 lb. lean beef, weighed free of skin, etc.	1 dessertspoon salt
1 onion	½ teaspoon pepper
¼ lb. medium fat bacon or ham, raw or cooked	2 beaten eggs
12 oz. fresh breadcrumbs	1 wineglass white wine, cider, or stock (more if necessary)
1 tablespoon chopped parsley	a small plateful of flavouring vegetables
1 dessertspoon chopped mixed herbs	a bouquet garni
a good pinch each of mace and mixed spice	meat glaze

Mince the beef, onion, and bacon together. Put into a bowl with the crumbs, parsley, herbs, spice, and seasoning. Bind with the eggs and liquid—add a little more if necessary to make the mixture hold together. Shape into a roll on a wet board, place on a double piece of grease-proof paper, roll up and tie securely at each end. Wrap in a piece of clean scalded cloth, tie as before, or sew or pin with safety-pins once or twice in the middle. Put into a large pan containing boiling water, the flavouring vegetables, a bouquet garni, and salt. Cover the pan and simmer 2 hours. Lift out carefully, tighten the cloth as much as possible and leave till cold. It is really more satisfactory to place a board on the top with two 1-lb. weights in order to give the galantine a firmer pressure than can be obtained by tightening the cloth. The result is a slightly flat top to the roll, but the firmer consistency allows thin and more even slicing. The following day remove cloth and paper and glaze well with meat glaze, giving two or three coats.

VEAL GALANTINE

3 lb. breast of veal
salt
pepper
mixed spice
teaspoon chopped mixed herbs
1½ lb. pork sausage-meat
1 glass sherry

½ lb. lean cooked ham or tongue
2 hard-boiled eggs
½ oz. pistachio nuts
2–3 quarts stock, or water with
    vegetables and herbs to flavour
meat glaze

Bone the veal. Season well with salt, pepper, spice, and the mixed herbs. Prepare force-meat by putting sausage-meat in a bowl with more seasoning and moistening with the sherry. Spread this over the meat, leaving a margin of about an inch. Cut the ham into thick strips, lay down the meat with the eggs, whole, in the middle; scatter over the nuts and roll up tightly, sewing up with fine string. Wrap in grease-proof paper and then in a cloth, tying securely. Put into boiling stock and simmer for about 2 hours. Remove cloth, wrap in a fresh piece, and press with 2–3-lb. weights. Leave till next day. Glaze with meat glaze.

PORK (OR VEAL) AND HAM GALANTINE

1 lb. pork or veal, uncooked
1 lb. cooked ham or sausage-
    meat
3–4 shallots
2 cloves of garlic crushed with
    a teaspoon of salt
1 tablespoon salt
1 teaspoon freshly ground
    pepper
1 tablespoon French mustard
1 saltspoon crushed coriander
    seed (optional)

2 tablespoons finely chopped
    herbs (savory, marjoram,
    thyme, or others to taste)
1 egg lightly beaten (or white
    only)
1 gill béchamel sauce or cream
3–4 slices of larding bacon or
    fat rashers, very thinly cut
For boiling
    3 quarts water
    ½ gill vinegar
    3 teaspoons salt

Put meats, shallots, and crushed garlic through the mincing-machine, mix in the seasonings thoroughly and mince again, add egg, sauce or cream and mix well. Shape the mixture into an oblong loaf. In the middle of a clean cloth lay the larding bacon or rashers, place the galantine on these, roll up the cloth and tie firmly.

Put an upturned dish or plate in the bottom of a saucepan, lay the galantine on it and cover with the mixture of water, vinegar, and salt. Simmer gently 2½ hours. When slightly cooled tighten cloth, press under a dish with a weight on top and leave till next day.

Cut in wafer slices, and accompanied by potato salad, or forming part of a dish of cold meats, this is excellent.

GALANTINE OF CHICKEN EN CHAUDFROID

one 4–5-lb. bird, undrawn
carrot, onion, stick of celery,
    bouquet garni
3 oz. cooked ham
3 oz. cooked tongue
2 truffles, or débris of truffle,
    chopped

½ oz. pistachio nuts
salt and freshly ground pepper
chervil, tarragon, truffle, sliced
    mushroom, or cucumber skin
    to decorate
aspic jelly for coating and
    decorating

Farce

¾ lb. sausage-meat or lean
    minced pork
1 tablespoon finely chopped
    parsley

2 finely chopped shallots
1 glass Madeira

Chaudfroid sauce

¼ pint béchamel (see page 155)

¾ gill aspic jelly with scant
    ¼ oz. gelatine dissolved in it

Bone the bird (see page 77) and set on one side. Draw the carcass, reserving the liver, heart, and gizzard. Wash and break up the bones and neck, and put these with the gizzard (well cleaned), the heart, and the vegetables and bouquet into a large pan with water to cover well. Add salt and set on the fire to simmer. Prepare the farce by adding parsley and shallots to sausage-meat and moistening with the Madeira. Cut the ham, tongue, and truffle into fine strips, blanch the pistachios and leave them whole.

Spread the bird on a board, skin side down, and level out the flesh as much as possible. Spread with half the farce and scatter the ham, tongue, truffle, and pistachios down the centre. Season with salt and freshly ground pepper and cover with the remaining half of the farce. Fold over the sides of the bird to form a neat roll, stitch securely with fine string or coarse thread. Tie up in a cloth or piece of muslin and put into the prepared stock, making sure that the liquid covers it. Simmer 2–3 hours according to the age of the bird. Turn it over once during the cooking.

When cooked lift out the galantine, tighten the cloth (or change it for a clean one), and set it between two dishes with a 4-lb. weight on the top.

Leave until the next day. Then remove cloth and stitches, place the galantine on a wire rack. Coat over with the prepared chaudfroid sauce (see page 164), allow to set. Give another coat if necessary. Decorate with chervil or tarragon leaves, thinly sliced mushroom, truffle, or cucumber skin.

Coat with a cool aspic and allow to set. Then give another coat to ensure that every part of the chaudfroid sauce is well covered with the jelly. Leave for an hour or two to set completely.

To dish set the galantine on a bed of chopped aspic, and surround with triangular blocks of cut aspic.

GALANTINE OF PARTRIDGE

Preparations should begin a day in advance.

2 plump partridges	1 truffle, chopped
Madeira	salt and freshly ground pepper

Stock

1 oz. dripping	a stick of celery
1 small carrot	3–4 pints water
1 onion	a bouquet garni

Force-meat

4 oz. pork sausage-meat	$\frac{1}{2}$ clove of garlic
1 oz. minced fat bacon	1 teaspoon mixed chopped
partridge livers	herbs
2 shallots	Madeira

Jelly

gelatine if required	a glass of Madeira

Split the skin of the partridges down the back, then work the flesh off the carcasses until they are completely boned out.

Lay each partridge, skin side down, flat on a board, and carefully trim the surfaces of the meat to make them level. Reserve any pieces so cut off. Sprinkle well with Madeira, half the chopped truffle, salt and pepper. Leave to marinade while the stock and force-meat are being prepared. For the stock break the carcass bones up, brown the carrot, onion, and celery in the dripping. Add bones and water to cover, about 3–4 pints. Bring to the boil, add a bouquet, and simmer with the lid on for about 1 hour. Then uncover and continue simmering for another half-hour.

Strain, rinse out the pan, and return the stock. Put the sausage-meat in a bowl with the bacon, sliced livers, finely chopped shallots, crushed garlic, and herbs. Work together, moistening with Madeira. Spread on the birds, scatter over the rest of the chopped truffle and the trimmings of meat. Draw up the skin, sew up with coarse thread, roll and tie firmly in a piece of muslin. Put into the boiling stock, cover and simmer 30–40 minutes. Take up, tighten the cloth, press lightly and leave till next day.

Strain the stock and when cold skim to remove all fat. If the stock is not set to a jelly, measure (making allowance for the glass of Madeira) and add enough gelatine in proportion to make a jelly that will just set, approximately ½ oz. to the pint. Clarify (see page 120); just before running the jelly through the cloth, pour in a glass of Madeira.

To serve cut the birds in slices, after removing the thread. Lay overlapping down a deep dish, and pour over enough cool jelly just to set the slices (see note on aspics, page 737). When set fill up with the jelly to cover the galantine with ¼ inch coating. Alternatively the galantine may be coated with meat glaze or brown chaudfroid and served whole, garnished with aspic.

A recipe for cold pheasant with a purée of chestnuts and red wine, Faisan aux Oranges, will be found in the Winkfield chapter, page 1009.

JELLIED VEAL

Preparations must begin a day in advance.

1 lb. lean veal, from the shoulder or knuckle	2–3 peppercorns
½ lb. gammon rasher bacon	¾ oz. gelatine (approx.)
1 small onion, sliced	2 hard-boiled eggs, sliced
a bouquet garni containing a stick of celery	1 large tablespoon chopped parsley
a strip of lemon rind and 1 clove	freshly ground pepper
	salt

Trim the veal and tie up if necessary. Cut the rind from the bacon and blanch. Put both together into a pan with the onion, bouquet, peppercorns, lemon rind, and clove. Just cover with cold water, bring slowly to the boil, cover and simmer gently until the veal is perfectly tender. Cool slightly in the liquor, then remove the veal and bacon. Taste the stock, reduce if necessary until a good flavour, and salt lightly. Dissolve the gelatine in 1 pint of the stock and put aside to cool.

Meantime cut the veal into small squares and the bacon into strips. Fill a plain or charlotte mould, cake tin, or pudding basin with the meat and eggs in layers, adding parsley and seasoning. Ladle in the cool stock carefully until the meat is covered by about ½ inch. Use more stock and gelatine in proportion, if necessary.

Leave till the following day before turning out.

LAMB CUTLETS IN MINT ASPIC

1½–2 lb. best end neck of lamb	2 egg whites whipped to a froth
a few flavouring vegetables	1 tablespoon tarragon vinegar
water	garnish of tiny new potatoes in mayonnaise and cooked baby carrots and peas tossed in French dressing
1 pint stock	
¾ oz. gelatine	
1 bunch of mint	

Trim the meat. Simmer with the flavouring vegetables and water barely to cover until tender, about 50 minutes. Leave till quite cool. Then divide into neat cutlets and trim. Put the stock into a saucepan with

Plate 17. Puff pastry (see page 836)

1. This is an important stage, known as 'la détrempe,' the mixing of the flour and water to form a firm paste. Work from the centre, gradually drawing in the flour.

2. Here the paste is made and rolled to a square. Lay the butter in one piece in the centre and fold over the paste to form a parcel.

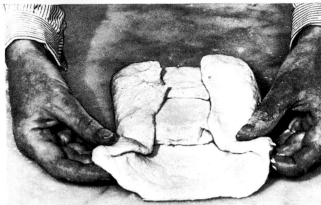

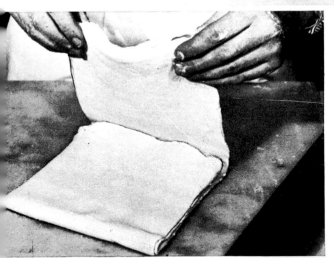

3. The paste is then rolled out away from you as directed in the recipe and folded in three as shown here. Accuracy in folding is important.

4. Mark the pastry lightly with the fingers to indicate the number of 'turns' or rollings given. This has had four. It is now in the correct position for further rolling.

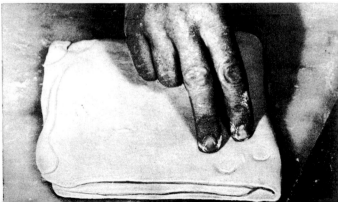

Plate 18. Making of brioche
(see page 791)

1. Here the flour is divided into four, and one part drawn aside. The yeast is creamed with the hot water and enough added to make a soft dough.

2. The completed yeast 'cake' with a cross-cut on the top is then slipped into the pan of hand-hot water.

3. The remaining flour has been mixed to a soft paste with the eggs, and milk if called for. The whole mass is then taken well up with a twist of the hand and thrown down on the slab.

Plate 19

4. This done, do not attempt to free your hand but keep in the position shown before gathering up the paste with the twisting movement. Continue until paste is thoroughly elastic.

5. When paste is well worked and glossy add the butter, and when thoroughly incorporated lift the yeast cake from the water with the hand, the fingers spread slightly open. Mix this well with the paste before putting into a floured bowl and into a refrigerator or cold place.

6. The next day, or when risen and firm, the paste may be shaped into brioches. The tops are lightly rolled into a 'tadpole' shape, ready to insert into the larger piece of paste to form a 'cottage' loaf.

7. Make three cuts with a small sharp-pointed knife round the 'tadpole'; this will have the effect of settling it in firmly. The brioches are then ready for proving, glazing, and baking.

Plate 20. Icing—various methods (see page 826)

1. *Showing the easiest method for icing éclairs or 'petits choux.'* Dip the tops into the prepared icing and reverse quickly.

2. *Method for icing small cakes.* Set on a palette-knife, the end of which is dipped into icing to prevent the cake from slipping off. Ice if possible in one movement. Push off on to rack with a small knife.

3. *Icing a large cake cooked in a moule à manqué.* The cake has been lightly glazed. Pour the prepared icing on to the centre. The knife is held in readiness to smooth round the sides of the cake if necessary.

4. The finished cake, Gâteau Cendrillon (see page 884), a génoise-filled coffee butter cream, iced with coffee fondant and decorated with grilled hazel-nuts.

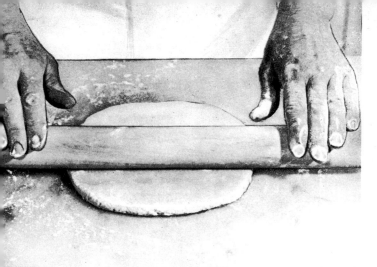

Plate 21. The process of lining a flan ring and baking blind (see page 843)

1. Rolling out pastry to an even round.

Laying it over the flan ring 'th the help of a rolling-pin.

3. Gently pressing up the edge, taking care to avoid any stretching.

(Continued overleaf.)

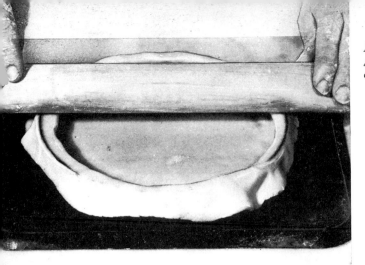

Plate 22.

4. Rolling off paste firmly and evenly with a floured rolling-pin.

5. Final pressing up of the edge to ensure a good case.

6. Lining the case with crump grease-proof paper before fil with beans, rice, etc.

Plate 23. Choux paste
(*see page 843*)

1. The weighed and measured butter and water are put together in the pan for boiling. The sifted flour is ready on a piece of paper.

2. When water and butter are bubbling fast, turn off gas or move from heat. Shoot the flour in quickly and all at once.

3. The mixture should be beaten until the paste comes from round the side of the pan. It is important not to continue beating once this stage is reached. Leave to cool slightly.

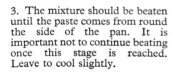

4. Beat the eggs and add about a third at a time to the mixture. Beat thoroughly until glossy. If eggs are large and paste is to be piped it may not be necessary to add all the beaten egg.

Plate 24. Lining small moulds (see page 844)

1. Lining the pastry into small moulds and pressing it well down with a small ball of paste.

2. Having rolled off paste, pressing it well up sides of mould to ensure a good shape.

Plate 25. Cutting of vol-au-vent and bouchées (see page 845)

Vol-au-vent

1. Roll out pastry to between ¼ and ½ inch thick. Using a lid or ring as a guide, cut out a round with a bevelled edge.

2. Turn it upside-down on to a damp baking-sheet. Mark the centre with cutter and the edge with a knife as shown. Always fold up trimmings evenly, ready for rolling out. (*Continued overleaf.*)

Plate 26. Bouchées (see page 846)

3. Here the pastry is rolled thinner than for a vol-au-vent. Brush the surface **lightly** with beaten egg before making the incision in the centre.

4. This picture shows the finished vol-au-vent and bouchées. Immediately they are baked remove the tops and scoop out any soft pastry from the inside. **They are then ready for use.**

Plate 27. *Making of génoise*
(*see page 848*)

1. This shows the mark of the whisk in the mixture and is the correct stage for the addition of the flour. The eggs and sugar have been whisked over gentle heat until thick, the bowl removed and the whisking continued for a further few minutes. This stage applies also to all sponges, whether the mixture is whisked by hand or mechanically.

. The flour is sifted in and the olding movement carried out ith a metal spoon. Reserve a uarter of the flour for the ddition of the butter.

3. Quickly pour the oiled butter on the last quarter of the flour sifted in on top of the mixture, Cut and fold as quickly as possible. When the butter is incorporated turn at once into prepared tin.

Plate 28. Pâtisserie—selection (see pages 864–875)

Big tray, left to right : Mokatines, Tartelettes aux Fraises (see Tartelettes aux Fruits), Langues de Bœuf, Mirlitons, Bateaux aux Raisins (see Tartelettes aux Fruits), Chocolatines.
Round tray at top : Sacristans.

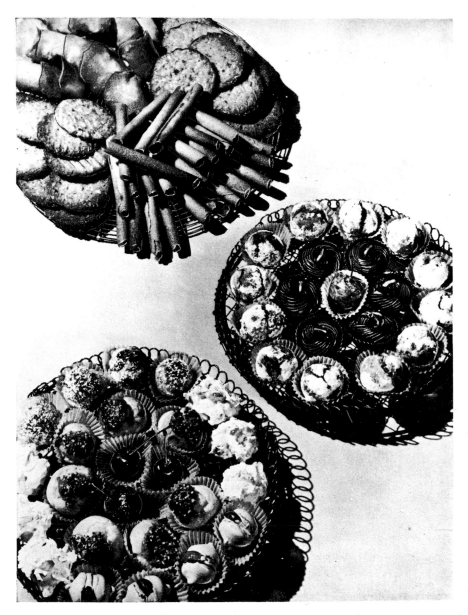

Plate 29. Petits fours secs (see pages 875–881)

Top tray: Tuiles d'Amandes, Oranginos, Cigarettes.

Middle tray: 'Pains de seigle' (*outer circle*), Colettes (*inner circle*), Fruit glacé (*centre*).

Bottom tray (*from left to right on outside circle*): Coquettes au Café (*bottom four*), Rochers aux Amandes (*at the side*), Suprêmes Pralinées (*at the top*), Salambos (*second circle*), Fruits glacés (*centre*).

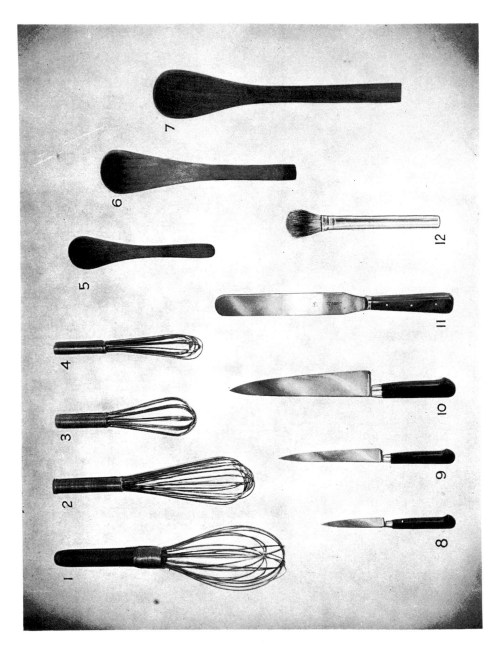

Plate 30 (see page 1151)

Plate 31 (see page 1152)

Plate 32 (see page 1154)

the gelatine and half the mint, well bruised. Whip whites to a froth and mix into the pan with the vinegar. Whisk over the fire until boiling. Then draw aside for 10 minutes. Strain through a wet cloth.

Pound or chop finely the remaining mint, add to one half of the jelly. Stir this over ice till on the point of setting, then pour into a shallow dish. When set arrange the cutlets on this and pour over the rest of the jelly, also stirred over ice until on the point of setting.

Serve with the garnish, slightly chilled.

The following Pâté of Veal and Beef is excellent. When ready it may be potted into a nice jar, such as is used for foie gras, or into a small, deep, brown, earthenware terrine. It is then put on the cold table with the terrine wrapped in a folded napkin. It is excellent served with fresh, hot toast.

PÂTÉ OF VEAL AND BEEF

1 lb. each of veal and beef	1 bay-leaf
½ oz. butter for cooking and an extra ½–1 oz. for working in after the meat has been pounded	salt and freshly ground pepper ground mace a little clarified butter to cover the top

Take a 7-lb. stone jam jar and into it put the meat, ½ oz. butter, bay-leaf, salt, and freshly ground pepper. Cover the jar and put it into a saucepan of water. Cook, preferably in the oven, for about 5 hours. Lift out the meat, pound well in a mortar. Flavour and season with more freshly ground pepper, a little salt, and a pinch of ground mace, and work in the extra butter to give a smooth and pleasant taste. Press into a jar or deep, brown terrine and cover with clarified butter.

TERRINE MAISON

Preparations must begin 2 days in advance.

6–8 rashers of streaky bacon	2 hard-boiled eggs
¾ lb. liver	1 teaspoon chopped herbs
1 small onion	¾ lb. lean veal or pork, or game
1 clove of garlic	1 bay-leaf
¾ lb. sausage-meat	flour and water paste
seasoning	jellied stock (approx. ½–¾ pint)

Take a small earthenware terrine. Line across the bottom and sides with bacon. Mince the liver with the onion and garlic and add to the sausage-meat. Season well, add the chopped eggs and herbs, and put a layer of this farce on the bottom of the terrine. Cut the meat into fine strips; arrange these in layers with the rest of the farce until the terrine is full. The top layer must be of farce, and the bay-leaf put on top of this. Put the lid on and seal round the edge with a paste of flour and water. Stand in a roasting-tin full of water and cook in a moderate oven for 1–1½ hours. Take out, remove the lid, and put a weight on the top (not more than 2 lb.). Leave until the next day, then fill up the sides of the terrine with good jellied stock. Leave until quite set and then turn out.

TERRINE OF HARE

Preparations must begin 2 days in advance.

1 good hare
larding bacon
marinade 4 (see page 732)
½ lb. fat or streaky pork (approx.)
finely chopped herbs (basil or thyme, marjoram)
a small glass of sherry or port
a good pinch of ground mace
salt and freshly ground black pepper

4–6 oz. tongue, cut in a thick slice
2 bay-leaves
flour and water paste
good jellied stock, made from bones of hare and trimmings of pork
gelatine if necessary

Choose a terrine or earthenware casserole. Remove the fillets from the back of the hare, lard them with the bacon, and put them into the marinade. Set on one side for a day or leave overnight.

Take all the meat from the rest of the hare, weigh it and take equal quantity of fat or streaky pork. Mince them twice together, then turn into a mortar and pound well, adding the herbs, wine, mace, salt, and freshly ground pepper to flavour well.

Cut the tongue into thick long strips. Lay these with the hare fillets in the terrine, then spread the farce over them. Press the bay-leaves on the top, cover with the lid and seal down with a flour and water paste. Stand the terrine in a bain-marie and cook in a slow to moderate oven about 1½ hours. Remove the lid, press with a good paper-covered weight and leave until the next day. Fill up with a good jellied stock (strengthened with gelatine if necessary) made from the bones of the hare and trimmings of the pork.

If the terrine is to be kept for any length of time, run clarified butter or melted lard over the top, and do not add any extra liquid.

Keep in a cool place or refrigerator and serve in the dish.

If no terrine is available make in a deep pie dish and cover the top with a lid of paste. When cooked remove the crust, press and finish as above.

WARWICKSHIRE PORK PIES

Preparations must begin a day in advance.

2 lb. fresh pork, lean and fat
1 small tablespoon salt
a pinch of cayenne and 1 small teaspoon ground pepper
Jelly
¾ lb. broken pork bones (approx.)
3 pints water

1 small pig's kidney (optional)
beaten egg

1 onion
a bouquet garni

Crust

2 lb. flour	1 gill milk
¼ lb. best lard	1 scant gill water

Prepare the stock for the jelly the day before in the following way. Put the bones into a thick pan with the water, salting very lightly, bring slowly to the boil, skimming well, then add the onion and bouquet. Cover and simmer very slowly all day (the slow oven of the Aga is excellent for this). When strong and of a good flavour strain and allow to get quite cold. Then remove the fat. There should be just under 1 pint of stock.

Cut the meat (and kidney if used) into small squares, mix well with the seasonings. Set aside. Warm the flour and rub in half the lard. Heat the milk with the water, adding the remaining lard. When melted cool to the temperature of new milk. Add to the flour and mix the whole to a smooth soft dough. Divide quickly into two pieces and mould each into a round pie, setting aside a small piece of dough for each lid. The moulding is most easily done round the base of a jam jar, pulling the paste up gently as you work (see note on moulding hot-water crust, page 841). Set the pies on a baking-sheet, fill with the seasoned meat, cover each with the remaining paste, decorate and brush with beaten egg. Bake 2 hours in a moderate to slow oven. After the first hour cover with a piece of wet grease-proof paper to prevent the crust hardening.

When the pies are cool fill up carefully with the stock with a funnel through a hole in the crust. The stock should be a firm jelly, and must be just melted, but not hot.

FRENCH RAISED PIE
a cold raised pie

use one batch pâte moulée (see page 842)

Farce

¾ lb. liver	¾ lb. sausage-meat
1 small onion	salt and pepper
a clove of garlic	

Filling

¾ lb. raw lean veal or game, cut in strips	1 teaspoon chopped herbs (parsley, thyme, and marjoram)
6 rashers of bacon	
2 hard-boiled eggs	1 bay-leaf

Line a raised pie mould (see page 842). (A cake tin with a loose bottom may be substituted.)

Line the bottom and the sides of the pie with the bacon, mince the liver, onion, and garlic and mix well with the sausage-meat to make a farce. Season highly, add the chopped eggs and the herbs and put a layer on top of the bacon. Arrange in layers of meat and farce until the pie is full, and on top of all lay the bay-leaf. Put on the cover, trim, and decorate as for Veal and Ham Pie (see page 630). Cook for at least 1½ hours in a moderate oven.

LAPEREAU SOUS CROÛTE (RABBIT PIE)

This dish should be prepared a day in advance.

2 young rabbits
12 prunes prepared and stoned
sweet chutney (optional)
salt and pepper
2 large onions
6 sage leaves or a few sprigs of
    savory

a little cooked bacon
2 or 3 hard-boiled eggs
finely chopped parsley
¾ pint good stock (jellied)
pâte moulée or pâte à pâté
    (page 842)
beaten egg to glaze

Steam the prunes till tender, but do not allow the skins to break. Take out the stones and stuff, either with a little sweet chutney or with the rabbit livers chopped and seasoned. Bone the rabbits, steep the pieces in water for an hour; put them into a pan and cover with fresh cold water, add salt and pepper, the onions, sliced, and the sage. Bring to the boil and simmer gently for half an hour. Take out the pieces of rabbit and put them into a pie dish with a little cooked bacon, slices of hard-boiled egg, and a good sprinkling of chopped parsley. Add the stuffed prunes, season well, and pour in the stock. Cover with the pastry, glaze with beaten egg, and cook in a fairly quick oven to a good brown. This will take about an hour. Leave until the next day before serving.

An excellent savoury flan may be made with meat, rabbit, fish, or left-overs of game and poultry. The choice of the accompanying ingredients is a matter of individual taste. This is a good way of using stewing or tinned steak to make an elegant dish. Suitable additions to the meat or fish element are as follows:

Blanched fresh, or tinned, cherries
Cooked stoned prunes
Cooked spring vegetables such as peas or beans
Tinned celery hearts
Asparagus tips
Shallots, baby carrots, or pickling onions, glazed
Button mushrooms cooked in a covered dish with milk and a nut of butter
Pickled walnuts, gherkins, or capers
Cucumber
Small decorative tomatoes

The following recipe, for 8–10, is given as an example for adaptation:

SAVOURY FLAN

1 large flan case of short crust,
    baked blind (see page 844)
1–1½ lb. stewing steak
fat for frying
1 onion
1 pint stock from the stewing
    steak (vegetable liquor will
    do if left-overs are used)
1 bay-leaf
seasoning

1 oz. (scant) gelatine
1 teaspoon lemon juice
8–10 glazed pickling onions
8–10 glazed baby carrots
a few large cherries, blanched
a few cooked peas
a sliced gherkin or pickled
    walnut
radishes for garnish

Wipe meat and cut into neat pieces, trimming away all fat and gristle. Heat fat in a saucepan, brown meat on all sides, add onion and allow to cook. Add stock, bay-leaf, and seasoning. Bring to boil, simmer very gently 2–3 hours till absolutely tender. Lift out steak, allow liquid to cool. Strain and skim off every vestige of fat. Soak gelatine in a little cold water, dissolve in a little of the warmed stock, then add to rest of stock, which should be made up, if necessary, to 1 pint. Adjust seasoning. Add lemon juice and taste.

Arrange the flan ingredients in the cooked pastry case. Pour over the almost set jelly and chill well. Garnish with slices or roses of radish.

In the above recipe the necessary stock is obtained from the stewing steak. When left-overs are used a separate stock is required.

CHICKEN MILLEFEUILLES

This is an alternative to bouchées of chicken and is a pleasant and attractive dish for a fork luncheon or buffet. The pastry is prepared and baked in exactly the same manner as for the sweet millefeuilles (page 888), but filled with a chicken or other savoury mousse, and glazed with a mayonnaise collée or chaudfroid.

puff paste made with 6 oz. flour
½ lb. finely minced cooked chicken
1–1½ oz. creamed butter
1½ gills well-flavoured béchamel sauce made with 1 oz. butter, 1 oz. flour, 1¼ gills milk (see page 155)

salt and pepper
1 large tablespoon lightly whipped cream
chaudfroid or mayonnaise collée (see pages 164 or 167)
truffle or mushroom for decoration
semi-liquid aspic jelly

Roll out the pastry thinly and cut into three strips about 3–4 inches wide and 8–12 inches long. Prick and bake to a good brown on baking-sheets moistened with water. Lift off and cool.

Pound the chicken, adding by degrees the butter, and when perfectly mixed the previously made cold béchamel. Season well and fold in the lightly whipped cream. Spread this mixture in layers between the strips of pastry, having first trimmed the edges of the strips. (The pastry should form three tiers.) Crumble these trimmings and set on one side. Coat the top of the millefeuilles with the mayonnaise or chaudfroid, decorate with truffle or mushroom (see page 655), and coat with semi-liquid aspic jelly. Press the crumbs along the top edge and set on a large silver dish or board covered with a napkin. The millefeuilles can then be cut in slices as required.

N.B. If for immediate serving the final coating of aspic may be omitted. In this case a mayonnaise collée is the better coating.

VEAL AND HAM PIE

8 oz. quantity flaky pastry	1 dessertspoon finely chopped parsley
1½ lb. shoulder of veal or pie veal	a little grated lemon rind
4 oz. lean ham or gammon rasher	salt and pepper
1 dessertspoon finely chopped onion	good jellied stock
	beaten egg containing a little salt

Cut veal in pieces 1–1½ inches square, and the ham into strips (if gammon is used remove rind, cut into strips, and blanch). Arrange meat, ham, onion, parsley, grated lemon rind, and seasoning in layers till pie dish is filled, doming the top slightly. Pour in enough stock to fill the dish three parts full. Cover in the following way: Roll out pastry just over ¼ inch thick, cut a strip from the edge about ¾ inch wide. Brush edge of pie dish and press on this strip. Brush strip with water, lay over the sheet of pastry. Press down well on the edge, then lifting the dish up on one hand cut off the paste round the circumference, holding the knife slantways under the dish. Mark round the edge with the tip of a knife, then with the back of a knife 'knock up' the edge. By this means the edge of the pastry is slightly raised and so will begin to flake readily when cooking. Make a hole in the centre of the pie; decorate. A simple way is to cut the rolled-out pastry into bands about 1 inch wide, then cut these diagonally into diamonds 3 inches long; with the back of the knife mark to represent the veins in a leaf. Arrange these on the pie. Brush with beaten egg containing a little salt. Put pie to cook in pastry oven (425° F.) for 30–40 minutes. Then wrap pie in a double sheet of wet grease-proof paper. Replace in oven but lower temperature to about 360° F. Leave for about another hour or until meat is tender when tested with the point of a knife or skewer. Remove.

This may be served cold or hot; if cold, add some stock to fill up through the hole in the crust.

Recipes for the following will be found in the appropriate chapters:

XX

Poultry and Game

GENERAL NOTES

Classification

Poultry is the name given to birds bred and nurtured in the farmyard for human consumption. Chickens, capons, ducks and ducklings, geese and goslings, turkeys and turkey poults, tame pigeons and guinea-fowl, are all included in this category. Tame rabbits are included also, although wild rabbits and wood-pigeons are considered game.

By reason of modern methods of preservation, for example deep freezing, it is possible to have poultry and game at all times of the year, and while this has obvious and important value, it is probable that no bird tastes quite so good as when it is killed and eaten in its proper season. A table of seasons for poultry and game is given at the end of this chapter (page 687).

Choosing poultry

In addition to being plump birds should be fresh and young, and the following points may be taken as a guide.

In a young bird

(*a*) The legs are smooth and pliable, the scales on them fine and only slightly overlapping, and the spurs of the male bird are hardly developed.

(*b*) The feet are supple, and the beak and breast-bone pliable; the tip of the latter, being gristle, bends easily.

(*c*) The skin is white and unwrinkled, the breast plump and white.

(*d*) The quills on the wings can easily be pulled out, and there should be no long hairs, especially on the thighs.

(*e*) There should be down under the wings and over the body, and the combs and wattles should be small.

If fresh

(*a*) There should be no unpleasant smell, and the flesh should be firm and show no greenish tinge.

(*b*) The eyes should be clear and not shrunk into the head.

(*c*) The feet should be soft and limp, and the feathers soft and full.

Poultry, like meat, should be hung. There is, however, a possible alternative. In an emergency a bird may be plucked and prepared immediately after being killed and before it has become cold.

If a bird bought from a shop is not to be used at once it should be hung by its feet in a cool, well-ventilated larder.

Poultry should not be over-hung. If by mischance this happens and there is the faintest suspicion of taint, wash out the body with cold water, to which a little salt and vinegar have been added; rinse and dry thoroughly with a dry cloth. It is, however, better not to use such birds.

Plucking and hanging

It is best to pluck the birds immediately they are killed, as the feathers pull more easily when the bird is warm. They should then be hung undrawn head downwards in a cool airy larder for 2–4 days, according to the weather and age of the bird, old birds being hung longer than young ones. Chickens are not drawn before being hung. After hanging for approximately 3 days, they are drawn and trussed for cooking.

The birds are plucked in the following way. Lay the bird on a board over a small dust-bin with the feet towards you, and begin plucking at the top of the breast, pulling out the feathers in an opposite direction to that in which they lie, and allowing them to fall straight into the bin. When it happens that the birds are to be plucked and cooked on the same day, the plucking, in particular of an old bird, may be facilitated by first dipping the bird for half a minute into boiling water. This greatly helps the removal of the feathers, but it must never be done unless cooking is to take place at once.

There is a strong note of warning to be sounded on this point. On the occasion of a big gathering here a dozen or so young birds were killed, and to save time the poultry-keeper plunged them into boiling water, plucked them, and hung them straight away in the larder. By the next morning they were in an advanced stage of decomposition, and all had to be destroyed at once.

The reasons for this were as follows:

The birds were young and the process really unnecessary.
They were not immediately drawn.
The weather was warm.
They were probably immersed for more than half a minute.

This keeping of food in a tepid or lukewarm state is always dangerous, and there is a note on it in the paragraphs on stock (page 116). In this case all the circumstances combined caused extremely quick decomposition.

After the bird has been plucked it is ready to be singed. This may be done in a variety of ways. The cleanest and simplest is to put a little methylated spirit into a tin plate. Light this and singe the bird over it. Alternatively a gas-lighter or a gas-ring may be used. But they are not so simple, practical, or clean as the methylated spirit. This will burn off all the down, hairs, and small bits of feather. If any quill ends remain, pull them out carefully with a pair of tweezers.

Drawing

Have two bowls of water at hand—one warm for cleansing the fingers, and the other cold to receive the giblets. Place a double thickness of kitchen paper on a board and:

1. With a sharp knife cut off the head, leaving 3–4 inches of the neck.

2. Turn the bird over on to the breast, insert a small sharp-pointed knife at the base of the neck, and slit up to the end. Pull away the loose skin which will form a flap to be folded over later, and gathering it up in the left hand cut off the neck very close to the top of the spine. From this end remove the crop and windpipe, and any fat which may be present.

3. Now turn the bird round and make a short cut between vent and tail (or pope's nose).

4. Place the first two fingers of each hand inside the bird at either end to loosen the inside, keeping the fingers high under the breastbone to avoid breaking the gall-bladder attached to the liver at the back of the bird. Withdraw the fingers of the left hand (at the neck end) and holding the bird firmly draw out the gizzard, the intestines, then the heart and liver with the gall-bladder attached.

5. Wipe out the bird thoroughly with a damp cloth. It is not normally necessary to put it under the tap and run water through it, and in the case of a young bird this may take away from the flavour.

6. Cut away the gall-bladder from the liver, taking great care to remove it whole, for if this is broken one has to discard the liver also. The intensely bitter flavour of the gall-bladder would spoil the taste of the whole bird. Dispose of the intestines. Place the liver, heart, neck, and gizzard, the latter split and cleaned, in the bowl of cold water. These are the giblets.

7. Cut the skin round the knee joint at the bottom of the drumstick. Twist and give the lower part of the leg a sharp pull. The sinews may come out easily, but if, in the case of an older bird, they do not come with this twist, take a skewer, catch them up in it, twist the skewer and jerk. This drawing out of the sinews makes the drumsticks much more tender when cooked. Cut off the feet, scald and scrape the scaly skin off the remaining piece of leg.

8. Scald the feet and strip off the 'stockings.' Put the feet with the giblets.

Stuffing

If the bird is to be stuffed this is done now before trussing.

Trussing

1. Fold the flap of skin smoothly over the back of the neck end, and fold the ends of the pinions backwards and under to secure this.

2. Place the bird on its back, and press the legs well down into the sides to plump up the breast. Pass the tail through the vent.

3. Place the bird with the neck end to the right. Thread a trussing-needle with stout thread or thin twine.

4. Pass the needle through the wing joint nearest to you and right through the body so that it comes out at the very top of the leg on the far side. Reinsert the needle on the far side into the wing joint. This should leave a stitch of about 1 inch showing. The needle passes back through the body, coming out at the top of the leg on the near side, and the thread is now tied off neatly and firmly.

5. Rethread the needle and pass it through the back of the bird under the drumsticks. Pass the string through the drumsticks and tie in a bow at the side.

N.B. There are other ways of trussing, but this is one of the easiest.

CHICKENS

Young birds (cockerels) weigh from $2\frac{1}{2}$ to $3\frac{1}{2}$ lb. These are best for roasting, sautéing, and frying. A $3\frac{1}{2}$-lb. bird serves 4–5 people.

Old birds. Boiling fowls weigh from $3\frac{1}{2}$ to 5 lb. and may be boiled or used for fricassées, casseroles, and similar dishes. A method for rendering an old bird tender is given below.

Poussins and spring chickens. Poussins are baby chickens 4–8 weeks old. Spring chickens are from 8 weeks to 4 months old. Poussins may be roasted, sautéd, or grilled, and, according to their size, are either served whole or split in two.

Capons. As the practice of caponizing the cock birds in domestic poultry yards has become more common recently, a note on it may be called for here. It is done nowadays by the introduction of capsules into the neck of the bird. If to be practised it is advisable that it should be done by a veterinary surgeon or skilled poultry-keeper to avoid pain to the birds. The effect is to increase the quality of meat, the birds becoming large and plump in a short time, and the flesh white and tender.

Stuffing

A chicken is usually stuffed in the breast; the stuffing is introduced through the opening at the neck end and it is convenient to do this with a spoon. The stuffing should not be packed in too firmly, allowance must be made for expansion; breadcrumbs, for instance, expand considerably. When the cavity is filled the flap of skin referred to earlier is folded over and secured as described. In some recipes a second stuffing for the carcass may be called for. This is put in through the opening and the same observation about expansion applies.

To make an old bird tender before the final cooking process

Take a thick saucepan, large enough to hold the bird. Lay on the bottom of it a sizable piece of rind of bacon, or a couple of fat rashers, just enough to keep the bird from touching the bottom of the saucepan.

Put in a sliced onion, some carrot, and no liquid whatsoever, but put a very tightly fitting lid on the pan, or put a lid on the pan and a heavy weight on top. You want as nearly as possible a hermetically sealed saucepan. Put the pan over very low heat and cook gently in this way for 20 minutes to half an hour, or in a slow oven 40–45 minutes, according to the size of the bird. At the end of 20 minutes take off the lid to see how things are progressing. The test that the bird is ready for cooking is that the flesh is white and swollen up and the whole has a pleasant smell. The bird is now ready for cooking in any way that may be required. If you are going to continue by braising, all you need do now is to add, after the pan has cooled off a little, the liquid and ingredients with which you are going to braise the bird. You may take it out and joint it, use it for curry, and in some cases it is even fit for roasting.

ROAST CHICKEN (ENGLISH METHOD)

The English way is to roast the bird, usually stuffed with force-meat or herb stuffing, in dripping or bacon fat, turning the bird over from time to time and basting well, for about 40 minutes. The bird is then taken out, the string removed, the chicken dished or carved and kept hot whilst the gravy is made. For this the dripping is poured off, a little sliced onion fried in the pan, giblet stock added, and the whole seasoned, boiled, and strained (see note on gravy, page 526).

Frothing

This is done by dredging the roasting bird lightly with flour 15 minutes before the end of cooking and basting the breast well with hot fat. It has the effect of making the breast brown and crisp. It is particularly suitable for game when the bird is roasted with dripping.

ROAST CHICKEN (FRENCH METHOD)

For the French method of roasting put 5 or 6 sprigs of tarragon or parsley inside the chicken with a small piece of butter and seasoning. Before trussing, the breast of the chicken is rubbed with butter or thickly brushed with melted butter. A slice or two of larding bacon is put on top, or failing this a piece of buttered paper. Set the bird in the roasting-tin, add ½ pint good stock made from the giblets and a few drops of lemon juice. Roast in a moderate oven 50 minutes to 1 hour. The bird must be well basted and turned over frequently so that the legs and back get well browned. During the last 15 minutes remove the paper to allow the breast to brown well. The gravy in the pan should reduce by about a quarter, and extra stock must be added during cooking if it reduces too much. The final amount should be 1–1½ gills. The gravy is made by straining off the juice into a small saucepan, skimming well, and boiling vigorously for a minute or two.

N.B. If it is inconvenient to make stock use instead the same amount of water.

Put the giblets, excluding the liver, either inside the bird with the herbs or, if preferred, in the tin. If desired, the gravy may be slightly thickened by working a small teaspoon of flour into the skimmings of butter and adding this to the gravy, which must then be reboiled and finished with a squeeze of lemon.

The advantage of the French method

Chicken is a delicately flavoured and rather dry meat, and in the ordinary method of roasting a high and sometimes fierce temperature is reached which may dry up the natural juices. The French method conserves these, the cooking is slower and longer, and on the whole the moistness of flesh and flavour is preserved by adopting this method.

Signs that birds are cooked:

(a) When the meat shrinks from the end of the drumstick.

(b) When a sharp fork or trussing-needle run into the thigh joint of the chicken will enter easily. If the juice that runs out is pink the bird is not quite cooked. Remember that the legs of the bird take longer to cook, so that when roasting they should be uppermost most of the time.

Carving

When possible this is better carried out in the kitchen, preferably on a board. The pieces can be kept hot and be properly arranged on the serving dish. In the kitchen too it is easier to cut the joints in the way to be described, which gives an even distribution of the various parts of the flesh. For example, the cutting through of the thigh-bone just above the joint ensures that the drumstick is served with a portion of the thigh or *cuisse*. Game or saw-edged kitchen scissors are valuable, but wanting these the bone may be cut by taking the thick part of the blade of a good knife near the handle, cutting through the flesh, and then giving a sharp tap with a wooden mallet.

Method of carving *

First cut off the legs. This is facilitated by pressing the thighs down outwards, away from the body, so that the joint is easily seen and may be readily severed. If the bird is well cooked each oyster will come away with the thigh (the oyster is a small oval of flesh lying next to the thigh joint on the back of the carcass). If the bird is very small the whole of the leg, both drumstick and thigh, is served in one piece. If not, the drumstick may be separated from the thigh; but where the carving is done in the kitchen the legs may be cut off in the way described with a portion of the thigh joint attached. The wings are taken off by taking a line from the top of the wish-bone and bringing the knife right down through the joint. The breast is then cut off horizontally in one piece in a small bird, or in a larger bird it is cut off in two or three slices from either side of the breast-bone.

For a spring chicken the breast and the wings may be sliced off in one piece.

* See plate 13

Chicken for sautéing or frying are cut up in the raw state and are jointed in the same way, except that when cutting off the wings the knife is carried right through the carcass bone. The pieces may then be trimmed with the scissors.*

Accompaniments to roast chicken

English fashion. Crisp rolls of bacon, good gravy, bread sauce.

French roast chicken. Good gravy, watercress, and green salad. See also Poulet Rôti à l'Estragon, page 646.

Fried and sautéd chicken have their own appropriate garnishes, which will be given with the recipes.

Boiled chicken may have parsley sauce and grilled bacon, cream sauce flavoured with tarragon, and velouté sauce and rice; and a fricassee of chicken implies cooked, shredded chicken warmed in a cream sauce.

'Poulet' indicates a young bird. 'Poule' an older fowl.

In the following section no special reference is made to the number of persons the dishes will serve. As a general guide it may be noted that a young bird, 3½ lb., will serve 4–5 and a larger bird 5–6 people. Much depends on the accompaniments, stuffing, etc.

To boil chicken

A large chicken takes from an hour to an hour and a quarter, even an hour and a half if very large; a moderate-sized one about three-quarters of an hour. These times are for young birds.

The bird should be put into cold salted water with carrots and onions cut up in it, brought to the boil and then simmered. At no time should it be allowed to boil rapidly. Old-fashioned cooks used, in order to keep the flesh very white, to lay slices of lemon over the breast, tying them in place and then wrapping the whole thing in linen. If this is not done, care must be taken to skim the water from time to time. If the birds are to be served cold, they may be masked in a really good cream sauce or a chaudfroid.

An interesting way of boiling a fowl is to cook it either *au riz* or *à l'estragon*.

The following recipe for Poule au Riz is a good way of using a large boiling fowl.

POULE AU RIZ

1 boiling fowl	a bouquet garni
1½ pints white stock, or a stock made of vegetables, giblets, and water	a sprig of rosemary seasoning
	6 oz. rice
1 onion stuck with 2 or 3 cloves	extra stock or water if necessary

Make the fowl tender in the way described earlier. Allow the pan to cool for a few moments, then add stock, to come three-quarters of the way up the bird, onion, bouquet, rosemary, and seasoning. The breast may be covered with a piece of grease-proof paper to keep it white. Put a very tight-fitting lid on the saucepan, bring to boiling-point and simmer either in the oven or over gentle heat for 1½–2 hours. It should never do more

* See plate 12

than simmer. If the bird is cooked on the top of the fire and not in the oven, it is advisable to turn it after half an hour's cooking. In the meantime, while it is cooking, prepare the rice (see preparation of rice, page 386). The rice should be added about half an hour before the end of the cooking. By this time the liquid will probably be reduced to about a pint, and it is in this liquid surrounding the chicken that the rice is sprinkled. If the amount of liquid is inadequate a little more stock or water must be added. When the chicken is cooked remove it, take out the onion and the bouquet and rosemary, and skim any superfluous grease that is on top of the rice. Satisfy yourself that the seasoning is correct. Serve the rice, which should be a little moist, round the carved bird.

POULET AU RIZ
a young chicken served with a pilaff

1 roasting chicken
1 onion
1 carrot

a bouquet garni
water

Pilaff
3 oz. onion or white part of leek
1 oz. butter or chicken fat
6 oz. rice

white stock—about 1–1¼ pints according to the type of rice used
2 tablespoons grated cheese
seasoning

Garnish
2 oz. mushrooms (preferably buttons)

4 oz. button onions
a nut of butter

Sauce
1 oz. butter
1 oz. flour
2 egg yolks

3 tablespoons double or single cream
a squeeze of lemon juice
bouillon from chicken

Into a saucepan put chicken, onion, carrot, and bouquet with water just to cover. Cover pan and simmer till tender, about 50 minutes.

Pilaff. Slice onion or leek, soften in butter, add rice, cook a few minutes. Add stock to cover well. Season well, bring to boil. Then set pan in oven or on very low heat on stove till rice is tender. Do not stir.

Garnish. Slice mushrooms, or if buttons leave whole. Cook quickly in butter. Blanch the button onions till tender. Set aside and keep warm. Drain chicken and reduce the bouillon. Carve chicken, set aside on covered dish and keep hot.

Sauce. Melt butter in pan, add flour and ¾ pint of the reduced bouillon. Stir till boiling, reduce till syrupy. Draw aside, adjust seasoning. Beat yolks in a bowl, add cream and a little of the hot sauce by degrees. Return gradually to pan, whisk over the fire, add mushrooms, onions, and lemon juice.

With a fork stir into the pilaff a little grated cheese, arrange it on a hot dish with chicken on top, spoon over the sauce with the garnish and serve at once.

POULET AU BLANC

A delicate dish for a bird of about 3½ lb. The bird may be cooked in veal stock or half stock and half water. Failing this a stock may be prepared in the following manner:

For the stock

1½ pints cold water	3 oz. turnip (optional)
the giblets of the chicken, previously blanched	a bouquet garni
	seasoning
½ lb. carrots	3 or 4 cloves
3 oz. onion	a sprig of rosemary

Let all these simmer for an hour.

For the dish

a bird about 3½–4 lb.	½ oz. butter
veal stock, or half stock and half water, or stock as above	lemon juice
	seasoning
6 oz. white button mushrooms	

For the roux

1¼ oz. butter	4–6 tablespoons cream, *or*
1¼ oz. flour, scant weight	2 egg yolks
¾ pint of liquid in which the bird has been cooked	

If necessary prepare stock as above. Put the bird in the pan with the stock to come about half way up. Cover the breast of the bird with a buttered paper. Put the lid on the saucepan very firmly, using a piece of grease-proof paper to make it fit as tightly as possible. Simmer gently for an hour or until tender.

Towards the end of cooking prepare the mushrooms; cook gently in a little butter with lemon juice and seasoning for 3–4 minutes. Set aside and keep warm.

When ready lift out bird and strain the stock. Make a roux with the butter and flour and dilute it with ¾ pint of the strained liquor. Add the cooked mushrooms, and either the cream or a liaison made with the egg yolks (see page 140; do not allow to boil); adjust seasoning and serve with the chicken. Or you may carve the chicken in the kitchen, and serve with this sauce over it.

POULET AU BLANC A L'ESTRAGON

a plump roasting chicken, 3½ lb., with the giblets (excluding the liver)	1 bunch of tarragon (about a dozen small sprays)
¼ oz. butter	1 oz. butter, good weight
3 oz. sliced carrot	1 oz. flour
3 oz. sliced onion	1 egg yolk
½ dozen parsley stalks (stems only)	½ gill cream or top of milk
	1 teaspoon chopped tarragon
salt, freshly ground white pepper	warm water to cover

Choose a pan that will just fit the chicken. Rub the bottom and sides with the butter. Add the giblets, vegetables, parsley stalks, and seasoning. Cover and cook gently for half an hour on a low heat. On no account must the vegetables be allowed to colour, and to avoid this add a spoonful or two of warm water two or three times during the half-hour. Now put in the chicken, and pour in enough warm water barely to cover.

Simmer slowly with the lid on the pan, skimming occasionally, until the bird is tender. This will take approximately 1–1½ hours.

Pour off about 1¼ pints of the stock into a saucepan, add the bunch of tarragon, and allow to boil rapidly until reduced to ¾ pint. In the meantime cover the pan with the chicken in it and set aside to keep hot.

Strain the tarragon-flavoured stock into a jug, make a roux with the butter and flour in the pan and pour on the stock off the fire. When thoroughly blended return to the fire and stir until boiling. Simmer a minute or two, then add the liaison of egg yolk and cream as described on page 140 and finish with the chopped tarragon.

Dish the chicken, either whole or jointed, but making sure that it is well drained. Coat over with the sauce and serve at once. Plainly boiled potatoes tossed in butter and chopped parsley are best with this dish.

TRADITIONAL ENGLISH BOILED CHICKEN

1 boiling fowl	1 oz. butter
1 onion, sliced	1 oz. flour
1 carrot, sliced	3–4 thin rashers of streaky
3–4 peppercorns	bacon
a bouquet garni	stock from the chicken
1 large handful of parsley	½ gill cream or milk

Simmer the bird in water barely to cover, with the onion, carrot, peppercorns, and bouquet. When absolutely tender draw aside and strain off a good pint of the liquor. Reduce this to about ¾ pint and skim well.

Meantime boil the parsley in water with a little salt until tender, about 7 minutes. Drain, press well, and rub through a sieve or strainer. Put aside.

Cut the rind and gristle from the bacon rashers, flatten out well on a board, cut in half and roll up each piece. Stick on a thin skewer, grill or cook in the oven 6–7 minutes.

Melt the butter in a saucepan, add the flour off the fire, cool the reduced stock slightly, then add and stir over the fire until boiling. Draw aside, add the parsley purée, beat well for a minute or two and finish with the cream or milk. Cover the pan and set aside in a bain-marie.

Carve the chicken, arrange on a hot dish, spoon over enough sauce to moisten well, and serve the remainder in a sauce-boat. Garnish with the bacon rolls. Serve the dish with a mousseline of potato.

The sauce may be made entirely with milk, which gives a creamier consistency.

CHICKEN COOKED IN COCO-NUT MILK
flavoured with herbs

½ lb. freshly grated coco-nut or
    4–5 tablespoons desiccated
    coco-nut
1½ pints boiling water (approx.)
a 3½-lb. chicken
1 teaspoon salt
½ teaspoon pepper
1 saltspoon cayenne

12 fresh coriander seeds
1 bay-leaf
a sprig of tarragon
a pinch of saffron (soaked in
    hot water)
2 egg yolks to each ½ pint of
    final liquid

The egg yolks may be reduced in number and be supplemented by a liaison of beurre manié of 1 oz. each of butter and flour to each pint of liquid.

Make the coco-nut milk in the way described on page 403. After the first infusion pour a little more boiling water on the grated nut for use if required.

Cut up the chicken into suitable pieces. Mix together salt, pepper, and cayenne and rub well into all the pieces.

Put the chicken into a pan with enough coco-nut milk to cover, using both brews if necessary. Now put in coriander, saffron, bay-leaf, and tarragon. Put on a tightly fitting lid and simmer very gently till ready. When the chicken is thoroughly cooked, lift out the pieces and put on a hot dish. Adjust the seasoning of the liquor and make the liaison of egg yolk (see liaisons, page 138). With this dish very well-dried boiled rice should be served. Or you may serve half plain boiled rice and half fried rice with herbs (see page 387).

CHICKEN WATERZOOI
a Flemish dish

1 roasting chicken
3 carrots, small to medium [1]
2 leeks [1]
1 onion [1]
1 oz. butter
a pinch of sugar
seasoning
¾ pint good veal or chicken
    stock or water
Garnish
    plain boiled potatoes

2 wineglasses white wine
4–5 parsley roots (Hamburg
    parsley) [2]
2 egg yolks or a level dessert-
    spoon arrowroot
¾ gill cream
chervil and tarragon

    croûtons

Cut the vegetables in julienne strips. Put into a small pan with half the butter, a pinch of sugar, salt and pepper. Barely cover with stock or water, cover with a piece of buttered paper, bring to the boil and cook in the oven until most of the liquid has evaporated. Spread the bottom and sides of a large casserole with the remaining butter. Put in the chicken, pour over the wine and stock, add the parsley roots well washed, scraped,

[1] Young spring vegetables should be used for the julienne.
[2] In place of the Hamburg parsley it is possible to use roots of the ordinary parsley, but they have not the same flavour.

and tied in a bunch. Scatter over the julienne, cover the whole with paper and then with a tight-fitting lid. Bring up to the boil, then cook in the oven about an hour, or until quite tender.

Take up, carve the chicken and arrange in a casserole or deep dish. Lift out the parsley roots and press through a strainer, rubbing through as much as is sufficiently soft. Put the purée back into the pan with the liquor and thicken it with the egg yolks and cream mixed together. (If arrowroot is used this should be slaked with the cream and then allowed to boil in the sauce.) Reheat carefully without boiling and pour over the chicken. Scatter over the chopped tarragon and chervil, and surround with fried croûtons. Serve the boiled potatoes separately.

If more convenient the chicken may be jointed before cooking.

POULET EN COCOTTE BONNE FEMME

An essential of this dish is that it shall have a garnish of lardons of bacon, mushrooms, potatoes, and onions.

1½ oz. butter or dripping	½ oz. flour
1 roasting chicken	1 pint stock
2 oz. bacon	salt and pepper
2 oz. mushrooms	a bouquet of herbs
12 little white onions	2 potatoes or 8–12 new potatoes

Melt the fat in a large stew-pan and brown the chicken slowly and carefully all over. Take it out and joint it. In the same saucepan brown the bacon cut in lardons and blanched, the mushrooms cut in quarters, and the small onions left whole; cook gently. Put the chicken and its juice into an earthenware *cocotte* with the bacon, mushrooms, and onions; dust with the flour and continue cooking for a few minutes. Pour on the stock, season, and bring to the boil. Add bouquet of herbs, cover and allow to simmer for an hour. About a quarter of an hour before the end of cooking add the potatoes, previously blanched, either small new ones or the larger ones cut into small olive shapes. Finish cooking and serve in the *cocotte*.

When it is necessary to use an older bird for this dish, the same ingredients may be used, but the preliminary process of making tender, given on page 634, should be carried out. Immediately after this process the chicken may be jointed and the pieces browned. The subsequent cooking will be longer, and again the potatoes should not be introduced until about a quarter of an hour before the bird is ready.

POULET PAYSAN

The word paysan indicates a garnish of thin rounds of onion, carrot, and turnip. Sometimes the vegetables are cooked with the chicken as for a braise. In this recipe they are cooked separately, which is the best way for an older bird, since as this takes longer to cook the vegetables would otherwise be overdone. So the method can be adapted according to whether you are using a young bird or a boiling fowl.

2 oz. butter
a boiling fowl made tender by the method referred to on page 634 (or a roasting chicken)
2 shallots

Garnish
6 oz. onions
6 oz. carrots
4 oz. turnips

1 clove of garlic crushed with salt
2 rashers of bacon
1 gill red wine or cider
1¼ pints stock
seasoning
a bouquet garni

¼ pint stock
chopped parsley

Melt half the butter in a casserole, put in the fowl or chicken and brown all over. Lift out the bird. Into the fat in the pan place the finely sliced shallots, the garlic crushed with salt, and the bacon cut into small pieces and blanched. Cook these gently until slightly brown, then add wine, stock, seasoning, and bouquet. Bring back to boiling-point, simmer for a few minutes, replace the bird and braise in the oven, basting frequently, for an hour or more until it is tender. This is shown by the shrinking of the meat from the end of the drumsticks. Remove, carve, and keep warm. The gravy should be strained, reduced to the consistency of a thin syrup, and reserved.

The garnish should be prepared while the fowl is cooking. Melt the remainder of the butter in a shallow pan, or small frying-pan, add the onions, carrots, and turnips, finely sliced into rounds, seasoning, and ¼ pint stock. Cover with a thickly buttered paper and simmer until the vegetables are just tender. This cooking may be done either in the oven or on top of the stove; in the latter case a plate or saucer should be used as a lid to the frying-pan.

To serve lay the vegetables in the middle of a round dish, arrange the carved bird on them, pour a small quantity of the gravy over, dust the dish with chopped parsley, and serve with the rest of the gravy in a sauce-boat.

Again the chicken may be jointed before being browned if this is more convenient.

CASSEROLE OF CHICKEN

1 roasting chicken or boiling fowl (if the latter is chosen first prepare it according to the method on page 634)
1½ oz. butter
½ pint good jellied stock (approx.)
1 clove of garlic crushed with salt

2 tablespoons each of finely chopped parsley and chives
1 dessertspoon finely chopped tarragon
1 teaspoon finely chopped thyme
4 oz. sliced mushrooms
the juice of 1 lemon
salt and freshly ground pepper

Brown the chicken slowly and carefully all over in the hot butter. Lift it out. Joint and carve it neatly, and break the back into two or three pieces.

Put the stock into the pan and bring to the boil, stirring it well round to remove any 'caramel.' Add the garlic. Now pack the chicken into a casserole with layers of the herbs, mushrooms, lemon juice, freshly ground pepper and salt. Keep the pieces of back for the top. Moisten with the stock, being careful to keep the level of the liquid below the top pieces of chicken.

Put on the lid and seal it with a flour and water paste if necessary. Cook in a slow to moderate oven $1\frac{1}{2}$–$2\frac{1}{2}$ hours.[1]

Other vegetables may be used in place of mushrooms.

POULET EN CASSEROLE NORMANDE

1 medium-sized chicken (if a boiling fowl is used first make it tender in the way described on page 634)	2 rashers of streaky bacon, cut in lardons and blanched
	2 well-flavoured apples
	seasoning
$1\frac{1}{2}$ oz. butter	$\frac{1}{4}$ pint cider, preferably draught cider (approx.)
1 medium-sized sliced onion or 1 dozen baby onions or shallots, left whole	a bouquet garni

Brown the chicken all over in the hot butter. Remove it, put the onions into the pan and sauter over a moderate heat. After a few minutes add the bacon, increase the heat, and when the contents of the pan are turning colour add the apples, peeled, cored, and cut in eighths.

Shake over a brisk heat for a minute or two. Now carve and joint the chicken neatly, and break the back into two or three pieces. Arrange the bird in a casserole in layers with the mixture from the pan, and plenty of seasoning. Rinse the pan out with the cider, which may be diluted with a little water if wished, and pour into the casserole. Tuck the bouquet down the side, lay the pieces of back on the top and cover tightly, sealing round the edges, if necessary, with a flour and water paste. Cook in a slow to moderate oven for $1\frac{1}{2}$–$2\frac{1}{2}$ hours,[1] according to the age of the bird.

POULET A L'ORANGE

1 roasting chicken	1 large orange
a bouquet garni	1 fresh sweet red pepper or tinned pimento
$1\frac{1}{2}$ oz. butter	
2 onions	1 heaped teaspoon arrowroot or beurre manié
salt	
freshly ground black pepper	paprika
1 gill red wine	chopped parsley
$\frac{1}{2}$ pint stock	

---

[1] When it is necessary to take so long a time for cooking in the oven it is a good plan to set the casserole in a tin of water inside the oven. This ensures that the heat shall not get so great as to dry up the contents of the casserole. Even when the casserole is sealed with flour and water it is difficult with prolonged cooking to prevent entirely the escape of moisture.

Put the bouquet of herbs inside the bird and over the outside rub half the butter. Fry the onions in the rest of the butter, put in a casserole with the bird, with salt and freshly ground black pepper. Heat the wine, flamber it, and pour round with the stock. Set to braise gently in the oven without the lid for about an hour, and baste every quarter of an hour. When half done add the orange blanched for 5 minutes, cut in half and finely sliced, and the pepper shredded and also blanched (if tinned do not blanch). Continue cooking. At the last take up the chicken, carve, reduce the gravy to taste, thicken it slightly with the arrowroot or beurre manié, add a good pinch of paprika, and pour over the chicken. Dust well with chopped parsley. Serve with crisp sauté potatoes or with Pommes Sicilienne (see page 204).

POULET CHASSEUR

1 roasting chicken, 3½ lb.	¾ pint stock
1¼ oz. butter	1 heaped teaspoon tomato purée
1 oz. onion, sliced	a bouquet garni
1 oz. celery, sliced	1 oz. butter (approx.) for
4 oz. mushrooms	cooking mushrooms
½ oz. flour	6–8 chipolata sausages
1 wineglass white wine or cider	chestnut croquettes (see below)

Brown the chicken all over in butter. Lift out and put into the pan the sliced onion and celery and the chopped peelings from the mushrooms. Allow to colour. Scatter over the flour, brown slightly, then add the wine or cider, the stock and the purée. Bring to the boil. Meantime joint the chicken, replace in the pan, add bouquet, cover tightly, and put into a slow to moderate oven for 35–40 minutes.

Take up, strain the sauce and reduce to a syrupy consistency. Cut mushrooms into four, sauter briskly in butter and add to the sauce. Sauter the sausages also and slice in two if over-long. Dish the chicken, spoon over the sauce, and arrange the sausages and croquettes around the dish.

Chestnut croquettes

1 lb. cooked sieved chestnuts	salt, pepper
2 celery stalks	milk if necessary
1 small onion	seasoned flour
1 oz. butter	beaten egg and dried white
1 small egg	crumbs

Chop onion and celery, soften slightly in the butter with the lid on the pan. Mix into the chestnuts with plenty of salt and pepper, add the beaten egg with a little milk if necessary, to make a stiff paste. Allow to cool, shape into small balls, roll lightly in seasoned flour, and coat with beaten egg and dried white crumbs. Fry in smoking hot fat till golden brown.

POULET PAPRIKA

1 chicken, 3½ lb.
salt and pepper
1 oz. fat
a level tablespoon paprika
3 or 4 small onions
1 large or 2 small cloves of garlic crushed with 1 teaspoon salt
a cup of water or stock

2 green peppers, finely sliced and blanched
3 or 4 tomatoes, peeled, pipped, and chopped
1 level tablespoon flour
1 gill sour cream (it is better if the cream has gone sour naturally, otherwise it may be soured by the addition of a little lemon juice)

Cut up the chicken as directed on page 636. Season with salt and pepper. Heat the fat in a pan, cook the onions and crushed garlic gently in this until a pale gold in colour. Add the paprika and continue frying for a few minutes. Add the stock or water and arrange the pieces of chicken in the pan. Add the finely sliced and blanched peppers and the tomatoes. Cover with a tightly fitting lid and cook gently for an hour (1½ hours for an older bird). Mix the flour with a little of the cream, stirring gradually to a smooth mixture. Pour into the pan over the chicken off the fire, then bring back to the boil. Boil for a minute or two to cook the flour, add cream and serve. A fresh salad made from fruit, say plums or ripe pears, is excellent with this, as is a cucumber salad.

See also Poulet Rôti Paprika, page 647.

CHICKEN COOKED IN MILK

The following method is good for invalids. Put a sprig of French tarragon inside the bird and cook it very gently in milk. The milk should come half way up the bird. Poach or simmer it for 20 minutes. Take out and put a nut of butter in the chicken, and a well-buttered greased paper over the breast. Roast for about an hour, basting with butter. A little of the milk may go in the bottom of the pan.

POULET RÔTI A L'ESTRAGON (FAÇON SIMPLE)

1 roasting chicken
3 or 4 sprigs of tarragon, and a little chopped tarragon for the gravy

2 fat rashers
a little stock for the gravy

Put the sprigs of tarragon inside the bird, cover the breast with the rashers, wrap in well-buttered paper and roast, taking away the paper towards the end of cooking. To the gravy made in the usual way with stock add a little chopped tarragon.

POULET VÉRONIQUE
delicate dish with tarragon and muscat grapes

1 roasting chicken
2 oz. butter
tarragon
¾ pint chicken or veal stock

½ lb. muscat grapes
lemon juice
2 or 3 spoonfuls thick cream

Rub the chicken well with butter and put the remainder with a small bunch of tarragon inside the bird; cover with buttered paper, pour ½ pint stock into the tin and roast 40 minutes to an hour. Meantime peel and pip the grapes, squeeze over them a few drops of lemon juice and keep covered. Take up the chicken, carve and keep hot. Strain off the juice into a small saucepan, déglacer the roasting-pan with the remaining stock, add to the contents of the saucepan and reduce well. Add cream to the gravy, add the grapes at the last moment and spoon over the chicken.

POULET RÔTI PAPRIKA

1 chicken roasted by the French method (see page 635)

2 tablespoons cream, approx. (sweet or sour)
French or potato gnocchi (see page 427) or nouilles

Sauce

1 onion
1 oz. butter
1–2 teaspoons paprika
¾ oz. flour
¼ pint stock

1 lb. tomatoes
salt and ground black pepper
a clove of garlic
1 bay-leaf

Roast the chicken in the French way. Carve and put into a casserole. While the chicken is roasting prepare the sauce as follows: Chop the onion, soften in butter in a saucepan, add the paprika, cook for a minute, add the flour off the fire, the stock, and the tomatoes, cut in half and lightly squeezed to remove the seeds. Bring to the boil, add the salt, ground black pepper, garlic, and bay-leaf. Simmer till well reduced, then strain.

Cover the chicken with the sauce and simmer the whole for 15 minutes before serving. At the last moment pour over a spoonful or two of cream, and serve with French or potato gnocchi or nouilles.

POULET ROMARIN

See Winkfield chapter, page 1003.
See also almond sauce for roast chicken, page 173.

POULET SAUTÉ A L'ESTRAGON

1 young tender chicken, 2½–3 lb.
1½ oz. butter
salt and pepper
¼ pint strong veal or chicken stock

a bouquet of 3 sprigs of tarragon tied together
2 or 3 tablespoons chicken or veal velouté sauce (see page 152) or cream
a little chopped tarragon

Joint the chicken as for a sauté (see page 637).   Brown the pieces slowly and well in the hot butter in the sauté pan, add salt and pepper, stock and bouquet.   Cover and simmer for 20 minutes.   Dish.   Add the sauce or cream to the liquor in the pan, boil up very well and strain.   Add the chopped tarragon, pour over the chicken and serve.

POULET SAUTÉ CHASSEUR

1 chicken, 2½–3 lb.
seasoning
1 dessertspoon olive oil
1 oz. butter
2 tablespoons brandy or sherry
    may be used
1 chopped shallot
6 button mushrooms

1 wineglass white wine
½ pint brown stock
2 tomatoes, peeled, seeded,
    and chopped
a good pinch of chopped tarra-
    gon and chervil
heart-shaped croûtons of fried
    bread

Cut up the chicken as for a sauté and season the pieces.   Heat the sauté pan, put in the oil and butter and when foaming add the pieces of leg. Sauter gently 5 minutes, then add the white meat and continue cooking slowly until turning a good colour.   Cover the pan and put into the oven for 10 minutes.   Remove and flamber with the brandy.   Take out the pieces and put into a clean pan.   To the first pan add the chopped shallot and the mushrooms, sauter 4–5 minutes, then moisten with the wine. Reduce to half, then add the stock and tomatoes and continue cooking until syrupy in consistency.   Add the tarragon and chervil, pour over the chicken, set on a low heat and simmer 5–6 minutes.

Serve in a hot dish and surround with heart-shaped croûtons of fried bread.

POULET SAUTÉ PARMESAN

See Winkfield chapter, page 1006.

POUSSINS SAUTÉS AU CITRON

See Winkfield chapter, page 1007.

POULET VALLÉE D'AUGE

2 spring chickens
1 oz. butter
2 oz. onion
2 sticks of celery
2 apples

½ oz. flour
¼ pint cider
½ pint good stock (approx.)
¼ gill or more cream

Garnish
    fried apple rings

    château potatoes

Joint the chickens.   Flour lightly and sauter in the butter until golden brown.   Remove, add the onion, finely sliced, to the pan.   Sauter 4 or 5 minutes, then add the sliced celery and apples.   Sauter for another 5 minutes. Add the flour, cider, and stock. Bring to the boil, replace the meat, cover and simmer 15–20 minutes. Then remove lid and continue until meat is cooked and sauce well flavoured. Dish the meat, strain the sauce, return to a pan and boil up well. Whisk in the cream, then pour over. Garnish with fried apple rings and serve château potatoes separately.

FRITOT DE POULET AUX FINES HERBES

1 young chicken, about 3 lb., gently poached in water with vegetables and herbs to flavour
vinaigrette dressing

fresh herbs (parsley, mint, marjoram, tarragon, etc.) in sprigs
French dressing
quarters of lemon
sauce poulette (see below)

Batter
4 oz. flour
1 tablespoon oil
1 gill milk

1 egg yolk
1 egg white
salt and pepper

Make the batter in the usual way (see page 432), but add the egg white whipped to a stiff froth just before using, and after the batter has stood for an hour or so. Cool the chicken in the liquid before draining and carving into neat joints. Marinade in the vinaigrette, also marinade the herbs in French dressing. Drain both the chicken and the herbs, dip into the prepared batter and fry at once in deep smoking hot oil. Drain, dish on a napkin, and surround with quarters of lemon. Serve a sauce poulette separately.

The batter may also have a teaspoon of savory or thyme and a heaped dessertspoon of finely chopped parsley mixed into it.

Sauce poulette

For ½–¾ pint sauce take just over ½ oz. butter, ½ oz. flour for the roux, ½ pint good white stock, and make up in the usual way (velouté sauce, see page 152). To this add a liaison of 2 egg yolks and 1–2 tablespoons cream. Finish with 1 tablespoon mushroom juice, 1 oz. butter added in small pieces off the fire, a good squeeze of lemon juice, and a teaspoon of chopped parsley.

A SECOND MARINADE (SUITABLE FOR FOREGOING DISH)

1 dessertspoon salt
½ teaspoon pepper
1 teaspoon finely chopped summer or winter savory (thyme may be used instead of this, but it has not such a delicate flavour)

1 heaped tablespoon finely chopped parsley
1 heaped tablespoon mint
1 small saltspoon cayenne
1 tablespoon lemon juice or vinegar; possibly a little more may be required

Mix the ingredients together, rub them all over the pieces of chicken and allow them to stand for an hour or more before coating and frying.

The classic accompaniments to the next two dishes are corn fritters and fried bananas.

CHICKEN MARYLAND (1)

1 young chicken	fat for shallow frying
1 tablespoon flour seasoned with salt, pepper, and paprika	sour cream (optional)
egg and breadcrumbs	gravy or jus

Garnish

corn fritters (see page 244)	bananas, sliced lengthways and fried in butter

Joint the chicken as for a fricassée and dip in seasoned flour. Egg and breadcrumb and fry in a frying-pan, allowing at least an inch depth of fat. Butter is good, but American recipes recommend also bacon dripping or fat pork which has been desalted. It takes from 35 to 45 minutes to cook and the cooking should be gradual. Sour cream may be added to the gravy. Garnish with the bananas and surround with the corn fritters.

CHICKEN MARYLAND (2)

The following may be accompanied by a sauce crème (see page 156) flavoured with horse-radish, or a tomato sauce (see page 178).

1–2 young roasting chickens, according to size	beaten egg
seasoned flour	fresh white breadcrumbs
	3 oz. clarified butter

Garnish

grilled rashers of bacon	bananas, sliced lengthways and fried in butter
corn fritters (see page 244)	potato croquettes (see page 209)

Joint the chicken as for a sauté, trim, roll in the seasoned flour, brush with egg, then roll in the crumbs, pressing them on firmly. Heat the butter in a large sauté or frying-pan, arrange the pieces in this and fry gently, turning occasionally so that the pieces are well coloured on all sides. When cooked arrange in a hot dish and garnish with the bacon and bananas. Surround with the corn fritters and potato croquettes.

SPATCHCOCK CHICKEN

An excellent luncheon dish.

spring chickens, 2–4 according to size	dust of cayenne
2–3 oz. butter, oiled	watercress
lemon juice	French dressing
grated Parmesan cheese (optional)	pommes paille (straw potatoes)
	1 lemon
salt	sauce Robert (page 148) or barbecue sauce (page 728) or a
freshly ground pepper	good gravy

Split the birds down the back, using scissors. Flatten well on a board and run a small wooden, plated, or silver skewer through the legs to keep them in place. Season well and sprinkle with lemon juice. Leave for half an hour.

Brush well over with some of the butter and set under a previously heated grill with skin side uppermost at a moderate distance away, taking care that they are not too close. Grill to a good brown, approximately 7 minutes, brushing with more of the butter half way through. Turn over and grill for about another 7 minutes, making sure the chicken is absolutely cooked and brushing with butter in the same way.

Now turn over again, brush once more with butter and sprinkle with Parmesan. Sprinkle with the remaining melted butter and grill until crisp. Serve in a large very hot earthenware dish, garnished with lemon quarters, bunches of watercress dipped in French dressing immediately before serving, and pommes paille. Hand the gravy or sauce separately.

If the Parmesan cheese is omitted, dried white crumbs may be used instead, or the surface of the chicken may simply be brushed with butter.

FRICASSÉE OF CHICKEN
with cream sauce and devilled bones

1 cooked boiling fowl	½ pint milk
2 oz. butter	2 rashers of streaky bacon
2 tablespoons each of Harvey and Worcestershire sauce	2 tomatoes, peeled and cut into thick slices
mustard, cayenne, and a dash of anchovy sauce	chopped parsley
¾ oz. flour	salt and freshly ground pepper
	watercress to garnish

Cut the legs off the chicken and if large, and game scissors are available, divide into three joints, otherwise cut into two. Score the surface. Cut the white meat off the carcass and cut into large shreds. Melt a good ½ oz. of the butter in a flat dish, add the sauces, anchovy, mustard, and seasoning to taste. Allow the leg joints to marinade in this for at least an hour.

Melt ¾ oz. of the butter in a saucepan, add the flour (off the fire), dilute gradually with the milk and stir until boiling. Add seasoning and the white meat, then cover the pan and leave on the side of the fire. Melt the rest of the butter in a frying-pan, fry in this the bacon and the prepared tomatoes, and when cooked remove from pan and keep hot. Put in the chicken legs and fry until a rich brown, then pour the marinade in which these legs were soaked into the pan and let all simmer for a minute or two.

Arrange the devilled bones round a fireproof dish for serving, put the white meat in the centre and garnish with the bacon and tomatoes. Strain over the juice from the pan and dust with chopped parsley. Garnish with watercress.

Another good way of using cooked chicken is à la King, which is diced chicken in a cream sauce with various additions. It may be dull or good depending on the flavouring of the sauce and on the additions.

Early recipes for this dish, dating back to the days of King William, said that breast of chicken only might be used, but later recipes indicate the whole of the bird, provided it is young and tender.

CHICKEN A LA KING (1)

cold chicken meat finely diced (about ¾ lb.)

Sauce
2 oz. butter
2 green peppers blanched, sliced, and finely minced
1 oz. flour
1 saltspoon paprika

½ lb. mushrooms (optional but good) and a little butter
lemon juice

2 saltspoons salt
¾ pint good milk or half chicken broth and half milk or cream

Melt the butter and soften in it the finely minced green peppers. Add the flour and seasoning and continue cooking, then dilute with the liquid. Bring to boil and add the diced cooked chicken. Peel the mushrooms, put them in a deep plate or dish with a little dab of butter on each, and seasoning, and just enough butter in the dish to prevent them from sticking. Cover over and cook in the oven. When soft add the mushrooms, the juice in which they were cooked, and a dash of lemon juice to the chicken. This may be served in a fireproof dish, or portions may be served on slices of toast, or suitably sized croûtons. It is perhaps better as a filling for rolls of which the crumb has been taken out, the shell brushed with butter, and the whole baked in the oven, the advantage being that these do not get so soft as toast.

The following recipe from New York is, I believe, one of the earliest for this dish.

CHICKEN A LA KING (2)

cold chicken, diced
1 oz. butter
1 small green pepper, seeded, blanched, and finely sliced and minced
¼ lb. white button mushrooms, finely sliced
½ oz. flour
2 saltspoons salt

1 pint milk, or chicken stock and cream mixed
3 yolks
2 teaspoons onion juice
1 tablespoon lemon juice
2 saltspoons paprika
2 saltspoons celery salt
sherry (optional)

Heat butter, soften green pepper and mushrooms in it. Sprinkle in flour and salt, continue cooking for a few minutes. Add liquid gradually. Add chicken and heat gently without allowing to boil. Beat yolks, add onion and lemon juice, paprika and celery salt. Dilute with a little hot liquor from pan. Pour all back into pan, cook a few more minutes but on no account allow to boil. Add a little sherry if liked.

N.B. This sauce is most safely made in a bain-marie or double boiler.

CHICKEN PIE (1)

1 boiling fowl
seasoning
¼ lb. thinly cut bacon rashers,
  or sliced ham
1 large tablespoon chopped
  parsley

1 medium-sized onion, finely
  chopped
flaky pastry made with ½ lb.
  flour (see page 835)
water and flavouring vegetables
  (1 carrot and 1 onion, both
  sliced)

For a pie the chicken may either be boned and the meat cut into con-
venient-sized pieces, or jointed in the usual way and the pieces cut again.
In either case make a good strong broth from the carcass and/or bones,
water, and flavouring vegetables, strain it off and allow it to cool before
making the pie.

Well season the pieces of chicken, pack them into a pie dish with layers
of the bacon cut into lardons and blanched (or the ham shredded), the
parsley, and the onion. Fill up the dish with the broth, cover with the
pastry, trim and decorate as for meat pies. Bake in a hot oven, i.e. 400° F.,
for about 30–40 minutes. Wrap a piece of wet grease-proof paper round
the pie, decrease the heat of the oven and continue cooking for a further
1–1¼ hours. Take out and fill up with more of the chicken broth.

If to be served cold, make sure that the broth will set to a jelly when cold,
or adjust accordingly with a small quantity of gelatine.

CHICKEN PIE (2)

1 large fowl
1–1½ pints stock or water
3 medium onions, sliced
1 head of celery, sliced, or teaspoon celery seed
1 carrot, sliced
a bouquet garni
1 whole bay-leaf
12 peppercorns, 1 teaspoon
  allspice, and a blade of
  mace, all tied in muslin
½ oz. fine sago or tapioca

4–5 tablespoons white wine or
  stock
seasoning
1 oz. butter
1 egg yolk
1 teaspoon lemon juice
2 hard-boiled eggs
2 or 3 rashers blanched and
  cut in lardons
½ lb. flaky pastry made with
  ½ lb. flour (see page 835)

Make the fowl tender (see page 634). Cut up as for a fricassée and
simmer in stock with the vegetables, bouquet, bay-leaf, and spices 45–60
minutes or until cooked. Pour the broth from the chicken, strain and
return to pan, add sago, wine, adjust seasoning, add butter. Continue
cooking 10–15 minutes. Lift out pieces of chicken and arrange in a pie
dish. Make a liaison with egg yolk, lemon juice, and about ¾ pint of the
hot broth. Add the hard-boiled eggs, cut in two, to the pie dish with the
bacon. Fill up with the thick gravy, taking care not to fill too full or it
will overflow in the baking. Cover with the pastry and bake in a moderate
oven for about an hour, lowering the heat after about 40 minutes.

SUPRÊMES DE VOLAILLE

These appear in more than one form, the word suprême indicating that only the choicest part of the bird is used, that is to say the white meat only. Sometimes the bird, preferably a capon, is cooked as poulet au blanc; the white meat is then carved off and served in a sauce suprême. In another form the meat may be made into a mousse or cream as in the following recipe.

¾ lb. raw minced chicken

Panade

1½ oz. butter	a blade of mace
1½ oz. flour	a slice of onion
1½ gills milk	2 eggs
1 bay-leaf	2 tablespoons cream
1–2 peppercorns	

Sauce

¾ oz. butter	½ gill cream or top of milk
½ oz. flour	1 egg yolk
1½ gills strong chicken stock	

Garnish

2 oz. sliced mushroom	French beans, finished with a
a squeeze of lemon juice, a nut	little butter and a squeeze of
of butter, and seasoning	lemon juice
pommes rissolées or château	

Make the panade as follows: Infuse the bay-leaf, mace, peppercorns, and onion in the milk. When it is well flavoured strain and cool slightly. Melt the butter, add the flour, and pour on the milk. Stir until boiling. Turn on to a plate to cool. Pound chicken well, add the cold panade by degrees. Pass through a wire sieve. Beat the eggs and beat into the mixture. Adjust the seasoning and stir in the cream. Fill into well-greased cutlet or dariole moulds. Poach or steam until firm to the touch, 15–20 minutes.

Meantime make the sauce: Melt ½ oz. of the butter, add the flour, pour on the stock, stir until boiling, add the cream to the egg yolk, add to the sauce as for liaisons, and finish with the rest of the butter.

Cook the mushroom with a squeeze of lemon juice, a nut of butter, and seasoning. Turn out the 'cutlets' and arrange *en couronne* with the mushroom on the top. Coat with the sauce and fill the centre of the dish with the beans, finished with a little butter and a squeeze of lemon juice. Hand the rissolé potatoes separately. If dariole moulds are used, arrange the garnish at each end of the dish.

CHAUDFROID OF CHICKEN

1 plump roasting bird or boiling fowl	truffle for the garnish, or thinly sliced button mushrooms
vegetables and bouquet for flavouring	lightly cooked in a spoonful of water and a squeeze of
¾ pint chaudfroid sauce (see page 164)	lemon juice
2 pints aspic jelly (see page 736)	watercress or fine cress

If a boiling fowl first treat it as on page 634 before simmering. Simmer the bird in water just to cover with the vegetables and herbs until tender. Allow to cool in the liquid. Take up, strain and remove all grease from the stock and use the latter to make the aspic. Also prepare the chaud-froid. Skin the chicken and carve neatly. For this it is usual to cut the 'suprême' (i.e. the breast and wing meat) off in one piece from each side, and then slice each slantwise into three pieces. Take off the legs, remove the bone carefully and cut the leg meat into two neat pieces. If too large divide into three. Lay all the pieces on a wire rack with a tray underneath.

Have the chaudfroid just cool and about to set. Coat over each piece, leave till firm, then give a second coat if necessary. Have ready the garnish, usually slices or motifs of truffle, or button mushrooms cut into thin slices and lightly cooked in a spoonful of water and a squeeze of lemon juice. Lay three or four of these slices overlapping. Arrange the garnish on each piece of chicken when the chaudfroid is set.

Coat over with some of the cool aspic, making sure that every bit is covered and giving an extra coat or two if necessary. Leave till quite set.

Chop the remaining aspic, cover a glass or silver dish with it, making a slight dome in the middle. Arrange the chaudfroid carefully on this, and decorate all around with the cress.

CHICKEN SALAD (1)

1 boiled chicken, cold
3–4 hard-boiled eggs
2 celery hearts or fresh green peppers
½ lb. grapes (muscat for choice)
3 oz. blanched almonds, either salted or devilled

French dressing well flavoured with mustard
sour cream dressing (see page 367)
freshly ground black pepper

Carve chicken and taking meat from bones cut into thin strips. Separate yolks and whites of the hard-boiled eggs, wash and chop whites. Cut celery into strips, or seed, blanch, and slice green peppers. Pip and peel grapes.

Mix these ingredients (except egg yolks) in a bowl and toss them well in a good French dressing, well flavoured with mustard. Arrange in a serving dish and cover with the yolks pressed through a fine wire strainer. Sprinkle with freshly ground black pepper and cover with the nuts roughly chopped. Serve with the cream dressing.

CHICKEN SALAD (2)

1 cold cooked chicken: this may be a boiling fowl, simmered gently in water with vegetables and herbs to flavour; allow to cool in the liquor

¼ pint boiled or cole-slaw dressing (pages 369 and 370)
½ pint mayonnaise (1 egg yolk, 1½ gills oil, salt, pepper, mustard, 1–2 tablespoons vinegar)

Salad

4–6 oz. rice, boiled, drained, and dried	French dressing
	½ lb. firm ripe tomatoes
3 oz. diced French beans or peas, cooked	watercress
	2 hard-boiled eggs
4 oz. diced carrots, cooked	

Carve or slice the chicken neatly, set on one side. Mix the cream dressing and mayonnaise together, lightening them with a little real cream if wished. Mix the rice and vegetables together and moisten well with the French dressing. Scald tomatoes, peel and quarter. Arrange the chicken on top of the rice mixture and coat over with the cream dressing. Garnish the dish with the tomato quarters, the watercress, and the egg, using the sieved yolks and shredded whites separately.

Chicken Millefeuilles. See 'Pièces Froides,' page 629.

Chicken Mousse. See Ham Mousse, page 734.

Chicken curries. See curry chapter, pages 406–11.

Chicken Koulibiaca. See Chapter X, page 279.

See also Winkfield chapter (pages 1003–7) for other chicken recipes.

DUCKS AND DUCKLINGS

Ducklings are from six weeks to three months old, and both ducks and ducklings should have flexible beaks and pliable breast-bones. They are drawn and trussed as for chicken.

Ducks are usually stuffed before roasting. Ducklings will be moister and most tender if stuffed, even though the stuffing is not required for eating.

To roast choose a young bird, use a small quantity of good dripping, and allow 40 minutes to 1 hour according to size. Ducks should not be underdone like wild duck, but must be well cooked. Use young ducks only for roasting, old ducks for braising, or for pâtés. An older bird may be made more tender in the same way as chicken by the method given on page 634.

A 4-lb. duck will serve 4–5 people.

Classic accompaniments

Apple sauce with sage and onion stuffing: from ½ to ¾ lb. stuffing required for each bird.

Orange salad with a liver and sausage-meat stuffing.

Sauce bigarade (orange and red wine) for roast or braised duck.

Green peas, rissolé potatoes, braised celery, are good vegetables to serve with duck.

The classic English way of serving roast duck

Choose young birds, stuff them with sage and onion stuffing. Roast carefully, basting every 15 minutes and turning every time you baste so that the duck is thoroughly cooked all over. Serve with apple sauce, young green peas, and new potatoes.

To carve *

The wings are first removed, only a small portion of the breast being taken with them. The breast is then carved in slanting slices, starting from the wing and working upwards to the breast-bone. When both sides are carved the legs are removed.

ROAST DUCK
with fried apple and salted nuts

1 roasting duck	1 teaspoon flour
orange or anchovy stuffing, or	1 wineglass sherry
other force-meat	grated rind and juice of ½ lemon
butter, bacon fat, or dripping	1 teaspoon chopped parsley
1 cup stock	2 firm medium-sized apples,
2 shallots, finely chopped	preferably Cox's
a dozen or more fresh walnuts	1 bunch of good watercress
salt and pepper	

Stuff the duck, set in a roasting-tin with the dripping. Roast in a moderately hot oven 40–50 minutes, basting well. Remove the duck to a hot dish, keep warm. Pour off the fat from the pan, déglacer with a little of the stock, pour off and reserve it. Now put a spoonful of the fat into a saucepan, heat, add the shallots and fry with the walnuts until turning colour. Salt and pepper well. Add the flour, colour to a delicate brown, and pour on the remaining and the reserved stock. Bring to the boil and simmer to a syrupy consistency. Now add the sherry and lemon rind and juice and simmer again. Finish with the parsley. Wipe the apples, core, and cut into rings. Fry quickly in some of the duck fat to a good brown on both sides.

Carve the duck, arrange in a dish, garnish with the apple rings and watercress, pour some of the gravy round and serve the rest in a sauce-boat. If wished the duck may be sent to the table whole and the gravy and garnish served separately.

Canard aux Navets is a particularly good dish. The classic recipe calls for much butter; nevertheless it is given here and may be regarded as a party dish. An alternative recipe is also given.

CANARD AUX NAVETS (1)

1 good-sized fat duck, or 2	1 oz. onion
smaller ones, with the giblets	2 dozen young, baby turnips,
a carrot	washed before peeling and
the white part of a leek	dried after peeling in a clean
a bouquet garni	cloth so that they brown well
1 pint water	1 tablespoon sugar
seasoning	1 tablespoon flour
5 oz. butter	

* *See plate 15*

Slice the carrot and leek finely.   With these and the giblets, a bouquet garni, water, and seasoning, make ¾ pint good stock.   Heat 2 oz. butter in a large saucepan and brown the duck all over.   Season with salt and pepper, add the finely sliced onion and cook all together, very slowly, for ¾ hour to 1 hour according to the size of the duck.   Cover the pan. Wash, peel, and dry the turnips, which should be small (if not, they must be halved), and cook with the remainder of the butter, very gently, for half an hour with the lid off the pan.   About 10 minutes before they are soft sprinkle them with the sugar so that they brown well.   Take a little of the butter in which the duck was roasted, and mix it to a roux with the flour.   Add the stock gradually and bring to boil.   Put the duck, turnips, and sauce all together.   Adjust the seasoning, continue simmering for about 5 minutes, remove as much fat as possible.   Both duck and turnips should be a rich brown.   Carve or joint the duck and serve surrounded by the turnips.

CANARD AUX NAVETS (2)

1 large or 2 small ducks	a bouquet garni
1 oz. fat, lard, butter, or the fat part of bacon chopped up	seasoning
	1–1½ lb. small turnips
1 heaped tablespoon flour for the roux	1 oz. good fat for frying the turnips (butter preferably)
1 pint stock, which may be made from the giblets	2 teaspoons sugar

Melt the fat.   Put in the duck and colour on every side, cooking gently for about 15–20 minutes.   Take out from pan and put on a plate or dish. Sprinkle the flour in the fat in the pan and brown well.   Dilute gradually with the stock.   Season well.   Simmer for 10 minutes and skim off the fat.   Now strain the sauce into a bowl.   Rinse the pan, put back the sauce, bring back to boiling-point, put in the duck and the bouquet, cover with a grease-proof paper close down over the bird, put on a tightly fitting lid and cook in moderate heat for about 25 minutes, allowing it to simmer steadily and gently.   If this can be done in an oven so much the better.

The turnips are prepared as follows.   Very small ones may be left whole, but big ones should be cut, either in slices or shaped like olives.   They should be washed before peeling, not after they have been peeled, or they will not brown well.   Peel thinly, dry with a clean cloth, heat the ounce of butter and cook the turnips, so that their surfaces become brown. Sprinkle with sugar during cooking to increase the depth of colour. Put the turnips round the duck in the pan and continue simmering for 35–40 minutes.

Lift out the duck, lay it on a flat dish, and arrange the turnips round it. The remaining sauce in the pan should measure not more than a good ½-pint.   If it is more than this it must be reduced.   Skim off all the grease and pour a little of the sauce over the duck, serving the rest separately.

The following recipe calls for an experienced cook:

CANETON AUX CERISES

1 plump duckling
butter

½ pint good strong stock
giblets

Demi-glace

¾ oz. good dripping
mirepoix of 1 oz. each of carrot, onion, shallot, and ½ oz. celery
¾ oz. flour
1 pint good stock

1 dessertspoon chopped mushroom stalks and peelings (duxelles)
a bouquet garni
1 teaspoon tomato purée
1 wineglass burgundy or claret
salt and pepper

Garnish

1 lb. perfect red cherries
1 good orange
3–4 lumps of sugar

1½ oz. castor sugar
1 wineglass port

Rub the duckling well with butter. Set in a roasting-tin with half the stock and the giblets, reserving the liver. Roast in a hot oven, basting well, about 25 minutes. The flesh must be pink. Remove the legs from the duck, and cut the flesh from each side of the breast down to the wing. Lay these two pieces skin side down (this is important or the juice will run out) with the legs on a warm plate. Cover with another plate and set aside. Cut away the top part of the carcass, i.e. breast and wing bones, and set aside also. Break the back up and pound with the liver. Skim as much fat as possible from the liquor in the tin, add the pounded backbones to it with the remaining stock. Boil up, simmer 5 minutes, strain and reserve.

Have ready the demi-glace sauce which should have passed the 'dépouiller' stage and is made as follows: Brown the mirepoix slowly in the dripping, add the flour and brown also. Draw aside, add remaining sauce ingredients with the exception of the wine, season lightly, cover and allow to simmer for about an hour. Now dépouiller the sauce (see page 144), then add the wine and the reserved juice from the dripping pan. Continue simmering with the lid off the pan until a good syrupy consistency.

Meantime prepare the garnish. Stone the cherries. Rub the zest from the orange on to the lumps of sugar. Put the latter into a pan with the castor sugar, port, and the strained juice of the orange. Allow to dissolve, then add the cherries. Cover and shake over a moderate fire for about 5 minutes or until the cherries are just cooked.

Choose an entrée or flat silver dish, arrange the breast-bone in the centre with the legs divided in two, and the wing bones, on each side.

Cut the pieces of breast into slices and arrange on the breast-bone. Spoon enough sauce over to moisten well and arrange the cherries at either end of the dish. Serve the remaining sauce in a boat.

SALMIS OF DUCK (FOR 6)

1 good plump duck, 4–5 lb., with the giblets	1 dessertspoon tomato purée
good dripping for roasting	6 oz. button mushrooms
a good ¾ oz. flour	1 wineglass port or Madeira
1 oz. clarified butter	¾ oz. butter
1¼ pints good, well-flavoured brown stock	seasoning
	lemon juice
	stale bread

Roast the duck with the giblets (reserving the liver) in a little good dripping for about 25–30 minutes. Do this in good time so that it is cool before carving. The duck must be well browned all over.

Prepare the sauce by browning the flour slowly in the butter to a nut-brown. Add the stock and tomato purée and simmer with the lid on the pan about three-quarters of an hour. Carve the duck, removing the breast portions in two pieces, and jointing the legs. Set aside. Break up the back of the carcass and add to the sauce with the giblets, skin, and wing bones. Reserve the breast-bone. Simmer for a further 15–20 minutes. Cool slightly.

Trim the mushrooms, sauter briskly for 3–4 minutes in a sauté pan or casserole in a tablespoon of duck fat; draw aside and add the legs of the duck cut in two or three pieces. Add the pieces of breast and the wine. Cover and reheat very gently. When quite hot strain over the sauce, reheat again and skim well. Allow to simmer gently while doing so, then draw aside. Lightly cook the liver of the duck, pound till smooth with the butter, seasoning, and a squeeze of lemon juice.

Cut croûtons, heart-shaped or triangular, from the bread, fry until golden brown, then spread with the liver paste. Adjust the seasoning of the salmis, adding a squeeze of lemon juice. Set the breast-bone on the serving dish, take out the pieces of breast and quickly cut in slices. Arrange these on the bone with the other pieces of meat round. Boil up the sauce and spoon with the mushrooms over the dish. Surround with the croûtons.

CANARD A LA ROUENNAISE

This is a classic, but not a dish for the inexperienced cook. It is included here with some misgivings as to its practicality. It should be noted that in France the duck for this dish is killed by strangulation so that all blood is retained, and in consequence the flesh is very dark in colour.

1 good duck	1 oz. butter
1 rasher of larding bacon or ½ oz. butter	1 gill demi-glace sauce (see page 143)
salt and pepper	1 gill good red wine, burgundy preferably
4–6 oz. foie gras or liver pâté	
2 shallots, finely chopped and softened in the butter	

Carve the legs off bird and prepare for roasting with the rasher of bacon or the butter spread over the breast. Season with salt and pepper and put to roast in a hot oven (450° F.). Roast for 20–25 minutes only. (The bird should be slightly underdone.) Fifteen minutes before the end of the roasting time grill the two legs, brushing them with the duck fat. (These are not roasted on the bird as the short roasting does not allow sufficient cooking time for the legs.)

When the duck is cooked remove the liver and pound in a mortar with the finely chopped shallots, the butter in which they were softened, and the pâté. Spread this mixture down the centre of a fireproof dish, carve the breast off the duck into long thin slices and arrange on the farce. Cut the legs into two and place at either end. Keep the dish hot. Break up the bones of the carcass, put in a press or mortar to crush to extract all the juice; failing that, place in a colander and press with a weight. Mix with the demi-glace and red wine and reboil. Pour over the duck. Return to the hot oven for 5 minutes before serving.

Croûtons may be used as a garnish.

For duck served with lemon compôte, and Caneton Sauvage à la Fenouil, see Winkfield chapter, pages 1007 and 1008.

GEESE AND GOSLINGS

Geese and goslings (called green geese until they are three months old) have yellow feet and bills when young. As the birds grow older the feet and bills become reddish in colour. The feet should be soft and moist, the flesh rosy, and the fat a pale yellow. In this country they are usually sold when ready for cooking, but if they are home-killed they should hang for 5–7 days according to the weather.

ROAST GOOSE

A 10-lb. goose serves eight people. It may be stuffed and roasted and takes about 2 hours. Goose can be very tough, and if the bird is not of the youngest and tenderest it may be treated in the same way as is recommended for older fowls on page 634. To roast: Stuff, truss, and sprinkle with flour, put for the first 15–20 minutes in a hot oven, about 400° F., and then reduce to 350. Baste every 20 minutes. Put a sour apple into the pan to flavour the gravy (see stuffing chapter, page 688). Crab-apples roasted whole or sliced make an excellent garnish, or fried slices of apple are also good. In this case a herb stuffing or one containing fruit may be chosen (see stuffing chapter, page 688).

The left-overs of goose are best used up in a devil, devilled bones in other words, and these may be served with stuffed prunes. They may also be pounded and used in the making of pâté. Cold goose, thinly sliced, with cranberry sauce is excellent.

SALMIS OF GOOSE A LA GRECQUE
salmis of goose with red wine sauce and dolmas

1 goose or duck, with the giblets	1 glass or more red wine
dripping	½ pint stock

Sauce

1 oz. butter	1 tablespoon chopped mush-
¾ oz. flour	room stalks and peelings
mirepoix: 1 oz. each of carrot,	a bouquet garni
onion, shallot, and celery	½ teaspoon tomato purée
¾ pint stock	1 glass red wine
	salt and pepper

Dolmas

1 dozen small blanched vine or	1 chopped onion
cabbage leaves	½ oz. butter
2 tablespoons boiled rice	chopped herbs
the liver and cooked gizzard of	1 egg
the goose or duck	tomato-flavoured stock

Garnish

¼–½ lb. button mushrooms	½ lb. button onions, and sugar,
	salt, and a nut of butter for
	finishing

Set goose in roasting-tin with the stock and dripping, reserving the wine, and roast in a moderate oven for about an hour. Meantime make the sauce. Brown the mirepoix in the butter, add flour and brown also. Add all the remaining ingredients and simmer 30–40 minutes. Meantime, for the dolmas, soften the onion in the butter, add the diced raw liver, cook a few minutes and add the finely diced gizzard, herbs, and seasoning. Add to the rice, and bind with the egg. Fill into the cabbage leaves, roll up and lay in a shallow pan or casserole. Moisten with a tomato-flavoured stock and simmer 20 minutes. Now sauter the mushrooms quickly, and blanch the onions. Finish the latter in a nut of butter, salt, and sugar in order to glaze them. Strain the sauce, reserving the vegetables. Carve the bird, pound the carcass with the reserved wine and sauce vegetables, and bring up to the boil. Strain and add the liquor to the sauce. Add mushrooms to the sauce, carve the goose and dish with dolmas and onions. Spoon over the sauce. Set dish in oven for a quarter of an hour before serving with a mousseline of potatoes.

A recipe for Goose Pâté will be found in the Winkfield chapter, page 977.

TURKEYS

Turkeys, when young enough, are called turkey poults, and they should have smooth black legs. They are then tender for roasting. Freshly killed turkeys have bright full eyes, the flesh should be white, and the cartilage at the end of the breast-bone pliable. They are usually sold ready for roasting, but home-killed birds should hang for a week or longer in cold weather, and from 3 to 4 days in mild weather. Approximately 2 quarts of stuffing are required for a large bird, but usually two kinds are used, say sausage-meat for the carcass and prune and apple in the breast.

The drawing and preparation of bigger birds such as geese and turkeys is difficult to do at home, and as in this country they are usually bought ready for cooking, details of preparation are not given. The local poulterer will prepare home-killed birds for the table for a small fee.

BOILED TURKEY

Choose a moderate-sized hen turkey, tie in a clean cloth, or failing this skim well during the first quarter of an hour of cooking. Cover the bird with warm water, salted, and simmer for $1\frac{1}{2}$–$1\frac{3}{4}$ hours. Serve with celery or mushroom sauce. The celery sauce is made by the addition of cooked celery in purée to a good béchamel. Take 3 heads of celery or 2 roots of celeriac and cook till tender, putting into the water 1 onion stuck with 2 or 3 cloves and the necessary seasoning. Make into a purée. For the mushroom sauce take half a dozen good-sized mushrooms, peel, cook in a little milk, chop finely, and add to the béchamel sauce.

ROAST TURKEY

Choose a medium-sized bird, about 10–12 lb. A turkey is easier to cook if not too big, and is a better fit in the average oven. A hen turkey is supposed to have more delicate and tender flesh than a cock bird.

Alternative methods of roasting

English fashion. Use a good beef dripping, and if possible have a good proportion of bacon or ham fat mixed with it. This not only gives a good flavour, but a brown and glistening finish to the bird.

Heat the fat first in the roasting-tin, which should be large enough to hold the turkey comfortably and leave room to baste easily. The fat should cover the bottom of the tin to a depth of about 1 inch. Set the bird, after stuffing, in the tin, baste, then cover with paper and put into a moderate oven, 350°–400° F.

Roast, allowing approximately 10 minutes to the pound, and basting every 15–20 minutes. Take the paper off while doing so and replace it until about the last half-hour, when it may be removed for the final browning.

Turn the bird over fairly frequently during the roasting to ensure that the legs get a thorough cooking, and as much of the top heat of the oven as possible. So often the breast of a turkey, and particularly that of a large bird, gets stringy and overcooked, while the legs remain underdone. This can be avoided by cooking the bird for a greater part of the time on its side and turning it over as described.

An indication that the bird is cooked is the tendency of the meat to shrink away from the knuckle end of the drumstick. The flesh should not crack or split; this means that the heat has been too great and the roasting too rapid. During the last half-hour remove paper and baste well for the final browning. Then dish; remove the trussing and stuffing threads. Prepare the gravy as for an ordinary roast. Be careful to add very little flour (if any) to thicken, and use a good stock made from the giblets in preference to water or vegetable stock.

French fashion. The advantage of this method of roasting is that the flesh of the turkey (always inclined to be on the dry side) will remain succulent and tender, and the gravy will be rich and full of flavour. It is a specially good method to use if the turkey is to be eaten cold.

For roasting allow between 4 and 6 oz. of butter according to the size of the turkey. Rub the butter well over the breast and legs of the bird, season well with freshly ground black pepper and a touch of salt, cover with paper and set in a roasting-tin. Put the giblets in the tin with a pint or more of hot water or stock, or alternatively use a well-flavoured stock previously made from the giblets. The liver is kept on one side for frying later; it is then thinly sliced or diced and added to the gravy.

Cook as for the first method in the same oven temperature, but allowing about 20 minutes to the pound and removing the covering paper half way through the cooking. It may be necessary to lower the heat a little at this stage. Care must be taken to see that the liquid in the tin does not reduce too much; water or stock should be added to keep it to about ¾ pint.

When the turkey is well browned and thoroughly cooked, dish and strain off the liquid from the tin into a saucepan.

Skim off some of the butter and mix it with a heaped teaspoon of flour. Work it to a creamy paste, then add it to the gravy. Stir, boil up well, skim, adjust the seasoning, and add the liver before serving.

N.B. If no stuffing is to be used a bunch of parsley and a little of the butter may be put inside the bird.

The following is a good way of cooking a small turkey. Simmer it for half an hour in water or stock, lift it out and rub all over, fairly thickly, with butter or margarine. Then cover with fine breadcrumbs and pat these in place. Finish roasting in the oven.

For Devilled Turkey Bones see page 725.

GUINEA-FOWL, OR PINTADE

In England the guinea-fowl has become a domestic bird; in its native haunts it is a wild fowl and its flesh has a slightly gamy taste, something between chicken and pheasant. The flesh of a young bird is tender but a little on the dry side. For this reason, when it is to be roasted, the stuffing should contain some fat and the breast be covered with a rasher of larding bacon or well buttered. If the bird is killed at home, in warm weather, it should hang at least 2 days, and in cold weather longer. It should not be plucked before hanging, but immediately before cooking. The best way to treat a young guinea-fowl is to roast it 45–60 minutes with the breast covered with larding bacon; it must be well basted. The gravy served with it should be from the pan in which it has been roasted, diluted with a little stock or vegetable water, and the addition of a little sour cream is excellent; alternatively it may be roasted in the French manner. It may well be served with a sweet compôte of cranberries or plums, flavoured with fresh tarragon leaves.

Guinea-fowl, of course, may be braised, grilled, or cooked *en casserole*, or in many of the ways recommended for pigeons, ducks, or chickens.

PIGEONS

Pigeons when young have a fat breast, flexible beak, thick neck, and supple breast-bone. The skin is rosy, the flesh red. When all these signs are present the birds are suitable for roasting. If the birds are old and tough they are only suitable for cooking in a casserole or for braising.

One can quickly get tired of pigeons and it is a good thing to vary the ways of cooking them. Where there is any question of the tenderness of the bird, it is as well to submit it to the preliminary dry cooking as for chicken (page 634).

ROAST PIGEON

This is perhaps the nicest way of serving tender young birds. Allow half a bird per person. The pigeon may be stuffed with its own liver, or any one of the mixtures used for duck. In particular those stuffings containing fruit are good, such as the raisin, apricot, and almond stuffing (see page 695).

Cover the breast with a piece of bacon tied in place with string, or brush with melted butter and dredge with flour. Roast in a hot oven for 25–35 minutes, baste well. After 15 minutes remove the rasher of bacon in order to brown the breast. But the bacon should be served with the bird. When roasted put on a hot dish, make the gravy with a little additional jus, pour around and garnish with bunches of fresh watercress which have been dipped in French dressing.

Very young tender pigeons may be grilled. They should be brushed over with melted butter on both sides and grilled under a hot grill until cooked through.

PIGEON CRAPAUDINE

pigeons	a good sauce such as rémoulade,
breadcrumbs	piquante, or devil (see pages
melted butter	168, 177, and 725)
seasoning	sliced gherkins

This is a dish for young and tender pigeons. Cut the pigeons right down the back and flatten them out. Have the breadcrumbs on one plate and the melted butter, seasoned with salt and pepper, on another.   Dip the pigeons first in the butter, brushing it into the crevices, then in the crumbs, covering well on each side.   With a palette-knife, or the blade of an ordinary knife, pat well to make the crumbs adhere to the surface. Have the grill hot, but to start with do not put the birds too near the heat or the crumbs will be burnt before the flesh is cooked through.   The time required is approximately 20–25 minutes.   Start to grill on the cut side.   The birds must be turned carefully so that the breadcrumbs remain undisturbed, and be basted from time to time with melted butter. Serve separately a good sauce, such as rémoulade, piquante, or devil sauce, and garnish with sliced gherkins.

This recipe may also be used for very small, very young rabbits.

PIGEON A LA FLAMANDE

2 pigeons	$\frac{1}{2}$–$\frac{3}{4}$ pint stock
1 oz. butter	salt and pepper
2 rashers of fat bacon cut in lardons	2 oz. raisins
6 or 8 small onions	beurre manié (see page 139) or arrowroot (optional)

Heat butter in a casserole, brown pigeons on both sides, lift out and put on a hot plate.   Brown the bacon and the onions in the same butter. Split pigeons and put with onions and bacon back into the casserole.   Add enough stock to come three-quarters of the way up the birds.   Season. Cook in a moderate oven for 1 hour.   While the pigeons are cooking soak raisins (stoned if necessary) in 2–3 tablespoons warm stock or water and add half an hour before end of cooking.   The gravy may be thickened slightly with beurre manié or, if a clearer gravy is preferred, a level teaspoon of arrowroot slaked first in a spoonful or two of water or sherry.

PIGEONS EN COCOTTE NORMANDE

2 pigeons	$\frac{3}{4}$ pint stock
1 oz. good dripping	$\frac{1}{4}$ pint cider
2 oz. onions, sliced	seasoning
3 apples (1 sliced and 2 cut in rings for garnish)	a bouquet garni
$\frac{3}{4}$ oz. flour	2 rashers of bacon
	chopped parsley

Brown the pigeons in the dripping in a casserole or *cocotte*, lift out and cut them in half.   Trim away the backbone with the scissors.   In the same fat brown the onion and the sliced apple.   Sprinkle in the flour, brown slightly, pour in the stock and cider and bring to the boil.   Season, add the bouquet and the pigeons.   Cover the *cocotte* tightly and put into the oven for about 1½–2 hours.   While this is going on cut the other apples into rings for frying.   Remove the pigeons, strain the sauce and reduce over a quick fire.   Arrange the pigeons in a dish, pour over the sauce and garnish with the apple rings fried quickly till brown.   Cut the rashers in half, fry or grill lightly and put on top of the pigeons just before serving.   Dust with chopped parsley.

PIGEONS WITH CHERRIES

2 good plump pigeons
1 oz. dripping or bacon fat
2 sliced shallots or large spring
    onions
1 oz. flour
1½ pints good stock

a bouquet garni
¼ lb. good red cherries, stoned
½ oz. butter
feuilletons and sour cream
    (optional)

Brown the pigeons slowly but thoroughly in the dripping in a casserole. Lift them out and in the same fat brown the sliced shallots. While the onions are browning split the pigeons in half and trim the backbone with the scissors. Sprinkle the flour into the pan and brown lightly. Add the stock, bring to the boil and add the pigeons with the bouquet garni. Cook in the casserole in a slow to moderate oven for about 1½ hours. Then remove the pigeons carefully and keep warm. Reduce the sauce by boiling quickly until it is of a syrupy consistency. Strain the sauce and replace in it the pigeons to reheat thoroughly. Sauter the stoned cherries quickly in the butter. Dish the pigeons, pour over the sauce and scatter over the cherries, which should be sizzling hot. This dish is sometimes served with crisp feuilletons of puff pastry, and a good addition is ¿ little sour cream beaten into the sauce after straining.

PIGEONS EN CASSEROLE A L'ITALIENNE

2 plump pigeons
8 pickling onions
salt and pepper
2 rashers of fat or streaky bacon

a small nut of butter if necessary
1 pint tomato sauce (approx.),
    well flavoured and seasoned
    (see page 178, recipe 1,
    double quantity)

Dice the bacon, melt it in a stew-pan over gentle heat to extract the fat. Add a small nut of butter if more fat is required. When the bacon begins to brown put in the pigeons with the onions and seasoning, cover and cook gently for half an hour, turning the pigeons from time to time. Meantime prepare the tomato sauce. Then split the pigeons in two, trim, and lay them in a casserole with the onions and bacon, pour over the sauce and cook in a moderate oven 20–30 minutes. Serve with a risotto, nouilles, or fried gnocchi.

Young tender pigeons may also be fried in the following way. Cut each bird into four pieces. Prepare a small quantity of marinade, using cider and white wine, chopped shallot, chopped parsley, a clove of crushed garlic, salt and pepper. Marinade the pieces in this for 2 hours, then drain and dry. Sprinkle with flour, dip in seasoned egg and breadcrumbs. Fry in shallow fat for approximately 15 minutes. Drain carefully, serve with fried parsley (see page 49). Garnish with eighths of lemon, and a highly seasoned tomato or vinaigrette sauce may be handed. The latter may have a dessertspoon of finely chopped mixed herbs added to it.

When pigeons are very plentiful the following is not too extravagant a dish.

Cut long, thick slices (each slice should be half the breast of a pigeon), make a long incision down the middle of each piece, without separating the two halves, stuff this opening with well-seasoned, chopped, cooked mushroom, season well, dip each piece into egg and breadcrumbs, pour over them a little melted butter, and grill gently until each fillet is thoroughly cooked.

PIGEONS A LA CAMPAGNE

A party dish, suitable for a shooting party, and may be put in a hay-box.

4 small pigeons	1 teaspoon sugar
4 oz. streaky bacon, in the piece	6 oz. small mushrooms
	¾ oz. flour
1 oz. butter	1 pint stock
2 dozen small pickling onions	1 gill white wine or cider

Cut the bacon up into small squares, blanch and drain. Take a casserole or stew-pan big enough to hold the pigeons and in it heat the butter. Put the bacon in this and cook gently until lightly coloured. Then remove with a skimmer and keep hot. In the same fat brown the onions gently, shaking the pan, but taking care not to break the onions up. Sprinkle with a teaspoon of sugar towards the end of cooking to help colour them. Lift out with a strainer and add to the bacon. Cut the mushrooms in halves or quarters, according to size, and cook them gently in the same butter. Lift out and add to the bacon and onions. Now put in the pigeons and allow to colour to a pale golden brown on both sides. Lift out, add the flour to the butter and allow to cook until pale brown. Dilute gradually with the stock and wine. Bring to boil and strain. Rinse the pan, put in all the ingredients, sauce, bacon, onions, mushrooms, and pigeons. Put on a tightly fitting lid, cook gently, never more than simmering-point, preferably in the oven. When done lift out the pigeons, onions, and mushrooms and arrange on a hot dish. Skim as much grease as possible from the sauce. There should be only about ¾ pint juice left. If there is much more than this it should be reduced over a good fire. Scrape the sides of the pan well and strain this sauce over the pigeons.

CASSEROLE DE PIGEONS LIÉGOISE

1 oz. good butter	1 dozen baby new potatoes
3 young plump pigeons	¼ pint shelled peas
4 oz. streaky bacon cut into lardons and blanched	2 sprigs of savory
	salt
1 dozen spring onion bulbs	freshly ground pepper
1 dozen baby carrots	4–5 tablespoons boiling water

Heat the butter in a casserole. Brown the birds slowly and thoroughly in this, then remove and add the bacon. Continue to rissoler gently until brown, then take out and put in the vegetables, well dried, all except the peas.   Continue to fry gently for 5–6 minutes.

Put the pigeons into an earthenware casserole, surround with the bacon, vegetables, and peas.   Season well, add the savory and moisten with the water.   Cover tightly and seal the edge with a flour and water paste. Cook in a slow oven 1¼–1½ hours.   Serve straight to table in the casserole, where the pigeons can be split on a hot plate before serving.

N.B. The onions used for this dish should be those with a very pronounced bulb, snow-white streaked faintly with green.

A salmis differs from a casserole in that the process is a mixture of roasting and braising, the roasting being done first and for a short time so that the flesh is *saignant*.   The sauce is added to the meat, together with all the juices from the bird.   It is a suitable process for young birds.   (See Salmis of Duck, page 660.)

SALMIS DE PIGEONS

2 young pigeons
dripping for roasting
1 oz. each of carrot, onion, and celery, cut into small dice (mirepoix)
1 oz. butter
¾ oz. flour, scant
¾ pint stock

½ teaspoon tomato purée
bouquet garni of ¼ bay-leaf, a sprig of thyme, 4–5 parsley stalks
seasoning
1 wineglass red wine
2–4 oz. mushrooms
6 croûtons of bread

Roast the pigeons lightly in a hot oven (about 15 minutes).   Take out and cool.   Meanwhile brown the mirepoix in the butter, reserving ¼ oz., then add the flour and allow to brown slowly.   Draw aside, add the stock, purée, and bouquet.   Season lightly and simmer, skimming occasionally, for 20 minutes.   Then strain.

Carve the pigeons and lay the pieces in a casserole.   Chop or pound the carcasses, add the wine and turn into a saucepan with the strained vegetables, etc.   Allow this to boil rapidly for a few minutes, then strain back again into the sauce, pressing well to extract all the juice.   Simmer the sauce for about 20 minutes, or until a syrupy consistency.   Adjust seasoning.

Pour half the sauce over the pigeons in the casserole, set on a gentle heat or in the oven for about 10–15 minutes.   Meantime sauter the mushrooms in remaining butter and fry the croûtons.   Add the mushrooms with the remaining sauce to the salmis, and continue cooking for a further 7 minutes.   Then dish and garnish with the croûtons.

PIGEONS FARCIS ALLEMANDE

2 pigeons
¾ oz. dripping
1 carrot, 1 onion
½ oz. flour

¾ pint bouillon
a bouquet garni
salt and pepper
croûtons of fried bread

Force-meat stuffing

1 large onion
the livers
3 oz. mushrooms
1 oz. butter
2 heaped tablespoons fresh
white breadcrumbs

1 dessertspoon finely chopped
parsley
a small beaten egg
a little stock if necessary

Split the flesh of the pigeons down the back and work loose so as to remove all the body bones, leaving the leg bones (this is usually done with a small knife known as a boning-knife). Prepare the force-meat as follows: Finely chop the onion, livers, and mushrooms. Sauter these lightly in the butter. Add, off the fire, the crumbs, parsley, egg, and a little stock if necessary to moisten. Flatten the birds on a board, spread the mixture on the inner surface and sew up firmly. Melt the dripping in a casserole and brown the birds all over, adding the sliced onion and carrot during the process. Add flour and brown slightly. Draw aside and add the liquid, bouquet, and seasoning. Braise slowly for 40–60 minutes. To serve cut the birds in half and arrange on croûtons of fried bread. Reduce the gravy, correct the seasoning, and strain over the birds. This dish is very good accompanied by a compôte of fruit—apricots, oranges, apples, plums.

PIGEON AND MUSHROOM PIE

Preparations should begin a day in advance.

½ lb. good rump steak
3–4 plump pigeons
1 dessertspoon chopped onion
1 tablespoon chopped parsley
grated rind and juice of 1
lemon
salt and pepper
a good pinch of ground mace
a nut of butter or fat

4 oz. mushrooms
seasoned flour
good stock made from the
bones, with vegetables and
a bouquet to flavour
½ lb. flaky pastry (page 835) or
pâte moulée (page 842)
beaten egg

Cut the steak into squares. Bone the pigeons, cut in pieces, reserving the livers. Sprinkle over the onion and parsley, add a little grated rind and juice of lemon with salt, pepper, and ground mace. Leave overnight. Meantime break up the bones and make some good strong stock with the addition of a few vegetables and a bouquet to flavour. Strain and cool. Sauter the livers in a nut of butter or fat. Chop the mushrooms. Roll the steak in seasoned flour and fill into a pie dish with layers of the pigeons and their marinade, the mushrooms and sliced liver. Add more seasoning if necessary. Fill up the dish with stock and cover with the pastry. Trim, decorate, and paint with beaten egg. Bake in a hot oven, first to cook the pastry, about 30 minutes, then lower the heat and continue cooking for another 1–1¼ hours. Half way through cooking wrap a piece of wet grease-proof paper over and round the pie to prevent the pastry hardening.

For a recipe for Spiced Pigeon and Rice see Winkfield chapter, page 1010.

RABBITS

All recipes given for rabbit may be used also for veal.

Rabbits are best from October to February.

Wild rabbits are 'paunched' or gutted immediately they are killed; they are then hung for 4 or 5 days before being skinned. In warm, moist weather they must be carefully watched, as they should not be used if in the least tainted.

A good-sized wild rabbit weighs approximately 2½ lb. and will feed 5–6 people. Tame rabbits bred for the table can weigh much more, between 5 and 6 lb. They have much more meat on them and the flesh is white. Ostend rabbits are tame rabbits specially bred for the market; they may weigh as much as 8 or 9 lb. The flesh is white and of delicate flavour.

If it is wished that the flesh of the rabbit shall be particularly white and of delicate flavour, the joints should be soaked for 12 hours in a marinade of water and vinegar, a teaspoon of vinegar to each pint of water. The following morning the water is thrown away and the pieces of rabbit washed and dried. Many people to whom rabbit is indigestible find that after this preliminary treatment it is so no longer. This treatment is suitable for all rabbits and in particular should be applied to imported ones. Frozen rabbits or those that have been in cold storage may need as much as 24 hours' soaking, and the water should be changed frequently.

Rabbits for roasting should be neatly trussed, but for casseroles, sautés, fricassées, etc., they should be jointed first and then soaked. Rabbits for roasting and for sautés or casseroles may be marinaded as for hare after soaking.

Roast rabbit is inclined to be dry, and should be stuffed with a good force-meat and well basted during cooking. Rabbits are really best done in other ways, *en casserole.* as sautés, fricassées, or devils.

To skin a rabbit

Cut off the four feet above the knee. Lay the rabbit on the table on its back, with the tail towards you. With a sharp knife make a cut about 1 inch long across the belly, near the thighs. Pull the skin thus disengaged off the thighs, turning them out of the skin as though pulling off a glove. Pull the skin towards the tail, until the whole of the lower part of the body is free from skin. Then turn the body over so that the head is towards you, take a firm hold of the skin and pull it as far as it will go. Turn out the legs, one by one, then cut round the head and pull the skin right off.

Another method of skinning

Hang the rabbit up on a meat hook forced through the skin of both back legs, put a basin below the head, which hangs downwards. Take a sharp-pointed knife and cut all round the skin of the legs just below the hook. Cut down the back of each hind leg, and pull the skin off. Now cut right through the skin just below the tail and the vent, take a firm hold of the skin and pull it right off the body—it comes off quite easily—as though pulling off a glove inside out. Turn the front legs out of the skin like the fingers out of a glove, easing off the fold of skin that holds them with the point of the knife. Pull downwards until the ears stop you. Cut off the ears and pull down until you come to the eyes. Take these right out and cut through the tissue that joins the skin to the head. This will allow you to pull the skin right off the muzzle.

To truss

When the rabbit is to be roasted whole, truss it by drawing the back legs forward and the front legs back, and run a skewer through the head into the back, so that the head is kept upright.

To joint

The legs are first chopped off, and the 'wings' cut away from the ribs. The back is chopped into three or four pieces, the head (split) and neck being used for stock.

Either red-currant or sharp elderberry and apple jelly may be served with roast rabbit. Onions with bacon, or pickled pork, are classic garnishes for a casserole, gibelotte, or fricassée.

Roast rabbit

A rabbit may be stuffed with any of the poultry stuffings, and sewn up and roasted whole. It requires to be well basted and takes from 45 to 50 minutes, according to its size. The flesh should be thoroughly well cooked throughout. It may be served with gravy and red-currant jelly. To some people a whole roasted rabbit is an unpleasant sight, because normally the head is left on, so if preferred either the back and the thighs may be stuffed and roasted, or the back only. If it is to be the back and thighs, stuff in exactly the same way as for whole roast rabbit.

The following is a good recipe when rabbits are plentiful, but extravagant in that the back only is dished.

LAPEREAU RÔTI

See note on preliminary treatment of rabbit on page 671.

2 young rabbits	a bay-leaf
2 rashers of bacon	seasoning and 2 cloves of garlic
2 carrots	an extra bouquet of herbs for
2 onions	the inside of the rabbit
a bouquet garni	1 tablespoon wine vinegar

Cut away the legs of the rabbits, leaving only the flesh of the back, and cook all the trimmings in water with the vegetables finely cut up, the herbs and seasoning. Simmer gently until all are tender. Add only enough water to cover these ingredients; by the time you have finished the cooking there should be about ½ pint of liquid. If there is more, reduce; if less, add a little water. Strain off the liquor, pressing to get all the juice possible. Inside body of the rabbit put the garlic, crushed, and the extra bouquet of herbs. Season well and cover with the bacon. Put in a roasting-tin and baste with the liquid that you have strained, adding the vinegar. Finish cooking and basting, undo the bacon, allow the rabbit to brown a little more. Skim off the grease and serve with the juice in the pan.

Grilling

Rabbit may also be grilled; it may be previously treated in the way described on page 671 for whitening the flesh. The grilling must be slow and thorough, so that the flesh is thoroughly cooked. The joints should be marinaded for an hour or so in oil, chopped parsley, chopped chives, and seasoning. They are then egged and breadcrumbed, grilled and basted as they grill with the marinade. They may be served with a sharp sauce such as a vinaigrette (page 367) or sauce tartare (page 168). The joints may also be spread with mustard worked into a little butter after they have been marinaded. They are then grilled and basted from time to time with melted butter.

RABBIT COOKED WITH PRUNES

Preparations should begin a day in advance.

1 rabbit	1 gill red wine
marinade	1½–2 gills stock
1 oz. butter	seasoning
½ oz. flour	⅓ lb. prunes

The day before this dish is to be eaten cut the rabbit in pieces and put them in the marinade given on page 671. Soak the prunes all night, preferably in warm tea. Next day lift the pieces out of the marinade, dry well. Heat the butter and colour the pieces on each side. Sprinkle with the flour and allow this also to colour. Moisten with the red wine and stock, add seasoning. Put in the stoned prunes. Bring to boiling-point, cover, and continue cooking very gently for about an hour, if not in the oven, then over gentle heat. At the end of the cooking there should be about ½ pint of liquid. If more it may be poured off and reduced.

LAPIN BRABANÇONNE

Begin preparations a day in advance.

1 young rabbit	mild ale
lard or dripping	bread
3 oz. pickled pork or streaky	French mustard
bacon, blanched and drained	seasoning
4 medium-sized onions, sliced	2 lumps of sugar

Soak rabbit overnight in salted water with a dash of vinegar, wash, dry, and joint. Heat the fat in a casserole, cut pork or bacon into short strips and brown in the fat with the onions. Then take them out and brown the pieces of rabbit well in the remaining fat. When a good brown drain off the fat, put the onions and bacon back on the top of the rabbit, and cover with a slice or two of bread spread generously with French mustard. Moisten up to the bread with a mild ale, season well, adding 2 lumps of sugar. Cover closely and set the casserole in a slow oven for 2 hours, or until perfectly cooked.

GIBELOTTE DE LAPIN

Preparations should begin a day in advance.

1 rabbit	1 teaspoon tomato purée
marinade of vinegar, salt, and water	a clove of garlic crushed with salt
1 oz. dripping	salt and pepper
1 oz. flour	3 oz. bacon, blanched
2 shallots or 1 small onion	20 small pickling onions (approx.)
1 pint stock (approx.)	12 croûtons (optional)
a bouquet garni	

Joint the rabbit and soak in vinegar, salt, and water overnight. (In addition to this the joints may afterwards be marinaded for an hour or two in a little vinegar with finely chopped parsley, onion, and a bay-leaf.) Dry the pieces thoroughly and brown well in hot dripping. Dust over with the flour, add the finely chopped shallots and continue cooking for a few minutes. Then add the stock, bouquet garni, tomato purée, the garlic and salt and pepper, and allow to simmer, preferably in the oven, for about an hour. In the meantime cut the bacon up in small pieces and cook it in a little dripping in a frying-pan. Lift it out and brown the onions in the same fat. When the rabbit is half cooked add the onions and the bacon. Finish cooking and serve in the casserole with croûtons arranged round.

LAPIN MOUTARDE

Begin preparations a day in advance.

1 rabbit	seasoning
2–4 oz. bacon or salt pork, if possible in one piece	1 heaped dessertspoon French mustard
2 oz. bacon fat or butter	a bouquet garni
4–6 onions according to size	½ gill cream or evaporated milk
1 tablespoon flour	1 dessertspoon chopped parsley
1¼ pints stock	

Joint the rabbit and soak it overnight in vinegar and salted water. Drain and dry thoroughly. Cut the bacon into dice, blanch and drain. Melt the fat in a casserole, add the onions cut into quarters lengthways and shake over the fire for about 3 minutes. Then put in the rabbit and bacon and sauter briskly to a golden brown. Shake in the flour and turn the pieces well about till flour is just coloured; pour on the stock, add seasoning, the mustard and herbs, and bring slowly to the boil. Simmer till quite tender, about 1–1¼ hours. If the sauce is rather thin pour it off and reduce rapidly, then add the cream and the chopped parsley. Pour back on to the rabbit and serve.

LAPIN SAUTÉ CHASSEUR

1 young rabbit cut up into suitably sized pieces
3 dessertspoons olive oil
1 dessertspoon clarified butter
1 tablespoon finely chopped shallot
1 teaspoon flour
1 teaspoon tomato purée

1 wineglass white wine
½ pint stock
3–4 oz. mushrooms
a little butter to cook mushrooms
fried croûtons
chopped parsley

Heat the oil and butter in a sauté pan, lay in the pieces of rabbit, scatter the chopped shallots into the pan and sauter over a moderate fire 15–20 minutes. Give a dusting of flour, add the purée, the wine, and lastly the stock. Cover and simmer gently three-quarters of an hour, or until the rabbit is tender. In the meantime wash and trim the mushrooms, cut into fine slices, sauter them lightly in butter and add to the pan 10 minutes before serving. Dish the rabbit, reduce the sauce to a syrupy consistency and spoon over, and serve garnished with the croûtons and a good dusting of chopped parsley.

RABBIT WITH LENTIL PURÉE

1 good rabbit, jointed
4 oz. lentils, soaked overnight
3 oz. onion, sliced
1 stick of celery, sliced
a bouquet garni
salt and pepper

nut of butter
beurre manié (page 139), in the quantity of ¾ oz. flour and ¾ oz. butter to a pint of liquid
croûtons of fried bread

Prepare the rabbit as on page 671. Rinse it well and put all, except the head, in a stew-pan with the lentils, onion, celery, bouquet, and seasoning. Just cover with water, put on the lid and simmer over gentle heat for 2 hours or until the lentils and rabbit are very tender. Put the rabbit in a covered bowl to keep hot. Strain off the vegetables, reserving the liquor, and rub them through a hair or nylon sieve. Return the purée to the rinsed pan, dilute with stock to bring to a quantity sufficient to coat rabbit well and allow enough for each helping. Reheat, add beurre manié in proportions given and adjust seasoning. Add nut of butter. The sauce should have the consistency of cream. Replace the rabbit and warm gently. Pile up in centre of a hot dish and serve croûtons of fried bread.

In late summer use dried peas instead of lentils, or ¾ pint shelled peas, or a tin of processed peas. A spoonful or two of thick cream added at the last is a great improvement, and makes the sauce particularly smooth and creamy.

RABBIT PIE
excellent hot or cold

2 young rabbits
seasoning
2 onions, sliced
a little sage or savory
cooked bacon
hard-boiled egg
chopped parsley

12 stuffed prunes (see page 705)
1 pint good jellied stock
pie pastry (flaky or rough puff, see pages 835 and 837)
beaten egg

Bone the rabbits, steep the pieces in salted water with a dash of vinegar for some hours, put them into a pan and cover with fresh cold water, add salt and pepper, sliced onions, and sage or savory. Bring to the boil and simmer gently for a good 15 minutes. Take out the pieces of rabbit and put them into a pie dish with a little cooked bacon, slices of hard-boiled egg, and a good sprinkling of chopped parsley. Add also about a dozen stuffed prunes, season well and pour in a bare pint of good jellied stock. Cover with a pie pastry, glaze with beaten egg, and cook in a fairly quick oven to a good brown for about an hour.

For Lapin à la Bressane see Winkfield chapter, page 1010.

GAME

August to March is, generally speaking, the season for game. It starts with grouse, black game, capercailzie, hazel hen, ptarmigan, quail, and wild duck. Partridge and pheasant follow in September and October. In addition to these there are also snipe, woodcock, teal, widgeon, plover, and ortolan.

Venison and hare are also forms of game, the best time for hare being August to February. After being shot game needs to be well hung; the actual time varies according to the type of game, the weather, the taste of those who are going to eat it, and, to some extent, the age of the bird. It is possible, therefore, to give only approximate times for hanging. Pheasant, partridge, and snipe are generally hung until the flesh is slightly high, and gain flavour and tenderness if this is done; but it should be remembered that the gamy flavour so much appreciated by some people is anathema to others.

In moist, thundery weather birds become high after hanging for only a short time, so in these conditions they should be watched. Birds should hang undrawn by the neck and should not be plucked until ready for cooking. They may be considered ready when the feathers just above the tail can be easily plucked out, but if required well hung they may be allowed a further day or two beyond this.

A sign of a well-hung bird is a greenish tinge on the thin skin of the abdomen. Water birds, such as teal, widgeon, and wild duck, are generally hung only for a day or two before being cooked.

After hanging, the birds are plucked, drawn, and trussed ready for roasting. Snipe, plover, and woodcock, however, may be served undrawn but with the crop removed, and these are not generally hung so long as birds which are to be drawn.

Young game is always roasted and older birds are used for casseroles, pies, and terrines.

To choose game

Young birds have soft, pliable feet and the tip of the breast-bone should also be soft and pliable. In old birds the feet are hard and scaly, and if pheasants or grouse they have sharp claws and the breast-bone is also hard.

Hares and wild rabbits should have sharp thin claws and soft thin ears. Dry rough ears and blunt ragged claws are signs of age; the teeth should be white and sharp.

Venison shows clear bright fat when the animal is young. The flesh is often marinaded before cooking.

Certain water birds, such, for instance, as wild duck, have sometimes a fishy taste which is not liked by everyone, and this may be removed by treating them in the following way. Into the roasting-pan put hot water, salt, and some sliced onion. Baste the birds with this for some minutes, then pour away the liquid and start roasting in the ordinary way.

For roasting, bacon or ham fat, good dripping or butter may all be used. Bacon fat gives a good brown colour as well as good flavour, and butter is used when possible for the more delicate birds. A piece of larding bacon laid over the breast of a bird before roasting keeps it from being dried up in the oven, and when the flesh is particularly dry a piece of butter may with advantage be put inside the bird. It may be borne in mind that there is not much gravy from game birds, and it is useful to have in reserve some game stock so that good gravy may be produced.

Marinades

Marinades for game will be found in the chapter on devils, barbecues, and marinades, pages 731–2.

GROUSE

In season 12th August to 10th December. Young grouse may be hung approximately a week in warm weather and longer in cold weather. Again this is a matter of taste. Young birds are roasted, old birds cooked in casserole or terrine. Birds should be well roasted but not overdone, and as the flesh is inclined to be dry a piece of larding bacon may be put over the breast and a nut of butter inside the bird. According to the heat of the oven cooking time may vary from 25 to 30 minutes.

To carve. Carve the breast and the wing off in one, and if too large a portion for one person it may be sliced again. Young grouse are usually cut in half, one half being allowed for each person.

Accompaniments. Grouse are usually served with fried breadcrumbs, bread sauce, and wafer potatoes. Watercress, slices of lemon, cranberry sauce, and apple and celery salad are also suitable accompaniments.

PARTRIDGES

Young birds are usually roasted, the breast covered with a rasher of fat bacon.   Old birds are cooked in casserole or terrine.   Hanging time about 7–8 days according to weather and taste.   Cooking time 20–25 minutes. Partridge is preferably eaten not too high, and when possible may be basted with butter with advantage.

The English partridge is superior in flavour to the French or red-legged bird.   The latter is larger and may well be boned, stuffed, and garnished.

To carve.   Split the birds in two, allowing half for each person.

Accompaniments.   Fried breadcrumbs, wafer or straw potatoes, water-cress, clear gravy, and an apple and celery salad are all suitable.

PARTRIDGES WITH QUINCE

3 good partridges	butter
2 rashers of streaky bacon	1½ gills good stock
1 medium-sized onion	2–3 tablespoons top of milk or
1 quince	cream
salt and freshly ground black	chopped parsley
pepper	castor sugar

Cut the rind off the bacon, flatten out and lay at the bottom of a stew-pan or casserole.   Slice the onion finely and lay it round the birds with half the quince finely sliced.   Season with salt and freshly ground black pepper.   Add about ½ oz. butter, cover the pan tightly and set on a low fire for about 30 minutes.   Remove the lid and sauter over a brisk fire to colour a nice brown.   Take out the partridges, split them, and return to the pan with the stock.   Bring to the boil and simmer until the birds are tender, allowing the stock to reduce a little by removing the lid.   Slice the rest of the quince and sauter in a little butter until brown.

Dish the partridges, strain and reduce the gravy, adding the cream and chopped parsley and adjusting the seasoning.   Pour it carefully over the partridges and garnish with the slices of quince.

N.B.   Add a little castor sugar to the quince for the garnish while sautéing, and also a pinch to the sauce if necessary.

Serve with château potatoes (see page 208).

PERDRIX AUX CHOUX
a French classic

2 medium-sized onions	4–6 oz. streaky bacon, in the
2 medium-sized carrots	piece
1 oz. good butter or bacon fat	¼–½ lb. good pork sausages
2 partridges—good, plump	a bouquet garni
birds	seasoning
1 medium-sized good-hearted	¼–½ pint good stock
cabbage	beurre manié, if necessary
	chopped parsley

Slice the onions and carrots in thin rounds and heat the butter in a thick pan. Brown the partridges slowly and thoroughly in the butter. Cut the cabbage in four and blanch 6–7 minutes in boiling water with the bacon. Take out the birds and put the onion and carrot into the pan to soften in the butter. Drain, refresh, and squeeze the cabbage; press out all the moisture and cut each quarter into 2 or 3 pieces. Cut bacon into strips, removing rind. Split the birds in halves or into smaller pieces if preferred. Take out the onion and carrot, lightly brown the sausages in the pan and take them out. Lay half the cabbage on the bottom of the pan, arrange on it the sausage, partridge, bacon, onion, and carrot, put the bouquet on top and season well. Cover with the rest of the cabbage, moisten with the stock, put a piece of paper under the lid, cover tightly and put in a slow oven for 1½–2 hours. After half an hour's cooking remove the sausages and put them aside. To dish remove the bouquet and arrange the cabbage in the centre of a fireproof dish with the onion and carrot; lay the partridge on top. Slice the sausages into 2 or 3 pieces and heat them, arrange them round the dish with the sliced bacon. Reduce the liquor in the pan and thicken it if necessary with a little beurre manié. Pour a little over the dish and serve the rest separately. Dust the dish with chopped parsley.

This is a simplified version of the classic dish. Often the onions, carrots, and bacon are left whole and extracted at intervals from the pan as they become ready. They are then sliced or quartered before dishing. The essential point is the long slow cooking of the cabbage to make it succulent and tender. The dish when finished must look rich and well garnished.

Neither a Savoy nor a very green cabbage is suitable for the dish. Choose a pale, hard, green and white kind.

SALMIS DE PERDREAUX

Perdreaux are birds under a year old.

2 plump young partridges	¼ pint good jus or stock
butter	1 teaspoon finely chopped
1 tablespoon finely chopped	thyme and parsley mixed
shallots	seasoning
olive oil or butter for frying	4 oz. button mushrooms
1 heaped teaspoon flour	lemon juice
½ glass each of red and white	stale bread
wine, or a glass of red wine	

Draw the partridges, replace the heart and the liver inside each bird and truss neatly. Rub over well with butter and roast lightly for about 15 minutes. Meanwhile soften the shallots in a tablespoon of butter or oil, add the flour, cook a minute or two and pour in the wine and stock. Add the herbs and seasoning and allow to simmer 7–10 minutes with the lid on the pan. Peel the mushrooms and cook 4–5 minutes in a spoonful or two of water and lemon juice and a nut of butter. Cut two large slices of bread, trim into two neat croûtes and fry golden brown in oil or butter. Carve the breast from each partridge in two neat pieces, put these into a shallow pan with the mushrooms. Pound or crush the carcasses, add to the sauce with the mushroom liquor and simmer 2–3 minutes. Pass this sauce through a fine strainer on to the partridge breasts. Reheat carefully and adjust the seasoning. The sauce should be thick enough to coat the meat lightly. Lay the croûtes on a hot dish, arrange the partridges on them, spoon over the sauce and mushrooms and serve very hot.

For a recipe for Partridges cooked in Vine Leaves, a cold dish, see Winkfield chapter, page 1009.

For Galantine of Partridge see page 623.

PHEASANTS

Pheasants should be well hung for a week to ten days according to the weather. They may be barded with bacon and should be well basted during cooking. Towards the end of cooking, when the barding bacon is removed, the final basting may well be done with butter. Hen birds usually have more flavour and are less dry than cocks, though smaller in size. A good pheasant should serve 4–5 people and should be cooked for 45–60 minutes, according to the oven and the taste of those who are going to eat it.

A good way to roast pheasants is to start roasting in the usual way, if possible with a little butter, and half way through the cooking to add a glass of red wine. At the end of cooking it will be found that the tin is practically dry—in fact glazed—so that it must be déglacéd to make an excellent gravy.

To carve. Cut off the wings and the legs and carve the breast into three or four slices.

Accompaniments. Pheasant may be served with bread sauce, clear gravy with a squeeze of lemon in it, fried breadcrumbs, wafer potatoes, braised celery or chestnuts, and quarters of lemon with a dust of cayenne; it is also excellent with oranges, and for this see recipe for Faisan aux Oranges in Winkfield chapter, page 1009.

Pheasant is excellent cooked in the same way as for Chicken Vallée D'Auge (page 648), but longer cooking time is required than for chicken.

CASSEROLE OF PHEASANT WITH CHESTNUTS

1 pheasant
1 oz. butter or 1 good table-spoon olive oil
½ lb. good chestnuts (weighed when peeled and skinned)
½ lb. button onions
¾ oz. flour (approx.)
¾–1 pint good stock

grated rind and juice of ½ orange
1 dessertspoon red-currant jelly
1 teaspoon red wine vinegar or glass burgundy
a bouquet garni
salt and pepper
chopped parsley

Brown the pheasant slowly all over in the hot butter or oil. Remove from the pan. Sauter the chestnuts and onions briskly until they begin to turn colour, shaking the pan frequently. Remove from the pan and add enough flour to take up the remaining fat. Mix well. Add the rest of the ingredients, except the parsley, and bring to the boil. Put in the pheasant, surround with the chestnuts and onions and cover tightly. Cook in a slow to moderate oven 1½–2 hours.

Take up, joint the bird, and place in a fresh casserole or deep dish with the chestnuts and onions. Remove the bouquet, skim the liquor and reduce if necessary. Adjust seasoning. Pour over the pheasant, dust with chopped parsley and serve.

SNIPE

Snipe are very small birds and are not drawn before cooking. They can be very lightly roasted and should 'fly through the kitchen,' 10–12 minutes being an approximate roasting time. They may be served on toast with a clear gravy, fried potatoes, and a salad.

WILD DUCK

This may first be blanched with salt water and onion. Put a bunch of parsley, the livers, and a nut of butter inside the duck before roasting. Cover the breast with buttered paper or larding bacon, which is removed before the end of cooking to allow the bird to brown. For an average-sized bird 30–35 minutes is about right. Serve with an orange salad, orange juice, and blanched shredded orange peel in the gravy. Wild duck is generally hung only 2 or 3 days.

CANETON SAUVAGE A L'ORANGE

a plump wild duck	freshly ground pepper
2 good seedless oranges	a small glass of port
butter	a few tablespoons strong jus
1–2 onions	or stock
salt	watercress

Pare the rind from half one orange, and squeeze out the juice. Cut the other orange, unpeeled, in thin rounds and set aside. Clean the duck well and wipe out with a damp cloth; do not wash. Rub over the breast well with butter and put a nut inside the carcass with the onion. Season lightly with salt and well with freshly ground pepper. Cover with a piece of grease-proof paper. Roast quickly in a hot oven. Wild duck should be served underdone, though this is a matter of taste; 20 minutes is usually considered enough. About 10 minutes before it is done remove the paper, pour over the juice of the orange, and baste frequently until the end of the cooking time. Meantime cut the pared rind into thin shreds and blanch. Fry the sliced orange quickly in butter until brown, dusting with castor sugar while turning. Dish the duck. Pour off any fat from the tin and déglacer with the wine and strong stock. Season and stir well to dissolve any caramel. Strain into a small saucepan. Reduce to a good flavour, thickening slightly if wished, and add the orange rind. Serve separately in a sauce-boat. Arrange the orange slices round the duck and a good bouquet of watercress at each end of the dish.

'Game' chip potatoes or pommes paille are correct with this dish, as also is a bigarade sauce (see page 145 in sauce chapter), which would then take the place of the gravy.

Orange salad or baked oranges may accompany the dish instead of fried oranges.

WOODCOCK

Woodcock are not hung so long as other birds which are to be drawn. They are plucked and trussed but not drawn before roasting, and each one may be set on a piece of bread which has been toasted or fried on one side. The birds are placed on the untoasted side so that while roasting the juice will run into the bread. Woodcock are moderately well roasted for about 20–30 minutes, and then are cut right through in half and served on the toast with a clear gravy flavoured with a squeeze of lemon.

Another, though less rich method is to roast them without the toast underneath. When cooked well through cut them in half, make toast separately, spread the 'trail' on the toast and on top of this serve half the bird.

HARES

There are two kinds of hare, the English brown hare and the Scotch or blue hare. The brown is larger and better altogether. Young hares are called leverets. A good-sized hare is enough for 9–10 people, leverets and blue hares for 6–8.

Hares should be hung head downwards for a week to ten days and not drawn until ready for use. They should then be skinned and the blood carefully kept. This collects under a piece of membrane in the ribs and care must be taken when breaking it. The blood is used to thicken the gravy when the hare is roasted or 'jugged.' The back, being the best and thickest part of the hare, can be stuffed and roasted, and the legs and 'wings' (the forelegs) either jugged or made into a casserole or pie.

A hare should never be washed, but wiped thoroughly with a damp cloth after skinning. To joint, first cut off the hind legs, chop them in two, then do the same with the forelegs. If the back is not for roasting, chop it into 4–6 pieces and trim off the surplus skin.

Hare is often marinaded for a day or two before being roasted or put into a game pie. Marinading adds to the flavour of the meat, and helps to make it more tender.

Roast hare is generally stuffed or has force-meat balls served with it, and a good gravy thickened with the blood. The stuffing must be well flavoured; this can be a herb, chestnut, or sausage stuffing with the addition of the liver of the hare. Force-meat balls are rolled in flour and lightly fried before being added to the roasting-pan about half an hour before the hare is done. A sprig or two of rosemary in the roasting-pan gives a good flavour.

When the back and legs only are to be roasted it is sometimes a good plan to stuff after marinading. The inside of the back and loins is lined with thin slices of fat bacon before the stuffing is put in.

Red-currant jelly is served with both roast and jugged hare.

In the recipe which follows it will be seen that the saddle of the hare only is used. For reasons of economy the whole of the hare may be used, or the legs and 'wings' may be used for Hare Pudding.

A sauté pan or a shallow stew-pan is the best utensil for the cooking of this dish.

RÂBLE DE LIÈVRE A LA CRÈME

1 good plump hare	1 oz. butter
French mustard	1 gill good jus or strong stock
1 gill cream	(approx.)

Marinade

2 small onions	salt
2 small carrots	1 tablespoon red wine
3 tablespoons olive oil	2 bay-leaves
vinegar	½ sprig rosemary
a good sprig of thyme	6 peppercorns

To make the marinade. Slice the vegetables and cook them in the oil until soft but not coloured. Add the remaining ingredients and simmer 7 minutes. Pour into a basin. Cool.

Joint the hare carefully, leaving the back whole. Put the whole of it into the marinade and leave for 36 hours, turning and basting occasionally. Remove the back, spread lightly with the mustard. The rest of the hare may be put aside and jugged separately. Brown the back slowly in hot butter, then add the strained marinade and allow it to reduce by about a third. Pour on the stock; the hare should be barely covered with liquid. Bring to boil, cover the pan tightly and cook in a moderate oven until absolutely tender. Dish the hare, which may be carved as for a saddle, the slices being laid across the backbone. Add the cream to the pan, boil up well for a minute or two, strain the sauce, spoon enough sauce over the hare to moisten it well and serve the rest in a sauce-boat.

Serve pommes paille and haricots verts as an accompaniment.

HARE PUDDING

An excellent substitute for beefsteak and kidney pudding, in which the 'wings' and legs can be used up if the back has been taken for a roast.

¾ lb. quantity good suet crust (see page 841)	1 dessertspoon mixed chopped herbs
3–4 rashers of streaky bacon	1 tablespoon sharp red-currant jelly
hare cut into medium-sized pieces	salt, freshly ground pepper
seasoned flour	1 small tea-cup good stock
1 dessertspoon finely chopped onion	1 small glass port (optional)

Line a pudding basin fairly thickly with three-quarters of the crust. Flatten out the bacon and line round the sides and bottom of the basin. Fill in with the pieces of hare rolled in the flour. Add onion, herb, and seasoning. Moisten well with the liquor. Roll out the remaining paste, cover and trim round. Tie down with a paper and cloth and boil (or steam) for 4 hours. A little boiling water or stock may be poured in just before serving as in a steak and kidney pudding.

Serve in the basin with a folded napkin tied round, accompanied by red-currant jelly.

For Terrine of Hare see Pièces Froides, page 626.

JUGGED HARE

One of the best of the English dishes. The essential part of a jugged hare is that, after long slow cooking, the liquor be thickened with the blood of the hare and enriched with port; force-meat balls should accompany the dish.

The French version is a 'civet,' which again implies that the sauce should be thickened with a blood liaison. Their garnish for a civet consists of button onions, button mushrooms, and croûtons of fried bread. Diced bacon is also cooked with the hare.

1 hare, cut into neat pieces
marinade 2 (see page 731)
1 large tablespoon bacon fat
2 large onions stuck with 1 clove each
4–5 peppercorns
1 stick of celery, sliced
1 carrot, quartered
1 teaspoon spiced pepper or allspice
a bouquet garni
a good pinch of salt

the juice of a lemon or of a Seville orange, and a strip of the rind
1–2 pints stock
1 large glass port or a glass of the marinade
1 dessertspoon red-currant jelly
beurre manié (see page 139)
blood of the hare
force-meat balls (see page 692), fried in butter or deep fat

Soak the pieces of hare in the marinade for several hours. Dry well and fry quickly to a nice brown in the bacon fat. Then pack into a deep casserole or earthenware pot with the vegetables, spices, bouquet, salt, and lemon rind and juice. Pour in enough stock barely to cover the meat, cover the pot tightly, seal round the edge with a flour and water paste. Cook in a slow oven about 3 hours. If the oven is a little too hot, stand the pot in a deep tin of hot water. Then remove lid, pour off all the gravy into a pan and take out vegetables and bouquet. Thicken the gravy with enough beurre manié to give it the consistency of very thin cream, allow it to boil, then draw aside and make the liaison with the blood. Add several spoonfuls of the gravy by degrees to the blood, then pour it back carefully into the pan, with the port and red-currant jelly. When the latter has quite melted strain back on to the hare through a tammy strainer. At this point the hare may be redished into a fresh casserole. Reheat carefully, gently shaking the casserole. Avoid stirring as this may break up the pieces of hare. The sauce should be rich and very smooth. Adjust seasoning and serve very hot with force-meat balls fried in butter or deep fat. (For the latter, egg and crumb before frying.)

The above recipe can be made richer by the addition of more port and a 4-oz. slice of raw gammon of bacon. This latter should be cut into strips and rissoléd gently in the fat, then removed before the hare is fried. It is then added to the pot with the vegetables, etc.

Most game 'jugged' in this way makes an excellent dish; extra beurre manié should be added to replace the blood liaison.

CIVET DE LIÈVRE

marinade, which may be marinade 2 on page 731 or more simply marinade 4 on page 732

1 hare	salt, pepper, grated nutmeg
2 oz. butter	1 clove of garlic
2 medium-sized onions	½ lb. button mushrooms
4–8 oz. streaky bacon, in the	blood of the hare
piece	½ lb. button onions, glazed
2 scant oz. flour	(see page 200)
2½–3 pints stock	8 triangular croûtons of fried
½ pint good red wine	bread

Cut the hare up into even-sized pieces. Put into the marinade for some hours. Take up and dry thoroughly. Cut the bacon into large dice or lardons, after removing rind. Blanch. Heat the butter in a thick *cocotte*, put in the bacon and rissoler gently till turning colour. Lift out and put on a plate. Now add the 2 onions cut in quarters and allow to colour. Then remove on to the plate with the bacon. Add the flour and allow to colour to a nut-brown. Now put in the hare and rissoler well, turning the pieces about and shaking the pan constantly. This will take 7–10 minutes. Draw off, add the stock and wine, stir well and bring to the boil. Add the crushed clove of garlic, seasoning and nutmeg, the onions and bacon, all the marinade if using 2, otherwise a little of the cooked marinade.

Put a piece of paper under the lid. Cover well and cook gently and steadily for about 1½ hours either on the stove top or in the oven. Then take out the pieces of hare with the bacon and put into a casserole. Strain the sauce through a tammy strainer on to the hare, add the mushrooms, unpeeled, well washed, dried, and cut into four if on the large side. Cover again and simmer for another 20 minutes or so, until thoroughly cooked.

Take up and add the blood liaison (see previous page). Garnish with the button onions and arrange the croûtons round the edge of the casserole.

VENISON

Venison is the meat of red deer, and generally speaking comes from Scotland. It has little fat and therefore is better for careful preparation and cooking. The best parts are the loin and haunch, either of which may be sautéd, grilled, roasted, or braised. All venison is improved by marinading in various ways and should also be hung for 7–10 days, or longer, after killing.   If home-killed it may be cooked while still fresh, though most people prefer it well hung and gamy.

Roe deer is also excellent, with whiter and less gamy meat than the red. The same treatment may be applied.

Usual accompaniments to venison or roe deer are red-currant or Rowan jelly, a poivrade sauce or the gravy with the addition of sour cream, and braised chestnuts or a purée of chestnuts.

BRAISED VENISON

Take a nice joint of venison, preferably from the haunch.   Have ready this marinade:

4 oz. carrots, sliced	6 juniper berries, crushed, or
4 oz. onions, sliced	Jamaican pepper (allspice)
2 oz. celery, sliced	a sprig of rosemary
¾ gill oil	a clove of garlic
¼ pint wine vinegar	6 peppercorns, crushed
bouquet garni (thyme, parsley	1 pint wine, wine and water
stalks, and bay-leaf)	mixed, or cider

Brown vegetables in the oil, add remaining ingredients.   Bring to the boil and simmer 30 minutes.   Draw off and leave until cold.   Pour over the joint and leave for as long as desired, basting twice a day.   (Marinading should be done in a deep dish.)   When ready for cooking take up the meat and wipe dry.   Braise according to the directions given on page 66, using a mirepoix of vegetables and a little of the marinade.   Take good stock to moisten.   When the meat is tender take up, slice, and arrange in the serving dish.   Strain gravy, reduce, skimming meanwhile.   Thicken slightly if necessary with a little beurre manié or arrowroot and add a spoonful of red-currant jelly.   When dissolved, rectify the seasoning and spoon over the dish.   Serve with potato purée or purée of celeriac and potato.   Green beans to accompany and red-currant jelly on the side.

SAUTÉD VENISON

For this choose part of a loin or a tender piece from a well-hung haunch of venison.

Marinade

2 shallots	celery salt
a strip of lemon rind	2 wineglasses red wine, bur-
salt	gundy for preference
freshly ground black pepper	
butter or bacon fat	slices of lemon
5–6 juniper berries	château potatoes (see page 208)

Remove any bone and cut the venison into ½–¾-inch slices, allowing one slice per person.   Lay in a dish, season well with salt, pepper, and celery salt, and add the finely chopped shallot with a strip of lemon rind.   Pour over the wine, cover and leave for some hours, or a day or two.

Heat a large sauté or deep frying-pan, and put in enough butter or bacon fat to cover the bottom.   Have ready the meat, well drained from the marinade and lightly dried on a piece of muslin.   Lay in the meat and cook over a slow to moderate fire until turning a nice brown on one side, then turn and brown on the other.   This process should take about 20 minutes.   Lower the heat, cover the pan and, if possible, put it into a slow to moderate oven until the meat is meltingly tender (about 20 minutes), otherwise leave on a slow fire for the same length of time.   Lay the slices overlapping down a long dish, strain the marinade into the pan and boil up briskly.   Adjust the seasoning and add the juniper berries crushed.   Spoon the gravy over the meat and garnish with slices of lemon and château potatoes.   A little lemon juice may also be added to the gravy with the crushed berries.

For Gougère de Gibier and Mazagrans de Gibier see Réchauffés, page 722.

SEASONS FOR GAME AND POULTRY

The following list gives the normal seasons for game and poultry.   The advent of cold storage and deep freezing makes it possible for us to have them at other times, though in the opinion of epicures they are never quite so good as when eaten in season.

Black game	20th August to 10th December
Chickens	All the year round
	Petits poussins: March to July
Ducklings	March to July
Ducks	All the year round, but the best time is from July to February
Geese	October to March
Goslings	April to October
Grouse	12th August to 10th December
Hares	1st August to last day in February
Partridges	1st September to 1st February
Pheasants	15th October to 1st February
Pigeons	All the year round
Rabbits	September to February
Turkeys	November to April
Wild birds	1st August to 1st March

XXI

Force-meats, Farces, Stuffings, and accompaniments for Poultry, Game, Fish, and Meats

ALTHOUGH the words force-meat, farce, and stuffing may all seem to mean much the same thing, it is easier for the student if some differentiation is made in writing of them.

The word force-meat to most of us would suggest such things as force-meat balls to accompany hare, to introduce into a meat pie, or perhaps to be served with a fish soup. It may cover, too, certain mixtures containing meat, fish, or game with which we stuff a bird, fish, or joint, but equally we use the word stuffing for these, as for other less rich mixtures. I do not think the English domestic cook would think of the word as covering the quenelles, mousselines, and creams which may properly come under the designation of farces.

It is dangerous, from the point of view of accuracy, to simplify too much, but roughly one might say that force-meats and stuffings in English are mixtures used as accompaniments to and fillings for certain main foods, such as poultry, game, fish, meat, and vegetables, while the French farces are extended to cover, for instance, quenelles, mousselines, and creams, which may accompany an elaborate dish or be served as a course apart.

The more elaborate farces which played a part in the *haute cuisine* of the past must, perhaps, be regarded as out of date to-day, but a book for students would be incomplete if the subject was not discussed, and on page 698 there will be found a short note on farces mousselines and those made with a panade, followed by recipes for fish and meat creams which are made on the same principles. More practical for us at the moment is the matter of stuffings, for in these we have the means to improve and stretch certain main foods which may be expensive.

The virtues of stuffings and force-meats for birds, fish, meats, and vegetables may be summarized, but it must be remembered that primarily they should create harmony of taste and lend contrast of flavour, and to this end should be concocted with imagination.

To make a good stuffing which blends perfectly with the meat or fish for which it is intended takes a little care. A too highly seasoned stuffing

688

will kill the delicately flavoured meat, while a bland stuffing with a spicy meat—hare, for example—would be pointless.   A good stuffing should be like a good sauce: it should bring out and enhance the flavour of the dish which it accompanies.   Consistency is important: the stuffing should not be stodgy or wet or too dry and crumbly, nor should there be too much in proportion to the remainder of the dish.   The fault of most stuffings is that they are either too bready or, perhaps more usually, do not contain enough fat.   The proportion of fat should be very much the same as in pastry-making, that is to say half as much fat as breadcrumbs.   Force-meat balls, which are so often served with hare, may well be used with other meat dishes, ragoûts, roasts, or braises.   They may be made quite small, no bigger than a walnut, and fried and served as an accompaniment to beef, mutton, or pork.

1. They may be used to add flavour where this is desirable.   Guinea-fowl and veal, for example, may be improved by a well-flavoured stuffing.

2. They help to preserve moisture.   The flesh of birds, small ones in particular, is apt to become dry in cooking.   Ducklings may with advantage be stuffed, even if the stuffing is not to be eaten.

3. They may serve to reduce richness, as in the case of goose and pork. With this object sour apples are sometimes used to stuff goose, not necessarily to be eaten but to counteract the richness of the flesh.

4. They may be used to make certain staple foods go further, so effecting economy without austerity.

In the story of 'The Seven Young Goslings,' an enchanting nursery book of my youth, the wolf, perpetually trying to cheat his way into the house while the mother goose is out, finally succeeds.   Patty-pans on feet, tongue plastered with chocolate and curd, paws covered in flour, he deceives the goslings and in answer to their cry 'Who's there?' replies: 'Me, your mamma, with the sage and onions, my just-about-done-ones.' In this way was underlined, in our nursery at any rate, the idea that sage and onions was a classic of all time.   Quite a few English cooks have taken this view too, and in overstating the sage element have sometimes prejudiced those with sensitive palates.   The making of stuffing is an opportunity for the inventive and imaginative amateur cook, because to the basic ingredients there are so many possible additions.

Bases of stuffing

The first thing is to consider the various bases to which one adds seasoning, flavouring, and other important items.   These in the main are bread, potatoes, rice, onions, chestnuts, and apple, to which we may add sausage-meat and possibly veal, pork, and oysters.   Oatmeal is sometimes used, especially in the north and midlands, and sweet corn, straight from the cob and prepared in a way which will be given later, makes one of the most delicate stuffings for chicken.

Bread.   This may be in the form of crumbs from a stale loaf, either rubbed through a wire sieve or pulled in small pieces with the fingers, which gives a more open result but a less smooth filling. Or the bread may be torn into small pieces and lightly browned in the oven; this will give a drier, lighter stuffing. Sometimes it is soaked in stock, milk, or water and creamed thoroughly; this gives a more compact stuffing and it is the method adopted when rolls of French bread are used with the crust included. Sometimes the crumbs of plain biscuits are used in conjunction with breadcrumbs.

Rice.   When rice is used as a base it must be properly boiled, well salted, refreshed, and dried before being incorporated with other ingredients.

Potatoes.   These may be used either raw, in which case they are cut up, minced, or grated, or they may be cooked, mashed, well seasoned, and mixed with other ingredients.

Apples.   These are usually peeled and chopped or grated and used either in conjunction with breadcrumbs or with dried fruits, or with both.

Onions.   Onions are generally parboiled or chopped and softened in butter and associated with crumbs and other ingredients.

Chestnuts.   These may be used in the form of a purée, or better still, many people think, they may be cooked and roughly broken.   In some cases they may even be used whole.

Sausage-meat.   This is sometimes considered to be the poor man's version of a proper hachis of pork and veal.   It is better to buy sausage-meat rather than to have to skin the sausages.   This meat is generally mixed with chopped onion and herbs, and moistened with stock or wine, preferably sherry.   This treatment makes it a better stuffing than when it is used as received from the butcher.

Veal.   The veal may be finely minced twice, then mixed with herbs and softened onions and breadcrumbs, or with French bread that has been soaked in a mixture of milk and beaten egg.   Or it may be mixed with crumbs and bound with egg.   Lemon or orange rind is a popular flavouring with veal stuffing.

Pork.   This is used in the same way as veal, but in this case a larger proportion of herbs is generally added.

Chicken liver.   When using chicken liver for stuffing or hachis, do not cut up before sautéing, but brown quickly and lightly while whole, then cool slightly and dice.   This rule applies also when chicken liver is to be added to a complete sauce or gravy.   Livers are sometimes used raw as a farce for a terrine, but when used as a force-meat they should be treated as above.   The pan in which they were browned, and the fat used for browning, are then employed for sautéing onions, mushrooms, or whatever else is called for in the recipe.

Oatmeal.   Usually medium or coarse oatmeal is taken, mixed with softened onion and chopped herbs, moistened with milk and bound with egg.   This is a stuffing which swells very much when cooked, so extra room has to be left with this in mind. A little fat, sliced bacon, butter, or lard is generally added with oatmeal stuffing.

Generally speaking, it may be said that the above form the bulk to which other ingredients are added, and the range of these others may vary according to the dish in hand, the occasion, and the length of your purse.

The possibilities are wide and embrace the contents of the herb garden, sweet peppers, fruits (fresh, dried, and tinned), chestnuts, almonds, olives, mushrooms, truffles, oysters, liver, kidney, sausage-meat, and pâtés, zest of orange, lemon, and lime, fruit juices, chutneys, chopped pickles and so on, up to the gargantuan extravagance of stuffing a turkey with a capon, a capon with a chicken, a chicken with a pheasant, right on down to the final quail, a recipe, by the way, that on the whole R. H. and I think may be excluded for the moment.

Fat in some form or another is generally a component of stuffing, and it is chosen to fit the dish in hand. Suet, bacon fat, butter, or dripping may all be used. Beef suet will probably, for instance, be taken for force-meat balls for a stew, although butter will take its place for fish or chicken.

It would be a waste of paper to give all the possible combinations, and this chapter will include comparatively few recipes, but here is an opportunity to let your fancy roam, not to be content with plain herb stuffing, and not to forget what a lift the addition of fruit can give to this article of food. Not to forget, either, that a well-stuffed bird goes further than a hollow one, and that if the stuffing is a really good affair it will pay you to make plenty of it, and having filled the bird to bake some of it apart in a baking-tin for extra helpings, though this will be a waste of time if the stuffing is dull, soggy, half seasoned, or over-flavoured with strong herbs.

Roughly speaking $\frac{1}{2}$ pint of stuffing is allowed for each pound of bird, but that is only to be taken generally; some birds will contain more, some less, and it is advisable not to pack the stuffing too tightly.

In addition to the recipes that follow it should be noticed that others are given in the meat, fish, game, and poultry chapters for stuffings appropriate to the dish in hand.

FORCE-MEATS (SIMPLE)

ANCHOVY AND HERBS FOR MUTTON, VEAL, OR HARE

5 oz. fresh crumbs
1 oz. fat bacon, chopped
1½ oz. butter or shredded suet
3–4 shallots, finely chopped
1 large tablespoon chopped parsley and chives mixed
1 teaspoon lemon thyme
stock to moisten, if necessary

6 fillets of anchovy, diced, *or*
1 large teaspoon anchovy essence
the grated rind of ½ orange
juice of an orange (Sevilles are good if a pungent stuffing is required)
1 beaten egg
salt and freshly ground pepper

Mix all the dry ingredients thoroughly in a bowl, season well, and bind with the liquids.

Good for a shoulder of mutton, breast of veal, etc.

FORCE-MEAT BALLS
for hare, rabbit, and veal

1 small onion, finely chopped
1 rasher of bacon, chopped
4 tablespoons fresh breadcrumbs
1 tablespoon chopped suet
2 teaspoons chopped parsley

1 tablespoon lemon thyme or
   marjoram, chopped
seasoning
beaten egg
brown breadcrumbs and deep
   fat for frying

Cook the onion with the bacon until the onion is soft. Add the rest of the ingredients and bind together with beaten egg. Shape into balls. Dip the balls into egg and breadcrumbs and fry in deep fat until golden brown.

SAUSAGE OR PORK FORCE-MEAT
for turkey or goose

This force-meat is a classic and is used mostly for the carcass.

$1\frac{1}{2}$ lb. sausage-meat, *or*
$1\frac{1}{2}$ lb. freshly minced pork or
   veal
3 oz. fresh white breadcrumbs
1 dessertspoon chopped mixed
   herbs

1–2 onions, finely chopped
3 oz. minced fat bacon
1 beaten egg
a little stock, if necessary

Mix the ingredients all together, moistening with a little stock if necessary.

The quantities given are enough for a 10-lb. bird and may be altered according to the size of the turkey or goose to be stuffed.

VEAL FORCE-MEAT
for turkey, veal, or mutton, or force-meat balls

$\frac{1}{2}$ lb. veal, weighed when free
   from skin and gristle
6 oz. lean raw bacon, ham, or
   pork
3 shallots, finely chopped
6 oz. stale white bread, without crust, and soaked in
   milk for $\frac{1}{2}$ an hour
2 oz. creamed butter

2 large mushrooms, unpeeled,
   well washed, dried, and
   chopped
1 dessertspoon finely chopped
   parsley
salt, pepper, and a dust of
   cayenne
a pinch of mace
1 large egg

Mix the veal and bacon and pass twice through the mincer. Pound well in a mortar, or put through a wire sieve. Soften the shallots in $\frac{1}{2}$ oz. of the butter and when cool add to the meat. Place the soaked bread in a piece of muslin and wring out as much liquid as possible. Remove from the muslin and crumble. Add the crumbled bread to the meat and pound well. Add the mushrooms and the rest of the creamed butter gradually, together with the seasoning, parsley, mace, and lastly the beaten egg.

If no mortar or sieve is available beat well in a bowl.

N.B. Rabbit may be used in place of veal.

If the mixture is too stiff and solid in consistency, it can be lightened by the addition of a little cream or the milk in which the bread was soaked.

Mushrooms may be omitted, and a dozen or more sauce oysters added (or the oysters may be added as well as the mushrooms). If the mushrooms are omitted a good dash of anchovy essence is an improvement.

STUFFINGS

APPLE AND POTATO STUFFING
for goose

1 lb. apples
1 lb. onions
a few spoonfuls of orange juice and water
2 sprigs of lemon thyme
2 sprigs of savory

grated rind of 1 orange
seasoning
3 or 4 boiled potatoes put through a ricer and well seasoned

Peel and slice finely apples (cored) and onions. Put in pan with just enough orange juice and water to cover. Add herbs whole and seasoning to taste. When cooked remove herbs, press the mixture through a sieve. Add grated orange rind and sufficient potato to make a firm stuffing. Other herbs may be substituted, e.g. parsley, sage, chervil, etc.

STUFFING FOR BAKED HADDOCK

2 hard-boiled eggs
4 oz. fresh crumbs
1½ oz. beef suet, chopped or shredded
1 medium-sized onion, finely chopped
1 tablespoon chopped parsley
1 tablespoon chopped mixed herbs (thyme, marjoram, savory, etc.)

grated rind and juice of a lemon
1 tablespoon anchovy essence
1 beaten egg
milk
salt and pepper
lemon quarters and anchovy sauce to accompany

Chop the eggs coarsely and put with all the dry ingredients into a bowl. Mix well and bind with the lemon juice, anchovy essence, and egg, adding enough milk to bring the mixture to a good consistency.

N.B. This was enough for a 2½–3-lb. fresh haddock. The haddock was stuffed, sewn up, and roasted in the oven with bacon fat to baste well. It was served with lemon quarters and anchovy sauce.

HERB AND ORANGE STUFFING
for loin of mutton, fresh haddock, poultry, and rabbit

4 large tablespoons fresh white crumbs
2 large tablespoons chopped herbs (parsley, thyme, chives, and marjoram)
2 tablespoons finely chopped onion
1–1½ oz. butter

grated rind and juice of 1 large orange
1 egg
salt
pepper
extra orange juice or stock if necessary

Put the crumbs into a bowl with the herbs and plenty of seasoning. Soften the onion in the butter without colouring, add all to the mixture with the grated orange rind and juice. Bind with the egg. If the mixture is too dry and crumbly add a little extra orange juice or stock to bring it to a nice moist consistency.

ORANGE STUFFING

9 oz. chopped onion	a pinch of ground mace
4 oz. chopped celery	salt
3 oz. butter	a dash of cayenne
5 oz. stale bread, cut in dice	freshly ground black pepper
2 lemons	1 beaten egg
4 oranges	

Soften the onion and celery without colouring in 2 oz. of the butter. Toast the bread in the oven to a golden brown. Put into a basin, add the grated rind and juice of the lemons and the grated rind and juice of 1 orange.

Cut the peel and pith from the other 3 oranges and cut out the sections. Add to the basin with the seasonings and beaten egg. Mix thoroughly.

Put in a buttered dish, brush over with melted butter and bake in a hot oven 10–15 minutes.

OYSTER STUFFING
for fish or veal

½ cup picked shrimps	1 teaspoon chopped lemon thyme or savory
3 oz. fresh crumbs	
1 dozen sauce oysters and their liquor	grated rind and juice of ½ a lemon
3 shallots, finely chopped and softened in ½ oz. butter	1½ oz. butter
1 tablespoon chopped parsley	1 egg, beaten, or a little cream
	salt and pepper

Soak the shrimps in a little milk or water to remove any excess of salt. Put the crumbs into a bowl with the oysters, shrimps, drained and dried, shallots, parsley, herbs, and lemon. Mix well. Season well with pepper and very lightly with salt. Bind with the melted butter, oyster liquor, and egg, or, if the egg is omitted, add a little cream.

APPLE AND PRUNE STUFFING

6 oz. fresh breadcrumbs	seasoning
12–15 prunes, steamed, stoned, and split in two	grated rind and juice of ½ a lemon
2 large apples, peeled, cored, and roughly chopped	1 egg, beaten
2 oz. nut kernels, chopped	2 oz. butter, melted

Mix dry ingredients, add seasoning, and lemon rind and juice. Bind together with melted butter and egg.

RAISIN, APRICOT, AND ALMOND STUFFING
for ducks

1 oz. butter or dripping from duck
2 large onions, sliced
2 oz. raisins, pipped
1½ oz. almonds, blanched and split
1 tablespoon chopped parsley

2 tablespoons tinned apricots, sliced
salt, freshly ground black pepper
grated rind and juice of ½ a lemon

Slice the onions and fry in the butter or dripping till they begin to turn brown. Add raisins and almonds and continue frying for a few minutes. Turn into a bowl, add the remaining ingredients and mix lightly with a fork. Stuff into a duck.

This is also suitable for other fowl and for veal or pork.

RAISIN AND NUT STUFFING
for birds or veal or pork

6 oz. fresh breadcrumbs
2–3 oz. each of stoned chopped raisins and nuts
1 heaped tablespoon chopped parsley

2–2½ oz. butter or other appropriate fat
freshly ground black pepper, salt
1 egg

Mix all ingredients thoroughly.

SAGE, ONION, AND PICKLED WALNUT STUFFING
for goose and pork

½ lb. onions
8–10 sage leaves
4 oz. fresh crumbs
1 large apple, peeled, cored, and diced
cider or stock, if necessary
salt and freshly ground black pepper

1 egg
1½ oz. butter
grated rind of ½ a lemon
a squeeze of lemon juice
3–4 pickled walnuts

Chop the onions, put into a pan with cold water to cover well, bring to the boil and simmer 4–5 minutes. Drain and wring dry in a piece of muslin. Pour a small quantity of boiling water on the sage leaves and stand for 5 minutes. Drain, dry, and chop finely. Put the crumbs into a bowl with the onions, sage, and apple and season highly. Beat the egg and stir in with the melted butter and lemon rind and juice. Lastly add the walnuts cut into four.

If the mixture is too dry, add a spoonful or two of cider or stock to make it bind nicely.

SIMPLE STUFFING FOR PORK, GOOSE, AND DUCK

1 onion, finely chopped
1 dozen sage or savory leaves,
    finely chopped
4 oz. fresh breadcrumbs

1 oz. suet or butter
1 egg
seasoning

Mix well together.

SWEET CORN STUFFING FOR ROAST CHICKEN
(3-lb. bird)

3–4 cobs of fresh sweet corn to
    yield 3 full tablespoons of
    kernels
1 medium-sized onion
1 oz. butter

1 tablespoon chopped parsley
grated rind of 1 small lemon
a squeeze of lemon juice
1 beaten egg
salt and freshly ground pepper

Boil the cobs in the ordinary way, drain, and with the back of a knife scrape off the kernels. Cut the onion in half, and cut each half downwards in thin slices. Melt the butter in a frying-pan, add the onion and cook slowly until turning colour. Then add the corn and continue frying gently, seasoning well, for 4–5 minutes. Draw aside, add the parsley, lemon rind and juice, and lastly the egg. Fill into the breast of the bird. If for the carcass, double the quantity.

EXCELLENT STUFFING FOR TURKEY

the liver of the turkey
2 oz. butter
¼ lb. chipolata sausages
stock or water
½ lb. chestnuts (weighed when
    peeled)

6 large French plums, scalded,
    stoned, and halved
4 small pears, peeled, cored,
    and cut in quarters
1 wineglass white wine
salt and pepper

Brown the liver quickly and lightly in a third of the butter. Put on one side to cool. Simmer the sausages in stock or water 5–7 minutes, drain, cool, and skin. Simmer chestnuts in stock or water until tender, drain, put into a bowl and break up in pieces with a fork. Oil the remaining butter, add to the bowl with the sausages, each cut in half or in three pieces, the plums, pears, and liver cut in dice, and any remaining juice from the pan. Season well and moisten with wine.

Half this quantity is really enough for the breast of an average-sized turkey. The whole is about right for a carcass stuffing.

Ripe dessert pears answer very well for this, but excellent results may be had with hard stewing pears cooked in the oven as for a compôte with lemon rind and cinnamon, and then well drained before using. In this case the pears may be slightly under rather than over cooked.

TURKEY STUFFING WITH TWO KINDS OF FARCE

A smooth mixture for the crop and whole chestnuts and sausages for the main filling.

For a 10–12-lb. turkey

2 lb. chestnuts (weighed when peeled)	2 eggs
the liver of the turkey	½ lb. chipolata sausages
3–4 sprays of parsley, chopped	stock in which there is a piece
seasoning	of celery and some salt

Prepare the chestnuts as follows: Put them in a pan and cover with cold water. Bring the water to boil, then immediately lift the pan from the fire, lift out the nuts one at a time, keeping the pan covered meanwhile, and peel, removing both inner and outer shells. As the water begins to cool and the chestnuts become more difficult to deal with, put the pan back on the fire and reboil quickly, but do not leave it on the fire or the chestnuts will become soft. If too many are dealt with at the same time there is also a danger of this. When all the chestnuts are peeled, cook till tender in stock.

Take about a quarter of the cooked chestnuts and pound them. Chop liver and parsley finely, add to the chestnuts, season well and bind with the slightly beaten eggs, and use this to stuff the crop. Fry the sausages and add to the remainder of the whole chestnuts. Season well and stuff the body with these.

STUFFING FOR TURKEY

Celery, French plum, and chestnut stuffing used for the breast of the bird is excellent with a veal force-meat.

12 fine, large prunes or French plums, soaked overnight in ¼ pint red wine, or wine and water mixed	the grated rind of ½ a lemon
	½ lb. chestnuts, weighed when peeled and cooked until tender
1 oz. butter	salt and pepper
1 head of celery, chopped	1 small beaten egg
1–2 oz. onion, finely chopped	
1 dessertspoon chopped mixed herbs	

Simmer the plums in the wine in which they have been soaked, allowing it to reduce well, until they are just tender. Stone and cut each into four. Melt the butter in a pan, add the celery and onion and allow to soften slightly. Add the plums, herbs, lemon rind, and chestnuts, broken into pieces. Stir lightly with a fork, season well and add the juice from the plums. Draw aside and when thoroughly cool stir in the egg.

CHESTNUT STUFFING (1)
for turkey

Chestnut is the classic stuffing for turkey and is generally used for the breast of the bird.

1 lb. chestnuts (weighed when peeled)	1 dessertspoon mixed chopped herbs
stock	salt and pepper
1–2 oz. onion, finely chopped	2 eggs
1 oz. melted butter	

Cook the chestnuts in stock until tender. Strain and sieve. Add the onion to the purée with the butter, herbs, and plenty of seasoning. Moisten if necessary with a little of the stock in which the chestnuts were cooked. Bard with beaten egg. Fill the breast of the bird and sew up with a coarse thread.

CHESTNUT STUFFING (2)

¾ lb. chestnuts (weighed after peeling)	1 tablespoon chopped parsley
milk or stock	1½ oz. melted butter
3 oz. fresh breadcrumbs	1 beaten egg
1 large onion, finely chopped or minced	seasoning

Simmer chestnuts in milk or stock until tender. Drain and sieve. Mix with the breadcrumbs, minced onion, parsley, butter, and egg. Season well and mix to a good consistency with a little of the stock or milk in which the chestnuts were cooked.

WATERCRESS STUFFING
for lamb or chicken

1 heaped tablespoon chopped onion	3 oz. watercress, cut finely with scissors, using as much of the stem as possible
3 heaped tablespoons chopped celery or a good pinch of celery salt	seasoning of salt and freshly ground black pepper
2 oz. butter	5 oz. breadcrumbs
1 level teaspoon salt	1 egg
	a little milk if required

Mix all dry ingredients together and bind with egg and if required a little milk.

For rice stuffing see Shoulder of Lamb à la Turque, page 558.

FARCES MOUSSELINES AND PANADES

A farce mousseline may be described as a delicate mixture of which the main component is a finely pounded base of fish, meat, or poultry, worked with egg whites and cream and appropriate seasonings and flavourings.

The resulting mixture may be used as a stuffing for certain dishes or may be formed into quenelles, small creams, which are poached or steamed.

The making of these farces mousselines is considered to belong to the higher branches of cookery, not so much by reason of any great difficulty or highly complicated process, as by the importance of meticulous attention to detail. This is an occasion when short cuts will not work and it is essential that each process shall be properly carried out.

1. Mincing. It is advisable to mince meat twice, fish once, and it is of benefit if meat can also be pounded in a mortar. This preliminary mincing makes the base more friable and easier to work.

2. The egg whites are only broken up sufficiently to make it possible to add them gradually, as gradually as one adds oil to eggs in mayonnaise. It is required that the mixture shall thicken and become firm as they are added and it is important to be able to judge to a nicety the amount required to avoid slackening the mixture too much.

3. Sieving. When the whites are incorporated the mixture is passed through a sieve. At one time a hair sieve was considered essential, but modern cooks use a wire sieve of fine mesh.

4. The cream. This should be double or thick, although single may be used at need; top of milk will not serve. The use of this or of a too thin cream renders the texture rubbery, and when cooked the farce is covered with little bubbles of curd. Evaporated milk may be used to eke out the cream, but owing to its pronounced taste it is better not to use it exclusively. Half the quantity of cream called for is vigorously beaten in after the sieving, and as in the case of the egg white the addition is done gradually.

5. Seasoning. When half the cream has been incorporated the mixture may tend to slacken. At this point the addition of salt will cause it to thicken again. So the salt and pepper called for in the recipe should now be put in.

After this the second half of the cream is beaten in a little more quickly. A final adjustment in seasoning may now be made. Meat mousselines should be well seasoned, those of fish more delicately.

6. Texture and testing. The consistency now is that of very well-whipped cream, so firm that it can be moulded into the shapes required. It is now ready for testing for setting qualities and for texture after cooking, which should be that of a light, cream sponge which leaves the serving spoon clean.

Into boiling salted water a piece of the farce the size of a pea is dropped; the pan is immediately drawn aside from the fire, and in 1–2 minutes the cooking should be completed. If the test shows the mixture to be too soft or slack a little more egg white may be added. If, as may be the case if double cream has not been employed, the consistency is too firm and rubbery, additional cream is required. Testing should be carried out until the right consistency is achieved.

7. Proportions. The proportion of egg white and cream to meat or fish varies a little in certain recipes. To ½ lb. of meat or fish 2–3 egg whites may be called for, and 1½–2 gills of cream and approximately ½ teaspoon salt.

8. Cooking. Fill well-buttered cutlet or quenelle moulds with the farce, smoothing over the surface with a palette-knife and pressing the mixture well down into the moulds, leaving no cracks on the surface. Have ready a shallow pan (a sauté pan is ideal) two-thirds full of boiling salted water. Drop the moulds into this in a single layer, immerse completely, and poach 7–8 minutes. Shake the pan gently, and when the creams are cooked they will detach themselves from the moulds and float to the surface. Lift them carefully from the water with a slice and drain on a muslin before dishing and covering with the appropriate sauce.

MOUSSELINE FARCE (CHICKEN OR VEAL)

½ lb. white meat, chicken or veal, weighed when minced	½ teaspoon salt (approx.)
	a pinch of white pepper
3 egg whites	a grating of nutmeg or a small
1½ gills–½ pint cream	pinch of ground mace

Mince the meat twice, taking care not to lose any in the mincer. Break the whites with a fork. Work into the meat by degrees. Rub through a wire sieve. Return to the bowl and add some of the cream little by little, beating vigorously all the time. Add the seasoning and nutmeg, add the remaining cream and taste to make sure it is well seasoned. The farce is now ready for poaching, steaming, or for use as a stuffing.

MOUSSELINE FARCE FOR FISH

A friable fish is best for this, such as whiting or haddock. Abroad, brochet (pike) is highly esteemed.

½ lb. fish, weighed after mincing (once through mincer is enough)	1½ gills cream
	½ teaspoon salt, a dash of white pepper, and flavouring according to purpose
2 egg whites	

Flavouring, added with the egg whites, may, for example, be reduced tomato pulp, lobster coral, preferably raw, or duxelles. Testing should be carried out in the way described, bearing in mind that fish usually makes a less firm farce than meat.

FARCES MADE WITH PANADE (OR PANADA)

Panade (or Panada) is a term given to a thick paste made of flour and water or milk and a small quantity of butter. To this base raw fish or meat is added to make the farce. For a vegetable farce a thick béchamel replaces the heavier panade. The panade, cold, is worked into the minced raw meat or fish before sieving, then further ingredients, butter and eggs as called for in the recipe, are added.

An old-fashioned panade is made of bread well soaked in milk, squeezed dry, and worked over the fire with cream or milk to a stiff paste, in the following way:

Bread panade. Cut stale bread in cubes. Soak in milk, squeeze in muslin till dry. Put in a pan with a nut of butter, a little milk or cream, and seasoning. Work over the fire till it leaves the side of the pan.

A panade is usually called for by weight as in the recipe for Veal or Chicken Cream. The following is a simple basic recipe given primarily to indicate method; but it will be seen, for example, that in the recipe for Fish Farce with Panade milk and not water is used, and that proportions of other ingredients vary. It is the method that remains the same.

PANADE

1½ gills water	4 oz. flour
1 oz. butter, good weight	a pinch of salt

Put water, salt, and butter in pan and bring to boil. Take from fire, add flour all at once, mix well, return to the fire and beat well until mixture is smooth and leaves the sides of the pan clean. Spread on a greased plate to cool.

VEAL OR CHICKEN CREAM WITH PANADE

7 oz. raw minced veal or chicken	3½ oz. butter
3½ oz. panade	2 small eggs
	salt and pepper

Pound minced meat and panade thoroughly together and rub through a sieve. Return to a bowl and add creamed butter and eggs by degrees. Season.

FISH FARCE WITH PANADE

¾ lb. whiting or haddock (weighed when minced)	salt
2 eggs	pepper
½–¾ gill cream	a pinch of ground mace

Panade

½ pint milk	2½ oz. flour
2 oz. butter	

Prepare the panade by boiling the milk with the butter, add the flour, off the fire, and beat until smooth. Put aside to cool. Beat the panade into the fish, add the eggs, and when thoroughly mixed rub through a wire sieve. Season liberally, add the spice and finally the cream.

This farce is suitable for using as a filling to a mould with fillets of fish, or as a cream steamed, or poached in a ring mould, coated with an appropriate sauce, and garnished.

ACCOMPANIMENTS

Apart from sauces, salads, and all the classic accompaniments to meat, poultry, game, and fish, there are various other small side-dishes of value which may serve to bring out the flavour of the principal dish, to refresh the palate or, more materially, to make a main and possibly expensive ingredient go further. In this there is much room for imagination and inventiveness. Primarily it is a matter for niceness of judgment in combining flavours rather than for great culinary skill, so it is particularly a field for experiment by the amateur.

It may also be said that certain accompaniments are greatly appreciated by the over-sensitive palates of some children. A child who proves difficult in the matter of food can often be coaxed to eat by such simple and refreshing additions to ordinary diet. It is only proposed to make here a few suggestions to be used as spurs to the imagination of the student who has so far not explored this avenue.

I should like, for example, to draw attention to the lemon fritters given with the poussins in the Winkfield chapter on page 1007, which are also excellent with fritto misto, with curry, or with barbecued meat. These were the outcome of a discussion on the value of sharpness in accompaniments to roast meats generally. They were well liked, but since they involved deep-fat frying an alternative was called for, and R. H. then disappeared into the kitchen and produced lemon toasts, which, in turn, proved so successful that we eat them with roasts and with curries, and sometimes serve them alone as a first course.

With rich meats such as pork, goose, and ham this sharpness—this agreeable sweet-sour—may be supplied by serving grilled peaches, baked oranges, or crab-apples, and old-fashioned cooks used to serve spiced prunes with Irish stew; the stuffed prunes given in this chapter are good and may well accompany rabbit or hare. As for the Stuffed Spiced Peaches given on page 1037, they are for high days and holidays as accompaniment either to hot or cold dishes.

I remember a summer dish of grilled petits poussins—tender birds, if a little flavourless—being served round a centre of a hot compôte of fresh fruits cooked in syrup and reduced to a point of rich stickiness. Peaches, cherries, and apricots I remember, but other fruits would serve.

Cranberries, commonly associated with cranberry sauce to serve with turkey, may be more originally used by being made into a sort of fresh chutney, mixed with orange rind and juice, well sweetened, and allowed to soften for some hours before being eaten. It is necessary to remember that, not being a sweet fruit, they require a good deal of sugar. Morello cherries may be used in the same way.

Fried or baked bananas are good with chicken and particularly so with fish. Fish dishes call for delicate accompaniments. The herb fritters on page 277 may well be part of a fritto misto of fish or be used to accompany other fish dishes, while horse-radish cream, usually considered in connection with roast beef, is good with fish and, served in small cucumber cups, is a classic accompaniment to smoked trout; it is also very good with other fish dishes, and in particular with rich fish such as herrings, mackerel, and salmon.

A long, a very long time ago, when banquets and ceremonial dinners were of a length and richness quite startling to our minds to-day, it was customary to serve half way through the meal—probably before the roast —a water-ice or sorbet. This might be made of simple fruit juice or of a syrup flavoured with liqueur or wine made acid with lemon or orange juice. Such mixtures, lightly frozen, were mushy rather than firm, and smooth in texture, and their object was to refresh the palate. They were also intended to act as aperitif for the further rich dishes to come. Nowadays such stimulus to appetite is hardly necessary, but the refreshment of the palate is another matter. It is, of course, an affair of individual taste; some people can eat rich food such as goose or duck or hot food such as a curry or a barbecue and find no need of a cool or refreshing accompaniment; others like a cool respite. In America I met a sharp cranberry waterice served with roast goose and a mint lemon ice with roast lamb—met and liked very much these modern adaptations of the old-fashioned sorbet.

In serving such an accompaniment certain conditions must be observed: the main dish, if it is to be hot, must be piping hot, and the water-ice served in a separate dish. As examples I suggest orange cups—halves of orange carefully divested of flesh—one for each person, filled perhaps with a tomato ice; or, to be handed round, the larger grape-fruit cups—two of them will probably be required—filled with a pale green mint or parsley ice. Glass plates or little dishes, well chilled, must be at each place, for in no circumstance should this accompaniment be put on the main plate.

Muscat grapes, peeled, pipped, chilled, and dressed with lemon juice, generally please the most fastidious palate. The frozen fruit juices mentioned on page 1188 are also suitable.

In addition to the fruit preserves and jellies suitable to accompany a savoury course given in the appropriate chapters, certain sauces such as mint and orange or cranberry sauce are sometimes solidified—but lightly— with gelatine, and are good. The fact is that there are endless combinations and variations with which to enliven routine and add interest to sessions in the kitchen.

HORSE-RADISH CREAM IN CUCUMBER CUPS

1 gill whipping cream
lemon juice or wine vinegar (about 1 dessertspoon vinegar or the juice of $\frac{1}{2}$ a lemon is about right, but it should be adjusted to taste)
1 dessertspoon sugar, or to taste

salt
2 good tablespoons finely grated horse-radish
$\frac{1}{2}$ teaspoon French mustard
freshly ground pepper
cucumber cups

Cut slices of cucumber about 2 inches thick. Do not peel. Hollow out the top of each slice about half way down and season with pepper and salt. Beat the cream till fairly stiff and it will hold its shape. Season, add mustard, sweeten, and add the vinegar or lemon juice gradually, taste and adjust seasoning, then fold in the grated horse-radish. Pile this into the cups and chill.

LEMON TOASTS
to serve with roast birds, curries, or barbecues

thinly cut bread and butter
 (Procea bread for choice)
½ oz. butter

grated rind of 1 large lemon,
 and the pulp
castor sugar
cucumber pickle (see page 1112)

Toast half the bread on buttered side only until golden. Cream butter and add grated rind and a teaspoon of sugar. Cut pith from lemon and cut into quarters, then down into small pieces. Spread the toasted side of the bread with the pickle and cover with the pieces of lemon. Put remaining pieces of bread on top, buttered side down, spread the top side with the flavoured butter and dredge with castor sugar. Brown under the grill.

BAKED ORANGES

medium-sized oranges
1 teaspoon brown or white
 sugar to each orange

a nut of butter for each orange
1 good teaspoon sherry for
 each orange

Cut off the blossom end of each orange, leaving a hole about 1½ inches in diameter. With a sharp, curved knife remove the flesh to a depth of about 1 inch. Take out the pips from the rest of the orange, loosen the flesh from the peel and return removed flesh divested of pith and pips. Work the sugar and butter together and put a knob into each orange. Stand the oranges in a baking-dish, and pour round them enough water to reach one-third of the way up their sides. Bake in a slow to moderate oven for 45 minutes. Dish the oranges on a folded napkin, and just before serving put a good teaspoon of sherry in each.

BAKED APRICOTS

Cook a dozen or so tinned apricots with ½ oz. butter and a heaped teaspoon sugar, allow them to get sticky and finish with a squeeze of lemon. See also Apricot Salad in salad chapter, page 351.

GRILLED PEACHES OR APRICOTS
(tinned or fresh)

Put a speck of butter in the half of each peach, dredge lightly with sugar and glaze under the grill, sprinkle with lemon juice and serve.

FRIED BANANAS

Split bananas lengthwise, dust lightly with sugar, fry in butter, sprinkle with lemon juice and a pinch of salt.

BAKED BANANAS

Butter a baking-tin well, arrange the bananas split lengthwise and dot lightly with butter, bake in a moderate oven 20–30 minutes until tender. Sprinkle with lemon juice and a pinch of salt.

STUFFED PRUNES

Stuffed in the following way, prunes may be used as an accompaniment to hare, rabbit, and mutton or incorporated in a game or rabbit pie.

12 well-soaked prunes
½ oz. butter
3 shallots, finely chopped
the liver and kidneys of hare or
    rabbit, finely chopped
1 oz. fat bacon, finely chopped

seasoning
1 teaspoon each of well-
    chopped parsley and sage
1 egg yolk
a spoonful or two of stock

Heat butter in small sauté pan, add shallots, liver, kidneys, and the bacon, and simmer for about 5 minutes. Season well, add herbs, bind with the egg yolk, and stuff prunes with the mixture. Set in a buttered fireproof dish, add a spoonful or two of stock, cover with a buttered paper and cook 5–7 minutes in a moderate oven.

SPICED PRUNES

See page 1106.

COMPÔTE OF FRENCH PLUMS OR DRIED FIGS
to serve with roast birds

fruit
lemon rind, thinly pared
bay-leaf

claret
red-currant jelly
castor sugar

Take dessert plums or figs from jars or boxes, put in a saucepan with the lemon rind and bay-leaf and just cover with claret, add red-currant jelly to taste and castor sugar. Simmer with the lid on 20 minutes. Remove lid, continue simmering till the fruit is just covered with a rich sticky juice.

FRESH ORANGE AND CRANBERRY CHUTNEY

To be made some hours before it is required.

½ lb. ripe cranberries
1 ripe Jaffa orange
3–4 oz. sugar according to taste

1 dessertspoon tarragon vinegar
1 teaspoon finely chopped mint

Pare carefully the yellow part (the zest) of the orange rind and put with the cranberries; remove and discard the white pith of the orange, add the flesh to the cranberries. Mince these ingredients finely or put through the mincing-machine. Add sugar, vinegar, and mint and stir well for some minutes. When the sugar is thoroughly dissolved put the mixture in the ice-box where it will keep for a day or so.

COMPÔTE OF CHERRIES
as an accompaniment to cold ham, chicken, turkey, etc.

1 lb. red cherries	the zest and juice of an orange
1 wineglass claret or burgundy	1 tablespoon red-currant jelly
2 oz. lump sugar	

Stone the cherries, rub the zest of the orange on to 1–2 lumps of the sugar. Put the wine, sugar, and orange juice into a pan, bring to the boil, add the cherries, and simmer about 5 minutes, shaking the pan well, when the cherries should be done. Add the jelly and shake over the fire for another minute or two. Turn out into a bowl and chill before using.

Pippins in Orange Jelly, see page 1094.

Spiced Damsons, see page 1104.

APPLE AND MINT ICE (FOR 6)
suitable to serve with roast chicken, veal, or pheasant

4 large cooking apples	6–8 sprigs of mint
¼ pint water	1½ gills water
the finely grated rind and juice of 1 large lemon	6 oz. sugar
	green colouring (optional)

Wipe the apples, quarter and core them. Stew to a pulp with the water in a covered pan. Rub through a strainer. Add the lemon juice and rind. Pound the leaves of the mint in a mortar until fine.

Bring the water and sugar together to the boil, when dissolved boil rapidly for a minute or two. Cool slightly, add to the mint and blend together. Add this to the purée. Taste and adjust the flavouring, colour if you wish. Chill and freeze.

Though this can be frozen in refrigerator trays, one gets an infinitely better result in the churn-type freezer.

For the following water-ices, eaten as accompaniment to savoury courses, it is important that the liquid shall be particularly well seasoned and flavoured or the result will be insipid.

CUCUMBER ICE

For those who have an electric emulsifier, the best method of making this ice is to pulp the cucumbers and mint in the machine and then mix with the other ingredients before freezing. Otherwise treat as below.

2 cucumbers	1 dessertspoon sugar
2 sprigs of mint	green colouring if necessary
¼ pint water	salt
1 tablespoon white wine vinegar	a squeeze of lemon juice

Peel the cucumbers. Cut into small chunks and simmer in salted water until just tender. Drain well and rub through a hair or nylon sieve.

Strip the leaves from the stalks of mint, pound till smooth. Heat the water, vinegar, and sugar together, pour on the mint, add lemon juice, cucumber pulp, and salt to taste. Colour if necessary. Chill before freezing.

This makes a good first course when served seasoned with French dressing in hollowed-out tomatoes (fresh, ripe ones), with brown bread and butter as an accompaniment.

LEMON AND PARSLEY ICE

the pared rind and juice of 1 lemon
¾ pint water

2 oz. sugar
2 large handfuls of parsley

Pare the rind from the lemon. Put into the pan with the water and sugar, bring to the boil and infuse for 5 minutes. Add the lemon juice, strain and cool. Boil the parsley 5–10 minutes, drain, press and rub through a sieve. Add this to the lemon mixture and freeze.

TOMATO WATER-ICE OR SORBET

For a pint of liquid for freezing

1½ lb. good ripe tomatoes
2 or 3 shallots, finely chopped
mint or basil to flavour
salt and freshly ground pepper

sugar to taste
lemon juice to taste
1 gill water

Cut the tomatoes up, remove seeds, and stew the flesh with shallots, water, herbs, and seasoning to a pulp, rub this through a nylon sieve or aluminium strainer. Add sugar to taste (the amount depends on the ripeness of the tomatoes), add lemon juice to taste (at least the juice of 1 lemon), but bear in mind that it is better to over- than to under-flavour this liquid. Chill well before freezing in a churn-type freezer. Allow to ripen for an hour before serving. See page 960 (Ices).

JELLIED SAUCES

These are made by diluting slightly with water such sauces as mint, mint and orange, and cranberry and then adding gelatine in proportion of ¾ oz. to a pint of sauce. They should not be too solid in consistency; the original sauce may be fairly sweet and it is helpful in warm weather to chill them in the ice-box to accelerate setting. The liquid may be poured into dariole moulds, set, and turned out for individual helpings.

See also 'The Store Cupboard' (pages 1103–6) for Spiced Crab-apples, Spiced Oranges, and other spiced fruits to accompany meats both hot and cold.

XXII

Réchauffés

A RÉCHAUFFÉ is a dish made from cold cooked meat—a 'done-up' dish. It may be made of mutton, beef, veal, poultry, game, etc., and is prepared in various ways: it may be heated up in a suitable sauce, dipped in batter and fried, turned into rissoles, croquettes, savoury pancakes, cottage pies and so forth, but in whatever way the meat is used, it should not be subjected to a second thorough cooking or it will become tough and indigestible. For the most part it is a question of heating it up to boiling-point without allowing it actually to boil.

It may be argued that in the case of croquettes and rissoles the already cooked meat is subjected to far higher temperatures, but in these cases the covering of egg and crumbs or thin pastry takes the impact of the heat, the inside being merely heated through, while in the case, for instance, of a cottage pie a thick layer of creamed potatoes protects the meat from being overcooked in the baking. When reheating meat in a sauce, the sauce should first be slightly warmed, the meat put in and the whole brought slowly just up to boiling-point. The best way to do this is in a bain-marie or its equivalent of a pan of boiling water large enough to take the cooking-pan. Cooked meat put into boiling sauce will toughen and shrink, and the flavour of the sauce will not penetrate the meat. Cooked meat to be used for cottage pies or rissoles should first be finely diced or minced and mixed with a well-flavoured gravy or bound with suitable sauce.

Some dishes call particularly for one kind of meat; for instance, a miroton is made with sliced beef in a brown gravy with onions, cottage pie is best made with cold beef, though mutton may be used, and a moussaka is made of cold mutton diced with potatoes, aubergine (or Jerusalem artichokes as a substitute), tomatoes, and a cheese sauce.

Cottage pies, moussakas, mirotons, and fish or meat cakes fried in shallow fat may be regarded as homely dishes, simple to prepare but good only if proper care is taken with them. Croquettes and rissoles, however, call for greater skill and may take their place in more formal menus. Instructions for making these will be found later in this chapter, pages 716–19.

708

MIROTON OF BEEF

If properly made this is a really good dish.

¾ lb. cold roast or boiled beef
6–8 oz. onions
1 oz. good beef dripping
1 teaspoon flour
1½ gills stock
½ gill white wine or cider
1 clove of garlic and a bay-leaf

seasoning of salt and pepper
4 or 5 potatoes, scrubbed and freshly boiled in their jackets
a squeeze of lemon juice
1½ tablespoons breadcrumbs
a nut of butter

Trim the beef of fat and skin and shave it into very thin slices; chop the onions finely and blanch them in boiling water for 5 minutes, drain well and dry in a piece of muslin. Heat the fat in a frying-pan and cook onions over moderate heat until evenly coloured. Dust in the flour and allow to colour. Add stock, wine, salt and pepper, bay-leaf, and garlic. Stir until boiling, simmer 20 minutes, draw aside and allow to cool. Add the slices of beef and allow to heat through, 5–7 minutes. Peel the cooked potatoes and slice about ¼ inch thick. Arrange them *en couronne* in a fireproof dish, lift the slices of beef from the sauce and lay them within the ring of potatoes. Adjust the seasoning of the sauce, add a squeeze of lemon juice, reduce if too thin, and spoon over the meat. Sprinkle crumbs over the top, dot or sprinkle with butter, brown quickly on the top shelf of the oven about 10 minutes.

RUSSIAN BEEF

½ lb. cold boiled or roast beef
1 large onion, finely minced
¾ oz. dripping
3 oz. cooked, boned, skinned kipper
½ lb. freshly boiled potatoes

seasoning of salt and freshly ground pepper
1 egg
hot milk
browned crumbs

garnish of salt cucumbers (preferably cucumbers in dill pickle) or gherkins, with chopped dill

Soften the onion in the dripping without browning. Trim and mince the meat, pound the kipper and put the potatoes through a sieve. Mix well together, add the onion and seasoning. Whip the egg and beat into the mixture, adding enough hot milk to make it pliable and light. Grease a pie dish, fill with the mixture, smooth over, mark with a knife, dust with browned crumbs and bake in a hot oven 15–20 minutes. Serve a dish of sliced pickled cucumbers or gherkins with chopped dill separately.

BŒUF AUX PRUNEAUX

slices of cold beef
¼ lb. prunes (stoned)
1 glass red wine
4 large onions

salt and pepper
a little sugar
a nut of butter
chopped dill

Soak the prunes for half an hour or so in red wine.   Simmer 10 minutes.
Slice the onions very thinly, cook them very gently in a large pan with salt,
pepper, a dust of sugar, and the butter.   When they are soft add the
chopped dill, soaked prunes, and wine, lay the slices of beef on top, cover
and cook over gentle heat for half an hour.

The following is very good for a luncheon dish:

DEVILLED BEEF ROLLS

slices of cold roast or boiled
beef

Sauce
½ oz. butter
½ oz. flour, scant weight
½ pint stock or gravy
1 dessertspoon made mustard
2 dessertspoons red-currant
jelly (or crab-apple jelly)
seasoning

French mustard and chutney
or
mild horse-radish cream sauce

a little sweet chutney or horse-
radish sauce
¼ pint port or red wine
a little sugar to taste
2 spoonfuls cream for finishing
(optional)

Shave the beef into thin slices, spread with French mustard and chutney
(or the horse-radish sauce) and roll up, fastening with wooden toothpicks,
or tying with string.

Prepare the sauce: heat the butter in a saucepan, add the flour and
allow to colour nut-brown, add the stock and all the remaining ingredients.
Taste and adjust seasoning and flavouring generally.   Heat the rolls
gently in this in a fireproof dish, remove fastening and finish with the
cream if this is available.

BEEF ROLLS (2)

slices of very thinly cut cooked
beef
dripping for frying
3 or 4 shallots (according to
size), sliced or chopped
3 or 4 open mushrooms, finely
chopped

1 dessertspoon finely chopped
parsley and chives mixed, or
lemon thyme may be added
seasoning
1 tablespoon Worcestershire
or A1 sauce
1 dessertspoon French mustard
a little grated horse-radish
sauce (see below)

Heat the dripping, soften the shallots and mushrooms in it for a few
minutes, cooking very gently.   Add herbs, seasoning, sauce, mustard, and
horse-radish.   Continue cooking gently for a few minutes, merely enough
to mix all thoroughly.   Spread the slices of beef with this, roll up, tie with
string, and fry in a little hot dripping.   This should be served with a well-
seasoned sauce.   The following is excellent:

Sauce
Slice a few mushrooms and soften them in a little butter in a saucepan.
Add a few spoonfuls of tomato sauce and a cup of stock.   Add the juice of

half a lemon, test for seasoning. This sauce may be thickened with a little beurre manié (see page 139); alternatively a well-seasoned tomato sauce may be served.

Here is a recipe for a quickly made tomato sauce:

1 oz. fat	1 onion, sliced
½ oz. flour	1 bay-leaf
seasoning	a bunch of herbs
½ pint tomato juice	

Soften the onion in the fat, sprinkle in the flour and continue cooking. Add the tomato juice and seasoning with a whole bay-leaf and a bunch of herbs. Cook until reduced, adjust seasoning and serve.

CORNED BEEF HASH (1)

a good American classic

Of the many recipes for this popular dish those that appeal most to us are those in which raw potatoes are used, cooked slowly with the milk and onions and finally with the beef. Because the potatoes are diced one is apt to expect that the cooking time will be short; in fact this is not so. Another point to be observed is that potatoes vary much in their powers of absorption, and the quantity of milk given may have to be increased. The garnish of gherkins or walnut and the additional flavouring of chutney and French mustard may not be classic but are certainly good.

2 oz. margarine or beef dripping	1 1-lb. tin of corned beef
1 onion	4 pieces of hot toast
1½ lb. potatoes, diced	pickled walnuts or gherkins
½ pint milk	a little chutney and French
salt and pepper	mustard (optional)

Make the margarine hot in a deep frying-pan, chop the onion coarsely and cook until soft but not brown. Add the diced potatoes and stir well. Cook over moderate heat for 10 minutes, stirring from time to time. Pour in the milk, season with salt and pepper, cover and cook gently for three-quarters of an hour. Dice or chop the beef and add 10 minutes before serving. Chopped chutney and a little French mustard may be added to taste, although not usually called for. Divide in four and spread on pieces of hot toast. Decorate each with a piece of pickled walnut or two small gherkins.

CORNED BEEF HASH (2)

dripping for frying	½ pint milk (approx.)
equal parts of corned beef	seasoning
and raw potatoes, chopped	rounds of buttered toast (optional)
up	a spiced pickled mushroom, sliced
1 small onion or 2 shallots	pickled gherkin, or teaspoon of
to each pint of above	chutney for each helping

Heat the dripping, add potatoes, allowing them to soften a little.   Then add the minced shallot and seasoning.   Continue cooking very gently for a few minutes until the shallot is soft.   Then add the corned beef.   Stir and continue cooking.   Now add gradually the boiling milk, a little at a time, until the whole is well mixed and soft.   As the potatoes cook they will absorb the milk, and it is advisable to keep a pan of hot milk at hand, adding a little from time to time until the potatoes are softened.   The whole may then be browned under the grill in the frying-pan, or portions may be put on rounds of buttered toast and these browned under the grill.

A good finish is to lay a pickled mushroom or gherkin, finely sliced, or a spoonful of chutney on top of each helping.

The following may be made with a very small amount of meat:

CORNED BEEF GALETTE

Prepare a good potato purée (see page 203), and soften two small onions, chopped, in about an ounce of dripping, add to the freshly made purée of potatoes and season well.   In making the purée use only enough milk to make it fairly stiff.

Set aside and proceed with the following preparation:

¼ lb. corned beef	1 teaspoon chopped parsley
2 shallots	browned crumbs
½ oz. dripping	piquante or tomato sauce (see
1 teaspoon flour	pages 177 and 178)
seasoning	potato purée (prepared as
2 gherkins	above)

Dice the corned beef, chop the shallots, soften them slowly in the dripping, add the beef and cook for a minute or two on the fire, adding the flour.   Take off, season.   Chop the gherkins and add to the mixture with the parsley.   Grease a shallow cake pan very well with dripping, dust out with browned crumbs, fill in with a thick layer of the potato purée, put the corned beef mixture on this and fill up the tin with potato.   Smooth over and bake 40 minutes to 1 hour, or until well browned, in a moderate oven. Leave a few moments before turning out.   Serve with creamed cabbage or carrots Vichy (see page 193), and a piquante or tomato sauce.

It is only a modern practice to use cold cooked meat for the cottage pie; in days gone by fresh meat was used, finely minced by hand, added to a rich gravy with onions in it, surmounted by a fine mound of the lightest purée of potatoes containing butter and milk, dotted over with butter and crisply browned.

Now, more commonly, this dish is a réchauffé; even so it need not be a Cinderella among dishes provided it is properly made, well seasoned and flavoured and covered with a really good purée of potatoes properly browned at the last.   Unfortunately the potatoes are often too casually prepared and are neither light enough nor sufficiently seasoned or browned.

COTTAGE PIE

¾ lb. chopped or coarsely minced cold beef from which fat and skin have been carefully removed
½ oz. dripping
1 onion, finely chopped

1 teaspoon flour
¼ pint good gravy or thin tomato sauce, more if required
seasoning

For the top
¾ lb. freshly boiled potatoes
seasoning

hot milk
butter or margarine

Make the purée of potatoes in the usual way (see page 203). Heat the dripping in a saucepan, add onion, cover, and allow to soften slowly. Add flour, allow to colour, pour on the gravy, bring to boil, season and simmer for a few minutes. Draw aside to cool. Mix in the meat, adding more gravy or sauce, if required, to moisten well. Turn into a pie dish, put the potatoes, which should be white, light and creamy, on top of the meat, pile high and leave with a rough surface. Dot with butter or margarine, sprinkle with a pinch of salt and pepper, and bake in a quick oven till brown and crusty.

This dish may be improved in the following ways:

Add a little mushroom ketchup to the gravy; glaze small pickling onions (see page 200), put some of them in the pie and reserve others for the crust.

Add a little butter to the mashed potatoes before adding the hot milk, and after baking arrange circles of glazed onions on top of the potatoes.

This recipe may be used also for cold mutton.

The following is a good homely dish and makes a small amount of meat go quite a long way.

SAVOURY HASH OF MUTTON WITH STUFFED TOMATOES

slices of cold roast mutton trimmed of most of the fat
butter, dripping, or oil for frying
2 shallots
a clove of garlic crushed with salt
1 level tablespoon flour

1 level tablespoon tomato purée
1 teaspoon chopped parsley
1 level teaspoon paprika
seasoning
a good ½ pint water
1 tomato for each person (4–5 in this case), and butter for the top

Stuffing
1 onion, chopped
a little butter or oil for frying
2 oz. mushrooms washed and chopped

4 oz. sausage-meat
chopped thyme or basil
seasoning

Heat the fat and brown the slices of mutton. Lift them out and brown the shallots and garlic. Cook gently for a few minutes, then add flour, purée, parsley, paprika, and seasoning. Add water and bring to boil, add the meat and reheat slowly. Slice the tops thinly off the tomatoes and with a small pointed spoon scoop out the pips and juice and some of the flesh, but leave a good thick wall. Rub the pulp through a strainer, add a little seasoning. Season well the insides of the shells of tomato. Brown the onion in the fat, add mushrooms, cook for a few minutes. Draw aside, add sausage-meat, herbs, and seasoning, moisten well with the sieved tomato purée. Fill the tomato shells, dot the top with butter, bake in moderate oven for about 10 minutes. Dish the meat, if necessary reduce the gravy, surround with the tomatoes and serve.

MOUSSAKA

¾ lb. cold cooked mutton cut in dice
1½ oz. butter or 1½ tablespoons oil
2 shallots or 1 small onion, finely chopped
seasoning
any good bottled sauce, soy, or ketchup
½ lb. raw sliced potatoes

1 large aubergine, sliced, salted, and left for ½ an hour [1]
a clove of garlic crushed with salt
a good ½ lb. tomatoes, peeled, pipped, and sliced
¼ pint mornay sauce (see page 156)
1 egg yolk (optional)
grated cheese

Heat ½ oz. of the butter or a third of the oil in a thick frying-pan. Add shallots or onion, allow to colour, then add the meat and shake over a brisk fire for a few minutes; draw aside. Season well and add enough of the bottled sauce to flavour and moisten well. Turn into a hot fireproof dish and keep warm. Heat the remaining fat in the pan, put in the potatoes and fry until brown. Then take out and arrange them on top of the meat. Add the aubergine to the pan and cook 5–7 minutes. Add the garlic with the tomatoes and cover the pan, continue cooking for a further 5 minutes. Cover the potatoes in the dish with this mixture. Have ready the mornay sauce, beat the yolk into it and spoon over the dish. Sprinkle over with cheese and bake in a quick oven 15–20 minutes until well brown.

The following is an excellent dish and may be made with or without the liver or kidney. It is a light loaf flavoured with garlic, made crisp in the oven, and filled with a savoury salpicon.

PAIN FARCI

a Procea or light milk loaf
a little oil or butter

Salpicon

2 onions
2 mushrooms
¾ oz. dripping
¾ oz. flour
1½ gills bouillon or stock
seasoning

a clove of garlic crushed with salt

diced, cooked meat or ham and, at option, a little liver or kidney
1 large teaspoon chopped parsley or mixed herbs
2 or 3 large tomatoes, peeled, pipped, and sliced

[1] Sliced, blanched Jerusalem artichokes may be used as a substitute for the aubergine, as may marrow or zucchini; the zucchini do not require blanching.

Crush the garlic and work it well into butter or oil. Slice a thin piece off the top of the loaf, and with a sharp spoon remove the crumb of the bread, leaving a wall of about half an inch. Brush thoroughly inside and out with the garlic butter, not omitting the removed top slice. Make the salpicon. Slice onions and mushrooms finely, and brown in the melted dripping with the diced liver or kidney. When lightly brown add flour and allow this to brown also, add stock, stir till boiling. Reduce for 5–6 minutes, season well. Draw away from fire and add diced meat, parsley, and tomatoes. Mix well and fill the loaf. Replace the top slice to form a lid, leaving it half open. Wrap round with greased paper, put in a fire-proof dish, and cook in a moderate oven 30–40 minutes.

SLICED BEEF WITH CABBAGE

A good recipe for cold boiled or roast beef. Tinned luncheon meat is satisfactory and blends well with the cabbage.

6–8 slices of meat	1 heaped teaspoon flour
2 lb. cabbage	1½ gills stock
¼–½ oz. butter	2 tomatoes, peeled, pipped,
seasoning	and chopped
½ oz. good beef dripping	chopped parsley
2 oz. onion, finely chopped	

Trim the beef, sprinkle with salt and pepper. Cut the cabbage into quarters, removing the hard core, and wash it well. Plunge into plenty of boiling salted water and boil 7–10 minutes. Drain, squeeze, and chop. Return to the pan with the butter, season well, cook over gentle heat 4–5 minutes. Set aside. Heat dripping in large frying-pan and when lightly smoking lay in slices of beef, fry quickly 1½–2 minutes on each side. Lift out on to a hot plate and keep warm. Pour off a little of the surplus fat, add the onion to the pan and allow to brown gently. Add the flour and continue to brown for a minute or two. Pour on the stock, add the tomatoes, seasoning, and parsley. Stir until boiling, then simmer for 1 minute. Arrange the cabbage down a long dish. Lay the slices of beef on the top, and carefully pour over the gravy. Serve plain boiled potatoes with this dish.

SLICED BEEF IN BATTER

Also good with tinned luncheon meat and may be used for cold mutton.

cooked meat	tomato sauce (see page 178), or
seasoning	coulis (see page 179), or
fritter batter (see page 441)	sauce piquante (see page
dripping for shallow frying	177)

Prepare the batter. Cut the meat in fairly thick slices, up to ¼ inch, and season. Heat the dripping in the pan, dip the slices of meat in the batter, and when the fat is lightly smoking lay them carefully in it. Allow to brown first on one side and then on the other. Drain well on rack or crumpled paper. Serve on a hot dish and hand the sauce or coulis separately.

Other accompaniments suitable to the meat used may be served, for example horse-radish sauce or prunes stuffed with chutney or a sharp mint jelly and so forth.

CROQUETTES, RISSOLES, MEAT AND FISH CAKES

CROQUETTES

Just as it is a practice in some eating-places to call any sort of stew a braise, so are the words croquette or rissole often given to flat cakes of meat or fish cooked in shallow fat. This is probably done for snobbish reasons, but it is incorrect. A flat cake containing a main cooked ingredient, bound together perhaps with potato or rice and moistened with milk, sauce, or egg, then fried in shallow fat, may be, and often is, a good homely dish, but it is neither a croquette nor a rissole. Croquettes are an altogether lighter and more delicate dish and may easily replace an entrée on less homely occasions. They are not expensive; they are a particularly suitable way of using left-over meat, fish, game, or fowl, but are not entirely easy to make and require some care and practice. Their texture should be such that when the fork enters the crisp, perfectly fried covering the inside presents a rich, creamy mixture.

THE MAIN INGREDIENT

This may be fish, meat, fowl, game, hard-boiled eggs, or mushrooms, all cooked and diced, or chopped, seasoned, and possibly flavoured with chopped herbs. When these have been cut up or flaked they should be kept covered till the sauce is ready. They are then bound evenly together with a sauce, usually a thick béchamel or velouté, or sometimes a brown sauce, and with egg yolk. The mixture, quite cold, is then shaped, egged and crumbed (or in the case of rissoles contained in a pastry case), and fried in deep fat.

THE BINDING SAUCE

This sauce, thicker than a coating sauce, must be of a texture which will hold the main ingredient evenly distributed and which, when cold, will set sufficiently firmly to enable the croquettes to be shaped. Approximately 1 gill is required for 7 oz. solid ingredients, though this may vary according to the absorbent qualities of the main ingredient. In the recipes which follow, the ingredients for the binding sauce are given in suitable proportions, but it is perhaps as well to bear in mind that as flours differ in their thickening power it may, on occasion, be necessary to make adjustments in one's recipes; so the general point to remember is that if the croquettes are heavy and sticky in consistency the probability is that the binding sauce was too thick, and conversely if the croquettes are difficult to form into suitable shapes the sauce has been too thin.

When the principal cooked ingredient has been bound together with the sauce and egg yolk, well seasoned and well flavoured, the whole must be allowed to get absolutely cold before being formed into the required shape, which may be in the form of a cutlet, an oval, in a roll like a cork, or in a ball.

There is another point about the binding sauce which may be of interest to those who have had a little experience and who enjoy the finer points of flavour in cooking. The quantity of liquid called for in the recipes is generally the right amount, in proportion to the flour, to make a sauce of the required consistency after a short time of cooking. An experienced cook, accustomed to judging accurately the texture of her sauce, may prefer to compose it in a different manner. Taking a somewhat larger proportion of liquid she will, by a process of long and gently cooking, effect the necessary reduction so that her sauce will still be of the right texture to bind properly, but will be more concentrated in flavour. Anyone who has tried making a béchamel sauce first by the short and then by the long method will appreciate this point concerning flavours. It is too difficult for a beginner to judge the exact amount of reduction required, and so, in the average recipe, the amount of liquid indicated is that which will give the right consistency without serious reduction.

The principal ingredient is mixed with the sauce in the saucepan, but cooking is not then continued, the whole is merely kept warm for a short time to allow the flavours to interpenetrate. The raw egg yolk is then added to the mixture and the whole is spread out evenly on a buttered dish in a layer $\frac{1}{2}$ inch thick. A little melted butter should be brushed over the top of it, and it should be covered with a plate and left to get absolutely cold. When you are ready to make the croquettes the mixture should be divided into regular portions and cut with a knife. A good average weight for each croquette is 2 oz. A pastry board is now dusted with flour and each croquette rolled lightly in it. They are then shaped according to taste.

The next point of importance in making croquettes is the proper coating with egg and breadcrumbs. If this is not carried out adequately and carefully some of the mixture may escape from the cover, and if any crack is left and the mixture oozes out, not only will the croquette be ruined, but the frying fat may boil over. It is advisable to have plenty of properly dried white breadcrumbs. To run short is to court failure. These should have been prepared in the way given on page 37, and there should always be a jar full of them in the kitchen. A double handful will be about the right amount for normal purposes. Put these on a piece of strong kitchen paper large enough to allow each croquette to be gently rolled by a movement of the paper, as they should not, at this stage, be touched with the hand. Have the beaten egg in a plate, season well, dilute with a little oil (in the proportion of 1 teaspoon oil to 2 beaten eggs), which is recommended for a crisp coating.

Lay the lightly floured croquettes into the egg, with a palette-knife turn and brush them over, lift on to the paper of crumbs and roll each gently by a movement of this; avoid touching them with the fingers. Now turn the board over or wipe the floured surface clean and lay the croquettes on this. Make quite certain that the whole of the surface is properly covered with egg and crumbs.

The croquettes are now ready and may be left for $\frac{1}{2}$–1 hour before frying. Arrange them in a frying basket, have your fat smoking, put the basket into the fat, which, if hot enough, will cause a crust to form immediately. (A cube of bread dropped into the fat should brown in 40 seconds.) As soon as the croquettes are a good golden colour lift them out and drain them on crumpled kitchen paper or a fine wire rack. They may be arranged *en couronne* round a purée of suitable vegetables or, if in the shape of rolls and to be served alone, piled up one on top of the other. The accompanying sauce should be served in a sauce-boat. The choice of vegetables, which are often in the form of a purée, should be made with discretion, and should have some relationship to the principal elements of the croquette, and as this is a fried dish the accompanying sauce may suitably be of a somewhat piquante nature.

RISSOLES

The mixture for rissoles is made in the same way as that for croquettes, the difference being that rissoles are enveloped in a thin sheet of pastry, either short crust or puff paste. These also are deep fat fried. Because the mixture is to be thus contained it is possible to use a slightly less thick sauce for binding than in the case of croquettes, and the yolk of egg is not required for binding and is only added if wanted for richness. In some cases the contents of a rissole are not bound with a sauce. For example, a rissole may be made with a filling of foie gras or certain types of pâté, or for a sweet rissole one may use a firm, sweet apple purée; but whatever the filling, the essential part of a rissole is that it shall be contained in pastry and fried in deep fat.

To make rissoles, roll out the pastry $\frac{1}{8}$ inch thick, cut in rounds and put a teaspoon of whatever mixture is to be used in the centre. Damp round the edge of the pastry with water or beaten egg and fold over in two, pressing the edges tightly; or smaller rounds may be cut, a teaspoon of the mixture put in the centre, and the second round of pastry put over the top. But whichever shape is chosen the important thing to observe is that the edges are well damped and well pressed together, because if the mixture escapes into the fat it will not only ruin the rissole but it may cause the fat to boil over.

The following is an attractive-looking and quickly made variation. Cut the pastry into rounds, placing a teaspoon of the mixture in the centre of each. Damp the edges and gather up in the shape of a 'money bag.' Hold firmly with the fingers of the left hand where the string would normally be tied and turn on to its side, the drawn-up edge towards the left. With the edge of the right hand roll the rissole lightly forward so that it is twisted slightly and made firm at the gathers.

The fat for cooking rissoles should be slightly less hot than that for croquettes, 375°–380° F. as against 385°–390° F. The rissoles, as in the case of croquettes, are laid in the frying basket and lowered into the fat. The heat of the fat may be increased a little after the rissoles have been added. They should be cooked to a good golden brown and then drained on kitchen paper or a wire rack. A garnish of fried parsley is suitable for many savoury rissoles.

An additional crispness to the surface is sometimes given by the use of vermicelli. This is used only when a short crust is employed. The pastry is brushed over with seasoned egg and the rissoles are then rolled in the vermicelli.

MEAT OR FISH CAKES

The fish or meat cakes referred to earlier are not necessarily fried in deep fat. Fish or meat, flaked, diced, or chopped, and well seasoned, is bound together with a well-dried purée of potato or with rice, to either of which a beaten egg may be added. The cakes are shaped and dipped in beaten egg and crumbs. They are then fried in smoking shallow fat about an inch deep, first on one side, then on the other, and drained on crumpled paper.

It may be noted that coverings other than breadcrumbs are sometimes indicated. American books often recommend biscuit crumbs, and corn-flakes and oatmeal are sometimes used with fish or meat cakes for shallow frying.

RECIPES FOR CROQUETTES

It will be observed that the proportion of sauce to solid ingredients varies a little in certain recipes. This may be because certain solids are more absorbent or because some croquettes need to be more creamy than others. Egg croquettes are usually liked best if fairly creamy and liquid in consistency. In the case of fish it is possible that the amount of flour in the sauce may be slightly modified; for a wet fish such as cod the 1½ oz. to 1½ gills of liquid will probably be right, whereas for a drier fish such as salmon you will probably use very slightly less.

CHICKEN CROQUETTES

10 oz. chopped white meat of chicken
2 small mushrooms cut in small pieces
1 teaspoon finely chopped onion
½ oz. butter
salt and pepper

1 dessertspoon finely chopped parsley
1–2 yolks of egg
1½ gills béchamel or velouté sauce (approx.) (see below)
egg and breadcrumbs
deep fat for frying

Binding sauce

1 oz. butter	seasoning
1 oz. flour	1 teaspoon lemon juice
1½–2 gills milk or chicken stock, or a mixture of these	

Make the sauce in the usual way (see pages 152 or 154) and reduce until rich and creamy and about 1½ gills in all. Add lemon juice. Cut the mushrooms in small pieces and sauter in a little butter, together with the chopped onion. Mix with the chicken meat also cut in very small squares or fine dice, and leave in the pan with the sauce so that the flavours may mingle; adjust seasoning and add parsley. When the whole is cool add yolk, spread the mixture smoothly on a plate and leave to get quite cold. Divide in equal portions, form into shapes, coat with egg and crumbs, and fry in deep fat. Serve hot with a garnish of green peas or asparagus tips.

Veal may be used in exactly the same way as chicken.

CROQUETTES OF CHICKEN WITH PINEAPPLE

The sharpness of pineapple is pleasantly refreshing with many réchauffés. In the following recipe it is used as a base for reheated chopped meat, bound together and formed into cakes and baked, not fried.

8 oz. chopped cooked chicken, turkey, or veal, marinaded for an hour or so in pineapple or lemon juice	4 slices of pineapple
	1 dessertspoon grated lemon rind
2 oz. breadcrumbs	1 oz. butter
1 tablespoon finely chopped spring onions, onion tops, or chives	3 level tablespoons brown sugar
1 large egg	2 tablespoons pineapple juice
	a dash of lemon juice

Make four small cakes of chopped meat, crumbs, rind, and onion, bind with the egg. Arrange these on the pineapple and set on a greased baking-tin. Melt the butter in a saucepan, add sugar and pineapple and lemon juice. When blended pour over the cakes. Bake for about 35–40 minutes in a moderate oven, basting well.

EGG CROQUETTES

4 hard-boiled eggs	a squeeze of lemon juice
1½ oz. butter	1 yolk
1½ oz. flour	seasoning
½ pint milk	egg and breadcrumbs
1 tablespoon chopped mint or parsley	deep fat for frying

Garnish

crisply grilled bacon rolls and parsley or watercress

Chop the hard-boiled eggs in small pieces, make a sauce with butter, flour, and milk, reducing to a thick creamy consistency, mix the chopped eggs, parsley, lemon juice, and raw yolk with the sauce, season. Spread it on a plate and allow to get cold and firm. Divide in equal portions, shape into croquettes, egg and crumb and fry in deep fat to a golden brown. Serve garnished with crisply grilled bacon rolls and a bunch of fresh parsley or watercress.

CROQUETTES DE POISSON A LA CRÈME

1½ gills milk	8 oz. flaked cooked fish
1 slice of onion	(smoked haddock is ex-
1 bay-leaf	cellent)
1 blade of mace	seasoning
1½ oz. butter	1 egg
1¼ oz. flour, scant weight (but	dried white breadcrumbs
see note on page 719)	1 beaten egg for coating
	deep fat for frying

Bring the milk slowly to the boil with the onion, bay-leaf, and mace. Melt the butter in a small saucepan, add the flour, off the fire. Allow the milk to cool slightly, strain all at once over the contents of the pan. Bring back to boil and allow to simmer for a minute or two. Add the fish gradually, beating well. Adjust the seasoning, then add the egg. When thoroughly mixed turn on to a plate and allow to get quite cold. Divide into equal portions, roll and shape on a floured board, brush with egg, roll and press slightly in the crumbs, fry in deep fat. Drain well. Serve with piquante sauce such as tartare or tomato, or with quarters of lemon.

CROQUETTES OF MEAT

½ lb. cold minced meat	a dust of nutmeg
2 oz. minced ham or bacon	seasoning
1 teaspoon chopped parsley	yolk of egg

Sauce

1 oz. fat, oil, or dripping	1½ gills good stock
1 oz. flour	

Garnish

fried parsley

Make a brown roux with fat and flour, add stock and allow the sauce to reduce slightly. Allow to cool, add the meats, parsley, and nutmeg and adjust seasoning. Bind with egg yolk. Turn mixture on to greased plate, cover with greased paper and leave till absolutely cold. Divide into equal portions, flour and egg and breadcrumb as already described. Fry in deep fat, drain well and garnish with fried parsley.

FISHCAKES

½ lb. cooked white fish, free	1 teaspoon chopped parsley
from skin and bone	seasoning
½ lb. freshly boiled well-dried	egg for coating, and dried
mashed potato	white breadcrumbs
½ oz. butter	fat for frying
1 beaten egg	

Flake the fish well with a fork. Put the potatoes through a sieve or ricer, add to the fish with the butter, beaten egg, parsley, and seasoning. Mix thoroughly and leave for some hours before shaping. Put the mixture in dessertspoons on to a floured board, shape into cakes, brush over with beaten egg, roll in crumbs. Fry in smoking fat, turning when brown, drain on crumpled paper. It should be noted that some recipes call for crushed vermicelli in addition to or in place of breadcrumbs. Many American recipes call for rolled biscuit crumbs (cracker crumbs). Oatmeal or cornflakes may also be used.

MAZAGRANS DE GIBIER

6 oz. cooked game, rabbit, hare, pheasant, etc.	beaten egg
½ oz. butter	2 tablespoons grated cheese if wished
½ oz. flour	extra grated cheese for dusting
1½ gills stock	browned crumbs
1 tablespoon sherry	a few pickled walnuts or gherkins, or failing these a tablespoon of good chutney
salt and pepper	
1 lb. freshly boiled potatoes	
a little milk and butter for purée	

Finely dice the meat. Melt the butter in a saucepan, add the flour, mix and allow to brown lightly. Pour on the stock, stir until boiling and simmer until thick; add the sherry and the meat, but do not reboil. Season. Have the potatoes just cooked; strain and dry. Push at once through a wire sieve or ricer on to a cloth, as for mashed potato. Return to the pan and beat up over the fire to a firm creamy consistency, using a little hot milk and butter. If wished the mixture can be finished off with beaten egg and a spoonful or two of grated cheese. Butter some scallop shells or other small moulds, line with the potato purée, put a spoonful of the game mixture in each and cover with a layer of potato. Smooth off and mark in ridges with a knife, brush over with beaten egg and dust with cheese and browned crumbs. Bake for 10–15 minutes in a hot oven. Put a slice of pickled walnut or gherkin on each and serve. If using chutney put a small teaspoon on the potato of each mould before browning.

GOUGÈRE DE GIBIER

Choux paste (see page 843)

2 oz. butter	2 oz. finely diced cheese
¼ pint water	salt and pepper
2½ oz. plain flour	mustard
2 eggs	
game salpicon (see next page)	browned breadcrumbs
grated cheese	chopped parsley

Well butter a pie plate or small fireproof dishes, fill the pie plate with two-thirds of the choux paste, or put a dessertspoon of paste into each small dish.   Dip the fingers in warm water and hollow out the centre of the paste.   Fill with the game salpicon, partially cover with the remainder of the paste, scatter over with grated cheese and browned breadcrumbs, and bake in a moderate to hot oven 30–45 minutes, or 15–20 minutes for the small dishes.   Serve at once, well dusted with chopped parsley.

Game salpicon

3–4 oz. cooked game, chicken, or ham	1 level dessertspoon flour
1 medium-sized onion	1 large mushroom or tomato
1 dessertspoon butter or dripping	¼ pint stock
	salt and pepper
	1 teaspoon chopped mixed herbs

Finely dice the meat and slice the onion as thinly as possible.   Melt the butter in a small sauté pan or saucepan, put in the onion and sauter slowly until soft and 'melted.'   Add the flour off the fire with the chopped mushroom or sliced tomato; pour on the stock.   Bring to the boil and reduce until syrupy-looking.   Season well, add the herbs and the meat. Stand on the side of the stove to allow the meat to absorb the flavour of the sauce.

XXIII

Devils, Barbecues, and Marinades

PEOPLE of sensitive and unadventurous palate or of delicate digestion might regard with apprehension dishes with such filibustering and satanic names. Yet the bark, if I may so express it, of barbecues and devils is generally fiercer than their bite. The truth is that with one or two exceptions the finished dish might be described as aromatic rather than peppery; even when the initial ingredients sound fiery the final dish often presents a spicy and agreeable flavour without any tongue-burning propensities. Take, for example, that best of Christmas-time dishes, devilled turkey bones, one of the high lights, it might be said, of this type of dish. The flesh, marinaded in a bath of hot-sounding liquid, ends up with an appetizing and agreeable flavour and certainly without any real fire. The mushrooms in a creamed devilled sauce, again, are quite bland and pleasing to a delicate palate.

For barbecues, too, the meat, fish, or poultry may be soused and basted with fiery liquid during the cooking, but any real pepperiness must appear in the accompanying sauce, and this is something that you have under your control. As this method of cooking has manifold and good uses, it would be a pity, under misapprehension of their nature, to set such dishes aside. The word barbecue is associated with outdoor meals and has its origin in gargantuan feasts for which whole beasts, spitted from 'barbe to queue,' were roasted over outdoor fires of hickory wood. It is said that this fashion of cooking was introduced to America by French hunters or buccaneers.

The pit dug, the fire started many hours ahead of time so that the roasting might be done over glowing, smokeless heat, the meat, first marinaded, was basted during its cooking with long mops and brooms dipped into buckets of salted water. This basting prevented the outside of the meat from becoming too scorched. Later, as pieces were carved from the beef, they were dipped into a hot barbecue sauce and quickly clapped on to chunks of home-made bread. Enormous, appetizing feasts, hardly belonging to the world of to-day, and yet for picnics, for outdoor and for some indoor meals, the principles of making a barbecue may with advantage be applied. A leg of mutton barbecued is quite delicious, and so are chops, and chicken and fish served in a barbecue

724

sauce. Ham, grilled or fried perhaps out of doors for a picnic, may be finished off with a barbecue sauce to lend it a particularly appetizing flavour.

DEVILLED TURKEY BONES

Make a marinade of the following ingredients:

1 gill salad-oil
2 tablespoons Worcestershire sauce
2 tablespoons tomato ketchup
1 dessertspoon each of English and French mustard

1 teaspoon sugar
a dash of anchovy essence
salt, pepper, and a dash of paprika

Cut up the joints into suitably sized pieces, skin them and score them deeply with a knife; lay them in the marinade and with a spoon pour the liquid into the cuts that you have made in the meat, working it well in. Leave for several hours, basting from time to time, then fry the pieces in a little hot dripping, or cook them under the grill, and serve like a grill with fried tomatoes, bacon, watercress for garnish, and an accompanying sauce, such as devil sauce 2 or 3.

DEVIL SAUCE (1)

for fish, chicken, and eggs

1 gill cream
1 teaspoon anchovy essence
1 tablespoon Harvey sauce
1 dessertspoon Worcestershire sauce

1 dessertspoon mushroom ketchup
1 dessertspoon mango chutney
salt, pepper, mustard, and a dash of cayenne

Whip the cream till stiff, add the remaining ingredients (except the chutney) by degrees, whisking gently to keep the sauce as thick as possible. Fold in finally the chutney, spread on the top of cooked fillets of fish, chicken, or poached eggs in a gratin dish, bake in a hot oven 5–10 minutes and serve at once.

DEVIL SAUCE (2)

3 tablespoons Worcestershire or Harvey sauce
2 tablespoons mushroom ketchup
1 tablespoon tarragon vinegar
1 tablespoon onion, finely chopped
2–3 thin slices of lemon cut in two

1 clove of garlic crushed with a level teaspoon salt
1 cup strong chicken broth or gravy
1 cup tinned or fresh tomatoes, skinned and chopped
freshly ground black pepper
1 bay-leaf
salt

Simmer all ingredients together for 10 minutes and serve hot.

DEVIL SAUCE (3)

2 oz. butter
1 dessertspoon sugar
1 teaspoon dry mustard
a pinch of salt and pepper
a dash of cayenne or tabasco
1 teaspoon Worcestershire sauce

a pounded yolk of hard-boiled egg
1 tablespoon finely chopped chives
2 tablespoons wine vinegar
1 tablespoon cream

Cream together butter and sugar, add remaining ingredients, cook in a double saucepan till well blended.   Good for vegetable dishes.

CHUTNEY DEVIL SAUCE

3–4 tablespoons gooseberry, apple, or red-currant jelly
1 teaspoon lemon or 1 tablespoon orange juice

grated rind of an orange and a little of its flesh skinned and broken in pieces
4–5 tablespoons good chutney, pepper, salt, and paprika

Mix all the ingredients together and heat gently.   This is refreshing and useful and may be varied by the addition of herbs and made as peppery as taste dictates by the addition of cayenne.

DEVILLED LIVER KEBABS

liver, sage leaves, and mushrooms

a little butter

Cut liver in squares, slice the mushrooms, marinade in a similar mixture to that given for turkey bones.   Drain and arrange liver, sage leaves, and mushrooms on little skewers.   Brush with melted butter, grill, and serve with one of the devil sauces.

MUSHROOM DEVIL

1 lb. freshly gathered mushrooms of even size

1 oz. butter
pepper, salt, and lemon juice

Sauce
1 gill cream
1 tablespoon tomato ketchup
freshly grated horse-radish
1 tablespoon Harvey sauce

1 dessertspoon tarragon vinegar
freshly grated nutmeg
mustard and lemon juice

Peel the mushrooms and cut the stalks level with the cups; do not pull them out.   Heat a frying-pan and drop in half the butter, when foaming add half the mushrooms, sauter over a very hot fire for 2 or 3 minutes. Remove and lay the mushrooms in a casserole or deep dish, sprinkle liberally with pepper, salt, and lemon juice.   Put the remaining butter into the pan, sauter the remaining mushrooms, add to the dish, seasoning in the same way.   Whip the cream stiffly, beat in ketchup, vinegar, salt, seasonings, and nutmeg.   Make the sauce piquante and aromatic, spread it thickly over the mushrooms, bake quickly, without a lid, to golden brown in a hot oven, 5–10 minutes.   It is important to sauter the mushrooms quickly to prevent the juice from running out.

DEVILLED CHICKEN (COLD OR HOT)

For a picnic where transport is not a problem or for a supper dish.   It must be prepared a day in advance.

Serve in a casserole with an accompanying casserole of cold boiled rice, dry and flaky.

Simmer a boiling fowl till tender with vegetables and a bouquet garni. Leave in cooking liquor until cold; then skin, joint, slice into convenient pieces, brush over with melted butter, and grill quickly on both sides until well browned.   Lay in a casserole, pour over while hot devil sauce 2 to moisten nicely.   Leave until the next day to allow the flavour to soak into the chicken.

You may with advantage heat up cooked chicken in a sauce made as follows:

1 gill cream	2 teaspoons dry English mustard
1 tablespoon curry-paste	seasoning
1 teaspoon French mustard	

Heat ingredients gently without allowing them to boil.

DEVILLED VEGETABLES

This dish is made with potatoes and aubergines, but tomatoes or tomatoes and outdoor cucumbers may replace the latter.

4 medium-sized raw potatoes	2 teaspoons dry mustard
2 aubergines or a pint of peeled tomatoes and diced cucumbers combined	½ teaspoon turmeric
	¼ saltspoon cayenne or a small hot chilli, fresh or from
1 medium onion, finely chopped	those preserved in sherry
2 tablespoons olive oil	a good pint water or chicken stock
1 dessertspoon salt	a little coco-nut milk or cream
½ teaspoon ground ginger	

Sprinkle the prepared slices of aubergine (see pages 232–3) with salt and leave half an hour, then pour off the liquid.   Dice potatoes.   Heat oil and cook onion in it till soft and lightly coloured.   Add vegetables and all other ingredients except liquid and cook gently in the hot fat.   Add water and simmer gently until all moisture is absorbed and the vegetables tender. Add coco-nut milk or cream and cook for a few minutes more.

This really is a devil and hot for the sensitive palate.

BARBECUE SAUCE
for serving with meat, devils, etc.

1 onion, chopped
1 clove of garlic crushed with teaspoon salt

Soften these in a small nut of margarine or butter, or 1 teaspoon olive oil, then add the following:

1 lb. skinned chopped tomatoes (or tinned tomatoes)
2 or 3 stalks of celery, chopped (or celery salt)
2 or 3 thin slices of lemon
2½ tablespoons vinegar
2 tablespoons tomato ketchup or A1 sauce

1 tablespoon Worcestershire or Harvey sauce
½ pint fruit juice or water
1 good tablespoon sugar
a bouquet of herbs and 2 bay-leaves

Cook gently 20 minutes, strain and if too thin reduce. Finish off with 1½–2 oz. butter.

BARBECUED MUTTON

a leg of mutton
1 teaspoon each of dry mustard, ginger, salt, and freshly ground pepper

2 cloves of garlic
a little flour for dredging

Basting sauce

4 tablespoons each of Worcestershire sauce, A1 sauce, and mushroom ketchup
2 teaspoons sugar
1 tablespoon vinegar
a dash of cayenne

1 oz. butter, melted
extra fat for baking if meat is lean
1 onion, sliced
2 cloves of garlic crushed with salt

Rub mustard, ginger, salt, and pepper well into the surface of the meat. Split the garlic cloves and insert into the lean part of the meat. Dredge with flour. Bake in a sharp oven for 30 minutes, then pour in the sauce and start basting. Watch that the liquid does not dry up and add water or vegetable stock if required. The gravy should be rich and brown and may be strained over the meat; extra liquid may be added if the gravy is to be served apart.

If the gravy is too rich some of the fat may be skimmed off. This is good hot or cold.

BARBECUED DUCK

a good-sized duck
2 oz. butter
2 tablespoons olive oil
½ teaspoon dry mustard
½ teaspoon freshly ground black pepper
a pinch of cayenne
1 tablespoon Worcestershire sauce

1 tablespoon tomato ketchup
1 tablespoon chilli sauce
1 tablespoon red wine
1 tablespoon mild vinegar
1 tablespoon water
grated rind of ½ orange
juice of ½ lemon
½ teaspoon sugar
small clove of garlic, crushed

Rub mustard, pepper, and cayenne, mixed together well, into the duck. Put in pan with water and pour over the olive oil. Begin to roast. Mix remaining ingredients and add to pan. Then baste at 10-minute intervals while cooking. Add extra liquid, water or wine, if sauce reduces too much. Serve sauce apart.

BARBECUED POUSSIN

A suitable way of cooking poussins.

a whole or ½ a poussin per person

melted butter for brushing

Sauce

2 oz. butter, melted	1 teaspoon onion juice
5 tablespoons mild vinegar	2 tablespoons red wine
a bouquet garni	1 large clove of garlic, crushed
1 tablespoon Worcestershire sauce	1 teaspoon paprika
1 tablespoon tomato purée	½ teaspoon salt
	¼ teaspoon pepper

Mix the ingredients for the sauce together. Split the poussins down the back, wash and dry thoroughly. Grease the grill rack. Brush the poussins with the butter and grill under a hot grill till brown. When golden brown reduce heat, then start basting with the sauce and continue till birds are well cooked. Reduce sauce if necessary, strain and serve apart.

BARBECUED PORK

Rub the surface of a piece of pork weighing 2–3 lb. with a mixture of:

1 teaspoon salt	1 teaspoon freshly ground pepper
1 teaspoon sugar	1 teaspoon ginger

Brown the meat in a little hot fat, drain off and pour over the following mixture. Cover tightly and cook in a moderate oven for 1–1½ hours, basting occasionally.

3 tablespoons tomato chilli sauce	2 tablespoons A1 sauce or home-made plum sauce
2 tablespoons mushroom ketchup	1 tablespoon sugar
3 tablespoons Worcestershire sauce	a dash of vinegar
	2 cloves of crushed garlic
	2 bay-leaves

To serve carve the meat, dish; skim gravy and strain over. Serve potatoes sautéd with sprigs of rosemary separately.

BARBECUED PORK CHOPS

Grill the chops. Baste with the sauce given for poussins, but add 2 teaspoons French mustard.

BARBECUED FISH

Slices of halibut, cod steaks, or large fillets of plaice are particularly suitable. Heat butter in a frying-pan. Dip fish in flour, cook and brown on both sides. Put on a dish, keep hot. Add to the butter in the pan:

2 gills boiling water or wine and water	juice of ½ lemon
salt and pepper	a good pinch of sugar
½ teaspoon French mustard	a few capers, and if possible a good-sized leaf of fennel
1 dessertspoon A1 sauce	

Bring to the boil, reduce a little, and pour over the fish.

BARBECUED HAM OR BACON

thick gammon rashers or slices of ham	1 pickled gherkin or onion or a few capers finely chopped
2 tablespoons bacon fat	1 tablespoon Worcestershire sauce
1 tablespoon chopped onion	
1 small green pepper, seeded and finely chopped	1 tablespoon chilli sauce
½ cup vinegar	2 slices of lemon

Soften onion and green pepper in bacon fat, add the remaining ingredients (except the bacon) and bring to the boil. Fry bacon or ham, push to one side of frying-pan, add the sauce and baste.

MARINADES

A marinade is a highly seasoned liquid in which meat, fish, or game may be soaked as a preliminary to cooking. The object is to impregnate the meat with certain flavours to make it tender, or in some cases to make it keep. A marinade may be cooked or uncooked and the time involved anything from an hour or so to a few days. The amount of liquid used is not generally sufficient entirely to cover the meat, which has to be turned and basted from time to time. An example of a quick uncooked marinade is seen in the use of sherry or brandy in the preparation, say, of a special tournedos, when a few spoonfuls of either are poured over the meat, which is then left for an hour or two and turned from time to time. The liquid may afterwards be incorporated with the sauce accompanying the dish. Lemon juice is often used in the same way, particularly for fish. An uncooked marinade may call for wine, brandy, lemon juice, oil, seasonings, and aromatic flavouring ingredients, such as parsley, thyme, bay-leaf, mixed herbs and whole spices, juniper berries, rosemary. Which of these may be used and the proportions of them depends on the dish in hand, those of stronger and more pungent flavour being generally reserved for such meat as venison, beef, and certain dishes of game.

In Provence they add a strip of orange rind to the marinade or foundation for a braise. This gives a delicate individual flavour which is very good.

Here is an example of a quick uncooked marinade. To the meat on a dish add the following: a little onion or shallot, very finely sliced, a bouquet of herbs, lightly bruised, salt and crushed peppercorns.   Sprinkle with lemon juice or vinegar and several spoonfuls of oil.   Leave for 1 hour before proceeding with the cooking.   Madeira may be used for marinading dark meat and brandy for either dark or white.   An uncooked marinade may be used for steaks and cutlets and also for meat which is to be used for terrines and pâtés.

A cooked marinade is more commonly used for large joints, and in the interests of economy any liquid left over may be reboiled and reserved for further use.   It will probably keep about a week.   The aroma and flavour of the vegetables, herbs, and spices are extracted by cooking.   Generally speaking, the liquid is not used until quite cold.

For these marinades an earthenware vessel should invariably be employed.   The piece of meat should be turned two or three times a day and basted with a wooden spoon.   In very hot weather, if meat is to be kept in the liquid for more than a day or so, it may become necessary to take precautions against fermentation.   For this the meat is removed and the liquid reboiled (a few spoonfuls of additional vinegar and wine may at option be added), the whole allowed to cool again and the meat replaced in it.

Here is an example of a cooked marinade, suitable for certain meats:

MARINADE (1)

a bottle of white wine (cider, draught for preference, is sometimes used in place of wine)	2 onions, 2 carrots, 2 shallots, all roughly chopped
	a large bouquet of herbs
	5–6 peppercorns
¼ pint wine vinegar	5–6 juniper berries and a bay-leaf

Boil all ingredients together for half an hour, allow to get thoroughly cold.   Add 2 or 3 spoonfuls of oil.   Allow the meat to remain in this for at least 12 hours, basting and turning from time to time.

Sometimes for a large piece of venison a boiling marinade is called for, either when the meat is on the coarse side or when time is short.   On page 558 will be found a marinade for a leg of mutton to be treated as venison, and on pages 571 and 540 particularly good mixtures for Daube Avignonnaise and Daube Marseillaise.   On page 554 will be found a marinade for saddle of lamb.

MARINADE (2)
for hare, rabbit, grouse, venison, etc.

¼ pint red wine	freshly ground black pepper
2 tablespoons salad-oil	a few crushed juniper berries
a sliced shallot	salt
2 bay-leaves	

Put all together, bring to the boil, take off, cool.   When cold pour over the meat, cover and leave 12–24 hours, turning the pieces over occasionally. The marinade can be reduced to half quantity and added to the gravy or sauce.

MARINADE (3)

for cutlets, steaks, pigeon, game, and rabbit

1 large onion
¼ pint brandy (or sherry as a substitute); dry white wine or a good red wine may also be used
1 level teaspoon dry powdered thyme

1 small bay-leaf
4–5 parsley stalks, bruised
2 shallots, chopped
2 large tablespoons good olive oil
4–6 bruised peppercorns or all-spice (Jamaican pepper)

Cut onion in thin slices, mix with the other ingredients. Use as it is for cutlets, steaks, veal, game (pigeons especially), and rabbit, and strain it when it is to be added to the gravy. The quantity of oil may be decreased according to taste, though the presence of this helps to soften and flavour the meat and makes it more juicy, particularly that which has little or no fat.

MARINADE (4)

Here is a marinade for hare, game, and for cooked meat to be made into a réchauffé:

1 tablespoon red-currant jelly
3 liquid oz. each of mushroom ketchup, port, and wine vinegar

1 dessertspoon mixed thyme and marjoram, chopped
1 medium-sized chopped onion
a good pinch of salt
1 teaspoon Jamaican pepper

Warm the jelly, dissolve in it the ketchup, add to the other ingredients. This marinade may be strained and added to the sauce or gravy in which the meat is being cooked or reheated.

MARINADE FOR FISH

The following marinade for fish may be spicy rather than hot:

a pinch of saffron soaked ½ hour in a tablespoon boiling water
2 cloves of garlic crushed with salt
a good pinch of ground coriander or cumin seed

1 tablespoon finely chopped parsley
2 tablespoons tomato ketchup
1 gill wine vinegar
a little lemon juice
seasoning of salt and freshly ground black pepper

Mix all together, adjust seasoning and add if liked a dash of cayenne or chilli vinegar, or the sherry from a bottle of chillis preserved in sherry (see page 1108).

Marinade the fish for some hours in this before draining, drying, and coating for frying or preparing for grilling. With fried fish a little of the sauce may be sprinkled over the fillets immediately before serving. For baked fish a gill or so of the marinade with a nut of butter may be added, and the fish basted well during cooking.

XXIV

Cold Savoury Mousses, Soufflés, and Aspic

SAVOURY mousses and soufflés are not properly part of the classic cold table, but find their place on the party buffet. They are an economical way of using expensive materials, 1 lb. of meat serving 10–12 people when made up in this way. A mousse or a soufflé is also a palatable dish to be made from left-overs of chicken, game, veal, ham, and salmon.

Such dishes are made from the cooked meat minced, then pounded with butter, béchamel or velouté sauce, and finally mixed with liquid aspic and whipped cream, these last two ingredients having the effect of lightening the consistency. If a mousse is to be turned out for serving, a little gelatine is often added, and for a soufflé stiffly whipped whites of egg.

It is possible to make a mousse from pounded meat, butter, and cream alone, but this is less economical of materials and proves too rich for many palates. Certainly when the mousse is to be served as a main course it is more usual to employ sauce and aspic in the making.

General proportions for mousses

To each 1 lb. meat allow ½–¾ pint sauce, which when cold should have the consistency of thick cream. Allow also 2–3 oz. butter (creamed), ¼ pint aspic jelly, ¼–½ oz. gelatine, and 2 or more tablespoons lightly whipped cream.

For soufflés allow approximately the above proportions, but adjust a little so as to produce a slightly slacker mixture, and use the full quantity of gelatine. To these quantities allow the whites of 4 eggs stiffly beaten. Incorporate them immediately before turning the mixture into a soufflé dish round which a band of paper rising above the rim has been tied.

The difference between a cold soufflé and a mousse is primarily one of texture, the mousse being, as its name implies, soft and smooth, and the soufflé more airy and spongy. A soufflé contains egg whites and cream while a mousse contains butter and cream but no egg whites.

Mousses may be dished in various ways. For formal functions, the following procedure, not very often seen to-day, may be carried out:

1. A mould, usually a charlotte mould, is decorated and lined with aspic (see page 737). An aspic cream is then sometimes used as a second lining, which has the effect of throwing the decoration into relief, if this is not

733

effected by the colour of the mousse itself. The mousse, turned out, is surrounded with chopped aspic, and cubes or triangles of aspic jelly. Small individual moulds may be treated in the same way.

2. A second method, in which the mousse is served in a soufflé dish, is simpler.

Fill a soufflé dish three parts full with the mousse. Smooth over the surface. Run a little cool aspic over the surface to form a clear covering. When this is set a decorative garnish is arranged and a little more cool aspic run over it. When this is quite set the dish is filled to the brim with aspic.

3. A simpler method still, suitable for the less rich party mixtures and for a veal mousse.

Take a plain charlotte mould, soufflé dish, or small dariole moulds and either oil or rinse out with cold water. Fill with the mousse, allow to set, turn out and cover with a mayonnaise or cream dressing, finishing with a suitable garnish.

Garnishes

Truffle, sliced, chopped, or cut into shapes
Tarragon and chervil
Cucumber
Quartered tomatoes
Sliced button mushrooms

HAM MOUSSE (1)

1½ gills béchamel sauce (see page 155) made with:
  1 oz. each of butter and flour
  1½ gills milk
½ lb. lean cooked ham
1 oz. creamed butter or margarine
¼ oz. gelatine dissolved in 4 tablespoons melted aspic jelly

salt, pepper, mustard, cayenne
carmine
2 large tablespoons lightly whipped cream
aspic
cucumber or tomato for garnish

First make the béchamel and set on one side to get cold. Mince the ham twice and pound well with the butter. Gradually incorporate the béchamel and when smooth and creamy add the gelatine and aspic. Do this with care, for if it is worked too much it is liable to curdle. Add the seasoning to taste, colour delicately, fold in the whipped cream and turn into a soufflé case, which should be a little more than three parts full. Smooth the top, run over a little cool aspic, and when set cover with thin slices of cucumber, slightly overlapping, or skinned, quartered, and pipped tomatoes. Pour in enough aspic to set it, then fill to the top with aspic.

HAM MOUSSE (2)

½ lb. ham
1 teaspoon tomato purée
¼ pint aspic
½ oz. gelatine
¼ pint béchamel sauce (see
    page 155)

seasoning
¼ pint partially whipped cream
2 egg whites
extra aspic for coating

Mince ham and pound with the purée. Rub through a wire sieve. Dissolve gelatine in the aspic and add when cool to the ham, first mixing in the béchamel sauce and seasoning. As the mixture begins to thicken fold in the cream and stiffly whipped whites. Pour at once into a prepared soufflé case. When set remove paper and cover with a thin layer of cool aspic. When firm decorate with chopped aspic or other garnish.

The above is strictly speaking more a soufflé than a mousse; it calls for aspic jelly in the mixture, but it is possible, particularly if method 3 is adopted, to replace this with stock. If this is done the amount of gelatine must be increased (¼ oz. gelatine to 1 gill stock).

Both the above recipes may be taken for chicken, veal, or rabbit. A recipe for Salmon Mousse will be found on page 517, and one for a cold cheese soufflé on page 755.

ASPIC JELLY

Since aspic is called for in many cold dishes, either as an ingredient or an accompaniment, some directions for making and clarifying the jelly will now be given.

Aspic jelly is made from a good, strong stock—chicken, veal, beef, or fish. This base should be so rich in gelatinous matter that it is not necessary to add gelatine to it, but if for reasons of time-saving or economy it becomes needful to set the jelly more firmly, the proportion of gelatine should never be more than 2 oz. medium strength gelatine to the quart.

The base for a good jelly should contain a fair proportion of bone and gelatinous meat; shin of beef, knuckle of veal, a calf's foot, and veal bones are all good to use for the purpose, as all have a high proportion of gelatine. After the stock has been prepared it must be carefully strained and every particle of grease removed. It may be slightly acidulated by the addition of a little wine vinegar, some lemon juice, or in some recipes red or white wine may be added. It must, however, always be remembered that although aspic is often used as a decoration, like all other garnishes it ought to be pleasant to eat. It should not be over-sharp in taste, and the stock should be good enough to give it a well-seasoned, slightly piquant flavour.

Since, however, it is used for decorative purposes, the appearance and consistency of the aspic must be good. This exacts from the cook both time and care; the final result, however, is well worth the trouble.

Herbs are frequently used in dishes coated with aspic. Sometimes whole sprays or separate leaves are laid on the food before coating; for example, tarragon leaves are often arranged along a whole salmon trout, or sprays of fennel and tarragon on eggs.   In this way flavour is imparted while the clearness of the aspic is preserved.

Mint aspic is very good, and for this the mint is finely chopped.   Cutlets in mint aspic is a good cold dish.

A tomato aspic may be made on the same principle as consommé madrilène, that is by adding tomatoes when clarifying, and is good with eggs.

Special stock for meat aspic

2 rashers of streaky bacon	3 pints water
3 oz. onion	½ stick of celery, 1 leek, and
1½ oz. good red carrot	bouquet garni tied together
1 lb. shin of beef	(bouquet should include
1 small calf's foot	tarragon and in the case of
1 set of chicken giblets or	fish a sprig of fennel)
small chicken carcass	1 teaspoon salt
2 wineglasses white wine or	
water	

Lay the bacon on the bottom of a thick pan, slice the onion and carrot, arrange over the bacon, put the meat on the top with the calf's foot split in two and the giblets.   Cover and 'sweat' on a low fire or in the oven 15–20 minutes; this is in order to draw out the juices from the meat and vegetables and must be done slowly and carefully.   Do not stir or disturb the meat in any way during this operation.   Then add a wineglass of white wine or water, bring to the boil and reduce until there is about a tablespoon of honey-coloured liquid or jus at the bottom of the pan.   Add a further wineglass of wine or water and repeat the process.   This is known as *tomber à glace* and again helps to extract the juice from the meat; it also strengthens it.   Now add the water, vegetables, bouquet garni, and salt. Bring to the boil, skimming well.   To make this easier add a few spoonfuls of cold water when it comes to the boil, skim and bring again to the boil. Repeat this until no more scum will rise.   (See recipe for Pot-au-feu, page 116.)   Simmer on a low fire steadily and continuously for 2–3 hours, taking great care that it does not boil hard.   The surface of the liquid should just move.   Then strain off and allow to get cold.

ASPIC JELLY
for 1 quart aspic

This aspic is suitable for all meat, game, and chicken dishes.   When a more delicately flavoured aspic is wanted, for certain egg dishes or whole chicken in jelly, use chicken or veal only for the stock and flavour with a dry white wine in preference to the sherry.

1¾ pints good well-flavoured stock (made with meat, fish, or game)	½ gill sherry
	1–2 tablespoons vinegar
	1¾–2 oz. gelatine
½ gill white wine	2 egg whites

Put the cold stock, wines, vinegar, and gelatine into a pan and dissolve over gentle heat.   Add the egg whites whipped to a froth and whisk until boiling-point is reached.   Allow the mixture to boil undisturbed to the top of the pan, draw aside, boil up twice more, allow to settle for 5 minutes and then strain through a scalded cloth.   (See note on clarifying, page 120.)

To pour over a mousse or coat a galantine

When the jelly has been clarified let it cool to the point of setting, that is allow it to become quite cold.   Then pour a small quantity into a very clean small pan (either enamel or tin-lined copper); set the pan on ice and stir slowly with a silver or metal spoon until the jelly begins to thicken. Use at once for coating over the mousse or galantine.

The same method is followed when aspic is run over the top of a mousse served in a soufflé case.

1. The soufflé dish is filled two-thirds or three-quarters full with the mousse, the surface is smoothed over, and the mousse is left in a cool place to become firm.

2. A small quantity of cool aspic is run over the top to the depth of $\frac{1}{4}$ inch and is left to set.

3. The garnish or decoration is then put on, and a small quantity of cool aspic is spooned over to set it.

4. When the jelly over the decoration has set firmly, fill to the brim with cool aspic.

A galantine is covered and decorated in the same way.

A mould that is lined, decorated, and then turned out makes a good show for a cold table or a buffet supper.   The dish, when finished, is garnished with cut and chopped aspic.

To line a mould

1. Choose a plain mould such as a charlotte or bombe and see that it is perfectly clean.

2. Have ready a bowl of ice (a handful of freezing salt added to it will make setting quicker); set the mould comfortably in this.

3. Pour a small quantity of cool aspic into the mould, and at once turn it round and round with a smooth steady movement so that the jelly runs over the sides and bottom.   As soon as the jelly begins to set or thicken pour it quickly out and begin again.

4. Continue the process until there is an even lining not less than $\frac{1}{4}$ inch thick on the sides and about $\frac{3}{8}$ inch on the bottom.

5. Be careful that each layer of aspic that goes into the mould is cool, and that it is not allowed to lump on the sides and pull off the lining already there.   As soon as it begins to thicken too much pour it out.   Concentrate first on the sides; when they are satisfactorily coated the bottom of the mould can always be finished off with a little more aspic run in to set in an even layer.

6. Decorate by dipping each piece of garnish, tarragon, truffle, etc., in a little cool aspic before setting it in with the point of a small vegetable or garnishing knife.   When the decorations are in place reline the mould as before to set the garnish.   This layer should only be half as thick as the first, and may consist of aspic cream instead of jelly to make a white or cream background for the decoration.   The mould is now ready to fill with the mousse and must be filled to the brim and left to set quite firmly before it is turned out.

To turn out

Have ready a large bowl full of hand-hot water, and a clean cloth.   For small moulds (lined and decorated in just the same way as the large) have ready a double piece of grease-proof paper lightly smeared with cold water. Pick up the mould with the palm of the hand over the top, dip it into the water—for small moulds, dip right in and out again with a slow, sweeping movement; dip a large one in on a level with the top of the mould.   Wipe the outside of the mould with the cloth and shake it gently; turn it upside-down and let it slide out on to your hand and so to the dish in one movement.   If the mould does not move dip it again into the water.   Small moulds are slid on to the grease-proof paper one by one, and then transferred to the dish with a palette-knife.

To chop aspic

Turn out on to wetted grease-proof paper and chop with a large knife. Do not hold the point of the knife down with the other hand, as is usual, and avoid touching the jelly with your fingers.

To keep aspic

If perfectly clear, the jelly may be melted down and put into a bowl. Set, and run a little cold water over the top.   Pour off the water before using.   The aspic will keep for 2–3 days.

To cut blocks of jelly

To cut squares, triangles, etc., for garnishing pour the cool jelly into an oblong tin, quite free from grease—a refrigerator ice tray is convenient— and leave it to set.   Cut into the required shape with a wetted knife.

For setting eggs, cutlets, prawns, tomatoes, etc., in aspic, pour a small quantity of cool aspic into the mould or moulds chosen to the depth of $\frac{1}{4}$–$\frac{3}{4}$ inch and allow it to set.   Then lay in the eggs, cutlets, etc., and leave round them a space of $\frac{1}{4}$–$\frac{3}{4}$ inch.   Carefully spoon in enough cool aspic to come level with the food in the mould and leave it to set.

When presenting a *pièce froide,* such as a chicken chaudfroid or salmon trout, run a little cool aspic over the bottom of the dish to the depth of about $\frac{1}{4}$ inch and allow it to set firmly before placing the *pièce* on it.   A silver dish is the most effective for such *pièces.*

N.B. Cool aspic means jelly that is on the point of setting.

XXV

Milk and Cheese

MILK

THE way in which young people to-day will drink milk in season and out of season never ceases to surprise me, nor can I get acclimatized to milk-bars. This is because I can remember the days when milk, in careful nurseries boiled for safety and in consequence unpleasant to our young palates, was for the invalid rather than the healthy. I wonder what you would have thought, accustomed as you are to the hygienic fashion of delivering milk in sealed bottles, had you watched a good-natured milk-man, as he decanted the milk at the kitchen door, pause to give some passing urchin a drink from his measure. All we thought about it was 'What a nice milkman,' nor did it occur to us to ring the bell to warn some careless housewife that a stray cat was drinking from the open bowl which she had left on the step for the milkman to fill. As a matter of course you accept pasteurized milk or milk from tuberculin-tested herds, hardly realizing how safeguarded you are. I remember the great anti-tuber-culosis campaign and the struggle that was waged to get clean and pure milk, even if only for babies and little children. Sometimes the work of these campaigns was uphill indeed, for, though it seems hard to believe, opposition was strong and every weapon was brought to bear, and mockery not the least among them, even down to the poorest and meanest of argu-ments on the lines of 'What was good enough for my father is good enough for me' and 'Unnatural, I call it.'

Such a retrograde attitude seems strange to us to-day, but it is only fair to remember what tradition and memory of hard work might have in-fluenced a dairy farmer in those days. There is an interesting sidelight on this in a book called *A Hundred Years in the Highlands*.[1] The author, Osgood Mackenzie, is quoting from the highland memories of an uncle, covering a period between 1803 and 1860.

And now as to the dairy. No finery of china or glass or even coarse earthenware was ever seen in those days; instead of these there were very many flat, shallow, wooden dishes and a multitude of churns and casks and kegs, needing great cleansing, otherwise the milk would have gone bad. And, big boilers being also unknown, how was the disinfecting done, and how was hot water produced?

[1] Osgood Mackenzie, *A Hundred Years in the Highlands* (Geoffrey Bles).

Few modern folk would ever guess. Well, the empty wooden dishes of every shape and size were placed on the stone floor, and after being first rinsed out with cold water and scubbed with little heather brushes, they were filled up again, and red-hot 'dornagan' (stones as large as a man's fist), chosen from the seashore and thoroughly polished by the waves of centuries, which had been placed by the hundred in a huge glowing furnace of peat, were gripped by long and strong pairs of tongs and dropped into the vessels. Three or four red-hot stones would make the cold water boil instantly right over, and the work was then accomplished. But oh, the time it took, and the amount of good Gaelic that had to be expended and more or less wasted before the great dairy could be finally locked till evening came round again.

That, of course, was written a long time ago, but even in much later years many of the poorer farmers lived without any of the convenient conditions that we take so much as a matter of course, and it is no wonder perhaps that they became neglectful and were afraid of innovation.

The anti-tuberculosis campaigns laid great emphasis on the dangers of dirty milk, and men as well as women worked to arouse public opinion, and to find remedies for what was certainly a bad state of affairs. Serious as these campaigns were, they had their lighter moments, and dear me, what mockery of laughter sometimes greeted recommendations about keeping cows, byres, and milk-cans clean, particularly cows. Some of us were asked to help by educating schoolchildren in this matter, and I laugh still when I remember the intelligent child who ended her essay on the need for clean milk for babies with a strong recommendation in favour of mother's milk, because, as she so rightly said, 'the cat could not get at it.'

I remember too a sad personal story which haunted me for many a long year, and made me, I must admit, reluctant to drink milk at all. A chief official in the Public Health Service lost his daughter in a violent and rapid consumption. One summer, as they were about to start a prolonged stay in their country house, he bought for her a small and very pretty cow. This was her own pet, and she would drink no other milk but what it gave. At the end of the summer she was dead, and the cow was found to be suffering from advanced tuberculosis affecting the milk glands. That is what this sad and pathetic man told me. Although it affected then my appreciation of milk as a beverage, it also interested me later in the reform-ation which has come to bring us safe and clean milk. Later on, but still many years ago, when civic and other responsible authorities were waking up to the dangers of dirty milk, a large meeting was convened. To this many important people were invited, and in particular one eminent and witty politician. It was hoped that a final and rousing speech from him would stir everyone to activity and incite the press to campaign for the cause. His speech was to be the last, the apotheosis. As one earnest speaker after another said his say, repeating, with slight variations, as is often the case on such occasions, what had already been said, it was observed that the great man was gradually overcome with sleep. To the general relief, at the appropriate moment he sprang into vivacious con-sciousness and, addressing the gathering in formal fashion, opened his speech in an arresting if unexpected manner: 'My Lords and Ladies,

ladies and gentlemen. Without doubt I think we must be all agreed that milk is a very dry subject.'

Whatever you may think of its dryness, you will agree if you consider the next few sentences that it is at least full of contradictions.

Milk can be a dangerous carrier of disease; it may also be the sole supporting food of a sick person.

It is sometimes described as a complete food, easy of digestion; some people find it highly indigestible.

As a beverage it is nectar to some, anathema to others.

It will on occasion turn sour for no apparent reason, or, on the other hand, cannot be induced to do so quickly when cheese-making or a cremet is in hand.

In old books one learns that for a proper sillabub the milk must be milked straight into the sillabub bowl, innocent of any preliminary straining and with no inkling of the need for pasteurization or indeed of any precautions whatsoever.

After all this you will, I believe, agree that one must understand something about this staple and temperamental food.

PASTEURIZED MILK

A good deal of the milk sold in big towns is 'bulk' milk, collected from a number of dairy farmers. In the interests of safety this is pasteurized, that is to say brought up to a certain temperature and maintained at this long enough to destroy germs. This is a valuable safety precaution, but it affects certain reactions of milk in cooking. For example, pasteurized milk will not sour naturally like untreated milk.

TUBERCULIN-TESTED MILK

This, generally more expensive, milk is from certain tested and controlled herds. It is usually distributed to the public non-pasteurized and the natural properties of the milk are retained. This is the most satisfactory milk to set for cream and to use for cheeses and junkets. The necessary process of souring proceeds quickly and naturally.

Hand-skimmed milk is a very different substance from that treated in a separator. The milk left after domestic skimming is suitable for many culinary purposes, and for this reason it is a sensible practice to set aside a certain amount of household milk to give a small supply of cream.

To set milk for cream

Pour new non-pasteurized milk into shallow bowls or preferably milk pans (which are to be bought cheaply from any dairy supplier). Allow to stand for 12–24 hours according to the weather, but allow a minimum of 12 hours. The same amount of cream is not to be obtained by syphoning this off the top of milk bottles.

To skim

Use preferably a proper skimmer; failing this a large metal spoon may be used, but should first be dipped into cold water.

To sour milk

Non-pasteurized milk usually becomes sour after 2–3 days, depending on the weather, the place where the milk is kept, and whether it has been cooled after milking.

Milk for souring should be left in warm room temperature, and the quicker it becomes sour the more palatable is the result. Milk that has formed a natural curd generally makes a more pleasantly flavoured milk cheese than one to which rennet has been added. Sometimes to induce milk to turn sour quickly a 'starter' is employed, that is to say a small quantity of sour milk left over from a previous batch is stirred into the fresh milk; this produces a lightly set and not over-acid curd. In commercial cheese-making special 'starters' are used, but they are of a different kind. Properly soured milk is used in a variety of ways, and in Sweden a bowl of it is a popular first course. A bowl of sour milk lightly set is served for each person, accompanied by thin ginger biscuits. This is prepared by putting a good spoonful of sour milk into each bowl of new-warm milk, which is kept in a warm place until set, probably for 6–8 hours, and is then moved to a cool place until wanted. This way of treating it produces a pleasant, light, and not over-acid curd.

Methods of making sour-milk cheese will be given later on in this chapter.

Uses of sour milk

Sour milk is used for the making of cheeses, various sweet and savoury dishes, cakes, scones, and salad-dressings.

Evaporated milk

This is tinned, unsweetened milk, and may in certain dishes replace cream. As it has a pronounced taste, care must be taken when it is used in this way, and one usually adds less than the amount of cream called for in the recipe. It is possible to whip evaporated milk, but it becomes foamy rather than solid and when whipped cannot be successfully piped, although it may be made slightly more solid by the addition of a little gelatine. For whipping evaporated milk see page 43.

Condensed milk

This is tinned, sweetened milk. It is useful in certain sweets when sugar is short, but again care must be taken when this is used as the flavour is pronounced and it is very sweet.

Buttermilk

This is the liquid left after butter has been churned. Sometimes it is rich with minute particles of butter. If used for drinking it should therefore be strained, but it is admirable as it is for scones and soda bread.

Boiling milk

For this a thick pan should be taken, preferably one kept exclusively for the purpose. First rinse it out with cold water. Do not fill the pan to the brim. Although milk saucepans are generally sold without lids, R. H. reminds me that if you wish to prevent the early formation of skin you will put a lid on the pan, in which case it will be necessary to watch it with great care. If the milk is being heated for drinking it should be brought very quickly to the boil and not allowed to simmer, as this detracts from the flavour. If it must be kept it should be put into a bain-marie, or kept warm in a double saucepan. After the milk is poured out the pans should go straight into cold water, as this greatly facilitates cleaning.

Reducing milk

It is not often in English recipes that one finds an instruction to reduce milk, but some French cooks recommend it. This means that the milk is simmered until it is reduced in quantity, probably by half. This gives a creamy finish, and reduced milk is useful for certain sauces.

JUNKET

1 pint warm new milk	1 small teaspoon rennet
1 dessertspoon sugar (or to taste)	a little thick cream

Ideally the milk should be warm from the cow, poured straight into a dish, sweetened, and the rennet added. But in the majority of cases to-day the milk has to be rewarmed. When this is done the milk should not be warmed beyond blood heat. Add sugar, if this is required, stir well, pour into a china dish, stir in the rennet and leave to set. Junket should not be kept in a refrigerator. When set a little thick cream is poured over the top, and sometimes ratafia biscuits are added. Junket should not really be flavoured, but some old recipes call for the addition of a little brandy. Nutmeg is a later and foreign addition, as, of course, is coffee essence, which takes us far beyond the original good old-fashioned junket.

CREMETS

These are a form of soured sweetened milk which have the appearance of rich, thick cream and are excellent to serve with fruit.

2 quarts milk	sugar to taste
1½ gills thick fresh cream	

Sour the milk quickly, in 24 hours if possible. For this a 'starter' is useful (see page 742). When set to a curd turn into a piece of muslin, tie the ends together and allow to drip 12–24 hours. When a fairly firm curd is achieved press it through a sieve, and beat in the cream by degrees, adding sugar to taste. When thick and creamy pile up in a dish and serve with fruit. An alternative is to finish this as cœur à la crème, and in this case the sugar is omitted, and the curd put into muslin-lined baskets and left to drain a further 2–3 hours before turning out.

CHEESE

Generally speaking, cheese may be considered under three categories, hard, medium, and soft.   It is inadvisable to keep cheeses in a refrigerator. They may suitably be served on a board, in assorted kinds, and be kept in the larder, covered with two or three layers of muslin.

ENGLISH CHEESES

Caerphilly.   A Welsh cheese, medium hard, white in colour, with a slight bite in the taste.   Similar to a Swedish cheese which is now on the market.

Cheddar.   A solid, mellow cheese.

Cheshire.   A solid cheese, stronger in flavour than Cheddar and redder in colour.   More crumbly and piquant in flavour.   Blue Cheshire is a refined version of the red: a connoisseur's cheese.

Stilton.   A rich, blue-veined cheese.   As this cheese becomes dry, or as a means of hastening its ripening, it is sometimes fed with small quantities of port or Madeira, and even, sometimes, with ale.

Wensleydale.   A pure cheese large in size, very white, slightly veined with green.   Semi-creamy in texture and generally on the market at Christmas-time.

FRENCH CHEESES

Brie.   A large, flat, round cheese, creamy, of delicate flavour.   It does not keep well.

Camembert.   In small, thick rounds.   At its best when soft and nearly *coulant.*

Coulommier.   A firm, rich, and creamy cheese.

Fromage de Monsieur.   Small, like a Camembert, but richer and more delicate in flavour.

Pont l'Évêque.   A much stronger cheese than Camembert, not quite so soft, though of similar consistency, and square in shape.

Port Salut.   A soft cheese of good flavour, full of little holes.

Roquefort.   A fine, green cheese, strongly flavoured, but not so strong as gorgonzola.

Tôme.   Like a Port Salut, but whiter.   The outside is covered closely with grape pips taken from the wine press.

ITALIAN CHEESES

Bel Paese.   Soft cheese, full of flavour.

Gorgonzola.   Veined with green, a strong cheese.

Parmesan.   Only for cooking.   Very hard, of incomparable flavour, and usually mixed with gruyère for cooking.   The gruyère gives the smoothness and richness, and the Parmesan the flavour.

SWISS CHEESES

Gruyère. A firm, pale yellow cheese, with large holes, which should be moist and milky at the edges when freshly cut—'a tear in each eye.' When it has become hard and shiny it is not nearly such a good cheese.

DUTCH CHEESES

Edam. Round, red-rinded cheese, generally bought by the piece. Slightly harder than Gouda.

Gouda. Very good, golden cheese, short in texture. A large cheese, bought by the pound.

DANISH CHEESES

A Danish Port Salut is now being imported and is of slightly fuller flavour than the French cheese of this name.

Danish gorgonzola or 'blue cheese.' A cheese of good flavour.

Samsoe. Like a Dutch Gouda.

SWEDISH CHEESE

We import now a hard Swedish cheese, dry and pleasant in flavour, not unlike Caerphilly.

CREAM OR MILK CHEESES

Demi-sel. Milk.

Petit Gervais. Cream.

Petit Suisse. Cream.

These cheeses do not keep.

In addition to these well-known cheeses there are many local cheeses which are beginning to come back. During the war, when the price of cheese was controlled, many dairy farmers did not make their special cheeses.

HOME-MADE SOUR-MILK CHEESE

For this the milk is soured as quickly as possible, and when a good firm curd is obtained it is put into muslin to harden and drain for anything from 12 to 24 hours, depending on the hardness of the curd and the consistency of cheese required. If the curd is hung too long too much of the whey will be drawn out, leaving the curd dry and crumbly. Ideally it should be firm but moist. The curd is then sieved, seasoned well, and either served as it is, shaped into cakes, or flavoured in various ways and mixed with other ingredients such as cream, butter, and in some cases with bought cheese which has been pressed through a sieve and beaten to a cream.

These home-made sour-milk or sour-cream cheeses are excellent. When once the curd is made in the way given above, the flavouring, seasoning, and final texture are a matter of taste. Freshly ground black pepper, salt, paprika, celery salt, anchovy essence, and Worcestershire sauce are all possible ingredients, and chopped herbs in variety, or chopped capers, sweet pickles, gherkins, onion juice, garlic, and so forth. The range is wide. The texture of the curd may be improved by beating it up with cream or butter or with bought hard cheese, sieved and beaten. Although one or two recipes are given, the possible variations are so great that they must depend on the individual cooks.

CHILLED CREAM CHEESE

household cheese
chopped herbs: chives, chervil, mint, thyme, savory; any or all in mixture are suitable
a small piece of butter or margarine

seasoning
milk or beer for moistening
caraway, sesame, or coriander seed (coriander must be crushed) are good additions

Grate the household cheese and either pound in a mortar or press through a fine wire sieve; beat well, add all other ingredients and beat to the consistency of thick clotted cream. Heap roughly on a dish and set this in a circle of ice. On the ice arrange radishes, olives, gherkins, pickled walnuts; whichever of these are available or all in mixture.

Serve with fresh biscuits hot from the oven, or hot garlic loaf (see page 359).

GOOD LUNCHEON CHEESE

This is particularly good.

3–4 tablespoons chopped cashew kernels, walnuts, or almonds, and a little butter for browning them
a good oz. butter or margarine
4 oz. strongly flavoured cheese, such as Danish Blue
1 heart of celery, chopped, or a pinch of celery salt

¾ oz. shallots or mild onion, grated, or chopped spring onions
1 tablespoon chopped parsley
freshly ground black pepper and salt
cream or top of milk if required

The chopped nuts are put with a little butter into a frying-pan, lightly browned, and tossed in salt and set aside. Press the cheese through a fine sieve. Beat well with the butter. Incorporate the other ingredients (except the nuts). Add a little cream or top of milk if required. The mixture should be light and creamy. Season well. Press into suitable shape, cover well with the chopped nuts, and serve.

LIPTAUER CHEESE

This is a much more highly flavoured cheese and is more suitable for cocktail savouries than for eating in quantity.

4 oz. curd or cottage cheese
4 oz. butter, well creamed
2 fillets of anchovy, well drained from the oil and finely chopped
1 level dessertspoon caraway seeds
1 level dessertspoon chopped capers

1 level dessertspoon chopped chives
1 level dessertspoon paprika
1 teaspoon made English mustard
½ teaspoon salt
a pinch of celery salt

Sieve the curd, beat into the creamed butter gradually. When whipped-looking add the rest of the ingredients. When thoroughly incorporated pile up in a dish and serve.

N.B. The finished cheese must be piquant and savoury, and more seasonings such as mustard and paprika added if necessary. Liptauer may be kept for several days in a covered jar.

SAVOURY CREAM CHEESE

4 oz. curd or mild cheddar cheese
4 oz. butter or margarine, well creamed
1 dessertspoon chopped chives

1–2 pickled walnuts
salt, freshly ground pepper
radishes
watercress

Sieve the curd or grate the cheese. Work into the butter gradually. When well beaten add the chives, sliced walnuts, and seasoning; stir just enough to mix. Pile up in a dish and surround with cut radishes (see page 48) and bouquets of watercress.

N.B. If using cheddar cheese a little less butter may be put in, say 3 oz., and 1–2 tablespoons boiling milk. This will make the mixture light and creamy. Additions other than walnuts may be put in to taste.

SOUR-MILK CHEESE (ANOTHER METHOD)

Some recipes call for the sour milk to be scalded.

2 pints thick sour milk
1 nut of butter
2 dessertspoons salt

¼ gill cream
seasoning
chopped herbs to taste

Put the sour milk into a saucepan and scald till the curd separates from the whey, but do not allow it to boil. Add the other ingredients except the herbs and beat well together. Adjust seasoning, add chopped herbs to taste.

FROMAGE AUX CIBOULETTES

2 Petit Gervais or demi-sel cheeses	salt and freshly ground black pepper
1 oz. butter	sugar to taste
¼ pint yoghourt or 'jellied' sour milk (approx.)	1 tablespoon chopped chives

Sieve the cheese and cream the butter well. Beat the two thoroughly together, seasoning well. Now stir in the yoghourt or milk, adding only enough to make it of a pleasant sharp flavour and a soft creamy consistency. Adjust the seasoning, adding sugar to taste. Add the chives and leave an hour or two before using.

CREAM CHEESE (FROMAGE A LA CRÈME FONTAINEBLEAU)

Preparations must begin a day in advance.

½ pint double cream	a pinch of salt
¼ pint creamy milk	fresh cream (optional)

Mix cream and milk together. Leave on ice for half an hour. Add salt, whip until light and creamy, but not to the stage of whipped cream. Line a wicker basket or strainer with a piece of muslin, first scalded and then wrung out in cold water. Put in the mixed cream, leave in a cold place until firm, approximately 12 hours. Then turn out. Pour over fresh cream. Serve with sugar or salt.

For other cheeses of this type see also Chapter I, 'The Cocktail Party,' pages 6–8.

CŒUR A LA CRÈME

Small heart-shaped baskets are needed for this dish. Preparations must begin a day in advance.

2 quarts new milk	salt
2 small tablespoons rennet (approx.)	½ pint cream (approx.) fresh cream

Warm milk and add rennet. When a firm curd is obtained break it up and sprinkle it with a little salt. Fill it into a wicker basket or strainer lined with muslin. Leave to drain for 8 hours, then press through a fine sieve. Put into a bowl, add the ½ pint cream very lightly whipped and more salt if necessary. Fill into small heart-shaped baskets and leave to drain again. At the end of 2–3 hours turn on to a dish, pour fresh cream over them. Eat with sugar or salt.

N.B. 1. Enough rennet should be added to the milk to make a firm curd.

2. The amount of cream may be increased depending on how rich you wish the 'cœur' to be.

From Camembert cheese an excellent iced after-dinner savoury is to be made, and the recipe for this will be found in Chapter II, 'Hors-d'œuvre, First-course Dishes, and After-dinner Savouries' (see page 34).

Camembert Croquettes are another excellent savoury. A recipe will also be found on page 34.

To pot cheese

Certain of the harder cheeses may be improved by potting. For this one pounds the cheese in a mortar or presses it through a sieve and beats it, adding about a third of its weight in fresh butter. In addition to this a spoonful or two of white wine is added, and sometimes a little powdered mace or other suitable spice. This mixture, well beaten together, is pressed into a pot and covered with melted butter. The process is admirable for using, for instance, the last of a Stilton cheese which has begun to get dry, or even one which is beginning to get over-ripe. For the stilton port or red wine may replace the white. The cheese may be served in the pot or taken out and sliced. Treated this way it will last a long time.

Now we come to dishes made with cheese, and the best of these, perhaps, is a proper Swiss fondue. I think I should like to start by giving you the recipe for the real thing. This dish is eaten in the most friendly and unconventional manner; a supply of bread is cut into small pieces, each *convive* takes a piece on the end of a fork, and all dip into the dish of fondue together. You may see it is hardly the dish for a conventional luncheon, but it is perfectly delicious. Nor is it an economical dish: more economical versions of it will follow.

SWISS FONDUE (1)

For each person allow approximately 4 oz. cheese, $\frac{1}{2}$ glass white wine, and $\frac{1}{4}$ glass kirsch. A good pinch of corn-flour or potato flour is used to bind the fondue, and a little nut of butter may be added, but this is optional.

For four persons

Rub the bottom of a shallow earthenware casserole with garlic. Mix 2 glasses white wine and 1 lb. rich cheese, grated (gruyère, for example). Place over a medium flame and stir continuously until a thick paste is obtained. Then add a glass of kirsch, in which the corn-flour has been mixed, and then a nut of butter.

The fondue is served in the casserole in which it is mixed and cooked. The cooking generally takes place over a spirit-lamp which is gradually lowered and finally extinguished when the dish is nearly empty.

FONDUE (2) (FOR 6)

1½ lb. cheese, grated	1 clove of garlic
¾ pint white wine	

Crush garlic and rub it thoroughly all round the inside of a casserole. Put in wine and grated cheese and stir over a fire until creamy. Take the casserole on to the table, have ready a dish full of slices of French bread, which should be dipped into the fondue.

Here is another recipe with less wine but including eggs:

FONDUE (3)

a clove of garlic, salt and pepper	one-third their weight in
1 glass white wine	gruyère
6 fresh eggs	one-sixth their weight in butter

Bruise garlic in a saucepan, heat wine, add cheese, grated, and stir over gentle heat till creamy. Add beaten eggs and butter and cook 7 or 8 minutes till thick. Season highly and serve in hot buttered dish.

If you have a chafing-dish both these dishes can be served at table. While cooking they must not be left for a moment and you must not stop stirring.

MOCK FONDUE (4)

1 oz. butter	salt, pepper, mustard, cayenne
½ oz. flour	hot buttered toast cut into
¼ pint rich milk	squares
1½–2 oz. grated cheese, gruyère or cheddar	

Melt butter in a saucepan, add the flour. Pour on the milk and stir until boiling. Simmer a minute or two, then draw aside and beat in the cheese by degrees with plenty of seasoning.

Have ready the toast arranged in a hot dish. Pour over the cream when perfectly smooth and serve at once. Sliced cooked mushroom can be scattered over the toast before pouring over the fondue.

It may be said that quite a good homely fondue is to be made with odds and ends of various cheeses, both hard and soft. The great thing is to have a little white wine with which to mix them and to cook them in the saucepan. When a fondue is made in this way we usually pour it over slices of bread, if it has not got that rich and sticky quality of the real thing.

A more economical dish may be made by the following recipe. This is an American dish, and is really more like a simple form of soufflé. It is made with a foundation of breadcrumbs instead of the more usual panade or thick sauce.

CHEESE FONDUE

¾ pint milk	6 oz. breadcrumbs
1 oz. margarine or butter	4 oz. grated cheese, gruyère
1½ teaspoons salt	for preference
¼ teaspoon freshly ground black pepper	a clove of garlic crushed with a little salt
a pinch of cayenne	4 eggs

Bring the milk to the boil, add to it the butter or margarine, salt, pepper, and cayenne, and pour it over the breadcrumbs. Add the garlic, crushed with a little salt, and the grated cheese, and stir until the cheese is melted. Separate the eggs and beat in the yolks. Cool a little. Whip the egg whites stiffly and fold them into the mixture. Pour into a buttered pie dish or soufflé case (which should not be more than three-quarters filled) and bake for 40 minutes in a slow oven (375° F.).

WELSH RABBIT

Welsh rabbit is the English version of a fondue. The cheese used should be a dry 'flavoury' cheddar. Ale replaces the kirsch, otherwise rabbit is made in much the same way as a fondue. Ideally it should be made on the table in a chafing-dish, hot toast and hot plates being provided and the rabbit poured bubbling on to them. Buck rabbit is a Welsh rabbit with a poached egg on the top.

4 oz. dry well-matured cheddar cheese	½ gill brown ale salt, pepper, cayenne
1 oz. butter	hot buttered or plain toast

Thinly slice or grate the cheese. Put into a shallow saucepan or chafing-dish with the butter, ale, and seasonings, set over a gentle heat and stir continuously until melted. Do not allow to get too hot. When smooth and creamy pour immediately over the toast. Dust with cayenne and eat at once.

QUICK RABBIT

This is not a true rabbit but more of a toasted cheese. It is easy and quick to make.

3 oz. grated cheese	salt, pepper, cayenne
1½ oz. butter	slices of crisp toast
1–2 tablespoons boiling milk	

Work the cheese and butter together, adding the milk by degrees and the seasonings. When a creamy consistency spread thickly on the toast, arrange in a shallow dish and brown quickly under a hot grill. Serve at once. A good variation is to spread the toast with anchovy paste before putting on the cheese mixture.

SWISS RABBIT

1 egg	3 oz. grated gruyère cheese
1 oz. fresh white breadcrumbs	a little nutmeg
3 tablespoons single cream	salt, pepper
1 oz. butter	hot buttered toast

Beat the egg, add the breadcrumbs and cream. Melt the butter in a saucepan, add the cheese, egg mixture, spice, and seasoning. Stir over gentle heat until hot and creamy. Arrange toast in a serving dish and pour over the mixture. Serve at once.

GOLDEN BUCK

4 oz. cheddar cheese
1 oz. butter
½ gill brown ale
a pinch of celery salt or ordinary
    salt
a pinch of paprika pepper
freshly ground black pepper

2 beaten eggs
1 tablespoon cream or milk
½ teaspoon Worcestershire
    sauce
4 rounds of freshly made toast
    with crusts removed

Grate cheese and put into a saucepan with the butter, ale, salt, and peppers. Heat gently until the cheese begins to melt, add the eggs and cream. Stir over the fire until thick and creamy. Add the Worcestershire sauce. Have ready the toast, cut rounds in half and arrange on a hot dish. Pour over the mixture and serve at once.

SALÉ

This is a rich cheese tart and though good made with ordinary cheese should be made with gruyère. It is excellent hot or cold.

rich short crust made with
    6 oz. flour (see page 835)
¾ pint béchamel sauce (see
    page 155)

3 eggs, well beaten
½ gill thick cream
5 oz. grated gruyère cheese
salt, pepper, grated nutmeg

Line the pastry into a 7-inch flan ring. Make sure it is well lined and has a good edge. Crimp the border with the pastry pincers or with finger and thumb. Prick the bottom. Have the béchamel ready and cool, add the eggs by degrees, then the cream and cheese. Adjust seasoning and flavour delicately with nutmeg. Pour mixture into the pastry and bake in a fairly hot oven, 400° F., for 25–35 minutes. If getting a little too brown cover with a piece of paper. Set flan in the middle of oven to get bottom as well as top heat. Remove ring a few minutes before taking finally from the oven to ensure that the pastry is thoroughly cooked.

N.B. This is an occasion when the previously well-heated baking-sheet should be put on the oven rack to receive the flan ring; the additional starting heat secures a crisp case of pastry.

GANNAT

A variety of cheese brioche—excellent for a luncheon bread or for a picnic, sandwiched with cream or Liptauer cheese.

8 oz. flour	¾ gill milk
1 level dessertspoon salt	2 eggs
½ oz. yeast	4 oz. grated gruyère cheese
1 level teaspoon sugar	salt, pepper, cayenne pepper
2 oz. butter	beaten egg or milk to finish

Sift flour with salt into a bowl. Cream yeast with the sugar. Slice the butter into the milk and warm gently to melt. Pour on to the yeast and add the eggs, well beaten. Stir, then add to the flour and mix up to a soft dough. Cover the bowl and set to rise for about an hour. Then work in two-thirds of the cheese and plenty of seasoning. Knead just enough to mix thoroughly. Put into a large sandwich tin or flan ring; pat out with the fist to flatten well. It should be about 1 inch thick in the tin. Brush lightly over with beaten egg or milk, scatter over the rest of the cheese. Prove for 7–10 minutes, then bake in a quick oven 20–25 minutes.

Short, rich biscuits made with cheese, called sablés, are excellent as cocktail savouries or may be served as a luncheon dish. A recipe for them as cocktail savouries is given in the appropriate chapter, but I am putting one here so that it may be seen how they are served as a luncheon dish.

SABLÉS

4 oz. flour	salt, pepper
4 oz. butter	a small pinch of cayenne
4 oz. grated cheese	beaten egg

This recipe, by reason of the fact that the quantities of butter and flour are equal, requires no liquid.

Sift flour into a bowl. Rub in the butter, not too thoroughly. Add cheese and seasoning. Work up quickly to a paste. Roll out about ¼ inch thick and cut into rounds or triangles. Brush lightly with beaten egg and bake in a moderately hot oven until golden brown. Cool slightly before taking off the tin. Serve either as a cocktail savoury or as a luncheon dish. For the latter arrange the sablés *en couronne* in a fireproof dish. Pour a good sauce mornay or sauce aurore (see pages 156 and 155) in the middle, and serve hot with a watercress or green salad.

N.B. When cooking sablés or rich pastry line the baking-sheets with grease-proof paper. Arrange the biscuits, etc., on this and bake. In this way the butter in the pastry is not so liable to burn, and moreover the edges of the paste will not take colour so quickly. (See page 831, pastry chapter.)

ALMOND SABLÉS

Paste

6 oz. plain flour	½ teaspoon paprika
4 oz. butter	1 yolk of egg
1½ oz. ground almonds	1 tablespoon water
3 oz. grated cheese	beaten egg for gilding
salt, pepper	

Filling

1 teaspoon arrowroot or corn- flour	salt and pepper
	1 gill warm milk
1 small egg	1½ oz. grated cheese
1 level teaspoon paprika	

Pastry. Sift flour into a bowl, rub in the butter. Mix in the almonds, grated cheese, and seasonings. Beat the yolk, adding half the water. Pour into the bowl and work up quickly to a firm paste, adding remainder of water if necessary. Roll out a little more that ⅛ inch thick. Stamp into rounds of about 1½ inches in diameter. Brush one half of the batch with the beaten egg. Bake all in a moderate oven until a pale golden brown. Allow to cool slightly before lifting off on to a rack. Meantime prepare filling; put a teaspoon on each sablé not painted with egg and cover lightly with the gilded halves. Serve hot for a savoury. Half the above quantity is enough for 4 people, but the sablés keep well, unfilled, in a tin. The surplus filling may be kept in the refrigerator.

Filling. Put the arrowroot, egg yolk, paprika, and seasoning into a bowl, mix and add milk and cheese by degrees. When blended stir continuously over moderate heat and bring to boil. Draw aside, whip white to a firm snow, mix into the sauce, taking the same precaution as for an egg yolk liaison (see page 140). Return to the heat and cook for a minute or two, stirring slowly with a folding movement.

BEIGNETS SOUFFLÉS AU FROMAGE

Choux paste

1½ gills water	3¾ oz. sifted flour
3 oz. butter	3 eggs
2 oz. grated Parmesan cheese, or gruyère and Parmesan mixed	a small pinch of cayenne deep fat grated Parmesan and paprika
English mustard	for the top
salt, pepper	

Make up the choux paste as directed on page 843. When thoroughly beaten work in the cheese and seasonings. The mixture must be highly seasoned. Put out on to a baking-sheet or large dish in small teaspoonfuls. Heat fat bath to approximately 320° F., or until a very slight haze will rise from the surface. Lift the teaspoonfuls of paste one at a time with the end of a palette-knife dipped into the hot fat, and slide them gently into the fat bath. Do not fill it too full, but allow them room to swell. Cook 7–10 minutes, increasing the heat very gradually. At the end of that time they should be well puffed out, firm to the touch, and golden brown. Drain thoroughly on kitchen paper, sprinkle well with Parmesan cheese and paprika pepper. Pile up in a hot dish or on a napkin and serve at once.

The following recipe is for a cheese mousse dish made with gruyère. It is an excellent form of cold soufflé and makes a first-class luncheon dish.

MOUSSE DE FROMAGE (GRUYÈRE SOUFFLÉ) (FOR 6)

½ pint well-flavoured béchamel (see page 155), made with ½ oz. each of butter and flour and ½ pint milk
1 egg yolk
4 oz. grated gruyère cheese
salt, pepper, a little mustard
1 rounded dessertspoon gelatine
2–3 tablespoons stock or water

a squeeze of lemon juice
¾ gill whipped cream or evaporated milk
3 egg whites, whipped to a firm snow
watercress, or tomato salad
quarters of peeled and pipped tomatoes
grated cheese

Make béchamel sauce, allow to cool slightly. Beat in the yolk and grated cheese by degrees. Season highly. Warm the gelatine in the stock and add to the sauce when melted with the lemon juice. When quite cool fold in the cream and lastly the stiffly whipped whites. Have ready a soufflé dish with a band of oiled paper round it. Stand an oiled pound jam jar in the middle of the dish and pour the mixture round to fill and to come about 1 inch above the edge. Leave to set.

Carefully peel off the paper, gently twist and lift out the jar. Immediately fill the space with the watercress, arranged in a bouquet, or if preferred a tomato salad. Arrange the quarters of tomato on top of the soufflé and press the cheese round the sides. Serve well chilled.

A recipe for cheese soufflé, Soufflé au Fromage, will be found on page 330.

XXVI

Bread and Bread-making

CHILDREN of to-day have many pleasures which were denied to us, but there is one, well remembered, that does not often fall to them: the fragrance and taste of new home-made bread.

I wish I could conjure up the smell that greeted us on baking days as we came in from a frosty walk, or which hung on the summer air round the open kitchen window. I wish I might hand you a crust pulled from a new-baked loaf with the butter quickly disappearing into it, because, if I could do this, I believe I could convert you beyond all argument of time and trouble into enthusiastic bread-makers. There is no difficulty in baking at home, indeed all the old problems have been smoothed away. You need no longer rise early to fill a brick oven with red-hot embers to heat it ready for the dough, or bank up a kitchen range. Yeast is easy to get and you can keep dough in an ice-box, and yet many of us accept without question the monotony of bought bread.

Bread takes a short time to mix and a long time to rise, and if you organize things well bread-making can be accomplished with very little strain or trouble. Certainly nothing comparable with the pleasure and benefit to be derived, unless of course you take the view sometimes expressed that it is a waste to spend time in preparing food which is eaten so quickly, in which case you will not, I am sure, be reading this book.

HOUSEHOLD BREAD

When I first set up housekeeping I lived quite a few Irish miles from a shop, always excepting of course the ubiquitous public-house. Even at the end of those miles there was precious little to buy; there was a butcher who killed at very long intervals, a grocer with most limited stock, and, inevitably, more public-houses. Our bread came from the local pub, and very dubious stuff it was both in colour and content: one never quite knew what one might find in the way of odds and ends in a loaf; their presence there was always ascribed to some unaccountable malignancy by the ingenuously surprised publican. New at the game, unlearned in the domestic arts, I was taken aback and really did not know what to do, unless to abstain from eating bread at all. A relative from the north country took me in hand, bade me make bread three times a week in a tone of voice that suggested it was just done by a flick of the wrist, and then mitigated what seemed to me in my ignorance to be a sentence of hard labour by presenting me with a bread-making machine. This consisted of a pail with handle, ratchet, and mixing-rod, and was called the Three-Minute Bread-Maker. That 'three-minute' euphemism won me over and from that day forth I baked all our bread. I am going to tell you about this machine because it broke down my resistance to bread-making: all those inhibitions about the time it takes, the amount of work involved, and the undeserved reputation that yeast has for being a temperamental raising agent. So much did that machine do for me that I bought one of them not so very long ago, in order to illustrate to students how childishly simple and foolproof an affair is the making of bread in its simplest form. The instructions were quite briefly: 'Take 4 lb. flour, 1 oz. yeast, 1 teaspoon sugar, 1½ tablespoons salt, a quart of warm water. Put liquids in first and solids next.' Yeast, sugar, and a little of the warm water were mixed in a basin and put to prove for a quarter of an hour in a warm place —our yeast was of more variable quality in those days—then in went all liquids, then flour and salt and one turned the handle for three minutes. This turning of the handle was the only three-minute part about it, for of course the bread had to rise for the proper length of time. When the dough, thoroughly mixed, left the sides of the pail and gathered itself together round the mixing-rod, it was ready for rising, the lid was put on and the tin set in a warm place. Then, when the dough had risen to the top of the pail, it was turned out, shaped into loaves, put in tins, proved, and baked.

You will see that none of the refinements of bread-making entered into this, no sponging, no double kneading and rising, no addition of fat, nothing indeed but the simplest basic bread; but it was good, crusty, and fresh, so that one never really got tired of it, and it is on such very simple first principles that all the frills and improvements are built. Flour, salt, liquid, and a raising agent are the basic materials of bread, and the refinements, variations in ingredients and in method that one may choose, are matters of taste.

Before giving the recipes for the many different kinds of bread, it is worth while considering each of the basic ingredients used in bread-making: the flour, liquid, yeast, and other additions.

The flour

The basis of English bread-making is generally speaking good, household flour, but even under this heading flours vary in their powers of absorption, and for this reason it is sometimes necessary to vary the amount of liquid given in a recipe. Flour should be kept in a dry, well-ventilated place and it is advisable to sieve and dry it before using. There are various additions which may be made to the basic flour, such as wholemeal flour, oatmeal, semolina, and potato, to produce different types of bread; the salt called for in the recipes should be sieved with the flour so as to be evenly distributed.

For those who bake regularly it is well worth while to buy stone-ground flour. This is white flour but with a high percentage of wheat and of good nutty taste. Stone-ground flour is obtained from special mills which specialize in it.

Self-raising flour is not used for household bread-making.

Brown bread is often made with a mixture of one part of white flour to two parts wholemeal. The addition of the white flour prevents the bread from being too close in texture, and the proportion is varied according to the coarseness of the wholemeal flour and how brown a bread is wanted.

The leavening agent

As will be seen later, baking-powder is used for certain types of bread, though loaves made with this shortening are suited to occasional rather than to everyday use, and daily bread is most suitably made with yeast as its leavening agent. I can remember the time when a kitchen-maid used to be dispatched to the nearest brewery to bring back a jug of barm for bread-making, and in old-fashioned books one comes across recipes for home-made yeast; but now we use a very convenient form known as compressed yeast which keeps well for a week and more in an ice-box. It is only necessary to understand what yeast is to be able to avoid such accidents as will kill it and render it useless. Yeast is a living plant which, under certain circumstances, will grow and multiply and act as a leavening agent; it needs both air and moisture to do this and grows best in a warm temperature. In fact, up to a point, its action may be accelerated by an increase in temperature, but at a certain stage, somewhere around 115°–120° F., heat will kill the action of the yeast, so that if you use water which is too hot, or put your bowl of dough in too hot a place, you may render the yeast ineffective; but when you consider that it will keep fresh for many days in a refrigerator and will continue to grow and act even with a certain amount of inexperienced treatment, it is clear that it is by no means so temperamental as some people consider. In the old days we used to put yeast, sugar, and warm water together to prove at the back of the stove; after a while the yeast would bubble up and increase greatly in volume and so reassure the bread-maker that it was fresh and fit for use. Nowadays the compressed yeast is more ordinarily creamed with a teaspoon of sugar until it becomes liquid. Within certain limits the amount of yeast to be used should depend on the length of time that the dough can be left to rise, but it cannot be too strongly said that one never gets such good bread if one hurries the process by using a larger proportion of yeast to flour. The best results are obtained by long, slow rising and a minimum amount of yeast. Here is a rough indication of the amount of yeast in relation to the time of rising: If it is possible to allow the dough to rise for as much as 12 hours, 1 oz. of yeast will raise 5–7 lb. of flour. A more convenient proportion is 1 oz. of yeast to 4 lb. of flour and 2–3 hours' rising. The actual time may vary by reason of the temperature of the surroundings. When light rolls and buns of very open and spongy texture are required, then 1 oz. of yeast may be suitably allowed to 1 lb. of flour.

To keep yeast

1. Yeast may be kept in a screw-top jar in a refrigerator, but it should be remote from the ice tray.

2. Another method is to press the yeast firmly into the bottom of a jam jar and then invert the jar and stand it in a saucer of cold water. No part of the yeast must come in contact with the water.

Liquids

Water is most suitably used for regular everyday household bread-making. Bread made with water has a crisp crust. Excessively soft water deficient in mineral content will sometimes produce a sticky dough, and where such water is the only supply a small amount of additional salt may be added to the bread. The addition of milk or the use of milk alone will produce a smooth crust and a soft rich loaf of particularly golden colour. Potato water adds flavour and may be used in place of water. In some breads, generally those made with baking-powder, fruit juices are used as part of the liquid. The addition of too great a proportion of liquid will give bread a spongy and open texture. It is generally considered that good bread should be moderately close and even and have a crisp crust. On the other hand, rolls or buns should be spongy and open in texture and a slacker dough is required, and therefore a greater proportion of liquid and yeast is used. The liquid is used lukewarm.

Fat

The addition of lard or butter to the dough produces a smooth top, a soft crust, and helps to keep the bread fresh and soft for a longer time. Some people consider it improves the flavour of the bread; others prefer the crisper crust of fatless bread. But in rolls and various sweet breads fat is essential and is used in larger quantities than for household bread. Eggs and fats are both added to bun loaves to make them richer.

THE PROCESS OF BREAD-MAKING

Mixing and sponging

If the bread is not to be sponged the ingredients are mixed together either in a bowl or on a floured board and then kneaded.

The process of sponging is considered to give a lighter bread and is carried out before the mixing proper. Flour and salt are sifted into a warm basin, the yeast is creamed with sugar and water added. This is poured into a well in the flour. Enough flour from the sides of the well is drawn into the liquid to form a thickish batter, and more flour is dusted thickly over the top. The bowl is then covered with a cloth and left in a warm place 20–30 minutes until the yeast has bubbled and broken through the crust of flour. The whole is then mixed and turned on to a floured board for kneading.

Kneading

The process of kneading is a difficult one to describe, but it may be said that it should be done with rhythm, evenly and regularly, the dough being gathered towards one with the fingers bent, and pushed away with the fingers closed and the base of the palm in action. It is this process that distributes the yeast and produces an even-textured bread. Some recipes call for more than one kneading, the object being to produce a bread of particularly fine texture. In such cases the kneaded dough, which is put to rise in a warmed floured bowl, is allowed to double in bulk and is then turned out again on to a board, kneaded again, replaced in the bowl, allowed to rise again, and then shaped and proved.

Rising

For this process the 'warm place' may be a protected and draught-proof corner of a warm kitchen, or an airing cupboard, or the bowl may be placed on a cake rack at the back of the Aga. I used to put my bread-making pail in the corner of a big fire-place covered with a thick blanket. Steady moderate warmth is all that is required.

Proving

This is the final process before baking. The risen dough is turned from its bowl on to the floured board, kneaded gently for a minute or so, divided into portions of a size that will three-quarters fill a tin, then each loaf is shaped a little and put into the tin. The tins are then set in a warm place for about 15 minutes until the bread has risen well. The dough is now ready for baking.

For the first process of sponging and the final one of proving the dough should be near more direct heat: the plate oven of the Aga, the grid over the gas cooker with a pan of hot water on the stove below (this is especially good as yeast responds to moist heat), or the back of the stove.

Baking

New tins bought for the baking of bread should be baked empty in a hot oven before they are put into use. Old-fashioned cooks considered it quite unnecessary to grease their shining bread tins, though they did sprinkle them lightly with flour, and I well remember the row of tins, never washed but always softly bright, that caught the light in our kitchen. They acquired a patine rather than a shine and were, quite simply, things of beauty. It is a modern practice to brush bread tins inside with melted lard.

Baking is carried out in a hot oven (450°–500° F.). When cooked the bread shrinks away from the side of the tin and when the loaf is knocked out—this is done by turning the tin upside-down and giving the corner a sharp rap on the edge of the table—it should sound hollow when rapped with the knuckles. Many people return loaves to the oven after they have been turned out of the tin so that the sides and bottom of the loaf may become crisp. After baking the loaves should stand on a wire rack till cool.

In the manufacture of bread steam plays a part which is not possible in the domestic kitchen. On this point, however, a member of the teaching staff at Winkfield, Mrs Chaplin, told me of something she saw in a kitchen in Vienna. The cook, who was making rolls, put her tray of these into a hot oven and immediately flung ½ cup cold water into the oven, so that it hit the hot sides and turned to steam, and then quickly shut the door. This was done to produce a crisp crust. It seems a good trick used with care in the oven of an Aga or similar type of stove. I should be afraid of advocating it with gas or electric stoves.

Steaming bread

Just as rich plum cake is sometimes steamed so the process may be used for loaves. Use a steamer or large saucepan with well-fitting lid and cover the bread with greased paper, or put it in a pudding mould with a lid. Steam for 1½–2 hours according to size and finish off 15 minutes in the oven to dry off and harden the crust. This is considered a good way of cooking brown bread.

Glazing

When household bread is taken from the oven the top crust may be rubbed over with buttered paper to improve its appearance. Loaves and rolls are sometimes finished off with a sprinkling of aromatic seeds, poppy, cardamon, caraway, and sometimes with a little rock-salt. For this they should first be brushed over with a glazing medium before baking.

A good pinch of salt added to a beaten egg gives a good shiny glaze and this is generally used for milk bread. Milk is used for twists and rolls; buns and tea bread are brushed with well-sweetened milk (1 tablespoon of sugar to 3 of milk, warmed till sugar is dissolved). A sugar icing for sweet buns will be found on page 784.

Crusty bread

Bread made with water and without the addition of any fat generally has the crispest crust, but this quality may be increased by two simple processes. When a loaf is baked and ready to come out of the oven it may be brushed all over with cold water and put back in the oven for a few moments longer; or the process described in an earlier paragraph of throwing water into the oven at the beginning of baking may be adopted if a suitable oven is used.

The following list of possible causes of failure may be useful for reference:

1. If the yeast is not fresh the bread may taste bitter and sour.
2. Cold basins and ingredients and draughts will check the rising of bread.
3. If the dough is mixed with too hot a liquid or left in too hot a place to prove the yeast may be killed.
4. If the bread rises very much and is uneven in texture, being full of holes, it is likely that the bread was put in too cool an oven so that the yeast

continued to grow after proving instead of being killed immediately by the heat of the oven.

5. If the oven is too hot the outside crust will be hard and dark before the bread is cooked through.

6. If the oven is too cool the bread will be pale, dry, and hard.

A GENERAL NOTE ON BREAD-MAKING

Quantity to make

Although there are occasions when one wants to make a single loaf quickly, to make bread in very small quantities is not really satisfactory; 4 lb. of flour is, I think, the smallest reasonable amount even for a very small family, but there is no wastefulness in this nor any real disadvantage because the dough may be used in various ways:

1. A portion of it may be set aside and turned, by the adding of butter, eggs, fruit, and sugar, into a bun loaf.

2. Some of it may be made into bread sticks and kept in tins for weeks.

3. A portion of dough may be put in the ice-box where it will keep for a week or more. It should be put in a bowl and covered by a plate. When required it is taken out and allowed to rise. If during its time in the ice-box the dough rises it may be cut through with a knife and re-covered.

To refresh stale bread

Moisten lightly with cold water and put into a hot oven, or place the moistened bread in a paper bag and put in the oven until crisp. A whole loaf may be dipped into a bowl of cold water for 2 minutes and then put in a slow oven for 45–60 minutes.

To cut new bread

Dip knife into hot water before cutting.

YEAST BREADS

HOUSEHOLD BREAD

4 lb. flour	1 oz. yeast
1½ tablespoons salt	2 pints lukewarm water
1 teaspoon sugar	

Warm the flour, sift it with the salt into a large warm basin and make a well in the middle. Cream yeast and sugar and add warm water. Pour into the well in the flour. With a wooden spoon stir gently from the centre so that flour from the sides of the well falls into the liquid till a fairly liquid batter is formed. Sprinkle the top of the batter thickly with flour taken from the sides of the bowl. Cover with a cloth and leave in a fairly warm temperature until the batter has broken through the surface of the flour. This is known as sponging and should take place fairly rapidly (about 20–30 minutes). A satisfactory way is to put the bowl on the stove rack with a large pan of boiling water underneath. When well risen beat and knead well with your hand, first in the bowl and then on a floured board. When well worked put back into a floured bowl, cut a cross on the top and cover with a cloth and thick piece of blanket. Allow to stand in a warm room away from draughts to rise (a cupboard is excellent). Allow about 2 hours for this. Take up, shape into loaves, either in tins or 'cottage' shape,[1] cover with a cloth and prove, i.e. stand in a fairly warm temperature 15–20 minutes until the loaves have risen well. The temperature is the same as for sponging. Bake in a hot oven until a good brown, about 40 minutes to 1 hour.

PLAIN LOAF

The following recipe makes one good cottage loaf or two small tin loaves, and may be made in about 2 hours:

1½ lb. flour	1 teaspoon sugar
3 teaspoons salt	¾ pint warm water
½ oz. yeast	

Sieve flour and salt into a warm basin. Cream yeast with sugar and add the warm water. Make a well in the flour, pour in the liquid, sprinkle over the top with a little flour from the sides. Allow to sponge 7–10 minutes. Mix, knead, allow to rise in a warm place for an hour. Shape into a cottage loaf, put on a floured oven sheet, prove for 15 minutes. To give extra edges of good crust take a pair of scissors and make a series of snips round the edges of the loaf. Bake 35–40 minutes according to the heat of the oven. If extra crispness is wanted use one of the processes given on page 761.

WHOLEMEAL BREAD

This may be made entirely with wholemeal, in which case the amount of yeast used is fairly large, otherwise the bread may be over-solid. Many recipes for wholemeal bread call for a proportion of white flour, sometimes one-third white, sometimes half white and half wholemeal, in which case the amount of yeast may be modified. Wholemeal varies considerably in its powers of absorption and it is useful to reserve a little of the flour, say a quarter of the whole amount to be added, when the liquid is being stirred and worked into it. In this way it is more easy to control the consistency of the dough, which should be soft.

---

[1] *To shape a cottage loaf.* Take two-thirds of the dough for the bottom of the loaf and one-third for the top. Make both pieces of dough into rounds, put the smaller piece on top and then make a hole with two fingers right through the top and well down into the lower part of the loaf.

For loaves of coarse texture:

3 lb. coarse wholemeal flour	1¼ oz. yeast
1 tablespoon cooking salt	approximately 1½ pints milk and
1 dessertspoon Barbados or moist brown sugar	water, warm

Mix salt thoroughly with flour in a warm bowl, draw aside to make a well in the middle of it. Cream sugar and yeast together, add the warm liquid and stir well to mix. Pour into the well, and with your hand mix the flour into the liquid, gradually drawing it from round the sides of the bowl. It should be a soft dough. Cover the bowl with a thick cloth and leave to rise in a warm place 1–1½ hours. Turn on to a floured board and knead well until the dough will leave both board and hands clean. Divide into two and knead each piece until there is no trace of stickiness. Shape each into a round loaf and put on a floured baking-sheet or into a large sandwich tin, but be careful that the sides of the loaf do not touch the tin. Allow to rise again for another half-hour, then bake in a moderately hot oven for about 1 hour.

RYE BREAD

This is a close-textured dark loaf.

1½ lb. rye flour	1 teaspoon sugar
1 lb. white flour	¾ oz. yeast
1 oz. butter or lard	¾ pint warm milk and water
1 level tablespoon salt	mixed (approx.)
1 heaped teaspoon caraway seeds (optional)	beaten egg or white for glazing

Mix the flours and salt together in a warm bowl. Rub the fat in finely with the finger-tips. Add caraway seeds. Cream yeast and sugar together, add half the liquid and stir thoroughly. Make a well in the flour, pour in the yeast mixture and with the hand gradually draw in the flour, adding enough liquid to make a firm dough. Knead until smooth, make a cross-cut on the top of the dough, cover bowl with a thick cloth and leave in a warm place to rise about 1½ hours. Take up and knead for about 5 minutes on a floured board. Divide into two and shape each piece into an oval loaf, rounded on the top and tapering slightly at the ends (like a French loaf only fatter). Alternatively shape each piece into a plain round—a cob loaf. Set on a floured sheet and prove 15 minutes. Bake in a hot oven 40–50 minutes. At the end of 30 minutes draw to the mouth of the oven and paint quickly with the glaze. Return to oven to finish baking and to take a deep brown colour.

N.B. The amount of white flour added to rye can be adjusted to taste, after a trial baking. As a rule rye bread tends to get dry and hard rather quickly. The fat here helps to prevent this.

PULLED BREAD

On baking day a fresh white loaf may well be used for this crisp and delicious item of food. The soft part of a quite new loaf is pulled apart with two forks. This must be done lightly, stretching each piece a little. The pieces are put in the oven until golden brown and very crisp.

TRIMMING FOR BREAD AND ROLLS

Various aromatic seeds are used in European countries for this finishing of rolls. The best, I think, is poppy seed, for this has a subtle nut-like and not too strong flavour. The bread or rolls are glazed at the end of cooking and the seeds thickly scattered over the surface. Cardamon, coriander, and caraway seeds are sometimes used, but call for moderation, and crushed rock-salt is used to finish off onion breads and bread sticks.

BREAD STICKS

Bread sticks may be made with a portion of ordinary dough. These should be baked slowly. They should snap in two when ready. The following recipe for a slightly richer dough is probably better for this purpose.

1 lb. flour	1 oz. butter
1 teaspoon salt	½ pint milk
¼ oz. yeast creamed with 1 tea-	
spoon sugar	

Sieve flour and salt into warm bowl. Make a well, add a little of the milk to the creamed yeast and pour in; stir in a little of the flour. Allow to rise 20 minutes; add remaining milk with butter melted in it. Allow to rise again 10 minutes, cut dough in small pieces, roll into sticks 6–8 inches long and no thicker than your little finger. Put on baking-tin and prove 20 minutes, bake in moderate oven.

These keep well in tins. If to be salted they should be brushed with milk or water and sprinkled with a little crushed rock-salt. See also Potato Sticks in cocktail chapter, page 16.

POTATO BREAD (1)

This is an old-fashioned type of bread and needs about 4 hours' rising in all. Potatoes are more often used to-day in the making of rolls, and then fat and milk are usually added.

Sponge

¾ lb. potatoes, freshly boiled and hot	1½ oz. yeast creamed with a teaspoon of sugar
1¾ pints tepid water	¾ lb. flour
1 pint tepid water	1½ oz. salt
5 lb. flour	

Press the potatoes through a wire sieve on to a dry cloth and then beat them. Add 1¾ pints tepid water to the creamed yeast and incorporate this with the beaten potato. Add ¾ lb. flour to form a fairly liquid batter. Set this to work in a warm place for about 2 hours.

Meanwhile sift 5 lb. flour and salt and put to warm. After the sponge has risen add to it the pint of warm water called for and then the flour. Mix, knead, and allow to rise for 2 hours (a medium soft dough is required, so if flour is very strong, i.e. absorbent, the amount of liquid must be adjusted). Then knead and shape into loaves, prove and bake.

POTATO BREAD (2) (WITH SULTANAS)

3 oz. boiled potatoes pressed through a wire sieve and beaten
12 oz. flour
a pinch of salt
1½ oz. yeast
2 tablespoons tepid milk
3 oz. butter

2 egg yolks
1½ oz. sultanas
½ oz. sugar
1 gill extra milk (approx.), if necessary
a little extra beaten egg for glazing

Sieve flour with salt and warm; put into a large bowl and make a well in the centre. Dissolve the yeast in a little tepid milk, pour into the well and mix to a paste with a little of the flour; cover and leave to rise. When the yeast paste has risen mix in melted butter and egg yolks, sultanas, sugar, and mashed potatoes. Knead all together to a firm dough and, if necessary, add the milk. The amount of milk depends upon the quality of the flour and potatoes. Cover dough and leave to rise in a warm place. Knead and make into loaves. Brush with egg and leave to rise.

ONION BREAD (1)

This is good to eat with cheese. It may be made quite simply as follows:

Soften in butter or margarine thinly cut slices of onion, season well. Drain them free of fat. Before baking plain bread dough glaze the loaves well with egg and salt and arrange the rings on top. A little egg may be put between the rings where they overlap. If towards the end of baking the onion slices are getting too brown, a greased paper may be laid over them.

In the second method a mixture of egg and onion is made and spread on top of the loaves. This, of course, gives a soft top.

ONION BREAD (2)

A more complicated way.

1 oz. yeast
2 tablespoons tepid water
1 pint milk (hot), and extra warm milk if required
2-3 oz. lard
1 tablespoon sugar
2 teaspoons salt

2 lb. flour
6 medium onions, finely sliced
3 oz. butter or margarine
seasoning
2 eggs
4 tablespoons sour cream (or milk)

Break the yeast up in the tepid water and stir till dissolved. Bring milk almost to boiling-point, add sugar and lard (reserving a teaspoon for brushing over dough), put into a large bowl and set aside to cool. When reduced to blood heat add the yeast to it. Sift flour with salt. When milk is cool add the flour, mix and knead in the usual way, using extra liquid if required. When the dough is well kneaded and smooth set it to rise till doubled in bulk. Turn on to a floured board and knead again. Put back into a warm greased bowl, brush top lightly with lard and allow to double again. Cook the onion rings gently in butter till soft but not brown; season well. Beat eggs, add cream and onions. Prepare bread tins by lining with oiled paper which comes above the rim of the tin by an inch or so. Knead the dough once more for a minute or two. Shape into loaves. Put into tins, not more than three-quarters full. Spread the onion mixture thinly on top and bake about 30–35 minutes.

Another method makes a more rustic and hearty type of bread of peasant origin. In this the softened and seasoned onion is laid in a shallow, greased baking-tin, and a soft dough is patted or rolled out quite thinly—not more than $\frac{1}{2}$ inch—and laid over the onions. A mixture of egg yolks, sour cream or milk, and seasoning, as in the foregoing recipe, is poured over it before baking in a hot oven.

For a cheese bread called Gannat see page 753 in the milk and cheese chapter.

SEMOLINA BREAD

A good light tea bread.

1½ oz. sugar	6 oz. flour sieved with a teaspoon
¼ oz. yeast	of salt
1 oz. butter or margarine	rind of 1 lemon, grated
¼ pint milk	1 oz. raisins
1 egg	4 oz. mashed hot potato
6 oz. semolina	egg glaze

Cream the sugar and yeast. Add the butter to the hot milk and allow it to become tepid. Add this and the beaten egg to the yeast, then add to the dry ingredients. Beat until smooth, knead on a floured board until it leaves your fingers clean. Put to rise till double in bulk, knead lightly, put on a greased baking-tin, prove, brush with egg glaze and bake in a hot oven 30–40 minutes.

The following is a quickly made very light bread with a soft dough. It may be made after lunch and be in time for tea. Suitable for a plaited loaf.

QUICKLY MADE LOAF

1 lb. flour (warmed)	½ oz. yeast
1 teaspoon salt	1 teaspoon sugar
1½ oz. butter or margarine	1 egg
¼ pint tepid milk (approx.)	

Sieve flour and salt and make a well. Heat milk, melt butter in it, and allow to cool till tepid. Cream yeast and sugar. Beat egg well. Mix milk and egg and creamed yeast and pour into well in flour. Mix, knead till smooth; the dough should be soft. Put to rise in a warm place for about 1 hour. Form into small loaves or plaits, place on a greased baking-sheet. Prove 15 minutes. Bake in a quick oven 20–30 minutes.

This bread is suitable to form into plaits and twists:

BREAD TWISTS AND PLAITS

Make a soft dough (the recipe above is suitable). After the dough has risen divide it into three equal portions and roll out on a floured board into three long strips, then plait them together, pointing them at both ends. Put on a greased baking-sheet and glaze, then prove and bake. The plait may be finished with poppy seeds.

BUN LOAF

Properly this is made from bread dough with additions. It may be as plain or as rich as you wish. Eggs, fat, sugar, and fruit are beaten into the dough after the first rising. The enriched dough is put into tins, which must not be more than half full, proved till the mixture fills the tins, and then baked.

Before the war we made a very rich mixture which was popular. To 2 lb. dough we added ½ lb. butter, 1 lb. sugar, 2 lb. sultanas or mixed dried fruits, 2 oz. candied peel, 6 eggs, a good pinch of mixed spice, the rind of a lemon, and 3 drops of lemon essence. These ingredients were all beaten together, kneaded, and a small amount of extra flour added as one worked it. This is too extravagant now but the necessary modifications still give a good bun loaf. Good and reasonable proportions are:

To 2 lb. dough add after the first rising:

3 eggs, beaten	8 oz. dried fruit
4–6 oz. butter, softened	a pinch of spice
4–6 oz. sugar	the grated rind of 1 lemon or
2 oz. chopped candied peel	2–3 drops of lemon essence

If it is required to make a bun loaf from scratch, so to speak, with no dough prepared, here is a recipe:

1 lb. plain flour	2 oz. sugar
a pinch of salt	3 oz. butter, creamed
1 teaspoon sugar	6 oz. mixed dried fruit (sul-
¾ oz. yeast	tanas, glacé cherries, mixed
2 eggs	chopped peel)
1 cup warm milk and water,	a little extra milk for brushing
more if necessary	castor sugar for dusting
grated rind of 1 lemon	

Sift flour and salt into warm bowl. Cream yeast with sugar, add to beaten eggs and liquid. Pour into flour and work up to a soft dough, add more milk and water if necessary. Knead well. Cover with a cloth and leave to rise in a warm place till double its bulk. Then work in remaining ingredients, turn into a greased tin to a little more than half full. Prove in a fairly warm place 10 minutes or until mixture has risen well, brush over with milk, dust with castor sugar, and bake in a moderately hot oven 40 minutes to 1 hour.

GUGELHOPF (KUGELHOPF)

A rich Austrian bun loaf.

12 oz. flour	1 oz. castor sugar
a pinch of salt	4 oz. butter, oiled
1 oz. yeast, scant weight	4 oz. raisins or currants
1½ gills warm milk	a small handful of almonds,
3 small eggs, well beaten	blanched and split or shredded

Sift flour and salt together. Add sugar. Dissolve yeast in the warm milk. Stir into the flour with the eggs and butter. Lastly add the fruit. Butter a fluted mould well and strew it thickly with the almonds, which may be shredded or split. Dust the mould with sugar and three-quarters fill with the mixture. Allow to rise in a warm place until the dough reaches the top of the tin. Stand the tin on a thick baking-sheet and bake in a moderate oven 40 minutes to 1 hour.

KUCHEN

This is a soft yeast bread of German origin, a counterpart of our bun dough. It is made up in a variety of ways, usually with some form of 'topping,' such as slices of apple, cinnamon, and sugar, or fried crumbs, raisins, cinnamon, and sugar. A popular covering is a 'streusal,' which is a mixture of butter and flour rubbed together (a variant of 'crunch'). For kuchen dough (which may vary in richness) take:

½ lb. flour	1 beaten egg
½ teaspoon salt	1–2 oz. butter, oiled
½ oz. yeast	¼ pint warm milk
1 oz. sugar	

Sift the flour and salt. Cream yeast with the sugar. Mix into the flour with the egg, milk, and butter. Beat thoroughly, then leave to rise in a warm place until double its bulk. Turn out on to a floured board and knead lightly. The dough is now ready to be made up in various ways. For an apple kuchen work 2 oz. well-cleaned raisins into the dough. Shape into a large bun with the hand and put into a lightly greased cake or deep sandwich tin. Flatten top with your fist and cover with quartered sliced apple, pressing the sharp edge of the slices into the dough. Brush lightly with a thin syrup or water, sprinkle thickly with castor sugar mixed with a little cinnamon, and leave to prove 20 minutes. Bake in a moderately hot oven 40–45 minutes.

STREUSAL KUCHEN

Flavour the kuchen dough with grated lemon rind. Roll out about 1 inch thick, set on a baking-sheet, brush over with milk and sprinkle with the 'streusal.' Prove 15 minutes, then bake in a hot oven 20–25 minutes. Slide on to a rack to cool. Cut into squares.

'*Streusal*'

| 2 oz. flour | 1 oz. sugar | 2 oz. butter |

Mix the flour and sugar together. Heat the butter and pour into the mixture. Stir until it breaks up into fine crumbs, then use.

The following recipe for Selkirk Bannock is an old one. It is of course a type of bun loaf. R. H. remarks that in a Scottish house where she visited often as a child it appeared at every meal, even at breakfast; that it was eaten with cheese at luncheon, buttered in thin slices for tea, and was cut—as all such fruit breads—in slices and never in wedges. It may be as rich as you wish; the following is not a rich bannock.

SELKIRK BANNOCK

The word bannock is usually applied to a dough baked in one large round about the size of a meat plate, or even larger.

4 oz. butter or lard	4 oz. sultanas
1 pint warmed milk (approx.)	2 oz. currants
¾ oz. yeast	2 oz. candied peel
1 teaspoon sugar for creaming yeast	4 oz. castor sugar
2 lb. flour	a little milk and sugar for glazing
1 teaspoon salt	

Melt butter or lard, add ½ pint of the milk warmed to blood heat; cream yeast with the teaspoon of sugar, add milk and fat. Warm and sieve flour and salt. Make a well in the centre and pour in the liquid to make a batter. Sprinkle top with flour from sides and leave to sponge as for bread, about half an hour. When sponge has worked add as much of the remaining warmed milk as is required to make soft dough. Knead well, put to rise till doubled in bulk. Knead in fruit, slightly warmed, and sugar. Shape into a large flat round. Prove 20–30 minutes. Brush with milk in which a little sugar is dissolved. Bake 40–45 minutes.

The Irish barm brack as delivered by the baker in my young days was a fruit loaf on plainer lines: fruit and candied peel being added to a yeast dough with a little sugar and spice and sometimes butter.

I remember in particular its speciality on All Hallows E'en, when, in the hope of coming on the ring, the horse-shoe, or the thimble concealed within it, one was apt when unlucky to eat too much in search of these treasures.

BAPS, CRUMPETS, MUFFINS, AND PIKELETS

Many years ago there used to be in the middle of the town of Derby a little house with a front door rather high up in the wall, and outside it a stone platform approached by a flight of stone steps.   On the platform stood a large table covered in a snowy sheet on which were arranged high piles of crumpets, pikelets, and muffins.   The whole was presided over by a wrinkled old woman enveloped in a gathered apron and wearing a white bonnet.

In spite of my extreme youth—for I used to be pushed there in a 'mail-cart'—I still remember the delicious smell of baking, the general sense of snowy whiteness, and my excitement in carrying the purchases home, and ever since I have wanted to be able to achieve such beautifully made crumpets and muffins; but I never have.

In old recipes for bread and muffins and baps one generally finds that the dough is left to rise all night, which involves kitchen activity late in the evening.   It is taken for granted that the cook will put down a dough about tea-time which will be ready for half an hour's kneading around 10 p.m., and will then work on it again for half an hour or so the next morning before baking rolls for breakfast.   We have found quicker and easier ways, but not always are the results so good.

BAPS

1 lb. flour mixed with a tea-spoon of salt, warmed and sifted
2 oz. butter or good lard
$\frac{1}{2}$ oz. yeast if to be raised over-night, or 1 oz. if to be raised quickly

1 teaspoon sugar for creaming the yeast
$\frac{1}{2}$ pint milk and water (more if necessary) mixed and warmed to blood heat
a little extra milk for glazing

Rub the fat into the flour.   Make a well; cream the yeast, add liquid and pour in.   Mix to a slack dough adding extra warm liquid if required. Allow to rise till doubled in bulk (if $\frac{1}{2}$ oz. yeast leave all night, if 1 oz. an hour or two according to temperature it stands in).   Knead, divide in eight even pieces.   Knead each into a ball about the size of a goose egg and flatten with the hand.   Then lightly roll to an oval with a rolling-pin. Put on a well-floured tin.   Prove 15 minutes.   Brush with milk, bake till firm, 15–20 minutes.   Serve fresh and hot with butter.

CRUMPETS

New home-made crumpets freshly toasted are generally particularly light and good.   It is desirable to have crumpet rings and a metal plate or girdle; without rings the batter spreads too much and one does not get the same results.   Here is an old household recipe:

2 lb. flour warmed and sifted with a good teaspoon salt

1 quart milk warmed to blood heat (more if required)
1 oz. yeast

Dissolve yeast in a little of the lukewarm milk. Have the warmed sieved flour and salt in a large bowl. Make a well and pour in the milk mixed with the yeast. Mix to a thin batter (if more liquid is required because of the strength of the flour it should be warm). Set aside in a warm place to rise for half to three-quarters of an hour. Have metal sheet or girdle hot and rings greased and hot on the sheet. Pour in enough batter to fill each ring about ½ inch deep. Cook till set, then turn and finish. For serving, toast the bottom well, the top lightly. Butter and pile in a hot dish.

Another recipe calls for a mixture of milk and water and adds a pinch of bicarbonate of soda.

When during the war I found myself spending a great deal of time in the kitchen I was fired with a wish to make muffins, though I cannot think where I hoped to find butter to put on them. I had some good American books and found lots of recipes made with all manner of ingredients, nuts and fruit, eggs and sugar, but they were not at all what I wanted. I was after the muffin of the muffin-man, the floury, yeasty affair that has to be properly toasted and buttered before it is eaten. I do not suppose I have ever got them to quite the point of perfection of those the old lady sold outside her funny little house. I have never let them rise all night, but we do make very good muffins with the following recipe:

MUFFINS

The mixture required for muffins is of the same ingredients as for crumpets, except that the mixture is a soft dough rather than a batter. The crumpet dough is poured into the rings for cooking while muffin dough is generally shaped lightly with the hands, as in the case of baps. Indeed, the bap recipe may also be used, but muffins are cooked on a metal sheet and not in the oven. Take the same mixture as for crumpets but add a little extra warmed flour and salt to the liquid to make a soft dough, so soft that it can only just be handled with well-floured hands. Cover and allow to rise. Then divide in even pieces, shape them into rounds lightly and place them on a very well-floured board to rise. When ready they are cooked on a hot-plate or girdle on top of the stove. It helps to keep the shape if they are dropped into crumpet rings, but this is not essential. They should be baked to a light brown on each side. To prepare for table open all round the edge of the muffin very nearly to the centre with the fingers. Toast well on either side and slowly enough for the heat to penetrate to the centre. Then pull apart, butter each piece and put together again. Cut in halves and pile on a hot dish.

PIKELETS

The pikelets I remember were only about as thick as pancakes and bigger than either crumpets or muffins. We were not allowed to buy these very often, and I am sure this was because traditionally they were buttered on both sides and this was extravagant. Piled up and buttered in this way they cannot have been easy to eat very tidily. The memory of them in some remote way makes me think of Mr Chadband, whose unctuous speeches we used almost to learn by heart for schoolroom mimicry and entertainment.

½ lb. sifted warmed flour	2 eggs
½ teaspoon salt	warm milk, enough to make a
1 oz. yeast dissolved in a little	thin batter
warm milk	

Mix the batter as for crumpets, adding beaten eggs to a little of the milk. Have the girdle very hot and well greased. Spoon on the batter, which should spread like a pancake. Turn. Make one at a time.

ROLLS

YEAST ROLLS (ENGLISH METHOD)

The average English roll is made with a bread dough with a bigger proportion of yeast and made richer with extra fat and milk in place of water. For example:

1 lb. flour	¾ oz. yeast
¼ teaspoon salt	an egg (optional)
1 oz. butter or margarine	½ pint milk (approx.)

Mix as for bread. Let the dough rise for not less than an hour, shape, prove, and bake in an oven hotter than that for big loaves.

American cooks are particularly rich in lore in all matters concerning cookies, rolls, biscuits, and cakes, and no cook would willingly be without some of the best American publications. Our students at Winkfield constantly use a recipe for Standard Rolls taken from Fannie Merritt Farmer's *The Boston Cooking School Cook Book* (Little, Brown & Co., Boston). Mrs Wilma Lord Perkins has recently revised the ninth edition of this most valuable book, and has given me generous leave to quote from it. I am taking as well as the Standard Roll recipe her note on, and recipe for, Refrigerator Rolls, and the two recipes for Potato Biscuits. We in England are not so familiar as her compatriots with this use of the ice-box, and it is a most helpful practice.

STANDARD ROLLS

1 cup milk [1]	1 yeast cake softened in ¼ cup
2 tablespoons butter	lukewarm water
1 tablespoon sugar	2½–3 cups all-purpose or bread
1 teaspoon salt	flour

[1] See American measures, page 60.

'Scald milk. Add butter, sugar, and salt, and cool to lukewarm. Add yeast and 1½ cups flour. Beat thoroughly 5 minutes or 2 minutes if you use an electric beater. Add enough more flour to make the dough just barely firm enough to handle.

'Knead. Shape immediately ... or let rise about 1 hour before shaping. The second rising makes rolls of finer grain, especially if you are using bread flour.

'Arrange in buttered pans. Brush with melted butter. Cover with cloth. Let rise until double in bulk (about 1 hour).

'Bake at 425° until well browned (12–20 minutes). Makes about 18.'

REFRIGERATOR ROLLS

'You do not need a special recipe for Refrigerator Rolls, although Potato Biscuit, below, is especially successful. A rich, sweet dough slows up the action of the yeast, so use ¼ cup each, sugar and butter, in making Standard Rolls. Double the entire recipe, except the yeast, to have enough for 3 or 4 dozen rolls. Put in well-buttered bowl, turn dough so that top is greased, and cover tightly so that a crust will not form on top. Store in refrigerator. If the dough rises, cut through it with a knife, and cover it again. Set a plate on top to help hold it down.

'Cut off a part of the dough, knead and shape.'

POTATO BISCUIT[1]

½ cup milk [2]	¾ teaspoon salt
4 tablespoons shortening	1 yeast cake [3] softened in ¼ cup
¼ cup sugar	lukewarm water
½ cup hot riced potatoes	2½ cups ... flour

'Scald milk. Cool to lukewarm. Stir in shortening, sugar, potatoes, salt, yeast, and ½ cup flour. Cover. Let rise until light. Add 2 cups flour, cover and again let rise.

'Turn on to floured board, pat, and roll ¼ inch thick. Shape.... Let rise.

'Bake at 425° F. 12–20 minutes according to size of biscuits. Makes about 18.'

RICH POTATO BISCUIT

'After adding yeast add 1 egg, yolk and white beaten separately.'

POTATO ROLLS

1 lb. flour	1 gill each of milk and water,
4 oz. freshly boiled mashed	warmed
potatoes	1 teaspoon salt
1 oz. yeast	2 oz. butter or margarine
2 oz. sugar	1 egg
	milk (or egg and salt) to glaze

---

[1] 'Biscuit' in this case indicates a rich roll.   [2] See American measures, page 60.
[3] A yeast cake—½ oz.

Warm the flour, cook the potatoes with a little salt and press them through a fine wire sieve on to a clean cloth, keep covered and warm. Cream the yeast with a little of the sugar and add a spoonful or two of the liquid. Sieve flour and salt into a large bowl and rub in the butter or margarine. Add rest of sugar and mashed potatoes. Add a little milk and water to the liquid yeast and the beaten egg. Add this to the flour with more milk and water to make a soft dough. Knead well. Cover and allow to rise till doubled in bulk. Turn out on to floured board, cut up and shape. Prove 15–20 minutes. Brush with milk or with egg and salt and bake in a hot oven.

BRIDGE ROLLS FOR A PARTY
quantities for about 4 dozen

2 lb. flour warmed and sieved	4 eggs
with $\frac{1}{2}$ oz. salt	$\frac{1}{2}$–$\frac{3}{4}$ pint milk
2 oz. sugar	3 oz. yeast
2 oz. butter or margarine	egg and salt to glaze

Heat milk, dissolve butter in it, and allow to cool to blood heat. Cream yeast with a little of the sugar. Beat eggs and add the warm milk. Sift flour and salt, add remaining sugar, make a well. Add liquids. Mix and knead. Leave to rise $\frac{3}{4}$–1 hour. Knead lightly and shape at once into small fingers. Arrange on greased baking-sheets fairly close together. Brush over with egg and salt. Prove 20–30 minutes till well risen. Brush again and bake in a hot oven (440° F.).

SODA AND BAKING-POWDER BREADS

When an article of food has become part of national diet it is more often than not an honest-to-goodness product, and generally speaking it is well to look at the original ways of making before accepting whole-heartedly all the modern 'improvements.' This is true enough of soda bread, a staple Irish food. To the Irish wife the use of yeast for bread came slowly, and even now soda bread is preferred by the old country people. Flour, salt, baking soda, and good buttermilk were the ingredients as I knew them long ago. The acid of the buttermilk in conjunction with baking soda was sufficient to release the necessary carbonic acid gas to make the bread light. Nowadays in most recipes one sees that a mixture of soda and cream of tartar is called for. Buttermilk of the kind that we had then is less plentiful or procurable now, so one must accept modifications. Even so, bread and scones made with sour milk and a modified amount of cream of tartar are better, I think, than the more modern baking-powder bread mixed with sweet milk. To make good soda bread of a light and melting texture buttermilk or sour milk is essential. When sweet milk is used the amount of cream of tartar is generally twice that of bicarbonate of soda; if sour milk is used one may reduce the amount of cream of tartar to equal to or even less than that of bicarbonate of soda.

For this type of bread no rising is called for; the moment soda bread is mixed it must be oven cooked. Only the lightest kneading, enough for shaping, is required; anything more makes the bread heavy.

Three kinds of soda bread were common, white, fly, and brown, the fly variety containing currants in rather exiguous quantities. Ours, of course, was baked either on a girdle or in the oven, but up in the hills the farmer's wife used either her girdle or her pot-oven, and the loaves or farls to be cooked on the former might be 1½–2 inches thick, and were started off on moderate heat so that they were cooked through before the browning process began. When baked and brown below the loaves were turned and finished off. What we liked best in those far-off days were the loaves of the wife who cooked them in her Irish pot-oven. These had a thin skin-like crust, a brownness and flavour all their own, a perfection achieved by no written rules but by years of practice. The dough was put into the heated, floured pot with room left for rising, the upturned lid was put on and a few hot turfs set in it, then the pot was set in the hot ash at the side of the fire. It is a long time since I or any of my contemporaries watched this being done—we only remember it.

We bake our soda bread now sometimes in the oven but preferably on a girdle, and this must be heated to the right degree. A common mistake is to get this too hot to begin with, and then the crust of the bread cooks too quickly while the inside remains uncooked. A good test is that when flour is dusted on to the greased girdle it becomes light brown in colour in about 3 minutes. It is desirable to turn the loaves only once, baking as far as possible on one side before turning. If the girdle overheats this point may have to be disregarded. The dough is shaped with the hands into a large flat round and then with a sharp knife cut across into four; these are called farls.

We still make all three varieties, using half brown and half white flour for brown loaves and 1½ oz. currants per pound of flour for the fly variety.

SODA BREAD

This is without doubt the most delicate of soda breads, but can only be made when good rich buttermilk is available.

2 lb. flour	1½ oz. butter or margarine
1 teaspoon bicarbonate of soda	1 pint (approx.) buttermilk
1 heaped teaspoon salt	

Sift flour, salt, and bicarbonate of soda together. Rub in the butter. Mix with buttermilk to a good soft dough. Shape rapidly on a floured board into a large round about 2 inches thick. Cut into four. Put these quarters or farls on to a hot ungreased girdle. Cook on low steady heat about 12–15 minutes on each side.   When the bread is done it will sound hollow when lightly tapped.

1. For brown and fly breads 1 dessertspoon sugar is added.

2. If the buttermilk used is not rich and good, or if it is replaced by sour milk, a small teaspoon of cream of tartar should be added to the above recipe.

3. Fat in soda bread is optional; it certainly makes the bread keep better.

4. If the loaves are to be baked they should be put in a moderate oven for approximately the same time as is taken on the girdle, 25–30 minutes.

5. If sweet milk is used for mixing, the proportions of soda and cream of tartar are two of cream of tartar to one of bicarbonate of soda, as in recipe for Brown Soda Bread.

Brown soda bread may be made as for previous recipe, using half wholemeal, half white flour.   If the bread is to be made with sweet milk the following recipe may be used:

BROWN SODA BREAD

1 lb. 6 oz. wholemeal flour	4 level teaspoons cream of tartar
12 oz. white flour	2 level teaspoons salt
2 level teaspoons bicarbonate of soda	2 level teaspoons sugar (optional)

1½ pints milk or milk and water (approx.), according to the strength of the flour

Mix and shape, divide and bake as above, but allow 30–35 minutes. This makes four good-sized farls.

BAKING-POWDER BREAD

2 lb. white flour	2 oz. butter or lard
4 heaped teaspoons baking-powder	a good pinch of salt
	fresh or sour milk

Sift the baking-powder with the flour, add salt and rub in the fat.   Add approximately 1¼ pints milk and mix up quickly and lightly.   Shape on a floured board to a thick round, cut in four, and bake in a moderate oven (400°–450° F.).   Three ounces of currants can be added to the flour after rubbing in the fat, making fly bread.   Halve the quantity of flour if for scones.   Use a small round cutter for stamping out, not more than 2 inches diameter.

SINGIN' HINNY OR NORTHUMBERLAND FARMHOUSE GIRDLE CAKE[1]

¾ lb. flour	1 oz. lard
3 oz. currants	1 teaspoon salt
2 oz. ground rice	2 teaspoons baking-powder
2 oz. sugar	½ pint liquid (½ cream, ½ milk)

[1] Taken from *Come into the Garden, Cook*, for which permission was given for its use by the publishers of *Farmhouse Fare*, Farmers' Weekly, 43 Shoe Lane, E.C.4.

Mix flour, ground rice, salt, sugar, and baking-powder. Rub in lard. Mix in currants which have been previously washed and dried. Then add the liquid and mix to a moderately soft dough. Roll this out to $\frac{1}{4}$ inch thickness. Prick all over with a fork and bake on a fairly hot girdle until nicely browned on both sides. It can be cut in halves or quarters for convenience in turning. This cake is delicious split and buttered and eaten hot.

SCONES

It is interesting to read in old-fashioned books recipes for scones containing no leavening agent. Most of them were rolled thin, handled quickly, baked on a hot girdle, and served at once. Flour, butter, salt, and cream are the ingredients for one recipe; for another sago boiled in milk, salt, and flour. Others were made with barm or yeast. The lightest scones are those made with sour cream, sour milk, or buttermilk.

For 1 lb. flour and 1 teaspoon salt use:

$\frac{3}{4}$ teaspoon bicarbonate of soda and the same quantity of cream of tartar, with enough buttermilk to mix to a soft dough

or

if to be mixed with sweet milk use $2\frac{1}{2}$ teaspoons baking-powder, or $\frac{3}{4}$ teaspoon bicarbonate of soda with $1\frac{1}{2}$ teaspoons cream of tartar

Other additions to each pound of flour may be:

1–2 oz. sugar	1–2 eggs may replace part of
2 oz. fat	the liquid
2 oz. fruit	

The soda and cream of tartar should be free of lumps, and these and the flour should be sieved before mixing. Fat is rubbed in with the fingers. The dough should be soft and moist and must be mixed in a bowl, turned on to a floured board, kneaded very lightly, pressed out to the required thickness (generally about $\frac{3}{4}$ inch), and then cut in triangles or circles. The scones should be cooked on a girdle or in the oven. Time 7–15 minutes.

GIRDLE SCONES

$\frac{1}{2}$ lb. flour	1 teaspoon golden syrup or
$\frac{1}{2}$ teaspoon bicarbonate of soda	treacle
$\frac{1}{2}$ teaspoon cream of tartar	$\frac{1}{2}$ oz. butter
$\frac{1}{2}$ teaspoon baking-powder	1 tablespoon sugar
	a short $\frac{1}{2}$ pint milk

Mix all dry ingredients with sifted flour, rub in the butter, add syrup and milk and mix with a knife to a fairly stiff dough. Handle as little as possible and roll out very lightly to approximately $\frac{3}{4}$ inch thick. Cut into rounds and bake on a hot, greased girdle, turning once, till brown on both sides.

OLD-FASHIONED PLAIN SODA SCONES

$\frac{1}{2}$ lb flour, dried and sieved with a pinch of salt
$\frac{1}{2}$ teaspoon bicarbonate of soda
1–2 gills buttermilk

Warm the buttermilk in a bowl in the oven, add bicarbonate of soda. This will effervesce and at this moment should be mixed with the flour. Roll out, dust with flour, cut in rounds and cook on clean, ungreased girdle.

DROP SCONES

½ lb. flour
½ teaspoon bicarbonate of soda
½ teaspoon cream of tartar
½ teaspoon baking-powder
1 tablespoon syrup

a nut of butter
1 tablespoon sugar
1 egg
½ pint fresh milk (approx.)

Mix all the dry ingredients, rub in the butter and add syrup. Add half the milk, mixing well with a wooden spoon, then break in the egg and beat well. Then add the remaining milk. The mixture should just drop from the spoon. Allow to stand 10–15 minutes, not more. Heat a well-greased girdle and when really hot drop the mixture in spoonfuls and bake for about 3 minutes on each side till golden brown.

To keep the scones warm and soft wrap in a clean cloth.

Potato scones or cakes were very popular in our schoolroom both for tea and with the breakfast bacon. They are not easy to eat politely for they should be very soft and buttery. They are thin, soft, brown little cakes. The potatoes must be freshly boiled and sieved and not allowed to get cool before mixing.

POTATO SCONES

1 lb. potatoes cooked in salted water and put through a wire sieve while hot
4–5 oz. flour sieved with a teaspoon of salt

1½ oz. butter (or very good dripping if to be eaten with bacon for breakfast)

Work all ingredients together without liquid. Roll out lightly with a well-floured rolling-pin. Cut and bake on an ungreased girdle, turning once. Serve hot and buttered, or fried with fried bacon for breakfast. Some cooks advocate ½ teaspoon baking-powder with this mixture.

R. H., recalling the ways of an old Irish house she used to visit in her childhood, adds a note on potato cakes, giving both an Irish and a Scottish recipe.

POTATO CAKES (1)

These were really more like scones than the usual potato cake. They were made on special occasions when an important visitor was expected to tea. They were the size of scones, round, about ¼ inch thick, a rich brown on both sides, piping hot, and swimming in butter.

1 lb. freshly boiled floury potatoes (approx.)
salt

a small handful of flour, warmed and sifted

Well dry the potatoes after draining. Crush with a 'beetle' on a floured board or push through a wire sieve. Avoid rubbing in any way. Add plenty of salt and scatter the flour over. Knead gently and quickly to a light dough (about 1–2 minutes). Roll out about ¼ inch thick, stamp into rounds about 2½ inches across and slip on to the girdle. Cook about 12 minutes, turning once only; each side should be a good brown. Butter thickly immediately they come from the girdle, stack on a hot dish and eat at once.

POTATO CAKES (2)

A Scottish recipe.

These are different in shape and texture. Made in large farls they are thin and flexible and are equally good eaten cold or fried with the breakfast bacon.

1½ lb. freshly boiled floury potatoes	6 oz. flour
	salt

Crush or sieve potatoes on to a floured board, add salt, work in the flour by degrees, kneading lightly and carefully. Then roll out as thinly as possible. Cut into rounds the size of a dinner plate, then cut each round into four. Bake on a rather hot girdle for 7–10 minutes, turning once only.

WELSH GIRDLE SCONES

3 oz. butter	3 oz. currants
¾ lb. flour sieved with 1 level teaspoon bicarbonate of soda, ½ teaspoon cream of tartar, a pinch of salt	2 oz. sugar sour milk or buttermilk

Rub the butter into the flour. Add the rest of the dry ingredients and mix thoroughly. Stir in enough sour milk or buttermilk to make a light dough. Roll out to about 1 inch thick, stamp out into rounds, and cook 5–7 minutes on each side on a hot girdle. The scones should be well browned.

HOME-MADE BAKING-POWDER

For immediate use one may mix 4 level teaspoons cream of tartar to 2 of bicarbonate of soda and this will raise 1 lb. flour mixed with 1 teaspoon salt. If required for keeping, a proportion of ground rice is added, for instance:

2 oz. bicarbonate of soda 4 oz. cream of tartar	4 oz. ground rice

Sieve several times and keep dry.

TEA-CAKES

TEA-CAKES (PLAIN)

¼ lb. flour warmed and sieved
with 1 teaspoon salt
⅜ oz. yeast creamed with 1 teaspoon sugar

2 oz. butter or margarine
¾ gill milk
2 eggs
sweetened milk for glazing

Heat the milk, add the butter, and allow to melt and cool to blood heat. Beat eggs and mix with yeast and milk and butter mixture. Have warmed, sieved flour in a warm bowl, make a well and pour in the liquid. Mix and turn on to a floured board. Cut in pieces and knead lightly into shape. Put each piece in a greased ring on a greased baking-sheet. Cover and put in a warm place until well risen. Bake in a hot oven approximately 15 minutes. Glaze with sweetened milk and return to the oven for the glaze to dry. (See Glazing, page 52).

TEA-CAKES WITH FRUIT

1½ lb. flour, sieved and mixed
with 1 teaspoon salt
6 oz. butter or margarine
2 oz. sugar
3 oz. dried fruit

½ oz. chopped candied peel
1½ oz. yeast creamed with 1
teaspoon sugar
2 gills warm milk
1 gill warm water

Rub the fat into the flour. Add fruit, peel, and sugar. Make a well and pour in the yeast mixed with the warm milk and water. Beat well with the hand. Cover, set to rise in a warm place till doubled in bulk. Turn on to a floured board, knead lightly and shape. Set on greased baking-tins to prove and bake in a hot oven.

SALLY LUNNS

These very light tea-cakes are called after the woman who invented them. She lived, I believe, in Bath and is said to have made them for the Prince Regent. One recipe I find dated *c.* 1770. They used to be baked in thick, round, flat loaves on a baking-sheet, but more often now are dropped into greased cake tins. One recipe says that when baked the cakes should be sliced, toasted, and buttered, shaped again into a cake and cut in quarters. Another recommends that the cake be torn open and buttered and replaced in the oven till the butter is melted. They are often sliced horizontally twice, i.e. the cake is divided into three slices, toasted, and buttered. But whatever way you choose it is heavy on butter.

SALLY LUNN (1)

¾ lb. flour warmed and sieved
with ½ teaspoon salt into a
warm bowl
¾ oz. yeast creamed with 1 teaspoon sugar

1½ gills milk
1 oz. butter
1 egg
milk and sugar for glazing

Prepare two warmed, greased 5-inch cake tins. Heat the milk and dissolve the butter in it, then allow to cool to blood heat. Sieve the warm flour and salt into a warm bowl. Beat the egg and add the tepid milk. Cream the yeast and sugar and add egg and milk to it. Make a well in the flour and strain in the liquid, mix to a dough, turn on to floured board and knead lightly for a few minutes. Put half the dough into each warm cake tin, cover, set in a warm place, and allow to rise until doubled in bulk, about half an hour. Bake in a hot oven about 15–20 minutes. Brush with sweetened milk and put back in oven to dry the glaze.

SALLY LUNN (2)

A rich recipe requiring cream.

1 lb. flour warmed and sifted
    with 1 teaspoon salt
1 oz. yeast creamed with 1 tea-
    spoon sugar
3 egg yolks

2 egg whites
½ pint cream
water
milk and sugar for glazing

Beat yolks and whites and pass through strainer. Add to creamed yeast and cream and beat. Add about a gill of tepid water. Mix the liquid with the flour, adding extra water or milk if necessary (this depends on the thickness of the cream and the strength of the flour). Mix, cover, and put in a warm place to rise for about 1½ hours. Then knead lightly and shape. Drop into greased tins and bake 20–25 minutes. Glaze as in the previous recipe.

PENNY BUNS

2½ lb. flour, warmed and sieved
1 oz. yeast creamed with 1 tea-
    spoon sugar
up to 2 pints warm milk
6–8 oz. butter or margarine
2 eggs

4–6 oz. currants, cleaned by
    being rubbed with a little
    flour on a wire sieve
4 oz. sugar
sweetened milk or sugar syrup
    (page 784) for glazing

Into a warm bowl put 1¼ lb. flour; make a well and pour into it the yeast and about a quarter of the milk, enough to make a soft dough; add a little more if required. Mix well and beat with the hand. Cover and let this sponge rise for 30–40 minutes. Warm the remaining milk and melt the butter in it. Pour into this the beaten eggs. Mix with the risen sponge, fruit, remaining flour, and sugar. Beat and set to rise in a warm place, covered, for an hour or two. Bake in a hot oven for 10–15 minutes. When cooked take from the oven, glaze well with sweetened milk or sugar syrup, and replace for a moment or two for glaze to dry.

SULTANA TEA-CAKES

1 lb. flour warmed and sifted
    with 1 teaspoon salt
1 oz. yeast creamed with 1 tea-
    spoon sugar
1 egg

½ pint milk
2 oz. sugar
1 oz. butter
4 oz. sultanas

Put flour and salt into a warmed basin. Cream the yeast, beat the egg and then whisk together. Heat the milk, add sugar, allow butter to melt in milk, and cool to blood heat. Mix this with the yeast and egg. Pour into a well made in the flour; mix. Put to rise, covered. When risen knead lightly, adding sultanas. Shape, prove, and bake.

BATH BUNS

1 lb. flour and 1 teaspoon salt (warmed and sifted)	3 small eggs
½ pint warm milk	4 oz. sultanas
¾ oz. yeast creamed with 1 tea-spoon sugar	1½ oz. candied lemon peel
¼ lb. butter	1–2 oz. crushed lump sugar (for finish)
¼ lb. castor sugar	sweetened milk or egg for glazing

Add creamed yeast to tepid milk. Pour into well in warmed sieved flour and salt; knead lightly. Cream butter, work in sugar, beat eggs. Work these into the dough with sultanas and 1 oz. of the peel. Put to rise another 40 minutes. Shape into buns. Put on a lightly greased baking-sheet. Brush with egg or sweetened milk and sprinkle with the crushed lump sugar and remaining peel. Bake in a moderate oven 20–30 minutes.

CHELSEA BUNS (1)

A fairly rich mixture.

1¼ lb. flour warmed and sieved with a teaspoon of salt	a scant gill of warm milk
5 oz. butter	4 eggs
4–5 oz. castor sugar	4–5 oz. currants, cleaned
1 oz. yeast creamed with a tea-spoon of sugar	1 small teaspoon mixed spice
	a little castor sugar for finishing

Rub half the butter roughly into the dried, warmed flour and salt and add half the sugar. Beat the eggs, add the tepid milk to the creamed yeast and mix with them. Make a well in the flour and pour in the liquid. Mix thoroughly and knead until smooth. Put to rise, covered, for about an hour and a half, until doubled in bulk. Then knead lightly into shape on a floured board and roll out to a square. Soften the remaining butter and spread over the dough with some of the remaining sugar, then fold and roll out again. Sprinkle with the rest of the sugar, the fruit and spice. Now, with the hands, roll up like a Swiss roll. Cut this into slices of about 1½ inches. Lay the slices flat close together on a warm, greased tin and prove for 15–20 minutes. Sprinkle with sugar. The buns should now touch. Bake in a quick oven and leave until cool before separating the buns. A small Swiss roll tin is convenient as this confines the dough to a limited space.

CHELSEA BUNS (2)

A less rich mixture may be made with:

1 lb. flour	1 egg
1½–2 oz. butter	about 1½ gills of milk
3 oz. castor sugar	½ teaspoon spice
½ oz. yeast, creamed with 1 teaspoon of sugar	2 oz. sultanas and currants

Proceed as in foregoing recipe.

These may be finished with bun glaze:

Sugar syrup for glazing buns

Enough for approximately 12 buns.

2 oz. sugar ½ gill water

Boil together for a few minutes and brush over sweet buns.

ROCK BUNS

To get really short rock buns no liquid beyond eggs and possibly a spoonful of cream should be used. For economy many modern recipes give milk as an ingredient. This will make a bun, but it will lack the characteristic friable quality of a good rock bun. An old-fashioned and good recipe follows, which at need may be modified.

ROCK BUNS (1)

½ lb. flour sifted with ½ teaspoon salt and 1 level teaspoon baking-powder	4 oz. currants (or mixture of currants, sultanas, and chopped peel)
4 oz. butter	grated rind of ½ a lemon
4 oz. sugar	a little extra liquid if necessary
3 eggs	(preferably 1 tablespoon cream)

Cream butter and sugar, beat in the eggs, sift in the flour, add fruit and grated rind and blend together with the fingers. The mixture should be very firm. If a little extra liquid is essential, use for choice a tablespoon of cream, but blend thoroughly before concluding this is necessary. Form the mixture into small rough lumps with two forks and bake on a greased sheet in moderate oven.

ROCK BUNS (2)

A different method of mixing.

8 oz. self-raising flour	1 oz. finely chopped candied peel (optional)
a pinch of salt	2 beaten eggs, or 1 egg and 2–3 tablespoons milk
4 oz. butter or margarine	a little milk if necessary
3 oz. castor sugar	
4 oz. currants and sultanas mixed	

Sift the flour and salt and rub in the butter finely. Add the sugar, cleaned fruit, and peel. Mix in the eggs with a fork, adding a little milk if necessary, but keeping the mixture very stiff. Using two forks, divide it out into pieces the size of a small egg, and arrange on a greased baking-sheet. Bake in a fairly hot oven 15–20 minutes.

If a more economical recipe is called for, cut the fat by 1 oz. and the fruit by half. Use only 1 egg and milk, as indicated in ingredients.

DOUGHNUTS

¼ lb. flour warmed and sieved with ½ teaspoon salt	1½ oz. sugar
1 oz. butter	1 gill milk
2 egg yolks	castor sugar or a mixture of cinnamon and sugar for dusting
¼ oz. yeast creamed with 1 teaspoon sugar	deep fat for frying

Rub butter into flour, add sugar, make a well. Add warm milk to creamed yeast and egg yolks and put mixture into well. Mix and beat well till smooth. Set in a warm place to rise, 30–45 minutes. Knead well, turn on to a floured board and roll out ½ inch thick. Cut in small circles. Put on a greased tin and allow to prove till doubled in size. Fry in deep fat till golden brown. Drain and sprinkle with sugar.

American cook books give recipes for doughnuts made with baking-powder. These are good, though not the classic that we know.

AMERICAN DOUGHNUTS

8 oz. flour (more if necessary)	2 oz. sugar
½ teaspoon salt	1 egg
2 flat teaspoons baking-powder	1 gill warm milk
2 oz. butter	castor sugar

Warm the flour and sieve with salt and baking-powder. Melt the butter and add to well-beaten egg, sugar, and warm milk. Add the prepared flour. The dough should be soft but just firm enough to handle, so if a little extra flour is needed this must be added. If the dough can now be chilled in the ice-box for 20 minutes or so it will help in handling. On a floured board roll to ½ inch, cut into small rounds and allow to stand for a few minutes. Fry in deep fat and dredge with castor sugar.

OATCAKES

1 lb. oatmeal (medium), and extra oatmeal for dusting	½ teaspoon bicarbonate of soda
1 oz. bacon fat (lard or margarine may be used instead	½ teaspoon salt
	¼ pint hot water

Melt bacon fat with the hot water. Add baking soda and salt to the oatmeal. Make a well in the centre of the oatmeal, pour in the melted fat and water and, using a palette-knife, mix to a fairly moist dough. On a board well dusted with oatmeal roll out as thinly as possible to an even round, dusting with oatmeal during the rolling to prevent sticking, and rubbing in more oatmeal with the palm of your hand.

Cut in farls (Scotch for quarters) or rounds with a pastry cutter. Place on a baking-sheet, ungreased, and bake in a moderate oven, turning several times to prevent steaming. Bake for approximately 20 minutes, until the oatcakes are crisp and faintly golden.

They may equally well be baked on a girdle, but must be toasted finally either in front of an open fire or in the oven.

BISCUITS

Plain Biscuits

For the most part plain biscuits made at home are best served straight from the oven, and so may well be made in small quantities. If they are stored they need to be re-crisped in the oven before serving. The most popular of our recipes is the one for 'Last-Minute' Biscuits, which do keep quite well. If biscuits are to be kept they should be put in tins the moment they are cool and before they have had time to absorb moisture from the air. A piece of grease-proof paper should be put right over the top of the tin and the lid fitted over it.

ORFORD'S WATER-BISCUITS

$\frac{1}{2}$ lb. flour	2 oz. fat
$\frac{1}{2}$ teaspoon salt	a little water
1 teaspoon baking-powder	ground rock-salt

Sift the flour with the salt and baking-powder and rub in the fat finely. Moisten with water to a firm dough. Roll out very thinly, prick all over and stamp into large rounds. Sprinkle with ground rock-salt and bake in a slow to moderate oven until a pale golden colour.

THIN BISCUITS

4 oz. flour sifted with a good pinch of salt and $\frac{1}{2}$ teaspoon baking-powder	$\frac{1}{2}$ oz. butter 2 eggs

Rub butter into flour, mix to a stiff paste with beaten eggs. (If flour is very strong a few drops of water may be added, but a stiff dough is needed.) Cut in rounds and bake in a slow oven till blistered.

These should be served fresh from the oven.

'LAST-MINUTE' BISCUITS

This is a misnomer, for it suggests that they are made in a twinkling. They are very quickly baked, but the beating and rolling take time. They should properly be made with flour, salt, and cream. If cream is not possible a little fat is rubbed into the flour and milk is used for mixing. The stiff paste is well beaten with a rolling-pin for 8–10 minutes, and this is important. The biscuits are rolled out to paper thickness, are large and irregular in shape and very brittle.

4 oz. flour sieved with a good pinch of salt
a few spoonfuls of cream, only just enough to mix to a thick paste; or use instead of cream ½ oz. butter rubbed in, and mix with milk

When mixed turn on to a marble slab and beat with the rolling-pin, regularly and steadily working over the dough and turning. After beating the dough may rest 20–30 minutes. Break up into quite small pieces and roll out till paper thin. Prick all over. Leave them in irregular shapes. Bake in a quick oven, generally 3–4 minutes.

They are quite delicious and may be used in place of poppadums with curry, or served with cheese or with fruit. If a sweet biscuit is wanted they may be brushed with a little sugar syrup (page 784) and dried in the oven. They keep well, but should be warmed up before being served.

WATFORD WAFER BISCUITS

8 oz. flour
1 teaspoon ground ginger
a pinch of salt
4 tablespoons milk (more if necessary)
2 oz. castor sugar
1 oz. butter

Sift flour, ginger, and salt. Scald milk, add sugar and butter. Cool slightly and mix into the flour to form a stiff paste. More milk may be added if necessary. Divide into pieces the size of a walnut. Roll each wafer thin; when quite cold trim with a large round cutter, prick well and bake in a slow oven. This wafer biscuit may be varied by adding a teaspoon of caraway seeds in place of the ginger.

Sweet Biscuits

SHORT DIGESTIVE BISCUITS

6 oz. wholemeal flour
1 oz. oatmeal
½ teaspoon salt
1 oz. white flour
3 oz. butter or margarine
sugar to taste
¼ teaspoon each:
bicarbonate of soda
cream of tartar
or
1 teaspoon baking-powder
enough milk to bind

Rub fat into the dry ingredients and add just enough milk to bind. Knead. Roll out thinly, cut, prick, and bake. (Do not overbake.)

GERMAN BISCUITS

3½ oz. flour	1 egg yolk
2½ oz. butter	vanilla essence to taste
1¼ oz. sugar	

Cream the butter with the sugar until white, add the vanilla and yolk and beat.　Work in the flour to make a light soft dough.　Roll out thinly and cut into shapes.　Bake in a slow oven to a pale golden colour.

These are usually cut into fancy shapes—crescents, stars, etc.

BRANDY-SNAPS (1)

¼ lb. flour	juice of ½ a lemon
¼ lb. butter	whipped cream sweetened and
¼ lb. sugar	flavoured with brandy or
¼ lb. syrup	vanilla
¼ oz. ginger	

Melt sugar, butter, and syrup, add the warmed flour, ginger, and lemon. Stir well and put out on a well-greased baking-sheet in teaspoonfuls, 6 inches apart.　Bake in a moderate oven until golden brown, leave for a few moments to cool, then roll up over the thick handle of a wooden spoon and fill with whipped cream.

BRANDY-SNAPS (2)

¼ lb. butter	3 oz. syrup
6 oz. sugar	2 teaspoons ground ginger
¾ lb. self-raising flour	1 teaspoon bicarbonate of soda
1 egg	

Cream the butter, beat in the sugar and ginger, add the syrup with the egg and enough of the flour to prevent curdling.　Beat well.　Stir in remaining flour with soda.　Divide into small pieces, roll into balls, flatten out and put on greased baking-sheets.　Bake in a moderate oven, when they will spread out quite thinly.　Take off quickly and roll up on the handle of a wooden spoon.

GINGERBREAD NUTS (AUNT NELLIE) 1879

1½ lb. flour ('seconds' is best)	½ lb. moist sugar
1 oz. ground ginger	1 lb. black treacle
1 teaspoon bicarbonate of soda	6 oz. clarified butter or fat
3 oz. mixed chopped candied peel	a little milk if necessary

Mix the dry ingredients in a bowl.　Warm the butter until just melted, add the treacle and stir well.　Add to the dry ingredients and knead well. If the paste is not wet enough add a little milk.　Shape into nuts the size of a large walnut and flatten slightly; set on a buttered baking-sheet and bake for half an hour in a slow to moderate oven. If biscuits are preferred, roll the paste out thinly and cut into rounds, arrange on a buttered tin, and bake for half an hour in a slow to moderate oven.

CHOCOLATE BISCUITS

8 oz. butter	8 oz. self-raising flour
4 oz. castor sugar	2 oz. powdered chocolate
1 teaspoon vanilla essence	

Filling (*optional*)

2 oz. powdered chocolate	sugar and vanilla or rum to
strong coffee	taste
2 oz. butter	

For the biscuits. Cream the butter, beat in the sugar and essence, then work in the chocolate and flour by degrees. When a paste, divide into pieces the size of a walnut. Roll into balls and put out at regular intervals on a buttered tin. Flatten each one with a fork dipped in water and bake in a moderate oven for 12 minutes. Lift off carefully and serve as they are or sandwich them with the filling.

For the filling. Cook the chocolate with the coffee to a thick cream, beat in the butter in small pieces off the fire, add the sugar and flavouring. Leave till cold before using.

FORK BISCUITS (PLAIN)

5 oz. self-raising flour	flavouring (grated lemon or
4 oz. margarine	orange rind, or powdered
2 oz. castor sugar	chocolate)

Soften the margarine, add sugar by degrees, beating until smooth; add flavouring, gradually work in the flour. Form into balls the size of a walnut, flatten out on to a baking-sheet, using a fork dipped in water. Bake in a moderate oven, 350° F., 15–20 minutes.

N.B. If chocolate flavouring is used, take 1 oz. less of flour and replace by 1 oz. powdered chocolate.

SHORTBREAD

Good shortbread must be made of the finest ingredients, fresh butter, castor sugar, and white flour. Traditionally shortbread is decorated with orange or candied peel and almonds. It needs lightness of hand and nice judgment, for if the ingredients are worked too much together the result is tough and chewy, instead of being short and melt-in-the-mouth.

SCOTS SHORTBREAD

4 oz. fresh butter	orange or citron candied peel
2 oz. castor sugar	blanched split almonds
4 oz. fine flour	castor sugar
2 oz. rice flour or fine semolina	

Cream butter, beat in the castor sugar. Add flours by degrees, working quickly and lightly. Immediately they are incorporated pat out with the fist to a cake about ¾ inch in thickness and 8 inches in diameter. Pinch round the edge with pastry pincers or with the fingers. Prick the middle and decorate with strips of the peel and the split almonds. Dust over with castor sugar. Slide on to a baking-sheet covered with a piece of paper dusted with flour and bake in a moderately hot oven 15–20 minutes. The shortbread must be a pale biscuit colour.

ICE-BOX BISCUITS

A delicious biscuit, and a particularly useful type for the cook-hostess, is the ice-box biscuit. For this a rather rich dough or paste is made up, rolled in wax paper, and kept in the ice-box. When biscuits are required thin pieces are shaved off—the chilling of the paste makes this easy—and quickly baked. One achieves rich, thin, crisp biscuits. They may be varied in flavour or filled with various fruit and nut filling. The paste, being rich, is too soft to cut thinly before chilling, and the inexperienced are sometimes tempted to add extra flour. This detracts from the texture of the biscuit.

This seems to be another suitable moment to take advantage of Mrs Irma S. Rombauer's permission to quote from her book *The Joy of Cooking* (J. M. Dent & Sons Ltd), because it was from American friends that I first learned this trick of using the refrigerator for making very thin biscuits, something I had not been able to do before. Ice-box biscuits are a boon to the busy woman.

RULE FOR ICE-BOX COOKIES

'Combine the ingredients as directed and shape the dough into long rolls about 2 inches in diameter. If the dough is too soft to roll, chill it until it can be handled easily. Do not use additional flour. Cover the rolls with waxed paper and place them in the refrigerator for about 24 hours (until they are thoroughly chilled). Cut the rolls into the thinnest possible slices. Bake them on a greased sheet in an oven heated to 400° for about 10 minutes. The whole nuts may be combined with the dough or they may be used to garnish the slices.

VANILLA ICE-BOX COOKIES
about 40 2-inch cookies

Sift: 1 *cup sugar*

Beat until soft: ½ *cup butter*

Add the sugar gradually. Blend these ingredients until they are very light and creamy.

Beat in: 1 *egg*

Add: 1 *teaspoon vanilla*
      ¼ *teaspoon grated lemon rind (optional)*
Sift before measuring: 1¾ *cups bread flour*
Resift with: ¼ *teaspoon salt*
           2 *teaspoons baking-powder*
Stir the sifted ingredients into the butter mixture.
Add: ½ *cup nuts (optional)*

Follow the preceding rule for ice-box cookies. Sprinkle the cookies with:
Sugar (optional)
(this makes them sandy) and with:
Chopped or half nuts (optional)
Bake them as directed.'

CONTINENTAL BREADS *

When you become expert in making English bread almost certainly you will want to make those richer breads often classed together under the generic term 'French' bread.

The long rolls and flutes sold in the French bakeries are beyond the scope of the domestic kitchen; the baking of them is done by a special process that would prove too difficult for us. On the other hand, the rich doughs used for croissants and brioches are quite satisfactorily made at home, but the process is more complicated than in the case of household bread, and great attention has to be paid to detail in the early stages of one's experiments. The method of mixing and making these doughs, the way in which the yeast—very high by the way in proportion to the flour—is sponged is different from English bread-making. The rich mixture of flour, eggs, and butter is worked on a slab, and the way in which it is treated may strike the novice as recklessly vigorous, for, apparently in rough fashion, the paste is lifted up with the fingers of one hand and thrown down again with a flick of the wrist, and this is continued until gradually the dough becomes less sticky and detaches itself from the hands and slowly acquires the right elastic consistency. The yeast, mixed with a small part of the total amount of flour and a little warm water, is made into a soft dough or yeast cake and then dropped into a pan of warm water where it is left to grow and develop, rather in the form of a cauliflower, doubling in volume, and continuing to develop and rise for about 7 or 8 minutes. Sometimes another method is adopted and the dough is put into a small warm basin, covered, and left to rise, but on the whole the warm water method is the safer one, providing as it does a more even temperature. After 7 or 8 minutes, when the dough is ready, it is lifted by putting the hand, fingers spread out, underneath, and is laid on a piece

* *See plate 18*

of muslin or clean cloth to drain for a minute or two; this is then mixed with the paste on the slab. The paste for brioches, when finished and before rising, is of the consistency of stiffly whipped cream, and it would be hard to shape were it not chilled thoroughly after it has been mixed. Some cooks make the mixture the day before and so are able to keep the paste overnight in an ice-box or other really cold place. On the other hand, if the paste is made up by say ten o'clock in the morning, left to rise in a warm place for about 1 hour, then put in the ice-box for an hour, the brioches may be ready for lunch. (See recipe for Brioches Clothilde, page 794.)

The following recipes for brioches range from the simple to the rich classic form. The novice is advised to become expert in the less rich mixtures before attempting the others.

The following recipe, which sets out method in detail, is for moderately rich brioches:

BRIOCHES

½ lb. flour	3 oz. butter, well creamed or
½ oz. yeast	softened
1 level teaspoon salt	2–3 tablespoons milk
2 level teaspoons sugar	warm water
2 eggs	beaten egg for brushing

Sieve the flour into a heap on the pastry slab. Divide with a palette-knife into four equal portions and draw one portion away. Make this fourth section into a little heap and make a hole in the centre, and into this crumble up the yeast, mixing the whole with 2 tablespoons warm water, using your fingers and gradually drawing in the flour. Mix this until it is smooth, using extra warm water if needed. You should now have a little ball of soft dough. Snip a cross on the top with scissors, drop into a pan of warm water (see note, page 793). The dough will at once sink to the bottom, but as it begins to develop it will rise again to the surface. Sprinkle salt and sugar into the remaining three parts of flour on the slab and draw up into a heap; make a well in the middle and break in the eggs. Mix together, adding milk as required to make a fairly firm paste. Now the beating process begins, and this is to some degree a knack. At first the sticky paste will adhere to your fingers, but do not try to wipe it off, simply carry on with the process and gradually the paste will become more liquid and detach itself. With a twisting movement lift up the paste with the fingers of one hand, then with a flick of the wrist throw it down again and repeat this again and again with vigour and dispatch, not troubling, as has already been said, to get your fingers free of the mixture, because it will detach itself, and you will find that you have a fine elastic paste ready now to have the softened butter worked into it. The butter is also worked in with the fingers until thoroughly incorporated.

Now lift out the yeast dough in the way described on the previous page. (The synchronizing of the preparation of the mixture on the slab and the readiness of the yeast cake is a matter of practice, see note, page 793.) Now

mix all together.   Lift the paste off the slab with a palette-knife and put
into a clean, lightly floured bowl large enough to permit rising.   Cover
with a cloth and either allow it to rise in the way described, that is 3–4
hours in a warm room, after which it is pushed down and put in a cold
place, or if more convenient put it away into the ice-box for 12 hours or
more.   After this time the paste will be firm enough to handle.   It should
be noted that the minimum time to be allowed in the ice-box—and this is a
makeshift—is 4–6 hours.

The brioches are now shaped, proved, and baked in a very hot oven.
It is possible now to buy the deep, fluted, proper moulds, like tartelette
tins, which are the conventional shape for brioches.   Turn out the dough,
now cold, firm, and easy to handle, knead lightly, form it into a roll with
your hands, and divide evenly into pieces about the size of an egg.   Cut
off about a third of the 'egg,' roll the remaining two-thirds into a ball and
put each into the little greased tins.   In the centre of each make a small
incision, enough to form a small hole.   Now take the small pieces of
dough—the thirds that you cut off the 'eggs'—roll them into little balls and
shape them into short tails (R. H. says 'like a tadpole').   This may conveniently be done with the side of the hand on the edge of the slab.   Then
push the tail into the hole that you have cut into the brioche, so that each
has a firmly fixed topknot.   Prove for 10–15 minutes in a warm place: the
plate oven in an Aga, for instance, or on an oven rack over a tin of boiling
water.   Brush each with beaten egg (see note on glazing with eggs on
page 38), bake in a hot oven (425°–450° F.) to nut-brown, about 15
minutes.

Warm water.   This should be comfortably warm but not hot.   R. H.
mentions that students will bring her a pan of water for this purpose so hot
that you cannot bear your hand in it, and this, of course, would kill the
yeast.   If, on the other hand, some unexpected delay occurs and the
water gets too cool, they will put the pan back on the stove with the yeast
in it, and this again is fatal because the cake drops to the bottom, comes
in contact with the hot-plate, and is destroyed.   If you need, for any
reason, to increase the heat of the water, this should be done by the
addition of more hot water, and R. H. describes the temperature by saying
that it is as warm as you would bath a baby in.

Synchronizing.   Although the yeast cake must be removed when doubled
in bulk, it is a convenience if this moment synchronizes with the readiness
of the dough.   It may take a little practice to get this timing perfect, but
it is not really difficult.   When you are working with a small quantity of
dough the water used for the yeast cake may be a little warmer than for a
large batch, because you will be ready for it sooner and you want to hasten
development, while with a large batch of dough the working will take
longer, so the yeast development may be slowed up a little.   If your
dough is not quite ready when the yeast cake is risen, do not prolong the
time in water, but take it out and cover till ready.

BRIOCHES CLOTHILDE (A LARGE BRIOCHE)

Simpler and quicker than the classic recipe which follows it.

1 lb. flour (good weight)	1 glass of milk (a little less than
a pinch of salt	½ pint) (approx.)
2 tablespoons sugar	3½ oz. butter
3 eggs	½ oz. yeast

Sift flour with salt, mix to a dough with the sugar, beaten eggs, and about three-quarters of the milk. Work the paste very well. Use some of the remaining milk (or all if it will not make the dough too wet) to dissolve the yeast. Add to the paste with the softened creamed butter at the last. Mix well together. Half fill a large brioche mould (or two) with the mixture. Allow to rise 1–2 hours at room temperature (65–70° F.). Bake in a moderate oven.

N.B. The original recipe has more sugar—up to 5 tablespoons. This is intended to be a tea brioche, but even so is a little on the sweet side.

BRIOCHES (CLASSIC RECIPE)

The butter here is very high in proportion to flour, and this makes it difficult to handle. R. H. says do not start a novice on this one. Preparations must begin a day in advance.

8¾ oz. flour	3 small eggs
scant ¼ oz. salt	7 oz. butter (this may be cut,
scant ½ oz. yeast	and if margarine is used it is
¾ oz. sugar	advisable)
tepid water	egg for glazing

Take about a quarter of the flour and make a soft dough with the yeast dissolved in tepid water, and put to rise (see first brioche recipe, page 792) until twice its size. Make a well in the remaining flour and in it place the salt, sugar, and eggs; beat on the slab to give it elasticity as described in the first brioche recipe. Add the risen yeast cake. Cream the butter thoroughly, mix into a little of the dough and then mix all together. Put to rise at room temperature for an hour or more. Push down, cover the bowl with a plate, and put into the ice-box for 12 hours. The next day shape (have hand floured, but not the board). Prove, brush with egg, and then bake in a medium oven.

BRIOCHE (CRÈME DE LAIT)

A large brioche made with cream and no butter.

9 oz. flour	3 small eggs
¼–½ oz. yeast	3 tablespoons single cream
a pinch of salt	egg for glazing
1–3 tablespoons sugar	

Take a small quantity of the flour. Make up into a yeast cake (see first brioche recipe), set aside to sponge in hot water. Beat the remaining flour, the salt, sugar, eggs, and cream together till thoroughly elastic. Well drain the yeast cake and work into the mixture. Turn into a bowl and allow to rise for 2 hours. Shape into a large brioche, set in a brioche tin. Prove, brush with egg, and bake in a moderate oven.

If the dough is not for immediate use, cover the bowl with a plate and set it in a cold place overnight.

CROISSANTS

The mixture for these is really a type of flaky pastry made with yeast, and they may be plain or rich within reason.

The paste is made in the same way as a brioche paste, but is firmer. Flour, yeast, and liquid, together with one-third of the butter called for, are made into a paste. This is put into a bowl in the ice-box to get firm. It is then finished off with the remaining butter as for flaky pastry. For method of rolling see Puff Pastry (page 836).

CROISSANTS (1)

A simple type for general use. Good for 'bread and cheese' lunch. Started the day before baking.

1¼ lb. flour	½ oz. yeast
¾ pint milk	½ oz. salt
4 oz. butter (or 3 oz. butter and	egg for glazing
1 oz. margarine)	

Warm a quarter of the milk to blood heat. Mix this with the yeast with your fingers in a bowl and add as much flour as it will absorb to make a dough slightly softer than a pastry dough. Place the dough in a greased bowl, cover with a cloth and leave in a warm place to rise to double its size. (This will take approximately 1 hour.) When risen add the rest of the milk all at once, the salt and all the flour, and knead gently as for ordinary bread to make a firm dough. Do not overwork as this will tend to make the dough sticky. (The quantity of flour needed may vary slightly according to the quality used; if using fine white flour you may need less than the 1¼ lb. indicated.)

Roll out the dough into an oblong about ⅓ inch thick and spread half of it with the whole 4 oz. of butter as though spreading bread and butter. Fold over the plain half, seal the edges with a rolling-pin and continue as for puff pastry (page 836), giving five turns only. Leave overnight in a refrigerator or on a cold slab in the larder.

Roll out into a strip 10 inches wide and ¼ inch thick, cut into 5-inch squares, then cut these diagonally across into triangles. (This makes a large breakfast croissant; a smaller size more suitable for tea is made by cutting the triangles in half.) Roll up the paste from the base of the triangle and seal the point with a little water or beaten egg. In rolling keep the middle of the roll fairly thick, pulling out the ends and giving them a twist as you shape into a crescent, then lightly join the ends to prevent them opening out during proving.

Leave to rise until double in bulk, about half an hour, pull the joined ends slightly apart, glaze with beaten egg and bake in a hot oven 20–30 minutes.

CROISSANTS (2) (CLASSIC)

Preparations must begin a day in advance.

7 oz. flour	a good pinch of salt
¼ oz. yeast	warm (blood heat) milk and
3½ oz. butter	water

Take one quarter of the flour and make into a soft yeast cake (see first brioche recipe, page 792). Mark or snip a cross on the top with scissors and drop into a pan of hot water. Mix remaining flour with half the butter, the salt, and enough milk and water to make a fairly firm dough. Beat well on the slab or board. Drain the yeast cake thoroughly and mix into the dough. Put into a floured bowl, cover, and leave in a cold place 12 hours. If not in a refrigerator, the paste must be pushed down about twice during that time. Turn on to a floured slab, roll out to a round and set the rest of the butter in the middle. Fold up like a parcel, roll out, fold in three and leave 15 minutes. Now give it two more turns and set aside for 15 minutes. Repeat this once more and set aside to get thoroughly firm. Make up into croissants (see previous recipe).

CROISSANTS (3) (MRS CHAPLIN'S RECIPE)

1 oz yeast	1 lb. flour
½ lb. butter	salt
¾ oz. sugar	½ pint milk (approx.)

Make a dough with the yeast, sugar, salt, milk, and flour. Work until smooth and allow to rest in the ice-box. Roll out the dough, slice the butter thinly and lay over half of it. Fold over the other half and roll out again. Give the dough three double turns, i.e. 6 rolls, resting it 15 minutes between every two. If possible leave overnight. Then give one single turn and make up and finish as for first recipe.

In the above recipe the yeast need not be sponged. It is simply creamed with the sugar and added to the milk, about ½ pint in this case.

CROISSANTS (4)

½ lb. flour	milk
3–4 oz. butter	water
¼–½ oz. yeast, according to richness (if margarine has to be used in place of butter more yeast is called for)	salt and a pinch of sugar
	beaten egg for brushing

Proceed in the same way as in first brioche recipe (page 792), but working only one-third of the butter called for into the paste before the yeast cake is added. When the paste has risen and is firm roll out into a strip. Now divide the remaining butter into half and finish as for flaky pastry (see page 833), giving it three to four turns, with two waits of 15 minutes in the ice-box in between. To shape the croissants roll to a wide thin strip (about $\frac{1}{4}$ inch thick, not more) and with a large knife cut into triangles. Roll from the wide base to the tip and touch the tip with beaten egg to hold it firm. Turn into a horse-shoe (see instructions on page 796), prove on a baking-sheet, brush with egg and bake.

CROISSANTS DE BOULANGER

6 oz. flour sieved with a pinch of salt	$\frac{1}{2}$ oz. yeast
hot water	3 oz. butter
	1 wineglass milk and water

Make a yeast cake (see first brioche recipe, page 792) with a quarter of the flour and a little hot water. Slip into a pan of hot water. Mix the remainder of the flour with half the butter and the liquid. Beat well. Set aside to rise 5–6 hours in room temperature. Turn on to the slab, flatten out with the hand to about $\frac{3}{4}$ inch thick, put on the rest of the butter in small pieces and fold in three. Put in the ice-box to firm, then give four turns with the rolling-pin with a 15-minute rest after the second turn. Set aside for about an hour, then make up into croissants (see recipe 1, page 795).

DANISH PASTRY

Resembles a sweet croissant dough; used for Danish almond buns, pin-wheels, Swedish tea wreath.

12 oz. plain flour	1–1$\frac{1}{2}$ gills slightly tepid milk
a good pinch of salt	(not from refrigerator—
$\frac{1}{2}$ oz. yeast, good weight	room heat)
1$\frac{3}{4}$ oz. castor sugar	7 oz. fresh butter

Sift flour and salt together. Cream yeast with a teaspoon of the sugar. Add remainder to the flour. Pour 1 gill of the milk on to the yeast mixture, blend and add to the flour, working it to a smooth dough. Add rest of milk if necessary.

Beat and knead well on the board. When thoroughly smooth roll out to $\frac{1}{2}$ inch thickness. Divide the butter into pieces the size of a small walnut. Press all over the surface of the paste. Fold in three and roll out away from you as for puff pastry (see page 836). Fold in three and set aside 15 minutes. Then give the paste two or three turns until the butter is well worked in, and the paste does not look streaky. Chill 1 hour (until firm) or leave overnight.

DANISH ALMOND BUNS

Danish pastry (see page 797) flaked browned almonds
glacé or fondant icing (see
  pages 827 and 862)

Filling

1½ oz. butter   1 oz. ground almonds
1½ oz. icing sugar   vanilla

Cream the butter, add the sugar by degrees. Add the almonds and a few drops of vanilla.

Roll out the pastry ½ inch thick and spread the filling over. Roll up like a Swiss roll. Cut into pieces 1–1½ inches wide. Lay on a lightly buttered baking-sheet about 2 inches apart. Prove 10–15 minutes. Bake 15–20 minutes in a hot oven. When cool coat each with the icing and sprinkle with the almonds.

Alternative shapes

Roll out the pastry ½ inch thick, stamp out into rounds, brush lightly with water. Put a spoonful of the filling into the middle of each round. Fold lightly over, prove and bake as before. When cool coat with the icing and sprinkle with the almonds.

Pinwheels

Roll out the pastry to between ¼ and ½ inch thick. Cut into squares of about 2½–3 inches. Make a cut starting ¼ inch from the middle to each corner of the square. Put a small piece of the filling in the middle, bend each corner of the square over and press down lightly to hold it in position. Prove and bake. Ice as before.

The following recipe, which comes from a village baker near Angers, is for a wonderfully light galette for tea. It is large and round, about the size of a meat plate, and is best eaten warm with butter and honey.

GALETTE DE SAVENNIÈRES

10 oz. flour   ¼ glass warm milk (2½ fluid oz.)
⅛ oz. yeast   2 eggs
½ glass warm water (5 fluid oz.) extra flour or milk as required
2 oz. butter   beaten egg or sugar and milk
1 oz. sugar   to glaze
a pinch of salt

Put about 3 oz. of the flour into a small basin, make a hole in the middle and crumble in the yeast. Add slowly the warm water, mixing in the flour and the yeast and smoothing away any lumps. Cover the basin and set to sponge 15–20 minutes.

Meanwhile melt the butter, sugar, and salt in the warm milk. Put the remainder of the flour in a mixing bowl. Beat in the eggs and pour in the warm milk and the yeast mixture. Mix all thoroughly with the fingers, then, tilting the bowl, beat the batter to incorporate air, allowing it to flop against the side of the basin. Continue for about 3 minutes; the batter should be fairly thick. Add extra flour or milk according to the consistency of the batter. Cover with a cloth and let it rise for 20 minutes in a warm place. Turn out on to a greased baking-sheet, spreading it into as even a circle as you can. (It should be about 1 inch thick in the middle and firm enough to retain its round shape on the baking-sheet without spreading itself too thinly.) Let it rise again about 20 minutes, uncovered. With the back of a long knife make three or four lines about 2 inches apart both ways across the top, and bake in a hot oven about 20 minutes. Almost at the end of cooking glaze with beaten egg or sugar and milk.

XXVII

Cakes

ENGLISH CAKES

CAKE-MAKING always seems to have played an important part in the English kitchen, to say nothing of English history. Our cakes differ from the French gâteaux and from the European coffee cakes; the old-fashioned customs of offering a light fruit cake at the end of luncheon and plum cake for five o'clock tea both have an English feeling.

I think we may roughly classify English cakes as follows: (1) plain cakes which may be made with butter or dripping, may have few eggs or none, and in which a small quantity of fruit or peel may or may not appear; (2) rich cakes which call for a greater proportion of butter and eggs, and where fruit cakes are concerned a plentiful addition of fruit and peel; (3) sponge mixtures of English sponge cakes, Swiss rolls and suchlike; and (4) gingerbreads, which range from the homeliest to rich mixtures, and are really in a class by themselves. All these have classic ingredients and methods which distinguish them and which are worth considering in detail.

Nearest to our English cakes are those of the United States of America; some of the old and treasured recipes may well have been carried over there by the Pilgrim Fathers and later emigrants, and the American woman has built up a magnificent tradition of cake-making from which we may borrow and use many ideas. Two books referred to in other chapters, *The Boston Cooking School Cook Book* and *The Joy of Cooking*, are full of excellent information about cakes and, in particular, of practical and delicious icings, and so these books are much appreciated in England.

The French gâteaux and the proper French génoise, which is the lightest and perhaps the most perfect of delicate cake mixtures, will be discussed in a later chapter.

Before dealing with the various methods of mixing which control the type of cake, a word should be said about individual ingredients.

1. The flour. White flour is generally used and should be of the best, and be dried, warmed, and sifted for use.

2. The fat. This may be butter, margarine, dripping, or, on occasion, lard. It is usually incorporated by being rubbed into the flour; for certain types of cake it is melted and added with the warm liquid, or it may be creamed and beaten with castor sugar.

3. The sugar. This may be castor, granulated, or brown. If brown sugar is used the dark brown Barbados or the paler sand sugar is generally taken in preference to demerara.

4. Dried fruit. Many fruits obtainable to-day are carefully prepared, cleaned, and packed before distribution. Then all that is required is to separate them and, when the recipe calls for it, dust them lightly with flour. Fruit sold loose, currants in particular, is put into a fine sieve, washed by being rubbed gently to and fro with the hand, and then dried, or it may be cleaned by being rubbed in flour in the sieve. Sometimes the currants are put into cold water and just brought up to boiling-point. This has the effect of plumping up the fruit.

5. Liquids. These are best used at room heat and not freshly taken from the refrigerator.

6. Baking-powders and baking-soda. Baking-powder is generally employed in the making of scones and small cakes, but even in the following recipes for larger cakes it is on occasions called for, though more often one finds bicarbonate of soda enumerated in the ingredients. This alkali, when mixed with an acid, gives off carbonic acid gas and therefore becomes a leavening agent. For scones, breads, and so forth the acid is generally cream of tartar, but bicarbonate of soda, together with, say, lemon or fruit juice or sour milk, will also have a raising power. Bicarbonate of soda used alone also has an effect on the texture and colour of the cakes, softening and darkening, and is therefore good for plain fruit cakes. Baking-powder and sometimes bicarbonate of soda may be added by being sieved with the flour, but frequently bicarbonate of soda is added at the end of the cake-mixing with a couple of tablespoons of lukewarm liquid taken from the amount called for in the recipe. After the soda has been stirred into the lukewarm liquid the mixture is immediately added to the cake mixture as a final process. Care should be taken not to add soda in excess of the amount called for, for not only will this, if acid is also present in the cake, cause it to rise too much and then to fall down in the baking, but the taste of excessive soda is unpleasant.

7. Eggs. These may be hens', ducks', or goose eggs, and if it is borne in mind that a hen's egg weighs approximately 2 oz. the necessary adjustments may be made if other types of egg are used. Duck eggs are less satisfactory for mixtures calling for separate beating of the whites. Vinegar is sometimes taken in place of eggs in the interests of economy.

The following list of proportions of ingredients for plain cakes is offered as a guide:

Per pound of flour:

Butter or margarine	6–8 oz.
or	
Margarine and lard mixed	6 oz.
or	
Dripping	4–6 oz.

Dried fruit	6–12 oz.
Sugar, brown	6–8 oz.
Eggs	2–3
or	
Vinegar	3 tablespoons
Milk	1½ gills to ½ pint
Baking-soda	1 teaspoon, slightly rounded
Spices	1 teaspoon, slightly rounded

METHODS OF MIXING

Method 1.   *The rubbing-in method*

In this the fat is lightly rubbed into the flour with the tips of the fingers before other ingredients are added.

Method 2.   *The heating method*

In this the fat, together with the liquid, is heated before being cooled and added to the dry ingredients.

Method 3.   *The creaming method*

In this the butter is first creamed alone and then beaten with the sugar, before other ingredients are added.

Method 4.   *The sponge method*

In this either the eggs and sugar are beaten together or the yolks and sugar worked together and the whipped whites added at the last.

The first two methods, rubbing in the fat and heating it with the liquid, are applied to the simpler kinds of cake, the creaming method to rich mixtures, and the fourth to sponge cakes. Each method should be examined in detail, and perhaps attention should first be drawn to the matter of mixing with the fingers or with the hand. When fat is to be rubbed into the flour, coolness is an asset, so the hands are first well washed in warm water and then rinsed in cold. When the butter is to be creamed, the natural warmth of the hand facilitates the process, so washing and rinsing in warm water is suitable.

Method 1

In this the fat, varying in kind and proportion according to the type of cake in hand, is rubbed in with the fingers; this should be done thoroughly so that it is evenly distributed throughout the flour. When properly done the fat is no longer distinguishable and the flour acquires a rougher, somewhat crumbly appearance. During the process the flour should be raised with the fingers and allowed to drop down into the bowl from time to time: this keeps it cool and aerated. If this process is carried out too heavily or continued for too long the mixture, instead of being light, firm, and crumbly, becomes moist. After the incorporation of the fat is completed other dry ingredients are added, sugar and fruit, etc., then the eggs (or vinegar in their place) and finally the milk and the baking-soda. After the addition of liquid the mixture is not beaten but merely stirred thoroughly and then turned into a cake tin.

The following summing-up of rules for the above method will serve for reference:

1. Sift the flour with the spices into a bowl.

2. Rub the fat well into the flour, lifting the flour up all the time, and rubbing and sifting it through the fingers.

3. Mix in the sugar, cleaned fruit, chopped peel, nuts, etc.

4. Beat the eggs until frothy, and mix them with a good three-quarters of the milk. If using vinegar in the place of eggs, pour the milk on to the vinegar in a deep bowl or jug.

5. Heat the remaining milk until barely lukewarm, then add the soda.

6. Mix the eggs and milk (or vinegar and milk) quickly and lightly into the dry ingredients, then lastly add the milk and soda.

N.B. Sour milk may be used with advantage, and if this is done a smaller amount of soda is required.

7. Stir only enough to mix thoroughly. Do not beat vigorously as this toughens the mixture and makes the cake heavy. The consistency of the mixture should be moist without being wet; it should just drop from the spoon.

8. Turn immediately into a prepared cake tin, i.e. greased, papered, and floured, and bake in a moderate oven, 350°–380° F., 40 minutes to $1\frac{1}{2}$ hours according to the size of the cake. Rock-cakes, plain fruit, vinegar, eggless, and dripping cakes are made by this method.

Method 2

This is employed for purposes of economy, usually for those cakes requiring no eggs and for some of the simple gingerbreads.

The dry ingredients are put all together into a bowl, and the fat, water, syrup, etc., are heated together, and sometimes actually boiled. They are then well cooled before being stirred into the dry ingredients. This is important, because otherwise the flour would start to cook and the mixture become tough and rubbery. Again, the mixture is stirred and not beaten. In this method baking-soda and baking-powder are sometimes used together, and are sifted into the flour, the soda being used to darken the cake. The proportion of raising agent is rather higher than in cakes containing eggs. (Bicarbonate of soda and cream of tartar, mixed in the proportion of one part soda to two parts cream of tartar, form a leavening agent. For keeping purposes these are mixed with rice flour, see Baking-powder, page 801.)

Method 3

This forms the basis of many cakes, from an English génoise or Victoria sponge sandwich to rich fruit cake.

For this the butter or margarine is first creamed with the hand, then the sugar—castor sugar in this case—is beaten in by degrees. After this the remainder of the mixing is carried out with a spatula, or, in default of this, with a wooden spoon. The eggs are added, in some cases whole, in some cases the yolks only, the whites being whipped and added at the last. A small quantity of flour is beaten in with each egg to prevent curdling and then the other ingredients are added. Baking-powder is the most commonly used raising agent for these cakes, but if six eggs or more to each pound of flour are employed this may be omitted, as for example for a rich Madeira cake, where a smooth close texture is wanted. Sometimes the recipe specifically calls for the eggs to be added whole, otherwise the procedure is as follows: Beat the yolks well into the creamed butter with a small spoonful of flour for each yolk, then whip the whites stiffly and fold them into the mixture with the remaining flour.

Proportions for a creamed sponge cake

For this allow equal quantities of butter, sugar, and flour, one egg to every 2 oz. of each ingredient, and no other liquid. The result of this mixture without any raising agent will be close-textured, like the Madeira cake already mentioned, but if baking-powder is added, or if self-raising flour is used to these proportions, a light, spongy, English génoise or Victoria sponge is the result; when baking-powder is employed it is taken in the proportions of two level teaspoons to every pound of flour.

Proportions for a plainer cake

For a less rich cake the flour, instead of being equal in proportion to butter and to sugar, may be increased by half—that is to say 6 oz. flour to 4 oz. sugar and 4 oz. butter. For this mixture a raising agent becomes necessary, so 1 teaspoon baking-powder is mixed in with the flour (or self-raising flour is used), and the recipe would then be:

4 oz. butter or unsalted margarine	6 oz. plain or self-raising flour
4 oz. castor sugar	1 level teaspoon baking-powder if plain flour is used
2 eggs	½ gill milk

and the mixture should be of dropping consistency.

GENERAL RULES FOR THE MAKING OF CAKES BY THE CREAMING METHOD

1. The butter or unsalted margarine must be reasonably soft before creaming, that is to say at room temperature and not straight out of the refrigerator.

2. The butter should be creamed without the sugar first until it is light and white-looking; it will take at least 5 minutes for a small cake, and, as has already been said, is best done with the hand, although if the quantity is less than 4 oz. a small wooden spatula is to be preferred as being less wasteful. If the weather is very cold the bowl may be warmed first; this

should be done by filling it with hot water, then emptying and drying; the bowl should not be put into the oven, either with or without the fat in it.

3. Having creamed the butter thoroughly, clean off your hand with a palette-knife and change to a wooden spatula; add the sugar by degrees and continue beating until all is soft and white.

4. Now add the eggs, one at a time, with a spoonful of the sifted flour. If the eggs are to be separated, beat in the yolks only.

5. Beat thoroughly, adding flavouring or fruit at this stage: glacé cherries (halved and rolled in flour), stoned raisins, currants, sultanas, grated orange rind, caraway seed, and so on.

6. If liquid is called for it is added now with a small proportion of the flour—the flour serves to prevent the mixture from curdling.

7. Add now the remaining flour (sifted with the baking-powder if this is required), and, if the eggs have been separated, the stiffly beaten whites should be folded in with the flour.

8. It is important that all the beating should be done at the initial stages of mixing, and not after flour has been added. If flour is beaten too much it becomes elastic and gives the cake a tough and unpleasant texture. Failure to cream the butter properly and then to beat in the sugar thoroughly will result in a dry and uninteresting cake. It is the initial beating that makes a cake light and gives it a damp and moist texture which it will keep for some time.

Sometimes rich fruit cakes are steamed for the major part of their cooking, and dried off and coloured by a final spell in the oven. This produces a moist cake and is a favourite method for Christmas and similar fruit cakes. The approximate division may be taken as two-thirds of the whole time for steaming and one-third for finishing in the oven.

Method 4. Sponge cakes

The ingredients for sponge cakes are eggs, sugar, and flour. Generally speaking no baking-powder is called for, although it is included in certain American recipes. Its effect is to make the cake rise very much, and unless eaten at once it is apt to become dry and unpalatable, whereas a sponge cake made with adequate eggs and sugar and flour, and without baking-powder, will remain fresh for many days.

There are two types of sponge cake, (I) in which the whole eggs and the sugar are whipped together over a gentle heat till thick, with the flour sifted and folded in at the last, and (II) in which the eggs are separated, the yolks creamed and beaten with the sugar, the whites stiffly whipped and folded into the mixture with the sifted flour. The first method makes a damp, soft, and slightly sticky sponge without a crust and is suitable for Swiss rolls or sponge sandwich to be filled with jam or fruit and cream, the second method gives a more spongy and a firmer consistency with a definite crust on the top of the cake, though this also depends to some extent on the proportion of sugar to eggs; this may be served to eat with fruit or as a tea-time cake. For both methods the following proportions may be taken as a guide: to each egg 1½–2 oz. sugar and ¾–1¼ oz. flour. Sometimes fécule (potato flour or arrowroot) is mixed with a proportion of plain flour and used in method II; this gives a cake with a shorter and more fluffy consistency. Sponge cakes are usually flavoured with lemon rind or orange-flower or rose-water added to the mixture, or with rose geranium or lemon verbena leaves laid in the bottom of the cake tin.

GENERAL RULES FOR SPONGE CAKES

1. Use castor sugar and the finest flour available, sift this well and dry it before using.

2. Remove the thread from the egg yolks before beating.

Method I

1. Whisk the whole eggs and sugar over gentle heat. If using a copper bowl set this over a large pan of very hot water or over gentle direct heat. If a china bowl is used, stand in a large bowl of boiling water.

2. Use a balloon or fine wire whisk [1] for beating and start to whisk slowly and steadily with an upward movement all the time, gradually increasing the speed of whisking as the mixture thickens. This process will take 10 minutes and the time should not be curtailed.

3. When the mixture is really thick, take the bowl away from the heat and go on whisking for another 5 minutes. By this time the mixture should have the consistency of softly whipped cream.

4. Remove the whisk and sift in the flour through a round wire strainer, folding it in with a large metal spoon. As soon as this is done turn the mixture into a prepared cake tin.

Method II

For this the yolks and sugar are beaten together and the whites whipped separately and folded in with the flour. For the beating of yolks and sugar take a heavier type of whisk or a wooden spatula. Beat until thick and pale in colour. The beating is properly effected when some of the mixture, lifted on the spatula, will fall from it in a smooth, steady ribbon. See the whipping and beating of eggs, page 287. The whipped whites are then added two tablespoons at once, a sifting of flour is sprinkled over them each time, and both are folded in.

A slow oven is essential for a sponge cake (see oven temperatures on page 60). For Swiss roll or small cakes the top shelf is used, a larger cake should be put on the middle or bottom shelf. Average baking time for a 4–6-egg sponge is 40 minutes to 1 hour, a Swiss roll takes 15–20 minutes, and a sponge sandwich 20–30 minutes.

---

[1] Students often ask whether a rotary whisk is not equally suitable; a rotary whisk serves several useful purposes, but for the whipping of whole eggs and for egg whites a balloon whisk is more effective. By the movement of the whisk, the lifting of the mixture, air is incorporated and a lighter cake is achieved.

Before giving recipes for the various types of cake the method of preparing cake tins must be dealt with.

A perfectly smooth, shining interior surface is required for cake and bread tins, and this may be preserved by the use of fine metal wool when washing up.

The preparation of the tins

A fine film of grease is required over the whole interior surface; this is best obtained by using, for plain and fruit cakes in particular, melted lard. A pot of this, together with brush, should be kept for this special purpose. The melted lard should be spread evenly and thinly over the surface, and care taken to leave no surplus. When the directions call for a dusting of flour, this is then sprinkled in, the tin turned from side to side to distribute the flour over the side and the bottom, and then turned upside-down and gently knocked to remove any surplus.

If a cake calls for fairly long baking—a plain or rich fruit mixture, for example—the instructions may call for the tin to be lined with paper, and this is done in the following manner: Cut a strip of grease-proof paper for the sides, to come about 2 inches above the edge of the tin, and cut a circle for the base of the tin. Turn up about 1 inch of the side paper along the edge and snip this hem with slantwise cuts, so that the side strip of paper will remain firmly in place when it is used to line the tin. This cut hem of paper lies flat on the bottom of the tin.

First of all brush the tin evenly with melted lard; arrange the side paper and the circle at the bottom, then brush the paper over with melted lard, and if the tin is to be floured this is done now. When very large, rich fruit cakes have to be baked, in addition to these precautions a thick band of brown paper may be tied round the outside of the tin; the tin may also be set in a pan or roasting-tin of rock-salt while baking takes place. These precautions are to prevent burning.

Preparing a tin for a sponge cake

For this purpose olive oil may be used, clarified butter, or, at need, clarified unsalted margarine, but it should be noted that excess of salt or water in either of these two latter may cause the cakes to stick; lard may also be used. For a sponge cake the sides of the tin may be left unlined and only a round of paper for the bottom of the tin used. The preparation of the tin is carried out in the same way as for an ordinary cake, except that a little castor sugar is added to the flour for the dusting, and for flavouring a few leaves of rose, geranium, or verbena, or scented mint leaves, may be arranged on the bottom of the tin. Again, if a very large cake is in hand, a thick band of brown paper tied round the outside of the tin is a sensible precaution. It should be noted that some cooks and cookery books call for the process of greasing to be done with the tips of the fingers, and if this is done great care should be taken to ensure that the distribution of the butter, oil, or lard is even.

Preparing a cake tin for a Swiss roll

The sponge for a Swiss roll may be baked in a special Swiss roll tin, which varies in size from 10–12 inches in length and about 5–9 inches in width. The tin is well brushed with melted lard, the bottom only lined with grease-proof paper, and the whole rebrushed and dusted out with flour, sometimes with flour and sugar. A Swiss roll may also be baked in a paper case, which is convenient when a tin of the right size is not available. This case is made from either thick grease-proof or cartridge-paper in the form of a rectangle. A plain sheet of paper approximately 9–10 inches long by about 7–8 inches wide is taken, the sides are folded in to the depth of approximately 1–1¼ inches, and the corners are mitred and fastened with a paper clip. The inside of the case is then brushed with melted lard or oil and lightly dusted out with flour. The case should be laid on a baking-sheet before the mixture is poured in.

The turning out of a Swiss roll sponge

Dust a sheet of grease-proof paper well with castor or icing sugar; reverse the cake tin on to this sheet of paper, tear away the paper in strips. If the sponge has been baked in a paper case, remove first the corner clips and press the sides carefully down, then proceed as before.

The filling of a Swiss roll

Immediately the cake has been turned out on to the sugared paper and the edges have been trimmed, the jam, slightly warmed, should be spread on fairly thickly. If jelly is to be used this may be thoroughly broken up with a fork. The cake is then rolled up lengthwise. If the jam or jelly for some reason is not ready, the sponge may be rolled up with the paper still inside and left until the filling is prepared. Equally, if it is to be filled with whipped cream or butter cream it is rolled up with the paper inside and left until cold, and then gently unrolled and spread with the cream.

Testing to see if a cake is sufficiently cooked

The first indications that cooking is completed is that a certain amount of shrinkage has taken place, and this will be noticed round the sides of the tin. A further test is to take a fine warm skewer or steel knitting-needle and push it gently into the cake; if it comes out absolutely clean the cake may be assumed to be cooked through. This is a test to use with discretion in the case of sponge and génoise mixtures, for if a hole is made in a partially cooked cake of this type, the whole may fall. A little experience will indicate when a cake of this kind is ready.

Baking temperatures

A list of these will be found on page 823.

The keeping of cakes

Cakes if properly made should for the most part keep a week if in an air-tight tin. The richer the cake, that is to say the greater the proportion of butter, eggs, and fruit to flour, the longer it will keep, and fruit cakes in particular will improve with keeping.

DRIPPING CAKE

1 lb. flour	½ pint milk (approx.)
6 oz. good dripping	1 large tablespoon black treacle
2 oz. candied orange peel	2 eggs
½ lb. raisins	1 teaspoon bicarbonate of soda
6 oz. sugar (pieces or Barbados)	

Sift flour and rub in the dripping thoroughly. Chop the candied peel and stone the raisins. Add to the flour with the sugar. Beat the eggs to a froth and stir into the mixture with enough cold milk to make a stiff paste. Warm ½ gill of the milk with the treacle, mix with soda and add. The mixture should drop easily from the spoon. Turn into a greased and papered cake tin, and bake in a moderate to slow oven 1½–2 hours.

This is a good well-keeping cake, suitable for lunch or country tea.

VINEGAR CAKE

This is a plainish cake, without eggs, and suitable for picnics or packed lunch, eaten with cheese.

6 oz. butter or dripping	¼ lb. stoned raisins
1 lb. flour	3 tablespoons vinegar
½ lb. sugar	just over ¼ pint milk
¼ lb. currants	1 teaspoon bicarbonate of soda

Rub the fat well into the flour, add the sugar and cleaned fruit. Put the vinegar into a large jug and add the milk, reserving a spoonful or two. Warm this slightly and mix it with the soda. Add quickly to the jug, being careful to hold it over the bowl as the mixture will froth up.

Stir it at once into the mixture and turn into a prepared tin. Bake in a moderate oven for the first 20 minutes and then lower the heat slightly for the next 40–50 minutes.

LORRIMER PLUM CAKE

This should not be eaten for at least a week after being made.

½ lb. butter, dripping, or margarine	1 large teaspoon mixed spice
1 lb. flour	grated rind of 1 lemon
¾ lb. brown sugar	1 bottle stout (½ pint)
½ lb. currants	4 eggs
½ lb. raisins, stoned, or sultanas	1 teaspoon bicarbonate of soda
¼ lb. candied peel, chopped	

Rub fat into sifted flour, add sugar, fruit, peel, spice, and lemon rind. Whisk the stout for a minute, add the beaten eggs and soda. Pour on to the dry ingredients and mix thoroughly. Turn into a prepared cake tin and bake in a slow to moderate oven 1½–2 hours. Keep for at least a week in an air-tight tin before cutting.

LUNCHEON CAKE (1)

An economical cake. It should be made at least a day before required.

2 oz. butter or margarine
1 lb. plain flour
½ lb. brown sugar
2 level teaspoons mixed spice
¾ lb. stoned raisins or sultanas

1½ level teaspoons bicarbonate
   of soda
½ level teaspoon salt
½ pint sour milk
2 tablespoons salad-oil

Rub butter into flour, add the sugar, spice, and fruit, mix the soda and salt with the milk. Make a well in the dry mixture, pour in the milk and oil and stir well together. Immediately it is mixed turn into a greased and papered cake tin. Bake in a moderately slow oven, 375° F., for 1–1½ hours. Keep at least a day before cutting.

This is a good plain cake, and keeps moist and good for picnics where a good wedge of cake is called for.

LUNCHEON CAKE (2)

Very good; eggless; as rich as you like in fruit.

¾ lb. flour
¼ teaspoon each of ground cin-
   namon and nutmeg
½ teaspoon mixed spice
a pinch of salt
2½ oz. butter, margarine, or
   dripping
6 oz. soft brown sugar

6 oz. currants
10 oz. sultanas and raisins mixed
1 oz. finely chopped candied peel
1–2 oz. cherries
grated rind of ½ a lemon
½ cup apple juice or cider
1 cup milk
¾ teaspoon bicarbonate of soda

Sieve the flour with the spices and salt, rub in the fat finely, add sugar, the cleaned sultanas and currants, peel, cherries, and lemon rind. Mix thoroughly. Make a well in the middle of the ingredients, pour in the apple juice. Warm 2 tablespoons milk with the soda and add to the well with the remaining milk. Stir until well mixed, turn into a prepared cake tin and leave to stand 12 hours. Bake in a very moderate oven (350° F.) for 1–1½ hours.

This cake keeps well and is surprisingly good for an eggless cake. It was a great stand-by in the war as a Christmas cake, and most popular. The amount of fruit can be varied according to taste and availability.

LUNCHEON CAKE (3)

Very good; suitable for a birthday cake.

¾ lb. butter or margarine
¾ lb. castor sugar
1 lb. plain flour
½ lb. currants
4 oz. sultanas
2 oz. glacé cherries
2 oz. dates
6 oz. raisins

1 teaspoon bicarbonate of soda
½ teaspoon mixed spice
a pinch of ground nutmeg
3 eggs
½ tea-cup of orange or lemon
   squash
1 dessertspoon caramel
a little cider or milk to mix

Cream the butter or margarine, add the sugar, beat thoroughly. Divide the flour into three parts; mix the fruit into one part, the soda and spice into another, and leave the third part plain. Beat the eggs into the creamed mixture, adding the plain flour.

Mix in the fruit and flour with the squash and caramel, lastly the soda and flour with enough cider or milk to make a soft mixture. Turn into a buttered and papered tin and bake slowly 1½–2 hours. The cake may be baked in one large tin or two smaller ones.

SPICE CAKE

3 oz. margarine	¼ teaspoon nutmeg
3 tablespoons golden syrup, *or*	¼ teaspoon cinnamon
6 oz. sugar	¼ teaspoon ginger
1 egg	1 tablespoon lemon juice
6 oz. self-raising flour	1 tablespoon water
a pinch of salt	12 oz. sultanas
	grated rind of 1 lemon

Topping

2 tablespoons flour	¼ teaspoon ginger
2 tablespoons brown sugar	1 oz. margarine
¼ teaspoon nutmeg	1 oz. shelled walnuts

For the cake. Brush a cake tin with melted lard and line with grease-proof paper. Cream the margarine with the golden syrup or sugar and beat in the egg. Beat well, until the mixture is light and fluffy. Sift the flour with the salt and the spices, and add to the mixture alternately with the lemon juice and water, mixed together. Lastly stir in the sultanas and the lemon rind. Put into the prepared tin and smooth flat.

For the topping. Mix together the flour, brown sugar, and spices and cut the margarine into the mixture with a fork. When the mixture is crumbly scatter it over the top of the cake. Add the shelled walnuts, roughly chopped. Bake for 1 hour 10 minutes in a moderate oven. This can be served hot as a sweet or cold as a cake.

PLUM CAKE

An excellent old-fashioned plum cake; keeps well.

½ lb. butter	4 oz. mixed peel, finely chopped
½ lb. moist sugar	grated rind of ½ a lemon
½ lb. currants	3 eggs
½ lb. sultanas	½ lb. flour
½ lb. raisins, stoned	½ teaspoon baking-powder
2 oz. ground almonds	2 tablespoons sherry
2 oz. shredded almonds	a little milk

Cream butter, add sugar and beat thoroughly. Clean fruit, add with almonds, peel, lemon rind, eggs, and a little of the flour to prevent the mixture curdling. Sift baking-powder with rest of flour and stir in with the sherry and enough milk for the mixture to drop from the spoon when finished. Turn into a paper-lined tin and bake in a slow oven, 375° F., for 1–1½ hours.

Spice may be added if wished, but it is not used unless the cake is required for a Christmas or birthday cake.

RICH PLUM CAKE (1)

Suitable for a wedding or Christmas cake.

½ lb. butter
½ lb. brown sugar (Barbados)
6 eggs
grated rind and juice of 1 lemon
¼ teaspoon each of ground cinnamon, ground cloves, mixed
  spice, and ground nutmeg
½ cup black treacle
¾ lb. plain flour

2 lb. dried fruit: 12 oz. currants, 8 oz. sultanas, 8 oz.
  stoned raisins, 2 oz. glacé
  cherries, 2 oz. candied orange
  peel
1 cup fruit juice, cider, or milk
1 level teaspoon bicarbonate of
  soda
¼ cup rum

Cream the butter, add sugar, and cream again. Beat in egg yolks with lemon rind and juice, spices, and treacle. Work in half the flour with half the fruit, with enough liquid to moisten. Add bicarbonate of soda to remaining flour and add with rest of fruit. Before it is completely mixed, whip whites stiffly and fold in, adding remaining liquid and rum. Bake in a slow oven 2–3 hours.

The following cake is given as an example of a steamed cake:

RICH PLUM CAKE (2)

½ lb. butter
½ lb. sugar (brown is best)
5 eggs
½ lb. flour
2 teaspoons mixed spice
½ oz. grated nutmeg
2 or 3 lb. mixed fruits in
  variety
as much home-made candied
  peel as you like (page 1131)

½ cup golden syrup, failing this
  milk or milk and honey
a glass of sherry, brandy, cider,
  or beer
a pinch of bicarbonate of soda
  dissolved in a spoonful of
  water

Cream butter and sugar, beat well. Beat eggs and add, still beating. Sift flour, keep back a little to dredge over the fruits. Mix flour and spices and add to mixture. Add cleaned, floured fruit and liquids. Steam 3½ hours and finish off with 1½ hours in slow oven.

GUERNSEY CAKE
Miss Hay Newton, 1879

This is an old family recipe and very good.

¾ lb. butter
¾ lb. castor sugar (or brown if
  preferred)
¾ lb. dried cherries, slightly
  chopped
2 oz. sweet almonds, blanched
  and pounded
2 oz. orange candied peel, finely
  chopped or sliced

2 oz. angelica, chopped
8 egg yolks, well beaten
¼ lb. ground rice
2 tablespoons brandy or sherry
½ lb. dried and sifted flour
3 egg whites whipped to a firm
  snow

Cream butter, then mix in the ingredients in the order mentioned, folding in the whites at the last. Turn into a paper-lined tin and bake in a slow oven for approximately 1 hour 20 minutes. Above quantity makes one large cake, or two of smaller size.

DUNDEE CAKE

6 oz. butter	3 oz. glacé cherries, halved
6 oz. castor sugar	grated rind and juice of ½ a
4 small eggs	lemon
1 oz. ground almonds	6 oz. flour
8 oz. sultanas	1 level teaspoon baking-powder
8 oz. currants	½–1 oz. split almonds
3 oz. mixed peel, chopped	heavily sweetened milk

Cream butter thoroughly, work in the castor sugar, when white and creamy beat in the eggs one at a time, with a good dusting of flour for each egg, and the ground almonds. Add the sultanas and currants, well cleaned, and the peel, cherries, and lemon. Stir in the remaining flour sifted with the baking-powder. Turn into a prepared cake tin and bake in a moderately slow oven about 1½–2 hours. When the cake is half cooked scatter the split almonds over the top. Five or ten minutes before taking out of the oven brush over with heavily sweetened milk.

LEMON WHISKY CAKE

Preparations must begin the day before the cake is wanted.

R. H. says: 'This was always the favourite cake made for shooting parties (and eaten freshly made for tea) at the big house in Ireland we used to visit when I was a child.'

3 eggs, their weight in butter, castor sugar, and flour	1 large lemon
	¾ gill whisky
6 oz. sultanas	1 teaspoon baking-powder

Pare off the rind of the lemon very thinly. Put it into a wineglass with the whisky. Do this the day before making the cake.

Cream the butter, beat in the sugar until white. Separate the eggs and sift the flour. Add the yolks one at a time with a spoonful of the flour, beating thoroughly. Mix the sultanas in with the strained whisky and a little more of the flour. Whip the whites stiffly and fold into the mixture with the remaining flour and the baking-powder. Turn into a greased and papered tin and bake in a moderate oven 1–1½ hours.

This mixture makes an excellent seed cake, using a dessertspoon of caraway seeds in place of the sultanas.

VICTORIA SPONGE SANDWICH

3 eggs, their weight in butter, castor sugar, and self-raising flour (or 1½ teaspoons baking-powder and plain flour)	good jam
	icing or castor sugar

Cream the butter until it looks like whipped cream. Add the sugar and beat until white. Add the eggs one at a time with a good spoonful of sifted flour. Beat thoroughly. Sift the baking-powder with the remaining flour, stir quickly into the mixture. Turn into two sandwich tins 7 inches across, well buttered and floured; bake in a moderate oven 20–30 minutes. Turn out when cool, sandwich well with a good jam. Powder with icing or castor sugar.

The following is a good old-fashioned seed cake:

SEED CAKE

8 oz. flour	a good pinch of grated nutmeg
8 oz. butter	1 teaspoon caraway seeds
8 oz. castor sugar	2 tablespoons brandy
5 eggs	about a handful of caraway
3 oz. candied orange peel	comfits [1]

Sift and dry the flour, beat the butter to a cream with the hand, add the sugar gradually and beat to a fine white cream. Separate the yolks from the whites, beat in the yolks one at a time, with a teaspoon of flour added before each yolk. Add the candied peel, the grated nutmeg, the caraway seeds, and fold in the whisked whites of the eggs and the remaining flour. Lastly stir in the brandy and put the cake into a prepared tin. Strew over the comfits and bake in a moderate oven (360° F.) for an hour.

ORANGE CAKE

Very popular with children. R. H. says: 'Was always our choice for tea.'

2 eggs, their weight in butter, sugar, and flour	the finely grated rind and juice of 1 orange
1 teaspoon baking-powder	

Icing

4 oz. icing sugar	1 tablespoon stock syrup or
the juice of 1 orange	water
small quantity of apricot glaze (see page 856) or puréed jam	orange candied peel

Cream the butter, beat in the sugar until white. Separate the eggs and add the yolks one at a time with a dessertspoon of the flour and the orange rind and juice. Sift the remaining flour with the baking-powder. Whip the whites stiffly and fold in with the flour. Turn at once into a small prepared cake tin or sandwich tin, flatten and hollow slightly on the top. Bake in a moderate oven 20–30 minutes. Turn out and cool. Brush or spread the cake with a thin layer of apricot glaze or puréed jam; sieve the icing sugar, put into a small pan with the orange juice and work with the stock syrup or water to make a thick cream. Warm slightly and pour over the cake. Decorate with the peel, softened in a little hot water.

[1] Caraway comfits are sugared caraway seeds and may sometimes be bought at the confectioner's. They may be replaced by roughly crushed lump sugar.

HONEY CAKE

3 eggs	grated rind of ½ a lemon
2 tablespoons castor sugar	2 oz. corn-flour (good weight)
3 tablespoons honey	2½ oz. flour

Separate eggs, cream yolks with sugar, honey, and lemon rind 7 minutes until white. Sift in corn-flour and mix thoroughly. Fold in stiffly whipped whites with the flour, turn into a greased and sugared shallow cake tin and bake in a moderately slow oven for 35–40 minutes. It is advisable to line the tin with paper.

HONEY BREAD

8 oz. flour	1 tea-cup hot water
4 oz. sugar	1 teaspoon baking-powder, *or*
4 oz. honey	1 teaspoon bicarbonate of soda

Mix flour with the sugar in a bowl, melt honey in the water, add and mix thoroughly, sprinkle baking-powder or bicarbonate of soda on top and stir in. Turn into a loaf tin, bake slowly for about 1 hour. Spices or grated lemon rind may be added.

This type of cake should be served in thin buttered slices.

CHEESECAKE (CURD)

2 oz. butter	grated rind and juice of 1
4½ oz. sugar	lemon
10 oz. curd	2 oz. semolina (fine)
2 oz. ground almonds	2 oz. stoned raisins (optional)
	2 eggs

Cream the butter, add sugar and curd (sieved), beating well. Beat in the almonds, lemon rind and juice, semolina, raisins, and yolks of egg. Whip whites, fold into the mixture and turn into a shallow tin, well greased and floured and the bottom lined with paper. Bake in a moderate oven about 1 hour.

Curd may now be bought by the pound, and both best cream and cooking curd are obtainable. When it is not available a good substitute is bought milk cheese.

GINGERBREADS

These can be made by both the boiled and creamed methods. The finished mixture, really a batter, is much slacker than the ordinary cake mixtures. Gingerbread definitely improves by keeping. A slack oven should always be used for baking, because of the high proportion of treacle or syrup used.

Note on weighing treacle

The best method to weigh treacle is as follows: Weigh a cup or measure, leave on scales and add extra weight according to the amount of treacle called for. Pour treacle into the cup until the correct weight is reached. Warm the cup or measure first. This is a less messy way than flouring the scale pan and weighing treacle direct.

SPONGY GINGERBREAD

6 oz. flour
1½ teaspoons ground ginger
1½ teaspoons mixed spice
a pinch of salt
1 good teaspoon bicarbonate of soda
a pinch of cayenne
6 oz. wholemeal flour
12 oz. golden syrup

4 oz. castor sugar
6 oz. butter
1 large dessertspoon orange marmalade
2 eggs
1½ gills milk
sliced blanched almonds and sliced preserved ginger to finish (optional)

Sieve the flour with spices, salt, bicarbonate of soda, and cayenne. Add the wholemeal flour and mix together well. Warm the syrup, sugar, butter, and marmalade together until melted. Beat eggs with milk, pour into a well made in the flour, add warmed ingredients and mix together until a smooth batter is formed. Turn into a prepared tin and bake in a very moderate oven 1½ hours. Makes one large cake or two small ones. It is improved by sliced blanched almonds and sliced preserved ginger scattered over the top when baking is half done.

EVERYDAY GINGERBREAD

¼ lb. butter
6 oz. treacle
2 oz. golden syrup
¼ pint milk
2 eggs
½ lb. flour
2 oz. sugar

½ teaspoon mixed spice
½ teaspoon ground ginger
½ teaspoon bicarbonate of soda
1 oz. each of sultanas, sliced ginger, and shredded almonds (optional)

Warm together butter, treacle, syrup, and milk, allowing the mixture to get just hot enough for the ingredients to blend well. Add to the beaten eggs, mix with the dry ingredients, turn into a prepared tin and bake in a cool oven for 2 hours.

SPICED GINGER ROLL

4 oz. flour
a pinch of salt
1 level teaspoon ground cinnamon, mixed spice, and nutmeg mixed
1 teaspoon ground ginger
2 tablespoons golden syrup, good measure

2 tablespoons black treacle, good measure
2¼ oz. butter or margarine
1 egg
½ cup (4 liquid oz.) warm water
1 teaspoon bicarbonate of soda
red-currant jelly or apple purée

Sift flour, salt, spices, and ginger together. Melt syrup, treacle, and butter together. Whisk egg, add water and soda. Add quickly to the syrup mixture, then pour into the flour. Whisk lightly for about half a minute. Turn into a greased and paper-lined Swiss roll tin or paper case (11 × 9½ inches). Bake in a moderate oven 12–15 minutes. Turn out on to a paper well dusted with castor sugar, spread with warm red-currant jelly or a well-reduced apple purée. Trim edges and roll up carefully.

Whipped cream or coffee- or caramel-flavoured butter cream may also be used for filling.

Better used hot as a sweet, though not to be despised for a picnic or schoolroom tea.

BELVOIR GINGER CAKE

This must be made at least a day or two before required.

4 oz. butter	½ lb. plain flour
4 oz. brown sugar	½ teaspoon bicarbonate of soda
4 oz. sultanas	2–3 tablespoons milk
10 oz. (or a breakfast-cup) black treacle	a few blanched split almonds or 1 piece of stem ginger
1 teaspoon ground ginger	drained from syrup and
2 eggs	sliced

Cream butter, add sugar, cream again thoroughly. Then add fruit, treacle, ginger, and the eggs one at a time with about half of the flour. Mix thoroughly. Then add remaining flour with the soda warmed in the milk. Turn at once into a papered, greased, and floured tin (8-inch). Bake in a slow oven about an hour or more. When two-thirds baked scatter the top of the cake quickly with the almonds or preserved ginger. Finish baking.

This cake is excellent for a picnic eaten with a wedge of cheese, Cumberland fashion.

See also Ginger Sponge Cake, page 1029.

PARKIN

This must be made a day or two before required.

¾ lb. medium oatmeal	¼ lb. margarine or dripping
6 oz. flour	1 lb. treacle
1 tablespoon sugar	½ gill milk
¼ teaspoon ground ginger	½ teaspoon bicarbonate of soda
¼ teaspoon salt	

Mix first five ingredients thoroughly. Warm treacle and fat together, but do not allow to get too hot. Warm milk to blood heat, add soda, and mix into dry ingredients with the treacle mixture. Have ready a Yorkshire pudding or roasting-tin, well greased and floured and the bottom lined with paper; pour in the mixture. Bake in a moderate oven, 375°, for approximately 40 minutes or until firm to the touch. Flaked or shredded almonds can be scattered over the cake after the first 15 minutes in the oven.

Keep a day or two before use, then cut into squares as required. This recipe may be doubled if one wants to keep a supply in hand. Up to a point parkin improves with keeping. Excellent eaten with cheese, for 'elevenses' or lunch.

Chocolate Cakes

CHOCOLATE SPONGE CAKE

1 oz. sweetened chocolate	4½ oz. castor sugar
1½ oz. unsweetened chocolate	2¼ oz. flour
3 eggs	chocolate cream (see below)

Cook the chocolate with water to a thick cream, put aside to cool. Whisk the eggs with the sugar until thick. Stir in flour and chocolate. Turn into a greased and floured shallow tin. Bake 20–30 minutes (375° F). Sandwich with chocolate cream.

Chocolate cream

2 oz. sweetened chocolate	1 small beaten egg or ½ a large
scant ½ gill coffee or water	egg
½ oz. butter	1 dessertspoon rum or brandy

Put chocolate and liquid into a small pan. Heat over a slow fire to a thick cream. When little more than lukewarm draw aside to beat in butter and egg together. Flavour with the rum or brandy.

RICH CHOCOLATE CAKE

6 oz. sweetened block choco-late	1 coffeespoon sal volatile
6 oz. butter	2 oz. flour
3 oz. castor sugar	white fondant or glacé icing
3 oz. ground almonds	(see pages 862 and 827),
5 eggs	flavoured with rum

Break up chocolate and melt it over gentle heat. Cream the butter, add the sugar, and beat until soft and white. Beat in the chocolate with the almonds and egg yolks. Whip the whites stiffly and fold in with the sal volatile and flour. Bake in a slow oven 45–50 minutes.

Ice with a white fondant or glacé icing flavoured with rum.

CHOCOLATE CAKE (LADY PORTARLINGTON)

4 oz. sugar	½ oz. unsweetened block choco-late
3 eggs	
2½ oz. sweetened block choco-late	1½ oz. arrowroot or corn-flour

Work the sugar and yolks together until white. Grate and sift the chocolate and mix with the arrowroot. Sift again. Whip the whites stiffly and mix into the creamed yolks with the arrowroot and chocolate. Put into a well-buttered and floured shallow tin, approximately 6½ inches in diameter, and bake for 45 minutes in a slow oven. (This has been tried with 2 duck eggs and 1 hen's egg and the result was excellent and very light.)

On page 1027 of the Winkfield chapter will be found a recipe for a chocolate roll and another for a chocolate filling.

NUSSKUCHEN

3 oz. butter	2 tablespoons milk
3 oz. sugar	1 level teaspoon baking-powder
1 egg	1 white of egg
1½ oz. ground hazel-nuts	lightly whipped cream
3 oz. flour	chocolate marquise (see page
1 tablespoon coffee essence	863)

Bake nuts in oven till brown. Rub in a rough clean cloth to remove skins. Then grind in nut- or cheese-mill. Cream butter well, add the sugar, and beat until white. Beat in the egg, nuts, flour, and coffee essence; stir in the milk, baking-powder, and lastly the stiffly whipped white of egg. Turn into a greased and floured shallow cake tin and bake in a moderate oven 20–30 minutes. Turn out and when cool split and fill lavishly with lightly whipped cream. Just before using pour over it a chocolate marquise.

N.B. For a winter sweet fill with cooked apple:

Apple mixture

1 lb. apples	2 tablespoons apricot jam
rind and juice of 1 lemon	

Peel, core, quarter, and thickly slice the apples. Put them into a pan with the grated rind and juice of the lemon and the apricot jam. Cook fairly quickly till just soft without breaking the apples; avoid stirring, but shake the pan. Turn on to a plate to cool before using.

Sponge Cakes

PLAIN SPONGE CAKE

A useful all-purpose sponge, suitable for a sponge sandwich or a Swiss roll.

4 eggs	6 oz. castor sugar
3 oz. flour	a grating of lemon rind

Break the eggs into a bowl, add the sugar, and beat until thick over a gentle heat. Remove and continue whisking for another 5 minutes. Then add the lemon rind and fold in the sifted flour. Turn at once into a prepared cake or sandwich tin. Bake in a slow to moderate oven (350°–375° F.). For a firmer consistency add an additional ounce of flour; do this if the cake is to be iced.

The following recipe is for a firm sponge with a crust; it is particularly suitable for serving with fruit compôtes, etc., and keeps well.

OLD-FASHIONED SPONGE CAKE

5 eggs, their weight in castor sugar, and the weight of 3 eggs in flour	1 tablespoon orange-flower water

Separate the yolks from the whites. Take 1 tablespoon of sugar away from the total quantity for every egg white. Put the remaining sugar into a bowl with the egg yolks. Whisk over gentle heat until white and mousse-like. Add the orange-flower water. Whip the whites stiffly, incorporate the remaining sugar, and fold into the mixture with the sifted flour. Turn at once into a greased and sugared cake tin, and bake in a slow to moderate oven 40 minutes to 1 hour.

OLD-FASHIONED NORFOLK SPONGE CAKE

A good keeper and excellent for icing, being firm and smooth when baked.

4 eggs	½ lb. lump sugar
2 yolks	grated lemon rind to flavour,
6 oz. water	or orange-flower water
½ lb. plain flour	

Break eggs into a bowl, beat slightly. Dissolve sugar in water, then boil rapidly until the thread is reached (see page 860). Remove from fire and when off the boil pour in a steady stream on to the eggs, whisking all the time. Then whisk steadily until the mixture is very thick. Add the flavouring, then sift and fold in the flour. Turn at once into a prepared tin and bake in a moderately slow oven (375° F.) for about 1 hour. The above quantity makes two medium-sized cakes.

The following recipe is for a very soft, rich, sticky sponge, reminiscent of lemon curd. It keeps well.

GÂTEAU DE SAVOIE

3 eggs	grated rind and juice of a small
5 oz. castor sugar	lemon
2½ oz. fécule (potato flour) or 1¼ oz. each of arrowroot and flour	

Separate the eggs. Mix the sugar and fécule together and beat the yolks with a fork. Mix well into the dry ingredients with the lemon rind and juice. Whip the whites to stiff foam and fold into the mixture.

SWISS ROLL

4 eggs divided into yolks and whites	3½ oz. flour, less 1 tablespoon to be replaced by
a pinch of salt to add to whites	1 tablespoon corn-flour
6½ oz. castor sugar	1½ teaspoons baking-powder
1 tablespoon cold water mixed with	jam or jelly for filling and a little sugar for surface
1 teaspoon lemon extract or the same quantity orange-flower water	

Prepare oven sheet with greased paper turned up at edges to form a tray. Put in a few sweet geranium leaves if liked.   Measure all ingredients.

1. Sift mixed flours and baking-powder four times.

2. Sift sugar if uneven in texture and set aside 4 tablespoons to beat with whites.

3. Beat egg whites with salt till stiff, incorporate 3 spoonfuls of the sugar and add fourth at the last, folding it in.

4. Beat yolks to a ribbon, adding liquid gradually, and the remaining sugar.

5. Fold whites into yolks.

6. Fold in flour.

Pour on to tin moderately thinly, spread evenly.   Bake about 12 minutes in a moderate oven (350° F.).   Prepare jam or jelly by warming or beating so that it spreads easily.   Turn sponge on to paper or cloth sprinkled with sugar.   Remove greased paper quickly.   Spread jam and roll.

SWISS ROLL OR SPONGE SANDWICH (EASY)

4 oz. castor sugar	3 oz. flour
3 large eggs	½ teaspoon baking-powder
1 tablespoon tepid water	good jam for filling

Cream the sugar and yolks well together for at least 5 minutes.   Add water, then fold in the flour, sifted with the baking-powder, whip whites stiffly and fold them in a third at a time.   Turn into two sandwich tins and bake in a moderate oven 10–12 minutes.   Turn out, cool, sandwich together with a good jam.   Dust top with icing or castor sugar.

For a Swiss roll make a paper case (see page 808) or turn into a prepared Swiss roll tin.

SPONGE CAKE WITH FRUIT

A firm spongy cake with a crisp thick crust.

4 eggs, their weight in castor sugar, the weight of 1 egg in plain flour, and the weight of 1 egg in arrowroot or corn-flour	the grated rind of 1 lemon
	1 handful of currants or sultanas, previously cleaned and rolled in flour

Break 2 eggs and 2 yolks into a bowl, add sugar and whisk over hot water until very thick, 7–10 minutes. Remove from heat and continue whisking for another few minutes. Whisk whites stiffly, fold into the mixture with the sifted flours, the lemon rind, and fruit. Turn at once into a greased and floured cake tin and bake in a slow oven 40–50 minutes. N.B. It is advisable to line the bottom of the tin with greased paper before dusting the tin out with flour.

In the Winkfield chapter (page 1029) will be found a recipe for an admirable ginger sponge cake. It is a light sponge mixture containing chunks of preserved ginger; it is iced with fondant and decorated with thin slices of ginger. It contains no powdered ginger or spices and is pale gold in colour.

Small Cakes

COFFEE CAKES

Simple and good.

8 oz. flour	3 oz. castor sugar
2 heaped teaspoons baking-powder	1 large egg
	2–3 tablespoons milk
2 oz. butter	2–3 teaspoons coffee essence
2 oz. lard	

Filling

1½ oz. butter	coffee essence to flavour
2½ oz. icing sugar	

Sift flour and baking-powder together. Rub in the fats, add the sugar. Beat the egg with a fork, add milk and coffee essence. Pour into the middle of the bowl and stir with the fork, gradually drawing in the dry ingredients. When a stiff mixture put out on to a greased baking-sheet in about sixteen rough pieces. Bake about 15 minutes in a hot oven (400° F.). Take out, cool, split, and spread well with the filling towards the edge of each cake. Reshape and dust thickly with icing sugar.

For the filling, cream the butter very well and beat in the sifted icing sugar by degrees. Finish with the coffee essence and use while soft and creamy.

N.B. These are excellent small cakes for an emergency and should be eaten straight away. They are popular in the nursery or schoolroom, but lose their charm if kept.

Mixtures such as that for Victoria sponge may be used for small cakes to be cooked in patty pans or queen cake tins. The mixture may be changed by the addition of fruit, peel, or seeds; the Cream Sponge Cake mixture given on the next page is excellent for small cakes, and grated chocolate may be added as flavouring, but the best small cakes are made on the proper French génoise base and will be found in the chapter on pâtisserie, page 847.

As a general rule, small individual cakes are baked on the top shelf of the oven at approximately 375°–400° F.   Large cakes are put on the middle or lowest shelf and the temperature may begin at approximately 375° F. and be reduced to 350° F.   The arrangement of the oven shelves should be made before the cake is mixed.

BAKING TEMPERATURES

Type of Cake	Electric Stove	Radiation Stove Regulo Marks
Rich fruit	320°–340° F.	3
Madeira type	375°–380° F.	4–5
Sponge (large cake)	370° F.	4
in layer tins	390° F.	5
Large plain cake	350°–375° F.	4–5
Victoria sponge in sandwich tins	375°–400° F.	5–6
Small cakes	400° F.	6–7

AMERICAN CAKES

It is impossible, I think, to finish this chapter without discussing one or two American cakes, so I am again making use of the generous permission granted to me to quote from *The Boston Cooking School Cook Book*.[1]   It must, of course, be remembered in using these recipes that American measures differ from ours, their pints being 16 oz. instead of our 20 oz. They have properly regulated measuring spoons, and when they say a spoonful they mean a level spoonful.   In our kitchens we have tablespoons of more than one size and an English reference is generally to a rounded spoonful.   But in any case, before undertaking an American recipe you will do well to refer to the table of American measures on page 60.

I have chosen an American cream sponge containing baking-powder, and in this differing from our English sponge cake.   This is a good, smooth, creamy sponge and excellent for a Swiss roll.

CREAM SPONGE CAKE

4 egg whites
4 egg yolks
1 cup sugar
1½ tablespoons cold water
1½ tablespoons lemon juice

1 cup cake flour [2]
1¼ teaspoons baking-powder
¼ teaspoon salt
1 teaspoon vanilla

---

[1] Fannie Merritt Farmer, *The Boston Cooking School Cook Book* (Little, Brown & Co., Boston).

[2] In the U.S.A. it is possible to obtain various grades of white flour.   At the moment of writing we have not this facility and must use in cake-making the best white flour obtainable.

'1. Measure all ingredients. Sift sugar through fine sifter one to four times before measuring. Use pastry or cake flour and sift once before measuring. Separate yolks and whites of eggs. They will beat easily if at room temperature.

'2. Beat egg whites until stiff but not dry, and beat in gradually 1 tablespoon sugar for each egg white (out of sugar called for in recipe) and set aside. With sugar added, the whites will remain stiff for some time. It is unnecessary to wash beater before beating yolks.

'3. Add liquid to egg yolks and beat until lemon-coloured and so thick that rotary beater turns with difficulty. Beat in remaining sugar.

'4. Combine yolks and whites and fold together with spoon until mixture is even.

'5. Mix and sift remaining dry ingredients and cut and fold into egg mixture. Do not beat after adding flour, to avoid breaking air bubbles.'

This cake may be poured into two 8-inch sandwich tins and is baked about 25 minutes at 350° F.

The following Devil's Food Cake is another typical American cake, rich and very good, sometimes so soft it has to be eaten with a spoon.

DEVIL'S FOOD CAKE

Make the following mixture:

3 oz. unsweetened chocolate, shaved	1 gill milk
good 5 oz. brown sugar	1 teaspoon vanilla

Put chocolate, sugar, and milk into a pan and cook and stir them until they are quite smooth. Add the vanilla and cool.

Cake mixture

4 oz. butter	7 oz. brown sugar
2 eggs	1 gill milk
8 oz. flour sifted with 1 teaspoon bicarbonate of soda	

Cream the butter, add the sugar, and beat until light and creamy. Beat in the eggs. Add the cold chocolate mixture and beat again. Add the sifted flour and the milk and stir well. Bake in two sandwich tins, buttered and with the bottom lined with oiled paper. Cook in a moderate oven for about 20 minutes.[1] Turn out and allow to become quite cold, then fill with this mixture:

Filling

6 tablespoons shaved unsweetened chocolate	cream or top of milk to moisten
7 oz. sugar	vanilla and almond essence
	1 egg

---

[1] Care should be taken not to overcook, as the result should be soft, almost sticky.

Mix chocolate and sugar, add enough cream to moisten, stir over very gentle heat until the chocolate is melted. Beat the egg and add it. Cook over very slow heat until the egg thickens, add vanilla and almond essence and leave to get quite cool.

The following recipes have been collected by R. H., and she has translated the American measures into English terms.

AMERICAN UPSIDE-DOWN CAKE

2 oz. butter	½ teaspoon salt
5 oz. sugar	canned pineapple or peaches
1 egg	soaked dried apricots or stewed
1 cup milk (8 liquid oz.)	firm fruit
9 oz. flour	glacé cherries
4 level teaspoons baking-powder	French plums, etc.

Topping

3 tablespoons sugar (brown preferably)	3 tablespoons butter

Cream the topping and spread the bottom and sides of the tin and arrange the drained fruit on this. Cream the butter, add the sugar and continue creaming, beat in the egg. Sift the flour with the baking-powder and salt and add alternately with the milk. Turn into the prepared tin and bake about 1 hour, at 350° F. Turn out while hot.

This may be served hot as a sweet, cut into portions and accompanied by a hard sauce, or be allowed to cool and be served as a cake.

FROSTED WALNUT CAKE

7 oz. flour	½ cup milk (4 oz. liquid measure)
2¾ level teaspoons baking-powder	2 egg whites
½ teaspoon salt	vanilla frosting (use seven-minute frosting, page 829, twice the quantity given)
2¾ oz. butter	
½ teaspoon vanilla	
8 oz. sugar	a handful of coarsely chopped walnut kernels for the filling
2 egg yolks	
¾ cup walnuts	

Sift flour with baking-powder and salt. Cream butter thoroughly, add vanilla and sugar by degrees. Beat till fluffy. Add yolks, walnuts, and ½ cup flour mixture with ¼ cup milk. When mixed stir in ½ cup flour, then the rest of the milk and flour. Stir to blend well. Whip whites till stiff but not too dry and fold into mixture.

Pour into a buttered bread tin or two 8-inch layer pans (sandwich tins). Bake 20–30 minutes at 375° F. Layer with walnut filling (for this take half the frosting and add the kernels). Reshape and cover with the rest of the frosting.

ANGEL CAKE

1¾ oz. fine flour sifted with ¼ oz. corn-flour 5 oz. castor sugar 5 egg whites or 4 large whites beaten with a pinch of salt and ½ teaspoon cream of tartar	1 tablespoon water 1 teaspoon vanilla essence white glacé or thin fondant icing (see pages 827 and 862), flavoured with vanilla

Sift the flour five times and spread it out to dry. Sift the sugar twice and add 1 oz. of it to the flour before the last sifting. Beat the egg whites with salt, cream of tartar, and cold water in a copper bowl with a balloon whisk until they are stiff enough to stand up in peaks, but not dry. Fold in the sifted sugar a good tablespoon at a time, then add the vanilla essence and fold in the sifted flour gradually, a tablespoon at a time, sifting it once more over the mixture. Pour the mixture into an ungreased angel cake tin and bake in a very slow oven for 35 minutes (275° F.). Increase the heat slightly (325° F.) and bake 10 minutes longer. Leave in the tin until cold before turning out and covering with white glacé or thin fondant icing, flavoured with vanilla.

ICINGS *

The simplest and quickest forms of icing for cakes are glacé or water icing and American frosting. Fondant icing is the finest and probably the most economical on sugar, but it is a little more complicated to make and involves the use of the sugar thermometer. Directions for the making of fondant icing will be given in the chapter on pâtisserie, page 862.

To prepare a cake for icing

The cake should be twelve hours old or at least should be completely cold and set. This applies to cakes other than rich fruit cakes, wedding or birthday cakes; for these the interval between baking and icing should be much longer. Sponge or chocolate cakes which are to be iced should first be split and filled with whatever filling may be called for; the cake is then reshaped and turned upside-down, because the base of the cake presents a smoother surface for icing. Cakes intended for icing should have the mixture well flattened and slightly hollowed in the middle when in the tin before baking. This applies in particular to cakes containing butter, for most sponge cakes rise fairly evenly.

Set the cake on a small rack or on to a marble slab, or in the absence of either of these on an inverted plate. It may be noted that a cake with short, sloping sides is the easiest type to ice (see *moule à manqué*, page 849). Brush the cake over evenly and thinly with a warm apricot glaze (see page 856). Allow this to set. The object of this protective coating is to avoid any crumb getting into the icing and also to prevent the cake absorbing

* *See plate 20*

moisture from the icing and so rendering it dull. The icing is now run or spread over the surface of the cake, according to the type of icing selected. If glacé or fondant is used, the cake must be decorated immediately; this applies particularly to marbling or decorations with cherries, nuts, peel, etc. Royal icing, which is used on wedding and birthday cakes, must be left to harden before the final decoration is added.

Almond paste or marzipan

This is put on to fruit cakes after they have been glazed lightly in the way described above. For a small cake the paste may be put on in one piece in the following way: Roll out the paste to a thick round, 1–1½ inches. Set this carefully on the top of the cake, allowing it to project about 2 inches all round. Then with the flat of your hand rub the top in small circular movements; as the paste is smoothed out, press and smooth it round the sides. When completely and evenly covered take a bottle and, keeping it in an upright position, roll it round the sides of the cake; this will give a good edge and smooth sides. For a large cake the sides and top may be covered separately with the paste, and in this case the paste on the top is thicker than that on the sides, ¾–1 inch on top, and ½–¾ inch on the sides. For this a round of paste is rolled out, set and pressed on the top of the cake and then trimmed; the remaining paste is rolled out comparatively thinly and cut into a wide strip to fit the sides. It is then pressed round and trimmed, the bottle being used as before. The cake is then ready for royal icing and is best left for a day or so before this is put on.

GLACÉ ICING

This is made with icing sugar moistened with stock syrup (see page 860). Water is sometimes used in the place of syrup but the icing is neither so smooth nor so glossy in surface. If water must be used, a few drops of oil may be added when the icing is being mixed. When a chocolate icing is required, the addition of a little apricot glaze gives an especially glossy finish.

For a medium-sized cake take:

> ¾ lb. icing sugar
> stock syrup or water to moisten
> a few drops of oil if water is used
> vanilla or coffee essence to flavour
> If chocolate is used, take block chocolate, half sweet and half
> unsweetened, cook to a very thick cream with a little water, and
> allow to cool completely before using. About 1–2 oz. of this may
> be added to the icing according to taste. An alternative method
> is to grate or shave the chocolate finely and to melt it on a plate
> over gentle heat.
> a little apricot glaze (see page 856) for a chocolate filling

Set the icing sugar into a pan or bowl, add by degrees the stock syrup or water and bring it to the consistency of thick cream, working well with a wooden spatula. Add the flavouring while doing this, and the oil if called for. Add the chocolate and glaze if required. Stand the bowl or pan in a bain-marie and stir the icing until just over lukewarm. Have the cake ready, pour the icing on to the middle of it; if the right consistency it will run over the top and down the sides. It is as well, as a precaution, to reserve about a quarter of the icing in the pan. If necessary the icing may be helped to run off easily by being spread gently over the top of the cake with a palette-knife, and the sides may be touched up by spooning the remaining icing round the edge, although a better effect is achieved if the icing will run naturally and need not be spread by the palette-knife. If a palette-knife is used a jug of warm water should be kept at hand to dip it into during the process. When the icing runs over the top and sides and spreads on to the slab or plate it may be scraped off with a knife and melted and used again.

The decoration of a cake iced with a soft icing has to take place before the icing has hardened: it is a great help if the trimming is first arranged on the base of an upturned plate, and then it can be transferred to the top of the cake quickly and without hesitation.

ROYAL ICING

This is a hard icing used for rich fruit cakes. For a cake weighing 2–3 lb., the whites of 4 eggs, the juice of half a lemon, and approximately $1\frac{1}{2}$ lb. of sifted icing sugar are used. Put the egg whites into a bowl, beat in the sugar and lemon juice by degrees, working the whole thoroughly and beating until the icing is smooth and white. When complete the icing should be white and stiff. If it is not for immediate use, clean down the sides of the bowl, remove the spoon or spatula, cover the bowl with a damp cloth. If required for piping decoration, have the mixture slightly slacker than that used for spreading on the cake. For thinning use lemon juice or egg white, not water. Some confectioners choose acetic acid rather than lemon juice as this has a purer colour. For coating a cake have it ready covered with marzipan, put on the icing and spread evenly over the top and sides with a palette-knife. When quite smooth, and not before, dip the knife in a jug of tepid water and smooth over the top and sides once again. This accomplished, no further smoothing should be done. When perfectly hard and set the decoration is piped on.

For a description of piping decorations see 'The Forcing-bag' in 'Kitchen Knowledge' (page 53). Perhaps too you will like to take warning from the following story told me by a pupil at one of the adult courses held here:

Her native cook liked to pipe, in sugar or cream, the name of the sweet he was serving—Lemon Mousse, Chocolate Soufflé, or whatever it might be. To encourage his interest in cooking she gave him an English cookery book. At her next dinner party the sweet appeared with the following legend: 'This is a very economical recipe.'

MARBLING

Before a soft fondant icing has set have ready a small paper cornet filled with coloured royal or fondant icing or melted chocolate. Whipped cream is sometimes used in place of the fondant icing, as is red-currant jelly, beaten until smooth. Pipe across the surface of the cake or sweet already iced or spread with cream in straight lines about ¾–1 inch apart. Then with the point of a knife lightly draw the same number of lines at the same distance apart at right angles to the lines already piped. In between these lines repeat the process, drawing the knife point in the opposite direction. The knife point should be wiped before each line is drawn.

AMERICAN ICINGS

Here is a useful frosting suitable for many cakes. It comes from *The Boston Cooking School Cook Book* (see footnote, page 823).

SEVEN-MINUTE FROSTING

¾ cup sugar	few grains salt
2 tablespoons water	1 egg white
⅛ teaspoon cream of tartar, *or*	flavouring (vanilla, coffee es-
1 teaspoon light corn syrup (glucose)	sence, peppermint)

'Mix sugar, water, cream of tartar, salt, and egg white in double boiler top. Stir to dissolve sugar. Set over boiling water and beat with rotary beater until stiff enough to stand up in peaks. With an electric beater the frosting may be stiff enough in 4 minutes. Remove from heat and continue beating until thick enough to spread. Add flavouring.

'Add other ingredients to half the frosting, reserving other half to frost top and sides of cake.'

The following American icings are also derived from *The Boston Cooking School Cook Book*, but have been translated into English measures and the instructions slightly elaborated.

AMERICAN ICING

6 oz. castor sugar	a small pinch of salt
2 tablespoons water	a few drops of vanilla or other
¼ teaspoon cream of tartar	flavouring
1 egg white, unwhipped	

Mix all ingredients together in a double boiler, stir until the sugar is dissolved; whisk with a rotary whisk until stiff, keeping the sides of the pan cleaned down with a rubber spatula. When ready the mixture will stand up in peaks. If the icing is to be used for filling as well as icing, for which it is entirely suitable, a double quantity of the above recipe must be made. Nuts, glacé fruits, and other trimmings may be added.

AMERICAN BOILED FROSTING

This is in effect an Italian meringue in that the sugar and water are boiled to a certain degree and poured on to whipped egg whites. The proportions are as follows:

½ lb. granulated sugar	½ gill water
1 whipped egg white	a pinch of cream of tartar
flavouring to taste	

Dissolve the sugar in the water, add the cream of tartar, and boil rapidly until 238° F. Remove from the fire and when just off the boil pour slowly and steadily on to the beaten white, whisking all the time. Continue whisking until the mixture is stiff enough to spread. Flavour to taste. This also may be used as a filling.

FUDGE FROSTING

1 level tablespoon butter	a good ½ gill top of milk
½ lb. sugar	1 oz. chocolate
a small pinch of salt	½ teaspoon vanilla

Simmer sugar, milk, chocolate, and salt till the chocolate is completely melted. Boil without stirring till 234° F., or the soft ball stage. Remove from the heat, add butter and stand until cool and thick. Add vanilla and pour over the cake.

ALMOND PASTE (MARZIPAN)

1 lb. ground almonds	1 tablespoonful sherry or rum
¼ lb. icing sugar (finely sieved)	1 teaspoonful orange flower
¼ lb. castor sugar	water
2 small eggs	few drops almond essence
juice of half a lemon	

Mix the castor sugar, the icing sugar, and the almonds thoroughly together in a bowl. Pour in the lightly beaten eggs, add the other liquids, and work to a smooth paste.

XXVIII

Pastry

PASTRY-MAKING would sometimes seem to be invested with a halo. 'A light hand with pastry,' 'Such a wonderful cook, you should just try her pastry,' and the adage 'Better some of a pudding than none of a pie'—all this sets the pie high in the kitchen hierarchy. This is discouraging for the easily depressed, who may gain an idea that here is something that comes only by chance and good fortune, and so be led to anticipate failure. Some degree of good fortune may be admitted for argument; if you have by nature cool, firm fingers and a natural ability to use them you may get there more quickly, but the truth is that pastry-making, like most other things in cooking, is a matter of knowing how and why and sticking to the rules. Some kinds of pastry are more difficult to handle than others, certain of them are not easy to make in hot weather unless you have uncommonly perfect conditions, others exact more patience, and naturally each one of them is at the mercy of the usual kitchen hazards, an intractable oven or a fall in the gas pressure.

There are a good many kinds of pastry to consider even in the domestic kitchen: short crust, rich short crust, flaky pastry, rough puff pastry, puff pastry, pâte sucrée or French flan pastry, pâte à tartelettes, pâte frolle, and pâte brisée; then there are suet crust, strudel paste, choux paste, pâte moulée, hot-water crust, and American short crust, so it may be as well to study what factors are likely to control the quality of the work.

CONDITIONS

1. A cool, airy room is ideal.

2. A marble slab or slate shelf is the best possible surface for rolling and making pastry, as it is smooth, solid, and cool.

3. The ingredients, the fat and water in particular, should be cool, the water well chilled, but the fat itself not too hard, otherwise it will not blend properly with the flour.

4. All pastry should be handled lightly but firmly with sure and certain movements; too much handling will give a greasy and heavy result.

5. The mixture for pastry should be neither too wet nor too dry: too much water or other liquid will make the paste difficult to handle and,

when baked, the result will be tough and hard and it may shrink and lose shape in the baking; too little liquid also makes the paste awkward to handle, and the whole mass is not properly bound together and will crack frequently while it is being rolled out.

6. Pastry is baked at a temperature of 400°–440° F.

7. The flour must be dry and well sifted and should usually be plain flour except in the circumstances to be mentioned in a moment. Flour containing baking-powder or self-raising flour will render the pastry spongy in texture. The exceptions to this are that if for reasons of economy in the making of short crust you must reduce the quantity of fat to less than half the amount of flour, then the addition of baking-powder or the use of self-raising flour may help to soften and lighten the result. Sometimes, also, in the making of a cheese short crust, the use of self-raising flour may help to lighten and offset the excess of grease caused by the presence of the cheese, which might otherwise make the pastry heavy. With these exceptions plain flour should be used.

8. The fat should be butter, margarine, or butter, margarine, and lard mixed. Pastry made entirely with lard is greasy and inclined to be strong in flavour and very crumbly and difficult to handle.

BAKING TEMPERATURES

Type of Pastry	Electric Stove	Radiation Stove Regulo Mark
Short crust, pâte brisée	400° F.	6
Rich short crust	400° F.	6
American pastry	400° F.	6
Pâte à pâté	400° F.	6
Pâte à tartelettes	400° F.	6
Pâtes sucrées, 1, 2, and 3	350°–400° F.	4–6
Pâte frolle	350°–400° F.	4–6
Flaky	425° F.	7
Rough puff and puff	425°–450° F.	7–8
Strudel	450° F.	8
Choux	430° F.	7
Suet crust	400°–425° F.	6–7
Hot-water crust	400° F.	6
Pâte moulée	400° F.	6

Short crust

For an ordinary short crust plain flour is used, and a proportion of half fat to flour. For a rich short crust approximately two-thirds of fat to flour may be taken, but generally no lard is used for this. Water is generally used for mixing, though if a softer pastry is required milk may be employed in its place. An egg yolk or a small quantity of beaten egg will help to enrich and bind the pastry and will sometimes be called for in a recipe where a fairly high proportion of fat to flour is used, as in the case of a rich short crust.

The method. The fats, which should be firm but not too hard, and certainly not too soft, are cut into the sifted flour with a palette or round-ended knife. As soon as the pieces are well coated with flour they are rubbed in with the finger-tips, and this should be done above the bowl so that the crumbs fall back into it. This movement of lifting up the flour and rubbing in the fat from a height helps to lighten and aerate the pastry. This process should not be overdone and, particularly in warm weather, the fat should not be rubbed too heavily into the flour. When the mixture looks like fine breadcrumbs it is ready for mixing with the liquid, and this is done with a palette-knife until the moment when the mixture begins to form into small lumps of dough; then it is better to use the hand to knead all together into one ball of paste, because it is easier to judge accurately with the hand the exact amount of liquid required. This depends on the proportion of fat called for in the recipe, and to make a firm dough may vary from 4 to 5½ tablespoons to each half-pound of flour; the higher the proportion of fat the less liquid will be necessary. The texture of the flour has also some influence on this, as the finer it is the more liquid it will absorb. Short crust is used for fruit pies, open tarts, flans, and for ordinary everyday puddings.

Rich short crust

This is used for flans, tartlets, fruit pies and so forth when a richer pastry is wanted, and particularly if the dish is to be eaten cold. It may also be used for savoury flans and pies and is useful when the weather is too warm for making flaky pastry. The method is the same as for short crust.

Flaky pastry

This is a combination of two methods of making pastry, the short crust and the puff pastry methods. Only a portion of the fat is rubbed into the flour, a firm paste is made with cold water, the paste is rolled out and then the remaining fat is pressed on to it in small pieces; the paste is then folded and rolled as for rough puff or puff pastry. The fat used should be half lard and half butter or two-thirds butter and one-third lard. Only by a proper rolling of the paste will success be achieved, and in hot weather it is difficult to control the fat and to prevent it from coming through the pastry, so it will be seen that cool weather is best for this work. Flaky pastry is used particularly for meat pies, jam puffs, sausage-rolls, etc.

Puff pastry

This is generally considered the finest of all pastries, and as there are several special points to be considered in puff pastry-making, further notes will be given with the recipes.

Rough puff pastry

This is very like puff pastry, though the method is simpler and the proportion of butter or margarine to flour is not so high. It should be flakier than, and not quite so firm as, flaky pastry, and as a rule has no lard in it.

Pâtes sucrées

The various pâtes sucrées, forms of sweet short pastry, are widely used in the making of flans and tartlets and form the basis of certain pâtisseries. Details about the making will be given before the recipes.

Pâte à tartelettes

This is a slightly more economical paste than the foregoing.

Pâte frolle

This is a pastry containing pounded or ground almonds.

Pâte brisée

This is the equivalent of our short pastry, but is made by French methods. It is used for either sweet or savoury dishes.

Strudel paste

This is a type of paste peculiar to certain sweet or savoury rolls; it is a Hungarian speciality and details about its making will be given with the recipe.

Suet crust

The method of making suet crust is different from that for short pastry. Self-raising flour or baking-powder and flour should be used, and a certain proportion of fresh white breadcrumbs may well be added to the flour to give a light and fluffy result. Finely chopped or shredded suet in the proportion of a third to half the amount of flour is used, and water, or occasionally milk, for mixing. The consistency should be that of a light scone dough.

Hot-water crust

For raised pies such as pork, veal and ham, and game the crust is made in a different way. The whole process has to be carried out with speed. Recipe and method are given on page 841.

Pâte moulée

A type of short crust suitable for French raised pies. It is made up in the French fashion and left in a cool place for two hours before using.

Pâte à pâté

A somewhat similar paste but slightly richer. Made up in the same way as pâte moulée.

American short crust

This differs from the English in method; the fat or shortening is chopped and blended into the flour instead of being rubbed in. The reason for this is that often vegetable fats resembling lard are used, and the warmth of the hand used for blending might produce a sticky paste. American short crust is of a more crumbly texture than ours, and is in fact more like a shortbread than our pastry.

Choux paste

This, used for éclairs, cream buns, and similar light confections, is made by an entirely different method. The flour is mixed with boiling liquid and the eggs added subsequently. The details of the making of choux paste will be found with the recipe.

RECIPES

SHORT CRUST PASTRY

6 oz. plain flour
a pinch of salt
2¼ oz. butter
¾ oz. lard

1 small dessertspoon castor sugar for sweet pastry, or salt and pepper for savoury
2 to 2½ tablespoons cold or iced water (approx.)

Sift the flour with the salt, rub in the fat in the way described; add the sugar, mix to a firm dough with the water, using a palette-knife and finally the hand. This paste may with advantage be left in a cool place half an hour or more before being rolled out.

N.B. The proportion of lard alters if margarine is used. When butter is used a small proportion of lard is suitable; when margarine replaces the butter then the proportions may be half and half.

RICH SHORT CRUST PASTRY

8 oz. plain flour
a pinch of salt
5 oz. butter
1 dessertspoon castor sugar

a squeeze of lemon juice
2–3 tablespoons iced water
1 egg yolk or ½ a beaten egg

Make up as for short pastry, mixing the egg with a spoonful of water before adding to the flour. Chill slightly before rolling out.

FLAKY PASTRY

For this the method must be carefully followed and the pastry rolled correctly. Butter is the most suitable fat, but margarine may be taken as a substitute.

6 oz. plain flour
a pinch of salt
2 oz. butter

2 oz. lard
3–4 tablespoons cold water

Sift the flour and salt into a bowl, divide the fat into four; rub one part of this into the flour and mix to a firm dough with the cold water. Roll out into a strip approximately 5 inches wide, put a second portion of fat on two-thirds of the pastry in small pieces. Dust with flour and fold in three; leave in a cool place 15 minutes, then roll out, pressing it away from you. Put on the third portion of fat, fold in three, and roll out again, then add the fourth portion and roll out once more; give final rolling out if the paste appears streaky. Chill before use and wrap in a clean cloth if not to be used immediately.

N.B. Both the fats must be firm but pliable enough to blend well with the paste, otherwise the pastry will tend to be greasy when cooked. If margarine has to be used in place of butter, it is advisable to use this rather than the lard for rubbing into the flour at the start.

PUFF PASTRY *

The flour for this should be the best pastry flour available, the butter fresh or slightly salted and of firm and non-sticky texture. Puff pastry made with butter has an incomparable flavour and texture. A satisfactory pastry may be made with margarine, although it is inclined to be a little on the tough side. Margarine of a kind specially manufactured for the purpose and not available to the public is sometimes used commercially for the production of puff paste.

The following points are to be observed in puff pastry-making:

1. An equal weight of flour and butter is used. The water should be as cold as possible, preferably iced; a squeeze of lemon juice is usually added.

2. The flour and water is made up into a paste before the butter is added; the consistency of this paste is important: it should be firm enough to hold the butter but not so firm as to be tough and difficult to roll. It should not be elastic, and in order to avoid this consistency the dough should be mixed as rapidly as possible and overkneading avoided. Some recipes indicate that a piece of the butter the size of a walnut be rubbed into the flour first. This also is a means of avoiding elasticity. If a fairly large quantity is to be made up, it is a good plan to mix only half the flour and water at a time.

3. The butter should be firm but not soft. The instruction sometimes given in a recipe to beat the fat on the slab to make it pliable should only be carried out when the texture of the fat renders this necessary; in particular does this remark apply to margarine. The butter and the paste should be of the same consistency. If this is so, the blending of one with the other will be easy. The firmer, within reason, that they are, the more easily they will roll.

4. Rolling must be carried out with a special movement; the rolling-pin, a heavy one for preference, is brought down firmly on to the pastry and

See plate 17

then given a quick, short roll, lightly but firmly back and forth. The pin is then lifted and the process repeated; no pushing movement should be given, for if this is done the butter will be pushed out of place and the pastry will not rise satisfactorily. With each turn (or rolling) the pastry becomes a little thinner; for example, after the first turn it is left about $\frac{3}{4}$ inch thick and after the last about $\frac{1}{4}$ inch. Care must be taken during the first two or three turns that the butter does not come through the paste, for this would give a sticky surface and so call for the undesirable use of extra flour; flour, when rolling, must be used sparingly since too much spoils the pastry.

5. It is not easy to make puff pastry in hot weather; the process of rolling becomes difficult and the pastry consequently rises very little. Good puff pastry should rise at least twice the thickness of the raw paste.

6. Uncooked puff paste will keep for two to three days if wrapped in a cloth in a cool place; the pastry should be completed, however, and not left after the first two or three turns.

| 6 oz. plain flour | 6 oz. butter |
| a pinch of salt | a good gill of iced water |

Sieve flour and salt into a bowl, rub in a nut of the butter. Mix to a firm dough with the water. Roll out into a rectangle about $\frac{1}{2}$ inch thick. If necessary beat butter on slab two or three times to make it pliable (but see note 3 above). Put the butter in a whole slab, shaped roughly like a $\frac{1}{2}$ lb. block, in the centre of one half of the dough (keeping the dough in one piece). Fold over the other half and press the edges together. Allow to stand 15 minutes. With the sealed ends towards you roll away from you. Fold in three. Turn the paste round so that the open edge faces you and roll again. Repeat the process twice more so that in all the paste has six turns of rolling and resting. Leave 15 minutes before use. If the pastry shows streaks of butter an extra turn may be given. If it is to be kept the paste should be wrapped in a clean cloth.

PUFF PASTRY (AN ALTERNATIVE METHOD)

Sieve flour and salt on to a slab, scoop a hollow in the middle, and add water by degrees. Work up quickly into a firm but pliable dough. Roll out into a square, put butter in middle. Fold over the sides and ends like a parcel, pressing firmly into position. Wrap in a cloth and leave 15 minutes. Then give the paste six or seven turns as above.

ROUGH PUFF PASTRY

6 oz. plain flour	3–4 tablespoons chilled or iced
a pinch of salt	water
5 oz butter or margarine	

Sift flour in bowl with salt; break or cut butter into pieces the size of a large walnut. Mix into the flour, leaving fat in lumps, add water to bring to a fairly firm dough. Wrap in a cloth and set aside 10 minutes in a refrigerator, then roll on a floured slab to a strip about 6 inches wide and 1 inch thick, using the puff pastry method of rolling (see note 4). Fold in three, turn round and bring the open edge towards you; roll out once more, this time rolling the paste to about ½ inch thick if possible. Fold in three and set aside in a cool place 15 minutes. Repeat this process, that is to say two rollings and one rest, twice more; by this time the paste should be uniform in colour and show no signs of streakiness. Chill again before using.

PÂTE SUCRÉE OR FRENCH FLAN PASTRY *

This crisp, short, sweet, and melting pastry, not one of the easiest to make, is employed for flan cases and tartlets, and the secret of its success lies in the careful blending of the ingredients and the lightness of handling. The method is different from the English pastry-making; the flour is sifted on to a marble slab or board, a well is formed in the centre of it by pushing the flour gently aside, and into this well the butter is put (lard is not used for this pastry), together with the sugar and egg or egg yolk. No other liquid is employed in mixing, and this ensures that the pastry will neither shrink nor lose shape during cooking. Either castor or icing sugar may be used: the finer the sugar, the more melting the paste. If, however, this pastry is to be moulded, for example for the lining of large flans or moulds, castor sugar is to be preferred, because icing sugar may cause the pastry to spread a little. The butter, sugar, and egg are blended together in the well before the flour is gradually drawn in; the butter and sugar are not creamed together, for this would give the pastry a somewhat cake-like consistency, spongy rather than soft and melting. During the process of blending only the finger-tips of one hand should be used, and the mixture should not be drawn up on the fingers beyond the second joints. As soon as all the flour has been drawn in, the fingers should be cleansed with a palette-knife, and then the paste is smoothed out with the 'heel' of the hand on the slab. When a small quantity of paste is in hand this process should not be repeated more than half a dozen times, and should cease immediately the paste binds together. If it is carried out unneccessarily long, the paste will become a sticky mass difficult to handle, and necessitating more flour which will spoil it. Now the paste is formed quickly into a ball, wrapped in paper and set aside in a cool place, and it should not be used for at least half an hour and preferably longer. Pâtes sucrées, like other pastries made by the French method, may be made at least a day before they are required, and the butter or margarine for this type of pastry should be moderately soft. If more convenient, whole eggs may be used rather than yolks only; 1 small egg is generally considered the equivalent of 2 yolks.

* See plate 16

FRENCH FLAN PASTRY (PÂTE SUCRÉE) (1)

This pastry should be made directly on a board or marble slab.

4 oz. plain flour	2 egg yolks (or, for economy,
2 oz. butter or unsalted mar-	1 yolk and 1 dessertspoon
garine	cold water)
2 oz. castor sugar	a few drops of vanilla essence
	or a little grated lemon rind

Put the flour on to the slab, make a well in the centre, and put the other ingredients in the middle. Work butter, sugar, and yolks together with the finger-tips of one hand; when blended mix in the flour and work up to a paste by smoothing it out on the slab in the way described with the 'heel' of the hand. As soon as the mixture will form into a ball, the pastry is ready and should be put away in a cool place for at least half an hour before being used. No extra liquid should be added.

PÂTE SUCRÉE (2)

4 oz. flour	2 yolks of egg
2¾ oz. butter	vanilla either in the form of
1½ oz. icing sugar (good weight)	essence or of vanilla sugar

Make up according to the directions given for pâte sucrée 1.

PÂTE SUCRÉE (3)

8 oz. flour	2 egg yolks
6 oz. butter	vanilla essence to flavour
2½ oz. icing sugar	

Make up as above.

PÂTE A TARTELETTES

This is a slightly more economical paste than the foregoing pâtes sucrées. It is sometimes preferred because it is a little crisper and slightly more flaky. It is used almost entirely for fruit flans and tartlets.

4 oz. flour	½ oz. castor sugar
2½ oz. fresh butter	¼ gill cold water
a pinch of salt	

Sift flour on to slab with the salt. Scoop a hollow in the centre. Put in the sugar, butter, and water; blend together, then gradually draw in the flour to make a firm but pliable paste. Leave at least half an hour wrapped in a cloth, roll out into a strip, fold into three, turn the paste round to bring the open edge towards you, and repeat once more. Set aside at least an hour before using. Roll this paste thinly for use and prick the bottom of the flan to prevent blistering.

PÂTE FROLLE (ALMOND PASTRY) (1)

8 oz. flour	3 oz. ground almonds
6 oz. butter	a few drops of vanilla essence
3 oz. castor sugar	or orange-flower water
1 egg	

Sift flour on to board or slab; make a well in the centre and put in the sugar, egg, and vanilla or orange-flower water, sprinkle the ground almonds on to the flour. Mix the egg and sugar together with the finger-tips until light and creamy, add butter and continue working, gradually drawing in the flour and almonds. When a paste is formed leave in a cool place for half an hour or more before using. Use for flans, tartlets, or as a basis for petits fours.

PÂTE FROLLE (2)

6 oz. flour	1 yolk
3 oz. butter	2½ oz. almonds (ground)
3 oz. castor sugar	grated rind of ½ a lemon
1 small egg	

Make up as above.

PÂTE BRISÉE

For this, the French equivalent of our short pastry, mixed fats, for instance butter and lard, may be used. For binding, water and egg are employed. The French method of mixing applies, that is to say the fats and liquid are worked simultaneously into the flour. The paste is then left for an hour or two in order to rest and lose elasticity. This is used for flans, sweet and savoury, and can also be used for a pâte moulée (see page 625 in 'Pièces Froides').

½ lb. flour	1 egg
a large pinch of salt	1 oz. sugar
3½ oz. butter	scant ¼ pint water

Make up as for pâte sucrée, working as little as possible, and leave for 2 hours before using. The above recipe makes a good ordinary crust; it may, of course, be made much richer by using the same proportions as for English rich short crust. It is in the method that it differs.

STRUDEL PASTE

To be thoroughly successful only the very finest white flour should be used for this. In pre-war days Hungarian flour was famous, and it was no doubt this that gave the strudel the fine wafer-like crispness which is essential. A reasonably good strudel paste may be made from present-day flour, though its success is variable. Apple strudel is probably the best known, but cream cheese strudel may be served with a hot cherry sauce, and some of the savoury strudels are well liked and popular. Strudels are economical to make, useful as a luncheon dish, and substantial in character.

The following note may help the beginner: The cloth called for should be a large one, an old apron or a small table-cloth is excellent. Before rolling up the strudel paste after the filling has been put on to it, the edge of the paste should be pulled off, because this is usually a little thick in texture (in the form of a slight rim). To accomplish the rolling movement, the cloth is tilted and the strudel pressed lightly together from underneath the cloth as it rolls up. When a big strudel is made it may be curved into a horse-shoe shape when it is tilted on to the baking-sheet.

½–¾ lb. plain flour	2 tablespoons browned crumbs
a good pinch of salt	filling
1 small egg (optional)	a small quantity of oil added
¼–½ pint tepid water	to the water and egg (about
oil for brushing	a dessertspoon) is an im-
2 oz. butter (approx.) melted	provement

Beat the egg and add about ¼ pint of the water. Put the flour into a bowl, add salt, and mix quickly with the liquid to make a soft dough, adding more water if necessary. Beat as for brioche paste (see page 792) on a floured board till thoroughly elastic. Put into a clean, floured basin, cover and put into a warm place for about 15 minutes; meanwhile prepare the filling. Roll the pastry on to a floured board as thinly as possible, then lay on a floured cloth, brush with oil and leave till elastic, about 10–15 minutes. Pull gently from all sides until the paste becomes as thin as paper. Brush well with some of the melted butter, scatter over the crumbs, then add the filling. Roll up, slide on to a baking-sheet, brush again with melted butter and bake for about 30 minutes in a moderate to hot oven. Serve on a board and cut in wide slanting slices.

SUET CRUST

½ lb. self-raising flour, or 1	¼ lb. finely chopped or shredded
teaspoon baking-powder and	suet
½ lb. plain flour	cold water to mix
a pinch of salt	

Two ounces of the flour may be replaced by 2 oz. fresh white bread-crumbs for an extra light and spongy crust, and for a sweet pudding a small amount of sugar, either white or brown, may be added to the flour.

Sift the flour and salt together. Add the suet and rub in lightly with the finger-tips for a minute. Mix to a light and spongy dough with the liquid. Toss and pat lightly on a board to a smooth ball, roll out, then use immediately. The method of lining a pudding basin will be found on page 535 (Beefsteak and Kidney Pudding).

HOT-WATER CRUST FOR PORK PIE

1 lb. flour mixed with a pinch	1½ gills water
of salt	¼ lb. lard

Bring the lard and water to boiling-point in a saucepan. Pour immediately on to the flour. It is necessary that the action should be quick, for the paste must be moulded into shape before the lard has time to set and the paste become brittle. First set aside about a third of the paste for the top crust or lid, then roll out the remaining paste, or pat it out with the fist. In the middle of it set a wide-bottomed jam jar or small casserole of about 4–5 inches diameter across the base, round which to shape the paste. Then with the hand push and pat and lift the paste into position, working as quickly as possible.

PÂTE MOULÉE

10 oz. flour	5 oz. butter or butter and lard
1 teaspoon salt	mixed
4–6 tablespoons very cold water	1 egg

Sift the flour on to a marble slab, make a depression in the middle, add the salt, water, butter, and egg. Allow salt to dissolve in the liquid, mix in the butter, and then gradually work in the flour. Knead the paste until smooth, and put away in a cold place for 2 hours.

PÂTE A PÂTÉ

10 oz. flour	2–3 tablespoons water
a pinch of salt	2 egg yolks
7 oz. butter or margarine	

Sieve the flour with the salt on to a pastry board, make a well in the centre, and in this place the butter and egg yolks; work the yolks and butter together, adding the water, and gradually pull in the flour. Chill before using.

To line a raised pie mould

For veal and ham and game pies, either round or oval.

Make pâte moulée or pâte à pâté in the way described above and cut out a third of it for the top. Roll out the remainder to ¾ inch thick, making it round or oval as required, then lightly flour the surface and fold over double. You will now have in front of you a half-circle of double pastry. With your hands gently pull at the two ends of the base of your semicircle, pulling away from you in an upward direction, the object being to form this double paste into a sack. Roll lightly (away from you), taking care not to press the paste too much, for the layers must not stick together. When you have finished the double paste should be about ½ inch thick. Now open out gently and the paste should be in the shape of a bag. This is slipped into the pie mould. Use the reserved third of the paste for the lid. The same sort of method is used as for suet crust for steak and kidney pudding, as may be seen on page 535.

By this method of moulding there will be no folds in the finished crust. The flour laid on the surface of the paste prevents the two surfaces from sticking.

AMERICAN SHORT CRUST

As has been mentioned, the method here differs from our method in that the fat or shortening is cut and blended into the flour instead of being rubbed in. The following recipe is one adapted to English measures from an American recipe:

5 oz. shortening	3 large tablespoons cold water
a pinch of salt	8 oz. self-raising flour

Put flour and salt into a mixing bowl, add shortening. Cut the fat well into the flour with a palette-knife or pastry blender, sprinkle water in, gradually mixing with a fork. Gather lightly into a ball. Chill in the refrigerator at least half an hour before use.

CHOUX PASTE*

1. The flour must be sifted and dried, and it is convenient if it is put on to a piece of paper so that it is easier to shoot it all into the boiling liquid at once.
2. The beating of the mixture should not be more than is just enough to bring the paste away from the sides of the pan, a condition which indicates that the flour is cooked. If beating is continued beyond this point the paste will fail to rise properly and become cake-like in consistency, and this indeed is a common fault in the making of choux paste.
3. Thorough beating must be given when the eggs are added.
4. For baking choux paste the oven should be hot, average temperature 430° F., and the paste should on no account be taken from the oven until it is quite firm to the touch. If this rule is not observed, the pastry will fall immediately it is taken from the oven. Choux pastry should always be well baked and freshly made.

1½ gills water	3¾ oz. plain flour
3 oz. butter	3 eggs

Bring the butter and water to the boil together. When bubbling draw aside and immediately add the flour all at once. Beat until smooth and the paste will leave the sides of the pan. Leave to cool. Whisk the eggs lightly and add by degrees, beating thoroughly. If the eggs are exceptionally large retain the last spoonful until you have ascertained whether it is required, or whether you may get too wet a mixture. When finished the paste should be smooth and shiny-looking.

TO LINE A FLAN RING †

The same method is employed when either short crust pastry or pâte sucrée is used. It will be found, however, that pâte sucrée, which has none of the elasticity of short crust pastry and does not spring back when rolled thinly, is easier to handle; this is particularly so when tartlet moulds are being used and a more thinly rolled pastry is being handled.

* *See plate 23*   † *See plate 21*

It is unnecessary to grease rings or tins before lining and the method of working is as follows: The pastry is first rolled out into a round about $1\frac{1}{2}$ inches bigger than the ring and about $\frac{1}{4}$ inch thick. The ring should be set on a thick baking-sheet. The pastry should be lifted on to a rolling-pin and laid right over the ring. The edges of the paste should be lifted slightly so that they may be pushed gently against the sides of the ring, then, with a small piece of paste cut from the sides, rolled into a ball, and dipped into flour, the paste is pressed closely round the bottom edge. The finger and thumb should then be used to press back and flatten the top edge, and a slightly floured rolling-pin should be rolled across the edge to remove surplus paste, after which the edge should be pressed up once again by the finger and thumb. A beading round the edge should then be made with pastry pincers or with the tip of the fingers and thumb, unless the flan is to have a lattice finish, when this is unnecessary. The bottom of the flan should be pricked and it is ready to be baked blind or filled with fruit or savoury or sweet custards. If a sweet custard filling is used it is not usual to prick the pastry until the custard has begun to set, usually after about 5 minutes in the oven; for this the flan is drawn to the mouth of the oven and the bottom lightly pricked with the point of a warm knife.

TO LINE SMALL MOULDS, TARTLETS, BOATS, ETC. *

The moulds should be laid on the table close together, about six at a time. The paste should be rolled out thinly, lifted on to a rolling-pin, and laid over all the tins together. A small piece of paste rolled into a ball and dipped into flour should be used to press the paste into the moulds, and surplus paste removed by rolling a well-floured rolling-pin over them, first one way and then the other. The trimmings should then be rolled out again and more moulds lined in the same way. Each mould should be taken separately, the edges lightly pressed up with the thumb and the bottoms lightly pricked.

Alternatively a fluted cutter may be used in lining tartlet moulds. The cutter should be about 1 inch bigger in diameter than the moulds. The number of rounds required should be stamped out with the cutter and the paste pressed down into each mould with the thumbs; the cases may then be baked blind or filled as required.

If a paste difficult to handle, such as a pâte frolle, is being used, or if the weather is particularly warm, the paste should be divided into small pieces and pressed into and round each mould with the thumbs; when the necessary thickness of paste on the mould has been reached, the surplus should be trimmed off with a sharp knife.

TO BAKE BLIND

This is a term which indicates the baking of unfilled flans and tartlet cases, when the filling ingredient requires no further cooking.

The flan ring or moulds should be lined with paste in the way described, and if possible chilled for a short time afterwards to ensure that the paste

* See plate 24

is well set. A piece of grease-proof paper should then be pressed into the flan, care being taken to see that it fits well round the sides. Rice, beans, or broken macaroni, which may be kept specially for the purpose, should be used to fill the ring approximately three-quarters full, and the flan may then be baked. The paper and contents should be removed about 5 minutes before cooking is completed, and the flan returned to the oven to finish cooking. The rice, beans, or whatever has been used as a filling should be replaced in a jar for future use.

Tartlets or small moulds, after being lined with paste, should have laid in them small rounds or ovals of grease-proof paper which have been first touched on the bottom with a spot of grease to enable them to stick well; filling is thus made easier.

Sometimes the inside surface of the finished flan case is glazed to prevent penetration of moisture from the filling (see page 855).

LATTICE FINISH FOR A FLAN

Flans that are to have a lattice finish call for an extra amount of pastry; the additional quantity of flour and fat is generally given in individual recipes.

After the flan has been lined and filled the trimmings of the pastry are gathered together, rolled out, and cut into narrow strips; these are then laid at regular intervals across the top of the flan. The ends of the pastry are firmly pressed against the flan ring and the edges thus cut off by pressure. A second set of strips is laid over the first at similar intervals but from a different angle. The top of the flan is now brushed with water or beaten egg and finished with a strip of pastry pressed all round the edge.

Alternative method

For this, instead of strips of paste, long thin rolls of pastry are used; a small ball of pastry is taken and rolled on the board with the fingers until it becomes elongated and thin. When you have a long rolled strip as thin as a pencil this is ready for use in the same way as the strips of pastry. (See Tartes aux Pommes Grillés, page 872.)

TO PREPARE VOL-AU-VENT AND BOUCHÉE CASES

*Vol-au-vent cases.** Roll out the paste to a thickness of $\frac{1}{2}$ inch. With a saucepan lid of suitable size, 5–6 inches in diameter, make a light impression on the paste. Hold the lid lightly in place, and with a knife held at an oblique angle cut round, producing a bevelled edge. Turn the paste upside-down on to a wet baking-sheet, so bringing the wider surface uppermost. The bevelling of the edge helps to produce even rising of the paste. Place a smaller lid, of a size which will leave a 2-inch border of paste, and with the point of a knife make a slight incision all round, taking care not to cut right through. Mark the border in the way illustrated (see plate between pages 832–3) and the inner circle in a criss-cross pattern. Brush

* *See plate 25*

over the whole lightly with egg-wash, avoiding the bevelled edge and taking care that the wash does not overrun this; the effect of sealing this cut edge with the wash would be to prevent the pastry rising. Bake in a hot oven. When the paste is baked and risen the marked incision will be emphasized. Cut shallowly round this clear marking and lift off the criss-crossed circle of paste. This thin crisp layer will form a lid for the case when filled. Below this layer will be found some partially cooked paste; pull this out gently. The shell is now ready for the chosen filling and the replacement of the lid.

*Bouchée cases.** For these the paste may be rolled out to about $\frac{1}{4}$ inch thickness. Small fluted cutters are generally used, the oblique cutting desirable for the vol-au-vent cases being unnecessary. Choose cutters of suitable relative size, marking the centre ring as before without cutting through the paste. If a number of small cases are being cut from a sheet of paste the brushing over with egg-wash is done before the shapes are cut.

PASTRY QUANTITIES

When a recipe calling for pastry says 'Take 6 oz. pastry,' it means the amount of pastry obtained by using 6 oz. flour. Sometimes the expression used is 'quantity pastry': '6 oz. quantity puff pastry,' for example. It does not mean 6 oz. of the prepared paste.

* *See plate 26*

XXIX

Pâtisserie, Petits Fours, Petits Gâteaux, and Gros Gâteaux

THIS chapter on pâtisserie and petits fours carries the cook into a realm of her work sometimes labelled 'high class.' While there are recipes, some of them among the petits fours glacés, which call for especial neatness and dexterity, there is little here that cannot be accomplished by a student of cookery, provided she pays real attention to every simplest direction. There is less margin here for 'getting by.' If the recipe says 'Beat the meringue till thick' that, and just that, must be done and nothing less will serve—however tired your arm may be. These attractive and popular little cakes and sweetmeats call for a high degree of attention to detail. In particular sugar boiling calls for meticulous care and the icing of small cakes requires practice, but it would be a pity to forgo the pleasure of making these things under the mistaken idea that they are only to be accomplished by the professional cook. The recipes for the foundations make the processes clear, we hope, but there are one or two general recommendations which may be offered.

A good many of the petits fours may be made when one is making puff or flaky pastry or meringue, when by making a little more than is needed for the general dish in hand there will be plenty left over for this extra purpose. By planning intelligently it is easy to have pleasant additions to the menu and at the same time be economical of labour and materials. Another point too is this: if you are making these items for a party and must therefore make special provision of foundations, it is well to restrict your range to a series of items made on a similar base. You may with advantage choose, say, a génoise and a meringue or a choux paste and a pâte sucrée, and on either of these bases concoct a wide variety of cakes. It would be unnecessary to extend the range of bases beyond two for most occasions.

Another point here is that in selecting the final uses for the base, variety must be considered. Choose contrast of soft and crisp, plain and rich, and in the final setting up of a tray or dish see that this contrast of taste and texture is well represented. There are many variations of the foundations beyond those given here, but we have included a representative selection of the classics. In this respect it may be said that when a classic is being made, the decoration should follow tradition or the result should not bear

847

the name.   Petits fours should be very small, literally of a size to be eaten in one mouthful, and they should be uniform in size; for petits fours glacés it is correct to use paper bonbon cases, which in itself is an indication of the size they should be.

GÉNOISE *

French génoise is a rich firm type of sponge cake containing butter.   It is lighter, or more spongy, than the English génoise or genoese, but nevertheless ices well.

The method is that of a whipped sponge, in that the whole eggs and sugar are whisked together over heat until thick, then removed and the whisking continued for a further 3–4 minutes.   Flavouring is added, the flour sifted and folded in, and then the melted butter swiftly incorporated. The mixture must be turned at once into a prepared tin and baked in a moderate oven, 350°–370° F.

It is wise to melt the butter in a bowl in a bain-marie to prevent it from becoming too hot and separating.   Care should also be taken not to stir the mixture one second longer than is absolutely necessary whilst adding the butter, for if over-worked the whole liquefies and turns a greenish colour.   When this happens it is useless and must be thrown away.

There are two kinds of génoise, 'fine' and 'commune.'   As the name indicates, the 'fine' is richer than the 'commune'; it has approximately equal quantities of butter, sugar, and flour, while the 'commune' has only half the amount of butter to the other ingredients.

All the ingredients for génoise should be of the finest—castor sugar, white flour, and unsalted butter.   It is quite possible to make a good génoise commune with the standard flour and margarine, but it is wiser not to attempt the 'fine' unless white flour and butter can be used.   Margarine has a fair amount of water in it, so if a high proportion is added to a soft mousse-like mixture it tends to make it heavy.

Génoise forms the base of many iced cakes and petits fours.   Madeleines, the traditional small cakes baked in the form of a shell, in varying sizes, are an example of a génoise fine.

GÉNOISE FINE

4 eggs	3½ oz. flour
4½ oz. castor sugar	3½ oz. butter
flavouring	

Break the eggs into a copper or china bowl, add the sugar and flavouring, and whisk over a gentle heat until the mixture has doubled in bulk.   Take the bowl from the heat and continue whisking for another 3–4 minutes. Sift and fold in the flour, previously dried and sifted, then add the butter, melted but not hot, when most of the flour has been added.   Mix as rapidly as possible, then turn at once into a prepared cake tin, drawing the spatula through the middle of the mixture as it pours into the tin, to complete the mixing.   Bake in a moderate oven for 20–30 minutes.

* See plate 27

GÉNOISE COMMUNE

4 eggs	4½ oz. flour
4½ oz. sugar	2 oz. butter
flavouring	

Use method as for Génoise Fine.

BISCUIT FIN AU BEURRE

This cake is very like a génoise, but of a slightly firmer consistency when baked. It is used largely for icing, both with fondant and crème au beurre, as it gives a firm and even surface. The method of making is slightly different from that of a génoise. The eggs are separated and the yolks well beaten with the sugar. The whites are then beaten stiffly and folded into the mixture with the sifted flour.

It is perhaps the easiest to make of the French types.

4½ oz. castor sugar	3½ oz. flour
4 eggs	2 oz. butter

Put the sugar in a bowl with the egg yolks, and work well with a wooden spatula until white and mousse-like. Whip the whites to a firm snow and fold into the mixture, sifting the flour in at the same time. Then quickly add the butter and turn at once into a greased and floured cake tin. A *moule à manqué* is the most suitable.

N.B. The quantities of the above recipes may of course be altered for making smaller or larger cakes.

The above cake mixtures are best baked in a shallow rather than a deep cake tin; the ideal type is a *moule à manqué*. This is a round tin with sloping sides, and 1½–2 inches deep, which when turned upside-down enables the icing to run easily over and down the sides of the cake. The moulds may be had in varying sizes. If difficult to obtain, a good iron-monger will make them for a small charge.

FRANGIPANE

This is used as a filling in conjunction with pastry of some kind, e.g. gâteau Pithiviers or gâteau frangipane.

4 oz. butter, unsalted	1 oz. flour
4 oz. castor sugar	lemon juice, vanilla, or orange-
2 eggs	flower water for flavouring
4 oz. ground almonds (see page 853)	

Cream the butter, add sugar by degrees. Beat in the eggs one by one. Add flavouring. Lastly work in the almonds and flour. Use as required.

CRÈMES AU BEURRE (BUTTER CREAMS)
for filling and decorating

There are three varieties of butter cream:

1. Crème au beurre mousseline
Creamed butter to which is added a whipped egg mousse.

2. Crème au beurre meringuée
Creamed butter to which a cooked meringue is added.

3. Crème au beurre
Creamed butter into which a heavily sweetened custard is beaten.

The choice of these butter creams is determined by two factors, the type of cake or sweet for which they are intended, and the ingredients available, and the choice will be helped if their different consistencies are understood.   Crème 1 is rich and creamy and calls for egg yolks; crème 2 has meringue cuite mixed with the butter and is of lighter texture: the whites of egg only are included; crème 3 is firm but still creamy, is perhaps the most economical and certainly the easiest to make.   It is even possible to use a custard made of custard powder for this.

CRÈME AU BEURRE MOUSSELINE

3 oz. lump or granulated sugar	flavouring: sweetened choco-
½ gill water	late, coffee essence, zest of
2 egg yolks	orange, or lemon rind
4–6 oz. unsalted butter	

Dissolve sugar in water.   Boil to the short thread (see page 860) and test between the finger and thumb.   Take off the heat at once, cream yolks and pour the syrup on to them in a steady stream, whisking well. Then whisk until thick and mousse-like.   Cream butter thoroughly until white and whipped, then whisk in the mousse by degrees.   Flavour to taste with melted sweetened chocolate, coffee essence, the zest of orange, or lemon rind.

PRALINE BUTTER CREAM

Make as above, but add 1–2 tablespoons crushed praline in place of other flavouring (see page 854).

CRÈME AU BEURRE MERINGUÉE

2 egg whites	4–6 oz. unsalted butter
4 oz. icing sugar, sifted	flavouring

Put the whites and sugar into a copper bowl, whisk over gentle heat until very thick and the meringue will hold its shape.   Remove from heat and continue whisking for a few more minutes.   Cream the butter thoroughly and beat the meringue into it by degrees.   Flavour as in first recipe.

CRÈME AU BEURRE

2 oz. sugar	6–8 oz. unsalted butter
¼ pint milk	flavouring
2 egg yolks	

Add the sugar to the milk, boil. Pour on to the well-creamed yolks, blend and return to the pan. Thicken over the fire without boiling, strain and cool. Well cream the butter and whisk in the custard by degrees. Flavour as before.

N.B. If the butter cream curdles this may be remedied by slightly warming the bowl containing the mixture. This applies to all the butter creams.

CRÈME PATISSIÈRE

This is much used in the sweet course and for cakes. There are two slightly different types or methods of making.

1. In this the whipped egg white is added to the hot cream and cooked slightly so that the cream when cold will remain firm but mousse-like.

2. The whipped white, to which a certain proportion of the sugar in the recipe is added to form a meringue, is folded into the cream after it is cooked and cool. The result is a softer cream.

The former type is used for éclairs, fillings for cakes, sponge, or génoise; the second when it can suitably replace whipped cream, for example in a flan (Abricots Bourdaloue) or Polkas.

Both varieties may be flavoured as called for. Flavouring such as orange or tangerine is imparted by removing the zest of the fruit with 2 or 3 lumps of sugar; these are then crushed or dissolved in the milk and the cream is thickened as directed in the recipe. Coffee essence is added when the cream is completed. Chocolate may be added either by boiling the chocolate in the milk before thickening, or when the cream is made by beating in the melted chocolate as the mixture cools.

CRÈME PATISSIÈRE (1)

2 egg yolks	1 egg white
2 oz. castor sugar	a few drops of vanilla essence,
½ oz. corn-flour	or the sugar called for in the
¾ oz. flour	recipe to be flavoured with a
½ pint milk	vanilla pod (see page 44)

Break yolks into a bowl, add sugar by degrees, and cream well. Add the sifted flours with about ½ gill of the milk. Bring remainder of the milk to the boil, pour on to the yolks, blend, return to the pan, and stir over heat until at boiling-point. Draw aside. Whip the white stiffly, put about a quarter of the cream into a basin, fold in the white by degrees, then return this mixture to the pan. Cook over gentle heat for a few minutes, folding the mixture over occasionally, and adding vanilla essence. Then turn into a basin to cool.

CRÈME PATISSIÈRE (2)

Same proportions of ingredients as in preceding recipe, though the thickening may be all corn-flour.   Use only 1 spoonful of sugar to cream with the yolks.   Cook the cream as above and turn into a basin to cool. Now whip the white stiffly, whisk in a spoonful of the sugar and when the meringue is smooth fold in the remainder.   Whisk the cream and carefully incorporate the meringue.   Flavour to taste.

In some recipes all the remaining sugar is added to the white and the white is whipped until stiff, as for a meringue cuite.

MOCK CRÈME PATISSIÈRE

A useful cream when both eggs and time are short.

½ pint thick custard made with ¼ pint milk, 1 tablespoon custard powder, 1 dessert-spoon sugar, and a little extra milk if necessary

2–3 tablespoons whipped cream
vanilla essence to flavour

Have custard made and cool, whisk well, fold in the cream and add the vanilla.

N.B. If custard is too solid add a little extra milk; though it must hold its shape, it must not be so stiff that the cream when added loses its light and creamy quality.

Meringues

MERINGUE SUISSE

This is the more ordinary meringue, used for meringues 'à la chantilly' and as a finish for various sweets and puddings.   Proportions are:

4 whites of egg   8 oz. castor sugar (2 oz. per egg
                               white)

Whip whites stiffly until they will form a peak on the whisk (see page 287 for whisking of egg whites).   Now beat in 1 good tablespoon of the sugar. This will make the mixture smooth and satiny.   After half a minute remove whisk and fold in the remaining sugar, half at a time.   Use immediately.

MERINGUE CUITE

Used mostly for meringue baskets, piping and so on.   Its advantage is that it will stay up and remain firm for some little time after it is made. Very useful for commercial purposes as it may be whipped in a mixer without heat.   Icing sugar is used here with the object of obtaining a smoother finish, but when made in a machine castor sugar is perfectly satisfactory.

4 egg whites	a few drops of vanilla or other
9 oz. sifted icing sugar	flavouring

Put the whites, sugar, and vanilla into a copper bowl. Whip over gentle heat until very thick. Use for meringue baskets, etc.

MERINGUE ITALIENNE

8 oz. sugar	3 egg whites
¾ gill water	a few drops of vanilla

Boil the sugar and water together to the ball, 298° F. Whip whites to a stiff snow, pour on the syrup in a steady stream, whisking all the time. Add vanilla. Use when cold for cake fillings or to replace whipped cream.

N.B. The above mixtures are best made in a copper bowl and beaten with a balloon whisk. (See page 287 for whisking of whites.)

THE PREPARATION OF ALMONDS FOR PÂTISSERIE

To blanch

Have ready a pan of fast-boiling water, remove pan from direct heat and immediately put in the almonds. Stir round two or three times, cover the pan and leave 3–4 minutes. Test a nut to see that the skin may readily be removed, then drain off hot water and rinse the nuts in cold. Drain, turn on to a board, and press the skins off with the ball of the thumb or between finger and thumb. Rinse again and dry thoroughly on a cloth.

Shredded almonds

Blanch and skin the nuts and split in two; cut each half lengthwise in fine pieces. The shreds may be used as they are or sprinkled with castor sugar and browned in the oven, or they may be browned without the addition of the sugar, depending on the use to which they are to be put.

Flaked almonds

Blanched, skinned almonds are cut horizontally into flakes with a small sharp knife.

Chopped almonds

Blanched, skinned almonds are chopped and usually browned in the oven; used for decoration or for nougatine.

Ground almonds

With the object of saving time and labour it is a common practice to buy almonds ready ground. It is true that these bought almonds may be used for a variety of recipes, but to get the true flavour and the perfect texture it is infinitely better to prepare the ground almonds at home. By this means one obtains a richer and more flavoured ingredient and one which more readily forms a soft paste. Blanched, skinned almonds are chopped and pounded, and such sugar as may be called for in the recipe added gradually during the pounding.

THE USE OF HAZEL-NUTS IN PÂTISSERIE

The term grilled when applied to hazel-nuts is a little misleading. Though the nuts may be grilled in order to get them thoroughly toasted and brown, a better result is obtained by baking them in the oven for 5–6 minutes. The browning is more even and there is less risk of the nuts catching. The nuts are not blanched, as are almonds, but turned on to a rough cloth, such as an oven cloth. They are rubbed briskly in the cloth, which will remove fine fibres of skin. The nuts are then picked over and set aside, or turned on to a wire sieve and rubbed gently to free them from remaining skin.

PRALINE

This is an almond preparation made with whole unblanched nuts and castor sugar. It is largely used for adding to, and flavouring, soufflés, creams, and ices, butter creams and so on. It may be used well crushed, or pounded, and then sifted to remove the larger pieces, or it may be pounded until it will form a paste.

Praline keeps quite well provided it is put immediately it is made into an air-tight jar or tin. It may then be pounded as required.

3 oz. almonds, unblanched   3 oz. castor sugar, good weight

Put together into a pan. Set on low heat until sugar melts. When turning a pale brown stir with a metal spoon and continue cooking until a good nut-brown. Turn on to an oiled slab or plate; leave until hard, then crush into coarse powder or pound to a paste.

WHITE PRALINE

Used largely as a finish for cakes, Japonais for example.

6 oz. lump sugar   3 oz. ground almonds
$\frac{1}{2}$ gill water

Dissolve sugar in water, boil syrup to 248°–250° F. Take off the fire, add almonds and stir until crumbly and sandy. Shake through a wire sieve and store at once in an air-tight tin.

NOUGAT

There are two kinds of nougat, nougat Montelimart, white, with nuts and cherries, which is served purely as a sweetmeat, and nougat parisien or nougat brun, made with almonds and caramelled sugar. This too is a sweetmeat, but it also appears in the sweet course and as cakes moulded in the shape of baskets, cornets, leaves, etc. It must be shaped or moulded whilst it is still hot and malleable, as it hardens very quickly. For the amateur nougat in this form is rather difficult to handle. Nevertheless it is worth attempting.

8 oz. castor sugar	4 oz. almonds finely chopped
1 good teaspoon glucose	and baked to a light nut-
	brown, then kept warm

Put the sugar and glucose into a pan, allow to melt on slow heat. When a golden brown add the nuts (warm) and continue to cook, stirring occasionally, for a few minutes. When a rich brown turn on to an oiled slab. Turn over several times with a palette-knife to cool it slightly, then roll out as thinly as possible with an oiled rolling-pin or oiled lemon. Cut into shapes, leaves, diamonds, crown and so on, or mould into a basket or baskets.

If it hardens too quickly slip on to a lightly oiled baking-sheet and put into a warm oven until pliable. Hard nougat (i.e. completely set) may be softened down in this way.

MARMELADES

Marmelade is the term given to well-reduced purées of various fresh or dried fruits. It implies a fruit purée which, when cold, will set to a firm paste or fruit 'cheese.'

For this the fruit is stewed to a pulp, usually without sugar; it is then sieved and cooked again with sufficient sugar to sweeten well, until it will just come away from the sides of the pan. It is then turned on to a plate to cool before use.

MARMELADE DE POMMES

Wash the unpeeled apples, wipe, quarter, and core. Rub over the bottom and sides of a stew-pan with butter. Slice the apples thickly into the pan, add strip of lemon rind, cover and cook very gently, stirring occasionally, until completely soft. This part of the cooking may be done in the oven. Rub through a sieve. Rinse out the pan, return the purée to it, and sweeten with not less than 2 oz. brown sugar to each pint of purée. Cook rapidly, stirring continuously until the mixture drops easily from the spoon; this may take 4–5 minutes.

TO GLAZE PASTRY

There are two kinds of glaze, a dry glaze for use on the pastry covering a pie or flan, and a jam glaze which should be used on fruit in a pastry case.

Dry glaze

The pastry should be brushed lightly with water and well sprinkled with castor sugar before baking. Alternatively, lightly beaten egg white and sugar may be used, either before the pastry goes into the oven or a few minutes before baking is complete; for the latter the pie is removed from the oven, lightly brushed over with the egg white, sprinkled with sugar, and returned to the oven.

Jam glaze

If possible apricot jam should be used for yellow fruit and red-currant or gooseberry jelly for red fruit. While still hot the glaze should be painted or dabbed over the fruit with a soft brush (badger hair is the best). Care should be taken to coat the fruit completely and to fill in any cracks or gaps round the edge of the flan or tartlet. The glaze should be practically set on the fruit when cold.

If the fruit has been cooked in the pastry it should be glazed while still warm. If the flan case or tartlet has been baked blind, it should be brushed out with glaze before it is filled with fruit. In this way a protective coating is formed which helps to prevent juice from soaking into the pastry. The flan may then be filled with fruit which should be brushed over in the way described.

APRICOT GLAZE

4 large tablespoons apricot jam	a squeeze of lemon juice
½ gill water	

Put the jam into a pan with the water; boil and cook for 5–6 minutes. Add the lemon juice, stir and strain well. Reduce again if necessary; the glaze should just drop from the spoon while still hot.

It is a good plan to save time and trouble by making a pound or two of jam into glaze at a time; the surplus glaze may be poured back into the jars and used as required.

RED-CURRANT JELLY GLAZE

Red-currant or gooseberry jelly will give the best colour and flavour for red fruit. Normally water should not be added to the jelly, which should be allowed to melt slowly in the pan; it should be used before boiling-point is reached, and strained if not perfectly smooth. If a firm jelly is used a very little water may be added and the whole whisked to bind while heating. The jelly should not be allowed to boil down or colour and flavour may be spoilt.

Raspberry and red-currant jam are sometimes used. The jam should be heated with 3–4 tablespoons water to 1 lb. jam. This should be allowed to boil a minute or two before being well rubbed through a strainer. It should then be returned to the pan, reduced briskly for 4–5 minutes, and stirred occasionally; care should be taken to see that it does not discolour. It should be noted that this type of glaze cannot be boiled down so much as apricot.

Another type of glaze may be made from the juice of the fruit used to fill the flan. A little jam or jelly should be added to this and the whole reduced to a good flavour. It should be thickened with a small quantity of arrowroot (about 1 teaspoon per ¼ pint, depending on the thickness of the juice). This should be slaked with a dessertspoon of cold water. Arrowroot gives a clearer result than corn-flour.

CHOCOLATE CARAQUE

For this good block chocolate or couverture should be used. Melt grated chocolate over gentle heat—on a plate over warm water is best. Work with a palette-knife while melting. Then spread thinly on a marble slab, working a little with the flat of the knife. Leave until practically set. Then with a long, sharp knife shave it off the slab slant-wise, using a slightly sawing movement and holding the knife almost upright.

The chocolate will form long scrolls or flakes. These will keep quite well in a tin, but look better freshly made.

SUGAR BOILING

Sugar boiling is not one of the simpler kitchen processes. In its more complicated manifestations, the use of boiled sugar for forming flowers, baskets, ribbons, and other decorative objects, it belongs to the art of the *confiseur*. Many of us have spent our kitchen life without any of the special equipment used by him and have managed to make home-made sweets, syrups, ices, and fondants in a fairly satisfactory way. But on the other hand, most of us have failures to record: the day when a water-ice simply would not freeze because unknown to us the density of the syrup was too heavy; the time when the fondant ran off the cake or the fudge was too soft because the temperature of the sugar had been inadequate. If it is fairly usual for your cooking to include items calling for sugar boiling, you will achieve more uniform success and avoid mishap if you equip yourself properly, and this is no very great affair. Certainly if you have in mind to make the petits gâteaux and petits fours discussed in this chapter you will need the simple equipment given here.

1. A suitable pan, which may be either a scrupulously clean and well-polished saucepan or a special pan. A proper sugar pan is made of copper, is unlined, and has a sharp lip and a fairly long wooden handle.

2. A sugar-boiling thermometer; this registers very high temperatures. It is best to have one with a clip which secures it to the side of the saucepan, so keeping it upright; this ensures accurate reading. The thermometer when in use is kept in a vessel of hot water; this not only mitigates the shock of the high temperature of the sugar when the thermometer is put in, but keeps it free of clinging sugar grains.

3. A *pèse-sirop* or saccharometer. This is an instrument for measuring the density of a syrup, that is to say the relative proportions of sugar and liquid. It is usually employed for syrups boiled to the lower temperatures and is useful when candied fruits, water-ices, and syrups are made. The *pèse-sirop* is not used to measure temperature. It must float in the liquid

before the test can be made, so that it is necessary to place the liquid for testing in a tall, narrow vessel.   This should be of glass so that the reading is facilitated.   The syrup may be cold or hot, but not of so high a temperature that it will crack the container in which you are testing.   Certain accurate recipes will indicate the density required, and if the *pèse-sirop* indicates that this has not been achieved the syrup should either be diluted with more water or reduced by further boiling.   There is a point sometimes confusing to the beginner.   A *pèse-sirop* measures density, a thermometer temperature, but there is a relationship between the two.   A syrup boiled to 220° F., for example, will be found to register 28° on the *pèse-sirop*.   When a syrup is to be boiled to a higher degree than this the *pèse-sirop* is not employed, the thermometer being now an adequate guide. See also note below.

4. A sugar scraper.

5. One or two wooden spatulas kept specially for the purpose.

6. A marble slab.

7. A set of candy bars (four short steel bars used to keep the syrup in place on the slab).

8. A large hook fixed to wall or shelf for pulling candy.   These last two items are for sweet- or candy-making; Edinburgh rock is an example of a pulled candy.

N.B.   In the absence of a *pèse-sirop* it is possible to achieve approximately the right density of syrup without any continued boiling provided the proportions laid down are adhered to.   The table on page 859 may be taken as a general guide.

The sugar is dissolved completely in the water, which is then brought up to boiling-point; the density will then be approximately correct without any further boiling.

RULES FOR SUGAR BOILING

These are important, and must be observed with real care and carried out accurately, for when sugar is boiled to high temperatures it may be regarded as temperamentally tricky.

1. The sugar should preferably be cane loaf, because this gives a clearer syrup; granulated sugar may also be used.   The proportion of sugar is usually twice that of water.

2. When a syrup is being made, the sugar should always be allowed to dissolve completely before the liquid is brought to boiling-point.

3. While the sugar is dissolving in the liquid the contents of the pan are stirred, the spatula being drawn gently from side to side across the base of the pan so that the sugar is prevented from settling in a cake at the bottom. A gentle tap or two made with the spatula on the bottom of the pan will help the sugar to dissolve more quickly.

4. Immediately the sugar is dissolved the liquid glucose or cream of

tartar, whichever is called for, is added, the lid put on the pan and the contents brought to boil. The steam in the covered pan will wash down any crystals of sugar that may have formed on the sides of the pan. When the liquid boils remove the lid and skim well.

5. The thermometer, ready warmed in a pan of hot water, is now lifted out and put into the syrup in an upright position. The temperature is taken at eye level.

6. The syrup is now boiled rapidly without shaking or stirring till the required temperature is reached.

7. The thermometer is now removed and replaced in its pan of hot water.

8. The right temperature achieved, boiling must not continue; remove the pan from heat and if a thick-bottomed pan has been employed the base of the pan may be dipped for a moment in cold water to check boiling. The syrup is now ready for use.

9. During the boiling process sugar crystals may form on the sides of the pan; if these are allowed to remain they may cause the sugar to 'grain,' or crystallize. They must be removed by brushing down the sides of the pan with a pastry brush dipped in hot water.

10. Graining or crystallizing is also caused by stirring the syrup as it boils. The presence of glucose or cream of tartar is a deterrent; the amount used will depend on the purpose for which the sugar is being boiled. Glucose and cream of tartar both help to produce a fine grain and are used, for example, in the making of fondant. For crumbly sweetmeats such as certain types of fudge these ingredients are not used. Liquid glucose is the kind employed; this is extremely sticky and difficult to extract from the jar. The easiest way is to dip the fingers into cold water and then pull the glucose out. If the fingers are kept well moistened the handling of the glucose is made easy.

TEMPERATURES AND DENSITY DEGREES OF SUGAR BOILING

Pèse-sirop or saccharometer

Water-ices	17° of density of sugar				(6 oz. sugar to 12 liquid oz. water)
Fruit compôtes	20° „	„	„	„	($\frac{3}{4}$ lb. sugar to 1 pint water)
Babas and savarins	22° „	„	„	„	(6 oz. sugar to $1\frac{1}{2}$ gills water—$7\frac{1}{4}$ liquid oz.)
Stock syrup	28° „	„	„	„	or 220° F. (1 lb. sugar to $12\frac{1}{2}$ liquid oz. water). Syrup boiled to this degree of heat will prove to have acquired a density of 28°.

Thermometer

Short thread	215°–220° F.
Long thread or feather	225°–230° F.
Soft ball (fondant)	240° F.
Hard ball	245°–250° F.
Crack	310° F.
Hard crack	325° F.
Caramel	380°–390° F.

STOCK SYRUP

This is the name given to a thick syrup which may be kept and used as required and is useful for many purposes; among others it may be used to dilute and work into a fondant to bring it to the right consistency; it may be used for water-ices, for fruits rafraîchis, and be diluted to produce a fairly light syrup. It should be stored in a jar and covered with a piece of paper, and should not be tightly stoppered. If it is intended that it shall be kept for some time, a good teaspoon of liquid glucose may be added; this will prevent the sugar from graining while in the jar.

2 lb. sugar   1 pint water

Dissolve sugar in water, follow the rules for sugar boiling, boil to the thread, 215°–220° F., skimming well while boiling. Draw aside, cool slightly, and strain through muslin.

SPUN SUGAR

This, a web of finest threads of cooked sugar, is used for the decoration of cold sweets, in particular for ices and soufflés. In the domestic kitchen it may be made in a small quantity, just enough for the dish in hand, at the last moment. It may even be achieved without the use of a sugar thermometer. If, however, it is used frequently it may be made in moderately large quantities and kept. For this it should be made with the greater degree of accuracy secured by the use of a thermometer. It is kept in a box which has a layer of quicklime laid at the bottom; the box is then carefully lined with paper and the spun sugar put in. The quicklime is used to absorb moisture.

If the sugar is not boiled to the right degree, two things may happen. The sugar will either fail to spin properly, or, having spun, will not remain dry and brittle but subside into a sticky mass. For the spinning itself two forks held together will serve, but when spun sugar is required often a sugar-spinner should be acquired; this piece of equipment resembles a biscuit-pricker.

The spinning may be carried out over an oiled rolling-pin held in the left hand—a convenient method for a small quantity—or over the handle of a spatula for larger amounts. For this the broad end of the spatula is laid on the table, weighted with a heavy baking-sheet, and the handle, oiled, is allowed to project beyond the edge of the table. On the floor below, paper or baking-sheets should be laid.

SYRUP FOR SPUN SUGAR

4–6 oz. loaf sugar   1 small tablespoon liquid glucose
½ gill water

Put the ingredients into a pan, allow sugar to dissolve over low heat, then bring to boil and allow to cook rapidly, without shaking or stirring, to the hard crack, 320° F. Check the boiling, set pan on the table on a board or thick cloth. Dip the spinner or forks lightly into the sugar; only a very small amount of the syrup is required, and when a thread begins to run as the spinner is raised begin to throw. This is done with a loose movement of the wrist to and fro over the handle of the spatula. If too much syrup is taken up you will get drops of the syrup instead of a thread. Continue in this way until all the syrup is used up. Carefully draw the sugar off the handle or rolling-pin and use or store as may be required. The best spun sugar should be white or at most of the palest cream colour.

CARAMEL

The two following methods for making caramel are suitable for decoration of gâteaux and sweets; the caramel may be put straight on to a cake, be used for dipping, or poured on an oiled sheet for breaking up.

Method 1

4–6 oz. castor sugar

Put the sugar in a small heavy saucepan, place over gentle heat, and allow to dissolve slowly without stirring. Boil steadily to a rich brown (or 380°–390° F.) and use as required.

Method 2

4–6 oz. loaf sugar   ½ gill water

Put the sugar and water into a pan. Allow to dissolve over gentle heat without stirring. Bring to the boil and cook steadily until brown as in above recipe.

CARAMEL (BLACK JACK)

This is used for colouring or browning. Caramel formed the base of Parisian Essence, which was the finest quality of gravy browning. Home-made browning may be easily made and is satisfactory. Allow syrup to boil until really black, when it will become thin and will smoke freely. At this stage remove from heat and pour into it gradually and carefully about ½ cup hot water. Reboil; the burnt sugar will dissolve and a thin syrup form. Pour this off when cool and bottle for use.

Be careful not to add too much water to the caramel, otherwise it will be weak in colour.

FONDANT

1 lb. loaf or granulated sugar	a good pinch of cream of tartar
1½ gills water	or 1 teaspoon liquid glucose

Put sugar and water together in a scrupulously clean thick-bottomed saucepan.   Allow sugar to dissolve on slow heat, add the cream of tartar dissolved in a spoonful of water, cover pan and bring to the boil.   Remove lid, put in the thermometer, previously heated (see note 5 on sugar boiling, page 859), and boil rapidly to 238°–240° F.   Brush the sides of the pan down from time to time as directed on page 859.   Stop the boiling immediately the proper degree is reached, by dipping the bottom of the saucepan in cold water.   Pour out the syrup in a steady stream on to a wetted marble or slate slab.   Sprinkle the surface lightly with water, and allow to cool for a few moments.   Then draw the edges of the syrup together towards the middle with a sugar scraper, and start to work the fondant with a wooden spatula held in one hand and the scraper in the other.   Continue working without stopping, being careful to draw in all the syrup, until the fondant 'turns,' i.e. becomes white and opaque.   Knead well, a small piece at a time, and put into a bowl.   Cover with a piece of damp clean cloth and leave to mellow for an hour or two before use, or it may be put into a screw- or clip-top bottling jar and stored away for future use.

N.B. The higher the degree of density to which the syrup is taken, the harder the fondant is to work.   If inclined to be lumpy, knead as thoroughly as possible and put aside to mellow.   Many of the lumps will disappear during this process.   Do not start to work the syrup whilst still very hot; this will cause the fondant to be rough and sugary.   The working of the fondant may be done in a large bowl if a slab is not available, but both working and preliminary cooling will take longer.

Fondant is used for icing cakes, petits fours, etc., and also as a base for chocolate truffles and marzipan, and in sweet-making.   The temperature which the syrup should reach varies from 238° F. to 242° F.   The highest degree is used mostly for fondant centres, whilst for ordinary purposes (icing and so on) 239°–240° F. is the most satisfactory.   Generally speaking the firmer the fondant is the more economical, as it will require more 'letting down' or diluting.   This should be done with sugar (stock) syrup and the flavouring called for.   Water, of course, can be used in place of the syrup, but the gloss is not so good, nor the consistency of the icing so smooth.   When adding the liquid to the fondant, work well with a small wooden spatula and stand bowl or pan in a bain-marie.   Avoid overheating; the temperature of the icing or fondant should be just over lukewarm.   For orange or lemon flavouring add juice to taste.

It is convenient to have at hand in the store cupboard not only a jar of white but also one of chocolate fondant.   When chocolate is added to fondant already prepared it has to be melted and is worked into the fondant with a little stock syrup.   This is a little more trouble than making a chocolate fondant.

CHOCOLATE FONDANT

1 lb. loaf or granulated sugar
1½ gills water
1 teaspoon liquid glucose or a good pinch of cream of tartar

a few drops of vanilla essence
1½ oz. unsweetened chocolate
1 oz. sweetened chocolate

Make fondant as directed. Melt chocolate on a plate over gentle heat. Add it and the vanilla to the syrup while working it on the slab, before it has turned. Store and dilute as for white fondant.

If fondant is wanted darker in colour, use 2 oz. unsweetened chocolate and only ½ oz. of the sweetened.

CHOCOLATE MARQUISE

This is a form of icing suitable for immediate use. It will keep but loses its gloss when thoroughly set.

4–6 oz. best block chocolate or couverture
2–3 tablespoons coffee or water

½ oz. unsalted butter
vanilla or rum to flavour

Break up or grate the chocolate. Put into a pan with coffee or water. Melt over gentle heat (or in a bain-marie). When a thick cream remove from heat and add the butter in small pieces. Flavour and pour over the cake.

To ice a cake or cakes with fondant

Turn the cake upside-down after sandwiching it, etc. Brush top and sides over thinly with apricot glaze. Allow to set. Put cake on wire rack over marble slab or plate, or put directly on the slab.

Warm the fondant, working in the flavouring and syrup, and when a good coating consistency pour on the middle of the cake. Allow to run over the top and down the sides. Take up, with a palette-knife, any that falls on to the slab and return it to the pan. The glazing of the cake prevents any crumbs from entering the icing, and also ensures that no moisture from the fondant will be absorbed by the cake, so spoiling the gloss of the icing.

For small cakes, éclairs, etc., dip the end of the palette-knife in the icing, set the cake on it, and with a large spoon coat the icing over in one movement. With the back of a knife push the cake off on to a wire rack to set. Finish off with piping or other decoration. (See notes on piping under 'The Forcing-bag,' page 53.)

To ice petits fours arrange them in rows on a pastry rack, standing on an enamel tray. Then pour the fondant over them.

Take care not to overheat the fondant or it will lose its gloss.

PETITS GÂTEAUX AND PETITS FOURS [*]

MADELEINES

These are a classic of the génoise type of gâteau; they are baked in shallow, shell-shaped moulds which may be bought in various sizes.

2 oz. castor sugar	1¾ oz. flour
2 eggs	1¼ oz. unsalted butter
vanilla or vanilla sugar or orange-flower water	

Put sugar and eggs in a basin with the vanilla, or a small spoonful of orange-flower water, and whisk until a thick mousse. Remove the whisk and, using a wooden spatula, fold in the finely sifted flour and lastly the melted butter. Three parts fill greased and floured madeleine tins and bake in a moderate oven about 7–10 minutes.

BISCUITS A CUILLER (ENGLISH SPONGE FINGERS)

3 eggs	flavouring of orange-flower water or vanilla
2½ oz. castor sugar	
	2½ oz. flour

Separate the yolks from the whites of egg. Cream yolks with sugar till white and fluffy. Add flavouring. Whip whites to a firm snow and add from a quarter to a third of the quantity to the yolks with the flour, sifting the latter in. Fold in the remaining whipped whites with care, working quickly. It is important that at this stage the mixture should be firm yet fluffy. Put the mixture into a bag fitted with a medium-sized plain pipe. Pipe out in finger lengths (as for éclairs) on to greased, floured baking-sheets. Dust very well with castor sugar, tilting the sheet over a clean piece of paper to remove the surplus. Bake in a very moderate oven, 350°–370° F., for 5–7 minutes.

This mixture may also be put out in small rounds or 'drops' and finished as above. These are usually sandwiched together with a little butter cream, sharp jelly, or whipped cream lightly sweetened and flavoured with vanilla.

CHOCOLATINES

These cakes of génoise, cut into squares or rounds, are split, filled and spread all over with chocolate butter cream, and rolled in browned almonds.

Cut a génoise commune, baked the day before, into small squares or rounds. Fill with a thin layer of chocolate butter cream (see butter creams, page 850), and also spread the sides and the top with the cream. Roll in browned ground or finely chopped almonds and pipe a small rose of butter cream on the top.

[*] See plates 28 and 29

MOKATINES

Prepare a génoise commune and cut into small rounds. Fill with a thin layer of coffee butter cream (see page 850), and then spread the top and sides with the same cream. Roll in chopped browned almonds and pipe a small rose of coffee butter cream in the centre.

Alternative

Another variation is to split the génoise and fill with coffee butter cream (see page 850). Cut it into fingers, approximately $1\frac{1}{2}$ inches wide by $3\frac{1}{2}$ inches long. Brush with apricot glaze (see page 856) and coat with coffee-flavoured fondant (see the making of fondant, page 862).

When set, pipe down the centre of each with coffee butter cream, using a fine rose icing pipe and a side to side movement of it.

MIRLITONS

These little cakes have a rich génoise mixture containing crushed macaroon in a pastry case.

Line tartelette moulds with pâte brisée (see page 840) or trimmings of puff pastry (see page 836). Prick well and put $\frac{1}{2}$ teaspoon apricot marmelade (see page 855) into the bottom of each. Fill with this mixture:

2 eggs	vanilla
$3\frac{1}{2}$ oz. castor sugar	blanched split almonds (3 for
4–5 large macaroons, firm and	each mould)
well dried (see page 868)	icing sugar

Whip eggs with the sugar over gentle heat until thick. Remove and whisk for a further few minutes. Crush the macaroons and fold into the mixture, with vanilla to flavour. Fill into the moulds, decorate each with three split almonds in the shape of a trefoil. Sprinkle well with icing sugar. Bake for about 15 minutes in a moderate to hot oven. See that the baking-sheet is so placed in the oven that it gets more heat below than on top.

The next four recipes are useful when puff pastry is on hand; they all call for trimmings of it. By making a little extra paste work may be saved— R. H. calls it 'working in one thing with another,' adding that it is not always easy to get this idea adopted. The first recipe is for Palmiers, leaf-shaped pieces of flat, sticky, sweet puff pastry, which may be served plain and are very good, or two may be put together with whipped cream in a sandwich. Excellent to serve with compôte of fruit.

PALMIERS

Roll and fold puff pastry trimmings, using castor sugar in place of flour and giving one turn. Roll into an oblong and trim the edges. Fold each side to the centre and then on to itself. Press firmly. Cut into pieces 1–$1\frac{1}{2}$ inches wide and set these on their sides on a damp baking-sheet. Flatten slightly and bake in a hot oven (400° F.), turning when one side has caramelized, and allowing the other side to caramel.

LANGUES DE BŒUF

Roll out the trimmings of puff pastry and cut into rounds about $2\frac{1}{2}$ inches in diameter with a fluted cutter. Put a handful of castor sugar on the marble slab and roll out the rounds into very thin ovals on the sugar, one at a time. Turn the ovals over so that the sugared side is uppermost and bake on a wet baking-sheet in a moderately hot oven 7–8 minutes.

These are good served with fruit compôte.

SACRISTANS

Roll out the trimmings of puff pastry thinly to a rectangle 5–6 inches wide and brush with beaten egg. Sprinkle a wide band in the centre (running lengthwise) with finely chopped almonds and icing sugar. Cut into strips about $\frac{1}{2}$–$\frac{3}{4}$ inch wide and twist. Bake on a damped baking-sheet in a hot oven about 5 minutes.

These also are good to serve with fruit compôte.

ALLUMETTES GLACÉES

Roll out trimmings of puff pastry thinly to a rectangle about 4–5 inches wide and spread with royal icing (see page 828), with a pinch of flour added. Cut into fingers with a floured knife and bake in a moderately hot oven about 12 minutes.

These become Condés if the icing is sprinkled with shredded almonds before baking.

The next five recipes have choux paste as a foundation:

ÉCLAIRS

Take the basic quantity of choux paste (page 843), pipe out in finger or éclair shapes on to lightly greased baking-sheets. Bake until firm. Split and fill with crème chantilly (page 42) or crème patissière (page 851), coffee, chocolate, or plain, and ice with the appropriate flavoured icing, glacé or fondant (see pages 827 and 862).

PARIS-BREST

Choux paste piped in rings, sprinkled with almonds, baked, split, and filled.

basic quantity choux paste (see page 843)
icing or castor sugar
flaked almonds

crème patissière (see page 851), well flavoured with ground praline (see page 854)

Prepare choux paste. Fill into a bag with a large plain pipe. Pipe out in circles the thickness of two fingers and $3\frac{1}{2}$ inches in diameter. Sprinkle with flaked almonds and dust with sugar. Bake in a hot oven until crisp and dry. Cool, split, and fill with the crème patissière, which may be enriched with a little whipped cream or creamed butter. Dredge with icing or castor sugar.

The next recipe is for one of the best of all petits gâteaux; little cups of choux paste are filled with crème patissière and finished on top with burnt icing sugar. These are not too sweet and of excellent flavour.

POLKAS

basic quantity choux paste (see page 843)
apricot purée flavoured with orange (see note at end of instructions)

crème patissière (see page 851)
icing sugar

Line buttered, deep tartlet tins with the paste, using a bag and small plain pipe, or the mixture may be spread over the insides of the moulds with wetted fingers. Bake in a hot oven till firm to touch and golden brown. Take from the moulds; put ½ teaspoon orange-flavoured apricot purée at the bottom of each, fill well with crème patissière, powder thickly with icing sugar, and touch the top of each with a red-hot flat-iron or spoon.

N.B. The apricot purée mentioned is made from cooked dried apricots, well sweetened and flavoured with the zest of an orange and a little of the juice. This is a variation of our own and does not belong to the true gâteaux Polkas, which do not usually contain such a purée. We consider, however, that the apricot gives this rather bland filling the character it lacks.

PAINS DE MECQUE

These are made with plain choux paste put out in the form of small eggs. They are hollowed slightly, baked brown, and the depression filled with a sharp jelly.

basic quantity choux paste (see page 843)
castor or icing sugar

red-currant, gooseberry, or apple jelly

Make the choux paste. Lightly grease a baking-sheet. Put out the paste in dessertspoons, taking care to keep an oval shape.

Dip a finger into egg white or water and make a deep depression along the top of each. Dust heavily with sugar, and bake in a moderately hot oven until firm and well risen. These 'pains' should be well browned in colour. Cool slightly, then fill the depression with a small spoonful of the jelly.

MADELONS

These resemble the preceding Pains de Mecque, but are of different shape. They are piped out in the form of an S. Not too sweet, they are excellent to serve with coffee.

basic quantity of choux paste (see page 843)
castor or icing sugar

sharp jelly, such as red-currant, gooseberry, etc.

Make the choux paste, fill into a bag with vegetable rose pipe, 7–8 cut. Pipe out on to lightly greased baking-sheet in the form of an S.   Dust with castor or icing sugar and bake in a hot oven until firm and well coloured. Take off sheet and cool.   Split one side and fill with the jelly.

Serve the above gâteaux with coffee or afternoon tea.

Egg whites, nuts, and sugar are the principal ingredients in the following six recipes:

MACAROONS (1)

An ordinary and useful recipe.

6 oz. ground almonds	vanilla essence
10 oz. castor sugar	rice-paper
3 egg whites	split almonds
¾ oz. flour or arrowroot	

Mix almonds and sugar, add egg whites and cream very well together. Add the arrowroot or flour and flavour to taste with the vanilla.

Fill mixture into a forcing-bag with a plain pipe.   Spread rice-paper on to baking-sheets and pipe out into rounds about 2 inches across.   Alternatively, use a teaspoon to spread out the mixture.   Press a split almond on to the centre of each macaroon.   Bake for approximately 20 minutes in a slow to moderate oven, 375° F.   Cool thoroughly before storing in a tin.

MACAROONS (2)

4½ oz. almonds	whites of 3 eggs
½ lb. icing sugar	vanilla essence

Blanch almonds (see page 853).   Put through a grater, then turn into a mortar.   Pound thoroughly, add the sugar by degrees, then turn into a pan.   Now work in the egg whites gradually, a little at a time, over gentle heat, in order to keep the paste fairly firm.   Add vanilla essence.   When just hot pipe out the macaroons on to rice-paper or buttered and floured baking-sheets.   Leave 1½ hours before putting into the oven.   Cook in a moderate oven 10 minutes.

MACAROONS (3)

A more laborious recipe, producing well-flavoured macaroons of good texture.

6 oz. whole almonds	6 oz. icing sugar
3–4 bitter almonds, or to taste	5 egg whites
6 oz. loaf sugar	

Blanch the almonds (see page 853).   Spread out on a piece of kitchen paper and dry on the rack over a gas or electric stove, or on top of an Aga stove.   Break in half; when this can be done with ease the almonds are dry enough.

Put all the nuts into a mortar with 2 oz. loaf sugar and pound thoroughly. Turn on to a wire sieve and sift on to a big sheet of paper. Repeat this process with the fragments of almond that will not go through the sieve, adding more loaf sugar each time, pounding thoroughly and getting the fragments as fine as possible, until all the sugar has been used and the fragments of almond have all been passed through the sieve.

Into the mortar put the almonds and sugar, 4½ oz. icing sugar, and 3 unbeaten egg whites, one at a time, working well after the addition of each white. When the paste is firm and easy to work fold in the meringue, spoonful by spoonful, made by whipping the 2 remaining egg whites stiffly and folding in 1½ oz. icing sugar. With a large plain pipe fill a bag with the mixture and pipe out in rounds about 3 inches across and 1¼ inches apart on to a baking-sheet, greased and lightly floured, or on to a plain baking-sheet on which a sheet of rice-paper has been laid. Bake 16–18 minutes in a very moderate oven (340° F.). Remove carefully and cool on a wire tray. If rice-paper has been used cut round each macaroon with kitchen scissors.

DUCHESSES PRALINÉES

Crisp wafers, sandwiched with praline butter cream.

3½ oz. sugar	1 oz. butter
1 oz. ground almonds	3 egg whites
1 oz. ground grilled hazel-nuts	praline butter cream (see page
1 oz. flour	850)

Whisk the egg whites stiffly, mix in with a metal spoon the sugar, nuts, and flour, and lastly the melted butter. Spread into thin ovals (using a cardboard or metal stencil) and bake in a very hot oven 4–5 minutes. Sandwich together with a little praline butter cream.

N.B. The cream should be piped slightly towards one side of each biscuit, so that on the opposite side the edges gape a little.

CHAMONIX

Meringue, chestnut purée, and cream—like a mont blanc but with a meringue instead of a sponge base.

Make either a Swiss meringue or a meringue cuite. For meringue use:

2 whites	2 drops of vanilla
4 oz. sugar	

For a meringue cuite beat whites and sugar together over gentle heat until quite firm. For Swiss meringue whip the whites stiffly and fold the sugar in quickly; add vanilla.

Pipe out on to a greased and floured baking-sheet in rounds. Set in a moderate oven. Using a bag and small plain pipe, pipe a purée of chestnut (see page 71) on to each round. Fill the centres with whipped cream and dust over with grated chocolate.

GALETTES MUSCATS

Almond biscuits covered with chocolate and veined like oak leaves.

4 oz. ground almonds	vanilla
4 oz. castor sugar	covering or couverture choco-
whites of 2–3 eggs, beaten	late
lightly with a fork	

First make a drawing on a piece of cardboard of a large oak leaf. Cut out the parts between the lines to form a stencil (a tinsmith will make and cut a stencil for you). Mix the almonds and sugar together, work in the egg whites to form a smooth moist paste. Flavour with vanilla. Butter and flour some baking-sheets. Spread the mixture on the sheets through the stencil. Bake in a slow to moderate oven (375° F.) until a pale brown. Take off and cool.

Break up the chocolate, warm to blood heat on a plate over hot water, working well. Spread the chocolate fairly thickly on one side of the leaves. When setting, mark in the veins of the leaves with the back of a knife; allow to set before serving.

Nearly all the following recipes call for pastry in various forms as a foundation:

PONTS NEUFS

Little tartlets of pâte brisée filled with a mixture of choux paste and crème patissière.

pâte brisée (see page 840)	crème patissière (see page 851)
choux paste (see page 843)	vanilla or rum

Line tartlet tins with pâte brisée, prick the bottom lightly and fill with a mixture of choux paste and crème patissière in equal proportions and flavoured with vanilla or rum. Paint with egg and place two bands of pâte brisée on the top. Bake in a fairly hot oven 12–15 minutes.

ANTILLES

Little pastry boats holding a purée of banana and thin rum-flavoured icing.

Line boat moulds with pâte sucrée (see page 838) and bake blind. When cool brush with warm apricot glaze (see page 856) and leave to cool and harden. Fill with a purée of raw banana flavoured with a little heavy orange syrup. Glaze and ice with a thin rum-flavoured fondant icing (see page 862).

SAINT-ANDRÉS

Little boats filled with an apple marmelade and covered with royal icing.

pâte brisée (see page 840) or	apple marmelade (see page 855)
pâte sucrée (see page 838)	royal icing (see page 828)

Line boat-shaped moulds with pâte brisée and fill with an apple marmelade well reduced and cold. Spread each with royal icing and lay two narrow bands of pastry slantwise across the top. Bake in a moderate oven about 10 minutes.

LISETTES

Pastry boats filled with almond and egg white mixture decorated with diamonds of glacé orange peel.

pâte sucrée (see page 838)	2 oz. ground almonds
apricot jam	vanilla if castor sugar is used
2 egg whites	candied orange peel (see page
2 oz. castor or vanilla sugar	1131)

Roll out the pastry very thinly and line into boat-shaped moulds, using a fluted cutter. Put a spot of apricot jam into the bottom of each. Beat the whites of egg very stiffly and fold in the sugar and ground almonds. Flavour with vanilla or use vanilla sugar. Fill into the moulds, put a diamond of candied orange peel on the middle of each, dust over with icing sugar, and bake in a moderate oven 10–12 minutes.

CELESTINS

Simple pâte sucrée boats filled with génoise and iced with orange glacé or fondant.

Line boat moulds thinly with pâte sucrée (see page 838), put a spot of apricot jam at the bottom, and fill with madeleine mixture (génoise fine, see page 848). Bake in a moderate oven. When cool brush with an apricot glaze (see page 856) and ice with the orange icing on page 814 or an orange-flavoured fondant (see page 862).

TARTELETTES AUX FRUITS

These are among the prettiest of petits gâteaux.

pâte sucrée or pâte à tarte-lettes (see pages 838–9)	wood strawberries, raspberries, etc.
black and white grapes	apricot or red-currant glaze
sections of tangerine	(see page 856)

Make pastry and leave to rest for an hour or so. Roll out very thinly and line into deep tartlet tins or boat moulds. Bake blind.

Have ready the appropriate glaze. Brush out the cases while the glaze is still hot. Leave to set. Prepare the fruit. Arrange in the cases and brush over with the glaze.

Tartlets can also be made for petits fours by using very small moulds. They give colour to any arrangement of fours glacés or to a cake tray.

TARTELETTES AUX POMMES GRILLÉES

pâte sucrée (see page 838)   hot apricot glaze (see page 856)
apple marmelade (see page 855)

Roll out pastry thinly, line into tartelette moulds, fill with the marmelade, and make a fine lattice-work of long rolled strips (see page 845).   Bake in a hot oven (400°–425° F.) for 12–15 minutes.   Remove from moulds, brush over with hot apricot glaze.

For a large flan make in the same way.

In the Winkfield chapter (page 1023) will be found a recipe for Tartelettes aux Fraises des Bois à la Crème.

FINANCIÈRES

Frangipane type.   Rich mixture with fruits confits, iced with rum-flavoured fondant.

2½ oz. butter   1¾ oz. mixed glacé fruits
2 oz. ground almonds   rum
2 oz. castor sugar   apricot glaze (see page 856)
a bare ounce of potato flour or   fondant icing (see page 862)
   fécule   flavoured with rum
1 egg   glacé cherries

Cream the butter, add almonds, sugar, potato flour, and egg.   Chop the fruit and macerate well in rum before adding to the mixture.   Grease and flour some boat moulds, fill level with the mixture, bake 7–10 minutes, then turn out.   Brush over with apricot glaze, then coat with a white fondant icing flavoured with rum.   Put half a glacé cherry on each one.

FRANGIPANES

A rich almond mixture in flaky or puff paste cases.   Iced with thin white fondant or glacé icing.

flaky pastry (see page 833) or   white glacé or fondant icing
   trimmings of puff pastry (see   (see pages 827 and 862)
   page 836)   stock syrup (see page 860)
frangipane (see page 849)   vanilla
                                        glacé cherries

Roll out the pastry thinly.   Line into deep tartlet moulds.   Prick the bottom.   Fill to just below the top with the frangipane; this is best done with a bag and plain pipe if a number are to be filled.   Bake in a moderately hot oven (400° F.) until well browned, 20–30 minutes.   Turn out and cool.   Warm the fondant and work to a thin icing with the syrup.   Flavour with vanilla.   Brush each cake with the icing; press a half-cherry in the middle of each and coat again with icing, using a spoon.   Leave to set. The icing should be thin enough to form more of a glaze than an icing, so that the brown of the cake shows through.

VÉNITIENS

Pâte sucrée coated with royal icing, piped with a well-reduced apricot glaze, and baked. Plain, slightly sticky. Good for tea and to serve with fruit.

pâte sucrée (see page 838)
royal icing, 1 egg quantity (see page 828)

apricot glaze, well reduced (see page 856)

Roll out the pastry thinly to a large square. Trim the edges. Have the icing slightly softer than for piping. Spread over the surface of the paste. Cut into small squares with a floured knife, arrange on a baking-sheet. Put the glaze into a paper cornet and pipe on each square, from corner to corner and from side to side, a Union Jack. Bake in a fairly hot oven (400° F.) until nicely brown. Lift off and cool.

GALETTE BRETONNAISE

Not unlike a biscuit containing currants; they keep well in a tin.

4 oz. flour
2 oz. butter
3½ oz. castor or icing sugar
5 oz. well-cleaned currants
2 small eggs

a few drops of vanilla essence or the grated rind of ½ a lemon
egg-wash

Make up as for pate sucrée (see page 838), adding currants. Set aside for half an hour or more. Divide into even-sized pieces, the size of a bantam's egg. Arrange at regular intervals on a lightly greased baking-sheet. Flatten out by pressing with a floured thermos cork or the base of a small mould. Brush with egg-wash, mark with a knife, and bake in a fairly hot oven (400° F.).

GALETTES NAPOLITAINES

Rich almond biscuits coated with a mixture of royal icing and shredded almonds and baked.

Roll on a floured marble slab balls of pâte frolle (almond pastry, see page 840) the size of a small egg. Place on a buttered tin and flatten well. Cover each biscuit with a little of the following mixture:

3½ oz. icing sugar
1 egg white

a large pinch of flour
1¾ oz shredded almonds

Work together in the order named; the mixture should be of a good spreading consistency. Dust with icing sugar and bake in the centre of the oven to ensure a good bottom heat for about 10 minutes or until a pale golden brown.

TOMMIES

Hazel-nut pastry sandwiched with honey and coated with chocolate.

3 oz. hazel-nuts
4 oz. butter
2½ oz. castor sugar

5 oz. flour
couverture chocolate
honey

Brown nuts in oven.   Rub in a cloth to remove skins.   Grind through a mill or cheese grater.   Cream butter, add sugar, work in the nuts and flour with the hand.   Immediately a paste is formed, set aside to chill for half an hour.   Roll out thinly, stamp into rounds, and bake 12–15 minutes in a moderate oven.   Take off and when cool sandwich together with honey.

Melt chocolate to blood heat, coat the biscuits, and when chocolate is on the point of setting fill a little extra into a paper cornet.   Pipe over each biscuit in lattice fashion.

If wished the biscuits may be coated with a chocolate marquise (see page 863), but the piping should still be done with the plain couverture.

FOURRÉS AU MIEL

Pâte sucrée, fruits confits, and honey.   Sweet and sticky, a good use for scraps of pâte sucrée and a few fruits confits.

Prepare a pâte sucrée (see page 838) and work in fruits confits finely chopped and soaked in rum for half an hour or so.   To 4 oz. flour quantity of pâte sucrée use $3\frac{1}{2}$ oz. fruits confits.   Roll out fairly thinly and cut into rounds about 3 inches in diameter with a plain cutter.   Cook in a hot oven on buttered baking-sheets.   When cool sandwich with a little honey and powder with vanilla sugar.

The following is a recipe for a well-known pâtisserie.   The mixture given below is for a baba and is that used for a savarin.   A recipe for the latter will be found in the chapter on sweets.

BABAS

These are commonly made in dariole moulds.   If made in rings the currants are omitted and whipped cream fills the centres.

$4\frac{1}{2}$ oz. flour	$\frac{3}{4}$ oz. yeast
a pinch of salt	2 eggs
1 wineglass (décilitre) warm milk	2 oz. currants, well cleaned
$1\frac{3}{4}$ oz. butter	sugar syrup 22° *pèse-sirop* (see Sugar Boiling, page 857)
$\frac{1}{2}$ oz. sugar	rum

Sift the flour and salt into a warm bowl.   Cream the yeast and sugar together and pour in the milk.   Blend well together and add to the flour with the beaten eggs.   Beat vigorously with the hand for 5 minutes, then cover the bowl and leave in a warm place $\frac{3}{4}$–1 hour until well risen.   Cream the butter until soft and beat thoroughly into the mixture.   Add the currants.

Well grease dariole moulds, pour in the mixture, three parts fill, and leave to prove 5–10 minutes in a warm temperature.   Bake in a hot oven until a good golden brown, approximately 15–18 minutes.   Turn out carefully on to a pastry rack, soak with syrup.   Sprinkle each baba well with rum just before serving.

The following may be regarded as petits gâteaux or petits fours, according to the size they are made:

MACARONS AU CHOCOLAT

4½ oz. ground almonds	2½ oz. melted chocolate
7 oz. castor sugar	split almonds
2 whites of egg	

Work ingredients well together; roll into small balls and put on to greased and floured baking-sheets. Flatten out, put an almond on to each, and bake in a slow oven 20–30 minutes.

These macaroons may be baked on paper, and then taken off by means of water run under the paper whilst the tins are still hot.

LANGUES DE CHATS

2 oz. butter	2 egg whites
2 oz. castor sugar	a few drops of vanilla, or use
2 oz. flour	vanilla sugar

Cream the butter and when thoroughly soft beat in the sugar. Whip the whites to a snow and add to the mixture alternately with the flour, beating it vigorously and adding the vanilla essence. Fill into a forcing-bag with an éclair pipe.

Grease and flour a thick baking-sheet, pipe out the mixture in the shape of éclairs. Bang the tin smartly on the table once or twice to flatten the biscuits slightly. Bake in a fairly hot oven for 10–12 minutes. The biscuits should be a very pale golden with the edges deeply tinged with brown.

TUILES D'AMANDES, OR DENTELLES

Curled wafer biscuits, very thin and very good.

2 whites of egg	½ teaspoon vanilla essence
4 oz. castor sugar	1 oz. blanched shredded almonds
2 oz. flour	2 oz. butter

Break the whites into a bowl, beat in the castor sugar with a fork, add the flour, vanilla, almonds, and butter, melted but not hot. Grease some baking-sheets and spread out the mixture in teaspoons in a circle. Bake to a golden brown in a moderate oven, then lift off carefully and lay over a rolling-pin to cool. Store immediately in an air-tight tin.

The size of these is determined by what they are intended for, i.e. petits gâteaux or petits fours.

ORANGINES

Flat, thin rounds, with orange candied peel and almonds.

2 oz. blanched almonds	1½ oz. flour
2 oz. butter	a few drops of carmine
2 oz. orange candied peel	a spoonful of milk if necessary
2 oz. castor sugar	

Chop the almonds and peel finely. Cream the butter, add the peel and almonds, then the sugar, flour, carmine, and a spoonful of milk if necessary.

Butter some baking-sheets, put out the mixture in half-teaspoons, then flatten out with a wet fork. Bake till well tinged with brown, then leave for a few minutes before taking off the tin.

BERRICHONS

Rather like macaroons; may be filled with butter cream and iced.

4 egg whites	4½ oz. castor sugar
4½ oz. ground almonds	1¾ oz. flour

Whip the egg whites until stiff and firm, fold in the almonds, sugar, and flour. Pipe on a buttered and floured tin into small rounds like macaroons, or long as for Langues de Chats. Bake in a moderately hot oven 7–8 minutes. These may be filled with butter cream, decorated, and iced. They also form the base of several petits fours.

CIGARETTES RUSSES

To serve with ices or as petits fours. Like tuiles but rolled into cigarettes.

2 egg whites	1½ oz. flour, well sifted
3½ oz. sugar	1¾ oz. melted butter

Whisk the egg whites until stiff, mix in very lightly, using a wooden spoon, first the sugar, then the flour, and lastly the butter. Spread fairly thinly, in oblongs the size of a cigarette paper, on a buttered and floured tin, and bake in a hot oven 5–6 minutes. Remove from the tin, quickly lay upside-down on the table, and roll round a pencil, holding it firmly with the hand. Slide off the pencil and leave to cool.

N.B. Bake one or two first to test the mixture; if too thin and difficult to handle add a pinch of flour, if too firm or hard add a spoonful of melted butter. Store at once in a tin.

The ends of each cigarette may be dipped in melted chocolate and then chopped pistachios or chopped browned almonds.

PETITS FOURS GLACÉS

These are tiny cakes of génoise fine or commune, split and filled with apricot jam or butter cream. A slab of cake is cut up into appropriate sizes and each small piece is individually iced. The cake should not be iced before being cut up.

COQUETTES AU CAFÉ

Tiny rounds of cooked coffee-flavoured meringue cuite, sandwiched with meringue and with half a glacé or crystallized cherry inside.

Prepare a meringue cuite (see page 852) and flavour with a strong coffee essence.   Pipe out into very small meringues (boutons) and bake in a cool oven 8–12 minutes, or until firm to the touch, on a greased and floured baking-sheet.

When cool, sandwich two together with a little uncooked meringue and half a crystallized or glacé cherry in the middle.   Serve in small paper cases.

SUPRÊMES PRALINÉES

Tiny marbles of choux paste, filled with praline cream.

Bake 'petits choux' as for Salambos, and *before* baking brush with beaten egg and sprinkle with very finely chopped almonds and sugar. Bake in a hot oven.   When cool, fill with praline butter cream (see page 850) and dust lightly with icing sugar.

SALAMBOS

Choux paste filled with whipped cream (crème chantilly) or crème patissière, and the tops dipped in caramel or sugar boiled to the crack.

Pipe out choux pastry into small balls, using a plain éclair pipe.   Bake in a hot oven.   When cool fill with crème chantilly (see page 42) or crème patissière (see page 851).

Dip the tops in sugar boiled to the crack (see page 860), or caramel (see page 860), and dip again in finely chopped pistachio nuts.   Serve in small paper cases.

POTS-POURRIS

Tiny tartlets filled with glacé fruit, soaked in rum.   Iced with thin fondant.

pâte sucrée (see page 838)
mixed glacé fruit or fruits confits
trimmings of génoise (see page 848)

rum
thin, warm, fondant icing (see page 862) flavoured with rum

Line small tartlet tins with pâte sucrée.   Bake blind.   Finely chop the glacé fruit and macerate in a little rum.   Leave as long as possible.

Take about one quarter of génoise to the quantity of fruit.   Crumble it into a bowl and moisten with a little rum.   Mix with a fork, adding the fruit.   When thoroughly mixed and well moistened fill level into the cases.

Ice with a thin warm fondant flavoured with rum.

CROISSANTS DE PROVENCE

Tiny croissants made of almond paste, flavoured with vanilla or orange-flower water.

5½ oz. freshly blanched almonds	vanilla or orange-flower water
5¼ oz. castor sugar	beaten egg
2 egg whites	shredded almonds
1 spoonful apricot marmelade (see page 855)	sweetened milk

Pound the almonds well, adding the sugar by degrees.   Then mix in the apricot marmelade, adding the egg whites a little at a time, and only enough to make a paste that can be rolled in the hand.   Flavour to taste.

Divide the mixture into pieces the size of a nut and roll with a little flour to the size and shape of your little finger.   Brush with beaten egg and then roll in shredded almonds (they should be well covered).

Place on paper to bake in the shape of a croissant, gild with egg, and bake in a moderate oven 10 minutes.   When they are. cooked brush them lightly with sweetened milk and return to the oven for a few minutes to make them shiny and sticky.

PAIN DE SEIGLE

4½ oz. blanched almonds	scant 1 oz. flour
4½ oz. castor sugar	2 small egg whites
2 oz. praline (pounded and sieved)	

Grind and pound the almonds with the sugar to a paste, add flour, and moisten with the egg whites.   Add the praline.   Divide the mixture into small pieces the size of a walnut, roll in very slightly beaten egg white and then in sifted icing sugar.   The best way to do this is to moisten the palms of the hands well with the white and roll the pieces of mixture between them.   Then roll the pieces in a piece of paper well covered with the sugar.   Bake on rice-paper in a moderate oven 15 minutes.

ROCHERS

Little rocks of almond-filled meringue.

Prepare a meringue cuite as on page 852, add 4 oz. finely shredded almonds and flavour with vanilla.   Place in small rough teaspoons on a buttered and floured baking-sheet and bake 8–10 minutes in a moderate oven.

These can also be flavoured with coffee, strawberry, chocolate, etc.

The following petits fours are a type of confiserie and may be offered as bonbons:

FRUITS GLACÉS

Fruits glacés or glazed fruits are fruits dipped in syrup boiled to the crack. The syrup then sets on the surface of the fruit, giving a hard and shiny surface. They are served as petits fours, or may form part of the dessert for dinner.

Choose fruit that is perfectly dry: this is important, otherwise the syrup will not adhere; small clusters of grapes, both black and white, sections of orange or tangerine, fine ripe, dry strawberries and cherries, are the most suitable.

First prepare the fruit, and lightly oil the marble slab or baking-sheet together with a dipping fork or ordinary table fork. Prepare a syrup with:

4 oz. loaf sugar	½ teaspoon liquid glucose
½ gill water	

Boil to the crack, following directions for sugar boiling (see page 858). Check boiling when correct stage has been reached. Prop the pan in a tilted position at side of slab, then quickly dip in the fruit. Put at once on the oiled slab and leave to set (about 5 minutes).

If a fair amount of fruit is to be dipped, have ready another lot of syrup about to reach the crack stage. It is easier to dip a small quantity at a time. Any syrup left over may be burnt for caramel.

These fruits will not keep satisfactorily above an hour or so. Serve in small paper cases.

FRUIT DIPPED IN FONDANT

Fruit dipped into fondant should be, like fruits glacés, as dry as possible. Brandied cherries or other fruit preserved in syrup must be drained thoroughly before dipping. The fondant should be taken to 240°–242° F. to ensure a firm coating when set, and be diluted with stock syrup before warming and flavoured with brandy, kirsch, etc.

Fruit so treated may be strawberries (fresh or candied), physalis (fresh), cumquats (preserved), brandied cherries, greengages and so on.

PHYSALIS (CAPE GOOSEBERRIES)

physalis fondant icing (see page 862)	rum

Cut the 'petals' or covering capsules of the physalis in three places up to the stalk and fold these carefully back. Warm the fondant in a bain-marie, working it with sugar syrup or water and rum to flavour. It must be thick enough to coat nicely. Dip in the physalis, holding them by the 'petals.' Set on a marble slab dusted with icing sugar. When firm put into small paper cases.

CUMQUATS 'DÉGUISÉES'

Drain cumquats well from their syrup.   Dip into warm fondant (see page 862) flavoured with rum, using a dipping fork or ring.   Put to set on a marble slab well dusted with icing sugar.   Serve in small paper cases. Fresh cumquats may be treated in the same way and are refreshing and less sweet.

CERISES MARQUISES

For these use brandy cherries well drained on a wire rack.   Dip each one by the stalk into warm fondant (see page 862) flavoured with kirsch. Put to set on a marble slab well dusted with icing sugar.   Serve in small paper cases.

CHOCOLATE TRUFFLES (1)

½ oz. unsweetened chocolate
¼ lb. couverture or best block
  chocolate
3 oz. fresh butter, well
  creamed

2 oz. fondant (see page 862)
rum, or vanilla or coffee essence
melted couverture and un-
  sweetened chocolate powder
  or cocoa powder for rolling

Melt the unsweetened and the sweetened chocolate over gentle heat after cutting up.   While lukewarm work well into the fondant, then work in the butter.   Flavour to taste.   Divide into small teaspoons and put on to waxed or grease-proof paper to harden.

When firm have ready the melted couverture; put a little on the palms of the hands and lightly roll the truffles between them.   Toss into a paper of unsweetened chocolate or cocoa powder.   Brush off the surplus and put on racks to dry.

Truffles are always nicer if eaten freshly made.

CHOCOLATE TRUFFLES (2)

¼ lb. best couverture or block
  chocolate
water or strong coffee
3 oz. good fresh butter
2 tablespoons cream or evaporated milk (optional)

3 oz. finely crushed praline
rum or vanilla essence to flavour
couverture and cocoa powder
  for finishing

Melt the chocolate over gentle heat to a thick cream with the water or strong coffee.   Draw aside, stir in the butter by degrees, then add the cream and praline.   Flavour to taste.   Put out in small teaspoons on to waxed or grease-proof paper.   When set finish as in the preceding recipe.

COLETTES

Tiny cases of chocolate filled with rich chocolate cream (crème ganache).

3–4 oz. couverture or good block chocolate	small paper sweet cases

Crème ganache

5 oz. couverture or block chocolate	2 egg yolks
½ gill cream or strong coffee	rum to flavour
2 oz. butter	shredded pistachios or gold-leaf

Cut up chocolate and melt over gentle heat. With the tip of your little finger or the handle of a teaspoon line into the paper cases. Leave to set. Meantime make the crème ganache. Break up the chocolate, put into a pan with the cream or coffee. Cook until thick, draw aside, cool, and beat in the butter in small pieces, add yolks and flavour with rum. Leave until quite thick, stirring occasionally. Fill into a bag with a rose pipe. Carefully peel off the paper from the cases, pipe in the 'ganache,' and decorate each one with a few shreds of pistachio or a touch of gold-leaf.

PÂTE D'AMANDES FONDANTES

take equal proportions of fondant and freshly blanched almonds
 (say ¼ lb. of each) (best quality ground almonds may be used, but
 the resulting flavour is not so good)
flavour to taste—vanilla, rum, coffee and so on
dates, walnut kernels, glacé cherries

Grind and pound almonds to a paste.

Work into the fondant; do this on a slab. When thoroughly incorporated divide paste into three. Flavour one piece with coffee, one piece with rum, and a third with vanilla; the rum-flavoured portion may be coloured pink or green.

Divide into *small* pieces. Roll the coffee-flavoured into balls, the pink or green into ovals, and the white into oblongs. Stone the dates and cut cherries in half. Press a half-walnut on each side of the coffee fondants, insert a piece of the rum-flavoured into each date. Reserve the white for the cherries which are pressed on to each end of the oblong.

These are usually glazed, i.e. dipped into sugar boiled to the crack (see page 860), then put when set into paper cases.

GROS GÂTEAUX

These large cakes are enough for 6–8 people except when another number is specified. They are classics, bearing classic names. They may be served for tea, for afternoon parties and buffets, and now, since convention is relaxed, are often offered for the sweet course, accompanied perhaps by fruits rafraîchis or compôtes.   Some are more difficult to make than others, but none is really outside the possibility of a student who has mastered the principles of cake- and pastry-making and of icings.

Gâteau Praline is a light génoise mixture, filled with praline butter cream and finished off with a white praline.

GÂTEAU PRALINE

Génoise

4 eggs	3½ oz. flour, sifted
4¼ oz. castor sugar	3½ oz. butter, melted
praline butter cream (see below)	white praline (see page 854)

Break the eggs, add the sugar gradually, and whisk over heat until thick. Remove and continue beating until the bowl is cool, then quickly fold in the sifted flour and melted butter.   Bake as for Gateau Mousseline aux Noisettes.

When cold cut in two and sandwich with praline butter cream.   Spread the cake top and sides with the same cream and cover with white praline.

Praline butter cream

For the butter cream add crushed praline to taste—about 2 tablespoons —to the basic quantity of butter cream (see page 850).

Gâteau Mousseline aux Noisettes has nuts incorporated in the cake itself and is dredged with icing sugar, but not iced.   It is really a plain nut sponge, good for serving with fruit compôtes and fruits rafraîchis.

GÂTEAU MOUSSELINE AUX NOISETTES

4½ oz. castor sugar	1¾ oz. flour
1¼ oz. ground grilled nuts	1¾ oz. fécule or arrowroot
4 yolks, 3 whites of egg	

Put the sugar and ground nuts in a basin, add the egg yolks, and work with a spatula until creamy and white.   Fold in the sifted flours and lastly with great care the stiffly whisked egg whites.   Turn into a buttered and floured *moule à manqué* and bake in a very moderate oven about 40 minutes.   When cold dredge heavily with icing sugar.

Gâteau Nougatine also has nuts in the cake itself and is covered with butter cream and crushed praline and decorated with thin leaves of nougatine.

GÂTEAU NOUGATINE

4 eggs	2 oz. butter, melted but not
4¼ oz. castor sugar	hot
3½ oz. flour	2 oz. ground browned almonds
	filling (see page 883)

Separate the eggs. Beat the yolks thoroughly with the sugar. Whip whites to a stiff snow. Fold into the yolks and sugar alternately with the flour, butter, and almonds. Mix as quickly as possible and turn at once into buttered and floured *moule à manqué* or a square tin. Bake in a moderate oven 40–50 minutes. When cooked turn out and cool. Split and fill with the following:

Filling

To a 6–8 oz. quantity of the crème au beurre mousseline (see page 850) add 2 oz. baked hazel-nuts, ground and pounded. (Praline may be used instead.) Fill the cake and spread the cream over the top and sides, press crushed praline round sides. Nougatine rolled out thinly and cut into leaf shapes or diamonds is used to decorate the top of the cake.

Gâteau Pain de Gênes is a rich moist cake in which ground almonds predominate. It is neither iced nor decorated and it keeps well.

GÂTEAU PAIN DE GÊNES

5 oz. castor sugar	3 eggs
4 oz. butter	a liqueur glass of kirsch (or use
3½ oz. ground almonds	another flavouring)
1½ oz. flour or fécule	

Cream the butter, add the sugar and cream until white. Add the ground almonds and continue working 2 or 3 minutes. Beat in the eggs and then fold in the flour and lastly the kirsch or other flavouring chosen. Turn into a prepared tin and bake in a very moderate oven 40–45 minutes.

In Gâteau Japonais ground almonds and sugar are mixed with white of egg and no flour or fécule is used. It is therefore an almond meringue biscuit and it is filled with coffee butter cream. It may be served with fruit or the layers may be filled with sliced strawberries or raspberries and whipped cream.

GÂTEAU JAPONAIS

6 oz. ground almonds	coffee butter cream (see page
¾ lb. castor sugar	850)
6 egg whites	white praline (see page 854)

Mix the sugar and almonds and sift together. Beat the whites very stiffly, fold in the almonds and sugar. Place the mixture in a piping bag with a plain pipe. Pipe out two or three rounds in a spiral to the required diameter on a buttered and floured baking-sheet. Cook in a slow oven ¾–1 hour, as for meringues. When cooked allow to cool completely.

When cool, sandwich together with coffee butter cream and spread top and sides with the same cream. Cover with white praline and score the top with a knife.

Coffee butter cream and browned chopped almonds are the important points of Gâteau Moka:

GÂTEAU MOKA

Prepare a biscuit fin au beurre (see page 849) and bake in a *moule à manqué* in a very moderate oven 35–40 minutes.   When cool split into two or three rounds, fill with coffee butter cream (see page 850), and reshape. Spread the top and sides with a layer of the cream (keeping a little back), then cover with browned, finely shredded or chopped almonds.

Decorate the cake with the remaining butter cream piped through a vegetable rose pipe.

Gâteau Cendrillon is one of the best of coffee cakes.   It is composed of the lightest génoise mixture, flavoured with coffee, filled with coffee butter cream, iced with a coffee fondant, and finished with browned almonds or hazel-nuts.

GÂTEAU CENDRILLON

Génoise fine

4 eggs	3½ oz. flour
4½ oz. sugar	3½ oz. butter
coffee essence	coffee fondant or glacé icing
coffee butter cream (see page 850)	(see pages 862 and 827)
	browned almonds or hazel-
apricot glaze (see page 856)	nuts

Prepare a génoise fine (see page 848) and flavour lightly with coffee essence.   Bake in a *moule à manqué* in a moderate oven for 40 minutes. When quite cold, preferably the following day, cut in two and fill with coffee butter cream.   Brush the cake with apricot glaze, ice with a coffee fondant or glacé icing, and decorate the top with halved browned almonds or browned whole hazel-nuts.

In Doboz Torte we have a famous cake made with several layers of sponge biscuit with chocolate butter cream between each and a top of caramel; butter creams of other flavours may replace the chocolate, and alternate layers of coffee and chocolate butter cream are good.

GÂTEAU DOBOZ (DOBOZ TORTE)

4 eggs	butter cream (¾ lb. quantity
6 oz. castor sugar	approx., see recipe 1 or 2,
5 oz. flour	page 850) flavoured with
	melted chocolates
	grated chocolate or crushed
	cake or biscuit crumbs

Caramel (see page 861)

4–6 oz. lump or castor sugar

Butter and flour five baking-sheets.   Whisk the eggs, add the sugar gradually and whisk over hot water until thick.   Fold in the flour and spread the mixture out in large rounds, approximately 8½ inches across. Bake until golden brown. Loosen from the tin and trim round with a saucepan lid and a sharp knife; lift off the tin on to a rack to cool.

Take one round with the best surface. Lay on an oiled pastry rack or tin and pour over a caramel; when just about to set mark into sections with the back of an oiled knife. Trim round the edge.

Sandwich the rounds together with chocolate butter cream, put the caramel-covered round on the top, spread the sides with butter cream (keeping a little back) and press round with grated chocolate or crushed cake or biscuit crumbs. Pipe remaining butter cream round the top edge.

Gâteau Caraque is a rich chocolate sponge filled and spread with chocolate butter cream and decorated with caraque chocolate. It keeps well.

GÂTEAU CARAQUE (FOR 6)

3 eggs	basic quantity of butter cream,
4½ oz. castor sugar	recipe 1 or 2 (see page
1 oz. sweetened block chocolate	850) flavoured with melted
1½ oz. unsweetened chocolate	chocolate
2¼ oz. plain flour	caraque chocolate

Break up the chocolate and melt with a little water or coffee to a thick cream. Set aside to cool. Whisk the eggs with the sugar until really thick. This will take about 7 minutes and is best done over hot water. Whisk for another minute or two after removing from heat, then sift in the flour, folding it in quickly and carefully with the chocolate.

Turn at once into a greased and floured shallow cake tin, round or square, and bake in a moderate oven 30–40 minutes. It is advisable to line the bottom of the tin with grease-proof paper. Turn out and when cold split and sandwich with chocolate butter cream; spread the sides and top with the cream (keeping a little back) and cover the top with the caraque chocolate. Dust lightly with icing sugar and pipe large roses of cream at intervals round the edge.

For Gâteau Mexicain any good form of chocolate sponge will serve. It must be dark and rich. The chocolate fondant icing should be marbled with royal icing.

GÂTEAU MEXICAIN

Make a good chocolate cake such as a Gâteau Négresse (see page 886) and bake it in a deep sandwich tin or *moule à manqué*. Turn out and when cold sandwich with chocolate butter cream (see page 850), brush lightly with apricot glaze (see page 856), and ice with chocolate fondant (see page 863). Pipe at once across the cake with royal icing (see page 828) in straight lines about 1–1½ inches apart, before the fondant has time to set. Then immediately, with the point of a knife, draw lines across the piped lines at the same intervals apart. Then draw the lines across the opposite way. (See Marbling, page 829.)

Gâteau Négresse is a rich damp chocolate cake. It may be iced with a marquise or filled with chocolate butter cream.

GÂTEAU NÉGRESSE

4 oz. sweetened block choco- late	3 eggs
	2 oz. ground almonds
4 oz. butter	2½ oz. fresh white breadcrumbs
5 oz. sugar	½ teaspoon vanilla essence

Cut up chocolate and melt in a little water to a thick cream. The amount of liquid depends on the chocolate and may vary from 1 tablespoon to as much as 3. It is wiser to start with the smaller amount and add more if necessary.

Cream the butter well, beat in the sugar gradually. Add egg yolks and almonds and continue to beat. Then stir in the chocolate, crumbs, and vanilla. Whip whites to a snow and fold into the mixture. Turn into a shallow cake tin, well greased, the bottom lined with paper, and dusted out with flour. Bake in a moderate oven, 370° F.–400° F., for about 45 minutes to 1 hour, or until cooked. Leave a minute or two before turning out. Turn out, dust with icing sugar or coat with a marquise icing (see page 863), or fill with chocolate butter cream (recipe 1 or 2, page 850, flavoured with melted chocolate).

The following is a delicious orange cake and is quoted in its classic form. We have sometimes, when the season was right, taken a few cumquats (tiny Japanese oranges), pounded, sieved, and sweetened them and spread them on the split surface before filling with the crème patissière; then, as R. H. remarked, we must not call it 'viennois.' The fresh taste of this unusual fruit made the sacrifice of the name worth while.

GÂTEAU A L'ORANGE VIENNOIS

Prepare a génoise fine or commune (see pages 848–9). When cooked and cold split and fill with orange-flavoured crème patissière (see page 851). Reshape and pour over a white fondant or glacé icing (see pages 862 and 827) to which has been added a little finely shredded blanched orange rind.

The following pineapple gâteau may be made with biscuit fin or génoise fine and is filled with cream, reshaped, and covered with sliced fresh or frozen pineapple, then glazed. It makes an excellent summer luncheon sweet. This recipe shows a sponge mixture.

GÂTEAU ANANAS

3 eggs	rum
4½ oz. castor sugar	icing sugar
3 oz. plain flour	whipped cream or crème patis-
1½ oz. glacé pineapple or mixed glacé fruit (optional)	sière 2 (see page 852)
	hot apricot glaze (see page 856)
slices of frozen or fresh pine- apple	

Whisk the eggs and sugar together over hot water until very thick. Remove the bowl from the heat and continue whisking for another few minutes. Then fold in the sifted flour with the diced glacé fruit and turn at once into a shallow cake tin or *moule à manqué*. Bake in a slow to moderate oven, 375° F., for 30–40 minutes.

Cut pineapple into thin slices. Sprinkle with rum and a little icing sugar. When the cake is cool split and sandwich with the whipped cream or crème patissière. Brush the outside of the cake lightly with hot apricot glaze, then cover the top with the sliced pineapple. Brush again *thickly* with glaze and leave to set. It is important that the glaze should set fairly firmly when cold, so it must be properly reduced.

In Gâteau Lyonnais we have a chestnut cake finished with apricot glaze and fruits confits.

GÂTEAU LYONNAIS

4½ oz. castor sugar
4 eggs
vanilla

apricot marmelade or glaze (see pages 855 and 856), and extra glaze for brushing

9 oz. chestnuts, weighed when cooked and sieved
3½ oz. butter

fruits confits

Method as for biscuit fin au beurre (see page 849). Use chestnuts in place of flour, reserving 2 tablespoons to press round the sides of the finished cake.

Spread mixture about ½ inch thick on prepared baking-tin, bake 20 minutes. Cut in three, sandwich with apricot marmelade or glaze, and brush top and sides lightly with the glaze. Decorate the top with fruits confits and brush again with glaze. Press chestnuts round the sides and serve.

N.B. May be sandwiched with whipped cream in place of the marmelade.

In the Winkfield chapter (page 1026) will be found a recipe for a very good gâteau made with chestnuts and chocolate.

The rich and delicious Gâteau Amatio is made in a flan ring lined with almond pastry and filled with crème patissière flavoured with praline. The top is covered with almond pastry.

GÂTEAU AMATIO

Pâte frolle
6 oz. flour
2½ oz. ground almonds
3 oz. butter
3 oz. castor sugar

crème patissière, 1½ times the quantity given in recipe 1, page 851
1 coffee-cup crushed praline

1 egg
1 yolk
grated rind of ½ a lemon

1–2 tablespoons thick cream
a little rum (optional)
beaten egg for brushing

Make up the pâte frolle according to the directions on page 840.   Leave in a cool place at least half an hour.   Roll out three-quarters of the paste and line into a deep flan ring.   Chill and fill with the crème patissière into which the praline and cream have been stirred.   (The crème patissière may be flavoured with rum.)   Roll out the remaining paste, cover the top completely, trim, mark over with a knife, brush with beaten egg, and bake in a moderately hot oven 35–40 minutes.   Serve freshly made, but cold.

Four gâteaux made with puff pastry follow.   Probably the best known is the popular millefeuille.

GÂTEAU MILLEFEUILLE (1)

puff pastry (see page 836), made with ¾ lb. flour
apricot glaze (see page 856)

pâte sucrée (see page 838) made with 6 oz. flour
fruit and cream for the filling

Roll out the puff pastry fairly thinly and cut into five or six rounds about 10 inches in diameter.   Remove the centre of each round with a cutter about 3–4 inches in diameter, so leaving a large ring of pastry about 3 inches wide.   Prick and bake on a damp baking-sheet in a hot oven.   Roll out the pâte sucrée into a round a little thicker and larger than the circles, prick and bake in the same way.   When they are all cool mount one on top of the other on the round of pâte sucrée, brushing each ring with glaze and pressing lightly together.   Brush the top and sides again with glaze and decorate the sides with tiny shapes of puff pastry (stars, diamonds, etc.) and the top with, say, glacé fruits and split blanched almonds.   The cake should be decorated, but the method of decoration is a personal choice and is not governed by any set rule.

At the moment of serving the gâteau is filled with fruit (peaches, raspberries, strawberries) and a cream of some sort (patissière, bourdaloue, etc.); the best of all fillings is a crème chantilly layered with Alpine strawberries.

GÂTEAU MILLEFEUILLE (2) (FOR 8–10)

This is another version of the millefeuille, and in some ways is more convenient to serve than the other as it can be cut into slices.

puff pastry (see page 836) made with 8 oz. flour
½ pint quantity pastry cream (see basic recipe, page 850) or crème chantilly (see page 42)

raspberry or strawberry jam
8 oz. icing sugar, with syrup or water, *or*
thin white fondant icing (see page 862)
rum or vanilla to flavour

Divide the pastry into three and roll out each piece into a strip about 4 inches wide and as long as possible.   Place on a wet baking-sheet and bake until brown and well risen.   When cool trim the edges and spread a layer of jam on one strip, cover with pastry cream and place another piece of pastry on the top. Spread again with jam and cream and cover with the third piece, the smooth side uppermost. Press lightly but firmly together. Put the icing sugar into a pan with the flavouring and enough syrup or water to mix to a cream (or use thin white fondant). Warm and coat over the top of the pastry. Crush the trimmings and press along the top edge of the millefeuille. Serve on a long board or cut into slices with a sharp knife.

An alternative filling is a light purée of chestnuts with crème chantilly, and a chocolate marquise may take the place of the glacé or fondant icing.

TARTE FRANÇAISE

puff pastry (see page 836) made with 6 oz. flour

egg-wash for brushing (see page 38)

dessert fruit such as black or white grapes, tangerines,

peaches, cherries, strawberries

apricot or red-currant jelly glaze according to the colour of the fruit (see page 856)

Roll out pastry to a long wide strip and cut out a piece approximately 12 inches long by 5–6 inches wide and $\frac{1}{4}$–$\frac{1}{2}$ inch thick. (The length depends on the size of your oven.) Lightly flour this piece and fold over on to itself lengthways. You now have a long double piece of pastry from which to cut a frame which will form the wall of the tart. With a sharp floured knife cut out a section of this double piece of pastry leaving three sides, one long and two short, all $1\frac{1}{2}$ inches wide. This will leave you with a narrow frame folded in two.

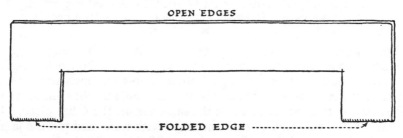

OPEN EDGES

FOLDED EDGE

Set this aside. Roll out the centre piece to the size of a 'picture' for the 'picture frame' that you have just made. Trim the edges, put on a wet baking-sheet. Brush round edges with water, carefully lift up the folded border and lay on one side of the paste. Now open it out, arrange it evenly, and trim off the bottom edge. With the back of the knife mark the border in zigzag, and prick the bottom of the tart. Brush border carefully with egg-wash, so that none will get on to the outside edge. Bake in a hot oven until golden brown. Slide off on to a rack to cool. Brush the bottom lightly with the glaze and arrange the fruit in rows of contrasting colour down the tart. Keep fruit whole and as dry as possible; peaches and tangerines, of course, must be halved or quartered. Brush the fruit thickly with the glaze and serve the tart on a long board.

GÂTEAU PITHIVIERS

puff pastry (see page 836)   crème aux amandes (see below)

Roll out the puff pastry and cut two rounds, one (the top) being slightly thicker than the other. Place the thinner piece of pastry on a slightly damped baking-sheet and spread the centre thickly with the almond cream, leaving a border 1–1½ inches wide.

Crème aux amandes

3½ oz. blanched almonds   vanilla or liqueur glass of
3½ oz. castor sugar   orange-flower water or rum
a good 1¼ oz. butter   beaten egg or lightly beaten
2 yolks   white for brushing

Pound the almonds to a paste, add the sugar and butter by degrees. Work in the yolks and flavouring until the paste whitens and is soft and creamy.

Brush round the edge of the pastry with water, and lay over the thicker round of pastry. Paint with beaten egg or lightly beaten white, and mark with a decorative pattern using the back of a knife. The correct decoration is the 'cart-wheel' usual for galettes.[1] Dust with castor sugar and bake in a hot oven 20–30 minutes.

GALETTE JALOUSIE

trimmings of puff pastry should be used for this galette, or flaky
pastry (see page 833), about 6 oz. quantity pastry for 4 people.
good firm jam or a purée of apples, apricots, etc.

Roll out thinly. Cut a strip 3½ inches wide and 8 inches long, fold over, trim neatly, and then with a pair of scissors cut along the whole length of the paste in narrow strips, leaving a border of about an inch along the top and at the sides, as you would cut a ham frill. Fold up the trimmings and roll out thinly to a long strip about the same size as the other piece. Put this on a wet baking-sheet, brush the edges with water and put the jam or purée down the middle. Now cover carefully with the top piece of 'jalousie,' press down round the edges and trim off. Brush lightly over with water, dust with sugar, and bake in a hot oven 20–30 minutes or until well browned.

The foregoing are representative of the many classic gros gâteaux. The student of cookery, having achieved mastery of these, may wish to extend her knowledge, and she will be wise then to acquire some of the many French books dealing with this subject.

[1] 'Cart-wheel' here means a circle with curved spokes.

XXX

Sweets, Hot and Cold

BOILED, STEAMED, AND BAKED PUDDINGS

Puddings made with Suet

Plum puddings. Plum or Christmas puddings are better boiled than steamed. The following are all well tried and tested recipes and vary only in richness. A plum pudding always improves with keeping, which allows the mixture to mature, and it is customary to make a batch of puddings rather than a single one. After the first boiling the cloths are removed and the puddings re-covered as directed in the first recipe, and they are then stored for future use. In the old days in some households puddings would be made in November or December with the new season's fruit and kept until the following year, so that the Christmas pudding was always a year old. R. H. says her grandmother always did this and would never eat a pudding less than a year old.

The Christmas pudding, stuck with a piece of holly, flaming with lighted brandy or rum, is served with brandy or rum butter or with cream.

Cold plum pudding is generally sliced and fried in butter, and served with powdered sugar and brandy or hard sauce. It is also good and unusual to serve very thin slices well frozen in the ice-box. These may have similar accompaniments.

CHRISTMAS PUDDING (1)

1¼ lb. sultanas	1 teaspoon mixed spice
1¼ lb. currants	1 teaspoon ground ginger
1 lb. raisins	2 lb. brown sugar
1 lb. mixed peel	1 lb. breadcrumbs
4 oz. sweet almonds	12 eggs
1¼ lb. suet	½ pint milk
1 lb. flour	½ gill brandy
2 nutmegs, grated	

Wash and dry fruits. Stone and chop raisins. Chop peel, almonds, and suet. Mix flour and spices, add prepared suet, fruit, sugar, and breadcrumbs. Beat eggs well and add them to dry ingredients with milk. Stir thoroughly and mix the ingredients well together. Add brandy; fill several well-greased pudding basins to the top and cover with greased paper and pudding cloths. Boil steadily for 7–8 hours. Fill up boiler from time to time with boiling water. Remove pudding from water. Take off wet cloth and cover again with a dry cloth. When cold, store in cool larder. When required for use, boil pudding for 2–3 hours, according to size.

Christmas Pudding (2) is a recipe from Miss Muriel Downes, deputy principal of the London Cordon Bleu School, where it is made every year. R. H. thinks it among the best.

CHRISTMAS PUDDING (2)

½ lb. self-raising flour
¾ lb. breadcrumbs (fresh white)
1 lb. currants
1 lb. sultanas
1 lb. stoned raisins
¾ lb. suet, finely chopped
4 oz. chopped candied peel
2 oz. shredded almonds
1 grated apple

juice and grated rind of an orange
1 teaspoon mixed spice
½ nutmeg, grated
1 teaspoon salt
6 eggs beaten to a froth
1 gill milk, ale, or stout (use brown ale)
1 lb. brown sugar

Mix all ingredients together. Turn into greased basins. Cover with greased papers and floured pudding cloths and boil 6–8 hours. Boil a further 3 hours before serving.

The following is R. H.'s grandmother's pudding, old-fashioned and rich:

CHRISTMAS PUDDING (3)

1¼ lb. plain flour
5 level teaspoons baking-powder
5 level teaspoons ground nutmeg
2½ level teaspoons salt
2½ level teaspoons cinnamon
5 dessertspoons mixed spice
1 lb. 14 oz. brown sugar

1 lb. 14 oz. fat
2 lb. 8 oz. breadcrumbs
10 level tablespoons marmalade
20 eggs
10 lb. dried fruit
2½ pints ale or stout

Makes ten 2-pint basins. Boil 6 hours. Second boiling 2–3 hours.

The following is a good plain ginger pudding:

GINGER PUDDING (FOR 4–6)

6 oz. fresh white breadcrumbs
6 oz. chopped or shredded suet
2 oz. flour
1 teaspoon ground ginger

1 level teaspoon bicarbonate of soda
2 small eggs
7 oz. golden syrup
custard sauce or extra syrup

Mix dry ingredients together. Add the eggs beaten with the golden syrup. Mix and turn into a well-greased charlotte mould or pudding basin, to a little more than three parts full. Tie down with a pleated paper and steam 3 hours. Turn out and serve with a custard sauce or warm golden syrup.

MARMALADE PUDDING (FOR 4–6)

3 oz. suet	1½ tablespoons marmalade (prefer-
3 oz. fresh breadcrumbs	ably home-made)
3 oz. castor sugar	1 teaspoon orange-flower water
	1 large or 2 small eggs

Mix suet, crumbs, and sugar together, stir in marmalade, orange-flower water, and beaten egg.   Put in a buttered mould and steam 3 hours.

The following is an excellent dark brown pudding:

BURBIDGE PUDDING, SOMETIMES CALLED GUARDS PUDDING (FOR 4–6)

6 oz. fresh white breadcrumbs	1 large egg
6 oz. chopped or shredded suet	1 level teaspoon bicarbonate
4 oz. brown or sand sugar	of soda
a pinch of salt	mousseline (page 187) or
3 tablespoons strawberry or	custard sauce
raspberry jam	

Mix dry ingredients together.   Add jam and the egg beaten up with soda.   Mix thoroughly, turn into a well-greased mould which should be only a little more than three parts full, and steam 3 hours.   Turn out and serve with a mousseline or custard sauce.

SIX CUP PUDDING (FOR 4–6)

Like a rich plum pudding, and much liked by the young, this is good on a cold day.   It is served with hot mousseline sauce (page 187) or rum butter (page 186).

1 tea-cup of each of the follow-	¾ cup milk
ing ingredients:	1 teaspoon bicarbonate of soda
plain flour	1 level teaspoon mixed spice
fresh breadcrumbs	a little grated lemon rind
brown sugar	1 egg
mixed dried fruit	mousseline sauce or rum
chopped or grated suet	butter

Mix all the dry ingredients together and mix soda in a little of the milk, warmed.   Beat the egg and mix into the pudding with the rest of the milk and the soda.   Turn into a well-greased pudding basin and steam for 3 hours.   Serve with sauce or rum butter.

TREACLE SPONGE (FOR 4–6)

½ lb. flour	¾ tea-cup milk
¼ lb. suet	¾ cup sugar
½ teaspoon ginger	¾ cup treacle
½ teaspoon bicarbonate of soda	custard sauce or cream

Mix all well together.   Pour into a greased mould.   Steam 2 hours. Serve with custard sauce or cream.

APPLE HAT (FOR 4–6)

Apple Hat is a classic English homely pudding, only pleasant if the apples are properly sweetened and of the kind that become *fondant* when cooked.

6 oz. self-raising flour	about 2 tablespoons brown
a pinch of salt	sugar
2 oz. fresh white breadcrumbs	1 strip of lemon rind
4 oz. suet, chopped or shredded	a cup of cold water
cold water or milk	brown sugar and cream
approx. 1 lb. cooking apples	

Sift flour and salt together into a bowl. Add crumbs and suet, rub together lightly. Mix to a light spongy dough with cold water or milk. Grease well a medium-sized pudding basin, cut off a good quarter of the paste, roll out the remainder into a bag shape (see Steak and Kidney Pudding, page 535) and with this line the basin. Fill with sliced apples layered with the sugar, add lemon rind, and pour in a small cup of cold water. Roll out remainder of paste to a round. Cover top of basin, press down round edge, and trim off; cover with a piece of pleated buttered paper and tie down. If to be boiled, cover again with a scalded floured cloth pleated in the same way. Steam or boil 3 hours. Lift out, stand a minute or two, then turn out and serve with brown sugar and cream.

Other fruit 'hats' are made in the same way.

The next pudding is made in a pie plate, has a toffee top, and is very popular in the nursery:

DUTCH APPLE PUDDING (FOR 4–6)

6 oz. quantity suet crust (see	lemon rind and juice
page 841)	brown sugar
1 lb. apples (approx.)	golden syrup

Divide the paste in two, roll out one half into a round and with it line a well-greased pie plate 9–10 inches in diameter. Cover with sliced apple to make a thick layer. Flavour with a little grated lemon rind and juice and sprinkle well with sugar. Roll out remaining pastry, cover the pie, and cover the top of the pastry with golden syrup. Sprinkle with brown sugar. Bake until a dark brown and the top is crisp and like toffee (30–40 minutes).

SUSSEX POND PUDDING (FOR 4–6)

½ lb. self-raising flour	2 oz. butter
4 oz. shredded or chopped suet	2 tablespoons brown sugar
a pinch of salt	a little grated lemon rind
water to mix	

Mix flour, suet, and salt together. Add water to make a soft light dough (about a tea-cup). Well grease a pudding basin. Roll out paste to a thick round and with it line the basin. Work the butter and sugar together.

Flavour with the lemon rind. Put into the middle of the pudding. Fold and press the paste over the top. Cover with a pleated buttered paper and steam 2½–3 hours. Turn out, serve plain or with brown sugar.

Sponge Puddings

These are light steamed puddings calling for butter, sugar, and eggs. The flavouring may be of vanilla, orange, coffee, or lemon; and sultanas, candied peel, sliced ginger, and glacé cherries are all suitable ingredients. The proportions for the pudding may be equal weight of butter, sugar, flour, and eggs, or, if a more economical pudding is called for, the flour may be increased by half as much again. Milk is required to bring the mixture to the right consistency, which is indicated when it will just drop from the spoon. The basin or mould is well greased and may be decorated before the mixture is put in with raisins, sliced ginger, or whatever fruit is called for. The bottom of the basin may also be lined with 2–3 tablespoons golden syrup or jam. Care must be taken when turning out the pudding. Generally speaking, the mixture should three parts fill the basin and be tied down with a pleated greased paper. (See Steaming, page 71.)

CANARY PUDDING (FOR 4–6)

2 eggs; their weight in butter, castor sugar, and self-raising flour

vanilla or lemon rind
hot jam

Cream butter, add castor sugar by degrees, beat thoroughly, add flavouring. Beat in a spoonful of the flour with the eggs, one at a time. Then fold in remainder and three-quarters fill the greased basin. Steam 1½–2 hours. Turn out and pour round the hot jam.

Small individual moulds may also be used. Baked in dariole or castle pudding moulds, this mixture makes what are known as castle puddings. These are turned out and the jam poured round as for Canary Pudding.

The above basic mixture may be used for:

1. Valencia Pudding

Here the basin is lined with split stoned raisings which are put with the split side against the basin and may be arranged in a pattern. The amount depends on the size of the basin, say about 4 oz. The mixture is put in and steamed as above. A mousseline sauce may be served as accompaniment.

2. Canton Pudding

Sliced glacé ginger is used to decorate the mould or basin and chopped ginger is put in the mixture. Say 2–3 oz. in all. Mousseline or ginger sauce may be served.

3. Orange Pudding

Chopped orange, candied peel, or pieces of spiced orange (see page 1105), approximately 2–3 oz., may be added to the mixture with a little grated rind, and the juice added to a mousseline sauce.

A more economical mixture may be:

4 oz. butter or margarine	flavouring
4 oz. sugar	6–8 oz. self-raising flour
2 eggs	½ gill milk (approx.)

The above is enough for 6 people and may of course be modified.

BELVOIR LEMON PUDDING (FOR 4–6)

This is steamed pudding with a taste of lemon curd and an unusual and attractive sauce. It is very good pudding.

4 oz. butter	4 oz. fresh white breadcrumbs
4 oz. castor sugar	grated rind and juice of 2 lemons
2 yolks of egg	½ teaspoon baking-powder

Sauce

2 whites of egg	1 dessert apple (large)
3 oz. castor sugar	

Cream the butter, add the sugar and beat thoroughly, add the yolks, crumbs, and rind and juice of the lemons. Lastly add the baking-powder. Turn into a well-buttered charlotte mould. Steam 40 minutes.

Just before turning out prepare the sauce. Whip the whites to a stiff froth, add the sugar, whip for a minute or two, and add the apple finely diced or chopped. Spread this thickly in a circle on the serving dish. Dust with castor sugar and set in a quick oven. Turn the pudding on to it and serve at once.

The following is a very light steamed sponge, excellent for using up egg whites:

ROXANE PUDDING (FOR 4–6)

3 oz. butter	3 level teaspoons baking-powder
4½ oz. castor sugar	3 egg whites
grated rind of ½ lemon	chocolate or hard lemon sauce
good ½ gill milk	(pages 184 and 185)
8 oz. flour	

Cream the butter, add sugar and whip until white. Add the lemon rind and the milk with the flour, sifted with the baking-powder. Whip whites to a stiff snow and fold into the mixture. Turn into a greased and floured mould. Steam 1 hour, then turn out and serve with hot chocolate or lemon sauce poured round and over.

CHOCOLATE SOUFFLÉ PUDDING (FOR 4–6)

1½ oz. each of butter and flour	1½ oz. castor sugar
3 oz. sweetened chocolate, block or powdered	2 whole eggs
½ pint milk	extra sugar for sauce

Melt the butter in a pan, add the flour off the fire. Stir until smooth, then boil 2 oz. of the chocolate in the milk and pour on to the butter and flour. Return to the fire and stir until it comes to the boil. Then beat in the castor sugar with 1 whole egg and 1 yolk. Lastly, add 1 stiffly beaten white. Butter well a charlotte mould; dust well with castor sugar, pour in the mixture, and steam in a double saucepan until set (about 45 minutes). Turn out on a dish for serving and pour over the following sauce:

Chocolate sauce. Cut up the rest of the chocolate and put it into a pan with a good gill of water and sugar to sweeten well. Simmer until the consistency of cream.

The following is a soufflé pudding with fried apple, pleasant and light:

SANS SOUCI PUDDING (FOR 4–6)

1½ oz. each of butter and flour	2 large dessert apples, peeled
grated rind of ½ a lemon	and diced
1½ gills milk	½ oz. butter
1½ oz. sugar	browned crumbs
2 eggs	sabayon or mousseline sauce
	(see pages 186 and 187)

Melt butter in saucepan, add flour, grated lemon rind, and milk. Blend and stir over fire until boiling. Draw aside, add the sugar and the yolks. Beat well. Fry the apple quickly in the butter until brown. Add to the mixture. Whip whites to a firm snow and fold in. Grease a large charlotte mould, dust with the crumbs, but in the mixture (three parts full only), and steam gently 40–45 minutes. Draw aside, leave 3–4 minutes before turning out. Pour round a sabayon or mousseline sauce.

SUET ROLY (WITH FRUIT) (FOR 4–6)

6 oz. self-raising flour	4 oz. mixed fruit, sultanas, and
2 oz. breadcrumbs	raisins
5 oz. chopped beef suet	1 oz. chopped candied peel
a little golden syrup, slightly	water to mix
warmed	a little grated lemon rind

Make suet crust as described on page 834. Roll out to a strip about 7–8 inches wide. Spread quickly and lightly with a thin layer of warm syrup. Sprinkle prepared fruit and peel on this. Roll up and wrap in a grease-proof paper to steam (3 hours), or in a scalded floured cloth to boil (2 hours). Serve with warm golden syrup with a little grated lemon rind in it.

BAKED ROLY-POLY (FOR 4–6)

8 oz. suet or short crust (pages 835 and 841)   jam

Roll out pastry to a strip 7–8 inches wide, spread with slightly warmed jam. Do not spread too near to the edge. Roll up. Press edges lightly together. Bake for 30–40 minutes.

BATTER PUDDING

An ordinary baked batter pudding is made with a Yorkshire pudding mixture (see page 434) to which a little melted butter has been added.

QUEEN OF PUDDINGS

½ pint milk	2–3 tablespoons strawberry
pared rind of 1 small lemon	or raspberry jam, slightly
½ oz. butter	warmed
1 oz. castor sugar	4 oz. castor sugar (for the
2 oz. fresh white breadcrumbs	meringue)
2 eggs	

Infuse lemon rind in milk in covered pan. Strain into a bowl, add the butter and sugar and, when dissolved, the breadcrumbs. Mix and leave to cool. Add the egg yolks, mix thoroughly, and turn into a lightly buttered pie dish. Stand 30 minutes, then bake in a moderate oven 25–30 minutes until set. Remove, cool slightly, and spread the jam over the top. Whip whites to a firm snow, fold in the sugar (keeping back a teaspoon) as for meringue (see page 852), and pile on the top of the pudding. Dust over with castor sugar, leave 5 minutes, then put into a slow oven until the meringue is set and straw-coloured.

REGENCY PUDDING

¾ lb. apples	2 eggs
2–3 oz. brown sugar	1 oz. corn-flour
strip of lemon rind	1 oz. castor sugar
2 tablespoons water	½ pint milk
3 oz. short pastry (page 835)	vanilla pod
2–3 tablespoons orange marmalade	4 tablespoons castor sugar

Peel, core, slice, and stew the apples with the brown sugar, lemon rind, and water. Roll out the pastry thinly; damp the edge of a medium-sized pie dish and line with a thin strip of pastry. Decorate the edge with small leaves cut from the rest of the paste, damping lightly before putting them on the strip of pastry. When the apples are soft put them through a sieve, and mix them with the marmalade. Pour into the pie dish. Cream the egg yolks with the corn-flour and sugar, bring the milk to the boil with the vanilla pod, remove the pod and pour the boiling milk over the egg mixture. Stir well, return to the pan and bring to boiling-point. Cook several minutes, then pour the custard over the apples and bake 30–35 minutes in a moderately hot oven (400° F.). Whip the egg whites stiffly, add the castor sugar gradually, pile the meringue on top of the pudding, and set in a cool oven (300° F.).

MILK PUDDINGS, SWEETS, AND CUSTARDS

RICE PUDDING

Most people have their own special recipe for rice pudding, and it is fair to say that it is a feather in anyone's cap to make a perfect one, soft and creamy in texture, with a brown and even skin.   The secret is long, slow, gentle cooking and a medium thick or thick-grained rice.   Carolina is the rice most suitable for puddings and creams.

Some cooks allow the rice to soak in the milk for half an hour before the dish is put in the oven.   Some like to stir once or twice during cooking, slipping a spoon carefully under the skin to do so.

a nut of butter	1 dessertspoon sugar
1 tablespoon rice (1¼ oz.)	1 pint milk

Rub the butter round a pie dish, put the rice and sugar at the bottom. Pour on the milk, stir, and put into a slow oven (300° F.).   Cook for about 3 hours.   The rice should be soft and the surface nicely browned.   Take from the oven.

If to be served cold, the skin may be removed, and the surface, dredged with sugar, glazed under the grill.

N.B.   A vanilla pod cooked in the pudding gives a delicious flavour; after use this should be washed, dried, and stored again.

SAGO AND TAPIOCA

Allow 3 tablespoons to a quart of milk, sugar to taste, and cook as above.

A shred of lemon peel or a little grated orange rind is an improvement to these puddings.

Rice Creams

CRÈME DE RIZ A LA CONNAUGHT

2½ oz. rice	1 egg white
1¼ pints milk	sugar to taste
1 vanilla pod	toasted almonds
¼ pint cream	

Sauce

6–8 oz. dried apricots, soaked overnight	lemon rind
	sugar syrup
sugar to taste	kirsch

Wash rice, add to milk with vanilla pod.   Simmer until the rice is soft and creamy, adding more milk if necessary.   Turn into a bowl to cool. Sweeten to taste.   Remove pod.

Meanwhile simmer apricots in the water in which they have been soaked.   Add a strip or two of lemon rind to flavour, and a little sugar. Rub through a wire sieve with a little of the juice.   Turn into a pan, dilute with sugar syrup if necessary, flavour with kirsch, and reheat to boiling-point. Whip cream until thick, whip egg white to a snow, mix the two together and whip until it will hold shape. Fold into the rice. Turn into a glass or china bowl and scatter with the toasted almonds. Serve the hot sauce separately.

RICE TYROLHOF

Rice Tyrolhof is made with a rice cream set with gelatine, which must not be too stiff, so if necessary more milk may be added while cooking, to preserve a creamy consistency.

2½ oz. thick-grained rice	3 oz. wood strawberries or
1 pint milk, more if necessary	grapes
1½ oz. sugar	1 dessertspoon rum (optional)
1 rounded teaspoon powdered	2 tablespoons whipped cream, *or*
gelatine	1 egg white, stiffly whipped
juice of an orange	sauce (see below)
1 sweet apple	

Simmer rice and milk until tender and creamy, adding a little extra milk if necessary. Add sugar, cool, add gelatine melted in the orange juice, the diced apple, and the strawberries or skinned and pipped grapes. Add the rum. Lastly fold in the whipped cream or egg white. Pour the mixture into a lightly oiled plain mould or cake tin. When set turn on to a serving dish and pour round a fresh raspberry or strawberry sauce.

Sauce

Crush about ¼ lb. picked fruit with a silver fork, rub through an aluminium strainer, and sweeten with icing or castor sugar.

TAPIOCA CREAM

2 oz. tapioca	¼ pint cream
1 pint milk	12 ratafias
vanilla pod	2 tablespoons sherry
1½ oz. castor sugar	pistachio nuts

Cook tapioca in milk with vanilla pod and sugar in double saucepan till quite soft. Pour into a basin, remove vanilla pod, and allow to get quite cold. Whisk cream slightly. Fold in. In the bottom of a glass bowl put 6 ratafias to soak in sherry, pour the tapioca mixture on to these. Decorate top with the remaining ratafias in a ring and chopped pistachios in the middle.

CUSTARDS

When making custards with fresh eggs, the following points should be observed:

1. Egg whites will set a custard and egg yolks give it a creamy texture.
2. For a crème à la vanille (English 'boiled' custard) yolks only should be used, in the proportion of 4 yolks to 1 pint of milk.

3. It is best to thicken the custard in a double saucepan because the heat is slower, the danger of curdling is less, and the custard will be creamier.

4. Curdling occurs if the custard is boiled, so as soon as the mixture coats the back of a wooden spoon it must be removed from the heat and strained into a bowl. Should the mixture curdle the mishap may be remedied provided the degree of curdling is not too great. For this the mixture is poured at once, and without straining, in a large, cold mixing bowl and whisked vigorously.

5. A small teaspoon of corn-flour per pint of milk added to the yolks and sugar will help to prevent curdling.

6. For a baked custard only a certain proportion of egg white is added, 2 whole eggs and 2 yolks to 1 pint of milk. If all whole eggs were used, the custard would be too firm and have a tendency to curdle.

7. Different flavours can be added to both types of custard and are usually infused in the milk while it is being heated, e.g. thinly pared orange or lemon rind, unsweetened chocolate, crushed coffee-beans, and vanilla.

CRÈME A LA VANILLE (ENGLISH BOILED CUSTARD)

Creme à la vanille seems a much better name than boiled custard.

2 yolks of egg	1 tablespoon sugar
¼ pint milk	½ vanilla pod, split

Beat the yolks with a fork. Put the sugar, milk, and pod together in a saucepan; bring slowly to the boil. Remove pod, pour on to the yolks, stir, and return to the pan. Stir over moderate heat to scalding-point or until the liquid will coat the back of the spoon. Pour off and cool.

Serve as a sauce with fruit or round a pudding.

PETITS POTS DE CRÈME

Petits Pots de Crème is a favourite French sweet, and the following recipe indicates different flavours. All three may be offered, or one flavour only. They are made in special little glazed earthenware or fire-proof china pots (with or without lids), which are useful also for a chocolate mousse.

just over 1 pint milk (22½ liquid oz.). This allows 1½ gills for each flavour	1 large egg or 2 small vanilla pod or essence coffee essence
4 egg yolks	1–1½ oz. melted chocolate
1 oz. castor sugar	

Scald milk with the vanilla pod and sugar. Remove pod and pour milk on to the yolks and egg, beaten together. Add vanilla essence if no pod available. Strain and divide into three equal parts. Flavour one with coffee, one with chocolate, and leave the third plain. Pour carefully into the pots, stand these on a shallow pan or tin filled with boiling water. Cover with a lid, or if the pots themselves have lids, put them on. Lift carefully into a slow to moderate oven and leave until just set. The time will vary from 12 to 20 minutes, according to the thickness of the china and the heat of the oven. Lift the pan or tin out carefully and remove the lid quickly (see Steaming, page 71) so that no water falls on to the creams. Remove them and cool.

CRÈME CARAMEL

Caramel

3 oz. castor sugar

Custard

2 whole eggs	vanilla to taste
2 yolks	1 pint milk
2 tablespoons sugar	

Put the castor sugar into a small saucepan and allow to melt without stirring. When it begins to change colour stir carefully from time to time until a good brown. Pour into a warmed soufflé case or cake tin. Turn it about to coat the caramel all over the bottom and sides.

Now break the eggs into a bowl, add the yolks, sugar, and vanilla, and beat up with a fork. Scald the milk and pour on to the eggs, stir and pour into the mould. Stand in a bain-marie (a roasting-tin containing hot water). Cover with a piece of paper and set the tin in a moderate oven until the custard is set. Then remove from the heat, and leave until cold before turning out.

For junkets and cremets, see chapter on milk and cheese, page 743.

BREAD AND BUTTER PUDDING

A simple, homely pudding and a favourite if well made. The amount of fruit may vary to taste.

2–3 rounds of thin bread and butter	a handful of sultanas or currants or a mixture of both
granulated sugar	a piece of candied peel (citron or orange)

Custard

1 egg	vanilla pod or strip of lemon rind to flavour
1 yolk	
1 tablespoon sugar	between ½ and ¾ pint milk

Butter a pie dish, cut each round of bread and butter in four; blanch or soak sultanas and thinly slice the peel. Put a layer of bread in the bottom of the pie dish. Strew it with sultanas, a little peel, and sugar. Repeat this and finish with a top layer of bread, buttered side uppermost. Pour in the custard, which should just fill the dish. Sprinkle well with sugar. Set the dish in the bain-marie and cook in a moderate oven until the custard is set and the top well browned and crusty. Serve hot in the dish.

It is important that the pudding should not be too 'bready.' If the dish is three-quarters full before the custard is poured in the proportion will be about right. Do not pour it in over the bread, but at the side of the dish.

To make custard. Beat egg and yolk lightly. Put sugar, milk, and vanilla pod or lemon rind into a pan and bring slowly to boil. Remove pod or peel. Cool slightly. Pour on to the beaten eggs, stir, and strain into the dish.

N.B. This pudding is improved if allowed to stand an hour or so before baking, and it may be enriched with extra eggs and cream in the custard and a larger proportion of fruit.

FRUIT SWEETS

STEWED FRUIT

Stewed fruit is a misnomer; fruit should be carefully poached in a small quantity of syrup. The quantity and richness of the syrup varies a little according to the juiciness or otherwise of the fruit. Fruits containing a good deal of juice (plums, greengages, cherries, raspberries, etc.) are best cooked in a small quantity of heavy syrup, while less juicy fruits (apples, pears, gooseberries, etc.) call for a thinner syrup, and for a greater amount. It is important that the syrup should be made before the fruit is added, and not fruit, sugar, and water put into the pan together. If this is done the fruit becomes overcooked, and a watery mass lacking in flavour may result, instead of a rich, syrupy compôte. The addition of arrowroot is optional, but with certain sour fruits—black-currants and damsons, for example—it has the effect of softening the flavour and the appearance of the juice is improved.

COMPÔTE OF FRUIT

1–1½ lb. fresh fruit
4–6 oz. sugar (according to the acidity of the fruit)
2 gills water

1 level teaspoon arrowroot
wine, cinnamon, or nutmeg to give flavour (optional)

Wash and prepare the fruit, remove stones from plums, cherries, damsons, and greengages, peel apples and pears thinly, top and tail gooseberries, pick currants and raspberries. Dissolve the sugar in the water, bring to the boil and boil 3–5 minutes, according to the thickness of syrup desired. Lay the prepared fruit in the syrup and cook gently until tender. Take the fruit out carefully with a spoon, blend the arrowroot with a tablespoon of cold water, pour it into the boiling syrup, stir for 1 minute, then strain the syrup over the fruit. If wine is used, add it after blending with arrowroot. Cinnamon or nutmeg should be put in the syrup with the fruit.

NOTE ON PREPARATION OF APPLES FOR COOKING

Apples for use in pies, flans, and compôtes should not be put into water after slicing; this is often done with the object of preserving their whiteness, but it detracts from their flavour. Often too when they have been soaked in water the slices are not adequately dried afterwards, so that the syrup of a compôte is weakened and the pastry of a flan or pie rendered soggy. The best plan is to have all other ingredients ready and preparations made: pastry prepared, flan case lined, syrup ready. Then the apples may be sliced at the last moment and no soaking in water is necessary. Where a large quantity of apples is being prepared, as for example for canning or drying, they are frequently put into a weak solution of salt and water to prevent discoloration. A plate must be laid on the surface to keep them under the water. On no account must the apples be left soaking for a long time in the water, as for example overnight, as the apples readily absorb the flavour of the salt.

FRUITS RAFRAÎCHIS (FRESH FRUIT SALAD)

A fruit salad usually implies fruit that is not cooked, for example a mixture of peeled and pipped grapes, sliced bananas, oranges, pears, pine-apple and so on, moistened well with a thick syrup. The syrup is prepared and allowed to cool. The fruit is sliced with a silver or stainless steel knife and put into the bowl or dish. Enough syrup is then poured over to moisten nicely, a good sprinkling of a liqueur added (kirsch or maraschino are the most suitable), and the whole carefully stirred. The dish may then be put into the ice-box to chill well before serving.

SUGARED FRUIT

Summer fruits, such as strawberries, raspberries, and currants both red and black, make a delicious dish if put into a bowl in layers with a good dusting of fine sugar, icing or castor, between each layer, and then set aside for some hours, preferably in a refrigerator, to allow the sugar to melt and the juice to run. It is best to slice the strawberries if large.

FRUIT FOOLS

A fruit fool is a simple sweet, popular with young people and quick to make. The main ingredients are fruit purée, fresh or tinned, and cream, to which may be added a thick custard for reasons of economy.

Strawberries, gooseberries, raspberries, black-currants, and apricots make perhaps the best fools.

Gooseberries, black-currants, and apricots should first be cooked before being turned into a purée; strawberries and raspberries are puréed raw.

The purée itself must have the consistency of thick cream, so if the fruit is previously cooked the syrup should be drained off before sieving. A little may be added to the purée to taste, and lightly whipped cream is then folded in.   If custard is added this is beaten in before adding the cream. The proportion of cream to fruit varies a little according to the kind, but as a general rule ¼ pint cream to ¾ pint fruit purée will give a good creamy mixture.

Freshly made sponge fingers are usually served with fools.

The addition of a few heads of elderflower to gooseberries or rhubarb while these are being cooked adds a delicious flavour.

RHUBARB

This may be very palatable if carefully cooked and sweetened.   It is at its best at the beginning of the season.   Early forced rhubarb is better cooked by the first method given below, i.e. carefully poached in a fairly thick syrup.   Later in the season the jam method or a compôte flavoured with ginger answers well.

RHUBARB COMPÔTE (IN SYRUP)

Wipe rhubarb, with a stainless steel knife cut off leaf and root end, then cut into short lengths 2–3 inches long.   Prepare a moderately heavy syrup: 1 cup of water to 1 of granulated or lump sugar (see Compôte of Fruit, page 903) is enough for 1 lb. rhubarb.   Add rhubarb, cover pan, and bring very slowly up to simmering-point.   Avoid stirring.   By this time the rhubarb should be tender but whole.   An alternative method is to put the pan into the oven.   Draw aside and allow to cool before sliding out the contents of the pan into a bowl.

RHUBARB COMPÔTE (JAM METHOD)

The advantage of this method is that the rhubarb invariably keeps whole without any special attention.   The amount of jam is added to taste and according to the acidity of the rhubarb, roughly 3–4 tablespoons to 1½ lb. rhubarb.   If raspberry jam is used, warm first and rub through a strainer to remove pips.

Wipe rhubarb, cut as before.   Spread a layer of raspberry or gooseberry jam in the bottom of a pie dish or casserole.   Cover thickly with rhubarb and add a little more jam.   Fill to the top with rhubarb, finish with a little more jam, and cover with paper or a lid and cook in a moderate oven 30–35 minutes.   Allow to cool in the syrup before turning into a glass dish.

RHUBARB AND GINGER COMPÔTE

This compôte is extremely good; the ginger gives just the right flavour of spicy sweetness to the rhubarb.

1–1½ lb. rhubarb	2 tablespoons ginger syrup, *or*
1 cup sugar	¼ teaspoon ground ginger
1 cup water	1–2 tablespoons thinly sliced preserved ginger

Trim and cut rhubarb as before. Put the sugar and water into a pan and boil rapidly 5 minutes, add ginger syrup or powdered ginger slaked with a little of the syrup from the pan. Draw aside, add rhubarb, cover, and poach very gently 5–7 minutes. Arrange rhubarb in serving dish, pour over the juice, and scatter with the sliced ginger. Chill before serving.

KISSEL WITH CINNAMON TOAST

Kissel can be made with stewed or bottled raspberries, cherries, or black-currants, either mixed or by themselves.

1¾ pints strong, well-flavoured and sweetened fruit juice	1 heaped tablespoon arrowroot
pared rind of an orange, and the strained juice	3–4 tablespoons of the stewed fruit, from which the juice has been drained
1 glass claret or burgundy	cinnamon toast (see below)

Put the 1¾ pints juice, rind, and wine into a pan and bring slowly to the boil. Slake the arrowroot with the orange juice. Take out the rind and add the arrowroot whilst on the boil, stirring vigorously; then remove from fire. Add the fruit and pour into individual cups or bowls. Dust the top lightly with sugar to prevent a skin forming and serve warm or cold, but not chilled. Eat with:

Cinnamon toast. Toast two or more rounds of a malt or honey bread on one side only, butter the other side and sprinkle thickly with castor sugar mixed with cinnamon. Grill rather slowly to a good even brown. Cool slightly before cutting into fingers. Make at the last minute and eat hot.

A PLAINER KISSEL

Take stewed fruit with a larger proportion of juice than usual. If using raw fruit, put it to cook with a little water. The fruit should be either cherries, black-currants, or red currants and raspberries mixed.

Have ready the fruit and sweetened juice in a pan. Bring to the boil. While on the boil, pour in potato flour or arrowroot slaked to a thin cream with water. Move off the heat at once, stirring vigorously with a wooden spoon. Pour off to cool and sprinkle the surface with sugar to prevent a skin from forming. Allow approximately 1 dessertspoon heaped arrowroot to a pint of fruit juice.

Kissel may also be thickened with sago or fine tapioca in place of the arrowroot: Danish Röd Gröd is made as above, but with sago used as a thickening.

SUMMER PUDDING

This may be made in two ways. In the first method the pudding is filled with fruits stewed whole, in the second with sieved fruit. This is sometimes preferred, because it is seedless.

Method 1. Line a china bowl or soufflé dish with slices of bread soaked in the juice of the stewed fruit. Fill the lined bowl with the fruit: blackcurrants, raspberries, red currants, or blackberries and apples mixed. Place one or two layers of bread in between the fruit and finish off with a round of bread soaked in juice on top. To press it lay a saucer or plate on it, with a 1 lb. weight on top. Leave in the ice-box or a cool place overnight. Turn out and serve with a whipped custard or plain cream.

Method 2. This is exemplified in the following recipe for Blackberry Summer Pudding.

BLACKBERRY SUMMER PUDDING (SEEDLESS)

2 apples	stale white bread
1¼ lb. blackberries	1 heaped teaspoon arrowroot
½ pint water	or corn-flour to ½ pint juice
1½–2 oz. sugar	

Peel, core, and thinly slice the apples; wash the blackberries. Put the water into a pan with the sugar, and when dissolved boil rapidly for 5 minutes. Add the fruit, cover, and simmer till pulpy, for approximately 10 minutes. Strain, reserving the juice, rub fruit through an aluminium strainer, then add half the juice, adding more sugar if necessary.

Slice bread very thinly, cutting off all the crust. Cover the bottom of a china soufflé case with the bread, then spoon in enough of the thin purée to cover completely. Continue like this, with layers of bread and purée, until the dish is well filled, making sure that each layer of bread is well soaked with the fruit purée. Lay a small plate on the top with a 1-lb. weight on it and leave overnight.

Meanwhile, add a spoonful or two of the remaining juice to the arrowroot. Put this and the juice into a pan and bring to the boil. It should have the consistency of thin cream. Leave till cold. Turn out the pudding, pour over a small quantity of the sauce, and serve the rest in a sauce-boat. Cream may be served separately.

If properly made there should be no trace of white bread, and the pudding itself should be quite short in consistency. This may well be made with damsons, fresh or bottled.

CHARTREUSE DE POMMES (1)

This is a chartreuse of apples set in their own jelly; that is to say, set with the natural pectin of the apples. It is well, if the apples are really ripe, to make the syrup not with plain water, but with water in which the peels and cores of the apples have been gently cooked, as this will extract the maximum amount of pectin from the fruit. See notes on pectin (page 1084). The best kind of apple to choose is the pippin type; Cox's

Orange Pippins are particularly good.   Apples which soften quickly when cooked are unsuitable.

10 oz. lump sugar
1½ gills cold water
½ teaspoon lemon juice
1¾ lb. firm-fleshed dessert
    apples

4 oz. preserved fruit (candied
    orange peel, glacé cherries,
    angelica, candied apricots,
    etc.)

Sauce

2 tablespoons red-currant or
    apple jelly or apricot jam

2 tablespoons water
1 tablespoon rum

Dissolve the sugar in the water, add lemon juice.   Bring to boil, boil 4–5 minutes.   Draw aside.   Peel, core, and quarter apples and slice them directly into the syrup.   Cook the apples gently in the covered pan 10–12 minutes.   Stir gently from time to time.   Uncover pan, continue cooking until the amount of syrup left is just sufficient to moisten the slices.   Put lid on pan, draw aside, and leave until slices are clear.   Meanwhile, cut the preserved fruits in small pieces and mix them together; add them to the cooked apple and stir carefully.   Pour the mixture into a wet cake tin and put it away in a cold place to set.   Make the sauce with the jam or jelly, water, and rum.   Unmould the chartreuse, pour the sauce over, and serve cold.

CHARTREUSE DE POMMES (2)

Hot sauce served separately makes a good contrast to this sweet: hot mincemeat sauce (see page 973) or a sabayon (see page 186).

7 even-sized dessert apples
1 pint water
a strip of lemon peel
½ lb. sugar

1 oz. candied orange peel
3 oz glacé cherries or glacé fruit
3 oz. raisins or sultanas
2 pints lemon jelly

Peel and core 6 apples.   Boil water with lemon rind and sugar in shallow pan.   Put in the 6 apples, cover, and simmer on low heat till just tender, turning once only.   Draw aside and leave to cool in covered pan.   Meanwhile chop remaining apple, orange peel, cherries, and sultanas.   Cook all together in a small pan with a spoonful or two of the syrup.   When soft and rich-looking, draw aside and cool.   Drain apples from syrup.   Fill centres with fruit mixture and arrange in a deep dish or shallow glass bowl.   Have a jelly made and when slightly cool pour this over apples, reserving about ½ pint.   Allow to set.   Chop reserved jelly coarsely and heap round edge of dish.

Jelly may be made from the apples.   In this case, to the syrup from the apples add the pared rind and juice of 2 lemons, an extra ¾ pint water, and more sugar as required.   Measure juice and add ¾ oz. powdered gelatine per pint.   It may then be clarified.

The following is a pleasant and refreshing sweet:

APPLES OR PEARS BRISTOL

4 large dessert or cooking apples or pears	3–4 oz. sugar
1½ gills water	2 large oranges

Caramel
2 oz. castor sugar

Peel apples or pears, quarter and core. Boil water and sugar 5 minutes. Add apples, cover, and simmer till just tender. Leave to cool in syrup with pan covered.

Pare rind from half an orange, cut into fine strips with scissors; simmer in water 5 minutes, drain and rinse with cold water. Put aside. Cut peel and pith from oranges and cut out sections (see page 47). Put castor sugar in small saucepan set on moderate heat and leave to dissolve without stirring. Boil rapidly until a clear golden brown, pour on to an oiled tin and leave to set. Then break caramel into small chips.

Arrange the apple in glass bowl with the orange on top. Pour on syrup, scatter with orange rind and caramel. Chill before serving.

The next recipe is a pleasant sweet served either hot or cold. It is good for a simple party, and well liked by children.

SCALLOPED APPLES

1–1½ lb. apples, of good flavour	thin bread and butter
brown or white sugar to taste	whites of 1 or 2 eggs
1 large lemon	2 oz. castor sugar to each
1–2 oz. candied or glacé fruit	white

Peel, quarter, and core apples. Arrange in a buttered pie or fireproof dish in layers with sugar, the grated rind of the lemon, its flesh cut into segments as for grape-fruit (see page 47), and the sliced fruit. When the dish is full, cover with a piece of buttered paper. Put into a moderate oven until the apple is soft. Take out, cover top neatly with squares of bread and butter, and put back to brown.

Whip whites, incorporate the sugar, and spread this meringue over the crisp brown top. Dredge with castor sugar, leave for a few minutes, then brown delicately in a cool oven.

POMMES GRATINÉES

These are good both hot and cold; for a party they may be served with a hot or cold sabayon or mousseline sauce.

4–5 large baking apples	brown sugar
a little butter	3 dessert apples or the equiva-
2 heaped tablespoons apricot	lent in other fruit (Victoria
or peach jam	plums, bananas, rhubarb,
	etc.)
grated lemon rind	syrup made with 4–6 oz. sugar
lemon juice	and 1½ gills water

Meringue

2 whites of egg	1 oz. ground almonds
4 oz. castor sugar	icing sugar

Peel, core, and slice the baking apples; rub a shallow stew-pan over with butter, add the apples, jam, lemon rind, juice, and brown sugar to taste. Cover and cook slowly to a pulp. Remove the lid and reduce rapidly to a thick purée. Cool slightly and then shape into a galette or flat cake in a shallow fireproof dish.

Meanwhile peel, core, and quarter the dessert apples (or prepare other fruit); cook gently in syrup until clear. It is best to do this with the lid on the pan. Then drain and arrange the quarters on top of the galette. Whip whites and sugar together until the consistency of very thick cream; stir in the ground almonds and spread over the pudding. Powder with icing sugar and colour a delicate brown in a slow oven.

DANISH APPLE CAKE (A TYPE OF CHARLOTTE)

There are several versions of this type of charlotte; this is probably one of the best. The crumbs should not be too fine, and they must be crunchy and buttery. For a special occasion use crushed macaroons.

1½ lb. apples	about 2 oz. butter
a little butter	crème chantilly (page 42) or a
lemon rind to flavour	hot or cold sabayon sauce
sugar to sweeten	(pages 186 and 187)
2 cups fresh white crumbs,	icing sugar
rather coarsely grated	strawberry jam (optional)

Peel, core, and slice the apples; rub a stew-pan round with butter, put in the apples with sugar to sweeten and a strip or two of lemon peel. Cover and simmer till soft, then remove peel. Avoid getting the apples too pulpy, and if they are very juicy remove the lid soon after they start to cook and boil rapidly to reduce.

Meanwhile dry the crumbs slightly in the oven, melt the butter in a frying-pan, and fry the crumbs to a golden brown. Arrange half the apples in a fireproof dish in the form of a cake. (If whipped cream is used a layer of strawberry jam may be put on the bottom of the dish, but it would be too sweet with the sabayon.) Put half the crumbs on the top, then the rest of the apple, and scatter over the remaining crumbs. Dust with icing sugar and pour round the sauce. Serve cold.

APPLE CHARLOTTE (FOR 5–6)

apple purée, made with 2 lb.	sugar
apples	bread
butter	2–3 oz. melted butter

Sauce

5 tablespoons apricot jam	a liqueur glass of rum, sherry,
3½ tablespoons water	or kirsch

Make a stiff apple purée or marmelade (see making of marmelade, page 855). Have it well flavoured and sweetened; cool. The addition of 2 tablespoons apricot jam and a little lemon rind to the marmelade improves the flavour.

Well butter a charlotte mould and dust it out with sugar. Cut slices of stale bread not more than ⅛ inch thick, remove the crusts and cut into fingers about 1½ inches wide and the height of the mould in length. Dip these into melted butter and arrange round the sides, overlapping them slightly. Then cut rounds to fit both top and bottom exactly. Dip these also into the melted butter, put in the bottom round, fill to the top with the purée, then lay the remaining round on top. Bake in a moderate oven for 40 minutes or until thoroughly brown. Prepare the sauce by mixing together ingredients and beating a little; it should be warm but not hot. When the dish is cooked leave for a minute or two, then turn out and pour round a small quantity of the sauce, serving the rest in a sauce-boat.

For greater economy the bread may be buttered before cutting, but the result is not so good as that obtained by dipping in the melted butter.

The following is another type of charlotte:

BROWN BETTY

butter	brown sugar or golden syrup
bread	custard or cream
raw fruit	

Raw fruit is used for this dish, and the best kinds are apple, apple and blackberry, young gooseberries, small red plums, and apricots.

Butter well 4 or 5 rounds of thinly sliced stale bread. Cut each round into four. The crust may be left on if the bread is not too well baked. Put a layer of the bread on the bottom of a pie or fireproof dish. Scatter with a thick layer of fruit: apple thinly sliced, plums or apricots halved and stoned. Sprinkle with a large spoonful of brown sugar or golden syrup (the latter always for apples), add one more layer of bread, then fruit to fill the dish full and sugar or syrup to sweeten. Lastly, arrange a layer of the bread squares slightly overlapping to cover the whole surface of the fruit. Add a final large spoonful of sugar or syrup over the top and bake in a moderate oven for 30–40 minutes.

Serve with custard or cream.

APPLES WITH CHOCOLATE (POMMES AU CHOCOLAT)

This sweet may be served either hot or cold, with or without the meringue. An apricot or raspberry sauce (page 184) may replace the chocolate.

Syrup

1 pint water	4–6 medium apples
4 oz. sugar, *or*	a strip of lemon rind
2 large tablespoons golden syrup	

Fruit Mixture

3 oz. mixed dried fruit	juice of ½ lemon or orange
a small piece of candied peel	a pinch of cinnamon
¼ oz. butter	

Meringue

1 egg white	2 oz. castor sugar

chocolate sauce (see page 184)

Make the syrup. Boil for a few minutes. Peel and core the apples, poach them in the syrup, turning and basting frequently. Then drain well and arrange in a fireproof dish. Fill the centres with the fruit mixture (see below). Make the meringue (see page 852). This quantity is just enough for 4 apples; for more use 2 whites and 4 oz. sugar. Pipe or pile meringue on the top of each apple, dust with sugar, and brown lightly in a cool oven. Pour round a chocolate sauce before serving. If the meringue is omitted altogether, pour the chocolate sauce over the apples.

To make the fruit mixture. Chop the fruit and peel and put together into a small saucepan with the other ingredients. Cook over a slow fire for a few minutes, working well until soft and rich-looking. Moisten with a little of the apple syrup if necessary. The rest of this syrup can be used for the base of a fruit drink or compôte.

TOFFEE APPLES WITH FRIED NOUILLES

This is a sweet much liked by children and a good way of using up batter or pancakes left over from a previous meal.

Batter

4 oz. plain flour	1 tablespoon melted margarine
a pinch of salt	or oil
1 egg	1 dessertspoon sugar
	½ pint milk

4–5 medium-sized apples	2 large tablespoons golden
1 tablespoon butter	syrup
	1 large tablespoon sugar
	½ a lemon

Make batter (see page 432) and stand for an hour. Fry about a dozen thin pancakes and set aside. Peel and core apples, cut in quarters. Melt butter in frying-pan, add syrup and sugar. Allow to boil to a light toffee, put in apples and cook fairly quickly until brown on both sides, turning once only. The toffee should now be a deep golden brown. Arrange apples overlapping down one side of a lightly buttered fireproof dish, pour over any remaining toffee, and sprinkle with lemon juice. Set in a slow oven 5–6 minutes.

Cut pancakes into thin strips, toss them about to separate the pieces. Fry in smoking hot fat (preferably deep fat) until golden brown and crisp. Drain well, then pile up in the dish on other side from apples. Dust with sugar and if liked a little cinnamon. May be served with yoghourt, cream, or custard.

MOUSSE D'ABRICOTS PROVENÇALE

This is a light and delicious sweet. Toasted almonds scattered over the dish make a good alternative to the chocolate rounds, or both may be used.

½ lb. dried apricots, soaked overnight
pared rind and juice of ½ lemon
2 medium-sized cooking apples, peeled, cored, and sliced

sugar to taste
whites of 2–3 eggs
1 oz. or more block chocolate

Stew apricots gently with lemon rind, juice, and apples. Drain from juice and rub through sieve or strainer. When cold, sweeten purée to taste. Whip whites stiffly, add by degrees to purée, continuing to whisk. Pile up in a serving dish and surround with chocolate rounds:

Cut small rounds from grease-proof paper about 2 inches in diameter. Melt chocolate on plate over gentle heat. Spread fairly thinly on paper rounds with knife. Leave to set, then peel off paper.

The syrup left from the apricots may be used in a fruit drink.

CHESTNUT AND ORANGE COMPÔTE

Chestnuts are a good addition to a fruit salad or compôte.

1 lb. large chestnuts, weighed when peeled, and water to cover
3 large oranges

1¼ pints water
6 oz. sugar
a few drops of vanilla essence

Put chestnuts into a pan and cover with cold water. Bring to boil, draw aside, and take out one at a time and remove both skins. If inner skin does not come off easily, return to the pan and reboil. Put sugar and water into a pan with vanilla. Dissolve sugar and boil 5 minutes. Add chestnuts, partially cover pan, and simmer gently about an hour or until nuts are semi-transparent and the syrup fairly thick. Cut the rind and pith from oranges and either cut out flesh from the sections or slice them. Draw chestnuts aside when done, cool and add oranges. Chill before serving.

This may be accompanied by small pâtisseries or cake.

BANANES GRATINÉES

6 bananas
4 good oranges
brown sugar

rum butter (page 186)
sweet short biscuits

Peel the bananas and cut them in long slanting slices. Grate the rind from one orange, then cut the peel and pith from all four. Work the grated rind into the rum butter. Cut the oranges in thin slices with a sharp knife, removing the pips. Arrange in layers in a fireproof dish with the bananas, sprinkling with the sugar. Dot the top with rum butter and bake in a moderate oven 10–15 minutes.

Serve very hot with rum butter and a sweet short biscuit, both handed separately.

CHERRY PAIN PERDU

2–3 slices of milk loaf or cake
1½ lb. cherries or 1 large can of
cherries
1 oz. butter

castor sugar
walnuts, toasted in oven and
coarsely chopped

Cut crusts off the bread, cut each slice into four. Stew cherries 5–6 minutes, drain, sweeten juice if necessary, and boil till thick. Spoon enough of this syrup over the bread to soak it well. Heat a frying-pan, throw in the butter and, when foaming, put in the bread; dust with sugar. Fry till brown on both sides, then arrange in the bottom of a lightly buttered china dish or bowl. Cover with the cherries, chill, then pour over the remaining syrup and sprinkle thickly with the toasted walnuts. Serve with cream or custard.

PASTRY SWEETS

N.B. The notes on pastry-making in Chapter XXVIII, page 831, should be read in conjunction with the following recipes. An explanation of quantity pastry will be found on page 846 and a note on baking blind on page 844.

CUSTARD TART

A good short crust or pâte brisée (see pages 835, 840) is best for this tart. The following recipe is a French one and very good:

ordinary or rich short crust pastry (6 oz. quantity) (see pastry notes,
page 831)

Custard filling

1 egg
2 yolks
1 oz. sugar
¼ oz. flour, scant weight

½ pint creamy milk, good measure
½ oz. melted butter
1 dessertspoon orange-flower water
or other flavouring

Work the egg, yolks, sugar, and flour well together. Add milk, butter, and flavouring. Roll out pastry and line into a flan ring, about 7 inches in diameter, making sure the flan case will have a good edge. Pour in the custard mixture to within $\frac{1}{4}$ inch of the top. Do this on the oven rack drawn slightly out so that none is spilt. Then slide back. Have the tart in the middle of the oven so that it may get bottom heat. Cook for 30–35 minutes in a fairly hot oven, 400° F. Once the custard has begun to set, the bottom of the flan may be lightly pricked with a fine knitting-needle to prevent blistering. If the tart colours too much before it is ready, cover with a piece of damp paper. Cool slightly before removing ring and sliding on to a tray.

The following is an old-fashioned rich short tart:

TREACLE TART

3 oz. butter	3–4 large tablespoons golden syrup
4 oz. lard	2 heaped tablespoons fresh white
8 oz. flour	crumbs
salt	a grating or two of lemon rind and a
1 teaspoon baking-powder	squeeze of lemon juice
water	

Rub the fats into the flour, sifted with a pinch of salt and the baking-powder. Be careful not to over-rub (see pastry notes, page 833). Moisten with 2–3 tablespoons cold water, enough to bind it firmly together. Roll out $\frac{1}{4}$ inch thick, line into a large pie or dinner plate, and trim round the edge. Fill with the syrup, crumbs, and lemon mixed together. Roll out the trimmings of paste, cut into strips, and lay them criss-cross, lattice fashion, on top of the syrup, pressing them down securely on the edge of the plate. Press one final strip round the edge. Bake in a moderately hot oven about 35 minutes.

NORFOLK TREACLE TART

4 oz. quantity rich short crust	2 tablespoons cream
(see pastry notes, page 831)	a little grated lemon rind
4 tablespoons golden syrup	1 small beaten egg
a pat of butter the size of a	
walnut	

Roll out the pastry, line a flan ring, flute or decorate round the edge. Warm the syrup gently, remove from heat, and add butter in small pieces. When dissolved add cream, lemon rind, and beaten egg. Mix thoroughly and pour into the pastry. Set in a moderate oven on middle shelf for 25–30 minutes or until the pastry is a pleasant brown and the filling is set. It is advisable to prick the bottom gently with a fine skewer or knitting-needle when the setting begins. Remove the ring carefully and slide tart on to a hot dish or board. This version of a treacle tart is good cold as well as hot. Black treacle, or a mixture of treacle and syrup, can, of course, be substituted for the golden syrup for those who like a treacly flavour.

APPLE FLORENTINE

A florentine is an old-time version of an apple pie.

firm cooking apples	flaky pastry (see page 835)
butter	spiced ale or cider
brown sugar	nutmeg, ginger, lemon, sugar,
ground cinnamon	cinnamon
lemon rind	icing sugar and thick cream

Peel and core the apples, cut them in quarters if large, otherwise leave whole. Fry or bake in butter until brown, then sprinkle liberally with the sugar, cinnamon, and grated lemon rind. Choose a deep dish, but not so deep as a pie dish; fill with the apples and cover with flaky pastry rolled out to $\frac{1}{4}$ inch thickness. Press round, trim, and decorate. Bake in a quick oven 25–30 minutes. Run a sharp knife round the edge to lift the crust, then cut it into pieces. Remove carefully and pour in enough hot spiced ale or cider to moisten the apples well. Lay the pieces of pastry back on top of the dish. Dust with icing sugar and serve hot with thick cream.

To spice the ale or cider pour about $\frac{1}{4}$ pint into a saucepan, add a grating or two of nutmeg, a quarter of a stick of cinnamon, a good pinch of ground ginger, and the pared rind of half a lemon. Heat slowly, add sugar to taste, then strain before using.

The following recipe is an example of a flan where the pastry and fruit are cooked together. The pastry used may be a rich short crust or pâte sucrée (see pages 835 and 838); hard fruits such as apples, small plums, and apricots are the most suitable.

When using plums or apricots the usual practice is to brush the inside of the flan with dry corn-flour; the split halves of the fruit, with stones removed, are laid in the flan cut side uppermost, and sugar dredged over the top. The flan is baked as described and finished with yellow or red glaze according to the colour of the fruit.

APPLE FLAN MÉNAGÈRE

Pastry

4 oz. flour	2 yolks of egg
2 oz. butter	a few drops of vanilla essence
2 oz. castor sugar	

Filling

1 lb. medium-sized apples	apricot glaze (see page 856)
castor sugar	

Make up pastry according to directions given for pâte sucrée (page 838). Leave at least half an hour before use. Mark or decorate round the edge. If pastry is at all soft, chill for about 15 minutes before filling with the apple.

Peel, quarter, and core the apples. Slice into the flan. When just below the level of the edge, spread evenly to make a flat surface. Continue to slice the apples, but arrange the slices overlapping in circles, starting the first on the outside edge. This is done for the appearance of the dish. Dust the top well with sugar and bake in a moderately hot oven on the middle shelf 25–35 minutes. After about 20 minutes, gently lift off the ring and return flan to the oven to finish cooking. Brush over well with the hot apricot glaze and slide on to a rack to cool. Serve on a wooden board.

APPLE AND ORANGE FLAN

sugar to sweeten, including 2 or 3 lumps of sugar
1 large orange
1½ lb. apples

4 oz. quantity pâte sucrée (see page 838) or rich short crust pastry (see page 835)
apricot glaze (see page 856)
sabayon sauce (see page 186)

Take the lumps of sugar and rub them over the rind of the orange until well soaked with the zest. Peel, core, and slice the apples. Put them into a thick pan with the lump sugar and a little extra sugar to sweeten. Simmer until well reduced, then turn out on to a plate to cool.

Line a 6-inch flan ring with the pastry, fill with the apple mixture, dust with sugar, and bake in a moderately quick oven 20–30 minutes; cool slightly. Cut the peel and pith from the orange, then cut flesh into thin slices. Arrange overlapping round the edge of the flan. Heat the glaze and brush well over the top and sides. Serve just warm with a sabayon sauce, hot or cold.

TARTE CANELLE

This is a black-currant flan flavoured with cinnamon, the two flavours going well together.

6 oz. flour
3 oz. butter
3 oz. sugar
2 yolks
1 tablespoon water

1 dessertspoon cinnamon
sugar to sweeten
about ½ lb. black-currants picked from their stalks

Make up the flour, butter, sugar, yolks, water, and cinnamon as for pâte sucrée (page 838). Leave half an hour in a cold place. Meanwhile prepare a marmelade of the currants (see page 855) by putting them into a pan with plenty of sugar, and cooking them slowly at first and then quickly, stirring frequently, until thick and rich-looking. Turn on to a plate to cool. Tinned or bottled black-currants may be treated in the same way, drained from their juice. Roll out pastry, line into a 6–7-inch flan ring. Roll off and gather up the trimmings. Roll these out, and cut into strips. Fill the marmelade into the flan and arrange the strips over the top, lattice wise. Put a further strip round the edge. Brush over with water and dust with castor sugar. Bake in a fairly hot oven (400° F.) 20–25 minutes. If tinned fruit is used some of the juice may be sweetened, reduced, and thickened slightly with arrowroot. It is then cooled before being brushed over the flan in place of the 'dry' glaze.

APRICOT TART BOURDALOUE

4 oz. quantity rich short crust
    pastry or pâte sucrée (see
    pages 835, 838)

tinned or fresh apricots
flaked browned almonds

Crème bourdaloue

2 egg yolks
2 oz. sugar
orange flavouring or the grated
    rind of an orange

1¼ oz. cream of rice
¾ pint milk
1 egg white

Cream the yolks with a spoonful of the sugar and the flavouring, add the cream of rice; beat well and pour on the milk which has been brought to the boil.   Return to the pan and stir until boiling.   Turn out and cool. Add the sugar to the white and whisk until stiff.   Fold this into the cream and use.

N.B. If cream of rice is unobtainable, use half flour and half corn-flour and ½ pint milk.   As will be observed, a bourdaloue is a crème patissière made with cream of rice in place of flour.

Line a 6-inch flan ring or pie plate with pastry, bake blind in a moderately hot oven for 30 minutes.   Remove paper and ring, and put back in oven for a few minutes.   Take out and cool.   Drain all the syrup from the apricots, reduce this till thick, then cool.   If fresh apricots are used, halve and stone, poach in syrup, then drain and reduce syrup as above.   Put crème bourdaloue into the case, forming it to a shallow dome; cover completely with the apricots, brush well with the syrup to glisten, and scatter with almonds.   Serve at once.

LA POIRAT (NORMANDY PEAR TART)

Pastry

8 oz. flour
4 oz. castor sugar
2 oz. butter
2 oz. lard

1½ oz. shelled chopped walnuts
vanilla essence or ¼ teaspoon cinnamon
2 egg yolks
½ gill cold water

Filling

5 medium-sized pears, Williams or a good stewing pear
2–3 tablespoons thick or clotted cream

Make up the pastry as for pâte brisée (see page 840).   Set aside for an hour.   Meanwhile prepare pears: William or dessert pears are peeled, quartered, cored, and poached 3–4 minutes in syrup, then drained and cooled.   If stewing pears are used they should be ready stewed (see page 903), quartered, and free from syrup.   Roll out approximately two-thirds of the paste; line a flan ring.[1]   Fill well with the pears.   Roll out remaining

---

[1] The inside of the pastry may be moistened with a little of the pear syrup mixed with a spoonful of apricot glaze (see page 856).   This is an improvement when dessert pears are used.

paste into a round that will just cover the flan. Stamp the centre out of this with a 2½- or 3-inch cutter. Lay this wide pastry ring over the flan, press round the edge, and mark the surface, lattice wise, with the point of a knife. Brush over with water or egg white and dust well with castor sugar. Bake in a hot oven (425°–450° F.) for 30–35 minutes. Take out when well browned, remove ring, and allow to cool.

For serving, slide on to a board and pour the cream into the middle of the tart. Serve just warm.

The following type of flan is one in which the fruit is sautéd first in butter before being put into the pastry. A cream mixture, or light batter, is poured into the case and the whole baked in the oven. Any firm fruit may be used. The tart is eaten cold.

TARTE NORMANDE

Use flaky or short crust pastry (see page 835) for this flan.

4 oz. quantity paste (see pastry notes, page 831)	½ lb. fruit (apples, gooseberries, etc)
1 oz. butter	glacé icing flavoured with rum or vanilla
1 oz. sugar	

Cream

½ oz. flour	¾ gill milk (approx).
1 egg	a few drops of rum or vanilla
1 oz. sugar	essence

Line a 6-inch flan ring with the pastry. Make sure there are no cracks in the paste and that the sides of the flan are high. Cut the apples into thick slices, leave gooseberries whole. Sauté the fruits quickly in the butter, sprinkling with sugar and allowing them to take colour. Arrange in the bottom of the flan. Put the flour into a bowl, add the egg and sugar and beat well. Dilute with the milk and flavour with the rum or vanilla. Pour carefully into the flan, and gently slide it into a moderate oven. Bake in steady heat 30–40 minutes until well coloured. Allow to cool before icing with the glacé icing.

GÂTEAU BASQUE

This is a covered jam tart, excellent for a picnic or luncheon-party; almonds or hazel-nuts are added to the pastry.

7 oz. flour	grated lemon rind
1½ oz. ground almonds or hazel-nuts	1 lb. apricot, cherry, or strawberry conserve
4 oz. butter	egg white
3½ oz. castor sugar	castor sugar
3 egg yolks or 2 *small* eggs	

Sift flour on to the slab or board; sprinkle the almonds on the flour and scoop a well in the middle. Put in the butter, sugar, eggs, and a little grated lemon rind. Work up to a paste (see directions for pâte sucrée on page 838). Set aside for an hour.

Cut off about a third of the paste, roll out the remainder just over $\frac{1}{4}$ inch thick, and line a shallow flan ring or pie plate. Roll or trim off the edges and add trimmings to reserved paste. Three-quarters fill with the conserve. Roll out remaining paste, cover the flan or plate, trim round with knife. With the point of the knife draw curved lines from the middle of the pastry so that they meet the edge at intervals of about an inch. Brush lightly over with the egg white and dust with castor sugar.

Bake in a moderately hot oven, 400° F., for about 25 minutes. Set in the centre of the oven.

CHAUSSONS

A chausson is the French equivalent of our turnover. It can be either oval or round in shape and is made of short or flaky pastry. The filling is of fruit.

APPLE CHAUSSON

6 oz. flour	1 teaspoon cinnamon
3 oz. butter	1 beaten egg
3 oz. castor sugar	a little extra castor sugar for glazing

Filling

1 lb. apples	grated lemon rind
$\frac{1}{2}$ oz. butter	brown or white sugar
1$\frac{1}{2}$ oz. each of currants and sultanas	

Make up pastry according to directions given for pâte sucrée on page 838. Leave to rest.

Peel, core, and quarter apples. Cut in thick slices. Rub the bottom of a stew-pan thickly with butter, put in the apples in layers with the fruit, lemon rind, and sugar to taste. Press a piece of grease-proof paper on to the fruit, cover the pan tightly and cook over moderate heat, shaking the pan frequently, for 5-6 minutes. The apples should be partially cooked. This may be done in the oven if more convenient. Turn on to a plate to cool.

Now divide the pastry in two, roll out to two large rounds. Lay one on a baking-sheet, pile on the apple mixture, leaving a margin of about $\frac{3}{4}$ inch, brush this with water, lay over the other round and press the edges down well. With the point of a knife draw curved lines from the middle of the chausson so that they meet the edge at intervals of about 2 inches. Make two circles with the point of the knife, near the edge and parallel to it, pressing in the point to make a sharp indentation.

Brush the chausson lightly with water, sprinkle with castor sugar, and bake on the middle shelf in a moderate oven 35–40 minutes.

CHOUX A LA CRÈME

Choux pastry

3 oz. butter	3 eggs
1½ gills water	3¾ oz. flour
icing sugar	hot chocolate or fresh fruit
crème chantilly (see page 42)	sauce (page 184)

Bring the butter and water to the boil together. When bubbling draw aside and immediately add the flour all at once. Beat until smooth, when the paste will leave the sides of the pan. Leave to cool. Whisk the eggs lightly and add by degrees, beating thoroughly. If the eggs are exceptionally large, do not add the last spoonful as it may make the mixture too wet. When finished, the paste should be smooth and shiny-looking.

Put out in teaspoons on a damp baking-sheet. Bake 20–30 minutes in a moderate to hot oven. When quite firm to the touch take out, put on to a rack, and cool. Fill with whipped sweetened cream (crème chantilly). Pile thickly into a serving dish, dust with icing sugar, and serve with hot chocolate or fresh fruit sauce.

CHOCOLATE PROFITEROLES

These are a variation on choux à la crème and very good.

Make a choux paste. Put out in teaspoons on a lightly greased baking-sheet. Bake 20–30 minutes in a moderate to hot oven. When quite firm to the touch take out and put on to a rack to cool. Fill with chocolate crème patissière, dust with icing sugar, and serve with a hot chocolate sauce. Crème chantilly is sometimes used in place of the crème patissière. The traditional way to serve these is to pile them up, when filled and dusted with sugar, in a pyramid in the dish, and at the last moment pour the boiling sauce over. Nowadays it is more usual to hand the sauce separately.

LINTZER TORTE

This is an Austrian sweet which is a cross between a flan and a cake. This English version has more fruit in it than the original.

¾ lb. fresh raspberries or good raspberry jam	1½ oz. almonds, ground, without blanching, through a nut-mill
sugar	grated rind of ½ lemon
6 oz. self-raising flour	½ teaspoon ground cinnamon
2½ oz. butter	½ teaspoon Nescafé
2 small eggs	
2½ oz. sugar	

Cook down the raspberries to a thick pulp or marmelade (see page 855) with plenty of sugar, and spread on a plate to cool. If using jam reduce a little. Sieve the flour on to the board, make a well in the centre, and put in the rest of the ingredients. Work up to a paste, then leave in a cool place for half an hour. Roll out or if sticky pat with your hand, and line a 6-inch flan ring thickly; trim off. Roll out the trimmings and cut into strips.

Fill with the raspberry marmelade and press the strips across lattice fashion. Brush with water and dust with castor sugar, and bake in a moderate oven 30 minutes. Serve cold.

APPLE STRUDEL

strudel paste (see page 840)
a little oil
2 lb apples
2 oz. each of currants and sultanas
brown or white sugar to taste

½ teaspoon each of cinnamon and mixed spice
3–4 tablespoons browned crumbs
2 oz. butter
icing sugar

Roll out the strudel paste, lay on a large, well-floured cloth. Brush with oil. Peel, core, and thinly slice the apples. Mix with the dried fruit, sugar, and spices and 2 tablespoons of the crumbs.

Pull the paste gently from all sides, until as thin as paper. Take enough of the melted butter to dab all over the paste, leaving a good margin round the edge. Strew over the remaining crumbs, then scatter with the apple mixture. Tear away the extreme edge of the paste from all round the sides. Hold the cloth by the two corners nearest to you, give a sharp flick to bring the edge of the paste over on to the apple mixture, then, tilting the cloth gently, roll up the strudel, pressing lightly on the outside of the cloth in order to roll it moderately closely. Be careful not to roll it completely off the cloth. Lift the cloth and tilt the strudel on to a large greased baking-sheet, curving it slightly while doing so. Brush with the rest of the melted butter and bake in a hot oven until golden brown. Take out, dust well with icing sugar, cut into pieces slantwise, and serve on a wooden board with cream or a whipped vanilla sauce.

This particular strudel is best served freshly made, hot or just warm.

CREAM CHEESE STRUDEL (1)

10 oz. white or milk cheese
1¾ oz. creamed butter
2½ oz. castor sugar
yolk of 1 egg or 1 small egg
vanilla essence to flavour
1 teaspoon lemon juice

2½ oz. sultanas
a little grated lemon rind
strudel paste (see page 840)
1–2 oz. melted butter
browned crumbs
icing sugar

Sieve cheese. Work in the creamed butter and sugar by degrees, add the egg and vanilla, beating thoroughly. Soak sultanas overnight in water with a squeeze of lemon juice. Then drain and add to the cream cheese mixture with the lemon rind.

Roll and pull the strudel paste as for Apple Strudel; brush or dab with the melted butter and sprinkle well with the crumbs. Put the mixture on in small pieces, then finish as for the Apple Strudel.

CREAM CHEESE STRUDEL (2)

strudel pastry (see page 840)

Filling

¼ lb. cream cheese	grated lemon rind
sugar to sweeten	2 oz. browned hazel-nuts
1 egg	hot cherry sauce

Cream the cheese with the sugar, beat in the egg, and add a grating of lemon rind. Chop the hazel-nuts and add to the mixture. Prepare and finish strudel as in first recipe (for Apple Strudel). Serve with a hot cherry sauce. Make this as for a kissel (see page 906), i.e. a compôte of cherries slightly thickened with arrowroot.

BAVARIAN STRUDEL

4 oz. butter	1¾ oz. sugar
6 oz. flour	3 tablespoons milk

Filling

1½ lb. apples	sugar
1 oz. sultanas	breadcrumbs
mixed spice	milk and sugar for glazing

Rub fat into flour. Add sugar and bind with milk. Peel, core, and slice apples, mix with sultanas, spice, and sugar to taste. Add a handful of dry crumbs. Now roll out the pastry into a long strip, about 4–5 inches wide. Put the apple mixture down the middle. Fold over the sides of the pastry towards the middle. Brush over with milk and dust with sugar. Bake in a moderate oven 30–35 minutes.

CHIFFON PIES

This is a popular American sweet, made in different flavours: coffee, orange, chocolate, etc. This recipe may be taken as a basic one. For chocolate use a slightly bitter chocolate and about an ounce less sugar. For a coffee chiffon pie use a pure and not too sweet essence and an ounce less sugar.

LEMON CHIFFON PIE

4 oz. quantity rich short crust	grated rind of ½ lemon
(see pastry notes, page 831)	1 teaspoon powdered gelatine,
2 eggs	dissolved in 1 tablespoon
3 oz. castor sugar	warm water
strained juice of 1 lemon	2 heaped tablespoons whipped
a pinch of salt	cream

Line a flan ring with pastry and bake blind. Separate the whites from the yolks of egg. Beat yolks with 2 oz. of the sugar, add lemon juice and salt. Turn into a double saucepan and cook over gentle heat until thick, whisking all the time. Then remove from the hot water, add the grated rind and gelatine. Continue whisking until light and fluffy and on the point of setting. Whisk whites with remaining sugar and fold into the mixture with the cream. When it will hold its shape, pile up into the pastry case. Chill. Slightly whipped cream may be poured over immediately before serving.

DEEP SOUTH APPLE PIE

Pastry

4 oz. lard or American shortening	approximately ¾ gill cold water
a pinch of salt	8 oz. self-raising flour
	icing sugar
1½ lb. cooking apples	½ teaspoon cinnamon
3–4 oz white or brown sugar (or to taste)	1 tablespoon orange marmalade
	½ oz. butter

Soften lard in a mixing bowl. Add salt and water. Sift flour over it, cut the lard into the flour and mix to a rough paste. Put in the refrigerator for at least half an hour. Peel, core, and slice the apples. Cook them slowly with sugar and cinnamon to a pulp. Add the marmalade and butter and beat well. Cool. Knead pastry lightly and divide into two. Line a pie plate, pour in apple mixture, cover with second round, and bake 30 minutes in a moderately hot oven (400° F.). The pie may be dry glazed before baking, i.e. brushed with water and dusted with castor sugar. Serve hot or cold, well dusted with icing sugar.

The pastry for the following Cherry Pie is made with lard; this gives a rich and very friable crust. If to be eaten cold a rich short crust (see page 835) may be preferred. The cup for measuring may be an ordinary large tea-cup.

CHERRY PIE

Pastry

4 oz. lard	a pinch of salt
5 tablespoons water	8 oz. self-raising flour

Filling

2½ cups stoned, stewed, drained cherries	⅛ teaspoon salt
1 cup cherry juice	2 drops of almond essence
½ cup sugar (or to taste)	1 dessertspoon tapioca (fine)
	1 tablespoon melted butter

egg white and castor sugar for glazing

Soften the lard, add the water and salt, sift in the flour. Cut the lard into the flour and mix to a rough paste. Put into the refrigerator for at least half an hour. Combine all the ingredients for the filling and allow to stand for about 15 minutes. Line a deep pie tin with two-thirds of the pastry, fill with the cherry mixture. Roll out the remaining pastry and cover. Make four slits on the top of the pastry, glaze with egg white and castor sugar. Bake approximately 35 minutes in a moderately hot oven.

ENGLISH FRUIT PIE OR TART

English fruit pies, or tarts as they are now more often called, are cooked and served in a pie dish. The fruit is usually put into the dish raw, well layered with sugar, brown or white, and with a top layer of fruit nicely domed above the dish. A little water is then poured into the dish and the whole covered with a short pastry crust (see page 835). The pastry is lightly brushed with water and dusted with castor sugar and is then ready for baking. Traditionally a fruit pie has little ornamentation, this being reserved for meat pies. Certain pies call for flavouring of some kind. Grated lemon or orange rind, cloves (not more than 2 to the dish), half a vanilla pod, a leaf or two of lemon verbena, a few slices of quince and so on are good in apple pies. A little elderflower syrup in gooseberry, or ginger or orange in rhubarb, all help to make the pie more interesting. See notes on preparation of apples for cooking, page 904.

APPLE PIE

Choose good cooking apples.

about 1–1½ lb. apples	water
brown or white sugar to taste	6 oz. quantity short pastry
flavouring to taste	(see page 835)

Peel, core, and slice apples into a medium-sized pie dish. Layer with the sugar and add the flavouring. Arrange the last layer of apples in a dome slightly above the dish. Add water to half fill the dish. Light syrup may be added instead, in which case decrease the quantity of sugar.

Have ready the pastry, roll out about ¼ inch thick, cut a band of paste very slightly wider than the edge of the dish. Brush edge with water and press the band round. Now lift pastry on rolling-pin and lay over the pie. Press down the edge and trim off the pastry with a sharp knife, holding up the dish in one hand and cutting with the other, holding the knife slant-wise slightly under the dish. Mark round the edge with the point of a kitchen knife and mark lattice fashion over the top with the back of the knife. Brush lightly with water, dredge with castor sugar, set the pie on a tin, and bake in a moderately hot oven (400° F.) 15–20 minutes. Then lower heat slightly and continue cooking a further 15–20 minutes.

LEMON MERINGUE PIE

Rich short crust pastry

5 oz. flour	3 oz. butter
1 teaspoon sugar	1 yolk and a little water to mix

Filling

1 oz. corn-flour	2 egg yolks
½ pint milk	grated rind and juice of 1
1 oz. sugar	lemon

Meringue

2 egg whites	4 oz. castor sugar

Line a flan ring with the short crust pastry and bake blind. Mix the corn-flour smoothly with a little of the milk and heat the remainder. Pour on to the mixed corn-flour, return to the pan, and boil 3–4 minutes, stirring continuously. Add the sugar, allow to cool a little, beat in the egg yolks, and the grated lemon rind and juice. Pour the mixture into the pastry case and cook a few minutes in the oven to set. Whip the whites until stiff and dry, whisk in 1 tablespoon of the sugar and then carefully fold in the remainder. Pile the meringue on the pie to cover the filling completely, dust with castor sugar, and set in a cool oven for 10–15 minutes.

BATTER PUDDING AND PANCAKES

For general notes on batters, pancakes, and fritters see chapter on batters (page 422).

STEAMED BATTER PUDDING

6 oz. flour	a little grated lemon rind
a pinch of salt	2 eggs
½ oz. sugar	6 liquid oz. milk (just over ¼ pint)

Sift flour with salt into a bowl. Add the sugar and lemon rind and make up into a batter (see page 431) with the egg yolks and milk. Allow to stand for at least 1 hour before cooking. Whip the whites stiffly and fold into the batter. Turn into a greased basin and steam 1½–2 hours. Turn out and serve with hot jam or marmalade, or brown sugar and butter.

SIMPLE PANCAKE BATTER

4 oz. plain flour	1 egg
1 dessertspoon castor sugar	1 yolk
½ oz. or more oiled butter	½ pint milk (approx.)
a pinch of salt	

Mix and cook according to instructions on page 431.

The ingredients given will make 12–16 quite small pancakes or 10–12 medium-sized ones. Even if this number is not required at one time, it is not uneconomic to make a full amount of batter. The extra batter may be made up into cassoulette cases, which keep for a short time in an air-tight tin; extra pancakes may be used for pancake chips, very popular with children.

CRÊPES FOURRÉES AUX POMMES

This is really a pile of thin pancakes sandwiched with a fruit mixture, looking like and being served in the same way as a pudding.

basic batter as above

Apple mixture

1½ lb. apples	½ oz. butter
brown sugar	apple jelly or apricot jam
cinnamon or lemon peel	(melted)

Mix the batter mixture as given above and allow to stand for about an hour. Peel, core, and rather thickly slice the apples, rub the butter over the bottom of a thick stew-pan, and put in the apples with layers of sugar and cinnamon or lemon peel to taste. Cover and cook very slowly, without stirring, on the stove or in the oven until the apples are soft and tender. Fry the pancakes as thinly as possible, lay them in a dish, sandwiching them with the apple one above the other. Spoon over the top a little melted apple jelly or apricot jam and put the dish in the oven for about 10 minutes. Pour round an apricot or other fruit sauce. For fruit sauces see sauce chapter, page 184.

CRÊPES AU CHOCOLAT

basic batter as above

Fruit mixture

6 oz. dried fruit (raisins, dates, apricots, prunes, etc.)	flavouring of rum, liqueurs, vanilla, etc.
1 oz. candied peel	½ oz. butter
a short ¼ pint of flavoured syrup or fruit juice	a squeeze of lemon juice

chocolate sauce (see below)

Shred the fruit and peel, macerate in the rum or liqueur for an hour or two, then put into the syrup and simmer until thick. Add a squeeze of lemon juice and the butter and use.

Make the batter in the usual way and allow to stand for half an hour; make the pancakes as thin as possible, diluting batter if necessary. Sandwich together one on top of the other with layers of the fruit mixture in between each. Brush over with a little melted butter, and dust well with sugar to glaze to a caramel under the grill. Cut before serving and pour round the chocolate sauce.

Chocolate sauce

2 oz. block chocolate	½ teaspoon vanilla
2 tablespoons sugar	yolk of 1 egg (optional)—this
1 teaspoon unsweetened chocolate powder or cocoa	gives a richer sauce, *or*
½ pint water	1 teaspoon arrowroot diluted
¼ teaspoon Nescafé	with 1 tablespoon water

Put the chocolate and chocolate powder, sugar and water into a pan together, bring to the boil, stir until dissolved, then simmer 15–20 minutes or until it has the consistency of thin cream. At this stage it should be syrupy and rich-looking. Add the vanilla and Nescafé. If the yolk is to be used, mix it with a spoonful or two of warm water, then add a little of the sauce to it by degrees. When thoroughly blended, whisk it into the remaining sauce in the saucepan and serve at once without reheating. If arrowroot is used in place of egg for thickening, the sauce must be brought to the boil in order to cook this ingredient.

APRICOT PANCAKES

basic batter as above	1 oz. almonds
1 lb. fresh apricots, or a tin of apricots	cream
sugar	

Make the pancakes. Prepare a syrup of $\frac{1}{2}$ pint water or apricot juice and 4 or 5 tablespoons sugar to taste. Cook the fresh apricots, halved and stoned, in the syrup, or heat up the canned ones in their own syrup with a little extra sugar to taste. Take out the fruit and reduce the syrup until thick. Blanch and shred the almonds, then toast in the oven until brown. Arrange the pancakes on top of one another in a shallow fireproof dish, sandwiching between them the apricot compôte and pouring the syrup over and around. Bake in a hot oven 15 minutes, cut into sections to simplify serving, scatter almonds over the whole together with 2 or 3 spoonfuls thick cream. Serve very hot.

PARTY PANCAKES

Here are some recipes for richer, party pancakes. It should be noted that these batters call for butter and not margarine. A good quality oil is the best substitute.

Richer batter (1)

4$\frac{1}{2}$ oz. flour	1 dessertspoon brandy or rum
a pinch of salt	1 tablespoon melted butter
1$\frac{3}{4}$ oz. sugar	12 liquid oz. cold boiled milk
2 eggs	lemon, orange, vanilla, etc., to taste

Make up according to the directions given for mixing batter (page 431). If flavouring with orange or lemon, it is best to rub a lump of sugar over the rind until it is soaked with the oil or zest.

Batter 2 is a richer batter to which crushed macaroons are added.

Richer batter (2)

4$\frac{1}{2}$ oz. flour	$\frac{1}{2}$ gill (2$\frac{1}{2}$ oz.) cream
a pinch of salt	7 liquid oz. milk
1$\frac{1}{4}$ oz. sugar	$\frac{3}{4}$ oz. crushed macaroons
1 tablespoon melted butter	flavour to taste
2 eggs	

CRÊPES SUZETTE

This is a classic dish about which little need be said, except perhaps that success depends on the pancakes being wafer thin and piping hot when served; they are flavoured with orange juice and curaçao, and are brought to table flaming in lighted rum

richer batter 1, with an extra $\frac{1}{4}$ oz. butter added in the way indicated on page 432

Orange butter

2–3 lumps of sugar	1 oz. castor sugar
1 large orange (or preferably 2 tangerines if in season)	1 tablespoon orange juice
1½ oz. butter	1 tablespoon orange curaçao

2–3 tablespoons rum

Make the batter as indicated and allow to stand (see batter notes, page 431). Take the zest of the orange by rubbing the lumps of sugar over the rind until these are well soaked with the orange oil. Crush the sugar and add to the butter. Work well together, adding castor sugar, orange juice, and curaçao. Cook the pancakes, using very little butter to grease the pan for the first pancake, and none subsequently: the pancakes should be thin and dry. Brush a shallow tin with butter, lay the pancakes on this, overlapping them, and brush again with a little melted butter. They are then ready for the final reheating in the oven. When required, put the tin into a hot oven for a few minutes, and when the pancakes are thoroughly hot take them off the tin and spread each with the orange butter. Roll up, lay in a hot dish. Warm the rum by holding the spoon for a minute or so over a flame, then set it alight and pour round the dish. With a chafing-dish, this process may be carried out at table; the hot orange butter is put into the dish, the pancakes added, and then the rum lighted and poured over the whole.

N.B. When tangerine oranges are in season, Crêpes Suzette are all the better for being made with tangerine butter rather than orange.

The Crêpes Fourrées Winkfield, given on page 1020, are an excellent and unusual dish for special occasions, and the following recipe is a slightly different version :

CRÊPES NAPOLITAINE

Batter

4 oz. plain flour	1 yolk
a pinch of salt	1 large tablespoon melted butter
1 level dessertspoon sugar	½ pint milk
1 egg	

Filling

cherry, raspberry, or apricot jam, slightly warmed

Meringue

1 egg white	vanilla
2 oz. castor sugar	1 dessertspoon ground almonds

sauce (see page 930)

Batter. Sift flour into bowl with salt and sugar, make a well in the centre, break in the egg and yolk, adding a little milk. Stir well, gradually drawing in flour and adding enough milk to make a thick cream. Add butter; beat well; add remaining milk, and set aside for about an hour. Heat a small thick omelet pan, put in a few drops of oil or melted butter. Pour in enough batter to coat thinly the bottom of the pan; allow to brown well on one side; lift edge of pancake, slide knife underneath, and turn or toss over. Cook about half the time on other side, slide or turn on to a rack, and continue until batter is finished. Lay one pancake in fireproof dish, spread it thinly with warmed jam, cover with another, then more jam and so on until there is a stack of about 8–10 pancakes.

Meringue. Whip white stiffly, incorporate sugar, vanilla, and almonds. Spread over the pancakes, dust with castor sugar, leave 10 minutes, then brown delicately in cool oven for 15 minutes. Pour sauce round and serve hot or just warm.

Sauce. This is whipped custard. If made with custard powder use a level tablespoon of powder to 1 pint milk and 1 dessertspoon sugar. Make in usual way and whisk till cool. If egg custard, use 1 egg, 1 teaspoon sugar, and ¼ pint milk. Mix yolk with sugar, pour on hot milk, return to pan, and stir until mixture will coat back of spoon. Whip white stiffly and whisk into custard whilst cooling. Flavour with vanilla.

CRÊPES A LA NORMANDE

2 large cooking apples, cinnamon and sugar to flavour, of which a small portion should be lump sugar
½ quantity of richer batter 1

1 oz. blanched or chopped almonds
zest of an orange rubbed off on to the lumps of sugar
crème chantilly (whipped, sweetened, vanilla-flavoured cream)

Cut up the apples and cook to a pulp. Rub through a strainer and return to the rinsed pan with the sugar (reserving a few lumps) and cinnamon to flavour. Reduce until the purée will just leave the sides of the pan. After the batter has stood for the required time (see batter notes, page 431) add the almonds and the crushed orange-flavoured sugar; then make the pancakes, using a little butter to grease the pan. When all are done, thinly spread the inside of each one with the apple purée, fold over, lay down on a dish, dust well with castor sugar, and glaze in a quick oven. Serve the crème chantilly separately.

CRÊPES PRALINÉES

richer batter 2

Praline butter

2 oz. butter
1½ oz. castor sugar

2 tablespoons praline powder (see page 854)
rum

Prepare batter and allow to stand (see batter notes, page 431).

Cream butter, beat in the sugar by degrees, and when white and whipped-looking mix in the praline and flavour well with rum.

Fry the number of pancakes required. Quickly spread the inside of each with butter, roll up in the shape of a cigar, heat for a moment in the oven, and serve at once.

These are good with Pêches Flambées, which are peaches poached in syrup, drained of all but a tablespoon, and flambéd with brandy or rum (see page 66).

SWEET FRITTERS

BEIGNETS DE NANCY

macaroons (see page 868)
apricot or quince marmelade
  (see page 855)
fritter batter 1 (see page 442)

kirsch
cream or sabayon sauce (see
  page 186)

Make a dozen or more small macaroons. Join them together with the marmelade flavoured with kirsch. Dip in the batter and fry at once in deep fat. Drain well, powder with sugar, and dish in a napkin. Serve with cream or a sabayon sauce.

BEIGNETS PICAYUNE

4 slices of pineapple
crème patissière (see page 851)
finely chopped citron peel

rum
fritter batter 2 (see page 443)

Cut the slices of pineapple in half. Have the crème patissière of a very thick consistency. Mix to taste with the citron peel and flavour well with rum. Spread a layer on each half-slice of pineapple. Dip into fritter batter 2 and fry until golden brown. Drain, sprinkle with sugar, and glaze in the oven.

BEIGNETS DE PRUNEAUX ET DE CHOCOLAT

16–20 good French plums or
  prunes
¼ stick of cinnamon
1 wineglass red wine (claret), or
1 cup of fairly strongly made
  tea
a strip of lemon rind

almonds
candied orange peel
fritter batter (see page 442)
grated chocolate
cream or sabayon sauce (see
  page 186)

Simmer the prunes with the cinnamon, wine or tea, and lemon rind for 10–15 minutes, or until tender. Drain and stone. Stuff with a blanched almond and a small piece of candied orange peel. Dip at once into fritter batter and fry in deep fat. Drain well and roll in grated chocolate. Serve at once with sabayon sauce or cream.

CRÈMES FRITES

This dish presents contrast in texture: pieces of smooth, firm crème patissière, usually highly flavoured with various liqueurs, vanilla, almond, or what you will, dipped in egg and breadcrumbs or covered in batter, then fried in deep fat. The fork breaks through a crisp covering to the flavoured creamy centre. This dish was a favourite in the days of professional cooks, for it indicated a measure of practice and skill; now that less experienced cooks have taken over one does not meet it so often.

A crème patissière in itself has so many uses that no reasonable cook will fail to master it, so she may as well go a step further and learn to make these Crèmes Frites. They call for attention to detail in the preparation of the crème, and as this is a case of a delicate mixture being subjected to several processes, light handling is essential. Should you fail to produce a perfect dish the first time you try them, do not condemn the recipe out of hand as being wrong or useless.

The following recipe is for a rather dry crème patissière, one which it is possible to cut in shapes with a knife and to coat and fry:

a good ¾ pint milk (17 liquid oz.)	2 yolks
a vanilla pod	¾ oz. butter
4 oz. flour	vanilla essence
2 oz. sugar	vanilla sugar
2 eggs	

Split the vanilla pod; put the milk in a double pan, reserving ½ gill, add the pod and infuse (see page 44) for 15 minutes. Sift flour and sugar into a bowl, separate the whites and yolks of the eggs, add all the yolks to the flour, and the reserved ½ gill of milk. Cream well. Remove pod and pour on milk, mix, return all to pan, and stir until the contents touch boiling-point. Draw aside, add butter. Whip the whites and add to the cream (see notes on crème patissière, page 851). Bring again to boiling-point. Allow to cool a little and strengthen flavour with the addition of a little vanilla essence. If liqueur is used as flavouring it should be added now. When quite cool, spread the cream 1 inch thick on a plate to get cold. When completely cold and set cut into shapes, crescents, or rounds, etc., and either dip into batter 2 (see page 443) or flour, then egg and breadcrumb (see page 38). Serve dusted with vanilla sugar and hand a fruit sauce separately, e.g. a peach sauce flavoured with kirsch (see page 185).

FRUIT AND FLOWER FRITTERS

Apple and banana fritters are generally popular, but other fruits may be used also, though some of the softer, juicier fruits are a little more difficult to handle. In addition to fruits certain flowers are used, elder and marrow flowers, for example, and in some countries orange and lemon flowers.

A fritto misto of fruits is an unusual dish, but once you have the batter mixed and the hot fat bath there is not much extra work involved, and you may choose three or four fruits which go well together, e.g. pineapple and strawberries, orange, apple, and banana and so forth.

Although the following recipes indicate the use of liqueurs, these, of course, are optional, and sugar only may be employed. The word macerate means to soften by steeping; the length of time for all fruits mentioned, except strawberries, is 30 minutes.

Apples. Peel, core, cut in rings $\frac{1}{4}$ to $\frac{1}{2}$ inch thick. Macerate in sugar and cognac.

Apricots. Choose them not too ripe, halve, stone, and macerate in kirsch and sugar.

Bananas. Peel, slice each into three slanting pieces, macerate in rum and sugar.

Oranges. Choose the best Jaffas. Peel carefully and divide into sections. Macerate in rum and sugar or curaçao.

Peaches. Choose firm, ripe peaches. Peel, halve, and stone (quarter if large). Macerate in brandy and sugar.

Pears. Choose firm, small, ripe pears, peel, quarter, and core. Macerate in sugar and kirsch.

Pineapple. Peel and slice the pine, cut each slice in two, remove hard core. Macerate in kirsch or rum and sugar.

Strawberries. Choose large, ripe, dry berries, hull, and macerate in kirsch and sugar 15 minutes.

Tangerines. Peel, divide in sections, remove pips by making a small slit in the skin, macerate in rum or curaçao.

Drain the fruit carefully from the liqueur, dip at once into the prepared batter (fritter batter 2, see page 443), fry in deep fat. Drain well, dust with icing sugar, and glaze for a few minutes in a sharp oven (this final glazing is optional). The flowers are treated in the same way with sugar and any suitable liqueur, but are not glazed after frying.

These fritters may be served with a sabayon sauce (see page 186).

BEIGNETS SOUFFLÉS

These are made with a choux paste. They are not easy to make without a little practice. The fat, if too hot to begin with, will cause a crust to form so that the beignet will not rise to the full extent. It is the proper manipulation of the fat that calls for practice. (See pages 73–4 on frying.)

The mixture is put out on a baking-sheet in even-sized spoonfuls, and a palette-knife dipped in hot fat is used to lift up each ball of paste. In this way they will slide into the fat without splashing or breaking. The second recipe (after Carême) is the richer of the two. (For Beignets au Fromage see page 754.)

BEIGNETS SOUFFLÉS (1)

1½ gills water	3 small eggs
3 oz. butter	½ oz. sugar
3¾ oz. flour	vanilla to flavour

Boil water and butter together, draw aside and immediately add the flour all at once. Beat till smooth. Cool. Beat in the eggs one at a time, adding the sugar and vanilla. Divide the mixture up into dessertspoons on a baking-sheet and drop carefully into a bath of hot fat, lifting with a palette-knife. (See notes on frying, pages 73–4.) Fry gently, gradually increasing the heat, for approximately 7 minutes. Drain, roll in castor sugar, and serve with a hot jam or fruit sauce.

BEIGNETS SOUFFLÉS (2) (AFTER CARÈME)

¾ pint milk	1½ oz. sugar
1¼ oz. butter	1 large egg white
3½ oz. flour	1 dessertspoon whipped cream
3 yolks of egg	vanilla pod

Boil the milk containing the vanilla pod until it is reduced by half (to 1½ gills); remove pod, add butter, reboil, and add quickly, off the fire, the flour. Cool, beat in the yolks and sugar, whip the white stiffly and fold in with the cream. Divide out into pieces the size of a green walnut and fry in not very hot fat (it should be hardly smoking), gradually increasing the heat, for about 7 minutes. Serve with jam or fruit sauce.

BEIGNETS SOUFFLÉS EN SURPRISE

prepare ½ quantity of crème patissière as given on page 851	No. 2 Beignet Soufflé mixture cherry, strawberry, or quince preserve

Have the crème patissière hot, light, and well made. Fry beignets according to directions in previous recipe; drain well. Split at side and insert a small dessertspoon of the crème patissière and a teaspoon of the preserve. Arrange at once on a hot dish on a napkin, dust thickly with icing or vanilla sugar. Serve very hot.

KAISERSCHMARREN

7 oz. flour	½–¾ pint milk
1 egg	1 yolk
vanilla	1 oz. sugar
½ oz. butter	

3 oz. sultanas or raisins	sugar
½ gill apple juice, cider, or white wine	1 oz. butter

Make up the ingredients for the batter into a thick cream, using the yolks only and reserving the white.   Add the butter melted at the last. Stand for half an hour.   Whip the white stiffly and add to the batter. Heat the pan, grease lightly, and fry the batter into about five thick pancakes.   Turn on to a rack and keep hot.   Meanwhile simmer the sultanas in the apple juice until well plumped out.   Melt the butter in the frying-pan.   Tear the pancakes into pieces using two forks, add them to the pan, and shake up over the fire, dusting well with sugar.   Pour in the sultanas and shake over the fire for a few more minutes.   Then serve at once piled up in a dish.

TOFFEE PUDDING

¼ lb. butter	½ pint milk
¼ lb. demerara sugar	fingers of bread
½ lb. golden syrup	whipped cream

Put the butter, demerara sugar, and syrup into a frying-pan, stir until melted over slow heat, then boil more rapidly until golden brown, stirring continuously.   Bring the milk up to boiling-point.   Arrange the fingers of bread in a large dish, pour over the milk.   Lift out the fingers at once and put them into the toffee sauce to coat them well.   Pile them up in a fireproof dish, and if necessary pour over a little extra toffee sauce.   Serve with whipped cream.

HOT SWEET SOUFFLÉS AND OMELETS

HOT SWEET SOUFFLÉS

To achieve a perfect hot soufflé requires technical skill and some practice: they are as temperamental as prima donnas, and if your aim is to produce classic perfection—a dish light and melting, the inside barely set —you must be patient.   Such a soufflé is made by the French methods, 1 and 2.   There are, of course, other methods producing soufflés of a type perfectly pleasing to many, but not perhaps such as would receive the unreserved approval of the professional.   Methods 3 and 4 are both easier for the less experienced cook, and by them it is possible to produce pleasing results; R. H. describes method 4 as foolproof.   Then there is also the American method, described in the part of this book dealing with savoury soufflés (page 321).

The novice will be wise to begin her hot soufflé-making by method 4, graduate to 3, and then, having become expert in these, go on to the more difficult processes of 1 and 2.

The following remarks on sweet soufflés should be read in conjunction with the general notes on soufflé-making in the egg chapter (page 320). It will be noted that there is a slight difference between the savoury soufflés described there and the sweet ones here in that the latter contain little butter and sometimes none.

Method 1. French in origin, this has a base of crème patissière to which yolks and whites of egg are added. The Soufflé à la Vanille is an example; the recipe given may equally well be used for lemon and chocolate soufflés.

Method 2. This is also French, and has a base of flavoured milk which is thickened with flour and arrowroot to make a light sauce. After the mixture has boiled a small amount of butter is added. This is a particularly delicate form of soufflé and requires that care shall be taken over every detail, and particularly that the oven temperature shall be correct. The flavours for this are vanilla, chocolate, and lemon.

Method 3. This is the one often used by the English cook. It has a panade for base and is easier than the foregoing, because the amount of flour used produces a firmer mixture, with consequently less risk of falling after cooking. The lemon soufflé given is an example of this.

Method 4. This is based on the soufflé omelet. It contains no flour, and while it makes a pleasant sweet its texture is firm and not so melting as that of the classic dishes. The quantity of egg white makes the mixture set readily and remain firm. The banana soufflé is an example. In Soufflé Rothschild there is no flour, but the cream gives the smooth texture.

The following recipes are intended as examples, and different flavours may be used to produce a whole range of sweet soufflés:

METHOD 1. SOUFFLÉ A LA VANILLE (HOT)

Crème patissière

½ pint milk	1 egg yolk
⅓ vanilla pod	1 egg
2 oz. vanilla-flavoured sugar (not essential but an improvement)	1¼ oz. flour or ½ flour and ½ corn-flour

Soufflé

3 yolks	4 whites of egg

First make the crème; infuse the pod in the milk, keeping saucepan covered. Meanwhile cream the sugar thoroughly with the egg and yolk, sift in the flour, and when well mixed pour on the milk, first removing the pod. Blend well, return to the pan, and stir over the fire till boiling, keeping the mixture very smooth. Draw aside, allow to cool, and beat in the yolks one at a time. Whip whites stiffly and fold into the mixture according to directions given for soufflés (page 320).

Turn into a prepared soufflé case, bake in a moderate to hot oven for about 15–16 minutes, draw out gently, quickly dredge with icing sugar, and slide back into the oven for a further 2–3 minutes.

N.B. When making a lemon or orange soufflé by this method, use 1 large lemon or orange in place of the vanilla. Take a proportion of the sugar in loaf sugar, and rub the lumps over the lemon or orange rind to remove the zest, making sure this is thoroughly done.   Then, in place of vanilla pod, dissolve the lumps in the warm milk when making the crème.   All other ingredients remain the same.

METHOD 2.   SOUFFLÉ AU CHOCOLAT (HOT)

This is particularly light and delicate.   All chocolate soufflés are better made with block chocolate, but a good quality powder may be used. Block chocolate may be previously melted before the milk is added, but powdered chocolate should first be well simmered in the milk.   An approximate quantity of chocolate only is given here, because the strength and flavour varies according to the quality.   The mixture should be tasted and more added if necessary; for those who like a fairly strong flavour, a small proportion of unsweetened chocolate or cocoa may be mixed with the sweetened chocolate.

3½ oz. block or couverture chocolate or 2½ oz. chocolate powder	1¼ oz. arrowroot or arrowroot and flour mixed (half and half)
1–2 tablespoons water	½ oz. butter
¾ pint milk	3 egg yolks
1½–2 oz. vanilla sugar	4 egg whites
	icing sugar

Take a saucepan which will be large enough to hold the mixture when the beaten whites are added.   If block chocolate is being used proceed as follows:

Shred or grate the chocolate and put into pan with water, melt over gentle heat to a thick cream.   Heat the milk, reserving 2–3 tablespoons, add sugar, and when dissolved add to the melted chocolate and stir well. Pour this on to the arrowroot (or arrowroot and flour) slaked with the reserved milk, return to pan, and stir till boiling.   Draw aside at once, dot the surface of the mixture with the butter in small pieces.   Cover.   Prepare the soufflé case.   Break the eggs.   When the mixture is cool, beat in the yolks one at a time, whip the whites and fold into the mixture.   Turn into the prepared case, bake in a moderate to hot oven 20 minutes.   After about 16–18 minutes slide soufflé out of the oven and quickly dust with icing sugar.   Put back immediately for a further 2–3 minutes.

If powdered chocolate is used, add the milk to it, reserving as before 2–3 tablespoons for slaking.   Simmer chocolate and milk together for a few minutes till smooth and creamy; add sugar.   Pour on to the arrowroot and proceed as for block chocolate.

METHOD 3.   LEMON SOUFFLÉ (HOT)

1½ oz. butter	finely grated rind of 1 large lemon
1½ oz. flour (or ½ flour and ½ cornflour)	juice of ½ lemon
¾ pint milk	3 egg yolks
1½ oz. castor sugar	4 egg whites
	icing sugar

Melt the butter in a large saucepan, add the flour off the fire, pour on the milk and stir until boiling. Draw aside, add sugar, lemon rind and juice, and when thoroughly mixed beat in the yolks one at a time. The lemon rind may be added in the form of the zest, i.e. rubbed on to lump sugar which is then dissolved in the milk. Whip whites and fold carefully into the mixture. Turn into a prepared soufflé case and bake in a moderate to hot oven approximately 25 minutes. After about 20 minutes dust with icing sugar and return to oven for a further 2–3 minutes.

METHOD 4. BANANA SOUFFLÉ (HOT)

Other fruit may be used in place of bananas.

6 bananas	1½ oz. shredded almonds or
grated rind and juice of 1 orange	coarsely chopped toasted walnuts
a squeeze of lemon juice	4 whites of egg
4 oz. castor sugar	a pinch of salt

Peel the bananas and crush with a fork. Mix with the grated rind, orange and lemon juice, sugar, and nuts. Whip whites to a firm snow with the salt and fold into the purée. Turn at once into a prepared soufflé case and bake in a moderate oven (about 350° F.) 25–30 minutes. Remove paper and serve.

SOUFFLÉ ROTHSCHILD

2–3 peaches or nectarines	3 yolks
ripe strawberries	1 tablespoon sugar
2 slices of pineapple	2 tablespoons whipped cream
2 liqueur glasses kirsch or Cointreau	4 whites
sugar to taste	icing sugar

Slice the fruit, which must be ripe and perfect, with a silver knife. Put into a soup-plate, pour over the liqueur, and dust with sugar to taste. Leave for an hour. Separate the eggs, cream yolks with a tablespoon of sugar, add 2 tablespoons of juice from the fruit, and the cream. Whip whites to a firm snow and fold and cut into the mixture.

Lightly butter a soufflé case, and tie a band of buttered paper round it. Pour a third of the mixture into the case, lay half the fruit, lightly drained, over the top, and cover with another third of the mixture. Finish with the remaining fruit and mixture. Cook in a moderately hot oven 15 minutes. At the end of 12 minutes, dredge quickly with icing sugar and put back for a further 2–3 minutes to caramelize. Remove paper and serve at once.

SWEET OMELETS AND OMELETTES SOUFFLÉES

Sweet omelets may be made in the same way as savoury omelets, but they may also be in the form of omelettes soufflées. The two following recipes for Omelette au Rhum illustrate the two methods:

OMELETTE AU RHUM

6 eggs	3 or 4 tablespoons rum
a pinch of salt	fine sugar to finish
2 tablespoons sugar	

Lightly beat the eggs in a bowl with salt, half the sugar, and 1 tablespoon rum. Cook the omelet, fold, place on a dish, sprinkle the surface well with fine sugar, and place for a moment under a red-hot grill to caramelize the surface of the sugar a little. This may also be done with a red-hot skewer, marking in criss-cross pattern. Add remaining sugar to 2 or 3 tablespoons rum, warming it slightly to dissolve the sugar. Pour it round the omelet and light.

OMELETTE SOUFFLÉE AU RHUM

Omelettes soufflées are, with some exceptions, baked in the oven and not cooked on top of the fire, and their preparation needs the same care as is given to a soufflé. The amount of white usually exceeds that of yolk. Here is a typical recipe:

3–3½ oz. sugar	a little icing sugar
4 yolks of egg	3–4 tablespoons rum
6 whites of egg	

Put the sugar in a bowl, make a little hole in the middle, add the yolks of egg and mix with a spatula. Beat until the mixture runs from the spatula or wooden spoon in a long, shining ribbon. Beat the whites of egg until stiff as described on page 287. Add a good spoonful of rum to the yolks, then a spoonful of the beaten white should be mixed in and the remainder of the white folded in. Put in a fireproof dish greased with butter with the fingers and sprinkled on the bottom with icing sugar; pile up, with a spoon, the mixture from the basin. Shape it into an oval about 3 or 4 inches in height, and lying horizontal. Smooth with a palette-knife, and with the flat blade of the knife make a depression about an inch deep the whole length of the omelet. With the point of the knife make a few slashes round the sides. The indentation and slashing facilitate the cooking of the inside of the omelet, and the indentation also makes a place for the rum, which is added at the end. Set the omelet dish for a minute or two on the hot-plate of the stove and then put into a medium oven. After about 5 or 6 minutes turn the dish so that the omelet cooks evenly all round. The cooking will take about 15–20 minutes, according to the temperature of the oven. If the oven is too hot and colouring too rapid, a sheet of grease-proof paper may be laid lightly over the omelet. About 5 minutes before the end of cooking, remove the dish from the oven, sprinkle the whole of the surface of the omelet with icing sugar, and brown under the grill for the remaining 5 minutes. Meanwhile warm the rum in a saucepan with a spoonful of sugar, and when the omelet is ready pour it round. Light the rum and serve immediately.

Recipes for sweet omelets and for omelettes soufflées vary in the proportion of egg whites to yolks. Here is one for an omelette soufflée in which six egg whites are used to three yolks, and this is followed by one in which yolks and whites are equal.

OMELETTE SOUFFLÉE

3½ oz. sugar	6 whites
3 yolks	a pinch of salt

Flavouring
> a few drops of vanilla, lemon, or almond essence.
> 1 tablespoon Cointreau, kirsch, or other suitable liqueur

Set aside 1 tablespoon of the sugar. Put the rest in a bowl, make a hole in the middle, and add the yolks. Beat with a wooden spoon or spatula as described on previous page. Add the flavouring to the yolks. Beat the whites stiffly with the salt. Add the spoonful of sugar set aside. Take about a quarter of the bulk of the whites and mix with the yolks. Then fold in the remainder of the whites. Butter a fireproof dish, sprinkle with sugar, and put the mixture into the dish. With a palette-knife shape it into a high oval. As before, make the depression and the slashes at the side. Proceed with cooking as in the previous recipe.

In the following recipe the whites and yolks are equal. A little flour is used. It is a simple and economical jam omelet for serving 5 people.

JAM OMELET

3 eggs	a little grated lemon peel
1½ oz. sugar	a pinch of salt
½ oz. sifted flour	½ oz. butter

Separate egg yolks and whites. Put sugar and yolks in basin and beat as described on previous page. Sprinkle in the flour and continue beating. Add the flavouring and a pinch of salt. Beat the whites stiffly, fold into the yolks. Heat the butter in an omelet pan, pour in the mixture. Put the omelet pan into an oven and cook the mixture for 12–15 minutes. Slide on to a heated dish, spread with jam, fold over, sprinkle the surface with sugar, mark with a red-hot skewer in a criss-cross pattern, burning the sugar, and serve immediately.

OMELETTE SOUFFLÉE DENTS DE LION (FOR 2)

2 eggs	¼ lb. strawberries
1 dessertspoon castor sugar	crème chantilly (see page 42)
1 tablespoon milk or cream	icing sugar
a piece of vanilla pod ½ inch long	red-currant or raspberry jelly glaze (see page 856)
½ oz. butter	

Separate yolks and whites. Cream yolks with sugar. Add the milk; scrape the seeds from the vanilla pod and add, retaining the pod (see note on page 44). Whip whites and fold into the mixture. Heat the omelet pan, drop in the butter, and pour in the egg mixture. Cook for $\frac{1}{2}$ minute on a moderate heat, then slip the pan into the oven for 4–5 minutes or until set. Remove, fill with the strawberries mixed with a little glaze. Fold over and turn out on to a dish. Dust well with icing sugar and mark criss-cross with a red-hot skewer. Serve a bowl of crème chantilly separately.

The filling may be of warm jam, melted chocolate with marrons glacés débris, cherry compôte, pêche flambée, etc., in place of the strawberries. The omelet itself may be flambéd with rum immediately before sending to table.

COLD SOUFFLÉS AND CREAM SWEETS

Most cream sweets have as their base a custard; this, generally speaking, may be set with gelatine, enriched with lightly whipped cream, and flavoured and moulded in various ways before being finished and decorated.

Cold soufflés may be roughly divided into three different types. In one the base is of custard made with egg yolks, flavoured, gelatine added, and the whole lightened with whipped cream and with stiffly whipped whites. In another, known as a milanese soufflé, the whole eggs and yolks are whisked together with the sugar, and gelatine added with the flavouring and whipped cream. In yet a third the yolks, flavouring, and sugar only are whisked together before the gelatine, cream, and stiffly whipped whites are folded in.

As a general rule a custard base is used for soufflés such as chocolate, coffee, vanilla, orange, praline, etc.; while for fruit soufflés, when fresh fruit purées are employed, either of the last two methods may be followed.

The recipes given here are representative of the different types of soufflé, the idea being that the cook can make her own variations and adaptations of them.

Many students ask the difference between a sweet soufflé and a mousse. Briefly, a mousse has a more velvety and creamy texture than a soufflé. This is produced by egg yolks, a good proportion of whipped cream, and little or no egg white, whereas in a soufflé whipped egg whites are always used.

In the instructions for cold soufflés there is often a direction to add an ingredient when the mixture is 'on the point of setting' or 'just beginning to set.' This point is most easily observed at the edges and base of the bowl, where, chilled by the ice, the mixture begins to solidify first.

CHOCOLATE SOUFFLÉ (FOR 5–6)

an example of the custard method

¾ pint milk
2 oz. unsweetened chocolate or
    cocoa
3 eggs

3 oz. sugar
½ oz. gelatine
3–4 tablespoons water or coffee
2–3 tablespoons whipped cream

Put the milk and chocolate into a pan, bring slowly to the boil and simmer 1 minute, whisking well. Separate the yolks from the whites, cream them with the sugar, pour on the flavoured milk, blend, and return to the pan. Thicken over the fire without boiling, strain into a pan and cool. Dissolve the gelatine in the water or coffee, add to the custard.

When cool, stand the pan in a bowl of ice and stir till the custard begins to set; take off the ice and quickly fold in the whipped cream and lastly the stiffly whipped whites of egg. Do not whip these until just before setting the custard on the ice.

Turn at once into a soufflé case that has a band of lightly oiled paper tied round it. The mixture should come about half an inch above the dish. Leave to set. When set, remove the paper and decorate with cream.

As chocolate and cocoa vary in strength, it is advisable to taste the milk after boiling with the chocolate; it can then be adjusted if necessary before the custard is made. If preferred, sweetened chocolate with a small proportion of cocoa may be used, in which case the sugar can be cut down in the recipe.

VANILLA SOUFFLÉ (FOR 5–6)

another example of the custard method

vanilla pod or orange rind
¾ pint milk
3 eggs
1½ oz. sugar
½ oz. gelatine
2–3 tablespoons water

¼ gill cream
strawberries, with kirsch or
    elderflower syrup to flavour
caraque chocolate or whipped
    cream

Split pod and scald in the milk. Cream yolks with sugar. Pour on milk. Thicken over heat without boiling, strain and cool. Dissolve gelatine in the water, add to custard. Stir over ice, and when beginning to set fold in the cream and lastly the whipped whites. Have ready a large soufflé case with a band of paper tied round it and a small oiled jam jar or bottle in the middle. Pour in the mixture and leave until set. Remove jar and immediately fill the middle with whole or sliced sugared strawberries flavoured with kirsch or elderflower syrup. Carefully peel off the paper and decorate with caraque chocolate or whipped cream.

An alternative flavouring and filling might be pared orange rind infused in place of the vanilla pod, the juice used to dissolve the gelatine, and sliced bananas replacing the strawberries.

TANGERINE SOUFFLÉ (FOR 6–8)

This is an example of a soufflé milanese. A purée made from fresh strawberries or raspberries may take the place of the tangerine juice. This soufflé should be kept in a cool place; it may be put into the ice-box for a final chill, but should not be kept there for long.

3 eggs	½ oz. gelatine
2 yolks	juice of 1 lemon
1½ oz. castor sugar	2–3 tablespoons cream
½ oz. lump sugar	crème chantilly (see page 42)
3 tangerines (or 2 oranges)	

Break the eggs and yolks into a bowl, add the castor sugar. Rub the lumps of sugar over the rind of the tangerines until they are soaked with the oil. Crush and add to the eggs. Whisk over hot water until thick. Remove from the heat and whisk a further 5 minutes until a close foam. Dissolve the gelatine in the lemon juice, add to the mousse with the juice of the tangerines (make up to 1½ gills with water), and stir over ice until on the point of setting. Quickly fold in the lightly whipped cream, and pour at once into a soufflé dish with a band of paper tied round it. The mixture should come about half an inch above the edge of the dish. Leave to set, then peel off the paper carefully and decorate with crème chantilly.

LEMON SOUFFLÉ (MOUSSE AU CITRON) (FOR 5–6)

This is a particularly light and delicious soufflé or mousse.

3 eggs	3–4 tablespoons water
6 oz. castor sugar	1½ gills cream, partially whipped
the grated rind and strained juice of 2 small lemons	a little extra whipped cream and chopped browned nuts for decorating
1 level dessertspoon gelatine (between ¼ and ½ oz.)	

Separate yolks and whites of the eggs. Work the sugar into the yolks by degrees, then add lemon rind and juice. Whisk over gentle heat until thick and mousse-like, remove and whisk for a few minutes longer. Then dissolve gelatine in the water, add to mixture. Whip whites to a firm snow. Fold the cream into the mousse and lastly the egg whites. Turn at once into a prepared soufflé case and put aside to set.

Peel off the paper carefully, spread or pipe the top with the extra cream, and press the nuts round the sides, which come above the case.

The following is a simple and popular sweet, generally made in special chocolate mousse pots (see Petits Pots de Crème, page 901):

MOUSSE AU CHOCOLAT BASQUE (FOR 4–6)

6 oz. good block chocolate	rum or vanilla
½ gill water	3 eggs
½ oz. butter	

Break up the chocolate and cook to a thick cream with the water. Draw off the fire, cool slightly, and beat in the butter. Add the rum to taste and the yolks of the eggs one by one. Whip the whites stiffly and stir briskly into the chocolate. When thoroughly mixed pour into small pots and leave overnight. This fills 6–8 pots.

The next is a rich and delicious sweet calling for the best dessert chocolate; this will ensure that the result is not too sweet.

SUPRÊME AU CHOCOLAT (FOR 4–6)

3 oz. sweetened, 1 oz. un-sweetened chocolate (or half and half
4 tablespoons sugar

4 eggs
3½ oz. butter
crème à la vanille

Melt chocolate and mix in with a fork the sugar, the yolks of egg, one by one, and then the slightly softened butter. Beat well. Fold in the whites of egg stiffly whipped and pour into an oiled mould, or, if you prefer, pile up the mixture in the serving dish. Allow to stand for 15 hours and serve with crème à la vanille (use the recipe on page 901, but take double quantities).

ZABAIONE (HOT)

This is an Italian sweet, literally 'egg punch.' It may be served warm or ice-cold. The methods are slightly different: the method for the cold one is given after that for the hot. The hot zabaione should be served immediately.

3 egg yolks
1 oz. castor sugar
2½ tablespoons Marsala

sponge fingers or ratafia biscuits

Put the yolks into a double saucepan with the sugar and Marsala. Whisk over gentle, then moderate heat until the mixture is very thick. Pour into small goblets. Serve with the sponge fingers. Alternatively, the ratafias may be put in the bottom of each glass and macerated with a little of the Marsala before pouring in the zabaione.

ICED ZABAIONE

2 oz. sugar
1 tablespoon water
1 whole egg

2 egg yolks
1 tablespoon Marsala

Place the sugar and water in a small pan and when sugar is dissolved boil quickly to 260° F. Beat the egg white until stiff, add the sugar syrup and mix quickly with the whisk until absorbed.

Place the egg yolks and Marsala into a bowl and whisk over heat until thick and mousse-like, then combine with the meringue mixture. Pour into glasses and place in the refrigerator to become ice-cold.

PRUNE MOUSSE

This is an exception to the rule that a mousse must necessarily contain egg yolks and cream; the thick, soft consistency of the sieved prunes should give the necessary mousse-like texture without the further enrichment of egg yolks.

½ lb. good prunes, soaked over-night in tea
sugar to taste
the pared rind of ½ a lemon
a good squeeze of lemon juice
¼ pint prune juice
a scant ½ oz. gelatine

2–3 tablespoons lightly whipped cream
1 egg white whisked to a firm snow
whipped cream or crème à la vanille (see page 901)

Simmer prunes till tender in the tea in which they have been soaked, adding sugar to taste and the lemon rind. When tender drain and sieve; add lemon juice. Take the prune juice, add the gelatine, and dissolve over gentle heat. Stir into the purée and sweeten again if necessary.

When quite cool, fold in the whipped cream and lastly the egg white. Turn into a soufflé dish or wet mould to set. Turn out and serve with whipped cream or a crème à la vanille.

FLAMRI DE SEMOULE

This is an adaptation of our English flummery, and makes a pleasant cold luncheon sweet. It should be light, spongy, and slightly sharp, and is a good sweet to make when egg whites are plentiful.

3 tablespoons semolina
½ pint water
¼ pint white wine, *or*
⅛ gill lemon juice and ⅛ gill water

a squeeze of lemon juice
1½ oz. castor sugar
2 egg whites
raspberry or strawberry purée or sauce (see page 184)

Bring the liquids to the boil, draw aside and sprinkle in the semolina. Simmer, stirring frequently, 5–7 minutes or until the semolina is cooked.

Draw aside, stir in the sugar and add a little extra water if necessary. The mixture should just drop easily from the spoon. When moderately cool, whip the whites to a firm snow and fold them into the mixture. Turn at once into a lightly oiled charlotte mould. Leave an hour or two before turning out, and then pour round a fresh raspberry or strawberry purée or sauce.

BAVAROISE

This is a good basic cream which lends itself to various flavours and decorations.

3 egg yolks	2 tablespoons whipped cream
1½ oz. castor sugar	unsweetened chocolate (about
¾ pint milk	1½ oz.) or orange rind or
½ oz. powdered gelatine	vanilla pod
3 tablespoons water or fruit juice	fruit, caramel, or chocolate sauce

Bring the milk to the boil with the chocolate, orange rind, or vanilla pod. Cream the yolks and sugar to the ribbon, pour on the boiling milk, return to the pan, thicken over the fire without boiling, strain off into a pan and cool. Dissolve the gelatine in the water or fruit juice over gentle heat. When melted, add to the custard and allow to cool. Set the pan on ice, and stir continuously until thickening. Then quickly fold in the whipped cream, pour at once into a lightly oiled charlotte mould or ring, and leave to set. Turn out, pour a fruit, caramel, or chocolate sauce over or round.

CRÈME BEAU RIVAGE (FOR 6–8)

This is a popular mousse or cream that can be adapted to any fruit in season.

3 egg yolks	2–3 spoonfuls water
1½ oz. castor sugar	1 white of egg
1 level teaspoon arrowroot	2–3 tablespoons whipped cream
½ oz. lump sugar	3–4 tablespoons red-currant
2 tangerines or 1 large orange	jelly or thickened fruit
¾ pint milk	syrup
1 dessertspoon gelatine	

Beat the yolks with the castor sugar and arrowroot. Rub the lumps of sugar over the tangerine or orange rind until well soaked with the zest. Add to the milk and scald. Pour on to the yolks, return to the pan and thicken over the fire without boiling, strain and cool. Dissolve the gelatine in the water, add to the custard, and whip the white. Set the custard on ice (do this in a pan, it is both quicker and easier) and stir until thickening. Now fold in the whipped cream and lastly the egg white. Turn into a glass bowl or soufflé dish to three parts fill it. Leave to set.

Put the jelly with 2 or 3 tablespoons water into a saucepan, boil up, strain and cool. Peel the tangerines or orange and cut into thin slices. Arrange on the top of the cream when set and spoon over the jelly sauce. In season, a fresh fruit sauce should be used in place of the jelly.

BROWN BREAD CREAM

This is a variation of the Beau Rivage.

2–3 tablespoons brown bread-crumbs	1 level tablespoon gelatine
3 egg yolks	lemon juice and water
1½ oz. sugar	2 large tablespoons whipped cream
¾ pint milk	fresh raspberry purée or sauce
vanilla or grated lemon rind to flavour	

Bake the crumbs until crisp.   Make a custard with the yolks, sugar, and flavoured milk.   Dissolve gelatine in lemon juice and a spoonful of water, and add to the custard.   Stir over ice until thickening, then fold in the crumbs and whipped cream.   Pour at once into a soufflé case or a mould to set.   Serve in the dish or turn out and pour over a fresh raspberry purée or sauce.

The following is a good luncheon sweet; it should be served chilled:

NORWEGIAN CREAM

2 large tablespoons apricot jam	¾ pint hot milk
3 eggs	3 tablespoons whipped cream
1½ dessertspoons sugar	caraque chocolate
½ teaspoon vanilla	

Spread the apricot jam over the bottom of a soufflé dish.   Break 2 eggs and 1 yolk into a bowl and cream them with the sugar and vanilla.   Pour on the hot milk, blend, and strain into the soufflé dish.   Stand the dish in a tin half full of hot water, cover with a piece of paper, and set in a moderate oven until firm to the touch (or the mixture may be gently steamed). Leave until cold.   Whip the remaining egg white stiffly and fold into the whipped cream.   Cover the dish with the caraque chocolate, pile the cream on top, and decorate with a little more chocolate.

MERINGUES CHANTILLY

These are so called because they are filled with crème chantilly (whipped, sweetened, vanilla-flavoured cream).   Meringues are nicer if made fairly small, and look more attractive if they are allowed to take a little colour in the oven and become a pale café-au-lait.   Care must be taken not to over-dry them, which makes them hard and brittle instead of being crisp and very slightly sticky on the inside.

4 whites of egg	8 oz. castor sugar
a pinch of salt	castor or icing sugar for dusting

Choose 2 or 3 thick baking-sheets, brush over with melted lard and sprinkle thoroughly with flour.   Tap the sheets on the table to ensure that the surface is completely covered with a light coating.   Add salt to whites, whip to a firm snow (see note on whipping of whites, page 287).   Have the sugar ready sifted, add 1–2 large tablespoons, and continue whisking for a further half-minute.   Then remove whisk quickly and fold in the remainder with a metal spoon.   Put out the meringue with a bag and plain forcing-pipe, or with a dessertspoon, in small half-shells.   Dust them well with castor or icing sugar and leave 5–7 minutes before putting into a cool oven (200° F.).   This delay gives a crisp, frosted surface to the meringues. Allow them to dry for about 1½ hours or until they can be easily detached from the sheet.   Then gently press the flat surface to hollow them slightly and replace on the sheet upside-down.   Put back into the oven for a further half-hour or so.   Store in a tin immediately they are cool.

N.B.   The general fault in the making of meringues is in the whipping of the whites and sometimes in the method in which the sugar is added. The rules about the whipping of egg whites should be carefully followed.

MERINGUE BASKETS

These are an example of a cooked meringue.   This is used for forming into shapes such as baskets and containers for fruit, as it is firmer than meringue suisse (the ordinary meringue) and pipes more easily and cleanly.

4 egg whites	rice-paper
8½ oz. icing sugar	strawberries or raspberries
vanilla	red-currant jelly

Whisk whites with sugar over heat until very thick.   Flavour with vanilla.   Pipe out with a rose vegetable pipe in swirls on rice-paper to form small baskets.   Set in a cool oven 1–1½ hours.   Take out, cool, and fill the centres with the raw fruit bound with a little red-currant jelly.

MARRONS MONT BLANC

This is a famous sweet, much appreciated by those who like chestnuts.

1 lb. chestnuts (weighed when peeled)	1½ oz. butter
½ vanilla pod or a small teaspoon vanilla essence	sponge cake
	rum
milk or milk and water	1 white of egg, whipped cream,
2½ oz. sugar	and a little vanilla essence
¾ gill water	and sugar
	grated chocolate

Blanch chestnuts and remove both skins (see page 48 for preparation of chestnuts).   Put them into a saucepan with vanilla or vanilla essence. Cover with milk or milk and water, simmer till tender, and drain well. Push the chestnuts through a wire or nylon sieve and put into a bowl.

Boil the sugar with the water to a thick syrup (just before it reaches the thread stage). Beat this with the butter by degrees into the chestnut purée. Enough syrup must be added to produce a pliable and soft paste. Have ready the sponge cake, broken into pieces and laid into the bottom of a flat glass dish. Sprinkle very well with rum. Take a cornet or bag with a small plain pipe and fill this with the purée. Pipe the purée neatly round the edge of the cake, continuing round and round in layers until a low wall is formed. Add the whipped white of egg to the whipped cream sweetened and flavoured with vanilla, and spoon it into the centre. Dust over with grated chocolate.

N.B. Sometimes the appearance of this dish is spoiled because a certain amount of liquid appears as the purée is piped. This is possibly because the nuts have been overcooked in the milk or have been insufficiently drained. There is an alternative method of cooking the nuts which obviates this. For this the outer skin of the nut is split, and the nut baked in the oven till soft and then peeled and sieved. The syrup is then added as before.

RICH AND PARTY SWEETS

GÂTEAU DIANE

Cake

4 egg whites	9 oz. castor sugar, scant weight

Filling

2 egg whites	3½ oz. chocolate
4 oz. icing sugar, good weight	chopped browned almonds
8 oz. unsalted butter	icing sugar for finishing

Whip the 4 whites stiffly, beat in a large tablespoon of the castor sugar, then fold in the remainder. Spread this mixture into four rounds, about ¼ inch thick, on a buttered and floured baking-sheet, and cook in a slow oven. Turn the rounds over and dry off in a cool oven.

Meanwhile prepare the filling. Whip the 2 whites with the icing sugar over gentle heat until thick. Cream the butter well, and if block chocolate is used melt on a plate over gentle heat. If chocolate powder is used, add a little coffee or water and cook to a thick cream. In either case cool before using.

Beat the meringue into the butter by degrees, then add the chocolate. Sandwich the rounds one above the other with the chocolate cream. Spread the sides and top with the cream as well, and cover with chopped browned almonds. Take three narrow strips of paper, lay them over the top of the cake at intervals, then dust well with icing sugar. Remove the paper. Serve the cake the following day.

BABA AUX FRAISES

This is a decorative centre-piece for a luncheon or supper table. Strawberries may also be heaped at each end of the dish to give more colour.

Baba paste

4½ oz. flour	½ gill warm milk
a pinch of salt	2 eggs
½ oz. yeast	1¾ oz. butter
½ oz. sugar	

Syrup

6 oz. loaf sugar	½ split vanilla pod
1½ gills water	

4–6 oz. small whole strawberries, which, some hours before, have been sugared, well sprinkled with kirsch or vanilla-flavoured syrup, and thoroughly chilled.

Syrup. Dissolve the sugar slowly in the water, add vanilla, and boil rapidly without stirring for approximately 5 minutes. This should bring it to just before the stage known as the short thread, i.e. when the syrup will form a short thread between the finger and thumb. Remove pod and use syrup while hot. If it seems too thick, dilute with a very little water. It must be thin enough to penetrate the baba, but not so thin that none remains on the outside.

To make the baba. Sift the flour and salt into a warm bowl. Cream the yeast and sugar together and pour in the milk. Blend well and add to the flour with the beaten eggs. Beat vigorously with the hand for 5 minutes. Cover the bowl and leave in a warm place until it has doubled its bulk (about 45 minutes). Cream the butter until soft, and beat it into the dough for 5 minutes. Well butter a large charlotte mould or cake tin, pour in the mixture, and leave to prove 10–15 minutes in a warm temperature. Then bake in a hot oven until a deep golden brown, about 30 minutes.

Turn out carefully on to a pastry rack, with a tray or plate underneath. While still hot baste thoroughly with the prepared syrup. The baba must be well soaked and should glisten with the syrup. Make an incision in the top with a large round cutter and scoop out the centre carefully with a metal spoon. Fill with the strawberries. Serve a bowl of crème chantilly (see page 42) or a cold sabayon sauce (see page 187) separately.

SAVARIN MONTMORENCY

Use for this the yeast mixture given for the baba, but turn it when completed into a well-buttered savarin mould. This is a ring mould with a rounded base. Prove, bake, and finish with the syrup as for the baba. Fill the centre with a compôte of cherries.

MARQUISE ALICE

This is a classic and *recherché* cream sweet. It looks pretty with chocolate cornets round.

¾ pint milk	2 large tablespoons praline
3 yolks of egg	3 tablespoons lightly whipped
2 oz. castor sugar	cream
1–2 oz. block chocolate	¼ pint lightly whipped cream
½ oz. gelatine	red-currant jelly
½ gill water	whipped cream for cornets
1 white of egg	

Scald the milk. Beat the yolks and sugar together, pour on the milk, return to the pan, and thicken over the fire without boiling. Strain and cool.

Meanwhile make some small cornets out of grease-proof paper. Melt the chocolate over gentle heat, and with the handle of a teaspoon spread it fairly thickly over the inside of the cornets. Leave to set. Melt the gelatine with the water, and add to the custard; when cool stir over ice until it begins to thicken. Whip the egg white. Add the praline to the custard with the 3 tablespoons of cream and lastly fold in the white. Turn at once into an oiled deep sandwich tin, or a French mould known as a *moule à manqué*, and leave to set.

Turn out on to the serving dish, and mask all over with ¼ pint lightly whipped cream. Beat a little red-currant jelly until smooth, then put this into a paper cornet, cut off the tip, and pipe across the top in straight lines about ½ inch apart. Then with the point of a knife draw lightly the same number of lines at the same distance apart across the lines already piped. In between those lines draw the knife point the opposite way. This makes the classic pattern on a Marquise Alice. Peel the paper off the cornets and fill them with whipped cream. Place a small Alpine strawberry in each, or a point of red-currant jelly, and surround the marquise with them.

BANANES A LA CREOLE

This is a light mousse in a pineapple-lined mould: a fresh-tasting cold sweet.

1–2 pineapples, according to size	4 ripe bananas
syrup flavoured with kirsch for poaching	

Mousse

2 eggs, 2 yolks	½ gill lightly whipped cream
1½ oz. castor sugar	orange rind or kirsch to flavour
a scant ½ oz. gelatine	angelica for garnish
a little orange juice	

Peel pines, and poach whole in the syrup. Drain and slice thinly. Poach bananas, slice in half. Set on one side whilst preparing the mousse.

If preferred pour the boiling syrup over the bananas instead of poaching them, and allow to cool. This gives them a better appearance and colour. Line a plain mould, either a dome or a shallow cake tin, with the pineapple slices.

To make the mousse whisk the eggs, yolks, and sugar over heat until thick. Remove from the heat and whisk till cool. Dissolve the gelatine in a little orange juice, add to the mousse with the flavouring and the cream. Stir over ice until setting, then turn at once into the mould. Leave till set, then turn out. Surround with the bananas and garnish with leaves of angelica.

VACHERIN MELBA

This is a meringue basket filled with ice and fresh fruit. Other fruit than peaches may be used.

peaches

vanilla-flavoured syrup for poaching

Meringue
    4 egg whites
    vanilla

8¼ oz. castor or icing sugar
rice-paper

Ice-cream
    2½ oz. sugar
    3 egg yolks
    vanilla pod

¾ pint cream
½ gill water

Melba sauce
    1 gill fresh raspberry purée

stock syrup or icing sugar

Whisk whites and sugar together until thick over gentle heat. Flavour with vanilla. Put in bag with large rose pipe. Pipe out on to rice-paper in the shape of a basket. Dust with sugar and dry in a cool oven. Meanwhile prepare ice-cream by boiling water and sugar to the thread. Pour on to beaten yolks and whisk until thick. Whisk cream lightly, flavour with vanilla pod. This is done by scraping a few of the seeds from the inside of the pod, allowing them to lie in the cream. Then pour into freezer. Churn till thick, remove dasher, and leave to mellow.

Peel peaches, poach lightly in the syrup. Cool, drain. For sauce, sweeten the raspberry purée with syrup or icing sugar. Fill the meringue case with the ice-cream, set the peaches on top, and pour over the sauce.

CROQUENBOUCHE

4 whites of egg
8 oz. castor sugar
about 6 oz. loaf or granulated
    sugar

crème chantilly (see page 42)
raspberries or strawberries

First make the meringues. Whip the whites and incorporate the castor sugar as on page 852. Take a bag with an éclair pipe and fill with the mixture. Have ready some greased and floured baking-sheets. Pipe out in small round meringues the size of a small walnut. Dust over with castor sugar and leave 5 minutes before putting into the oven to dry.

Now cut a round of grease-proof paper for the base of your croquen-bouche and brush with oil. (Alternatively a round of baked pâte sucrée may be used.) Approximately 8 inches diameter will be suitable, and allow a margin of 1 inch.

Put a third of the loaf sugar on to boil with $\frac{1}{2}$ gill water. Boil to the crack. Check boiling by dipping pan for a moment in cold water. Prop pan on the table so that it will remain tilted, then dip about half the edge of each meringue into the syrup and arrange in a ring round the edge of the paper or pastry, sticking the edges firmly together with the syrup. The circle completed, start another one on the top of the first and continue until you have five, six, or even more circles one on top of the other, each a little smaller than the last, so that a cone is formed. Fresh sugar may be boiled as required. The top of the cone may be open or completely closed. If the cone is to be filled with layers of fruit and cream, put these in before the opening becomes too small. If the croquen-bouche is filled it must be served as soon as possible after completion, and it may be garnished with spun sugar. Otherwise the fruit and cream may be served separately and the croquenbouche used for a centre-piece for a buffet.

Small choux filled with cream may be used in place of meringues.

CANTALOUPE EN SURPRISE

1 cantaloup melon	strawberries or red currants
castor sugar	sherry
a little egg white	

Cut the top off the melon and remove the seeds. Using a large vegetable scoop or spoon, carefully remove all the flesh of the melon; add two-thirds of the strawberries, sliced, and sprinkle with sugar and sherry. Chill the mixture, and the melon skin. Frost the remaining strawberries, i.e. brush with slightly beaten egg white, roll in castor sugar, and leave on a wire rack to dry. Put back the macerated fruit into the chilled melon skin and serve decorated with the frosted strawberries on the top. Set the melon on strawberry leaves on a dessert dish.

The following is a popular sweet: a rich nut biscuit with cream and peaches. It is a favourite for a luncheon party.

GALETTE AUX NOISETTES

3 oz. hazel-nuts	$4\frac{1}{2}$ oz. flour
a pinch of salt	$3\frac{1}{4}$ oz. butter
$2\frac{1}{4}$ oz. castor sugar	$\frac{1}{4}-\frac{1}{2}$ pint cream
fresh or canned peaches (rasp-berries or strawberries may also be used)	icing sugar for decoration

Toast the nuts in the oven and when nicely browned rub in a dry cloth to remove the skins, and then grind finely. Sieve the flour with a pinch of salt, make a well in the middle and in this put the butter and sugar. Sprinkle the nuts on the flour and work up as for pâte sucrée (see page 838). Chill in the refrigerator for at least 30 minutes. Divide the pastry into three, roll each piece into a round and bake in a moderate oven. When cool, sandwich with whipped cream and peaches and dredge the top with icing sugar.

POMMES CASTILLANE

6–8 even-sized dessert apples	4 oz. mixed glacé fruits
	rum

Syrup

1 pint water	vanilla pod to flavour
2 large tablespoons sugar	

Almond pastry

8 oz. flour	1 egg
3 oz. castor sugar	3 oz. ground almonds
6 oz. butter	

Sabayon sauce

2 egg yolks	1 tablespoon lightly whipped
1 tablespoon rum	cream

Core and peel the apples, and poach them in syrup. When quite tender drain well and fill with mixed glacé fruits, macerated in a little of the syrup flavoured with rum. When the apples are quite cold, arrange in a large flan case of almond pastry and coat with sabayon sauce.

To make the pastry. Sift the flour, make a well in the middle and in this put the sugar, butter, and egg; sprinkle the ground almonds on it. Mix the egg, butter, and sugar, then gradually draw in the flour. Leave in a cool place at least half an hour. Line the flan and bake in a moderate oven.

To make the sauce. Boil the remaining sugar syrup to the thread, pour on to the egg yolks, and whisk until thick and mousse-like. Add rum and continue whisking until quite cold. Finish with lightly whipped cream. Alternatively an iced zabaione (see page 955) may be used.

GÂTEAU DE PÊCHES MOUSSELINE

4–6 ripe peaches, according to size	syrup for poaching, flavoured with vanilla or liqueur

Génoise

3 eggs	2¾ oz. flour
3¾ oz. sugar	1 oz. butter

Mousseline

3 egg yolks	2 large tablespoons lightly whipped cream
1 tablespoon castor sugar	
2 tablespoons Marsala	

To prepare the génoise, break the eggs, add the sugar gradually, and whisk over gentle heat until thick. Remove from the heat and continue whisking until the bowl is cold. Fold in the flour and the melted butter, and bake in a prepared tin, square or *moule à manqué*, about 25 minutes. Meanwhile poach the peaches in the syrup and leave to cool.

Moisten the sponge with some of the syrup and arrange the halved peaches on the top, and when quite cold coat over with the mousseline.

Mousseline. Place the egg yolks, sugar, and Marsala in a bowl and whisk over hot water until thick. Continue whisking until quite cold, then add the cream.

CROISSANTS AUX PÊCHES ZABAIONE

This is a luncheon sweet of croissants fried and toffee-like.

3–4 large peaches	6 croissants
vanilla-flavoured sugar syrup for poaching	a good oz. butter

Iced zabaione

2 oz. sugar	3 egg yolks
1 tablespoon water	1 tablespoon Marsala or brown sherry
1 egg white	

Scald the peaches, skin, and poach in a heavy vanilla syrup until tender. Cool and then chill thoroughly. Thin a little of the peach syrup and dip in it the croissants, carefully split. Melt the butter in a frying-pan, add a little syrup, and cook together for a few minutes. Fry the croissants in this until golden brown. Remove and arrange round a serving dish.

Zabaione. Put the sugar and water in a small pan, and when the sugar has dissolved boil quickly to 250°–260° F., or until a little of the syrup will form a hard ball when dropped into cold water. Beat the egg white until stiff, add the sugar syrup, and mix quickly with a whisk until thick. Place the egg yolks and Marsala into a bowl and whisk over heat until thick and mousse-like; combine with the meringue and chill thoroughly. Arrange the peaches in the middle of the dish and pour over the zabaione.

N.B. It is necessary to add egg white to a cold zabaione, although the classic variety, served hot, is made with yolk alone. The whipped white holds the mixture together.

CRÈME BRÛLÉE

This is a speciality of Trinity College, Cambridge.

4 egg yolks	a vanilla pod, split, or a few drops of essence
a level tablespoon castor sugar	
1 pint cream	castor sugar

Mix the yolks well with the sugar. Put the cream and vanilla pod together into a double saucepan. Cover and bring up to scalding-point, then remove pod and pour on to the yolks, blending well. Add the essence at this stage if the pod is not available. Return to the pan and thicken very carefully over the heat, stirring constantly. On no account allow it to reach boiling-point, scalding-point should be enough. Strain into a pie dish or eared gratin dish and allow to stand for several hours or preferably overnight. Heat grill, and dust the surface of the cream with castor sugar so that it presents a uniformly white appearance, but avoid getting too thick a layer. At once push the dish gently under the grill. Allow the sugar to melt and take colour. Then remove from the heat and stand in a cold place for 2–3 hours before serving. It is usual to serve this with a dish of fruit, as it is a little rich on its own, though delicious.

TRIFLE AND TIPSY CAKE

A tipsy cake used to be made with a whole savoy cake soaked with sweet wine or sherry mixed with brandy. This was garnished with almonds and surrounded with custard. A variant of this contained jam. An old-fashioned trifle was made on somewhat the same lines and covered with a whip of egg white, sugar, and cream beaten with a little sherry made in the same way as a sillabub, i.e. as whipping proceeded the froth was skimmed and drained on a sieve. The trifle of to-day may be a combination of the two dishes.

TRIFLE

stale plain sponge cake	rich custard
sherry and, at option, brandy. A rich proportion would be 3 tablespoons brandy to each gill of sherry	whipped, sweetened, and van-illa-flavoured cream
strawberry or raspberry jam	almonds blanched and split angelica ratafia biscuits

Cut or break the sponge cakes into suitable pieces, soak each in the sherry and brandy (or sherry only). Spread each piece with jam, pile up in a dish. Leave to soak for an hour or two. Make a rich custard and while hot pour over the soaked cake. Leave until well chilled. Cover and pile up with the cream. Stick the split almonds thickly over the surface and decorate also with strips of angelica and ratafia biscuits.

In these decadent days sherry alone is generally used.

CHARLOTTE RUSSE

Sponge Fingers, page 864. A small quantity of Lemon Jelly (or any flavoured jelly), page 958. Rich custard made with: ½ pint milk; a vanilla pod; 3 egg yolks; 1 oz. castor sugar; scant ½ oz. gelatine; ¼–¾ gill water; 1½ gills cream.

Run a little of the cool jelly into a charlotte mould to cover the bottom by about ½–¾ in. When just about to set arrange the sponge fingers round the sides of the mould with their ends in the jelly. Prepare custard. Infuse the split vanilla pod in the milk. Cream yolks with sugar, pour on the milk, blend and return to the pan. Stir over gentle heat until thick, but do not boil. Strain and cool. Soak the gelatine, then dissolve over heat and add to the custard. Partially whip the cream and fold into the custard when on the point of setting. Turn at once into the prepared mould. Leave to set. To turn out, dip the mould into hot water.

JELLY-MAKING

Commercially prepared jelly squares, crystals, and the more expensive bottled jellies have rather put home-made jelly out of fashion. It is not to be wondered at when women have so many more preoccupations than once they had, but it is a pity to forget all about the subject. For those amateurs of cooking who like to know how things are best done, here are both notes and recipes. It may also be said that the flavour of a home-made jelly is particularly good.

The rules are simple and, beyond a jelly-bag for jellies that are to be cleared, no special equipment is needed. The jelly-bag used for the clearing of sweet jellies is made of flannel.

Clear jellies, such as lemon and certain other fruits, wine, and aspic, should be sparklingly clear. Others, such as milk, and orange and some other fruits, are, in the interests of flavour, left uncleared. A good jelly, when turned out of its mould, should really 'shiver like a jelly,' only just holding its shape.

GELATINE

Good gelatine is not cheap, but it is important that the best quality available be used. It is false economy to use an inexpensive one. The incorporation of gelatine with various liquids is much easier now that powdered or very fine leaf gelatine is sold. The old-fashioned heavy thick leaves were much less easy to use, and the variation in weight between leaf and leaf could be misleading. So we now use either:

(a) powdered gelatine

or

(b) fine French leaf gelatine.

Whichever is used, it is necessary to soak the gelatine first, the powdered variety in the liquid called for in the recipe. When the powdered gelatine is quite soft, the liquid is gently heated and the gelatine melts with ease. Leaf gelatine is soaked in a bowl of cold water, and when thoroughly soft is drained and either added to the main quantity of liquid called for in the recipe, or dissolved in a smaller quantity which has been set aside for the purpose.

Leaf gelatine is sold in both half and whole sheets. As a general guide it may be reckoned that five to seven whole sheets weigh approximately an ounce.

Gelatine may vary in strength to a small degree; the following proportions may be taken as a guide: A quart of liquid will require $1\frac{3}{4}$–2 oz. good quality gelatine for setting. For a quart of slightly thickened liquid, such as custard and thin fruit purée, $1\frac{1}{2}$ oz. gelatine is called for.

Before powdered gelatine came on to the market isinglass, a very pure form of gelatine, was much used. Agar-agar, made from seaweed, is another powerful setting agent and is sometimes used in invalid cookery.

RULES FOR JELLY-MAKING

1. Scald pan, cloth or bag, and whisk before use. Choose a large pan (preferably of thick enamel, and not aluminium) to allow plenty of room for the liquid to rise.

2. Measure and weigh all ingredients carefully; use loaf sugar for cleared sweet jellies, as this will give a more brilliant finish.

3. For the process of whisking and clearing see Lemon Jelly 1.

4. Care of cloth and bag is essential. A thick, coarse linen cloth should be chosen, and a flannel bag. Wash always in clear water and boil or scald before use.

The method of making is set out in the following recipe for lemon jelly:

LEMON JELLY (1)
to make 1 quart

1½ pints water	1½ gills lemon juice
1¾ oz. gelatine	2-inch stick of cinnamon
7 oz. loaf sugar	whites and shells of 2 eggs
thinly pared rind of 3 lemons	¼ gill sherry

Add about ¼ pint of the water to the gelatine, and set aside to soak. Meanwhile scald both pan and whisk. Pour into the pan the rest of the water, add the sugar, and set on low heat to dissolve with the lemon rind, juice, and cinnamon. Now add the gelatine and stir until all is melted. Then add the whites whipped to a froth, the lightly crushed egg-shells, washed, and the sherry. Whisk and allow to boil up. Draw aside, leave for a minute or two, then repeat twice more. Leave to settle, then pour through the scalded jelly-bag. Immediately a small quantity of jelly is through, take it up and pour it back again on the top of that in the bag. When the first of the liquid shows itself to be sparkling clear leave until all is through. To facilitate the process towards the end, when the jelly may be cool and on the point of setting, set a jug half full of boiling water upright in the bag, and lay a thick cloth over the top.

The jelly is then ready for use. This one is particularly lemony and most refreshing. It may be layered in a mould with fresh fruit, set before turning out, and served with whipped cream. (See also Austrian Jelly Tart, page 959.)

The following alternative recipe for lemon jelly calls for more lemons and is slightly more sharp in flavour. It also has more sherry.

LEMON JELLY (2)

2 oz. gelatine	10 oz. lump sugar
1¾ pints water	2 egg whites and shells
4 lemons	1 gill sherry

Put the gelatine and the water into a scalded pan and leave to soak. Take off the zest of 2 lemons on lump sugar and peel the other 2 lemons very thinly. Put the lemon peel, sugar, and the squeezed and strained juice of all the lemons in with the gelatine and stir over gentle heat until gelatine and sugar are dissolved. Whip the whites to a froth. Add the crushed egg-shells and sherry, and whisk the whites into the jelly mixture. Whisk until the liquid boils, boil up well and allow to settle. Repeat this process twice more, then pour through the scalded jelly-bag and clarify as indicated in the recipe for Lemon Jelly 1.

ORANGE JELLY

The following is an example of an uncleared jelly.

1 pint fresh orange juice	½ pint water
the pared rind of 1 orange	3 oz. sugar
the pared rind of ½ lemon, and	1¼ oz. gelatine
the juice	cream

Strain orange juice and set aside. Put orange rind, and lemon rind and juice, into a pan with half the water and the sugar. Set on low heat to infuse. Add rest of water to the gelatine and allow to soak 5–10 minutes. Add to the pan, stir, and when melted strain and cool. Now add to the orange juice, taste, and add more sugar if necessary. Turn into a glass bowl to set. Serve with cream.

AUSTRIAN JELLY TART

This is a decorative sweet and may have different varieties of fruit in season. The flan case may be made of pâte sucrée or rich short crust (see pages 838 and 835).

Flan case—pâte sucrée

4 oz. flour	1 egg yolk
2 oz. butter	1 dessertspoon water
2 oz. castor sugar	

Make up, line into a 6–7-inch flan case, bake blind.

Crème patissière. See page 851
Lemon Jelly. ½–¾ pint
Fruit. Cherries, bananas, black and white grapes

Make the crème patissière. Take a sandwich tin equal in size to the flan. Run cool jelly over this, and when it is just set put in the fruit. This may be arranged in a cart-wheel, making a contrast with the varieties chosen. Cover with jelly at setting point. Allow to set completely, then fill to the top with jelly.

Fill the pastry case with crème patissière. Dip the mould containing jelly and fruit into hot water and turn out on top of the crème. This is a dish requiring dexterity.

ICES

The first ice-cream I can remember was the delicious and utterly forbidden confection known as hokey-pokey. A kind, thoroughly badgered grown-up justified the ban on the grounds that it had probably been stored under the bed of the foreign itinerant vendor, a gay-looking fellow whom we found charming. Fortunate we thought him too, in that in the long night hours he could indulge in his own wares without effort. Hokey-pokey was nothing in the world but a sweetened custard containing gelatine, frozen, and packed in little boxes or handed out wrapped in wax-paper. As far as I can remember it was a halfpenny a piece. Ice-creams in those days were not nursery, not even schoolroom food, and it was a long time later that they were recommended by doctors for sick children who disliked milk in any form, and particularly for those with throat infections. When later it was given to me, suffering from a bad attack of tonsillitis, I felt it must be a prelude to death, a sort of penitential offering from remorseful grown-ups. But now what have you? Ice-cream cornets, stop-me-and-buy-ones, ice-cream bricks brought in from shops and packed for safe transport—and no minatory finger shaken or needed. All of these are practical, sensible, and wholesome, and clearly much appreciated by millions of people.

Nevertheless, if this range has been so far the limit of your ice-cream life, you have not lived, for you have yet to know the perfection of home-made ice-cream, water-ices, parfaits, ice-puddings, bombes, and soufflés. Properly made, churned to perfect texture, flavoured in many imaginative ways, these are, or may be, in a class by themselves.

You may buy bread and probably do all the time, but once you have eaten home-made bread you will become critical of the general run of bought loaves, and it is the same with ice-cream. Certainly if you become proficient you get, in both these culinary efforts, a good deal of praise and appreciation, often beyond the merit of the skill and work involved.

Ice-creams are not difficult to make, and have the great advantage that they are best made some hours before they are to be served: this is to give them time to mature. They provide a useful range of sweets for occasions ranging from nursery lunches to dance suppers. A simple custard ice pleases children and a really good ice or parfait lends a cachet to a party menu. A simple, homely ice may be and often is made in the drawer of the refrigerator, and a note on this will be given later; but one does not produce by this means the perfect texture of an ice made in a churn type of freezer in which the mixture is constantly beaten or churned during the freezing, and for this reason a good type of churn freezer should be part of the kitchen equipment of those who are interested in good food and cooking.

A churn type of freezer. A good machine of this type costs nowadays anything between £6 and £7, so if you think this exceeds your budget I would suggest you put it on your list of wedding presents. It consists of a wooden bucket with an inner metal container. The container is fitted with a dasher or churner and lid, and the whole held in place with a metal clamp with a ratchet and handle. The inner container holds the mixture to be frozen, the dasher keeps it moving whilst this process is going on, and between the inner container and the bucket the freezing mixture is placed.

Care of the ice machine. While the wooden pail is in constant use it may be emptied, rinsed, and turned upside-down for storing; it should never be dried near heat. Should it be left a long time out of action it may be filled from time to time with water to prevent the wood from shrinking. The metal container and dasher should be carefully washed and scalded before they are put away, and rescalded before use: in fact they should be treated as dairy equipment. The container should be put away uncovered; the wooden pieces of the dasher should be scrubbed and dried.

What a freezing mixture is. A freezing mixture is a combination of ice and salt. The former should be broken or chipped with an ice-pick into pieces of convenient size, but should not be crushed or pounded to slush. If no pick is available a sharp skewer or packing-needle is used; gently tapped with a hammer, either of these implements will cause the ice to split off easily into small pieces. The salt must be the freezing or rock-salt obtainable from any fishmonger. The proportion is three parts of ice to one of salt. The ice should not be broken up until it is to be used. A block of ice which has to be kept for a few hours should be well covered with a folded cloth (an old blanket is suitable) to keep it from the air.

How to use the freezer. Assemble all the parts together. Then set the metal container in place inside the pail. Put the lid on, preferably with a piece of grease-proof paper inside so that it is impossible for any salt to find its way in. Holding the container in place begin to pack with ice and salt in layers round the side, beginning and ending with a layer of ice. A convenient way of packing and measuring at the same time is to use a saucer. As the layers of ice and salt are packed round the sides the handle may be given an occasional turn to help to settle the ice in place, and the handle of a wooden spoon or an ice-pick may be used to push the mixture well down. The ice and salt must come well above the level of the mixture to be frozen. The whole may now be left about 10 minutes so that the container becomes thoroughly chilled. Now lift the lid carefully, watching that no salt or ice falls into the container, and pour in the mixture to be frozen which should be really cold. The container should never be more than three-quarters full. Replace the lid, fix on the clamp and start to turn; continue regularly until the mixture is properly frozen.

The resistance to the churning grows steadily, so that it is easy to know when the ice is ready. The freezing may take anything from 15–20 minutes, provided that everything has been thoroughly chilled before the operation is started.

The handle is now taken off and the lid wiped over and removed; the dasher is drawn out carefully, and scraped free of the mixture. The lid is now rinsed in cold water and replaced, the hole filled up with a cork or paper, and the water drained off from the pail. This is done by tilting so that the liquid runs through a hole which will be found high up in the side. The pail is now filled up again with ice and salt, covered with a thick cloth or blanket, and left for at least half an hour, often for longer. Care must be taken, if an ice is made particularly early in the day, that the freezing mixture is replenished whenever this becomes necessary.

MIXTURES. ICE-CREAMS

Cream ices may be made with an egg mousse base to which cream is added, or with custard in which a certain proportion of egg white is added to the yolks. Partially whipped cream is folded in when cold. Fruit purées may be added in varying proportions to these bases. The quantity will depend on the type of fruit chosen. Freezing has the effect of reducing sweetness and flavour, so mixtures made for this purpose are highly flavoured and sweetened. At the same time it is important to have the correct proportion of sugar in these mixtures; if under-sweetened the resulting ice is unpleasant, but if over-sweetened the mixture will not stiffen properly. Again, if there is not enough sugar the ice will be hard, rocky, and unpalatable. From 3–4 oz. sugar per pint of cream or custard is the maximum proportion for a plain vanilla ice. For a chocolate or coffee ice the sugar in the flavouring must of course be taken into account.

Fruit ices may be made with a moderately sweetened purée added to the mousse or custard. This again will affect the amount of sugar put into the custard itself. (See basic recipes, page 966.)

Cream. Single cream is specially suitable for all egg mousse bases. Whipped cream gives a richer and smoother consistency to a cream ice. Evaporated milk, scalded, chilled, and whipped, is a good substitute for cream provided it is used for a strongly flavoured fruit ice.

Water-ices. Water-ices are made from strong, well-flavoured fruit syrup. It is important to have the correct proportion of sugar for a smooth and soft-textured ice. If water-ices are often made it is worth while investing in a *pèse-sirop* (see page 857), which measures the density of the sugar in the syrup and secures perfection. On page 859 will be found a table of proportions giving the degree of density which may be achieved without boiling.

When a lighter, foamy ice is required a small proportion of whipped egg white is added to the half-frozen ice, after which churning continues.

A water-ice is finished and left to mellow like ice-cream.

GENERAL RULES

Here is a summing-up of the general rules for ice-making.

1. The mixture must be well flavoured, sweetened, and coloured. Freezing has the effect of diminishing these qualities and this must be taken into account.

2. The container for the ice mixture must be firmly placed in position before the freezing mixture is packed round it.

3. The salt that is used for freezing must be the proper rock-salt which is obtainable from any good fishmonger.

4. It is important to avoid getting any trace of salt in the mixture, for if this happens nothing can be done to remove it.

5. Ice is broken or chipped with an ice-pick into pieces of convenient size to go into the machine, and must never be crushed or pounded. If no ice-pick is available it may be broken by using a skewer and tapping this lightly with a hammer. A strong packing-needle is also suitable.

6. Proportions are three parts of ice to one of salt, and a convenient way of measuring is to use a saucer, which makes it easy to fill the machine and to measure at the same time.

7. The mixture should be chilled before it is put into the container, and it is churned immediately, and without stopping.

8. The container for the ice mixture must never be filled more than three parts full. When properly churned the mixture swells slightly, and if more than the quantity indicated is put in it will overflow.

9. After the dasher has been freed and removed and the lid replaced, the bucket is again packed down with the freezing mixture and the ice left to mellow or ripen; this improves both flavour and texture and the time may be from half an hour to several hours.

10. During both the freezing and the ripening process any water in the pail must be drained off, and as the freezing mixture becomes lower in the pail it must be replenished.

The following is a summing-up of the procedure for making ices:

1. Assemble the machine.

2. Fix the container in position.

3. Cover it with a piece of paper and the lid, to prevent any salt getting into it.

4. Surround with well-packed layers of ice and salt.

5. Pour in the mixture, filling not more than three-quarters full.

6. Churn steadily until stiff, replenishing ice in bucket if level falls too low. The level of the ice should be above that of the mixture in the container.

7. When set remove dasher, rinse lid and replace it. Lay a piece of grease-proof paper under the lid and fill up the hole with a piece of paper or a cork.

8. By tilting drain off any water in the pail through the hole which is found three-quarters of the way up the side. Fill up the bucket with ice and salt.

9. Cover the bucket with a thick blanket and set aside in a cool place to ripen.

THE SERVING OF ICES

1. When dishing an ice put the serving dish into the ice-box or on ice for some time before it is required.

2. The scoop or spoon with which the ice is dished should be dipped into cold water before each helping of the ice.

BOMBES AND ICE-PUDDINGS

These may be made with more than one kind of ice: two flavours of cream ice or an ice-cream and a water-ice. This is only possible if two freezers are available. Sometimes when there is only one freezer a cream ice is made, used to line a mould, and the centre then filled with a well-chilled mousse or with iced and sweetened fruit, such as raspberries, strawberries, or sliced fresh peaches. The most usual shape is a bombe mould; this has a tightly fitting lid and a screw at the base which when loosened allows air to enter the mould after freezing, and so facilitates unmoulding.

METHOD OF USING THE MOULD

1. Chill the mould thoroughly.

2. Have ready a pail of broken ice, freezing salt, lard, grease-proof paper, and the frozen mixture.

3. Fill the mould to the brim with the ice or ices to be used. Sometimes the inside of a bombe mould is just 'clothed' with an ice to the depth of one or two inches, and the ice is then smoothed out with the back of a spoon. The space left is then immediately filled up with a contrasting flavour. For example, the lining may be of coffee ice and the filling of banana ice, or of whipped sweetened cream or a mousse.

4. Cover the top with a piece of grease-proof paper. Fix on the lid.

5. Smear the joints with lard and make sure that the screw at the base of the mould is firmly screwed home.

6. Roll the bombe at once in a sheet of grease-proof paper and put it into the pail with a good layer of ice and salt at the bottom. Then fill up the sides and top of the pail with the broken ice and layers of salt.

7. Cover with a thick piece of cloth or blanket and leave at least two hours.

8. When turning out the bombe have ready a large bowl of cold water, a chilled serving dish, and a clean cloth. Remove the paper and plunge the mould into the bowl of cold water, lift out, dry, and loosen the lid. (If the ice is frozen very firmly a second dipping may be needed to loosen it.) Remove the lid and the paper. Turn upside-down on to the chilled serving dish. Unscrew the screw at the base, allowing air to flow into the vacuum. Lift off the mould and finish according to the recipe.

... For .Glace en Surprise, Omelette Glacée en Surprise, and Bombe Favorite, see recipes on pages 970–1.

A parfait is an ice-pudding made with an egg mousse and whipped cream which is turned into a bombe and frozen in the mould. The bombe, as before, is buried in ice and salt for some hours and then turned out. The consistency of this dessert should be that of a very thick fool. It is not frozen before being put into the bombe mould, and is really only sufficiently chilled for the mousse just to hold its shape when it is turned out. This is an elegant and delicious sweet and it may be made in many different flavours.

An iced soufflé. This is much the same as a parfait, but in addition to the cream it contains whipped whites of egg, or it may be made as a milanese soufflé mixture, without the addition of the gelatine. The mixture is poured into the soufflé case, which has a band of paper tied round it, and set in a deep freeze until quite firm. At one time an ice cave was employed for this: a large metal box, the double walls of the sides, bottom, and top being packed with ice and salt. The moulds or dishes were put into the interior, and the doors closed. After some hours the doors were opened and the contents found to be frozen.

REFRIGERATOR ICES

Many people now make ices of various kinds in the drawer of the refrigerator. The makers of refrigerators generally supply a book of instructions with the machine, and this should be studied and followed, for the performance varies with different machines. There are, however, certain general points applicable to all. The temperature control should be set to the maximum freezing power some time before the ice is to be made: a minimum of half an hour beforehand. Everything that is to be used should be well chilled: the mixture itself, the cream or egg white that may have to be added at some point in the freezing, and the bowl, whisk, and spoon used in beating the mixture at certain times during the process. The grids must be moved from the tray or drawer, which should be free of snowy deposit on the outside.

The mixture for freezing should be of thick consistency, achieved by the presence of whipped egg whites, beaten cream, or in some cases of gelatine.

The time of freezing depends on the machine; usually after the first half-hour the mixture is firm enough for a first beating in the chilled bowl, or in the drawer itself. After this it may be frozen for another 40 minutes or so. Sometimes the whole process may take from $2\frac{1}{2}$ to 3 hours, but a great deal depends on the preliminary chilling of ingredients and utensils.

Most ice-cream mixtures may be frozen in the refrigerator, but here are two suitable recipes to emphasize the method:

Simple Ices to be made in the Refrigerator

SIMPLE CUSTARD ICE-CREAM

1 pint milk	vanilla pod
1 tablespoon custard powder	1 egg
$1\frac{1}{2}$ oz. sugar (or to taste)	

Bring the milk to the boil with the vanilla pod. Remove pod, and pour the milk over the egg yolk creamed in a basin with the sugar and custard powder. Stir, return to rinsed pan, and cook in a bain-marie until thick. Chill thoroughly. Pour into the chilled tray, put into the freezer, and leave for about 30 minutes. Remove, break up the mixture with a fork, and turn into a cold bowl. Beat well with a rotary beater and fold in the stiffly beaten egg white. Put back into the tray and freeze again until firm. Take out again and beat well, return to tray and freeze for another hour, or until firm.

RED-CURRANT WATER-ICE

¾ pint syrup, made with:	2 cups red-currant juice
¼ pint water	a scant oz. gelatine
1 lb. sugar	

Dissolve the sugar in the water over low heat, bring to boil, boil 5 minutes. Strain and add red-currant juice, keeping back 2 or 3 tablespoons. Soak the gelatine in the juice, then dissolve over gentle heat and stir into the liquid. Allow to get quite cold. Pour into a well-chilled tray, put into freezer, and leave for 30 minutes or until stiff. Remove, turn into a bowl, and beat well with a rotary beater. Return to tray, put back into the refrigerator, and freeze 40–50 minutes. To give a creamier texture the beating process may be repeated after the mixture has been frozen again for 30 minutes. It should then be put back into the refrigerator for another 10–20 minutes.

ICE-CREAM MIXTURES

Before the two basic mixtures are described on which ice-creams are built into a range of sweets suitable for parties and other occasions, it should be noted that an ice-cream may be made from the simplest custard, well sweetened and flavoured, without the addition of cream or other enrichment. Such ice-creams are wholesome food, suitable for and acceptable to children.

There are two main basic mixtures, a custard and a mousse:

Method 1. In this a custard is enriched by the addition of cream, and egg white is included, giving a slightly thicker mixture than an ordinary custard. Sometimes a teaspoon of corn-flour is added to the yolks, not only as an economy measure but also to prevent curdling.

The mixtures for refrigerator ice-creams are frequently made thicker by this means. Custard mixtures may be flavoured in various ways. The recipe for Vanilla Ice (1) is a typical example of the custard method.

Method 2, with a mousse base. This produces a finer and more velvety texture and may well be used when egg yolks are available, e.g. when whites have been used for meringues. Again the base may be used for various flavours. The recipe for Vanilla Ice (2) is an example of this method.

VANILLA ICE (1) (FOR 1 PINT)
with a custard base

2 whole eggs	½ pint milk
2 yolks	1 vanilla pod
2 oz. sugar	½ pint cream, partially whipped

Beat eggs, yolks, and sugar together till well blended. Split vanilla pod and add to milk. Infuse the pod in the milk in a double boiler, covered, for 5–10 minutes (see note below). Strain on to the eggs, mix, and return to pan. Cook till thick and creamy. Strain again into a bowl. Whisk occasionally as it cools. When cool add cream. When quite cold turn into the freezer and churn.

N.B. It is advisable to use a double boiler for making the custard; the proportion of egg white renders the mixture even more liable to curdle than a custard made with yolks only. Even when thickened in this utensil care must be taken not to overcook, and the pan must be removed from heat the moment the custard has thickened.

VANILLA ICE (2) (FOR 1 PINT)
with a mousse base

2½ oz. sugar	¾ pint single or double cream
⅜ gill water	1 vanilla pod or 1 teaspoon
3 yolks of egg	vanilla essence

Put sugar and water into a small pan and set on low heat to dissolve sugar. Cream the yolks, split the vanilla pod and infuse in the cream over slow heat until well flavoured. Strain and cool. When the sugar is completely dissolved bring the syrup to boiling-point, and boil rapidly until a little of it will form a thread drawn out between finger and thumb. Remove from heat, leave half a minute, and pour on to the yolks, whisking all the time until the mixture is thick and mousse-like; cool, add cream, chill, and pour into freezer. Churn till thick. Pack down and leave to ripen. When the flavouring can be imparted without need for infusion, e.g. with an essence, the cream may be partially whipped before being added to the mousse, and this gives a thicker, creamier consistency. Essences may be added to the yolks before the syrup is poured on or when the cream is folded in.

The next ice is an example of a fruit-flavoured ice-cream:

RASPBERRY OR LOGANBERRY ICE

Here an egg mousse base will always give a more satisfactory result than a custard or the addition of cream. There is no risk of the acid curdling the milk or cream, and the result is smoother and more velvety.

Take a good pound of fresh raspberries or loganberries. Rub these through a nylon sieve, or failing this an aluminium strainer. Measure the purée, which will be about 1½ gills. To this add icing sugar or stock syrup (see page 860) to sweeten moderately. Now prepare the basic egg mousse given above, and combine this with the fruit purée, adding a squeeze of lemon juice and 1½ gills to ½ pint cream. This may be single cream or double cream lightly whipped. Now taste and rectify the flavour if necessary. Chill and freeze.

Treat gooseberry, strawberry, black-currant, plum, or damson ices in the same way. The proportion of fruit purée to mousse or cream will vary with the kind of fruit. For example, a strawberry ice may need more purée to the amount of cream or mousse to get adequate flavour than black-currant. The finished mixture should always be full-flavoured and well sweetened. Gooseberry ice may need a little colouring added.

The following is a delicate and delicious party ice, creamy both in texture and colour:

WHITE COFFEE ICE

¾ pint single cream	¾ gill water
2 oz. good weight coffee-beans, medium or French roast	4 yolks of egg
4 oz. loaf or granulated sugar	½ pint double cream, partially whipped

Infuse the beans in the single cream in a double saucepan until well flavoured. This may take 45 minutes to 1 hour. Do not take cream beyond scalding-point. Strain, measure, and cool. It should be reduced to about ½ pint.

Boil the sugar and water together to the thread. Pour on to the beaten yolks and whisk until thick and mousse-like. Add the coffee-flavoured cream and, when the mixture is quite cold, the partially whipped cream. Chill, then pour into the freezer and churn until firm. Remove dasher, pack down and leave to ripen.

A hot ginger sauce served with this is delicious; this is made with chopped preserved ginger heated up in some of its syrup; about 1 tablespoon per person is sufficient.

During the summer sugared raspberries or a mixture of red currants and raspberries make an excellent accompaniment.

POIRES BELLE HÉLÈNE

This is a delicious sweet. Choose William or Comice pears if possible.

3 large or 6 small fine whole pears	shredded almonds, well dusted with castor sugar and browned in the oven
vanilla-flavoured syrup	
vanilla ice-cream	chocolate sauce (see page 184)

Peel the pears with a silver knife and if large cut in half and core. Poach in thick syrup till tender and cool in the syrup. Prepare a vanilla cream ice and pile up in the chilled serving dish. Arrange the pears round and scatter over with almonds. Serve at once with a chocolate sauce separately.

BROWN BREAD ICE (GLACE AU PAIN BIS)

This was at one time a popular ice, and it is made like a praline ice-cream. Either a caramel sauce (see page 188) or sugared fruit is a good accompaniment.

basic quantity of vanilla ice (see page 967)
2–3 heaped tablespoons fresh brown breadcrumbs

1 tablespoon castor sugar
a little vanilla or rum

Prepare the ice-cream according to directions, set aside to ripen. Meanwhile put the crumbs on a baking-sheet, sprinkle with the castor sugar, and brown slowly and thoroughly in a very moderate oven. Turn on to a plate to cool. Stir these into the ice-cream, using a metal spoon and adding a little rum or extra vanilla to flavour. Set aside the freezer to allow the cream to harden slightly after the addition of the flavouring; then serve.

This ice may also be served as a coupe with the various sauces given on page 972 poured over.

The chief attraction of this ice is the contrast of the crisp crumbs and the soft ice-cream.

PRALINE ICE

This is one of the best of ices. A custard or egg mousse base may be used, but in either case the praline is added after the ice is frozen and just before the dasher is removed; it is given a turn or two to mix in the praline. If it were added earlier to the ice it would dissolve into the mixture. The same rule applies when 'fruits confits,' first macerated in rum or liqueur, or marrons glacés are added to an ice. The reason that these also are added at the last is that they contain a good proportion of sugar, which would make the ice difficult to freeze. When they are added in this way, the ice is already frozen and so the danger is removed.

3 yolks of egg
2½ oz. castor sugar
1½ gills milk

vanilla pod (split) or vanilla essence
1½ gills cream
2 tablespoons or more ground praline (see page 854)

Cream the yolks with the sugar until white. Scald the milk, with the vanilla pod, and pour on to the eggs and sugar. Return to the pan and continue cooking until the mixture coats the back of the spoon. When quite cold fold in the cream, partially whipped, and the vanilla if essence is used. Pour into the freezer, churn, and when frozen add crushed praline to taste.

CHOCOLATE ICE-CREAM

Care must be taken with this ice. It is easy to over-sweeten, and if this happens it will not freeze satisfactorily. For this reason a proportion of unsweetened chocolate should be used, and this also adds colour and flavour. Either a custard or egg mousse may be used as the base.

If a custard base is used take 2 oz. sweetened and $\frac{1}{2}$ oz. unsweetened chocolate to the basic recipe (page 966). Simmer the chocolate in the milk before making the custard, or if block chocolate is used, melt this and add to the made custard before folding in the cream.

For an egg mousse base (see page 966) take 1 oz. sweetened and 1 oz. unsweetened chocolate. If block chocolate is used, melt and add to the mousse before the addition of the cream; if powder, mix with 2 or 3 spoonfuls water and cook for a minute or two before cooling and adding. Then fold in the partially whipped cream. Freeze and ripen as before.

GLACE EN SURPRISE

This is a classic and popular with the young. It is sometimes known as Baked Alaska.

vanilla, chocolate, or straw-
　berry ice-cream
a round of sponge cake
3 whites of egg

6 oz. castor sugar
rum, or an appropriate hot
　fruit sauce

Prepare ice-cream and set aside to ripen. Have ready the serving dish, also a roasting-tin filled with ice and freezing salt, and a hot oven. Prepare a meringue with the whites and sugar, and with this fill a bag with a rose pipe. Set the cake on the serving dish. Pile the ice evenly on the top. Pipe the meringue over so as to cover completely. Dust with castor sugar. Put the dish on the ice in the roasting-tin and slide into the oven for 2–3 minutes. Heat the rum or sauce. When the meringue is well coloured remove the pudding, set light to the rum and pour round, or pour round the fruit sauce.

OMELETTE GLACÉE EN SURPRISE

This is somewhat similar to the Glace en Surprise, but a trifle more *recherché*.

praline or vanilla ice-cream
ripe strawberries or raspberries
　(about $\frac{1}{4}$–$\frac{1}{2}$ lb.)
stock or elderflower syrup

omelette soufflée mixture made
with 2 eggs, 1 white, 1 dessertspoon castor sugar, 1
tablespoon liqueur or cream.
Beat yolks thoroughly with
sugar and liqueur or cream.
Beat whites and fold and
cut them into the yolks.

Choose a large soufflé dish and have ready a tray of ice and freezing salt as before. Prepare ice-cream. Slice strawberries or use whole raspberries, sprinkle well with stock syrup or elderflower syrup. Chill.

Have ready a hot oven. Tie a band of greased paper round the soufflé dish and set firmly well down in the tray of ice. Prepare omelette soufflée mixture. Fill the dish half full with the ice-cream and cover top with the strawberries or raspberries (to about two-thirds full). Put the soufflé mixture on the top and dust over with the icing sugar.

Put into the hot oven for about 5 minutes until well browned and risen. Remove paper and serve at once.

BOMBE FAVORITE

This is an old and well-tried recipe; it is not, strictly speaking, an ice, but meringues and cream lightly frozen in a bombe mould.

8 half-shells of meringue	icing sugar or stock syrup
½ pint double cream, lightly whipped	¾–1 lb. fresh raspberries
1 liqueur glass kirsch or the seeds of a vanilla pod	spun sugar (optional)

Break each half-shell of meringue into three pieces. Put into a bowl. Fold the kirsch or vanilla into the cream, sweeten lightly with icing sugar. Add to the meringue and stir just enough to mix. Have ready a medium-sized to large bombe or plain ice mould, lightly oiled. Fill in the mixture to the brim. Cover and pack in ice as for bombe ices (see page 964). Leave for 2 hours in ice and salt. Then rinse the mould in cold water, remove lid, and turn out as described on page 964. Meanwhile press the raspberries through a nylon sieve, sweeten the purée with icing sugar or stock syrup. Chill. Pour this sauce round the bombe, which may be decorated or 'veiled' in spun sugar.

WATER-ICES

See preliminary notes on water-ices, page 962.

LEMON WATER-ICE

1 pint water	the pared rind and juice of 3 lemons
6 oz. loaf sugar	

Put the rind into a scrupulously clean saucepan with the loaf sugar and the water. Dissolve completely, then boil rapidly 5–6 minutes (or test by *pèse-sirop*, see page 859). Set aside, cool, add the juice of the lemons, mix and strain. Chill and freeze.

This water-ice may have the addition of from a third to a half of a stiffly whipped egg white, depending on personal taste.

A lemon water-ice is often used as a base for such ices as a black-currant leaf ice (see overleaf), or an elderflower ice (muscat) (see page 1024).

BLACK-CURRANT LEAF ICE

1 pint water	3–4 handfuls of black-currant
6 oz. loaf sugar	leaves
pared rind of 2 and juice of	a few drops of green colouring
3 lemons	

Prepare syrup as in previous recipe, but after boiling for 5 minutes add the leaves; cover pan and draw off the heat. Allow to infuse until well flavoured, then drain, squeezing the leaves well to extract all the syrup. Add the lemon juice, and the colouring. Freeze as before.

PINEAPPLE WATER-ICE

This makes an excellent dinner-party sweet; it may be served in the shell of the pineapple and may accompany strawberries, whole or sliced, in rich syrup. Crème chantilly (see page 42) may also be handed.

1 large pineapple, which should yield ¾ lb. pineapple pulp	pared rind and juice of 1 small lemon
6 oz. loaf sugar	⅛ of an egg white, stiffly
¾ pint water	whipped
	spun sugar (optional)

Split the pine completely in two without removing the leaves. Scoop out the flesh and shred finely with the help of two silver forks, excluding the core. Weigh pulp. After pulp is weighed the amount of syrup should be adjusted if necessary, taking the above proportions as a guide. Dissolve sugar in the water, add the core of the pineapple and the pared rind of the lemon. Boil rapidly for 5 minutes, draw aside and, removing rind and core, pour over the pineapple. Add the lemon juice and chill. Pour into the freezer. Churn to a slush, then add the egg white and continue churning until firm. Remove dasher and pack down; leave to ripen.

Set the pineapple shells on the serving dish, pile up the ice in each half and serve at once. Spun sugar may be used to garnish, and vine leaves may cover the serving dish.

For other water-ices see Winkfield chapter, page 1024.

The following sauces are good to serve with ice-cream. The first five sauces mentioned are best served hot, though chocolate and caramel may both be served cold.

SAUCES TO ACCOMPANY ICE-CREAM

Chocolate (page 184)
Caramel (page 188)
Walnut butterscotch (page 186)
Mincemeat (see page 973)
Pineapple (see page 973)
Strawberry and raspberry (see Fresh Fruit Sauces, page 184)

Sliced strawberries may also be served with ice-cream, after being flavoured with elderflower syrup and chilled.

PINEAPPLE SAUCE

Take 2–3 tablespoons crushed or shredded pineapple (this is nicer fresh, but tinned may be used); grated rind and strained juice of ½ lemon; stock syrup.

Mix the pineapple with the lemon rind and juice and moisten well with the syrup. Bring to the boil, simmer a few minutes, and then serve hot in small individual *cocottes*, or in a sauce-boat. Just before serving a little rum may be added.

MINCEMEAT SAUCE

The mincemeat given on page 1102 is suitable in smaller quantities to serve hot with ice-creams. Mincemeat made with suet is to be avoided. A fresh mincemeat may be made with white grapes, shredded almonds, and diced apple and banana, and is excellent with a vanilla or praline ice. Approximate quantities are:

4 oz. peeled and pipped white grapes	1–2 bananas, diced
½ oz. butter	1 oz. glacé cherries, thinly sliced
1½ oz. shredded almonds	juice of a lemon, and a little grated rind and sugar to taste
1 large dessert apple (Cox's), diced	rum or brandy to taste

Melt the butter, add the fruit and almonds, and fry quickly 3–4 minutes. Moisten with the juice of a lemon and add grated rind, sugar, and rum or brandy to taste. Simmer for a minute or two, then serve hot with vanilla or praline ice.

PÊCHE MELBA

A famous ice created by Escoffier for Madame Melba.

The classic ingredients are fresh peaches, vanilla ice made with cream, and a sauce made with fresh raspberries.

1 pint vanilla ice, page 967, No. 2	1 to 1½ lb. raspberries, fresh or frozen
4 to 6 (according to size) fresh peaches skinned and lightly poached in a vanilla-flavoured syrup	icing sugar to taste (about 4 oz.)

Prepare peaches, drain and chill. Rub the raspberries through a nylon sieve and to the resulting purée add enough icing sugar to sweeten well; this must be added by degrees or the sauce will not thicken properly. This raspberry sauce is known as 'Sauce Melba.'

To dish, pile the ice cream in a chilled bowl or dish, cover the top with peaches, whole or halved according to size. Coat the top with the sauce.

XXXI

Winkfield

THE idea for this oddly named chapter came one summer's day, when R. H. and I were talking, as usual, about the absorbingly interesting topic of cooking. Whatever ideas fell into our minds that afternoon were immediately noted down by her for experiment; there seemed to be a recurring motif throughout the conversation of 'Let's try it.' I do believe that a suggestion that we might try the golden apples of the Hesperides, cooked in all the wines and spices of Arabia, would have sent her off to the kitchen with the secret look in her eye which says 'Just wait and see.'

It was then that we decided to set one chapter aside for dishes that seemed to us to be worthy of particular attention. Because our minds at that moment were very much taken up with plans for Winkfield and its pupils, we began by calling it the Winkfield chapter, intending that it should contain principally those dishes evolved or designed for the special purposes and occasions of our students here. But as time went on we realized that this was too restricting altogether. Naturally R. H. does not reserve her inventive faculty for Winkfield alone; she and Miss Downes are for ever thinking out and contriving new dishes, and improving old, for the Cordon Bleu School in London, and for the Kitchen Restaurant which has become part of it. It was not likely that we would exclude such added richness from the pages of the book, and soon we were adding these, together with some of our own old and special favourites and the names of cookery-books that we use and enjoy both here and in London.

So in the following pages you will meet a somewhat miscellaneous assortment of recipes, names of books, and party menus. Although its contents long ago ceased to derive from Winkfield alone, the name of the chapter has remained in our minds, and I don't think that our friends who have sent us recipes or those of our teachers who have spent time in testing and inventing will mind if we let it go into print under the title first thought of.

SOME FIRST COURSES. A FEW SAVOURIES. VEGETABLE DISHES AND SALADS

The following is a very good dish if well made; it calls for simple materials and processes, but the frying must be done carefully.

CROÛTES MAINTENON

4 oz. mushrooms	(see page 154) or tomato or
1 oz. butter	brown sauce
4 oz. ham	8 small squares of bread
a few spoonfuls duxelles sauce	cayenne or Nepal pepper

Mornay sauce

¾ pint milk	scant oz. flour
a slice of onion and carrot	seasoning
a bouquet garni	3 oz. finely grated cheese
1 oz. butter	

Wash the mushrooms, slice, and cook until soft in the butter. Add the shredded ham and moisten with the sauce available. Fry the bread in hot fat until golden brown on each side, drain and keep hot.

Infuse the milk with the vegetables and herbs. Melt the butter, add the flour, and strain on the milk. Season and stir until the sauce boils. Allow to simmer for a few minutes and then remove from the heat and beat in the cheese a little at a time.

Place a good spoonful of the mushroom mixture on 4 squares of the bread and then cover lightly with the remaining squares. Coat with the mornay sauce and dust with cayenne or Nepal pepper.

The next recipe is for a simpler croûte which we have called Winkfield Toasts:

WINKFIELD TOASTS

½ oz. butter	1 dessertspoon chopped parsley
1 small onion, finely sliced	2 tablespoons diced ham
1 level teaspoon curry-powder or paste	2 hard-boiled eggs, coarsely chopped
½ oz. flour	8 rounds Procea bread
¼ pint milk, more if necessary	shallow or deep fat for frying

For the top

1 oz. butter	seasoning
2 oz. grated cheese	

Melt the butter in a small pan, add the onion and curry-powder, soften for a few minutes, then add the flour. Pour on the milk and stir until boiling, draw aside, add the parsley, the ham, and the eggs. Add more milk if necessary to make the mixture soft and creamy. Cut crusts off the bread and fry in deep or shallow fat until brown and crisp. Put a large spoonful of the mixture on half of the slices. Cream the cheese and butter together for the top. Season well, spread fairly thickly on one side of the other pieces of bread. Place lightly, cheese mixture uppermost, on the other halves and bake in a quick oven 5 minutes.

The next two recipes are for small savouries, the first a little rich, the second less so but very good:

PETITS CORNETS DE JAMBON OU SAUMON FUMÉ

Curl tiny triangles of ham or smoked salmon round your finger to make a cone and fill with cream cheese, creamed with a little fresh butter and seasoned with salt, a pinch of paprika, and a squeeze of lemon juice. Serve on a finger of short pastry spread with savoury butter.

TARTELETTES OF SMOKED COD'S ROE

short paste (see page 835)	fillets of anchovy
smoked cod's roe mixture (see below)	1 hard-boiled egg

Line some small tartelette moulds with the short pastry, fill with paper and rice and bake blind (see page 844). Fill with the savoury paste of cod's roe, slightly dome the top, and garnish with the fillets of anchovy and the hard-boiled egg yolk and white.

Smoked cod's roe mixture

4 oz. smoked roe	béchamel sauce (see page 155)
1 oz. butter	or cream

Pound the roe with the butter and rub through a wire sieve. Soften with a little sauce or cream.

COLD CHEESE SOUFFLÉS

3 oz. grated Parmesan	$\frac{3}{4}$ pint cream
2 oz. grated gruyère	2 teaspoons tarragon vinegar
salt, pepper, a grain of cayenne	browned crumbs
$\frac{1}{2}$ teaspoon French mustard	turned olives for decoration
$\frac{1}{2}$ pint good aspic jelly	

Prepare 6–8 small china soufflé cases by tying a piece of grease-proof paper firmly round the outside. Put the grated cheese and seasonings into a bowl and mix them well together. Add to them the aspic and vinegar, whipped until frothy when cool (but not set). Fold in the stiffly whipped cream. Fill into the soufflé cases, allowing the mixture to come a little above the rim. Chill well in the refrigerator. Take out, remove the paper, dust with browned crumbs, and decorate each with a turned olive.

BANANES GRATINÉES

Melt some butter in a fireproof dish, add salt and paprika, cook for a few minutes. Put in whole, peeled bananas and turn until well coated with butter. Sprinkle thickly with fresh white crumbs and grated Parmesan and gruyère cheese mixed in equal proportions. Add some extra shavings of butter and bake in a moderate oven until golden brown.

The following is one of the best of the stuffed savoury pancake dishes; it is suitable for a small luncheon-party:

CRÊPES FARCIES AU JAMBON ET AUX CHAMPIGNONS

Pancake batter

4 oz. flour	1 whole egg
salt and pepper	1 yolk of egg
1 tablespoon salad-oil or melted butter	½ pint milk

Sift the flour into a bowl with the seasoning. Make a well in the centre, put in the egg, yolk, and oil, add the milk gradually and beat until smooth. This should have the consistency of thin cream. Leave for ½–1 hour in a cool place.

Filling

1 oz. butter	1 gill stock
4 oz. mushrooms	1 thin slice of ham for each
1 finely chopped shallot	pancake
salt, pepper	1 teaspoon chopped parsley
¾ oz. flour	1 tablespoon cream
1 small tin asparagus tips or a small bundle of asparagus or sprue	grated Parmesan cheese a little extra melted butter

Melt the butter in a pan, slice the mushrooms and add to the butter with the shallot, salt, and pepper. Cover the pan with the lid and cook slowly 3–4 minutes. Remove and stir in the flour, then the stock. Bring to the boil over the fire. Add the parsley and the cream. Keep warm. Heat a pancake pan and brush over with a little melted lard. Cover the bottom of the pan with a thin coating of the batter. Brown carefully on one side; turn over and brown the other. Slide pancake on to a rack. Cook the remainder of the batter in the same way. Lay a thin slice of ham on each pancake, spread a spoonful of the filling in the middle, roll up and arrange closely in the serving dish. Arrange the asparagus tips over. Sprinkle well with the cheese and a little extra melted butter. Brown under the grill or in a quick oven.

The following recipe is for a rich goose pâté which will keep for a week at least. It should be served in its terrine. It is excellent as a first course eaten with hot toast. If required as a main course, it may have lean ham added in proportion of a third of the weight of the pounded goose.

GOOSE PÂTÉ

1 goose with giblets	bay-leaf
4–8 oz. butter	clarified butter or goose fat
1 large glass port	salt and freshly ground black pepper
ground mace	

Roast the goose and sauter the liver in a little of the butter. Simmer the giblets in a little water with salt and a bay-leaf until very tender. Allow all to get cold. Then pick the meat from the carcass, removing the skin, mince twice with the liver and giblets. Pound thoroughly and sieve. Pound again, adding the creamed butter by degrees with the port. Add all the cuisson or juice from the roasting-pan and from sautéing the liver, also a little of the fat if liked. Season highly and flavour with mace. Put into a terrine, smooth over the top, and run clarified butter over to cover. Keep in a cool place.

This pâté may be made with left-overs of roast goose or duck.

The following recipe is particularly good and will make an unusual first course, a refreshing salad, or an excellent hors-d'œuvre:

AUBERGINES CAVIAR

3–4 aubergines according to size	1 small finely chopped green pepper (optional)
1 large clove of garlic crushed to a cream with salt	salt, freshly ground pepper, dash of cayenne
1 shallot, finely chopped	lemon juice

Wrap each aubergine in oiled paper, set on a tin and bake in a moderate oven till soft, about 40 minutes. Cool, split, and scrape out the pulp carefully with a silver spoon. Chop slightly and turn into a bowl, add garlic, shallot, pepper, and plenty of seasoning. Sharpen well with lemon juice. Put into a refrigerator or on ice to chill thoroughly. Serve in one of the following ways:

As hors-d'œuvre

Serve in a china pot or bowl, sunk in crushed ice. Hand hot dry toast and pats of fresh butter. The contrast of temperature and texture is delicious.

As a first course

Skin large, ripe tomatoes, cut off the tops, scoop out the seeds and season inside with salt, pepper, and lemon juice. Fill well with the 'caviare,' replace the tops in a half-open position, and set each tomato on a round of toast spread with garlic-flavoured butter.

As a salad

Make a well-seasoned tomato salad and dress with French dressing, adding plenty of well-chopped herbs. Arrange the 'caviare' in an oval fireproof dish and surround with the salad. Eat with freshly made baps and butter.

BRAISED LETTUCES IN A CREAM SAUCE

lettuces	1 tablespoon lemon juice
2 egg yolks	salt, black pepper, a pinch of sugar
a good pinch of fécule or corn-flour	2 tablespoons thick cream
2 oz. butter	

Have the lettuces ready braised with their liquor. Strain it off and take ¾ gill.

Work the yolks and fécule in a bowl with a nut of the butter, add the lettuce juice, stand bowl in a bain-marie and stir continuously, adding the rest of the butter bit by bit. Add the lemon juice carefully and season to taste. When the sauce has the consistency of cream add the fresh cream; adjust seasoning and continue to stir over the heat for another 2 or 3 minutes. Pour over lettuces and serve.

The following is an excellent first course for luncheon or dinner. It is lighter than a dish made entirely of mushrooms, and although the taste of these predominates, the fennel has a pleasant sub-flavour.

MUSHROOMS AND FENNEL

1½ oz. butter	a dust of cayenne
2 oz. finely chopped onion	2 teaspoons chopped fennel
1½ oz. Florence fennel, chopped	leaves taken from the top of
or sliced thinly	the root
1 tablespoon chopped parsley	1 egg yolk
¼ lb. mushrooms, sliced	2 tablespoons sour or fresh
a little nutmeg	cream
salt	boiled rice
a pinch of Nepal or freshly	a little melted butter
ground pepper	

Sauce

¾ oz. butter	¼ pint milk
¾ oz. flour	

Melt the butter, add the onion, fennel, parsley, mushrooms, and seasonings. Cover pan and simmer 7–10 minutes. Meanwhile make the sauce in the usual way; when boiling add the fennel leaves and add to the mushrooms. Bring again to the boil, draw aside and at once add the yolk, first mixed into the cream, by degrees. Turn into a hot dish and serve with boiled rice tossed up with a little melted butter.

MUSHROOMS IN SCALLOP SHELLS

¾–1 lb. good mushrooms	1 clove of garlic crushed with
4 tablespoons fresh bread-crumbs	salt
	seasoning
1 oz. melted butter	a little good stock or gravy, or
2 egg yolks	mornay sauce (see page 156)
2–3 tablespoons cream	grated cheese, browned
1 heaped dessertspoon each of	crumbs, and melted butter
finely chopped parsley and	
chives	

Wash and peel the mushrooms, remove stalks, and set aside 3–4 for each person, chop stalks and peelings and any remaining mushrooms. Add crumbs and bind with the butter, yolks, and cream. Mix in the herbs, garlic, and seasoning. Fill the mushroom cups with this mixture, arrange in buttered scallop shells, spoon over a little good stock or coat with mornay sauce. Sprinkle with cheese, crumbs, and melted butter, and bake in a moderate oven 12–15 minutes. Serve very hot in the shells.

In Pommes Dauphine we have beignets made of a mixture of sieved potatoes and choux paste fried in deep fat.

POMMES DAUPHINE

2 oz. butter	4 medium-sized potatoes
¼ pint water	½ oz. butter
2½ oz. flour	grated nutmeg
2 eggs	deep fat for frying

Make a choux paste mixture with butter, water, flour, and eggs. Place the butter and water in a saucepan, when boiling draw aside and scoop in the flour. Beat till smooth and leave to cool. Beat in the eggs. Meanwhile cook the potatoes and dry them well, sieve and beat in the butter, grated nutmeg, and choux paste; sieved potato and choux paste should be equal in quantity. Cook in spoonfuls in hot deep fat, gradually increasing the heat as they cook (see cooking of beignets, page 74). Drain well, sprinkle with salt.

WINKFIELD ZUCCHINI OR COURGETTES

Choose small even-sized zucchini about the size of a thick cigar, allowing 3–4 per person.

1 oz. butter	1 dessertspoon chopped mixed herbs
salt	
freshly ground black pepper	brown bread and butter and
squeeze of lemon juice	quarters of lemon

Do not peel the zucchini, but plunge into boiling water for 2 minutes. Drain thoroughly. Heat a fireproof dish, put in the butter and allow to melt. Add the zucchini whole with plenty of salt and pepper, the lemon juice, and herbs. Cover with buttered paper and cook in a slow to moderate oven for 25–30 minutes, basting occasionally. Adjust seasoning before serving with brown bread and butter and quarters of lemon.

In hot weather there are certain forms of salad which may well replace soup as a first course. Some of them are suitable for adaptation to whatever fruit or salad material is in season. The seasonings and dressings may be varied to suit your taste.

The following recipe is for a summer evening first course of melon, cucumber, very small tomatoes, avocado pear, herbs, and a French dressing. It is served in a clear crystal bowl and thoroughly chilled. It is not unlike the Spanish soup Gazpacho, but more delicate in flavour.

It may be eaten with a spoon in a soup-plate and should be accompanied by slices of French roll and curls of butter.

MELON, CUCUMBER, TOMATO, AND AVOCADO PEAR
FIRST COURSE

The best tomatoes to use are the tiny ones generally grown for decoration, about the size of a cherry or small plum. If these are not available ordinary tomatoes may be used, but must be emptied of seed and liquid, peeled and quartered.

Scald and peel the tomatoes. Take an equal bulk of cucumber, tomato, melon, and avocado pear. The melon may with advantage be scooped out with a vegetable scoop and the cucumber peeled, split lengthwise in four, and then cut across into cubes. As far as possible all the fruits or pieces of fruit should approximate in size. The fruits are put in the bowl, seasoned, and sprinkled with plenty of finely chopped mixed herbs, generally a good tablespoon. The whole is then dressed liberally with a good well-seasoned basic French dressing containing a little sugar, and set in the ice-box for a few hours. At the end of this time the amount of liquid will have increased. The dish should be served with a ladle into the soup-plates.

The next recipe is a simpler and less liquid form of the above:

PEAR, MELON, AND CUCUMBER SALAD

Take equal parts of melon, pear, and cucumber (outdoor varieties are suitable) and cut into dice of approximately equal size. Marinade the fruit in the following dressing for at least 1 hour:

5 tablespoons oil	a few drops of onion juice
3 tablespoons lemon juice	freshly ground pepper
1 dessertspoon sugar	1 dessertspoon French mustard
1 teaspoon salt	

Lift out the fruit and arrange in small glass bowls. Test the dressing for seasoning and sharpness and make any necessary adjustments. If you like pour 2 tablespoons cream or cream dressing over the fruit. Serve very cold.

PINEAPPLE AND CUCUMBER

Allow half of a very small pine per person.

Cut pines in two, scoop out the flesh and break it up in small pieces, taking away the core. Mix the fruit with some small cubes of cucumber and a few blanched almonds. Replace this into the halves of pine and pour over a little cream dressing, made with fresh cream; add a few drops of lemon juice, a little sugar, and salt and pepper. Serve half a pine to each person and hand brown bread and butter.

The following is good as a first course for luncheons:

PEAR AND CREAM CHEESE SALAD

4 ripe dessert pears	seasoning
2 oz. Roquefort cheese	lettuce leaves (1 for each pear)
½–1 oz. butter	paprika
3–4 tablespoons cream cheese	rolled bread and butter, or hot
a little single cream or top of	home-made water-biscuits
milk	(see page 786)

Peel the pears and remove the core and pips from the centre. Cream the Roquefort cheese with the butter to the consistency of firm whipped cream and fill the middle of the pears. Whisk a little single cream or top of milk into the cream cheese till the mixture will just pour; season lightly. Place each pear on a lettuce leaf, coat with the cream cheese dressing, and dust with paprika. Serve very cold with rolled bread and butter, or with water-biscuits.

The next dish may be eaten alone with brown bread and butter or as an accompanying salad:

PLUM SALAD

ripe dessert plums	3 tablespoons tarragon vinegar
lemon juice and a little sugar	a little cream or top of milk
1 egg	a little chopped tarragon
2 tablespoons sugar	

Split the plums in half and remove the stones, sprinkle with lemon juice and a little sugar and leave for half an hour. Meanwhile prepare the dressing. Beat the egg and the sugar together, add the vinegar, and stand the bowl in a pan of boiling water, Stir until thick, then cool and dilute with cream or top of milk. Arrange the plums on individual plates and cover with a spoonful of the dressing. Scatter over the tarragon.

In Salade Niçoise we have a rustic and substantial dish:

SALADE NIÇOISE

1 lb. fine ripe tomatoes	2–3 oz. black olives, halved
1 small cucumber, sliced or	and shredded
diced	French dressing, strongly flav-
salt and freshly ground black	oured with garlic
pepper	8–10 fillets of anchovy
chopped herbs (basil, summer	brown bread and butter
savory, and parsley)	quarters of lemon
lemon rind (optional)	
½ pint cooked broad or French	
beans or peas	

Scald and peel tomatoes, cut into slices, or if preferred quarter them, and remove the seeds and water (this may be strained and the juice added to the dish afterwards). Lay the tomatoes and the cucumber in a small fireproof or hors-d'œuvre dish. Season very well and sprinkle liberally with the chopped herbs. Lemon rind may be grated over with the herbs.

Scatter over the beans or peas, then the olives. Season again and spoon over the dressing. Split the anchovy fillets in two and arrange lattice fashion on the top of the salad. Serve with brown bread and butter and quarters of lemon.

Use for a first course on a hot summer's day.

The following Tomato Ice is really a party dish. It is rich, and because of the mayonnaise and cream not over-cold. It may be served as an accompaniment or as a base for an elegant shell-fish cocktail.

TOMATO ICE (AMPLE FOR 6)

½ pint thick mayonnaise (see page 166)
½ pint tomato pulp, made from 1 lb. tomatoes stewed with a little garlic, bay-leaf, and lemon thyme or basil to extract juice, then sieved

1 teaspoon tomato purée, if necessary
the juice of 1 large lemon
the grated rind of 1 orange
½ gill partially whipped cream
a good pinch of sugar, salt, and pepper

Make mayonnaise, using lemon juice instead of vinegar to sharpen. Incorporate the ingredients in the order given. The tomato purée is added if the fresh tomatoes are poor in flavour or lacking in strength. Taste and adjust seasoning. Pour into the freezer and freeze in the usual way. As this is a thick and creamy mixture it is particularly suitable for freezing in the drawer of the refrigerator.

This may be used either as an accompaniment to grilled sole and turbot or as the base of a prawn cocktail. Fresh-chopped herbs as well as shredded or chopped lobster may be added to the mixture, together with a dash of brandy or sherry, so turning it into a lobster ice or frozen lobster cocktail.

MINT ICE

This, filled into the centre of grape-fruit, makes an excellent first course for lunch.

Allow one half of a grape-fruit for each person. Cut grape-fruit in half and cut round and between each section to remove the membrane (see preparation of grape-fruit, page 47). Dust lightly with sugar and set aside to chill.

For the ice take:

¾ pint water
4 oz. sugar
the pared rind and juice of 2 small lemons

1 large handful of mint leaves, picked from the stalks
green colouring (sap green)
chopped mint or crushed crystallized mint leaves for the top

Boil water, sugar, and lemon rind together for 5 minutes. Draw aside, add mint, and infuse 10 minutes. Then strain, add lemon juice and colouring. Cool then freeze until firm.

Serve a good spoonful in each grape-fruit, and sprinkle with chopped mint or crushed crystallized mint leaves.

BLACK-CURRANT LEAF ICE IN MELON

This is a delicious first course for a summer's day. Choose a small English hothouse melon or a sugar melon.

Prepare the ice (see page 972). Colour with a little sap green. The ice should be pale green and translucent.

If the melons are really small halve and remove the seeds, allowing one half to each person. If a larger melon is used cut into thick slices, removing the seeds, and put ice in the centre.

EGG DISHES

The following egg dishes are particularly suitable for luncheon, some as first, others as main courses. Œufs Pochés aux Concombres is a fresh and pleasant first-course dish for a summer luncheon:

ŒUFS POCHÉS AUX CONCOMBRES

trimmings of puff paste	a spoonful or two of béchamel
4 new-laid eggs	if wished
1 small cucumber	$\frac{1}{2}$ oz. butter
2–3 tablespoons picked shrimps	1 tablespoon lightly whipped
hollandaise sauce, bound with	cream

Line the paste into deep tartlet tins. Bake blind. Poach the eggs and keep in hot water until wanted. Cut cucumber into dice, blanch, drain, and sauter half in the butter with the shrimps. Add the remaining cucumber to the hollandaise with the cream.

Put a spoonful of the cucumber and shrimp mixture into each case, place an egg on top and coat over with the sauce. Serve at once.

Œufs à la Niçoise might be used as a first course or, by the adjustment of the number of olive beignets, become substantial enough for a main course. It makes a good luncheon dish.

ŒUFS A LA NIÇOISE

This is cooked *sur le plat* with garnish of ham and olive beignets.

2–3 oz. cooked ham	cream
1½ oz. sliced gruyère cheese	olives
4–5 eggs	anchovy fillets
melted butter	fritter batter (see page 442)

Well butter a gratin dish. Cover bottom with small slices of ham, scatter with the cheese and break eggs on the top. Sprinkle with melted butter and a little cream. Stone olives, stuff with an anchovy fillet, dip into fritter batter, and fry in deep fat till golden brown. Slip dish into oven 6–8 minutes to allow eggs to set, then surround with the olive beignets.

Two fairly substantial dishes follow, Œufs Frits Cubanos and Œufs Valenciana; both call for fried eggs:

ŒUFS FRITS CUBANOS

1 large onion, finely sliced	1¼ pints light stock
1 clove of garlic, chopped	4 bananas
2 oz. butter	sugar, lemon juice
6 oz. rice	4 eggs
salt, pepper, and 1 teaspoon paprika	devil sauce (see page 145)

Cook onion and garlic in half the butter until just colouring. Add rice and cook a further 3–4 minutes, adding salt, pepper, and paprika. Pour on 1 pint of the stock, bring to the boil, cover, and put the pan into the oven for 15 minutes. At the end of that time add the remaining stock if necessary, and put back the pan to finish the cooking.

Meanwhile peel the bananas, slice lengthways, and fry in remaining butter until golden brown, sprinkling with sugar, lemon juice, salt, and pepper.

Fry the eggs in deep fat, or in butter. Dish the rice and set round it the eggs and bananas arranged alternately. Serve the devil sauce.

ŒUFS VALENCIANA

1 oz. butter	almonds
4 oz. rice	raisins
½–¾ pint stock	2 green peppers, blanched
seasoning	2 bananas, sliced
2 onions	4 eggs
2 large tomatoes	

Melt the butter, add the rice, and stir for a few minutes. Add the stock, season, and bring to the boil. Cover tightly and put into a moderate oven for about 20 minutes. In the meantime have ready a savoury mixture of the fried onions, tomatoes, almonds, raisins, and green peppers, and stir this into the rice with a fork, adding the fried bananas. Fry the eggs in deep smoking fat and serve on the rice.

Three recipes calling for hard-boiled eggs follow, and the first two are good as a main course:

TIMBALE A L'INDIENNE

Rich short crust pastry

8 oz. flour	1 egg yolk
a pinch of salt	2–3 tablespoons water to mix
6 oz. butter	

Sieve the flour with a pinch of salt, rub in the butter until the mixture looks like fine breadcrumbs, and then mix with the egg yolk and water. Turn a deep sandwich tin upside-down, cover the outside all over with pastry, pricking the top, and bake until crisp and golden brown. Fill with the following mixture:

1¼ oz. butter	cream
1 large teaspoon curry-powder	3–4 hard-boiled eggs, quartered
1 oz. flour	
¾ pint milk	½ pint prawns, picked and washed
8–10 button or large spring onions	
lemon juice	boiled rice flavoured with a large teaspoon paprika

Melt butter, cook curry-powder in it for a few minutes, add flour, mix, pour on milk and stir until boiling. Simmer 4–5 minutes. Simmer onions until just tender. Drain well. Add to sauce. Simmer again for a minute or two. Finish with a squeeze of lemon juice and a little cream.

Add the eggs before filling into the case with the prawns. Serve in a hot dish surrounded with boiled rice flavoured with paprika, the paprika having been cooked in a little melted butter and stirred into the rice with a fork.

Vol-au-vent à l'Indienne is a luncheon dish of hard-boiled eggs in a rich creamy curry-flavoured sauce:

VOL-AU-VENT A L'INDIENNE

vol-au-vent of puff pastry, made with 8 oz. flour (see puff pastry, page 836)

Filling

1¼ oz. butter	lemon juice
1 finely chopped onion	1–2 egg yolks
1 teaspoon curry-powder	1½ oz. butter
1 teaspoon tomato purée	3 or 4 hard-boiled eggs, quartered
1 oz. flour	
¾ pint milk	

Melt the butter, add the onion, curry-powder, and tomato purée, and cook slowly for 4–5 minutes. Blend in the flour, add the milk and stir until boiling. Simmer 4–5 minutes. Finish with a squeeze of lemon, and the egg yolks and butter, added as for a liaison (see page 138). Add the hard-boiled eggs and reheat gently. Remove top of vol-au-vent, scoop out the inside, slide on to the serving dish, and fill with the mixture.

The last recipe for hard-boiled egg dishes selected for this chapter is a delicate light concoction of egg yolks crushed through a fine sieve, piled on the whites, and served with a rich creamy sauce. With this quarters of lemon and brown bread and butter are handed. Although simple this dish, served ice-cold and well seasoned and flavoured, is among the best of cold egg dishes, and suitable for a first course for a summer party luncheon.

ŒUFS DURS SOLEIL D'OR
Allow 1 hard-boiled egg per person

seasoning
rounds of buttered bread or croûtons
chopped chives

cold curry dressing as given on page 29 (sauce for Melon 2, about ⅓
    pint for 6 eggs), mixed with 1 tablespoon chopped mango chutney
or
⅓ pint whipped cream, flavoured to taste with the following:
  curry-paste   a touch of sugar
  French mustard   1 tablespoon mango chutney
  a dash of cayenne

thin brown bread and butter and quarters of lemon

Cut eggs lengthwise, press yolks through a fine wire strainer or small meshed wire sieve and season. Arrange whites in a dish on rounds of buttered bread or croûtons and spoon the yolks lightly over them. Sprinkle with chopped chives. Serve ice-cold with either of the sauces named and hand thin brown bread and butter and quarters of lemon.

The following sauce is an alternative:

¼ pint mayonnaise, made with   mustard
  tarragon vinegar   1 large teaspoon chopped dill,
juice of ¼ lemon   mint, tarragon, or basil
salt   2 tablespoons lightly whipped
pepper   cream
sugar

Mix the ingredients in the order given and serve the sauce separately, or it may be poured in the dish in which the eggs, arranged on rounds of buttered bread, have been laid.

Now follow two recipes for œufs mollets, the first with a delicately seasoned sauce:

ŒUFS MOLLETS A L'INDIENNE

4 eggs   a slice or two of lemon
1 teaspoon curry-powder   sieved apricot jam or jelly
1 finely chopped onion   cream
1 dessertspoon oil   boiled rice
½ gill strong tomato pulp   sliced pimento for garnish
½ gill white wine or water   paprika
salt, pepper   ¼–½ pint mayonnaise

Mayonnaise
1 egg yolk   a little dry mustard
salt   ¼–½ pint oil
pepper   vinegar or lemon juice

First prepare the mayonnaise: cream thoroughly the egg yolk and seasoning in a warm basin, using a small wooden spoon. Add the oil very slowly from the point of a teaspoon, beating continuously. When the mixture is really thick and about half the oil has been added, mix in the vinegar. Beat in the remaining oil, and if the mayonnaise is too thick to use add 1 tablespoon boiling water or a little whipped cream.

Place the eggs in boiling water and boil for 5 minutes from the time the water comes back to boiling-point. Put immediately into cold water and leave 7–8 minutes, then peel carefully and slip into fresh cold water until wanted.

Meanwhile cook the curry and onion in the oil until soft, add the tomato pulp, wine, seasonings, and lemon; continue cooking for a few minutes and then strain.

Add the curry sauce and apricot jam to the mayonnaise to taste, adding cream to mellow the flavour. Arrange the rice down the centre of a serving dish, dry the eggs and place on this. Spoon over the curry cream dressing and garnish with the pimento and a dusting of paprika.

The next recipe calls for particular care in seasoning. Œufs mollets in a soufflé might be cloying to the taste, were the latter not very well seasoned.

ŒUFS MOLLETS EN SOUFFLÉ EN SURPRISE

This party dish consists of œufs mollets in a delicate soufflé. It is excellent as a first course for luncheon.

6 eggs	2 egg yolks
¾ pint béchamel sauce, prepared by the long method (see page 155)	3 egg whites

The importance of this dish lies in the sauce, which must be perfect, delicately flavoured and the consistency of cream. Treat the 6 eggs as for Œufs Mollets à l'Indienne (see above). Butter well a deep gratin or large soufflé dish. Beat the 2 yolks into the béchamel, whip whites stiffly and fold into the sauce. Put about one-third of the mixture on to the bottom of the dish, arrange the eggs in a circle or oval. Cover completely with the rest of the mixture and bake in a hot oven 15–20 minutes. The soufflé should be well risen and soft and creamy inside. Serve at once.

The next recipe is popular with those who like mussels:

OMELETTE DIEPPOISE

Omelet

3 eggs	2 tablespoons water or cream
	½ oz. butter

Mussels

1 quart mussels	1 carrot
1 glass white wine	1 stick of celery
½ pint water	a bouquet garni
1 onion	6 peppercorns

Sauce

¾ oz. butter	seasoning
scant ¾ oz. flour	a little liquid from the mussels
1½ gills fish stock	1 egg yolk
½ gill white wine	2 tablespoons cream
2 peeled, seeded, and chopped tomatoes	chopped parsley

First prepare the mussels; wash well and remove all the weed. Place in a pan with the wine, water, and flavourings. Cover, bring slowly to the boil, and shake over the fire for 5 minutes.

Sauce. Melt the butter, add the flour away from the heat, and blend in the fish stock and wine. Stir until boiling, correct the seasoning, add a little mussel liquor to flavour, and then prepare the liaison. Beat the egg yolk and cream together. Add a little of the hot sauce and return slowly to the pan. Reheat carefully and keep in a bain-marie while preparing the omelet.

Take the mussels out of their shells, remove the beard, and mix them with a little of the sauce, the tomato, and the chopped parsley.

Fill the omelet with the mixture, coat with the remainder of the sauce, and glaze lightly under the grill.

SOUPS FOR SPECIAL OCCASIONS

The first of these is a delicate almond soup, which may be served hot or cold.

POTAGE CRÈME D'AMANDES (FOR 4–6)

1½ pints good jellied stock, veal or chicken, free from grease
4 oz. blanched almonds, well pounded or passed through a nut- or cheese-mill
¾ oz. butter
¾ oz. flour
milk if necessary

3 yolks of egg
¼ pint single cream
seasoning
ground mace (optional)
about ¼ pint freshly cooked green peas or blanched shredded cucumber

Put almonds and stock together. Cover the pan and simmer 15–20 minutes. When well flavoured strain through a muslin, squeezing the almonds well to extract all the liquid.

Make a roux with the butter and flour. Measure stock and make up to 1½ pints with milk if necessary. Stir over moderate heat until boiling. Cream the yolks well, add the cream and then add carefully to the soup (see adding of liaisons, page 138). Adjust seasoning and, if liked, flavour delicately with ground mace.

Stir over gentle heat or in a double saucepan to the consistency of cream. Do not allow to boil. Add the garnish and serve at once.

This soup is good cold.

The following cold soup has an excellent taste of fresh mushrooms:

CRÈME DE CHAMPIGNONS (COLD CREAM OF MUSHROOMS)

1¼ oz. butter
1¼ oz. flour
1½ pints strong well-flavoured chicken stock, free from grease

6 oz. white button or small cap mushrooms
½ pint single cream
tarragon leaves
rolled white bread and butter
a little extra melted butter

Melt butter, add flour, pour on the stock and bring to the boil. Wash mushrooms, but do not peel. Press through a fine wire sieve. Add this pulp to the soup with the cream. Simmer for 3–4 minutes, then pour off into a bowl, cover, and whisk occasionally whilst cooling. When quite cold, whisk again before serving with 2 or 3 tarragon leaves in each cup (these may be chopped if wished).

Have ready the rolls of bread and butter, lay on a baking-sheet and sprinkle over a little extra melted butter. Bake in a hot oven till golden brown and crisp; serve with the soup.

CREAM OF SORREL SOUP

2 double handfuls of sorrel	salt, freshly ground pepper
2 double handfuls of spinach	1 gill cream and a little extra
1–2 oz. onion, finely chopped	for finishing
1½ oz. butter	lemon juice, sugar
1¼ oz. flour	chopped chives
1¾ pints warm milk	

Pick over the leaves and wash thoroughly. Boil sorrel and spinach separately in water. Drain, press, and dry and rub through a fine sieve.

Soften the onion in the butter without colouring, add the flour off the fire, pour on the milk, blend, and return to the heat. Stir until boiling, add salt and pepper. Simmer 4–5 minutes. Then beat in the purées, add cream, and adjust seasoning, adding lemon juice and sugar to taste. Serve with the extra cream, lightly whipped, and a pinch of chopped chives in each soup-cup or plate.

The following Spinach and Sorrel Soup is extremely simple and has a fresh and good flavour:

SPINACH AND SORREL SOUP

1 medium-sized onion	1½ pints light stock
1 oz. butter	salt
4 handfuls of spinach	Nepal pepper
4 handfuls of sorrel	1 tablespoon horse-radish
¾ oz. flour	2 tablespoons whipped cream

Slice the onion and melt in the butter. Add the spinach and sorrel. Cook slowly until soft. Add the flour and the stock. Season, bring to the boil and sieve. Reheat, add horse-radish and whipped cream, and serve.

CREAM OF CURRY SOUP (HOT)

1 oz. onion, finely chopped	¼ pint coco-nut or almond milk
1½ oz. butter	salt, pepper, sugar, a pinch of
1 level dessertspoon curry-powder	ground coriander
	2 egg yolks
1¼ oz. flour	2–3 tablespoons thick cream
1 pint strong chicken stock, free from grease	thin slices of lemon and boiled rice, coloured with paprika
½ pint creamy milk	for garnish

Soften onion in the butter without colouring, add curry-powder, and cook for a few minutes. Stir in flour, pour on the stock and milk, and bring to the boil. Simmer 10–15 minutes. Meanwhile prepare nut milk by pouring a cup of boiling water on to 1 large tablespoon grated fresh coconut or ground almonds. Allow to stand 15 minutes, then drain and press through a piece of muslin or a strainer. Add to the soup with the seasonings. Prepare the liaison with yolks and cream, add to the soup, adjust the flavour, and run through a fine strainer or tammy.

Return to a clean pan to reheat carefully, or else serve at once with a slice of lemon in each plate and the boiled rice flavoured with a teaspoon of paprika, which has been cooked in a good nut of melted butter and stirred into the rice with a fork.

The next soup has a delicious flavour and is spicy and fresh rather than hot. It is one of the best soups for dinner on a hot summer evening:

ICED CURRY CREAM SOUP (CRÈME CONSTANCE)

4 oz. finely chopped shallots	1 strip of lemon rind
1 oz. butter	1 small bay-leaf
1 level tablespoon curry-paste	1 small dessertspoon arrow-
1 oz. flour	root
1¾–2 pints vegetable or chicken	cream (see below)
stock	

Soften shallots in ¾ oz. of the butter, then add curry-paste. Cook 4–5 minutes. Add the rest of the butter, then the flour, and pour on the stock. Bring to boil, add lemon rind and bay-leaf, simmer 20 minutes, strain, and return to the rinsed pan to reduce if necessary. Then add the arrowroot slaked with a tablespoon of cold water and reboil. Strain again, cool, then chill. Serve with a spoonful of the following cream in each cup:

Cream

1 wineglass port	1 good dessertspoon apricot
1 teaspoon curry-paste or	jam or purée from dried
powder	apricots
	2 tablespoons whipped cream
	or evaporated milk

Mix the port and curry-paste or powder together and simmer until reduced to half quantity. Leave till cold, mix with the purée or jam, strain, then beat into the cream.

ICED TOMATO SOUP (UNCOOKED)

3 lb. very ripe tomatoes	castor sugar
the juice of 1 orange and the	freshly ground black pepper
rind of ½	salt
the juice of ½ lemon	brown bread and butter

Scald the tomatoes, skin, cut in half, and remove the seeds. Strain these through an aluminium strainer, pressing gently to extract all juice.

Rub the flesh of the tomatoes through a nylon sieve. Mix with the tomato juice and the juice of the orange and lemon. Add the sugar, pepper, and salt to taste. This should make approximately 1½–2 pints. If too strong or thick, dilute with water or white wine and water. Chill thoroughly and serve with rolls of brown bread and butter. Remove the crusts before rolling. Mix the grated orange rind with the butter before spreading on the bread.

POTAGE DE TOMATES A L'ESTRAGON
(WINKFIELD TOMATO SOUP)

1 onion	½ pint tomato juice (this may
1 lb. ripe red tomatoes	be tinned)
¾ oz. butter	½ bay-leaf
¼ clove of garlic, crushed	1½ pints strong beef stock
½ teaspoon salt	a level dessertspoon arrowroot
1 dessertspoon tomato purée	a little extra stock or tomato
(if the strong Italian variety	juice
the quantity may be halved)	tarragon leaves

Slice the onion, wipe the tomatoes, cut in half and squeeze to remove the seeds. (Do not throw the expressed pulp away, as the juice from it is required.) Melt the butter in a stew-pan, add the tomatoes, onion, garlic, and salt. Cover and cook very slowly for about 40 minutes to 1 hour. Then rub through a nylon sieve, rinse out the pan well, put in the purée, tomato juice, together with the juice strained from the seeds, bay-leaf, and stock. Simmer 20 minutes to ⅓ hour. Adjust seasoning, remove bay-leaf; slake the arrowroot with a little extra stock or tomato juice and add with the tarragon leaves. Reboil and serve hot or cold.

TWO SAUCES FOR SPECIAL OCCASIONS

ALMOND SAUCE
for serving with roast chicken, turkey, rabbit, or veal, or with grilled fish

2 oz. blanched almonds	a little lemon juice
a good ½ oz. butter	salt, pepper, a pinch of ground
½ oz. flour	mace
¼ pint good stock, chicken or	2 tablespoons cream
veal	grated lemon rind (optional)

Chop almonds finely. Cook slowly until golden brown in the butter. Draw aside, add the flour and, when well mixed, the stock. Blend well and stir over moderate heat until boiling. Boil gently 3–4 minutes, add a squeeze of lemon juice, and seasoning and mace to taste. A little grated lemon rind may be added as well, but care must be taken not to spoil the delicate flavour of the almonds. Add the cream and boil rapidly to a syrupy consistency.

TAMARIND SAUCE
excellent with cold curry of chicken or lobster

4 oz. dried tamarind   a strip of lemon rind
½ pint water   3–4 tablespoons sugar

Put the tamarind and water together in an earthenware casserole.   Set
in a slow oven ¾–1 hour.

Remove and rub through a strainer into a pan; it should have the consistency of cream.   Add sugar and lemon rind, simmer 10–15 minutes.
Remove lemon rind and serve hot.

Tamarind is bought at shops that supply curry materials (see page 421).

FISH

A few fish dishes have been included in this chapter.   Three of these are
for lobster; they are followed by a simple spiced fish, good as a luncheon or
supper dish, a tourte or cold pie, not unlike a raised pie, and an unusual
recipe for Coquilles St Jacques.

LOBSTER '31' (COLD)

2 uncooked lobsters weighing   watercress
    about 1 lb. each   6 oz. boiled rice mixed with
court bouillon   chopped chives

Sauce
    ½ pint thick mayonnaise, well seasoned
    ¾ gill fresh strong tomato pulp or juice
    a few drops of tabasco
    salt, pepper, a squeeze of lemon juice
    2–3 tomatoes, according to size, peeled, quartered, pipped, and cut
        into shreds
    2 tablespoons lightly whipped cream

Plunge lobsters into the boiling court bouillon.   Simmer 15 minutes.
Draw aside and allow to cool in the liquor.   Mix the sauce ingredients in
the order given.   Lift out lobsters, drain, and split each in two.   Remove
bag from head, lift out tail meat, cut each piece into three or four, and
replace upside-down on opposite shell from which it was taken.   Crack
claws, remove meat, and lay in the heads of the shell.   Arrange lobsters on
serving dish, garnish with the cress.   Serve rice in a separate dish and the
sauce in a boat or bowl.

LOBSTER BARCELONA (HOT)

2 oz. butter   2 aubergines
3 oz. onion, finely sliced   oil for frying
6 oz. rice   1 good-sized lobster, freshly
salt, pepper, paprika   boiled
saffron to flavour, previously   ½ oz. butter
    soaked in a little water   1 glass sherry
1¼ pints light stock

Melt two-thirds of the butter, add the onion, cover, and cook slowly until soft but not coloured. Add the rice, sauter for a few minutes, then add seasoning, the saffron, and the stock. Bring to the boil, cover tightly, and put into a moderate oven for 20–25 minutes. Stir in lightly with a fork the remaining butter.

Meanwhile slice the aubergines slantwise and dégorger. Remove shell from lobster, cut the tail meat into thick scallops, and leave the meat from the claws whole. Melt the butter in a sauté or frying-pan, put in all the lobster meat and season highly. Heat sherry and flame; set aside. Fry aubergines in hot oil. Put the rice in the middle of a hot dish, pile the lobster on the top and pour over the juice from the pan. Arrange the aubergine round.

LOBSTER ARMORICAIN (HOT)

This is a classic dish from which Lobster Américain derives both its name and its appearance.

1 large uncooked lobster, 1¼–1¾ lb.	and water squeezed out, then roughly chopped
1½ tablespoons good oil	1 wineglass white wine
1 small glass brandy or dry sherry	1 large cup cooked vegetable mirepoix (beans, turnips, carrots)
2 oz. butter	
1 finely chopped small onion	1 wineglass stock, if necessary
1 clove of garlic, crushed	½ oz. flour
salt, pepper	1 teaspoon tomato purée
¾ lb. tomatoes, peeled, seeds	boiled rice

First kill lobster by putting the point of a knife through the head (see fish chapter, page 493), then cut up. Remove coral, sauter lobster in the hot oil 5–10 minutes. Flame with the brandy. Remove lobster from pan, add half the butter and the onion and garlic. Cook slowly. After 5 minutes add seasoning, tomato, and wine. Simmer 10 minutes. Add mirepoix, and stock if called for. Cream remaining butter with the coral, flour, and purée, add to pan off the fire and reboil. Add lobster, reheat, and dish with the boiled rice.

SPICED FISH

6 steaks or fillets of haddock or other white fish	½ oz. flour
oil	¾ pint vegetable stock
1 dessertspoon grated green ginger	1 teaspoon tomato purée
	coffee-cup coco-nut milk
4 shallots	coffee-cup cream
1 oz. butter	lemon juice
1 small teaspoon curry-powder or paste	seasoning
	chutney, poppadums, and boiled rice flavoured with a large teaspoon paprika
1 teaspoon each of turmeric and ground coriander	

Flour the fillets and fry quickly (or grill) until brown in hot oil. Lay in a deep dish and scatter over the ginger. Chop shallots, soften in butter, add curry and spices, fry a few moments, mix in the flour and fry again. Now add the stock and purée, simmer 20 minutes. Add the lemon juice and coco-nut milk, simmer another 7 minutes, then finish with the cream. Adjust the seasoning, spoon over the fish, and set in a moderate oven 20–30 minutes. Serve with chutney, poppadums, and boiled rice flavoured with paprika, the paprika having been cooked in a little melted butter and stirred into the rice with a fork. This dish is very good served hot or cold for supper.

TOURTE AU POISSON

1 batch of pâte à pâté (see page 842).

Filling

2 oz. boiled rice	a little beaten egg for binding
8–12 finely chopped spring onions	½ lb. fresh salmon, skinned and filleted
4 hard-boiled eggs	1 lemon
½ lb. minced raw hake or haddock (chicken, veal, or rabbit may also be used)	aspic jelly, or a little white wine and water mixed and stiffened with gelatine
salt, pepper, cayenne or Nepal pepper	

Make up the pastry and leave to rest for 1 hour. Line a deep flan ring; reserve the trimmings for the cover. (We usually bind two 6-inch flan rings together, one on top of the other, with fine string.) Mix the rice, onions, 2 finely chopped hard-boiled eggs, and the raw hake together, season highly and bind with a little beaten egg.

Place a little rice mixture at the bottom of the pastry case; put in the centre the salmon. Shape the remaining rice mixture into balls and arrange in the case with the remaining hard-boiled eggs, quartered. Place the finely sliced lemon over the top. Cover with pastry and decorate. Bake in a moderate oven for about 1–1½ hours. When cold fill up with aspic jelly.

Tourte au Poisson is best eaten cold.

The following is an excellent and unusual dish. It requires care and attention, particularly in the matter of the sauce.

COQUILLES ST JACQUES GRATINÉES DUXELLES

8 scallops	½ pint strong fish stock
a nut of butter	¼ pint white wine
a good pinch of paprika	cheese for dusting
	a little extra butter, melted

Duxelles

8 oz. mushroom stalks and peelings	grated rind and juice of 1 lemon
1 oz. butter	1 teaspoon finely chopped herbs
1 onion, finely chopped	1 tablespoon chopped parsley
2 shallots	salt and pepper

Sauce

2–3 egg yolks	salt and pepper
3 oz. butter	paprika
¼ pint strong fish stock from the scallops	2 or 3 tablespoons fish velouté (optional)
grated rind of 1 lemon, and the juice	

Have the scallops sent from the fishmonger freshly opened. Cut them from the shell, remove the beards and the coral. Wash scallops, beards, and coral in several waters, then drain well. Slice the scallops and put to cook with the beards and coral in the butter, paprika, stock, and white wine. Simmer gently 5–7 minutes. Draw aside.

Prepare the duxelles by chopping the mushrooms finely and cooking with the butter, onion, and shallots. After 4 minutes add rind and juice of lemon, herbs, parsley, and seasoning. Continue to cook until the duxelles is firm but moist. Set aside.

Prepare the sauce by beating the yolks well with a nut of the butter; add the fish stock strained through muslin, thicken over gentle heat, adding the rest of the butter gradually piece by piece. Add the rind and juice of the lemon and the seasoning. Strain. The fish velouté may be added here to help bind the sauce.

Line the bottom of each deep shell with a small quantity of duxelles. Three parts fill with some of the sauce and cover with the remaining duxelles. Arrange on each the slices of scallop, coat with the rest of the sauce. Set the coral upright in the centre of each scallop, dust with cheese and sprinkle with melted butter and brown quickly under the grill.

N.B.   The beards are not used but are included for flavouring.

MEAT DISHES

R. H. has made the following note on hot-pot to precede the recipe for a particularly good example of this essentially English dish.

'A hot-pot is always served in the dish in which it is cooked, and at one time special dishes were made. (We had a white-glazed hot-pot with HOT-POT written on it in black.) They have no lids, I imagine so that the potatoes can form a really crisp crust. Some recipes say the meat should be browned in dripping before being put into the pot, but I have always understood that in the traditional one the meat is not browned. My mother tells of shooting parties in Lancashire where the feature of the lunch was an enormous hot-pot "like a glorified Irish stew." Oysters are an important part of the hot-pot.'

LANCASHIRE HOT-POT

2 lb. lamb chops or best end neck of mutton	2 lb. potatoes
2 onions or 1 Spanish onion	about ½ pint good gravy or rich stock
4 oz. mushrooms	½ oz. oiled butter
2 kidneys	salt, pepper
8–12 oysters	

Trim chops or divide neck into neat cutlets, removing most of the fat. Use any bone or trimmings from the neck for stock. Slice the onions thinly, quarter the mushrooms or, if buttons, leave whole. Slice each kidney into four. Beard the oysters, reserving any liquor. Slice potatoes.

Take a hot-pot or deep baking-dish, brush out lightly with some of the oiled butter. Put a thick layer of potatoes on the bottom, arrange the chops on this, slightly overlapping one another, with a mushroom or two, a slice of kidney, and an oyster on each. Put the remainder of the oysters, mushroom, and kidney in the centre of the pot, scatter over the onion with plenty of seasoning. Add the rest of the potatoes, seeing that the last layer is neatly arranged. Pour in at the side of the dish about $\frac{1}{4}$ pint of the gravy to include the oyster liquor, and brush the potatoes well with the oiled butter. Cover with a piece of buttered paper, set in a moderate oven and cook for 2–2$\frac{1}{2}$ hours. A little more than half an hour before it is ready, make sure that the hot-pot is moist enough, adding more gravy if necessary, also remove the paper to allow the potatoes to brown well before serving.

MUTTON PIES

These are small pies which were favourites for picnics and point-to-point lunches. Freshly made and wrapped hot in a napkin, they were much in demand. The pastry was usually flaky, though at times they were made with a hot-water crust as for pork pies.

1 lb. lean mutton, preferably a piece from the leg	1 tablespoon chopped onion
a bouquet garni	1 tablespoon diced potato
an onion stuck with a clove	salt, pepper
a few peppercorns	flaky pastry made with 8 oz. flour
2 tablespoons diced carrot	egg-wash

Put the mutton into a stew-pan with the bouquet, the onion stuck with a clove, salt, and the peppercorns. Barely cover with cold water, bring to the boil, skim, and simmer until just tender. Allow to cool in the liquor. Put the carrot and onion into a pan. Strain in enough of the stock to cover, simmer 5 minutes, then add the potato. Continue until the vegetables are just cooked. Drain, keeping the stock, and turn into a bowl. Dice the mutton and add, with a little stock to moisten and seasoning. Have ready the pastry, divide in half, roll out one half and line into patty tins. Fill with the meat mixture, which should be cold. Roll out the remaining pastry, stamp out into rounds, and cover the pies, first wetting the edge of the pastry. Press round, decorate, and brush with the egg-wash.

Bake in a hot oven 20–30 minutes. Remove from the tins and cool slightly before packing.

In the section of this chapter dealing with parties, mention is made of a table labelled '1852 Plenty.' A highly decorative piece, suitable to the period, was needed. A boar's head was decided upon, and although a pig's head had to be used the result was fine. Interest in the decorative aspect of the dish was soon replaced by approval of the filling, which was excellent.

BOAR'S HEAD

a good pig's head	pepper, and Jamaica pepper
a brine bath (or the pig's head	(allspice)
may be salted by the butcher	1½ lb. lean veal or pork minced
for the time given in the	1½ lb. minced pork or sausage-
recipe, in which case bone	meat
out the head afterwards)	1 lb. liver, minced
4 young, tender rabbits	½ oz. pistachio nuts, blanched
1 gill sherry	and shredded
4 shallots, finely chopped	1 small truffle, shredded
2–3 bay-leaves, crushed	vegetables and bouquet garni
salt, freshly ground black	for stock

Wash the head thoroughly and split open from the back forwards, being careful to avoid damaging the forehead or snout. Remove the brain and tongue and bone out the head. Shape ears to points and immerse the head and tongue in a brine bath for 36–48 hours. Then lift out the tongue, put into cold water, bring to the boil, and simmer an hour or more or until it can be skinned. Meanwhile take out the head, rinse, and dry thoroughly. Put on one side. Using a sharp knife lift off the fillets from the back of the rabbits and strip the rest of the meat from the bones. Put the fillets in a dish with the sherry, shallots, bay-leaves, salt, and pepper. Marinade for some hours. Mince the rest of the rabbit meat, add to the minced veal, pork, and liver. Take up the tongue, plunge into cold water, then skin. Set aside to cool completely. Work the minced meats together, add the marinade (first removing the bay-leaves) with more seasoning if necessary. Cut the tongue into strips the same size as the fillets.

Lay the head on a board, spread the farce over it, and on this lay long-ways at regular intervals the rabbit fillets and tongue. Scatter over the pistachio nuts and truffle, then shape up the farce and head. Sew up securely, wrap up in a piece of muslin, binding the snout with tape and shaping the whole in its original form. Put into a large pan with the bones (or the stock made from the bones). Cover with water and vegetables and a bouquet garni to flavour. Bring to the boil and simmer 3–4 hours. Lift up, tighten the cloth, and press and hold securely with boards and weights to keep the shape. Leave until the next day. Remove cloth, glaze, and decorate.

Traditionally, in place of glaze the boar's head is finished with a mixture of lard and soot spread or rubbed on the skin in order to give it the correct grey-black colour. This is, of course, not edible, but is trimmed off a little at a time by the carver before slicing the head.

The decoration of the head is also traditional. Hard-boiled egg white and a small round of truffle are used for the eyes, the white tinged with a little carmine. The tusks can be represented by celery, and a bright flower should be stuck behind the ear. The head is raised up on a 'socle' of cooked rice (not of course to be eaten) covered with silver paper or with lard coloured green. It is surrounded with a wreath of bay or rosemary.

Nowadays the head is usually glazed with a meat glaze, though the decoration remains the same. This dish appears only at Christmas time on the cold table.

In another party menu the following Cornets de Jambon are mentioned. This is a first-class, popular dish for the cold table, called in France Jambon Roulé. It may be either simple or elaborate. The cornets contain a mousse of foie gras, and in the following recipe are made into a proper cold entrée.

CORNETS DE JAMBON

Allow a 1-oz. slice of ham, cut on a bacon slicer, for each cornet

Filling for 12 cornets

4 oz. pâté	1 tablespoon sherry
¼ pint béchamel sauce, made with 1 oz. each of butter and flour	1 tablespoon partially whipped cream
1 level teaspoon French mustard	seasoning

Garnish

sliced truffle, *or*	aspic jelly
button or sliced mushrooms, cooked in a little water and lemon juice, cooled, and drained	watercress

Curl each slice of ham into a cornet shape and slide into a cornet mould, or a cornet made of double thickness grease-proof paper or single cartridge-paper, then trim with scissors. Set cornets upright by sticking the points into holes made in a cardboard egg tray.

Mince the ham trimmings, avoiding most of the fat. Pound the pâté with the cold béchamel, the minced trimmings of ham, the mustard, and the sherry. When soft and creamy add the cream. Adjust seasoning.

Fill into a bag with a large plain pipe and pipe into each cornet. Press a mushroom (or a slice of truffle) on each cornet and set aside.

Melt a small quantity of the aspic and stir on ice until on the point of setting. Coat the top of each cornet with this. Leave to set.

Chop remaining aspic. Arrange in a semicircle on the serving dish; with the help of a small knife remove the cornets from the moulds and arrange on the aspic. Garnish the dish with watercress. Serve a tomato salad and a potato vinaigrette with it.

N.B. The aspic may be dispensed with and the cornets dished on shredded lettuce or on a vegetable salad. But the general effect is not so good.

The next recipe is for an extremely good entrée which may also be made with escalopes de veau in place of lamb:

CÔTELETTES D'AGNEAU NELSON

2 lb. best end of neck of lamb, chined only	2 oz. butter grated Parmesan cheese

Soubise purée

½ lb. onions	seasoning
1 oz. rice	a good nut of butter
½ tea-cup stock	

Duxelles

8 large mushrooms, with the trimmings and stalks	½ oz. butter cheese and a little extra melted butter
1 shallot, finely chopped	
sauce madère (see below)	

Make the soubise: chop the onions, blanch, drain, and simmer or cook in the oven with the rice and stock in a covered pan until both onions and rice are tender. Rub all through a fine sieve, season well, and add the butter.

Divide the meat into cutlets, trim, and cook the cutlets on one side only, in half the butter made hot. Drain and spread the soubise on the uncooked side. Lay the cutlets in a sauté pan or roasting-tin, dust with Parmesan, and baste well with the rest of the butter, melted. Continue cooking in the oven for 10–15 minutes.

Duxelles. Wash the stalks and peelings of the mushrooms in salted water and squeeze dry. Melt the butter, add the shallot, cover and cook until soft, add the chopped mushroom trimmings and continue cooking until all the butter is absorbed. Season. Fill into the mushrooms, lay in a buttered dish or tin, sprinkle over with the cheese and a little melted butter. Cook in a hot oven 5 minutes, then finish under the grill.

Dishing. Arrange *en couronne* with a little of the sauce madère on the dish and surround with the grilled mushrooms. Serve the remaining sauce separately.

Sauce madère

½ oz. dripping or butter	½ pint good stock
3 shallots, finely chopped	salt and pepper
1 rasher of bacon, finely chopped	1 teaspoon chopped mixed herbs
1 level dessertspoon flour	
small teaspoon tomato purée	1 sherry glass Madeira or sherry
a few mushroom peelings	

Heat the dripping in a small saucepan, add the shallots and bacon and cook slowly to a golden brown. Add the flour and allow to colour slowly. Draw aside, add the purée, peelings, stock, and seasoning, bring to the boil. Simmer 15 minutes, add the herbs, adjust seasoning, and boil for another 5 minutes. Strain. Reduce sherry in a saucepan to half. Add to the sauce, reboil, and simmer another 2–3 minutes or until syrupy.

Bœuf Braisé Frankfurt is an excellent and popular dish. This is a good way of cooking a whole piece of fillet of beef.

BŒUF BRAISÉ FRANKFURT

1–1½ lb. beef fillet

Marinade

1 sliced onion
1 clove of garlic, crushed
1 bay-leaf

2–3 parsley stalks
¼ gill each of red wine and sherry

1 oz. butter
seasoning
¼ lb. good spinach, blanched
3–4 thin rashers of bacon
2 onions, finely sliced
2 carrots, finely sliced
a few mushroom stalks and peelings

1 level dessertspoon flour
1 level teaspoon tomato purée
1½ gills stock
a strip of lemon rind
1 teaspoon red-currant jelly
a bouquet garni

Garnish

tomato coulis (see below)   carrots Vichy (see page 193)

Trim the meat. Put into a pie dish and add the marinade. Leave for an hour or longer, turning occasionally. Take up and drain well. Brown all over in the butter, drain the marinade, heat and flame the meat with it. Remove the meat, season, and cover with the blanched spinach leaves. Cover again with the bacon rashers and tie with cotton.

Add to the pan the onions, carrots, and mushroom peelings. Cook until turning colour. Stir in the flour and replace the beef. Add the purée, stock, lemon rind, jelly, and bouquet. Season, bring to the boil, cover tightly, and braise in the oven 45 minutes to 1 hour. Take up, carefully remove the cotton and bacon, and cut the beef in slices. Have ready the coulis and put it down the centre of a serving dish. Lay the beef on top, boil up the gravy and strain over. Arrange the carrots at each end of the dish.

Tomato coulis

6–8 tomatoes
salt
freshly ground black pepper

a little crushed gárlic or chives
½ oz. butter

Peel the tomatoes, cut in thick slices. Remove the pips. Put the seasoning and garlic into a frying-pan with the butter. Melt over a slow fire, then add the tomatoes. Cook quickly for a few minutes. Adjust seasoning and use.

N.B. When tomatoes are poor in flavour a little purée may be added.

If fillet is unobtainable a piece of good braising beef such as top rump or topside may be substituted, but with a less succulent result.

LANGUES D'AGNEAUX BRAISÉES AUX RAISINS

4–6 lambs' tongues	a bouquet garni
1 onion	salt
1 carrot	peppercorns

For braising

Mirepoix:	2 onions, diced	$\frac{1}{2}$–$\frac{3}{4}$ pint good stock
	2 carrots, diced	a bouquet garni
	1 small turnip, diced	2–3 rashers of bacon

Sauce brune

$\frac{3}{4}$ oz. butter or dripping	a few mushroom peelings
2 shallots	$\frac{3}{4}$ oz. flour
1 carrot	1 small teaspoon tomato purée
1 stick of celery	1 pint stock
1 small piece of turnip, finely diced	a bouquet garni
	1 glass sherry

Garnish

$\frac{1}{4}$ lb. peeled white grapes	potato purée flavoured delicately with nutmeg or mace
1–1$\frac{1}{2}$ oz. shredded almonds	

Blanch and refresh tongues. Then put to stew with the sliced vegetables, bouquet, salt, and peppercorns for about 1$\frac{1}{4}$ hours. Plunge into cold water, skin. Have ready the mirepoix. Put the bacon on the bottom of a casserole, add mirepoix, cover and cook gently 6–7 minutes. Moisten with the stock, add a fresh bouquet, cover and braise gently for half an hour.

Meanwhile prepare the sauce. Brown vegetables in the butter or dripping, add flour and colour also. Add chopped mushroom peelings, purée, and stock. Add bouquet and simmer for 35–40 minutes. Strain, return to rinsed pan. Reduce sherry and add. Continue simmering until syrupy in consistency. Then add the grapes and almonds. Have ready the potato purée, arrange down the serving dish, set the tongues on the top and spoon over the sauce.

ROGNONS D'AGNEAU MARSALA

6 lambs' kidneys	6 thin rashers of bacon
4 tablespoons fresh crumbs	beaten egg
1 tablespoon freshly chopped herbs	a nut of butter for each kidney
1 oz. butter or margarine	Marsala or sherry and good stock
1 onion, finely chopped and blanched	cream
salt, pepper	croustades

Remove the skins from the kidneys, split, but do not separate the two halves. Prepare a good farce with the crumbs, herbs, butter, and onion. Season well and mix with a little beaten egg to bind.

Fill the kidneys with this mixture, wrap each in a rasher of bacon and secure with a cocktail stick.   Place in a buttered baking-tin in a very hot oven with a nut of butter on each kidney: 5–7 minutes should be sufficient for lambs' kidneys.   Remove from the oven and arrange in a serving dish. Déglacer the pan with a little Marsala or sherry and good stock.   Thicken the jus with a spoonful or two of fresh thick cream, arrange each kidney on a croustade and pour over the jus.

POULTRY AND GAME

The flavour of certain herbs delicately imparted to chicken dishes may be excellent.   This has to be done with discretion.   Tarragon in association with chicken is generally accepted; the following dish is flavoured with rosemary.   This is a pungent herb, but used with care will lend aroma to the sauce.

POULET ROMARIN

2–3 sprigs of rosemary	3 mushrooms, thinly sliced
1 roasting chicken	4 tomatoes
1½ oz. butter (approx.)	1 teaspoon each of flour and
¼ pint giblet or chicken stock	butter
or water	extra stock or water
1 onion, thinly sliced	

Put the rosemary inside the chicken with a good nut of butter.   Spread well with the rest of the butter.   Put the stock or water into the roasting-tin, cover the chicken with paper, and roast, basting and turning frequently, for about 1 hour.   Remove from the roasting-tin, carve, and keep hot. Skim off a little of the fat from the pan into a saucepan, add the onion, mushrooms, and the chicken liver, diced.   Sauter for 5–6 minutes.   Add the tomatoes, skinned and cut in four, with the pips removed.   Work the flour and butter together (beurre manié).   Strain liquor from the chicken and add stock or water to make up to a good ½-pint.   Add the beurre manié, then simmer gently.   Spoon over the chicken.

The following is a delicious party dish of cold chicken:

CHICKEN WITH CHERRIES AND TARRAGON

roasting chickens	water and a little wine (optional)
2–3 sprigs of tarragon for each	lettuce
bird	toasted walnuts
¼ oz. butter	

Sauce

vinaigrette dressing	cream
gravy from the roasting-pan,	stoned cherries
strained and well skimmed	tarragon leaves

Put the tarragon and a nut of butter inside each bird.   Spread the birds with butter, and roast in the French fashion with water (or wine and water) in the pan. When cooked allow to cool. Carve neatly, arrange the pieces in a nest of crisp lettuce leaves and pour over the sauce.

Sauce. To a vinaigrette dressing add the gravy from the roasting-pan, and cream to taste. Add to this some stoned cherries and a few chopped leaves of tarragon. Spoon the sauce carefully over the chicken and scatter toasted walnuts over the surface.

POULET AUX QUATRE HERBES

1 small chicken	1 glass red wine
2 young, tender bay-leaves	1 tablespoon oil
4 leaves of fresh sage	1 oz. butter
6 sprigs of thyme	1 wineglass light stock
6 sprigs of tarragon	

Chop the bay-leaves finely and pound with half the herbs in a mortar. Pour the wine over and leave the herbs to macerate for an hour or two. Stuff the bird with remaining herbs. Make the butter and oil hot in a heated pan and brown the bird lightly all over. Pour the wine and the herbs into the pan, add the stock, and simmer the bird gently for 30–35 minutes. When it is quite tender lift it on to a hot dish, strain the liquor, reduce a little if necessary, and pour it round the bird or into a sauce-boat.

The almond sauce served with the following roast chicken is good also with turkey or guinea-fowl.

POULET RÔTI AUX AMANDES

1 roasting fowl	½ pint good chicken stock
2 oz. butter	salt
a sprig of tarragon	a pinch of sugar
¼ pint stock	ground mace
2 oz. blanched almonds	2 tablespoons cream
scant ½ oz. flour	

Garnish

2 red and 2 green peppers, sliced and sautéd in butter

Put ½ oz. of the butter and the tarragon inside the bird, rub another ounce over the bird, cover with paper, set in a roasting-tin with the stock, and cook in a moderate oven. Baste frequently and turn. After 20 minutes remove the paper and continue cooking until the bird is well browned, about 1 hour. Meanwhile chop the almonds as finely as possible, put into a frying-pan with the remaining ½ oz. butter, and cook slowly until pale golden brown. Blend in the flour, add chicken stock, season with salt, a pinch of sugar, and ground mace. Simmer for 5 minutes.

Carve the bird, arrange in a serving dish, add the cream to the sauce and spoon over. Garnish with the peppers.

Serve Pommes de Terre Château separately (see page 208).

In Poulet à la Mode de Kiev we have a delicacy for special occasions, and one which calls for skilful cooking. Though some part of the preparation may be done beforehand, the final cooking, i.e. the frying, must be done at the last minute.

The dish is rich and the accompanying sauce should be sharp, a demi-glace with a touch of sherry and lemon juice; or it may be served simply with quarters of lemon.

POULET A LA MODE DE KIEV

2 small plump chickens, *or*
1 large plump bird (capon type)
fresh butter
grated lemon rind and juice
salt
freshly ground black pepper
a pinch of ground mace

chopped parsley
seasoned flour
beaten egg
dried white breadcrumbs
watercress dipped in French
    dressing

Cut the flesh of breast and wing from the chicken in one piece. To do this keep the knife on the bone, but avoid cutting through the wing joint itself. Cut each piece through longways in half; if a large bird, get three pieces from each side. With a slightly damped heavy knife bat out each piece. Alternatively put each piece between waxed paper and beat flat with a rolling-pin. When very thin remove and set aside. Work butter on a plate, add the grated rind and enough lemon juice to sharpen, season well, add mace and parsley. Put into the refrigerator to harden. Cut into finger lengths. Put a piece on each slice of chicken, roll up, folding in the ends. Roll lightly in seasoned flour. Brush evenly with beaten egg, roll in the crumbs and allow to dry for an hour or two. Fry in deep fat until golden brown (allow 4–5 minutes). Drain and serve very hot with bouquets of watercress dipped into French dressing just before serving.

MANGO CHICKEN

1 roasting chicken
3 oz. butter
2 large onions
2 slices of tinned mango or 2–3
    peaches, peeled and sliced
nutmeg

1 lemon
½ pint stock or water
salt and freshly ground black
    pepper
½–1 gill cream

Pilaff

1–2 oz. onion
1 oz. butter
8 oz. rice
1 dessertspoon turmeric

paprika

1–1¼ pints chicken stock or
    water
salt and freshly ground black
    pepper
hard-boiled eggs for garnish

Joint the chicken neatly a few hours before cooking, so that the back and trimmings may be made into stock. Slice the onions finely. Fry the chicken slowly to a golden brown in half the butter. (It is important that butter and not margarine should be used.) Melt the rest of the butter in another stew-pan and fry the onions slowly. When turning colour add the mango or the peaches. Continue frying over quicker heat for a few more minutes. Join the chicken and onion mixtures together. Add a little grated nutmeg with 2 strips of pared lemon rind; then add the stock and seasoning. Cover the pan tightly and stew slowly (preferably in the oven) for about 1 hour.

Meanwhile prepare the pilaff. Chop the onion. Soften in the butter. Add the rice and fry with the turmeric. Pour on the stock, season well, bring to the boil, cover, and cook in the oven until the rice is tender and the stock absorbed.

When the chicken is very tender remove from the pan with the lemon rind. Boil up the sauce, adding the lemon juice to taste and adjusting the seasoning. Stir in the cream and boil rapidly to the right consistency. Dish the chicken, pour over the sauce, and serve the rice separately. Dust with paprika and garnish with hard-boiled eggs.

POULET SAUTÉ PARMESAN

1 young chicken (2½ lb.)	2 oz. Parmesan cheese
2 oz. butter	seasoning
scant ½ oz. flour	2 egg yolks
1½ gills top of milk or single cream	crumbs (dry white)
	fresh tarragon leaves

Joint the chicken, and sauter it for a good 20 minutes in about half the butter, then dust lightly with salt.

Melt the remaining butter in a saucepan, add the flour, cook for a minute or two without letting it brown, then pour in the milk. Stir very well over a slow fire and allow it to come just to boiling-point. Add ½ oz. of the cheese and the seasoning. Pour a little of this on to the egg yolks, return to the pan and thicken over fire without boiling.

Take a fireproof dish, put in half the cheese on the bottom, arrange chicken on this, mask with the sauce, mix the remaining cheese with the same quantity of crumbs, sprinkle over the chicken, and set in a hot oven for 5–7 minutes to brown. Scatter over tarragon leaves and serve at once. N.B. Any butter, etc., from the sauté pan should be poured over the chicken before it is masked with the sauce.

The pan may also be déglacéd with a spoonful or two of dry white wine. If cream is used add only a teaspoon of flour.

The following dish should be set in a clear glass bowl. It calls for tender chicken, and aspic flavoured with white wine and lemon juice. In the centre are 'truffles' of foie gras, rolled in real chopped truffle.

CHARTREUSE DE VOLAILLE CHAMBÉRY

1 medium-sized chicken or 2 young chickens	2 whites of egg
1 onion	2 oz. gelatine
1 carrot	1 dessertspoon lemon juice
a bouquet garni, including 1 stick of celery	½ gill sherry
3–4 peppercorns	4 oz. pâté de foie gras
1 glass white wine	1½ oz. butter
	1 truffle

Put the chicken into a pan with the vegetables, bouquet, peppercorns, and white wine. Barely cover with water and simmer gently 50 minutes to 1 hour according to size. Cool in the liquor, then lift out the bird, drain well, and leave until quite cold. Strain the stock, remove all grease and measure 1 quart. Whip whites to a froth, add to stock with the gelatine and lemon juice. Whisk over moderate heat until boiling. Add sherry. Boil up three times, draw aside to settle, and strain through a thick cloth or jelly-bag previously scalded (see directions for making aspic, page 735). Set aside to cool. Work the pâté and butter together. Chop truffle. Shape the pâté mixture into small balls, roll in the truffle. Set till firm in the refrigerator. Take a glass bowl, carve the meat off the chicken, arrange round the sides of the bowl, put the 'truffles' in the middle, and set the whole with the cool aspic. When firm fill up the bowl with the aspic, and garnish round the edge with chopped jelly. Chill slightly before serving.

Lemon fritters are given as an accompaniment to the next dish. They are also excellent with roast chicken and with duck.

POUSSINS SAUTÉS AU CITRON

2 poussins	a piece of glaze the size of a
1½ oz. butter	walnut
salt, pepper	lemon fritters (see below)
1 glass white wine	new potatoes tossed in butter
¼ pint strong chicken stock	chopped parsley

Split the poussins. Mèlt the butter in a sauté pan, put in the birds and allow to brown slowly on both sides. Then season well, add the wine and stock, cover and simmer a further 15 minutes. Dish the birds, add the glaze to the liquor in the pan, reduce and pour over the chicken. Garnish with lemon fritters, potatoes, and parsley.

Lemon fritters

Boil 1–2 lemons in lightly salted water with a pinch of baking-soda for 30–40 minutes. Drain them well and cut into quarters lengthwise. Cut away the white pith from the edge of the quarters, remove any pips and cut each again in half.

Dip each piece into fritter batter and drop at once into smoking hot fat. Fry until a deep golden brown, drain well and serve very hot.

The slices of lemon may be marinaded in French dressing before being dipped in batter. If this is done care should be taken to drain the pieces well on muslin after marinading, otherwise the dressing discolours the batter and is liable to get into the fat.

The following dish is of cold roast duck served with a lemon compôte. The acidity of lemons is an excellent offset to so rich a bird. The same idea may be applied to goose, pork, or any rich meat.

COLD DUCK WITH LEMON COMPÔTE

1 plump duckling	1–2 oz. butter
2 sprays of rosemary	salt and freshly ground pepper

Stuffing

liver of the duck	3 tablespoons chopped cooked
2 chickens' livers	mushrooms
1 chopped shallot	2 tablespoons minced bacon
1 tablespoon chopped parsley	1 breakfast-cup fresh crumbs
	1 beaten egg
watercress lightly dipped in	small new potatoes tossed in
French dressing	butter (or a potato vinai-
lemon compôte (see below)	grette)
	chopped parsley

Prepare stuffing by dicing the livers and mixing with the rest of the ingredients. Season well and bind with the egg. Fill into the bird. Spread the butter over the breast and legs of the bird. Season lightly with salt and pepper. Cover with paper, set in roasting-tin with the rosemary. Roast in a moderate oven 50 minutes to 1 hour, basting every 15 minutes. When well cooked, which in this case means cooked *à point*—that is to say delicately pink inside, and not brown—remove and cool. When quite cold carve and arrange on a dish with the stuffing. Garnish with bouquets of watercress. Serve with it a lemon compôte, potatoes, and parsley.

Lemon compôte

4–6 fine thin-skinned ripe	2½ oz. sugar
lemons	¾ gill water
3–4 sprays of tarragon	

Pare the rind from 1 lemon. Cut it into fine shreds. Blanch it for 5 minutes, drain. Slice the peel and white pith from the lemons, using a thin sharp knife. Cut the flesh across in thin rounds, removing all pips. Lay in a shallow dish or *compôtier*. Dip the tarragon sprays into boiling water. Pick off the leaves and scatter over the lemons. Boil the sugar and water together 2–3 minutes, or until a thick syrup. Cool slightly and pour over the lemons. Chill.

CANETON SAUVAGE A LA FENOUIL

1 wild duck	3 oranges
1 gill stock	½ oz. butter
1 head of Florence fennel	

Sauce

mirepoix: 1 oz. each of carrot,	1 tablespoon chopped mush-
onion, and shallot	room stalks and peelings
1 oz. butter or good dripping	½ teaspoon tomato purée
½ oz. flour	1 gill red wine
¾–1 pint stock	seasoning
a bouquet garni	
croûtes of fried bread	purée of potatoes lightly flav-
	oured with grated orange
	rind

Set the duck in a roasting-tin with the stock, reserving the liver; cover the breast with a rasher of bacon or with buttered paper and cook in a moderate oven 20–25 minutes according to size. The bird should still be *saignant*. Cook liver in the fat for the last few minutes, and pound it till smooth.

Sauce. Brown the mirepoix in the butter, add the flour and cook to a good russet brown. Pour on the stock, stir until boiling, add the herbs, mushroom, and tomato purée and simmer 30–40 minutes. Strain. Add the red wine, adjust the seasoning, and reduce until syrupy.

Joint the duck and leave in the hot sauce to absorb the flavour. Slice the fennel and oranges thinly and sauter quickly in a little butter, dusting with sugar before placing in the serving dish. Arrange the duck on this and spoon over the sauce. Garnish with croûtes of fried bread spread with the pounded liver. Serve with a purée of potatoes.

FAISAN AUX ORANGES

This is a *pièce froide* for the cold table, a change from roast pheasant. The base of purée of chestnuts and the red wine in the dressing are both good touches, and the garnish is crisp and appropriate.

1 pheasant	seasoning
butter	3 good oranges
1 gill sherry	1 gill French dressing
a bouquet garni	1 shallot, finely chopped
1¼ lb. chestnuts, weighed when peeled	½ gill red wine, flamed and reduced
1–2 tablespoons strong stock	curled celery and corn salad for garnish
1–2 tablespoons partially whipped cream	

Cook the pheasant in a covered pan with a little butter, the sherry, and the bouquet. Cool. Cook the chestnuts in the stock, drain and sieve, beat to a purée, season, and add cream. Spread this purée down the middle of the serving dish, carve pheasant and lay on top. Peel and slice oranges and arrange round. Add any juice from the pan to the French dressing with the shallot and red wine. Mix thoroughly. Spoon over the dish and garnish with celery and corn salad.

PARTRIDGES COOKED IN VINE LEAVES (COLD)

plump partridges	watercress or curled endive salad
3 vine leaves for each bird	
larding or streaky bacon	

Clean and wipe the birds well and then salt them well inside and out. Wrap each bird in vine leaves and roll up in the bacon. Tie securely with strong thread. Put into boiling unsalted water, simmer 35 minutes after boiling-point is resumed. Then plunge into ice-cold water; when cold remove, and untie coverings. Serve on a watercress or curled endive salad.

The birds may be accompanied by a garlic-flavoured French dressing, and by potatoes in their jackets.

If the long list of ingredients for the following pigeon dish discourages you, do not yield and pass it by. The list is long, but the dish is neither extravagant nor troublesome to prepare, and it is one of the very best ways of preparing pigeon. It has an exceptionally delicious and unusual flavour, making it acceptable to many who do not take particular pleasure in eating pigeons. For those allergic to this bird, this recipe may with advantage be applied to other fowl.

SPICED PIGEON AND RICE

3 good pigeons
2 cloves of garlic
2 teaspoons each of fennel seed and coriander
1 thick slice of onion
1 small piece of bruised ginger root
3 pints water

Tie the above spices, the ginger, and the onion in a piece of muslin, put into a pan with the pigeons and water. Simmer until pigeons are tender, then remove pigeons and continue to boil down the liquid until about 1½ pints remain.

Meanwhile prepare the following:

3 small onions, chopped
1½ oz. butter
1 clove of garlic, crushed with salt
1 dessertspoon chopped glacé ginger
a pinch of ground cloves
3 cardamon seeds, the shells cracked and the contents lightly bruised
1 teaspoonful cumin seed
4 oz. sugar
½ cup water
salt and Nepal pepper
½ lb. rice
½ oz. freshly grated coco-nut
2 oz. stoned raisins
2 oz. shredded almonds

Cook onions in butter until golden brown, then add garlic, ginger, spices, and 1 cup of the stock from the pigeons. Simmer for a few minutes. Now make a thick syrup of the sugar and the water. Pour into a casserole with the onion mixture, seasoning, rice, and coco-nut. Split the pigeons, trim away the backbone with the scissors and add the rest to the casserole. Cover with the remaining stock and a little water (about 1¾ pints in all). Put on the lid and simmer until the rice is tender, or cook in a slow oven. Stir in the raisins just before cooking is completed, and toast the almonds in the oven until a light brown. Serve in the casserole, scattering over the almonds just before sending to the table.

The next recipe is a good rabbit dish for luncheon:

LAPIN A LA BRESSANE

1 good rabbit, soaked for an hour or two in salt and water with a dash of vinegar
2 oz. butter or margarine
3 oz. streaky bacon cut into lardons and well blanched
1 dessertspoon flour
1 good tablespoon white wine vinegar
2 large onions, thinly sliced
1–2 cloves of garlic, crushed
a bouquet garni
salt, pepper, nutmeg
1 egg yolk
¾ gill single cream

Joint rabbit and dry the pieces thoroughly. Brown well in the butter with the lardons of bacon, dust with the flour, and moisten with a little water and the vinegar. Add the onions, garlic, bouquet, and seasoning. Cover and cook gently until the rabbit is tender. Draw aside, remove bouquet, dish the rabbit, and thicken the sauce with the yolk and cream, stirring well. Spoon over the rabbit and serve very hot. The sauce may be strained if wished.

The rabbit used here should be a domestic one. These may be bought under the name of Ostend rabbits. The flesh is exceptionally white and very tender, and does not require the long soaking applied to wild rabbits.

MIXED GAME IN ASPIC

This is a dish to make only for a large party or to divide into several portions, set in earthenware dishes as Christmas presents. It sounds lavish, but where game is available it is a practical dish, as a mixture of all sorts is suitable. The proportions given may be altered, diminished, or reproportioned; any one bird may be omitted, but the hare is important to give richness.

2 pheasants	2 partridges (old ones will
1 chicken (boiling fowl)	serve)
2 pigeons	1 hare
1 wild duck	1 rabbit

Jellied stock

1 large onion stuck with 2 cloves	seasoning
1 carrot	water and stock from the cooking
a bouquet garni	large glass port
2 bay-leaves	gelatine if required
thin strip of lemon rind	

Force-meat balls

1 lb. sausage-meat	2 tablespoons breadcrumbs
1 large egg white	grated lemon rind
4 teaspoons chopped parsley	

1 lb. ham, cut in shreds	pickled walnuts
pistachio nuts	salt, freshly ground pepper,
1 tin of truffles	and cayenne

Cut off the heads and feet from the birds and put them aside with the giblets. Put the birds, hare, and rabbit, whole, into a large stew-pan, cover with stock or water. Cook gently until so tender that the flesh leaves the bones easily. As the smaller birds are cooked lift them out. When all are cooked skin and bone the birds, and put aside the skin and bones. Put all the bones, skin, and giblets from the birds into a pan with the onion, carrot, bouquet, bay-leaves, lemon rind, and seasoning. Cover with the stock from the birds, etc., adding enough water to cover well the stock ingredients.   Cover, bring to the boil, and simmer for an hour or two, until well reduced.

Meanwhile prepare the remaining ingredients.   Make up the force-meat, seasoning well.   Make into marbles and fry lightly.   Blanch and split the nuts, slice the truffles and pickled walnuts.   Arrange in a suitable dish or dishes (game-pie dish or terrine) first a layer of mixed meats, game, force-meat balls, and ham, then a sprinkling of nuts, truffles, and seasoning.   Continue in layers until the dish or dishes is/are full.

When the stock is ready strain it, skim, allow to cool, and skim again. Add the port and adjust the seasoning.   It should set to a perfect jelly; to test this put a spoonful in a saucer in the ice-box.   If it does not set firmly a small proportion of gelatine must be added ($\frac{1}{4}$ oz. to a pint of liquid).   Dissolve this in a little warm water.   When the stock is on the point of setting, not before, pour it into the dish or dishes.   If any stock is left over allow it to set on a plate, chop, and put on top of each dish.

Blanched tarragon leaves are a good garnish, or a bay-leaf may be laid on top of each dish and set with a spot of liquid jelly.

A few of the spiced cherries on page 1104 may be used with the nuts in the layers.

CURRIES AND DISHES FLAVOURED WITH CURRY

One would not venture to serve, to a large number of guests of varying and unknown tastes, a curry dish in the generally accepted sense of this term.   Because it was difficult to draw a line of differentiation between what should and should not come within the category, we decided to include as curries all dishes in which curry-powder or paste formed an ingredient.   I doubt whether many of the three hundred odd guests at the coronation luncheon detected this ingredient in a chicken dish which was distinguished mainly by a delicate and nut-like flavour in the sauce.

CORONATION CHICKEN (COLD) (FOR 6–8)

2 young roasting chickens	salt
water and a little wine to cover	3–4 peppercorns
carrot	cream of curry sauce (see page
a bouquet garni	1013)

Poach the chickens, with carrot, bouquet, salt, and peppercorns, in water and a little wine, enough barely to cover, for about 40 minutes or until tender.   Allow to cool in the liquid.   Joint the birds, remove the bones with care.   Prepare the sauce given below.   Mix the chicken and the sauce together, arrange on a dish, coat with the extra sauce.

For convenience in serving on the occasion mentioned, the chicken was arranged at one end of an oblong dish, and a rice salad as given below was arranged at the other.

Cream of curry sauce

1 tablespoon oil
2 oz. onion, finely chopped
1 dessertspoon curry-powder
1 good teaspoon tomato purée
1 wineglass red wine
¾ wineglass water
a bay-leaf
salt, sugar, a touch of pepper

a slice or two of lemon and
  a squeeze of lemon juice,
  possibly more
1–2 tablespoons apricot purée
¾ pint mayonnaise
2–3 tablespoons lightly whipped
  cream
a little extra whipped cream

Heat the oil, add onion, cook gently 3–4 minutes, add curry-powder. Cook again 1–2 minutes. Add purée, wine, water, and bay-leaf. Bring to boil, add salt, sugar to taste, pepper, and the lemon and lemon juice. Simmer with the pan uncovered 5–10 minutes.   Strain and cool.   Add by degrees to the mayonnaise with the apricot purée to taste.   Adjust seasoning, adding a little more lemon juice if necessary. Finish with the whipped cream. Take a small amount of sauce (enough to coat the chicken) and mix with a little extra cream and seasoning.

This is an admirable sauce to serve with iced lobster.

Rice salad

The rice salad which accompanied the chicken was of carefully cooked rice, cooked peas, diced raw cucumber, and finely chopped mixed herbs, all mixed in a well-seasoned French dressing.

The recipe for the next chicken curry is labelled in my notes as 'new and good.'   This is quite definitely curry, and its pepperiness may be adjusted by varying the length of time the peppers are allowed to remain in the sauce.   The sauce, applied in this recipe to a lightly roasted chicken, is good for other basic ingredients, e.g. shell-fish, eggs, vegetables.

The following dish may with advantage be prepared a day before it is required:

ALMOND CHICKEN CURRY

roasting chicken   sauce (see below)

Lightly roast a chicken, carve, and lay the pieces in a casserole.   Prepare the sauce.

Almond curry sauce

50 almonds
½ a fresh coco-nut, grated
½ cup tamarind
1 oz. butter
4 medium-sized onions
1 tablespoon turmeric
1 tablespoon coriander

1 teaspoon good curry-paste
  or powder
½ oz. flour
3–4 medium hot peppers
lemon juice and red-currant
  jelly, and a little sugar if
  necessary
½ cup rich milk or cream

Blanch and grind, or pound, the almonds.   Steep the coco-nut in a cup of boiling water and do the same with the tamarind.   Melt butter, add sliced onions, and cook slowly until turning colour. Add turmeric and coriander, the curry-paste and almonds, fry 4–5 minutes. Add flour, the strained water from the coco-nut and tamarind (made up to 1 pint with water, if necessary), and the peppers. Bring to the boil and simmer for 20 minutes; now add the lemon juice and jelly to taste, with a little sugar if necessary. Finish with the milk or cream. Add this sauce to the chicken. Cover and continue cooking on a slow heat for another 40 minutes. Serve or keep to the next day, and unless a very hot curry is wanted remove the peppers after the final cooking.

The next two curries have fruit as a basic ingredient. Both are spicy rather than hot, and both are refreshing dishes. The first may be used as a first course or as an accompaniment to a more substantial curry. The second, accompanied by rice, makes a good light luncheon dish.

FRUIT CURRY

cherries, apricots, pears, peaches, bananas, mangoes (tinned, optional)
medium syrup (see Fruit Compôtes, page 903)
2 oz. butter
6 oz. onions
1 dessertspoon flour
1 tablespoon green ginger grated
1 teaspoon coriander, crushed
1 teaspoon black pepper
1 dessertspoon curry-powder
1 pint chicken or vegetable stock
juice of 1 lemon
1 heaped tablespoon coco-nut soaked in a coffee-cup of boiling water for at least 10 minutes and strained
1 coffee-cup cream

Poach fruit gently in a medium syrup. Melt butter, add chopped onions. Cook gently 4–5 minutes, add the dry ingredients, cook again 4–5 minutes. Add stock and simmer 30 minutes. Add drained fruit, lemon juice, coco-nut milk, and cream. Reheat without boiling. Serve either very hot or iced.

BANANA AND MELON CURRY WINKFIELD

Curry sauce

3 oz. butter
12 spring onions or 2 shallots, sliced
1 dessertspoon curry-powder
¾ oz. flour
a bouquet garni
1 twist of thinly peeled lemon rind
1 teaspoon curry-paste
¼ pint stock; vegetable water, or bean or potato water
seasoning
1 heaped teaspoon red-currant or crab-apple jelly
1 heaped tablespoon desiccated coco-nut or fresh almonds ground up or ground almonds (the first is better). If fresh coco-nut can be used it is of course better, and for this take 3 tablespoons
1 gill boiling water
a squeeze of lemon juice

Curry

6 medium-sized bananas or 5 large ones. The big, rather solid plantains are excellent for this dish

boiled rice

2 large slices of cantaloup melon or ½ a small melon
1 oz. butter for frying

Sauce. Heat the butter, fry the sliced onion, add the curry-powder, and continue cooking for a few minutes. Add the flour, continue cooking until slightly brown. Add the bouquet, the lemon rind, the curry-paste, and the stock and seasoning. Simmer for 15–20 minutes. Add the jelly, nut milk (made as directed for previous recipe), and lemon juice. Reduce to the consistency of cream. Strain, return sauce to the rinsed pan. Peel the bananas and cut each into three chunks. Cut the melon in chunks. Heat the butter, fry bananas and melon briskly for 4–5 minutes, shaking the pan and turning, so that they do not stick. When fried put them into the sauce, cover, and keep warm for half an hour, so that they may become slightly impregnated with the flavour of the curry sauce. Serve with boiled rice.

PINEAPPLE NUT RICE

½ lb. rice
2 medium-sized onions
1½ oz. butter
1½ oz. blanched almonds or cashew nuts

1 small pineapple, *or*
4–6 slices of canned pineapple
1 large seedless orange
castor sugar, salt and pepper
2 eggs, hard-boiled
chopped chives

Boil the rice in plenty of salted water. Strain, rinse thoroughly with hot water, and strain again; drain and dry thoroughly. Slice the onions finely and fry till slightly coloured in half the butter, adding the shredded almonds or split cashews when the onion is half cooked. Season highly. Turn the rice into a bowl and with a fork stir in the onion mixture, cover and set aside to keep hot. Have ready the pineapple, sliced, and the core removed with a small round cutter. Cut peel and pith from the orange and cut into slices. Fry both pineapple and orange quickly in the remaining butter to a golden brown, dusting as you do so with a little castor sugar. Pile the rice up in the middle of a hot dish, surround with the slices of orange and pineapple and quartered hard-boiled eggs. Scatter chopped chives over. Serve as an accompaniment to roast veal or chicken, or separately with a tamarind sauce (see page 993).

The rice may be flavoured with saffron or moistened with a little cream when the onion mixture is added.

The following is rich, but worth while on occasion:

CHICKEN CURRY FOR A PARTY

The risk in giving this recipe is that one is sure to be accused of being extravagant, but if I may say so, this seems at least as good a way of enjoying cream as by using it to enrich cakes and gâteaux.

roasting chicken, 1 large or 2 small	a bouquet with a sprig of tarragon
2 oz. onion	salt
2 oz. carrot	
6 oz. shallots or onions	salt
1 clove of garlic, crushed	½ pint cream
2–3 oz. butter	yolks of 4 eggs
2 tablespoons curry-powder	1 tablespoon chutney

Cut up the chicken, put it with the onion, carrot, bouquet, salt, and enough water just to cover. Bring to boil, put on lid, and simmer till chicken is just cooked but no more, then lift out chicken and set liquid to cool.

Cook the onions and garlic in butter, add curry-powder, continue cooking 3 minutes. Lift out the onions. Put the pieces of chicken into the same fat and allow to brown. Add about ½ pint of the chicken broth, season to taste, simmer 10 minutes. Beat egg yolks, add to cream. Lift the chicken on to the serving dish, and keep hot; add the cream and eggs to the liquid in the pan, cook without allowing to boil until the sauce thickens, add the chutney, pour over the chicken, and serve with rice and the usual accompaniments.

CURRIED EGGS (COLD)

6 eggs, hard-boiled	1 gill whipped cream
2 medium-sized onions, chopped	salt and pepper
¾ oz. butter	bread croûtes fried in butter, 1 for each egg
1 dessertspoon curry-powder	cream of curry sauce or mayonnaise (see page 1013)
2 tomatoes, skinned, pipped, and chopped	watercress or curled celery for garnish
2 tablespoons mango chutney, chopped	

Peel the eggs and split them in two lengthwise. Remove the yolks, sieve into a small bowl and cover. Slip whites into cold water.

Soften onions in the butter, add curry-powder, fry a minute or two, then add tomatoes and chutney. Cook to reduce for a few minutes, turn out and cool. Fold into the cream, lastly add the sieved yolks and seasoning. Dry the whites carefully, set one half on a croûte, first spreading the croûte with a little of the mixture. Fill whites well with the mixture and cover with the other halves. Coat over the dressing and garnish the dish with watercress or curled celery.

The next recipe was given to us by an Indian student, and the two following by a Persian one.   All three were made by them for us to taste. They are included here primarily for the benefit of students from eastern countries.   Shernaz set off for the Bombay Emporium in Grafton Way, Warren Street, London, W.C., to seek the strange-sounding ingredients she needed.   The dish she produced was very hot for English palates, but the recipe which follows has been slightly adapted.   Even so, this cannot be described as anything other than hot.

RED ALMOND CURRY (SHERNAZ ADAPTED)

50 almonds
½–¾ of a coco-nut
1 chopped onion
4 cloves of garlic
1 tablespoon clarified butter
   or ghee
1 teaspoon ground coriander
1 teaspoon kaskas

1 teaspoon jeeroo
8 goa chillis (medium hot)
1 teaspoon salt
prawns, mullet, or other fish
  (enough for 4 people)
small handful of dried tamarind soaked in a cup of
  boiling water

Grind, then pound to a paste the almonds and half the coco-nut.   Grind and pound the remainder and pour on 2 cups boiling water.   Infuse and strain.   Fry the onion and garlic in the butter, add the spices, fry again, then add the nut paste, chillis, coco-nut milk, and salt.   Bring to the boil, add prawns, mullet, or other fish and simmer till the fish is cooked. Strain the tamarind (to make about ½ cup liquid) and add to the curry. Simmer again until the oil begins to rise to the surface.

QORMA

2 teaspoons chana dal
1 onion
¼ lb. butter or cooking fat
½ lb. mutton
6 cardamons

salt
cayenne
juice of 1 lemon or 4 aloo
  bokhara

Use a deep pan with lid.   Soak chana dal for 1 hour.   Brown the onion (use entire fat), drain and crush.   Return to the pan.   Add meat and fry lightly, then add cardamons, salt, cayenne, and juice of lemon or aloo bokhara.   Add enough liquid to cook meat, allow to simmer gently till nearly all liquid is absorbed.   Serve with boiled rice as for Lawand.

LAWAND

2 cloves of garlic
¼ lb. yoghourt or jellied sour
  milk
½ lb. mutton
1 medium onion

¼ lb. butter or cooking fat
6 cardamon seeds
½ teaspoon each of cayenne
  pepper, salt, turmeric, and
  dry and crushed coriander

Use a deep pan with lid.   Cream garlic with a teaspoon of salt, beat into sour milk.   Soak meat in the flavoured sour milk for an hour (meat prepared in chunks about 2 inches in diameter). Chop onions in slices and brown evenly a light brown, drain, cool, and crush in a mortar. Mix turmeric, salt, cayenne, coriander, and cardamons in a little water, add to the cooking fat, cook till water is absorbed, add onion and meat, and fry slowly till evenly brown. Keep stirring. Add liquid, enough to cook meat (about 2 cups). Simmer gently in a covered pan or put in the oven. Cook until liquid is nearly all absorbed. If meat is not tender add more boiling water.

Rice. Boil rice, drain water, shake well with about 3 tablespoons of the gravy of the Lawand. Bake in the oven and serve with Lawand.

For English tastes the quantity of fat may be modified.

SWEETS AND ICES

The first recipe is for a rich steamed pudding. The quantities given make a large pudding, but any that remains may with advantage be packed in a basin and resteamed the following day. The general texture and flavour of a big pudding is better than that of one made with half quantities. A plain custard sauce may take the place of the sabayon given.

FIG AND GINGER PUDDING

6 oz. figs	½ teaspoon salt
6 oz. dates, weighed without stones	1½ teaspoons baking-powder
3 oz. raisins, stoned and roughly chopped	1 breakfast-cup breadcrumbs
3 or 4 tablespoons preserved ginger and syrup	1 breakfast-cup finely chopped suet
a little brandy or rum	⅓ cup fruit juice, orange or lemon
1 breakfast-cup flour, measured after sifting	2 eggs
	sabayon sauce (see below)

Cut up all the fruit roughly and leave to stand for 1 hour, covered with a little brandy or rum. Then sift flour and salt with the baking-powder, mix in the breadcrumbs and the finely chopped suet, and add the soaked fruit, the ginger, and the fruit juice. Beat the eggs well and fold them in. Butter a three-pint basin and fill with the mixture, which should not come more than two-thirds of the way up the basin, as it will rise in cooking. Cover the basin with a well-buttered paper and a pudding cloth and tie down firmly. Put in boiling water and boil gently for 3½ hours, or cover with buttered paper or with grease-proof paper and steam 4½ hours.

Sabayon sauce

2 tablespoons castor sugar	1 teaspoon vanilla or 2 tablespoons sherry
2 large eggs	grated rind of 1 lemon

Put the sugar, yolks, vanilla or sherry, and the grated rind of lemon into a bowl and beat them until the mixture is lemon-coloured and smooth. Put the basin over a saucepan of hot water, and whisk until the mixture is fluffy all through. Beat the egg whites stiffly and fold them in.

The next pudding is a particularly good type of batter pudding for special occasions:

WINKFIELD BATTER PUDDING (FOR 4–6)

1½ gills milk infused with lemon rind or vanilla pod	a handful of blanched shredded almonds
3 oz. butter	3–4 tablespoons good apricot jam and the juice of ½ lemon
3¾ oz. flour	
3 eggs	

Put milk and butter together, bring to the boil. Draw aside, add the flour immediately and beat until smooth. Cool. Beat in the eggs one at a time, reserving one white. Whip this stiffly and fold in at the end.

Well butter a pie dish or soufflé case, put in the mixture and scatter with almonds. Dust well with castor sugar and bake in a moderately hot oven for 40–45 minutes. Heat jam with lemon juice, and when pudding is well risen and firm to the touch pour it over. Serve at once.

ARD DARAICH TOFFEE PUDDING

This is a good pudding. We have two versions of it, one with a French pancake mixture, the second, and better, made with a castle pudding mixture. The sauce may be varied by using more lemon and lemon rind or by flavouring with rum or liqueur.

3 oz. butter	4 oz. self-raising flour
3 oz. castor sugar	½ pint milk
3 eggs	toffee sauce (see below)
a pinch of salt	

Cream butter thoroughly, add sugar, beat till white and fluffy. Add eggs one at a time with a spoonful of the flour and the pinch of salt, beating well. Add remainder of the flour and the milk. Stand batter half an hour. Well grease and dust with flour three sandwich tins of equal size (5–6 inches). Pour the batter into these and bake in a moderately hot oven (400° F.) 15 minutes. Turn out and layer together on a hot serving dish with a little toffee sauce poured between each layer. Pour the rest over and round. Serve at once.

Toffee sauce

3 tablespoons granulated sugar	grated rind and juice of ½ lemon
2 tablespoons golden syrup	
½ oz. butter	¼ pint water

Put sugar, syrup, and butter into a pan together. Cook on a moderate heat, stirring occasionally with a metal spoon until a good toffee. Draw aside, add the grated rind and lemon juice and the water by degrees. Reboil and use.

ARD DARAICH SPONGE PUDDING

3 oz. sugar	4 oz. flour
3 oz. butter	½ gill milk
3 eggs	sauce (see below)

Cream sugar and butter, beat in eggs one at a time, sift in flour and add milk. The mixture should be fairly liquid. Fill three greased sandwich tins and bake in a hot oven about 15 minutes.

Sauce

2 oz. butter	4 dessertspoons water
2 oz. sugar	juice of ¼ a lemon
4 dessertspoons syrup	

Melt butter and sugar till the butter is absorbed. Add syrup, water, and lemon juice and boil for 5 minutes. Pile sponges in a serving dish, placing brown side uppermost and pouring hot sauce on each one in turn, with the remaining sauce round the dish.

The following dish is for layered pancakes covered with meringue and lightly browned almonds. The pancakes, some of them dipped for a second in Cointreau, are sandwiched with specially flavoured jams or jellies. If no store of these is laid in, more conventional jams, with some additional flavouring, are used.

CRÊPES FOURRÉES WINKFIELD

Batter

2 oz. flour	1 level dessertspoon melted
1 egg	butter or oil
1 yolk	a pinch of salt
1 level dessertspoon castor	¼ pint milk
sugar	a little water

Mix in the way described (page 432) and leave for an hour. Thin down if necessary with about 2 tablespoons of water. The pancakes should be thin and lacy.

Flavouring
    a liqueur glass of Cointreau in a soup-plate

Filling
    a little rose petal jam
    crab-apple jelly flavoured with scented geranium. (Suitable substitutes would be cherry jam flavoured with a dash of kirsch, or marmalade sieved and flavoured with grated orange rind.)
    the peel of ½ a tangerine, finely shredded and chopped, and the pith removed

Finish
    2 egg whites
    4 oz. castor sugar
    12 almonds, blanched and shredded, and a tablespoon of icing sugar

Dip half the pancakes quickly in and out of Cointreau. Pile up in alternate layers of plain and flavoured and spread with fillings, first one of jam, then another of jelly, and sprinkle the shredded and chopped tangerine rind in every other layer. Beat the egg white until really stiff, fold in sugar. Spread this meringue over the pile of pancakes. Dredge with sugar, sprinkle with almonds, and return to oven for a few minutes until lightly browned.

FRESH STRAWBERRY AND RED-CURRANT FLAN

flan case (see page 843)
red-currant jelly
sweetened whipped cream
maraschino
strawberries

glaze of melted red-currant jelly
garnish of red currants frosted
  with castor sugar
white of egg

Make a flan case, bake blind, put in a layer of red-currant jelly broken up with a fork, and over this spread a thick layer of sweetened whipped cream flavoured with maraschino. Arrange strawberries on this. Melt a little red-currant jelly and pour over the top. Garnish with bunches of red currants brushed over with lightly frothed white of egg, dipped in castor sugar, and dried on a wire rack.

The above is a refreshing flan, both to look at and to eat. The Rum Pie which follows is sweet and rich. It is a chocolate and rum version of the popular Lemon Chiffon Pie.

RUM PIE

Make a flan case with short pastry (see page 843); bake blind. Make a custard in the following way. Take:

$\frac{1}{2}$ pint milk flavoured with a
  pinch of nutmeg
2 oz. sugar (short weight)
2 eggs

$1\frac{1}{2}$ teaspoons gelatine
1 teaspoon corn-flour or
  arrowroot
2 tablespoons rum

Separate the whites and yolks of the eggs. Beat the yolks with sugar and a pinch of salt till they form a ribbon. Stir in the corn-flour, heat the milk and add it gradually to this mixture. Return to pan (preferably a double boiler) and cook till thick. Strain in the gelatine, previously dissolved in a little water.

Allow to cool, fold in stiffly beaten whites of egg and add rum. Set in a cold place while you prepare the top of the pie in the following way. Take:

a few spoonfuls of cream
a little sugar for sweetening
a bar of chocolate

2 tablespoons water
a few drops of rum

Melt the chocolate in the water over gentle heat; mix cream, stiffly whipped, with sugar and rum and add cooled chocolate. Cover the pie with this and chill all well.

GÂTEAU ALLEMAND

4 eggs	¼ oz. ground almonds
6 oz. sugar	raspberry jam
grated rind and juice of a small	whipped cream
lemon	water icing
3 oz. fine semolina	

Separate the eggs and beat the yolks and sugar together until thick. Then add the rind and juice of the lemon, the semolina, and ground almonds. Whip the whites stiffly and fold into the mixture. Turn into a buttered and floured square or rectangular tin and bake in a moderately hot oven. The mixture should be about 1½ inches deep when cooked.

Cut in half and sandwich with raspberry jam and whipped cream. Coat the top with a thin water icing and cut in squares with a hot knife before serving, or leave whole. Fresh fruit may be used in place of the jam; the cake should then be filled with the cream and the top covered with raspberries.

MACARONS MONTMORENCY

This is delicious and fresh, and good also without the cream, which can be replaced by cold sabayon sauce flavoured with orange.

about a gill of sugar syrup (see	1 gill cream
stock syrup, page 860)	2 or 3 lumps of sugar
1–1½ lb. fine large red cherries	1 egg white, whipped
macaroons	½ teaspoon arrowroot
1 orange	kirsch to flavour

Make a thick syrup with sugar and water. Stone the cherries and poach gently in the syrup. When done, drain and reduce the syrup until thick. Cool. Pour a small quantity in the bottom of a glass dish, break the macaroons into medium-sized pieces and put half into the dish. Cover with the cherries and then with the remainder of the macaroons.

Rub 2 or 3 lumps of sugar on to the rind of the orange, and crush finely. Whip the cream to a light froth, add the sugar, beat until it will just hold its shape, fold in beaten egg white, then cover the whole dish with the cream. Chill well before serving. Mix the arrowroot with the orange juice; add to the remaining cherry juice. Boil up, cool, flavour with kirsch and serve with the pudding. Use a good canned or bottled cherry when fresh cherries are out of season.

For macaroons see recipe on page 868.

PINEAPPLE NINON

Choose a ripe pineapple, do not remove the leaves but split in two lengthways. Remove the inside of each half with care, leaving the outer skin as a case.

Cut the flesh of the pine into thin slices, removing the core. Powder with fine sugar and sprinkle with kirsch. Do the same to $\frac{1}{2}$ lb. good strawberries and 2 or 3 ripe bananas. Leave for an hour on ice, or chill in a refrigerator.

Fill back into the skin of the pine and serve surrounded by small tartelettes of almond pastry filled with whipped cream and garnished with a small strawberry. The dish may be decorated with spun sugar.

Almond pastry (pâte frolle)

4 oz. flour	2 yolks
2 oz. butter	2 oz. ground almonds
2 oz. sugar	

Sieve the flour, make a well in the centre and in it place the butter, sugar, and yolks. Sprinkle the almonds on the flour. Work up to a paste with the hand and chill before using.

STRAWBERRY GALETTE (GALETTE AUX FRAISES)

2 eggs	$\frac{1}{4}$ gill water
3 oz. castor sugar	$\frac{1}{2}$ lb. strawberries
2 oz. flour	a little maraschino or kirsch
a little grated lemon rind or vanilla	or Marsala
2 oz. loaf sugar	light fondant or water icing

Put the eggs and castor sugar together into a bowl and whisk over gentle heat until thick. Remove from heat and whisk till cold. Sift in the flour, add the lemon rind or vanilla. Mix all together lightly and quickly and turn at once into a deep sandwich tin which has been well greased and floured. Bake in a slow to moderate oven for 25–35 minutes. Turn out and cool. Cut the strawberries into thick slices. Boil the loaf sugar to the thread with water, cool a little and pour it over the strawberries. Flavour with the maraschino, kirsch, or Marsala. Split the cake, fill with the strawberries, and pour the syrup in and over it. About half an hour before serving pour over a light fondant or water icing.

TARTELETTES AUX FRAISES DES BOIS A LA CRÈME

This is a melting rich crust filled with cœur à la crème and finished with wild or Alpine strawberries, very pretty.

Pastry (pâte frolle)

$1\frac{1}{2}$ oz. almonds	2 oz. butter
$2\frac{1}{2}$ oz. castor sugar	grated rind of $\frac{1}{2}$ lemon
1 small egg	jelly to glaze
4 oz. flour	

Pound the almonds with the sugar, adding half the egg. Sift the flour on to a marble slab, make a well in the centre and in it place the butter, almond mixture, rest of the egg, and lemon rind. Work up together and chill 1 hour before using.

Now prepare the filling as follows:

¾ oz. butter	vanilla
1 oz. castor sugar	a little cream
4 oz. cream or milk cheese	

Cream the butter, add the sugar, and stir in the sieved cheese, adding vanilla to flavour; finish with a little cream.

Line pastry into tartelette moulds.   Bake blind, fill level with the cream mixture, cover with small ripe strawberries, and glaze with a red-currant or gooseberry jelly.

CHILLED PEARS

Sliced ripe William pears arranged in a dish in layers with crème patissière flavoured with zest of orange make a good cold sweet.   The whole dish should be well chilled.

The following Muscat Ice is one of the most delicious of water-ices. The lemon syrup flavoured with the flowers of the common elder has the flavour and scent of muscat grapes.

MUSCAT ICE

Make a lemon syrup as for Lemon Water-ice (see page 971).   After boiling the syrup for 5 minutes plunge in 3–4 heads of elderflower, and allow them to infuse until the syrup is sufficiently flavoured.   Strain the syrup before adding the lemon juice.

In winter elderflower syrup (see page 1098) may be used to flavour; in this case decrease the quantity of sugar in the lemon syrup by about a quarter to a third, and add the elderflower syrup to taste with the lemon juice.

These water-ices are largely determined by taste if no *pèse-sirop* is employed.   If the syrup is strong, well flavoured, and nicely sweet it will freeze satisfactorily.

As we grow a number of old roses, we find it simple to keep a few jars of the concentrated Rose Petal Jam given on page 1036.   One special use to which we like to put this is a Rose Petal Water-ice.

ROSE PETAL WATER-ICE

1 pint water	juice of 3 lemons (¾ gill)
5 oz. sugar	2 heaped dessertspoons rose
rind of 2 lemons peeled very thinly	petal jam

Put water, sugar, and lemon rind and juice into a pan and boil 5 minutes. Remove from fire and stir in the rose petal jam.   Strain.   When cold, freeze.

N.B.   For a more sherbet-like consistency, a quarter to a third of an egg white may be used.   This is added when the ice is half frozen, and freezing is then continued.

In the section on ices (page 968) will be found a delicate white coffee ice.
A plain vanilla ice is very good served with a hot mincemeat mixture
containing rum or brandy.   Recipes for both are given in the section on
ices (see pages 967 and 973).   Little copper or fireproof *cocottes* may be
used to contain the hot mincemeat.

CAKES

R. H. says that the following tea-cake was always on the tea table in an
Irish country house she visited as a child.   It was said that no one could
make it like the yard man.   So after sundry splashings and scrubbings he
was often brought into the kitchen to make it.

LEMON TEA-CAKE (LISSANOURE)

This should be eaten hot and running with butter.   For those who like
a seedy cake the lemon may be reduced by half and replaced by a teaspoon
of caraway-seeds; it may still be eaten hot and buttered.

2 eggs, their weight in butter, castor sugar, and self-raising flour	grated rind and juice of 1 lemon

Cream butter, beat in sugar thoroughly.   Add the egg yolks with the
lemon rind and juice and a tablespoon or two of the flour.   Whip whites
to a firm froth and fold into the mixture with remaining flour.   Turn at
once into a shallow greased and floured tin and bake in a moderately hot
oven 20–30 minutes.   Split whilst still hot and butter lavishly.

The brioche given below is good for a picnic or for tea at Christmas
time:

BRIOCHE LOAF (BRIOCHE MOUSSELINE)

½ lb. flour	a pinch of salt
½ oz. yeast	4 oz. butter
2–3 tablespoons tepid milk	grated lemon rind
3 eggs	dried and/or glacé fruit
1 oz. sugar	water icing flavoured with rum

Dissolve the yeast in the milk and add to 2 oz. of the flour to form a light
dough.   Set aside to rise for 10 minutes.   Meanwhile mix the remainder
of the flour with the eggs, sugar, and salt until thoroughly elastic.   Cream
the butter, add to the paste, and when thoroughly mixed work in the yeast
dough.   Leave in a cool place 3–4 hours, or overnight.   Then add the
grated rind of a lemon, raisins, cherries, sultanas, etc.   Fill into a fluted
mould or tin and leave to rise 20–30 minutes.   Bake in a hot oven 30–40
minutes.   Turn out and ice with a thin water icing flavoured with rum.

VIENNESE CROISSANTS

½ lb. flour	salt
½ oz. yeast	6 oz. butter
a little milk	almond filling (see below)
2 eggs	apricot glaze or vanilla fondant
1 oz. sugar	icing

Take about 2 oz. of the flour, mix to a stiff dough with the yeast and a little milk, and place in a pan of warm water to rise. Mix the remaining flour to a soft dough with the eggs, sugar, and salt and a little milk if necessary. Now work the two doughs together, adding two-thirds of the butter, and knead until smooth. Leave to rise overnight. Next day roll out the dough, spread the rest of the butter over half of it, and fold over. Give two more turns as for puff pastry.

Roll out and cut in strips 4½ inches wide and then in triangles. Put a little almond filling at the base of each triangle and roll up to form a crescent. Prove until nearly double in bulk, glaze, and bake in a hot oven (450° F.). When cooked and cool they may be glazed with apricot glaze or thinly iced with thin white vanilla fondant icing.

Almond filling

1½ oz. pounded or ground almonds	½–¾ oz. butter
1½ oz. sugar	vanilla

Pound the ingredients together to a stiff paste.

WALNUT BREAD

12 oz. flour	1½ gills black treacle or golden syrup
2 heaped teaspoons baking-powder	3 oz. walnuts
6 oz. sugar	3 oz. raisins or sultanas
1½ gills milk	2 small eggs or 1 large

Sift flour with baking-powder. Warm the milk, treacle, and sugar together. Make a well in the centre of the flour, add the walnuts, raisins, and beaten eggs. Pour in the liquid and stir only enough to mix. Turn into a greased and floured bread tin and bake in a very moderate oven for about an hour

The following Gâteau aux Marrons is made without flour. It should not be overcooked and should be moist and slightly sticky. It is good served as a sweet with a compôte of fruit.

GÂTEAU AUX MARRONS ET AU CHOCOLAT

4 eggs	½ lb. chestnuts (after cooking)
8 oz. castor sugar	chocolate filling (see page 1027)
3 oz. chocolate (1 oz. may be unsweetened)	

Beat the egg yolks and sugar until white, add the chocolate melted to a thick cream with a little water or strong black coffee. Make the chestnuts into a purée and fold in, together with the egg whites, whisked until stiff and dry.

Line two shallow cake pans with well-buttered paper, pour half the mixture into each, and bake in a moderate oven 30–40 minutes. When cool, sandwich with chocolate filling and pour a little over to cover.

Chocolate filling

3 oz. chocolate	sugar to taste
2 tablespoons water	¼ pint cream
2 yolks of egg	

Mix chocolate and water and melt slowly over gentle heat till thick. Add yolks, well beaten, and sugar. Stir till smooth. Allow to cool and mix in the cream. For a rich sweet a double amount of cream may be used.

N.B. Chocolate-flavoured crème patissière may be used in place of this.

CHOCOLATE ROLL

3 eggs	2 level tablespoons good cocoa
5½ oz. castor sugar	2 level teaspoons baking-
2¼ oz. potato flour or arrow- root	powder

Butter cream for filling

½ gill milk	4 oz. butter
2 oz. sugar	coffee essence
1 egg yolk	

Whisk eggs and sugar together over heat until thick. Whisk till cool, then fold in the flour, cocoa, and baking-powder, sifted together. Turn at once into a greased and floured paper case. Bake 5–6 minutes in a hot oven. Turn out on to a sugared paper and allow to cool.

For filling, heat the milk with the sugar, pour on to the yolk, return to the pan, and thicken without boiling. Cream the butter, work in the custard when cool, and flavour well with coffee essence. Spread the roll with this and roll up firmly.

When the edible Cape gooseberries (physalis) are to be bought in those shops that specialize in unusual fruits, the following is certainly a cake to make. It is delicious and refreshing.

GÂTEAU PHYSALIS

Biscuit fin au beurre

4 eggs	Cape gooseberry jam or butter
4½ oz. castor sugar	cream
3½ oz. flour	apricot glaze
2 oz. butter, melted but not hot	vanilla fondant icing
	physalis

Cream the egg yolks and sugar until white and mousse-like. Fold in carefully the finely sifted flour alternately with the egg whites whisked until stiff and dry; lastly fold in the butter. Pour the mixture into a prepared *moule à manqué* and bake in a moderate oven about 40 minutes.

Split when cool and sandwich with Cape gooseberry jam or butter cream. Reshape, brush with melted glaze, allow to set, then ice with a vanilla-flavoured white fondant icing. Just before it sets completely, arrange round the top edge physalis with the capsules cut and folded back. Unless the cake is eaten at once the physalis should be dipped in white fondant flavoured with vanilla and left to set.

The physalis make a delicious sweetmeat and are mentioned in Pâtisseries, page 879.

PETITS FOURS WINKFIELD

Make a génoise fine, bake in a rectangular tin. Turn out and leave to cool. Cut into small rectangles, brush over the top and sides with melted apricot glaze. Ice with fondant icing flavoured with orange-flower water.

Gâteau Bigarreau is made with fresh white heart cherries. These may be replaced by other summer fruits, raspberries being especially good.

GÂTEAU BIGARREAU (FOR 6)

Sponge cake

3 eggs	3 oz. fine flour
4½ oz. castor sugar	

Glaze

3 tablespoons apricot jam	½–1 gill water
2 tablespoons red-currant jelly	

1 lb. white heart cherries	a little sugar if cream is used
2 tablespoons praline (see page 854)	chopped browned nuts or praline for decoration
a good gill cream or crème patissière	

Break the eggs into a basin, whisk in the sugar by degrees. Stand the bowl over a pan of hot water and whisk steadily until the mixture is white and thick. Fold in the flour. Line the bottom of a shallow cake or sandwich tin with paper, well buttered, and dust out with flour. Pour in the mixture and bake in a moderate oven 20–30 minutes.

To make the glaze put jam and jelly into a pan with water. Simmer until the consistency of cream, strain and cool. Stone the cherries. Whip and sweeten the cream, fold in the praline. Split the cake, sandwich with the prepared cream mixture. Brush the sides and top with glaze, arrange cherries all over the top. Brush again thickly with glaze and press chopped browned nuts or praline round the sides of the cake.

One usually thinks of a ginger cake as dark in colour, sticky perhaps, and tasting of ground ginger. This Ginger Sponge Cake is really a light sponge cake holding chopped glacé ginger, and iced with fondant icing thickly covered with overlapping thin slices of ginger. It is generally liked by those who do not care for the usual gingerbreads or cakes.

GINGER SPONGE CAKE

4 eggs	1½ tablespoons lemon juice
7¼ oz. castor sugar	glacé ginger sliced thinly
4¼ oz. sifted flour	apricot glaze
1 rounded teaspoon baking-powder	fondant icing (about 1 lb.)
1½ tablespoons water	2 oz. or more glacé or crystallized ginger cut in pieces

Separate eggs. Cream yolks thoroughly with two-thirds of the sugar. Sift baking-powder and flour together. Whip whites to a smooth but firm snow, beat in the rest of the sugar. Add the water and lemon juice to the yolks and the ginger to the flour. Now fold the whites and flour into the yolk mixture, and when just incorporated turn into a prepared cake tin about 8–9 inches in diameter. Bake in a moderate oven (375° F.) for about 45 minutes to 1 hour. Turn out. When cold brush lightly with apricot glaze and ice with the fondant; decorate with the ginger.

N.B. If glacé ginger is used in the cake it must be well drained from the syrup before being cut into pieces and tossed in the flour. Crystallized ginger should be washed in hot water to remove the sugar crystals, then dried and cut in pieces.

The following is an excellent type of cheesecake:

CURD CAKE

Good short pastry

6 oz. flour	1 egg yolk
4 oz. butter	2–3 tablespoons water

Make up in the usual way and line into a sandwich tin or flan ring.

Fill with:

½ lb. good white cheese (milk or home-made sour milk cheese, see page 745)	1 oz. flour, good weight
	1 handful of stoned raisins
	2 tablespoons cream
1¾ oz. butter	3 yolks and 3 whites of egg
1¾ oz. sugar	

Sieve cheese. Cream butter, add sugar, beat well. Work in the flour, raisins, cream, and yolks. When thoroughly mixed fold in the whites, stiffly whipped. Turn into the pastry and bake in a moderate to hot oven, about 400° F. When cooked remove ring, or turn out of the tin when cool.

SOME SPECIAL PARTIES

The fun of preparing for even the simplest party is enhanced when there are enthusiastic students to help. Some of the Winkfield parties have been the high light of a student's year, and R. H. says she enjoys even the laborious preparations for large numbers because she is free to choose and plan the menus. Asked whether outside hostesses do not accord her such freedom, she answers, with no doubt a touch of exaggeration: 'They always seem to ask for mousse.' What she is really saying is that hostesses often play for what they think is safety, refuse to be adventurous, and in consequence do not inspire the cook to her best efforts.

The most exciting party was one given on Coronation Day, for which preparations were shared by the students and staff of the Cordon Bleu School in London and of Winkfield. This was a luncheon for the representatives of other countries invited by Her Majesty to be present in Westminster Abbey on the occasion of her coronation. It was held in the Great Hall of Westminster School. Sir David Eccles, the Minister of Works, paid us the unexpected compliment of asking us to undertake the luncheon, and then added 'and to serve it also.' Although we were simmering with excitement, R. H. and I let days go by before we allowed ourselves to make real plans, feeling that perhaps Sir David, remembering the youthfulness of our students, might modify his ideas about what we could accomplish. But nothing so discouraging happened.

Once the plan was firmly established we concerned ourselves exclusively with our problems, which in brief were these. The luncheon was for about three hundred and fifty people, the largest party to be seated in the Great Hall, the rest in a house some distance away. By two o'clock the guests would be very hungry and probably cold. There would be people of many nationalities, some of whom would eat no meat. Kitchen accommodation was too small to serve hot food beyond soup and coffee. The serving of the food would have to be simple because all the waitresses would be amateurs.

The menu chosen was as follows:

Potage de Tomates à l'Estragon (page 992)

Truite de Rivière en Gelée, Sauce Verte (page 507)

Poulet Reine Elizabeth (page 1012—Coronation Chicken)

ou

Cornets de Jambon Lucullus (page 999)

Cherry and Walnut Salad (page 1032)

Galette aux Fraises (page 1023)

Mousse au Citron (page 943)

Coffee, Petits Fours (page 876)

Potage de Tomate à
l'Estragon.

Truite de Rivière.

Poulet Reine Elizabeth
ou
Cornets de Jambon Lucullus

Salades.

Galettes aux Fraises
Roulade. Mousse au Citron

Café. Friandises.

Moselle Brauneberger '43
Champagne Krug '45.

For *Truite de Rivière* the trout, boned, was coated in a delicately flavoured aspic, decorated with fresh dill, and accompanied by sauce verte, brown bread and butter, and sections of lemon.

Poulet Reine Elizabeth was chicken, boned, and coated in curry cream sauce, with, at one end of each dish, well-seasoned dressed salad of rice, green peas, and pimentos.

The *Cornets de Jambon Lucullus* were filled with a rich pâté.

The *Cherry and Walnut Salad* was chosen in place of green salad because it was thought too difficult to keep the latter perfectly fresh, since so much preparation had to be done ahead of time, and the dishes taken into the building overnight. The Cherry Salad recipe on page 352 was used, but with walnuts in place of almonds.

In summer we usually have a party at Winkfield at which we and the students entertain the parents. In 1952 we had what we thought would be an amusing idea. Between us R. H. and I have quite a few old cookery-books which describe the parties and banquets of days gone by, and we thought it would be interesting for the students of the post-war era to prepare a buffet supper in the fashion of 1852, and to set beside it an austerity table in the fashion of 1952. And so, choosing one of the most elaborate and, to modern ideas, probably fantastic tables, we began preparations for the buffet, and this is what it held.

Consommé aux Paillettes d'Or (pages 119 and 1033)

Langouste Truffée (page 1033)

Truite Saumonée en Gelée aux Crevettes (page 472)

Boar's Head (page 998)

Raised Pies (page 626)

Crème de Veau en Aspic (page 1033)

Croquenbouche (page 952)

Bavaroises (page 946)

Gelée au Citron (page 958)

Trifle (page 956)

Melon

Les Friandises

Café

The consommé was flecked with gold-leaf, a fashionable trick of those days, with no real purpose except to be amusing, for it tastes of nothing, it just looks pretty.   There was a langouste rampant, looking extremely handsome.   For this a very large langouste of about eight to ten pounds was bought alive, cooked, decorated with truffles, and glazed with aspic, the tail meat being taken out and cut into slices, and each slice coated with mayonnaise collée.   The langouste was raised on a pale green 'socle' and the shell brushed over with oil so that it glistened.   The 'socle,' made of pounded cooked rice, was not to be eaten, it was merely a base to support the langouste.   Such a foundation was often covered with silver paper, but, copying an illustration, we spread this one with pale green-tinted lard. The escalopes were arranged around and the whole mounted on a silver dish.   It all looked very grand and decorative.

Then we wanted to have a stuffed boar's head—in the event it had to be a pig, for we did not think of it early enough to procure a real boar's head. But even this looked dramatic, blackened as it was with lard and soot in the traditional way.   This sounds unpleasant, but it reproduces the colour of a boar's head and serves to show up the white tusks, modelled in wax, and the traditional wreath of bay-leaves.   The filling, of a particularly good pâté, was delicious.   Typical mousses were made; on this occasion some were of veal and some of salmon.   The moulds were lined with aspic and decorated, and when turned out looked shining and attractive.

Then in the centre was the tall pyramid of the croquenbouche.   This consisted of tiny meringues stuck together with a syrup of sugar, i.e. the sugar boiled to the crack.   These were arranged in a pyramid and a fountain of spun sugar came from the top, and there was a circle of straw-berries round the base.   This sweet may also be made with little choux pastry cases.   These main dishes were surrounded by others suitable to the period, bavaroises, jellies, trifles, and others.   Melons were sliced, the seeds removed, the slices replaced, and the fruit tied up with ribbon. There were, of course, crystal jugs of claret cup.   And carrying the fun a step further, we copied an illustration and made a brilliantly coloured cockerel in painted cellophane, with a blue ribbon and 'A Votre Service' printed on it in gold.   Two fine swans, made in the same way, held sweet-meats.   The decoration for this table was a gigantic epergne, spouting a fountain of asparagus fern, and the inevitable garlands of asparagus fern round the edge of the buffet.

The 1952 austerity table was composed of many kinds of home-made bread, home-made cream cheeses, and a huge dish of raw vegetables, *les crudités*.   These were all arranged on a warm yellow Hessian table-cloth, and this table appealed quite as much to the eyes of some of us as the more elaborate one.

Before giving the menu for a subsequent year, I must confess that this was the occasion of the accident mentioned on page 632.   It might perhaps have been regarded as a salutary warning to students, but it involved some quick thinking about a change-over. The revised menu ran:

Spicy Tomato Soup (page 92)

Pâté Maison (see Goose Pâté, page 977)

Baked Ham with Cumberland Sauce (pages 579 and 165)

Salad of peaches and pears with delicate salad-dressing (page 369)

Galette aux Fraises (page 1023)

White Coffee Ice (page 968)

Coffee

Petits Fours (page 876)

On an occasion when the members of a catering committee (all men) came to luncheon the following menu was prepared:

Fritto Misto (page 520)

Sauce Tartare (page 168)

Lemon quarters and brown bread and butter

Cold Turkey

Salad of pears and peaches (page 369)

Pommes de Terre Sicilienne (page 204)

Gâteau Bigarreau (page 1028)

Coffee

Food for adult students at day courses calls for some thought because of limitations of time and space. Buffet luncheons prove successful, and food requiring a fork only is satisfactory. The following are some of the dishes that seem popular:

Bouchées filled with mushrooms, prawns, or chopped eggs in a good béchamel.

Well-seasoned ham or chicken mousse with tomato salad.

Cold gruyère soufflé.

Home-made rolls or croissants filled with a roll of thinly cut ham containing a little chutney.

Stuffed hard-boiled eggs on a rice salad.

Cherry or strawberry tartlets.

Tarte Française (page 889).

Sponge cake filled with whipped cream and fresh fruit (or tinned pears); chocolate icing (page 827).

Mince-pies with special mincemeat (page 1038).

The cold dishes are an attempt to get away from the too bready sandwich. If it is a cold day a hot soup of pronounced flavour, spicy tomato or cream of curry, is appreciated.

Here is a menu for a party buffet:

Spicy Tomato Soup (page 92)

Small slices of salmon garnished with asparagus tips

Chicken Millefeuille (a mousse of chicken in layers of crisp pastry) (page 629)

Ham and tongue arranged on a big dish, glazed all over with aspic to keep it looking fresh

Stuffed Eggs (page 313)

Celery stuffed with cheese (Céleri Farci, page 7)

Rose Petal Ice (page 1024)

Strawberries in Muscat Syrup

In planning a buffet it is important that the general appearance shall be pleasing, and cold food is best served on silver dishes, as has been said in the chapter on the presentation of food. The flowers should stand high, so that not only are they out of the way, but they can be seen even when there is a big group of people standing round the buffet.

Last of all I should like to mention the sort of party which appeals equally to the cook-hostess and to the shy guest—a kitchen party. For this the food, plain perhaps without being excessively so, is served simply. Copper dishes, wooden bowls and boards, clean nylon sieves, fireproof dishes—all look right. I think these parties are particularly good in summer, because then a certain amount of cold food is suitable, and the kitchen can be fresh and cool. Some hot food may be liked, and soup can be served easily in cups. A good curry is practical because it may with advantage be made the day before, and it should have its accompaniment of fresh chutney, poppadums, and rice. But I am really thinking of such items as the rustic gazpacho, the salade niçoise, a good terrine, and a dish of wafers of smoked ham with black olives and gherkins; of Dublin Bay prawns, cold turkey or roast beef with different salads; avocado pears, globe artichokes with vinaigrette dressing; asparagus; an assortment of cheeses on a board, sieves of home-made rolls and trays of biscuits, and a mound of Liptauer cheese with radishes, pickled walnuts, and gherkins round the edge. Bowls of fruit are the nicest of sweets, particularly ripe berries, strawberries or raspberries, with orange juice. Nothing 'minnie' in fact, and with the accent on food that can in no circumstances be eaten in the genteel manner. Wine as you like, but equally beer if you want it. The table may be scrubbed wood or covered with coloured Hessian, the napkins those coloured cotton squares sold for scarves. The centre-piece may be a basket of fruit or vegetables or a bowl of herbs. The aim, I think, is complete informality combined with a sort of simple elegance.

MISCELLANEOUS RECIPES

ROSE PETAL JAM

For a jam to be eaten at tea-time the recipe which follows is too sweet, and it is better to use a fruit jam or jelly flavoured with rose petals, made in the way described in the section on jams (page 1097).

The conserve made from Sir Kenelm Digby's recipe written in the seventeenth century has a particular value as a flavouring ingredient, and a very little of it goes a long way. By being, apparently, lavish with sugar, it is possible to have a small store of little pots of highly concentrated rose conserve. A spoonful or two of this added to a suitable jam or jelly will give a delicious perfume and flavour. It may be used to flavour ices and other sweets.

We use the thin, highly scented petals of the old roses, and often find it quite unnecessary to discard any part of them.

Four pounds of sugar to one pound of petals sounds a lot, but it is surprising what a quantity of petals are used to make up a pound.

It seems best to give Sir Kenelm Digby's recipe as it was written.

CONSERVE OF RED ROSES

'Boil gently a pound of red rose leaves (well picked and the nails cut off) in about a pint and a half (or a little more, as by discretion you shall think fit, after having done it once—the Doctor's Apothecary taketh 2 pints) of spring water; till the water have drawn out all the tincture of the roses into itself, and that the leaves be very tender and look pale like linen; which may be in a good half-hour, or an hour, keeping the pot covered whiles it boileth. Then pour the tincted liquor from the pale leaves (strain it out, pressing it gently so that you may have liquor enough to dissolve your sugar) and set it upon the fire by itself to boil, putting into it a pound of pure double refined sugar in small powder; which as soon as it is dissolved put into it a second pound, then a third, so that you have four pounds of sugar to every pound of rose leaves. Boil these four pound of sugar with the tincted liquor till it be a high syrup very near a candy height (as high as can be not to flake or candy). Then put the pale rose leaves into this high syrup, as it yet standeth upon the fire or immediately upon the taking it off the fire, and stir them—away from the fire—exceeding well together to mix them uniformly, then let them stand till they are cold, then pot them up. If you put your conserve into pots whiles it is yet thoroughly warm and leave them uncovered some days, putting them in the hot sun or store, there will grow a fine candy on the top, which will preserve the conserve without paper upon it from moulding till you break the candied crust to take out some of the conserve.

'The colour of the rose leaves and the syrup about them will be exceedingly beautiful and red, and the taste excellent, and the whole very tender and soothing and easie to digest in the stomack, without clogging it as doth the ordinary rough conserve made of raw roses beaten with sugar which is very rough to the throat. The worst of it is that if you put not a paper to lie always close upon the top of the conserve it will be apt to grow mouldy there on the top.'

Spiced peaches are excellent with ham and various meat dishes. Stuffed spiced peaches are a glorification of this favourite form of spiced fruit. Because one may use up the flesh of imperfect peaches and modify the ingredients to suit one's taste, I do not think they need be considered an extravagance. The candied peel may be the only addition to the chopped peach flesh, and this should be home-made. You may use as few or as many of the other items as you please.

The peaches should not be eaten until some little time after they have been preserved, as all the stuffing ingredients must soften and blend well together.

Soft, really ripe English peaches do not lend themselves to this preparation. The best kind for the purpose are those firm-fleshed golden yellow fruits imported to this country in early summer. They are known, I think, as Hale or Lemon Cling peaches.

STUFFED SPICED PEACHES

Peel the peaches, cut a slice off the top and with a pointed spoon remove the stone. Weigh the stoned fruit. For each 2 lb. of fruit allow:

½ pint French wine vinegar
1 lb. sugar

a few slices of preserved ginger, chopped, or a piece of bruised root ginger

Stuffing

chopped peaches
chopped candied peel (see page 1131)
preserved ginger

preserved pineapple and/or any other candied fruit, such as cherries, strawberries, figs
a few drops of kirsch or Cointreau (optional)

In addition, certain spices and herb seeds may be used to suit individual taste, and we add to the stuffing a little celery seed, a pinch of mace, and some fresh ripe coriander seed, crushed. This must be added judiciously. A little cinnamon is another possible addition. The stuffing should be luscious and spicy, and the flavouring adjusted by tasting.

Make a syrup of the vinegar and sugar, adding the chopped ginger (if bruised root is used it should be put in a muslin bag). Chop the stuffing ingredients and fill them into the stoned peaches, replacing the slice that was removed. With a piece of twine bind round each peach to prevent the top slice from slipping, or fasten with a cocktail stick. Arrange the peaches, so stuffed, close together in a deep dish. Pour the boiling syrup over them and leave overnight. Next day drain the syrup away carefully, boil it up, and pour again over the peaches. Do this for three days in all.

On the fourth day lift out the peaches with great care into a stew-pan, add the syrup, and simmer gently for about half an hour. The exact time must depend on the ripeness of the peaches, but they must not be cooked so that they fall to pieces. Pack in wide-necked jars, cover, and do not use for a month at least.

When the country hedgerows are laden with the cream-coloured, heavy-scented flowers of the wild elder, there is one kitchen activity that must not be overlooked. That is the making of 'muscatel' syrup, jam, and jelly. The use of elderflowers with gooseberries, either in syrup or jelly form, imparts a definite flavour of muscat grapes. This has already been mentioned in connection with muscat ices, but may well be emphasized here.

'MUSCATEL' FRUIT SYRUP

1½ lb. granulated sugar
¾ pint water

2 lb. green gooseberries, well washed
8–10 elderflowers

Make a syrup of the sugar and water, add the gooseberries, and simmer very carefully without breaking. Then add the elderflowers and continue for another 5 minutes. Strain on a piece of muslin over a sieve. Bottle the syrup and sterilize for 20–30 minutes. The gooseberries left may be made into a fool or a purée. A heavier syrup is given on page 1098.

The mincemeat given below has a fresh flavour and is juicy and re-freshing. We do not use it exclusively at Christmas time. A little of the mixture with the addition of rum, brandy, or a suitable liqueur is good served piping hot with a plain vanilla ice.

WINKFIELD MINCEMEAT

1¼ lb. currants
1¼ lb. sultanas
1 lb. raisins
¾ lb. mixed peel
6 large apples
¼ lb. almonds
rind of 1 lemon and juice of 2
¾ lb. brown sugar
1 teaspoon salt
½ teaspoon ground cloves

1 teaspoon allspice
1 teaspoon ground cinnamon
1 teaspoon freshly grated nut-meg
6 bananas
¼ lb. butter, melted
¼ lb. glacé cherries
brandy, sherry, or rum to moisten

Clean the currants and sultanas and pick them. Stone and chop the raisins. Chop the mixed peel. Grate the apples without removing the skins. Blanch and shred the almonds. Add lemon rind and juice, sugar, salt, and spices, then add brandy, sherry, or rum; peel and dice the bananas, fry quickly in a little of the butter; chop the cherries, add both these fruits, with the melted butter. Turn into a large covered jar. Do not keep more than 2–3 weeks.

BOOKS FOR THE HOME KITCHEN

This chapter would be incomplete without reference to cookery books. Any kitchen is incomplete without a small collection of these, and the cook who disregards them and does it 'all out of my own head' is merely limiting her knowledge and her repertoire in stupid fashion. There are the books of sheerly utilitarian recipes, the books of technical reference by the help of which one may diagnose one's mistakes, the narratives giving glimpses of regional manners and customs, and the books for hostesses which may be regarded as ideas books. There are certain volumes which the true student of cookery really ought to have; for the most part these are written in the French tongue. The collection of even a small library will involve some trouble: advertising for books out of print, or hunting them down in second-hand shops; looking through the shelves of Hachettes in Regent Street, or placing with them orders for books from France which they have not already got. It is possible now to order books from America through booksellers, and altogether library life is easier than it was a short while ago. It is almost certain that some of the books to be mentioned will be out of print, but this is no reason for omitting them from the list, since almost certainly they are to be obtained. If we were to restrict the list to current books it would not represent the books we rely on and use all the time at Winkfield.

We all have our favourite bookshops, and booksellers are notably helpful in finding what one wants. Some of us prowl among the old bookshops in Charing Cross Road, stopping at Foyles to browse among the endless shelves. I like any excuse to go to the enchanting shop of Mr Heywood Hill in Curzon Street, and driving west insist on stopping at Salisbury so that I can get inside Beach's famous bookshop there. Second-hand books are surprisingly cheap, and provided you have some idea of what you want you are seldom disappointed.

A glance at the rows of contemporary books on the shelves of a bookshop will underline the limitations of the list which is to follow. The respective quality of these you may judge for yourselves. I have tried to select a few indispensables which have stood (and will, I believe, continue to stand) the test of time.

RECIPE BOOKS (ENGLISH)

The Best of Boulestin (Heinemann).
Book of Menus by X. M. Boulestin (Heinemann).

The first of these contains the best recipes of this great culinary expert, and the second gives his menus for every day in the year, with recipes.

Good Foods by Ambrose Heath (Faber & Faber).
Good Soups by Ambrose Heath (Faber & Faber).
The Country Life Cookery Book by Ambrose Heath (Country Life).

These are only a few of the many books on cookery by this well-known author.

Farmhouse Fare, published and republished from time to time by the *Farmers' Weekly*.

This is an inexpensive and most useful book of simple country recipes.

The Joy of Cooking by Irma S. Rombauer (J. M. Dent & Sons).

This is an American book edited for the English market by Marjorie Baron Russell. It is certainly the most comprehensive book of recipes mentioned in the category of English books. In earlier chapters we availed ourselves of permission to quote from it.

Mme Prunier's Fish Cookery Book edited by Ambrose Heath (Nicholson & Watson), and recently reissued in paperback (Arrow Books).

This classic book on fish is an important volume for every collection of cookery books. On a later page I shall take advantage of Mme Prunier's leave to quote one or two recipes.

The Book of Vegetable Cookery by Errol Sherson (Frederick Warne & Co. Ltd).

This first-class and comprehensive book on vegetables may have to be bought second-hand.

Au Petit Cordon Bleu by Dione Lucas and Rosemary Hume, published and recently reprinted by J. M. Dent & Sons.

This is a book of first-class recipes best suited to cooks with some experience.

Party Food and Drink by Rosemary Hume (Chatto & Windus).
Sweets and their Sauces by Rosemary Hume (Chatto & Windus).

These two small and inexpensive books are full of first-class recipes.

Food in England by Dorothy Hartley (MacDonald).

A comprehensive survey of English food and methods of cooking throughout the ages.

Good Things in England by Florence White (Jonathan Cape).

This book is full of traditional English recipes.

Receipts and Relishes, 'being a vade-mecum for the epicure in the British Isles.' Introduced by Bernard Darwin (Whitbread & Co.).

An excellent book of regional recipes arranged under counties.

Common Sense Cookery by A. Kenney-Herbert (Edward Arnold).

This is an old-fashioned book; the third edition is dated 1894. Some of the menus are rich and strange to our eyes to-day, but the book itself is full of information of great practical value, and well worth finding.

I have recently had the privilege of seeing some part of the typescript of a book which I imagine will be published before this one appears. It is called *Cooking with Bon Viveur*. The recipes I saw all had the desirable touch of originality, and it is a book to acquire. It is to be published by the Museum Press.

From the same authority comes a book *An ABC of Wine Drinking* (Muller), which is a most useful book for students.

French Pastry, Confectionery, and Sweets.   Continental dishes by E. J. Kollist (Cassell & Co.).

RECIPE BOOKS (AMERICAN)

The Boston Cooking School Cook Book by Fannie Merritt Farmer (Little, Brown & Co., Boston).

Although American this fine book is easily obtainable in this country, and should by no means be omitted from any domestic bookshelf.   It is comprehensive, simple to follow, beautifully illustrated, and full of admirable recipes.   Particularly valuable is the chapter on cakes and icings.

Wilma Lord Perkins gave us generous permission to quote from the book, which we have accepted with gratitude.

RECIPE BOOKS (FRENCH)

Je Sais Cuisiner by Delage and Mathiot (Albin Michel).
An excellent book of standard French recipes.

Petits et Grands Plats by Laboureur and Boulestin (Au Sans Pareil).
An excellent source of good French bourgeois dishes.

Cuisine Provençale (Reboul).
Good and simple Provençal cookery.

BOOKS ON TECHNIQUE

The Complete Book on Home Food Preservation by Cyril Grange, F.R.H.S. (Cassell & Co.).

This is a comprehensive book on food preservation, which ought to be in every kitchen where even the simplest jams are made.   It covers a vast range of processes: canning, bottling, drying, pickling, and preserving.   A quotation from this book is made, with permission, in another chapter.

The Complete Book of Modern Pressure Cooking by Marjorie Baron Russell (Falcon Press).
Cooking by Magic by Marjorie Baron Russell (Falcon Press).

The first of these is a comprehensive work on cooking under pressure, containing explanations of the technique and giving tables and many recipes.   It is an essential book for teachers and demonstrators.

The second is a simpler and shorter book on the same subject, and does not contain so many recipes.

HOSTESS BOOKS

Lovely Food by Ruth Lowinsky (Nonesuch Press).

More Lovely Food by Ruth Lowinsky (Nonesuch Press).

You may have to look for these books, but they will reward your search. They are full of ideas and recipes which are better for the experienced cook than the novice, though the ideas may well be absorbed by all. Mrs Lowinsky says I may quote from her, and on a later page I shall try to give some idea of the charm of her books.

Lady Sysonby's Cook Book (Putnam).

This delightful book has a foreword by Osbert Sitwell and contains the accumulated lore of four generations; the illustrations are by Oliver Messel. In 1949 a new and revised edition was available. Lady Sysonby gave permission for quotations from her book to be made, and these too will be found on a later page.

Kitchen Essays by Lady Jekyll, D.B.E. (Thomas Nelson & Sons).

A charming book of the kind one takes to bed to read. The theme ranges from cottage hospitality to supper after the play, and food for travellers and for those too fat and too thin is discussed. It is now available in a new version re-edited by Lady Jekyll's daughter, Lady Freyberg (Collins).

Food for the Greedy, a collection of recipes, by Nancy Shaw (Cobden-Sanderson).

Caviare to Candy by Lady Martineau (Cobden-Sanderson).

Lady Martineau collected her recipes from many countries, and the pages of her introductory chapters in my copy of her book are worn thin because I have read them over and over again to students. The ideas, though considered simple in the day the book was written, are a little grander than we consider now for everyday use, but this does not lessen the value of what she writes about food.

Leaves from a Tuscan Kitchen by Janet Ross (J. M. Dent & Sons).

Another old book worth finding. It contains particularly good and original recipes for cooking vegetables.

The Epicure's Companion by Edward and Lorna Bunyard (J. M. Dent & Sons).

An entertaining narrative dealing with both food and wine.

A Book of Food by P. Morton Shand (Jonathan Cape).

A most interesting and amusing book on food and wine. The author has very downright opinions which, even though they may not invariably be shared by every reader, are provoking and entertaining.

The two foregoing books deal with both food and wine, the next two with wine only. The first, *The Complete Wine Book* by Frank Schoonmaker and Tom Marvel, was published by George Routledge & Sons in 1935, and therefore the list of vintages is not up to date; but the general information remains sound, and there is a most valuable chapter on wine in the kitchen.

The second is a little book called *A Wine Primer* by André Simon (Michael Joseph); it is described as a text-book for beginners on how to buy, keep, and serve wine.

There is a charming book called *The Country Kitchen* by Della Lutes, with an introduction by Florence White.   It is a narrative of life lived in a Michigan farmhouse fifty to sixty years ago, and was published in 1938 by George Bell & Sons.   Although it is a bit remote from a modern cookery book, it is full of good ideas, quite apart from its general interest.

FRENCH BOOKS FOR THE STUDENT OF COOKERY

For the student who has only schoolgirl French it is hard work to wade through French cookery books.   The effort, however, is well rewarded, for they give something of knowledge and inspiration not to be found elsewhere.   It is, perhaps, a comfort to reflect that a very limited knowledge of the language will, with perseverance, suffice.   You can get a long way to begin with with a smattering and a dictionary, and as the names of ingredients and processes begin to get familiar you will soon find the matter becoming easy.   It is, incidentally, a good way of increasing your familiarity with the language, the repetitive nature of the contents being helpful to the novice.

Ma Cuisine by Escoffier (Flammarion).   Now in English (Hamlyn).

A classic on cookery, excellent on all fundamental principles, a clear and concise guide to the professional cook.

Bons Plats et Bons Vins by Curnonsky (Maurice Ponsot).

This gives sound information, not only on cookery but on wines to accompany all kinds of food.   It is a book for the experienced cook.

Gastronomie Pratique by Ali Bab (Flammarion).

This is a tome, beginning with an account of gastronomy throughout the ages, and going on to give not only erudite and classic information on food and wine but hundreds of wonderful recipes.   The name Ali Bab is a clue to the fabulous quality of this book.

Abrégé de Cuisine (Flammarion).

A technical book for the professional, giving lists and descriptions of classic garnishes.

SELECTED QUOTATIONS

Last of all come the quotations from the books to which I have referred in this list.

I think her preface to Menu 1 gives the spirit and tempo of Ruth Lowinsky's book *Lovely Food*:

MENU 1

'Chosen to create a favourable impression on a father-in-law, who comes prepared to judge you as either the laziest housekeeper in Europe, or the most extravagant, or even a subtle combination of the two. On no account burst into caviare or pâté de foie gras to do him honour, but be very careful to bring in the fact that the sweets come from Fortnum & Mason, the fruit chosen by yourself, from Jesse Smith, and the coffee from Lyles, and he cannot, at any rate, accuse you of being lazy.

Clear Mushroom Consommé

Smelts à la Tartare

Romany Chicken

Meringues à la Suisse'

The consommé has fried mushrooms and a little hock added, the chicken, after light frying, is slowly cooked with 2 Spanish onions, 4 tomatoes, and a large glass of sherry, and served in the casserole. The meringues are mixed in a bowl with melted chocolate and whipped cream and decorated with chopped roasted almonds.

The fun continues through this book into *More Lovely Food*; here is the preface to Menu 2 in this second book:

MENU 2

'Everyone knows by now the complaint of an American woman, that anything she liked in London was either immoral, illegal, or fattening. Here is a luncheon which should avoid all these pitfalls.

Chou-fleur au Jus

Grilled Steak and Ginger

Black Coffee Jelly'

The cauliflower is cooked in stock and nutmeg grated over it, the steak has powdered ginger rubbed over it before it is grilled, and the coffee jelly is made with strong black coffee. You see it is a book of ideas and they range from rich to simple. I must, to finish, quote the remark of Mrs Lowinsky's little boy and her comment on it. 'My small boy grumbled: "I never like flavour, Mummy; I told her not to put it in but she always does." He would not have to reproach the majority of English cooks for this fault.'

It is for ideas too that an aspiring cook will make constant reference to Lady Sysonby's book. For many of the recipes I think one may need some practice in cooking, but I would give it to a girl who knew nothing at all in the firm belief that just reading it would make her want to learn. Books of inspiration are not always assessed at their true and great value by the more pedestrian among cooks.

And here, for example, are one or two of the ideas just to whet your appetite for the book and for the food:

SOUFFLÉ MONTE CRISTO

4 eggs	½ pint whipped cream
2 tablespoons castor sugar	vanilla essence
4 leaves of gelatine [1]	

'Beat yolks and sugar with vanilla essence for about 10 minutes, add cream and gelatine, and lastly the whites of eggs whipped stiffly.

Place a tumbler in the centre of a glass dish and pour this mixture in the dish in alternate layers with grated chocolate.

When set pour a little lukewarm water into the tumbler and remove, and fill the hole with ratafia biscuits soaked in kirsch, and cover the whole with whipped cream and chopped pistachio nuts.'

MOUSSE OF CRAB

'You want, for 4 people, a good-sized crab. Remove all the flesh, pound it thoroughly, and pass it through a fine sieve. Season it well with salt and pepper and a little cayenne pepper.

Take about ¾ pint cream and whip it to a stiff froth, and add it to the crab, also 4 leaves of gelatine [1] (dissolved in very little water). Mix well with the pounded crab, and work it a little in a saucepan or a bowl standing on ice.

Put the mixture in a soufflé dish, sprinkle on the top a little chopped parsley, and put the mousse to set and get really cold—3 hours on ice or in a refrigerator.

Serve in a soufflé dish, and with it a salad of cucumber and a vinaigrette sauce.'

ROQUEFORT TOAST

'Make a paste of Roquefort cheese with tomato chutney and Worcester sauce and a little onion. Spread thickly on squares of bread, and grill in the oven. Garnish with crisp bacon and serve very hot.'

Years ago when I was working on *Come into the Garden, Cook* I was given leave to quote from the earlier edition of Lady Sysonby's book and chose among others a dish she calls Poulet Crapaudine. The accompaniment of prunes and onions finished off in caramel is so popular with us that I am grateful for permission to quote it again here.

POULET CRAPAUDINE

'Roast the chicken in the ordinary fashion. Take about a dozen very small onions and put them in a stew-pan with a small piece of butter,

[1] Relative proportions of leaf to powdered gelatine will be found on page 44.

pepper, and salt.　Cover and let them cook, gently shaking them occasionally to prevent burning.　Stone 12 prunes, previously cooked, and put them in a stew-pan.　Put 2 tablespoons castor sugar into a pan and dissolve on the fire until it forms a light caramel.　Add 2 tablespoons of the best vinegar, and reduce till the caramel is quite dissolved.　Divide it between the onions and the prunes, and dish up in a sauce-boat to hand with the chicken.'

It is hard to choose from the richness of Mme Prunier's comprehensive book.　After much talk and turning the pages over once more, we have taken a recipe for red mullet, Rougets à la Livournaise, another for Sole au Gratin which is eminently good and simple, and her excellent Sauce Rémoulade.

ROUGETS A LA LIVOURNAISE

'Score and season the mullet; arrange them in a shallow fireproof dish, and cover them with chopped tomatoes which have been lightly stewed (*fondues*) in oil with chopped shallot, a tiny bit of crushed garlic, salt, and pepper.　Add a little good white wine, sprinkle with browned breadcrumbs and melted butter or oil, and cook in the oven for 15–20 minutes, according to the size of the fish.　When serving, sprinkle over a few drops of lemon juice and scatter over a few capers.'

SOLE AU GRATIN (WHOLE OR FILLETED)

'Cover the bottom of a shallow fireproof dish with rather thick duxelles sauce.　Lay the sole or the fillets on it, surround them with raw mushrooms cut in rather thick slices and overlapping each other, put on the sole itself a few cooked mushrooms, cover with duxelles sauce, sprinkle with browned breadcrumbs, dot with butter, and brown in the oven.　On taking from the oven add lemon juice and chopped parsley.'

SAUCE RÉMOULADE

'To ¾ pint mayonnaise sauce add a good dessertspoon of French mustard and 2 dessertspoons chopped gherkins, capers, parsley, chervil, and tarragon mixed together.　Finish with a few drops of anchovy essence.'

XXXII

Breakfast and Tea

A LIVELY discussion on the subject of breakfast led to the preparation by a member of the family of an amusing lecture entitled 'Now About Breakfast,' and I thought that the more salient points might prove useful to the young housekeeper. So here are a few extracts.

'Breakfast ought to be a comfortable affair—it should be hot, fresh, and easy to eat. . . . Having it in bed is usually thought of as a luxury, possibly as a trouble to the housewife, but it need not be so even if she has to prepare it herself, for a tray is little more trouble to prepare than a place to lay at table. By giving breakfast in bed she can inoffensively keep visitors out of her way while she gets on with her regular morning chores.' I think most of us who are busy in the morning agree about that. 'Don't allow the tray to be overcrowded. Look it over and see that everything required is on it. If you dislike getting up early there is quite a deal of preparation that may be made the night before. The table, or the trays, may be laid, the fish boned, the bacon trimmed.' After these and other remarks follow some very simple and what may appear to be obvious directions, but they are not perhaps quite so obvious or so automatically carried out by the inexperienced that they need be omitted. 'Do not make the tea early in the proceedings, but just a minute or two before everything else is ready. The toast must be crisp, and it also should not be cooked too early. Do not pile it up in a heap, but keep the slices apart and upright until ready to be put into the toast-rack. When bacon is to be grilled, lay the fat part of one rasher over the lean of the next so that the fat becomes crisp without the lean becoming hard.'

'Eggs. For boiling, put a large spoonful of salt in the water. This improves the taste and stops the white from flowing out of a possible small crack. For fried eggs do not put the egg into very hot fat or the white will frizzle; baste the egg gently with the fat.'

Many more instructions about the cooking of eggs are given in the chapter devoted to the subject, but these homely comments seem to find a suitable place here.

'Mushrooms and bacon. Do not fry the mushrooms in the bacon fat for this makes them too greasy. It is better to sauter them in butter.'

'Fried Bread. There are two methods of making good fried bread:

1. Take a plump piece of bread, dip each side slightly in the bacon fat in the grill and then toast.

2. Dip each side quickly into water without allowing the bread to soak. Fry in very hot bacon fat, pressing the middle of the slice down into it, and when the edges become brown turn the slice over. (The underside will be found to brown very quickly.) Again press the middle of the slice down into the fat. Drain on paper.'

The article then goes on to suggest some of the best breakfast dishes: grilled bacon, grilled kidneys, grilled or sautéd mushrooms, eggs fried, poached, scrambled, or boiled, kippers, finnan-haddock, kedgeree, fish-cakes, fried savoury drop scones, fresh fruit, baked apples, stewed fruit, orange, grape-fruit, and tomato juice, toast, brown bread, croissants, hot rolls, cereals, and porridge.

Before the war and beyond that again, when breakfasts were breakfasts indeed, and might even be an occasion for a social gathering, other and, to our impoverished view, grander dishes might be added to those already named—cold game, grouse in particular, a fine York ham and a glazed tongue, and to the toast would be added home-made breakfast rolls, baps, and scones, both wholemeal and white, all made that morning.

An egg might be served on a buttered, home-made crumpet. Flaked finnan-haddock, well seasoned, mixed with a little cream and served on a thick slice of well-buttered toast, was more popular than the ordinary finnan-haddock as we serve it often to-day. Fried prunes, or slices of dessert apple dusted lightly with sugar before frying, might be allowed to take the place of tomatoes with bacon on occasion.

Porridge. The following method gives good fresh-tasting porridge, and is simple and practical.

For 2 persons allow:

½ pint water	1 level teaspoon salt
2 oz. medium oatmeal (this is about 2 small handfuls)	

Bring the water to the boil in a saucepan, add salt, then sprinkle in the oatmeal, keeping the water on the boil and stirring all the time. When all the oatmeal is added allow to simmer gently 10–15 minutes, stirring occasionally. A little more water can always be added if the porridge thickens too much.

Some recipes call for 20 minutes for fine and 30 minutes for coarse oatmeal.

Rashers. A No. 3 cut gives a thin rasher. When preparing rashers for frying, do not blanch unless exceptionally salt. Cut rind off with kitchen scissors, and the bit of rust and bone which is on the other side of the rasher. This applies particularly to streaky bacon. Spread out on a board with a palette-knife or with an ordinary heavy knife.

SAVOURY DROP SCONES

To be made immediately before breakfast.

4 tablespoons self-raising flour	milk or equal parts milk and
salt and pepper and a pinch of	water, enough to make a
paprika	creamy mixture
(if liked, finely chopped chives	
or parsley)	

Combine flour, seasoning, liquid, and herbs if used. Mix to a batter of creamy texture. After cooking bacon or sausage drop the mixture a good teaspoon at a time into the hot fat; it rises quickly. When cooked on the bottom turn over and finish. These are very light and should be served at once.

KEDGEREE (FOR 6–8)

8 oz. rice	seasoning, including red pepper
8 oz. flaked cooked finnan-haddock	1–2 beaten eggs, *or*
	2–3 tablespoons cream
4 oz. butter	chopped parsley
3 hard-boiled eggs	

Boil the rice in plenty of boiling salted water. Drain thoroughly (see page 386). Melt the butter but do not brown, add the fish and chopped hard-boiled eggs. Mix well and heat thoroughly. Season well, add rice, and stir with a fork until very hot. At the last moment stir in the eggs or cream; cook for just 1 minute more, then turn into a hot dish and sprinkle with chopped parsley. The mixture must be creamy.

COFFEE-MAKING

A cup of good coffee seems to earn a considerable degree of appreciation, not perhaps entirely disproportionate, since the production of it does not necessarily come easily. There are certain preliminaries which have to be settled before you can be sure that you will produce uniformly good coffee day after day. For instance, it is advisable to choose a brand of coffee suited to the type of water in your locality, for the same brand of coffee may taste good in one place and poor in another. A good firm of coffee merchants will generally advise on this, as well as on the degree of roasting of the beans to suit your taste. 'French roast,' for example, produces a dark coffee and there are various degrees of colour in the finished bean. It is also necessary to decide to what degree of fineness your coffee is to be ground, and this will depend on the method you adopt for making. Your coffee merchant will also recommend a good breakfast coffee and another suitable for after dinner. If you are wise you will invest in a good coffee-grinder and grind the beans freshly for each meal. It is a matter of a few moments only, but it makes much difference in the result. If you like to warm the beans for a few minutes before they are ground (they must be kept in an air-tight container, by the way), so much the better. One small reminder about the coffee-grinder: no small portions of coffee previously ground should be left in the machine; this detracts from the flavour of the next batch of coffee. You will find for yourself the method of making coffee which suits you and your cooking equipment. With an Aga cooker and its cool oven the very simplest method seems good. Put coffee, ground to a medium degree, into a hot, dry jug, allow 3 to 4 table-spoons to each pint of water and add to the whole a pinch of salt. Then over this pour absolutely boiling water in exactly the right amount. Stir well for a moment, then set the jug in the oven so that the grounds can settle, giving an extra stir if part of the grounds rises to the surface. The coffee may then be poured off gently, a strainer only being used to catch any odd speck of the grounds which may have remained in suspension in the liquid. If you have no suitable cool oven for keeping coffee hot the jug may be put into a pan of hot water.

There are, of course, many machines on the market for making coffee, and while many of them are excellent a special machine is not absolutely essential. For example, you can make a very good coffee by the filter method by simply using filter paper on a strainer specially designed for this purpose. For this you should use filter-ground coffee which is very much finer. This produces a darker coffee with a somewhat different flavour. The reasons for the different degrees of fineness in grinding are, I think, obvious. By the jug method the liquid remains on the grounds, during which time the flavour continues to be extracted; the coarse grounds, holding no coffee dust, subside, leaving clear liquid. In the case of a filter the water simply passes through the grounds, so that it is necessary, in order to extract the greatest degree of flavour, that these shall be finer. Perfectly good coffee may be made in a saucepan, an enamel and not a metal one. Water is poured over the grounds, the whole just brought up to boiling-point, and then time allowed for settling.

Hot but not boiled milk should be served with breakfast coffee. If time in the morning is extremely limited, there is a method of making the latter which may appeal to you. For this a strong essence of coffee is made which will last satisfactorily for a few days. For a quarter of a pound of coffee take a pint of water and, if you like, a teaspoon of chicory; this, of course, gives a slightly bitter taste to the coffee. Make the coffee by the jug or saucepan method, stirring well, then strain carefully, put into a bottle, cork tightly. Add this essence to boiling milk in a quantity which suits your taste. Two tablespoons to half a pint of hot milk is a reasonable allowance.

A good deal is said on the subject of never allowing coffee to boil. While it probably will not be deleterious if freshly made coffee is allowed to boil for a moment or so, certainly continued boiling will destroy the flavour. This most often happens when sufficient coffee has been made for several meals, and then is allowed to boil when heated. It is the boiling of coffee previously made that is so bad.

Coffee should neither be made nor reheated in an aluminium pan, which gives it a metal taste. An enamel one should be used.

After-dinner coffee

As has already been said, a special brand of coffee should be obtained for this purpose, and a somewhat larger proportion of coffee to water should be allowed, say approximately a third more than is allowed for breakfast coffee.

During the war one accepted indifferent after-dinner coffee as a necessity, but when, after the war, one sought to find the coffee remembered of days gone by, one found disappointment. I was looking for the rich after-dinner coffee that literally curdled cream if anyone was foolish enough to spoil it with cream. Whatever I paid and wherever I looked I could not find it. Then I was told by an expert that this is what is sometimes known as acid coffee and it comes from finer and more expensive plantations, and is therefore not imported in any quantity, or rather I should say that such quantity of it as is imported is spread over too large an area.

When it is necessary to make after-dinner coffee in large quantities, say for a large party, it may be made in advance, but it should never be left uncovered, so after making it is strained, covered, allowed to get completely cold, and then may be warmed up. On no account should it be allowed to boil.

TEA-TIME

The very word tea-time has a nostalgic ring for those of us who remember the past with delight. In those days the disposition of a woman's time made tea-time possible, and the taste for, shall I say, the cosier figure gave no cause for apprehension. I have to admit that tea-time beyond the stimulant of the tea itself is not really necessary when other meals are adequate, but the hour, the association, and the food proper to it are all pleasant. So when, for example, on highland holidays tea-time falls naturally into place, it can be delightful. There is an argument concerning the serving of the tea itself that might be aired here. China tea offered plain or with thin slices of lemon is pleasant to many of us, and the connoisseur will not accept it in any other way, considering the addition of milk to so delicately flavoured a beverage as barbaric; even those who like to take it with milk insist that this shall be put in last. This brings us to the real argument. Leaving China tea out of the question, should tea be served with the milk poured in first or last? Those in favour of milk being put into the cup first will maintain, and rightly, I think, that the resulting cup of tea has a more blended taste. This is natural enough, because in pouring on to a small quantity of milk a larger quantity of scalding tea the milk becomes ever so slightly cooked. The difference in the taste of tea poured out in this way is less obvious in subsequent cups. Now those on the other side of the argument will say that in polite circles tea is poured first into the cups, and then they will add in good old-fashioned parlance 'and cream and sugar handed separately'; and it is when they use the word cream that they undermine their own argument. If you are serving tea with cream, then the cream should not be put first into the cup because the scalding of it spoils its flavour. In old-fashioned tea parties cream was *de rigueur* with tea and should certainly have been put in last, but a little ordinary milk, or milk, shall we say, on the thin side, poured into a full cup of tea does not really appeal to a discerning taste. In the old days, when it was correct to hand the cream after the tea had been poured out, there was another custom. The hostess would rinse out the tea-cups with boiling water from her silver kettle before pouring in the tea. This was not with the sole object of warming the cups, but also to prevent her delicate china from becoming cracked by the sudden impact of hot tea. Now we are no longer all of us so meticulous in the matter of pouring out, the putting in of the milk first will have the same advantageous effect.

As real tea-time belongs to conventional days, it is perhaps not out of place to discuss it in conventional fashion and to lay stress on the finer points of what was then considered *de rigueur*.

It was not then considered good taste to have too many small things— one good plum cake, one light cake, perhaps of the sponge or sponge-sandwich variety, or an orange cake, iced, might appear, and a hot dish of crumpets or buttered toast, anchovy toast or hot tea-cakes, and, in particular, that admirable hot cake described as Irish Sally Lunn. Even on the most elegant of tea tables it was then, and is now, permissible to leave jam in its pot set on a plate unless you possessed a nice, plain glass jam pot. It was the fancy dish that was inelegant. Then I hear the shadow of one old lady saying to me 'and never biscuits out of a tin, my dear!' although the same old lady would allow that for the country tea you might have a loaf of home-made bread, a pat of butter, watercress, radishes, and, if you were hungry from exercise, a boiled egg. If what I have just said sounds ridiculous and snobbish to you, and meaningless into the bargain, I will excuse myself by saying that as tea-time was in its glory in the old, conventional days, it is forgivable to report what was then *de rigueur*. This expression, which applies to far fewer things to-day than it did long ago, may be boring, as conventions can be. But when too many conventions disappear a certain grace goes with them.

Recipes suitable for tea-time are to be found in the bread, cake, and cocktail chapters, and I may be allowed to add the following suggestions for good tea-time food:

Home-made crumpets and muffins on pages 771–2.

Anchovy rolls, page 11.

Rock, Bath, and Chelsea buns for schoolroom tea (pages 783 and 784).

The rich chocolate cake on page 818.

A sponge sandwich (page 821), spread with the rose-petal jam filling given on page 1036.

Bun loaf (page 768).

Gügelhopf (page 769).

Selkirk bannock (page 770).

Singin' Hinny (page 777).

Potato cakes (page 779).

Sally Lunns (page 781).

Galette de Savennières (page 798).

Plain sponge cake with a crusty top (page 820).

The orange cake given on page 814.

And any one of the special jams and conserves given in the chapter on the subject.

If you want a particularly rich plum cake with an appeal to men, you may take a rich cake to begin with, make in it a discreet hole or two and feed it from time to time with a spoonful of brandy or rum, allowing the cake gradually to absorb this liquid. This cake has a curiously strong appeal to teetotallers who are unaware of the contents.

XXXIII

Garniture and Presentation of Food

'IT looked very nice but it tasted of nothing.' 'It looked an awful mess but it didn't taste bad.' Is there a familiar note in either of those remarks? There is to me. If you are not interested in cooking you will hardly be reading this book; if you are I shall be forgiven if I take time here to write a little about the presentation of food.

First of all, I am sure we are agreed that food should look pleasant, smell good, be harmonious to eye and palate. The appearance of the dish, too, should indicate the nature of the food being offered. It may be permissible in the more frivolous reaches of the subject to make gingerbread look like unhealthy babies, a sponge cake depict a crinolined lady, or little cakes simulate apples or mushrooms, but such disguises are entirely out of place in the serious side of cooking. This does not mean that such food shall not be decorative, only that it shall be decorative in quite a different way; for example, a sole meunière with its brown buttery surface contrasting with the rich colour of mushrooms, the rosiness of tomato and perhaps of orange is decorative, but it is not disguised, it is plainly fish; and since it looks and, we hope, smells and tastes good, it conforms to all the principles. Sole Colbert, too, with its contrast of golden crumbs and green butter, is another example, and so is a good cauliflower au gratin, milk-white, golden brown, with touches of tender green. I do hope I am making you feel hungry, for then all the points to be made will be half won.

Although it will have to be said with more emphasis in the later section of this chapter dealing with garnishing, it may also be observed here that whatever may appear on the dish as a garnish—in form of decoration—should not only be edible but should be intended for eating and should have special reason, of texture, flavour, contrast, for being associated with the main part of the dish. There should, in the interests of appearance, be harmony too between the food to be served and the dish used to hold it, so we may consider for a moment the question of dishes generally.

DISHES

R. H. and I were discussing the mistakes most commonly made by students in their examinations, and we agreed that generally speaking too small a dish is chosen and in consequence the food sometimes presents a crowded appearance; quite apart from appearance, it is difficult to serve without accident.   It is maddening, because a dish perhaps has been over-filled, to get a portion of food on to one's favourite dress; it is essential in the name of good manners to disregard this, for you neither wish to embarrass your hostess nor, in a restaurant, to make trouble for the waiter, but nevertheless it is annoying.   Naturally no one wishes to be the cause of such *contretemps*.   Choose, therefore, a dish which will hold with ease all that you intend to put on it.

Choose also a dish suitable to the type of food you are serving.   For example, a cauliflower au gratin does not look its best in silver, but calls for a brown fireproof dish.   A green salad dressed in a deep wooden bowl has an authentic look; arranged to look like a bouquet in a glass dish it reveals the hand of the inexperienced.   Aspic in any form calls for the shine of silver to reflect its lustre.   Fruit and ices generally look their best in glass, and an oval, shallow copper dish makes fish take on a party air.

Fireproof dishes

These are of comparatively recent introduction and have rightly become popular and universally used.   They give the desirable impression that the food is being served straight from the oven.   They are of particular value for serving homely dishes.   Before their advent silver was more extensively used, and since silver should not be put in the oven this was not so practical from any point of view.   Fireproof dishes should always be used for food that is cooked or finished in the oven, and the food should be served in these even if, for the sake of appearance, they are set on a silver dish.   One point may be noted here: These dishes sometimes come from the oven with dark marks produced by small portions of burned food; these marks may be quickly and easily removed with a damp cloth dipped in salt.   Fireproof is suitable for classic dishes of bourgeoise cuisine, for gratins, fried and grilled food, vegetable dishes, omelets, and some hot sweets.

Fireproof glass needs to be used with discretion to look well.   Not all foods baked in the oven look at their best in a transparent dish.   Individual dishes of fireproof or oven-proof glass are suitable for certain things: for baked eggs, for small cheese soufflés or gratins; but, while they make for economy of serving, they should be used in a limited way and with discretion, bearing in mind that generally speaking a portion of food from a large dish has better taste and consistency.

Of late it has been possible to obtain a type of pan new to many of us, a light pan of shining nickel.   These are really very pleasant for the serving of food which has not been cooked in them.   The few we possess are never darkened by being used for actual cooking but are reserved for serving vegetables.   These dishes may, of course, be put to heat on top of the stove, so that it is possible to keep the food they contain very hot.   When first I came to possess one or two I found myself longing to see once again certain lovely old Irish silver saucepans, the work of real craftsmen, with smooth, worn black handles, in which vegetables were handed in those days when economy had a less compelling stranglehold on us.

Copper dishes

These are fortunately once more obtainable. They are practical and lend an appetizing air to the food served in them. Food in a shallow copper dish is easy to glaze, moreover it may at need be set on direct heat, a proceeding which would cause a fireproof dish to crack. Except for saucepans used in the boiling of sugar, copper pans and dishes are tin-lined. They must, of course, be kept clean, but this does not present the labour that once was involved. Modern methods have reduced this, and notes for the cleaning of copper will be found in the chapter on the kitchen. Food served in shapely copper dishes, oval or round, has a professional air. These dishes are expensive, to be saved up for and acquired gradually, and very good as wedding presents.

For cold sweets, flat dishes of silver or china look good. Glass is difficult to use well and, of course, must be impeccably shining and free from the slightest suspicion of a smear. A plain, shallow glass dish is good for fruit salads to be served with the savoury course and for some cocktail savouries; glass bowls must be used for certain fruit dishes, punches, and fruit soups, but beyond this the usefulness of glass for serving is limited.

Silver dishes

For certain fine dishes and for party food, silver comes again into its own. Large, flat silver dishes are always in demand for buffet food, and silver is of particular value for food in which aspic is used. These dishes, like glass, must be faultless, and should be lifted or moved with a cloth and never with the bare hand, or inevitably the imprint of finger or thumb will give you away. Unfortunately silver does not retain heat for long, nor can it be started off very hot. Silver dishes are heated by being filled with boiling water, left for a few minutes, and then emptied and dried. Even this process is not looked on with favour by those who cherish the patine of old or much-cleaned silver, and the tendency now is to use it for cold food or as a container for fire or oven-proof or soufflé dishes.

R. H. recalls an occasion when, as yet new at the game, she went out to cook a dinner for some special occasion. Anxious to present food piping hot, she slipped the silver dish into the oven—not, she tells me, a particularly hot one—and what the butler said on the subject had moments of drama. I remember, too, a careless maid putting a silver dish into an oven so hot that one of the handles came off.

Soufflés or mousses should be served in the proper dishes made for them, or if a mousse is to be turned out it too may be served on silver.

TO DISH FOOD

'Do you think,' said R. H. to me, 'that we might have a little section of this book devoted to the process of dishing?' and then went on to say that students do quite often slip up over this: dishing up correctly for a party, but showing a tendency at other times to finish off a dish almost surreptitiously on a corner of the stove. A great deal of food preparation nowadays has to be done in a hurry, but the following remarks are addressed to the student of cooking who, having prepared a good and maybe not altogether simple dish, would like to finish off the job properly.   And again, it is always interesting to know how things should be done even if the knowledge has to be kept only for occasional reference.   Dishing up, then, is a process in itself to be carried out in an orderly and precise way. Not only do I listen to R. H. with avidity when she talks about food, but I think with lively appreciation of how she practises what she preaches; she can make a work of art out of simple food, and she can make dishes that I don't even like look entirely tempting.   So now I make no apology for going into quite elementary details about this important process.   First then, again, this is a separate process and the table should be made ready for it.   It will be easier if a specific and not too simple dish is taken to exemplify what has to be said, and we will choose chicken jardinière: a roast chicken surrounded with at least three and probably four or five different vegetables, all separately prepared, and with a small portion of gravy poured over the chicken.

First of all, then, clear the decks and on a reasonable area of kitchen table make ready for this important process of dishing.   Put in front of you a clear board with a serving spoon and fork on it; to the right other serving spoons and to the left the hot dish to contain the food: if this is of silver it should stand on a folded cloth.   Immediately beyond the board set pot boards or a board on which to place the bain-marie if this has been used.   Have everything hot.   Dish chicken hot and gravy hot.   (On this point see note below on reheating.)   Do not in an anxiety to feel unhurried start dishing too early so that you are faced with the tiresome problem of keeping things hot; with a garnished dish in particular this is not easy.   Rather have everything quite ready, then dish neatly and quickly and serve right away.   A professional cook will begin to dish up a main course while the first course is being eaten.   A cook-hostess will choose her menu carefully with not too many garnished dishes.

We will assume that the gravy has been made, the chicken carved, returned to the dry baking-tin, and moistened with a spoonful or so of gravy to keep it from getting dry.   We will also assume that the vegetables have been drained and finished off.   Arrange the saucepans of vegetables in front of you on the pot boards, lift from the oven and set on the board the baking-tin containing the pieces of chicken.   With a spoon and fork lift out the legs, divided in two (see carving, page 638), arrange these in the middle of the dish alongside each other, drumsticks in the centre, thighs on either side.   Now take the wing pieces and arrange on top, with the bone outside and the curved flesh in the centre.   Arrange the slices of breast in the middle between the pieces of wing.   Aim at keeping the arrangement high—a flat arrangement of such food looks less attractive.

Now arrange the garnish: Take off the pan lids; with a tablespoon lift out the vegetables and arrange them with an eye for good contrast of colour and shape.   Choose the vegetable of which you have the largest quantity and pile this at either end of the dish.   Arrange the others in little heaps.

Do not try to divide them up into small amounts, rather have one reasonable heap of each vegetable; this gives the least spotty effect. The heaps should just touch each other with no surface of dish showing in between. Now take the pan containing the gravy, put it in front of you and gently spoon the gravy over the chicken; do not, in an access of impatience, pour it over, or you will almost certainly disarrange what you have already done and you will probably add too much. The amount of gravy added to the dish should be but a few tablespoons, the rest is served apart.

Reheating

Before dishing you will ascertain that everything is hot. If the gravy has cooled it may be brought to boiling-point; if sauce is in question it may be heated up but probably must not reach boiling-point.

If chicken, meat, or fish needs reheating this may be done either in the oven carefully covered with a buttered paper, or if in a copper dish over direct heat.

A point about fried food may be noted here: to be at its best such food should be served immediately it is cooked. Should circumstances prevent this it is best not to keep it warm for any length of time but to allow it to get quite cold and then put it into a hot oven to reheat quickly, by which means it will regain crispness. The point is not to submit it to slow warmth over a length of time.

Generally speaking hot foods should be served really hot and cold foods be thoroughly chilled; pastry is not chilled and never put in an ice-box. There are, however, some foods which may be dangerous if sent to table too hot. Apple charlotte, for example, should be kept back for a few minutes after it has been turned out or it will be too hot to eat. Toffee sauces and puddings and mincemeat are further examples of what may be dangerously hot food. Jam and treacle sauces should not be served at boiling-point but should be heated just to melting-point.

A dish should be removed from the oven with a dry oven cloth, not with a tea or glass cloth and never with a damp cloth. Not only is it quite easy to burn yourself with the steam from a damp cloth, but it is also possible to crack even an oven glass or fireproof dish. A damp cloth may be used for wiping the sides and edges of the dish when dishing is completed.

Here are a few more notes concerning dishing up. If food is to be handed avoid dishing up in such a way that the portions are divided into exactly the number of persons to be served. Try to have at least one portion in excess. If this is inconvenient then serving should be done from a side table. If fillets of sole are to be masked with sauce this is done with the broad side and not the tip of a metal spoon. The quantity of sauce should be about two tablespoons for each fillet and a little to be poured round the dish.

Sauce in any dish should not be more than an eighth of an inch deep, but should cover the dish. The remainder is served apart. If a garnish, let us say, of cucumber is to be added to fillets of sole, a fresh spoon is taken and the pieces carefully arranged.

Rabbit is not an easy thing to dish, not easy to keep in place, but looks best if it can be carefully piled in the dish; a little of the sauce put in the dish first will help. Again R. H. comes with an illustration, relating to two students dishing up in an examination: both good cooks but one with a better sense than the other about how things should look. One lifted out the pieces of rabbit, balanced them neatly in a pile with the back pieces on top, spooned the gravy carefully over them, and presented an agreeable dish; the other turned out the perfectly good contents of the saucepan into the serving dish and produced something which R. H. graphically described as looking like a dead baby.

If slippery food such as fish cakes or cutlets is to be served with sauce in the dish a little may be put in first to prevent slipping. The food must not then be kept lying in the sauce but must be served immediately. When dishing cutlets *en couronne*, for example, the small amount of sauce laid in the dish will help to keep the whole in place.

Fried food used to be served on a napkin to prevent slipping; this has been followed by the paper doily which is to be avoided: it detracts from the appearance of well-cooked food and presents, to the person helped last, an unpleasing greasy piece of paper.

When food is dished *en couronne* the garnish, for example of peas with cutlets, is arranged in the centre; if in *demi-couronne* the garnish is arranged in the hollow of the crescent.

When food is dished fanwise, as for example sole Véronique, with all the points coming together, the garnish, in this case of grapes, is placed at the base of the fan.

The dishing of a few English foods has become common practice; for example, sea-kale after being well drained may be laid on a folded napkin and the sauce served apart. Asparagus is sometimes put on a napkin, sometimes on a plated rack on the dish. Toast should not be used as a bed for food unless it is to be eaten; it was an old-fashioned custom to dish such vegetables as sea-kale, celery, and asparagus on toast so that the toast could absorb any water which might flow from them. The vegetables if properly drained should not need this.

PRESENTATION OF FOOD

Although the way in which food is presented begins with the manner of dishing there are a few points to be observed apart from this aspect. The presentation of food for parties and special occasions is referred to in the appropriate chapter, but here a few simple suggestions are offered for your consideration.

The serving of food is subject like other things to the fashion of the day; and fashion to-day veers towards simplicity, a tasteful considered simplicity with an absence of unnecessary adornment. Food should never look over-handled and it certainly should not be over-trimmed. I can remember the days, now dead and gone, of tatted and tatty doilies, of ribbon-covered plate-handles which enabled the refined to pass the bread and butter daintily, with nothing so obvious and ordinary as holding the plate firmly by the rim. And I can remember the cake baskets of silver, now used by me very happily for flowers, and the monstrous cheese dishes for which, alas, I can find no such satisfactory use. Even bread was sometimes handed in a basket with a doily. Now we serve these things in, I think, a more practical and pleasing fashion.

Cheese, for example, looks at its best on a wooden tray, one or more kinds together; a Camembert looks pleasant laid in an inside cupped leaf of a Savoy cabbage placed on the tray. A Brie looks best on a straw mat such as those used for the purpose in cheese shops.

An assortment of bread and biscuits and rolls is attractive if arranged in lines on a wire cake rack, and rolls alone and unbuttered scones may be piled in a sieve kept expressly for the purpose. Small cakes too arranged formally on a wire rack have an unhandled fresh-from-the-oven look.

Jam looks best in a plain glass jam pot, and not spooned out into shallow dishes. The pot should be emptied, washed, and refilled each time it is used.

French mustard is served in its own pot with a wooden or horn spoon, and English mustard should be freshly made in small quantities every day.

Salt should frequently be freshly put out into cellars and the spoons taken out and rubbed up after every meal: salt so quickly spoils silver. Salt-cellars may be as simple and as capacious as you like, but I confess that I can never get used to sprinklers. I know they have their uses, particularly for large numbers, but not on the home dining table. Grinders for pepper and salt enable us to have freshly ground pepper and rock-salt.

Soup is more often served in soup-cups than in a tureen. If a hot vegetable is to be served with cold food, a hot plate, a salad plate if you like, should be provided. If you are wise and dress the salad yourself at table you will organize for your use a wooden tray containing all you need for the purpose. Baked potatoes, which long ago looked so beautiful in the lovely Irish silver potato rings, shaped like a huge napkin ring and pierced with intricate designs, look well in these lesser days in a substantial wooden bowl or rough earthenware casserole.

GARNITURES AND GARNISHES

In a minor way these two words seem to demarcate the points of view of two countries. The French garniture is an important affair from which a dish may take its recognized name. In England an idea is fixed in the minds of some people that the apotheosis of a garnish is the adornment of a dish of cold meat or of pats of butter with sprigs of parsley. It is, I am sure, this thought that sometimes prompts a waiter, serving English clients, to push aside the prepared watercress garnishing a grill. Provided the cook is a good cook, that watercress has been carefully prepared, dipped for a moment in French dressing, and is calculated to be a refreshment to the palate and a contrast to the richness of the meat. You are unlikely to find a person of epicurean taste rejecting such a garnish.

This, I think, brings us to discuss the essential nature of a garnish: what it should and should not be.

First, then, a garnish should never be an inedible frill. You may like the taste of raw parsley, which indeed is very good, but the pieces that adorn a dish of cold meat or pats of butter are not commonly eaten or intended for consumption. Better then take in their place what can be eaten, watercress perhaps, shredded horse-radish, radishes, sliced gherkins and suchlike. But indeed this is only the narrowest possible aspect of an important subject.

A garnish has the dual purpose of both looking and tasting good. In flavour it may be delicate and so bring out the equally delicate taste of the main part of the dish; or on the other hand it may be in startling contrast. Grapes or cucumber in association with sole exemplifies the first point, red-currant jelly or mint sauce with lamb the second, while in cauliflower with cheese sauce there is contrast of a strong-tasting sauce with a less highly tasting vegetable. The garnish may present contrast of texture, smooth sauce with crisp fried food. The flavour should not be overstated in such a way as to overwhelm the taste of the principal item of food.

In selecting the material for a garnish consider its good flavour, choose, for instance, vegetables which are at their best; generally speaking it is wiser to take those in season, for these usually taste the nicest. The garnish should be on the same scale, as it were, as the food, delicate garnish for delicate food; not truffle for cod, but for spring chicken. A few further examples may serve to point the matter.

Piquante sauce is served with fried food as an offset to its richness; mustard sauce with herring for the same reason. Horse-radish with roast beef, sharp sauce with mutton, each of these has a refreshing effect on the palate. With a dish of spring chicken the subtle flavour of truffles or tarragon may be introduced. In a delicate dish such as sole meunière two delicate tastes, that of the butter and of the fish, are united. Orange with fish, lemon with chicken, both lift the flavour of the main food. Contrast of texture is noted in the serving of smooth sauce with crisp food. Sauce tartare, for example, is smooth as well as piquante. One of the nicest ways of using prunes is to associate them with a savoury dish. Spiced prunes and onions together go well with chicken or lamb, as also do prunes stuffed with chutney. Bananas fried with fish or chicken, pineapple fried with roast chicken, game, or meat, both have their place.

You will have noticed from the few foregoing examples that a garnish or rather a garniture may be a sauce, a vegetable, of fruit or cheese, or, as we shall see from the list below, of shell-fish, and it will be clear too that these are far from being haphazard trimmings, but are carefully considered and sometimes integral parts of a good *plat*.

It would be outside the scope of this book to attempt an exhaustive list of classic garnitures. An advanced student of cooking wishing to know about these may obtain from France a book called *Abrégé de Cuisine* and published by Flammarion. The preparation of many of the dishes carrying great names is really the affair of highly trained chefs, and yet it is not a bad thing to know something about a few of them. It is useful even if only for choosing food from a menu in a restaurant to know what certain words indicate. For example, Crécy grows fine carrots, Périgord is famous for truffles, Nantua for shrimps, so that when such names are encountered you may know what to expect. I am sure some such knowledge would have helped the students wishing to earn approval with a dish of œufs benedictines who, instead of adding slices of ham to her dish, gently basted the eggs with the liqueur of that name.

It is in any case right and proper to treat these names with respect and not to use them indiscriminately. In some cases they derive from the names of famous chefs or from those of well-known people for whom the chefs created the dish. Sometimes, as has been said, they come from the names of places. Even a superficial study of the classic garnitures will make you agree, I think, that cookery really is an art—and not a chore.

A short list follows of a few standard names of dishes indicating certain garnishes. Quite apart from this rather specialized aspect of the matter, there are the correct accompaniments for simpler dishes. A list of cooking terms will be found in the chapter on general kitchen knowledge (page 53).

LIST OF NAMES DENOTING THE GARNISH AND METHOD OF COOKING

Anglaise	boiled vegetables: carrots, turnips, and quartered celery hearts; used for boiled salt beef, mutton, etc.
Aurore	denotes a flame-coloured sauce, the colouring obtained by using fresh tomato pulp; used for eggs, vegetables, or fish.
Bolognese	a rich sauce made with chickens' livers and flavoured with mushroom and tomato.
Bonne femme	lardons of diced bacon or pickled pork, button onions, mushrooms, and potatoes.
Boulangère	potatoes and onions cooked together in the oven, either sliced or whole; used with mutton or lamb.
Bouquetière	groups of carrots and turnips, cut in rounds (paysanne), French beans, cauliflower buds, button onions, and asparagus tips with jus lié or demi-glace sauce; for beef or lamb entrées.
Bourgeoise	diced bacon fried, glazed carrots, and small glazed onions, sometimes red wine in the sauce; used with liver or beef.
Bourguignonne	button mushrooms and onions with red wine sauce; used for beef or egg dishes.
Bretonne	flageolet or haricot beans, whole or in purée, or root vegetables, carrots, celeriac, onions.

Chasseur	sautéd mushrooms added to a sauté of game or chicken, veal, lamb, etc.
Dieppoise	mussels cooked in white wine, peeled shrimps and white wine sauce.
Dubarry	cooked cauliflower heads, masked with sauce mornay and browned; used for a meat entrée or tournedos.
Espagnole	rich demi-glace sauce, flavoured with sherry and finely chopped mushrooms.
Florentine	spinach in any form, purée or *en branches*, sometimes with a mornay sauce.
Indienne	curry-flavoured dishes.
Jardinière	groups of different vegetables, or a macédoine served with gravy or demi-glace sauce.
Joinville	slices of truffle, crawfish tails, and mushrooms; shrimp or lobster sauce.
Lyonnaise	usually onions in some form, fried or braised.
Meunière	fried in butter, with noisette butter sharpened with lemon juice poured over.
Milanese	Pasta with julienne strips of ham or tongue, grated cheese, and mushrooms, and mixed with tomato sauce.
Minute	food cooked very rapidly, e.g. fried or grilled; applied principally to entrecôtes.
Mornay	with cheese (a béchamel sauce flavoured with cheese).
Napolitaine	pasta with tomato sauce and Parmesan cheese.
Normande	garnish of mussels, oysters, shrimps, mushrooms, and fried smelts applied to a sole dish; also apple and cream when other dishes are in question.
Parmentier	potatoes, usually in the form of a purée; a typical example is the soup.
Portugaise	rich tomato sauce.
Printanière	an arrangement of early spring vegetables.
Réforme	julienne strips of truffle, carrots, and hard-boiled egg with finely chopped parsley
St Germain	garnished with peas, or a cream of pea soup.
Soubise	garnished with onion.
Vichy	garnished with whole or finely sliced glazed carrots and sprinkled with chopped parsley.

XXXIV

Menus, Parties, and Food for Special Occasions

To the experienced, the making of menus may appear a simple affair, a mere matter of common sense. There are, however, certain guiding principles which may be of use to the young housekeeper, and it seems worth while to set them out here.

In choosing dishes regard must be paid to the following points:

1. Suitability to the probable taste of your guests.
2. Propriety to occasion, of both the type and number of dishes served.
3. Suitability to the prevailing weather.
4. Contrast of texture.
5. The avoidance of exclusively cold dishes.
6. The choice of dishes both in type and number that have relation to the skill of the cook, the help available, and the equipment and space in the kitchen.

The compound of general sagacity and acuteness of discernment that goes to make up common sense is not possessed in equal degree by all, and is sometimes allowed, by a young cook, to be overlaid by other considerations, a not uncommon fault being a tendency for her to consider primarily her own taste, with an inclination to disregard food in which she personally is not interested.

At Winkfield we sometimes play a menu-making game, each member of a group suggesting an occasion, the guests, and the food she would choose to serve; it is then that a need for general guidance is observed.

Point one above was disregarded, for example, by the student who suggested a birthday dinner for a grandmother of advanced years and included corn-on-the-cob, fried fish and potato chips, toffee pudding and ice-cream, crediting the old lady with the teeth and digestion of Red Riding Hood's wolf.

Then there are generally a few who opine that mulligatawny soup, roast beef, and jam roly would not come amiss on the hottest summer day.

Exclusively cold food, even in hot weather, is not pleasing to everyone, and even cold Sunday supper, designed to lighten the work of the cook, may be relieved by a dish of baked potatoes or a cup of hot soup. Hot food stimulates the digestive juices, and hot soup is a definite stimulant.

It is possibly not safe to conclude that common sense will inevitably prevent an inexperienced cook from concocting a menu on the lines of one I came on in an American town where food is considered to excel: rich cream of mushroom soup, boiled turkey in cream sauce, creamed sweet potatoes and Zabaione; the memory of it has lasted over several decades.

In planning a menu, then, you will think about contrast of texture, occasion, the weather, the guests. If you are deciding what to prepare for dinner for your husband, you will think of what his day has been and whether he will be hungry from exercise or exhausted from mental effort. Never tolerate that nonsense about 'feed the brute'; men are often more discriminating about food than women are, and commensurately appreciative.

It is when you are your own cook, cook-hostess in to-day's language, with little or even no skilled help, that you have to be most clever in your planning. Whether you are cooking for two or for a party your aim should be to choose food and dishes that you can accomplish without overstrain and fuss. Think about the amount of time you are likely to have, the probable help, your space and equipment, and then choose what can be reasonably undertaken.

We enjoy comparative freedom from convention these days, but there are one or two points in this matter which are worth observing. For example, it is more usual to serve soup for dinner than as a first course for luncheon, though it is proper to serve a simple peasant broth for a homely midday meal. Plain grape-fruit, too, is more suitable for breakfast or luncheon unless it is somewhat glorified. Used as a basis for a mint ice it takes its place as first course for a dinner party. Then it is considered more conventional or shall I say a little more elegant on formal occasions to serve certain dishes as one large whole rather than in individual helpings. In small restaurants or cafés one sees individual dishes of salads, sweets, vegetable dishes, entrées, all so prepared for convenience of quick service; but it is a pity to let this way of serving food be adopted too freely in the home. Generally speaking one good dish both looks and tastes better than a lot of individual arrangements. There are of course exceptions to this; while a large soufflé is better than the same mixture put into custard glasses, petits pots à la crème are always made and served in individual pots, and while one would not serve a green salad or a salade niçoise in anything but a large bowl a salad of pears or peaches might be made in individual dishes. Mixed hors-d'œuvre, again, have a slight convention attached to them in that they are regarded as a luncheon rather than a dinner dish, although some of the individual items of which they are composed are suitable as a first course for a dinner party. It was once a usual practice to serve for dinner a separate vegetable course after the main course and before the sweet. This was of a dressed vegetable and might be asparagus, sea-kale, French beans, globe artichokes, petits pois à la française, or any delicate, carefully prepared vegetable. While this practice continues during the asparagus season it is not now perhaps so universally adopted with other vegetables.

Before setting out a few menus I should like to return for a minute to some general advice.

Do not be afraid of simplicity, no matter how important the occasion. If you are a busy person choose even for your principal dish something that may be made beforehand. If you are having several guests, choose certainly a preponderance of dishes that can be prepared either wholly or partly ahead of time, and do not elect to have too many garnished dishes. Leave yourself free to attend to one main dish. You can have even in this way elegant and unusual food. If you attempt too many dishes needing last-minute attention you may meet difficulties. All this does not, I hope, suggest taking the lazy or timid way. It is only interesting and exciting to cook if you stretch both effort and imagination.

Finally, if I may burden you with one more bit of advice, do most certainly plan the order of your preparation well before you are ready to start cooking, so that you begin early on those things that can safely be done ahead of time, only leaving to the last minute such operations as must be done immediately before serving.

SOME MENUS

To read through lists of menus can be deadening to the senses, but a few suggestions may prove useful on occasion, and the first are for small summer luncheon parties, with comments on the dishes named.

LUNCHEON MENUS FOR WARM WEATHER

(1)

(a)   Melon and cucumber, with delicate salad-dressing

(b)   Grilled Fish with Tomato Ice
                                    or
                    Omelette Fines Herbes with Green Salad

(c)   Pommes Rissolées

(d)   Cherry Pie
                                    or
                    Orange Gâteau and Fruit Compôte

(a) A refreshing dish with a light dressing delicately flavoured with tarragon.

(b) The tomato ice is served apart on a chilled ice plate and if well seasoned is delicious.

(c) Pommes rissolées, crisp on the outside and melting within, are suitable with both the omelet and the fish.

(d) The cherry pie has a thickened rich juice and a pastry top and bottom.

(2)

(a)   Œufs Durs Soleil d'Or

(b)   Fritto Misto of Vegetables
Lemon Quarters, Sauce Vinaigrette
Brown bread and butter

(c)   Iced Camembert

Hot Biscuits

(a) A delicate dish made from hard-boiled eggs with a rich cream sauce.

(b) The fritto misto has herb fritters with the vegetables and is a very good and economical dish.

(c) The iced Camembert is served with heated plain biscuits.

(3)

Small tomatoes stuffed with Petit Gervais cheese
Brown Bread and Butter
or

(a)   Salade Niçoise
French loaf and butter

Escalopes à la Crème
or
Grilled Lamb Cutlets

New Potatoes, Green Peas

Sugared Fruit
or
(b)   Strawberries with Elderflower Syrup

(a) This is a rustic salad and good for a simple luncheon. Crusty French bread with ice-cold pats of butter goes well with it.

(b) The elderflower syrup tastes of muscat grapes and is excellent with strawberries.

(4)

(a)   Tomato Salad, rolls and butter
or
Smoked Trout, Horse-radish Cream Sauce in cucumber cups

(b)   Hot Fruit Curry, 'Last-minute' Biscuits
or
Devilled Chicken

Strawberries with Grand Marnier
or
Strawberry Tartelettes with Cœur à la Crème

(a) The salad is best made with small whole tomatoes, well chilled. The rolls may well be starchless rolls called Energen. They are split, brushed over with butter (which may be very lightly flavoured with garlic or onion juice), and made crisp in the oven.

(b) The fruit curry is good but on the light side for a main dish.

Some suggestions for winter luncheon menus start with one suitable for a Christmas holiday luncheon.

(1)

Christmas Holiday Luncheon

Risotto
or
Potage Purée Bonne Femme

Cold Spiced Beef, Red Cabbage Pickle
or
Terrine and Salad

Pommes de Terre en Robe de Chambre Soufflées

Sticky Ginger Cake with Cheese
or
Mince Pies with Winkfield Mincemeat

(2)

(*a*)   Œufs en Cocotte à la Crème
                            or
(*b*)   Pâté, Toast

(*c*)   Carbonnade de Bœuf
              Purée of Potatoes and Celeriac
                            or
              Spaghetti à la Napolitana, Salad

                  Toffee Pudding
                        or
                    Apple Cake

(*a*) The eggs may be made more interesting by having under them a bed of mushrooms or shrimps first tossed in butter.

(*b*) The pâté may be bought by the pound or be from a tin, and it is worked up with a little butter and fresh herbs. It should be served very cold and accompanied by really hot fresh toast.

(*c*) The carbonnade de bœuf is a homely dish, but unusual and generally well liked.

(3)

(*a*)   Mushroom Devil
                        or
              Pain de Choux de Bruxelles

(*b*)   Kebabs and Rice
                        or
              Gougère, Raw Vegetable Salad

                 Apple Charlotte
                        or
                 Pommes au Beurre

(*a*) The devil is of field mushrooms under a spicy whipped cream.

(*b*) The kebabs may be of kidney or liver and bacon, of mutton, or of prunes, apple, and bacon.

(4)

Potted Shrimps
or
Œufs Mont d'Or

Devilled Turkey
Salad
Baked Potatoes
or
Choux Farcis aux Marrons

Ginger and Fig Pudding
or
Rum Pie

(*a*)

(*b*)

(*c*)

(*a*) Eggs baked on a mound of well-seasoned purée of potatoes.

(*b*) A very good dish of cabbage and chestnuts.

(*c*) The first is a rich steamed pudding and the latter a favourite sweet with men.

A bacon and egg luncheon can be popular, especially as a last-minute affair. Arrange on a large hot dish in rows:

Grilled bacon or ham
Poached eggs
Fried potatoes or potato croquettes
Little breakfast drop scones
Grilled tomatoes

Fried potatoes. Slices of boiled potato, egged, breadcrumbed, and fried. The seasoned crumbs should contain grated lemon rind and chopped parsley.

Lemon curd tart or custard tart makes a good finish.

There are times, particularly in the summer, when you like to see lots of friends but do not want to be preoccupied with cooking; that is the moment to institute bread and cheese lunches. I have never thought that my friends found these too casual or inadequate, and they can be, because of extreme simplicity, great fun.

To be successful there are points to be observed:

The bread. You will want, I think, a wire rack of fresh home-made rolls and twists, onion bread, home-made brown bread perhaps, bread sticks, pretzels, and an assortment of salted and water-biscuits; in this way you cater for those who can eat with pleasure a hunk of home-made hot crusty bread and those to whom this is, as R. H. says, death. But whatever of the foregoing you may choose, be sure to arrange to have on a long wooden board a golden, shining, savoury garlic loaf which, in spite of possible prejudice on the part of some of your guests, I guarantee will be eaten to the last crumb.

The cheese board. On the cheese board there should be a home-made cream cheese of the Liptauer type, a hard cheese, such as gruyère, Dutch, or Wensleydale, and one or two of the French cheeses, Port Salut, Fromage de Monsieur, Brie, or Camembert; if you like the very smelly cheeses, as most cheese-fanciers do, you may have a Pont L'Évêque or a St Paulin, and you may like to add a cream cheese such as Petit Gervais or Crème d'Isigny.

With this there will be black olives, radishes, Florence fennel cut in chunks, watercress, perhaps sliced pickled cucumber, and, I hope, guava jelly to eat with the Petit Gervais, celery or possibly chicory, and a large bowl of mixed green salad and a separate dish of tomato salad.   To this you may add a bowl of fresh fruit, treacle tart, or you might have apples fried in butter and sugar, Toffee Apples with Nouilles (see page 912).   If the weather is cold and you think the cheeses will be too chilly, you may like to have a really big dish of Fondue with large hunks of French bread. This may be followed by the same sweet.

DINNER MENUS

(1)

Potage Palestine, Potato Croûtons

(*a*)
(*b*)

Faisans aux Raisins
Salad

Gâteau Bigarreau

Mushrooms on Toast
or
Angels on Horseback

(*a*) Roast pheasant served with grapes.

(*b*) A salad of dessert apples, oranges, walnuts, and lettuce.

(2)

(*a*)

Consommé

Roast Fillet of Beef

(*b*)

Pommes Rissolées, Watercress Salad

Sea-kale or Asparagus au Beurre

White Coffee Ice

Tuiles d'Amandes

(*a*) If the consommé is served cold and jellied, quarters of lemon may be handed with it.

(*b*) The watercress should have a sharp French dressing.

(3)

(a)　　　　　　　Spinach and Green Pea Soup

　　　　　　　　　Roast Lamb
(b)　　　　　　　Mint and Horse-radish Cream
(c)　　　　　　　Pommes de Terre Siciliennes

(d)　　　　　　　Ripe Plum Salad
　　　　　　　　　Norwegian Cream

　　　　　　　　　Cheese Croquettes

(a) A particularly good soup made with tinned spinach, peas, and shredded horse-radish.

(b) The sauce is made with mint sauce, red-currant jelly, and cream horse-radish sauce, all beaten together.

(c) The potatoes are mixed with cooked Seville orange and are good and unusual.

(d) The salad is of ripe plums with a tarragon cream dressing.

(4)

(a)　　　　　　　Crème Constance

(b)　　　　　　　Sole Meunière Bretonne

　　　　　　　　　Roast Duckling
　　　　　　　　　Bigarade Sauce
　　　　　　　　　Orange Salad
　　　　　　　　Potatoes, Green Peas

(c)　　　　　　　Bombe Lychée

(a) An iced curry cream soup.

(b) Sole cooked à la meunière with rashers of streaky bacon between each fillet.

(c) A light cream ice, moulded, with the centre filled with lychées.

To end this array of menus here is one more for a specially hot summer day:

(5)

　　　　Cucumber, Melon, and Tomato Winkfield
　　　　　　　　　　　or
(a)　　　　　　　Soupe Vichyssoise

　　　　　　　　　Cold Roast Duck
　　　　　　　　　Lemon Compôte
　　　　　　　　　　　or
　　　　　　　　　Poulet Romarin
　　　　　　　　　Potatoes
(b)　　　　　Zucchini or Baby Marrows

　　　　　　　　　Muscat Ice
　　　　　　　　　　　or
(c)　　　　　　　Coupe aux Marrons

　　　　　　　　Hot Cheese Soufflé

(*a*) A delicious cold cream soup.

(*b*) The tiny marrows are cooked with butter, lemon juice, and herbs. The dish may be prepared and slipped into the oven at the last moment.

(*c*) A bowl filled with chestnut purée, hazel-nuts, raisins, and shredded tangerine rind, and covered with ice-cream.

In the Winkfield chapter will be found menus for some special parties.

MEALS BEFORE AND AFTER THE THEATRE

Dinner before the theatre is not altogether satisfactory, even when the play begins around eight o'clock.   The sense of hurry, of not wishing to go to one's seat after the curtain has gone up, the fear of fussing one's guests—these preoccupations are tiresome.   The ideal is, I think, a light meal before the theatre and supper afterwards.   The light meal before-hand may include glorified cocktail savouries, fishcakes, rather dry and flavoured with curry-powder, large cheese sablés, chipolata sausages, and a pizza (page 282).   The Potage Crème d'Amandes on page 989 is suitable and may be served hot or cold.

Many people like a plain really good chicken or turkey sandwich: fine white bread, adequately buttered, and white meat.   Smoked salmon is generally approved, or smoked trout, and, of course, short drinks.

The meal afterwards will depend on your cooking arrangements.   If the weather is warm you may be able to prepare it all beforehand.   A soup to be heated up if you like, and a cold dish, perhaps crab or lobster flaked, served on well-seasoned cold rice which has a flavouring of chopped herbs, dressed with the dressing for Lobster '31' (page 993), and with an accompaniment of lemon and brown bread and butter.   Cold curried chicken as on page 1012, or a plain cold roast bird of any kind and salad, are also acceptable.   Soupe à l'oignon is almost a classic after-theatre dish, as are spaghetti, bacon and eggs, grilled kippers, a good omelet, particularly omelet Arnold Bennett, and flaked finnan-haddock on fresh-buttered toast.   Scrambled eggs are good and so is the piperade on page 271.

Sweets may have refreshing qualities—fresh fruit salad or strawberry galette; and if coffee keeps you awake a tisane, particularly of mint or tilleul, is agreeable and soothing.

CHILDREN'S PARTIES

It is fortunate, I think, that children to-day are not so exclusively sweet-toothed as we were, and that while a children's party must include a certain number of traditional dishes—jellies, trifles, fruit salads and so forth—there is enthusiasm too for quite a number of savouries.   These may vary from the fairly substantial 'hot dog' or open sandwich to delicate cheese wafers or sticks.   It will be helpful, perhaps, to make a list of those things that we find well liked.   But first it may be generally observed that while whimsical ideas may be distasteful to epicures, food prepared with fantasy made up to represent other objects, is pleasing to the very young, and a children's party is justification for letting the fancy roam.

For example, there is a popular arrangement of apricots and cream on slices of sponge cake, representing poached eggs.   Then there is the ever-pleasing shallow dish of pale green jelly with a bosky surround and meringue swans floating on it.   Cakes made to look like pretty cottages or little boats, biscuits like stars or dominoes, and a 'scene' arranged on top of a cake are all allowable.   The food ought to look pretty, gay, and colourful.   But in spite of the tendency to-day to more savoury things than once were fashionable, certain traditional dishes must appear or it will not be quite a party.

Of sandwiches it is generally the open variety that make the biggest appeal.   Children are sometimes suspicious of hidden food.   A diagonal slice of a long French roll, buttered, with one half arranged with a slice of seasoned hard-boiled egg and the other with delicately flavoured cream cheese, will probably meet with more approval than a closed sandwich of the same material.   'Hot dogs' are popular and may be kept to reasonable size by using small rolls and chipolata sausages.   Potato sticks, cheese biscuits, ice-cream wafers buttered, sprinkled with cheese, and heated in the oven, bread and butter sprinkled with cheese, rolled up, and made crisp in the oven are all suitable.   It may be noted by nervous nannies that finely grated cheese used in moderation will not necessarily result in nightmares.

While jam sandwiches meet with modified favour, those made with chocolate and lemon curd are liked, as well as bread and butter sprinkled with hundreds and thousands.   Chocolate biscuits go well, and so does a simple hard sponge biscuit (I think it is called Casino) dipped into a chocolate coating.   Ice-cream, trifle, meringues, and éclairs are clearly desirable, as well as orange jellies in halves of oranges.   A good bowl of fruit salad is appreciated, and a light iced sponge cake soaked in fruit syrup, and filled with such fruit as cherries or strawberries and perhaps a little cream, is luscious, and harmless enough not to upset a delicate digestion.   To drink, simple old-fashioned lemonade is always accepted with pleasure, and milk shakes have become popular.   All these things are suitable for parties of quite young children.

One party trick is, I think, fairly safe for success: the provision of individual cherry or red-currant trees.   For these we cut little twiggy branches a few inches high, one 'tree' for each child, fix them in pots, and hang them with ripe cherries or with sugared currants as given on page 1021 under Fresh Strawberry Flan.   In winter you may adapt the idea for glacé cherries or sweets made to resemble fruits, but the fresh fruit is better.

Once a year we have a party of little boys from a home, and then our most popular menu is 'hot dogs,' egg sandwiches, doughnuts, ice-cream, jelly, milk shakes, and an individual iced cake for each boy with his name on the icing.   We also make a gingerbread house.

GINGERBREAD HOUSE

A biscuit mixture is used for this and the simplest way to deal with it is to cut paper patterns of walls and roof, to roll out the mixture and then to lay on it the patterns and cut round the edges with a sharp knife.   The paste is then baked and the edges trimmed while it is still hot.   The pieces are fixed together either with syrup of sugar boiled to the crack (see page 860) or with royal icing (see page 828).   The house is then decorated. Tiles on the roof are marked with icing pressed through a fine writing pipe, scrolls may outline the windows and door, and any other trimmings may be devised.   The house may be set in a snow scene or in any surroundings you may care to think out.

CAKE FOR GINGERBREAD HOUSE

4 oz. castor sugar or 'pieces,' i.e. sand sugar	3 teaspoons bicarbonate of soda
5 oz. black treacle or golden syrup	$3\frac{1}{2}$ oz. butter
1 teaspoon each of cinnamon and ginger	1 egg
	1 lb. 9 oz. white flour

Warm the syrup, spices, and sugar together to blood heat.   Add butter in pieces and when melted add soda.   Add this mixture quickly to the sifted flour in a bowl; add the egg beaten to a froth.   Stir well.   Knead on a lightly floured board, form into a ball and chill.   Roll out thinly and cut out as directed.

The above paste may also be used for biscuits and shaped into stars, crescent moons, and gingerbread men.

A solid house may be made with cake in the following way, and it may be covered with marzipan:

Bake a cake in a straight-sided bread tin, approximate size 9 x $4\frac{1}{2}$ inches, and another cake half the size (two cakes of the same size, though easier, are not so economical).   The larger cake is for the house itself and the smaller one, split, for the roof.   Trim the larger and level off the top. Trim the smaller cake also and shape into two triangles by cutting it across diagonally from corner to corner.   Lay these pieces cut side down on top of the other cake, cementing together with jam to make a gabled roof. The chimney-pot can be made out of marzipan.

Sometimes we have a party for young people, members of a junior hunt; for this we find all kinds of bouchées popular, stuffed-egg salad, cheese dreams, 'hot dogs' again, as well as the fruit salad and the sponge cake already mentioned, with meringues and éclairs in plentiful supply.

Recipes for sardine rolls, chipolata savoury, and sugared currants will be found in the appropriate chapters.

TRAIN FOOD

I well remember the first time I had a luncheon basket on a train; ordered ahead by wire it was brought to the carriage at some main-line station *en route*. Now, I thought, I really am grown up, no more packets of sandwiches for me. Someone must have tipped the guard, for I remember he brought in a fresh footwarmer and inquired if I was comfortable. Hair up, long skirts, luncheon basket, the *Strand Magazine*, on my way to my first house party—I was beginning life. In the basket was a wing of chicken, roll, butter, biscuits, cheese and, I think, celery and possibly cake or a jam tart and an apple, and I have an idea that it cost 2s. 6d., though it may have been less. Later, with less precision, I remember meals taken in restaurant cars, food of good quality with reasonable variety, albeit served in the somewhat regimented way adopted in railway dining-cars. In these paragraphs I should like to offer a few suggestions for those who wish to take food with them for long journeys.

The primary qualification about such food is that it shall taste fresh and be really appetizing. It should never bear the faintest trace of paper flavouring, something not so easy to avoid as one might think. Sandwiches or bread and butter, and chicken, may each be wrapped in lettuce leaves to keep them away from napkins or wrapping paper, and whenever possible special food cartons should be employed, and, for keeping salad fresh, Porosan bags. I should like to give you the details of a delicious meal made by one of the family for a small party going up to the far north.

Each of us was handed when we got into our sleepers a small, neat cardboard box containing two little screw-top cartons and other small packages. In one carton was a perfect freshly made lobster salad in a delicious dressing, the second carton contained fresh fruit salad of peaches, strawberries, and orange. Crisp poppy-seed-sprinkled rolls were quartered and buttered, and a Porosan bag held the crisp heart of a cos lettuce. There were small cream cheese rolls made by taking two short pieces of celery, filling the hollow made when they were put together with cream cheese, and rolling the whole in brown bread and butter. Porosan bags are a boon for carried meals; one heart of lettuce not used on this long journey was fresh and crisp when it was taken out of its bag eighteen hours or so after it had been packed up.

Thermos flasks, a commonplace to all of you, have brought about possibilities that would have seemed miracles to us: consommé, coffee, even toddy, all kept hot for many hours.

I asked R. H. to recall a train meal that she thought good, and she gave me this as one she remembered, commenting as she did so: 'Very good chicken, salad, and not too much bread.'

A small spring chicken was cooked in a pan with butter, a little white wine, and a small bunch of tarragon. When cold it had a light covering of jelly. It was split in four and wrapped in lettuce leaves. With this there were bread and butter sandwiches (French bread), lettuce and carefully picked watercress, salted water-biscuits, Camembert cheese, ripe pears, and a bottle of claret. R. H. mentioned another, remembered from schoolroom days: hard-boiled eggs, in their shells of course, French rolls with the centre scooped out, the shell buttered, and the hollow filled with a peeled and salted tomato, cold chicken (she said drumsticks were her demanded portion), buttered ginger cake, and cheese. We both remember a nasty one—hard-boiled eggs shelled so that they tasted unfresh, tin sandwich-loaf bread, buttered, tasting of paper, an un-English tomato tasting of nothing, cheese sandwich, and cake.

Lemon-cheese cakes, and good mince pies well flavoured with brandy or rum and made with fresh fruit mincemeat (page 1038), are good. If you are taking ham or hard-boiled eggs it is better to wrap these apart from the bread and butter. Hungry boys like 'hot dogs'; frankfurters poached in boiling water for seven minutes, drained, and put into a soft fresh roll or bap buttered, lavishly spread with French mustard and given a rub of garlic; or a grilled chipolata, surrounded by a thin grilled rasher in a French roll. Perhaps this is getting nearer to picnic food which properly comes in here, for train meals are of the nature of picnics.

PICNICS AND OUTDOOR MEALS

At about the same period as that of the luncheon basket, picnics were sometimes very grand—far too grand, I think, and the food too like what would have been eaten in the dining-room. In fact they seemed sometimes to be just transported meals—plate, food, champagne, and footmen all complete. This is not the best way to enjoy a picnic.

The nicest outdoor meals are those cooked on the spot, and some of the best among these are to be found in the chapter on barbecues.

When means of transport are available it is well to take along a frying-pan, possibly a primus stove, or if you plan a gipsy fire, and the weather is damp (or you live in the Highlands), a bundle of dry kindling and a fire-lighter. Then you will probably settle for a meal of bacon and eggs and sausages, or, if you have a cook among you, for an omelet, and you will certainly approve of the barbecued ham to be found on page 730. If you can be sure of a bonfire you will roast potatoes in the ashes, though they take at least an hour, and toast sausages on long sticks. I am not of girl-guide vintage, but I am told their suet treacle pudding, cooked for hours in a billy can, takes a lot of beating. But alas, time is often our enemy, and much outdoor food must be carried ready prepared. Some of the things found popular, in addition to those given under train food, are omelets in fresh rolls, hamburgers in baps, and Cornish pasties perfectly made with fresh meat and full of rich jellied gravy. For a long car journey in cold weather a good hot broth in a thermos is generally acceptable.

There is a refreshing filling for a long roll, of bananas and chutney, another of filleted bückling, and yet a simpler one of grated cheese and chopped pickled onions; and triple-decker sandwiches are substantial and good.

FILLINGS FOR ROLLS

Choose long French rolls. Slice a piece lengthwise off the top, about a third of the way down. Pull out part of the crumb. Soften the butter, adding a little salt, pepper, and lemon juice, and if liked (and suitable for the contents) a little crushed garlic or French mustard, and spread inside the roll.

Banana and chutney filling

Peel and split the bananas. Season with salt, pepper, and lemon juice. Chop some mango chutney and put a layer in the roll, then put in the banana, all or part according to the size of the roll. Put back the top.

Fillets of bückling

Line the rolls with thin slices of dill pickle cut lengthwise. Marinade the fillets in lemon juice and seasoning. Lay the fillets in the lined roll.

TRIPLE-DECKER SANDWICH

Cut three even-sized pieces of bread, butter two of them and spread the third on both sides with French mustard. Grill thin rashers, allow to cool and lay on the buttered pieces of bread. Put crisp watercress on the bacon. Use the piece spread with mustard for the centre layer of the sandwich. There are many other good, if less simple, triple-deckers. They may be made with bacon and mushrooms; chicken, mushrooms, and lettuce; asparagus, bacon, and toasted cheese. The bread itself may well be toasted. One thick slice of toast split in two makes a good top and bottom, the soft insides preventing the filling from slipping.

A small version of the Quiche given on page 283 is pleasant, and the devilled chicken on page 727 is good when there is no problem of transport. The cheese bread or Gannat given on page 753 may be split and filled with one of the home-made cheeses given in the cheese chapter, page 745.

OMELET IN A ROLL

Slice the top from a fresh oval-shaped roll, remove the crumb, butter the inside of the shell. Make an omelet with two eggs and turn it straight into the roll while hot. A long large roll may be used to contain a big omelet, which, when cold, may be cut in thick slices. You may like to have omelets of different flavour, perhaps one of fines herbes and one of cheese, and serve a thick slice of each. A good tomato salad packed in a bottling jar may be taken along to be eaten with the omelets.

CORNISH PASTY

4 oz. flour	1½-2 oz. beef dripping or
ice-cold water to mix	margarine
	a pinch of salt
4 oz. beefsteak	1 small kidney
1 small potato, raw	1 small carrot
salt and pepper	1 small onion

Make short pastry by rubbing the fat into the flour, sifted with the salt, and mixing to a firm dry dough with ice-cold water.   Roll out fairly thinly into a square and put aside.   Mince or chop the steak, skin and chop the kidney, peel and slice the potato and cut in dice, chop the onion and dice the carrot.   Mix the vegetables together and season them well.   Put a layer on one half of the pastry and cover with the meat.   Brush the edges of the square with water, fold them over and pinch them firmly together, so that no steam can escape.   Bake for half an hour in a hot oven (400° F.) to set the pastry, then reduce the heat and bake for a further three-quarters of an hour to cook meat and vegetables thoroughly.   This makes one large pasty.

HAMBURGER

1 lb. minced beefsteak	2 tablespoons chopped parsley
salt and pepper	or mixed herbs
1 tablespoon finely chopped	a little beaten egg and cream
onion or shallot	

Mix the dry ingredients together with a fork, bind with egg and cream, and shape into four large portions.   Brown in a frying-pan in hot bacon fat; turn and brown underneath, then reduce heat and cook slowly for 10-15 minutes.

The Belvoir Ginger Cake given on page 817 is good for picnics.

SHOOTING PARTIES

The tradition of food for shooting parties changes little, but varies according to the distances the food has to travel and whether it is to be eaten indoors, in a keeper's cottage perhaps, where facilities for keeping it hot are available, or whether it must be eaten in the open.   Sometimes the food is brought from the house by car, possibly in a hay-box.   One large and substantial dish is appreciated, and the following dishes recommend themselves: Lancashire hot-pot of the variety given on page 996, or a beefsteak and kidney pudding, or possibly a glorified Irish stew of mutton chops, mushrooms, and oysters.

Plum cake, mince pies, apple cake, fresh fruit, Stilton cheese and celery, cherry brandy and hot coffee are all part of such a meal.

R. H. remembers cooking for a party for Sandown races; it was classic either to the family or the races, she cannot remember which, that mutton pies containing both carrots and onions must be provided, and a recipe will be found on page 997.

She remembers another early assignment. For a large party for a race-meeting she had to prepare lunch to be eaten in the back of the shooting brake, and suggested a menu on the lines of a good straightforward shooting lunch; but she says, remembering: 'Nothing doing, everything had to be in aspic in silver dishes,' and adds: 'They hadn't really much taste.' She meant the people, not the dishes.

PARTY BEVERAGES

CIDER CUP

2 quarts cider
½ bottle orange squash
½ bottle lemon squash
1 or more pints other fruit juice
1 glass sherry

a good dash of bitters
cucumber rind
ice
a bunch of crushed mint in the jug

Mix an hour or two before serving.

HOCK CUP

Rub 2 oz. lump sugar on to the rind of 2 lemons, pound it and place it in a bowl with the strained juice, a liqueur-glass each of curaçao and chartreuse, and a quart of iced hock. Stir well, add 2 bottles of iced soda-water and serve.

MOSELLE SORREL CUP

1 bottle moselle, Sauterne, or
  Graves
2 bottles aerated or tonic water
juice of 3 oranges
juice of 2 grape-fruit

sugar or syrup to taste
slices of orange to float on top
ice
a good bunch of sorrel

Mix the wine and aerated water with the orange and grape-fruit juices, sweeten to taste, add the slices of fruit and a good lump of ice, float the bunch of sorrel on top and stand for several hours before serving. This is exceptionally good for dances, etc., and at all seasons.

RASPBERRY SHRUB

This must be made several weeks before it can be used.

1 quart good wine vinegar   4 quarts ripe raspberries
1½ lb. (approx.) granulated sugar

Pour the vinegar over 2 quarts of ripe raspberries and mash them with a wooden spoon. Put a cover over them and leave the basin for 48 hours. Strain off the liquid over another 2 quarts of raspberries and leave for another 48 hours. Mash well and strain again. Add the sugar, stir, and simmer over low heat for about half an hour, until the sugar is completely dissolved. Strain and bottle, cork and seal. Keep for 6 weeks and use with cold or iced water, or soda-water, as a refreshing drink.

SIMPLE CUP

Take a bottle of lemon or lime squash and one of orange or grape-fruit, pour into a big jug and add a cup of very strong tea.   Add what you can of any fruit juice from home-bottled fruit; you will need a little extra sugar.   Take both juice and grated peel of 2 or 3 oranges.   Add a few drops of almond, noyau, maraschino, or pineapple flavouring and a bottle or two of good cider or ginger ale.   This will do, but it will do better if you can add a little alcoholic note in the way of sherry, rum, brandy, or white wine; a little will go quite a long way in improving the taste.

WHITE WINE CUP

2 bottles dry white wine	strawberries
1 bottle soda-water	cucumber rind
1 wineglass brandy	borage
1 wineglass elderflower syrup	ice
sliced lemon	

Mix all together 1–2 hours before serving.

BISHOP PUNCH

½ teaspoon mixed spice	1 bottle sherry
2 lemons	2 oz. lump sugar
6 cloves	

Take the first lemon and stick 6 cloves into the rind.   Put it in a basin in a moderate oven for half an hour.   Boil a half-pint of water with the mixed spice and in a separate pan heat the sherry.   Pour spiced water and sherry into a bowl, add the baked lemon to the liquid and stand the bowl on top of the stove, at the back, for 20 minutes.   Meanwhile rub the lump sugar in the rind of the second lemon and add to the bowl with the squeezed juice of the second lemon.   Serve with a ladle into warmed glasses.

FRUIT PUNCH

Fruit juice from home-bottled fruit or tinned fruit can be used to make these fruit drinks, or orange, lemon, or grape-fruit squash, more economical, may be used for a large quantity.   The fruit juice, canned or fresh, tastes better and may be reduced with soda-water, fizzy lemonade, or ginger ale.

1. Equal quantities of orange juice and pineapple juice, one-eighth lemon juice, slices of orange and lemon, sprigs of eau-de-Cologne mint. Syrup or sugar to sweeten.

2. Lime juice cordial, ginger ale, orange juice, and slices of lemon or lime available.   Syrup or sugar to sweeten.

3. Apricot juice, lemon juice, fizzy lemonade, slices of apricot and apple, mint in sprigs.   Sugar or syrup to sweeten.

FRUIT PUNCH WITH TEA AND GINGER ALE

1 pint strong, hot China tea	1 pint orange juice
½ pint pineapple juice	juice of 3 lemons
1 quart ginger ale	ice
syrup or sugar to sweeten	pineapple mint

Mix the fruit juices with the tea, add syrup or sugar and ginger ale, cool and chill well. Serve with sprigs of pineapple mint.

ROYAL PUNCH

Make tea with 1 oz. China tea, 1 quart water, infuse 10 minutes. Strain the tea, pouring it on to 1 lb. loaf sugar. Add the juice of 8 good-sized lemons. Stir well with a silver spoon and when the sugar is dissolved add:

1 bottle burgundy	1 bottle rum
1 bottle champagne	½ bottle maraschino
1 bottle hock	

Mix everything well and let it draw in hot oven before serving.

SPICED FRUIT PUNCH

To 1 tumbler of port take:

¼ tumbler orange squash	2 strips of lemon peel
½ tumbler white wine	2 or 3 fragments of cinnamon
1 tablespoon sugar	stick

Put all together into a pan, bring to the boil and set light to it. Allow to burn out, remove peel and cinnamon and serve with a slice of lemon in each glass.

OLD-FASHIONED LEMONADE

3 lemons, unpeeled	a sprig of mint
3 tablespoons sugar	ice
1 quart boiling water	one or two extra slices of lemon

Wipe lemons and cut into dice, being careful not to lose any juice. Put into a jug with the sugar. Pour on boiling water, leave 15–30 minutes until strong without becoming bitter, then strain. Put the mint into the serving jug, with ice and one or two slices of fresh lemon, an hour before the lemonade is wanted.

ICED COFFEE

One of the devastatingly simple things so difficult to make. For this, freshly made extra strong coffee is essential. Chill it well, then mix with 'top' or very creamy milk. Keep it strong (iced liquids always lose a little of their flavour). Above all, do not put ice in the coffee, but keep it in the refrigerator until the last minute, then top the jug with thin cream whisked to a froth and very lightly flavoured with vanilla.

ICED TEA WITH MINT

Make strong tea with 1 teaspoon of tea for each person, infuse in boiling water and leave to stand in a warm place for 3 minutes. Strain and pour over crushed ice. Add thin slices of lemon or orange and crushed mint leaves.

ICED TEA WITH RUM

Make as above, serve with slices of lemon and a tablespoon of rum to each pint of tea.

ICED TEA WITH BRANDY

Make as above, add thin slices of orange and a tablespoon of good brandy to each pint of tea.

MILK SHAKES

Chocolate milk shake (1)

Shake in a cocktail shaker 2 tablespoons crushed ice, ½ pint milk, and 2½ tablespoons chocolate syrup. Strain into a glass and serve with a little freshly grated nutmeg on top.

Chocolate milk shake (2)

Shake in a cocktail shaker a good tablespoon of chocolate ice-cream and a half-pint of milk. Pour into a glass and serve with a spoonful of whipped cream on top.

STRAWBERRY OR RASPBERRY MILK SHAKE

This can be made in the same way, with strawberry or raspberry syrup or jam (a good tablespoon) shaken with crushed ice and a half-pint of milk; or with a tablespoon of strawberry ice-cream or raspberry water-ice shaken or stirred into a half-pint of milk. A sliced strawberry or one or two raspberries may be served on top of the glass.

COFFEE MILK SHAKE

2 tablespoons very strong coffee, freshly made	2 tablespoons crushed ice
a scant ½ pint milk	sugar to taste

Shake well, strain into a glass, and serve with a spoonful of whipped cream.

COFFEE-CHOCOLATE

Mix 1 pint strong black coffee with 1 pint milk, sweeten and pour from a height into a jug. Keep hot. Melt 2 bars of unsweetened chocolate with 2 tablespoons cold water. Boil 4 cups of milk with 3 tablespoons of sugar, and chocolate and vanilla, and pour from a height into the jug containing the coffee. Beat till frothy, serve with unsweetened whipped cream on top.

XXXV

The Store Cupboard

A REALLY good store cupboard needs careful building up, but when it is there, adequate, ordered, comprehensive, what a boon it can be, not only for everyday use but for sudden parties, emergencies, experiments, and for the immediate carrying out of a good idea. Of course this chapter must deal with jams and jellies, pickling and spicing and all the usual home-made stores, but it should also cover, I think, the subject of bought, tinned food: how to make the best of this when the occasion calls for its use, and what generally to buy.

To plan and build up such an adjunct to the kitchen is interesting and it is fun; it is also quite often an object of overweening pride. The only proper thing is to build it up to foolproof perfection and then emulate Tar Baby and Brer Fox, 'Tar Baby ain't sayin' nuthin' en Brer Fox he lay low.'

All that is intended in this chapter is to give a few general rules and recipes, together with some recipes that we think particularly good and out of the ordinary. If you have a garden, you may want more comprehensive information and you will be wise to acquire an admirable book, *The Complete Book of Home Food Preservation* by Cyril Grange, F.R.H.S., published by Cassell. Armed with this, a garden, time, and enthusiasm, you may acquire a very fine store cupboard.

JAM-MAKING

Home-made jam should be of refreshing taste and good colour. It should both set and keep well.

Equipment. The preserving pan may be of aluminium, stainless steel, or copper. An enamel pan, desirable for pickles, chutneys, and vinegar, may also be used, but must not be chipped or cracked.

It is convenient to know the weight of the empty pan. For certain preserves you may need to know the weight of a cooked pulp before the sugar is added, and weighing in the pan is sometimes an easy way.

The fruit. This should be dry, fairly ripe, and in good condition. Fruits for jam-making may be divided into those rich in pectin and those deficient in this. Pectin is a natural gum-like substance, present in most fruits before they are quite ripe. When they are absolutely ripe the pectin

1083

becomes pectose, which has not an equally effective setting quality. Fruits rich in pectin are black-currants, red-currants, gooseberries, Seville oranges, lemons, cooking apples, and plums. Examples of those with a low pectin content are strawberries, cherries, and marrow. The degree of pectin present in the fruit controls in some degree the quantity of sugar which may be added. For this reason it is useful to be able to gauge the pectin content, and the following may be regarded as a reliable test.

To test for pectin. After the fruit has been well simmered, a teaspoon of the juice is put into a small glass, and when cold three tablespoons of methylated spirit are added. This mixture is well shaken and the pectin will become concentrated. The appearance of a transparent jelly-like clot of reasonable size indicates the presence of an adequate amount of pectin in the fruit. If in place of this there appear small, broken-up clots, then the pectin content of the fruit is low.

To get the best results in jam-making the pectin in the fruit should be brought into solution before the sugar is added. To achieve this the fruit is simmered until soft, either with or without water, according to the kind of fruit, and then brought slowly to the boil, after which the sugar is added. This is the general rule, but sometimes the juice is drawn from the fruit by layering it with sugar and leaving it overnight.

Fruits deficient in pectin. To make jam successfully from such fruits certain additions to remedy the defect must be made. Juice from fruits high in pectin content may be employed, red currant, gooseberry, or apple, and now there are forms of commercially prepared pectin. Tartaric or citric acid and lemon juice are each sometimes called for.

It is also possible to prepare pectin at home, and the method is clearly described in the book already mentioned, *The Complete Book of Home Food Preservation* by Cyril Grange. I asked leave through his publishers to quote part of his notes on the subject, and this was generously given.

HOW TO MAKE PECTIN STOCK

'APPLE, GOOSEBERRY, OR RED-CURRANT EXTRACT. Use tart apples, green gooseberries, or just ripe red currants. Apples should be sliced thinly but not cored or peeled, for then the flavour is better. They must not be allowed to go brown after slicing but should be immersed in hot water at once.

N.B. Gooseberries and red currants also provide acid. . . .

'Wash and prepare fruit, place in pan and add $1\frac{1}{3}$ pints (nearly $1\frac{1}{2}$ pints) water to each 4 lb. fruit. Simmer tender and crush down at intervals. Strain firstly through hair sieve, and secondly flannel or felt. Next day put pulp back into pan, add $\frac{3}{4}$ pint water (to each 4 lb. fruit used at start) and simmer for $1\frac{3}{4}$ hours. Strain this and then add the two strained fruit juices together.

'Test for pectin . . . and if the clot is weak put the juice into a saucepan and heat to concentrate. Test again and when a firm whole clot is formed the pectin is properly prepared and can be used at once or stored for future use. A properly concentrated pectin should be moderately thick. To store, pour the fruit juice into *small* bottles or jars (screw-band or spring-clip type) and sterilize by boiling for 5 minutes. Do not use a pressure cooker, for high temperatures destroy the jellying power of the pectin. Seal air-tight.

'HOW TO USE PECTIN. The pectin has no distinct flavour and is invaluable for use for making jams or jellies from fruits which set badly or not at all. Shake the bottle before opening or stir the sediment as this is rich in pectin. The pectin extract can be used at the rate of from $\frac{1}{4}$ pint to 4 lb. fruit or juice according to the quantity required.

'If you wish to make a natural fruit jelly, then you add the necessary pectin after you have tested for pectin . . . in order to obtain a good set.

'If you are making *a pectin-base jelly* . . . then you may add as much as 2 pints pectin extract to 4 lb. fruit juice. In fact a general and safe guide to making fancy jellies, such as strawberry or cherry, is 3 lb. juice, 3 lb. sugar, and 1 pint of pectin.'

Water. Certain fruits call for the addition of water. The quantity varies according to the fruit in use and its juiciness and ripeness. It is simmered with the fruit before the sugar is added.

The sugar. This may be either loaf or granulated sugar, according to the type of fruit, and cane sugar is preferable. Loaf sugar is best for jellies and the harder fruits, but granulated is less likely to break up soft fruits such as strawberries and raspberries.

According to the variety $\frac{3}{4}$–$1\frac{1}{4}$ lb. of sugar for every pound of fruit is allowed. Fruit very acid and strong in pectin, such as black-currants, can take the maximum amount of sugar with advantage, and the resulting jam will be richer and juicier. Fruit naturally sweet such as cherries and strawberries calls for a smaller amount of sugar, unless extra acid in the form of red-currant juice is added. The sugar, first heated, is added when the fruit has been brought to boiling-point. The object of warming the sugar before adding it to the fruit is to avoid lowering the temperature. In this way the length of cooking is not extended unnecessarily.

The sugar is warmed in a baking-tin in a cool oven, and care should be taken that it is not overheated. The sugar, added to the jam when the fruit is soft, must be allowed to dissolve before the jam is boiled. If the fruit is not cooked before the addition of the sugar it will not be soft and clear, as sugar has a hardening effect, particularly on the skin of certain ripe fruits. The fruit cooked and the sugar dissolved, the jam is brought to the boil, and boiled rapidly until it will set. The shorter the time of boiling at this stage, the better the jam will be; too long cooking discolours it and destroys the fresh flavour. The time of boiling depends on the amount of pectin present and the amount of water that has been added. It may be as little as 1–3 minutes or as much as 20–30. Generally speaking each recipe indicates the length of time necessary, and it may be noticed that there is a certain kind of raspberry jam that is not boiled with the sugar at all, the fruit alone being brought to boiling-point, the warm sugar added, and the whole just brought again to boiling-point. This gives a jam of brilliant colour and fresh taste.

Skimming. This should be carried out only when necessary and towards the end of cooking; frequent skimming can be very wasteful. It is the scum and not the foam of the jam that should be removed.

To test for setting. Take a small quantity of the jam on to a small plate. Chill as rapidly as possible, then push the jam gently with your fingers. If it crinkles and a drop of the jam on the finger will not fall, then it is ready.

To pot jam. Have clean, warm, dry jam jars. Turn the jam into these, but do not fill too full, leave half an inch at the top of the jar or fill to the neck of a glass jam jar. Use a ladle, small jug, or cup, or proper jam filler, and wipe the jars while still hot with a hot, damp cloth, paying particular attention to the inside of the top of the jar.

To cover. The jars may be covered either while the jam is hot or after it has become cold. The advantage of the latter is that one can then ascertain that the jam has set. A small round of wax paper should first be put on top of the jam before putting on the outer cover. Then a vegetable parchment or cellophane cover is fastened down with fine string or a rubber band. The cover is trimmed, the jars polished, labelled, and dated and stored in a cool dry place. Too light a place is unsuitable as it may be detrimental to the colour of the jam.

If the directions given are disregarded, certain faults may appear in the jam. For example, crystallization may occur. This may be due to one of several causes: the jam having been boiled before the complete solution of the sugar; too large a proportion of sugar; too frequent stirring or too long boiling. This condition may be remedied by standing the jar in a moderately heated oven for half an hour. On the other hand, an inadequate proportion of sugar, too little boiling, or too hot a storing place may cause fermentation.

The appearance of mildew on jam is sometimes a cause for worry. If it appears soon after the jam is made, within a week or so, then something must be done. The recipe may be scrutinized to see if it is at fault, the jam, scraped free of the mildew, may be reboiled, and if necessary a little extra sugar added. Mildew may be caused by putting the jam into damp, unheated jars, by insufficient covering and sealing, or by storing in a damp place. If mildew makes its appearance only after some months, it is not likely to be the fault of the recipe. Provided it has not extended too deeply down into the jam it may be scraped off and the jam, perfectly wholesome, used. Jam kept for a considerable period should be watched for the appearance of mildew.

When mildew has made its appearance on a batch of jam it is a good thing if possible to change the storage place for a succeeding batch, because even though the conditions may otherwise be satisfactory, the air may have become overcharged with the mildew spores.

All these rules and regulations make jam sound temperamental, whereas we know that it is not so, at least not the ordinary household jam. Some of the less common fruits need a little more care. Perhaps the rules are worth a brief summing-up.

TO SUM UP THE PROCESS

1. Choose dry, sound, barely ripe fruit, wash if necessary, pick over, cutting out any defects with a silver or stainless steel knife.

2. Use loaf or granulated sugar and warm it before adding it to the fruit.

3. Add water or not, as the case may be, and generally speaking simmer the fruit until soft before adding the sugar; certain exceptions to this will be found in the recipes. Allow the sugar to dissolve completely in the fruit before bringing to boiling-point. Boil rapidly until the jam will set.

4. Skim only when necessary and towards the end of the cooking. Test the jam in the way described.

5. Have the jam jars perfectly clean, dry, and warm before filling. Wipe the jars with a cloth wrung out of very hot water, cover, tie down, and label.

N.B. In certain jams, such as strawberry and cherry, the fruit sometimes rises to the top of the pot; to avoid this the jam may be left to stand for 20–30 minutes after cooking, and then be stirred up and put into the jam jar.

SIEVED JAMS

These are suitably made with such fruits as apples, damsons, loganberries, raspberries, red-currants, and black-currants.

1. Prepare the required quantity of fruit and put it into a preserving pan with enough water to come very nearly to the top of the fruit.

2. Boil all together until well reduced and in a state of pulp. Rub the pulp through a sieve.

3. Measure the pulp and allow 1 lb. of sugar to each pint.

4. Dissolve the sugar, bring to boil, and finish in the way described for jam.

CONSERVES

To the mind of a cook there is a subtle difference between a jam and a conserve. It is true that the terms are not always used with precision. It may, perhaps, be fairly said that a conserve is often a rich kind of jam, with whole fruit preserved in syrup rather than a sweetened pulp of fruit. R. H. adds that a conserve is fit to be eaten straight, Russian fashion, with a spoon. Examples are to be found on page 1093.

Here are some typical recipes that will serve as a general guide to other household jams:

GOOSEBERRY JAM

3 lb. unripe green gooseberries   4 lb. sugar
1 pint water

Simmer the fruit till soft, 20–25 minutes. Add warmed sugar and allow to dissolve. Bring to boil. Test after 10 minutes; probably 15–20 minutes' boiling will be required.

1. Many varieties of ripe gooseberry have tough skins and so are less suitable for jam-making than unripe fruit.

2. The addition of elderflowers (see gooseberry jelly, page 1096) gives a good flavour.

BLACK-CURRANT JAM

2 lb. black-currants   3 lb. sugar
1½ pints water

Simmer the fruit in the water till quite soft, 50–60 minutes. Add warmed sugar and proceed as indicated above for gooseberry jam.

PLUM JAM (1)

4 lb. plums   4 lb. sugar
½–1 pint water, according to
    the juiciness of the plums

Stone plums. Break about half the stones, extract the kernels, and blanch. Tie remaining stones in muslin and cook with the jam. Simmer fruit till soft, add warmed sugar. Test after 15 minutes; it will probably require 25–30 minutes. When cooked add the kernels.

There is a particularly good greengage or plum, orange, and walnut jam given on page 1091.

PLUM JAM (2)

Choose sound medium ripe plums or greengages for this jam. Split plums with a stainless steel or silver knife and remove stones. Weigh the fruit and allow ¾ lb. granulated sugar to the pound. Put the fruit and half the sugar in layers into an earthenware bowl. Stand 12 hours. Turn into a preserving pan and bring slowly to the boil. Simmer until the plums are tender, add remaining sugar and boil rapidly until it will set, 20–30 minutes.

This recipe may also be used for damsons or bullaces; then the fruits are cooked whole and as many stones as possible removed during the process.

APPLE JAM

This can be dull and over-sweet. The following recipe produces a delicious lemony jam:

7 lb. apples, weighed when peeled and cored	preserving sugar, and a little lump, 5¼ lb. in all
4 lemons	4 oz. almonds, blanched and split

Rub zest of lemons on to the lumps of sugar. Rub round the preserving pan with butter (the apples are cooked without water and this will prevent them from sticking). Add apples cut up in fairly large pieces. Cook very gently over low heat till soft. Add zest of lemon and heated sugar, dissolve, bring to boil, add almonds. Cook 25–30 minutes and test.

PEAR AND APPLE JAM

3½ lb. pears, 3½ lb. apples, weighed after peeling and coring	4 oz. candied peel (home-candied orange or grapefruit is excellent, see page 1131)
rind and juice of 2 lemons	
5 lb. sugar, including a little lump	1 oz. almonds, roughly chopped

Rub the zest of the lemons on to the lumps of sugar. Cut up apples and pears and put in a large bowl. Add lemon juice and sugar and leave to stand all night. Next day add candied peel and almonds. Simmer till soft, bring to boil, test after 25–30 minutes.

APRICOT JAM
from dried apricots

1 lb. dried apricots	3 lb. sugar
2½ pints water	1½ oz. almonds

Warm the fruit and soak 48 hours in the water, which must cover it. Put fruit, the water it was softened in, and sugar into the pan. Bring gently to boil, taking care that the sugar becomes dissolved. Boil 1–1¼ hours. Blanch and split almonds and add 10 minutes before jam is finished.

BLACK CHERRY JAM

4 lb. cherries	1 rounded teaspoon citric acid
2¼ lb. sugar	

Stone the cherries. Crack about two dozen of the stones, add the kernels, blanched and skinned, to the fruit with the sugar and stand overnight. Barely cover the rest of the stones with water, boil 30–40 minutes and strain. Keep the water, add to the cherries with the acid and bring slowly to the boil. Then boil hard for about half an hour until set.

See note on stoning cherries, page 47.

SPICED BLACK CHERRY JAM

4 good seedless oranges	2 sticks of cinnamon
4 lb. black cherries	6 cloves
1 good gill lemon juice (6 oz.)	3½ lb. granulated sugar

Slice the unpeeled oranges thinly. Put into a pan with water to cover by about ¼ inch, and the spices tied in a muslin bag. Simmer until the oranges are really tender, then remove the bag. Meantime stone the cherries, crack a few of the stones, and blanch the kernels. Add them to the pan with the cherries, lemon juice, and sugar. Stir until the sugar is dissolved, then boil rapidly until thick.

The first of the following raspberry jams is brilliant in colour and fresh in flavour. As it is important that the fruit shall come exactly to boiling-point, it is desirable to use a thermometer for this jam. The fruit should not be very ripe.

RASPBERRY JAM (1)

1 lb. raspberries to 1 lb. sugar

Mash the raspberries lightly with a silver fork. Put into a preserving pan rubbed round with lemon. Bring to the boil, stirring fairly frequently. A thermometer is useful here as the fruit must *just* boil. Add at once the warmed sugar and when dissolved bring quickly to the boil. Remove at once from heat, pot immediately and when cold cover.

RASPBERRY JAM (2)

1 lb. raspberries to 1 lb. sugar

Heat fruit gently till juice flows. Add heated sugar, dissolve and bring to boil. Test after 3 minutes, which is usually adequate cooking time for freshly picked fruit.

UNCOOKED RASPBERRY JAM (1)

For this the fruit must be picked when absolutely dry or the jam will not keep. Allow 1¼ lb. sugar to each pound of fruit. Beat fruit and sugar together till the sugar is completely dissolved; this may take 40–50 minutes. When this is done pot and cover carefully.

UNCOOKED RASPBERRY JAM (2)

to each 1 lb. fruit allow 1 lb. castor sugar

Put fruit and sugar in separate dishes in a moderate oven for 15 minutes and allow to heat through without letting the sugar brown. Put all together in a bowl and stir for 10 minutes. Leave to stand 20 minutes. Carry out stirring and standing three times in all and put in one-pound jars. Put into a cool oven for 1 hour, then cover. If granulated sugar is used an extra stirring and standing will be required.

RHUBARB JAM

10 lb. rhubarb, weighed when cut up	3 oz. orange candied peel, thinly sliced
2 lb. cooking apples, weighed when peeled and cored	3 oz. glacé ginger
7½ lb. granulated sugar	grated rind and strained juice of 2 lemons

Arrange the rhubarb and sliced apple on a big dish or enamel tray, strewing the sugar in layers between the fruit. Leave 12–24 hours. Turn into a preserving pan, add the candied peel, ginger, and lemon rind and juice. Bring slowly to the boil, stirring frequently to dissolve the sugar, then boil rapidly until the jam will set, about 15–20 minutes.

RHUBARB AND ORANGE JAM

8 lb. rhubarb, trimmed and cut up in small pieces	5 oranges
	6 lb. granulated sugar

Spread the rhubarb on a dish in layers with the sugar and leave overnight. Boil the unpeeled oranges until they are just tender. Cut into quarters, remove the pips, then slice finely. Put them into a preserving pan with the rhubarb and sugar and stir over gentle heat. When the sugar is dissolved boil rapidly until the jam will set.

GREENGAGE OR PLUM, ORANGE, AND WALNUT JAM

This has a particularly good fresh flavour.

3 lb. greengages or plums	2 oranges
2½ lb. sugar	½ lb. shelled walnuts

Wash the unpeeled oranges and put them through the mincing-machine, cutting them just enough to enable them to pass through. Stone the greengages or plums and tie the stones in a piece of muslin. Put greengages and stones into a preserving pan with the oranges and sugar and simmer about 1½ hours. Add walnuts, roughly chopped, and continue cooking three-quarters of an hour.

Many people have a favourite recipe for strawberry jam. The three that follow are all good. A few heads of elderflower, tied loosely in muslin and plunged into the jam for a minute or so while it boils, give a delicious flavour. They should be removed as soon as the flavour is judged to be sufficient.

STRAWBERRY JAM (1)

Allow ¾ lb. granulated sugar to every pound of fruit, and the strained juice of 1 lemon to every 3 lb. fruit.

Crush a small saucerful of the berries and put into the preserving pan with a large spoonful of the sugar. Put over low heat till the sugar has dissolved, then add the rest of the fruit and bring slowly to the boil, stirring occasionally. Warm the sugar in the oven, add to the pan with the lemon juice. Boil rapidly 10–12 minutes, or until, on testing, the jam will set.

STRAWBERRY JAM (2)

A very good jam with whole fruits in a good thick syrup.

> 2 lb. strawberries   ½ pint red-currant juice
> 2 lb. sugar

Cover the hulled strawberries with sugar and leave overnight in a warm place to draw the juice from the fruit. (This can also be done in a cool oven in a few hours.) Put fruit and red-currant juice in a saucepan, bring to the boil, and boil rapidly till setting point is reached.

STRAWBERRY JAM (3)

This might be described as a conserve of strawberries, the fruit being plump and whole, and floating in rich syrup.

Choose dry, perfect strawberries, not overripe, that do not need washing. To 5 lb. strawberries, weighed after picking over and hulling, allow 5 lb. sugar and 1¾ pints water.

Dissolve the sugar in the water slowly, in a copper preserving pan. When it is completely dissolved, not before, bring it rapidly to the boil and boil to the soft ball degree (234°–238° F.). Add the strawberries, cover the pan, draw it off the heat, and let the strawberries soak in the hot syrup for a quarter of an hour. Put the pan back on the heat, bring rapidly to the boil, and let the syrup boil up over the fruit. Draw off the heat and let the syrup subside. Skim if necessary. Repeat this process of bringing to the boil, drawing off the heat, and skimming twice more. Lift out the strawberries with a pierced spoon and spread them in a single layer on a wire sieve, putting a large plate or a dish under the sieve to catch the syrup. Scrape all the syrup back into the pan and reduce by rapid boiling until a drop will set on a plate. Put back the strawberries and boil for 5 minutes. Put into hot, dry jars.

A few cloves tied in a muslin bag are sometimes cooked with this jam.

PINEAPPLE JAM

This is good and may well be made with the small, sweet pineapples that are sold cheaply.

Peel the pines in the way described on page 47. Slice and halve, remove any tough part of the core. To every pound of prepared fruit allow 1 lb. sugar and the pared rind and juice of 1 lemon. Tie the lemon peel in muslin, warm the sugar, add to the fruit, allow to dissolve, add lemon rind. Bring slowly to boil. Boil till fruit is clear, about 1¾–2 hours. Add lemon juice. Put a piece of the cooked lemon rind into each jar.

1. Grated lemon rind may be used instead of the pared peel.

2. A bunch of pineapple mint may be put in towards the end of cooking. This should be tied with string and hung in the jam, and removed when the flavour is sufficiently imparted.

A GOOD CHERRY CONSERVE

Morello cherries are the best kind to use, but lacking pectin they are cooked with red-currant juice.

To every pound of morello cherries, weighed after stoning, allow ⅜ pint red-currant juice and 1 lb. granulated sugar, dissolved in 1½ gills water.

Use a copper preserving pan, put the sugar into it with the water and dissolve it completely over very low heat. When it is completely dissolved add the stoned cherries and bring rapidly to the boil. Stir very gently with a wooden spatula, so that the fruit may not be bruised or broken. Boil for 8–10 minutes after the jam has come to boiling-point. Skim and pour the jam carefully into a kitchen bowl. Leave until the next day, so that the cherries may absorb the sweetness of the syrup. Put again into the preserving pan and add the currant juice. Bring up to the boil and boil fast for 3 minutes. Lift the cherries out with a wire spoon or fish slice and lay them in clean hot jars. Bring the syrup once again to the boil, and boil rapidly until it forms a large drop on the edge of the spoon— about 220° F. Fill the pots at once.

Now come some special conserves:

'TO PRESERVE APRECOCKS (RECIPE OF 1670)

'Take the fairest aprecocks and thrust out the stones at the head with a bodkin. Weigh them, and to a pound allow a pound and a quarter of fine sugar. Pare them very thin and lay them in a silver or earthenware basin and strew over sugar. Then a layer of aprecock and a layer of sugar, and so leave them covered at night. The next day preserve them with a very gentil fire, and when they are enough take them up clear from the sirup and put them in pots or glasses, and the next day put the sirup up on them and tye them up.'

R. H. says: 'Instead of paring the apricots I scald them to skin before stoning. It is a simple and delicious recipe.'

PEACH SLICES IN JELLY

apple jelly flavoured with lemon, rose geranium, or lemon verbena	thin slices of ripe peaches

Make a good apple jelly, flavoured with lemon or leaves of rose geranium or lemon verbena (for method see Quince Jelly, page 1097). Peel the peaches, slice thinly, and drop into the jelly when it is nearly at setting point (after about 15–20 minutes' boiling). Simmer gently for a few minutes, then boil rapidly till the peach slices are cooked and the jelly sets. The amount of peach slices to jelly is a matter of taste; it is better not to have the jelly too full of peaches, otherwise the appearance and flavour are spoilt.

GREEN FIG PRESERVE

small green figs, perfectly
sound
lime water made with 2 cups
slaked lime to a gallon of water

water
sugar
slices of ginger or strips of
lemon rind

Choose small green figs that are perfectly sound. Fallen ones may be used if they are firm and unblemished. Wipe them well and prick them. Soak them for 24 hours in lime water, then wash and drain them. Make a syrup of 1 pint water to ¾ lb. sugar. When it is boiling fast drop in the figs, but do not have too many at once in the pan. Boil gently until the fruit becomes clear and the syrup thickens. Slices of ginger or strips of lemon rind should be simmered with the figs during the last half-hour of cooking.

PIPPINS IN ORANGE-FLAVOURED JELLY

about 1 dozen pippins, Alling-
ton, Ribston, or Cox, small
and even-sized
about 6–7 lb. cooking apples
for the jelly

thinly pared orange rind
loaf sugar
flavouring, such as lemon verbena, rose geranium, or
scented mint leaves

Choose small, even-sized pippins, wash, pare, and core them carefully. Boil the peel and cores in water to make enough juice just to float the pippins. Poach them in this until tender. Take them out, cover and set aside. Well wash and cut up 6–7 lb. cooking apples, do not peel or core. Put them into a pan, add the juice from the pippins and enough water to come about an inch or so below the surface of the apples. Simmer to a pulp, strain through a cloth or nylon sieve. Measure the juice and allow 1 lb. sugar to 1 pint juice. Put together into a shallow pan, bring to the boil, skimming well, boil 2–3 minutes. Now carefully put in the pippins with a few leaves of rose geranium, lemon verbena, or mint tied in a muslin bag. Simmer very gently until the pippins become clear-looking (semi-transparent). Meantime simmer the orange peel in water until tender. Drain well.

Take out the pippins, wrap a piece of peel around each and pack carefully into wide-necked jars.

Boil the jelly rapidly, first removing the muslin, until it will just jell nicely. Pour into the jars to cover the apples. Leave till cold and tie down tightly.

A good rose petal jam will be found in the Winkfield chapter, page 1036.

JELLIES

There are two methods of extracting the juice from fruits for jelly-making. In the first no water is used. This is more extravagant but results in a better and finer jelly. In the second method water is added to the fruit and then all is simmered on low heat. This method is more suitable for the hard fruits such as apples, some plums, pears, and so forth.

Method 1. For this the fruit is put into a vessel and this set in a pan of water. A 7-lb. jam jar is a convenient container. A pan with a water jacket may also be used. The surrounding water is allowed to boil and the warmth causes the fruit in the inner vessel to render its juice. The fruit should be mashed a little from time to time. It is turned into a jelly-bag and allowed to drain overnight.

Method 2. In this case the fruit is put into a preserving pan and water added to about a quarter or a little more of the depth of the fruit, and then all is simmered until the fruit is pulpy. It is then turned into a jelly-bag or double linen strainer and allowed to drain all night.

Sometimes juice is extracted without heat, the raw fruit being crushed on a sieve. Red currants, for example, are sometimes dealt with in this way.

Fruit for jelly-making should not be overripe.

Sugar. One pound is generally allowed to each pint of juice, except for red- and black-currants, when as much as $1\frac{1}{4}$ lb. may be allowed, the reason for this being that the amount of pectin in these fruits is very high.

To make the jelly. Rub out a copper preserving pan with lemon. Mix the juice and sugar together, dissolving over slow heat. When dissolved bring to boiling-point, then boil hard and skim with a silver spoon. The time varies; when pure fruit juice is concerned, that is to say extracted by the first method, probably 3 or 4 minutes will be sufficient. In the second method, where the fruit has been simmered in water, 10 minutes may be required. If the proportions of fruit and sugar and water are correct, the jelly should not be required to boil for longer than this. Jelly must be put into warmed jars immediately it is cooked and covered as for jam. It should be noted that for jellies proper preserving sugar, that is to say loaf sugar, should be used, for this produces a clear and sparkling jelly.

Red-currant jelly ranks high among preserves, because of its individual tang and flavour. Crab-apple jelly, too, is popular. Apple and gooseberry jellies, apart from their general usefulness, are of particular value as media for other and special flavours.

RED-CURRANT JELLY

red currants   preserving or loaf sugar

Wash the fruit and, without taking from stems, put into a 7-lb. jam jar or large crock. Cover and stand it in a deep pan of hot water. Simmer this on the stove or put it into the oven for about an hour, to extract all the juice.

Turn on to a thick cloth or into a jelly-bag. Allow to drip through without pressing or squeezing in any way. Measure the juice and allow 1 lb. preserving or loaf sugar per pint. Dissolve the sugar in the juice over gentle heat, stirring with a silver spoon. Then boil rapidly until a little will set when tested on a plate. This sets quickly: usually 3–5 minutes' boiling is enough.

UNCOOKED RED-CURRANT JELLY

Squeeze currants through a fine cloth to extract juice. To each pint of juice add 1 lb. castor sugar, warmed in the oven. Stir juice and sugar together for half an hour. The jelly should be set by the following day.

GOOSEBERRY JELLY FLAVOURED WITH ELDERFLOWERS

Take green but nearly full-grown unripe berries and put them in a large jar. (Put a very little water in the jar if you think it necessary because the berries are hard.) Cover the jar tightly with a plate and tie down with a piece of linen. Set the jar deeply in a large pan of water (the water should come well up the sides). When the gooseberries are cooked—they will take at least 2 hours in the boiling bath—strain through a jelly-bag. Allow 1 lb. sugar to 1 pint juice. Boil and skim for 8–10 minutes and test. Allow 3 or 4 good elderflower heads to each pint of juice. Cut off the stems close to the flowers, tie these latter in muslin and put into the jelly when it comes to the boil. After 3 or 4 minutes taste for flavour and either remove the heads or leave them longer, according to your taste.

ELDERBERRY AND APPLE JELLY

3 lb. tart cooking apples (wind-falls answer well)	peeled rind of 1 orange and ½ a stick of cinnamon, tied
2 quarts elderberries, picked from their stalks	together with cotton
	water
	sugar

Wash the apples well and remove the blemished parts. Cut into pieces and put into a pan with the elderberries. Barely cover with cold water and simmer to a pulp. Turn into a jelly cloth or bag and leave until the next day. Measure the juice and allow 1 lb. sugar to each pint. Put together into a pan, stir over moderate heat until dissolved, then add the orange rind and cinnamon. Boil rapidly until a little will crinkle on a saucer when cold and pushed with the finger. Remove rind and turn into warm jars.

This jelly should be of soft rather than too firm consistency.

JELLY MADE FROM HIPS AND HAWS

Good as an accompaniment to cold meat or game.

3 lb. berries	sugar
3 pints water	lemon juice

Wash berries, simmer in water till soft, about an hour. Put in jelly-bag and allow to drain overnight. Allow 1 lb. sugar and juice of 1 lemon to each pint of juice. Boil till the jelly will set.

ROWAN JELLY

rowan berries	peeled rind of 1 lemon and 2
sugar	cloves (tied together in a
water	muslin) to 2 quarts of juice

Pick the berries from the stalks and wash. Put into a pan with water to come level with the fruit. Simmer until pulpy. Strain through a cloth or jelly-bag. Measure the juice and allow a pound of sugar to every pint. Put together into a copper preserving pan rubbed round with a piece of lemon. Bring to the boil, stirring occasionally, then add the flavouring and boil rapidly until a small quantity will crinkle when cold and pushed with the finger. Turn into small pots, first removing the muslin.

This jelly does not always have a firm and jelly-like set. It is excellent with game or rich meats.

QUINCE JELLY

To make a successful quince jelly it is advisable to add unripe apples to ensure a good set (unless quinces are unripe).

5 lb. windfall apples or crab-apples	pared rind and juice of 2 lemons
4 lb. quinces	sugar
water	

Wash apples and quinces and remove all blemished parts. Cut up and put into a pan with cold water to come level with the fruit. Simmer until pulpy. Turn into a jelly cloth or bag and leave overnight. Measure the juice and allow 1 lb. sugar per pint. Put together into a preserving pan rubbed round with a piece of cut lemon, add the lemon rinds tied together, and the strained juice of the lemons. Bring to the boil slowly, stirring from time to time to dissolve the sugar. Boil rapidly, skimming occasionally, until it will set lightly when tested. A piece of the lemon peel may be put into each jar if wished.

Make crab-apple, apple, and blackberry and apple jelly in the same way.

Flavoured jellies. Jelly flavoured with herbs makes an unusual and agreeable accompaniment to cold meats, poultry, and game: lemon thyme for a jelly to go with game; mint—one of the scented mints if available—for lamb, and tarragon for chicken. Good jellies for confectionery may be flavoured with elderflowers, rose petals, verbena, scented mints, and sweet geranium leaves.

One method of preparation is to extract the flavour into a small quantity of sugar and to add this to the jelly at the end of cooking. Petals of roses or scented leaves are crushed or bruised a little with a small quantity of loaf sugar. This may be done in a mortar or in a strong kitchen bowl. The sugar and leaves are then put with a few tablespoons of water in a covered fireproof dish and left for an hour or so in a cool oven; they may be brought to simmering-point, but not boiled. When it is clear that the sugar and water have absorbed the flavour they may be strained, the liquid added to the boiling jelly, and the whole brought back to boiling-point.

Sometimes, if the flavour is not adequate, the pulp of leaves or petals may be put into muslin and this submerged for a moment in the hot jelly.

The following recipe calls for the fresh leaves to be added direct to the jelly:

GERANIUM JELLY

This is a geranium-flavoured apple jelly, made with unpeeled apples and cooked for a very short time.

Fill an earthenware jar with unpeeled, uncored apples. If not hard the apples may go in whole, or they may be roughly cut up. Stand the jar in a pan of water and allow this water to simmer all day, or until the apples are reduced to pulp. Strain the pulp through a jelly-bag, adding about ¼ gill water at the last. Allow 1 lb. sugar to each pint of juice. Warm sugar in a cool oven. Boil juice 20 minutes with 8–10 sweet geranium leaves. Add warmed sugar, allow to dissolve, stirring gently all the time. Bring to boiling-point and test after 1 minute. This is quite adequate cooking time. Remove leaves, pot, and cover at once.

ROSE JELLY

For this the scented delicate petals of the old roses are best and may be used whole. If modern roses are taken the white tip of the petal is cut off, as it may prove bitter. The petals are pounded with the sugar in the way described, and the liquid added, but we generally find it necessary to plunge the petal pulp (contained in muslin) into the boiling syrup for a few minutes.

MINT JELLY

Use apple jelly as a base, as it is clear and has no pronounced colour or flavour.

1 large bunch of mint, preferably Bowles's round-leaved green colouring ¾ gill wine vinegar	pared rind and juice of 1 lemon 2 pints good apple jelly (see notes under Quince Jelly, previous page)

Pick the leaves from the stalks; tie stalks together and add to the jelly with the vinegar and lemon rind and juice. Boil for 5–7 minutes, test for setting. Meantime pound the finely chopped leaves, add 2 or 3 spoonfuls of them to the boiling jelly, taste and add more mint if necessary, then strain and add green colouring.

Elderflowers impart a subtle flavour to gooseberry jelly, and the following is excellent:

GOOSEBERRY AND ELDERFLOWER SYRUP

This is a delicious syrup tasting quite definitely of muscatel grapes, and it is described in some books as a muscat syrup. It makes the most delicious water-ice and is useful for flavouring fruit salads and summer drinks. For keeping purposes it must be sterilized after it is bottled.

The best bottles to use are those now sold for the purpose with rubber stoppers and clips.

4 lb. gooseberries, topped and tailed	1 pint water
3 lb. sugar	12 heads of elderflower

Put sugar and water into a pan, when sugar is dissolved add gooseberries, simmer very gently 5–10 minutes. Add washed elderflowers tied in a muslin bag. Allow to infuse until the syrup is well flavoured. Turn into a nylon sieve or muslin bag and allow to drain thoroughly. Strain again through a piece of muslin, pour into bottles and sterilize for 10 minutes (see page 1181). The remaining pulp may be used for gooseberry fool or for a fruit cheese.

ELDERBERRY SYRUP

5 lb. ripe elderberries, weighed when stripped from their stalks	1 small egg white, whipped to a froth
1 pint water	loaf or preserving sugar brandy

Wash the berries and crush or mash lightly. Put into earthenware jars with the water. Cover and stand in a deep saucepan of boiling water or in a slow oven. Keep on low heat until the fruit is pulpy. Then strain through a jelly cloth or bag. Measure the juice and allow ¾ lb. sugar per pint. Put the juice into a pan with the egg white and set the sugar to warm. Bring the juice to the boil, whisking occasionally. When boiling remove all scum and froth and add the sugar. Reboil, skimming frequently, and allow to simmer 3–4 minutes. Draw aside, and chill a small quantity to test the thickness of the syrup. Continue to simmer if necessary. Bottle, adding a teaspoon of brandy to each bottle. Seal and sterilize according to the directions given on page 1181.

If a very rich syrup is called for, use 1 lb. sugar to 1 pint juice; in this case, if the brandy is added and the bottles are sealed immediately, sterilizing can be dispensed with unless the syrup is to be kept for many months.

Make black-currant syrup in the same way, though here it is inadvisable to boil the syrup; merely heat to dissolve the sugar, bottle and sterilize.

FRUIT CHEESES

These are made with the fruit pulp and sugar and cooked to a thick consistency, so that when cold they are firm enough to be cut in slices. They make good, refreshing sweetmeats and suitably sized pieces may be cut and rolled in sugar. They are a good accompaniment to certain cold meats, and pieces of them may become one of the many accompaniments to curry.

Damson, quince, gooseberry, and apple are, among others, good fruits to use.   In cooking, care must be taken to stir constantly and thoroughly after the sugar has been added, for the thick mixture in the last stages of cooking may burn.

Three typical recipes will serve as a guide:

DAMSON CHEESE

damsons	water
sugar	

Put the clean fruit in the pan, add water about half way to the top of the fruit.   Simmer gently till fruit is thoroughly soft and pulpy.   This may take some time as damson skins are tough and must be thoroughly softened. Rub the pulp through a nylon sieve.   Weigh the pulp and allow 1 lb. sugar to 1 lb. pulp.   Now boil for 1–1¼ hours, stirring constantly and taking care to scrape the bottom of the pan from time to time.

APPLE CHEESE

apples	sugar
cider	lemon juice and grated rind

Wash and cut up unpeeled and uncored apples.   Put in pan with cider about half way up to the top of the fruit.   Cook to a soft pulp.   Put through nylon sieve.   Weigh pulp and for every pound allow 1 lb. sugar and juice and rind of 1 lemon.   Cook as for damson cheese.

The pulps left from certain fruit jellies are sometimes used for fruit cheeses, but may need additional flavouring, for example ratafia or noyau for plums and orange or ginger with apple pulp.

QUINCE CHEESE

9 lb. quinces	take the zest of orange and
water	lemon
preserving or granulated sugar,	2 lemons
with a little lump sugar to	2 oranges

Take 3 lb. of the less perfect quinces; do not peel or core.   Cut up. Put in pan with water barely to cover.   Simmer till soft and strain.   Peel, core, and slice thinly the remaining quinces.   Put into strained juice. Cover pan and simmer till quite soft; this will take some time and may be done in a slow oven.   Put all through a fine sieve.   Measure and allow 1 lb. sugar per pound of pulp.   Put in pan with the zest of orange and lemon rubbed on to lumps of sugar, and the strained juice.   Cook till thick, taking particular care in stirring.

MARMALADE, MINCEMEAT, ETC.

CHERRY BUTTER

A good preserve for immediate use.

8 lb. black cherries   4 lb. sugar
grated rind and juice of 2 lemons

Stone the cherries.   Crack a number of the stones, extract the kernels, blanch and skin.   Add to the fruit with the lemon and put into a bowl in layers with the sugar.   Leave overnight.   Bring to the boil, simmer 15–20 minutes, then boil rapidly until very thick.

MARROW GINGER

Choose the hard, yellow type of marrow.

8 lb. marrow, weighed after   pared rind and strained juice
   peeling and seeding   of 4 lemons
6 lb. preserving or granulated   ½ oz. ground ginger or 4 oz.
   sugar   crystallized ginger
                                   4 oz. walnuts

Cut marrow in inch cubes.   Put in a bowl with layers of sugar and leave 24 hours.   Turn into the preserving pan with lemon rind tied in a bundle, the juice, and the preserved ginger, cut up.   Bring slowly to boil. Take a little of the hot syrup and mix with the ground ginger (if used) to make a smooth paste.   Return to pan.   Boil gently, stirring carefully, taking care that the jam does not stick to the bottom of the pan.   Add the walnuts, chopped up, towards the end of cooking.   When the syrup is thick and the marrow clear and transparent it is ready for potting.

The following are two recipes from a family cook-book of R. H.'s:

ORANGE MARMALADE (MR RINGROSE'S)

Boil Seville oranges for an hour or until tender.   Cut in quarters and remove the pulp.   Remove pips and slice the peel.   Mix pulp and peel together and to each pound add 1 pint of water in which the oranges have been boiled.   Then weigh again and add to each pound 1¼ lb. sugar. Dissolve over slow heat, then boil rapidly for half an hour or until it will set.

ORANGE MARMALADE (COLONEL GORE'S)

Cut Seville oranges into four, remove pips and set aside.   Slice oranges, weigh, and to every pound of pulp take 3 pints cold water.   Mix and allow to soak 24 hours.   Before using the preserving pan rub it with a piece of lemon 'that the colour of the marmalade may be kept pure.'   Then simmer, with the pips in a muslin bag, approximately 4 hours or until the chips are quite tender. Turn into a basin, remove pips, and stand 12 hours or until the next day. Weigh and add 1¼ lb. sugar to every pound of pulp. Bring slowly to the boil, then boil rapidly until the syrup jellies and the chips are quite transparent. Cool slightly and pot with plenty of the jelly.

Any surplus jelly may be strained off and potted separately. Pot when very hot. This marmalade sets considerably more after a fortnight in the pots.

GRAPE-FRUIT AND PINEAPPLE MARMALADE

Equal weight of grape-fruit, pineapple, and lemon. Pare and shred the pineapple. Slice grape-fruit and lemon thinly. Allow 3 pints water to each pound of fruit. Cover the fruit with water and leave till next day. Boil till tender, approximately 3 hours. Measure and allow 1 lb. sugar to each pint of fruit. Cook together until the marmalade sets.

LEMON CURD

3 oz. butter	½ lb. lump sugar
2 large lemons	3 eggs

Put the butter into a double saucepan, then add the sugar (rubbed all over the lemon rind to extract the zest), the juice of the lemons, and the strained beaten eggs. Stir constantly over a moderate heat until thick. Store in a cool place.

MINCEMEAT (1)

½ lb. beef suet	½ lb. mixed peel, chopped
¾ lb. raisins	¼ lb. sweet almonds
½ lb. sultanas	grated rind and strained juice
¾ lb. chopped apple	of 2 lemons
¾ lb. brown sugar	a good pinch of mixed spice
¾ lb. currants	2 glasses of brandy

Chop suet finely. Wash fruit (see page 801). Shred almonds. Mix all together and moisten with the brandy. Keep a month before using.

The following juicy and fresh-tasting mincemeat is made without suet and is good to eat cold. It is best eaten within a few weeks of making, although I have known it keep well for many months.

MINCEMEAT (2)

2 lb. apples	rind and juice of 3 or 4 lemons
2 lb. raisins	½ lb. almonds
2 lb. currants	¼ lb. candied peel
1 lb. sultanas	2 lb. sugar
1½ lb. grapes	1 gill brandy or rum

Wash fruit (see page 801). Peel and core apples. Peel and pip grapes and chop roughly. Pare thinly the rind from the lemons and squeeze the juice. Blanch and chop roughly the almonds. Put apples, dried fruits, pared lemon rind, and candied peel through the mincer. Add roughly chopped grapes, almonds, lemon juice, and sugar and mix well. Add brandy or rum. Cover and allow to stand an hour or two, stirring from time to time.

Another mincemeat made without suet:

MINCEMEAT (3)

12 oz. chopped apples	1 level teaspoon ground nut-
12 oz. chopped raisins	meg
6 oz. cleaned currants	1 level teaspoon mace
3 oz. butter	½ gill boiled cider
6 oz. brown sugar	2 tablespoons golden syrup
2 level teaspoons cinnamon	grated rind and juice of 1 lemon
1 level teaspoon ground cloves	brandy or rum to moisten

Mix together and simmer 30–40 minutes. For those who do not like too sweet a mincemeat, omit the golden syrup.

SPICED FRUITS

These are an admirable addition to the store cupboard. They are only delicately acid and so are often liked by those who find many forms of pickle too much so. On the other hand they are not too sweet. The spiced cherries given are particularly good, and we use them not only as an accompaniment to cold food but for cake-making, to put in the middle of the cream filling of a meringue, and for cocktail savouries. The spiced crab-apples are good with such rich foods as goose or duck. Spiced fruits generally may suitably be served as one of the accompaniments to curry and may be used to garnish canapés and suchlike. The most luscious and *recherché* of all spiced fruits are the stuffed spiced peaches given in the Winkfield chapter. We usually keep a few jars of the latter for Christmas to be eaten with cold food, in particular with ham. Generally speaking, spiced fruits keep well for some months.

An instruction is usually given in the recipe to tie the spices in muslin; an alternative is to use, for a small quantity, a closed tea infuser, suspended from the side of the pan.

SPICED APPLES

3 lb. small firm apples, weighed after peeling, coring, and slicing	½ oz. cloves
	1 oz. stick cinnamon
	1 teaspoon allspice, whole
4 lb. sugar	1 teaspoon salt
2 pints vinegar	

Tie spices in a muslin bag. Put them with sugar, salt, and vinegar and bring to boil. Put in the prepared apples, cook till tender. Lift out apples and put in jars. Boil the syrup till thick and pour over the fruit. Tie down with care.

SPICED CRAB-APPLES

crab-apples	¾ gill wine vinegar
water	cinnamon stick
2 or 3 strips of lemon peel	1 or 2 cloves
1 lb. loaf sugar	peppercorns

These are crab-apples in a heavy spiced syrup. (Used as a flavouring they may be roasted in the pan with a goose or duck, or be put inside the carcass of the bird.)

Choose large, unblemished red crab-apples. Trim off the stalks and wash. Put them into boiling water with 2 or 3 strips of lemon peel. Simmer gently until barely tender. Remove a dozen or more of the perfect ones and set on one side.

On to 1 lb. loaf sugar strain 1½ gills of the water in which the crab-apples were boiled. Add ¾ gill wine vinegar and a small piece of cinnamon stick, one or two cloves, and a few peppercorns, all tied in a small piece of muslin. Put together in a pan. Stir until sugar is dissolved, then boil rapidly for 1 minute.

Draw aside and add the selected crabs, allowing only the barest movement of the liquid; the apples should just float nicely on the syrup. Simmer until the syrup has reduced enough to coat the crab-apples (about 30–40 minutes), but the spices should be removed after the first half-hour.

Put the crab-apples into pots, cover with syrup and seal.

SPICED CHERRIES

Take preferably morello cherries. Stone them and cover them with a good mild vinegar. Allow them to remain in this for 7 or 8 days, stirring them with a silver spoon twice a day. Now take out of the vinegar (keeping this for subsequent use in salad-dressing), drain well, and to each pint of cherries allow a pint of granulated sugar. Put back into an earthenware crock, leave for another 8 days, stirring twice a day as before, put into earthenware jars and seal. The vinegar used for these cherries is excellent for making the syrup for Stuffed Spiced Peaches (see Winkfield chapter, page 1037).

SPICED DAMSONS

2 quarts damsons	1½ gills vinegar (approx.)
2 lb. lump sugar	a few cloves and a little cinnamon

Prick the damsons well with a silver fork. Arrange in a pan in alternate layers with the sugar. Add vinegar to cover. Bring to boil slowly. Lift out damsons with a flat strainer or ladle, leaving liquid behind. Spread out the fruit on dishes to cool. Continue boiling the syrup with spices for 10–15 minutes. Pack fruit in stone jam jars, pour over boiling syrup. Leave several months to mature.

SPICED ORANGES

These are quite delicious to eat with hot or cold meat.

10 fine large oranges	1½ sticks of cinnamon
1 pint white wine vinegar	¼ oz. cloves
2¼ lb. cane or loaf sugar	6 blades of mace

Slice the oranges about ¼ inch thick, lay them in a pan and barely cover with water. Simmer with the pan partly covered until the peel is tender. Draw aside. Into another pan put the vinegar, sugar, and spices and boil well together for a few minutes.

Drain the oranges, carefully reserving the liquor. Lay half of them in the syrup, making sure that it will cover. Put the lid on the pan and simmer 30–40 minutes, until the oranges turn clear. Lift out into a shallow dish, put the rest of the oranges into the pan, and if not covered by the syrup add a little of the reserved orange liquor. Cook as before. Turn all into a bowl, cover and leave overnight. Then, if necessary, pour off the syrup and boil until thick. Add the slices and reboil. If the syrup is thick and well reduced, merely heat slowly to boiling-point with the oranges, then pot and tie down.

Should there not be sufficient syrup to cover, make fresh syrup in the above proportion of vinegar to sugar, boil till thick and fill up the jars. The spices may be left in the syrup, or put into a muslin bag and removed before potting.

It is important to keep this preserve 6–8 weeks before use.

SPICED PEARS

small pears, sugar and salt	1 or 2 sticks of cinnamon
4½ pints white distilled vinegar	a few cloves
1¼ lb. sugar	

Cook small peeled pears till tender in water with a little sugar and salt— 2 oz. sugar and ¾ oz. salt to each quart. Boil together sugar, vinegar, and spices. Put in the pears, bring back to boil. Set aside to cool a little. Bring back again to boil. Repeat this process three more times.

PLAIN SPICED PEACHES

2 pints vinegar (white wine or white distilled)	stick, and 1 teaspoon all-spice, tied in muslin
1 oz. cloves, ½ oz. cinnamon	4 lb. sugar
	7 lb. peaches

Bring vinegar, containing spices, to boiling-point, add sugar and dissolve. Peel the peaches; the golden yellow, thick-skinned imported peaches called Hale or cling are best for this, and these must be scalded for peeling. If garden peaches are used they should not be too ripe and may also need scalding. Ripe peaches may be skinned without scalding. Large peaches should be split and stoned. Drop the peaches into the boiling liquid. Cook till soft, taking care to see that they are cooked through. Lift out into jars. Boil the liquid to reduce a little and pour over the peaches. Tie down with care.

See also stuffed spiced peaches (Winkfield chapter, page 1037).

SPICED PLUMS
in black-currant leaves

Choose good, well-flavoured plums without blemish. Prick them all over with a wooden cocktail stick and pack them straight into wide-mouthed jars, with layers of black-currant leaves in between. Add a few cloves and 1 or 2 sticks of cinnamon to each jar. Allow ¾ lb. sugar to 1 pint vinegar and a level dessertspoon of salt. Boil together and pour over the plums. Tie down tightly and leave about 6–8 weeks before opening.

SPICED PRUNES

1 lb. prunes	½ lb. sugar
cold tea	mixed spice
¾ pint mild vinegar	

Wash prunes and soak overnight in cold tea. Boil together vinegar and sugar with the spice in a muslin bag. Cook the prunes in a little of the tea in which they were soaked for 10–15 minutes or until quite soft. Drain. Add ½ pint of the juice to the spiced vinegar. Pour liquid over the prunes. Put into jars, cover. They are fit for use after 24 hours.

SPICED MUSHROOMS

3 lb. button mushrooms	a few cloves
salt	a piece or two of root ginger,
½ pint wine vinegar (approx.)	bruised
½ pint port (approx.) (or red wine with a lump of sugar)	

Do not peel the mushrooms. Trim off the ends of the stalks, wipe well with a cloth dipped in salt. Lay the mushrooms on a meat dish, sprinkle with salt, and leave overnight. Put mushrooms and the liquid drawn from them into a shallow pan and cook gently, stirring constantly, until no liquid is left. Gauge the amount of liquid required barely to cover the mushrooms and make this of port and vinegar in equal proportions. Add liquid and spices in a bag to mushrooms and boil all together for a few minutes.

SPICED AND PERFUMED VINEGARS

A store of vinegars flavoured with herbs, spices, flowers, or fruits will save time and bring refreshing variety to salad-dressings, curries, chutneys and so forth.

Tarragon, mint, garlic, onion, chilli, rose petals, and spices are all good for salad-dressings, and the spiced vinegars may be used also for pickles and chutneys and for those chutneys which are made freshly to accompany a curry.

The vinegars are made in two ways. In one the flavouring ingredient, tarragon and mint for example, is allowed to steep for a certain length of time in the cold vinegar. In the second hot vinegar is used to extract the flavour. This method is used for garlic and spiced vinegars and suchlike.

For best and fruit vinegars white wine or white distilled malt vinegar should be used. For pickles, such as red cabbage, ordinary onions, and mixed pickles, brown malt vinegar is suitable.

TARRAGON VINEGAR

1 pint tarragon leaves   1 pint white wine vinegar

Immerse the leaves in the vinegar (a Kilner jar is a useful container) and leave for 5 or 6 weeks closely covered before using. There is no need to strain the vinegar, and after some of it has been used the jar may be filled up, provided the flavour is strong enough to take it. (See also bottled tarragon leaves, page 372.)

MINT VINEGAR

Fill a 7-lb. jam jar with sprigs of mint lightly bruised. Pour boiling vinegar over them and cover. Stir from time to time with a silver spoon. After a week or two strain and bottle it.

GARLIC VINEGAR

8 cloves of garlic crushed with salt   1 pint vinegar

Crush the garlic, bring the vinegar to boiling-point and pour over. Put in jars, cool, cover, and strain after 2 or 3 weeks.

MIXED HERB VINEGAR

For each quart of vinegar allow the following:

4 sprays each of thyme, summer savory, mint, rosemary
a good-sized plant of parsley, leaves, stems, and root (well washed)

a handful of tarragon sprays
½ a root of celeriac (celery may be substituted)
6 or 8 shallots
12 crushed peppercorns

If you grow it, and so can get fresh ripe seeds, 2 tablespoons coriander seeds may be added.

Lightly bruise the herbs, slice the celeriac and parsley roots and shallots. Steep all in the vinegar in a covered jar for 2 or 3 weeks in a warm place, stirring from time to time with a silver or wooden spoon, then strain and bottle.

SPICED VINEGAR (1)

For spiced vinegar it is necessary to heat the vinegar in order to extract the flavour of the spices. The following is a suitable selection for 1 gallon of vinegar:

1 oz. each of mixed allspice, celery seed, mustard seed, cloves, black pepper	1 oz. whole ginger 2 or 3 fresh or dried chillis 6 cloves of garlic

To this may be added ¾ lb. sugar, an improvement though not essential. Greater flavour is extracted from the spices by crushing them or by using them already ground, and the cloudiness of the vinegar resulting from doing this is of little inconvenience. Heat all together to boiling-point and simmer for 10 minutes. After 3 or 4 weeks the vinegar should be strained off and finally bottled. (As it is advisable to keep the vinegar closely covered all the time the spices are steeping, fruit-bottling jars may conveniently be used; the vinegar may then be put into narrow-necked bottles after the straining.)

SPICED VINEGAR (2)

4 quarts vinegar	3 cloves of garlic, bruised
¾ lb. sugar	

½ oz. each of the following spices, whole, but slightly bruised:

allspice	mustard seed
mace	peppercorns
cloves	root ginger
celery seed	coriander seed (¼ oz.)

Bring all very gently to boiling-point. Set aside and allow to infuse and cool slowly. Put into vessels without straining, and divide the spices so that each container has a portion. At the end of a month the vinegar should be well flavoured, but the spices may be allowed to remain.

CHILLI VINEGAR

One ounce dried chillis steeped in a pint of boiling vinegar for 5–6 weeks will give a hotly seasoned vinegar, a few drops only to be used for seasoning.

CHILLIS IN SHERRY

Fill a wine bottle with fresh chillis. Pour over them sherry. Cork securely. Keep a week or two before use. This will keep indefinitely and a few drops are excellent in curries, ragoûts, sauces, and salad-dressings. More sherry may be added from time to time.

ROSE PETAL VINEGAR

Fill a jar with rose petals, preferably those from damask roses, press them well down and cover with white wine vinegar. Leave for a month in a covered jar, then strain. Used for salad-dressings.

As well as using commercially prepared vinegar as a vehicle for flavouring, home-made vinegars may be made from fermented fruit. These are mild in flavour and suitable for salad-dressings but not for preserving purposes.

Here is a recipe for vinegar made with apples which appeared in *Farmhouse Fare* and was given again in *Come into the Garden Cook* by the kind permission of the editor.

VINEGAR FROM APPLES

Take a bushel of sour apples, cut them up and pound them. Place them in a large tub. They will shortly begin to ferment; then add some water which they will soon absorb. At the end of a month strain off the liquor into a cask; to every gallon of liquor add ½ pint vinegar (we find it best to use French red wine vinegar) that has been previously boiled and reduced from 1 pint. Let it remain for 6 weeks and there is an excellent vinegar.

Dregs of wine, strained, may with advantage be added to bought or home-made apple vinegar.

The following is a good recipe for vinegar to be made from nearly ripe gooseberries:

GOOSEBERRY VINEGAR

| 1 quart nearly ripe gooseberries | brown sugar |
| 3 quarts water | |

Crush the fruit well, add the water and allow it to stand for 24 hours before being strained. To each gallon of this liquid 1 lb. brown sugar should be allowed, and the whole then put into a cask and allowed to ferment; the liquid is then strained off for bottling. This is an old-fashioned household recipe which went out of fashion when sugar became scarce.

PICKLES

Some authorities on food and some epicures regard pickles with a certain amount of scorn, the suggestion, I think, being that the enjoyment of them indicates a jaded appetite, or that their use implies an inability to cook in that they may be used in the place of sauces. I am inclined to think that it all depends on the individual digestive power of the person

delivering the opinion, and, of course, on the quality of the pickles themselves.   I do not believe that the old-fashioned road-mender eating his
piece, bread, cheese, and pickled onion, suffered from a jaded appetite,
nor do I think that inability to acquire a good sauce is the cause of serving,
and successfully so, finely cut, crisp red cabbage pickle with spiced beef
around Christmas time.   There is indeed a sort of hierarchy of pickles:
walnuts, mushrooms, and small, sweet, silver-skinned onions enjoy a
certain prestige, the coarser varieties falling among the ranks of ill-bred
fellows.   I have noticed that one most critically epicurean host offers
sliced, sweet dill pickles among the things with drinks before dinner, and as
for me, I have always wanted to taste Amy's pickled limes so temptingly
described in *Little Women*.

Pickles belong to the tradition of the English kitchen, and the art of
making them should not be allowed to die out.   They are quite simply
vegetables or fruits preserved in spiced vinegar, usually receiving a preliminary treatment with brine.   They may be sweet or sour.   If the
vinegar is of good quality, the material treated fresh, the spicing carefully
judged, then the results may be excellent.   Coarse materials and rough
preparation, as in other branches of cookery, will give unsatisfactory
results.   The vinegar suitable for using in most pickles is a good brown
malt.   Piccalilli is made from assorted vegetables, but differs from other
pickles in that the preserving liquid is thickened spiced vinegar coloured
with turmeric.

A special mixture of spices is prepared and sold as pickling spice.   It
contains many of the necessary spices.

PICKLED RED CABBAGE

cabbage   spiced brown malt vinegar
salt   (see below)

Shred the cabbage finely, sprinkle with salt and leave 24 hours.   Pack
in jars and fill up with cold spiced vinegar.   This should be a crisp pickle
and be eaten 3 or 4 days after making; after a few months it becomes soft.

Spiced vinegar for this pickle: 2 oz. pickling spice to each quart of vinegar.
Bring to boiling-point and allow to cool.

CHOW CHOW OR MIXED VEGETABLE PICKLE

6 ridge cucumbers   salt
1 medium cauliflower   1 oz. turmeric
4 onions   ¼ oz. pepper
2 lb. tomatoes, green or red   2 oz. mustard seed
2 green peppers   ¼ oz. allspice
1 good head of celery   ½ gallon brown malt vinegar
1 lb. young runner beans

Prepare vegetables, cut in small pieces.   Sprinkle well with salt and
leave 24 hours.   Add spices in a bag to vinegar, bring to boiling-point.
Add vegetables.   Simmer till tender.

DILL PICKLE

50 small ridge cucumbers	1 pint vinegar
salt and water for soaking (in	8 oz. salt
the proportion of 1 lb. salt	1 big bunch of dill
to every 4 quarts water)	cherry leaves
5 quarts water	1 red pepper

Put cucumbers overnight in salt and water. Boil together water, vinegar, and salt and allow to cool overnight. Drain cucumbers, arrange in large jars with layers of dill and cherry leaves. Pack tightly, adding a small piece of red pepper to each jar. Cover with the cold vinegar and water and fasten down securely.

PICKLED EGGS

14 hard-boiled eggs	2 hot chillis
spiced vinegar	

For the spiced vinegar

1½–2 pints white wine vinegar	½ oz. white peppercorns
¼ oz. root ginger, bruised	

Simmer vinegar with ginger and peppercorns (in muslin) and allow to cool. Remove shells carefully from eggs. Arrange in jars, put a piece of chilli in each jar. Cover completely with the spiced vinegar. Tie down securely. Good for use after 4 weeks.

MARROW PICKLE

1 large marrow	¼ oz. chilli pods
1 lb. baby pickling onions	½ lb. sugar
1 oz. ground ginger	3 quarts vinegar
1 oz. ground turmeric	

Peel and remove seeds from marrow. Cut into small squares. Lay on a big dish, sprinkling salt between the layers. Treat onions in same way after peeling. Leave overnight. Drain well. Put remaining ingredients into a large pan, simmer half an hour, then add marrow and onions. Continue to simmer until thick.

PICKLED ONIONS

2 quarts peeled small pickling	¼ oz. each of cloves and pepper-
onions (silverskin)	corns
1½ oz. salt	2 oz. sugar
½ oz. pickling spice or allspice	1 quart good vinegar

Peel onions, sprinkle with the salt. Leave to stand overnight. Next day rinse well and dry. Put the spices, sugar, and vinegar into a pan and boil 5–7 minutes. Add onions and bring back to boil. Draw aside, take out onions and pack into jars. Reheat vinegar and pour over the onions to cover well. Cover when cold.

SWEET PICKLED ONIONS

small pickling onions   salt
tarragon   green or red pepper
mixed spice   white sugar
wine vinegar

Lay out the onions on a large meat dish and cover them with salt. Leave them overnight; in the morning wipe all the moisture off and pack them into jars with sprigs of tarragon, a piece of red or green pepper, and 1 teaspoon whole mixed spice to each 1-lb. jar. Boil sugar, in the proportion of 6 oz. white sugar to every 1¼ pints wine vinegar, or, if the vinegar is unusually acid, allow ½ lb. sugar to each 1¼ pints vinegar. Pour into jars and tie down at once.

PICKLED MUSHROOMS

mushrooms
vinegar spiced with, for each quart:
    3 blades of mace, bruised   ½ oz. peppercorns, bruised

Put the spices, in a muslin bag, in a pan with the vinegar. Bring just to boiling-point with the lid on the pan. Set aside and allow to infuse 2–3 hours. Peel the mushrooms, or rub off the peel. Cut the stalks level with the caps. Put in a pan. Sprinkle lightly with salt. Cook gently, shaking well, till the juice flows. Continue cooking till the juice has evaporated. Cover with spiced vinegar, simmer 2–3 minutes. Put carefully in jars and seal when cold.

SWEET CUCUMBER PICKLE

Excellent for sandwiches.

3 lb. ridge cucumbers, weighed   2 green peppers, halved, the
    when peeled and sliced   seeds removed, and shredded
1 lb. medium-sized onions,   1½ oz. salt (approx.)
    finely sliced

Pickle
10 oz. brown sugar   1 teaspoon turmeric
1½ oz. mustard seed   ½ teaspoon ground mace
1 teaspoon celery seed   1 pint white wine vinegar

Put the vegetables in layers in a bowl, sprinkling well with the salt. Cover and leave 2–3 hours. Drain, rinse with cold water, and drain again. Meantime put all the pickle ingredients together into a pan. Bring to the boil and boil for 2 minutes. Add the drained vegetables and bring again to boiling-point, stirring well from time to time.

The following is a sweet pickle of green tomatoes. It comes from Denmark and is often a component of their famous cold tables. It is **very** sweet, slightly sharp, and sounds to me as though it might come near to Amy's pickled limes in *Little Women*.

GREEN TOMATO PICKLE

4 lb. small green tomatoes, weighed after removal of specks

4 lb. sugar

¼ litre (1½ gills approx.) vinegar, and a little extra

1 stick of vanilla

brandy

Wipe tomatoes. Cut away any specks and weigh. Put into a pot with cold water and enough extra vinegar to make it slightly acid. Leave till next day. Put the vinegar into a pan with the sugar and boil until clear, stirring with a wooden spoon. Add some of the tomatoes and boil gently till soft. Take out and put into glass jars rinsed with brandy. Continue until all the tomatoes are done. Then boil juice slowly for 10 minutes, skim well, add the vanilla cut in four or five pieces and split. Boil for a minute in the juice and pour the latter over the tomatoes. Cover until the next day, then pot. Allow to mature a little before eating.

PICKLED PEARS 'SEVEN-DAY'

3½ lb. small pears

2 lb. sugar

½ pint white distilled vinegar

3 oz. mixed pickling spice

1 oz. whole ginger

Bruise spice and ginger and put in muslin bag. Peel pears and put all ingredients in pan. Bring to boil. Then pour into a stone crock and leave overnight. Next day pour off the liquor and boil it up. Return to pears. Do this every day for 7 days. At the end of this time there should be just enough liquor to cover the pears. Pot and tie down.

It is only in recent years that sweet peppers have become widely available in this country, but now their unusual and subtle flavour is becoming generally appreciated. At certain times of the year they become fairly inexpensive, and that is the moment to make the following pepper relish. The recipe has been adapted from *The Boston Cooking School Cook Book*.

PEPPER RELISH

12 large green peppers

12 large red peppers

12 medium-sized onions

2 pints white wine or white malt vinegar

1½ oz. salt

1 lb. granulated sugar

½ oz. mustard seed

Split the peppers and seed them. Chop finely or mince. Chop the onions. Put all into a basin and pour on boiling water to cover. Drain at once, then cover with cold water and bring to the boil. Drain thoroughly. Put the vinegar, salt, sugar, and mustard seed into a large pan, allow to boil, then add the pepper mixture. Reboil and boil hard for 1 minute, stirring continuously.

This pickle is suitable for immediate use, though like all pickles it is improved by keeping.

TOMATO AND CELERY PICKLE

1¼ pints tinned tomatoes	2 oz. sugar
1 large head of celery	¼ teaspoon ground allspice
2 green peppers	1 saltspoon cayenne
1 onion	1¼–1½ pints vinegar
1 tablespoon salt	

Chop or mince celery, green peppers, and onion. Put all the ingredients into a pan and simmer till soft, 1½–2 hours.

PICKLED WALNUTS

The walnuts must be picked about the end of June, before they become woody. They have to be pricked and the juice stains badly, with a stain that is most difficult to get rid of; in fact it has to wear off. It is best to wear new rubber gloves, taking care not to make holes in these, or to avoid handling the walnuts may be held with a sharp-pronged fork.

young green walnuts	peppercorns
salt	allspice
water	root ginger
malt vinegar	

Prick the walnuts all over with a long packing or carpet needle. Cover with brine—6 oz. salt to each quart of water. Leave in brine 5–6 days, then drain, cover with fresh brine, and leave another week. Drain and set out on tray in a sunny place, turning occasionally. When dry and black pack in jars and cover with spiced vinegar, made as follows:

Allow 1 oz. peppercorns, 1 oz. allspice, ¾ oz. root ginger to each quart of vinegar. Bruise the spices, put in a muslin bag and boil in the vinegar for 10 minutes. Allow vinegar to cool. Remove spices. Cover walnuts and tie down. Ready for use in 6–8 weeks.

TO PRESERVE HORSE-RADISH

In towns horse-radish is not always obtainable all the year round. It is easy to preserve it and to have a jar at hand in the store cupboard, ready for use.

Wash and peel the roots and grate at once. Fill small or medium-sized screw-topped jars two-thirds full. Add ½ teaspoon salt and ¼ teaspoon sugar to each jar. Cover with white distilled malt vinegar, put a piece of white paper under the lid and screw down tightly. If liked a piece of fresh chilli may be put into each jar.

This may be used for sprinkling on beetroot salad or as the basis of sauce.

PICCALILLI

Take a selection of vegetables such as sprigs of cauliflower, gherkins, pickling onions, green tomatoes, small green beans, etc. Sprinkle with salt, leave for 24 hours and drain. Cover the vegetables with clear, spiced vinegar and simmer 10–15 minutes. Drain away the surplus vinegar.

Add the thickened vinegar given below and cook 3–5 minutes. Pot and cover.

Thickened vinegar

4 oz. mustard seed, bruised	½ oz. whole peppers
3 pints vinegar	4 oz. turmeric
¼ lb. ginger root, finely sliced,	¾ oz. flour
or 1 oz. ground ginger	4 oz. sugar (optional)
¼ lb. garlic cloves, bruised	

Simmer all ingredients except flour in the vinegar. Allow to cool, leave for 24 hours. Strain, reserve a little liquid for mixing with the flour. Boil up again. Mix flour with cold reserved liquid, add to the boiling liquid and continue boiling for 5 minutes.

STORE SAUCES

In the Winkfield chapter I have mentioned Florence White's delightful book *Good Things in England,* but there is a quotation in it which is particularly apt to this chapter. It is from *The Quorn Hunt and Its Masters* by W. C. A. Blew, M.A.; it is headed 'Mrs Comber's Sauce.' It tells how Captain Charles Comber, born in 1752, gave a recipe for a sauce belonging to his mother to the keeper of the George Inn at Bedford, one Mr Harvey. In due course Mr Harvey, finding this sauce much liked by his clients, began to manufacture and distribute it as Harvey's Sauce, in time making from it a substantial income, and subsequently selling the recipe for an annuity of £400–£500 a year. She tells another story, too, of a sauce known for nearly a hundred years as Worcestershire sauce. It is said that the Lord Sandys of the day gave to the founder of the firm of Lea & Perrin a recipe which he had picked up when he was in India, but that it was not until 1838 that its owners began to make it on a large scale, selling it as Worcestershire sauce. Mr Lea, the head of the firm, died a millionaire.

I am afraid the market now is too full of proprietary sauces, and methods of modern merchandising are too complicated, for it to be fair to offer encouragement to any student to make her fortune in this way, but the two stories add a romantic touch to the subject of store sauces.

Certain proprietary sauces should find a place in any well-stocked store cupboard. It is true that a number of people use these to disguise the taste of disagreeable or indifferent food, and naturally an enthusiastic cook takes a poor view of this. But if she knows her job she will realize that she must have a certain range of store sauces; for example, she will require Worcestershire and Harvey sauces when she has a devil or a barbecue in hand, and she may, in an emergency, make a last-minute sauce with cream and a thick type of proprietary sauce such as A1. There is no need to enumerate all the occasions on which she will require these, but she will keep in her store cupboard a range of them and supplement them with her home-made sauces.   Of these I would say that primarily she should have perhaps a good tomato sauce and a savoury sauce made on a basis of fruit, such as plums or damsons, and she will certainly want one or two bottles of the ketchups to be mentioned later.

It may be useful to mention, perhaps, for those who have more leisure at one time of the year than another, that certain domestic sauces may be made and sterilized for winter use, such, for example, as mint sauce (or preferably mint-orange sauce), cranberry, and Cumberland sauce.   All that is required is that they shall be carefully bottled and sterilized for keeping.   I mention this casually as it is the true store sauces that are appropriate to this chapter.   I ought, perhaps, to have laid stress on the value of keeping a bottle of soy sauce in the store cupboard; it is the basis of many proprietary sauces and is particularly useful for incorporation with other ingredients in the composition of home-made sauces.

TOMATO CHILLI SAUCE

3½ lb. ripe tomatoes
2 large onions
1½ lb. apples
4 fresh green peppers
1 lb. brown sugar, good measure
1 heaped tablespoon salt
1 pint vinegar

½ teaspoon each of whole all-spice, ground cloves, and freshly ground pepper
1 teaspoon each of celery seed, dry mustard, and cardamon seed
1 saltspoon cayenne
2 cloves of garlic, crushed

Scald and peel the tomatoes, chop the onions finely, peel and core apples, seed and chop peppers.   Put all ingredients in an enamel or aluminium pan and cook till clear and thick, about 2–3 hours, stirring from time to time.   Towards the end of cooking guard against burning by constant stirring. Pot and seal well.

In certain seasons outdoor tomatoes give a very heavy crop.   It is then worth while to use them in quantity for making into a strong concentrated purée, and here is a recipe, from Tunis, where tomatoes abound.   It is really primarily suitable when outdoor ripe tomatoes are available in plenty.   The recipe may well be halved, but I give it in the quantities and wording sent to me.

TOMATO PURÉE (1) (ABOUT 25 LB. OF TOMATOES)

'Take ripe tomatoes, choosing the sort that have the most pulp.   Wash them in water.   Cut them in two and remove pips.   Put them in a vegetable pulper or *moulin* sieve.   Put them in by handfuls, well crush down and work them through.   This will remove the skins.   One should then have a thick juice which you mix well with 3 or 4 handfuls of fine salt. Put the salted juice into a clean cotton bag which you tie up and hang over a large basin.   Leave it all night to allow the water in the tomatoes to run out.   This should leave a red paste in the sack, which you again mix with enough salt to make it sting your tongue when you taste it; mix it in well.

Spread the paste on flat dishes (*not* metal) and let evaporate in the sun, or a cool oven, the rest of the water in it. The paste must not be allowed to dry and break, it must be still soft. Let it get completely cool, then put it into glass jars, cover with ½ inch of good oil and cover.

'This paste is highly concentrated, 1 teaspoon is enough to make a sauce for 4 people. As it is already salt, do not add any when you make a sauce. The 25 lb. of tomatoes should make about 2 lb. of paste.'

The following is a much reduced and rich tomato sauce; it may indeed replace condensed tomato purée in certain dishes. It may be poured into small pots, covered with a film of oil to preserve it, and then be kept for some time and used as required. For this purpose a larger quantity than that given below may with advantage be prepared.

TOMATO PURÉE (2)

24 lb. red ripe tomatoes	1 level teaspoon salt, 1 level
1 bunch of basil or lemon thyme	teaspoon sugar, per pint of purée

Wipe the tomatoes, cut in half and squeeze into a strainer to remove the seeds and water. Rub the contents of the strainer with a spoon to extract all liquid. Put this liquid into a preserving pan with the halved tomatoes and herbs. Simmer, remove herbs, and rub through a hair or nylon sieve. Measure the purée and add the salt and sugar in the proportion given. Return to the cleaned pan and boil gently and steadily until very thick.

For the last 15–20 minutes of boiling the purée must be continuously stirred, otherwise it will burn. Turn into small pots and wipe the edges round well. When cold run ⅛ inch olive oil over the top and cover with paper.

This is an easy and safe way of preserving the purée, but it must be really thick. When wanted for use pour off the oil, take what is required, smooth over the surface, and pour over fresh oil. An alternative method, suitable when the purée is on the thin side, is to can or bottle the purée in tins or Kilner jars.

TOMATO SAUCE (1)

good, ripe tomatoes
to every quart of pulp add:

1 pint vinegar	1 saltspoon cayenne
1 oz. sugar	4 oz. shallots, minced
1 oz. salt	4 cloves of garlic, minced
good ¼ oz. ground pepper, black or white	1 bay-leaf

Wipe the tomatoes, cut out any blemishes and cut in quarters. Pack into an earthenware crock or into jars, cover and bake gently in the oven until soft. Rub through a nylon sieve or aluminium strainer and measure the pulp. Add the other ingredients in the proportions given. Turn into an enamel pan and boil gently 40 minutes to 1 hour. Pass again through the sieve and return to the rinsed-out pan. Boil again until the consistency of cream, strain once more if not absolutely smooth and fill into sauce bottles. Screw or cork down securely.

TOMATO SAUCE (2)

A delicious sauce for spaghetti and pasta dishes or for adding to sautés and ragoûts.

2 lb. red ripe tomatoes	1 clove of garlic crushed with
a bouquet of a stick of celery,	salt
basil or lemon thyme, pars-	salt and freshly ground black
ley stalks, and ¼ a bay-leaf	pepper
	a nut of butter

Wipe the tomatoes and cut into small pieces. Put into a large saucepan with the remaining ingredients, cover and *simmer* for a good hour. Then remove the bouquet and rub through a strainer. Turn into a small saucepan, reheat, and reduce further if necessary. The sauce should be a dark rich red and just drop from the spoon.

PLUM SAUCE

4½ lb. red plums	½ lb. sultanas
6 onions	½ oz. chillis
2 quarts vinegar	1 oz. whole ginger
4 oz. salt	1 oz. allspice
1 lb. sugar	½ oz. turmeric
2 oz. mustard	1 nutmeg, ground

Wipe and stone plums, slice onions. Put plums, onions, sultanas, chillis, and crushed ginger into a pan with half the vinegar. Bring to boil and simmer 30 minutes. Strain and put back into the pan with sugar, salt, mustard, nutmeg, allspice, and turmeric. Add remaining vinegar and simmer 30–40 minutes. Bottle and keep at least a month before using.

SALAD-DRESSING

Excellent dressing to keep bottled.

2 eggs	1–2 teaspoons dry mustard
1 tablespoon castor sugar	salt and pepper
4 tablespoons white wine or	2 tablespoons good salad-oil
white distilled vinegar	

Beat eggs with a fork, strain into a double saucepan. Add sugar, vinegar, mustard, and seasoning. Mix thoroughly, then stir over moderate heat until thick and creamy. Remove from heat at once and allow to cool, beating from time to time. Then beat in the salad-oil by degrees and bottle. If for immediate use ½ gill cream may be added in place of oil. If kept this dressing should be diluted with a little milk or cream before use.

KETCHUPS

These are a thinner type of sauce than the foregoing. Mushroom and walnut are probably the most generally used. The former may be made with or without vinegar. That made without is perhaps the more useful.

MUSHROOM KETCHUP

Choose dry, open mushrooms. Weigh them and allow $1\frac{1}{2}$ oz. salt to every pound. Break up the mushrooms, put them in layers, sprinkled with salt, in a stone jar and leave 3–4 days. Stir and press them from time to time. At the end of this period press well, cover the jar and put it in a cool oven for 2–3 hours, according to the quantity used. Strain through a fine nylon sieve. Gently press to extract all juice. To each quart of liquor allow:

$\frac{1}{4}$ oz. allspice	a pinch of cayenne (optional)
$\frac{1}{2}$ root ginger	1 shallot, chopped
2 blades of mace	

Put all these in a muslin bag. Put the liquid and spice into a pan and simmer 2–3 hours till well reduced. Strain, put into proper sterilizing bottles and sterilize 15 minutes (see page 1181). This last is a precautionary measure. Some red wine, in the proportion of a quarter of the quantity of mushroom liquor, may be added and boiled with the liquid, or a few drops of brandy may be added to each pint.

TOMATO KETCHUP

8 lb. ripe tomatoes	$\frac{1}{2}$ oz. root ginger, bruised
salt	$\frac{1}{2}$ oz. Jamaica pepper (allspice)
$\frac{1}{4}$ lb. onions, chopped	2 bay-leaves
2 cloves of garlic, chopped	$\frac{1}{2}$ pint white distilled vinegar
$\frac{1}{4}$ oz. or blade of mace	1 oz. sugar (approx.)
$\frac{1}{2}$ oz. peppercorns	

Wipe the tomatoes and cut into thick slices. Arrange on a large dish or tray and sprinkle well with salt. Leave overnight. Turn into a preserving pan, add the onions, garlic, and the spices and bay-leaves tied in muslin. Simmer until very pulpy and well flavoured. Remove the muslin bag and rub the pulp through a nylon or hair sieve. Return to a clean pan with the vinegar and sugar. The sugar should be added to taste and the amount depends on the sweetness and quality of the tomatoes. Boil, stirring frequently, to the consistency of cream. Then pour, by means of a funnel, into warm, sterilized screw-top bottles. Screw down at once and store in a cool dry place.

N.B. As an extra precaution for keeping the bottles may be sterilized for 15–20 minutes after being filled and screwed down, though if the ketchup has been properly made and the vinegar is of good quality this is not, as a general rule, necessary.

WALNUT KETCHUP

50 green walnuts	1 teaspoon cloves
30 shallots	1 tablespoon peppercorns
4 oz. salt	3 blades of mace
4–5 cloves of garlic, crushed	2 anchovies
1 quart vinegar	

For this the green walnuts are gathered as for pickling, before a shell has begun to form, and this may be tested by piercing with a needle. Care must be taken in handling as they stain badly. Cut up the walnuts roughly and then crush or pound. Put into a pan with salt, crushed garlic, chopped shallots, and vinegar. Allow to stand for 10 days, stirring well every day. Strain, put liquid into a pan with spices and anchovies and simmer for 30 minutes. Strain again, or not, as you wish. Bottle and cork well.

If you do not strain for the second time, divide the spices and anchovies evenly between the bottles. A glass of port may be added when the liquid is simmered, but this is entirely optional.

Some recipes add ginger and horse-radish, some omit the anchovies, and the green covering of the ripened nuts may also be used, but needs to be thoroughly bruised, beaten, and stirred.

PONTACK KETCHUP OR SAUCE

This is an old recipe found in various forms in different books. It is a useful, highly seasoned store sauce.

ripe elderberries, picked from their stalks	best quality malt vinegar

to every quart of liquor take:

1 teaspoon whole cloves ($\frac{1}{4}$ oz.)	8 shallots
1 dessertspoon or blade of mace ($\frac{1}{2}$ oz.)	8 oz. boned anchovies (preferably), alternatively anchovy
1 tablespoon peppercorns (1 oz.)	essence to taste
1 dessertspoon allspice ($\frac{1}{2}$ oz.)	

Put the elderberries into a stone crock, or big jars. Cover with the vinegar, cover the crock or set lids on the jars and put into a slow to moderate oven for 2–3 hours to extract all the juice. Take up, strain while hot into a saucepan (enamel if possible). Now add the spices and shallots and boil until the liquor is well flavoured. Strain through a muslin, measure and return to the pan. Add the anchovies and simmer until they have dissolved. Take off at once and bottle. Seal or cork tightly. Allow to mature a month or two before using.

N.B. Anchovies in brine are the most economical to use here. They are usually preserved whole. Wash, bone, and soak in a little water to remove excess salt.

Anchovy fillets in oil are not so satisfactory: they do not dissolve so readily and they are more expensive. Anchovy essence can be used but only as a substitute.

QUIN'S KETCHUP

This sauce, like many of the bottled proprietary sauces, is a mixture of other ketchups or sauces with additional flavouring. It resembles Harvey sauce and is excellent for devils and fish.

1 pint pickled walnuts and their liquor	1 lb. shallots, chopped
1 pint (or ½ bottle) port	6 oz. boned anchovies, finely chopped
2 pints mushroom ketchup	1 teaspoon cayenne pepper
½ pint soy	

Break up the walnuts and put into an enamel stew-pan with the other ingredients. Cover and bring slowly to the boil. Simmer for 15 minutes. Turn into large bottling or Kilner jars, screw down and leave for a fortnight. Then take up, strain, and squeeze gently through muslin. Pour into small sauce bottles and cork down tightly.

FLAVOURING POWDERS

A recipe for curry-powder will be found on page 402.

The following seasoned salt is a useful thing to have. A small jar of it used to appear on old-fashioned tables. It has probably a greater value for use in the kitchen.

SEASONED SALT

1½ oz. dried thyme	1½ oz. paprika
1½ oz. dried bay-leaves	¾ oz. ground black peppercorns
¾ oz. dried marjoram	
¾ oz. dried rosemary	¼ oz. Nepal pepper
1½ oz. ground mace	¼ oz. celery seed

All these are well powdered, pounded, and put through a fine sieve. Allow 1 oz. of the mixture to 4 oz. salt.

CHUTNEYS

These may be sweet or semi-sweet, and hot—peppery, that is—or bland. Store chutneys may accompany cold meats and curries, and be used for sandwiches and canapés and other savoury fillings. Fresh-made chutney to be served hot or cold (in temperature) will be found in the chapter on curries. Of the recipes offered, the mint, apricot, plum, and apple are of particularly agreeable flavour, the Eastern chutney is as hot as mustard.

It is a perfectly simple matter to make up your own chutney recipes to suit the supplies of fruit and vegetables. The prescription is fruit or vegetables, sugar, vinegar, and flavouring ingredients, such as garlic, onion, spices, peppers, fresh, green, or dried ginger, chillis, cayenne, mustard seed and so forth, and long slow cooking is called for, up to 3 and 4 hours. Sometimes, particularly for the firmer fruits, this is carried out partially before the sugar is added. With softer fruits all the ingredients are often cooked together.

Roughly speaking the amount of sugar is half that of fruit; for example, 4 lb. fruit, 2 lb. sugar, and 1½–2 pints vinegar, 2–4 oz. garlic, 4 oz. green ginger, 4 oz. mustard seed, 2 lb. sultanas or seedless raisins, 1 lb. onions, 3 oz. salt. This is merely a rough indication.

One point should be made. If chutneys are to be kept for some time, they should be potted in a more liquid state than would be chosen for those to be eaten in a week or two. After a time they tend to become stiff and a little dry.

Equipment. The preserving pan for these preserved foods containing vinegar should not be of brass or copper. Enamel or aluminium are both suitable. A wooden spoon is used.

APPLE AND RAISIN CHUTNEY

4 lb. apples
1 lb. seedless raisins or sultanas
2 oranges, or 3 tangerines
2 lb. sugar, including some lump if the zest of orange is taken

1½ pints vinegar
a pinch of ground cloves
½ lb. chopped nuts

Peel, core, and chop the apples. Chop raisins, either chop the orange rind finely or take the zest on to some loaf sugar. Tie cloves in muslin. Cook apples, raisins, nuts, and spice with 1 pint of the vinegar and simmer in a covered pan till all is soft and thoroughly cooked. Pour remaining vinegar over the sugar and put in a warm place for the sugar to dissolve. When the fruits are cooked add sugar, vinegar, and orange juice and rind (or zest) and cook in an uncovered pan until thick.

APPLE CHUTNEY (1)

4 lb. sour apples
1 lb. sultanas
¼ lb. onions
1 tablespoon mustard seed

grated rind and juice of a lemon
1 dessertspoon ground ginger
1½ pints vinegar
2 lb. brown sugar

Mince peeled and cored apples, sultanas, and onions, crush mustard seed and add. Add rind and juice of lemon, ginger, and cook with 1 pint of the vinegar. Dissolve sugar in ½ pint vinegar and proceed as in foregoing recipe.

APPLE CHUTNEY (2)

3 dozen large apples
1½ lb. sultanas
3 lb. demerara sugar
4 oz. mustard seed
2 fresh red chillis, or 4–6 dried
1 rounded dessertspoon turmeric

2 oz. ground ginger
1½ lb. Spanish onions, cut in half and thinly sliced
6 cloves of garlic, peeled and crushed with a little salt
1 quart vinegar

Pare, core, and slice the apples, cut chillis if fresh into thin rings, put all together into a large pan. Simmer gently 1½–2 hours, until very soft and pulpy. Turn into a crock and leave overnight.

R. H.'s remark about the above is that a child could make it and that it always turns out well.

APRICOT CHUTNEY

2½ lb. apricots, weighed when split and stoned	1 dessertspoon salt
1½ lb. onions	1 pint malt vinegar
½ lb. raisins, stoned	grated rind and juice of 1 orange
1 lb. brown sugar	½ teaspoon cinnamon
1 tablespoon mustard seed	1 level teaspoon turmeric
1 level teaspoon chilli powder	2 oz. shelled walnuts
	grated rind and juice of 1 lemon

Put all the ingredients in the preserving pan with the exception of the walnuts. Simmer until soft and pulpy, add walnuts and pot.

APRICOT AND DATE CHUTNEY

with dried apricots

1 lb. dried apricots, or 2 lb. fresh	1 lb. sultanas or seedless raisins
2 lb. dates	1 lb. sugar, preferably brown
¼ lb. preserved ginger	4 tablespoons salt
3 cloves of garlic	white wine vinegar to cover

Soak apricots if dried, stone if fresh, stone dates. Crush garlic with a teaspoon of salt. Chop ginger. Cook all ingredients together till transparent, about 2 hours.

EASTERN CHUTNEY

This is as hot as mustard and to be eaten in small quantities. It is good to add to a devil sauce or curry.

3 lb. apples	½ lb. fresh chillis
1 quart French wine vinegar	½ lb. mustard seed
2 oz. garlic	1 lb. brown sugar
½ lb. green ginger	1 pint water
½ lb. seedless raisins	4 oz. salt

Peel and cut up apples and boil in half the vinegar or enough of it to cover them, crush the garlic, grate the green ginger, chop raisins and chillis (if you like the last four ingredients may be put through the mincing-machine). Crush the mustard seed either with pestle and mortar or with rolling-pin.

With a pint of water and the sugar make a syrup. Lay the cooked apples in a bowl, sprinkle with salt and other ingredients and add the syrup, the rest of the vinegar, and that in which the apples were cooked. Bottle and seal with a layer of paraffin wax and a cork or jam cover.

I have had this recipe as long as I can remember, and find it most useful for devils, barbecues and so on. It is best after keeping for a few months, as it mellows. The uncooked ingredients require this time to become blended and soft.

N.B. Green ginger is to be bought at shops which sell Eastern condiments, e.g. the spice counter at Selfridges and the Bombay Emporium, 70 Grafton Way, W.1.

DAMSON OR PLUM CHUTNEY

2 lb. damsons or plums
½ lb. apples
1 lb. seedless raisins
2 onions
1½ pints vinegar
1½ lb. brown sugar

1 tablespoon salt
2 cloves of garlic, crushed
a few chillis, fresh or dried
½ oz. allspice
½ oz. ginger

If plums are used they should be split and stoned, if damsons, as many stones as possible should be extracted after cooking.

Proceed as for apple and raisin chutney (see previous page), except that the onions are chopped and added to the fruit before cooking.

GREEN TOMATO CHUTNEY

6 lb. tomatoes, sliced
3 green or red peppers, chopped
1½ lb. onions, sliced
1¼ lb. apples, weighed when cored and sliced
¾ lb. sultanas
1½ oz. mustard seed

1½ oz. salt
1 large root of ginger, well bruised
¼ teaspoon cayenne
1½ lb. brown sugar
2 pints good vinegar

Put all the ingredients into a preserving pan. Simmer slowly 2–3 hours or until very soft. Remove the ginger before putting into pots.

TOMATO CHUTNEY

3 dozen fine large ripe tomatoes
6 large onions, cut in half and thinly sliced
6 green peppers, cut in half, seeded, and thinly sliced
2½ pints vinegar

4 oz. salt
8 oz. brown sugar
grated rind and juice of 2 lemons
½ teaspoon each of ground ginger, pepper, and mace

Scald and peel the tomatoes, cut into quarters, removing most of the seeds and water, strain juice and put tomatoes and juice into a large enamel pan. Add remaining ingredients and boil gently 1–2 hours. Turn into clean dry jars. Tie or screw down.

N.B. Apples may be used in place of peppers.

SWEET TOMATO AND PEPPER CHUTNEY

10 lb. good ripe tomatoes
8 large yellow or green peppers, seeded, cut in small shreds, and blanched
3 large onions, chopped and blanched
2 oz. salt
1 oz. mustard seed
3 pints good vinegar

¾ oz. celery seed, ¾ oz. whole allspice, ½ oz. root ginger, bruised, ½ oz. cloves, 4–5 cumin seeds, bruised, and 2 fresh bay-leaves, tied in a muslin bag
2 lb. brown or white sugar (brown gives more flavour, but white a better colour)

Scald and peel the tomatoes, cut in half, remove the hard piece of stalk and squeeze gently to remove the seeds and water. Strain off these and put the juice with the halves of the tomatoes into a preserving pan. Add the peppers and onions, salt and mustard seed and allow to simmer gently 20–25 minutes. Meanwhile boil the remaining spices with the vinegar for the same time, with the lid on the pan; remove the bag and add the vinegar to the tomatoes with the sugar. Continue to boil gently for 1–2 hours, stirring occasionally and then more frequently. If the chutney is to be well spiced, put in the muslin bag again when the vinegar is added and remove it as the mixture thickens. When fairly thick stir into an earthenware bowl. Leave overnight, pot and tie down.

INDIAN CHUTNEY

1 pint vinegar

½ pint sour apples, peeled, cored, and sliced

Boil together to a pulp. Cool.

Take:

¼ lb. stoned raisins
1 oz. mustard seed

1 oz. garlic

Chop raisins. Pound seeds in a mortar, add the garlic and when smooth add raisins.

Mix with:

½ lb. brown sugar
1 oz. ground ginger

1 oz. salt
½ teaspoon cayenne pepper

Add the mixture to the pulped apple and vinegar in an earthenware bowl. Stand overnight or for a day or two before bottling, and ripen at least 6 weeks.

MINT CHUTNEY

a good pint mint leaves
1 lb. onions
1 lb. apples
½ lb. tomatoes, green or red
1 lb. seedless raisins or sultanas

2 teaspoons salt
2 teaspoons mustard
1 pint vinegar
1 lb. sugar

Put leaves, onions, apples, tomatoes, and raisins through a mincer and cook with seasonings in ¾ pint of the vinegar till soft, about 20 minutes. Pour remaining vinegar over sugar. Add this after cooking and boil up.

PEAR CHUTNEY

7 lb. stewing pears, weighed when peeled, cored, and quartered	5 cloves of garlic crushed with a little salt
2 lb. onions, sliced and chopped	1½ oz. salt
1½ lb. raisins, stoned and chopped	grated rind and juice of a lemon
¾ lb. apples, weighed when peeled, cored, and sliced	1¼ lb. brown sugar
½ lb. sliced stem ginger	8 dried capsicums
	6–8 cloves tied in a muslin bag
	2 quarts good vinegar

Put the pears (if large the quarters may be halved) into an earthenware crock or bowl with the onions, raisins, apples, ginger, garlic, salt, and lemon. Put sugar, spices, and vinegar into a pan and boil for 3–4 minutes. Pour over the contents of the bowl and leave 12 hours or overnight. Boil gently 3–4 hours or until dark and rich. Remove bag of cloves half way through the boiling or when you have the right amount of flavour.

HOME-MADE BEVERAGES

The making of wine at home is, we think, outside the scope of this book. Those who wish to embark on this will be wise to read Chapter XVI in *The Complete Book of Home Food Preservation* [1] and perhaps study books devoted exclusively to the subject (see bibliography in wine chapter, page 1199). There are, however, one or two recipes which may suitably be included, those for instance for nettle and ginger beer, sloe and mulberry gin, and cherry brandy.

In my young days home-made nettle and ginger beer were considered wholesome and cooling summer drinks, although we were not allowed to have mineral waters. Nettle beer has a pleasant flavour and the fresh taste of lemons in ginger beer is good. These beers consist of flavoured, sweetened water made effervescent with yeast, brewers' barm being used in those days.

NETTLE BEER (1)

fresh-gathered nettles (about 2 gallons when lightly pressed down)	2 lb. sugar
	1¾ oz. cream of tartar
2 gallons water	1 oz. yeast

Boil the washed nettles in the water for 20 minutes. Put sugar and cream of tartar into a large earthenware crock and strain the nettle liquid over them. Stir until sugar is dissolved and allow to cool to new-milk warm. Add yeast well creamed. Cover the crock and allow the beer to work for about 24 hours. Skim and bottle. It is best to lift out the liquid with a jug or a measure so that sediment is left behind. Cork and tie down. It is ready for use in about 48 hours.

[1] Cyril Grange, *The Complete Book of Home Food Preservation* (Cassell).

Here is a second recipe, from *Come into the Garden Cook*:

NETTLE BEER (2)

Pick young nettles, as many as will half fill your preserving pan when pressed down. Fill up the pan with water and boil for 15 minutes. Strain off the liquid. You need 4 quarts in all, and you can add some water to the nettle liquid if you wish. Put into a large earthenware jar the following ingredients:

2 heaped tablespoons lemon crystals, or rind and juice of 3 lemons	1½ oz. bruised whole ginger 1 teaspoon cream of tartar 1 lb. sugar

and the following if you happen to have them:

orange rind crushed or cut up	pineapple mint or a bunch of balm well bruised

Pour on to this 4 quarts boiling nettle liquor. Allow to cool till new-milk warm, then add 1 oz. yeast, creamed. Leave for 24 hours, skim, strain, and put in screw-top bottles. It is ready for use in 2 or 3 days. In the old days we used to tie the corks with string, but unless we were fairly skilful the corks would escape and a few popgun explosions would warn us that our precious brew was being lost.

GINGER BEER

3 lemons	2 oz. cream of tartar
2 lb. sugar	2½ gallons boiling water
½ lb. root ginger	2 tablespoons yeast

Pare the rind from the lemons thinly; squeeze out and reserve the juice. Bruise the ginger. Put all the ingredients except the yeast and lemon juice into a crock and allow to cool till new-milk warm. Add the yeast, creamed. Allow to stand 12 hours. Strain, add lemon juice and bottle. Keep in a cool place. Ready for use in 2–3 days.

SLOE GIN

1½ pints sloes	a few bitter almonds, pounded,
¾ lb. sugar-candy or loaf sugar	or a few drops of almond
1 quart gin	essence

Prick the sloes and put into jars. Add other ingredients. Cover tightly. Shake from time to time and after 3 or 4 months strain, bottle, and keep. This improves with keeping. The sloes may afterwards be used for flavouring purposes.

Damson gin is made in the same way.

Mulberry gin is made with equal measure of mulberries and gin, and a little ratafia essence and sugar in similar proportions to the gin as the almond essence and sugar in the sloe gin.

CHERRY BRANDY

Cherry brandy is quite simple to make, the method being very like that for brandy cherries. In fact method 2 for brandy cherries gives a very good cherry brandy, though somewhat sweet. The following recipe has a more concentrated flavour and is not so sweet. Morello cherries are best, though black cherries are sometimes used, in which case spices should be added.

Recipe 1

> 5 lb. fine ripe morello cherries   brandy
> 1¾ lb. cane sugar

Pull out the stalks from the cherries, stone half of them and prick the remainder. Crack the stones, bruise the kernels slightly, and put these into a screw-topped or bottling jar with the cherries and sugar. Pour on enough brandy to cover. Screw down and leave at least a month. Strain through a fine muslin and bottle.

Recipe 2

> sound ripe morello cherries   strong syrup, i.e. stock syrup
> cloves, castor sugar, brandy   (see page 860)

Cut the stalks off the cherries about ½ inch from the fruit. Prick them over with a needle, pack them into bottling jars in layers, scattering a good tablespoon of sugar on each layer, and allowing 3–4 cloves to each jar. Fill jars with brandy and screw or clip down tightly. Leave 4–5 weeks. Drain the liquor from the jars and pour into each about ½ pint of the syrup, enough to come about a third of the way up. Fill up with the brandy liquor and screw down tightly. Shake jars gently to ensure thorough mixing, then leave for another month or more. Strain off if wished and bottle. Otherwise the brandy may be used direct from the jar.

FRUITS PRESERVED IN BRANDY

There are two principal methods of preserving fruits in brandy. The first and probably the simpler is to pack the fruit, first pricked to the stone with a needle, into jars, adding a small quantity of sugar for each jar. The jars are then filled with a good brandy and covered. They are left in a cool, dry place to mature for 4–6 months or longer. The second method is to poach the fruit carefully in syrup, pack it into jars, and cover with the syrup to which brandy has been added. The jars are then sealed and left as before. This method is perhaps the better as it makes a rich conserve suitable for serving as dessert and of course has a thicker juice.

Fruits most suitable for treating in this way are cherries, peaches, green-gages, and apricots.

The most suitable jars are wide-necked bottling jars with rubber bands and clip covers, or Kilner jars. Failing these, cover with parchment or bladder, or cork well.

BRANDY CHERRIES

Recipe 1

Choose large, firm, ripe morellos. Snip the stalks off to within $\frac{1}{2}$ inch of the fruit. Prick each cherry all over with a darning-needle. Pack into clean dry jars, with a large tablespoon or more of crushed lump sugar between each layer of fruit. Cover the fruit with brandy and cover securely to ensure that the jar is air-tight. Leave to mature 4–6 months.

Recipe 2

fine ripe morellos, loaf or cane sugar, brandy

Snip the stalks off to within $\frac{1}{2}$ inch of the fruit. Prepare a syrup with 1 lb. sugar to 1 quart water. Bring to the boil, skimming if necessary. When clear put in the cherries, comparatively few at a time. Leave for a minute or two. Take them out carefully before the skins can break and spread out on a dish to cool. Measure 1 pint of the thin syrup in which the cherries were blanched, add 2 lb. sugar. Allow to dissolve slowly, then bring to the boil, skimming well. Boil quickly until clear and to just before the thread stage (215° F.). Then draw aside, cool. Strain through a muslin. Pack cherries carefully in wide-mouthed jars (bottling or screw-topped honey jars). Measure syrup and add equal quantity of brandy. Mix well and pour into the jars, making sure that the syrup will cover.

PEACHES IN BRANDY

Treat peaches in the same way as for Brandy Cherries 2. Choose fine, ripe peaches, again the Hale variety is the best. Scald them in a boiling thin syrup or boiling water 4–5 minutes. Lift out and skin. Cut in half with a silver knife or if wished leave whole. Now slip them back into a fresh hot thin syrup made in the same way as the first syrup for the brandy cherries. Bring slowly to the boil, lift out carefully, drain well and cool. Arrange in wide-necked bottling jars. Then prepare the thick syrup as described for brandy cherries, boil to the long thread (230° F.), allow to get cold and add equal quantity of brandy. Pour over the peaches and seal down securely.

Apricots are treated in the same way.

A FEW SWEETMEATS FOR THE STORE CUPBOARD

Such sweetmeats as chocolate truffles, candied cumquats, and physalis coated in fondant are particularly delicious, but they cannot be kept for long. Recipes for them are to be found in Chapter XXIX. Here are recipes for a few sweets that will keep at any rate for a short time and need not be a last-minute effort.

The following sweetmeat is often spoiled by too much stirring while boiling. Slow cooking and a minimum of stirring should be observed; here are two recipes:

CHOCOLATE FUDGE (1)

1 lb. sugar
3 tablespoons good unsweetened chocolate or Van
Houten's cocoa

6 fluid oz. milk
2 oz. butter
vanilla essence

Stir together sugar, milk, and chocolate till the sugar is dissolved, then cook gently, allowing the temperature to rise gradually to the degree known as the thread (see Sugar boiling, page 858). Stir only if there is fear of the sugar burning. Drop in the butter off the fire, still do not stir. Cool. When nearly cold add vanilla and beat well. Pour on to an oiled dish, mark off in squares, and break up when cold.

CHOCOLATE FUDGE (2)

This fudge is slightly more granulated in texture than the foregoing.

2 lb. sugar, brown or granulated
½ pint milk
¼ lb. butter

3 tablespoons chocolate
a few drops of vanilla
grated rind and juice of an
orange

Put sugar and milk to soak for 1 hour. Bring to boil slowly with all other ingredients except vanilla. Once boiling, boil fast for 10–15 minutes. It will rise in saucepan; do not stir more than absolutely necessary to keep from burning. Take off when it begins to sink and crystallizes on edge of saucepan. Do not stir for 2 minutes, then add vanilla and beat with wooden spoon to the consistency of thick cream. Pour quickly on to well-buttered tin and allow to cool. Score when half cold.

HOME-MADE TOFFEE

¾ lb. demerara sugar
½ lb. butter

7 oz. golden syrup
grated rind and juice of ½ lemon

Boil all together and test for setting: a small quantity dropped into cold water should harden at once. Pour on to an oiled tin or plate. When barely set mark with a knife and loosen from the plate. Leave until firm before taking off and breaking into pieces. Store in an air-tight tin.

SPONGE CANDY

2 lb. brown sugar
1 cup cold water

2 level teaspoons bicarbonate
of soda

Choose a large pan, as the candy puffs up when the soda is added. Put sugar and water in pan. Boil for 20 minutes, then test in cold water. If it sets at once and cracks readily. it is done. Draw aside from heat. Add bicarbonate of soda. Pour on to a buttered tin. Mark while hot and cut up when half cold.

Fruit sweetmeats are wholesome and refreshing:

QUINCE SWEETMEAT

5 lb. ripe quinces, weighed when peeled and cored	rind and juice of 1 lemon
	preserving sugar
1 pint water	castor sugar for finishing

Cut quinces into small pieces. Cook them in the water until very tender. Rub through a fine sieve, then weigh the pulp and add an equal quantity of sugar. Return to the pan with the strained juice and grated rind of the lemon. Cook over gentle heat, stirring continuously until very thick. Cool slightly and pour into shallow tins lined with grease-proof paper. Leave in a warm place (an airing cupboard, stove rack, or cool Aga oven) for 2 or 3 days, or until dry and easy to handle. Peel off the paper and cut into rounds or crescents. Roll in castor sugar and store in a wooden or tin box with layers of grease-proof or waxed paper.

APRICOT SWEETMEATS

1 lb. good dried apricots	1 lb. granulated sugar
1 large orange	granulated sugar for finishing

Soak apricots overnight. Drain, steam until very tender. Boil orange unpeeled until tender. Pass all through a mincer or chop finely together. Put into a double boiler with the sugar. Allow to cook until the mixture will set when tested (as for the fruit cheeses, page 1099). Turn out and allow to cool before shaping into balls. Then roll in granulated sugar.

CANDIED GRAPE-FRUIT PEEL

Cut grape-fruit rind into strips ½ inch (or less) wide. Cut in 2- or 3-inch lengths. Drop in large bowl of cold water and soak overnight. The next day pour off water. Put fresh cold water over peel and cook until clear-looking and tender. Pour water off again. Allow 1 cup granulated sugar for each grape-fruit rind used. Pour fresh water over rind and sugar till just covered. Stir sugar till dissolved, then boil slowly until syrup is thick and looks slightly jellied on edge of rinds. It is best if all juice comes to be absorbed, but any surplus must be poured off. Dip each piece of rind in granulated sugar. Shake and place on tray, rind side down. Cover with wax paper and allow to stand at room temperature 12–24 hours.

CANDIED ORANGE PEEL (1)

Use skins with the juicy pulp removed, and preferably the thick-skinned variety of orange. To the skins of 3 large oranges allow:

6 oz. granulated sugar	1 large tablespoon golden syrup
¾ gill water	a pinch of bicarbonate of soda

Cover the skins with cold water. Bring to the boil, drain. Repeat this process twice more. With a sharp-edged spoon gently scrape out any remains of the orange pulp, leaving the white pith intact. Then cover afresh with cold water, adding a pinch of bicarbonate of soda. Boil uncovered until the skins are tender. Drain.

Put the sugar, $\frac{3}{4}$ gill water, and syrup into a pan. Dissolve and bring to the boil. Add the peels, simmer with the lid off the pan until all the syrup is absorbed and the peels are clear. Turn into a jar and tie down with paper or stopper closely. This peel will keep a comparatively short time, approximately 6 weeks. For longer keeping the peel should be candied properly, i.e. laid on wire trays and basted with the syrup, boiled down to the thread (see page 860). Put the trays in a slow oven to set the syrup.

N.B. Treat lemon peel in the same way, and if this recipe is used for grape-fruit double the quantity of sugar and other ingredients for 3 grape-fruit.

CANDIED ORANGE PEEL (2)

For general use.

1 lb. orange peel	$\frac{1}{2}$ teaspoon citric acid
$\frac{1}{2}$ pint of the water in which it is boiled	12–14 oz. loaf sugar

Soak the peel for 48 hours, changing the water constantly. Drain, put into boiling water, and simmer until quite tender. Drain well. Take the orange water and boil it with the sugar and citric acid to a clear syrup. Put in the peel, simmer until clear, then lift out and put into jars. If the syrup is still quite thin continue boiling until thick, then pour, boiling, over the peel when cold. Cover jars.

CANDIED ORANGE PEEL (3)

peel of 2 large oranges	granulated sugar or chocolate
$\frac{1}{4}$ cup water	coating for finishing
$\frac{1}{2}$ cup sugar	

Cut peel in strips. Cover with cold water, bring to boil. Drain. Repeat this four or five times, till quite soft. Make syrup of sugar and $\frac{1}{4}$ cup water. Boil softened peel in syrup, till latter is absorbed. Cool, roll in sugar, put on racks to dry, or allow to dry without rolling in sugar and dip in chocolate coating.

STUFFED DATES AND PRUNES

Prunes may be steamed for 10–15 minutes before being stoned, or the fruit may be marinaded for some hours in brandy or rum and then be allowed to dry. The stuffing may be of various candied or glacé fruits, also soaked in rum or brandy, together with various finely chopped nuts and marzipan. After stuffing roll the fruit in sugar.

PEPPERMINT CREAMS (1) (UNCOOKED)

1 lb. icing sugar, sifted fine	a few drops of peppermint
white of an egg	essence
½ gill thick cream	

Mix sugar with egg white and cream. Stir well to a smooth cream, adding essence as you mix. Dust a board with icing sugar, roll out the paste, stamp into rounds. Put on a wire rack and leave to dry about 12 hours.

PEPPERMINT CREAMS (2)

¾ lb. granulated sugar	4–6 drops of oil of peppermint
4 oz. water	

Cook sugar and water to 236°–238° F. Add flavouring. Allow to cool a little, pour on to an oiled slab and work with a spatula till creamy. Roll and shape and allow to set.

EDINBURGH ROCK

A good, useful, and easy-to-make sweetmeat. Use the same proportions as for fondant, namely:

1 lb. sugar	a good pinch of cream of
1½ gills water	tartar

flavours and colours to taste:

ginger	coffee
raspberry	pink
lemon	yellow
peppermint	green
vanilla	white

Make a good syrup, taking care to get proportions and method exact (see page 858). Boil to 259° F. Pour out on to oiled slab, using candy bars. (These are obtainable from shops selling confectionery equipment.) Cool slightly, remove bars and turn the edges to the centre with oiled scraper. Continue like this but avoid stirring. Directly syrup is cool enough to touch, pour whichever flavour and colour you choose into the middle, and continue turning the edges to the middle. Now take it up and pull it quickly and evenly over an oiled candy hook. Continue until the candy becomes cloudy and dull. Do this in a warm kitchen and if it becomes very stiff heat slightly over a gas-ring. Draw out the candy evenly, snip off into lengths with a pair of oiled scissors. Leave in a warm kitchen for about 24 hours, when the rock will become sugary and 'short' when broken. Put into a paper-lined air-tight tin to store.

The candy *must* be pulled sufficiently, otherwise it will remain sticky instead of becoming 'short.'

TURKISH DELIGHT

1½ lb. sugar	3 oz. corn-flour
1 lemon	1 oz. (good weight) gelatine
1 orange	colouring if wished
¼ pint water, and a little extra	icing sugar

Put the sugar, the pared rind and juice of the lemon and orange, and ¼ pint water into a copper pan, bring slowly to the boil, making sure the sugar is dissolved before boiling-point is reached. Test with thermometer and boil to the long thread (230° F.). Slake corn-flour with a little water and add to the syrup. Have ready the gelatine softened in a little water, add to the pan and boil until clear, stirring occasionally. Colour. Strain into tins about 1 inch deep and leave until the following day. Cut into squares and roll in icing sugar.

Chopped nuts, almonds, pistachios, etc., may be added to the mixture before pouring into the tins.

WHAT TO BUY FOR THE STORE CUPBOARD

If you live within a stone's throw of Soho or in the shadow of a multiple store this section of the chapter will have less interest for you than if your home is in the country. However, should you find it convenient to build up a store cupboard the notes may serve as reminders.

TINNED FOODS

The use of tinned foods has increased to a degree remarkable to those of us who can remember the old-fashioned store cupboard, which though it might fairly bulge with home-preserved foods might only contain a few tins of Italian tomatoes and maybe a tin or two of tongue. Conditions have changed and with the decrease of leisure much less preserving is done at home, and to the busy woman bought tins may be a life-line. So although it is painful for those of us interested in cooking to be told by some young thing, 'Oh, we live out of tins,' it is nevertheless suitable that tinned food should come under thoughtful consideration.

It is as well to bear in mind that a diet of tinned food is not necessarily economical, and attention may with advantage be paid to suitable ways of 'stretching' such foods; moreover it is possible to impart an added freshness of taste to foods preserved commercially. A few suggestions are offered on these matters and on some types of food that it is useful to keep in store. Generally speaking, it is wise to buy small tins of the best quality, so that the whole of the contents may be used up at once. It is desirable to follow the directions given on the tin, although when these indicate that the food is to be heated in the tin we like sometimes to depart from this and to empty the contents into a saucepan, test the flavour and seasoning, and make such additions as taste may direct.

Tinned tomatoes

These are of particular value because of their richness of flavour and colour, and indeed they often serve better for some dishes than the fresh fruit. The reason for this lies no doubt in the fact that tomatoes require plenty of sun to ripen thoroughly and develop their full taste. The Italian brands of tinned tomato, for example, are particularly rich; there is a special canning tomato grown in the hot sun of Italy, which I have tried to ripen over here, but with only a modified success: it is clearly a variety needing strong sun to bring it to perfection. Tinned tomatoes are valuable for soups, sauces, vegetable entrées, and particularly for spaghetti and other pasta dishes; they may also be used as a vegetable, and you may choose to add a pinch of sugar, salt, freshly ground pepper, a little chopped basil or mint, and if you like, as we do, a little grated orange peel or lemon rind. There is a simple nursery dish of potatoes and tomato mentioned on page 264 for which a good brand of Italian tinned tomato is really best. Small tins of tomato concentrate are essential and their value in the making of soups, sauces, and ragoûts brings them into continual use.

Tinned tomato juice

Again the extract of fruit ripened in hot sun has often a better flavour than a juice that can be made at home. The tinned juice is valuable not only for drinks and soups but also for savoury jellies and salads. We usually add orange juice to taste and plenty of seasoning. There is a suggestion among the recipes at the end of the section for its use with stock for a good iced soup.

Sauerkraut

Not a great many people have leisure to make sauerkraut at home, and the tinned variety is good and needs only about 10 minutes' cooking with a pinch or so of sugar and salt to season. If you appreciate a choucroute garnie you can have this dish—if you have a tin of frankfurter sausages—and the whole is prepared in a short time. Hot sausages are laid on the hot sauerkraut and the whole served with gravy or brown sauce, slices of grilled bacon, and possibly tomatoes.

Tinned peas

Of these the small garden peas are best; we like to open the tin, drain the peas (reserving the liquid for soups or gravy), and put them into a pan with a little butter, a pinch of sugar, salt, a squeeze of lemon juice, and some chopped mint. They are best eaten straight away and should not be kept waiting. Tinned peas are good also for a dish of petit pois à la française with the addition of spring onion and lettuce (see page 241). A small tin together with another of spinach is the basis of an excellent soup which will be given with the recipes later.

Pimentos

These are of special value in the preparation of pastas, risottos, and similar dishes; they are admirable for adding to curries, soups, and potato or rice salads and to give variation to a dish of mixed hors-d'œuvre.

Sweet corn

Tinned corn on the cob can be very good and may be eaten straight with fresh butter or with beurre noisette; but the cobs being of so large a size, few go to a tin and this is not an economical form of food. The corn mush, however, is particularly useful, either for fritters or for cream soups, and it may be mixed with cream, tomato, and smoked fish and added to baked potatoes, making in fact pommes de terre Monte Carlo. The corn may be gratinéd; for this it is put in a fireproof dish, seasoned well, dotted with butter, sprinkled with breadcrumbs, and browned in the oven. Or a sauce may be made with a little onion, butter, flour, and seasoning; to this are added the corn and egg yolk, and a few small croûtons fried in butter, and the whole is turned into a dish and gratinéd. In this way a small tin may be used to make a reasonably substantial dish.

Tinned fruit (grape-fruit, apricots, pineapple)

The sections of grape-fruit with apricots and bananas make an excellent salad to eat with a meat dish, and this is not an extravagant form of salad for winter use. Apricots and pineapple fried are both admirable accompaniments to various meats, particularly those rich in fat, such as ham, goose, pork, etc. Grape-fruit and orange juices are used as the basis for fruit drinks, and the orange in particular for mint sauce.

Tinned meat

Tins of tongue, brisket, and jellied veal are kept for emergencies and used, of course, just as they are straight from the tin, but tins of stewed steak lend themselves to extension. They may be used as a stuffing for baked potatoes; glazed onions and glazed carrots are a good addition to the stew; and the contents of the tin may also be used to make a meat sauce for a pilaff or a dish of spaghetti, so concocting from a tin a really substantial dish. Braised kidneys may be used in a similar way, used as a filling for a flan case, or served perhaps with pilaff of rice.

Fish

If salmon is to be eaten straight, a well-flavoured sauce such as Alabama is sometimes appreciated. This fish is useful as a basis for fishcakes and kedgeree, or it is eaten hot covered with a cheese sauce. Anchovies and sardines are both required for savouries and for egg dishes. Tins of crab and lobster are somewhat expensive and perhaps may best be used for the making of a pilaff or in a sauce. A useful recipe for using the shredded flesh will be given later.

Tinned soups

As it is possible to make a simple soup in a very short time, tinned soups may be regarded as primarily for emergency use. When the tin is opened we like to re-season, adding perhaps a squeeze of lemon juice or a dash of Worcestershire sauce or mushroom ketchup, chopped herbs, and a nut of butter and possibly a spot of cream. Your own taste will direct you what to add. Then it is a help of course if you have time to make a garnish. Certain soups may be diluted with milk in place of the water indicated on the tin. Never let tinned soups cook for a long time. It is well to open the tin, empty the contents into a pan, following the directions with regard to their dilution, and then judge what you will add of extra seasoning and flavour. A bay-leaf heated in a clear or in a potato soup gives a delicious fresh taste; a garnish of thin slices of orange is good with tomato soup, and a little Parmesan cheese may improve some of the meat soups. Onion juice, sherry, and curry-powder or paste are all possible additions. Consommé is a particularly useful form of tinned soup because the flavour may be varied in so many ways; diced cooked vegetables or breast of chicken, or other garnishes, may be added. Certain tins of soup mix well together —asparagus and green pea, celery and mushroom—and a recipe is given later for consommé and tomato juice.

Many of the foregoing might be regarded as utility numbers; for special occasions you may like to keep a tin or two of okra, small green pods of a West Indian plant, that may be served in sauce as a vegetable or more profitably added to soups or dishes of mixed vegetables, such as a casserole or a fritto misto. Tins of fonds d'artichauts, too, may be included, and are useful as a base for savouries. Tinned water chestnuts add an unusual touch to a chicken or curry dish. These may be regarded as an acquired taste, but we find them excellent served, for example, with chicken in a sour-sweet sauce. You can make your own sour-sweet sauce by mixing together a little soy, sugar, crushed garlic, mushroom or walnut ketchup, and tomato sauce or tomato ketchup. This is really a matter for invention, and when the sauce is as you like it you may heat the chestnuts in it and serve them with chicken, rice, or curry.

There are a few other tins which might be regarded as luxuries that we like to keep for special occasions. For example, tins of pâté de foie gras are useful for sandwiches and canapés; the contents may be worked up with butter, seasoning, and lemon juice. This treatment not only improves it but makes it go further, and it may be used as a first course with fresh hot toast. Lychees we regard as a particular luxury; they have an uncommon and subtle flavour. Sometimes we put one of them in the middle of the whipped cream in a meringue; the refreshing taste is much appreciated. We use them in a special fruit salad, sometimes as a sweet and sometimes as a savoury course. A few of the fruits added to a curry at the very last minute are excellent. Tinned mangoes and tinned peaches are useful in similar ways.

The following is a real store-cupboard dish, good for an emergency but not economical:

CANAPÉS OF TINNED LOBSTER, CRAB, OR CHICKEN

Take a tin of lobster, crab, or chicken.

Variant 1

½ oz. butter	parsley or a little tarragon,
½ oz. flour	chopped
½ pint rich milk or thin cream	small croûtons of fried bread
seasoning	

To this may be added, for a larger dish:

a tin of fonds d'artichauts	a little extra cream with an
seasoning	equal quantity of store sauce
rounds of buttered toast (in-	such as A1
stead of the croûtons)	

Make a sauce with butter, flour, and milk or cream, seasoning and herbs. Mix with shredded contents of tin. Adjust seasoning, pile on croûtons and serve hot.

For a larger dish season the fonds d'artichauts, lay them on rounds of buttered toast in a fireproof dish, pile up with the previous mixture. Mix cream and A1 sauce in equal quantities and pour over the contents of the dish. Heat up in the oven.

Variant 2

French dressing for marinade	grated horse-radish
mayonnaise or a good cream	finely chopped celery
dressing	small croûtons of fried bread
chilli sauce	

Marinade the shredded contents of the tin in French dressing for an hour or so. Mix with the dressing or mayonnaise flavoured with chilli sauce, horse-radish, and celery. Pile on croûtons and serve cold.

A vegetable casserole may be made by heating and draining the contents of say 3 tins of vegetables, sweet corn, spinach, and peas perhaps, pouring a good béchamel over them (see page 155), sprinkling the surface with grated cheese and butter, and finishing in the oven. Fried onion rings are a good garnish for this.

The following recipe makes an admirable soup, and one may use a packet of dried bouillon, or cubes, or a tin of consommé:

GREEN SOUP

1 oz. chopped sorrel	1 oz. flour
3 oz. chopped spinach	1 packet of dried bouillon, or
1 tablespoon chopped celery or	cubes, made up to 1½ pints
celery leaves	with water, or an equal
1 tablespoon chopped parsley	quantity of tinned consomme
1 oz. chopped onion, or spring	1 gill sour cream
onions	a bouquet garni
1 oz. butter	seasoning

Simmer sorrel, spinach, celery, and onion in half the butter for 7–10 minutes. Add parsley and remaining butter, stir in the flour. Pour on the hot bouillon, add bouquet, bring to boil, simmer a few minutes. Adjust seasoning, add sour cream, remove bouquet and serve. This is really very good indeed.

The following is also particularly good, fresh and unusual, and calling for tinned tomatoes, tinned spinach, and tinned peas; you can either use left-overs or open small tins.

SPECIAL SOUP

1 tablespoon chopped green pepper (optional but good)
1 tablespoon chopped onion
1 oz. butter
1 oz. flour
1 large beef cube mixed with 1½ pints water, or an equal amount of tinned bouillon

1 cup tinned tomatoes
1 cup tinned spinach
1 cup tinned peas
1 dessertspoon lemon juice
1 tablespoon grated horse-radish
2 tablespoons whipped cream

Soften the onion and green pepper in the butter, add flour, tinned vegetables, and bouillon and bring to boil. Sieve and reheat, add lemon juice, horse-radish, and cream. This soup has a subtle flavour difficult to define and is very good.

ICED TOMATO AND CHICKEN SOUP

1 sliced onion
½ stick of celery, sliced, or season with celery salt
6 fresh peppers, finely chopped
2 cloves
seasoning

1 small tin (¼ pint) chicken broth or stock
¼ pint water
1 tin tomato juice (½ pint)
slices of lemon

Simmer onion, celery, peppers, and seasonings gently in the chicken broth and water for about 20 minutes. Add tomato juice. Strain, chill thoroughly and serve with the lemon. It may be partially frozen in the tray of the refrigerator if this is liked.

The advent of emulsifying apparatus has added to the repertoire of cold soups, and reference is made to these in the chapter on modern appliances.

ICED BOUILLON

Take equal quantities of tomato juice and consommé or aspic, put these into a saucepan with a little sliced onion, a bay-leaf, peppercorns, and a pinch of curry-powder. Simmer half an hour, strain and re-season. Chill thoroughly either in a pail of ice and salt or in the tray of the ice-box. Serve with slices of lemon.

It would be possible to go on for a long time making suggestions for dishes made with tinned food, but these few will suggest others.

OTHER REQUIREMENTS FOR THE STORE CUPBOARD

Now for other desirable contents of the store cupboard. It is a good plan to keep a tin or two of evaporated milk and of cream; these are excellent to add to soups and for use in salad-dressings, and the cream is particularly useful for sweets.

Guava jelly is not only good to add to rice dishes and curries, but makes an unusual finishing course for luncheon with water-biscuits made hot in the oven, spread first with a good cream cheese and then with this jelly of individual flavour.

Anchovy essence is required for sauces and many dishes. Soy sauce, already mentioned, is generally useful; Harvey sauce, Worcestershire sauce, A1 sauce, tomato sauce or ketchup, French and English mustard are all essentials.

The ingredients of a home-made curry-powder have been mentioned in the curry chapter, and a small made-up portion will keep reasonably well if kept firmly air-tight. In addition to this, of course, a good proprietary brand of curry-powder should be kept, because this contains certain flavourings that cannot be obtained for the home-made variety. If you are addicted to curries you will want to have by you a tin of poppadums, perhaps Bombay duck, a jar of mango chutney, which has a special taste and texture of its own which cannot be produced at home, glacé ginger, such a good ingredient for a curry, and of course a good store of rice. Coriander seed is useful for curries and dill seed for various purposes; poppy seed we keep for sprinkling over the crust of home-made rolls and bread; vanilla pods, dried chillis, dried mushrooms, dried herbs—all have a useful place in the store cupboard, and orange-flower and rose water for flavouring. It is well to have reliable salad-oil—first-class oil for salads— and a good cooking quality of rape-seed or tea-seed oil for frying, as well as vinegar, malt and wine, olives, gherkins, and capers. Of spices and seasoning for everyday use we may list the following:

cinnamon, ground and stick	paprika
ginger, ground and root	cayenne (in small quantities)
nutmeg, whole and ground	rock-salt for use in a salt-
mace, blade and ground	grinder
allspice, not only for pickling,	whole black pepper
but to grind into the mix-	whole white pepper
ture for devils and grills	

This presents a formidable list, but it may be acquired by degrees, and what satisfaction it is to have materials at hand and not find oneself held up by the lack of small but important items, just at the moment when cooking is getting particularly interesting.

Sources of supply for unusual stores:

Bombay Emporium, 70 Grafton Way, W.1.
For all Indian curry stuffs and condiments.

Selfridges, spice counter.
For the average run of spices, both whole and ground, sold loose by ounce or upwards.

Parmigiani, 43 Frith Street, W.1.
For white and red wine vinegar and pastas and Italian cheeses.

Louis Roche, 14 Old Compton Street, W.1.
For French specialities.

King Bomba, 37 Old Compton Street, W.1.
For fresh pastas, wine vinegars, cheeses.

Ortega, 74 Old Compton Street, W.1.
For Massala powder, poppy seed, and various condiments.

N.B. Spices are best bought loose, in small quantities.
See also list in chapter on curries, page 421.

XXXVI

The Kitchen

THERE was a time when the kitchen was the heart of the house. Some interiors painted by early masters would indicate that it was also a centre of social life, farmyard activity, infant care, and musical diversion, and a children's playground: all very happy, jolly, and carefree; distracting perhaps for the cook.

A social history of our country might be written around English kitchens, from those of the great medieval castles built on a scale to feed a small army throughout a siege to the kitchenette of the modern working woman's flat.

In some of the great English houses one may still look down from a gallery and imagine the fever of activity that once was there: see perhaps the niches in the walls, built to protect the scullions that they too were not roasted as they turned the spits, see the whole magnificent *batterie de cuisine* and sense the lavish and spacious living of a bygone age. Kitchens with great dressers of china, brick bread ovens, shining ranges and burnished steel, lead-lined drawers for flour, kneading troughs, gargantuan dish covers and copper pans; all the implements of a serious art one may still sometimes see. Lavish, laborious, colourful; they have had their day.

An uglier era tolerated the basement kitchen, dark, labour-making, and disgraceful as a reflection on selfishness and indifference. There is, I think, nothing to be said in its favour.

With the advent of flats came the swing towards smaller and more compact kitchens. As long as the degree of smallness and compactness is controlled by necessity it is tolerable, but I should be sorry to see smallness in kitchens extolled as a virtue in itself.

One sees in magazines, especially in American publications, attractive illustrations of miniature kitchens and kitchenettes. In my view these are more alluring in theory than comfortable in practice. It takes as great a degree of skill and forethought to cook, really to cook, in them as it does to use successfully too small an ice-box or too small a cooking stove.

Flat-dwellers who must accept over-small kitchens are fairly well catered for in compact equipment, but may I offer advice. Have the largest ice-box you can manage for food storing. Don't, in the name of tidiness, overdo shut-in cupboards and dressers. Stagnant air smells unpleasant and I have known crockery and saucepans shut up too closely and too long to have a disagreeable smell; in cups this was noticeable when hot tea was poured into them—and this was not due to uncleanliness. Kitchen equipment is functional and not necessarily ugly, and need not all be hidden from the eye.

Although many people must accept and make the best of restricted space there are others who need not do so. The modern types of cooking stove, conserved heat, electric, and gas cookers, require less in the way of structural work to install than the old-fashioned ranges and the conversion of a room, not originally built as a kitchen, becomes possible. Changing over rooms to release a morning-room, perhaps, or a dining-room will sometimes give one a fine kitchen, and for anyone who really cares for cooking as an art or a hobby there is much pleasure and profit in having a good room.

There seems the possibility, even the likelihood, of a return to better kitchens, not the old unwieldy ones, of course, but something more suitable than many of us have tolerated for so long.

Is this part of a cycle?

In a bygone day the mistress of the house worked herself and trained her serving women; housewifery in all its manifestations was an honourable accomplishment. The old books show to what a high standard they worked and how little, compared with the housewife of to-day, they had to help in the more onerous activities.

Gradually, with greater freedom and expanding interests, there became less time for household work, and this was deputed to others. With an increase in the supply of prepared commodities less was made at home, and some of the collected lore of ages became neglected and then forgotten. Gradually there became fewer and fewer people who really possessed the wide and useful knowledge held by these great old housewives. Now very few remain and the whole status of housewifery is debased.

We seem to be starting again. Of necessity the mistress of the house has taken to her kitchen and naturally she is turning her mind to its improvement. Labour-saving devices, efficient equipment, interest in the preparation of food, and imagination in the use of a wider range of materials than our great-grandmothers ever dreamed of are all claiming the attention of intelligent women to-day.

Later in this chapter will be found details concerning kitchen planning and equipment, but before becoming categorical I should like to describe a kitchen that I enjoyed. By rigid conventional modern standards it would not perhaps rank as first-class, but it was cheerful, comfortable, and easy to run.

The walls were pale in colour, the window large. Fluorescent sunlight lighting was a joy. An Aga cooker simplified life for me; I found it economical, foolproof, easy to clean, and hot first thing in the morning. This meant that breakfast could be cooked before one had to stoke or clean. Supplementing this a gas cooker played its part on days when jam-making, bread-making, fruit-cake-making, or any prolonged activity had cooled down the Aga.

Along one wall was a glass-doored, glass-shelved, mirror-backed cupboard which held quantities of stores. Seasonings, flavourings, dried fruits, cereals, herbs: I could see at a glance what I wanted and when things needed replenishment. The mirror back reflected light. It was easy to clean and nice to look at. It was a real labour-saver. Another small glass cupboard was useful for any dish that had to stand for a while: an iced cake, fruit marinading in syrup, jam or jelly cooling—anything that was not ready to put away was temporarily protected in this from dust and, I had almost said, flies. The very mention of a fly in the kitchen would put me to shame with my American friends. In that kitchen-conscious country flies are not admitted to the house, and certainly not to the kitchen; but I confess I have never achieved their complete exclusion, nor ever shall until it is possible to buy the suitable fine wire gauze which can be mounted on frames to fit the windows and doors.

For the rest there was a capacious ice-box, a good flour bin, a dresser, a small double stainless steel sink, and a pyramidal saucepan stand. A broad shelf at convenient height held everyday commodities for immediate use, and the floor was covered with good lino; all this helped to make kitchen life easy and pleasant. I had not room unfortunately for a separate marble-topped pastry table (though I had a marble slab on the big table), or for a separate chopping-block. This latter is a useful piece of kitchen equipment; it saves separate boards, it almost eliminates noise, and it is easy to keep clean. I like the old-fashioned type made of an up-ended log of wood fixed on three solid legs. When chopping and meat-cutting have over-scarred the surface a thin layer is sawn off and one starts afresh on nice clean wood. If one cannot have this, a solid, thick, level, hardwood chopping-board is necessary.

The scullery attached to the kitchen I have just described has a stainless steel double sink with good draining-boards and a capacious plate rack above. These modern steel sinks have many advantages; the walls are resilient and this lessens the risk of breakages. They clean easily and look inviting, a word not usually associated with sinks. The second compartment makes thorough rinsing a matter of seconds, and the hot clean wet plates put up into the rack dry with a good polish.

An enamel-topped vegetable table and a vegetable rack for the day's supplies, and a cupboard for the larger utensils not in daily use, such as preserving pans, girdles, ice-machines and so forth were the main scullery items.

Views concerning kitchen floors must surely depend on up-to-date inventions, and new types of surface are always under consideration. Rubber and cork are being used in various ways, and floors of imitation tiles or flags, with many of the advantages and without the drawbacks of the real things, are also on the market. Since experiment and manufacture continue, it would be a mistake at any moment to hold fixed views.

Wood floors, unless of the parquet type and of extremely hard wood, present difficulties, in that they absorb grease and stain and require much scrubbing; dirt in cracks is hard to dislodge. They are, however, warm and not tiring to the feet.

Linoleum on a wood floor is easy to clean and comfortable for the feet. Cement or stone floors are, of course, cold and tiring to work on. Tiles are less cold and easy to keep clean, but they too are tiring and can be dangerously slippery if grease is dropped or if they are wet.

Tiled walls are easy to clean and light, but if they go all the way to the ceiling they have disadvantages. There is no place then where a nail or a screw may be put in, also I dislike their somewhat lavatorial appearance. I am unhygienic enough to have several pictures in my kitchen: one of a wedding cake, one of a pie, and one of a children's party, all by the late Rex Whistler and a constant source of pleasure. A half-tiled kitchen is convenient; the wall above needs to be of glossy washable paint for easy cleaning.

It will seem obvious to the modern woman to say that a kitchen should be reasonably near the dining-room. Her ancestors, however, do not appear to have subscribed universally to this idea, and a good line for an agent for a Georgian house might be 'fine kitchens within easy cycling distance of the dining-room.'

Some care needs to be taken to prevent the smell of cooking from straying into the dining-room, and a baize- or felt-covered door can sometimes be of use. The actual smell of food cooking in the kitchen is one thing—and can be a very good thing—but somehow diluted outside it has less appeal.

On the subject of that labour-saving device a dining-room kitchen hatch I find myself being illogical and prejudiced: I dislike it. My defence for a probably unreasonable point of view is this: if I do the cooking myself I like to have a pleasant kitchen and to eat in it, serving food piping hot from the stove. If I have staff I like to eat in peace in the dining-room undisturbed by the sudden surprising clatter of a hatch door and free from an unreasonable sense of a lack of privacy. But this is one-sided and I may be missing something by being so prejudiced.

Now to come down to the detail of kitchen equipment. The item of major importance is the stove. If one lives within reach of all public utilities one may choose between gas, electricity, conserved heat such as Aga or Esse stoves, and the closed kitchen range. Where possible the combination of a gas or electric cooker with an Aga or an Esse is ideal, giving as it does a high degree of economy with efficiency.

In the remoter country districts the supplementary range may be an oil or a Calor gas stove. Modern oil stoves are excellent for baking and boiling. They require the same meticulous care as any other oil lamp if they are to work perfectly. Some of the larger kinds now to be had are remarkably efficient.

A friend living in Eire was responsible for feeding large numbers of schoolchildren during the difficult years and described a device which is worth knowing about.

A cylindrical oil drum is used, open at the top and with a hole cut in the base large enough to take a broom handle. The drum is set on three or four bricks to lift it from the ground. A thick stick or broom handle stands down the centre of the tin and just through the hole at the base. The drum is tightly packed with sawdust, which should be rammed in. The broom-stick is then removed and the space left acts as a flue.

Paper lighted underneath starts the sawdust burning and soon great heat is generated. With a good-sized tin this goes on for hours. This is a useful trick for cooking chicken food, and I have known it used for bottling in a country house when fuel was short.

The virtues of conserved heat stoves, such as the Aga and Esse, are becoming more generally appreciated. To the cook accustomed to a large kitchener they present certain disadvantages. You can't pour in the coal and roar up the ovens; you can't grill over a clear red-hot fire; you can't let the flames lick round the sides of an omelet pan; you can't easily and quickly control the oven temperatures; you can't use a Dutch oven or heat up a salamander, and you can't sit in front of a glorious fire and toast muffins on a cold winter's afternoon. One can understand then the reluctance on the part of some cooks to discard the old-fashioned range with its quality of cosy cheerfulness and its response in performance (always provided it is possible to satisfy its insatiable maw).

With the present price of hard fuel I am daily thankful for my Aga cooker, and I wonder sometimes how a cook I know of is progressing at that very moment. Her reply to her mistress, who was proposing the installation of either an Aga or an Esse in place of the big range, was: 'You like my cooking, madam, and if you want me to cook you must give me the coal.' In arguing the case for a conserved heat stove it may be that less accent on the economy side and more on the many other advantages may be judicious.

Here are points which any cook might appreciate. No early morning lighting, stoking, or cleaning is necessary. The fire should only be let out at very infrequent intervals and in special circumstances. The stove, having been shut up all night, is at its hottest first thing in the morning. Stoking is required at most three times a day and sometimes less. Cleaning is very simple. One does not get scorched while cooking. There is no fear of fire. The heat is perfect for steady cooking and it is unusual to burn food cooked on the rings. On the other hand there is one minor matter concerning burning that should be indicated. The ovens are so well insulated that no smell of cooking escapes, and one cannot rely on the nose as a reminder that something is in the oven. Until one becomes accustomed to these stoves this sometimes leads to mishaps. One other point. A kitchen containing only a conserved heat stove may in some cases be too cold for comfort, and this should be borne in mind when plans are made. A supplementary source of general heat may on occasion be necessary. Beyond this there seems to me to be little to criticize, and I have found that provided one adheres to the very clear and simple instructions given, this type of stove combines high efficiency with real economy.

And what a comfort it is to have an orgy of baking, jam-making, bottling, or canning and not to have to think of the fuel bill.

The advantage of having a second string to one's bow in the shape of a gas or electric stove is this: the essential principle of an Aga or Esse is the conservation of heat, and the insulating lids must be kept down when the stove is not in use. If for prolonged cooking such as canning or preserving they remain open for hours the ovens cool down and take some time to heat up again, and this will also happen should stoking be forgotten or bad fuel cause clinker to form. Another point concerns toast. In some cases a wire toaster is supplied and slices of bread may even be put directly on the hot-plate, but the result is different in texture and taste from ordinary toast. I think that muffins and crumpets toasted directly on the hot-plate are particularly good, but then I like the underside of a crumpet to be slightly burnt. In any case it is a matter of taste, and for conventional toast one does better with other types of stove. For these reasons and for specially busy times it is an advantage, though by no means a necessity, to have a small supplementary stove available.

Gas cookers

The advantage of these is immediate quick heat. They are economical in that they are only in use when actually required for cooking.

The new types in particular are neat to look at and easy to keep clean, and there is now an eye-level grill which is very convenient. Regulo control lessens the necessity to keep a close watch on dishes being cooked. A list of regulo marks with their relative temperatures will be found on page 60.

Gas undertakings usually supply a card of instructions when a stove is installed, but it may be useful to mention that the gas flame should be confined to the base of the saucepan and should not lap round its sides. This is wasteful and does not expedite cooking to any degree commensurate with the waste.

Gas stoves should be wiped down with a cloth wrung out of hot soapy water at the end of the cooking of each meal. The inside of the oven door should be wiped with the cloth, and, as soon as the oven is cool enough, the sides of that also. The hot-plate requires the same treatment, and once a week the bars and burners should be rubbed with a paper pad, then taken out and washed in hot soapy water. They should be rinsed, dried thoroughly, and replaced. This cleaning is necessary, because now and again food will boil over on to the burners, and if these are not cleaned from time to time there will be unpleasant smells, and waste of gas.

Electric cookers

The electricity undertakings will supply instructions and these repay study, particularly by unaccustomed users, so that they may avoid wasting current. Oven heat should be fully used, and with careful planning a variety of suitable dishes may be cooked at the same time, for all parts of the oven can be used at once. It is useful to know where the electric elements are placed in the oven. If these are at the bottom the bottom shelf will give good strong heat. If placed at the side or at the top, the bottom of the oven will be cooler than the top or the middle shelf, and the lower shelf can then be used for slow cooking.

An electric oven takes 20–25 minutes to reach moderate heat. The switch should be turned to HIGH, and food, in most instances, should be put in when the thermometer on the oven door registers the degree called for in the recipe. When the food is put in the switch can be turned to MEDIUM or LOW, according to whether there are several dishes in the oven or only one. The heat remaining in the oven will be enough to finish the cooking in most recipes, but the oven temperature should be watched and regulated, particularly if the recipe gives a cooking time of more than three-quarters of an hour after the food is put in. The hot-plate can be treated in the same way. The switch should be turned to HIGH under a saucepan, then, when the contents of the pan come to the boil, to MEDIUM or to LOW, regulating the heat to simmering or boiling temperature as the cooking demands. The griller on a modern electric stove is particularly efficient.

Perhaps it should be added here that the latest type of electric oven is fitted with a thermostat. The dial is turned to the right temperature and then a small light appears, which goes out when the correct temperature is reached.

Electric cookers are easy to clean. The whole of the outside, as a rule, is enamelled, and can be wiped down every day, after cooking is over, with a cloth wrung out of hot soapy water; the oven and the oven door should be wiped while still warm. This removes all the grease, which if left will burn and make an unpleasant smell the next time the oven is heated. Shelves should be scrubbed, now and again, with hot water and soda. The white enamelled plate under the boiling plates should be wiped down after cooking has taken place on the top of the stove. Any marks that occur when food boils over on to the white enamel should be washed off before the metal is cool; if they are left and become burnt in it is difficult to remove them, and one must have recourse to a mild abrasive, although even this is not always adequate. In certain makes of stove it is possible to remove the elements from the oven, although it is generally considered that this is undesirable; in any case the elements should on no account be immersed in water.

Charcoal stoves are little known or understood in this country. The French appreciate the particular savour of food grilled over charcoal, and the Americans exploit this form of cooking for picnics and open-air meals, and have simple but clever types of stove made for the purpose.

The simplest of all is a bucket with holes in the sides like a workman's brazier; this is for outdoor use. Another American model has an open iron basket-grate on legs fitted with a grilling iron which catches the juices of the meat. This may be used indoors provided there is a suitable outlet for the charcoal fumes, which can be dangerous. Stoves of this kind are a frill rather than a necessity, but a very nice frill. I once had one made for me by a local blacksmith, but I have never asked a cook to use it as I felt it was regarded as my plaything.

Sinks

Earlier, reference was made to the advantages of a stainless steel sink with two washing compartments. Attention may well be drawn to the new types of sink now available.

The porcelain enamel sinks look pleasant and are easy to keep clean.

Saucepans

At this stage something may suitably be said about saucepans. For conserved heat stoves and for electric cookers it is essential, in order to keep perfect contact with the heat, to use ground base saucepans. Unless these are really well made and quite even, full use will not be made of the heat supply. This point is emphasized by the stove-makers. There is, however, another important consideration, and that is the false economy of buying cheap thin saucepans.

Before the war one could buy quite small attractive-looking saucepans for as little as sixpence, and big ones for two or three shillings. It may have seemed logical to the inexperienced housewife to buy these and discard them when worn for new ones. It is easier to spend money like this over an extended period than to save up and buy something expensive. But oh! what a difference there is in their use! Burnt sauces and burnt milk pans alone would argue the case for me. With good, thick, well-made pans one can almost eliminate this burning trouble. I have had good aluminium pans for about fifteen years and I only wish I had a daughter to inherit them. Every few years I send them to be refurbished, and they come home with every blemish removed and with a shine and patine that is the joy of any cook's heart.

In relation to their solidity aluminium pans are light in weight. They should never be washed in water containing soda or with proprietary mixtures containing soda; fine metal wool with a little soap is the best cleaner.

Should it be necessary to boil plain water in an aluminium pan a spoonful or so of vinegar should be added to avoid discoloration of the metal.

If eggs are boiled in an aluminium pan the latter turns black and is particularly difficult to clean; for this too vinegar should be put in the water.

A new and highly prized possession is a small set of stainless steel saucepans: shining, easy to clean, and nice to look at. A set of such pans is worth saving for.

Enamel pans look nice and are easy to clean; only those lined with heavy, good enamel are satisfactory. Once the enamel becomes chipped there is danger of burning food, and a splinter of enamel is not the best thing for the human alimentary tract. Heavy iron pans are useful for braising and long slow cooking. Tin-lined copper pans are cherished by those who love cooking; that they involve more cleaning than others is an unfortunate fact only gladly faced by amateurs in the French sense of the word.   They may be cleaned with fine wire wool and soap and should be watched for wear of the lining and sent for retinning when this becomes necessary. Unlined copper is the best type of pan for sugar boiling.

Saucepans should be kept on slatted shelves or open stands with the lids off.   It is a question of stagnant air again.

WASHING UP: A NOTE FOR BEGINNERS

This seems as good a place as any to slip in a note about washing up. In recent years a good many inexperienced washers-up have been shang-haied into lending a hand in this ever-recurring job.   Good nature has perforce taken the place of experience.

The following notes are not intended as an affront to the experienced housewife.   They are an offering to the young and perhaps newly married wife to enable her, should she so wish, to 'mug up' the subject privily.

Recently I had an opportunity to see at close quarters one or two of the magnificent silver cisterns and fountains that were used in the eighteenth century for washing the silver in the dining-room.   This was done, I learned, while the banquet was still in progress in order that the supply of table silver should be adequate.   The cistern or bath for the plates was a huge silver oval about 4 foot 6 long and 3 foot 6 wide.   Those I saw stood on low feet, bore elegant designs, and the insides were engraved with the owner's coat of arms.   The smaller cisterns were like large soup tureens—in fact we filled one of them with flowers for the centre of a banqueting table.   These were used for washing up the knives and forks. The fountain, a beautiful silver urn with a tap, looking like a large tea urn, held the water, and to judge by the respective sizes of cistern and fountain must have required several successive replenishments.

If it has not been your good fortune to watch a well-trained servant, an old-fashioned butler, or a Victorian maiden aunt performing the task of washing up, it is more than likely you will hold it in poor esteem.   Indeed, in the hands of the slovenly it can be an offensively unpleasant affair. There was nothing so about the way a good butler cared for his silver, washing one fork or spoon at a time, laying each piece down on a folded cloth, drying, polishing, and putting away with an almost brooding care for something worth looking after.   The washing up of old china cups and saucers which I once witnessed was carried out, as was their custom, in the drawing-room, after the visitors had departed, by the two charming though faded hostesses: warm soft water in a bowl and a snowy cloth having been brought in by the parlourmaid, with a dignity no whit less than that of her mistresses.   Then each beautiful bit of china was re-placed in the cabinet in the drawing-room of the lovely old Irish house. These refinements of washing up are, I know, but *souvenirs d'autrefois*,

KITCHEN EQUIPMENT *

The following pieces of equipment have been chosen for illustration (see also pages 1159–61) to avoid any confusion in the student's mind.   Much of the equipment in a kitchen is too well known for it to be shown here, and illustrations of it would take up valuable space.   These pieces, however, are not so easily recognizable.   They are all pieces of equipment mentioned in the book and necessary to the student.

1. *Balloon whisk.*   This is primarily for whisking egg whites, sponges, etc.   It has a wooden handle and is so curved that it will fit the copper bowl with which it should be used.   These whisks are sold in varying sizes also to fit the copper bowl.

2. *Fine wire whisk.*   Made from fine wire as the name implies, and should, therefore, be used for comparatively light mixtures—sponges, whisking egg whites, liquids such as cream soups or purées.   Sizes—medium to large.

3. *Heavy wire whisk.*   The wire of this whisk is thick and unyielding and may be used for thick mixtures.   Use it primarily for creaming egg yolks and sugar, working mousseline farces or creams, etc.   Made in small to medium sizes.

4. *Sauce whisk.*   Made of fine 'close' wire and as name implies used for all sauces. With all these fine wire whisks care must be taken to grasp them by the handle only. If the hand comes down over the wire of the whisk, it tends to pinch the wires together, and so in time destroys the efficiency of the whisk.

5, 6 & 7. *Wooden spatulas.*   Sold in varying sizes.   These spatulas are more efficient than the wooden spoon.   They are flat on both sides and have, therefore, no bowl in which food might collect.   They are easily scraped off against the side of the saucepan or bowl.   The best type should be comparatively thin, and made of boxwood or some other non-absorbing wood, so that the flavour of a mixture is not retained after the spatula has been washed.   Use for sauces, liquids, and mixtures of all kinds.

8. *French vegetable knife.*   Made in good steel with a black wooden handle. Essential for all 'small' preparation, boning, garnishes, etc.

9. *Filleting-knife.*   Thin and 'whippy.'   Used primarily for filleting and boning fish, and also for any process where a thin delicate knife is required.

10. *Chopping-knife or cook's knife.*   A heavier type of knife than the other two. Made in various sizes, measured by the length of the blade.   Used for chopping and all general purposes.

N.B.   All knives (and whisks) should be kept polished, i.e. well rubbed with wire wool or fine emery-paper.   Do this always after use.   During use, always wipe a knife immediately you cease to use it, for however short a period.   In this way a lot of unnecessary staining can be avoided.

11. *Palette-knife.*   A blunt round-bladed knife, also made in varying sizes.   Used for all general purposes, such as turning food while cooking, for dishing and transferring biscuits, etc., from baking-sheet to rack.

12. *Badger hair pastry brush.*   This is the best type of pastry brush to buy.   Made from badger hair securely fastened in to a metal handle, it lasts, with care, a very considerable time.   As the brush is soft and pliable, it does not easily disturb the decoration of, for example, fruit in a flan.

* *See plate 30*

KITCHEN EQUIPMENT *

1. *Copper whisking bowl.* Used primarily for the whisking of egg whites. Also employed for sponge cakes which need to be whisked over heat. The bowl may be put on low direct heat or set over a pan of hot water. Never use a metal cleaner. Polish outside with wire wool and soap, and clean inside immediately before use with a piece of lemon dipped in salt. Rinse in clean water and dry thoroughly.

2. *Churn-type freezer.* For making cream and water-ices. See page 961 (description of ice-machine). This picture shows the machine put together for use. When not in use remove lid of container and store in a cool dry place. During the winter it is advisable to fill the bucket occasionally with water, to prevent the wood from shrinking too much.

3. *Saucepan.* This shows a medium-sized pan for sauces. A saucepan proper is fairly deep, so that not too much surface of the sauce is exposed to the air, thus causing a skin to form. A deep pan is also easier for stirring.

4. *Chinese or conical strainer.* Made in varying sizes. The one shown here is the right size for straining a sauce. This type of strainer is especially for straining liquids or sauces. It gathers and controls the liquid so that it can be directed, and moreover avoids splashing. A tammy strainer is of the same shape, but made of gauze.

5. *Stew-pan.* Similar to a saucepan in shape but shallower. It is especially suitable for sauces of a certain type, i.e. tomato sauce or where vegetables have to be softened before flour and liquid are added, or for sauces that require quick reduction.

6 & 7. *Sauté pans.* These are of varying sizes and generally of copper. They are not easy to find and it is probably simplest to buy them second hand. If they are difficult to come by use a deep frying-pan. They are used principally for sautéing meat or chicken, and are shallow enough for frying and deep enough to hold the liquid for cooking. See sauté notes (page 64).

8. *Casserole (aluminium or other metal).* This is a most useful piece of kitchen equipment. It is suitable for ragoûts, small braises, etc., and can be used on the stove top or in the oven. Pans similar in type can be had in enamelled iron.

* *See plate 31*

sounding a bit nonsensical to you, and in any case taking no account of the more strenuous aspects of this task.

In that enchanting book *The Sword in the Stone* [1] there is proper appreciation of the value of magic; Merlyn the Magician is speaking:

'Excuse me a moment,' he added as an afterthought, and, turning round to the breakfast things, he pointed a knobbly finger at them and said in a stern voice: 'Wash up.'

At this, all the china and cutlery scrambled down off the table, the cloth emptied the crumbs out of the window, and the napkins folded themselves up. All ran down off the ladder, to where Merlyn had left the bucket, and there was such a noise and yelling as if a lot of children had been let out of school. Merlyn went to the door and shouted: 'Mind, nobody is to get broken.' But his voice was entirely drowned in shrill squeals, splashes, and cries of 'My, it is cold,' 'I shan't stay in long,' 'Look out, you'll break me,' or 'Come on, let's duck the teapot.'

This shows proper appreciation of what a nice bit of magic could do for us in these days. But I remember my surprise when I came on a description of this domestic ritual in one of Arnold Bennett's books. [2] In a passage between a young man and woman the whole affair is set out, and as it throws a light not only on washing up, but on the changes that have come into the lives of many of us, I venture to quote it:

Louis, lolling in the chair, and slightly rocking it, watched Rachel at her task. She completely immersed spoons and forks in the warm water, and then rubbed them with a brush like a large nail-brush, giving particular attention to the inside edges of the prongs of the forks; and then she laid them all wet on a thick cloth to the right of the basin. But of the knives she immersed only the blades, and took the most meticulous care that no drop of water should reach the handles.

'I never knew knives and forks and things were washed like that,' observed Louis.

'They generally aren't,' said Rachel. 'But they ought to be. I leave all the other washing up for the charwoman in the morning, but I wouldn't trust these to her.' (The charwoman had been washing up cutlery since before Rachel was born.) 'They're all alike,' said Rachel.

Louis acquiesced sagely in this broad generalization as to charwomen.

'Why don't you wash the handles of the knives?' he queried.

'It makes them come loose.'

'Really?'

'Do you mean to say you didn't know that water, especially warm water with soda in it, loosens the handles?' She showed astonishment, but her gaze never left the table in front of her.

'Not me!'

'Well, I should have thought that everybody knew that. Some people use a jug, and fill it up with water just high enough to cover the blades, and stick the knives in to soak. But I don't hold with that because of the steam, you see. Steam's nearly as bad as water for the handles. And then some people drop the knives wholesale into a basin just for a second, to wash the handles. But I don't hold with that either. What I say is that you can get the handles clean with the cloth you wipe them dry with. That's what I say.'

'And so there's soda in the water?'

'A little.'

'Well, I never knew that either! It's quite a business, it seems to me.'

---

[1] T. H. White, *The Sword in the Stone* (Collins).
[2] Arnold Bennett, *The Price of Love* (Methuen).

KITCHEN EQUIPMENT *

1. *Savarin mould.* So called because traditionally a savarin is made in a mould of this type. The difference between this and an ordinary ring or border mould is that a savarin mould has a domed top, and a ring mould a flat one. Both moulds are useful for creams both sweet and savoury, moulded pilaffs, etc.

2. *Fluted timbale mould.* Useful for sponge cakes, puddings, mousses, etc. Made in light aluminium.

3. *Charlotte mould.* A most useful mould, primarily intended for a charlotte russe—also used for apple charlotte. Steamed or baked puddings and sweet and savoury creams can be made in this.

4. *Brioche mould,* in which brioche mousseline is made. An enlarged version of the last mould on this page. Sometimes known as a Gugelhopf mould, but good for all yeast breads and cakes.

5 & 6. *Raised pie moulds* of varying shapes. The square is generally used for hare or game, and the oval for veal. These moulds have pins at the corners or ends which, when withdrawn, enable the mould to be easily detached. The square ones usually consist just of the sides without a bottom, and are put straight on to a baking-sheet before lining with pastry.

7. *Moule à manqué.* This resembles a deep sandwich tin, but with slightly sloping sides, and is principally for cakes which are to be iced. The sloping sides allow the icing to run down easily over the cake. The mould is also useful for cream sweets which are turned out and masked with cream, etc.

8. *Flan ring.* A most useful piece of equipment. The ring is put on to a baking-sheet and lined with pastry (see page 843). After cooking the ring may be easily removed.

SMALL MOULDS (Nos. 9–14)

9. *Madeleine or shell mould.* Used for cakes of that name, or for small sponge cakes. Made in varying sizes.

10. *Boat moulds.* For pâtisserie and for pastry cases for savouries, etc.

11. *Deep tartlet moulds.* For tartlets and small cakes. These are a more satisfactory shape than the shallow patty pan.

12. *Dariole mould.* Made in varying sizes. Sometimes known as a castle pudding mould. Used for puddings, aspics, fish or meat creams.

13. *Cornet mould.* Used for ham cornets, i.e. where the mould is lined with ham, or for cream 'horns' when the pastry is wrapped round the outside of the mould.

14. *Brioche mould.* See No. 4. The traditional shape for making brioches (see page 793). May also be used for small cakes, or pastry cases. May be had in varying sizes.

* *See plate 32*

Without doubt Louis' notions upon domestic work were being modified with extreme rapidity. In the suburb from which he sprang domestic work—and in particular washing up—had been regarded as base, foul, humiliating, unmentionable—as toil that any slut might perform anyhow. It would have been inconceivable to him that he should admire a girl in the very act of washing up. Young ladies, even in exclusive suburban families, were sometimes forced by circumstances to wash up—of that he was aware—but they washed up in secret and in shame, and it was proper for all parties to pretend that they never had washed up. And here was Rachel converting the horrid process into a dignified and impressive ritual. She made it as fine as fine needlework—so exact, so dainty, so proud were the motions of her fingers and her forearms. Obviously washing up was an art, and the delicate operation could not be scamped nor hurried. . . .

The triple pile of articles on the cloth grew slowly, but it grew; and then Rachel, having taken a fresh white cloth from a hook, began to wipe, and her wiping was an art. She seemed to recognize each fork as a separate individuality, and to attend to it as to a little animal. Whatever her view of charwomen, never would she have said of forks that they were all alike.

There is so much common sense in this that not a great deal remains to be said, except perhaps to make a summing-up of useful points.

If you have not a double sink, then supplement your single one with a rinsing bowl.

Use soap flakes rather than detergents, at any rate for delicate china and for tea-cups. If detergents are used take special care about rinsing, so that no smell is left behind.

A slice of lemon dipped in salt will remove tea stains from the inside of tea-cups.

Put a little vinegar in the water for rinsing glasses.

Old-fashioned housewives used to boil silver spoons and forks at least several times a week after washing, which took away the necessity of cleaning with plate powder and kept the beautiful patine of old silver. A big pan of water, large enough for the spoons and forks to be laid in gently, may be kept on the stove, and the silver is put carefully in this after washing. It is dried while still hot, and a final polish with a leather will finish off perfectly and eliminate the tiresome job of silver-cleaning.

The following is a recipe for a home-made cloth that polishes as it dries:

Mix 2 teaspoons each of Goddard's plate powder and cloudy ammonia with 2 tea-cups of water. Dip a small square of Turkish towelling into this mixture and hang up without wringing out. It should be allowed to drip until quite dry. Wash the silver in the usual way, dry with this cloth, and finish off with a final polish on a soft clean cloth.

A little dry mustard rubbed on the blade of a knife will remove traces of fish or onion.

Fine wire wool rubbed on soap is the best means of cleaning saucepans, and if the inside of a pan is rubbed with this every time it is washed up, a satin-like surface is produced in a good pan which not only makes it a pleasure to use, but reduces the need of any special cleaning.

Wire wool, when once it has been used, becomes rusty if left about; it may be kept in a jam jar of cold water. In this you may also put with advantage odds and ends of soap.

If you find that washing up is going to be part of your routine, you will be sensible to lay in the following equipment and to accept the routine:

Fairly loose-fitting, rough-surfaced rubber gloves.

One or possibly two papier-mâché bowls

A rubber scraper

A roll of rough *crêpe* paper, sold for the purpose of wiping crockery or cutlery clean before it is washed

Two or three mops

Tea and glass cloths

The routine

Scrape the plates free of all food, and stack.

Wipe knives and forks with the rough paper sold for the purpose.

Put knives in a jug of warm water and forks and spoons in a bowl of hot water.

Start with glasses, follow on with silver and cutlery, first in soapy then in clear water.

After forks and spoons are washed, put them into a capacious pan to boil while you finish the crockery.

Have a folded cloth on the draining-board to prevent chipping of china.

If possible, dry while the pieces are still hot.

When you have finished, put wire wool in jam jar of water, rinse mops in water containing a little soda or ammonia, shake out and put in a jar, head side up, to dry. Rinse the tea-towels and boil them for a few minutes each day.

It may be 'quite a business' as Louis said, but the unpleasant aspects of washing up are in this way largely eliminated.

The members of a brains trust were once asked what the cook-hostess should do about washing up; someone suggested that if she were well organized it might be done quickly between courses, another said leave it all till after the party. On the whole I think that if you stack carefully and properly it may be left till the next morning, when you are likely to be better equipped for the job.

THE REFRIGERATOR

The uses of a refrigerator for storing food are generally appreciated. As an adjunct to cooking, however, we possibly do not make full use of it yet. American books give many good recipes for rolls, breads, and biscuits, the dough of which may be kept for days in the refrigerator, to be taken out and used as required. It is a help for a busy woman to be able to make a batch of dough or biscuit mixture when she has an hour or two to spare, and to draw on it piecemeal for fresh rolls or sweet biscuits. Suitable recipes for this purpose are given in the bread chapter.

Many people use the freezing trays for making ices. The exacting cook prefers, I think, to make ices in an ice-machine, because in these the mixture is churned continuously during freezing. To this end if one lives in the country it is helpful to have a large refrigerator. One may then collect ice for two days if necessary, using this in the ice-machine. For this it is advisable to set the regulator to very cold, or the first batch of ice, removed from the drawers and stored in a bowl, may melt.

In a large house the refrigerator may be used for keeping immediately perishable goods, and it is probably supplemented by a cold larder or dairy. In a small house or flat it often has to take the place of larder and pantry.

There are several points of especial importance to be observed. Generally speaking all foods should be covered. Anything with a strong pungent smell will affect other foods stored at the same time. Such food, if it must be stored, may be carefully covered or wrapped in a cloth, but special bags and foil wrappings are now to be bought which are more practical.

Melon is an example of a food which affects other foods stored with it. Other fruits may be kept in cold storage, but if their stay in the cold is prolonged their flavour is diminished.

Milk and butter, in particular, absorb flavours easily and must be covered and kept on a shelf apart from other foods. Glass or plastic boxes are admirable containers for many foods. Paper affects the smell of the refrigerator disagreeably, and food should be unwrapped before storing. Salad, if to be kept so cold, should be put in a glass container, or failing this in a clean cloth or one of the patent bags already mentioned, and be kept far away from the ice chamber.

Refrigerators are easy to keep clean, and should be wiped over, inside and out, with a damp cloth every day, and thoroughly cleaned and defrosted at least once a week. If the freezing chamber is allowed to become thickly coated with 'snow' it will be difficult to remove the ice-trays and the 'snow' will absorb flavours, and may even develop an unpleasant flavour all its own, which will communicate itself to foods kept in the refrigerator. To defrost, disconnect and take everything out of the refrigerator, and leave the door open until the frozen covering of the ice chamber has melted completely. The refrigerator should then be well washed with hot, soapy water, with a little mild disinfectant in it, and then rinsed in clean water containing bicarbonate of soda, 2 tablespoons to 1 gallon of water. The enamel should be scoured with a mild abrasive, then washed again, wiped with a dry cloth, and left to become quite dry and cool before the foods are replaced. The ice-shelves with their cubed containers should be emptied, washed, and refilled with cold water. If the shelves lift out they should be taken out and washed in hot soapy water. If they are a fixture they must be washed along with the sides and bottom. Scientific cleanliness is necessary if the refrigerator is to give its best service.

The kitchen table should be as large as is reasonably possible. A too small table is particularly irritating at dishing-up time. It should be made of hard wood; metal-topped tables have their uses as subsidiaries but are not suitable as main tables, being too noisy and too slippery.

The introduction of formica for kitchen table tops is becoming popular, but is still expensive. It gives a highly resistant surface, easy to keep clean.

A rack or shelf below to hold sieves, rolling-pins, chopping-boards, and other impedimenta is desirable, and well-fitting, easily running drawers are essential.

To save the surface of the table from unnecessary dirt it is well to have proper stands on which to place saucepans taken from the stove. A piece of white lino or American cloth or a white enamel tray used when fruit is being peeled or poultry drawn will help to avoid stains.

The table should be scrubbed every day. Soda will turn the wood yellow, but a good cleanser may be made by mixing equal parts of pure soap powder, whitening, and silver sand.

A stool of convenient height is useful. Many cooking processes may be done sitting down provided that one has a seat of the right height. Cooking is tiring and there is no point in standing unnecessarily.

A card index for recipes is a real time-saver, in fact for the serious cook it is an essential. It takes time to find recipes in ordinary note-books, though they can be found more easily, of course, in the alphabetically arranged loose-leaved kind. But a card index is the most practical way of dealing with recipes. They are quickly found and as quickly replaced after use. When a recipe is superseded by a better one, it can be destroyed and the collection kept up to date.

Before adding a list of general kitchen equipment it may not be out of place to make reference to the advent at some future date of labour-saving devices for the kitchen. An exhaustive list would be impracticable here—and tantalizing—but there are one or two items which seem outstandingly desirable, and possibly public demand might expedite their importation or manufacture.

An American friend speaks glowingly of a small washing-machine attached to her sink for washing and drying tea-towels and dish-cloths. A small domestic engine with a buffer attachment which could be used, among other things, for cleaning and polishing aluminium or copper saucepans would be a great help. As well as time and energy this would save wear and tear on finger-tips.

Of small implements I would mention the value of a rubber spatula called a kitchen-aid which removes every scrap of mixture from a bowl, a wall tin-opener, and potato- or apple-peelers which can be adapted for left- or right-handed use. A grating machine on the lines of a nut-grater saves finger-tips. A French carving board with runnels and a little reservoir for collecting the gravy is useful, and there are no kitchen knives to compare with French chefs' knives.

The following list is offered as a guide and a reminder, and not with the idea that one must have every item suggested from the very outset. The inclusion of a set of French weights and measures and an American measuring cup and spoons may cause surprise. If, however, one is to make full use of French and American cookery books—and this is certainly desirable—these save a lot of confusion and calculation.

KITCHEN UTENSILS

Earthenware marmite, small stock-pot with lid, or enamel-lined boiler for stock-making

Copper or aluminium or enamel-lined saucepans from 4 to 12 inches in diameter, with lids

Double-handled aluminium casserole or stew-pan

Fish-kettle, with drainer and lid

Saucepan with steamer

Deep-fat iron frying-pan and a frying basket (French *bassin de friture* is best)

Copper preserving pan in two sizes (one quite small for small quantities)

Frying-pans in two sizes, in thick iron or aluminium if possible

Iron omelet pan—5 or 8 inches

Chopping-block or board

Marble slab (for pastry)

Wooden pastry board (for bread-making)

Rolling-pins (one light, and one heavy made of ironwood)

Scales and a set of weights

Mincing-machine

Pestle and mortar

Copper bowl for beating egg whites, sponges, etc.

Two spare thick baking-sheets to fit oven

Large metal spoon for skimming

Two ladles of different sizes

Two-pronged chefs' steel forks

Cooks' knives in varying sizes for carving, chopping, and filleting

Vegetable knife

Palette-knives in two sizes

Steel or carborundum

Meat chopper

Meat saw (small)

Trussing-needle

Larding-needle

Set of meat skewers

Wooden spoons in varying sizes }

Wooden spatulas (thin type) } boxwood if possible

Large wooden preserving spoon }

Stainless steel table, dessert, and teaspoons

Set of American measuring spoons

American measuring cup

Measuring jug with liquid ounce measures

Wire whisks in varying sizes

Balloon whisk
Rotary whisk
Two wire sieves in different size mesh
One nylon sieve
Two bowl strainers
One small and one medium Chinese or conical strainer
Wire salad basket
Colander
Vegetable scoop
Potato-peeler
Apple-corer
Grater
Tin-opener
Corkscrew
Tin funnel
Rubber 'kitchen-aid'
Pastry brush (badger hair is best)
Fish slice
Kitchen scissors
Sugar-boiling thermometer
Ice-pick
Pepper-mill
Nut-mill or grater for cheese, breadcrumbs, etc.
Sugar dredger
Flour dredger
Seasoning box
Spice box, or set of jars for spices
Bread pan, earthenware or enamel
Flour bin
String box
Jelly bag (flannel)
Set of vegetable forcing-bags and pipes, plain and rose, in varying sizes
Set of icing pipes
Charlotte mould
Savarin mould
French pie mould (for raised pies)
Small dariole moulds
Box of plain and fluted pastry cutters
Tartlet moulds, deep, French
Set of cake tins
Moule à manqué
Flan rings, 6, 7, and 8 inches
Yorkshire pudding tins
Assortment of fireproof dishes in earthenware, china, or glass
   „   „ pie dishes
   „   „ soufflé dishes (china)
   „   „ earthenware casseroles

Assortment of pudding basins
    „   „ mixing bowls
Cloths for straining, for galantines, and for covering steamed puddings
A piece of old linen kept exclusively for drying fish
A roll of butter-muslin
Drying cloths and swabs
Equipment for cleaning and disposal of refuse, such as brushes, brooms, dustbins, pig bucket, chicken bucket, pails, and cleaning cloths

To these may be added:
Pressure cooker for quick cooking and for extracting vegetable and fruit juices
Ice-cream machine
Bombe mould
Wooden tub for packing moulded ices
Set of French weights and measures
Coffee percolator
Electric coffee grinder
Electric beater
Emulsifying machine

In conclusion a point concerning the cleaning of certain utensils may be made.   Fine wire wool for cleaning saucepans, tins, knives, cooking forks, palette-knives, and all metal equipment has superseded the old, more laborious and destructive methods.   It is best used with soap or soap powder and can also be obtained in the form of a pad with soap already incorporated.   If metal surfaces are treated in this way after every washing up, the surfaces will always stay bright and clean.

XXXVII

Modern Kitchen Appliances

Pressure Cookers — Deep-Freezing — Bottling Equipment — Electric Mixers — The Blender

PRESSURE COOKERS

IN THE matter of pressure cooking we have in our midst at Winkfield two protagonists, one, A, championing this method of cooking, the other, B, seeing its virtues as through a glass darkly. As in other arguments, things go well as long as we all cling firmly to 'the silken string of moderation,' but once hold on this is loosened then the innocent onlooker might gather either that you could grill a tournedos, make spun sugar, or prepare a seven-course dinner in as many minutes provided you used the cooker properly; or, on the other hand, that you might as well subsist on compressed tablets as live by pressure cooking. In the early stages of discussion, before, that is to say, enthusiasm on either side leads to overstatement, there is much to be learned, and it seems to me to be worth while setting out the pros and cons here.

A is a pressure-cooking enthusiast and an expert, and briefly she says this: You must thoroughly understand your cooker and read and remember the instructions. You should apply your knowledge of cooking to those processes you carry out under pressure: for example, remembering to soften the vegetables in fats in the cooker before making a soup. If you observe these matters you may save time and fuel in considerable degree by using a pressure cooker. She instances her own case of having to cook dinner after a day's work for four men. She says that in the morning the daily help will cut up for her a boiling fowl and prepare vegetables. On her return in the evening she cooks the fowl in 20 minutes with vegetables, has a second cooker with potatoes, has time to make a velouté sauce with the chicken stock, and there is the main part of the meal ready very quickly. Or she says she might grill cutlets and then cook her potatoes in the cooker, which takes 5 minutes, provided they are cut in quarters, turn them out, and put into the cooker frozen peas and perhaps beans too, which take 1½ minutes at most to cook, so that by the time she has mashed the potatoes the other vegetables are ready to be strained, tossed in hot butter, and served. She goes on to point out with what rapidity stock is to be prepared under pressure. We are all agreed upon that and argument flows quietly for a moment, only to start again when she says she prefers her Brussels sprouts, cabbage, and other vegetables cooked in this way, and that fruit cooked so quickly retains its delicate, fresh flavour. Then there is the peace of unanimity once more when she points out that an excellent chutney is made in 15 minutes instead of the usual 1½–2 hours.

Half time, and B takes up the argument. 'Too hit and miss for me,' she says, adding that there are too many factors to consider concerning the materials you are using. As she points out, birth certificates are not supplied by the poulterer; not all old birds are the same age, and the cooking time that might reduce one old fowl to rags may be insufficient to soften the muscular fibre of another—and the cook can't look and see. No subtlety of flavouring, she says, no touch of this and that and no pinch of the other; the careful eye becomes useless, since you cannot see what is going on inside the pan. Then A and B come into harmony again over certain braises and stews which they agree need slow cooking, not under pressure, if the meat is to be impregnated with the flavour of vegetables.

It really amounts to this. If you are an amateur of cooking, regarding it as an art, liking to experiment and invent, you will use pressure only for certain basic purposes: for stock, for extracting juice say from tomatoes, and for chutney (though not for jams, since for these a certain amount of reduction is required). For the rest you will follow B, considering time and effort well spent when you are concocting a dish. But if you are bound to cook utility fashion, in the shortest possible time, then you will have not one but two pressure cookers, thanking the inventors for their ever-increasing cleverness, and conditioning yourself to a little extra noise in the kitchen—and noise, after all, is very much a part of modern life.

Sensing a certain tension on the point of noise, A emphasizes that the slight hissing issuing from the steam-escape valve should be regarded as reassuring, since it indicates that all is going well. Knowing this to be true a mischievous remark that something on these lines was also said of doodle bugs is made in low voice for the ears of B only.

If the points which are to follow are accepted, it will be agreed, I think, that a pressure cooker is really a precision instrument with the advantages and disadvantages inherent in such. Used precisely it will give precise results in an economical and labour-saving way, but it is not convenient equipment for the slap-dash or absent-minded; food can so quickly be overcooked if the cooker is forgotten or if the rules are disregarded. To those who take trouble to understand it—and no very great trouble is involved—it is a valuable ally; the novice may approach it in timid spirit, but the feckless and the dreamers and those who wander away and forget what is in hand should, in the interests of everybody, leave it alone.

What pressure cooking is

Pressure cooking is cooking done in superheated steam, that is to say in steam under pressure.

There are several types of pressure cooker now on sale. The manufacturers supply with each a book of instructions which should be kept for reference, and the rules should be observed exactly. Replacements of such spare parts as safety-valves and the rubber rings surrounding the lid should be made immediately they become necessary.

Although the principles of pressure cooking remain the same, the various cookers may differ in construction, and in every case the instructions for use should be observed. Pressure cookers vary in size; for a family of four one holding from 4 quarts is reasonable. If the cooker is required for purposes of bottling and canning then a much larger size holding at least 8 quarts is called for.

Every pressure cooker has, in addition to a steam-escape valve, a safety release valve which represents security. If, owing to mismanagement or carelessness, the pressure within should become too high, this safety-valve will blow out. With it will probably also issue a thin stream of food. With proper care such accidents are avoidable. So long as a small, steady flow of steam comes from the escape valve, all is well and there is no danger. If this flow should stop while heat is being maintained, then you will know that the escape valve is blocked. The cooker must then be taken off heat and pressure reduced by the application of cold water in the way to be described later. Pressure reduced, the lid is removed and the fault remedied by the clearing of the entrance to the steam-escape valve. An accident of this nature may happen with certain types of food: apples, dried peas, and possibly rice and pastas, such as macaroni—a thickened liquid from such food rising and clogging the escape valve. Some manufacturers advise against the cooking of these foods under pressure, while other experts consider that this may be done if proper precautions are taken.

Another possible cause of mishap is the overfilling of the cooker. It should be filled three-quarters full only, and for soup or stock, which create a considerable volume of steam, the cooker should be only half filled. A too rapid escape of steam caused by failure to remove the cooker from high heat when the proper pressure has been reached may result in burning, and the rules regarding this point must be observed. A further note on this will be found in the paragraph on liquid.

The methods of cooking for which a pressure cooker is suitable are those involving moisture: steaming, braising, stewing, or boiling. It is possible, of course, to make certain elaborations of preparation. For example, meat, fish, and vegetables may all be subjected to a preliminary browning before pressure cooking starts, or, after such cooking, a bird may be browned under a hot grill before it is served.

Although the book which accompanies the cooker gives the necessary information, the following *résumé* of points concerning its care will serve to underline the matter.

It is essential to keep the steam-escape valve entirely clean. Every time the cooker is used, water from the hot tap must be allowed to run freely through the valve. To ensure that no speck of dried food remains unmoved by the hot water, the valve may be cleaned from time to time with a pipe cleaner. For a cooker used every day, this may be done once a week.

Before the cooker is used it must, as in the case of a new saucepan, be thoroughly washed out in hot soapy water; this prevents the possibility of any of the polishing material used in manufacture remaining inside and discolouring the first dish cooked in it. After use the cooker is always washed in hot soapy water, but never with water containing soda: soda discolours aluminium. If stains appear they may be removed with a mild abrasive, and obstinate stains should yield to a polishing of fine wire wool, rubbed with soap. Another way of removing stains is to make a solution of 2 tablespoons cream of tartar or 1 tablespoon vinegar to 1 quart water, and put this in the cooker, bring it up to pressure, leave for 5 minutes, and wash out with warm water.

Another way of removing stains is to put a handful of apple peelings or rhubarb with $\frac{1}{2}$ cup water into the cooker and bring it up to pressure. Although stains from fruit and vegetables are harmless, it is disagreeable to cook with a stained saucepan of any kind, and a pressure cooker is no exception. When not in use, the cooker should be put away with the lid turned upside-down to allow access of air, and the steam-escape weight may be kept inside it or be hung up by its handle if there is one.

A pressure cooker is supplied with a rack or trivet for use in certain cases. The object of the rack is to keep the food from being immersed in liquid, and it is used primarily for steaming. Soups and stews are put directly into the cooker without the rack.

For a little extra cost it is generally possible to get a set of separators, which, fitting inside the cooker, serve to keep different vegetables apart. This is not essential, because it is possible to cook more than one vegetable at a time in the cooker without the flavours intermingling because they are cooked in steam. If they were immersed in water this would not be so.

A summing-up of the points may be taken as:

1. Read the instructions in the book supplied with the cooker carefully.

2. Wash the cooker before putting it into use.

3. Make sure that the steam-escape opening is quite clear at all times and contains no trace of foreign matter.

4. Lay the food in, either with or without the rack mentioned. Add the liquid in the amount specified and be sure that the cooker is not filled beyond the degree indicated and that it is impossible for the food to impede the escape valve.

5. Seasoning as called for is added, but it may be observed that much less is used than in general methods of cooking, because of the comparatively small amount of liquid used. For example, in the cooking of vegetables half a flat teaspoon of salt will be found adequate.

6. Fix on the lid, leaving open the steam-escape valve. Put the cooker over strong heat to begin with. When a steady stream of steam issues from the steam-escape, fix on the regulator weight and wait until 15 lb. of pressure is registered. For this you will observe the remarks made in the instruction book.

7. Heat must now be reduced; very little is required for the continuation of cooking. On an electric stove, for food that requires say 5–10 minutes' cooking, the current may be switched off entirely. The flame of a gas-ring will be lowered, and the cool ring of the Aga or the back of a coal range will suffice to complete the process.

8. Begin to count the cooking time from the moment when, the required pressure achieved, the cooker is set on low heat. If you have a time indicator, set it now. If you are timing by the clock, note down the time when cooking will be over.

9. Take care not to overcook, which may happen more easily with pressure cooking than with ordinary methods. This will be readily appreciated when it is realized that 1–2 minutes under pressure are equal to 5–10 minutes of ordinary cooking.

10. Cooking time expired, turn off heat, remove cooker, and cool by either (a) setting the cooker in a basin of cold water for 10 seconds or (b) allowing cold water to run freely over the sides and bottom of the cooker (but not over the top) until pressure has been reduced. Thirty seconds should suffice.

N.B. If water is allowed to run over the lid, some portion of it may find its way inside and so dilute the contents.

11. Remove lid and serve food. If the lid is left on or replaced, the contents will continue to cook.

12. Wash the cooker in hot soapy water and run hot water through the escape valve.

The liquid in the pan after pressure cooking is concentrated and good, and should be used—the liquid from vegetables for stock, soup, or gravy; the juice from a bird may be served with it.

Liquid used in cooking

The amount of liquid is usually indicated in the recipe, but some general indications may be found useful. First let me remind you that steam should escape from the cooker in a small steady stream; the important word here is 'stream': if the cooker is left too long on strong heat after the required pressure has been reached, the rate of escape will increase, and instead of a small steady stream there will be a hissing, puffing volume. This will be hint enough that you must reduce the heat, for if steam escapes at such an excessive rate, in 5 minutes about a gill of water will have become exhausted. For the plain cooking of vegetables, $\frac{1}{2}$ cup water is all that is called for, and although the time of cooking may be a few minutes only (and probably 10 minutes at most) it will be clear that steam escaping too fast may result in drying and burning. For all foods taking between

10 and 20 minutes to cook, ½ gill water is enough, and for foods taking longer than 20 minutes, say 30–35 minutes, ½ pint is the usual amount called for. For food which requires 35–40 minutes, ¾–1 pint will be needed.

FOODS THAT MAY BE COOKED UNDER PRESSURE

All foods susceptible of moist cooking may be pressure cooked: stocks and broths, soups and in particular vegetable soups, where quick cooking may be regarded as an advantage; fish, particularly that to be cooked in a court bouillon, tough meat, old birds, either poultry or game, rabbits, hares, and venison; and many vegetables, except possibly some of those of particularly delicate flavour, such as young French beans and small globe artichokes. Fruits may be cooked in light syrup.

Earlier an observation was made about the possibility of accident if rice and pastas are cooked in this way; some manufacturers advise against this, other experts in the use of these machines maintain that it may be done if proper precautions are taken.

The preliminary breaking down of fruit for jam- or jelly-making may be carried out in a pressure cooker, and fruit juice is very thoroughly extracted by this means.

Oranges and grape-fruit for marmalade, cut up and soaked overnight, may be cooked under pressure for 10 minutes and are then ready to be simmered, but this subsequent simmering must be done with the lid off the pan, so that the necessary reduction may take place. A pressure cooker is hermetically sealed and no evaporation takes place during the cooking.

Chutneys and pickles may be speeded up under pressure without loss of flavour, particularly where sweetness rather than sharpness is wanted.

Although the arguments for and against this method of cooking were outlined earlier, a few further points may be added in conclusion. A good deal of the smell of cooking is eliminated, and this is of special advantage when fish or fish stock is in hand. When chicken food or meat for dogs or cats is cooked indoors, a pressure cooker should be set aside exclusively for the purpose. A point sometimes pressed by enthusiasts is the better conservation of vitamins, but this is a matter better left to scientists and medicos. A commonly expressed disadvantage is that the methods of cooking are limited to those involving moisture, but no one would cook exclusively with a pressure cooker, or, it is to be hoped, with a frying-pan either.

BOOKS OF REFERENCE

Marjorie Baron Russell, *The Complete Book of Modern Pressure Cooking* (Falcon Press); *Cooking by Magic* (Falcon Press).

The following good American books can sometimes be procured:

Leone Rutledge Carroll, *Pressure Cooking* (M. Barrows & Co. Inc.).

Ida Bailey Allen, *Pressure Cooking* (Garden City Publishing Co.).

RECIPES, TIME-TABLES, AND COOKING DIRECTIONS

Recipes for ordinary cooking, provided they are for a moist process, may often be adapted for pressure cooking. The cooking time is cut down by two-thirds; for example, if the time given for ordinary cooking is 1½ hours, pressure-cooking time will be half an hour. Often, too, it is necessary to reduce the amount of liquid given in the recipe, remembering that no evaporation takes place.

The following is a small selection of recipes suitable for the process:

STOCKS AND BROTHS

Stock-making in a pressure cooker is rapid, and there is no offensive smell in the kitchen such as is produced by a stock-pot. Recipes for small amounts only are given, for it is assumed that the pressure cooker will be used when stock is wanted in a hurry; moreover, the usual size of cooker will not hold a large amount of stock, since, as has been emphasized, it must be filled only half full. It is understood that the cooker should be covered and brought up to pressure before the cooking time is reckoned.

HOUSEHOLD STOCK
cooking time 30 minutes

2–3 lb. bones from cooked meat, with scraps of under-done beef
4 stalks of celery, cut small
2 onions, each stuck with a clove
1 carrot, sliced

1 crushed clove of garlic (if liked)
a bouquet garni
2 teaspoons salt
9 peppercorns
2–3 pints hot water

Break the bones as small as possible, cut up the meat and remove fat. Put meat, bones, vegetables, garlic, bouquet, salt, peppercorns, and water into the cooker, cover and bring to pressure. Pressure cook 30 minutes. Reduce pressure with cold water, or stand 10 minutes off the heat. Remove lid. Strain, pour into a basin, remove fat from the surface when cold.

CHICKEN STOCK
cooking time 20–30 minutes

bones and carcass of a cooked chicken
1 sliced carrot
½ head of celery, sliced, or outside stalks cut small
1 onion stuck with a clove

bouquet of parsley, thyme, and bay-leaf
thin strip of lemon rind
1 teaspoon salt
6 peppercorns
1½ pints hot water

Put chicken carcass, broken up as small as possible, chicken bones, vegetables, bouquet, lemon rind, salt, peppercorns, and water in the cooker. Cover, bring to pressure and pressure cook 20–30 minutes. Reduce pressure with cold water, strain into a basin and leave to get cool. Remove fat before using.

MINESTRONE

cooking time 8 minutes

1 oz. butter or bacon fat
2 oz. small haricot beans, soaked overnight
1 tomato, peeled and finely sliced
1 carrot, diced small
1 potato, diced
1 large leek, white part only, shredded
1 onion, chopped
3 outside sticks of celery, cut small
½ heart of cabbage, shredded
2 oz. green peas
1 clove of garlic crushed with salt
1 quart water
2 oz. vermicelli or spaghetti
salt and pepper
1 tablespoon chopped parsley

Make the fat hot in the cooker, add the tomato and all the other prepared vegetables, and the crushed garlic. Cook gently all together for 5 minutes, with the cover off the pan. Add the water, hot, the salt and pepper, and the vermicelli or spaghetti. Cover, bring to pressure and pressure cook 8 minutes. Reduce pressure with cold water, pour into a hot soup tureen and sprinkle with chopped parsley.

N.B. Be careful not to add too much seasoning; 1 teaspoon salt and ¼ teaspoon pepper will probably be enough. Taste after cooking and add more seasoning if required.

TOMATO SOUP

cooking time 5 minutes

1 lb. tomatoes
1 oz. butter
2 tablespoons carrot, diced
2 stalks of celery, cut small
2 tablespoons chopped onion
2 cloves
1 clove of garlic crushed with salt
bouquet of parsley, thyme, and bay-leaf
1 pint water
1 oz. flour
2 tablespoons cold milk
salt and pepper to taste
1 small teaspoon sugar
cream

Peel and quarter tomatoes. Heat the butter in the cooker, add carrot, celery, and onion and cook gently 5–10 minutes. (Do not cover the cooker for this process.) Add tomatoes, cloves, garlic, bouquet, and water and cover. The water may be hot or cold. Pressure cook for 5 minutes. Reduce pressure with cold water, sieve the soup, blend the flour with the cold milk, mix in a little hot soup, then add the blended flour to the rest of the soup, return to the cooker and bring to the boil. Cook for 3 minutes, stirring, with the lid off the cooker, to cook the flour. Season with salt, pepper, and sugar, and serve with a spoonful of lightly whipped cream on each plate or cup.

TIME-TABLE FOR FISH

Fish should be cooked on the rack, wrapped in muslin or in grease-proof paper, to facilitate removal from the cooker. Season first with salt, pepper, dusted on both sides, and the juice of half a lemon.

Fish	Minutes at 15 lb. Pressure	Amount of Water
Steaks of cod	6 per lb.	$\frac{1}{4}$ pint
Haddock	6 „ „	$\frac{1}{4}$ „
Halibut	6 „ „	$\frac{1}{4}$ „
Herrings	10 if cooked whole 5 if boned and spread flat	$\frac{1}{4}$ „ add dash of vinegar
Mackerel	10 if cooked whole	$\frac{1}{4}$ „
Mussels	$2\frac{1}{2}$	$\frac{1}{4}$ „ add white wine
Plaice	5–6 according to thickness	$\frac{1}{4}$ „
„ fillets	3–5 „ „ „	$\frac{1}{4}$ „
Salmon or turbot (3 inches thick)	6	$\frac{1}{4}$ „
Scallops	5	$\frac{1}{4}$ „
Sole	5–6 according to thickness	$\frac{1}{4}$ „
Whiting	5	$\frac{1}{4}$ „

$\frac{1}{4}$ pint water is $\frac{1}{2}$ tea-cup.

COURT BOUILLON FOR FISH
cooking time 10 minutes

1 small sliced carrot
bouquet of parsley, thyme, and
    bay-leaf, tied together
6 peppercorns

$\frac{1}{2}$ pint white wine and water
1 sliced onion
1 teaspoon salt

Put all together into the pressure cooker, cover, bring to pressure and pressure cook for 10 minutes. Reduce pressure with cold water and allow the court bouillon to become lukewarm. Lay in the fish and cook according to the time-table above.

TIME-TABLE FOR MEAT

Meat	Minutes at 15 lb. Pressure	Amount of Water
Salt beef	25 per lb.	Enough to cover meat ($\frac{1}{2}$ pint)
Beef stew	15–20	Meat browned first, 1 tea-cup
Irish stew	15	$\frac{1}{2}$ pint
Haricot mutton	15	meat browned first, 1 tea-cup
Ox tongue	15 per lb. (fresh) 20 ,, ,, (smoked)	1 pint
Tripe (prepared)	15	$\frac{1}{4}$ pint and $\frac{1}{4}$ pint milk
Veal (blanquette)	15	$\frac{1}{2}$ pint

Any tried recipe may be used, provided the time is reduced to that given in this time-table and that the liquid is also reduced. Thickness of meat is the deciding factor; if meat is cut in thick squares it will take longer to cook.

IRISH STEW
cooking time 15 minutes

1½ lb. best end of neck of mutton
1½ lb. potatoes, peeled and cut in thick slices
1 flat teaspoon salt
¼ teaspoon pepper
2 tablespoons chopped parsley
1 lb. mild onions, sliced
½ pint vegetable stock

Trim the meat in neat pieces and put into the cooker, in layers, potatoes, onions, and meat. Season lightly between each layer with salt and pepper, but be careful not to overseason. Add the stock, cover and pressure cook 15 minutes. Reduce pressure with cold water, turn out on a hot dish and sprinkle with parsley.

VEAU PROVENÇALE
cooking time 25 minutes

2–3 lb. knuckle or shoulder of veal
1½ oz. butter
2 onions, chopped
2 carrots, diced
3 tomatoes, peeled
¼ a head of celery, cut small
1 pint vegetable stock or water
a small sprig of rosemary
bouquet of parsley, thyme, and bay-leaf
2 thin shreds of orange rind
1 teaspoon salt
6 peppercorns
1 oz. flour
the rest of the orange rind, grated and soaked in the juice of ½ a lemon

Cut the veal in neat pieces, suitable for serving. Make ½ oz. butter hot in the cooker, add the onions, carrots, tomatoes, and celery and cook them over very gentle heat, with the cooker uncovered, for 10 minutes at least. Then put in the veal, add the stock or water, hot, the rosemary, bouquet, the 2 thin shreds of orange rind, the salt and peppercorns. Cover, bring to pressure and pressure cook for 25 minutes. Reduce pressure with cold water, lift out the veal, strain off the stock and make a velouté sauce (see page 152) with this and the remaining butter and the flour made into a blond roux. Simmer and skim, taste for seasoning, and add the grated orange rind soaked in the lemon juice. Pour over the veal and serve very hot with a dish of boiled rice as accompaniment.

N.B. This dish can also be made with a young rabbit, soaked overnight in acidulated water and very well washed the next day.

TIME-TABLE FOR POULTRY AND GAME

Pressure cooking is good for tough birds, old birds, old rabbits and hare, and tough venison. The times here are for mature poultry and game.

Meat	Minutes at 15 lb. Pressure	Amount of Water		
Duck	10–12 per lb.	½–¾ pint		
Fowl, mature	10–12 ,, ,,	½–¾ ,,		
,, old boiler	12–15 ,, ,,	½–¾ ,,		
Grouse	10 in all	½ ,,		
Guinea-fowl	10–12 per lb.	½–¾ ,,		
Hare	20–30 ,, ,,	½–¾ ,,		
Partridge	20 in all	½ ,,		
Pheasant	10–12 per lb.	½–¾ ,,		
Pigeon	15–20 ,, ,,	½ ,,		
Ptarmigan	10–12 ,, ,,	½–¾ ,,		
Rabbit, young	10 ,, ,,	½ ,, soak beforehand		
,, old	12–15 ,, ,,	½ ,,	,,	,,
Venison	14 ,, ,,	½ ,,		

All the birds, etc., mentioned above should be stewed or braised rather than roasted.

TIME-TABLE FOR FRESH VEGETABLES

Use the rack. Cook in ¼ pint water, with a small flat teaspoon of salt only, no matter what the amount of vegetables may be.

It should be remembered that opinions vary on the amount of cooking that vegetables should have. Some people will not eat a cauliflower unless it is soft all the way through; others prefer it almost crisp. The time-table below gives the *average* time required in each case, and where the extremes vary very much alternative times are given. Again, vegetables fresh from the garden take less time to cook, as a rule, than those bought from a shop. Old or mature vegetables (carrots, for example) may vary quite a lot from young or immature vegetables in the time they take to cook. Use these tables as a *guide* only. Experience and your own taste will tell you how to use them to advantage.

It is taken for granted that all the necessary preparation has been carried out for each vegetable. It must, however, be remembered that vegetables cook much more quickly in a pressure pan when they are cut up. Large potatoes, for example, may easily take 10–15 minutes to cook, and even then they may be hard in the middle while their outside is soft and mushy. It is much better to halve or quarter them before cooking. Also they taste much better cooked in their skins, even when cut up. In some cases times are given for cooking vegetables diced.

Vegetables	*Minutes at 15 lb. Pressure*	*Observations*
Artichokes, globe	(Not recommended)	
„ Jerusalem	3–4	Halve or quarter
Asparagus	2–4	Stand upright if possible
Broad beans	1½–2	
French beans	2–4	
Beetroot, up to 4 oz.	15	Use ½ pint water
„ „ „ 8 „	20	„ ½ „ „
„ „ „ 16 „	35–40	„ 1 „ „
Sprouting broccoli	2–4	
Brussels sprouts	2–3	
Cabbage, shredded coarsely	1–1½	
Cabbage, quartered	2–3	Cut out hard core
Carrots, small and young	5–6	
„ large, left whole	8–10	
„ quartered lengthwise	4–5	
„ sliced or diced	2	
Cauliflower, whole	3–5 according to size and age	
„ divided into flowerets	1½–2½	
Celery, in 1½-inch pieces	2	
Celeriac in 1-inch cubes	3	
Chicory	6	Add lemon juice or vinegar
Kohlrabi, whole	8	
„ in ¼-inch slices	4	

Vegetables	Minutes at 15 lb. Pressure	Observations
Leeks, cut lengthwise	2–3	
Marrow, sliced	2–3	
Mushrooms, sliced	1	Do not peel
„ whole caps	2	„ „ „
„ „ „ large	4	„ „ „
Onions, whole	6–7 according to size	
„ sliced	2–3	
Spring onions	2–3	
Parsnips, cut lengthwise in quarters	7–8	
„ in dice or cubes	3	
Peas	1–4 according to size and freshness	
Potatoes, new, small	5–7	
„ „ large	10–15	
„ whole, medium size	8–10	
„ „ small	5–7	
„ large, quartered for mashing	4–6	
Salsify	5	
Sea-kale	6 exactly, overcooking makes it tough	
Spinach	1½	
Swedes in 1-inch cubes	3–5	
Tomatoes, whole	½–1	
Turnips, small and young	5–8	
„ older, cut in cubes	3–5	
Zucchini, whole	2–3	

FROZEN VEGETABLES

Put on in boiling water, adding only ½ gill; the ice from the vegetables melts and supplies the rest. Put on still frozen, broken in pieces.

Vegetables	Minutes at 15 lb. Pressure
Asparagus	1½
Broad beans	½–1
French beans	½–1
Brussels sprouts	1–1½
Cauliflower	½
Peas, English	½–1
„ foreign	1–2
Spinach	½–1
Macédoine	½–1

DRIED VEGETABLES

These cook more quickly if they are soaked overnight in warm water. Salt should not be added until the cooking is finished, as it makes the skins tough. Cook on the rack. Every pound of dried vegetables requires 1 pint water for pressure cooking. Peas are not recommended. After cooking, leave pressure to reduce at room temperature for 10 minutes, unless the vegetables are to be sieved and used for soup. In that event reduce the pressure with cold water, which makes the vegetables more inclined to break up.

Vegetables	Minutes at 15 lb. Pressure
Butter beans	30
Haricot beans, small	30–35
„ „ large	35
Lentils	15

TIME-TABLE FOR FRESH FRUITS

Many fruits are better cooked in a light syrup (see Compôtes of fruit, page 903). The liquid given in these time-tables may be either syrup or water, as desired. It is assumed that all fruit will be prepared in the usual way before pressure cooking.

Pressure cooking is particularly good for extracting juice from fruits for jelly-making, or for breaking down fruits for jam. See next page for the amount of water to be used, etc.

Fruit	Minutes at 15 lb. Pressure	Observations
Apples, whole	4–6	$\frac{1}{4}$ pint liquid is put in the cooker in each case
„ for sauce	1	Fruit peeled, quartered, and cored
Apricots	$\frac{1}{4}$	
Blackberries	Bring to pressure	
Cherries	Bring to pressure only	
Cranberries	$1\frac{1}{2}$	Add extra sugar for sauce
Currants	Bring to pressure	
Gooseberries	„ „ „	
Greengages	„ „ „	
Nectarines	„ „ „	

Fruit	Minutes at 15 lb. Pressure	Observations
Peaches	Bring to pressure	Pour hot water over to peel; halve and stone
Pears, ripe	2–3	Halve, if large
„ for stewing	5–6	
Pineapple	10	Peel and cut in slices or cubes
Plums, hard or unripe	1½–2	
„ ripe or Victoria	Bring to pressure	
Raspberries	„ „ „	
Rhubarb	*Nearly* bring to pressure	

Dried fruits

Apple rings	4–6
Apricots	1
Figs	10
Peaches	5–7
Pears	9–10
Prunes	10

All these dried fruits should be soaked overnight in hot water and cooked in the water they soaked in. If the water has been absorbed, add enough to make ¼ pint; the liquid in any case should not exceed this amount.

JAM- AND JELLY-MAKING WITH A PRESSURE COOKER

A pressure cooker is excellent for the preliminary processes of jam- and jelly-making, although, as has already been explained on page 1167, the final cooking must be done with the lid off the pan, or in a preserving pan.

To extract juice for jelly, put the fruit in the cooker with just enough water to show through the top layer. Cover, bring to pressure, and pressure cook 5 minutes. The juice can then be strained off and measured as usual.

To break down fruit for jam or marmalade, generally speaking ¾ pint water for every pound of fruit is enough. Use less for very juicy fruit. Put fruit and water in the cooker, cover and bring to pressure, pressure cook (usually) 5 minutes.

Oranges or grape-fruit should be sliced and soaked overnight, then put in the cooker (1½ pints water to every pint of pulp). Bring to pressure and pressure cook 5 minutes.

For red-currant jelly, pressure cook for 1 minute only.

The cooker must not be more than three-quarters full.

DEEP-FREEZING

Of all modern household gods among the most revered are deep-freezers: their praises are so highly sung that it might seem almost a hardship to be without one. A freezer can be a comfort if to have food in reserve at home, possibly a lot of it for long periods of time, will simplify house-keeping. Tidy, methodical systems of buying suitably for it and of packing and recording its contents, will repay the effort of adopting them. This point is emphasized later by Rosemary Hume, on whose long experience the following information is based.

There are various shapes and sizes of machine but, because there are new developments from time to time, there is little to be gained by descriptions of them here. Incidentally by housing a freezer in a shed or a garage, so that the surrounding temperature on the whole is low, running costs can be minimized, and this may influence one's choice of size perhaps. Here is a list of foods that can well be subjected to deep-freezing, with an indication (in brackets) of the number of months they can be expected to keep satisfactorily. They are put in raw.

Beef (9–12), Chicken, Duck and Game (8–12), Lamb, Pork and Veal (6).
White Fish (3), Mackerel (3), Salmon, which freezes rather better cooked than raw, (4–6), Smoked Salmon (6–8).
Beans—French, Broad and Runner (6–9), Mushrooms (3).
Egg whites (8–12), Egg yolks (mixed with a pinch of salt) (8–12).
Fruit in syrup, e.g. sliced pineapple (6–8).
Cream, whipped only (3).

There are one or two items for use in various dishes or as accompaniments to dishes which are worth noting, such as:
Fresh white breadcrumbs made in the blender. Put them into 2 or 4 oz. bags.
Chopped onions; cook these in butter and pack them into small cartons for use in stuffing or for the base of a sauce.
Mint sauce—in small cartons and snipped chives in small cartons.
Raw egg whites.
Demi-glace sauce in small cartons.
Boned and stuffed meat, shoulder or loin of lamb.
Bread and rolls.

The following are not recommended for deep-freezing:
Boiled rice.
Whole eggs (unless yolks and whites are separated), Stuffed eggs.
Anything with a high water content, e.g. cucumber.
Raw ham, because the saltpetre in the cure makes the meat taste rank after a short period of time.

Everything that is put into a freezer should be wrapped, labelled and neatly packed in. Insufficient wrapping, incidentally, may cause what is known as 'freeze burn' of poultry or meat, and this spoils their appearance and flavour. You should always wear gloves when handling things in the freezer, for you too can suffer from 'freeze burn' if you don't.

Baskets made of plastic-covered wire are invaluable for keeping certain types of food apart; meat, chicken, cakes, for example. On account of their pungent smell, fish, prawns, crab meat and things of this kind advisedly are kept, wrapped of course, in boxes at the bottom of the freezer; no matter how carefully they are packed they should not be cheek by jowl with anything which has a more delicate flavour than they have. It goes without saying that raw food of any kind must be of first quality and absolutely fresh at the time it is put into the freezer, and that it should be frozen as quickly as possible. Cooked dishes should be cooled as quickly as possible before freezing and then turned into foil containers and put into polythene bags. Bags must be tied up and all the air pressed out of them in the process.

One must always allow for the fact that liquids will swell when freezing and that therefore it is advisable when putting, say, soups or egg whites into cartons to fill these to within 2 inches of the top, in other words leaving room for expansion. One should not put any glass bottle or container in a freezer, for liquid inside it is likely to swell and shatter the glass.

It is advisable to keep a box file with a record of the contents of the freezer to remind you what food is cooked and what isn't, how much of it is ready for what number of people to eat, and the date of its consignment to the freezer.

When raw food is taken out of freeze it must be allowed to thaw out gradually, preferably in the refrigerator. It may be necessary to let things thaw for 4 to 20 hours; the extent of time needed depends of course on the type of food concerned.

Notes on buying and preparation of food for the freezer. Many butchers will allow one a reduction in price when a reasonably large quantity of meat, e.g. half a side of lamb or pork, is bought at any one time. They will arrange to divide it into cuts and joints ready for your purpose. A good buy for a small family, for it contains both roasting and stewing cuts, is a fore-quarter. The hind-quarter is all meat for roasting and, in the case of pork, it has the crackling. So far as beef is concerned aitch-bone, topside or top-rump are useful cuts, and 8 to 10 lb. will give 3 to 4 good-sized joints for braising. Cuts from the shoulder (chuck steak) cut into pieces and packed in amounts of $1\frac{1}{2}$ to 2 lb. are sufficient for four. Skirt and ox kidney are useful for pies. It is an advantage to have small packs of this sort of meat so that two packs can be taken out to make a double quantity of stew and one half put back cooked ready for another meal. Sirloin or rolled ribs, which are the best cuts for roasting, can also be divided into convenient joints of about 4 lb. in weight, and the same applies to grilling meat such as fillet steaks, rump steak and tournedos. Raw meat, game, poultry and fish, once frozen and later thawed out, should never be re-frozen; but they can of course safely be re-frozen if they have first been cooked. The meat and the game require to be hung for an appropriate period of time before they are frozen.

Soft fruit and vegetables freshly picked from the garden have the advantage of any bought from a shop. Stoned fruit (plums, damsons, apricots) freeze well if they are put into containers and provided that they are fresh and perfectly sound. Vegetables must be washed well, prepared and blanched before being packed and put down to freeze.

Freezing, it must be emphasized, will not improve the quality or the taste of anything; it merely holds in suspension anything which is subjected to the process. For some people, the anticipation of being able to enjoy some garden product out of season, tasting as fresh as the day it was picked perhaps, seems an overwhelming argument in favour of deep-freezing. Nevertheless for other people, even more pleasure is to be had in taking what the seasons bring as they come, and now I come to think of it, this was so for Constance Spry. On the other hand, when she and Rosemary Hume first were working on this cookery book, deep-freezers were not among the appliances that one could seriously think of having at home. Now that it is possible for so many people to have them, ideas on the whole subject seem to be changing every day.

BOTTLING

Equipment. Fruit may be bottled in a hot-water bath or in the oven. Vegetables should be bottled with the aid of a pressure cooker. In both cases equipment should be overhauled before the process begins.

Jars should be examined to see that they are not cracked or nicked at the edge.

Covers must fit perfectly; snap closures, if used, should be tested.

Rubber rings should be pulled out to double their length, or folded in two, to make sure that they do not crack, and that their elasticity is all it should be, they should be soaked in water for 10 minutes before use. Never use old rings.

Imperfect items should be discarded and fresh equipment bought; it is possible to buy covers, jars, and rubber rings separately.

Sterilizers. Complete sterilizers can be bought, with a false bottom, and provided with a handle and a thermometer; or a large fish-kettle will answer the purpose, especially one that has a false bottom (a necessity to prevent the jars from cracking when they come in contact with the heated bottom of the pan). Or a clothes-boiler can be used, if this also is provided with a false bottom: three thicknesses of wire netting folded together, for example, put in before the jars are carefully laid in. Even a bucket, with a false bottom of newspaper, will serve. In every event there must be plenty of room all around the jars: they should not touch one another anywhere, or there is a danger of cracks.

There are several varieties of jar: the Kilner jar, with a glass cap and a brass band to screw round it over a rubber ring; the snap-closed jar, with a metal or glass cap fixed on with a spring clip; and the jar with a Porosan metal cap, which is pressed on to the hot jar after sterilizing. For full directions on how to use all of these methods of closing, see the booklets issued by the makers of them.

Ordinary 1- or 2-lb. jam jars can also be used with metal snap closures, as well as with adequate covers of parchment, Porosan skin, or bladder, provided these can be affixed to make an air-tight seal. A recipe for cement to put over such jars is on page 1183.

N.B. *The Complete Book of Home Food Preservation* by Cyril Grange, F.R.H.S. (Cassell), gives exhaustive particulars of sterilizing methods.

Fruit, including tomatoes, should be ripe but firm. Tomatoes may be bottled in water, with a teaspoon of sugar and a teaspoon of salt to every pound. Fruits can be bottled in water or syrup; syrup is recommended, for if bottled in water some acids develop which make the fruits need more sugar than they should before they can be eaten with pleasure. Syrup may be thin, $\frac{1}{2}$ cup sugar (about 4 oz.) to each pint of water; medium, 1 cup (8 oz.) to each pint; or thick, 1 lb. to each pint of water. Half a pound to a pint of water is the average strength; it is suitable for all but very acid fruits, e.g. black-currants, green gooseberries, damsons and so on.

Vegetables should be bottled in a pressure cooker. Food experts agree that to use an ordinary hot-water sterilizer is not safe. The temperature reached is not high enough to kill spores and the bacteria that cause botulism, which can easily prove fatal.

Preparation. Fruit should be carefully graded; every fruit in the bottle should be, as far as possible, of the same size. Pick over the fruit with care, wash it if necessary and prepare it as if for cooking.

Raspberries, blackberries, and loganberries often contain grubs or maggots. Soak them for half an hour in salt solution ($\frac{1}{2}$ oz. salt to 1 quart water) to draw these out. Then wash carefully in a sieve or colander dipped in and out of cold water.

Plums, apricots, and nectarines may be left whole if small, or they may be halved and stoned. More fruit goes into a bottle if it is stoned first. A few stones may be cracked and the kernels added to the bottle to give flavour. Peaches may be skinned and halved before stoning.

If there are small quantities of fruit to be used up, they may be arranged in layers and sterilized together.

The liquid used, whether water or syrup, should be cold, except that for apples and pears, which keep their colour better in hot syrup.

To make syrup dissolve the sugar in water, then boil for 3–5 minutes and strain before use.

HOT-WATER STERILIZATION

1. Wash the bottles in hot soapy water, rinse in cold water, drain and leave wet inside.

2. Fill with prepared and graded fruit, packing the bottles with care, shaking down the fruit and packing it in with a packing stick or the handle of a wooden spoon. Leave $\frac{1}{2}$ inch space between the top of the fruit and the cover.

3. Pour cold syrup or water slowly into the bottles. Dispose of any bubbles that occur with the handle of a spoon.

4. Put on the rubber bands (previously soaked for 10 minutes in warm water) and the lids or the snap closures. Screw on brass bands, then turn back $\frac{1}{4}$ inch.

5. Stand the bottles on the false bottom of the sterilizer, pour in cold water until it comes above the shoulder of the bottles. Put on the lid.

6. Heat the water very slowly to 160° F. This should take 1 hour. Draw the pan off the heat and allow it to cool to 155° F. Keep between 150° and 155° F. by the thermometer until the time is made up to 2 hours.

7. Remove the bottles with great care, using a pair of tongs or a cloth folded in three; tighten the screw bands and stand the jars carefully on a wooden table or on thickly folded paper to cool. Leave for 48 hours. Test by unscrewing the screw bands or removing the snap closures and lifting the bottles by their lids. If the lids and the bottles part company they must be sterilized again.

OVEN METHOD (1)

1. Fill the jars with fruit as before. Fill with cold water or syrup.

2. Put on rubber rings and covers, but do not secure with screw bands or clips.

3. Put the jars in the oven on the bars of the shelf, or in a shallow baking-tin a quarter filled with warm water. See that the jars do not touch.

4. Have the oven at 250° F. or Regulo Mark $\frac{1}{2}$. Heat for $1\frac{1}{2}$–$2\frac{1}{2}$ hours. The time depends on the number of bottles being sterilized at once. Average time is about 2 hours for most fruits. Apples and pears may take longer.

5. Take from the oven one at a time with tongs or a folded cloth, screw or clip down and allow to cool on a wooden table or several layers of folded cloth or paper. Test for sealing.

OVEN METHOD (2)

1. Fill the jars to the brim. Cover each jar with its lid to prevent scorching. Add no liquid, and do not put on screw bands or clips.

2. Put on oven shelf or in baking-tin, as before.

3. Oven heat should be 240° F.   Leave the jars in for 1 hour, or until the fruit has shrunk slightly in the jar and has begun to change colour.

4. Have boiling water or syrup ready.   Fill jars to the brim and cover with lids and screw bands or snap closures.

5. Cool as before and test.

N.B. It is a good plan to have a spare jar of fruit with which to fill up the jars as the fruit shrinks.   The juice from the spare jar may be added to the boiling syrup.

TOMATO BOTTLING

Tomatoes may be bottled (*a*) whole, skinned or unskinned, in brine or tomato juice; (*b*) skinned and pulped in their own juice; (*c*) as purée.

Whole

1. Pack with care, filling the bottles as much as possible.   Pack skinned or unskinned; if the latter, prick the skins well so that the fruit does not burst.

2. Pour in brine, hot or cold (1 oz. salt dissolved in 2 quarts water), or tomato juice, seasoned.   Sugar may be added to the brine in the same proportion as the salt.

3. Put on lids, etc., in the way described above.

4. Sterilize (*a*) in hot-water bath, heat so that a temperature of 190° F. is reached in not less than 1½ hours.   Keep at this temperature for 30 minutes; or (*b*) in the oven, heat at 250° F., until the fruit has shrunk and changed colour.

Skinned and pulped

1. Skin, cut in pieces, and pack tightly.

2. Add salt (1 teaspoon to 1 quart jar) and an equal quantity of sugar. Add no water.

3. Sterilize in hot-water bath or in the oven, as for whole tomatoes.

Purée

1. Cook skinned tomatoes until soft, seasoned as above with equal quantities of salt and sugar, and flavoured, if desired, with crushed garlic or very finely grated onion and chopped herbs.

2. Rub through a fine sieve.   Reduce for 10 minutes and pour into hot jars.   Seal at once and cool.

VEGETABLES

Vegetables must be very carefully chosen and washed with particular care.   Peas, French beans, asparagus, mushrooms, and new potatoes are the more popular, but all these are more easily canned than bottled, as the process must be carried out in a pressure cooker, and to keep the bottles from cracking is not easy.   A large cooker must be used, and it must not be overfilled; ample space between the bottles should be allowed, and the bottles must be raised on the rack provided with the cooker.   It is advisable to read with care all the directions given by the pressure cooker manufacturers for bottling and canning and to follow them exactly.

In a pressure cooker a temperature is reached that is high enough to destroy all micro-organisms and bacteria. If no pressure cooker is available, vegetables should not be bottled, or canned, at home.

Vegetables need preliminary blanching or cooking. They should be prepared as for cooking, and dropped into boiling water according to the following time-table:

Asparagus. Boil for 5 minutes, pack into bottles and seal.

French beans. Drop 1 quart at a time into boiling water. Bring the water to the boil again and pack at once into hot jars and seal.

Peas. Drop into boiling water and cook 3 minutes. Drain and pack at once into hot jars and seal.

Mushrooms. Wash and peel, drop into boiling water, drain, pack into hot jars and seal.

New potatoes. Wash, drop into boiling water and cook 5 minutes. Skin and remove eyes or blemishes. Pack while hot and seal.

The times for pressure cooking are as follows:

Asparagus	40 minutes at 10 lb. pressure
French beans	45 ,, ,, 10 ,, ,,
Peas	60 ,, ,, 10 ,, ,,
Mushrooms	35 ,, ,, 10 ,, ,,
New potatoes	70 ,, ,, 15 ,, ,,

In every case the jars should be at least 2 inches apart; they should be carefully lifted from the cooker as soon as sterilizing is over, stood on a wooden table or on several layers of cloth or paper, out of a draught, and left to cool for 48 hours before they are tested for sealing.

TO CLOSE BOTTLES WHEN NO PATENT CLOSURE IS AVAILABLE

Make cement, according to the recipe which follows:

$\frac{1}{2}$ lb. black resin	$\frac{1}{2}$ lb. red sealing-wax
$\frac{1}{4}$ oz. beeswax	1 tallow candle

Heat all except the tallow candle together in an iron or earthenware pot. When the mixture froths up, before all the solids are melted, and before the mixture begins to boil up, stir it with a tallow candle, which will settle the froth until all is melted and fit for use.

N.B. This is useful when a small jar is used, as for the preservation of tarragon in brine.

ELECTRIC MIXERS

The modern electric mixer is a first-class labour-saving device. It carries out with great thoroughness the beating of many mixtures. It is admirable for making mayonnaise, for beating potatoes to a light purée, and for certain cake mixtures; with a proper attachment it may be used for mincing. It is of tremendous help to the beginner, to the busy housewife, and to the cook who has to provide food on a large scale. In addition to the mixing-machine there is also a portable electric beater which may be used in any bowl or saucepan. The makers of these admirable labour-saving devices supply instruction books which should be read and obeyed. R. H. asks for a rider here; she says that for a student whose arm and spirit are likely to fail when it comes to the beating of cake mixtures for a long time the electric beater is salvation, but that for her own part she would always choose to beat by hand when she was making a meringue suisse [1] or sponge or génoise mixture. She can tell more exactly, she says, the degree of beating, and she reserves the mechanical aids for work when there is less need for such precision. Mechanical aids to cooking are after all an element in mass production; mass-produced cakes, especially those involving the finer mixtures, have not quite the quality of the hand-made produce of an expert, so that in the higher reaches of cooking it is a mistake perhaps to be too exclusively wedded to these admirable labour-saving devices.

THE BLENDER

This is a small but not inexpensive piece of electrical equipment. Revolving at great speed, fine blades set inside the container reduce the contents to the finest of fine pulps in a matter of seconds.

It was a particularly velvety cream sauce served with salmon that crystallized my half-formed intention to acquire a blender, and I have never regretted it. I think it should come early on the list of wedding presents even for the bride who hopes and believes she will find and keep a good cook. It is of the greatest help in the preparation of small quantities of soup, of cold sauces and fruit cocktails, and though I believe it has several other possible uses, it is for these purposes that we particularly value it. Because of the extraordinary power of emulsification, it makes the smoothest of cream soups which may be served hot or cold and may be prepared from fresh or previously cooked food. Cold soups

---

[1] The meringue suisse is that used for meringues filled with crème chantilly; for this the whites are beaten alone and it is easy to overbeat. R. H. says that even in the restaurant, where these are made in quantity, she does not use a mechanical beater. On the other hand, for meringue cuite (used for shaping into baskets, etc.), in which the egg whites are beaten with the sugar, the mechanical beater may with advantage be used.

prepared from uncooked ingredients have a fresh and delicious flavour. Fruit and vegetable juices, either as cocktails or for other purposes, are made from fresh materials and taste quite different from juice extracted by cooking. We had occasion to make a number of different cocktails of this kind, and portions of each were left for some time in the ice-box. In this way we discovered that these extracted juices make excellent sorbets and savoury ices. In hot weather a frozen mush of fruit or tomato juice is excellent to serve with fish or poultry or as a separate course. For example, any one of those given might be served as a first course, put into half a prepared grape-fruit or in the hollow of a slice of melon. They are not so smooth or elegant as a proper lemon mint ice, given on page 983, but for everyday hot weather use they are admirable.

Before beginning to use this invaluable appliance, it is as well again to consult the accompanying booklet and to read with care all the instructions given. In addition, experience has shown:

(a) that all solid or semi-solid ingredients liquefy more easily if they are first cut in small pieces, e.g. oranges, tomatoes, slices of canned fruit;

(b) that it is as well, in all recipes, to switch to HALF first, then if necessary to FULL. The blender ought not to be run at FULL for more than 2 minutes at a time;

(c) it is as well not to have the goblet more than two-thirds full—half full for complete safety. If the container is overfilled it may splash the contents over the table. Treated with care the blender is clean and easy to use.

Before giving a few recipes it may be said that for soups in particular an exhaustive set of recipes is unnecessary. The ingredients for such soups as purée of sorrel, spinach, potatoes, or peas may all be emulsified in the blender. After the soup is made, instead of being put through a sieve it is put, in batches, into the blender. This produces an absolutely smooth, creamy purée, quite delicious, admirable for certain diets where smoothness is essential, and good for young children.

CRÈME VICHYSSOISE

12 small leeks, white part only	4–5 sprigs of parsley, roughly
1½ oz. butter	chopped
3–4 potatoes	½ pint cream
1 quart chicken stock	chopped chives
salt and pepper	

Cut the white parts of the leeks in thin slices, put them in a pan with the melted butter and cook them gently for 15 minutes. Dice the potatoes, add them with the stock, salt and pepper, and roughly chopped parsley and simmer until the vegetables are soft (about 30 minutes). Cool the mixture slightly, then pour, ½ pint at a time, into the electric blender, switch to HALF and run for 2 minutes after each fresh addition. Allow to become ice-cold (in hot weather put in the refrigerator) and serve with cream and chopped chives.

CELERY CREAM SOUP

1½ oz. butter	½ bay-leaf
½ cup onion, roughly chopped	1 pint milk
2 cups celery, cut in thin slices	chopped parsley
2 medium potatoes	a few tablespoons of cream, if
½ pint water	possible
salt and pepper	

Melt the butter, add the chopped onion and soften slowly without colouring. Add celery, diced potatoes, water, salt and pepper, and bay-leaf. Cover and simmer until the vegetables are soft, about 30 minutes. Add the milk and pour, ½ pint at a time, into the container of the electric blender, switch to HALF and run for 2 minutes after each fresh addition. Reheat, add chopped parsley and if available a few tablespoons of cream.

POTAGE BRUXELLES

½ cup chopped onion	2 cups chopped cooked Brussels sprouts
1 oz. butter	1½ cups cooked potato
1 pint milk	salt, pepper, and freshly grated nutmeg

Soften the onion in the hot butter for 10 minutes, warm the milk, mix with the cold vegetables and the cooked onion, put ½ pint at a time into the container of the electric blender, switch to HALF and run for 1½–2 minutes after each fresh addition, until all the mixture has been blended. Season with salt, pepper, and nutmeg and bring to boiling-point before serving.

CREAM OF CARROT SOUP

½ cup chopped onion	¾ cup cooked potato
1 oz. butter	2 cups chopped cooked carrots
½ pint milk	salt and pepper
½ pint water	½ teaspoon sugar

Soften the onion in the hot butter for 10 minutes, warm the milk and water together and add to the cooked vegetables. Add the onion, the seasoning, and the sugar, stir well and put into the container of the electric blender, ½ pint at a time. Switch to HALF and run for 1½–2 minutes after each fresh addition, until all the mixture has been blended. Bring to boiling-point before serving. A tablespoon or two of cream is an improvement.

GREEN SOUP

5 oz. spinach	1–2 spring onions, sliced
½ a peeled cucumber, cut up	½ apple, cut up
juice of 1 lemon	2–3 sprigs of mint
1 pint water	salt and pepper
1 oz. watercress	

Put all together through the electric blender with the indicator at HALF for 2 minutes. Take care not to have the container more than half full. Adjust seasoning and serve very cold.

CARROT AND APPLE SOUP

4 oz. carrots, sliced	2 oz. apple, cut up
1 handful of watercress	½ pint water
1 cup canned tomato	salt, pepper, and sugar

Mix all together, dividing the watercress in sprigs, and put in the container of the electric blender ½ pint at a time.   Switch to HALF and run for 2½–3 minutes after each fresh addition.   Adjust seasoning and serve very cold.

COLD TOMATO AND PINEAPPLE SOUP

½ lb. tomatoes, cut up	water of coco-nut, or 1 cup
1 cup pineapple juice	coco-nut milk (see page 403)
small cup canned tomatoes	small cup of water
	seasoning if necessary

Peel and cut up the fresh tomatoes, put all ingredients into the container of the electric blender, taking care not to have it more than half full, switch to HALF and run for 2 minutes.   Adjust seasoning if necessary and serve cold.

FRUIT COCKTAILS

¼ cucumber, cut up	2 sprigs of mint
½ handful of watercress	2 gills water
juice of 1 grape-fruit	sugar, salt, pepper, lemon juice

Peel and cut up the cucumber, pick the watercress into sprigs, squeeze the juice from the grape-fruit and put all ingredients into the container of the electric blender, taking care not to have it more than half full.   Switch to HALF and run for 2–3 minutes.   Makes 4 glasses.

1½ gills tomato juice	juice of ½ lemon
¼ sliced apple	½ teaspoon salt
2 teaspoons sugar	sprig of mint for jug
2 gills pineapple juice	

Put all together through the electric blender as above.   Makes 4–5 glasses.   Serve in a jug with a sprig of mint.

4 tomatoes, cut up, or 1 tea-cup canned tomatoes	juice of 1 lemon
	salt, sugar to taste
1 cup coco-nut milk (see page 403)	

Put all together through electric blender as above.

2 cups tinned pimento	2 cups tinned tomato
salt and sugar	

Make as above in good time and allow to stand before serving.

1 apricot	1 slice of pineapple
juice of 1 orange	1 gill pineapple juice
1 gill tomato juice	

Cut up the apricot and the pineapple in small pieces, put all the ingredients in the electric blender, taking care not to have it more than half full, and turn the indicator to HALF. Run for 2 minutes. Chill well before serving. This is also very good frozen.

1 apple, cut up	1 slice of pineapple
rind of $\frac{1}{2}$ orange	5 leaves of eau-de-Cologne mint
2 gills orange juice	1 teaspoon honey

Peel and core the apple, and cut up in small pieces, cut up the pineapple, cut the rind in thin strips and shred. Put all the ingredients except the honey into the electric blender, taking care not to have it more than half full, turn the indicator to HALF and run for 2 minutes. Add honey and chill. Smooth, and excellent frozen.

two-thirds tomato juice	1 whole sprig of apple mint
one-third pineapple juice	1 slice pineapple, cut up

Add to the juices the pineapple cut in small pieces and the apple mint stripped from the stalk and roughly shredded. Put into blender $\frac{1}{2}$ pint at a time, turn the indicator to HALF and run each $\frac{1}{2}$ pint for 2 minutes. Chill well. Rough, but excellent frozen.

1 peach (tinned may be used)	juice and rind of 1 orange and
1 apricot (tinned may be used)	$\frac{1}{2}$ lemon
2 teaspoons honey	1$\frac{1}{2}$ gills fruit juice

Cut up the peach, peeled if fresh, and the apricot. Pare the orange and lemon finely and shred the rind. Put all ingredients into the blender except the honey, taking care not to have it more than half full, turn the indicator to HALF and run for 2$\frac{1}{2}$ minutes. Add the honey and stir well. Chill before serving.

equal quantities of tomato and orange juice and one-third their combined quantity of lemon juice	1 sprig of apple mint
	salt to taste
	sugar

Put all ingredients into the blender, $\frac{1}{2}$ pint at a time, stripping the leaves from the apple mint and shredding roughly; turn the indicator to HALF and run for 2$\frac{1}{2}$ minutes after each fresh addition. Chill very well. Rough, but good frozen.

Appendix

WINES, THEIR CHOICE AND SERVING

THIS is not intended as a treatise on wines, but to be of practical help to our students, and to those who are interested in and wish to know a little about the subject.

Wine, like bread, is one of the basic things of life, and so is the right accompaniment to food. Like food it has its own rules for treatment and serving, simple and easy to memorize. Moreover, good wine is in harmony with good food, and those who are interested in one will undoubtedly be interested in the other. Wine, too, is not only a compliment to food but a complement as well, containing food other than alcohol, notably Vitamin B, and it makes an admirable natural tonic.

The study of wine, the various types, growths, and vintages, is both an interesting and fascinating one; many books have been written on the subject and are to be recommended to the student as a follow-on to this chapter. Before describing the various kinds of wine, their choice and treatment, there are one or two points worth bearing in mind. Perhaps the most important is that when in any doubt as to what wine to buy go to a wine merchant for advice (*not* the little grocer round the corner). If he is a good one he will not only be interested in what you want but will appreciate your tastes. Here, too, a little knowledge of geography is a help to the understanding of wine, and finally care must be taken to choose the right type of glass to use and to ascertain the serving temperature of the wine itself.

These details do much towards the proper appreciation and enjoyment of wine. Nowadays good wines are within reach of everyone; good wine is not necessarily the most expensive, or from those vineyards or châteaux that carry well-known names. Many excellent table wines are comparatively inexpensive and may come from a little-known vineyard, but are none the worse for that.

Claret at one time was a most popular drink in England, being cheap and plentiful, and so called as being a lighter, 'clearer' wine than the heavier, richer burgundies. So to-day an excellent table wine may well be a claret; they are often cheaper and better value for money than a burgundy.

One final point: remember that the only way to get to know wine is to drink it, and certainly for those who wish to learn more about wine this is an admirable way to study.

1189

FRENCH WINES

The wines of France are perhaps the best known throughout the world. Bordeaux, Burgundy, Champagne are household words where wine is concerned, and are, of course, the districts where the vines are grown and the wine produced.

Bordeaux

The red wines of the Bordeaux are known in England as claret. This term is only applied to a red wine; a white claret does not exist, though, of course, a white Bordeaux does.

The Bordeaux region is divided and again subdivided into districts and 'communes' or parishes, producing both red and white wines. The most important of these districts, and therefore the best known as producing some of the finer wines, are five in number: Médoc, Graves, Sauternes and Barsac, St Emilion, Pomerol. Under these in turn are listed the various communes or parishes; under Médoc, for example, St Julien, St Estèphe, Margaux, Pauillac, to quote the better known. These five districts produce, according to the soil and kind of vine, wines of varying quality and type. For example, the Médoc produces most of the great red wines; Graves is best known for its white wines, though it has one or two red wines of great quality; Sauternes for sweet white dessert wines; St Emilion and Pomerol for red wines like the Médoc, but slightly heavier and less well bred.

In the latter half of the last century the wines of the Médoc were classified into five various growths or 'crus,' 1st, 2nd, 3rd and so on, in order of their general excellence. It does not follow that a 4th or 5th growth is a poor quality wine, but merely that the 'class' and bouquet do not equal those of the 1st growth. Wines of the 1st growth are the aristocrats: Ch. Margaux, Latour, Lafite-Rothschild. In course of time the quality of certain growths has changed, so at the present time a 4th or 5th growth may contain a wine of excellent quality and bouquet.

Apart from the classified growths of the Médoc, there are some excellent bourgeois wines which are of sound value and good to drink after two to three years in bottle.

The vineyards growing and producing the wine are named after the 'château' or country house in whose grounds they lie and which usually owns them. This should be on the label of the bottle, together with the district or commune and the year or vintage. Thus: Ch. Leoville Barton, St Julien (denoting the commune), 1949. Some of the better wines are château bottled; this also is clearly stated on the label, and also branded on the cork, and denotes that the wine is bottled at the château instead of being dispatched in bulk for bottling in the country where it will be drunk.

It is impossible and indeed unnecessary to learn the various growths and the wines that are classified under them. If you wish a wine merchant will guide you here, and a book on wines will give full details. It is,

The chief wine-growing districts of France

however, useful to know or memorize from what district or commune the wine comes, as the quality and type of the wine will vary, and such knowledge is an added guarantee of satisfaction.   For example, a bottle labelled Bordeaux or even Médoc will be of more doubtful content than one labelled St Julien of the Médoc—a commune that produces many fine wines.

The year or vintage is also important, and wines above a certain price should always have the year on the label.   The quality of wine produced every year varies considerably, some years being great, some good, others indifferent, some vintages maturing more quickly and so on.

Moreover, a good year for claret may not be so good for burgundy, and vice versa; the same rule applies also to white wines.   It must, however, be remembered that there is always some good wine in bad years, just as there is bad wine in good years.

Bordeaux, white

The wines that come under this heading are those of Graves, Sauternes, and Barsac.   The first district also produces red wines of quality, but is perhaps better known for its white wines.   These are comparatively dry light table wines and are classified like the wines of the Médoc, though not officially.

Sauternes, a comparatively small region tucked down below the Médoc (in fact the town has given its name to the district), produces exclusively white wines.   They are pre-eminently sweet dessert wines, the most famous of which is Château d'Yquem.   Because of its name this wine is fabulously expensive, and certainly out of the reach of most people. There are, however, other excellent sweet wines from this district, at a reasonable price, for example Château Climens and Château Rieussec. Here again consult your wine merchant, for a good Sauternes is never cheap, and many that are sold cheaply lack the proper quality and bouquet that this wine should have.

Burgundy

The red wines of this district are of a heavier, richer type than the clarets, and the growths have not been classified in the same way, but take their name from the district, or from the commune.

Good burgundy is always in short supply owing to the comparatively small district from which it comes and consequently its small production. Burgundy is nearly always a blended wine, and therefore it is all the more important to rely on your wine merchant when buying it.   Much dishonest wine, owing to a greater demand for burgundy than can be supplied, is sold under this name.   Claret, on the other hand, is much more plentiful, so that one can be certain of getting the genuine article.   The most famous burgundies come from the Côte d'Or.   This soil produces some wines of superb bouquet and flavour, which have no equal.   Famous wines such as Romanée Conti, Nuits St Georges, and Pommard come from the Côte d'Or.   Other excellent wines, though perhaps not quite in the same class, come from the regions of Macon and Beaujolais, though these regions are not within the confines of Burgundy proper.   Wines of superior quality to remember from this area are those of Fleurie and Morgan, sound wines of moderate price.

Burgundy, white

These wines are classed among the greatest white wines of the world and carry such famous names as Puligny-Montrachet, Montrachet, Meursault, and Corton-Charlemagne.   Like the red they are in short supply and are, therefore, not cheap, though the lesser growths are often very moderately priced.

Chablis

This is another well-known white wine and comes from a region some miles north-west of the Côte d'Or.   Chablis is noted for its dry, flint-like flavour, and is the palest green-gold in colour.   It is pre-eminently a wine to serve with oysters and fish.

Another excellent white wine and comparable at its best to a Chablis is:

Pouilly and Pouilly-Fuissé

This comes from the Macon area and is much the same colour as the Chablis, but a little sharper and fresher to the taste.   It also is a wine to be served with fish.

Other white wines, though perhaps not so well known in this country, are those from the Loire Valley, the best known of which are those from Vouvray, Anjou, and Saumur.   Vouvray is perhaps the most famous and like those from Anjou has a fragrant bouquet, and it is one of the sweeter wines.   Muscadet is another pleasant white table wine and one which has become popular in recent years.   It comes from a region just north of the Loire.

Côte de Rhône

This part of France lies further south, and produces red wines, the most famous of which is Hermitage, in comparatively small quantities.   Well known, and more easily procurable, are Châteauneuf-du-Pape and another excellent wine, Côte Rôtie.   The Rhône wines are like a light burgundy, smooth and with a good bouquet.   Apart from the reds there is a very good white Hermitage.   Rhône wines are not expensive, and are excellent and a very good buy.

Rosé wines

These are wines of a rose-pink colour, light, refreshing, and inexpensive. The best of them come from the Rhône, Tavel being recognized as the best of them all.   They are pre-eminently table wines, and should be drunk young.

Champagne

Champagne is a wine known the world over, and is the only 'natural' sparkling wine.

Champagne is a 'made' wine, one reason which makes it so expensive, as it needs expert care in the blending and making. The sparkle is produced by the addition of sugar to an already fermented wine. This causes a second fermentation in the bottle and so gives it a 'natural' sparkle. There are many well-known firms producing excellent champagne, Krug, Perrier-Jouet, Mumm, Bollinger, to mention only a few, but here again consult your wine merchant and be guided by him. Vintage champagnes are expensive, and most shippers produce good non-vintage wines which are popular for wedding receptions and parties of that kind.

In France champagne is drunk towards the end of a meal, being considered more of a dessert wine, and therefore it is usually sweeter than that imported into England.

In this country the champagne may be dry, or very or 'extra' dry.

ALSATIAN WINES

Alsatian wines have become increasingly popular during the past few years. White, clean-tasting, and with a good bouquet, they resemble the wines of the Rhine and Moselle. Some, in fact, are made with the famous Riesling grape, with which the best German wines are made. The name of the grape is shown on the label, and the bottle itself is that of a moselle, green and shapely. The names of the different varieties of grape are distinctive, the best known being the Riesling, Sylvaner, and Traminer, the last slightly heavier and more perfumed than the other two.

GERMAN WINES

Hock and moselle

These fine wines have always been popular in England, particularly hock, and since the war they are again being widely drunk. They are, of course, white, and among the former are wines comparable to a Montrachet at its finest: clean, dry, and with a delicate and flowery bouquet. The Moselle wines have the same quality, but are lighter. In fact, being green-gold in colour, they can be compared to a Chablis rather than a Montrachet. The finer hocks and moselles are indubitably expensive, but an excellent table wine, particularly from the Moselle, can be bought quite reasonably.

Hock has come to represent Rhine wines in general, but its name is in fact an anglicized abbreviation of Hochheim, a town near the confluence of the Maine and the Rhine, on the edge of the Rheingau, the most famous and the finest of the wine-producing areas of the Rhine. The other two important areas are mostly further up-stream and on the other bank—Rheinhessen and Rheinpfalz (the Palatinate).

In order to understand hock and its terminology, it is necessary to realize that the German vineyards are the furthest north of all the great wine-producing areas in the world, and therefore the most dependent on the autumn weather.   This is the reason both for the comparatively small percentage of 'great' years in the Rhine and the Moselle, and for the technique of harvest and labelling.   In many years, owing to insufficient ripeness, a great deal of the wine from these areas has to be 'sugared'—that is, artificially sweetened—so that it will ferment properly.   Any wine treated in this way can only be table wine at best.   Even if this is not so, and the weather is good, the grapes ripen at different stages of the harvest, and the earlier the gathering, the drier the resultant wine will be.   The labelling is a logical conclusion of this technique, and that is why the labels on the brown bottles of hock or the green bottles of moselle show such words as 'auslese,' 'spatlese,' etc., indicating the degree of dryness or sweetness of the wine and incidentally its quality and cost.

OTHER WINES

Sherry.   The most famous of the Spanish wines is, of course, sherry, though Spain does produce sound red and white wines.   These are of the robust type and are best drunk in their own country.

Sherry is a 'fortified' wine, so called because at a certain stage of the fermentation it has brandy added to it.   There is no such thing as a vintage sherry.   This is because the sherry you drink is the result of expert blending of the harvest of several years.   There are several different varieties or types; Manzanilla, Amontillado, Fino, and so on.   These vary from very dry to dry and medium dry, and there are also the darker rich dessert sherries.

South Africa also produces good sherries.   They are less expensive than the Spanish owing to preferential duty.   The flavour and bouquet are not so fine, though this may be due to the longer Spanish tradition of blending.

Port is also fortified with brandy and is a product of Portugal, where most of the vineyards are situated on the slopes of the Douro.   It is exclusively a dessert wine and may be divided into two categories, wood and vintage port, the former being like sherry, a blend of many wines, whereas vintage port is the production of a single great year and is usually bottled after about two years, maturing in about twelve, and remaining at its best for about another twenty-five years.   It therefore achieves most of its maturing in bottle.   Wood port, on the other hand, matures, as its name implies, in cask.

Vintage port, because of its maturing in bottle, does not lose colour or strength, and must always be kept in the same position on its side, because of the casting of the sediment (see Decanting, page 1197).   A splash of whitewash is often put on the bottle to denote the proper position.

Tawny port, so called, is a blended wine and gets its name from the brownish colour which it absorbs from the oak of the cask.

Ruby port is a further blend of tawny port with younger and therefore redder wines; hence the name.

Madeira is usually drunk in this country as a dessert wine. It comes, of course, from the Portuguese island of Madeira and, like the so-called 'East-India' sherry, is said to be improved by a sea voyage.

Other wines worth noting are those from Italy; the ones most met with over here are Chiantis, both red and white, and Orvieto, a dry or medium dry white wine. They are essentially table wines, sound and robust.

Marsala is another Italian wine, hailing from Sicily. It is dessert wine and in this country is used almost exclusively for the flavouring of sweet and savoury dishes.

GENERAL RULES ON THE SERVING OF WINE

Temperature

This is a most important point in the serving of wine. As a general rule red wines should be served at room temperature or, as the French term it, *chambré*. The gentle warmth brings out the bouquet or flavour of the wine, and this process of warming must be done gradually. A bottle must never be put into hot water or stood in front of the fire as a last-minute effort. The bottle, whether it be claret or burgundy, should be brought into a warm room at least a day before serving. When taking it straight from the cellar or rack where it has been laid in a horizontal position (to keep the wine in contact with the cork), stand it upright in the room. When carrying keep it steady to avoid shaking. In the case of a good claret the cork should be drawn 5–6 hours before serving in order to allow the wine to 'breathe' and have contact with the air. The stronger and more robust the wine the longer beforehand it can be opened, with the exception of burgundy. This wine does not require aeration to the same extent and is usually opened just before serving.

As a general rule all white wines should be served at cellar temperature, i.e. fresh to well chilled. There are certainly exceptions to this rule in that some wines should be served colder than others. For example, a white Bordeaux is at its best when well chilled while a white burgundy or hock is usually served 'fresh.'

To chill, the best method is to draw the cork, wipe out the neck of the bottle with a clean napkin, and lightly recork. Plunge into an ice-bucket containing a mixture of ice and water and leave for 7–10 minutes, or put into a refrigerator 20–30 minutes, longer if necessary.

The same treatment applies to champagne, though here the cork is not drawn until just before serving. It should, of course, be well chilled, and in general it is colder than the still white wines.

A vin rosé should also be served fresh or slightly chilled. Port should be drunk at room temperature, as should a brown dessert sherry. Dry sherries are best at cellar temperature.

Decanting

Certain red wines, notably Bordeaux, are best decanted: some clarets throw a sediment or what is called a deposit in the bottle, which decanting removes.   Moreover, it is a method of allowing the wine to breathe and it also helps it to take the temperature of the room.   Care must be taken over this operation.   The cork should be drawn carefully and inspected to see that it is sound; if defective in any way the wine may be 'corked,' in which case it is undrinkable.   The signs of corked wine are a 'spongy' cork, damp with wine throughout its length; and wine which, not having been protected by the air, looks muddy and smells and tastes sour.

Wipe the neck of the bottle carefully inside.   Have ready the decanter and, holding the bottle by the neck, slowly pour in the contents through a piece of clean muslin—a wine funnel is useful here.   (The bottle is held by the neck because the angle is less disturbing to the sediment than if it were held by the body.)   Stop when about an inch from the bottom, though this level depends a little on the amount of deposit thrown.   Then stand the decanter in a warm room.   If by chance the wine has to be brought straight from the cellar to the table, or if the process of 'chambré-ing' has been too slow or insufficient, the following is an approved method. Pour hot water into the decanter to warm it thoroughly (or warm in a hot closet).   Drain off all water, uncork the bottle and pour about 2–3 table-spoons of the wine into the decanter.   Gently swill it round, then pour in the rest of the bottle.   This will give the necessary warmth and so release the bouquet in the wine.

White wines are never decanted.   Sherry is usually decanted and port always, owing to the 'crust' or deposit in the bottle.

Glasses

These are an important item in the serving of wine.   Authorities agree that the glass should be a plain white one and of the correct size and shape for each wine.   Most wine merchants nowadays sell fine glass and one cannot do better than buy glasses from them.   Generally speaking, the best shape is the cross between the goblet and the tulip shape, swelling out well above the stem but narrowing slightly at the top.   The bouquet or fragrance of the wine can then expand in the main body of the glass and is held there by the narrowing top.   The size of glass varies with the wine.

Sherry.   A small glass containing about ½–¾ gill.

White wine.   A medium-sized glass holding about 1–1½ gills.

Claret or red wine.   Nowadays the same sized glass is generally used for red as for white, but correctly red usually requires a slightly larger glass.

Champagne.   Best drunk in a goblet-shaped glass, rather than the open type known as a champagne glass.

Brandy.   This may be drunk in ordinary small glasses or in 'balloons.' The glasses should be warmed before pouring.

Liqueurs.   A thimbleful, i.e. about a tablespoon.

Port. Between a sherry and a claret glass.

Most wine merchants will hire glasses for functions.

Corkscrews

One of the lever type is the most satisfactory. It will then open the bottle without jerking it.

Finally, never fill a glass right to the top. Three parts full is ample, so that the bouquet of the wine may be concentrated by the shape of the upper part of the glass.

WINES TO SERVE WITH FOOD

The following are the wines that should be served, and that go best, with certain foods and made dishes:

As a general rule certain wines follow one another through the menu. For formal and special occasions three or even four wines may be drunk at one meal, or more informally one wine throughout. In this case care must be taken when choosing the menu to see that all the dishes will 'mate' with the one wine chosen. Where more than one wine is served it is customary to serve a dry sherry with the soup, a dry white wine with the fish course, a claret or burgundy with meat or game, and a white dessert wine or a medium dry or sweet champagne with the sweet course. Port can accompany the savoury or dessert. A brown or dessert sherry may also take the place of port.

The following list gives more details of the wines that go best with certain dishes.

Certain dishes or foods kill the flavour or taste of wine, and these dishes should of course be avoided when wine is to be served. Mint sauce is particularly harmful, and a salad with a vinegary dressing will destroy the flavour of any red wine.

Egg dishes also have a reputation for not going well with wine, though this may be a matter of individual taste.

APPROPRIATE WINES TO SERVE WITH VARIOUS DISHES

White Wines	*Dishes or Foods*
Chablis	Oysters and shell-fish generally
Other dry white wines	Fish, grilled, fried, or in mayonnaise
	Egg dishes
	Baby lamb
	Spring chicken
Wines not so dry	Fish with sauces
	Chicken sauté (light red wine is also suitable)
	Vol-au-vents, bouchées
	'White' entrées
Sweet dessert wines	Any sweet or dessert

Champagne may be drunk throughout the meal.

Red Wines	Dishes or Foods
Light wines such as Bordeaux or Côte de Rhône	Roast veal Saddle of lamb, or grilled cutlets Roast turkey, partridge, or chicken Casserole of chicken Pâtés and pâté de foie
Burgundy or more 'robust' or heavier wine	Game such as hare, grouse, venison, pheasant Roast beef Steaks, tournedos

Index

International Conversion Tables

The weights and measures used throughout this book are based on British Imperial standards. However, the following tables show you how to convert the various weights and measures simply.

International Measures

Measure	U.K.	Australia	New Zealand	Canada
1 pint	20 fl. oz.	20 fl. oz.	20 fl. oz.	20 fl. oz.
1 cup	10 fl. oz.	8 fl. oz.	8 fl. oz.	8 fl. oz.
1 tablespoon	$\frac{5}{8}$ fl. oz.	$\frac{1}{2}$ fl. oz.	$\frac{1}{2}$ fl. oz.	$\frac{1}{2}$ fl. oz.
1 dessertspoon	$\frac{2}{5}$ fl. oz.	no official measure	—	—
1 teaspoon	$\frac{1}{5}$ fl. oz.	$\frac{1}{8}$ fl. oz.	$\frac{1}{8}$ fl. oz.	$\frac{1}{8}$ fl. oz.

Conversion of fluid ounces to metric

1 fl. oz.	= 28·4 ml
35 fl. oz. (approx. $1\frac{3}{4}$ Imperial pints)	= 1 litre (1000 ml or 10 decilitres)
1 Imperial pint (20 fl. oz.)	= approx. 600 ml (6 dl)
$\frac{1}{2}$ Imperial pint (10 fl. oz.)	= 300 ml (3 dl)
$\frac{1}{4}$ Imperial pint (5 fl. oz.)	= 150 ml ($1\frac{1}{2}$ dl)
4 tablespoons ($2\frac{1}{2}$ fl. oz.)	= 70 ml (7 cl)
2 tablespoons ($1\frac{1}{4}$ fl. oz.)	= 35 ml ($3\frac{1}{2}$ cl)
1 tablespoon ($\frac{5}{8}$ fl. oz.)	= 18 ml (2 cl)
1 dessertspoon ($\frac{2}{5}$ fl. oz.)	= 12 ml
1 teaspoon ($\frac{1}{5}$ fl. oz.)	= 6 ml

(All the above metric equivalents are approximate)

Conversion of solid weights to metric

2 lb. 3 oz. = 1 k (kilogramme)
1 lb.   = 453 gm (grammes)
12 oz.   = 339 gm
8 oz.   = 225 gm
4 oz.   = 113 gm
2 oz.   = 56 gm
1 oz.   = 28 gm

Equivalents

1 U.K. (old B.S.I. standard) cup equals 1¼ cups in Commonwealth countries
4 U.K. tablespoons equal 5 Commonwealth tablespoons
5 U.K. teaspoons equal 6 New Zealand or 6 Canadian or 8 Australian
1 U.K. dessertspoon equals ⅔ U.K. tablespoon or 2 U.K. teaspoons

In British cookery books, a gill is usually 5 fl. oz. (¼ pint), but in a few localities in the U.K. it can mean 10 fl. oz. (½ pint).

Other non-standardized measures include:
Breakfast cup = approx. 10 fl. oz.
Tea cup   = 5 fl. oz.
Coffee cup   = 3 fl. oz.

Oven temperatures

Description	Electric Setting	Gas Mark
Very cool	225° F. (110° C.)	¼
	250° F. (130° C.)	½
Cool	275° F. (140° C.)	1
	300° F. (150° C.)	2
Very moderate	325° F. (170° C.)	3
Moderate	350° F. (180° C.)	4
Moderately or	375° F. (190° C.)	5
fairly hot	400° F. (200° C.)	6
Hot	425° F. (220° C.)	7
	450° F. (230° C.)	8
Very hot	475° F. (240° C.)	9

These temperatures are only an approximate guide as all ovens vary slightly, according to the make and country of manufacture.

Additional Recipes

ADDITIONAL RECIPES

ADDITIONAL RECIPES

ADDITIONAL RECIPES

ADDITIONAL RECIPES

ADDITIONAL RECIPES

ADDITIONAL RECIPES

ADDITIONAL RECIPES

ADDITIONAL RECIPES

ADDITIONAL RECIPES

ADDITIONAL RECIPES

ADDITIONAL RECIPES

ADDITIONAL RECIPES

ADDITIONAL RECIPES

ADDITIONAL RECIPES

ADDITIONAL RECIPES

ADDITIONAL RECIPES

ADDITIONAL RECIPES

ADDITIONAL RECIPES

ADDITIONAL RECIPES

ADDITIONAL RECIPES

ADDITIONAL RECIPES

ADDITIONAL RECIPES

ADDITIONAL RECIPES

ADDITIONAL RECIPES

ADDITIONAL RECIPES